Construction Codes and Inspection Handbook

Construction Codes and Inspection Handbook

GIL L. TAYLOR

McGraw-Hill

New York   Chicago San Francisco Lisbon London
Madrid   Mexico City Milan New Delhi San Juan
Seoul Singapore Sydney Toronto

The McGraw·Hill Companies

Library of Congress Cataloging-in-Publication Data

Taylor, G. L. (Gil L.), date.
    Construction codes and inspection handbook / Gil L. Taylor.
            p.   cm.
    Includes index.
    ISBN 0-07-146825-0
    1. Building inspection—Handbooks, manuals, etc.   2. Buildings—Specifications—
Handbooks, manuals, etc.   I. Title.

TH439.T39   2006
690.02'18—dc22   2005054521

1 2 3 4 5 6 7 8 9 0   QPD/QPD   0 1 2 1 0 9 8 7 6

ISBN 0-07-146825-0

*The sponsoring editor for this book was Cary Sullivan, the editing supervisors were
Caroline Levine and Stephen M. Smith, and the production supervisor was Richard C.
Ruzycka. It was set in ITC Century Light by MidAtlantic Books & Journals, Inc. The art
director for the cover was Anthony Landi.*

Printed and bound by Quebecor/Dubuque.

McGraw-Hill books are available at special quantity discounts to use as premiums and sales
promotions, or for use in corporate training programs. For more information, please write to
the Director of Special Sales, McGraw-Hill Professional, Two Penn Plaza, New York, NY
10121-2298. Or contact your local bookstore.

This book is printed on acid-free paper.

Contents

5 Masonry 143

Appendices 507

1
CHAPTER

General Information

Quality assurance monitors and confirms quality, but the contractor is responsible for providing it.

THIS CHAPTER COVERS CONSTRUCTION procedures and established construction standards. It is not intended to replace any of the model codes and or specific specifications in the contract documents. The goal is for the Inspector and or project site management to use this guide as a base to establish his or her own inspection guidelines and to provide the client with a well built project meeting the specifications. Our intent is for this reference tool to be instrumental in better buildings and projects being constructed and to be a valuable training guide for those just entering the construction field.

INTRODUCTION

As an Owner's Representative and/or the project Resident Inspector you should be thoroughly familiar with all the contract documents, including the plans with all changes and specifications as well as the contracts submittals such as shop drawings. Plans and specifications should include all revisions, changes, and amendments.

In addition, you should be thoroughly familiar with the reporting requirements as well as the specific duties and responsibilities (as well as the limits) that this particular project requires. Procedures and responsibilities will differ from project to project. It is crucial that the Inspector have a clear understanding of the project responsibilities as well as all reporting required prior to the start of the project.

RESPONSIBILITY

Inspectors have different responsibilities and authorities, dependent on the organizational setup and the size and scope of the project. Each Inspector should review the following:

a. Do I understand the limits of my responsibility?

b. Do I have the technical knowledge? Are gaps effectively covered with the help of other inspection staff and/or consultants?

c. Do I fully understand all reporting procedures?

d. Do I fully understand where I fit in the organization chart and to whom I report?

☐ One or more International Codes currently enforced statewide

▨ One or more International Codes enforced within state at local level

■ Adopted statewide with future enforcement date

Fig. 1-1 *International Code Council (ICC) code adoption (by state).*

e. Am I given sufficient authority to carry out my duties and responsibilities?

AUTHORITY

a. Make sure you know the extent of your authority. Your authority should as a minimum be to inspect all work and insure that it is accomplished in accordance with the contract plans and specifications.

b. Check with your supervisor on policies with respect to your authority to stop Subcontractor operations for such things as safety violations as well as construction deficiencies.

QUALITY CONTROL

a. Subcontractors may also be required to provide additional inspectors, either part time or full time depending on the requirements placed on the project. This is especially true for Government projects.

b. As the project's primary Inspector, it should be your responsibility to oversee any additional Inspectors and to determine their qualifications and ability to perform their duties.

c. The main role of the Inspector is to be able to assure the owner, that the quality requirements of the contract have been satisfied.

d. Some projects will require a Subcontractor Quality Control Program (Inspectors). It requires that the Subcontractor implement that part of the construction program such as the masonry, HVAC, electrical, etc., and control the quality of that trade in the daily work. Although they work for the contractor you should develop a close working relationship and in some cases they will report directly to you.

e. Effective project inspections require a serious and concentrated effort on the part of all the Inspectors as well as all site management personnel.

f. Contract requirements provide the tools for the accomplishment of the goals, as follows:
   1. Before start of construction, the Project Manager shall conduct a meeting with all contractors and discuss their individual quality control plans and procedures. Construction will not start until after the meeting and submittal/acceptance of at least the Project Quality Control plan. Project staffing should be sufficient to obtain the quality of construction designed in the plans and specifications.
   2. *Preconstruction meetings.* These meetings will be held before each type of work, such as the start of foundations, masonry work, slab on grade, plumbing grounds, etc., to ensure that the requirements are understood, documentation is complete, materials are on hand, and the people who are to perform the work understand what will be considered satisfactory workmanship. Both the contract specifications and those referenced in the contract specifications must be in the Job Site Trailer library and available to the inspectors. For instance, the welding specifications will depend entirely on the American Welding Society (AWS) Specifications for all requirements. If the Inspector does not have the AWS specifications, then he cannot know or enforce these provisions. Project Architects and Engineers can be helpful in obtaining referenced specifications.
   3. *Initial inspections.* These inspections must be conducted in a timely manner at the beginning of a definable feature of work.
   4. *Follow-up inspections.* These inspections also occur daily when work is in progress and are for the purpose of assuring that the controls established in the earlier phases of inspection continue to provide work that conforms to the contract requirements.

In all projects there is work that is eventually covered and cannot be inspected after the fact. This includes concrete, where the size, number, and location of reinforcing steel cannot be readily determined after the concrete is placed. Underground utilities cannot be inspected after covering. Work of this nature must be closely controlled and monitored during construction. If the contractor was notified to not cover until you have completed your inspection but does so anyway, then you can direct him to uncover the work at his expense!

- Situations may occur and the Inspector has a vital role in assuring that these and similar situations do not become Standing Operating Procedures (SOP). Responsibility for compliance should be a total team effort.

PLANS AND SPECIFICATIONS
(see Chapter 2)

a. Make a thorough review of plans and specifications during the bidding period.
   1. Watch for omissions.
   2. Watch for discrepancies between plans and specifications.

3. Check plans and specifications against requirements with which you have had problems on similar jobs.
4. Verify that the correct Geographic Design Criteria are used.
5. Compare elevations, grades, and details shown on plans, with those at the actual site.
6. Report all errors, omissions, discrepancies, and deficiencies to the Project Manager.

b. Always keep a posted and marked up set of plans and specifications convenient for ready reference.

c. Make sure that the Subcontractor has this same information.

d. Anticipate work operations by reviewing the plans and specifications for each operation before it begins.
1. Discuss Contract requirements with the Subcontractor before each construction begins.
2. Highlight and/or make notes of those provisions which need special attention, such as:
    (a) Unusual requirements
    (b) Provisions that other Subcontractors have overlooked
    (c) Repetitive deficiencies
    (d) Conflicting specifications, guidelines
    (e) Code violations
    (f) Use the checklists in this guide to help find significant items in the plans and specifications

Required Geographic Design Criteria

(These values are determined by the local code-administering jurisdiction.)

```
Ground Snow Load
Roof Snow Load
Wind Speed
Seismic Zone
Weathering Zone
Frost Line
Termite Zone
Decay Zone
Flood Zone
Winter Design Temperature
Heating Degree Days
Cooling Degree Days
Radon Zone
Exposure Profile
January Average Temperature
```

SHOP DRAWINGS

a. Review the prepared subcontractor submittal register, plans, and specifications. Check submittal register for inclusion of all shop drawings required including layouts of equipment, equipment rooms, etc. The Inspector must have copies of all shop drawings!

b. The Subcontractor is required to enter his or her data onto the submittal register and submit it to the Project Control Administrator. Compare this submittal with your check list.

c. The Project Manager is required to periodically review and update the submittal register. The Inspector should monitor each change.

d. Make checks of the submittal register to avoid untimely and omitted submittals so as to avoid delay of construction. Check specifications for required turnaround time.

e. Compare the shop drawings to the contract requirements and report apparent differences to your supervisor. (Approved shop drawings do not constitute a waiver of a contract requirement.)

f. Make sure each detail on the shop drawing is clearly detailed and understood.

g. It is the responsibility of the subcontractor to make notes on his submittal of items which deviate from contract requirements.

h. Check material being installed against the approved shop drawing. (If the Subcontractor installs unapproved material, inform him in writing that the material, if not subsequently approved, will be removed and replaced at his expense.)

INSPECTION REPORT

a. Prepare a complete daily report. Modify the form to reflect all requirements. Check specifications and contract documents. Check for inclusion of the following:
1. *Conditions*: Weather, moisture, soil conditions, etc. (*Note when and how adverse site condition hampered or shut down a particular operation.*)
2. *Activities*: Work phases, including locations and description of each activity and the inspection.
3. *Issues*: Disputes, questionable items, etc. (Also, note if they were settled and, if so, how they were settled.)

Fig. 1-2 *Sample of Weekly Inspection Report (page 1).*

4. *Deficiencies and violations*: Description, location, and corrective action.
5. *Instructions*: Given and received—identify recipient and source.
6. *Progress information*: Report all delays, anticipated and actual, and action taken or action contemplated.
7. *Equipment*: Report arrival and departure of each major item of equipment by manufacturer, model, serial number, and capacity. Report equipment in use and idle equipment.
8. *Reports*: Make sure reports are identified, dated, and signed.

• Check all past daily reports each day to ensure that issues are not lingering and that instructions received are noted and properly acted upon.

NOTES/COMMENTS:
MONTHLY PROGRESS MEETING - STATE/CLIENT DID NOT WISH TO CLASSIFY THE ROCK EXCAVATION.
MEETING WITH GAS/ RICHMOND UTILITIES ON SCHEDULE FOR COMPLETION.

THURSDAY						WEATHER	SUNNY	
PORTION OF SCHEDULED DAY SUITABLE FOR OPERATIONS						TEMPERATURE		
ROCK EXCAVATION 100 %	BORROW EXCAVATION WET 0 %	BUILDING PAD WET 0%	CONCRETE N/A	STRUCTURE N/A		MINIMUM	MAXIMUM	87

HAS ANYTHING DEVELOPED ON THE WORK WHICH MIGHT LEAD TO A CHANGE ORDER OR FINDING OF FACT?	■ NO ☐ YES *(Explain)*	24 HOUR PRECIPITATION	
		INCHES NONE	ENDING

NUMBER OF D W WILBURN EMPLOYEES

SUPERVISORY	OFFICE	LAYOUT	INSPECTION	TOTAL	LABOR		
1			1				

NUMBER OF CONTRACTOR'S EMPLOYEES				NUMBER OF SHIFTS x 1 ☐ 2						
CONTRACTOR HAMILITON	SKILLED 1	LABORERS 0	TOTAL 1	FROM	TO	FROM	TO	FROM	TO

Attach list of the folowing: (a) Major items of equipment either idle or working, and (b) Number and classification
Note: If the contractor's Daily Construction Report contains the information it need not be repeated.

WORK PERFORMED TODAY: *(Indicate location and description of Work performed.)*
STARTED HOE RAMMING ROCK (PICTURES)

NOTES/COMMENTS:

FRIDAY						WEATHER	THUNDER SHOWERS	
PORTION OF SCHEDULED DAY SUITABLE FOR OPERATIONS						TEMPERATURE		
ROCK EXCAVATION 100%	BORROW EXCAVATION 100 %	BUILDING 100%	CONCRETE %	STRUCTURE		MINIMUM	MAXIMUM	86

HAS ANYTHING DEVELOPED ON THE WORK WHICH MIGHT LEAD TO A CHANGE ORDER OR FINDING OF FACT?	■ NO ☐ YES *(Explain)*	24 HOUR PRECIPITATION	
		INCHES SOME	ENDING

NUMBER OF D W WILBURN EMPLOYEES

SUPERVISORY	OFFICE	LAYOUT	INSPECTION	TOTAL	LABOR		
1			1				

NUMBER OF CONTRACTOR'S EMPLOYEES				NUMBER OF SHIFTS x 1 ☐ 2						
CONTRACTOR HAMILITON	SKILLED 1	LABORERS 1	TOTAL 1	FROM	TO	FROM	TO	FROM	TO

Attach list of the folowing: (a) Major items of equipment either idle or working, and (b) Number and classification
Note: If the contractor's Daily Construction Report contains the information it need not be repeated.

WORK PERFORMED TODAY: *(Indicate location and description of Work performed.)*
ONLY ONE TRACKHOE AND OPERATOR- SPENT MOST OF DAY CLEARING WHAT HE RAMMED YESTERDAY - PILING IT UP!

NOTES/COMMENTS:
GAS LINE 99% FUZES- WAITING ON ROCK TRENCHER- SHOULD BE DELIVERED NEXT MONDAY.

Results of QA activities and tests, deficiencies observed, actions taken and corrective action of contractor,

CONTRACTOR HAS ALL LAW ENGINEERING INSPECTION REPORTS TODATE- ALL ARE ACCEPTABLE AS PER WILBURN
LAW ENGINEERING AND DESIGN ENG. (RON SMITH) OK'ED POSITIONING OF ROCK WASTE AS DEEP FILL IN PARKING AREA.

VERBAL INSTRUCTION GIVEN TO CONTRACTOR

NEED COPIES OF ALL REPORTS.
NEED ELECTRIC TO TRAILERS / AND OR MOVE / AND AN INSPECTORS OFFICE.

HAS ANYTHING DEVELOPED ON THE WORK WHICH MIGHT LEAD TO A CHANGE ORDER OR FINDING OF FACT?

STILL PENDING-THE REROUTING OF THE GAS LINE MAY COST ADDITIONAL MONIES. THIS IS TO BE CONFIRMED BY RICHMOND UTILITIES.

Fig. 1-3 *Sample of Weekly Inspection Report (page 2).*

PRECONSTRUCTION MEETING

1. Both the Quality Assurance Representative and the Project Manager should attend this Conference as well as all contractors' representatives associated with the project.

2. Minutes of the meeting should be available to each of the assigned quality assurance control representatives present.

3. The subject of the proposed Quality Control Plan should be well documented.

EQUIPMENT PROPOSAL

1. Have daily/weekly equipment rates been approved?

2. Does equipment proposed by the Subcontractor have proper approval for use?

3. Certain equipment requires a safety test or check before initial operation at the site.

4. Some equipment requires a permit or license before use.

5. Has equipment been recently inspected?

6. Do not allow the discarding of any oils, lubricants, or their containers on the project.

CLAIMS

1. Always be alert to possible claims or matters of possible dispute.

2. When you discover that a claim or dispute is in the making, notify the project manager and record all facts in your (Inspector) daily reports.

3. Make sure that adequate and accurate records of facts, materials, labor, and equipment associated with the claim or dispute are on file.

4. Photographs may be appropriate to supplement the record.

5. Differing site conditions may be cause for a claim. Subcontractors must notify the PM in writing before disturbing conditions.

PROGRESS SCHEDULES

a. Provide necessary assistance to the Subcontractor for his preparation of initial and revised progress schedules.

b. Encourage the contractor to submit timely updates.

c. Be familiar with the approved progress schedule and carefully watch for any slippage in progress.

d. Anticipate slowdowns and delays affecting progress.

e. Promptly report to the Project Manager and record in the daily reports all indications of any slippage in progress. Perform manpower analysis as needed.

f. When construction falls behind schedule, carefully examine the construction operations for ways progress can be improved and relay this to the Superintendent and Project Manager.

g. Be very careful not to direct or dictate the Subcontractor's operation (the PM/Superintendent is responsible for directing the contractor to take steps to improve his progress).

h. Keep informed of the required contract milestones and the final completion date.

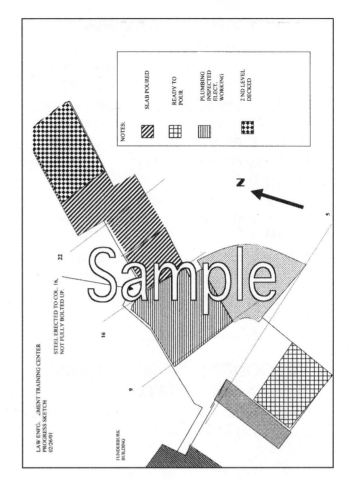

Fig. 1-4 *Sample of simple progress diagram.*

LABOR ENFORCEMENT

a. Keep informed of the labor requirements of the contracts.

b. Avoid taking part in any labor disputes. Inform the Project Manager of any labor problems and disputes.

c. Check that antidiscrimination posters and minimum wage rates are kept in a conspicuous place.

d. Assist office personnel in ensuring that:
   1. The worker-hours are accurately shown on payrolls.
   2. Payrolls are submitted as required from each sub-subcontractor who worked on the job.
   3. Each laborer and each piece of equipment are classified in accordance with the particular work function.

e. Make spot checks with sub-subcontractors' employees to verify that Davis-Bacon wage rates are being paid for the work classification being performed (if required).

STORAGE OF MATERIALS

a. Check to see that adequate space is available for the subcontractors' operations and storage areas (before the materials are scheduled for delivery).

b. Check that approval has been obtained for temporary sheds, buildings, etc., which the subcontractor proposes to install.

c. See that material and equipment are properly stored and protected.

d. Make sure that safety requirements, especially in the storage of flammable or explosive materials, are adhered to.

e. Make sure that temporary structures are secured against wind damage.

f. Ensure that the necessary heating and ventilating are provided.

SUBCONTRACTORS' PAYMENT ESTIMATES

a. Check specifications for method of measurement and payment for each item of work to be accomplished.

b. Review the schedules of values and methods of measurement for payment.

c. Assist the Project Manager in preparation of partial pay estimates.
1. Make timely measurements of work completed and work accomplished each pay period. It is usually a good idea to seek the contractor's concurrence.
2. Keep orderly, neat, and accurate records of measurements.

d. Check material on hand for which payment is being made for:
1. Fair market value of materials
2. Conformance with contract requirements (see submittal)
3. Proper storage and protection
4. Reduction in quantity by amount of material placed in the work

e. Monitor all increases or decreases in the quantity of work shown on the unit price schedules.
1. Make as accurate an estimate as possible of variations in quantities.
2. Report these variations in quantities promptly to the Construction and/or Project Manager.
3. Keep all estimates for future record.

RIGHTS-OF-WAY

Check that all rights-of-way are obtained prior to the start of any construction and entrance on property.

a. Require written evidence if Subcontractor-obtained.

b. Know the limits of rights-of-way and locations of benchmarks that may be used to determine location and elevations.

c. Post signs for workers and drivers to mark limits of operational area.

PHOTOGRAPHS

a. If allowable, check photographs for:
1. Views of major construction projected during various stages of progress.
2. Materials or construction related to changed conditions, claims, or potential claims.
3. Work in place for which removal has been ordered because of noncompliance with plans and specifications.
4. Photos of technical interest.
5. Bad and good safety practices by the contractors.
6. New methods of construction.
7. Property or material damages.
8. Manufacturer's Labels and Installation instructions.
9. Emergency conditions and safety violations.
10. Accident scenes.
11. Defective work.
    - **(a)** Check that each picture taken is completely described, identified, and dated.
    - **(b)** When possible, use tape measures or other readable measurement devices with pictures to show actual sizes and distances.

RECORD DRAWINGS

a. The Record Drawings should be reviewed monthly by the Project Manager to ensure they are correct.

b. Ensure that as soon as a change or addition is made in construction it is noted on the Record Drawing. This is the responsibility of the Site Superintendent and/or Project Manager. But in some cases it may be the Inspector's responsibility. Good inspection practice dictates that the Inspector keep good record drawings whether or not they are the set to be turned over to the client or owner.

c. See that the following items are considered in the changes for Record Drawings:

1. Size, type, and location of existing and new utility lines.
2. Layout and schematic drawings of electrical circuits and piping. Include sleeve drawings and diagrams.
3. Dimensions and details transferred from shop drawings.
4. Final survey records of cross sections, borrow pits, and layout of all earthwork.
5. Actual locations of anchors, construction, and control joints, etc., in concrete, where they are different from those shown on contract drawings.
6. Changes in location of equipment and architectural features.
7. Any and all Change Orders and Field Directives pertaining to the project.

PROJECT TURNOVER

The Inspector may have the responsibility of providing the client or owner the official turnover documents or, as they are sometimes called, the OEM manuals. The following records and materials will be needed as a minimum:

1. Record of property name, make, and model number of each piece of equipment.
2. All equipment test reports.
3. Approved shop drawings.
4. Operating and maintenance instructions.
5. Spare parts and tools.
6. Keys.
7. Guarantees with required contract and expiration date.
8. Record (as-built) drawings.

Check meeting minutes and contract documents for any additional requirements.

QUALITY CONTROL

- Remember that Inspector responsibilities begin at the inception of construction and end only with the final acceptance by the owner. The Inspector's main concern is to verify what has been done as well as what may have been left out as per the contract.

SAFETY

a. The overall Project Safety Programs as well as each individual contractor's safety program must be approved and enforced each and every day. This enforcement is usually not one of the duties of the Inspector, unless specifically called for in the contract. Large projects will have a full-time Safety Inspector, who may or may not report to the Resident Inspector.

b. Fully assess all work or operations for safety compliance before proceeding with inspecting for the technical compliance.

c. Be familiar with each contractor's accident prevention programs. These plans should be discussed and finalized before any construction begins.

d. Attend a different contractor's weekly safety meeting. Stand ready to evaluate and give advice as needed.

e. Mandate that applicable Occupational Safety and Health Act (OSHA) regulations be enforced.

INSPECTION FILES

The list below is a suggestion as to what files the Inspector will require for a project. Depending on the size and complexity of the project, the Inspector may need to add additional files as appropriate to ensure adequate documentation for the project.

1. General
   - **1.1.** Project Contract
   - **1.2.** Contractor's Contract
   - **1.3.** Clarifications
   - **1.4.** Request for Change Orders
   - **1.5.** Approved Change Orders
   - **1.6.** Field Directives
   - **1.7.** Claims
   - **1.8.** Schedule of Values
   - **1.9.** Request for Payments
   - **1.10.** Owner-furnished Labor/Materials
   - **1.11.** Selections
   - **1.12.** Shop Drawings
2. Correspondence
   - **2.1.** Architect/Engineer
   - **2.2.** Client
   - **2.3.** Contractor
   - **2.4.** Testing Labs
   - **2.5.** Consultants
   - **2.6.** Others/Misc.

3. Government Agencies
   3.1. Permits
   3.2. Fire Marshal
   3.3. Certified Payrolls
   3.4. Special
4. Field
   4.1. Transmittals
   4.2. Sketches
   4.3. Request for Information (RFI)
   4.4. Meeting Minutes
   4.5. Schedules
   4.6. Issues Log
   4.7. Daily/Weekly Reports
   4.8. Safety Plans/Reports
5. Technical Information
   5.1. One file per CSI Division
6. Closeouts
   6.1. MSDA Sheets
   6.2. Equipment Instructions
   6.3. Certificate of Occupancy
   6.4. Code Inspection Reports
   6.5. Warranties/Guarantees
   6.6. Record Drawings

RECOMMENDED EQUIPMENT

1. 12-ft steel tape measure
2. 100-ft cloth/plastic tape measure
3. 4-ft level
4. 8-ft level
5. Scales (architect/engineer)
6. Pocket calculator
7. Flashlight
8. Penlight
9. Camera
10. Speed square
11. Magnifying glass
12. Thermometer
13. Thickness gauge
14. Protective clothing
15. Hard hat
16. Safety glasses
17. Spud wrench
18. Circuit tester
19. Voltmeter
20. Ammeter
21. Wire gauge
22. Depth gauge

Construction Specification Institute (CSI) Numbers for Construction Projects

0200 Site Work
   Subsurface investigation & demolition
   Site preparation and excavation support
   Earthwork
   Tunneling piles and caissons
   Railroad & marine work
   Paving and surfacing
   Piped utilities
   Sewerage & drainage
   Site improvements
   Landscaping

0300 Concrete
   Concrete formwork
   Concrete reinforcement
   Cast-in-place concrete
   Precast concrete
   Cementitious decks and toppings
   Grout
   Concrete restoration and cleaning
   Mass concrete

0400 Masonry
   Mortar and masonry accessories
   Unit masonry
   Stone
   Masonry restoration, cleaning, and refractories
   Corrosion-resistant masonry

0500 Metals
   Metal materials, coatings, and fastenings
   Structural metal framing
   Metal joists
   Metal decking
   Cold-formed metal framing
   Metal/sheet metal fabrications
   Ornamental metal
   Expansion control
   Hydraulic structures

0600 Wood & Plastics
   Fastenings and adhesives
   Rough carpentry
   Finish carpentry
   Wood treatment
   Architectural woodwork
   Structural plactics (prefabricated)
   Plastic fabrications

0700 Thermal & Moisture Protection
   Waterproofing and dampproofing
   Insulation and fireproofing
   Shingles & roofing tiles
   Preformed roofing and siding
   Membrane roofing
   Flashing and sheet metal
   Roof specialties and accessories
   Skylights
   Joint sealers

0800 Doors & Windows
   Metal doors and frames
   Wood and plastic doors

Special doors
Entrance and storefronts
Metal windows
Wood and plastic windows
Hardware
Glazing
Glazed curtain walls

0900 Finishes
Metal support systems
Lath, plaster, and gypsum board
Tile
Terrazzo
Accoustical treatment and wood flooring
Flooring and carpet
Special flooring and floor treatment
Special coatings
Painting and wall coverings

1000 Specialties
Visual display boards, compartments, and cubicles
Louvers, corner protection, and access flooring
Fireplaces, exterior specialities, and flagpoles
Identifying and pedestrian control devices
Lockers, protective covers, and postal specialties
Partitions and storage shelving
Telephone specialties
Toilet and bath accessories and scales
Wardrobe and closet specialties

1100 Equipment
Maintenance, security & vault, teller & service, ecclesiastical, and library equipment
Theater & stage, instrumental, registration, and checkroom equipment
Mercantile, commercial, and detention equipment
Water supply and treatment equipment/hydraulic gates and valves
Fluid waste treatment and disposal equipment
Food service, residential, darkroom, athletic equipment
Industrial and process equipment
Laboratory, planetarium, and observatory equipment
Medical equipment
Navigation equipment

1200 Furnishings
Fabrics
Artwork
Manufactured casework
Window treatment
Furniture and accessories
Multiple seating
Interior plants and planters

1300 Special Construction
Special construction
Pre-engineered structures, aquatic facilities, ice rinks, and nuclear reactors
Tanks, tank covers, filtration equipment
Utility control systems
Industrial and process control systems
Recording and transportation control instrumentation
Solar energy systems
Wind energy systems
Building automation systems
Fire suppression and supervisory systems

1400 Conveying Systems
Dumbwaiters
Elevators
Escalators and moving walks
Lifts
Material handling systems
Hoist and cranes
Turntables
Scaffolding
Transportation systems

1500 Mechanical
Basic mechanical materials and methods
Mechanical insulation
Fire protection
Plumbing
HVAC/heat generation
Refrigeration
Heat transfer
Air handling and distribution
Controls, testing, adjusting, and balancing

1600 Electrical
Basic electrical materials and methods
Power generation
High-voltage generation
Service and distribution
Lighting
Special systems
Communications
Electric resistance heating
Controls and testing

REFERENCES FOR THE INSPECTOR

All references including Code Editions are to be the correct year as approved by the parties having jurisdiction.

- *International Residential Code* (Current Edition)
- *International Building Code* (Current Edition)
- *Building Officials and Code Administrators International*
- *BOCA National Codes* (Current Edition)
- *Southern Building Code Congress International Codes*
- *Uniform Building Codes*
- *National Electrical Code* (*NEC*)
- *International Fuel Gas Code* (Current Edition)
- *National Fire Protection Codes* (Current Edition)
- *International Energy Conservation Code* (Current Edition)
- *International Mechanical Code* (Current Edition)
- ACI 318-02/318R-02, *Building Code Requirements for Structural Concrete and Commentary*
- ACI 530/530.1-02/530R/530.1R-02, *Building Code Requirements and Commentary for Masonry Struc-*

tures and Specification for Masonry Structures and Related Commentaries

- ACI 301-99, *Specifications for Structural Concrete for Buildings*
- ACI 306.1-90, *Standard Specification for Cold Weather Concrete*
- ACI 305R-99, *Hot Weather Concreting*
- ACI 302.1R-96, *Guide for Concrete Floor and Slab Construction*
- ACI 117-90/117R-90, *Standard Tolerances for Concrete Construction and Materials (ACI117-90) and Commentary (ACI117R-90)*
- ACI SP-2-99, *Manual of Concrete Inspection*
- ACI 311.4R-00, *Guide for Concrete Inspection*
- American Concrete Institute (ACI) 347R, *Formwork for Concrete*

- *Corps of Engineers Specification Guide (COE)*
- Americans with Disability Act of 1990 (ADA)
- American Forest Association
- American National Standards Institute (ANSI)
- American Society for Testing and Materials (ASTM)
- American Wood Preservers Association (AWPA)
- APA—The Engineered Wood Association (EWA)
- Factory Mutual (FM)
- Truss Plate Institute (TPI) HIB-91
- OSHA Safety and Health (29 CFR 1926)
- Portland Cement Association (PCA), *Design and Control of Concrete Mixtures*
- American Society of Concrete Contractors (ASCC), *Contractor's Guide to Quality Concrete Construction*

2
CHAPTER

Design Quality Control Checklists

DURING DESIGN

Items listed in this chapter represent problems and/or situations that have a tendency to be prevalent on every project. As with all lists and checklists, it is not intended to be all inclusive; however, it is designed to assign accountability. The checklist should be incorporated into the actual contract with the Design Firm.

The Inspector of the Project should:

- Get on board early.
- Be an active participant in all design meetings.
- Anticipate problems and address them early.
- Provide guidance as required.
- Develop a team spirit with the designers.
- Provide advisement to the owner.

Communication is key to every successful building project.

> ## The 6 "P's" of Construction
> ### Prior Proper Planning Prevents Poor Performance

Identify all the main designers assigned to the project

Establish procedures to be used if a designer who worked on the project leaves the firm or is transferred

Credentials of Architect of record should be verified:

- Experience level
- Special certifications
- Work load
- *Stamps all drawings*

Other items that require review:

Keep team together throughout the project!

Retain design total compensation until project completion!

Résumés of all designers

Certification of all designers

Experience level of all designers

List of similar projects the firm has completed. Call them!

Establish language to be used on "Stamps" for Contractor.

Submittals—do not allow nebulous or imprecise language.

Go through the following lists on a repeated basis (all design meetings). Add to them accordingly!

Project:
Location:
Review Date:

NOTE: All items must be initialed either by the Discipline Design Chief or the Design PIC or Project Manager.

General Items

	Comments	Initials
"Work by others" and "work this contract" are clearly differentiated and interface points identified.		
All known existing features and improvements are properly and completely delineated and dimensioned.		
Orientation, horizontal coordinate systems, elevations, and vertical data are properly shown and referenced.		
Adequate subsurface investigations of the site have been made and logs and notes thereof are clearly shown on plans and referred to in specifications. Are boring locations adequate?		
The recommendations of *Geotechnical Report* have been considered in establishment of control elevations, foundation treatment, design, and assignment of bearing values for footing design. *Verify who will be responsible!*		
Adequate provisions have been made in the specifications for protection and maintenance of, access to, and utility services for existing facilities.		
All documents have been logically ordered and a table of contents provided.		
All documents, specifications, and plans have been dated and stamped. *Do not allow multiple documents to have the same date. (Track any and all changes from the Contract Set—even those that have been deleted!)*		
The scale and orientation of the drawings are consistent throughout the complete set of drawings.		
SOW shown in the RFQ has been "passed through" the current design directives to the individual subcontractors.		
Annotated, approved comments from previous reviews, as well as all correspondence and meeting minutes, are included in the design.		
List of the Building Codes and year that the design was based upon! Current?		
All required Permits—Local, State, and Federal—have been identified and responsibility assigned to the appropriate party.		

Functional Adequacy and Technical Feasibility of Design

	Comments	Initials
The functional and technical design requirements are in full accord with the RFQ directions. The applicable written guidance has been referenced in the design narratives (space allocations for buildings, per capita quantities for utilities, load capacities for floor or pavements, areas for hardstands, widths and lengths of runways, flow rate for fueling systems, etc.).		
All reasonably possible conditions of grading, loading, operations, utilities, and combinations thereof have been considered in the design and evidenced by the narrative and calculations.		
The design is based on use of *economical* and proven materials and equipment throughout.		
All required ADA design elements are clearly defined and shown. This includes all assembly points and ramps, as well as handrail locations.		

Sufficiency of Plans and Specifications as Contract Documents

	Comments	Initials
All necessary details, notes, schedules, and dimensions are shown on the drawings and are fully consistent throughout.		
Civil Details Required		
Soils testing (check locations)		
Gutter		
Storm drainage		
Existing utility locations		
Drainage schedule		
Erosion control		
Manholes		
Meter/water vault		
Gas lines		
Oil separator		
Fire loop w/PIV, hydrants		
Steam/condensation lines		
Area to be cleared (protection of existing features)		
Fence and gates (size of post, gate type, and widths)		
Demolition areas		
Typical pavements		
Bollard locations		
Misc. concrete pads		
ADA requirements and details		
Landscape plan and schedule		
Title blocks, drawing titles, drawing scales, and specification subtitles and section identification markings are shown and referenced.		
Requirements for installation of Owner-furnished equipment are clearly delineated.		
Ample space allowances are available for installation and servicing of equipment.		
The terminology used on the drawings agrees with that used in the specifications and does not repeat requirements stated in the specifications.		
Finish and color schedules have been coordinated with drawings.		
When drawings are printed at full size, all lettering, dimensions, symbols, wiring, and piping runs, etc., are clear and distinct.		
The drawings and specifications for all disciplines have been properly reviewed and coordinated to preclude conflicts.		
Complete legends for each discipline, including all symbols, are shown on the plans.		
North arrow and graphic/bar scales are shown correctly on all site plans.		

Civil/Site Design Checklist

	Comments	Initials
Existing and finished grades are shown.		
Haul routes, disposal/borrow sites, construction contractor's storage area, construction limits, and construction staging area are shown.		
Existing utilities, sizes, and materials are accurately surveyed and shown.		
New underground utilities have been checked for conflicts against the site plans. Who pays for additional expenses if utilities are not shown correctly ?		
Utility tie-in locations agree with mechanical stub-out plan.		
Profile sheets show underground utilities and avoid conflicts between new and existing.		
Property lines and limits of clearing, grading, turfing, or mulch have been shown and are consistent with architectural and/or landscaping plans.		
Fire hydrant and power/telephone pole locations correspond with electrical and architectural drawings.		
Basis of horizontal and vertical control is given and the control points are located properly with pertinent data shown: i.e., BM's/CP's elevations, coordinates, stationing, and/or start of construction.		
Top of valve boxes and manholes match finished grades, pavement, swales, or sidewalks.		
Boring locations, soil classifications, water table, and depth of rock are shown on the plans or in the write-ups, and are consistent with the building location.		
Rigid pavement joint plans are shown with reasonable spacing.		
Foundation coordinates are shown on the foundation plan and coordinated with architectural drawings.		
Finished floor elevations match on architectural and structural drawings.		
Civil specifications are coordinated with plans.		
Storm and sewage drains from the facility have adequate capacity.		
Directions to contractors are not duplicated in plan notes and in the specifications.		
Removal, demolition plan(s) is (are) complete.		
Construction limit line is shown, including removal of existing pavements when required.		
Sufficient attention has been given to preserving the natural terrain and tree cover.		
Sufficient general notes, dimensions, and elevations are shown for proper construction layout—construction base line (B/L) on finish grade spot elevations is indicated on graded earth areas and along pavements on "Grading and Paving Plan."		
Slopes of paved surfaces and graded earth areas are satisfactory and within criteria of maximum and minimum grades to prevent ponding and ensure positive drainage to the desired surface inlet or drainage outlet.		
Typical full and partial sections through site are sufficiently detailed to show relationship of finished floor elevation of building(s) to outside finished grades of both grassed and paved areas.		

Civil/Site Design Checklist

	Comments	Initials
The following typical sections are provided and adequately dimensioned:		
Concrete pavement		
Bituminous pavement		
Sidewalks, entrance drives, and roads		
Ramps/ADA requirements		
Other sections, as required		
All applicable detail sketches and construction notes are shown for curb and gutter, storm drain inlets, manholes, headwalls, painting pavement markings, riprap, erosion control measures, and other required items of sitework. Appropriate specification sections are referenced when applicable.		
If design includes concrete pavement, then the following are shown:		
Concrete joint layout plan		
Concrete joint details, and spacing		
Type of joint material, as per specifications		
Reinforcement/dowel locations		
Special details for reinforced concrete slab around storm drain inlets, when required		
Reinforcement of odd-shaped slabs, as applicable		
Tie-down anchors, when required		
ADA requirements (details, sections)		
Other details, as required		
"Storm Drainage Pipe Structures Schedule" shown in drawing detail(s) agrees with the drainage plan, drainage design analysis, and pipe profile(s) regarding inlet numbers, invert elevations, etc.		
Plant list agrees with the landscape plans.		
Locations of all soil borings, test pits, etc., correctly shown on the Grading Plan, and appropriate symbols included in legend.		

Storm Drainage Design Analysis

	Comments	Initials
Analysis contains an introductory page giving a brief description of the general terrain and/or site soil conditions, drainage patterns, basis of technical requirements, and other pertinent data affecting the proposed storm drainage system (formulae, appropriate rainfall, and runoff criteria, etc.).		
Drainage area map is complete, with subareas outlined, including possible "offsite" drainage, and all necessary "existing" and "new" drainage pipe and structures are indicated.		
Drainage tabulation forms are complete, and calculations are included for: ditch flow and culverts, when required; capacity and spacing of inlet openings; and correct pipe strength(s) (gauges/D-loads).		

Pavement Design Analysis

	Comments	Initials
Discussion of site conditions, etc., indicates that borings logs have been reviewed to ensure there are no unsuitable soils (heavy clays/organic soils) which would require removal and replacement in areas to be paved or in other critical areas. If these conditions exist, then provisions have been made for removal of same, and limits are shown on the drawings.		
Classifications of road usage, vehicle category, CBR/K values, and method of determining required pavement thickness and depths of compaction are satisfactory.		
For airfield pavements, characteristics of the subgrade and correct aircraft classification and wheel load are given, as well as other pertinent data necessary for determining the required pavement thickness.		
Assumptions used in the pavement foundation analysis are consistent with the CBR values specified in the final foundation report.		

Landscape Design Analysis

	Comments	Initials
The sprinklers, lighting, landscape, etc., correspond with the site limits, including the building and civil plans.		
Maintenance of landscape has been provided for in the design documents.		
Where applicable, appropriate "General Notes" are provided on the drawing(s) indicating trees to remain within the designated grading limits.		
All required plant items are included, and shrubs, etc., comply with approved plant list in the original Request for Proposal and/or other documents.		
Planting details are provided.		

Civil/Sanitary Design Checklist

	Comments	Initials
A. Sanitary Sewers		
Utility plan(s) show all existing and new sanitary sewers including manholes and cleanout locations. Are they compatible with the Landscaping Plan?		
Sizes of sanitary sewers are shown and all work can be located in the field from established BM's or baselines.		
Sanitary sewers are profiled, including building connections, and show pertinent data (existing and final grades, top and invert elevations, size, length, pipe crossing).		
Building connections have been coordinated with interior plumbing size and inlet elevations and locations.		
Sanitary sewers do not conflict with other underground utilities.		
Sewers are laid at sufficient slope to provide minimum velocity of 2 fps when flowing full.		
Minimum size sewer lines are shown for building sewers and for mains.		
Adequate cover for frost protection has been provided.		

Civil/Sanitary Design Checklist (*Continued*)

	Comments	Initials
Determination made to maintain flow in existing sewer system during construction of new sewers.		
Abandoned sewers are shown as plugged or removed.		
Sanitary sewer appurtenance details are provided.		
B. Water		
Pipe size is adequate for domestic water demand.		
Gate valves and valve boxes are properly located.		
Pipe size is adequate for fire flow demand.		
Number and location of new and existing fire hydrants are sufficient for adequate fire protection.		
Fire line entering building agrees with interior sprinkler plan P.I.V. shown.		
C. Design Analysis		
Domestic water line(s) are sized on correct fixture unit basis.		
Velocity and head loss are computed.		
Sanitary and waterline specifications include all items, sizes, and work shown on the contract drawings. Inapplicable paragraphs are indicated as "Not Used" and inapplicable reference publications have been deleted.		
All allowed pipe material options have been retained and correct strength of pipe has been selected.		
Special construction requirements shown on details are properly covered in the specifications.		

Architectural Design Checklist

	Comments	Initials
Site property lines and existing conditions match with survey or civil drawings.		
All dimensions are consistent, i.e., center to center, or face to face, etc.		
Building location meets all setback requirements, zoning codes, and deed restrictions.		
Building limits match with civil, plumbing, and electrical on-site plans.		
Locations of columns, bearing walls, grid lines, and overall building dimensions match structural drawings.		
Locations of expansion joints, all floors, match with structural drawings.		
Demolition instructions are clear on what to remove and what is to remain, and are coordinated with design documents.		
Building elevations match floor plans and have the same scale.		
Building sections match elevations, plans, and structural drawings.		
Building plan match lines are consistent on structural, mechanical, plumbing, and electrical drawings.		
Structural member locations are commensurate architecturally.		
Elevation points match with structural drawings.		

	Comments	Initials
Chases match on structural, mechanical, plumbing, and electrical drawings.		
Section and detail call-outs are proper and cross-referenced.		
Large-scale plans and sections match small-scale plans and sections.		
Reflected architectural ceiling plans are coordinated with mechanical and electrical plans.		
Columns, beams, and slabs are listed on elevations and sections.		
Door schedule information matches plans, elevations, fire rating, and project manual.		
Cabinets or millwork will fit in available space.		
Flashing through the wall and weep holes are provided where moisture may penetrate the outer material.		
Flashing materials and gauges are indicated or specified.		
Fire ratings of walls, ceilings, and fire and smoke dampers are indicated or specified.		
Miscellaneous metals are detailed, noted, and coordinated with the Project Specs.		
Equipment room or areas are commensurate with mechanical, electrical, and plumbing. Are they large enough? Doors? Venting? Future expansions?		
Limits, types, and details of waterproofing are coordinated with design documents.		
Limits, types, and details of insulation are coordinated with design documents.		
Limits, types, and details of roofing are coordinated with design documents.		
Skylight structures are compatible with structural, mechanical, and electrical designs.		
Piping loads hang from the roof or floors and are coordinated with the mechanical and structural drawings, and proper inserts are called for on the drawings.		
Mechanical and electrical equipment is properly supported and all architectural features are adequately framed and connected.		
All drawings showing monorails, hoists, and similar items have support details, notes, and the locations are coordinated with the architectural, structural, mechanical, and electrical drawings.		
Walls, partitions, and window walls are not inadvertently loaded through deflection.		
All window walls, expansions, and weeps are provided.		
All physically disabled requirements are coordinated with plumbing and electrical plans.		
Architectural space requirements are commensurate with duct work, conduit, piping, light fixtures, and other recesses.		
Architectural space requirements are commensurate with elevators, escalators, and other equipment.		
Dew point in walls, roof, and terraces, and vapor barrier has been provided as required.		

Architectural Design Checklist (*Continued*)

	Comments	Initials
Concealed gutters are properly detailed, drained, waterproofed, and expansion provided for.		
Grading around perimeter of building is compatible with civil drawings.		
Color finish schedules are on drawings.		
Interior valleys for buildings having large flat roofs are provided with saddles or crickets to eliminate formation of bird baths.		
When doing additions to existing structures, elevations of features such as doors and windows are exacting to the existing building. Brick veneer courses are made to line up perfectly. Color? Texture?		

Structural Design Checklist

	Comments	Initials
The design load conditions meet or exceed the Building codes and the Design Standards.		
The column orientation and grid lines on the structural and the architectural drawings match.		
The load-bearing walls and the building column foundation locations match with architectural drawings.		
The slab elevations match the architectural drawings.		
The depressed or raised slabs are indicated and match the architectural drawings.		
The limits of slabs on the structural drawings match the architectural drawings.		
The expansion joints on the structural drawings match the architectural drawings.		
The footing depth and cover are shown with the existing and final grades.		
The foundation piers, footings, and grade beams are coordinated with schedules.		
The footing and pier locations do not interfere with new and existing utilities, trenches, and tanks.		
The foundation wall elevations are the same as on the architectural drawings.		
The location of door and roof framing column lines and column orientation match the foundation plan column lines and column orientation.		
The structural perimeter floor and roof lines match the architectural drawings.		
The section and detail call-outs are proper and cross-referenced.		
The columns, beams, and slabs are listed in schedules and are coordinated.		
The column length, beam, and joist depths match with the architectural drawings.		
The structural dimensions match the architectural drawings.		
The drawings do not conflict with specifications.		
The architectural construction and rustication joints are correct.		

Structural Design Checklist (*Continued*)

	Comments	Initials
The structural openings are coordinated with the architectural, mechanical, electrical, and plumbing drawings.		
How will design errors and omissions be handled?		
The structural joist and beam locations do not interfere with water closets, floor urinals, floor drains, and chases.		
The structural design of roof and floors considered the superimposed loads, including the HVAC equipment, boilers, glass walls, etc.		
Cambers, drifts, and deflections have been coordinated with the architectural drawings.		
The concentrated load points on joists do not conflict with design by other disciplines, i.e., large water lines or fire main lines.		
Horizontal and vertical bracing, ladders, stairs, and framing do not interfere with doorways, piping, duct work, electrical, equipment, etc.		
The structural fire-proofing requirements are coordinated with the architectural requirements.		
Rock excavation is a base bid or a unit price.		

Mechanical Design Checklist

	Comments	Initials
A. Mechanical Design		
Mechanical plans match architectural and reflected ceiling plans.		
HVAC ducts are commensurate with architectural space and are not in conflict with conduit, piping, etc.		
Mechanical equipment fits architectural space with room for access, safety, and maintenance. Future expansion is allowed for.		
Mechanical openings match architectural and structural drawings.		
Mechanical motor sizes match electrical schedules.		
Thermostat locations are not placed over dimmer controls.		
Equipment schedules correspond to manufacturer's specifications and design documents.		
Mechanical requirements for special equipment; i.e., kitchen, elevator, telephone, transformers.		
Fire damper located in ceiling and fire walls.		
All structural supports required for mechanical equipment are indicated on structural drawings.		
All roof penetrations are shown on roof plans.		
Seismic bracing details are provided for all platforms which support overhead equipment and seismic flexible coupling locations and details are shown.		
B. Fire Protection Design		
Fire Alarm Plan (Building Code Required Elements) 1. Floor plan 2. Locations of alarm-initiating and notification equipment. 3. Alarm control and trouble signaling equipment.		

	Comments	Initials
4. Annunciation.		
5. Power connection.		
6. Battery calculations.		
7. Conductor type and sizes.		
8. Voltage drop calculations.		
9. Manufacturers, model numbers, and listing information for equipment, devices, and materials.		
10. Details of ceiling height and construction.		
11. The interface of fire safety control functions.		
Waterflow testing for all new sprinkler systems conducted and waterflow test data are indicated on drawings or in specifications.		
Detailed hydraulic calculations provided verifying that water supply is sufficient to meet fire protection system demand.		
Complete riser diagram is shown and checked.		
All piping from the point of connection to existing, to the top of the sprinkler riser(s), is shown on the drawings.		
All valves, fire department connections, and inspector's test connections are indicated on the drawings.		
Sprinkler main drain piping and discharge point are shown and detailed, and main drains discharge directly to the outside.		
The extent or limit of each type of sprinkler system, each design density, each type and temperature rating of sprinkler heads, and location of concealed piping are clearly specified or shown.		
Water-filled sprinkler piping is not subject to freezing.		
Detail of the sprinkler piping entry into the building is provided and includes details of anchoring and restraints.		
Aesthetics considerations are incorporated in the design of the sprinkler system; e.g., sprinkler piping is concealed in finished areas and recessed chrome-plated pendent sprinkler heads are used in finished area.		
Paddle-type waterflow switches are only used in wet-pipe sprinkler systems. The other sprinkler systems use pressure-type flow switches.		
The main sprinkler control valves are accessible from the outside.		
Fire ratings of fire-rated walls, partitions, floors, shafts, and doors are indicated.		
If spray-applied fire proofing is specified, the fire rating of the steel structural members is indicated.		
Location of required fire dampers is shown.		
Locations of all fire alarm indicating devices, pull stations, waterflow switches, detectors, and other fire alarm and supervisory devices are indicated on the drawings.		
The connection of the fire alarm and detection system to the installation-wide fire alarm system is clearly shown and detailed.		
C. Plumbing Design		
Plumbing plans match architectural, mechanical, and structural drawings.		
Plumbing fixtures match plumbing schedules and architectural locations.		

Mechanical Design Checklist (*Continued*)

	Comments	Initials
Compatibility of site piping limits interfaces with building piping.		
Roof drain locations coordinated with roof plan.		
Subsurface drains are located and detailed.		
Roof drain overflows are provided.		
Piping chase locations match architectural and structural drawings.		
All hot and cold water piping is insulated per the contractor's approved piping insulation display sample.		
Piping is commensurate with architectural space and not in conflict with conduit, duct, and structure.		
Piping openings match architectural and structural drawings.		
Structural design is compatible with plumbing equipment and piping requirements.		
Plumbing equipment schedules correspond to manufacturers' specifications and design documents.		
Floor drains match architectural and kitchen equipment plans.		
Site utilities have been accurately verified and site water and gas service requirements are met by supply utilities.		
Floor openings, i.e., drains, water closets, do not conflict with structural beams, joists, or trusses.		
Limits and confines where piping may be run are shown.		
Seismic bracing details are provided, and seismic flexible coupling locations are shown.		
Roof drain details are coordinated with other trades to show the installation of sump pans in ribbed sheet metal decks and the placement of roof insulation in and around the drainage fitting.		

Electrical Design Checklist

	Comments	Initials
Electrical plans match architectural, mechanical, plumbing, and structural.		
Location of light fixtures, speakers, etc., match with reflected ceiling plans. Checked with Fire Code, NEC.		
Electrical connections are shown for equipment, i.e., mechanical motors, heat strips, architectural, overhead doors, stoves, dishwashers.		
Locations of panel boards, transformers are shown on architectural, mechanical, and plumbing plans.		
Conduit chase locations match with architectural and structural drawings.		
Compatibility of conduit and light fixtures with architectural space and no conflicts exist with duct, piping, or structure.		
Electrical equipment structural requirements are met.		
Electrical equipment room fits architectural space, with clearance for safety and maintenance.		
Electrical voltage and phasing for all motors match on mechanical and architectural designs.		
Fixtures, speakers, clocks, etc., schedules correspond to a manufacturer's description and design documents.		

Electrical Design Checklist (*Continued*)

	Comments	Initials
Light fixture spacing and location to eliminate dark spots.		
Location of duplex outlets, telephones, fire alarms, clock outlets, etc., with architectural millwork and finishes.		
Limits and confines where conduits may be run are verified.		
Site utility service requirements are verified with supply utility.		
Seismic bracing details are provided, and seismic flexible coupling locations are shown.		

Drawing Checklist

	Comments	Initials
The checklist acquaints A–E's with printing and storage requirements for preparing contract documents. It is intended as a guide and does not replace detailed criteria provided elsewhere.		
All work depicted on drawings is readable at full size.		
A *minimum* of 1/8-in. height text is used within the body of drawing.		
New work is shown three pen weights heavier than existing (or clearly identified).		
Overlays and base sheet are composited to check for duplication or overprinting of features, notes, plans, sections, details.		
Titles, subtitles, scales, title block, and revision block information are complete and accurate.		
Titles of drawings agree with the titles listed on the Index of Drawings.		
The total number of drawings is shown only on the first sheet of the set.		
The signature block is on the first sheet of each discipline.		
Drawings are consecutively numbered in the rings beside title blocks.		
Site-adapted drawings have the appropriate notation in each revision block.		
Amended or modified drawings have the appropriate notation in each revision block.		
Symboling on drawings are standard and accompanied by the complete legend.		
The use of cross-referencing bubbles for locating sections, details, and elevations has been coordinated.		
On the Final Design submittal, all title block numbering (Plate no., File no., Sheet no., and Ring no.) is in place.		
All final contract drawings are free of tape, appliques, and shading.		
Colored ink is not used on plotted drawings.		
Multiple drawing layers are composited into a single reproducible sheet, or into one reproducible sheet per color overlay where color reproduction is planned.		
All basics and overlays are submitted in order; printing information appears below the cut line in the right-hand bottom corner.		

Checklist for Final Specification Preparation

	Comments	Initials
Project name, location, and project number are inserted as a header at the top of each heading on the first page of each section.		
Index on the first page of each section has been edited to correspond with paragraph titles in the narrative. For instance, if main paragraphs have been omitted they are shown "NOT USED" in the Index.		
All "gaps" have been eliminated where material has been omitted from the text.		
Other technical section(s) referenced within a section have been included, and either the section has been added or the paragraph rewritten to eliminate the reference.		
Omitted main paragraphs indicated as "NOT USED," and omitted subparagraphs indicated as "Not used."		
Omitted paragraphs are identified.		
All blanks are filled in, and all brackets are removed.		
All tables have been printed on one page (unless it is physically impossible to fit the table on one page).		
If tables require more than one page, headings have been duplicated on the second page.		
Margins are properly set a minimum of 25 mm (1 in.) on all four sides of sheet (right, left, top, and bottom).		
Page numbers are shown at least 12 mm (1/2 in.) from bottom of page and prefixed with the section number (C-15400-1, C-15400-2, etc.). All are counted and deemed correct.		
Paragraphs numbers are connected and made clear.		
Submittal Register has been fully edited and checked.		
Measurement and Payment paragraphs been properly edited on bid item projects or "Not Used" on "Lump-sum" bid projects.		
Verify that *all* required sections of the project specifications are included by comparing each division of the index to the drawings.		
Verify that the appropriate review level is indicated for all submittals listed on the Contractor Submittal Register, and that the Register agrees with edited technical specification sections.		

Fire Protection Checklist

	Fire-rated Assemblies
	1. Have you determined all required fire-rated assemblies from the plans?
	2. Do you have the accredited testing agency's specifications for the fire-rated assemblies?
	3. Are the rated assemblies constructed as specified?
	4. Are the fire-rated assemblies penetrated with either structural items, piping systems, or ducts?
	Fire-rated Doors
	1. Are they labeled as specified on the drawings? (Check label, hourly rating and temperature rise.)
	2. Does the self-closing device operate by closing and latching the door?
	3. Are the door sizes and direction of swing as shown on the drawings?
	4. Is the amount of glazing in the door as specified?

Fire Dampers	
1. Does the fire-rated construction enclose the sleeve?	
2. Has ⅛" to ½" been allowed between the sleeve and structure for expansion and construction? Is the fire damper sleeve not physically attached to the structure?	
3. Does the size of the retaining angle comply with the specifications?	
4. Is the connection between the duct and the sleeve a breakaway-type connection?	
5. Does the gauge of the damper sleeve comply with the plans?	
6. Is a damper access door provided?	
7. Is the fusible link listed (UL)?	
Construction Type	
1. Do you know the classification of the type of construction for the building?	
2. Do you know what fire ratings and structural materials are permitted for the building classification?	
3. Do you know the percent of openings in the exterior walls permitted for the construction type?	
Interior Finishes	
1. Have you verified that all ceiling and wall finish materials are in accordance with the plans?	
2. Have you verified the flamespread and smoke development of interior finish materials?	
3. Have you verified the critical flux index rating of flooring materials in the exits and exit accesses?	
Fire Stopping and Draft Stopping	
1. Have you verified that all fire stopping between floors is complete?	
2. Have you verified that draft stops are provided in all concealed combustible spaces as required?	
3. Are fire stopping materials as per specs? Approved?	
Exit Design	
1. Are travel distances to exits in accordance with the plans? Is the number of exits in accordance with the plans?	
2. Do corridors have minimum widths as shown on the plans? Are exit doors sized in accordance with the plans?	
3. Are dead ends limited to 20 ft?	
4. Are exit enclosures properly constructed?	
5. Are guard railings provided for balconies and are they structurally adequate?	
6. Are exit discharges clear and unobstructed?	
7. Have you checked tread depth for stairs?	
8. Have you checked riser height for stairs?	
9. Have you verified handrails as required for stairs?	
10. Have you verified guardrails as required by plans and specifications?	
11. Have you verified head clearance on stairs?	
12. Have you checked stair landing dimensions and door swing onto landing for reduction in width? Have you verified that stair width is in accordance with approved plans?	
13. Have you verified that all exit door hardware is in accordance with the approved plans?	
14. Have you verified access to the roof is in accordance with the approved plans?	
15. Does all door hardware operate?	
16. Are ramps sloped as shown on the approved plans?	
17. Are ramp widths as shown on the approved plans?	
18. Are exit lights located as required by the approved plans and as needed?	
19. Do the exit lights operate?	

20. Does the emergency system for the exit lights operate?
21. Is egress illumination properly installed?
22. Does the egress illumination operate properly?
23. Is the fire alarm system installed in accordance with the plans?
24. Does the fire alarm operate?
25. Have you operated the alarm from the sending stations?
26. Are egress windows in sleeping rooms provided with minimum clear openings?
27. Are smoke detectors installed in every dwelling, dwelling unit, and sleeping or guest room of a motel or hotel?
Sprinkler System
1. Is the sprinkler system installed in accordance with the approved plans?
2. Is the water pressure as specified in the approved plans?
3. Do all valves operate?
4. Have you followed the inspector's test?
5. Has paint been inadvertently applied to the sprinkler heads?
6. Is shelving, a structure, or a fixture obstructing any sprinkler head?
7. Are tamper switches and flow detector switches electrically connected to the fire department?

IBC CODE REQUIREMENTS AFFECTING PLAN REVIEW

Table 2-1   *Classifications*

Assembly	Group A
Business	Group B
Educational	Group E
Factory	Group F
High-hazard	Group H
Institutional	Group I
Mercantile	Group M
Residential	Group R
Storage	Group S
Utility and miscellaneous	Group U

Table 2-2   *Fire Alarm Plan (ICC Code Requirements)*

1. Floor Plan.
2. Locations of alarm-initiating and notification equipment.
3. Alarm control and trouble-signaling equipment.
4. Annunciation.
5. Power connection.
6. Battery calculations.
7. Conductor type and sizes.
8. Voltage drop calculations.
9. Manufacturers, model numbers, and listing information for equipment, devices, and materials.
10. Details of ceiling height and construction.
11. The interface of fire safety control functions.

Common path of egress travel. In occupancies other than Groups H-1, H-2 and H-3 (see Table 2-4), the common path of egress travel shall not exceed 75 ft. In occupancies in Groups H-1, H-2, and H-3 the common path of egress travel shall not exceed 25 ft.

Exceptions:

1. The length of a common path of egress travel in an occupancy in Groups B, F, and S shall not be more than 100 ft, provided that the building is equipped throughout with an automatic sprinkler system installed in accordance with Section 903.3.1.1 of the International Fire Codes.

2. Where a tenant space in an occupancy in Groups B, S, and U has an occupant load of not more than 30, the length of a common path of egress travel shall not be more than 100 ft.

3. The length of a common path of egress travel in occupancies in Group I-3 shall not be more than 100 ft.

Table 2-3 *Room and Area Firewall Separation Requirements*

Room or Area	Separation
Furnace room where any piece of equipment is over 400,000 Btu per hour input	1 hour or provide automatic fire-extinguishing system
Rooms with any boiler over 15 psi and 10 horsepower	1 hour or provide automatic fire-extinguishing system
Refrigerant machinery rooms	1 hour or provide automatic sprinkler system
Parking garage	2 hours; or 1 hour and provide automatic fire-extinguishing system
Hydrogen cut-off rooms	1-hour fire barriers and floor/ceiling assemblies in Group B, F, H, M, S, and U occupancies. 2-hour fire barriers and floor/ceiling assemblies in Group A, E, I, and R occupancies.
Incinerator rooms	2 hours and automatic sprinkler system
Paint shops, not classified as Group H, located in occupancies other than Group F	2 hours; or 1 hour and provide automatic fire-extinguishing system
Laboratories and vocational shops, not classified as Group H, located in Group E or 1-2 occupancies	1 hour or provide automatic fire-extinguishing system
Laundry rooms over 100 sq ft	1 hour or provide automatic fire-extinguishing system
Storage rooms over 100 sq ft	1 hour or provide automatic fire-extinguishing system
Group 1–3 cells equipped with padded surfaces	1 hour
Group 1–2 waste and linen collection rooms	1 hour
Waste and linen collection rooms over 100 sq ft	1 hour or provide automatic fire-extinguishing system
Stationary lead-acid battery systems having a liquid capacity of more than 100 gal used for facility standby power, emergency power, or uninterrupted power supplies	1-hour fire barriers and floor/ceiling assemblies in Group B, F, H, M, S, and U occupancies. 2-hour fire barriers and floor/ceiling assemblies in Group A, E, I, and R occupancies

Where an automatic fire-extinguishing system is provided, it need only be provided in the incidental use room or area.

Table 2-4 *Maximum Allowed Egress Routes per Occupancy*

Occupancy	Without Sprinkler System (ft)	With Sprinkler System (ft)
A, E, F-1, I-1, M, R, S-1	200	250
B	200	300
F-2, S-2, U	300	400
H-1	Not permitted	75
H-2	Not permitted	100
H-3	Not permitted	150
H-4	Not permitted	175
H-5	Not permitted	2000
I-2, I-3, I-4	150	200

See IBC Code and IFC Codes for special circumstances

Table 2-5 *Maximum Floor Area Allowances per Occupant*

Occupancy	Floor Area (in sq ft per occupant)
Agricultural building	300 gross
Aircraft hangars	500 gross
Airport Terminal	
Concourse	100 gross
Waiting areas	15 gross
Baggage claim	20 gross
Baggage handling	300 gross
Assembly	
Gaming floors (keno, slots, etc.)	11 gross
Assembly with fixed seats	IBC Sec. 1003.2.2.9
Assembly without Fixed Seats	
Concentrated (chairs only—not fixed)	7 net
Standing space	5 net
Unconcentrated (tables and chairs)	15 net
Bowling centers, allow 5 persons for each lane including 15 ft of runway, and for additional areas	7 net
Business areas	100 gross
Courtrooms—other than fixed seating areas	40 net
Dormitories	50 gross

Table 2-5 *Maximum Floor Area Allowances per Occupant (Continued)*

Occupancy	Floor Area (in sq ft per occupant)
Educational	
Classroom area	20 net
Shops and other vocational room areas	50 net
Exercise rooms	50 gross
H-5 fabrication and manufacturing areas	200 gross
Industrial areas	100 gross
Institutional Areas	
Inpatient treatment areas	240 gross
Outpatient areas	100 gross
Sleeping areas	120 gross
Kitchens, commercial	200 gross
Library	
Reading rooms	50 net
Stack area	100 gross
Locker rooms	50 gross
Mercantile	
Basement and grade floor areas	30 gross
Areas on other floors	60 gross
Storage, stock	300 gross
Parking garages	200 gross
Residential	200 gross
Skating Rinks, Swimming Pools	
Rink and pool	50 gross
Decks	15 gross
Stages and platforms	15 net
Accessory storage areas, mechanical equipment room	300 gross
Warehouses	500 gross

Table 2-6 *Minimum Loading per Occupancy*

Occupancy/Use	Uniform Load (psi)	Concentrated Load (lb)
Apartments (see Residential)	—	—
Access Floor Systems		
Office use	50	2,000
Computer use	100	2,000
Armories and drill rooms	150	—
Assembly Areas and Theaters		
Fixed seats (fastened to floor)	60	
Lobbies	100	
Movable seats	100	
Stages and platforms	125	—
Follow spot, projections, and control rooms	50	
Catwalks	40	
Balconies (exterior)	100	
On one- and two-family residences only, and not exceeding 100 sq ft	60	—

Table 2-6 Mimimum Loading per Occupancy (Continued)

Occupancy/Use	Uniform Load (psi)	Concentrated Load (lb)
Decks	Same as occupancy served	—
Bowling alleys	75	—
Cornices	60	—
Corridors, except as otherwise indicated	100	—
Dance halls and ballrooms	100	—
Dining rooms and restaurants	100	—
Elevator machine room grating (on area of 4 sq in.)	—	300
Finish light floor plate construction (on area of 1 sq in.)	—	200
Fire escapes	100	
On single-family dwellings only	40	—
Garages (passenger vehicles only)	40	
Grandstands (see Stadiums and arenas, Bleachers)	—	—
Gymnasiums, main floors, and balconies	100	—
Hospitals		
Operating rooms, laboratories	60	1,000
Private rooms	40	1,000
Wards	40	1,000
Corridors above first floor	80	1,000
Hotels (see Residential)	—	—
Libraries		
Reading rooms	60	1,000
Stack rooms	150	1,000
Corridors above first floor	80	1,000
Manufacturing		
Light	125	2,000
Heavy	250	3,000
Marquees	75	—
Office Buildings		
File and computer rooms shall be designed for heavier loads based on anticipated occupancy		
Lobbies and first-floor corridors	100	2,000
Offices	50	2,000
Corridors above first floor	80	2,000
Penal Institutions		
Cell blocks	40	—
Corridors	100	
Residential		
One- and two-family dwellings		
Uninhabitable attics without storage	10	
Uninhabitable attics with storage	20	
Habitable attics and sleeping areas	30	
All other areas except balconies and decks	40	—
Hotels and multifamily dwellings		
Private rooms and corridors serving them	40	
Public rooms and corridors serving them	100	
Schools		
Classrooms	40	1,000
Corridors above first floor	80	1,000
First-floor corridors	100	1,000
Scuttles, skylight ribs and accessible ceilings	—	200
Sidewalks, vehicular driveways and yards, subject to trucks	250	8,000

Table 2-6 *Mimimum Loading per Occupancy (Continued)*

Occupancy/Use	Uniform Load (psi)	Concentrated Load (lb)
Skating Rinks	100	
Stadiums and arenas	100	
Bleachers	100	
Fixed seats (fastened to floor)	60	
Stairs and Exits	100	
One- and two-family dwellings	40	
All other	100	
Storage warehouses (shall be designed for heavier loads if required for anticipated storage)		
Light	125	
Heavy	250	
Stores		
Retail		
First floor	100	1,000
Upper floors	75	1,000
Wholesale, all floors	125	1,000
Walkways and elevated platforms (other than exit ways)	60	—

Table 2-7 *Common Path, Dead-End, and Travel Distance Limits (by Occupancy)*

Occupancy	Common Path Limit		Dead-End Limit		Travel Distance Limit	
	Unsprinklered (ft)	Sprinklered (ft)	Unsprinklered (ft)	Sprinklered (ft)	Unsprinklered (ft)	Sprinklered (ft)
Group A (Less than 50)	20	20	20	20	200	250
Group A (50 or More)	75	75	20	20	200	250
Group B	75	100	50	50	200	250
Group E	75	75	20	20	200	250
Groups F-1, S-1	75	100	50	50	200	250
Groups F-2, S-2	75	100	50	50	300	400
Group H-1	25	25	0	0	75	75
Group H-2	50	100	0	0	75	100
Group H-3	50	100	20	20	100	150
Group H-4	75	75	20	20	150	175
Group H-5	75	75	20	50	150	200
Group I-1	75	75	20	20	200	250
Group I-2 (Health Care)	NR	NR	NR	NR	150	200
Group I-3 (Detention and Correctional-Use Conditions II, III, IV, V)	100	100	NR	NR	150	200
Group I-4 (Day Care Centers)	NR	NR	20	20	200	250
Group M (Mercantile)	75	100	50	50	200	250
Group R-1 (Hotels)	75	75	50	50	200	250
Group R-2e (Apartments)	75	75	50	50	200	250
Group R-3e (One Family)	NR	NR	NR	NR	NR	NR
Group R-4 (Residential Care/ Assisted Living)						
Group U	75	75	20	20	200	250
Group M (Covered Mall)	75	100	50	50	200	400

NR = No requirements.

3
CHAPTER

Sitework

LAYOUT AND QUANTITY SURVEYS

It is usually the responsibility of the contractor to establish the base lines, control points, and benchmarks necessary to completely lay out the work. The Subcontractor is required to utilize these established points to perform the necessary survey to execute his work.

a. Check that the established survey points have been found, and that they are protected from damage.

b. Confirm that the layout work is accurately performed by qualified personnel and that complete notes are maintained.

c. Ensure that adequate stakes and markings are provided and understood by all Subcontractors involved.

LAYOUT PROCEDURES

General

The Superintendent or Project Manager must establish the required order of accuracy of the layout surveys, if not stated in the specifications, prior to the start of any work.

Note: The layout surveys must be made with sufficient accuracy so that the construction that follows can be held within the specified tolerances. For example, if the specifications require a wall to be constructed within ½ in. of the location shown on the drawings, the work line laid out by the survey party will have to be correctly located within a much smaller margin of accuracy, say ⅛ in. or ¹⁄₁₆ in., to leave room for normal variations that must be expected in the construction work. On the other hand, the specified tolerances for the surface of a heavy rock fill might be 1 in. above and 6 in. below grade, in which case an error of as much as an inch in the layout would not be significant.

Deviations from Plans

If it is necessary or desirable to make changes in the location or dimensions of any part of the work, in order to rectify an error in the drawings or for any other reason, the Inspector must report the circumstances promptly to the Project Manager. The contractor suggesting the changes should summit the necessary documentation to the Project Architect or Project Manager for approval. Make sure that any approved changes are recorded on the record drawings.

QUANTITY SURVEYS

General

The surveying contractor is usually responsible for the original and final survey and for the compilation of quantities of work performed or finally in place where estimated quantities are included in the unit pricing. Surveyed quantities of certain materials and equipment may be required by the contract documents. The Inspector should have a copy for the files as well as for billing purposes.

Controls

Work should be tied into the same controls used for the construction layout. There must be a sufficient number of safely located reference points to ensure that the controls can be re-established in the event of any disturbance.

Instruments and Equipment

1. Are all instruments and equipment of a type and quality such that they are capable of maintaining the required degree of accuracy?

2. Have levels and transits been checked before starting work, to ensure they are in adjustment? When was the last calibration?

3. Does the contractor have a procedure for checking instruments periodically during the course of the work and having them sent in for calibration?

4. If adjustments are necessary at frequent intervals, this may indicate that an instrument is not in an acceptable condition.

5. Are tapes and rods checked for accuracy before starting work?

6. Does the contractor verify and understand metric (if used)? Are tapes in metric?

7. Are tapes and rods checked during the course of the work for damage or wear? Do not permit the use of tapes or rods which are difficult to read due to worn or damaged markings.

Measuring Procedures

General

Such items as orientation of the cross-sectional base line, frequency (spacing) of cross sections and individual shots, accuracy of tape and rod readings for individual shots, and required degree of precision in orienting the cross sections perpendicular to the base line all depend on irregularity of the terrain, shape of the excavation, fill, or other volume to be measured, and on the unit prices of the payment items involved. These standards must be established at the outset of the work, usually by the Superintendent or Project Manager.

Checking

a. Is all required leveling checked by closing on benchmarks?

b. Are distances checked at the end of each cross section?

Cross sections

a. Have specifications been reviewed and lists made of all payment items for which surveys will be needed to measure quantities?

b. Are sufficient intermediate cross-sections being taken to catch abrupt changes in slope of terrain?

c. Are plans referred to frequently enough to ensure that cross-sections are taken where needed.

d. Make sure a chart or marked drawings are being maintained to show locations of cross-sections taken to show the work in progress, and to ensure that cross-sections will be taken in advance of the work. All individual charts must be dated!

e. As surveys are taken, the Inspector must identify where actual conditions differ from those shown on the drawings. Share this information with the site management.

Examples:

- Ground surface differs from that indicated.
- Boulders or ledge rock occurring at locations or elevations are different from those indicated.
- There is evidence of ground water.
- Man-made objects such as well heads, fences, etc.
- Underground or overhead utilities.
- There is evidence of pollution or contamination.
- Archeological items of significance.

Report the existence of any of these conditions to the Project Manager. They may indicate substantial changes in contract payment quantities, or claims by the subcontractor due to differing site conditions.

Recording

a. Are all quantity measurements accurately recorded?

b. Is the record understandable to re-evaluate or examine all measurements and computations by a third party? Make sure dates and pictures are used where applicable.

CLEARING AND GRUBBING

Preconstruction Actions

Erosion and Sedimentation Control

Eroding construction sites are among the leading causes of water quality problems. For every acre under construction without a plan and controls, about a dump truck and a half of soil washes into a nearby lake or stream.

Problems caused by this sediment include:

1. *Dredging.* The expense of dredging sediment from lakes and ponds is a heavy burden for either owners, associations, or taxpayers.

2. *Lower property values.* Neighboring property values are damaged when a lake or stream fills with sediment. Shallow areas encourage weed growth and create boating hazards.

3. *Poor fishing.* Muddy water drives away fish like northern pike that rely on sight to feed. As it settles, sediment smothers gravel beds where fish like smallmouth bass find food and lay their eggs.

4. *Nuisance growth of weeds and algae.* Sediment carries fertilizers that fuel algae and weed growth.

5. *Road hazards.* When wet conditions cause traffic moving hazards.

6. *Local taxes.* Cleaning up sediment in streets, sewers, and ditches adds extra costs to local government budgets.

Preventing Erosion Is Easy

Erosion control is important for homes of any size or location. The materials needed are easy to find and relatively inexpensive—straw bales or silt fence, stakes, gravel, plastic tubes, sod, grass seed, rip-rap, and mulch.

Putting these materials to use is a straightforward process. Only a few controls are needed on most sites.

- *Silt fence* or *straw bales* to trap sediment on the downslope side of the lot and/or at yard inlets.
- *Soil piles* located away from any roads or waterways.
- *Gravel drive* used by all vehicles to limit tracking of mud onto streets.

- *Cleanup* of sediment carried offsite by vehicles or storms.
- *Downspout extenders* to prevent erosion from roof runoff.
- *Preserving* existing trees and grass where possible to prevent erosion.
- *Revegetating* the site as soon as possible.
- *Grassed* waterways and diversions.

Additional controls may be needed for sites that have steep slopes, and are adjacent to lakes and streams, receive a lot of runoff from adjacent land, or are larger than an acre. Most communities will require developing an erosion control plan that is subject to approval.

Erosion Control Measures

Straw bale or silt fence
- Put up before any other work is done.
- Install on downslope side(s) of site with ends extended up sideslopes a short distance.
- Place parallel to the contour of the land to allow water to pond behind fence.
- Entrench 4 in. deep.
- Stake (2 stakes per bale or 1 stake every 3 ft for silt fence).
- Leave no gaps between bales or sections of silt fence.
- Inspect and repair once a week and after every ½ in. of rain. Remove sediment if deposits reach half the fence height.
- Maintain until a lawn is established.

Soil piles
- Locate away from any downslope street, driveway, stream, lake, wetland, ditch, or drainageway.
- Temporary seed such as annual rye is recommended for topsoil piles.

Gravel drive
- Install a single access drive using 2- to 3-in.-sized aggregate.
- Lay gravel 6 in. deep and 7 ft wide from the foundation to the street.
- Use to prevent tracking dirt onto the road by *all* vehicles.
- Maintain throughout construction.

Sediment cleanup
- By the end of each work day, sweep or scrape up soil tracked onto the road.
- By the end of the next work day after a storm, clean up soil washed offsite.

Downspout extenders
- Not required, but highly recommended.
- Install as soon as gutters and downspouts are completed.
- Route water to a grassed or paved area.
- Maintain until a lawn is established.

Revegetation
- Seed, sod, or mulch bare soil as soon as possible.

Seeding and mulching
- Spread 4 to 6 in. of topsoil
- Fertilize according to soil test (or apply 10 lb/1000 sq ft of 20-10-10 or 10-10-10 fertilizer).
- Seed with an appropriate mix for the site.
- Rake lightly to cover seed with ¼ in. of soil. Roll lightly.
- Mulch with hay or straw (70–90 lb or one bale per 1000 sq ft).
- Anchor mulch by punching 2 in. into the soil with a dull, weighted disk or by using netting or other measures on steep slopes.
- Water gently every day or two to keep soil moist. Less watering is needed once grass is 2 in. tall.

Sodding
- Spread 4 to 6 in. of topsoil.
- Fertilize according to soil test (or apply 10 lb/1000 sq ft of 20-10-10 or 10-10-10 fertilizer).
- Lightly water the soil.
- Lay sod. Tamp or roll lightly.
- On slopes, lay sod starting at the bottom and work toward the top. Peg each piece down in several places.
- Initial watering should wet soil 6 in. deep (or until water stands 1-in. deep in a straight-sided container). Then water lightly every day or two for 2 weeks.

If construction is completed after the growing season, such as in September, seeding or sodding may be delayed. Applying mulch or temporary seed (such as rye or winter wheat) is recommended (or required). Straw bale or silt fences must be maintained until final seeding or sodding is completed in the spring.

Preserving existing vegetation

- Wherever possible, preserve existing trees, shrubs, and other vegetation.
- To prevent root damage, do not grade, place soil piles, or park vehicles near trees marked for preservation.
- Place plastic mesh or snow fence barriers around trees to protect the area below their branches.

Temporary Gravel Construction Entrance and Exit for Project Sites

Definition. A graveled area or pad located at points where vehicles enter and leave a construction site.

Purpose. To provide a buffer area where vehicles can drop their mud and sediment to avoid transporting it onto public roads, to control erosion from surface runoff, and to help control dust.

Conditions where practice applies. Wherever traffic will be leaving a construction site and moving directly onto a public road or other paved off-site area. Construction plans should limit traffic to properly constructed entrances.

Design criteria (typical). Aggregate size—Use 2- to 3-in. washed stone.

Dimensions of gravel pad

- *Thickness*: 6-in. minimum.
- *Width*: 12-ft minimum or full width at all points of the vehicular entrance and exit area, whichever is greater.
- *Length*: 50-ft minimum.
- *Location*: Locate construction entrances and exits to limit sediment from leaving the site and to provide for maximum utility by all construction vehicles. Avoid steep grades and entrances at curves in public roads.

CLEARING, GRUBBING, AND DISPOSAL WORK

Begin with a thorough review of the contract plans, specifications, and by walking the area with the Excavation Contractor and site management. Review all applicable restrictions.

Contract Schedule

1. A copy should be obtained and studied. Identify any areas that require revision.

Work Area

1. Determine whether limits have been established in agreement with plans and specifications.
2. Ensure that the area to be cleared and grubbed is marked.
3. Check the cut-off elevations.
4. Check depth and size of trees to be removed.
5. Make sure that utility lines are clearly identified and that the contractor verifys their locations.
6. Ensure that monuments, markers, and special trees are properly marked for protection.

Easements

1. Do not permit any contractors to enter any land where easements have not been received or when satisfactory agreement to enter has not been made, even if the land is only used as access to the project site.
2. Determine from the Project Manager that the rights-of-way are available for construction.
3. Mark all trees and vegetation that are to be undisturbed.
4. All access roads require signage for "Construction Entrance."
5. Do not allow contractors to exceed any weight limits.

Safety

1. Identify and post existing and potential hazards, including poison oak, poison ivy, and poison sumac.
2. Be sure that hospitals and clinics are identified to all contractors and their numbers are posted for all workers.
3. Check the contractor's accident prevention plan for each particular phase of operation *before* each phase begins.
4. Check personal protective equipment: hard hats, gloves, boots, etc.
5. Check that the contractor has fire fighting equipment on hand and it is operational.
6. Check that all equipment used on the project has had a recent safety check and that operators have been properly trained.

Power Lines and Other Utilities

1. Note whether they are properly posted, protected, relocated, or removed as required.
2. Do not allow unprotected work in and around "hot" power lines; arcing of electricity is possible.

Work Requirements

1. Verify the requirements and limitations for the different areas (especially on large projects).
2. Check the terrain, soil conditions, and foliage.
3. Ensure that Subcontractor has proper controls for erosion and drainage. Ensure that the Environmental Protection Plan, if required, has been approved and the contractor(s) is (are) familiar with its requirements.

Clearing

Swamping

1. Check removal of underbrush, vines, and small trees that will interfere with the later felling operations.
2. Determine the number and spacing of workmen in the area engaged in hand-clearing work (brush hook and axe operations) to ensure safe working conditions.
3. Inspect the operation of equipment (power saws, dozers, etc.) for sufficient clearance.
4. Check that workers are qualified to use special tools and that they do so in a safe manner.
5. Check protective devices and warning signals of equipment and operators.
6. Establish that the piling of material does not interfere with other planned stockpiling locations.

Felling Trees

1. Check all equipment.
2. Contractor fuel tanks must have containment for spills and adequate fire protection equipment available. Do not set the fire extinguisher next to the tanks!
3. Mark and protect trees to be left standing.
4. Check trimming of trees to be left standing.
5. Use approved tree wound paint on scars 1½ in. in diameter and larger caused by other falling timber.
6. If a tree professional is required, consult the Site Superintendent.
7. Ensure that felled trees are kept inside work limits.

8. Check rigs for topping operations.
9. Determine that workmen are kept properly positioned, within sight or hearing range, during tree felling operations.
10. Bulldozers and other heavy equipment must have overhead protection.
11. Check contractor's methods when hazards exist such as slopes, slippery terrain, rock, or outcrops.
    a. Check undercutting and wedging.
    b. Inspect the condition of such equipment as axes, crosscut saws, power saws, dozers, and winches.
    c. Prevent damage to trees to be left standing, existing structures, and/or structures under construction.

Stacking Felled Trees

1. Identify marketable logs (if required).
2. Inspect hand and power equipment used for bucking operations and the protective equipment required for operators.
3. Check stacking methods for pile locations, distribution of brush and logs in piles, compaction, and safe heights. Locate piles above high water level.
4. Make sure location will not create any water damming.
   a. Observe removal depths of all stumps and matted roots.
   b. Determine maximum size of roots and other materials that may remain in the area.
   c. Check method of measurement and payment.
   d. Cut stumps to ground level in revetment areas.
   e. See that depressions from grubbing are filled and compacted with approved materials.
   f. Inspect operation of equipment.
   g. Ensure that blasting procedures for stump removal are in accordance with approved methods. Check contractors' permits and/or licenses.
   h. Do not allow grading of hillsides during rainy weather if contractor is not ready to immediately reseed or sod.

Disposal

Determine the requirements for disposal and ensure that the operations are timely.

a. Check disposal of unsalvageable material. Debris must not be allowed to run off into streams, lakes, or adjacent properties.

b. Check piling and disposal equipment and procedures and the protective devices.

c. Check arrangements made by the Subcontractor for piling and storage of cleared debris on private lands.

    1. Check that the Subcontractor has a signed letter from the owner verifying arrangements made. Get a copy for your files.

    2. Report any unwarranted entry by the Subcontractor or unauthorized disposal of material on privately owned lands. Take pictures.

d. Locate debris areas above high water flow lines.

e. Check local fire district, county, state, Environmental Protection Agency, and U.S. Forest Service and all other requirements prior to burning. Obtain all necessary permits as required.

    1. Location and size of piles.

    2. Time of year burning is permitted.

    3. Standby fire-fighting equipment as required.

    4. Assigned fire watch (24 hours a day) until the fire is out.

Burning is not allowed in areas where it might cause damage to construction in progress, trees, existing structures, and others, or where the presence of heavy smoke may hinder traffic.

f. Check burning schedule for interference with other operations.

g. Do not permit burning in high winds. Check the local weather forecast.

h. Check suitability and safety of operations for periodic bunching of materials during burning.

i. Ensure that sufficient fire-fighting equipment and personnel are supplied by the subcontractor.

j. Ensure burning is complete. Reduce materials to ashes. Assign a person to watch. If in a remote area the watch is required to have means such as a cellular phone or radio for emergencies.

k. No burning is permitted on the surface of revetments, or roads unless specifically approved. Do not allow burning over buried utility lines, fuel, communication, storm drainage, etc.

Fig. 3-1 *Rock excavation.*

Cleanup

Thoroughly check final cleanup.

EARTHWORK

General

Scope

This section covers excavation, filling, and backfilling for building construction, embankments, grading, and preparation of subgrade for roadways, railroads, and other earthwork structures of similar nature.

Survey and Soils Control

1. A survey crew is generally assigned to conduct surveys or to check contractor's surveys. Soils testing is to be performed by an approved geotechinical firm.

2. The Inspector normally is not responsible for the performance of surveys or soil testing (unless qualified). However, he or she must be able to read and interpret the surveys and soil testing to determine that job requirements are met, and to make sure that the surveying and testing meet the specifications. All tests made and any action taken as a result of the tests are required to be documented and the Inspector is to have all copies.

3. Establish liaison with the Superintendent, survey personnel, and Project Manager, so that all concerned will be continually informed of the various surveys and soil tests. Also identify the standards and nature and scope of records, reports, and other construction data required, as well as individual assignments for obtaining data, and preparation and submission of reports.

Fig. 3-2 Soil technician checking soil compaction and moisture.

Samples of Material

Most contract specifications require that samples of certain types of soils, such as capillary water barriers under floor slabs and base material for roadways, are required to be tested by the contractor prior to use in the work. Use only tested and approved materials in the work.

Field Testing Soils

- Take a handful of the soil that you want to test. Spread it over your hand. If you can readily see the particles, chances are that it is sand or gravel. If it appears that more than half of the particles are more than ¼ in. in diameter, then it would be classified as gravel. If less than half are ¼ in. in diameter, then it is sand.

- Next take a handful of soil and wet it and then mold it into the shape of a cube. Then using only the pressure from your fingers, try to break it. If it makes a sound when breaking and/or cannot be broken easily, then the sample is more than likely a plastic clay soil type. If it breaks easily, then it is organic or a nonplastic clay type of soil. If, after the sample breaks, it crumbles easily, then it is a plastic silt or an organic silt.

The thread test

- Wet a handful of soil just enough to pat the soil in the palm of your hand. Add just enough water so that the soil will not stick to your hand. Next roll the soil into

Table 3-1 *Properties of Soils Classified According to the Unified Soil Classification System*

Soil Group	Unified Soil Classification System Symbol	Soil Description	Drainage Characteristic	Frost Heave Potential	Volume Change Potential Expansion
Group I	GW	Well-graded gravels, gravel–sand mixtures, little or no fines.	Good	Low	Low
	GP	Poorly graded gravels or gravel–sand mixtures, little or no fines.	Good	Low	Low
	SW	Well-graded sands, gravelly sands, little or no fines.	Good	Low	Low
	SP	Poorly graded sands or gravelly sands, little or no fines.	Good	Low	Low
	GM	Silty gravels, gravel–sand–silt mixtures.	Good	Medium	Low
	SM	Silty sand, sand–silt mixtures.	Good	Medium	Low
Group II	GC	Clayey gravels, gravel–sand–clay mixtures.	Medium	Medium	Low
	SC	Clayey sands, sand–clay mixtures.	Medium	Medium	Low
	ML	Inorganic silts and very fine sands, rock flour, silty or clayey fine sands, or clayey silts with slight plasticity.	Medium	High	Low
	CL	Inorganic clays of low to medium plasticity, gravelly clays, sandy clays, silty clays, lean clays.	Medium	Medium	Medium to Low
Group III	CH	Inorganic clays of high plasticity, fat clays.	Poor	Medium	High
	MH	Inorganic silts, micaceous or diatomaceous fine sandy or silty soils, elastic silts.	Poor	High	High
Group IV	OL	Organic silts and organic silty clays of low plasticity.	Poor	Medium	Medium
	OH	Organic clays of medium to high plasticity, organic silts.	Unsatisfactory	Medium	High
	Pt	Peat and other highly organic soils.	Unsatisfactory	Medium	High

Table 3-2 Soil Types

Gravel	Particles over 2 mm in diameter.
Sand	Particles between 0.05 and 2 mm in diameter.
Silt	Particles invisible to the eye but can be felt—0.002 to 0.05 mm.
Clay	Flour-like texture, sticky and plastic when wetted, crumpy when dry.
Organic	Vegetation that has decomposed.

a hotdog-like shape about ⅛ in. in diameter and then roll it into a ball. Repeat this several times; if the sample does not crack, then it is a plastic clay. If it cracks, then it is a nonplastic clay. If it cannot be rolled into the ball, then it is plastic silt. If it cannot be rolled into the hotdog shape, then it is a nonplastic silt. If the soil feels somewhat spongy, then it will probably fall into an organic class of soil.

- Need acceptable drainage to at least 5 ft from the foundation wall if soils are expansive or collapsible, i.e., clay.
- Three clays that can cause foundation problems:
  1. Kaolinite
  2. Montmorillonite
  3. Illite

Standards

1. Quality earthwork construction is required for all projects both small or large. Each procedure involved must be as per plans and specifications.

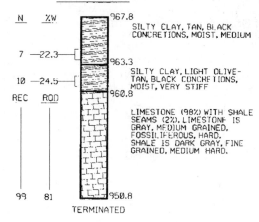

BORING 15

Fig. 3-4 *Sample of a soil boring.*

2. For large projects several classifications of excavation and of embankment materials are generally involved.

Note: Maintaining a chart or tabulation of quantities and distribution of materials may help the Inspector keep accurate records.

3. If the Subcontractor fails to operate according to specification requirements, notify the Site Superintendent or Project Manager. Keep a record of any recommendations and corrective actions taken in the daily report.

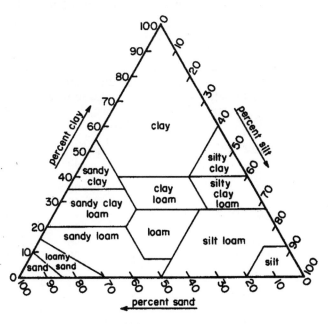

Fig. 3-3 *Soil pyramid.*

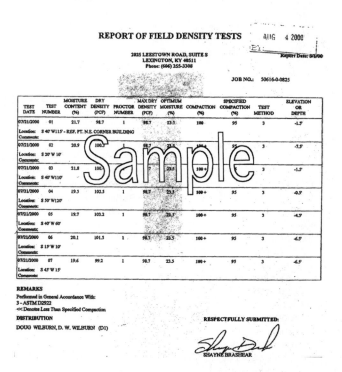

Fig. 3-5 *Sample soil density report.*

Table 3-3 *Soil Classifications*

Soil Grouping	USCS Symbol	Description of Soils	Volume of Expansion
Group I	GW	Gravels/gravel–sand mixtures/little fines	Low
	GP	Poorly graded gravel/gravely sands/little fines	Low
	SW	Well-graded sands/gravelly sands/no or little fines	Low
	SP	Poorly graded sands or gravelly sands, no or little fines	Low
	GM	Silty gravels, gravel–sand–silt mix	Low
	SM	Silty sand, sand–silt mix	Low
Group II	GC	Clayey gravel, gravel–sand–clay mix	Low
	SC	Clayey sands, sand–clay mix	Low
	ML	Inorganic silts and very fine sands, rock-flour, silty or clayey fine sands/clayey silts	Low
	CL	Inorganic clays of low to med. plasticity, gravelly clays, sandy clays, silty clays, lean clays	Med. to low
Group III	CH	Inorganic clays of high plasticity, fat clays	High*
	MH	Inorganic silts, micaceous or diatomaceous fine sandy or silty soils, elastic silts	High*
Group IV	OL	Organic silts and organic silty clays of low plasticity	Medium
	OH	Organic clays of med. to high plasticity, organic silts	High
	Pt	Peat and other highly organic soils	High

* Dangerous expansion possible!

Topsoil

Stripping

1. Check the contract requirement for stripping of top-soil.

2. Verify that the topsoil to be stripped meets the definition of topsoil. Verify the depth of stripping of topsoil.

3. Check that the stripped topsoil is not contaminated with unsuitable contaminants.

4. Be on the look-out for any potential signs of past pollution such as old fuel lines that have leaked!

5. Establish and maintain erosion control measures as required. In very windy areas it is necessary to cover the stockpiles to eliminate blowing dirt (or seed).

Stockpiling

1. Review and mark locations for stockpiles. Stockpiles must be planned for and not in the way of future construction efforts. In the way of future work?

Table 3-4 *Soil Lateral Loads*

Soil Description	Unified Soil Classification	Design Lateral Soil Load (psf)
Well-graded clean gravels; gravel–sand mixes	OW	30
Poorly graded clean gravels; gravel–sand mixes	OP	30
Silty gravels; poorly graded gravel–sand mixes	OM	45
Clayey gravels; poorly graded gravel–sand–clay mixes	OC	45
Well-graded clean sands; gravelly sand mixes	SW	30
Poorly graded clean sands; sand–gravel mixes	SP	30
Silty sands; poorly graded sand–silt mixes	SM	45
Sand–silt–clay mix with plastic fines	SM–SC	45
Clayey sands; poorly graded sand–clay mixes	SC	60
Inorganic silts and clayey silts	ML	45
Mixture of inorganic silt and clay	ML–CL	60
Inorganic clays of low to medium plasticity	CL	60
Organic silts and silt–clays, low plasticity	CL	Check codes
Inorganic clayey silts; elastic silts	MH	60
Inorganic clays of high plasticity	CH	Check codes
Organic clays and silty clays	CH	Check codes

2. Ensure the stockpiling is kept neat, well-drained, and in a safe condition at all times. It may be necessary to seed piles to keep wind erosion to a minimum.

3. Do not allow weeds to grow and seed on the stockpiles.

Spreading

1. Verify requirements for topsoil. Check that the quality of topsoil meets the specifications. Testing may be required.

2. Check for favorable soil and weather conditions.

3. Verify the scarifying depth of subgrade.

4. Check the method and required depth of placement for even distribution of topsoil.

5. Check the stripped topsoil to see that it is free from stones, sticks, roots, trash, or other material larger than ½ in. diameter, and free from all organics.

6. Topsoil is not to be compacted.

Excavation

Earth Excavation

1. Before starting excavation operations, photographs need to be taken of the construction area; also make sure that sufficient survey sections have been taken, and continue to take progress photographs during construction.

2. Review the log of borings to determine the rock shelfs, water tables, and to determine if unsuitable soils are likely to be encountered. Dewatering equipment may be necessary.

3. Unsuitable material must be identified and disposed of.

4. Check utilities and make sure the contractor has had them properly marked by the controlling authorities.

5. Evaluate materials being excavated against logs of borings. If differences are noted, notify the Project Manager.

6. Check that approved disposal areas and haul roads are used. Does the contractor have a water truck to control dust?

7. Check for location of required protection to sanitary and storm drains, electrical cables, communications cables, and gas lines subject to damage by heavy earth-moving equipment.

8. Ensure the utilization of only satisfactory materials from excavations.

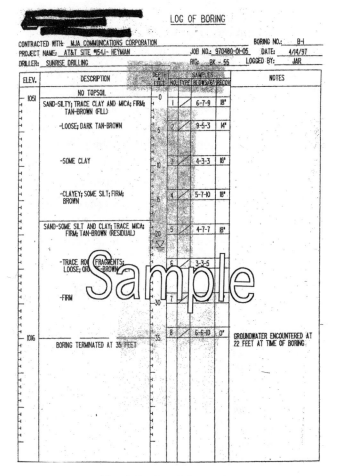

Fig. 3-6 *Sample boring log.*

9. Have a geotechnical firm verify moisture condition of suitable excavated materials in advance of the materials being used.

10. Ensure that excavation is performed in preplanned sequence.

11. Ensure that drainage is provided continually as excavation progresses.

   a. Do not permit ponding water in any construction area.

   b. Be sure that drainage ditches are maintained free flowing. Check erosion-control measures.

   c. Protect excavations from running ground water and topsoil contamination from rains.

12. Ensure that required tests for soil bearings are made upon completion of excavation.

13. Inspect borrow pits for:

   • Adequate stripping

   • Orderly removal of materials

   • Satisfactory drainage

   • Contractor safety measures

- Proper containment and posting of signs to prevent children or others from entering

14. Check borrow pit areas for conformance with final shaping and drainage requirements.

15. Determine average volume hauled for each type of hauling equipment. Record daily load count for various classifications of excavation when required for partial payments and or unit pricing. Make sure final cross-sectional surveys are taken and dated.

16. Review quantity surveys for payment purposes.

17. Examine all excavating equipment for compliance with prescribed safety requirements. All operators should have an equipment operations checklist and not rely on memory.

Earth Excavation for Buildings

1. Check for location and identification for site utilities before operations begin. Call the utility companies and have them marked.

2. Excavated material intended for use as fill must be free of all organic materials, and debris from building foundations, pavements, utilities, etc.

3. Ensure geotechnician verifies the foundation bearing and materials meet or exceed the contract specifications.

4. Check for the proper fill of all depressed areas or holes.

5. Correct any disturbed areas damaged from the operations.

Note: Fill is not permitted beneath footing to correct over-excavation unless approved by the geotechinician and compacted accordingly.

6. Inspect sides of excavations for safe slope (angle of repose) or if sides are made vertical, check OSHA requirements for bracing to safely retain the sides from possible cave-ins.

7. Check contractors' provisions made for preventing damage to adjoining property.

8. Observe methods of de-watering excavations and water disposal. Obtain permissions for runoff on adjoining property.

9. Ensure that footing beds in de-watered areas are not disturbed or softened.

10. See that proper sequence of excavation is as planned.

11. Inspect footing and foundation excavations for clearances sufficient to permit erection of forms, installation of services, and inspection.

12. Identify corrective methods used in cases of over-excavation.

   a. Never modify or change established elevations without written approval of the designing Engineer or PM.

   b. Correct over-excavation by placing approved, compacted backfill or concrete fill, depending on location.

   c. Keep a detailed record showing exact locations of any such corrective work.

13. Have contractor make provisions for preventing surface drainage into the excavated area.

14. See that footing drains are installed and sloped properly.

15. Check safety requirements for heavy equipment and operators working close to deep excavations.

Soil Poisoning

1. Check the specifications for soil poisoning under and around building structures.

2. Check for approval of material to be used and watch specifically for required concentration.

3. Check that the contractor had the MSDS advailable on the site.

4. Check application for coverage and quantity of material used.

5. Do not apply if rain is forecasted.

6. Use in or around waterways is prohibited.

7. Check EPA and local restrictions.

8. Keep and safeguard all certificates and warrantees for client handover.

Rock Excavation

1. Inspect Subcontractor's procedures for compliance with proposed and/or approved plan of operation.

   a. Drilling and blasting are the commonly used methods for rock excavation. However, picking, hoe-ramming, and wedging are also used.

   b. Check methods proposed for use in rock excavation for a safe operation (see below).

2. When covering soils have been removed, and prior to rock excavation, see that necessary surveys are made to determine pay quantities.

3. Determine compliance with all safety regulations.

   a. Carefully inspect handling, storage, and use of explosives (if used).

   b. Ensure compliance with City, County and/or State regulations relative to explosives.

c. Abide by provisions made for warning notices prior to blasting, including: curtailment of radio transmission, protection at highway and railroad crossings, and warning system for personnel.

d. Check compliance with restrictions on blasting near fresh concrete.

e. Check that requirements for monitoring of blasts are being carried out.

4. Check qualifications of Subcontractor's supervisor, drillers, and powdermen assigned to blasting operations.

Fig. 3-7 *Rock excavation with top laid back for safety.*

5. Inspect drilling and blasting equipment. Do not permit use of unsafe work or obsolete equipment.

6. Check drilling depth, materials encountered in drilling, and water in or flowing from holes. Indications of seams or faults can be shown by drill drop or changes in the rate of drilling.

7. Verify drilling pattern for blasting, quantity, and firing sequence of explosives.

8. Keep records of the quantities of explosives used.

9. Check results of each blast, particularly as final excavation lines and/or grades are approached.

a. Look for overbreak, damage to adjacent features, and safety. Drilling pattern and/or quantity of explosives should be modified if unsatisfactory conditions result.

b. Observe and record overbreak that results from structural weakness of rock for which payment will be made.

c. Have contractor correct unstable rock on sides of completed excavation.

d. Evaluate installation of necessary rock supports and recheck periodically to see that they are secure.

e. Ensure compliance with restrictions on blasting as final grades or excavation lines are approached.

f. Review all safety procedures with all trades working in and around the area.

g. Inspect scaling and removal of loose material from slopes.

h. Make sure that rock foundations are marked down to a satisfactory bed and side wall to receive concrete.

(1) Smooth, sloped surfaces are to be cut into rough steps or benches. Vertical height of steps or benches should be limited to 3 ft. Check OSHA requirements.

(2) Smooth, flat surfaces are to be roughened.

10. Evaluate trench excavation.

All excavations 20 ft or less in depth that have vertically sided lower sections shall have a maximum allowable slope of ¾ : 1. The trench shield must extend at least 18 in. above the top of the vertical sides.

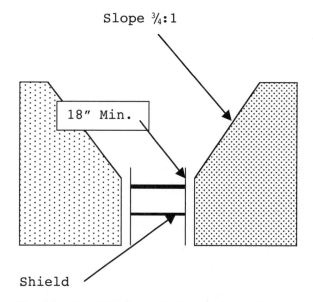

Fig. 3-8 *Typical OSHA sample of excavation requirements (based on soil types).*

a. Determine from codes if separate trenches are needed for water and sewer lines; also verify specifications.

b. Ensure that trenches are excavated to the minimum required depth below the bottom of pipe and to the required gradient.

c. Examine for and correct unstable rock on sides of trench.

d. Observe the drainage of excavated areas.

e. Check the disposal of material from rock excavation. Be sure that satisfactory rock is handled and used as required.

f. Watch for the excavation of trenches too far ahead of pipe laying.

g. Make sure that the specified density is obtained when backfilling trenches.

h. Maintain a complete record of all unusual conditions encountered.

i. Maintain a good photographic record of the excavation work and all backfilling operations.

j. Verify the contractor is following required OSHA trenching procedures. See Chap. 14 for additional information.

Foundations

Foundations Other Than for Buildings

1. Refer to previous sections for checking items relative to clearing and grubbing.

2. Observe depth of stripping and disposal of stripped material.

3. Examine earth foundation areas for evidences of peat, mulch, humus, organic materials, and other unsuitable material. Make sure they are removed.

4. Inspect filling and compacting of foundation depressions.

5. Evaluate densities of earth foundation materials prior to constructing embankment.

6. Check the drainage of the foundation area. Do not allow water to remain in footer excavations.

7. Ensure that rock foundations to receive impervious fill have all loose rock and other foreign material removed by specified methods. Similarly, check rock foundations to receive concrete.

8. Define special foundation treatment required.

9. Inspect marking and protection of all features that are to remain in the construction area, such as trees, poles, and structures. Taking pictures is a good method of recording their condition.

10. Record all cracks or faults, actual or possible, by taking pictures and/or plot maps, calling them to the Site Superintendent's attention.

Building Foundations

1. Check the actual foundation conditions with conditions shown on the drawings.

2. Check the layout. Make sure the foundation is in the correct place.

3. Make note of unsuitable materials in the foundation bed. Remove unsuitable materials and backfill with suitable materials. Keep accurate records of any such work.

Fig. 3-9 *Flooded foundation. The contractor did not allow for drainage.*

4. Review grade, slope, smoothness, and compaction of bottoms of excavations.

5. See that final grade for foundations in rock is carefully excavated so as not to cause breaking or shattering.

6. Consider the order of footing excavation. Lowest footing areas are usually dug first.

7. Check the effectiveness of de-watering excavations. Pump all water in footing excavations ASAP; do not allow the water to set.

8. Ensure that provisions are made to prevent surface water from entering excavations. Sump pits may be required.

9. Over-excavation at footings shall be filled with concrete during footing placement, not fill material. In some circumstances, if fill is used it must be compacted as per specs and inspected and tested by an approved geotechnical firm.

Caissons

1. Check for correct diameter and reamer, if belled bottoms are required.

Table 3-5 *Minimum Specified Compressive Strength of Concrete*

Locations of Concrete	Weathering Potential		
	Negligible	Moderate	Severe
Basement walls, foundations, and other concrete not exposed to the weather	2,500	2,500	2,500*
Basement slabs and interior slabs on grade, except garage floor slabs	2,500	2,500	2,500*
Basement walls, foundation walls, exterior walls, and other vertical concrete work exposed to the weather	2,500	3,000*	3,000*
Porches, carport slabs, steps exposed to the weather, and garage floor slabs	2,500	3,000*	3,500*

*Concrete in these locations that may be subject to freezing and thawing during construction shall be air-entrained concrete. Total air content (percent by volume of concrete) shall not be less than 5% or more than 7%.

2. Check the material removed with the soils report.

3. Are sufficient lengths of casings available?

4. Verify depths of hole. Record each with location and diameter and concrete test.

5. Check re-bar cages and clearances on the sides. Check plumbness and level of re-bar.

6. Check for correct elevation for the top of the caissons.

7. Make sure holes are dry. What plan does the drilling contractor have if water is encountered?

8. Check slump and strength of concrete.

Fig. 3-11 *Re-bar cage inserted for concrete. Note the small test hole at the bottom.*

Fig. 3-10 *Drilling rig.*

9. Do not allow for holes to be left in an unsafe manner overnight.

10. Do plans call for anchor bolts? Dowels?

Footer Design (Typical)

Questionable Soil

Where the bearing capacity of the soil is not definitely known or is in question, the Building Inspector may require load tests or other adequate proof as to the permissible safe bearing capacity at that particular location. To determine the safe bearing capacity of the soil, it shall be tested at such locations and levels as conditions warrant by loading an area not less than 4 sq. ft. to not less than twice the maximum bearing capacity desired for use. Such double load shall be sustained by

Table 3-6 *Minimum Width of Footings (in.)*

	Load Capacity of Soils (psf)			
	1,500	2,000	2,500	3,000
Conventional Light Frame				
1 Story	16	12	10	8
2 Story	19	15	12	10
3 Story	22	17	14	11
4″ Brick over Light Framing				
1 Story	19	15	12	10
2 Story	25	19	15	13
3 Story	31	23	19	16
8″ Hollow CMU				
1 Story	19	15	12	10
2 Story	25	19	15	13
3 Story	31	23	19	16
8″ Solid or Fully Grouted CMU				
1 Story	22	17	13	11
2 Story	31	23	19	16
3 Story	40	30	24	20

Table 3-7 *Soil Capacities for Design Width of Typical Spread Footers*

Materials	Load Bearing (psf)
Crystalline bedrock	12,000
Sedimentary and foliated rock	4,000
Sandy gravel, gravel (GW and GP)	3,000
Sand, silty sand, clayey sand, silty gravel, and clayey gravel (SW, SP, SM, SC, GM, and GC)	2,000
Clay, sandy clay, silty clay, clayey silt, silt, and sandy silt (Cl, ML, MH, and CH)	1,500

the soil for a period of not less than 48 hours with no additional settlement taking place.

EMBANKMENTS AND BACKFILL

Survey Control

1. Be familiar with locations of established benchmarks and base lines. Be sure that all control points are protected from damage during construction.

2. Determine that the Contractor's layout of work complies with the schedule requirements.

3. Check that all original ground surveys necessary for use as basis of payment to the Subcontractor are made in the project area, borrow areas, etc.

4. Ensure that surveys are made as each phase of the work is completed and as required in the specifications.

5. Review elevations of all completed excavations and embankments for compliance with specifications and drawings.

Preparation

Prior to the placement of embankment or backfill, check:

1. Removal of required vegetation, such as roots, brush, heavy sods, heavy growth of grass, decayed vegetable matter, rubbish, and other unsuitable material.

2. Plowing, stepping or benching of sloped surface steeper than 1 vertical to 4 horizontal. Check OSHA requirements.

3. Determine the Site Contractor's plans for the installation of all drainage and drainage structures before placing embankments.

4. Enforce all erosion control measures.

Haul Roads and Ramps

1. Inspect haul road layout. Restrictions on haul road type and haul routes may be imposed. If so, make sure signage and flagmen are positioned.

2. View construction ramps. Do not permit cutting through a compacted embankment; construct ramps out from the embankment.

3. Provide that original moisture content of haul road surfaces within permanent fill and excavation areas is maintained.

4. Periodically re-route vehicular traffic on embankment sections so that compacting effort will be uniformly distributed over the area.

5. Ensure that established roadways used for hauling are kept clean and smooth at all times, and that dust is kept to a minimum. Make sure Contractor has the use of a water truck on an as-needed basis.

Ditching

1. Maintain control of ditching operation with timely spot cross-sectioning, and the checking of grades, shapes, and slopes.

2. Areas of excessive excavation should be immediately backfilled and compacted.

3. Inspect for the complete removal of all roots, stumps, rocks, and foreign matter inside the excavated area.

4. Ensure the adequate disposal of excavated material.

5. Inspect the maintenance of the ditch. It is the Subcontractor's responsibility to maintain ditches until final acceptance of the work.

6. Be sure that the excavation is carried out in such a manner as to prevent surface water from flowing into a trench or other excavation.

7. Verify that OSHA requirements are followed.

Embankments

1. Meet classification of the soils being used for embankment formation. Dispose of all unsuitable material rapidly and check that it is not deposited in the embankment.

2. Evaluate Subcontractor-provided hauling and compacting equipment for safety, quantity, type, and general condition.

3. Check soil moisture requirement by determining that workable moisture content ranges are specified in the plans and specifications.

4. Determine that adequate, timely testing is performed and that results indicate that satisfactory moisture and density are obtained.

5. Determine the need for wetting, drying, or mixing of fill obtained from excavations or from borrow pits. Ensure that provisions are taken to uniformly check moisture condition of the soils in advance of needs.

6. Note controls for spreading embankment material.

    a. Ensure adequate mixing equipment (plows, discs, etc.) on-site for the mixing and breaking up of material and to provide uniformity of moisture distribution and material.

    b. Measure lift thickness; do not allow lifts in excess of 6–8 in. Check specifications.

    c. Notice uniformity of materials and moisture content.

    d. Ensure that there is a geotechnical technician making all required tests while work is progressing.

7. Note compaction of the material and record results.

    a. Start compaction operations as soon as possible after soil has been placed and satisfactorily conditioned with the specified moisture content.

    b. Check rollers and roller coverage.

    c. Check for tearing action in roller turn areas. Re-roll the area as necessary to obtain required density.

    d. Check roller action for evidences of excessive moisture content in the soil or for evidences of exceeding the soil bearing capacity. Soil densities should increase with an increase in the number of roller passes to the point of maximum density for a fixed moisture content.

    e. Evaluate operation of hand-manipulated tamping equipment for complete compaction coverage at optimum water content.

    f. Measure compacted layer thickness.

    g. Determine uniformity of density.

8. Check for surface drainage of each lift.

9. Ensure removal of oversize stones, roots, and debris from materials as they are placed.

    a. Check connections and plumbness of each section as progressively installed.

    b. Obtain and record readings each time the tubes are extended.

10. Determine that required record tests are taken.

11. Observe final alignment, section, and grade.

12. Seal each layer with light pneumatic equipment to preserve the moisture.

13. Have contractor proof roll final compaction and record findings.

14. Scarify and wet each layer prior to placing each succeeding layer, and check bonding between layers.

Backfill of Trenches and Building Excavations

1. Analyze condition of material at bottom of trenches and/or excavations. Remove wet or unstable material and replace with compacted, suitable material.

2. Evaluate material employed for pipe bedding. A minimum overdepth and bedding are required for rock trench bottom.

3. Look into the shaping of pipe beds for bottom of gravity storm and sanitary pipe. See that bell joint holes are being excavated so that pipes are uniformly supported over their entire length at the required grade. Grading should precede bell hole excavation.

4. Check the material for plasticity, gradation, and frost susceptibility, and see that the proper material is placed in the correct section.

5. Check width of trench bottoms for sanitary and storm drains. Width should not be greater than the dimensions specified.

6. Examine materials to be used for all backfill. Ensure that material is compacted under pipe haunches.

7. Inspect all excavations for removal of all debris and frozen material prior to backfilling.

8. Notice placement of layers and conformity of compaction and density results.

   a. Ensure that precautions are observed in backfilling against walls, and that sufficient time has elapsed for curing of concrete or block.

   b. Ensure de-watering of excavations to be backfilled.

   c. Ensure that material is placed at optimum moisture content.

   d. Observe all cold weather placing requirements.

9. See that sufficient depth of fill is over the pipe prior to permitting heavy equipment to pass.

10. Report to the Site Superintendent all indications of damages to walls or structures by backfilling operations, and determine if corrective action is required.

11. Check that proper safety precautions as per OSHA are taken for workers in the trench.

FINAL GRADING AND SUBGRADE PREPARATION

Final Grading

1. Check conformance to required lines and grades.

2. Ensure uniformity of smoothness and compliance with surface smoothness requirements.

3. Check drainage of finished surfaces.

4. Erosion controls are to be maintained.

5. Check for damaged stub-ups, clean-outs, drains, etc.

6. Observe the functioning of ditches and drainage structures.

Subgrade Preparation

Note: Subgrade is defined as that portion of the surface of any embankment, fill, or excavated area on which protective or base course materials are to be placed and all areas are to be topsoiled and seeded.

1. Check lines, grade, and shaping of subgrade.

2. Check for evidence of soft, yielding, or otherwise unsatisfactory material. Remove and replace as necessary.

3. Check for boulders and ledges in cut areas. Remove or break off to required depth.

4. Check moisture content and compaction immediately prior to placement of protective or base course materials.

DRAINAGE FILLS FOR SLABS AND STONE PROTECTION

Drainage Fills for Slabs

1. Check material for compliance.

2. Check rolling and/or operation of hand-operated tamping equipment for complete and uniform compaction coverage. Particularly watch compaction adjacent to walls, columns, and other similar areas.

3. Check layer thickness. Each layer of fill should not exceed 8 in., and 4 in. for hand-tamped areas.

4. Check for uniform required compaction.

5. Check shaping of surface for conformity with line, grade, and surface tolerances.

Stone Protection

1. Check approval of materials.
2. Check uniformity of stone size and/or gradation prior to and after placement.
3. Check equipment used and placement procedures.
4. Check thickness of protection.
5. Check lines and grades for conformity with tolerances.

UNDERGROUND PIPE SYSTEMS

Fig. 3-12 *Excavation for piping.*

General

This section covers excavation, trenching, backfilling, and laying of underground pipe systems. The types of underground pipe systems are as follows:

- Water
- Storm drainage
- Sanitary
- Fuel
- Steam and high- and low-temperature hot water.

Plans, Specifications, and Layout

Prior to the start of field construction, the plans and specifications should be thoroughly reviewed. The Inspector must check and review isolation of any utility lines that are to be worked on. Also, check and review the permanent disconnection and capping of critical utility lines, such as natural gas, fuel oil, or LPG that are to be abandoned.

Make sure contractor purges all fuel lines before they are abandoned.

1. Observe existing utilities and all possible interference with existing systems.
2. Confer with local utility companies to ascertain that all utilities are indicated on the Contract drawings. Utilities not shown on contract drawings should be entered on record drawings.
3. Check all electrical facilities, both aerial and underground, in accordance with the NEC.

Accessibility of Valves, Hydrants, and Manholes

All valves, hydrants, and manholes should be constructed in such manner that they can be utilized with ease when the project is complete. Hydrants should be accessible for operation. If possible, make the fire water system operational during the construction.

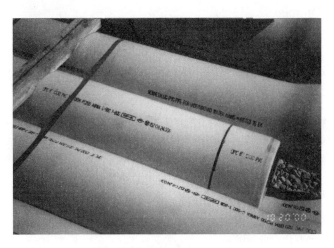

Fig. 3-13 *Check pipe grades.*

Lines and Grades

Lines and grades should be established and staked, and reference benchmarks should be set before any excavation or pipe-laying operations.

1. Check each type of utility being installed within a project for conflict as to the layout and elevations at each point of crossing.
2. Check for conflict with existing utilities.
3. Review codes for possible conflicts with specifications and plans.

Connections to Existing Utilities

Plan and coordinate connections to existing utilities. Under no conditions will an existing utility service be interrupted without full coordination with the owners and utility company involved.

Interference

Hold traffic interference to a minimum when installing utilities in or under walks, streets, or railroads. The contractor should ensure that jacking and boring of pipe, where required by the contract, are carried out in a manner so as not to disrupt traffic or other activities.

1. Determine that materials are on hand and that work is organized, so that interference will be held to a minimum.
2. Ensure that warning signs, barricades, and obstruction lights are placed and that regular traffic flows smoothly.
3. Traffic interruptions and detours must be coordinated with the proper road departments. Give plenty of advance notice.

Damages

See that completed pipe installations are not damaged by movement of construction equipment over or near the pipe during or after construction.

Testing

Pressure tests shall be performed prior to backfilling for visual inspection of joints. Alignment tests on all pipes and drain lines are made before backfill is completed. Test results shall be recorded.

1. Inspect every joint.
2. Ensure that corrective action is in accordance with requirements.
3. Do lines require flushing and cleaning after testing?

Pipes and Fittings

Material Compliance

1. Determine the quality of all material delivered to the work site for specification compliance.
   - Pipe, pipe fittings, valves, and other components should be checked to ensure that they carry the appropriate stamp and standards organization designations such as ASTM or ASME.
2. Compare official submittals with material brought to the job. Check labeling for type, grade, strength, and classification, and determine size and condition of materials. Make sure that pipe fittings, such as tees, ells, and couplings, are as on approved shop drawings.
3. Verify the quality of miscellaneous items such as valves, service boxes, stops, special connections, tapped tees, etc.

Handling and Storage

1. See that pipes and fittings are handled with the proper tools and equipment. Do not permit dragging and handling of pipe with chains, wire ropes, etc.
2. Check for damaged pipes, fittings, and pipe coating. Reject all damaged materials promptly, and have rejected materials removed from the job site immediately.
3. Make sure an adequate and accessible storage area has been provided.
4. Determine requirements for repairing damaged surface coatings.

Field Coating

1. Check the availability of an approved coating test device.
2. Check for breaks and abrasions of pipe coating.
3. Implement requirements for cleaning of surfaces before coating.
4. Follow the requirement for painting with primer and sealer.
5. Check for the requirement to coat edges or ends of pipe and bolt threads.
6. Check that temperature requirements are met. Follow manufacturers' instructions.

Laying Pipes—General

1. Check the gradient, line, and grade of the pipeline trench or bed before laying proceeds and after completion of each section.
2. Observe method of jointing permitted.
3. Use pipe manufacturers' installation information. Where there is a difference between this information and the contract specifications, this difference should be called to the attention of the Project Manager.
4. Check for cleanliness of the pipe (especially joints) during placement. Cover the pipe openings with temporary protection.
5. Ensure that all pipe to be placed on the earth is placed on dry, firm soil.
6. Check for obstructions in pipe, such as pipe plugs, and debris.
7. Do not allow for pipes to be left open overnight.

Water lines

1. Avoid high points as much as possible. Where high points occur, check specifications for requirements for vacuum and relief valves.

2. See that fire hydrants are plumb with the pumper nozzle facing the roadway. Check location of hydrant shut-off valve and post indicator valve (no shutoff valve between the PIV and the building it serves).

3. Measure height of the lowest nozzle above finish grade. An 18-in. clearance is usually required.

4. Check that fire hydrant threads conform and fit the hose or fire fighting equipment which will be connected to them.

5. Observe the hydrant barrel drain.

   a. Plug the drain in locations of high ground water where the hydrant is specified to have no drain. Check the hydrant valves to see if they are required to sit on a 4-in.-thick concrete pad.

   b. In the area where the ground water is low, the drain plug must be removed and drainage aggregate (18 in. of crushed stone) provided.

      • Reduce by 100 ft for dead-end streets or roads.

• Where streets are provided with median dividers which can be crossed by fire fighters pulling hose lines, or where arterial streets are provided with four or more traffic lanes and have a traffic count of more than 30,000 vehicles per day, hydrant spacing shall average 500 ft on each side of the street and be arranged on an alternating basis up to a fire-flow requirement of 7,000 gal/min and 400 ft for higher fire-flow requirements.

• Where new water mains are extended along streets where hydrants are not needed for protection of structures or similar fire problems, fire hydrants shall be provided at spacing not to exceed 1,000 ft to provide for transportation hazards.

• Reduce by 50 ft for dead-end streets or roads.

• One hydrant for each 1,000 gal/min or fraction thereof.

Table 3-8 *Minimum Required Fire Flow and Flow Duration for Buildings Type IA and IB*

Type IA and IB		
Fire Area (sq ft)	Fire Flow (gal/min) Measured at 20 psi	Flow Duration (hr)
0–22,700	1,500	
22,701–30,200	1,750	
30,201–38,700	2,000	
38,701–48,300	2,250	2
48,301–59,000	2,500	
59,001–70,900	2,750	
70,901–83,700	3,000	
83,701–97,700	3,250	
97,701–112,700	3,500	3
112,701–128,700	3,750	
128,701–145,900	4,000	
145,901–164,200	4,250	
164,201–183,400	4,500	
183,401–203,700	4,750	
203,701–225,200	5,000	
225,201–247,700	5,250	
247,701–271,200	5,500	
271,201–295,900	5,750	
295,901–Greater	6,000	4
—	6,250	
—	6,500	
—	6,750	
—	7,000	
—	7,250	
—	7,500	
—	7,750	
—	8,000	

Table 3-9 *Minimum Required Fire Flow and Flow Duration for Buildings Type IIA and IIIA*

Type IIA and IIIA		
Fire Area (sq ft)	Fire Flow (gal/min) Measured at 20 psi	Flow Duration (hr)
0–12,700	1,500	
12,701–17,000	1,750	
17,001–21,800	2,000	
21,801–24,200	2,250	2
24,201–33,200	2,500	
33,201–39,700	2,750	
39,701–47,100	3,000	
47,101–54,900	3,250	
54,901–63,400	3,500	3
63,401–72,400	3,750	
72,401–82,100	4,000	
82,101–92,400	4,250	
92,401–103,100	4,500	
103,101–114,600	4,750	
114,601–126,700	5,000	
126,701–139,400	5,250	
139,401–152,600	5,500	
152,601–166,500	5,750	
166,501–Greater	6,000	4
—	6,250	
—	6,500	
—	6,750	
—	7,000	
—	7,250	
—	7,500	
—	7,750	
—	8,000	

Table 3-10 *Minimum Required Fire Flow and Flow Duration for Buildings Type IV and V-A*

Type IV and V-A		
Fire Area (sq ft)	Fire Flow (gal/min) Measured at 20 psi	Flow Duration (hr)
0–8,200	1,500	
8,201–10,900	1,750	
10,901–12,900	2,000	
12,901–17,400	2,250	2
17,401–21,300	2,500	
21,301–25,500	2,750	
25,501–30,100	3,000	
30,101–35,200	3,250	3
35,201–40,600	3,500	
40,601–46,400	3,750	
46,401–52,500	4,000	
52,501–59,100	4,250	
59,101–66,000	4,500	
66,001–73,300	4,750	
73,301–81,100	5,000	
81,101–89,200	5,250	
89,201–97,700	5,500	
97,701–106,500	5,750	
106,501–115,800	6,000	4
115,801–125,500	6,250	
125,501–135,500	6,500	
135,501–145,800	6,750	
145,801–156,700	7,000	
156,701–167,900	7,250	
167,901–179,400	7,500	
179,401–191,400	7,750	
191,401–Greater	8,000	

Table 3-11 *Minimum Required Fire Flow and Flow Duration for Buildings Type IIB and IIIB*

Type IIB and IIIB		
Fire Area (sq ft)	Fire Flow (gal/min) Measured at 20 psi	Flow Duration (hr)
0–5,900	1,500	
5,901–7,900	1,750	
7,901–9,800	2,000	
9,801–12,600	2,250	2
12,601–15,400	2,500	
15,401–18,400	2,750	
18,401–21,800	3,000	
21,801–25,900	3,250	3
25,901–29,300	3,500	
29,301–33,500	3,750	
33,501–37,900	4,000	
37,901–42,700	4,250	
42,701–47,700	4,500	
47,701–53,000	4,750	
53,001–58,600	5,000	
58,601–65,400	5,250	
65,401–70,600	5,500	
70,601–77,000	5,750	
77,001–83,700	6,000	4
83,701–90,600	6,250	
90,601–97,900	6,500	
97,901–106,800	6,750	
106,801–113,200	7,000	
113,201–121,300	7,250	
121,301–129,600	7,500	
129,601–138,300	7,750	
138,301–Greater	8,000	

(a) Check thrust blocking and/or tie rods.

(b) Check for movement at joints, bands, dead ends, and hydrants.

6. Require the hydrostatic pressure test and specified leakage tests.

7. Ensure that the contractor sterilizes all phases of water lines that the construction work may have contaminated—not just the new piping runs.

  a. Main lines require thorough flushing with water until all mud and debris have been removed.

  b. Add disinfecting agent as required and in recommended quantities.

  c. Solution to remain in the line at least 8 and preferably 24 hr.

  d. There should be no less than 10 ppm residual at extreme end of line at end of contact period.

  e. Flush entire system thoroughly.

8. Ensure that valves are accessible; check the valve nut after backfilling is completed.

9. Check distance requirements between parallel and crossing water and waste piping.

Fuel Gas Lines

1. Do not permit lines to be buried under buildings, nor in trenches with other utilities, unless the Project Manager is aware of this.

2. *Enforce safety regulations rigidly during construction of gas and all other fuel lines.*

3. Continuously check the area with a detector for an explosive atmosphere. Record all readings!

4. When there is indication of an explosive condition, do not commence work until the explosive condition has been identified and cleared.

5. Install gas pipes above other utilities which they cross, and with a minimum cover of 2 ft. Pipe under

Table 3-12 Minimum Required Fire Flow and Flow Duration for Buildings Type V-B

Fire Area (sq ft)	Type V-B Fire Flow (gal/min) Measured at 20 psi	Flow Duration (hr)
0–3,600	1,500	
3,601–4,800	1,750	
4,801–6,200	2,000	2
6,201–7,700	2,250	
7,701–9,400	2,500	
9,401–11,300	2,750	
11,301–13,400	3,000	
13,401–15,600	3,250	3
15,601–18,000	3,500	
18,001–20,600	3,750	
20,601–23,300	4,000	
23,301–26,300	4,250	
26,301–29,300	4,500	
29,301–32,600	4,750	
32,601–36,000	5,000	
36,001–39,600	5,250	
39,601–43,400	5,500	
43,401–47,400	5,750	
47,401–51,500	6,000	4
51,501–55,700	6,250	
55,701–60,200	6,500	
60,201–64,800	6,750	
64,801–69,600	7,000	
69,601–74,600	7,250	
74,601–79,800	7,500	
79,801–85,100	7,750	
85,101–Greater	8,000	

Table 3-13 Number and Distribution of Fire Hydrants

Fire Flow Requirement (gpm)	Minimum Number of Hydrants	Average Spacing Between Hydrants (ft)	Maximum Distance from Any Point on Street or Road Frontage to a Hydrant
1,750 or less	1	500	250
2,000–2,250	2	450	225
2,500	3	450	225
3,000	3	400	225
3,500–4,000	4	350	210
4,500–5,000	5	300	180
5,500	6	300	180
6,000	6	250	150
6,500–7,000	7	250	150
7,500 or more	8 or more	200	120

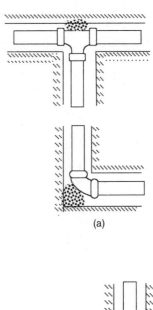

(a)

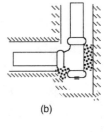

(b)

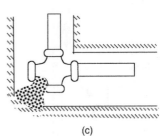

(c)

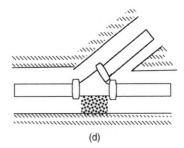

(d)

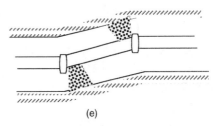

(e)

Fig. 3-14 Thrust blocks.

Table 3-14 *Minimum Required Area of Blocking*

	Thrust Block Area of Bearing			
	Square Feet of Bearing			
Pipe Size (in.)	**¼ Bend**	**⅛ Bend**	**1/16 Bend**	**Ts, Caps, Plugs**
6 or less	6	3	2	4
8	10	5	3	7
10	15	8	4	11
12	21	11	6	15
14	28	15	8	20
16	36	19	10	25
18	44	24	13	32
20	53	29	15	38
24	75	41	21	53

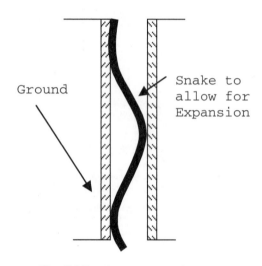

Fig. 3-15 *Plastic pipe in utility trench.*

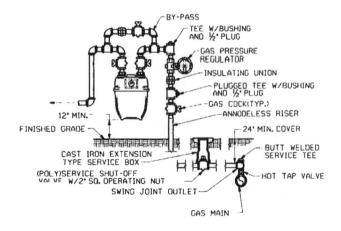

TYPICAL GAS SERVICE

Fig. 3-16 *Typical gas service installation.*

pavements or heavily traveled areas will be encased or located deep enough so that there will be no damage from heavy traffic. Verify local codes!

6. Check cleanliness of pipe before lowering into trench.

7. Check pipe coating for damage during connection, laying, and backfilling operations. Permit coated piping to be handled only by hand or with non-metallic flexible slings.

8. Keep pipe clean during installation by careful handling and by keeping ends of pipe closed.

9. Make sure contractor uses the correct marking tape over the pipe to identify the danger for anyone excavating in the future.

Fig. 3-17 *Gas line pressure test.*

Sanitary Sewers

1. Check distance separating sewers from water line. Always install sewer or force main below water line if the lines are within 6 ft horizontally, unless special provisions are taken at crossings; otherwise spacing must be at least 10 ft horizontally. Check for special code requirements where sewer lines or force mains cross above water lines. Require leakage tests for sanitary sewers and force mains. Check to see that spigot end of pipe is pointed downstream in pipeline.

2. Check that the designed grade is maintained between manholes.

3. Ensure that top elevation of manhole is flush with paving grades or higher than finished grade of ground surrounding area, as specified.

4. Check that the contractor is following specific safety precautions to be taken when working in sewers. Sewer gas is extremely dangerous. Review the contractor's Safety Plan.

Storm Sewers

1. Check that installation is performed by proceeding upgrade with spigot or tongue end of pipes pointing in the direction of flow.

2. Check the installation of all fittings, joints, connections at manholes, and connections to existing facilities.

3. Check grade, elevation, and finish of paved inverts.

4. Check that elliptical pipe sections are handled carefully in transporting, storing, and installing.

5. Check for installation of all subdrainage tile as shown on plans.

6. Where watertight joints are required, see that hydrostatic test requirements are met, and that rubber gaskets are not affixed more than 24 hr prior to pipe installation and are protected from sun, dust, and other deleterious agents.

7. Cover openings to prevent the entrance of dirt, debris, or animals into the pipe.

8. Require shaping the trench bottom as detailed in either the plans or shop drawings.

9. In rocky soils, over-excavate at least two pipe diameters and fill with suitable backfill material before placing pipe.

Heat Distribution Lines

1. All heat distribution piping is subject to expansion and contraction. Check that all lines are straight, both vertically and horizontally.

2. Expansion of piping will be absorbed by expansion joints or fabricated pipe loops. There must be room for the pipe loop to move as well as for maintenance.

3. Verify strength, security, and proper placement of anchors and supports.

4. Inspect rigid installation of anchors.

5. Require uniform pitch of steam pipe. *Trap all low points.*

6. Follow the manufacture-recommended installation procedure for the insulation materials, unless there are specific changes on the approved shop drawings. Log and report all discrepancies to the Project Manager.

7. Store and protect insulation from the weather.

8. Keep underground pipe conduit system dry during and after construction.

9. Examine waterproofing carefully. Check shop drawing details for both field-applied and factory-applied waterproofing to protect the insulation.

10. Valve pits should be watertight and have sumps or drains. Check for proper valves, fittings, supports, seals around pit openings, casing, drain, vents, sump, aluminum jacketing over insulation, ladder, etc.

11. Valve pits should also be checked to ensure that they are of the required size and that valves, flanges and other components have been located as to be accessible and to provide sufficient space for ease of maintenance. Is there a requirement for future work?

12. Check welding of pipe lines for compliance with specification requirements and the applicable codes.

13. Ensure that all changes in direction are done with approved type fittings.

14. Check welds or metal casing on underground steam lines for leaks or damaged asphalt coatings.

15. See that the proper class of underground system materials have been tested for acceptability.

16. *Require that all low points in the system are drained and high points are vented.*

17. Ensure that the field testing is satisfactorily performed, including hydrostatic, visual, and holiday detector tests.

18. Check for drainage of ground water from system.

Fuel Lines

1. Fuel lines in this section pertain to underground liquid petroleum systems.

2. Check drain connections at low points and air releases at high points.

3. Check that field application of covering on joints is not done until the pneumatic pressure test has been conducted.

4. Check if screens and filter elements are installed; check mesh and material; check installation for proper direction of flow; and check clearances for removal of screen and access to drain connection.

5. Check with an approved instrument for fuel vapors that may accumulate in pits or enclosed areas and can cause explosions.

   a. Provide adequate ventilation during operation in a liquid fuel area.

   b. Prohibit open fires, sparks, or static electricity in the vicinity of vapors which may be explosive.

   c. Check by use of a detector for explosive atmosphere.

JOINTING OF PIPES

General

- Check to see that all jointing surfaces are kept clean. Check to ensure that pipes of different materials, densities, or manufacturers can and are being properly joined. For example, heat fusion of plastic pipe of different densities is problematic. This piping should be joined with mechanical couplings to ensure a leak-proof connection. Also be aware of metal piping of different materials for cathodic protection.

   a. Do not join pipes in mud and water or while raining.

   b. Check tightness of joints.

Hot-Pour Joints

1. Hot-pour joints must be clean and dry. The presence of moisture may cause explosion and possible injury.

2. Check for uniformity of annular space.

3. Check method of application and make sure all joints are adequately filled.

4. Check temperature of the compound.

Poured Lead Joints

1. Check packing for uniformity and tightness.

2. Check depth and amount of lead being placed in joints.

3. Check the pouring operation; it should be done in *one continuous pour*.

4. Check driving during caulking. If lead is permitted to be displaced to a depth greater than 1/4 in., the joint should be remade.

Flexible Joints

1. Check for approved material, make, type, and number of splices.

2. Check placing and positioning of flexible gasket.

3. Check depth of gasket with a gauge.

4. Check use of approved lubricant.

5. Do not cover until a hydrostatic test is conducted as soon as possible.

Tapered End Couplings

- Drive tapered end couplings up tight when joining bituminous fiber pipe.

Cement Mortar Joints

1. Determine specific requirements for types of joints, whether oakum, diaper band, etc.

2. Ensure that mortar meets requirements of contract specifications.

3. Observe that the jointing operation will completely fill joints and form a bond on the outside.

4. Cure cement mortar joints.

5. Remove excess grout from inside and outside of pipe.

6. Protect from weather conditions until fully cured.

Pipe Threads

1. Cut pipe threads with the appropriate tools.

2. Provide proper length thread; the pipe taper is lost by overlength threading.

3. Ream pipe flush on the inside surface.

4. Apply joint compound to the threads on the pipe, not to the fittings.

5. Make up all joints tightly.

Copper Tubing Joints

1. Check types of pipes and fittings used against types required.

2. Ensure clean tubing before fluxing and soldering.

3. Cut copper tubing off square and remove burrs.

4. Check type of tools used for flaring compression type joints.

Welded Joints

1. Inspect contractors' qualifications and approved procedures.

2. Fabricate and weld as much as possible before lowering pipe into trench.

3. Check against possible cave-in when in trench.

4. Explore for explosive gases within pipes and before welding in fueling areas.

5. Check pipe ends for bevel.

6. Make a very careful inspection of welds in hard to reach areas.

7. Remove all welding slag before visual inspection.

Mechanical Joints in Manholes

- Install in accordance with manufacturer's instructions.

Flanged Joints in Manholes

Install gaskets and bolts and ensure that flanges are not damaged. Use proper bolt torquing procedures.

Corrugated Banding

1. Laps of all circumferential joints in the pipe should provide that the outside lap be on the *downstream side* of the joint with the longitudinal laps on the side of the in-place pipe.

2. All markings indicating the top of the pipe should coincide with the specified alignment of the pipe.

3. While the connecting band is being placed, ensure that the band is adjusted correctly.

4. Check the specifications, or the necessity, to use bituminous material at the joint after jointing.

Caps or Plugs

1. Close open ends of pipe when work is not in progress, and always at the end of each work day.

2. Keep pipelines clean of all debris, rodents, or water. Do not allow them to stay open overnight.

MANHOLES, CONCRETE CRADLES, AND ENCASEMENTS

a. Materials—Check material requirements with delivered materials at the preparatory inspection.

b. Construction

1. Check dimensions and layout.

2. Check placement of material such as concrete, reinforcement, brick, block, plaster, frames and covers, and rungs.

3. Check invert elevations and details of the invert channels in manholes.

4. See that manholes are not obstructed by dumped waste concrete or other construction material.

EXCAVATION, TRENCHING, AND BACKFILLING

a. Excavation—Existing underground utilities will be carefully marked by the appropriate utility company before excavation. Keep them protected for the duration of the work. Existing utilities will be suitably supported to prevent damage to them.

1. Check need for shoring or excavate to required side slope as per OSHA.

2. Report all damaged existing utilities immediately.

3. Note location of all unverified or unreported utilities for inclusion on record drawings.

4. Determine that access steps or ladders are provided in trenches, where necessary, and that they are maintained in safe condition. Check that all OSHA guidelines are strictly followed

b. Trenching

1. Begin trench excavation for sewers at the lower end of the line and proceed upgrade to protect the work from possible flooding, unless job conditions prohibit.

2. Check specifications and job requirements for maximum width of trench and minimum depth of pipe.

3. Check bed of the trench for grade and suitability of materials before any pipe is laid. If the trench is over-excavated, bring the bed to grade and compact. When encountering rock excavations, check the minimum over-depth specified and check that backfilling is performed with select bedding material.

4. Keep water from the trenches during construction. Use pumps or a well point system.

5. Check that final hand grading precedes pipe laying by no more than the amount of pipe that can be installed the same day.

6. Check excavation of bottom of trench. Is it graded and shaped to bottom quadrant of sewer pipe, and has excavation under all bells been performed as specified? Has approved gravel bedding material been used?

7. Inspect distance between potable water lines and sanitary sewer trenches for minimum allowable clearance.

8. Check pipe-handling procedures and do not allow loads being swung over the heads of workmen.

9. Are thrust blocks being used? Are they in the correct locations?

c. Backfilling—Ensure that special care is taken when backfilling around ductile iron. Recheck alignment after backfill operations.

d. Polyethylene sleeve

   1. Require leakage tests for sanitary sewers. Verify that specific backfill and compaction requirements for plastic pipe have been followed.

   2. Permit placement of backfill only between pipe joint locations until all lines have been tested and/or approved, unless job conditions require otherwise. In the case of pressure testing, place sufficient backfill material to prevent pipes from moving out of place. In the case of wrapped and coated piping, do not permit any backfilling until the coating at welds and fittings has been completed and the entire coating tested for holidays. Ensure that backfill in contact with the piping does not damage protective coatings. Make sure that all lines are located on as-built drawings before backfilling.

   3. Check backfill material, and inspect the placement operation for uniform layers (6–8 in.) on each side of the pipeline.

   4. Check that the contractor keeps foreign materials and large stones out of the backfill material.

e. Backfill operation check

   1. Thickness of each layer for moisture content and compaction.

   2. Do not allow machine compacted fill on top of a pipeline until required minimum cover has been placed.

   3. That there are no large or sharp rocks used.

   4. Have contractor check soil density testing as required.

Fig. 3-18 *Backfilling of storm pipe. The contractor has not adequately installed a bed under the pipe.*

5. Check sewer lines to manhole after the backfilling operation. Check from manhole for broken pipe, settlement in the line, lateral movement, and cleanliness.

SUMMARY OF SITE PIPING

a. The plans and specifications must always be followed unless the change has been approved by the Project Architect or Project Manager.

b. The Inspector must ensure that the contractor redlined as-built drawings and system O&M manuals are submitted to the owner as soon as possible after completion of all sections, or each section of the system if the construction is phased. In any case the appropriate (recorded) redlined drawings and O&M manuals should be given to the owner before any portion of the system is placed in operation by the client or the facility is occupied.

c. All items that are questionable should be reported to the Project Manager or appropriate site management. Follow up on their directives.

d. Maintain records of all training classes and attendees, and give to the client and owners.

PAVING

General

The objective in constructing any pavement is to provide a pavement satisfying design criteria and possessing such uniform characteristics of quality that it will have maximum serviceable life with minimum maintenance. This objective may be achieved only through painstaking attention to each step in the construction of a pavement. This check list will call to your attention items requiring careful thought and consideration relative to preparation of subgrade, construction of sub-base and base courses, priming of prepared base course, tacking bituminous binder course, and placement and finishing of the pavement surfacing.

Control Testing—General

1. The determination of satisfactory materials on the basis of samples submitted prior to construction and the design of starting mixes for bituminous and portland cement concrete pavements is normally a function of the design civil engineer.

2. Modify concrete batch weights to maintain uniformity of grading and to adjust for free moisture on the aggregates.

3. An approved geotechnical firm is usually required to conduct soils tests and to control mixing plant production. The inspector normally will not physically conduct tests, but he must be familiar with the tests and significance of tests results. The Inspector must have copies of all tests.

4. Minimum frequency of control testing is generally established by the contract specifications and as required by the Inspector.

5. Confer with subcontractor, engineer, Architect, and Project Manager and agree on how information is shared and how all concerned will be kept informed of test results, changes in character of materials, mix changes, behavior of mix, etc. During this conference, arrive at a understanding of the nature and scope of records, reports, and other construction data required, as well as individual assignments for obtaining data, and preparation and submission of reports.

Subcontractor Proposals

1. The specifications require the Subcontractor to submit samples of soils, aggregates for pavement surfacing, bitumen, concrete curing compound, joint-sealing compounds, etc., for testing prior to use in the work.

   a. Be familiar with arrangements for testing the materials.

   b. See that materials are submitted far enough in advance so as not to delay construction.

   c. Verify and maintain test results.

2. Obtain a copy of the minutes of all construction meetings and review their contents.

3. Check that all equipment used by the Subcontractor has the approval of the PM/Architect.

4. All equipment should have undergone a safety inspection before being allowed to operate on the job site.

5. Contractor fueling tanks for their equipment must have approved containment plan in case of leaks and spills. Fire-fighting equipment must also be on hand.

Preparation of Subgrade

Planning

1. Review the contractor's plan of the project construction area including clearing, grubbing and stripping requirements, location and extent of cut and fill areas, and nature of soils anticipated.

2. Is the planned order of work for handling, disposing, and using excavated materials suitable?

3. Determine that Subcontractor layout of work complies with specification requirements. Be familiar with required grades of finished subgrade.

4. Be certain that all original ground surveys, necessary for use as a basis of payment to the Subcontractor, are made in the project area, borrow areas, etc.

5. Check all drainage features and all embedded items that may be existing or are to be installed below top of subgrade.

6. Verify requirements for soils and compacting for various features of the work in cut and fill areas.

7. Is Subcontractor:

   • Using approved equipment?

   • Providing sufficient number of personnel?

   • Working in scheduled time?

Construction

1. Are the materials encountered of the same soils classification as those indicated on the geo-tech reports? If not, notify the Site Superintendent or Project Manager.

2. Is suitable material from excavations being used to the maximum extent practicable instead of being wasted?

3. Is excavation being performed to provide drainage from the excavated area at all times?

4. Are all pockets of soft, yielding, or otherwise organic material being removed and replaced with suitable material? If in doubt concerning removal of unsatisfactory material, consult the Project Manager and mark the locations on your set of drawings.

5. Have ground surfaces to receive subgrade embankment material been prepared?

6. Are embankments being constructed in the specified layer thickness of suitable material and compacted? Are geotechnicians present during testing?

7. Are embankment surfaces (subgrade) struck-off leveled and compacted to grade and surface smoothness tolerances?

8. Are surfaces in cut areas being compacted with suitable equipment to obtain the specified depth and degree of compaction? Are geotechnicians present during testing?

9. During the compaction of each layer of embankment, check to see if the moisture content of the soil

is being maintained at or near the optimum moisture content. If not, require drying by aeration or moistening by watering, as the case may be.

Fig. 3-19 *Soil compaction.*

10. Do prepared surfaces of cut areas (subgrade) meet grade and surface smoothness tolerances?

11. Is finished subgrade protected from traffic or other operations until the sub-base or base is placed?

12. Are subdrains required? If so, are they being installed at the required locations and grades?

13. Is trench backfilling being performed as required, using satisfactory materials compacted in specified layer thickness?

14. Is control testing of the subgrade and subgrade materials being performed in accordance with the sampling schedule?

15. Is contractor performing work on weekends unsupervised?

16. Do test results indicate that materials meet all specification requirements? If not, has action been taken to correct any deficiency? Where action has been taken to correct deficiencies revealed by tests, have retests been made, recorded, and cross-referenced to test failure?

17. Are all test results properly recorded on established reporting forms and adequate project records maintained?

Sub-base and Base Courses

Review Prior to Construction

1. Review project specifications.

   a. Verify requirements for the types of base course materials.

   b. Verify the maximum and minimum compacted layer thicknesses permitted.

   c. Verify the compaction requirements for each type of base course material.

   d. Verify acceptable construction procedures.

   e. Verify grade control and surface smoothness requirements.

   f. Check the specifications for items that may amplify or supplement the plans.

2. Review project drawings

   a. Review the type or types of base courses required for the various pavements involved.

   b. Verify the location and extent of the various types of pavements.

   c. Verify the total thickness of each base course type.

   d. Be familiar with grades to which the base courses are to be constructed.

   e. Be sure you are familiar with the location and nature of all utilities in place or to be constructed. You should plan to have offset reference stakes set so that the position of utilities may be determined after the area has been worked

   f. Verify the nature and location of all drainage features. Use flaggings or other visible markings to avoid any damage.

   g. Verify the location of all handholes, manholes, observation risers, and other structures or features to be installed within the pavement area.

3. Review proposed source or sources of base course material.

   a. Check with the Project Manager on status of materials approval and obtain copies of approval letters.

   b. Final approval is based on tests of material in place and compacted. Be familiar with results of tests on samples submitted which were the basis for approval.

4. Inspect approved source or sources of material.

   a. If material is bank run, be sure pit is stripped of all unsatisfactory material and that excavation will result in obtaining a uniformly acceptable material.

   b. If bank run materials are to be stockpiled, check that stockpile area is cleared and leveled as required and that proposed methods of stockpiling are satisfactory.

c. If material is plant processed, inspect plant and determine that processing, handling, and stockpiling methods established will produce uniformly acceptable material at a rate to satisfy approved construction progress.

5. Check all equipment brought on the job by the Subcontractor.

   a. Be sure that specified and approved equipment types are available.

   b. An adequate number of units in good mechanical condition must be furnished to perform the work in accordance with approved construction progress schedules.

6. Determine proposed procedures of handling high-quality base course materials.

   a. Some high-quality base course materials are required to be furnished in two or more size groups and blended by means of a mixing process.

   b. Check that equipment for mixing is on hand and is adequate to produce acceptable material at a satisfactory rate.

7. Determine that the necessary equipment is available for quality control of soils and for checking lines, grades, and smoothness of base courses as they are constructed.

Construction

1. Are the weather and temperature within the limitations specified?

2. Are the safety requirements met?

Hauling Equipment

1. Do not permit vehicles to continually follow in the same tracks in areas to be paved.

2. Spread out the tracking over the area insofar as possible.

3. See that hauling equipment complies with the safety requirements.

4. Determine if backup alarms are in good working order.

5. Check methods being employed to spread the material.

6. Methods differ for different types of base courses.

7. Check method of mixing.

8. Check method specified.

9. Check equipment used.

10. Check result being obtained.

11. Check to see that base and sub-base materials do not become mixed.

12. Check thickness of layers. Do they meet limitations on maximum and minimum layer thickness?

13. Check compaction of each layer of sub-base and/or base course.

14. Is approved equipment used and is uniformity and complete coverage of the area attained?

15. Watch for change in types of materials in that different types of materials may need to be compacted with certain types of equipment and different compactive effort.

16. Check equipment for conformance with specification requirements.

17. If approved equipment types or procedures do not produce the specified results, consult the Site Superintendent.

18. Check for ruts or soft yielding spots produced during rolling. Has proper action been taken to correct such weak spots either through stabilization procedures or removal and replacement of materials?

19. Is water being added to the base course material or is the material being aerated to obtain optimum moisture content and maximum compaction?

20. The contractor should provide the project with a geotechnical representative to make tests and to monitor them. Ensure that the site visits are timely and satisfy the needs of the project.

21. The specifications will adequately cover any special procedures necessary for the soil type used.

22. Be alert for poorly compacted material near manholes or other embedded items and along rows of grade stakes. It may be necessary to move or reset grade stakes.

23. Check each layer of material in place to determine compliance with thickness, density, and crown requirement.

24. Check the elevation crown and surface smoothness of the completed sub-base and base courses.

25. Check that sampling of in-place materials has been done in accordance with minimum sampling requirements and that test results are suitable. Verify with QA tests.

26. If failure to meet specification requirements is indicated by a test or tests, has the area involved been determined and immediate appropriate action taken to correct the deficiency?

27. Evaluate density tests daily.

28. Require that the specified width of shoulder be placed and compacted along with and at the edges of each layer of sub-base and base course.

29. Is grade control being performed by the Subcontractor, and has the work been spot checked by a survey party?

30. Proof-rolling base courses and tops of sub-base is necessary for some portions of flexible pavements. Check proof-rolling requirements.

31. Check that the edges of sub-base and base courses or shoulders are being treated as specified. Check requirements for forms.

32. Check for adequate maintenance of sub-base courses.

Granular Bases

Introduction

Aggregates are used in granular base and sub-base layers below the driving surface layer(s) in both asphalt concrete and portland cement concrete pavement structures. The aggregate base layers serve a variety of purposes, including reducing the stress applied to the subgrade layer and providing drainage for the pavement structure. The granular base layer is directly below the pavement surface and acts as the load-bearing and strengthening component of the pavement structure. The granular sub-base forms the lowest (bottom) layer of the pavement structure and acts as the principal foundation for the subsequent road profile, provides drainage for the pavement structure, and protects the structure from frost.

Granular bases are typically constructed by spreading the materials in thin layers of 150 mm (6 in.) to 200 mm (8 in.) and compacting each layer by rolling over it with heavy compaction equipment.

Materials

Aggregates used in granular base and sub-base applications generally consist of sand and gravel, crushed stone or quarry rock, slag, or other hard, durable material of mineral origin. The gradation requirements vary with type (base or sub-base).

Granular base materials typically contain a crushed stone content in excess of 50% of the coarse aggregate particles. Cubical particles are desirable, with a limited amount of flat or thin and elongated particles. The granular base is typically dense-graded, with the amount of fines limited to promote drainage. Granular sub-base is also dense-graded, but tends to be somewhat more coarse than granular base. Crushed content for granu-

lar sub-base is not required by many agencies, although provision of 100% crushed aggregates for base and sub-base use is increasing in premium pavement structures to promote rutting resistance.

Material Properties and Testing Methods

The granular base and sub-base generally make up the greatest thickness of the pavement structure, and provide both bearing strength and drainage for the pavement structure. Hence, proper size, grading, shape, and durability are important attributes to the overall performance of the pavement structure. Granular base and sub-base aggregates may consist of durable particles of crushed stone, gravel, or slag capable of withstanding the effects of handling, spreading, and compacting without generation of deleterious fines.

Some of the more important properties of aggregates for granular base and sub-base include:

- *Gradation*—A wide range of aggregate sizes and gradations are used depending on the pavement type and the conditions to which the granular base and sub-base will be subjected. The aggregate grading markedly influences the base stability, drainage (permeability), and frost susceptibility. Aggregates for use as granular base tend to be dense-graded with a maximum size of 50 mm (2 in.) or less, while granular sub-base can have a nominal maximum size commonly up to 100 mm (4 in.). The percentage of fines (-0.075 mm (No. 200 sieve)) in the granular base is limited, for drainage and frost-susceptibility purposes, to a maximum of 8%, with up to 12% permitted in granular sub-base.

- *Particle shape*—The use of angular, nearly equi-dimensional aggregate with rough surface texture is preferred over rounded, smooth aggregate particles. Thin or flat and elongated particles have reduced strength when load is applied to the flat side of the aggregate or across its shortest dimension and are also prone to segregation and breakdown during compaction, creating additional fines.

- *Base stability*—Granular base should have high stability, particularly in a flexible asphalt pavement structure. Large, angular aggregate, dense-graded and consisting of hard, durable particles, is preferred for stability. For maximum base stability, the granular base should have sufficient fines to just fill the voids and the entire gradation should be close to its maximum density. However, while base density maximizes at fines content between 6 and 20%, load-carrying capacity decreases when the fines content exceeds about 9%. Stability also increases with the percentage of crushed particles and increasing coarse aggregate size.

- *Permeability*—Since the granular sub-base provides drainage for the pavement structure, its grading and hydraulic conductivity are important. The fines content is usually limited to a maximum of 10% for normal pavement construction, and 6% where free-draining sub-base is required.
- *Plasticity*—The presence of plastic fines can significantly reduce the load-carrying strength of the granular base and sub-base.
- *Abrasion resistance*—Particles should have sufficient strength to resist degradation or breakdown during construction, under compaction or under traffic.
- *Resilient modulus*—Can assist in providing design coefficients for multilayered pavements by defining the relationship between stress and the deformation of granular base and sub-base layers.

Table 3.15 provides a list of standard test methods to assess the suitability of conventional materials for use in granular base applications.

REFERENCE FOR ADDITIONAL INFORMATION

- American Association of State Highway and Transportation Officials, *AASHTO Guide for the Design of Pavement Structures,* Washington, DC, 1993.

BITUMINOUS PRIME AND TACK COATS

Planning

1. Review project plans and specifications and then verify the following:

   a. Grades of bitumen specified for the prime and tack coat

   b. Quantity limitations of bitumen application for both the prime and tack coats

   c. Requirements for sampling, testing, and approval of the bitumen

   d. Application requirements and limitations

Table 3-15 Granular Aggregates Test Procedures

Property	Test Method	Reference
General specifications	Graded aggregate material for bases or sub-bases for highways or airports	ASTM D2940
Gradation	Sizes of aggregate for road and bridge construction Sieve analysis of fine and coarse aggregate	ASTM D448/AASHTO M43 ASTM C136/AASHTO T27
Particle shape	Flat and elongated particles in coarse aggregate Uncompacted voids content of fine aggregate (as influenced by particle shape, surface texture, and grading) Index of aggregate particle shape and texture	ASTM D4791 AASHTO TP33 ASTM D3398
Base stability	California bearing ratio Moisture–density relations of soils using a 5.5-lb (2.5-kg) rammer and a 12-in. (305-mm) drop Moisture–density relations of soils using a 10-lb (4.54-kg) rammer and an 18-in. (457-mm) drop	ASTM D1883/AASHTO T193 ASTM D698/AASHTO T99 AASHTO T180
Permeability	Permeability of granular soils (constant head)	ASTM D2434/AASHTO T215
Plasticity	Determining the plastic limit and plasticity index of soils Plastic fines in graded aggregates and soils by use of the sand equivalent test	ASTM D4318/AASHTO T90 ASTM D2419/AASHTO T176
Abrasion resistance	Resistance to degradation of large-size, coarse aggregate by abrasion and impact in the Los Angeles machine Resistance to degradation of small-size, coarse aggregate by abrasion and impact in the Los Angeles machine	ASTM C535 ASTM C131/AASHTO T96
Resilient modulus	Resilient modulus of unbound granular base/sub-base materials and subgrade soils—SHRP Protocol P46	AASHTO T274

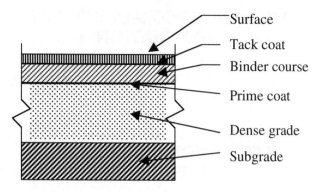

Fig. 3-20 *Bituminous pavements.*

Labels in figure: Surface, Tack coat, Binder course, Prime coat, Dense grade, Subgrade

2. Determine proposed sources of bitumen. Determine that test samples have been submitted, tested, and approved as required.

3. Check Subcontractors' equipment.

   a. Does distribution equipment conform to requirements for proper heating and circulation of bitumen, for control of spreading rate and uniformity of application, and for measuring and indicating devices?

   b. Is specified power equipment available and in good operating condition for the cleaning of surfaces to be primed or tacked?

   c. Verify requirements for equipment that will be needed to store materials.

4. Check with field geotechs to ensure that base course to be primed or pavement course to be tacked has met all test requirements.

5. Inspect base course and/or pavement course to be sure it is clean and free of foreign material or free water.

6. Check temperature and weather outlook to be certain that the bitumen will be applied in accordance with specified weather limitations.

Application

1. Is the area to be primed well defined by using strong lines to ensure sufficient primed area with true lines and neat edges?

2. Is surface ready to receive primer or tack?

   a. Is it cleaned of objectionable substances?

   b. Is it too wet or too dry for primer?

3. Check weigh bills and delivery tickets to be sure that the required and approved bitumen is being applied.

4. Make a continuous check on functioning of distributor.

   a. Is rate of bitumen application as specified?

   b. Does the amount of prime applied completely seal the surface voids of base courses without a surplus remaining on the surface after the curing period?

   c. Does the amount of tack applied appear to be sufficient for bonding but not in excess of the minimum necessary for bonding?

   d. Is application of bitumen uniform?

   e. Take prompt corrective actions in the event of unsatisfactory distribution.

5. Check to ensure that the bitumen has adequately cured in the minimum time or whether additional time is necessary for proper curing.

6. Is the primed or tacked area being protected prior to and during paving operations?

7. Record quantities of bitumen used each day.

8. Check that proper protection is provided to keep bitumen off posts, bollards, guard rails, and other structures during spreading operations.

9. Are junctions satisfactory?

Initial Checks

1. See that adequate fire protection is provided.

2. Review project plans and specifications.

   a. Verify the specification requirements for aggregates, aggregate handling, mixes, mixing plant, and hauling, placing, and rolling equipment.

   b. Verify construction procedures for spreading and rolling of the mix and preparation of joints.

   c. Verify requirements for grade control and surface smoothness.

   d. Be thoroughly familiar with physical location of pavements, thickness, and number of pavement courses required, and finished pavement grades and curb type and locations.

3. Aggregate submissions and mix designs

   a. Has approval of proposed materials and development of the starting job-mix formulas been made?

   b. Review and become familiar with aggregate and mix test data developed at time of approval.

4. Aggregate storage facilities

   a. Make sure the required separate stockpiles are provided.

b. Check preparation of area proposed for stockpiling of aggregates to ensure against contamination of aggregates.

c. Review stockpiling methods on transferring facilities. Check for segregation, contamination, and/or intermixing of the different aggregate sizes.

5. Check bituminous liquids storage facilities.

   a. Is storage tank capacity sufficient for at least a one day's run?

   b. Are pipe lines and fittings insulated?

   c. Are storage tanks equipped with heating facilities?

   d. Has a system been provided for circulation of bituminous liquids between the storage tank and the mixer?

Transporting, Placing, and Finishing Equipment

a. Check trucks that are hauling mix.

   1. Are truck beds tight, clean, and smooth?

   2. Have suitable covers been provided to protect the mix?

   3. Have facilities been provided for cleaning the inside of truck bodies and coating with a minimum amount of a concentrated solution of hydrated lime and water?

   4. If long hauls are contemplated, have the truck bodies been insulated to ensure that delivery temperatures of mix are within the range specified?

b. Check spreaders.

   1. Inspect for overall condition and freedom from obvious damage or fault.

   2. Stringline screed for correct alignment. Slight camber in the order of ⅛ in. is recommended on front screed.

   3. Check for indented and irregular area. This is a sign of a defective spreader.

   4. Check functioning of screed heating system.

   5. Inspect tamping bar for wear and proper movement and clearance from screed.

   6. Inspect hopper, barfeeders, distributor screws, and similar devices for ability to prevent segregation.

   7. Check controls for speed of motion and guidance.

c. Check rollers.

   1. Determine that the minimum number and types of rollers required have been provided.

   2. Check roller weights.

   3. Inspect roller wheels for smoothness. Check scrapers, sprinklers, and water-spreading pads for even wetting of wheel surfaces.

   4. Check operation of rollers for range of speeds and capability for changing direction smoothly.

   5. Inspect pneumatic-tired rollers for tire sizes, number of tires, tire pressures, tracking, weights, and wetting devices to properly moisten the tire surfaces. If not self-propelled, be sure towing unit is adequate and smooth-tired.

d. Check handtools.

   1. Necessary and specified rakes, shovels, and other hand tools must be available.

   2. Equipment for maintaining small tools in a hot condition must be provided.

   3. Material and equipment must be on hand for painting cold joints.

e. Sampling schedule for materials and mixes.

   • Prior to full-scale paving operations, it may be required that a quantity of mixture be produced to construct a test section. Observe all operations in connection with the test section as this is the basis of final determination of adequacy of materials, equipment, and construction procedures.

Paving Operations

1. General placing and finishing operations for hot and cold paving mixtures are essentially the same, except that the control of temperatures on delivery and during rolling is not required for cold mixtures.

2. Layout

   a. Check the Subcontractor's operation at the beginning of placement.

   b. Has he started at the highest lane in the area, and is he moving in the direction of the main traffic flow?

   c. Is the operation laid out so as to maintain a uniform surface?

   d. Will the lanes be placed so the joints will have required texture, density, and smoothness?

   e. Have the necessary stringlines been established?

   f. Stringline parallel to centerline of full pavement width should be used to align first lane. Pavement must be laid parallel to the centerline and excessive edge irregularities should not be tolerated.

Production Control

- Test methods to be followed are incorporated in the project specification by reference to appropriate Federal, Corps of Engineers, ASTM, etc., standards. Copies of all standards, together with current codes, should be on file in the Project Manager's and Site Superintendent's office and available as reference.

Placement of Mix

a. Check temperature of mixture (hot-mix) as delivered. Specifications prescribe minimum acceptable placing temperatures for hot-mix. Reject mixtures arriving at the spreader having temperatures less than the specified minimum.

b. See if weather limitations are being met.

c. Appearance of mixture should be noted as indication of properly batched and mixed material.

d. Plant Inspector should be notified immediately if mix is found unsatisfactory for any reason.

   1. Reject any unsatisfactory mix delivered and instruct Subcontractor to suspend placing operations until necessary corrections are made.

   2. Report such action to the Superintendent immediately.

   3. Record details of suspension of operation in the project log.

e. Hopper surfaces, tamper, screed, and other contact surfaces of spreader will be maintained in a clean condition.

f. Set screed on board of approximate thickness of new pavement at start of run (or lanes), or start off previously placed lane.

g. Check adjustment of screeds to lay course of desired thickness; make further adjustments if course thickness varies excessively.

h. Screed contour will be straight on rear (trailing) edge, crowned approximately ⅛ in. on front (leading) edge.

i. Check spreader operation frequently to prevent overloading and spilling, segregation, and irregularity in alignment and grade.

j. Check rate of feed of mixture from hopper, operation of distributing devices, and screed adjustment and take corrective measures promptly when irregularities in thickness, surface smoothness, or width of laid mixture are found.

k. Check irregular spots.

   1. Rakers will level off any irregular spots, but avoid excessive raking.

   2. Do not permit raked-out material to be cast over the fresh surface.

   3. See that all coarse particles unavoidably raked out to the surface are removed from the mat.

l. Preparation and placing of paving mixture at joints should be checked to ensure well-bonded and dense joint areas and even surfaces after rolling. Lane widths and layout of longitudinal joints for multiple course pavements must be planned so that joints of completed pavement courses will break by at least 1 ft.

m. Stop placement of paving mixture when weather conditions preclude laying down of pavement in a satisfactory manner. It is customary to permit loads in transit to be placed unless conditions are so severe that satisfactory results appear unattainable. Loads wet excessively by rain should be rejected.

n. Record of location of truck loads should be kept so that identity can be correlated with in-place samples subsequently taken for tests.

o. Keep weigh tickets of material placed as a basis for payments and to account for rejected loads.

p. Check yield twice daily by measuring area of lanes laid and comparing with weigh tickets of material delivered.

q. Check roller operation and rolling procedures.

   1. Rollers and rolling requirements are specified. Determine the precise rolling pattern and method to be followed during placement of the required strip. Check requirements for vibratory rollers.

   2. Are rollers being operated within specified speed range? Do they reverse without backlash? Are drum scraping and wetting devices functioning to keep wheels clean and moist?

   3. Keep rollers moving; do not permit them to stand on freshly placed mix. Be certain the rollers make the required overlap.

   4. Rubber-tired rollers are effective only on warm mixture; such rolling is not effective when the pavement temperature is below 130°F.

   5. Roll longitudinal joints while the mix is hot to produce a tight, well-bonded joint.

   6. Straight-edge check for surface smoothness compliance after the first roller coverage.

- The time to correct smoothness and grades is when rolling first begins.
  - To correct depressions, loosen material by raking to a depth of ½ in. and add necessary hot material by shoveling and raking.
  - To correct humps, loosen by raking to a depth below final grade, remove excess material, and rake smooth.

7. Check for compliance with smoothness requirements immediately following completion of tandem rolling. Take necessary corrective action.

8. Surface checking and movement of the mat on the first or second pass of the roller may be caused by one or more factors. Check base course surface for loose fines, moisture, or excessive primer, and the binder course surface for cleanliness and excessive tack coat.

9. Transverse and longitudinal cracks occurring under rolling usually result from soft base conditions but may be a result of inadequate control of mix temperatures and mix proportioning. Removal and replacement of pavement and base courses are generally necessary in the case of soft base conditions.

10. Check final finish of pavement to ensure that voids or scars are not left in the pavement surface.

r. Strict adherence to the grade and surface tolerances for all courses is mandatory.

s. Spot check daily finish grade and smoothness of pavement as a guide to continuing operations. Determine that complete grade and surface smoothness checks are made and recorded by the contractor responsible.

t. Finish shoulder adjacent to finished pavement as soon as possible.

u. Safety requirements should be rigidly enforced. See that the necessary respirators are used around toxic fumes.

v. Check for special requirements.

1. Check requirements for joints between old pavements and new ones, or for cutting into old pavements. Cold joints require different treatment than hot joints.

2. Check requirements for any special treatment required at edges of pavement.

3. Check requirements for any patching of existing pavements.

Check Sampling and Testing

Although the plant control laboratory is responsible for control, the Inspector has certain related responsibilities and must be familiar with sampling and testing procedures to determine that the pavement is properly constructed. The frequency of a complete coverage series of tests during a production run normally will be one set of samples for about each 200 tons produced. Check the contract specifications. A complete coverage series will normally include the following, but additional or repeated tests may be required:

1. Specific readings for temperatures of bitumen and aggregate on discharge from hot bins or dryer.

2. Samples from each hot bin for gradation tests and moisture determinations.

3. Samples of bituminous mixture after discharge from pug-mill.

4. A series of compaction tests (not less than four specimens per test) of the bituminous mixture sample for the determination of Marshall stability, flow, voids (total mix), voids (filled with asphalt), and unit weight.

5. An asphalt cement extraction test on the sample of bituminous mixture.

6. At the completion of determinations in the Complete test series, the laboratory posts results on trend wall charts. These charts should be reviewed frequently by the Inspector.

7. Check if plant control laboratory personnel will inspect batching and mixing operations for accuracy and at what intervals.

8. Sufficient cores (4 in. in diameter) or sawed samples for determining thickness, density, and composition should be taken and tested daily to determine conformance with the specification requirements.

Note: One-half the number of all density samples should be taken at a joint, so that the joint is approximately in the center of the sample to be tested. Corrective measures in rolling and placing methods will be taken immediately in the event density of samples does not conform to specification requirements. Check the specifications for nondestructive test methods such as the nuclear density meter test.

- Exchange of information and test data between placing Inspector and field laboratory should be ongoing during the operation. Coordination between the Inspector, the technician, and the paving engineer or his equivalent is a must.

SPECIAL APPLICATIONS OF ASPHALT

a. Check for special applications of asphalt such as for athletic facilities or special use material such as epoxy asphalt. A manufacturer's technical representative may be required at the site during mixing and laydown.

b. Check for gradation requirements and special mixes.

c. Check for special density and smoothness requirements.

d. Check for color coating.

  1. Check curing time of bituminous surface prior to applying coloring.

  2. Check rate of application of color coating.

  3. Check material being applied for required characteristics.

  4. Check application of line paint.

  5. Check for crazing, peeling, and bleeding of asphalt through the coatings.

  6. Check for testing requirements.

Concrete Pavement

Items to Check Prior to Beginning of Pavement

1. Review plans and specifications.

  a. Become familiar with location, extent, and grades of all pavement features.

  b. Become familiar with requirements for survey control.

  c. Verify required thickness of pavement and the required jointing system. Become familiar with the various types of joints required.

  d. Verify location and nature of embedded items within and below the pavement and of all structures within the pavement.

  e. Verify requirements for materials, plant, and equipment.

  f. Verify specified construction procedures.

  g. Determine the number of test specimens required. Review test specimen curing procedure.

2. Materials.

  a. Acceptance or approval of cement, air-entraining admixtures, concrete curing compounds, and joint-sealing compounds is based on tests of samples taken at origin of shipment. Each shipment to a project is inspected at origin and sealed or otherwise identified as accepted material. Determine through the Site Superintendent that sources of materials have been proposed by the Subcontractor and that arrangements have been made for sampling and testing.

  b. When above-mentioned materials arrive on site, check approvals and identifications to be certain that materials have been shipped from pretested stock.

  c. Determine that proper storage facilities for the above-mentioned materials have been provided.

  d. Check on concrete aggregate.

    (1) Have samples been submitted for acceptance tests and mix designs in accordance with specification requirements? Study aggregate approvals as available and be familiar with the source and type of aggregate and results of tests on samples submitted.

    (2) Determine that the aggregate storage area has been prepared to avoid inclusion of foreign material with the aggregate and that the area is graded to provide drainage.

    (3) Give particular attention to initial aggregate shipments to determine that the materials furnished are similar in every respect to samples submitted for approval.

  e. Check to see that miscellaneous materials, such as reinforcements, tie bars, dowels, joint fillers, and water, have been approved.

  f. Check requirement for obtaining approval of the design mix for the concrete which will be used. Make sure that exact proportions of materials composing the concrete mix have been approved.

Air-Entrained Concrete

Entrained air must be used in all concrete that is subject to freezing and thawing as well as deicing chemicals. Concretes with air is accomplished at the mixing plant by either using an air-entraining portland cement to the mix or by adding an air-entraining admixture. The amount must be closely monitored to ensure the concrete meets the project specifications. Air-entrained concrete is generally easier to work with and can be used even if not specifically called for in the plans and specifications.

Table 3-16 Recommended Air Contents

Exposure	Max. Aggregate Size (in.)				
	$\frac{3}{8}$	$\frac{1}{2}$	$\frac{3}{4}$	1	$1\frac{1}{2}$
Mild	4.5	4.0	3.5	3.0	2.5
Moderate	6.0	5.5	5.0	4.5	4.5
Severe	7.5	7.0	6.0	6.0	5.5

Exposure Definitions (ACI 211.1)

Mild. Indoor or outdoor concrete in an area where it will not be exposed to freezing, thawing, or deicing chemicals.

Moderate. Freezing is expected, but the concrete will not be continually exposed to moisture or free water for long periods prior to freezing; and it is not exposed to any deicing chemicals.

Severe. Concrete that is directly exposed to freezing and is subject to becoming saturated by moisture or free water and deicing chemicals.

Fig. 3-21 *Testing concrete on the job site.*

Mixing Plant

General

a. Inspect plant for general overall compliance with specification requirements.

b. Is the plant capable of batching at the minimum rate or at a rate consistent with proposed construction progress? Can the plant maintain the accuracy required?

c. Check aggregate bins or compartments for condition and size. Is the arrangement of the bins and provisions for loading the bins such that there will be no intermixing of the various aggregate sizes?

d. Check linkages of weighing devices for condition, cleanliness, and freedom of movement.

e. Check cement and aggregate scales for accuracy.

f. Has provision been made for interlocking batching controls?

g. Check recorders and their operation.

h. If a central mix plant is employed, check water batcher for accuracy of batching and interlock of filling and discharge valves; also check air-entraining admixture dispenser.

i. Have facilities been provided for obtaining samples of aggregate from each bin?

j. Does the plant conform to all safety requirements?

Concrete Mixing Plant

a. Check mixers for general condition, cleanliness, blade wear, and mixing capacity.

b. Are timing devices provided on stationary mixers, and are they interlocked with the discharge mechanism?

c. Are truck mixers, if permitted, equipped with accurate revolution counters?

d. Are batch-counters provided?

e. Check water batcher for accuracy.

f. Check air-entraining admixture dispenser.

Check Paving Equipment and Tools

a. Is all paving equipment on the job and in good operating condition?

b. Have the machines been adjusted and checked for accuracy of strike-off, screeding, and floating?

c. Do the vibrators comply with specification requirements?

d. Check hand tools such as edging tools, hand floats, and straight edges for required dimension and condition.

e. Are all necessary materials and equipment on hand for curing the pavement?

f. Is all necessary equipment for construction or forming of all types of joints on hand and in good condition?

g. Is adequate equipment on hand for sealing joints?

h. Has the Subcontractor provided and set up adequate facilities for making and curing test beams, if required?

Check Base Course Surface Preparation

a. Is approved equipment being operated in a manner to properly fine-grade the base course?

b. Is the base course prepared to produce a smooth, compacted surface conforming to grade and smoothness requirements?

c. Is the base course surface being maintained in a firm, moist condition?

d. If paving is carried on during cold weather, is the base course being properly protected against freezing and have you checked to ensure that base materials are entirely free of frost when concrete is placed?

e. Is base preparation and form setting being performed sufficiently in advance of concrete placement? Note minimum specification requirement.

Prior to setting forms, determine that the surface of the base course has been constructed to or slightly above required grade and that the material meets all test requirements. Check forms:

a. Are the forms identical in all respects to the form or forms approved for use on the work?

b. Are the forms free of warps, bends, and/or kinks and are they free of battered top surfaces and distorted faces and/or bases? Remove damaged form sections from the project.

c. Check forms as they arrive on the job site. Check straight-edge tops and vertical faces of forms after setting for deviations. Sight along forms to detect major deviations from true alignment.

d. Check dimensions, position, and securing of the metal keyway forms.

e. Does the base of each form section have full bearing for its entire length and width on fully compacted material?

f. Be sure that form pins are of adequate length, are properly wedged in the pin pockets, and are free from mushroomed heads.

g. Check locking devices between form sections for secureness and freedom from looseness or play. Are they properly spaced?

h. Make sure contractor is using a bonding agent on existing concrete surfaces that will be joined with new concrete.

i. Determine that forms have been set to required grades. If correction of grade is necessary, remove form sections, adjust the grade, and thoroughly recompact base material prior to resetting forms.

j. Properly clean and oil forms after each use.

k. Set forms well in advance of paving operations. Recheck alignment before start of pouring operations.

Check Grade Surfaces between Forms

a. Check to see that subgrade, base course, or filter course is free of foreign matter, waste concrete, cement, loose aggregate, or other debris.

b. Check scratch template and template operation to ensure that the rods are obtaining the required results.

c. Check the prepared surface with the approved scratch template immediately ahead of the paving operation.

d. Check the setting of the rods on the scratch template to ensure that proper thickness of concrete will be obtained.

Check Embedded Items

a. Are dowels provided of the required diameter (or diameters) and length (or lengths)? Correct spacing?

b. Are dowels clean, straight, and smooth with ends free from burrs or distortion?

c. Is the dowel basket and/or expansion joint assembly identical to the basket approved for the project?

d. Have means been provided for anchoring the dowel assembly securely in its required position?

e. Has a template been provided for checking dowel position?

f. If reinforcing steel is required, check type, dimension, and cleanliness. Also check spacing, clearance, and method of securing in place during the paving operation.

g. Check tie-down anchors and, if grounding electrodes are required, see that they meet the specified resistances.

h. Check all other embedded items for location and proper installation.

Check Area and Grade Control

a. Determine that adequate plans for area and grade control have been formulated by the Subcontractor and that plans have been made for checking the Sub's control of the grades of the concrete as placed.

b. Be sure that control is set up to maintain pavement joint alignment.

c. Determine that all utility lines within a paved area have been properly referenced so their position may be readily reestablished if necessary.

Inspections during Paving

Paving Operations

a. Check placing, spreading, and vibration of concrete as follows:

1. Slow down or stop placement of concrete if for any reason subsequent operations lag behind sufficiently to affect the quality of the concrete.

2. Be sure that concrete placement and vibration in the vicinity of embedded items are performed in such manner that they will not be disturbed.

Transverse dowel assemblies should be covered carefully so as not to disturb the cage position.

3. Adjust spreader to strike-off concrete at a level such that when vibrated, the proper amount of concrete will remain for finishing.

4. In the case of reinforced pavement, adjust spreader to strike-off concrete at the proper depth.

5. Check that protection is provided on the newly placed slab when the spreader is operated on a previously constructed slab. Make sure the slab is strong enough to support traffic.

6. Check operation of vibrators for effectiveness in consolidating the concrete. Check frequency of vibration and that they are operated at proper depth and that vibration is completely effective including vibration along the forms. Do not allow vibration in one location for more than a 20-sec duration.

7. Do not allow the use of vibrators to spread the concrete. Insert and withdraw vertically. Place vibrators to rapidly penetrate the freshly placed layer and at least 6 in. into the preceding layer. Do not allow in lower layers that have already begun to set up.

8. See that an extra vibrator, or sufficient parts for replacing and repairing a vibrator, is maintained on the job.

9. Prevent workmen from unnecessarily walking on fresh concrete.

b. Check embedded items as follows:

1. Reinforcing steel, if necessary, must be of required size and spacing, properly cleaned and set in the required position.

2. Reinforcing steel mats must be lapped a minimum of one full stay plus 2 in. Be certain that the reinforcing is not extended through a pavement joint.

3. Is one end of each dowel painted and greased?

4. Are the dowel assemblies being maintained in correct position and alignment during placement and finishing operations?

5. Are electrical and plumbing "stub-ups" adequately protected from damage? Are these two trades monitoring the pour in progress, to recheck alignments?

c. Check machine finishing as follows:

1. Periodically check adjustments of the transverse and longitudinal finishing machines on the slip-form paver. Need for change of adjustments may be determined by visual observations and straight-edge and/or string-line checks of the pavement surface left by the machines.

2. Forward screed of transverse finisher should carry a uniform roll of concrete of about 4 to 8 in. in diameter; rear screed should carry a uniform roll of concrete of about 2 in. in diameter.

3. If transverse finishing machine produces a slurry ahead of the screed after the first pass, concrete mix should be adjusted. Slight reduction of water will often correct this condition.

4. Transverse finishing machine should leave the concrete surface at proper grade and essential proper smoothness.

d. Check hand finishing as follows:

1. Use hand-manipulated floats sparingly. Hand floating should be necessary only to remove small surface irregularities.

2. Majority of hand-finishing should be performed with straight-edges.

3. Check all straight-edges for trueness.

4. Check surface of plastic concrete with a straight-edge, including check across longitudinal joints as straight-edge finishing is completed.

5. Surface of plastic concrete must fit straight-edge without deviation except at crowns and other planned breaks in grade.

6. Final surface finish is generally required to be produced by burlap dragging.

7. Timing of burlap dragging is important to produce the required surface texture drag when most of surface sheen has disappeared but while the concrete at the surface is in a plastic state.

8. Be sure the burlap drag is constructed and operated as required and that it is kept moist and clean.

9. Joints requiring hand tooling should be carefully formed. Check that edging tools are of required dimension and that the edging tool is not tilted during tooling of the joint or otherwise improperly manipulated to result in surface irregularities at the joint.

10. Do not permit use of soupy mortar to fill out depressions along joints during hand tooling; use fresh concrete.

11. Check that all spillage of grout and concrete on adjacent concrete surfaces is cleaned up imme-

diately. Particularly watch for removal of mortar accumulations on radius and sides of that part of a longitudinal joint formed in the previously placed, adjacent lane.

12. Eliminate tool marks by burlap dragging along joint with a small, hand-operated drag.

13. Filler-type or sawed transverse contraction joints are generally required. It is important to insert or cut the joint at the correct time.

14. Install filler strip of filler-type joint exactly as specified. Check that the filler strip as installed is properly aligned, is vertical, and is set flush with or slightly below the pavement surface.

15. Carefully observe finishing in the vicinity of the filler-type joint and immediately after finishing, check across the joint with a straight-edge. If depressions are found, fill out with freshly mixed concrete and refinish the surface.

16. Re-check pavement with a straightedge upon completion of finishing while concrete is plastic and make necessary corrections.

17. Dowel transverse construction joints as required for a properly aligned and smooth joint. Check plan details.

e. Check curing as follows:

1. Make sure that effective curing is maintained for at least seven days.

2. Check to see that unhardened concrete is always protected from rain and flowing water.

3. Make sure that the necessary materials and equipment for the curing are on the job prior to beginning the paving operation. See that necessary stand-by equipment is also at the site.

4. Check that curing procedures are suited to prevailing climatic conditions.

Table 3-17 *Concrete Insulation (Placed at 50°F) per Mix Designs; Minimum Air Temperature (°F)*

300 lb/cu. yd.

Thickness of Concrete	Thickness of Batt Insulation			
	0.5 in.	1.0 in.	1.5 in.	2.0 in.
6 in.	45	41	33	28
12 in.	41	29	17	5
18 in.	35	19	0	−17

Table 3-17 *(Continued)*

400 lb/cu. yd.

Thickness of Concrete	Thickness of Batt Insulation			
	0.5 in.	1.0 in.	1.5 in.	2.0 in.
6 in.	46	38	28	21
12 in.	38	22	6	−11
18 in.	31	8	−16	−39

500 lb/cu. yd.

Thickness of Concrete	Thickness of Batt Insulation			
	0.5 in.	1.0 in.	1.5 in.	2.0 in.
6 in.	45	35	22	14
12 in.	35	15	−5	−26
18 in.	37	−3	−33	−65

600 lb/cu. yd.

Thickness of Concrete	Thickness of Batt Insulation			
	0.5 in.	1.0 in.	1.5 in.	2.0 in.
6 in.	44	32	16	6
12 in.	32	8	−16	−41
18 in.	21	−14	−50	−89

5. Make sure the method of curing used provides complete and continuous protection of the concrete against cracking.

6. When forms are used, check within 1 hour after removal to see that sides of slabs are protected.

7. Check the initial curing for proper method, timely application, and duration.

8. Check final curing for type of covering used, method of applying the covering, and wetting of surface before the application of one of the optional coverings specified.

(a) Check weight of burlap and lap of edges.

(b) Check the wetting operation.

(c) Check method of holding down the waterproof paper covering and the cementing or taping operation. Make sure continuous cover with completely closed joints is provided.

(d) Re-checks are required for timely repairs to damaged coverings.

(e) Check application of curing compound. The compound is not to be sprayed on a dry surface and must be applied at the proper time. Check the manufacturer's application procedures.

(f) Check equipment/machine used to apply membrane. It should be able to provide continuous and uniform coverage of compound of the same consistency.

(g) Check for overlap coverage to ensure that two-coat application is being obtained and the coverage is no more than 200 sq ft per gallon for both coats.

(h) Carefully check for any defects, pin holes, or abrasions and have these surfaces recoated immediately.

(i) Check that joints to receive joint sealing are protected from membrane curing.

9. Check for any special requirements for curing concrete placed during cold weather. Refer to *ACI 306.*

f. Pavement protection: See that curing compound or covering is protected during the curing period. Check on the erection and maintaining of barricades to exclude all unnecessary traffic from the pavement for at least 14 days after the concrete paving.

g. Jointing of old pavement to new:

1. Check the conditions for continuous bond between old pavement and freshly placed pavement.

2. Check surface against which the new material is to be placed. It should be clean and properly coated with the approved bonding material specified.

h. Inspections subsequent to paving:

• Form removal: Do not permit removal of forms until maximum time after placement has elapsed. See that proper care is exercised to prevent injury to the concrete by form removal.

Sawed Contraction Joints

1. Determine that sufficient equipment is on hand and that satisfactory provisions have been made to carry on the sawing operation day or night as necessary.

2. Determine that alignment of joint is properly established prior to sawing to ensure straight and continuous joints.

3. Determine proper time for sawing by field trial. Sawing should be performed as soon as the concrete may be cut without excessive tearing and raveling of the concrete and without damaging the sides of the cut.

4. Check width and depth of cut.

5. Thoroughly flush saw cut and adjacent concrete surface with water immediately after each cut is made.

6. Insert cord to prevent entry of foreign objects into cut until widened.

7. Examine concrete surface in vicinity of planned joint location prior to sawing. If an uncontrolled crack has occurred, do not permit sawing of the joint. Discontinue sawing if crack forms ahead of the cut during the sawing operation.

8. See that curing coverings removed to permit sawing are replaced immediately after each joint is sawed.

9. If curing compound is used, check to see that joints are cured as specified and that curing compound does not enter the joint.

Joint Types (Typical)

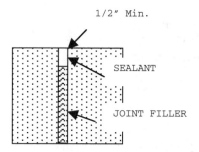

Fig. 3-22 *Expansion joint.*

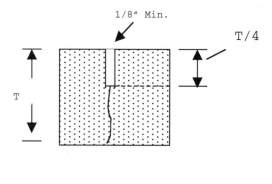

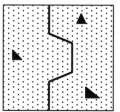

Fig. 3-23 *Contraction joint.*

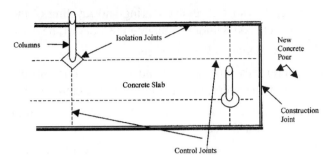

Fig. 3-24 *Typical joints and locations in concrete.*

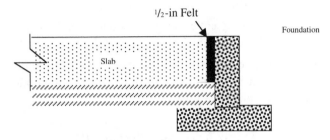

Fig. 3-25 *Isolation joint.*

Joint Sawing

1. Saw filler-type joints to width and minimum depth required. Carefully examine sides of cut to be certain that all traces of the filler strip have been removed.

2. Check to see that all joints, longitudinal and transverse, are sawed out to the required joint dimensions prior to joint sealing.

3. *Sawing must be done as soon as possible.* Waiting too long will allow cracking to develop.

Joint Cleaning

1. Check joint cleaning operation for required performance and sequence in preparation for joint sealing.

2. Check to see that concrete saws, saw blades, sandblasting equipment and sand, air compressors, air nozzles, and accessory small tools are available, suitable, and in good working condition.

3. Check sand-blasting operation to ensure that the proper nozzle or nozzles are used and that they are positioned and aligned to obtain satisfactory results.

4. Carefully examine final results to determine that the joint walls, joint bottoms, and ½ in. of adjacent pavement surfaces have been thoroughly cleaned and the joint is free of all foreign materials that would prevent bonding of the joint sealer to the concrete.

Joint Sealing

1. Determine that the correct type of joint sealing compound and the specified equipment for the joint sealer employed is being used. Sampling and testing may be required.

2. Do not permit sealing of joints under weather conditions outside specification limitations unless by approval from the Project Manager.

3. If two component sealants are used, check that proportions in place are correct. Have Subcontractor read and follow instructions on pails without exception. Check that placing equipment is suitable for materials used.

4. Nozzle for sealer application must be of such dimension that it can be inserted well into the joint groove to effect filling the groove from the bottom up without formation of voids.

5. Fill the joints to within ¼ in. to ⅛ in. of the pavement surface. Remove excess and spilled material from the pavement surface and waste.

6. Maintain complete records of the sealing operation.
   - Time of first pour
   - Time of sealing application
   - Time of second application (if required)
   - Method of application
   - Temperature
   - Site conditions
   - Area sealed

Hardened Concrete Check

1. Is the Subcontractor straightedging the finished pavement in the specified manner and within the specified time?

2. Check to see that the Subcontractor is taking required action to correct deviations outside smoothness tolerances.

3. If rubbing is performed to correct minor deviations during curing period, flush rubbed area with water and continue effective curing without delay.

4. Straight-edge check the finished surface for acceptance or rejection of the pavement.

5. If subsequent grinding of deficient pavement is approved, determine that limitations on area corrected by grinding are not exceeded.

Finished-Grade Checks

Normally, finished-grade surveys will be made by the contractor's survey party. The Inspector should be familiar with survey results. In the event deficiencies are found, he will be responsible for assuring work is corrected. A report is required on finish grade surveys.

Pavement Thickness Checks

Pavements will be checked for thickness by means of coring. The coring program normally is set up and performed by the Geotech contractor.

Common Pavement Deficiencies Corrections

1. When pavement areas are removed for replacement, check adjacent pavement or damage such as cracking, breakage of concrete at the edges, and damage to keyways or other load-bearing equipment. Such damage may necessitate further concrete removal and/or limiting the weights for a time as required by the Project Manager (PM).

2. Replacement slabs shall conform to minimum dimensional requirements and otherwise conform to all specification requirements.

3. Most random cracks occurring in pavements may be repaired. If there is no provision in the contract for repair of such cracks, check with the PM and or Design Engineer. Be sure that specified and/or proper equipment is issued and that repair methods are followed.

4. Control tests: These tests are the responsibility of the contractor's site quality-control testing technicians.

Table 3-18 *Common Concrete Problems*

Problem	Cause	Prevention and Corrections
Excessive bleeding	Excess water in the mix Not enough fines in the mix	Reduce water content Increase the cement, fly ash, or sand. Add air entrainment
Aggregate segregation	Too high slump Overvibration Not enough vibration Too long of drop for placement Lack of homogeneity in the mix	Add superplasticizer Reduce vibration in each location Insert vibrator at closer intervals Use appropiate drop chutes Increase mix time, add air entrainment
Sticky finish	Too much air entrainment Surface drying too fast	Reduce air and/or fines Spray water on subgrade and forms. Fog spray
Setting too fast	High temperatures High cement content Trucks getting hot from sun	Use cooler water/ice in mix. Use retarder additives. Cool aggregate with water Add water reducing retarder Sprinkle mixing drums during wait Reschedule deliveries for min. wait time
Setting up too slow	Mix too lean. Too much fly ash or slag Cold/wet subgrade	Increase cement content. Use accelerator Heat water and/or aggregates Insulate and or protect before placement of concrete
Plastic shrinkage cracking	Too rapid loss of water. High winds, heat or low humidity	Fog spray at curing. Reduce air or fines. Do not use vapor retarders. Use less mix water. Set up wind breaks. Lower concrete temperature.
Low yield	Low air content Wrong ratio of water cement and aggregates	Increase air Have test run
Flat Slabs		
Shrinkage cracks	Wrong spacings and depth of contraction joints Late joint sawing No isolation joints at walls or columns Excessive shrinkage	Cut joints ¼ the depth of slab. Space joints at 2½ times the thickness in feet Plan to saw the same day as pour, within 4 hours Install isolation joints Reduce water in mix. Cure ASAP after finishing

Table 3-18 *Common Concrete Problems (Continued)*

Problem	Cause	Prevention and Corrections
Hairline cracks	Too high slump of concrete Too early troweling or too much troweling Rapid surface drying	Reduce water Reduce the methods of troweling by contractor Cure concrete immediately after finishing
Blistering	Slab closed too soon, trapping air and water	Delay floating and troweling. Using wood floats helps.
Curling	Uneven drying between top of slab and lower parts	Use lower slump. Cure ASAP and as long as possible. Reduce space between joints
Scaling	Exposed to freeze thaw and chemical deicers Too much finishing on wet surfaces Chemical deicers applied before adaquate curing time.	Use air entrainment of 5–8% Use min. slump on 4. Protect from rain. Wait a min. of 30 days for normal curing.
Walls		
Honeycomb	Not enough vibration	Add superplasticizers. Reduce height of the pour. Insert vibrator more often.
Surface voids	Air or water trapped against formwork	Reduce air entrainment. Vibrate as close to form as possible.

Aggregate

1. Run sieve analysis of aggregate size at least twice daily for a full day's paving operation.

2. Test for surface moisture at start of paving and periodically during each day's operation, depending on changes in moisture condition.

3. Organic impurities test (color test) for each shipment of sand, or more frequently if deemed necessary.

4. Specific gravity test about weekly (check specifications), or when visual check indicates a change in the material.

Concrete

1. Supervise the making of test specimens by the contractor or his approved testing firm or techinicians. Take specimens at about 4-hour intervals on large pours or as prescribed in the specifications or as per ACI. Determine slump, entrained-air content, and temperature of concrete from same sample.

2. Make and record periodic slump or Kelly Ball penetration tests and entrained air tests during the day. Frequency of testing should be in the specifications.

3. Measure and record ambient air and concrete temperatures at hourly intervals (if required).

4. Determine that test specimens are cured and tested in strict accordance with standard procedures.

CONCRETE SIDEWALKS, CURBS, AND GUTTERS

Fig. 3-26 *Concrete damage due to freeze thaw and chemicals.*

General

The construction of concrete sidewalks, curbs, and gutters, in general, requires the same procedures in inspection as a large-scale paving operation.

Subgrade and Base Course

1. Check in-place materials and/or fill materials for bearing quality and compactibility, especially over utility trenches.

2. Check results of rolling for firmness of compacted subgrade; check compaction with density tests as required.

3. Check subgrade for correct grade and cross section.

4. If a base course is required, check materials, compaction, and surface grade and cross section for conformity with requirements.

5. Check moisture content of subgrade prior to concrete placement.

Forms, Concrete Placement, Finishing, and Curing

1. Check forms for condition, cleanliness, rigidity, and conformity with required dimension of the structure.

2. Check form setting including full bearing of form bases on prepared subgrade or base course, securing forms in place, adequacy of clamps, braces, and spreaders as applicable, provision for removable form sections, adequacy of forms for curb returns, and alignment and grade.

3. Check location, grade, and dimensions between forms.

4. Check the oiling and cleaning of forms and the time the forms are to be removed.

5. Check that the contractor has on hand the approved materials required to form contraction and/or expansion joints. Check location and spacing of joints.

6. Check to see that concrete mix is correct. Check slump and entrained-air content of the concrete.

7. Check placement and consolidation of concrete to ensure that segregation does not occur and that honeycombing or "bug holing" does not result.

8. Observe forming of contraction and expansion joints for proper installation and finishing of the exposed joint edges.

9. Check that exposed surfaces are finished by required methods.

10. Inspect tops and faces of curbs, surfaces of gutters, and surfaces of sidewalks for conformity with surface smoothness and shape requirements.

11. Ensure that an approved curing method is employed and that the curing is performed in accordance with the method, and that curing is started immediately after the finishing operations. Check that curing is continuous for the required curing period.

12. Verify protection of concrete against damage during backfill or other operations. Damaged concrete shall be repaired and/or removed and replaced as required.

13. Check cleaning and sealing of expansion joints in curbs and gutters, and expansion and contraction joints in sidewalks. Clean joints thoroughly immediately prior to sealing, and fill joints with approved material.

Note: Require cleaning of surfaces where spillage has occurred or excess sealer has been applied.

ADA REQUIREMENTS

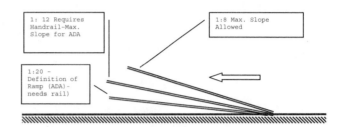

Fig. 3-27 *New Federal Register, Vol. 56, No. 144: ADA Rules and Regulations.*

New Construction

- Any route with a slope greater than 1:20 is considered a ramp.
- Maximum slope is 1:12 (for ADA).
- Maximum rise for any run is 30 in.
- Handrails are required for:
  a. Any horizontal rise greater than 6 in.
  b. Any horizontal projection greater than 72 in.
- Handrails on ramps must be 34 to 38 in. in height.
- Cross slope cannot exceed 1:50 (approx. ¼ in. per foot)
- Changes in level cannot exceed ½ in.
- Clear width of ramp must be a min. of 36 in.

Renovation/Existing Construction

- Slope between 1:10 and 1:12 for a maximum 6-in. rise.
- Slope between 1:8 and 1:10 for a maximum 3-in. rise.
- Slope greater than 1:8 is not allowed.

Landings

1. Must be as wide as the ramp leading to it.
2. Length must be at least 60 in. clear.
3. When the landing is used to change direction of the ramp, then it must be at least 60 in. by 60 in.

Handrails

1. Handrails are required if the rise is greater than 6 in. or the run is longer than 72 in.

2. Clear space between the handrail and wall is to be 1½ in.

3. Top of handrail to be mounted between 34 in. and 38 in.

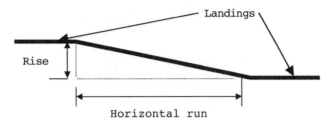

Fig. 3-28 *Ramp requirements.*

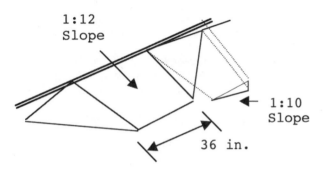

Fig. 3-29 *Built-up curb requirements.*

COMMON ADA ERRORS AND OMISSIONS IN NEW CONSTRUCTION AND ALTERATIONS

Introduction

The ADA requires that new construction and alterations to existing facilities comply with the ADA Standards for Accessible Design. ADA requirements for new construction and alterations include detailed provisions for elements, spaces, and facilities. Successful accessibility is often measured in inches, so attention to detail can make the difference between achieving access and excluding or injuring someone. When the ADA's minimum requirements are not met, the results can limit or exclude a person with a disability and can be dangerous. For example, when a curb ramp extends into an access aisle at an accessible parking space, a person using a wheelchair may not be able to get out of

the car or van. When the slope of a sidewalk that is an accessible route becomes steeper than 1 to 20, railings and edge protection are required for safe use. Objects that project into circulation spaces from the side or that do not provide at least 80 in. of head clearance can be extremely hazardous to people who are blind or who have low vision.

This section lists a sampling of common accessibility errors or omissions that have been identified through the Department of Justice's ongoing enforcement efforts. The specific requirement of the Standards that has not been met follows each error/omission. All references to figures can be found in the Standards. The list of errors/omissions provides examples of common deficiencies. It is not intended to be comprehensive or exhaustive. Any failure to comply with the Standards violates the ADA.

Fig. 3-29a *ADA ramps with handrails require a guard at the bottom of the ramp.*

For additional information about the design and construction requirements of the Americans with Disabilities Act (ADA), contact the Department of Justice ADA Information Line. This free service provides answers to general and technical questions about ADA requirements and is a source for free ADA materials including the ADA Standards for Accessible Design. You may reach the ADA Information Line at: (800) 514-0301 (voice). ADA information is also available on the Department's ADA Home Page on the World Wide Web at http://www.usdoj.gov/crt/adal adahoml.htm.

Parking

Error/Omission The built-up curb ramp projects into the access aisle. The accessible parking space and access aisle are not level in all directions.

Result When an access aisle has a sloped surface, a wheelchair may roll away from a car or van, preventing the wheelchair user from getting out of the vehicle. The sloped surface also prevents a van-mounted wheelchair lift from being fully lowered to the access aisle surface.

Requirement *4.6.3 Parking Spaces.* Parking spaces and access aisles shall be level with surface slopes not exceeding 1:50 (2%) in all directions.

Error/Omission There is no accessible route from accessible parking to an accessible entrance.

Result A person using a wheelchair, scooter, or walker has no way of getting from the accessible parking space to the building entrance. Often when there is an inaccessible walkway provided for others, wheelchair users must use a roadway or vehicular route, which can be dangerous.

Requirement *4.6.3 Parking Spaces.* Parking access aisles shall be part of an accessible route to the building or facility entrance and shall comply with 4.3.

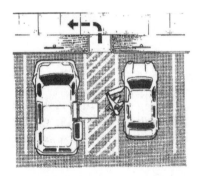

Fig. 3-29b *Allow room for handicap-equipped vehicles.*

Error/Omission No van-accessible spaces are provided in the parking area.

Result A person who uses a van equipped with a wheelchair lift has inadequate space to lower the wheelchair lift and get out of the vehicle.

Requirement *4.1.2 (5)(b).* One in every eight accessible spaces, but not less than one, shall be served by an access aisle 96 in. (2440 mm) wide.

Requirement Shall be designated "van accessible" as required by 4.6.4. The vertical clearance at such spaces shall comply with 4.6.5. All such spaces may be grouped on one level of a parking structure.

Accessible Route—Exterior

Error/Omission The pedestrian routes on a site from public transportation stops, accessible parking spaces, passenger loading zones, and public streets and sidewalks to the accessible entrance(s) are not accessible.

Result People with disabilities cannot travel from the site entry points to the accessible entrance(s). In some cases, people must use vehicular routes, which can be dangerous.

Requirement *4.1.2 (I).* At least one accessible route complying with 4.3 shall be provided within the boundary of the site from public transportation stops, accessible parking spaces, passenger loading zones if provided, and public streets or sidewalks to an accessible building entrance.

Curb Ramps

Error/Omission Curb ramp that is located across a circulation path has steep unprotected side flares.

Result People walking across the curb ramp may trip and be injured. People who use wheelchairs can tip over if they accidentally roll over the nonflared sides.

Requirement *4.7.5. Sides of curb ramps.* If a curb ramp is located where pedestrians must walk across the ramp, or where it is not protected by handrails or guardrails, it shall have flared sides; the maximum slope of the flare shall be 1:10. Curb ramps with returned curbs may be used where pedestrians would not normally walk across the ramp.

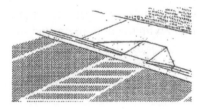

Fig. 3-29c *Wheelchair ramp.*

Ramps

Error/Omission Landing areas where ramps change direction (e.g., switchbacks or 90° turns) are too small.

Result Wheelchair users are unable to go up or down the ramp because there is not enough space to turn on a level surface. This makes the ramp unusable.

Requirement *4.8.4(3).* If ramps change direction at landings, the minimum landing size shall be 60 in. by 60 in. (1525 mm by 1525 mm).

Stairs

Error/Omission Parts of an accessible route with slopes that exceed 1:20 (0.6:12) lack required features including handrails and edge protection.

Result When a walkway or other pedestrian surface has a slope greater then 1:20, it is more difficult to maintain control of a wheelchair. Wheelchair users may also not be able to climb up the sloped route without railings. Lack of edge protection may result in injury if a wheelchair user rolls off the side of the route. People who use a mobility device such as crutches, a cane, or a walker may lose their balance or fall while using a sloped section that does not have handrails or edge protection.

Requirement *4.8.1. General.* Any part of an accessible route with a slope greater than 1:20 shall be considered a ramp and shall comply with 4.8.

Error/Omission Handrail extensions are not provided at the top and bottom risers.

Result People who use crutches or a cane or who have limited balance may fall at the top or bottom of the stairs because they have no railing to hold onto as they make the transition from the steps to the landing.

Requirement *4.9.4(2).* If handrails are not continuous, they shall extend at least 12 in. (305 mm) beyond the top riser and at least 12 in. plus the width of one tread beyond the bottom riser. At the top, the extension shall be parallel with the floor or ground surface. At the bottom, the handrail shall continue to slope for a distance of the width of one tread from the bottom riser; the remainder of the extension shall be horizontal. Handrail extensions shall comply with 4.4.

Fig. 3-29d Handrail requirement.

Doors

Error/Omission Adequate maneuvering clearance is not provided at:

- Stairs (residential exterior)
  1. At least 36 in. in width.
  2. With one handrail at least 32 in. in width.
  3. Risers not more than 7¼ in. in height.
  4. With two handrails 28 in. min. 7¼ in. in width.
  5. Treads not less than 11 in. in depth greatest vs. lessor by no more than ⅜ in.
  6. Handrail is required if three or more risers are used.
  7. All stairs must be provided with lighting.
  8. Landings must be minimum of 3 ft by 3 ft.
  9. Nosing must be ¾ in. to 1¼ in. except when depth of tread is at least 11 in.
  10. Handrails
      (a) 34 in. to 38 in. in height
      (b) Space next to wall not less than 1½ in.

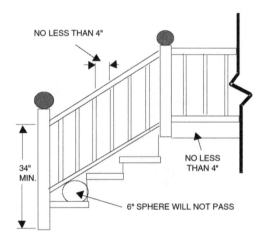

Fig. 3-30 Stairs.

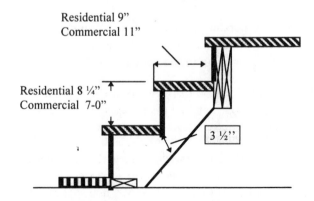

Fig. 3-31 Stair treads and risers (residential).

(c) Grip size 1¼ in. to 2 in.

(d) Openings less than 4 in. apart

(e) Need to withstand a 200-lb force (from all directions)

(f) Needed if platform is more than 30 in. above grade

Stairs for Commercial Use

Width. Minimum of 44 in. if more than 50 occupants; 36 in. if 50 or less.

Headroom. Must have a minimum headroom of 80 in.

Risers. Minimum of 4 in. and maximum of 7 in.

Treads. 11 in. minimum.

Vertical rise. Limited to 12 ft.

Ramps for Commercial Use

If used as an egress must have maximum slope of 1 in 12.

All others ramps should have maximum slope of 1 in 8.

Ramp runs should have maximum rise of 30 in.

Ramps must have a handrail on both sides if the rise is greater than 1 in 6.

Ramps must have landings at the top and bottom and all turns.

Ramps are to be slip resistant (no trowel finish).

PATCHING PAVEMENTS

Materials

1. Check both coarse and fine aggregate for conformance with requirements.

2. See that epoxy resin has been approved and that the proper type is being used for the atmospheric temperature conditions.

3. Verify other miscellaneous materials, such as those to be used in curing the portland cement, air-entraining admixture, joint-sealing materials, and water.

Storage

1. Check aggregates to ensure no breakage, segregation, or contamination by foreign material.

2. Check the epoxy storage area to see that it will be in compliance with requirements. Also check to see that the material has been maintained at a temperature between 70 and 85°F for 48 hours prior to use.

3. Ensure the cement is being maintained dry.

Mix

1. Check for approval of mix.

2. Check to make sure that control can be maintained.

3. Continue to check result of mix for workability and strength.

Equipment

1. Check for approval of all equipment which will be used in the operation.

2. Check to ensure that the equipment is being maintained in good working and safe condition.

Preparation for Placement

1. Check the removal of existing pavement to the depth specified and to a depth where surface to be paved will be sound and free of unweathered concrete.

2. Check sandblasting procedures when this operation is necessary.

3. Check for removal of all joint filler and sealants which will prevent bond between concrete and the patch.

4. Ensure that necessary fiberboard fillers are used to prevent the closing of any existing joints.

5. In order to provide adequate bonding of old and new surfaces prior to placing of epoxy, check that the surface has been blasted with both a high-pressure water jet and an air jet to remove free water.

6. Observe the application of a thin film of epoxy resin grout on the freshly cleaned surface.

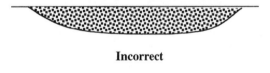

Incorrect

Sides cut and cleaned

Correct

Fig. 3-32 *Patching concrete.*

a. Verify mixing of material for the grout.

b. Check safety of the operation. Require full face shields, coveralls, and protective cream on workmen, and check adequacy of fire protection.

c. Check thickness of film.

d. Check number of coats.

Placing

Check the following:

1. Batching and mixing of materials.

2. That the initial epoxy grout is still tacky when fresh concrete is placed.

3. Handling and placing of the concrete.

4. Atmospheric and material temperatures.

5. Consolidation of concrete.

6. Making the necessary tests.

7. Finishing and curing.

8. Finished grade and alignment of joints to see that they match the grade and alignment of the adjoining surface.

9. For protection of patched areas.

10. The resealing of joints as required.

Safety

1. See that all workers are provided with:

    a. Rubber or neoprene gloves.

    b. Face shields or goggles.

    c. Protective creams.

2. Ensure that manufacturer's recommendations are followed.

3. Ensure proper ventilation when using epoxy in an enclosed area.

4. Avoid contact with skin and follow treatment/emergency methods recommended by manufacturer.

5. Are Material Safety Data Sheets available?

4
CHAPTER

Concrete

CONCRETE FOR STRUCTURES

General

This chapter covers commonly encountered concrete work other than concrete paving, which is covered in Chapter 3.

Inspectors are cautioned that contract requirements for concrete for a given job are contained in the drawings and specifications prepared for *that job* only. Also, that contract requirements may change from job to job. There are many differences between the concrete requirements for large jobs and for small jobs.

Types of Concrete

- Concrete is basically a mixture of Portland cement and aggregates. The chemical reaction between the cement and water bonds the aggregate to its hardened mass. We refer to this as concrete. There are many different types and forms of concrete, depending on the required strength desired and its exposure to the elements. The process of hardening of the cement when water is added is called *hydration*. Special attention needs to be taken if Codes or the Plans and Specifications require that the mixture be air-entrained.

Table 4-1   *Types of Concrete*

Type I	General purpose
Type IA	General purpose, air-entrained
Type II	Moderate sulfate resistance
Type IIA	Moderate sulfate resistance, air-entrained
Type III	High early strength
Type IIIA	High early, air-entrained
Type IV	Low-heat hydration
Type V	High-sulfate resistance

EFFECTS OF WATER ON CONCRETE STRENGTH (NON AIR-ENTRAINED)

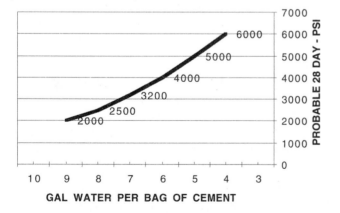

Fig. 4-1   *Effects of the amount of water in concrete mixes.*

Concrete Strength Test

Because Type I concrete reaches 46% of full strength at 3 days, 67% at 7 days, and full strength at 28 days, it is mathematically possible to determine the approximate strength at 28 days by using the 7-day test results. As we know, construction will continue, and it is critical to know if a concrete pour will have to be broken out and replaced.

$$S28 = \text{28-day compressive strength}$$
$$S7 = \text{7-day compressive strength}$$
$$S28 = S7 + 30 \times \sqrt{S7}$$

Example:

$$\text{Test at 7 days} = 890 \text{ psi}$$
$$\text{Anticipated 28-day test will} = 890 + 30 \times \sqrt{890}$$
$$= 890 + 30 \times 29.8$$
$$= 890 + 894$$
$$= 1784 \text{ psi}$$

Air-Entrained Concrete

Entrained air must be used in all concrete that is subject to freezing and thawing as well as deicing chemicals. Concrete with air is accomplished at the mixing plant by either using an air-entraining Portland cement to the mix or by adding an air-entraining admixture. The amount must be closely monitored to ensure the concrete meets the project specifications. Air-entrained concrete is generally easier to work with and can be used even if not specifically called for in the plans and specifications.

The following are properties of air-entrained concrete:

Workability. The improved workability of air-entrained concrete greatly reduces water and sand requirements, particularly in lean mixes and in mixes containing angular and poorly graded aggregates. In addition, the disconnected air bubbles reduce segregation and bleeding of plastic concrete.

Freeze-thaw durability. The expansion of water as it freezes in concrete can create enough pressure to rupture the concrete. However, entrained air bubbles serve as reservoirs for the expanded water, thereby relieving expansion pressure and preventing concrete damage.

Deicers resistance. Because entrained air prevents scaling caused by deicing chemicals used for snow and ice removal, air-entrained concrete is recommended for all applications where the concrete contacts deicing chemicals.

Table 4-2   *Maximum W/C Ratios for Various Exposure Conditions*

Exposure Condition	Normal-Weight Concrete (Absolute W/C Ratio by Weight)
Concrete protected from exposure to freezing and thawing or the application of deicer chemicals	Select a W/C ratio on the basis of strength, workability, and finishing needs
Watertight concrete* In freshwater In seawater	0.50 0.45
Frost-resistant concrete* Thin sections; any section with less than a 2-in. cover over reinforcement and any concrete exposed to de-icing salts	0.45
All other structures	0.50
Exposure to sulfates* Moderate Severe	0.50 0.45
Concrete placed underwater	Do not use less than 650 lb of cement per cubic yard
Floors on grade	Select W/C ratio for strength, plus minimum cement requirements.

*For the properties of watertight concrete, frost-resistant concrete and exposure to sulfates, use designing strength for air-entrained concrete.

Table 4-3   *Minimum Compressive Strength of Residential Construction Concrete (28-Day psi)*

Type	Weathering Potential		
	Neg	Mod	Severe
Basement walls, foundations not exposed to weather	2,500	2,500	2,500[a]
Interior slabs and basement slabs	2,500	2,500	2,500[a]
Basement walls, foundations, walls exposed to weather	2,500	3,000[b]	3,000[b]
Porches, carports, garage slabs, and steps exposed to the weather	2,500	3,000[b]	3,500[b]

[a]If subjected to freezing in construction then it must be air-entrained 5–7%.
[b]Must be air-entrained 5–7%.

Sulfate resistance. Entrained air improves concrete's resistance to sulfate. Concrete made with a low water/concrete (W/C) ratio, entrained air, and cement having a low tricalcium-aluminate content is the most resistant to sulfate attack.

Strength. The voids-to-cement ratio basically determines air-entrained concrete strength. For this ratio, voids are defined as the total volume of water plus air (both entrained and entrapped). When the air content remains constant, the strength varies inversely with the W/C ratio. As the air content increases, you can generally maintain a given strength by holding the voids-to-cement ratio constant. To do this, reduce the amount of mixing water, increase the amount of cement, or both. Any strength reduc-

tion that accompanies air entrainment is minimized because air-entrained concrete has lower W/C ratios than non-air-entrained concrete having the same slump. However, it is sometimes difficult to attain high strength with air-entrained concrete, such as when slumps remain constant while the concrete's temperature rises when using certain aggregates.

Abrasion resistance. Air-entrained concrete has about the same abrasion resistance as that of non-air-entrained concrete of the same compressive strength. Abrasion resistance increases as the compressive strength increases.

Watertightness. Air-entrained concrete is more watertight than non-air-entrained concrete because entrained air prevents interconnected capillary channels from forming. Therefore, use air-entrained concrete where watertightness is a requirement.

Air-Entraining Materials

Air-entraining admixtures are usually liquid derivatives of natural wood resins, animal or vegetable fats or oils, alkali salts of sulfated or sulfonated organic compounds, and water-soluble soaps intended for use in the mixing water. The manufacturer provides instructions to produce a specified air content. Some manufacturers market automatic dispensers that accurately control the quantities of air-entraining agents in a mix. Air is incorporated in concrete by using air-entraining cement, an air-entraining admixture at the mixer, or both methods. Air-entraining cements should meet the specifications in ASTM C175. Add commercial air-entraining admixtures at the mixer. They should comply with *ASTM C260*. Use adequate controls to always ensure the proper air content. Factors affecting air content are:

Aggregate gradation and cement content. Both significantly affect the air content of both air-entrained and non-air-entrained concrete. For aggregate sizes smaller than $1\frac{1}{2}$ in., the air content increases sharply as the aggregate size decreases due to the increase in cement volume. As cement content increases, the air content decreases but remains within the normal range of the cement content.

Fine aggregate (FA) content. This affects the percentage of entrained air in concrete. Increasing the FA content incorporates more air in a given amount of air-entraining cement or admixture.

Slump and vibration. These affect the air content of air-entrained concrete because the greater the slump, the larger the percentage reduction in air content during vibration. At all slumps, even a 15-second vibration causes reduced air content. However, properly applied vibration mainly eliminates large air bubbles and little of the intentionally entrained, tiny air bubbles.

Concrete temperature. Its effects become more pronounced as slump increases. Less air is entrained as the concrete's temperature increases.

Mixing action. This is the most important factor in producing air-entrained concrete. The amount of entrained air varies with the mixer type and condition, the amount of concrete mixed, and the mixing rate. Stationary and transit mixers may produce concrete having very different amounts of entrained air. Mixers not loaded to capacity can increase air content, whereas overloading can decrease air content. Generally, more air is entrained as the mixing speed increases.

Admixtures and coloring agents. These can reduce the amount of entrained air, particularly fly ash having high percentages of carbon. To prevent a chemical reaction with certain air-entraining admixtures, you must add calcium-chloride solutions to the mix separately.

Premature finishing operations. This can cause excess water to work itself to the concrete surface. If this occurs, the surface zone may not contain enough entrained air and be susceptible to scaling.

CONCRETE PRACTICES, TEST METHODS, AND REPORTING STANDARDS

Test ready-mixed concrete in accordance with the following methods:

1. *Compression test specimens*—Practice C 31/C 31M, using standard moist curing in accordance with the applicable provisions of Practice C 31/C 31M.

2. *Compression tests*—Test Method C 39.

3. *Yield, mass per cubic foot*—Test Method C 138.

4. *Air content*—Test Method C 138, Test Method C 173, or Test Method C 231.

5. *Slump*—Test Method C 143/C 143 M.

6. *Sampling fresh concrete*—Practice C.

7. *Temperature*—Test Method C 1064.

8. The testing laboratory performing acceptance tests of concrete shall meet the requirements of Practice C 1077.

9. Laboratory reports of concrete test results used to determine compliance with this specification shall include a statement that all tests performed by the laboratory or its agents were in accordance with the applicable test methods or shall note all known deviations from the prescribed procedures. The reports shall also list any part of the test methods not performed by the laboratory.

10. Tests of concrete required to determine compliance with this specification shall be made by a certified ACI Concrete Field Testing Technician, Grade I, or equivalent. Equivalent personnel certification programs shall include both written and performance examination as outlined in ACI CP-1.

11. Samples of concrete shall be obtained in accordance with Practice C 172, except when taken to determine uniformity of slump within any one batch or load of concrete.

12. Slump, air content, density, and temperature tests shall be made at the time of placement at the option of the Inspector as often as it is necessary for control checks. In addition, these tests shall be made when specified and always when strength specimens are made.

13. Strength tests as well as slump, temperature, density, and air content tests shall generally be made with a frequency of not less than one test for each 150 yd^3. Each test shall be made from a separate batch. On each day concrete is delivered, at least one strength test shall be made for each class of concrete.

14. If the measured slump or air content falls outside the specified limits, a check test shall be made immediately on another portion of the same sample. In the event of a second failure, the concrete shall be considered to have failed the requirements of the specification.

Strength

1. When strength is used as a basis for acceptance of concrete, standard specimens shall be made in accordance to Practice C 31/C 31M. The specimens shall be cured under standard moisture and temperature conditions in accordance with the applicable provisions of Practice C 31/C 31M. The technician performing the strength test shall be certified as an ACI Concrete Laboratory Testing Technician—Grade I or II or by an equivalent written and performance test program.

2. For a strength test, at least two standard test specimens shall be made from a composite sample. A test shall be the average of the strengths of the specimens tested at the age specified. If a specimen shows definite evidence, other than low strength, of improper sampling, molding, handling, curing, or testing, it shall be discarded and the strength of the remaining cylinder shall then be considered the test result.

3. Note—Additional tests may be made at other ages to obtain information for determining form removal time or when a structure may be put in service.

4. The representative of the purchaser shall ascertain and record the delivery-ticket number for the concrete and the exact location in the work at which each load represented by a strength test is deposited.

5. To conform to the requirements of this specification, strength tests representing each class of concrete must meet the following two requirements:

   a. The average of any three consecutive strength tests shall be equal to, or greater than, the specified strength, $f'c$, and

   b. No individual strength test shall be more than 500 psi below the specified strength, $f'c$.

Tests for Air Content

Tests that determine air entrainment in freshly mixed concrete measure only air volume, not air-void characteristics. This indicates the adequacy of the air-void system when using air-entraining materials meeting ASTM specifications. Tests should be made regularly during construction, using plastic samples taken immediately after discharge from the mixer and from already placed and consolidated concrete. The following are the standard methods to determine the air content of plastic concrete.

1. *Pressure method.* This method is practical for field testing all concrete except those containing highly porous and lightweight aggregates.

2. *Volumetric method.* This method is practical for field testing concrete, particularly concrete containing lightweight and porous aggregates.

3. *Gravimetric method.* This method is impractical for field testing because it requires accurate knowledge of specific gravities and absolute volumes of concrete ingredients. It is satisfactory for laboratory use.

Admixtures

Following are admixtures that modify concrete:

- *Water-reducing admixtures.* These reduce the quantity of mixing water required to produce concrete of a given consistency. The slump is increased for a given water content.

- *Superplasticizers.* These are high-range water reducers and are added to concrete with a low-to-normal slump and water-cement ratio to make high-slump flowing concrete. Flowing concrete is a highly fluid but workable concrete that can be placed with little or no vibration or compaction and can still be free of excessive bleeding or segregation.

- Flowing concrete is used

   1. In thin section placements

   2. In areas of closely spaced and congested reinforcing steel

3. In tremie pipe (underwater) placements

4. In pumped concrete to reduce pump pressure, thereby increasing lift and distance capacity

5. In areas where conventional consolidation methods are impractical or cannot be used

6. For reducing handling costs

The addition of a superplasticizer to a 3-in. slump of concrete can easily produce a concrete with a 9-in. slump. Flowing concrete is defined as having a slump greater than 7½ in., yet maintaining cohesive properties.

The effect of most superplasticizers in increasing workability or making flowing concrete is short-lived, 30 to 60 min, and is followed by a rapid loss in workability (slump loss). Due to this slump loss, these admixtures are often added to the concrete at the job site. Extended-slump-life high-range water reducers added at the batch plant help reduce slump-loss problems.

- *Retarding admixtures.* These are sometimes used to reduce the rate of hydration to permit placing and consolidating concrete before the initial set. They also offset the accelerating effect of hot weather on the set. These admixtures generally consist of fatty acids, sugars, and starches.

- *Accelerating admixtures.* These hasten the set and strength development. Calcium chloride is the most common. Add in solution form as part of the mixing water, but don't exceed 2% by weight of cement. Do not use calcium chloride or other admixtures containing soluble chlorides in prestressed concrete or concrete containing embedded aluminum, in permanent contact with galvanized steel, subject to alkali-aggregate reaction, or exposed to soils or water containing sulfates.

- *Pozzolans.* These materials contain considerable silica or much silica and alumina. They are combined with calcium hydroxide to form compounds having cement-like properties. Pozzolans should be tested first to determine their suitability, because the properties of pozzolans and their effects on concrete vary considerably.

- *Workability agents.* These improve the workability of fresh concrete. They include entrained air, certain organic materials, and finely divided materials. When used as workability agents, fly ash and natural pozzolans should conform to ASTM C618.

- *Damp-proofing and permeability-reducing agents.* These are water-repellent materials that are used to reduce the capillary flow of moisture through concrete that contacts water or damp earth. Pozzolans are also permeability-reducing agents.

- *Grouting agents.* These are various air-entraining admixtures, accelerators, retarders, and workability agents that alter the properties of portland cement grouts for specific applications.

- *Gas-forming agents.* When added to concrete or grout in very small quantities, they cause a slight expansion before hardening in certain applications. However, while hardening, the concrete or grout decreases in volume in an amount equal to or greater than that of normal concrete or grout.

Recommended Air Contents

Table 4-4   *Recommended Air Contents*

Exposure	Max. Aggregate Size (in.)				
	⅜	½	¾	1	1½
Mild	4.5	4.0	3.5	3.0	2.5
Moderate	6.0	5.5	5.0	4.5	4.5
Severe	7.5	7.0	6.0	6.0	5.5

Exposure definitions (ACI 211.1)

Mild. Indoor or outdoor concrete in an area that it will not be exposed to freezing, thawing, or deicing chemicals.

Moderate. Freezing is expected, but the concrete will not be continually exposed to moisture or free water for long periods prior to freezing; and it is not exposed to any deicing chemicals.

Severe. This is concrete that is directly exposed to freezing and is subject to becoming saturated by moisture or free water and deicing chemicals.

Grouts

- *ASTM C476.* Requires a minimum compressive strength of 2000 psi at 28 days.

- *Slump.* Needs to be in the range of 8 to 11 in. to ensure all cavities (in CMUs) are filled.

- *Type M or S.* Mortar to which sufficient water added can be used as grout.

For moderate and severe locations that are exposed to the weather, air-entrained must be not less than 5% and no more than 7%.

Table 4-5 Minimum Required Concrete Strength

% Concrete Strength					
Cement Type	3 Days	7 Days	14 Days	28 Days	60 Days
I	40	60	80	100	100
II	33	55	65	80	100
III	60	80	100	120	100
IV	20	40	55	75	100
V	20	40	60	80	100

JOB SITE CONCRETE MIXING

Table 4-6 Job Site Concrete Mixing

Max. Water/Cement Ratio			
Strength	Min. Number Sacks per Cu. Yd.	Ratio by Weight	U.S. Gal. per Bag
2,500	5	0.67	7.6
3,000	5½	0.58	6.6
3,500	6	0.51	5.8

Field Test for Moisture on Sand

Sands used as the fine aggregate in concrete may contribute a significant amount of moisture to the concrete mix. This moisture should be accounted for by decreasing the amount of water added to the dry materials in order to maintain the WIC ratio that is a part of the concrete design. The following procedure can be used as a field test for estimating the amount of moisture in sand. The procedure allows for some variation in estimating; therefore, the percentage of moisture determined is somewhat judgmental.

The samples used for this test should be taken from a depth of 6 to 8 in. below the surface of the piled sand. This negates the effect of evaporation at the surface of the pile. Squeeze a sample of sand in the hand. Then, open the hand and observe the sample. The amount of free surface moisture (FSM) can be estimated from the following criteria:

- *Damp sand (0–2% FSM).* The sand will fall apart. The damper the sand, the more it tends to cling together.
- *Wet sand (3–4% FSM).* The sand will cling together without excess water being forced out.
- *Very wet sand (5–8% FSM).* The sand ball will glisten or sparkle with water. The sand will have moisture on it and may even drip.

Fig. 4-2 *Damp sand.*

Fig. 4-3 *Wet sand.*

Fig. 4-4 *Very wet sand.*

The percentage of FSM determined by this method approximates the amount of water by weight on the sand. Use these estimates to adjust the mix design as indicated below.

Step 1. Determine the approximate FSM of the fine aggregate (FA) (sand) by the squeeze test.

Step 2. Estimate the FSM of the coarse aggregate (CA) by observation. Usually, 2% FSM is the maximum amount that gravel will hold without actually dripping.

Step 3. Multiply the percentages of FSM on the aggregates by their respective weights per cubic yard. This will yield the weight of the FSM on the aggregates.

Step 4. Divide the total weight of the FSM by 8.33 lb/gal to determine the number of gallons of water. Subtract those gallons from the water requirements in the original mix design.

CONCRETE REINFORCEMENT

Table 4-7 *Reinforcing Bar Sizes*

Re-bar Size and No.	Nominal Diameter
2	¼"
3	⅜"
4	½"
5	⅝"
6	¾"
7	⅞"
8	1"

Note: An easy way to determine the diameter—take the number of the bar and divide by 8.

Fig. 4-5 *Tying reinforcing bar on large wall.*

Steel Grading Authority

- *ASTM A615.* Billet steel, made from old car bodies, Grades 40 and 60
- *ASTM A616.* Rail steel (Made from old rail tracks), Grades 50 and 60
- *ASTM 617.* Axle steel, Grades 40 and 60
- *ASTM A706.* Low allow steel, Grade 60

Table 4-8 *Reinforcing Bar Strengths (Minimum Yield)*

Grade	MPa	psi
300	300	43,511
420	420	60,916
520	520	75,420
49	276	40,000
60	414	60,000
75	517	75,000

Note: The minimum strength for residential foundation use is usually Grade 60.

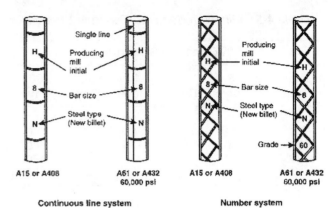

Fig. 4-6 *Re-bar grade markings.*

Table 4-9 *Metric Re-Bars and Inch-Pound Equivalents*

Metric Bar			Inch-Pound Bar		
No.	Dia. (mm)	Mass (kg/m)	No.	Dia. (in.)	Wgt. (lb/ft)
10	9.5	0.56	3	0.375	0.376
13	12.7	0.994	4	0.5	0.668
16	15.9	1.552	5	0.625	1.043
19	19.1	2.235	6	0.75	1.502
22	22.2	3.042	7	0.875	2.044
25	25.4	3.973	8	1	2.67
29	28.7	5.06	9	1.1128	3.4
32	32.3	6.404	10	1.27	4.303
36	35.8	7.907	11	1.41	5.313
43	43	11.384	14	1.693	7.65
57	57.3	20.239	18	2.257	13.6

Table 4-10 *Recommended Clearances for Reinforcement*

Application	Minimum Protection
Footings	3 in.
Concrete exposed to weather	1½ in.
Slabs	¾ in.
Foundation walls	¾ in.
Columns	1½ in.

Note: Check "undisturbed fill" requirements for more code requirements in foundation and basement wall re-bar placement.

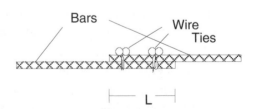

Fig. 4-7 *Proper lapping for re-bar.*

Table 4-11 *Reinforcing Bar Lapping*

Dia.	#11	#10	#9	#8	#7	#6	#5	#4	#3
12D	1-5	1-3	1-2	1-0					
15D	1-9	1-7	1-5	1-3	1-1		Minimum of 1-0 lap.		
17D	2-0	1-11	1-7	1-5	1-3	1-1			
20D	2-4	2-1	1-11	1-8	1-6	1-3	1-1		
24D	2-10	2-6	2-3	2-0	1-9	1-6	1-3	1-0	
27D	3-2	2-10	2-6	2-3	2-0	1-8	1-5	1-2	
30D	3-6	3-2	2-10	2-6	2-2	1-11	1-7	1-3	
35D	4-1	3-8	3-3	2-11	2-7	2-2	1-11	1-6	1-1
40D	4-8	4-3	3-9	3-4	2-11	2-6	2-2	1-8	1-3
45D	5-3	4-9	4-3	3-9	3-3	2-10	2-4	1-11	1-5
50D	5-11	5-4	4-8	4-2	3-8	3-2	2-7	2-1	1-7
60D	7-1	6-4	5-8	5-0	4-5	3-9	3-2	2-6	1-11

Lap (L) for tension bars = 25 times bar dia.

Lap (L) for column bars = 20 times bar dia.

Lap (L) for vertical bars = 40 times bar dia.

Note: If less than 12 in., lap bars 12 in.

Table 4-12 *Reinforcing Bar Tolerances*

Depth of Bar	Depth Placement	Tolerance of Min. Concrete Cover
Less than 8 in.	±⅜ in.	−⅜ in.
More than 8 in.	±½ in.	−½ in.

SOIL CAPACITIES

Footers (Code-Required Widths per Soil Conditions)

Table 4-13 *Soil Capacities for Design Width of Footers*

Wood Frame Construction				
Soil-bearing (psf)				
1,500	**2,000**	**2,500**	**3,000**	**3,500**
1-story 16	12	10	8	7
2-story 19	15	12	10	8
3-story 22	17	14	11	10

4″ Brick Veneer or 8″ Hollow CMU				
1,500	**2,000**	**2,500**	**3,000**	**3,500**
1-story 19	15	12	10	8
2-story 25	19	15	13	11
3-story 31	23	19	16	13

High chair (HC)

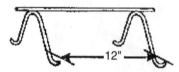

Continuous high chair (CHC)

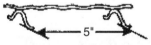

Slab bolster (SB)

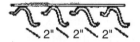

Beam bolster (BB)

Fig. 4-8 *Reinforcement supports.*

- Slope for footers: *Top must be level;* bottom slope <1 in 10 (10% slope).
- At least 12 in. below grade. Needs to be below frost level in your region.
- Spread footings at least 6 in. thick.
- Foundation walls shall extend at least 6 in. above at all points when brick veneer is used 4 in.

Note: See Chapter 3, Sitework, for soil classifications.

Fig. 4-9 *Large machine foundation.*

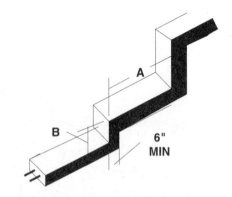

Fig. 4-10 *Step-down footer. Step-down B should not exceed three-fourths of step A.*

TESTING CONCRETE AT THE SITE

Concrete Slump Test

- The purpose of the slump test is to determine and check the consistency and uniformity of the concrete used from batch to batch. Different concrete placements require a specific slump to ensure that the intended strength and workability of the concrete is what the designers required. The standards for the test are from *ASTM C 143 Standard Method of Test for Slump of Portland Cement.*

- From the same truck, take two or more samples from the middle of the discharge. Never take samples from the beginning or the end. Obtain the samples in 15 min. or less (slump test must be made within 5 min. after taking samples.

- Place the samples in a wheelbarrow and remix them before taking the test. Make sure that you have enough to totally fill up the test cone.

Table 4-14 *Soil Lateral Loads*

Soil Description	Unified Soil Classification	Design Lateral Soil Load, psf
Well-graded, clean gravels; gravel-sand mixes	OW	30
Poorly graded, clean gravels; gravel-sand mixes	OP	30
Silty gravels; poorly graded, gravel-sand mixes	OM	.45
Clayey gravels; poorly graded, gravel-sand-clay mixes	OC	45
Well-graded, clean sands; gravelly sand mixes	SW	30
Poorly graded, clean sands; sand-gravel mixes	SP	30
Silty sands; poorly graded, sand-silt mixes	SM	45
Sand-silt-clay mix with plastic fines	SM-SC	45
Clayey sands; poorly graded sand-clay mixes	SC	60
Inorganic silts and clayey silts	ML	45
Mixture of inorganic silt and clay	ML-CL	60
Inorganic clays of low to medium plasticity	CL	60
Organic silts and silt-clays; low plasticity	CL	Check codes
Inorganic clayey silts; elastic silts	MH	60
Inorganic clays of high plasticity	CH	Check codes
Organic clays and silty clays	CH	Check codes

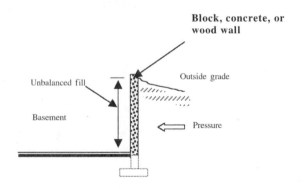

Fig. 4-11 *Unbalanced Fill.*

Table 4-15 Minimum Foundation Wall Widths for Plain Concrete Walls

Wall Height	Max. Unbalanced Backfill	Soil Types		
		GW, GP, SW, SP	GM, GC, SM, SM-SC, ML	SC, MH, ML-CL, Inorg. CL
6	4	6	6	6
	5	6	6	6
	6	8	8*	8*
7	4	6	6	6
	5	6	6	8*
	6	6	8	8
	7	8	8	10
8	4	6	6	6
	5	6	6	8
	6	8	6	10
	7	8	10	10
	8	10	10	12
9	4	6	6	6
	5	6	8*	8
	6	8	8	10
	7	8	10	10
	8	10	10	12
	9	10	12	†

*May be 6 in. if 4000-psi concrete is used.
†Check codes.

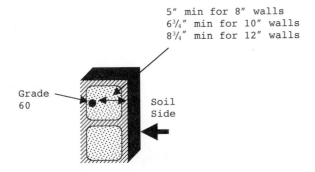

5″ min for 8″ walls
6¾″ min for 10″ walls
8¾″ min for 12″ walls

Grade 60

Soil Side

Fig. 4-12 Reinforcement for concrete and masonry foundation walls.

- Place the test cone on a moistened, level, nonabsorbent surface and fill to approximately one-third the volume of the cone or about 2½ in. high. Use a 24-in.-long, ⅝-in.-dia. steel rod. And with a "bullet"-shaped nose begin to stroke the concrete, first starting along the cones edges. Then, using a spiral-type pattern, progress to the center of the cone for a total of 25 strokes. Make sure each stroke is consistent.

- Next fill the cone to two-thirds full or about half the test cone's height; using the rod, stroke the concrete in the same manner as before. Do not stroke all the way down to the first layer of concrete; stroke just enough to penetrate the layer but not to the bottom.

- Fill the remainder of the cone to overflowing and repeat the strokes as before, making sure not to disturb the second layer of concrete. Using the rod, strike off the top of the test cone to make the concrete level.

- Clean away any overspill from the outside of the cone.

- Immediately after the overspill has been removed, gently lift the cone, being careful not to shake or twist the cone. It is important that all the steps up to now have been done in 2½ min. or fewer and with no interruptions. Place the inverted cone next to the concrete pile, lay the rod across the top of the cone, and measure to the nearest ¼ in. the difference (how much the concrete has fallen). This is the slump.

Fig. 4-13 Measuring the "air content."

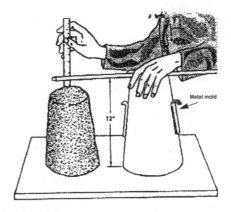

Metal mold

12″

Fig. 4-14 Measuring the slump.

Table 4-16 *Recommended Slumps*

Construction Application	Amount of Slump
Footings	4″ to 6″
8-in. basement wall with moderate ground water	4″ to 6″
8-in. basement wall with severe ground water	3″ to 5″
10-in. basement wall with moderate ground water	4″ to 6″
10-in. basement wall with severe ground water	3″ to 5″
Basement slab	2″ to 4″
Floor slab	2″ to 4″
Steps and stairs	1″ to 4″
Sidewalks, driveways, patios, and porches	2″ to 4″

Fig. 4-16 *Water stop installed in foundation.*

FOOTERS/FOUNDATIONS

Typical Footer Sizes

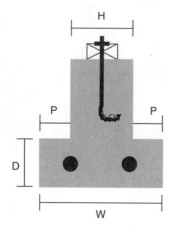

W   Based on the load-bearing capacity of soils and standard engineering practice.
D   A minimum of 6 in. thick.
P   A minimum of 2 in. and not to exceed the dimension of D.
H   Based upon loads, lateral loading, and standard engineering practice.

Fig. 4-15 *Typical inverted "T" footer.*

Table 4-17 *Recommended Footer Tolerances*

Variarion from plans	Minus ½ plus 2″
Forms/misplacement	2% of footing width, but less than 2″.
Thickness	Minus 5% of plan specification

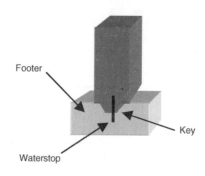

Fig. 4-17 *Foundation keyway with waterstop.*

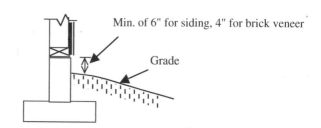

Fig. 4-18 *Foundation heights in respect to exterior veneers.*

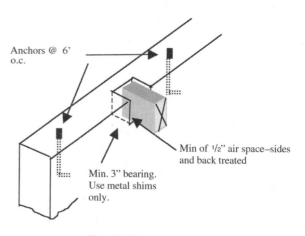

Fig. 4-19 *Beam pockets.*

Minimum Width of Footings

Table 4-18 Minimum Footer Width (in.) Based on Load Capacity of Soils (psf)

	1,500	2,000	2,500	3,000
Conventional Light Frame				
1 story	16	12	10	8
2 story	19	15	12	10
3 story	22	17	14	11
4″ Brick over Light Framing				
1 story	19	15	12	10
2 story	25	19	15	13
3 story	31	23	19	16
8″ Hollow CMU				
1 story	19	15	12	10
2 story	25	19	15	13
3 story	31	23	19	16
8″ Solid or Fully Grouted CMU				
1 story	22	17	13	11
2 story	31	23	19	16
3 story	40	30	24	20

Table 4-19 Load-Bearing Values of Soils

Materials	Load Bearing (psf)
Crystalline bedrock	12,000
Sedimentary and foliated rock	4,000
Sandy gravel, gravel (GW and GP)	3,000
Sand, silty sand, clayey sand, silty gravel, and clayey gravel (SW, SP, SM, SC, GM, and GC)	2,000
Clay, sandy clay, silty clay, clayey silt, silt, and sandy silt (CI, ML, MH, and CH)	1,500

CONCRETE SLABS

Questionable Soils

Where the bearing capacity of the soil is not definitely known or is in question, the building official may require load tests or other adequate proof as to the permissible safe bearing capacity at that particular location. To determine the safe bearing capacity of soil, it shall be tested at such locations and levels as conditions war-

rant by loading an area not less than 4 sq. ft. to not less than twice the maximum bearing capacity desired for use. Such double loads shall be sustained by the soil for a period of not less than 48 hours with no additional settlement taking place.

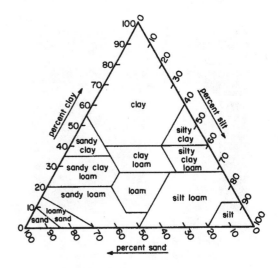

Fig. 4-20 *Soil pyramid.*

MONOLITHIC SLAB

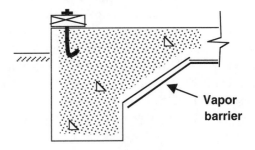

Fig. 4-21 *Monolithic slab with integral footing.*

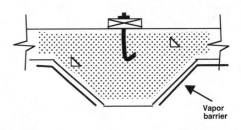

Fig. 4-22 *Monolithic thickened slab for interior footing.*

PIERS (CMU)

- *Unsupported* height less than *10 times* their *least* dimension.

- *Hollow units* must be filled solid with *type M or S* mortar.
- *Unfilled units* may not exceed *4 times* their *least* dimension.
- *Hollow units* must be capped with *4 in.* of solid units or top course *filled solid.*

Fig. 4-23 *Pier with numerous problems including exceeding the height-to-width requirements.*

RECORDS

1. Generally, the records required will be prescribed by the contract requirements and as required by any local or state jurisdiction. Some modifications of the record-keeping system may be in order because of conditions distinctive to a given project, but no such modifications should be made without the full knowledge and approval of the Construction Manager. On large projects or even small ones, it is impossible to be able to go back and review a particular construction event or problem without good records.

Fig. 4-24 *Piers installed incorrectly.*

2. Check with the Project Architect/Manager and contract documents to be sure that you know what records you will be required to keep and that you fully understand the preparation of the various forms involved.

3. If records are being kept with a computer, the Inspector must make sure that they are periodically transferred to a protected disk, CD, or tape for back-up in case of a hard drive failure.

4. It is crucial that you enter information accurately, completely, and promptly in all records. If you are to be absent, make sure that another team member takes the necessary notes for you.

CONCRETE MATERIALS

Preconstruction

1. Before starting concrete work have an on-site meeting and discuss the following:,

   a. Has Contractor given advance notice of source of materials?

   b. Have samples been furnished?

   c. Have mixes been established?

   d. Have tests been completed on air-entraining agent? On curing compound? Concrete placement conditions may be such as to require admixture other than air-entraining agent or calcium chloride. Has this admixture been tested and approved? Reduction of cement content for basic design mix is never permitted. Review plans and specifications.

Table 4-20 *Concrete Water Strength Ratios*

Compressive Strength (psi)	Water/Cement Ratio by Weight
2000	0.8
3000	0.69
4000	0.57
5000	0.47
6000	0.4

   e. Have shop drawings for steel reinforcement and embedded items been approved?

   f. Does the aggregate meet the contract requirements?

   g. Has cement been tested?

2. Check as work proceeds. Are test reports, certificates, and other documents of compliance on hand for all materials being used?

3. Is cement the type specified?

4. Has a trial mix been tested?

Fig. 4-25 *Termite treatment.*

Storage and Handling

1. *Do not* use concrete that is older than *1½ hours* or *has had over 150 rotations* after water has been added. This time may be less during hot weather.

2. Is oldest cement used first?

3. Has over-age cement, if any, been tested?

4. Have arrangements been made to secure all cement from one manufacturer?

5. Are admixtures correctly added at the site or are they specified to be added at the plant?

6. Is the cement on large multiple trucks being used in the same sequence as it is being delivered?

7. If there are *two* separate pour operations going on at the same time with different design mixes, verify the driver's trip ticket.

8. Has an area been designated for trucks to clean up?

CONCRETE PLACEMENT
Forming Concrete

1. General

   a. Use specified wood or metal prefabricated or job site fabricated units.

   b. Check fit-up and bracing to prevent deflection from line and grade.

   c. Check if forms are readily removable, as required.

2. For concealed surfaces, the concrete forms must be tight and sound.

3. For exposed surfaces the forms will be:

   a. Made of approved plywood of proper grade (i.e., BB or BC) or equivalent material in *4 × 8* ft sections.

   b. Same for form lining. Linings shall have solid backing.

c. Are forms treated?

d. Round column forms shall be the prefabricated seamless type. Check form-panel sizes when joints must be located for architectural alignment.

Fig. 4-26 *Braced concrete form wall.*

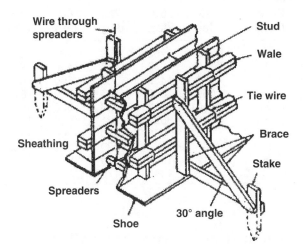

Fig. 4-27 *Typical wall bracing terminology.*

1. Metal forms retained in place for slabs:

   a. Factory-fabricated units are required.

   b. Check shop drawing information on deflection against allowed maximum deflection. Chamfer required?

   c. Are forms hot-dip galvanized?

   d. Are forms ventilated type as required for light-weight concrete?

2. Pan-form units for slabs:

   a. Is type of material approved? Use either prefabricated steel, hardboard, or fiberglass of specified thickness.

   b. Check for damaged units that would affect finished appearance of exposed surfaces.

Concrete Protection

Table 4-21 *Recommended Protection Periods for Air-Entrained Concrete*

Exposure to Freeze-Thaw	Normal Concrete	High-Early Concrete*
No exposure	2 days	1 day
Any exposure	3 days	2 day

*Type III or with an accelerator.

Concrete Rates of Pours

Table 4-22 *Maximum Rate of Pour for Concrete Walls*

	Max. Laterial Pressures (psf)				
Rate of Pour (ft/h)	90 deg	80 deg	70 deg	60 deg	50 deg
1	250	262	278	300	330
2	350	375	407	450	510
3	450	488	536	600	690
4	550	600	664	750	870
5	650	712	793	900	1050
6	750	825	921	1050	1230
7	850	938	1050	1200	1410
8	881	973	1090	1246	1466
9	912	1008	1130	1293	1522
10	943	1043	1170	1340	1578

Table 4-23 *Maximum Rate of Pour for Concrete Columns*

	Max. Laterial Pressures (psf)				
Rate of Pour (ft/h)	90 deg	80 deg	70 deg	60 deg	50 deg
3	450	488	536	600	690
4	550	600	664	750	870
5	650	712	793	900	1050
6	750	825	921	1050	1230
7	850	938	1050	1200	1410
8	950	1050	1178	1350	1590
9	1050	1163	1307	1500	1770
10	1150	1275	1435	1650	1950
11	1250	1388	1564	1800	2130
12	1350	1500	1693	1950	2310
13	1450	1613	1822	2100	2490
14	1550	1725	1950	2250	2670
16	1750	1950	2207	2550	3000
18	1950	2175	2464	2850	3000
20	2150	2400	2721	3000	3000
22	2350	2625	2979	3000	3000
24	2550	2850	3000	3000	3000
26	2750	3000	3000	3000	3000
28	2950	3000	3000	3000	3000
30	3000	3000	3000	3000	3000

Maximum Rate of Concrete Pour Is Affected by

1. Height of pour
2. Rate of pour
3. Weight and type of concrete
4. Outside temperature
5. Amount of vibration
6. Concrete slump
7. Chemical additives

Form Ties

1. Must be removable or snap-off metal tie.
2. Check for ties that will leave a conical hole 1 in. deep at least 3/8 in. but not more than 1 in. in diameter into the concrete from its surfaces.
3. Snap tie break-back from concrete surface will be at least 1 in. when surface is exposed, painted, or given other treatments.

Concrete Column Bracing

Chamfering

1. Check for corner molding in the form at exposed areas.
2. A chamfer strip should be used. Verify what is required in the plans and specifications.

Miscellaneous Material

1. Have the necessary materials such as inserts, slots, clips, anchor bolts, etc., been approved and are they on the job site prior to starting the concrete placement?
2. Contractor must receive approval on materials used for:
   - Capillary water barrier
   - Vapor barrier
   - Waterproofing
   - Reinforcing steel
   - Expansion joint material
   - Joint sealer
   - Forming
   - Curing compound

Table 4-24 Spacing Yokes on Concrete Column

Column's Largest Dimension (in.)						
Height	16	18	20	24	28	30
3						20
4	31				20	19
5		28	26	23	18	18
6					15	12
7	30		24	22		
8		26			13	
9	29		19	16	12	10
10		20			10	9
11	21		16	14		
12		18	15	13	9	8
13	20	16	14	12		
14		15	12		8	7
15	18	13	11	10	7	
16	15			9	6	6
17		12	10			
18	13			8		
19		11				
20	12		9			

Table 4-25 Concrete Tie-Rods and Wires

Steel Wire—Double Strand	
Gage of Wire	Breaking Load (lb)
8	1,700
9	1,420
10	1,170
11	930
Tie-Rods (Typical)	
Snap ties	3,000
Pencil rod ties	3,000

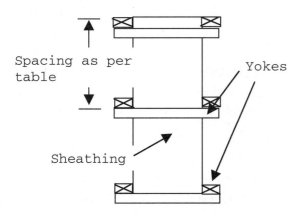

Fig. 4-28 *Parts of a concrete wall or column form.*

(Diagram labels: Spacing as per table; Yokes; Sheathing)

Stockpiles

1. Are aggregate stockpile areas graded, drained, and stabilized so that contamination will not occur?

2. Are aggregate stockpiles separated so that intermixing does not occur? Are they built up to avoid segregation and contamination?

3. Are aggregates conveyed from stockpiles to batching equipment by means that will avoid segregation and intermixing? Do not allow use of bulldozers or similar equipment.

Water

Is the supply of water for mixing and curing protected against contamination?

Note: An increase or decrease of water per cubic yard of concrete by 3% will increase or decrease the slump by 1 in.

Note: A good rule of thumb is not to use water that you wouldn't drink!

Admixtures

1. Is air-entraining admixture protected against freezing during storage?

2. Has over-age admixture, if any, been retested? *Do not use!*

3. Check accuracy of dispenser and correct dispersion of admixture (if done on-site).

Check slump and entrained-air contents as often as necessary to provide record data prescribed by specifications ASTM standards, and as required by the contract documents.

Table 4.26 *Wood Framing/Forming for Concrete Representative Working Stress Values (psi) for Visually Graded Lumber at 19 Percent Moisture Content, Continuing or Prolonged Reuse*

Species and Grade	Extreme Fiber Bending	Compression to Grain	Compression to Grain	Modulus of Elasticity $\times 10^6$
Douglas Fir–Larch				
Range, all grades	275–2450	625–730	475–1850	1.3–1.9
No. 2, 4×4 and smaller	1450	625	1000	1.7
Constr., 4×4 and smaller	875–1050	625	1150	1.5
Eastern Spruce				
Range, all grades	175–1400	390	300–1050	1.0–1.5
No. 2, 4×4 and smaller	975	390	650	1.4
Constr., 4×4 and smaller	700	390	750	1.2
Southern Pine				
Range, all grades	200–2600	375–660	400–2300	1.2–1.9
No. 2, 4×4 and smaller	1150–1400	375–565	650–975	1.4–1.6
Constr., 4×4 and smaller	825–1000	375–565	725–1100	1.2–1.4
Hem-Fir				
Range, all grades	100–1650	405	375–1300	1.1–1.6
No. 2, 4×4 and smaller	1150	405	825	1.4
Constr., 4×4 and smaller	700–825	405	925	1.2
California Redwood				
Range, all grades	225–2300	425–650	500–2150	.9–1.4
No. 2, 4×4 and smaller	1400	650	1100	1.25
Constr., 4×4 and smaller	665–825	425	925	.9
Adjustment for moisture content greater than 19%: Use percentage shown (also applies to wood used wet)	86	67	70	97
Increase for load duration of 7 days or less: Permitted for lumber and plywood	25%	25%	25%	0
Plywood sheathing used wet: Plyform B-B, Class I (grade stress level 5-2)	1545	(Bearing on face) 210	—	1,500,000

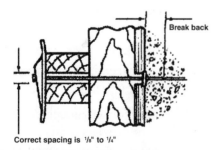

Fig. 4-29 *Concrete wall tie.*

Preplacement Inspection

Check all of the following prior to each placement placing should not be permitted to start until all are satisfactory.

Sample Concrete Panel

The approved panel should be of the same quality required for actual construction. It should include:

- Formed surfaces and joints

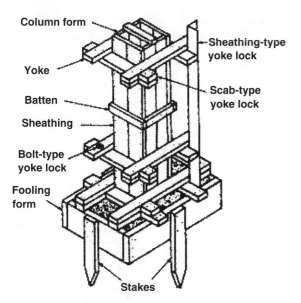

Fig. 4-30 *Typical concrete column bracing.*

Table 4-27 *On-Site Mixing*

Concrete Strength	Bags of 94-lb Concrete	Ratio by Weight	Gal. Water per Bag
2500 psi	5	0.65	7.3
3000 psi	5½	0.58	6.6
3500 psi	6	0.51	5.8
4000 psi	6½	0.44	5
4500 psi	7	0.38	4.3
5000 psi	7½	0.31	3.5

MAX. ALLOWED PRESSURE
POUNDS PER SQ. FT

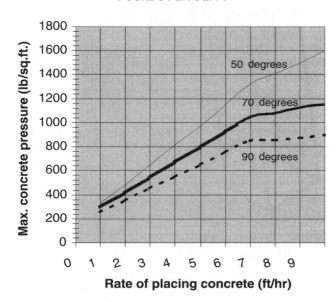

Fig. 4-31 *Concrete pressures at various temperatures and rate of placement.*

Table 4-28 *Pounds of Water per Cubic Yard of Concrete*

Aggregate Sizes				
Non-Air-Entrained Concrete				
Slump	⅜	½	¾	1	1½
1 to 2	350	335	315	300	275
3 to 4	385	365	340	325	300
6 to 7	410	385	360	340	315
% air	3%	2.50%	2%	1.50%	1%
Air-Entrained Concrete				
Slump	⅜	½	¾	1	1½
1 to 2	305	295	280	270	250
3 to 4	340	325	305	295	275
6 to 7	365	345	325	310	290
% air	8.00%	7.00%	6.00%	5.00%	4.50%

- Type of form ties
- Patching, including color match
- Smooth finish or special treatment
- Structural joints and flashing treatment

1. Erect with job mix design before structural formwork begins. Designate a protected location.

2. Reject if unaccepted/approved in writing with minor correction noted, as applicable.

3. Review procedures with all trades concerned.

Footings and Foundations

1. Have location, dimensions, and grade been checked? Use grade stakes in unformed footings. (Remove after pouring.)

2. Has all reinforcement been installed and inspected? Clearances? Laps?

3. Has fill and/or capillary water barrier been compacted to specified density? Fill is prohibited to remedy overexcavation; thicken the footing/foundation. However, never widen the footer without the PM's approval.

4. Mud sill may be required as a working surface.

5. Are foundation excavations free from frost, ice, rocks, or mud; free from standing or running water?

6. Have all penetrations been correctly identified, marked, and blocked out of sleeves installed?

7. Has waterproof paper or polyethylene covering been applied to dry or pervious soils (if specified)?

Table 4-29 *Water Cement Ratios by Weights*

Water/ Cement Ratio, by Weight	Maximum Aggregate (in.)	Air Content	Water, lb/cu. yd. Concrete	Cement, cwt./ cu. yd. Concrete
0.4	⅜	7.5	340	8.5
0.4	½	7.5	320	8
0.4	¾	6	300	7.5
0.4	1	6	280	7
0.4	1½	5	270	6.8
0.45	⅜	7.5	340	7.6
0.45	½	7.5	320	7.1
0.45	¾	6	300	6.7
0.45	1	6	280	6.2
0.45	1½	5	270	6
0.5	⅜	7.5	340	6.8
0.5	½	7.5	320	6.4
0.5	¾	6	300	6
0.5	1	6	280	5.6
0.5	1½	5	270	5.4
0.55	⅜	7.5	340	6.2
0.55	½	7.5	320	5.8
0.55	¾	6	300	5.5
0.55	1	6	280	5.1
0.55	1½	5	270	4.9
0.6	⅜	7.5	340	5.7
0.6	½	7.5	320	5.3
0.6	¾	6	300	5
0.6	1	6	280	4.7
0.6	1½	5	270	4.5
0.65	⅜	7.5	340	5.2
0.65	½	7.5	320	4.9
0.65	¾	6	300	4.6
0.65	1	6	280	4.3
0.65	1½	5	270	4.2
0.7	⅜	7.5	340	4.9
0.7	½	7.5	320	4.6
0.7	¾	6	300	4.3
0.7	1	6	280	4
0.7	1½	5	270	3.9
0.75	⅜	7.5	340	4.5
0.75	½	7.5	320	4.3
0.75	¾	6	300	4
0.75	1	6	280	3.7
0.75	1½	5	270	3.6

Does not include aggregate weight per cubic yard.

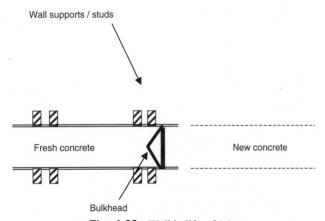

Fig. 4-32 *Wall bulkhead joint.*

8. Have precautions been taken to keep soil from contaminating concrete placed in unformed (neat cut) footing trenches?
   - Is the ambient temperature in the permissible range?
   - Are protections measures available in case of sudden bad weather?

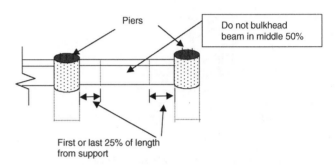

Fig. 4-33 *Grade beam breaks.*

Other Concrete Wall Systems

Insulated concrete form (ICF) systems fall into three categories: monolithic, waffle-grid, and screen-grid.

ICF—monolithic. Monolithic ICFs comprise a constant thickness concrete wall (a monolith) with the additional feature of insulation on each side. The advantage of these systems is their inherent strength, which surpasses that of the other two categories. The major disadvantage is that the amount of concrete used in a monolithic ICF is more than a waffle-type ICF and far more than in a screen-grid ICF.

Waffle-grid ICF. The waffle-grid type, like monolithic systems, forms a continuous wall, but has a narrower cross section in places. The narrower sections result in less concrete usage, at the cost of decreased strength.

Screen-grid ICF. The third type of ICF, the screen-grid, is so named because it comprises a post and beam system with open spaces in between. This type of system has a lower strength rating than monolithic and waffle-grid systems, but they are still extremely strong.

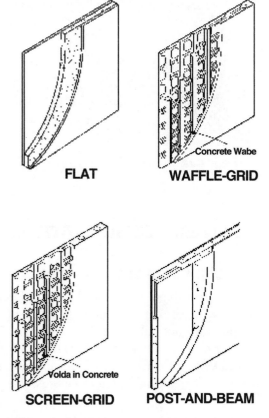

FLAT   **WAFFLE-GRID**

Concrete Wabe

SCREEN-GRID   **POST-AND-BEAM**

Volda in Concrete

Fig. 4-34   *Insulated concrete form (ICF) systems.*

ICF Wall Types

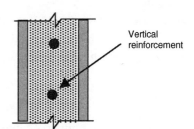

Vertical reinforcement

Fig. 4-35   *Flat ICF.*

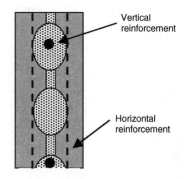

Vertical reinforcement

Horizontal reinforcement

Fig. 4-36   *Waffle ICF.*

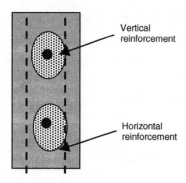

Vertical reinforcement

Horizontal reinforcement

Fig. 4-37   *Screen-grid ICF.*

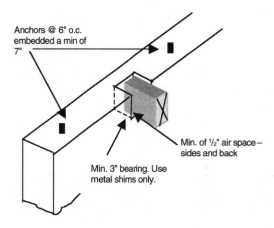

Anchors @ 6" o.c. embedded a min of 7"

Min. of ½" air space— sides and back

Min. 3" bearing. Use metal shims only.

Fig. 4-38   *Beam pockets.*

Slabs on Grade

1. Check for a capillary water barrier.
2. Runs for electric conduit and piping systems must be located *below* the slab.
3. Mud sill may be required as a working surface.
4. Is the vapor barrier membrane of specified thickness? Are the joints lapped at least 6 in.? Is it sealed with tape at laps and penetrations?
5. Check slump and entrained-air contents as often as necessary to provide record data prescribed by the job policy, and more often if necessary to confirm visual checks.
6. Check the placement of the specified reinforcing steel. Are concrete blocks or chair rails being used? Do they allow for the proper clearance?
7. All trades with under-slab work should have one person standing by to repair and inspect all stubouts during and after the concrete pour.

Welded Wire Fabric

- Welded wire mesh is to be lapped at least one full stay of spacing plus an additional 2 in. Thus for 6×6-in. fabric the lap must be at least 8 in.

- Lap all reinforcing bars a minimum of 24 times their diameter and never less than 12 in.

- Aggregate size is to be limited to ¾ the size of the minimum spacing between the reinforcement and forms.

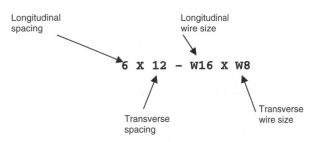

Fig. 4-39 Welded wire markings.

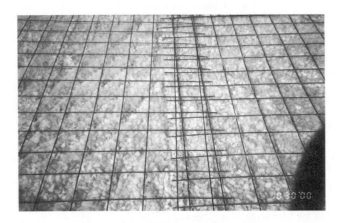

Fig. 4-40 Welded wire fabric/mesh.

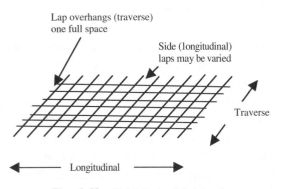

Fig. 4-41 Welded wire fabric/mesh.

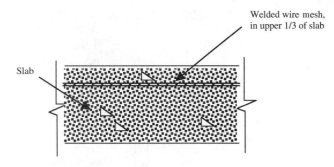

Fig. 4-42 Wire fabric/mesh placement.

WEATHER CONSIDERATIONS

Cold Weather Concrete

- When preparing to pour concrete in cold or freezing temperatures it is extremely important that protection is provided not only for the concrete itself, but for the formwork and re-bars as well. At no time should concrete be placed on frozen subgrade. This will result in cracks and possible failures when the subgrade thaws.

- Concrete should be between 50 and 70°F. While the hydration process does generate some heat, it still may need additional heating and protection. At no time should the materials be heated to the point that the concrete is above 70°F. This will seriously reduce the strength.

- Moisture is very important in cold weather placement. Keep the concrete moist, especially if heating. It is recommended to keep fresh concrete at 70°F for

Table 4-30 *Recommended Concrete Temperatures (°F) for Cold Weather Construction*

Condition	Temp.	Temperatures		
		Thin	Moderate	Mass
Min. temperature of fresh concrete as mixed	>30	60	55	50
	0–30	65	60	55
	<0	70	65	60
Min. temperature of fresh concrete as placed		55	50	45
Maximum allowable for gradual drop in first 24 hr after end of protection		55	40	30

3 days or at 50°F for 5 days. If high-early concrete is used, keep at 70°F for 2 days or at 50°F for 3 days. Never allow the concrete to freeze for the next 4 days.

Concrete Insulation

Table 4-31 *Concrete Insulation per Mix Designs*

Insulation Required for Concrete Placed at 50°F (300 lb/cu. yd.)				
	Thickness of Batt Insulation			
Thickness of Concrete	0.5 in.	1.0 in.	1.5 in.	2.0 in.
6 in.	45	41	33	28
12 in.	41	29	17	5
18 in.	35	19	0	−17

Insulation Required for Concrete Placed at 50°F (400 lb/cu. yd.)				
	Thickness of Batt Insulation			
Thickness of Concrete	0.5 in.	1.0 in.	1.5 in.	2.0 in.
6 in.	46	38	28	21
12 in.	38	22	6	−11
18 in.	31	8	−16	−39

Insulation Required for Concrete Placed at 50°F (500 lb/cu. yd.)				
	Thickness of Batt Insulation			
Thickness of Concrete	0.5 in.	1.0 in.	1.5 in.	2.0 in.
6 in.	45	35	22	14
12 in.	35	15	−5	−26
18 in.	37	−3	−33	−65

Insulation Required for Concrete Placed at 50°F (600 lb/cu. yd.)				
	Thickness of Batt Insulation			
Thickness of Concrete	0.5 in.	1.0 in.	1.5 in.	2.0 in.
6 in.	44	32	16	6
12 in.	32	8	−16	−41
18 in.	21	−14	−50	−89

Fig. 4-43 *Slab concrete pour protected with "blankets."*

Hot Weather Concrete

Concreting in hot weather poses some special problems such as strength reduction and cracking of flat surfaces due to too-rapid drying.

Concrete that stiffens before consolidation is caused by too-rapid setting of the cement and too much absorption and evaporation of mixing water. This leads to difficulty in finishing flat surfaces. Therefore, limitations are imposed on placing concrete during hot weather and on the maximum temperature of the concrete; quality and durability suffer when concrete is mixed, placed, and cured at high temperatures. During hot weather take steps to limit concrete temperature to less than 90°F, but problems can arise even with concrete temperatures less than 90°F. The combination of hot dry weather and high winds is the most severe condition, especially when placing large exposed slabs.

Effects of High Concrete Temperatures

Three common things affect high concrete temperatures.

1. *Compressive strength of concrete.* Figure 4-44 demonstrates the effect of high concrete temperatures on compressive strength. Tests using identical concretes having the same *W/C* ratio show that while higher concrete temperatures increase early strength, the reverse happens at later stages. If water content is increased to maintain the same slump (without changing the cement content), the reduction in compressive strength is even greater than that shown in Figure 4-46.

2. *Water requirements.* Because high temperatures accelerate hardening, a particular concrete consistency generally requires more mixing water than normal. Figure 4-45 shows a linear relationship be-

tween an increase in concrete temperature and the increase in mixing water required to maintain the same slump. However, increasing water content without increasing cement content results in a higher *W/C* ratio, which has a harmful effect on the strength and other desirable properties of hardened concrete.

3. *Cracks.* In hot weather the tendency for cracks to form increases both before and after hardening. Rapid water evaporation from hot concrete can cause plastic shrinkage cracks even before the surface hardens. Cracks can also develop in the hardened concrete because of increased shrinkage due to a higher water requirement, and because of the greater difference between the high temperature at the time of hardening and the low temperature to which the concrete later drops.

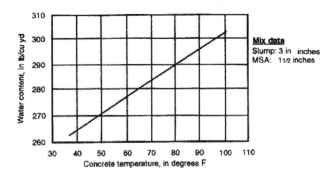

Fig. 4-44 *Concrete temperature and the increase in mixing water required to maintain the same slump.*

Cooling Concrete Materials

The most practical way to obtain a low concrete temperature is to cool the aggregate and water as much as possible before mixing. Mixing water is the easiest to cool and is also the most effective, pound for pound, in lowering concrete temperature. However, because aggregate represents 60–80% of the concrete's total weight, the concrete temperature depends primarily on the aggregate temperature. Figure 4-45 shows the effects of the mixing water and aggregate temperatures on the temperature of fresh concrete. Lower the temperature of fresh concrete by:

• Using cold mixing water. In extreme cases, add slush ice to chill the water.

• Cooling CA by sprinkling, thereby avoiding too much mixing water.

• Insulating mixer drums or cooling them with sprays or wet burlap coverings.

• Insulating water supply lines and tanks or painting them white.

• Shading those materials and facilities not otherwise protected from the heat.

• Working only at night.

• Sprinkling forms, reinforcing steel, and subgrade with cool water just before placing concrete.

Special Precautions

High temperatures increase the hardening rate, thereby shortening the length of time available to handle and finish the concrete. Concrete transport and placement must be completed as quickly as possible. Take extra care to avoid cold joints when placing concrete. Proper curing is especially important in hot weather due to the greater danger of crazing and cracking. But curing is also difficult in hot weather, because water evaporates rapidly from the concrete, and the efficiency of curing compounds is reduced. Leaving forms in place is not a satisfactory way to prevent moisture loss when curing concrete in hot weather. Loosen the forms as soon as possible without damaging the concrete and cover the concrete with water. Then use frequent sprinkling, wet burlap, or other similar means of retaining moisture for longer periods.

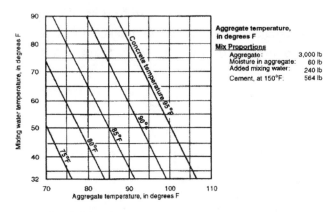

Fig. 4-45 *Effects of the mixing water and aggregate temperatures on the temperature of fresh concrete.*

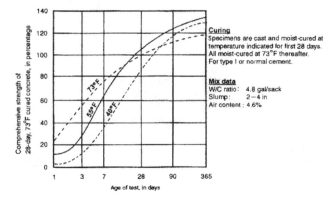

Fig. 4-46 *Comparison of compression strengths of varying concrete temperatures.*

PREPLACEMENT INSPECTION

Check all of the following prior to each placement; concrete placing should not be permitted to start until all are satisfactory. Plan ahead!

Sample Concrete Panel

Approved panel will be representative of quality required, including:

- Formed surfaces and joints
- Type of form ties
- Patching, including color match
- Finish specifications or special treatment
- Structural joints and flashing treatment
- Erect with job mix design before structural form work begins
- Designate a protected location

Footings and Foundations

1. Have location, dimensions, and grade been checked?
2. Has fill and/or capillary water barrier been compacted to specified density? Loose fill is prohibited to remedy overexcavation; thicken the footing/foundation. Check with the Site Superintendent if it is excessive.
3. Are foundation excavations free from frost, ice, mud, or standing water?
4. Is bottom of excavation frozen?
5. Check all reinforcements and embeds.
6. Has waterproof paper or polyethylene covering been applied to dry or pervious soils? Check specifications.
7. Cold joints prepped?
8. Are all sleeves in place and correct?
9. Have precautions been taken to keep soil from falling in on the concrete?
10. Have all reinforcements been inspected for proper grade, clearances?
11. Have all insulations been inspected and correctly spaced? Checked for correct thickness and type?

Foundation Insulations

1. Vertical insulation should be expanded polystyrene or extruded polystyrene. (Check specifications.)
2. Horizontal insulation is to be extruded polystyrene.

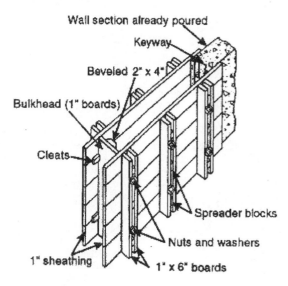

Fig. 4-47 *Typical forming (cold joint) in concrete wall forming.*

3. Horizontal insulation placed less than 12 in. below the ground or the portion extending outward from the foundation edge more than 24 in. requires protection.
4. Protection consists of:
   a. Concrete slab
   b. Asphalt paving
   c. Cementitous board
   d. Rated plywood
   e. Other approved materials
5. Insulation in "heavy" termite-infested areas. Extruded and expanded polystyrene, polyisocyanurate, and other foam plastics are not to be installed on the exterior face or under interior or exterior walls or slab foundations located below grade.

The clearance between the foam plastic installed above grade and exposed earth is to be at least 6 in.

Fig. 4-48 *Foundation wall insulation.*

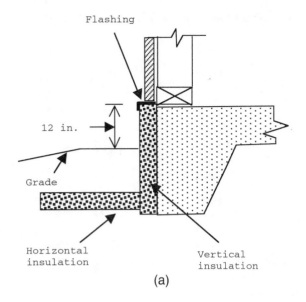

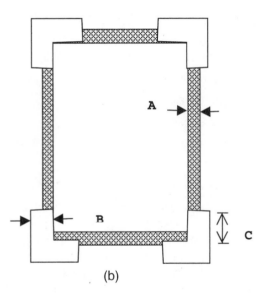

Fig. 4-49 *Typical foundation insulation.*

Table 4-33 Minimum Required Insulation for Figure 4-49

Air Freezing Index	Horizontal Insulation Dimensions		
	A	**B**	**C**
1,500 or less	NR	NR	NR
2,000	NR	NR	NR
2,500	12	24	40
3,000	12	24	40
3,500	24	30	60
4,000	24	36	60

Note: See Appendix for air freezing index.

Unbalanced Backfill

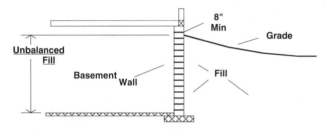

Fig. 4.50 *Unbalanced fill.*

Table 4-34 *Concrete/CMU Walls Maximum Height of Unbalanced Fill*

Wall Height	Max. Unbalanced Backfill	Soil Types		
		GW, GP, SW, SP	GM, GC, SM, SM-SC, ML	SC, MH, ML-CL, Inorg. CL
6	4	6	6	6
	5	6	6	6
	6	6	8*	8*
7	4	6	6	6
	5	6	6	8*
	6	6	8	8
	7	8	8	10
8	4	6	6	6
	5	6	6	8
	6	8*	8	10
	7	8	10	10
	8	10	10	12
9	4	6	6	6
	5	6	8*	8
	6	8	8	10
	7	8	10	10
	8	10	10	12
	9	10	12	Design req.

*OK if 4000 psi is used.
Concrete walls: Maximum height of unbalanced backfill per soil type.

Table 4-32 Minimum Required Insulation

Air Freezing Index	Vertical Insulation R-value	Horizontal R-value along Walls	Horizontal R-value at Corners
1,500 or less	4.5	NR	NR
2,000	5.6	NR	NR
2,500	6.7	1.7	4.9
3,000	7.8	6.5	8.6
3,500	9.0	8.0	11.2
4,000	10.1	10.5	13.1

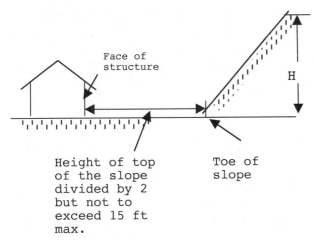

Height of top of the slope divided by 2 but not to exceed 15 ft max.

Face of structure

Toe of slope

H

Fig. 4-51 *Foundation clearance from slopes.*

Table 4-36 *Crawlspace Vents (with Vapor Barrier)*

Underfloor Area (sq. ft.)	With Vapor Barrier Sq. Ft. Required	Number of 7-in. × 15-in. Vents Required
1200	0.80	2
1400	0.93	2
1600	1.07	2
1800	1.20	2
2000	1.33	2
2200	1.47	3
2400	1.60	3
2600	1.73	3
2800	1.87	3
3000	2.00	3
3200	2.13	4
3400	2.27	4
3600	2.40	4

CRAWLSPACE VENTING

Ventilation

The underfloor space between the bottom of floor joist and the earth requires ventilation openings through the foundation walls. Without a vapor retarder the ratio is 1 sq. ft. of ventilation for every 150 sq. ft. of underfloor area. The ratio is 1:1500 if the underfloor area is protected by an approved vapor retarder.

Table 4-35 *Crawlspace Vents (No Vapor Barrier)*

Underfloor Area (sq. ft.)	Square Feet Required: No Vapor Barrier	Number of 7-in. × 15-in. Vents Required
1200	8.00	12
1400	9.33	14
1600	10.67	16
1800	12.00	18
2000	13.33	20
2200	14.67	22
2400	16.00	24
2600	17.33	26
2800	18.67	28
3000	20.00	30
3200	21.33	31
3400	22.67	33
3600	24.00	35

Slabs on Grade

1. Check for a capillary water barrier.
2. Runs for electric conduit and piping systems must be located below the slab.
3. Mud sill may be required as a working surface.

4. Is the vapor barrier membrane of specified thickness (minimum 6 mil)? Is it sealed with tape at laps (a minimum 6 in.) and penetrations?
5. If a series of braces originate from the same anchor point, are the braces tied together vertically halfway between anchor form?

ADA REQUIREMENTS (FLATWORK)

Ramps

1. Any route with a slope greater than 1:20 is considered to be a ramp, and must meet all ADA requirements.
2. The maximum slope allowed for ramps is 1:12, one unit of rise for every 12 units of run.
3. The maximum rise for any run is 30 in.
4. The minimum clear width of ramps is to be 36 in.
5. Cross slope of ramps maximum of 1:50.

Landings

1. Must be as wide as the ramp leading to it.
2. Length must be at least 60 in. clear.
3. When the landing is used to change directions of the ramp, then it must be at least 60 in. × 60 in.

Handrails

1. Handrails are required if the rise is greater than 6 in. or the run is longer than 72 in.
2. Clear space between the handrail and wall is to be 1½ in.
3. Top of handrail to be mounted between 34 in. and 38 in.

SHORING ELEVATED SLABS

Check that they are tied off in four directions at enough points to prevent bending or movement. After leveling the forms, have the shore wedges been secured in position?

Fig. 4-52 *Incorrectly placed shoring (notice the bent 2 × 4 supports).*

1. *General:* Shoring installations constructed in accordance with this standard shall be designed in accordance with American National Standard Recommended Practice for Concrete Formwork, ANSI-(ACI 347-78), Formwork for Concrete ACI 318-83, or with the following publications of the Scaffolding & Shoring Institute: Recommended Standard Safety Code for Vertical Shoring, 1970; Single Post Shore Safety Rules, 1969; and Steel Frame Shoring Safety, Safety Rules, 1969.

2. All shoring equipment shall be inspected prior to erection to determine that it is as specified in the shoring layout.

3. A shoring layout shall be prepared or approved by a person qualified to analyze the loadings and stresses that are induced during the construction process.

4. A copy of the shoring layout shall be available at the job site.

5. The shoring layout shall include all details of the specification, including unusual conditions such as heavy beams, sloping areas, ramps, and cantilevered slabs, as well as plan and elevation views.

6. Shoring equipment found to be damaged such that its strength is reduced to less than that required shall not be used for shoring.

7. Erected shoring equipment shall be inspected immediately prior to, during, and immediately after concrete placement.

8. Upon inspection, shoring equipment that is found to be damaged or weakened shall be immediately removed and replaced.

9. The sills for shoring shall be sound, rigid, and capable of carrying the maximum intended load without settlement or displacement.

10. All base plates, shore heads, extension devices, and adjustment screws shall be in firm contact, and secured when necessary, with the foundation and the form.

11. Eccentric loads on shore heads and similar members shall be prohibited unless these members have been designed for such loading.

12. The minimum total design load for any shoring used in slab and beam structures shall be not less than 100 lb/sq. ft. for the combined live and dead loads regardless of slab thickness; however, the minimum allowance for live load and formwork shall be not less than 20 lb/sq. ft. in addition to the weight of the concrete. Additional allowance for a live load shall be added for special conditions other than when placing concrete for standard-type slabs and beams. Shoring shall also be designed to resist all foreseeable lateral loads such as wind, cable tensions, inclined supports, impact of placement, and starting and stopping of equipment. The assumed value of load due to wind, impact of concrete, and equipment acting in any direction at each floor line shall not be less than 100 lb per lineal foot of floor edge or 2% of total dead load of the floor, whichever is greater.

13. When motorized carts are used, the design load shall be increased 25 lb/sq. ft.

14. The design stresses for form lumber and timbers shall be within the tolerance of the grade, condition, and species of lumber used.

15. The design stresses used for form lumber and timber shall be shown on all drawings, specifications, and shoring layouts.

16. All load-carrying timber members of scaffold framing shall be a minimum of 1500 f (stress grade) construction grade lumber. All dimensions are nominal sizes, except where rough sizes are noted, only rough or undressed lumber of the size specified shall satisfy minimum requirements.

17. When shoring from soil, an engineer or other qualified person shall determine that the soil is adequate to support the loads which are to be placed on it.

18. Precautions shall be taken so that weather conditions do not change the load-carrying conditions of the soil below the design minimum.

19. When shoring from fill or when excessive earth disturbance has occurred, an engineer or other qualified person shall supervise the compaction and reworking of the disturbed area and determine that it is capable of carrying the loads that are to be imposed upon it.

20. Suitable sills shall be used on a pan or grid dome floor or any other floor system involving voids where vertical shoring equipment could concentrate an excessive load on a thin concrete section.

21. When temporary storage of reinforcing rods, material, or equipment on top of formwork becomes necessary, these areas shall be sufficient to meet the loads.

22. If any deviation in the shoring plan is necessary because of field conditions, the person who prepared the shoring layout shall be consulted for approval of the actual field setup before concrete is placed.

23. The shoring setup shall be checked to ensure that all details of the layout have been met.

24. The completed shoring setup shall be a homogenous unit or units and shall have the specified bracing to give it lateral stability.

25. The shoring setup shall be checked to make certain that bracing specified in the shoring layout for lateral stability is in place.

26. All vertical shoring equipment shall be plumb. Maximum allowable deviation from the vertical is ⅛ in. in 3 ft. If this tolerance is exceeded, the shoring equipment shall not be used until readjusted within this limit.

27. Upon inspection, shoring equipment that is found to be damaged or weakened shall be immediately removed and replaced.

28. Shoring equipment shall not be released or removed until the approval of a qualified engineer has been received.

29. Removal of shoring equipment shall be planned so that the equipment that is still in place is not overloaded.

30. Slabs or beams that are to be reshored should be allowed to take their actual permanent deflection before final adjustment of reshoring equipment is made.

31. While the reshoring is underway, no construction loads shall be permitted on the partially cured concrete.

32. The allowable load on the supporting slab shall not be exceeded when reshoring.

33. The reshoring shall be thoroughly checked to determine that it is properly placed and that it has the load capacity to support the areas that are being reshored.

Metal Tubular Frames

1. Metal tubular frames used for shoring shall have allowable loads based on tests conducted according to the *Recommended Procedure for Compression Testing of Scaffolds and Shores*, Scaffolding & Shoring Institute, 1967.

2. Design of shoring layouts shall be based on allowable loads obtained using the test procedures of subsection (1) of this section and on at least a 2½:1 safety factor.

3. All metal frame shoring equipment shall be inspected before erection.

4. Metal frame shoring equipment and accessories shall not be used if heavily rusted, bent, dented, rewelded, or having broken weldments or other defects.

5. All locking devices on frames and braces shall be in good working order, coupling pins shall align the frame or panel legs, pivoted cross braces shall have their center pivot in place, and all components shall be in a condition similar to that of original manufacture.

6. When checking the erected shoring frames with the shoring layout, the spacing between towers and cross-brace spacing shall not exceed that shown on the layout, and all locking devices shall be in the closed position.

7. Devices for attaching the external lateral stability bracing shall be securely fastened to the legs of the shoring frames.

8. All baseplates, shore heads, extension devices, or adjustment screws shall be in firm contact with the footing sill and the form material, and shall be snug against the legs of the frames.

9. Eccentric loads on shore heads and similar members shall be prohibited unless the shore heads have been designed for such loading.

10. When formwork is installed at an angle or sloping, or when the surface shored from is sloping, the shoring shall be designed for such loading.

11. Adjustment screws shall not be adjusted to raise formwork after the concrete is in place.

Tube and Coupler Shoring

1. Tube and coupler towers used for shoring shall have allowable loads based on tests conducted according to the *Recommended Procedure for Compression Testing of Scaffolds and Shores,* Scaffolding & Shoring Institute, 1967.

2. Design of shoring layouts shall be based on working loads obtained using the test procedures of subsection (1) of this section and on at least a 2½:1 safety factor.

3. All tube and coupler components shall be inspected before being used.

4. Tubes of shoring structures shall not be used if heavily rusted, bent, dented, or having other defects.

5. Couplers (clamps) shall not be used if deformed, broken, or having defective or missing threads on bolts, or other defects.

6. The material used for the couplers (clamps) shall be of a structural type such as drop-forged steel, malleable iron, or structural grade aluminum. Gray cast iron shall not be used.

7. When checking the erected shoring towers with the shoring layout, the spacing between posts shall not exceed that shown on the layout, and all interlocking of tubular members and tightness of couplers should be checked.

8. All baseplates, shore heads, extension devices, or adjustment screws shall be in firm contact with the footing sill and the form material, and shall be snug against the posts.

9. Eccentric loads on shore heads and similar members shall be prohibited unless the shore heads have been designed for such loading.

10. Special precautions shall be taken when formwork is at angles, or sloping, or when the surface shored from is sloping.

11. Adjustment screws shall not be adjusted to raise formwork after the concrete is in place.

Single-Post Shores

1. When checking erected single-post shores with the shoring layout, the spacing between shores in either direction shall not exceed that shown on the layout, and all clamps, screws, pins, and all other components shall be in the closed or engaged position.

2. For stability, single-post shores shall be horizontally braced in both the longitudinal and transverse directions. Diagonal bracing shall also be installed.

Such bracing shall be installed as the shores are being erected.

3. Shore spacing assumes dead load of 50 lb/sq. ft., 4 × 4 or larger shores.

Table 4-37 Shore Loading

Uniform Load in lb/lin. ft.	Supported Structural (Single) Member (Spacing in Inches)				
	2 × 4	2 × 6	3 × 6	4 × 4	4 × 6
100	60	95	120	92	131
125	54	85	440	80	124
150	49	77	100	75	118
175	45	72	93	70	110
200	42	67	87	65	102
225	40	62	82	61	97
250	38	60	77	58	92
275	36	57	74	55	87
300	35	55	71	53	84
350	32	50	65	49	77
400	30	47	61	46	72
450	28	44	58	43	68
500	27	41	55	41	65
600	24	38	50	37	59
700	22	36	46	35	55
800	21	33	43	32	51
900	20	31	41	30	48
1,000	19	30	38	29	46
1,200	17	27	35	27	42
1,400	16	25	33	25	39
1,600	15	23	31	23	36
1,800	14	22	29	22	34
2,000	13	21	27	21	32
2,200	13	20	26	20	31
2,400	12	19	24	19	30
2,600	12	19	24	18	28
2,800	11	18	23	17	27
3,000	11	17	22	17	26
3,400	10	16	21	16	25
3,800	10	15	20	15	23
4,500	9	14	18	13	21

4. Devices that attach to the external lateral stability bracing shall be securely fastened to the single-post shores.

5. All baseplates or shore heads of single-post shores shall be in firm contact with the footing sill and the form material.

6. Whenever single-post shores are used in more than one tier, the layout shall be designed and inspected by a structural engineer.

7. Eccentric loads on shore heads shall be prohibited unless the shore heads have been designed for such loading.

8. When formwork is at an angle or sloping, or when the surface shored from is sloping, the shoring shall be designed for such loading.

9. Adjustment of single-post shores to raise form-work shall not be made after concrete is in place.

Respecting fabricated single-post shores, the following shall apply:

1. The clamp used for adjustable timber single-post shores shall have working load ratings based on tests conducted according to the standard test procedures for fabricated single-post shores in *Recommended Procedure for Compression Testing of Scaffolds and Shores*, Scaffolding & Shoring Institute, 1967, and on at least a 3:1 safety factor.

2. Shoring layouts shall be made using working loads that were obtained using the test procedures.

3. All fabricated single-post shores shall be inspected before being used.

4. Fabricated single-post shores shall not be used if heavily rusted, bent, dented, rewelded, or having broken weldments or other defects. If they contain timber, they shall not be used if timber is split, is cut, has sections removed, is rotted, or is otherwise structurally damaged.

5. All clamps, screws, pins, threads, and all other components shall be in a condition similar to that of original manufacture.

Adjustable Timber Single-Post Shores

1. The clamp used for adjustable timber single-post shores shall have working load ratings based on tests conducted according to the standard test procedures for fabricated single-post shores in *Recommended Procedure for Compression Testing of Scaffolds and Shores*, Scaffolding & Shoring Institute, 1967, and on at least a 3:1 safety factor.

2. Timber used shall have the safety factor and allowable working load for each grade and species as recommended in the tables for wooden columns in the *Wood Structural Design Data Book*, National Forest Products Association, 1970.

3. The shoring layout shall be made using the allowable load obtained by using the test procedure for the clamp or tables for timber referred to in (1) and (2) of this subsection.

4. All timber and adjusting devices to be used for adjustable timber single-post shores shall be inspected before erection.

5. Timber shall not be used if it is split, cut, has sections removed, is rotted, or is otherwise structurally damaged.

6. Adjusting devices shall not be used if heavily rusted, bent, dented, rewelded, or having broken weldments or other defects.

7. All nails used to secure bracing on adjustable timber single-post shores shall be driven home and the point of the nail bent over.

Respecting timber single-post shores, the following shall apply:

1. Timber used as single-post shores shall have the safety factor and allowable working load for each grade and species as recommended in the tables for wooden columns in the *Wood Structural Design Data Book*, National Forest Products Association, 1970.

2. All timber to be used for single-post shoring shall be inspected before erection.

3. Timber shall not be used if it is split, is cut, has sections removed, is rotted, or is otherwise structurally damaged.

4. All nails used to secure bracing on timber single-post shores shall be driven home and the point of the nail bent over.

Nailing

Check that enough nails have been used to hold each board or panel of the form of sheathing tight against studs or joists. Do not allow nailing from the inside out of forms—these could become lodged in the concrete with the point sticking outward.

Final Checks

1. Have forms been oiled, wetted, or sealed as required? Check to see that surplus oil has been removed from forms and that there is no oil on steel reinforcement, construction joints, or other surfaces where bond is required. Are forms clean prior to placing concrete?

2. Check forms for movement which may occur during placing operation. Have measuring devices or reference lines been set up?

3. Are all required chamfer strips and grade strips accurately aligned and securely fastened and protected?

4. Have necessary clean outs been provided for in the bottom of the forms? Are forms clean of debris? Check the grade of forms required in the specifications.

5. Has all standing water been removed?

6. Have all embeds and sleeves or blockouts been inspected and placed in the correct positions?

METAL DECKS

Table 4-38 Metal Decking Spans

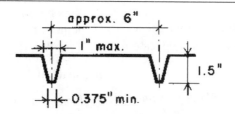

Deck Type/ Gage	Span Type	Weight (psi)	Total (Dead/Live) Safe Load for Spans Indicated in ft-in. (lb/ft^2)												
			4-0	4-6	5-0	5-6	6-0	6-6	7-0	7-6	8-0	8-6	9-0	9-6	10
NR22	Simple	1.6	73	58	47										
NR20		2.0	91	72	58	48	40								
NR18		2.7	121	95	77	64	54	46							
NR22	Two	1.6	80	63	51	42									
NR20		2.0	96	76	61	51	43								
NR18		2.7	124	98	79	66	55	47	41						
NR22	Three or more	1.6	100	79	64	53	44								
NR20		2.0	120	95	77	63	53	45							
NR18		2.7	155	123	99	82	69	59	51	44					

Table 4-39 Metal Decking Spans

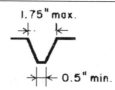

Deck Type/ Gage	Span Type	Weight (psi)	Total (Dead/Live) Safe Load for Spans Indicated in ft-in. (lb/ft^2)												
			4-0	4-6	5-0	5-6	6-0	6-6	7-0	7-6	8-0	8-6	9-0	9-6	10
IR22	Simple	1.6	86	68	55	45									
IR20		2.0	106	84	68	56	47	40							
IR18		2.7	142	112	91	75	63	54	46	40					
IR22	Two	1.6	93	74	60	49	41								
IR20		2.0	112	88	71	59	50	42							
IR18		2.7	145	115	93	77	64	55	47	41					
IR22	Three or more	1.6	117	92	75	62	52	44							
IR20		2.0	140	110	89	74	62	53 46		40					
IR18		2.7	181	143	116	96	81	69	59	52	45	40			

Table 4-40 *Metal Decking Spans*

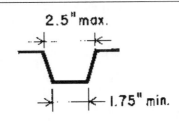

Deck Type/ Gage	Span Type	Weight (psi)	Total (Dead/Live) Safe Load for Spans Indicated in ft-in. (lb/ft^2)										
			5-0	5-6	6-0	6-6	7-0	7-6	8-0	8-6	9-0	9-6	10
WR20	Simple	1.6	89	70	56	46							
WR18		2.0	112	87	69	57	47	40					
WR22		2.7	154	119	94	76	63	53	45				
WR20	Two	1.6	98	81	68	58	50	43					
WR18		2.0	125	103	87	74	64	55	49	43			
WR22		2.7	165	137	115	98	84	73	65	57	51	46	41
WR20	Three or more	1.6	122	101	85	72	62	54	46	40			
WR18		2.0	156	129	108	92	80	67	57	49	43		
WR22		2.7	207	171	144	122	105	91	76	65	57	50	44

CONTROL AND CONSTRUCTION JOINTS

Control Joints

Table 4-41 *Metal Decking Spans Load Capacity of Typical Steel Roof Deck*

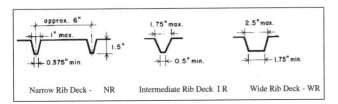

Table 4-42 *Spacing of Control Joints*

Slab Thickness, in Inches	Less Than ¾-in. Aggregate Spacing, in Feet	Larger Than ¾-in. Aggregate Spacing, in Feet	Slump Less Than 4-in. Spacing, in Feet
5	10	13	15
6	12	15	18
7	14	18	21
8	16	20	24
9	18	23	27
10	20	25	30

Note: Spacing also applies to the distances from the control joints to the parallel isolation joints or to the parallel construction joints.

Construction Joints

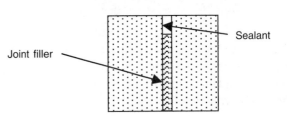

Fig. 4-53 *Expansion joint.*

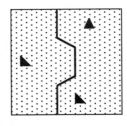

Fig. 4-54 *Keyed construction joint.*

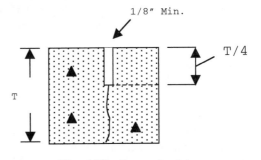

Fig. 4-55 *Contraction joint.*

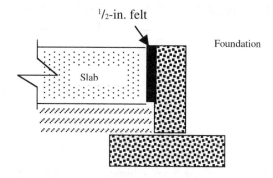

Fig. 4-56 *Isolation joint.*

Typical Joint Types and Locations

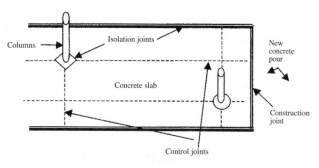

Fig. 4-57 *Typical joint types and locations.*

The criteria for location of joints are shown on the contract drawings. The specification limits the area for slabs on grade and the length for walls that can be placed continuously without joints.

Fig. 4-58 *This crack is a result of the contractor not installing a control joint in a timely manner.*

1. Are all joints (expansion, contraction, construction) located as shown on contract drawings or as otherwise approved?

2. Have construction joints at fresh concrete been prepared as required? Check requirements for air-water cutting, wet sand blasting, roughening, wetting, etc.

3. The location of bulkheads for construction joints in structural members, such as columns, beams, or slabs, should be checked with the design engineer.

4. Have the insert-type contraction joints been coated with approved materials and methods to break bond?

5. Has preformed filler been installed and securely fastened in expansion joint locations?

6. Are expansion joints free from irregularities or debris that would interfere with free movement?

7. Check all joints that are intended to allow for expansion or contraction. No reinforcement or other fixed metal will be continuous through this type of joint.

8. Are water stops firmly secured in correct locations, undamaged, and *spliced properly*?

9. Are contraction joints sawed after the concrete has set, usually within 12 hours? Check arrangements made to have the locations of the joints laid out accurately, and to have equipment available at the proper time? Extra blades?

10. Have the horizontal construction joints at fresh concrete been cleaned and dampened or treated with an approved bonding agent just prior to next placement?

Table 4-43 *Vertical Contraction Joints*

Wall Height	Joint Spacing
2–8 ft	3 × wall height
8–12 ft	2 × wall height
Less than 12 ft	1 × wall height

REINFORCEMENT

1. Is all reinforcement positioned in accordance with approved shop drawings? Check bar diameters, bar lengths, lengths of splices, bar-to-bar spacing, and clearances. *Face tie wire ends away from forms.*

2. Watch for specialty items such as wall intersection bars, and additional bars around corners and at openings.

3. Has reinforcement been cleaned of all loose, flaky, rust and scale, dried concrete, oil, grease, or other foreign material?

4. Is reinforcement tied and supported securely so that displacement will not occur during concrete placement?

5. Are reinforcement spacers, ties, concrete blocks, plastic covered chairs, and supports as specified or approved?

Minimum Bend Diameters for Reinforcement

Type/Size	Diameter
#10 through #25	6
#29, #32, and #36	8
#47 and #57	10
Stirrups and ties	4
ACI 318	

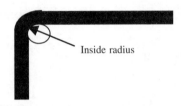

Inside radius

Fig. 4-59 *Minimum bend diameters for reinforcement.*

1. Precast concrete supports with tie wires will be used against the ground. Check for the specified clearance.

2. Dowels will be positioned before concrete placement and not stuck in or positioned after placement.

Reinforcing Bars

Table 4-44 *Metric Re-Bars and Inch-Pound Equivalents*

Metric Bar			Inch-Pound Bar		
No.	Dia. (mm)	Mass (kg/m)	No.	Dia. (in.)	Wgt. (lb/ft)
10	9.5	0.56	3	0.375	0.376
13	12.7	0.994	4	0.5	0.668
16	15.9	1.552	5	0.625	1.043
19	19.1	2.235	6	0.75	1.502
22	22.2	3.042	7	0.875	2.044
25	25.4	3.973	8	1	2.67
29	28.7	5.06	9	1.1128	3.4
32	32.3	6.404	10	1.27	4.303
36	35.8	7.907	11	1.41	5.313
43	43	11.384	14	1.693	7.65
57	57.3	20.239	18	2.257	13.6

Table 4-45 *Reinforcing Bar Strengths (Minimum Yield)*

Grade	MPa	psi
300	300	43,511
420	420	60,916
520	520	75,420
49	276	40,000
60	414	60,000
75	517	75,000

Embedded Items

1. Unless otherwise provided or approved, embedded items are to be fixed firmly in correct location before the concrete is placed and are to be embedded by placing the concrete around them. Boxing out or "pushing" in embeds will not be permitted unless specifically called for by the drawings, specifications, or special approval.

2. In case of a conflict in locations of embedded items with steel reinforcement, the relocation of embedded items or cutting, bending, addition, displacement, or omission of steel reinforcement will only be permitted with the approval of the Architect or Engineer. Keep a record of them in reports as well as in the Design Change Log (DCL).

3. Are all embedded items in place? Check mechanical and electrical drawings and approved shop drawings for the equipment for requirements for anchor slots, end bolts, piping, sleeves, conduits, boxes, reglets, etc., which do not often appear on architectural or structural drawings.

4. Are embedded items protected against damage during or subsequent to placement of concrete?

   Examples:

   • Bolt threads

   • Machine or polished surfaces covered

   • Steel mounting plates for precast installation

   • Light metal sleeves or boxes braced internally

   • Open pipes or conduits capped or plugged

   Contractor should always recheck after concrete pour.

5. Use a checklist when checking for embedded items. A sleeve placement schedule is a good idea to avoid costly errors.

Miscellaneous Preparations

1. Have arrangements been made to get concrete into all parts of the placement without segregation, loss

of ingredients, formation of air pockets or cold joints?

2. Check for vertical drops in excess of permissible limit.

3. Do not permit running of concrete by means of the vibrator.

4. Check for placement within the maximum time allowed after mixing. Usually 1½ hours (or 300 truck rotations) during normal temperatures. *But cut in half for hot days!*

5. Is conveying equipment (i.e., crane, buggies, truck mixers, pumpcrete pipe) capable of reaching all areas of the placement?

   a. Are temporary form openings, tramies, chutes, conveyors or other special equipment provided as necessary and approved?

   b. Are pockets vented so that air will not be trapped?

   c. Is there a written concrete placement plan? Are all parties briefed and aware of the schedule of pour?

   d. Are sufficient personnel available? Are the concrete testing agency alerted and standing by?

   e. Are all necessary tools on hand and in working conditions? Check especially: vibrators, generators, including a standby vibrator and finishing tools.

   f. Have arrangements been made, and is all necessary equipment on hand and in working order to provide curing and protection including cold/hot weather protection if needed?

   g. Are safe access and footing provided by means of ladders, platforms, walkways and staging conforming to safety requirements?

   h. Review the testing plans to be made and concrete placement plan during placement operation.

   i. Establish procedures for follow-up testing should a failure occur in the initial test.

   • Test to be used

   • Basis for acceptance/rejection (i.e., 85% at 28 days, etc.)

   • Who pays for additional cost

6. The rate of placing the concrete will be directly dependent on the preparations made before the pour. The placement shall not be permitted to start if it is evident that the preparatory work will not ensure placement of each batch of concrete within the specified time after mixing, and at such a rate as to prevent the formation of cold joints, or otherwise unsuitable.

7. Has the contractor made arrangements to make cylinders or beams to test the strength of the concrete at least once a day, and have provisions been made to properly make, handle, and cure the specimens?

8. Are the testing technicians and lab ACI certified to perform the required test?

CONCRETE TESTING

Concrete Quality Consulting, Inc.
1403 North Forbes Road

CONCRETE TEST REPORT

Project Law Enforcement Training Center Addition, EKU   Job No. 2078
Client D. W. Wilburn, Inc.   Client Ref. No PBCJ0010
Contractor D. W. Wilburn, Inc.
Field Testing: Date 03/19/01 Time 9:30 AM   By CQC: Teresa Johnson
Placement Location Slab; 2nd floor 22 to 18
Weather sunny   Air Temperature (°F) 43
Concrete Supplier Central Ky. Mixed Concrete   Plant Richmond   Type transit
Truck No. 96   Ticket No. 47461   Batch Size (CY) 10   Time Batched 8:58 AM
Mix ID 3000sp, Lightweight 1%

Specified Strength (PSI) 3000   Specified
Concrete Temperature (°F) 64   Measured Slump(In.) 9.0   Air Content (%) 6.0 +/- 1.5
Field Curing curing box   Measured Air Content(%) 7.75
Date Received In Laboratory 03/22/01   Cylinders Transported By CQC
Remarks Set #2 this date   Laboratory ID Number 13904

CYL. NO.	DATE TESTED	AGE (DAYS)	WEIGHT (LBS)	AREA (SQ IN)	DEFECTS OBSERVED	TOTAL MAXIMUM LOAD (LBS)	COMPRESSIVE STRENGTH (PSI)	BREAK TYPE
LE74A	03/26/01	7	22.6	28.13	none	58,940	2100	A
LE74B	04/16/01	28	22.5	28.18	none	103,370	3670	A
LE74C	04/16/01	28	22.7	28.18	none	103,100	3660	A
LE74R	04/16/01		22.4	28.18				N

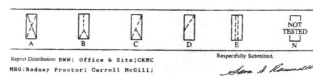

					NOT TESTED
A	B	C	D	E	N

Report Distribution DWW: Office & Site;CKMC   Respectfully Submitted,
MHG:Rodney Proctor; Carroll McGill;

Fig. 4-60 *Sample concrete testing report.*

CONVEYING AND PLACING

Equipment

1. Is equipment clean and checked for safe operation?

2. Are the pump and hose attachments of proper type/length and do they have required capacity and material?

3. Is there a chute and/or baffle present if needed?

4. Are there the required screeds and strike-offs?

5. Does the contractor have a contingency plan if a piece of equipment fails?

6. Is a 10-ft straight-edge or laser available to check finish slab tolerances?

Operations

1. Does the contractor have sufficient personnel available? For placing? For finishing?

2. Check requirements pertaining to placing fresh concrete on concrete which has set. Usually it is required that the old surface be covered by a layer of fresh mortar, or that the old surface receive a slush coat of neat cement grout followed by specified topping. Follow all manufacturer's instructions for any approved chemicals.

3. Is the time between completion of mixing and placement in final position in the form within the time allowed by the specifications? Is the concrete temperature at placement within the specified limits?

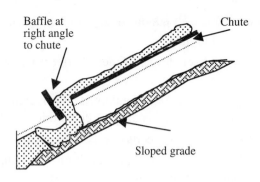

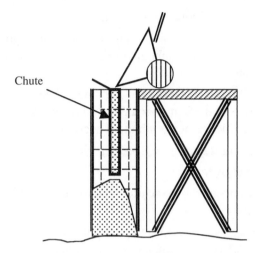

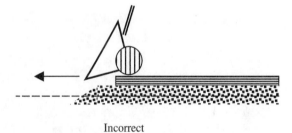

Incorrect

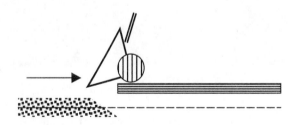

Correct

Fig. 4-62 *Placing concrete.*

Fig. 4-61 *Placing footer concrete. This method of re-bar placement is not usually acceptable and is considered poor quality workmanship.*

4. Check method of placement during handling of concrete to prevent segregation. Check height concrete is allowed to drop freely, and method used to guide concrete into place.

5. Is concrete placed rapidly enough to avoid formation of cold joints?

6. Job-site-made chutes and slides are not permitted for use in conveying concrete.

7. Are layers of concrete maintained approximately horizontal and not exceeding specified thickness?

8. Are form ties and supports checked frequently?

9. Is rate of placement within safe limits, such that forms will not be overstressed (see chart)?

10. Is each layer of concrete vibrated?

11. Is contractor "sounding" each new pour on high forms to ensure the subsequent layer is setting up (wall pours)?

12. Insert vibrators vertically, through the full depth of each layer, at uniformly spaced points so circles of visible influence of the vibrators overlap.

    a. Does contractor have a backup vibrator?

    b. Do not overvibrate.

    c. Vibrators are not to be used to move concrete in the forms.

    d. Ensure the correct length is available.

    e. Do not allow vibration too close to the forms.

Fig. 4-63 *"Honeycombing" concrete.*

13. The use of form vibrators is prohibited by some specifications and permitted by others, subject to specific approval. Do not allow their use except as approved.

14. Check use of hand compaction tools as practicable to assist in obtaining smooth, dense surfaces. Use hand compaction or vibrating screeds to consolidate thin slabs. Unless high-slump concrete is specifically designed and approved, such as for thin reinforcement walls, all concrete must be consolidated by hand compaction tools or a vibrator.

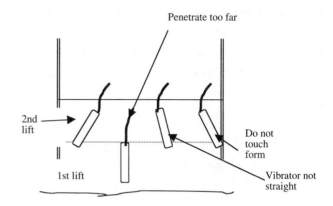

Fig. 4-64 *Improper placement of concrete vibrators.*

15. Do not allow excessive working of the concrete surface in completing a lift. Allow only enough to completely embed the coarse aggregate.

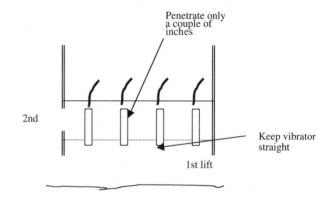

Fig. 4-65 *Proper placement of concrete vibrators.*

16. When pump delivery is used, concrete mix must be designed accordingly and conform to the design specifications.

Removal of Forms

Inspection Practice

1. Is care being taken to ensure that concrete is insufficiently hard and strong before removal of forms? Check specifications for minimum time and strength requirements.

2. Check to see that forms used for curing are left in place until expiration of required curing period. Forms shall be maintained snug against concrete surfaces at all times while using as curing means.

3. For best patching results, forms should be removed as soon as practical and patching should immediately be accomplished so that patches cure with parent concrete. *Specifications usually limit the time for* *fin removal and patching to first 24 hours after form removal.*

4. Check to determine that form-removal operation does not damage the concrete.

5. Be certain that all wood forms (and nails) are being removed, especially in hidden places.

Methods of Removal

1. Is spalling of concrete being avoided during the form removal operation? Use methods which will avoid spalling, chipping, and gouging.

2. See that form removal operations are performed in a safe manner.

Finishing

Formed Surfaces

1. Check the type of finish required.

2. Has the contractor constructed and received approval of sample panels to show the surface finishes required? Note that the placing of concrete represented by each sample is not to proceed until sample panel has been approved.

3. Repairing of defective areas and removal of fins, form marks, and holes are required to be done immediately upon removal of forms.

4. Check the cleaning of areas to be patched. Have honeycomb and rock pockets been cut back to solid material and cleaned before patching?

5. Check the requirements for the treatment of areas containing defective concrete.

6. Check for complete curing of patched areas.

7. Check surface for specified smoothness tolerances. Require rough areas and high spots to be ground smooth.

Fig. 4-66 *Concrete finishing.*

TYPICAL TOLERANCES

Footings

- Variations in length and width $-\frac{1}{2}$ to $+2$ in.

- Misplacement -2% of the footing width in the direction of the error but not more than 2 in.

- Thickness -5% on the specified thickness.

Walls

- Variations for plumb to be not more than ± 1 in. for walls up to 100 ft in height.

- Wall openings should not be more than $-\frac{1}{4}$ to $+1$ in.

- Variations in thickness:
  - $-\frac{1}{4}$ to $+\frac{3}{8}$ in. for 12 in. thick or less
  - $-\frac{3}{8}$ to $+\frac{1}{2}$ in. for walls 12 to 36 in. thick
  - $-\frac{3}{4}$ to $+1$ in. for all walls over 36 in. thick

Columns

- Variations of 1 in. from plumb for columns up to 100 ft in height.

- Variations in cross sections:
  - $-\frac{1}{4}$ to $+\frac{3}{8}$ in. for 12-in. thickness or less
  - $-\frac{3}{8}$ to $+\frac{1}{2}$ in. for 12- to 36-in. thickness
  - $-\frac{3}{4}$ to $+1$ in. for thickness over 36 in.

Beams and Girders

- Variations from level or grade should not exceed $\pm\frac{3}{4}$ in.

- Variations for exposed parapets should not exceed $\pm\frac{3}{4}$ in.

- Deviations from cross section not to exceed:
  - $-\frac{1}{4}$ to $+\frac{3}{8}$ in. for 12-in. thickness or less
  - $-\frac{3}{8}$ to $+\frac{1}{2}$ in. for 12- to 36-in. thickness
  - $-\frac{3}{4}$ to $+1$ in. for thickness over 36 in.

Elevated Slabs

- Variations from specified elevation should not exceed $\pm\frac{3}{4}$ in.

- Variations in slab thickness:
  - $-\frac{1}{4}$ to $+\frac{3}{8}$ in. for 12-in. thickness or less
  - $-\frac{3}{8}$ to $+\frac{1}{2}$ in. for 12- to 36-in. thickness
  - $-\frac{3}{4}$ to $+1$ in. for thickness over 36 in.

CONCRETE FINISHES

Unformed Surfaces

1. Check the plans or specifications for the type of finish required.

2. The working of the concrete surface should be the minimum that is necessary to produce mortar which is just sufficient for finishing.

3. Ensure that the screed runs are set to correct grade.

4. Check to see that floating is started as soon as the screeded surface has stiffened sufficiently to permit floating without drawing excessive mortar to the surface. (*There should be no free water on the surface at the start of floating. Dusting with cement or other material to dry the surface or to enrich the mortar will not be permitted.*)

5. Troweling should be done as soon as the floated surface has hardened sufficiently to prevent drawing more mortar to the surface but while the surface is still workable.

6. Check to see that marks left on the surface by edging tools are erased.

7. Ensure that the screed-run supports are removed to proper depth.

8. Make sure the screed-run voids are filled with good concrete and compacted.

9. Straight-edge the plastic concrete after filling screed runs, just prior to initial floating.

10. Check the surface for required smoothness tolerance.

Smooth Finish for Formed Surfaces

1. Check the contract specifications for areas requiring a smooth, slick finish.

2. Make certain that cement grouting operation is not delayed, thus allowing the grout to age with the concrete.

3. Has the contractor planned his operations whereby he can completely finish areas to natural breaks in the finished surface each day?

4. Has the proper mixture of cements (regular and white) been used in the grout mixture to blend with color of the finished surface?

5. Do the specifications require a hardener to be applied?

6. Is grout being applied so as to fill all pits, voids, and surface holes solidly?

7. Is the excess grout being scraped off at the proper time with a trowel and is the flush surface then cleaned to remove any visible grout film?

8. Is curing being planned so as not to allow grout to become dry during the setting period?

9. Has any loose dry grout been left on the surface?

F-Numbers (Standards)

The F-Number System is the new *American Concrete Institute* (#117) and *Canadian Standards Association* (#A23.1) standards for the specification and measurement of concrete floor flatness and levelness. F-numbers replace the familiar "⅛ in. in 10 ft" type specs that had proven unreliable, unmeasureable, and unrealistic.

The new standards include two F-numbers: F_F for flatness and F_L for levelness. Flatness relates to the bumpiness of the floor, while levelness describes the tilt or pitch of the slab. The higher the F-number, the better that characteristic of the floor.

F-numbers are linear, so an F_F 20 is twice as flat as an F_F 10, but only half as flat as an F_F 40. Slabs-on-grade are usually specified with an F_F number and an F_L number (the F_F is always listed first), such as: F_F 25/F_L 20. Because of deflection, elevated slabs are usually specified using only F_F. When a floor is described as an "F 25", it usually means "F_F 25".

The ACI/CSA F-Number System applies to 99% of all floor slabs. In the tiny percentage of floors that have defined traffic, where vehicles are restricted in their movement by wire or rail guidance, a different F-number, F_{min}, is used.

Most superflat floors should use the F_{min} system, since most of these slabs support defined traffic.

Rubbed Finish

1. Check for exterior exposed-to-view areas requiring rubbed finish.

2. Rubbed finish is performed after the surface has received a smooth finish. Rubbed finish is performed by rubbing with carborundum stones and water.

3. Check to see that no mortar or grout is being used during rubbing, and that all grout which has worked loose during rubbing is removed.

4. Check to see that the rubbing operation removes all form marks, small pits, and other blemishes.

Monolithic Finish

1. Most plans require the finish for floors and roof slabs to be the monolithic finish.

2. Make sure that all coarse aggregate has been forced away from the surface before screeding and straight-edging begins.

3. The timeliness of the floating and of the troweling is important. Make sure the surface is floated as soon as it will bear the weight of a man without deep imprint, and that it is troweled as soon as the moisture that was worked up from the floating operation has disappeared. Do not allow the addition of water or of dry cement.

4. Check to see that the surface is steel troweled to a smooth, even, impervious finish, free from trowel marks.

5. Check the requirement for the number of steel-trowelings.

6. The specifications may require a separate concrete wearing course such as for industrial use, with the rough slab terminated below finish grade. Check for the specification requirements for the wearing course design mix, placement, and finishing.

7. Do not permit use of trowels cleaned in form oil, silicone, or similar bond-breaking materials unless such materials have been removed from the trowel.

8. Check that troweled-in, abrasive aggregates are applied at required locations for the nonslip finish.

9. Do the specifications and or plans require any hardeners, decorative finishes, etc.

CURING, PROTECTION, AND FINISHING

General

1. Check the details of permissible methods and the number of days required for curing. Curing is the treatment given the concrete to ensure that adequate moisture is available for hydration of the cement, with consequent gain in the strength and durability of the concrete.

2. Protect fresh concrete from running water, premature or excessive loading, freezing, excessive heat, excessive temperature differentials within the concrete, etc.

Curing

1. Is the approved curing medium being properly applied immediately after placing and/or finishing?

2. Prevent use of membrane compound on concrete that is to receive paint, tile, roofing, hardener, etc. unless the curing compound is approved for this use (see specs).

3. Where moist curing is being used, is it continuous, not intermittent?

4. Are wood forms that are left in place kept wet for the duration of the curing period?

5. When waterproof paper or other approved covering is used, are laps and edges sealed? Is paper in full contact with surfaces being cured?

6. Check when curing compound is used for adequate mixing and uniform coverage.

7. Is the sprayed membrane:
   • Continuous for full coverage and without discontinuities that will permit loss of moisture?
   • Reapplied if subjected to heavy rainfall within 3 hours after application, or when damaged by subsequent construction operations at any time during the curing period?
   • Protected, to avoid damage from pedestrian and vehicular traffic or any other cause that would disrupt the continuity of the membrane?

8. Do not allow surfaces to dry. If concrete is surface dry, require moistener with fine spray of water before spraying curing membrane.

9. Are joints to receive sealant plugged to prevent coating with membrane curing compound?

10. Make sure the contractor follows the manufacturer's instructions and applies the compound accordingly.

Joints

1. Observe joints for proper depth, width, and location.

2. Make sure that the joints are clean and dry prior to sealing.

3. Inspect the sealing of the joints. See that the joint is completely filled with sealer to finish flush with the surface and that all defects are corrected.

Protection

1. Are precautions taken to protect surfaces from rain, snow, blowing debris, or flowing water until they can resist damage?

2. Is air entrained concrete being used in areas as required. ACI requires that concrete that during construction is exposed to freezing and thawing require air entrained concrete even if the final use is not intended to be exposed.

Wait Time of Form Removals

1. Determine requirements to remove forms and supports, and obtain instructions from the project manager or site superintendent as to special conditions which may govern, such as strength of control spec-

Table 4-46 Curing Methods

Method	Advantage	Disadvantage
Sprinkle with water or cover with wet burlap	Excellent results if constantly kept wet.	Likelihood of drying between sprinklings. Difficult to position on vertical walls.
Straw (wet)	Good insulator.	Can dry out, blow away, or burn.
Moist earth	Cheap, but messy and slippery to walk or work on.	Stains concrete. Can dry out. Removal problem.
Ponding water on flat surfaces	Excellent result, maintains uniform temperature.	Requires considerable labor. Undesirable in freezing weather.
Curing compounds	Inexpensive, easy to apply.	Sprayer needed. Inadequate coverage allows drying out. Film can be broken or tracked off before curing is completed. Unless pigmented, concrete can get too hot.
Waterproof paper	Excellent protection, prevents drying.	Heavy cost can be excessive. Must be kept in rolls; storage and handling problem.
Plastic film	Watertight, excellent protection. Light and easy to handle.	Pigmented for heat protection; requires reasonable care and tear; must be patched; must be weighted down to prevent blowing away.

Concrete Curing Rates

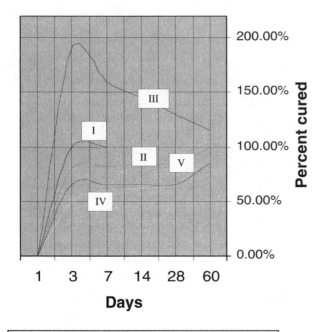

Fig. 4-67 *Concrete curing rates for each type of mix.*

Legend: Type I — Type II — Type III — Type IV — Type V

imens, special approval for earlier removal, or special requirements dictated by the project engineer or architect.

2. Is adequate covering provided to protect concrete from damage by other construction activities? Corners, edges, and projections?

Table 4-47 Recommended Protection Periods (for Air-Entrained Concrete)

Exposure to Freeze-Thaw	Normal Concrete	High-Early Concrete*
No exposure	2 days	1 day
Any exposure	3 days	2 days

*Type III or with an accelerator.

Table 4-48 Wait Time for Form Removals

Placement Area	Days
Walls (only)	1 to 2
Columns (only)	1 to 2
Beam/girder sides	1 to 2
Joist, beam	
Under 10′ span	7
10′ to 20′ span	14
Over 20′ span	21
Floor slabs	
Under 10′ span	4
10′ to 20′ span	7
Over 20′ span	10
Pan joist forms	
Less than 30″ wide	3
More than 30″ wide	4
Post-tensioned slab	As soon as full tension has been applied
Elevated slabs	Depends on reshoring; not later than same day of stripping forms

3. Loading of construction materials needs to be controlled so that new concrete is not stressed beyond its current strength? Examples: backfilling against new walls; storage of heavy materials on new floors.

4. Check for coverings and heating equipment in cold weather as necessary to maintain temperatures. Temporary combustible coverings, including tarps, must be clear of any heating equipment. Heater fuel storage and fire safety arrangements for refueling should be carefully checked.

5. Are min–max thermometers used to determine actual temperatures and to ensure that temperatures for concrete protection are within required range?

6. Heaters need to be vented to the outside in closed enclosures *due to the carbon monoxide and carbon dioxide that cause the concrete to dust severely.*

7. Check the removal of protection. Do not permit concrete to be subjected to sudden extreme change in temperature. A 25°F differential in temperature between the concrete and the surrounding air is considered the maximum.

Lightweight Concretes

General

1. Design mix required. Check aggregate requirements in the approved submittal information.

2. Check the special tests required for unit weights fresh and dry, for density control.

3. Check for special mixing cycle and placing requirements.

Lightweight Structural

1. Mostly the same procedures apply as for normal-weight concrete.

Fig. 4-68 *Tilt-up concrete wall construction.*

2. The aggregate manufacturer's qualified representative may be required at the worksite to assist in adjusting procedures to obtain the specified product.

3. Check for the required control tests.

Lightweight Roof Fill

1. This is used only over structural concrete decks. Check specifications for lightweight cast-in-place roof deck systems.

2. Check for light steel trowel finish and curing as for normal weight concrete.

Lightweight Insulating Portland Cement Fill

1. Check for required thickness and density to produce specified thermal "U" value.

2. Is edge vented at perimeter of slabs?

3. Are ventilating expansion joints provided at specified intervals? At edges and junctions with vertical surfaces and penetrations?

4. Check required curing; membrane curing compound is prohibited.

NONDESTRUCTIVE TESTING (NDT) OF CONCRETE

1. *Rebound hammer.* The rebound number is obtained from a hammer that consist of a steel mass and a tension spring. When the plunger of the hammer is pushed against the concrete surface, the steel mass is retracted, and a spring compressed. When the steel mass if fully retracted, the spring automatically releases causing the steel to be driven against the plunger causing the hammer to "rebound." The rebound is measured by a pointer on a scale and is usually graduated from 0 to 100. The reading is referred to as the *R-value*. The manufacturer will supply a chart showing the relationship between the R-values read and the compressive strength of the concrete. Not considered that accurate.

2. *Penetration test (Windsor probe).* This is a special powder-fired gun that fires a high-strength steel probe into the concrete. Usually, a sample of three probes is fired and the length of each probe extending from the concrete is then measured and averaged together. The manufacturer provides a set of five calibration curves, each corresponding to a specific hardness for the aggregate used in the concrete, which are converted to the estimated concrete compressive strength.

Table 4-49 *Common Concrete Problems*

Problem	Cause	Prevention and Corrections
Excessive bleeding	Excess water in the mix.	Reduce water content.
	Not enough fines in the mix.	Increase—cement, fly ash, sand. Add air entrainment.
Aggregate segregation	Too high slump.	Add superplasticizer.
	Overvibration.	Reduce vibration in each location.
	Not enough vibration.	Insert vibrator at closer intervals.
	Too long a drop for placement.	Use appropriate drop chutes.
	Lack of homogeneity in the mix.	Increase mix time, add air entrainment.
Sticky finish	Too much air entrainment.	Reduce air and or fines.
	Surface drying too fast.	Spray water on subgrade and forms. Fog spray.
Setting too fast	High temperatures.	Use cooler water/ice in mix. Use retarder additives. Cool aggregate with water.
	High cement content.	Add water reducing retarder.
	Trucks getting hot from sun.	Sprinkle mixing drums during wait. Reschedule deliveries for minimum wait time.
Setting up too slow	Mix too lean. Too much fly ash or slag.	Increase cement content. Use accelerator. Heat water and/or aggregates.
	Cold/wet subgrade.	Insulate and or protect before placement of concrete.
Plastic shrinkage cracking	Too rapid loss of water. High winds, heat, or low humidity.	Fog spray at curing. Reduce air or fines. Do not use vapor retarders. Use less mix water. Set up wind breaks. Lower concrete temperature.
Low yield	Low air content.	Increase air.
	Wrong ratio of water cement and aggregrates.	Have test run.
Flat Slabs		
Shrinkage cracks	Wrong spacings and depth of contraction joints.	Cut joints ¼ the depth of slab. Space joints at 2½ the thickness in feet.
	Late joint sawing.	Plan to saw the same day as pour; within 4 hours.
	No isolation joints at walls or columns.	Install isolation joints.
	Excessive shrinkage.	Reduce water in mix. Cure ASAP after finishing.
Hairline cracks	Too high slump of concrete.	Reduce water.
	Too early troweling or too much troweling.	Reduce the methods of troweling by contractor.
	Rapid surface drying.	Cure concrete immediately after finishing.
Blistering	Slab closed too soon, trapping air and water.	Delay floating and troweling. Using wood floats helps.
Curling	Uneven drying between top of slab and lower parts.	Use lower slump. Cure ASAP and as long as possible. Reduce space between joints.
Scaling	Exposed to freeze thaw and chemical de-icers.	Use air entrainment of 5–8%.
	Too much finishing on wet surfaces.	Use minimum slump on 4. Protect from rain.
	Chemical de-icers applied before adaquate curing time.	Wait a minimum of 30 days for normal curing.
Walls		
Honeycomb	Not enough vibration.	Add superplasticizers. Reduce height of the pour. Insert vibrator more often.
Surface voids	Air or water trapped against formwork.	Reduce air entrainment. Vibrate as close to form as possible.

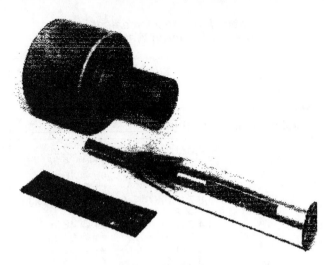

Fig. 4-69 *Rebound hammer.*

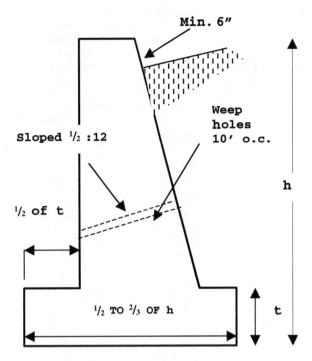

Fig. 4-71 *Concrete retaining walls (typical dimension ratios).*

3. *Ultrasonic pulse-velocity method.* This method involves the measurement of the time of travel of pulsed compressional waves through a known thickness of concrete. Concrete with excessive cracks may produce higher or lower readings and may give faulty strength of the concrete tested. One main consideration when using this method is that the concrete must be accessible on both sides.

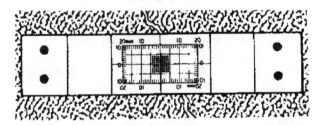

Newly Mounted Monitor

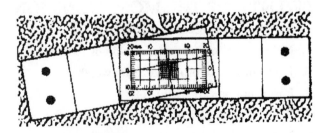

Monitor After Crack Movement

Fig. 4-70 *Crack monitoring gage.*

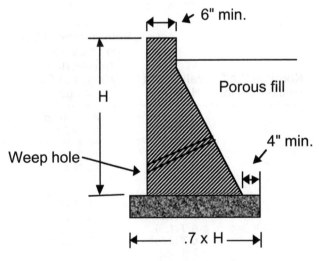

Fig. 4-72 *Gravity retaining wall.*

Table 4-50 *Reinforcement for Masonry Retaining Walls (30 psf)*

Nominal Wall Thickness, in.	Wall Depth H, ft (m)	Reinforcement Size and Spacing for Equivalent Fluid Weight of Soil, 30 psf
8	4.0 (1.2)	#4 @ 64 in.
	4.7 (1.4)	#4 @ 40 in.
	5.3 (1.6)	#4 @ 24 in.
	6.0 (1.8)	#5 @ 24 in.
	6.7 (2.0)	#5 @ 16 in.
10	4.0 (1.2)	#4 @ 72 in.
	4.7 (1.4)	#4 @ 56 in.
	5.3 (1.6)	#4 @ 40 in.
	6.0 (1.8)	#4 @ 24 in.
	6.7 (2.0)	#4 @ 16 in.
	7.3 (2.2)	#5 @ 24 in.
	8.0 (2.4)	#5 @ 16 in.
12	4.0 (1.2)	#4 @ 72 in.
	4.7 (1.4)	#4 @ 72 in.
	5.3 (1.6)	#4 @ 48 in.
	6.0 (1.8)	#4 @ 32 in.
	6.7 (2.0)	#4 @ 24 in.
	7.3 (2.2)	#4 @ 16 in.
	8.0 (2.4)	#5 @ 24 in.
	8.7 (2.7)	#5 @ 16 in.
	9.3 (2.8)	#6 @ 16 in.

Table 4-52 *Reinforcement for Masonry Retaining Walls (60 psf)*

Nominal Wall Thickness, in.	Wall Depth H, ft (m)	Reinforcement Size and Spacing for Equivalent Fluid Weight of Soil, 60 psf
8	4.0 (1.2)	#4 @ 32 in.
	4.7 (1.4)	#4 @ 16 in.
	5.3 (1.6)	#5 @ 16 in.
	6.0 (1.8)	#8 @ 16 in.
	6.7 (2.0)	Check codes/design
10	4.0 (1.2)	#4 @ 48 in.
	4.7 (1.4)	#4 @ 24 in.
	5.3 (1.6)	#4 @ 16 in.
	6.0 (1.8)	#5 @ 16 in.
	6.7 (2.0)	#6 @ 16 in.
	7.3 (2.2)	#6 @ 8 in.
	8.0 (2.4)	Check codes/design
12	4.0 (1.2)	#4 @ 64 in.
	4.7 (1.4)	#4 @ 40 in.
	5.3 (1.6)	#4 @ 24 in.
	6.0 (1.8)	#4 @ 16 in.
	6.7 (2.0)	#5 @ 16in.
	7.3 (2.2)	#6 @ 16in.
	8.0 (2.4)	#7 @ 16 in.
	8.7 (2.7)	#7 @ 8 in.
	9.3 (2.8)	Check codes/design

Table 4-51 *Reinforcement for Masonry Retaining Walls (45 psf)*

Nominal Wall Thickness, in.	Wall Depth H, ft (m)	Reinforcement Size and Spacing for Equivalent Fluid Weight of Soil, 45 psf
8	4.0 (1.2)	#4 @ 40 in.
	4.7 (1.4)	#4 @ 24 in.
	5.3 (1.6)	#4 @16 in.
	6.0 (1.8)	#6 @16 in.
	6.7 (2.0)	#6 @ 8 in.
10	4.0 (1.2)	#4 @ 64 in.
	4.7 (1.4)	#4 @ 40 in.
	5.3 (1.6)	#4 @ 24 in.
	6.0 (1.8)	#4 @16 in.
	6.7 (2.0)	#5 @16 in.
	7.3 (2.2)	#6 @16 in.
	8.0 (2.4)	#6 @ 8 in.
12	4.0 (1.2)	#4 @ 72 in.
	4.7 (1.4)	#4 @ 48 in.
	5.3 (1.6)	#4 @ 32 in.
	6.0 (1.8)	#4 @ 24 in.
	6.7 (2.0)	#4 @ 16 in.
	7.3 (2.2)	#5 @ 16 in.
	8.0 (2.4)	#5 @ 16 in.
	8.7 (2.7)	#7 @ 16 in.
	9.3 (2.8)	#7 @ 8 in.

STUCCO

Table 4-53 *Stucco Curing Times*

Coat	Keep Moist	Set (days)
Scratch	12 hours	2
Brown	12 hours	7
Finish	12 hours	2

TWENTY OF THE MOST COMMON CONCRETE PROBLEMS

1. Not reading the specifications/plans in detail.
2. Excavations not protected from weather.
3. Forms not braced adequately.
4. Pouring too high a lift for strength of forms.
5. Not enough workers, especially finishers.
6. Free-falling concrete.
7. Wrong slump (water usually added at the site).
8. Not following hot or cold weather concrete methods.
9. Pouring too late in the day, resulting in finishers working at night.

Stucco Mix

Material	Cubic Feet	Gallons	Pounds
Sand	2	15	200
Portland Cement	1/2	3 1/2	47
Lime	1/3	2 1/2	12
Water	3/4	6	48

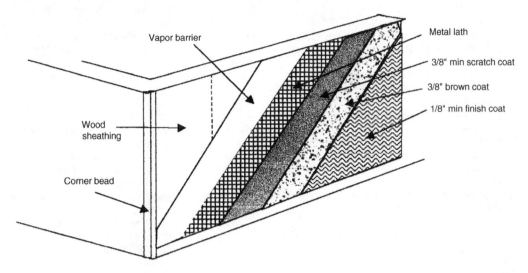

Fig. 4-73 *Stucco layers and required thicknesses.*

10. Not properly curing.
11. Control joints missing or not "cut" in a timely manner.
12. Wrong placement of anchor bolts.
13. Not testing concrete.
14. Not using the correct admixture especially air entrainment.
15. Incorrect shoring for multiple floors.
16. Damaging and displacement of stub outs.
17. Allowing excessive loads on "green" concrete.
18. Removing forms too early.
19. Not properly compacting base.
20. Incorrectly placement of welder wire mesh.

ASTM CONCRETE STANDARDS

American Society for Testing and Materials documents related to aggregates, cement, and concrete are as follows:

C 29-87	Test Method for Unit Weight and Voids in Aggregate
C 31-87	Practice for Making and Curing Concrete Test Specimens in the Field
C 33-86	Specification for Concrete Aggregates
C 39-86	Test Method for Compressive Strength of Cylindrical Concrete Specimens
C 40-84	Test Method for Organic Impurities in Fine Aggregates for Concrete
C 42-85	Method of Obtaining and Testing Drilled Cores and Sawed Beams of Concrete
C 70-79	Test Method for Surface Moisture in Fine Aggregate
C 78-84	Test Method for Flexural Strength of Concrete (Using Simple Beam with Third-Point Loading)
C 85-66	Test Method for Cement Content of Hardened Portland Cement Concrete
C 87-83	Test Method for Effect of Organic Impurities in Fine Aggregate on Strength of Mortar
C 88-83	Test Method for Soundness of Aggregates by Use of Sodium Sulfate or Magnesium Sulfate
C 91-87	Specification for Masonry Cement
C 94-86	Specification for Ready-Mixed Concrete
C 109-86	Test Method for Compressive Strength of Hydraulic Cement Mortars (Using 2-in. or 50-mm Cube Specimens)
C 114-85	Methods for Chemical Analysis of Hydraulic Cement
C 115-86	Test Method for Fineness of Portland Cement by the Turbidimeter
C 117-87	Test Method for Materials Finer than 75-Jlm (No. 200) Sieve in Mineral Aggregates by Washing
C 123-83	Test Method for Lightweight Pieces in Aggregate
C 125-86	Definitions of Terms Relating to Concrete and Concrete Aggregates
C 127-84	Test Method for Specific Gravity and Absorption of Coarse Aggregate

C 128-84 Test Method for Specific Gravity and Absorption of Fine Aggregate

C 131-81 Test Method for Resistance to Degradation of Small-Size Coarse Aggregate by Abrasion and Impact in the Los Angeles Machine

C 136-84 Method for Sieve Analysis of Fine and Coarse Aggregates

C 138-81 Test Method for Unit Weight, Yield, and Air Content (Gravimetric) of Concrete

C 141-85 Specification for Hydraulic Hydrated Lime for Structural Purposes

C 142-78 Test Method for Clay Lumps and Friable Particles in Aggregates

C 143-78 Test Method for Slump of Portland Cement Concrete

C 150-86 Specification for Portland Cement

C 151-84 Test Method for Autoclave Expansion of Portland Cement

C 156-80 Test Method for Water Retention by Concrete Curing Materials

C 157-86 Test Method for Length Change of Hardened Hydraulic-Cement Mortar and Concrete

C 171-69 Specification for Sheet Materials for Curing Concrete

C 172-82 Method of Sampling Freshly Mixed Concrete

C 173-78 Test Method for Air Content of Freshly Mixed Concrete by the Volumetric Method

C 174-87 Test Method for Measuring Length of Drilled Concrete Cores

C 177-85 Test Method for Steady-State Heat Flux Measurements and Thermal Transmission Properties by Means of the Guarded-Hot-Plate Apparatus

C 183-83 Methods of Sampling and Acceptance of Hydraulic Cement

C 184-83 Test Method for Fineness of Hydraulic Cement by the 150-μm (No. 100) and 75-μm (No. 200) Sieves

C 185-85 Test Method for Air Content of Hydraulic Cement Mortar

C 186-86 Test Method for Heat of Hydration of Hydraulic Cement

C 187-86 Test Method for Normal Consistency of Hydraulic Cement

C 188-84 Test Method for Density of Hydraulic Cement

C 190-85 Test Method for Tensile Strength of Hydraulic Cement Mortars

C191-82 Test Method for Time of Setting of Hydraulic Cement by Vicat Needle

C 192-81 Method of Making and Curing Concrete Test Specimens in the Laboratory

C 204-84 Test Method for Fineness of Portland Cement by Air Permeability Apparatus

C 215-85 Test Method for Fundamental Transverse, Longitudinal, and Torsional Frequencies of Concrete Specimens

C 219-84 Terminology Relating to Hydraulic Cement

C 226-86 Specification for Air-Entraining Additions for Use in the Manufacture of Air-Entraining Portland Cement

C 227-87 Test Method for Potential Alkali Reactivity of Cement-Aggregate Combinations (Mortar-Bar Method)

C 230-83 Specification for Flow Table for Use in Tests of Hydraulic Cement

C 231-82 Test Method for Air Content of Freshly Mixed Concrete by the Pressure Method

C 232-87 Test Methods for Bleeding of Concrete

C 233-87 Test Method for Air-Entraining Admixtures for Concrete

C 243-85 Test Method for Bleeding of Cement Pastes and Mortars

C 260-86 Specification for Air-Entraining Admixtures for Concrete

C 265-83 Test Method for Calcium Sulfate in Hydrated Portland Cement Mortar

C 266-87 Test Method for Time of Setting of Hydraulic Cement by Gillmore Needles

C 270-86 Specification for Mortar for Unit Masonry

C 289-87 Test Method for Potential Reactivity of Aggregates (Chemical Method)

C 293-79 Test Method for Flexural Strength of Concrete (Using Simple Beam with Center-Point Loading)

C 294-86 Descriptive Nomenclature for Constituents of Natural Mineral Aggregates

C 295-85 Practice for Petrographic Examination of Aggregates for Concrete

C 305-82 Method for Mechanical Mixing of Hydraulic Cement Pastes and Mortars of Plastic Consistency

C 309-81 Specification for Liquid Membrane-Forming Compounds for Curing Concrete

C 311-87 Test Methods for Sampling and Testing Fly Ash or Natural Pozzolans for Use as a Mineral Admixture in Portland Cement Concrete

C 330-87 Specification for Lightweight Aggregates for Structural Concrete

C 332-87 Specification for Lightweight Aggregates for Insulating Concrete

C 341-84 Test Method for Length Change of Drilled or Sawed Specimens of Cement Mortar and Concrete

C 342-79 Test Method for Potential Volume Change of Cement-Aggregate Combinations

C 348-86 Test Method for Flexural Strength of Hydraulic Cement Mortars

C 359-83 Test Method for Early Stiffening of Portland Cement (Mortar Method)

C 360-82 Test Method for Ball Penetration in Fresh Portland Cement Concrete

C 387-87 Specification for Packaged, Dry, Combined Materials for Mortar and Concrete

C 403-85 Test Method for Time of Setting of Concrete Mixtures by Penetration Resistance

C 418-81 Test Method for Abrasion Resistance of Concrete by Sandblasting

C 430-83 Test Method for Fineness of Hydraulic Cement by the 45-μm (No. 325) Sieve

C 441-81 Test Method for Effectiveness of Mineral Admixtures in Preventing Excessive Expansion of Concrete Due to Alkali-Aggregate Reaction

C 451-83 Test Method for Early Stiffening of Portland Cement (Paste Method)

C 452-85 Test Method for Potential Expansion of Portland Cement Mortars Exposed to Sulfate

C 457-82 Practice for Microscopical Determination of Air-Void Content and Parameters of the Air-Void System in Hardened Concrete

C 465-85 Specifications for Processing Additions for Use in the Manufacture of Hydraulic Cements

C 469-87	Test Method for Static Modulus of Elasticity and Poisson's Ratio of Concrete in Compression	C 778-80a	Specification for Standard Sand
C 470-87	Specification for Molds for Forming Concrete Test Cylinders Vertically	C 779-82	Test Method for Abrasion Resistance of Horizontal Concrete Surfaces
C 490-86	Specification for Apparatus for Use in Measurement of Length Change of Hardened Cement Paste, Mortar, and Concrete	C 786-83	Test Method for Fineness of Hydraulic Cement and Raw Materials by the 300-μm (No. 50), 150-μm (No. 100), and 75-μm (No. 200) Sieves by Wet Methods
C 494-86	Specification for Chemical Admixtures for Concrete	C 796-87	Test Method for Foaming Agents for Use in Producing Cellular Concrete Using Preformed Foam
C 495-86	Test Method for Compressive Strength of Lightweight Insulating Concrete	C 801-81	Practice for Determining the Mechanical Properties of Hardened Concrete Under Triaxial Loads
C 496-87	Test Method for Splitting Tensile Strength of Cylindrical Concrete Specimens	C 803-82	Test Method for Penetration Resistance of Hardened Concrete
C 511-85	Specification for Moist Cabinets, Moist Rooms, and Water Storage Tanks Used in the Testing of Hydraulic Cements and Concretes	C 805-85	Test Method for Rebound Number of Hardened Concrete
C 512-87	Test Method for Creep of Concrete in Compression	C 806-75	Test Method for Restrained Expansion of Expansive Cement Mortar
C 513-86	Test Method for Obtaining and Testing Specimens of Hardened Lightweight Insulating Concrete for Compressive Strength	C 807-83	Test Method for Time of Setting of Hydraulic Cement Mortar by Modified Vicat Needle
C 535-81	Test Method for Resistance to Degradation of Large-Size Coarse Aggregate by Abrasion and Impact in the Los Angeles machine	C 823-83	Practice for Examination and Sampling of Hardened Concrete in Constructions
C 566-84	Test Method for Total Moisture Content of Aggregate by Drying	C 827-87	Test Method for Change in Height of Early Ages of Cylindrical Specimens from Cementitious Mixtures
C 567-85	Test Method for Unit Weight of Structural Lightweight Concrete	C 845-80	Specification for Expansive Hydraulic Cement
C 586-69	Test Method for Potential Alkali Reactivity of Carbonate Rocks for Concrete Aggregates (Rock Cylinder Method)	C 856-83	Practice for Petrographic Examination of Hardened Concrete
C 595-86	Specification for Blended Hydraulic Cements	C 869-80	Specification for Foaming Agents Used in Making Preformed Foam for Cellular Concrete
C 597-83	Test Method for Pulse Velocity Through Concrete	C 873-85	Test Method for Compressive Strength of Concrete Cylinders Cast in Place in Cylindrical Molds
C 617-85	Practice for Capping Cylindrical Concrete Specimens	C 876-87	Test Method for Half-Cell Potentials of Uncoated Reinforcing Steel in Concrete
C 618-85	Specification for Fly Ash and Raw or Calcined Natural Pozzolan for Use as a Mineral Admixture in Portland Cement Concrete	C 878-87	Test Method for Restrained Expansion of Shrinkage-Compensating Concrete
C 637-84	Specification for Aggregates for Radiation-Shielding Concrete	C 881-78	Specification for Epoxy-Resin-Base Bonding Systems for Concrete
C 638-84	Descriptive Nomenclature of Constituents of Aggregates for Radiation-Shielding Concrete	C 900-87	Test Method for Pullout Strength of Hardened Concrete
C 641-82	Test Method for Staining Materials in Lightweight Concrete Aggregates	C 917-82	Method for Evaluation of Cement Strength Uniformity from a Single Source
C 642-82	Test Method for Specific Gravity, Absorption, and Voids in Hardened Concrete	C 918-80	Method for Developing Early Age Compression Test Values and Projecting Later Age Strengths
C 666-84	Test Method for Resistance of Concrete to Rapid Freezing and Thawing	C 928-80	Specification for Packaged, Dry, Rapid-Hardening Cementitious Materials for Concrete Repairs
C 671-86	Test Method for Critical Dilation of Concrete Specimens Subjected to Freezing	C 937-80	Specification for Grout Fluidifier for Preplaced-Aggregate Concrete
C 672-84	Test Method for Scaling Resistance of Concrete Surfaces Exposed to Deicing Chemicals	C 938-80	Practice for Proportioning Grout Mixtures for Preplaced-Aggregate Concrete
C 682-87	Practice for Evaluation of Frost Resistance of Coarse Aggregates in Air-Entrained Concrete by Critical Dilation Procedures	C 939-87	Test Method for Flow of Grout for Preplaced-Aggregate Concrete (Flow Cone Method)
C 684-81	Method of Making, Accelerated Curing, and Testing of Concrete Compression Test Specimens	C 940-87	Test Method for Expansion and Bleeding of Freshly Mixed Grouts for Preplaced-Aggregate Concrete in the Laboratory
C 685-86	Specification for Concrete Made by Volumetric Batching and Continuous Mixing	C 941-87	Test Method for Water Retentivity of Grout Mixtures for Preplaced-Aggregate Concrete in the Laboratory
C 688-77	Specification for Functional Additions for Use in Hydraulic Cements	C 942-86	Test Method for Compressive Strength of Grouts for Preplaced-Aggregate Concrete in the Laboratory
C 702-87	Practice for Reducing Field Samples of Aggregate to Testing Size		

C 943-80 Practice for Making Test Cylinders and Prisms for Determining Strength and Density of Preplaced-Aggregate Concrete in the Laboratory

C 944-80 Test Method for Abrasion Resistance of Concrete or Mortar Surfaces by the Rotating-Cutter Method

C 953-87 Test Method for Time of Setting of Grouts for Preplaced-Aggregate Concrete in the Laboratory

C 979-82 Specification for Pigments for Integrally Colored Concrete

C 989-87 Specification for Ground Granulated Blast-Furnace Slag for Use in Concrete and Mortars

C 995-86 Test Method for Time of Flow of Fiber-Reinforced Concrete through Inverted Slump Cone

C 1012-87 Test Method for Length Change of Hydraulic-Cement Mortars Exposed to Sulfate Solution

C 1017-85 Specification for Chemical Admixtures for Use in Producing Flowing Concrete

C 1018-85 Test Method for Flexural Toughness and First-Crack Strength Fiber-Reinforced Concrete (Using Beam with Third-Point Loading)

C 1038-85 Test Method for Expansion of Portland Cement Mortar Bars Stored in Water

C 1040-85 Test Methods for Density of Unhardened and Hardened Concrete in Place by Nuclear Methods

C 1059-86 Specification for Latex Agents for Bonding Fresh to Hardened Concrete

C 1064-86 Test Method for Temperature of Freshly Mixed Portland Cement Concrete

C 1073-85 Test Method for Hydraulic Activity of Ground Slag by Reaction with Alkali

C 1074-87 Practice for Estimating Concrete Strength by the Maturity Method

C 1078-87 Test Methods for Determining Cement Content of Freshly Mixed Concrete

C 1079-87 Test Methods for Determining Water Content of Freshly Mixed Concrete

C 1084-87 Test Method for Portland Cement Content of Hardened Hydraulic-Cement Concrete

D 75-82 Practice for Sampling Aggregates

D 98-87 Specification for Calcium Chloride

D 345-80 Methods of Sampling and Testing Calcium Chloride for Roads and Structural Applications

D 448-86 Classification for Sizes of Aggregate for Road and Bridge Construction

D 558-82 Test Method for Moisture-Density Relations of Soil-Cement Mixtures

D 632-84 Specification for Sodium Chloride

D 2240-81 Test Method for Rubber Property-Durometer Hardness

D 3042-86 Test Method for Insoluble Residue in Carbonate Aggregates

D 3963-82 Specification for Epoxy-Coated Reinforcing Steel

E 11-87 Specification for Wire-Cloth Sieves for Testing Purposes

E 380-84 Metric Practice

CONCRETE INSPECTION FORMS AND WORKSHEETS

Concrete Pour Worksheet

CONCRETE POUR WORKSHEET							
PROJECT				PROJECT NO.			
SUPPLIER				TESTING CO.			

LOCATION	FOOTER				TEST RESULTS		
DATES / AREA	DESIGN MIX/PSI	SLUMP	ADMIXTURES (AIR)	WEATHER: (AIR) TEMP (°F)	3 DAY	7 DAY	28 DAY

LOCATION					TEST RESULTS		
DATES / AREA	DESIGN MIX/PSI	SLUMP	ADMIXTURES	WEATHER: (AIR) TEMP (°F)	3 DAY	7 DAY	28 DAY

LOCATION					TEST RESULTS		
DATES / AREA	DESIGN MIX/PSI	SLUMP	ADMIXTURES	WEATHER: (AIR) TEMP (°F)	3 DAY	7 DAY	28 DAY

LOCATION					TEST RESULTS		
DATES / AREA	DESIGN MIX/PSI	SLUMP	ADMIXTURES	WEATHER: (AIR) TEMP (°F)	3 DAY	7 DAY	28 DAY

LOCATION					TEST RESULTS		
DATES / AREA	DESIGN MIX/PSI	SLUMP	ADMIXTURES	WEATHER: (AIR) TEMP (°F)	3 DAY	7 DAY	28 DAY

LOCATION					TEST RESULTS		
DATES / AREA	DESIGN MIX/PSI	SLUMP	ADMIXTURES	WEATHER: (AIR) TEMP (°F)	3 DAY	7 DAY	28 DAY

Concrete Form Inspector's Report

Project		Date	
Job location		General Contractor	
Placement description		General Contr. Supt.	
Floor			
Placement number			
Column line references			

Starting time of placement	
Completion time of placement	
Concrete placing equipment	
Concrete conveying equipment	
Type of work being poured	
Scope of subcontractor's work	
Type of formwork or structure to which Subcontractor's work is framed	
Comments on General Contractor's framing	

List of points to check out before and during concrete placement (depending on the type of pour, make your own checks; always check specifications).

	Form details for job			Check for possible exit routes; in case of trouble, have at least two such routes available wherever possible
	All shores in place			Prearranged signal with concrete-placing foreman to stop pour in emergency
	Wedges under shores tight & nailed			Know placing crew's sequence of pour
	Shoring hardware secured			Check for placing deep beams or drops before main deck
	Sills solid on ground or slab			For walls: Know rate of placement for which forms designed and protest if exceeded
	Lacing installed, when required and nailed			
	Check for spreaders when required			Clean out holes patched
	Joist pans			Chamfer and grade strips in place
	Plywood joints flush			Equipment available in case of need for adjustment or reinforcement
	X bracing installed where lateral movement could occur			**Others**
	Beam spreaders in place			
	Hardware tight			
	Tighten wedges under shores along construction joint of previous pour			
	Check shores for plumb (per plans)			
	Telltales in place and marked where required by Superintendent			
	Camber installed			
	Extra jacks Extra bracing Extra shores Wedges			

Comments	

Date		Inspector Signature	

5

CHAPTER

Masonry

GENERAL

This chapter covers brick, concrete masonry units (CMU), tile, stone, and reinforcements and other masonry construction.

SAMPLES

Have samples of all materials and certificates of compliance been submitted and approved by the Project Architect and Owner?

1. Check progress schedule for dates materials are needed.
2. Is contractor submitting samples early enough to avoid construction delays?
3. Are reference specifications available for review?
4. Are required certificates being submitted with samples and or shop drawings?

Sample Panels

1. Have sample panels been erected?
2. Are they located so as to be close enough to structure to provide ready access for comparison purposes? Do not permit sample panels to be incorporated in the structure. Only approved materials will be used in sample panels.
3. Have precautions been taken to prevent damage to sample panels?
4. Masonry construction shall not begin until the "mock-up" panel for the work has been approved. Record minor deficiencies and other comments for clear understanding on how to correct them. All embedded items, a control joint, flashings, weep holes, and other features will be included in the panel.
5. Check masonry against sample panel. The materials, workmanship, and finished appearance must be equal.
6. Sample panels should be cleaned to demonstrate effectiveness of the cleaning solution proposed for the work.

TESTS

The following listed tests will be required in most contracts; other tests may be specified in some contracts. (For all tests, the Inspector's responsibility is the same—to ascertain that the tests have been performed and that results are satisfactory before allowing the use or installation of materials.)

Concrete Masonry Units (CMUs)

Drying–Shrinkage Test

1. Specifications limit shrinkage of units
2. The design of control joint reinforcing was based on the specified limit of shrinkage.
3. This test determines if the shrinkage of units to be used is within the specified limits.
4. Test results must be submitted for approval by specified time.

Air–Dry Condition Test

1. CMU passing this test have a proper moisture content and will not shrink excessively from loss of moisture to the air.
2. The Inspector will require that the specified number of representative samples are delivered to the laboratory from each lot. Check the job specifications for compliance.
3. Samples must be sealed in lab-furnished, air-tight containers if testing lab is not in the immediate vicinity of the job site.

Concrete Block Grades

ASTM classifies concrete masonry units into two grades, N and S, and into two types, Type I and Type II.

Grade N units are to be used either below or above ground and where they will be directly exposed to moisture penetration and freezing and thawing. Minimum compressive strength is *800* pounds per square inch.

Grade S units are to be used above ground and where they will not be directly exposed to moisture penetration and freezing and thawing. They require weather-protective coatings when exposed. Minimum compressive strength is *600* pounds per square inch.

Type I units have established moisture limits depending on the average relative humidity at the manafacturer's location. *Type II* units have no specified moisture content and are used where the humidity is moderate to high.

Brick Grades

SW—Have a high resistance to freezing. Usually used for foundations and retaining walls. Used where they are exposed to wetness and subject to freezing.

MW—Used in freezing weather but do not get exposed to water. Safe to use in moderate climate conditions.

NW—Mainly used as interior walls and partitions. Not to be used in areas with a lot of annual rainfall and not subjected to frost or freezing conditions.

Table 5-1 *Brick Types*

Type	Uses
HBS	General use in exposed and interior walls and partitions; has a wider range of colors and size than HBX.
HBX	Same as the HBS, but has a high degree of mechanical perfection. Limited color range and sizes.
HBA	For architectural effects has nonuniformity of colors, sizes, and texture in each individual unit.
HBB	For general use where color and texture are not a consideration. Used in walls and partitions.

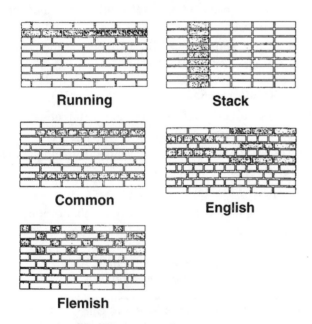

Fig. 5-1 *Typical masonry bonds.*

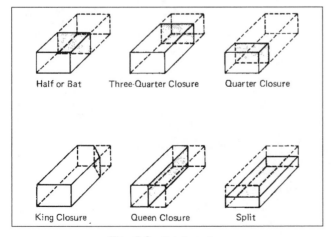

Fig. 5-2 *Brick sections*

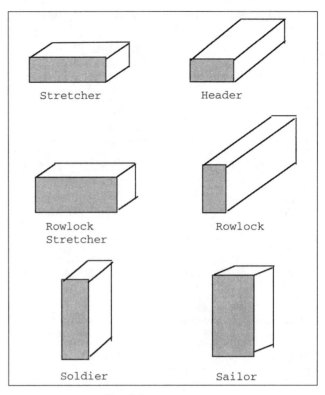

Fig. 5-3 *Brick positions*

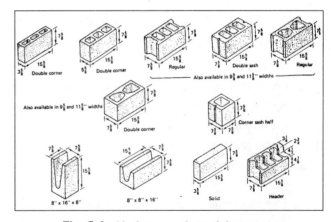

Fig. 5-4 *Block types and actual dimensions.*

Mortar

Tests for Mortar

1. Contractor is required to have mortar proportions established and tested by an approved laboratory for each type of mortar specified.

2. Check for approved batch proportions and mixing operations.

3. No change in proportioning or source of materials will be allowed without additional tests and/or Project Architect's or Engineer's approval.

Table 5-2 *Strengths for Masonry Mortars*

Type	Average Strength— 2-in. Cube at 28 Days
M	2500
S	1800
N	750
O	350

Table 5-3 *Proper Selection for Masonry Mortars*

Location of Mortar	Part of Structure	Recommended Type/*(Alternates)
Exterior above grade	Load-bearing wall, non-load-bearing parapet wall	Type N/*Type S or M Type O/*Type N or S Type N/*Type S
Exterior at or below grade	Foundation wall, retaining wall, walks, pavements, patios	Type S/*Type M or N
Interior	Load-bearing wall, non-load-bearing wall	Type N/*Type S or M Type O/*Type N
Fireplace	Flue liners or masonry exposed to heat	Refactory mortar

Materials

General

1. Do materials on site match the approved samples for:
   a. Color or range of colors?
   b. Texture?
   c. Grade (SN grade brick always used below grade)?
   d. Are steel door and window frames on the site before masonry is started?
2. Are sizes and defects within permissible tolerances?
   a. Obtain copies of referenced ASTM or other materials specification; tolerances are spelled out.
   b. Use these tolerances as basis for accepting or rejecting units.
   c. Typical defects to look for are: cracks, chips, checks, crazing, crawling, pop outs, and warped or misshapen units. *Defective units must be marked to preclude their inadvertent use!*
3. Are storage facilities adequate?
   a. Are units stored off ground and *completely* covered?
   b. Are coverings waterproof, such as tarps, polyethylene sheeting, or other waterproof material?
   c. Are coverings secured in place at the end of every work day?

Anchors: Ties and Joint Reinforcement

1. Do materials on site match the approved samples?

2. Is nonferrous metal specified or must the steel be galvanized?
3. On wall and partition intersection ties, check both specifications and plans for specific details as to type, size, shape, and material.
4. Check for omission of anchorage, especially at doors, windows, and other wall openings.
5. The bent ends of anchors must be set into masonry cells filled full with mortar.
6. Cavity-wall ties
   a. With hollow masonry in either wythe, i.e., in either or both the face and backup masonry, rectangular wire ties are required.
   b. Is length such that end anchorage occurs in specified face-shell-mortar beds?
   c. Are ties crimped for moisture drip at center of cavity space (after insulation) so no moisture will pass?
   d. Is the reinforcing $\frac{1}{16}$-in. wire either zinc-coated or copper-clad steel?

Joint Reinforcement

1. Is wire zinc-coated and do the different coating weights comply with specifications?
2. Are cross-wires spaced as specified for smooth and for deformed longitudinal wire?
3. Is specified gauge wire being used?
4. Is configuration acceptable with number of longitudinal wires, with box ties?

Table 5-4 *Spacing of Vertical Bars for Load-Bearing Masonry Walls*

Wall Thickness	#5 Bar	#4 Bar	#3 Bar
8 in.	48-in. O.C.	34-in. O.C.	22-in. O.C.
10 in.	45-in. O.C.	30-in. O.C.	16-in. O.C.
12 in.		48-in. O.C.	27-in. O.C.
14 in.		42-in. O.C.	24-in. O.C.

Lintels:

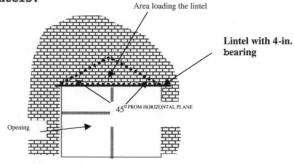

Fig. 5-5 *Lintel loading.*

Table 5-5 *Lintels*

Size of Steel Angle (in.)	No Story Above	One Story Above	Two Stories Above
3 × 3 × ¼	6 ft–0 in.	4 ft–6 in.	3 ft–0 in.
4 × 3 × ¼	8 ft–0 in.	6 ft–0 in.	4 ft–6 in.
5 × 3½ × ⁵⁄₁₆	10 ft–0 in.	8 ft–0 in.	6 ft–0 in.
6 × 3½ × ⁵⁄₁₆	14 ft–0 in.	9 ft–6 in.	7 ft–0 in.
(2)-6 × 3½ × ⁵⁄₁₆	20 ft–0 in.	12 ft–0 in.	9 ft–6 in.

No. of #4 or Equivalent Reinforcing Bars	No Story Above	One Story Above	Two Stories Above
1	6 ft–0 in.	4 ft–6 in.	3 ft–0 in.
1	8 ft–0 in.	6 ft–0 in.	4 ft–6 in.
2	10 ft–0 in.	8 ft–0 in.	6 ft–0 in.
2	14 ft–0 in.	9 ft–6 in.	7 ft–0 in.
4	20 ft–0 in.	12 ft–0 in.	9 ft–6 in.

Note: Long leg is always in the vertical position.

Brick

1. Has certificate of compliance been received?
2. Do color range and texture match approved samples?
3. Have broken, cracked, chipped, warped, spalled, oversized, and undersized units been rejected?

4. Obtain copy of ASTM C-26, C-216, or other reference specifications on tolerances contained therein.
5. Is an efflorescence test required?
6. Make sure masons protect brick from rain splashings that cause staining.

Brick Sizes

Nominal dimensions are most often used by the Architect in modular construction. In modular construction, all dimensions of the brick and other building elements are multiples of a given module. Such dimensions are known as nominal dimensions. For brick masonry the *nominal* dimension is equal to the specified unit dimension plus the intended mortar joint thickness. The intended mortar joint thickness is the thickness required so that the unit plus joint thickness match the coursing module. In the inch-pound system of measurement, nominal brick dimensions are based on multiples (or fractions) of 4 in. In the SI (metric) system, nominal brick dimensions are based on multiples of 100 mm.

Portland Cement, Masonry Cement, and Lime

1. Check containers to be sure materials received are the same as specified and tested.
2. If containers are broken or damaged, reject cements or lime. (Mark them and have them moved from the site immediately!)

Standard Nomenclature for Brick Sizes[1]

	Modular Brick Sizes							
Unit Designation	Nominal Dimensions (in.)			Joint Thickness[2] (in.)	Specified Dimensions[3] (in.)			Vertical Coursing
	w	h	l		w	h	l	
Modular	4	2-⅔	8	⅜, ½	3-⅝, 3-½	2-¼, 2-¼	7-⅝, 7-½	3C = 8 in.
Engineer Modular	4	3-⅕	8	⅜, ½	3-⅝, 3-½	2-¾, 2-¹³⁄₁₆	7-⅝, 7-½	5C = 16 in.
Closure Modular	4	4	8	⅜, ½	3-⅝, 3-½	3-⅝, 3-½	7-⅝, 7-½	1C = 4 in.
Roman	4	2	12	⅜, ½	3-⅝, 3-½	1-⅝, 1-½	11-⅝, 11-½	2C = 4 in.
Norman	4	2-⅔	12	⅜, ½	3-⅝, 3-½	2-¼, 2-¼	11-⅝, 11-½	3C = 8 in.
Engineer Norman	4	3-⅕	12	⅜, ½	3-⅝, 3-½	2-¾, 2-¹³⁄₁₆	11-⅝, 11-½	5C = 16 in.
Utility	4	4	12	⅜, ½	3-⅝, 3-½	3-⅝, 3-½	11-⅝, 11-½	1C = 4 in.
	Nonmodular Brick Sizes							
Standard				⅜, ½	3-⅝, 3-½	2-¼, 2-¼	8, 8	3C = 8 in.
Engineer Standard				⅜, ½	3-⅝, 3-½	2-¾, 2-¹³⁄₁₆	8, 8	5C = 16 in.
Closure Standard				⅜, ½	3-⅝, 3-½	3-⅝, 3-½	8, 8	1C = 4 in.
King				⅜	3, 2-¾	2-¾, 2-⅝	9-⅝, 9-⅝	5C = 16 in.
Queen				⅜	3, 2-¾	2-¾, 2-¾	8, 8	5C = 16 in.

[1] 1 in. = 25.4 mm; 1 ft = 0.3 m.
[2] Common joint sizes used with length and width dimensions. Joint thickness of bed joints vary based on vertical coursing and specified unit height.
[3] Specified dimensions may vary within this range from manufacturer to manufacturer.

3. Pay particular attention to sack- or bag-type containers for evidence of dampening, hardening, or setting up cement or lime.

4. Any other evidence that material does not meet specifications is cause for investigation and possible rejection.

5. Is the mortar of correct consistency to better adhere to the masonry?

6. If mortar is used with reinforcing steel, make sure no accelerating admixtures with salt such as calcium chlorides have been used.

Concrete Brick, Split Block, and Concrete Masonry Units (CMUs)

1. Have certification of compliance or certified laboratory test reports been received? (Fire rating required?)

Table 5-6 Fire Ratings for Masonry Units

Size	% Solid	Thickness	Rating
3 × 8 × 16	100	2.625	<1 hour
4 × 8 × 16	71.2	2.581	<1 hour
4 × 8 × 16	100	3.625	1.5 hour
6 × 18 × 16	52.9	2.975	1 hour
6 × 8 × 16	100	5.635	3.5 hours
8 × 8 × 16 (2 core)	53.2	4.056	2+ hours
8 × 8 × 16 (3 core)	54.7	4.170	2+ hours
8 × 8 × 16	66.7	5.090	3 hours
8 × 8 × 16	75	5.718	3.5 hours
8 × 8 × 16	100	7.625	4+ hours
12 × 8 × 16 (2 core)	47.9	5.568	3.5 hours
12 × 8 × 16 (3 core)	53.4	6.207	4+ hours

2. Have units passed the required tests for drying shrinkage and air–dry condition? Air–dry condition tests are made on units selected from the worksite stockpile. Were solid units presoaked in water with their surfaces dry before using?

3. Are all units to be used in any one structure of the same appearance (especially textured units)?

4. Have sizes of units been spot-checked? No overall dimension (width, height, or length) shall differ more than the deviation allowed from the specified standard dimensions.

5. Do specifications state location where bullnose units are required?

Coping Tile

1. Do tiles overhang parapet on both sides to provide for drip?

2. Are drip grooves provided?

3. Are flashings installed, as detailed, under copings?

Fireclay and Refractory Brick

1. Should be compact of homogeneous structure, free from checks, cracks, voids, or soft centers.

2. Do the units carry the required rating or are there a testing agency and statement of results of test required?

3. The sizes and allowable tolerances for firebrick shall be in accordance with applicable ASTM standards as follows:

  a. Dimensions of 4 in. and over shall not vary more than +2% from that specified.

  b. Dimensions under 4 in. shall not vary more than 3% from the contract specifications.

  c. The standard shown in the ASTM standards shall be for low-duty refractory brick.

Flue Linings

1. Is size of flue lining as specified and per code?

2. Does thimble size match size of boiler connection or smoke pipe?

3. Mortar joints must be smooth on the inside of the flue tiles (refractory mortar only).

4. Is the hard-burned fireclay or shale free from blisters and warping?

5. Codes require care to be taken in the lengths of linings as well as termination points for differing fuel types (such as for liquid fuels vs. solid fuels).

6. Check for correct fire separation distances.

Insulation

1. Either loose-fill or board-type insulation is specified—loose fill in CMU cells or board inside the cavity.

2. Loose-fill type must be treated for water repellency.

3. Board type must be closed-cell plastic treated for fire resistance.

4. Limit board insulation installed to allow a 1-in. air space in cavity walls.

5. Is material protected from weather during construction?

Mortar Materials

1. Are materials delivered to site as specified, tested, and approved? Check that only one brand of one type of cement and aggregate from only one source is used. Do not allow careless mixing procedures, including variations in mortar proportions. Variations tend to produce differing colors of the mortar when dry.

2. Type N mortar can be used for all nonreinforced masonry unless otherwise specified.

3. Pointing mortar has smaller-size aggregate and a waterproofing additive. Check the specifications for correct use.

Precast Concrete Trim

1. Has certificate of compliance been received, and does unit pass absorption test?

2. Have sills been cast with washes and drip grooves?

3. Are lintel units labeled to show top of each unit?

4. Is there a joint in the sill at every mullion? (Check plans and specifications.)

5. Inspect for crazing; pour water over precast trim; if present, crazing will be apparent. Evidence of excessive crazing is cause for rejection. Dusting, spalling, and/or use of surface coatings is also cause for rejection.

6. Have units weighing over 80 lb been provided with built-in loops of galvanized wire?

Prefaced Concrete Masonry Units

1. Have certificates and all required current test results been furnished for units?

2. Check units for bond between facing and concrete masonry units. Facing must turn over edges and ends for ⅜ in. in ⅛-in. thickness.

3. Check unit for chips, cracks, crazes, blisters, crawling, holes, and other imperfections detracting from appearance.

4. Check dimension, tolerances, and requirements.

Reinforcing Bars

1. Are shape, spacing, and size of bars as detailed? Are proper clearances being maintained?

2. Are bars free from scaly rust, oil, dirt, and grout splashes?

3. Are splices the same length as specified in contract drawings and specifications?

Stonework

1. Do specifications require shop drawings for stonework?

2. If shop drawings are not required, it is particularly important that a sample panel be erected and approved by all concerned before starting stonework.

Fig. 5-6 *Reinforcing bars in CMU wall. Check minimum clearances to outside of wall (see Figure 5-12).*

3. Reject stone with stains, cracks, chips, or seams.

4. Check all work against shop drawings and/or sample panels.

5. Check anchors, clamps, and dowels for specified type of materials, size, shape, spacing, and proper installation.

Structural Clay Facing Units

1. Are the units of the proper finish, texture, and color range?

2. Are bodies of units free from cracks or strength-impairing defects?

3. Are finished faces covered with ceramic glaze of uniform quality, free from defects which would detract from appearance *when viewed from a distance of 5 ft*?

4. ASTM C-126 or other referenced specification is to be used and as a basis of acceptance or rejection.

5. Have units been checked for nonstaining properties?

ERECTION AND PLACEMENT
Protection

1. Is the temperature above the minimum temperature allowed?

   a. For temperature below the minimum temperature specified, contractor shall submit a written proposal of methods of protecting masonry against cold weather.

   b. Frozen materials shall not be installed or built upon.

Fig. 5-7 *CMU wall protection from freezing and water.*

c. Work becoming frozen after installation shall be removed and replaced.

d. Mortar must be kept continuously above freezing for at least *48 hours* after units are laid. A copy of the IMIAWC (International Masonry Industry All-Weather Council) publications on cold weather masonry construction should be available.

2. Waterproof covering is required for top of unfinished walls, including the cavity spaces. Water entry through the top of unfinished walls contributes to efflorescence stain on the face of finish wall surfaces.

a. Use waterproof building paper, canvas, polyethylene sheeting, and similar materials.

b. Tie or weight in place; do not just drape.

c. Are coverings provided at the end of each work day?

d. Are coverings provided during inclement weather?

e. Is block corbeling within acceptable limits?

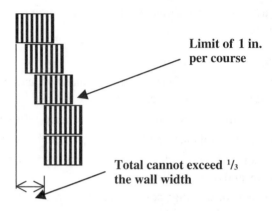

Limit of 1 in. per course

Total cannot exceed $^1/_3$ the wall width

Fig. 5-8 *Corbeling.*

f. Protect tops of complete walls from entrance of water, frost, and snow until roof is in place and tight.

Backfill Adjacent to Masonry Walls

1. Is parging required and applied to exterior concrete masonry walls below grade for basement spaces at

Table 5-7 *Weather Recommendations for Masonry Construction*

Air Temp., °F	Materials	Protection
Above 100 or above 90 with wind greater than 8 mph	Limit open mortar exposed to no longer than 4 ft and set units within 1 minute of spreading mortar. Store materials in cool or shaded area.	Protect wall from rapid evaporation cover, water fogging, damp curing, etc.
90 to 40	Normal masonry procedures.	Cover masonry construction with plastic or canvas at the end of workday to prevent rain from entering masonry.
Below 40	Heat mixing water. Maintain mortar temperature between 40 and 120°F until placed.	Cover masonry construction and materials with plastic or canvas to prevent rain, snow, water from freezing for 24 hours.
Below 32	In addition to the above, heat the sand. Frozen sand and frozen wet masonry units must be thawed.	When wind exceeds 15 mph, provide windbreaks during the workday and cover construction and materials at the end of each day to prevent wetting and freezing. Maintain heat above 32°F by using heat or insulated blankets for 24 hours after laying masonry units.
Below 20	In addition to the above, dry masonry units must be heated to 20°F before using.	Provide enclosures and supply sufficient heat to maintain masonry enclosure above 32°F for 24 hours after laying masonry units.

least *3 days* before backfilling against it? Check the plans and specs.

2. Carry backfill up evenly and compact in 6- to 8-in. lifts on both sides of walls.

3. For masonry walls in basements and crawl spaces, wait until floor slab or framing is in place before backfilling. If not, then temporary bracing may be required. Check restrictions on amount of "unbalanced fill" allowed per wall type and size.

CMU FOUNDATIONS

Foundation Drains

- Not required if well-drained soils. Check soils table.
- Gravel fill to be 1 ft beyond footer and 6 in. above the top.

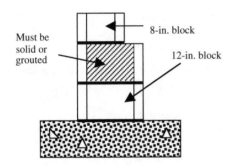

Fig. 5-9 *Changing CMU thickness.*

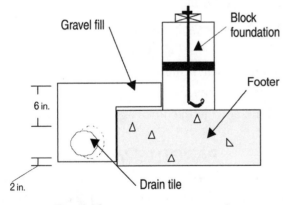

Fig. 5-10 *Drainage using drain tile.*

Damp-proofing

- Damp-proofing—⅜-in. portland cement and a bituminous coating, 3 lb of acrylic mortified cement, or ⅛-in. surface-bonding mortar.

Waterproofing

- Two-ply hot mopped felts, 55-lb roll roofing, 6-mil polyethylene or polyvinyl chloride, or 40-mil polymer-modified asphalt (all joints need to be sealed).

Unbalanced Fill

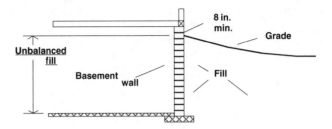

Fig. 5-11 *Unbalanced fill.*

Note: Concrete masonry unit (CMU) walls (either basement or retaining wall) require engineering design if over 4 ft, if there is not permanent lateral support.

Note:

- Soils deliver a pressure of around 30 psf; when wetted this figure can double.
- Retaining walls have the same requirements and considerations. Need to be engineered if over 4 ft.
- Never allow backfilling until wall is either temporarily supported or permanently supported.

Table 5-8 *Max. Height of Unbalanced Fill and Reinforcement for 8-in. Block Walls*

Wall Height	Max. Unbalanced Backfill	Soil Types		
		GW, GP, SW, SP	GM, GC, SM, SM-SC, ML	SC, MH, ML-CL, Inorg. CL
6	5	#4 @ 48	#4 @ 48	#4 @ 48
	6	#4 @ 48	#4 @ 40	#4 @ 40
7	4	#4 @ 48	#4 @ 48	#4 @ 48
	5	#4 @ 48	#4 @ 48	#4 @ 40
	6	#4 @ 48	#5 @ 48	#5 @ 40
	7	#4 @ 40	#5 @ 40	#6 @ 48
8	5	#4 @ 48	#4 @ 48	#4 @ 40
	6	#4 @ 48	#5 @ 48	#5 @ 40
	7	#5 @ 48	#6 @ 48	#6 @ 40
	8	#5 @ 40	#6 @ 40	#6 @ 24
9	5	#4 @ 48	#4 @ 48	#5 @ 48
	6	#4 @ 48	#5 @ 48	#6 @ 48
	7	#5 @ 48	#6 @ 48	#6 @ 32
	8	#5 @ 40	#6 @ 32	#6 @ 24
	9	#6 @ 40	#6 @ 24	#6 @ 16

For 8-in. CMU.
Note: Special reinforcement is required for earthquake-prone zones D1 and D2.

Table 5-9 *Max. Height of Unbalanced Fill and Reinforcement for 12-in. Block Walls*

Wall Height	Max. Unbalanced Backfill	Soil Types		
		GW, GP, SW, SP	GM, GC, SM, SM-SC, ML	SC, MH, ML-CL, Inorg. CL
7	4	#4 @ 72	#4 @ 72	#4 @ 72
	5	#4 @ 72	#4 @ 72	#4 @ 72
	6	#4 @ 72	#4 @ 64	#4 @ 48
	7	#4 @ 72	#4 @ 48	#5 @ 56
8	5	#4 @ 72	#4 @ 72	#4 @ 72
	6	#4 @ 72	#4 @ 56	#5 @ 72
	7	#4 @ 64	#5 @ 64	#4 @ 32
	8	#4 @ 48	#4 @ 32	#5 @ 40
9	5	#4 @ 72	#4 @ 72	#4 @ 72
	6	#4 @ 72	#4 @ 56	#5 @ 64
	7	#4 @ 56	#4 @ 40	#6 @ 64
	8	#4 @ 64	#6 @ 64	#6 @ 48
	9	#5 @ 56	#7 @ 72	#6 @ 40

For 12-in. CMU.

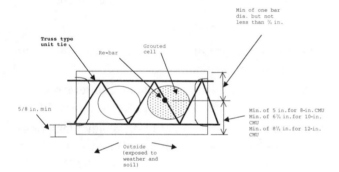

Fig. 5-12 *Reinforcement requirements for CMU.*

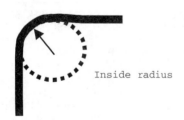

ACI 318: Reinforcing Bar Tolerances

Type/Size	Diameter
#10 through #25	6
#29, #32, and #36	8
#47 and #57	10
Stirrups and ties	4

Fig. 5-13 *Minimum bend diameters for reinforcement.*

Veneer Ties

- Must be minimum of No. 22 gauge × 7/8 in.
- In wind areas of 30 psf or less, one tie per 2 sq. ft of wall area.
- Ties around openings, 3 ft O.C. and not more than 12 in. from the edge of opening.

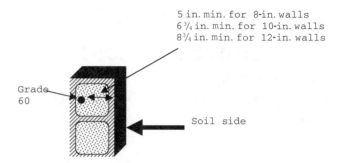

Fig. 5-14 *Reinforcement for concrete and masonry foundation walls.*

Foundation Damp-proofing

Masonry to be parged with 3/8-in. portland cement; then one of the following is to be applied:

1. Bituminous coating.
2. Acrylic modified cement – 3 lb per sq. yd.
3. 1/8-in. surface-bonding mortar.
4. Any approved waterproofing method below.

Foundation Waterproofing

One of the following:

1. Membrane of 2-ply hot mopped felts
2. 55-lb roll roofing
3. 6-mil polyvinyl chloride
4. 6-mil polyethylene
5. 40-mil polymer-modified asphalt

PARGING WALLS

Always give exterior concrete masonry basement walls two 1/4-in.-thick coats of parging, using either portland cement mortar (1:2½ mix by volume). The building code requires a 3/8-in.-thick coat, which can be divided into the first coat of 1/4-in.-thick and the last coat of a minimum of 1/8-in.-thick for optimum results.

Step 1. In hot, dry weather dampen the wall surface very lightly with a fog water spray before applying the first parging coat.

Step 2. Roughen the first coat when it partially hardens, to provide a bond for the second parging coat.

Step 3. Wait for the first coat to harden for 24 hours; then dampen it lightly just before applying the second coat. Keep the second coat damp for at least 48 hours following application.

Step 4. For below-grade parged surfaces in very wet soils, use two continuous coatings of bituminous mastic brushed over a suitable priming coat. Make sure that the parging is dry before you apply the primer and that the primer is dry when you apply the damp-proofing or waterproofing mastic.

Do not backfill against concrete masonry walls until the first floor is in place.

Erection Procedures

1. Check masonry dimensions against existing foundations and structural framing.
   a. The two must coincide.
   b. Bring any discrepancies to the attention of your supervisor immediately.
   c. Has tie-in to reinforced concrete structural frame been provided for?

2. Check vertical coursing against dimensional wall heights. Minor changes in joint width could eliminate a course.

3. Check horizontal layout by either a dry run or by tape.
   a. Is layout accurate to avoid fractional length units?
   b. Are openings located so units are of same length against both jambs? (Occasionally, openings can be slightly adjusted.)
   c. Check for conflicts between openings and partitions or equipment locations.
   d. Check that minor adjustments are made in width of head joints to keep bond plumb.

4. Check control joints for type and location.
   a. When control joints in concrete masonry units, concrete brick, and split block are spaced more than 30 ft apart for exterior walls and more than 38 ft apart for interior walls, notify the Project Manager. This is the maximum permitted with joint reinforcement in each masonry course.
   b. Control joints should be located at jambs of openings.
   c. With control joint at jamb, is bond barrier provided under lintel bed joint? Is bond barrier made of 16-oz sheet copper? Check specs.

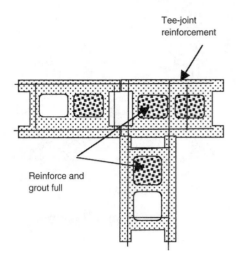

Fig. 5-15 *Intersection of structural CMU wall.*

   d. Joint reinforcement does not pass through control joints.
   e. Check drawings for control joints that pass through bond beams.
   f. Is contractor erecting leads at corners and jambs?
   g. Is contractor using a story-pole to establish coursing in leads?
   h. Are masons using levels to check plumbness and face alignment?

5. Is cutting of CMU and tile being done by power masonry saw? Are CMUs being wet cut? If so, they must be *surface dry* when used in the wall.

6. Are all joints in similar walls being finished with same-size tools?

7. Are masons waiting for initial set of mortar before tooling joints? A good rule to follow on the job is that mortar be "thumb-print" hard when tooling is done.

Fig. 5-16 *Typical flashing.*

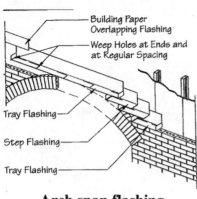

Arch span flashing
(a)

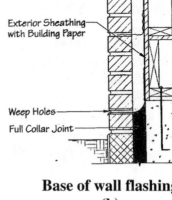

Base of wall flashing
(b)

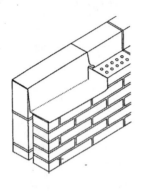

End dam flashing
(c)

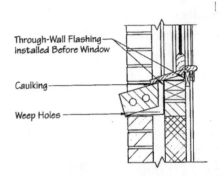

Window sill flashing
(d)

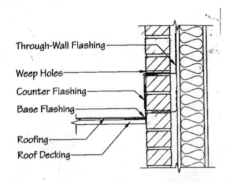

Roof intersection flashing
(e)

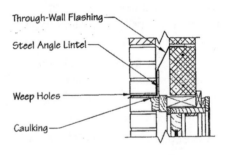

Window head flashing
(f)

Fig. 5-17 *Typical flashing details.*

8. If units are moved after mortar takes initial set, remove and replace them, using fresh mortar.

9. Has excess mortar been removed from faces of units and joints before setting up?

10. Are flashings installed in base courses, under sills and copings, and over lintels and bond beams?

See sheet metal specifications for additional guidance on flashing.

11. Is joint reinforcing called for? Continuously around building? Under sills? Over lintels?

12. Are bond beams called for?

   a. At floor levels?

   b. Under sill?

   c. Above lintel level?

   d. At top of wall?

   e. Is reinforcement the correct size? Spacing?

   f. At intermediate locations?

Fig. 5-18 *Reinforcing at metal door jamb.*

13. Does brick pattern call for header courses?

14. Cavity or composite construction may be laid up together so that the inner and outer wythes level off at all bed joints where ties or joint reinforcing occur.

15. Are steel strap anchors installed across chase walls as stiffeners at wall-mounted fixtures, two above and two below each fixture?

16. Are weep holes required wherever through-wall flashing is used, such as at base of cavity walls, over lintels, and over bond beams?

Door and Window Frames

1. Are the specified numbers of anchors provided for each jamb?

2. Have hollow door frames been filled *solid* with mortar?

3. Is hollow masonry at jambs filled with mortar for embedment of anchors?

4. Check dimensions of approved sash and sills.

Fig. 5-19 *Saw toothing: Not allowed and considered poor workmanship and quality.*

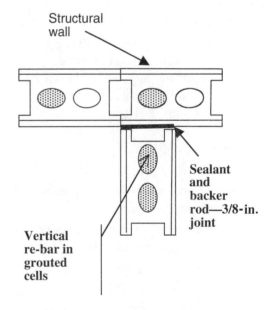

Fig. 5-20 *Partition wall abutting structural wall.*

Embedded Items

1. Check mechanical and electrical drawings for equipment, piping, wiring, and conduit locations. Shop drawings with the sleeve location are very useful.

2. Sleeves and equipment will be built in as masonry is erected, not cut in afterwards.

3. All cutting and fitting of masonry around equipment pipe lines, etc., shall be done by masons.

4. Set flush-type electric boxes so that bottoms of boxes are at *bed joints*. This may mean a slight adjustment to given height for some boxes where the height from FF is crucial.

5. Check for piping in exterior walls. Is there room for insulation?

Caulked or Sealed Joints

1. Are control joints being raked out uniformly and to the proper depth?

- Rake out ¾ in. on exterior.
- Rake out ¼ or ½ in. (square end CMU) on interior.

2. Check requirements for brick expansion joints.

3. Are wash-surface joints in precast sills being raked out?

4. Is caulking being accomplished around framed openings as required?

5. Usually, interior CMU control joints are raked out but not caulked. Use approved caulking compound where required.

6. Toothing is allowed only with Architect's or Project Manager's approval.

Incomplete walls, not capable of self-support, will be temporarily braced against wind pressure.

Check masonry abutting steel and other rigid construction. Provision for expansion and contraction or other movements must be detailed.

Batching and Use of Mortar

1. Is mortar accurately proportioned?

  a. Check for use of approved proportions. *Type N mortar* is usually required.

  b. Contractor must provide an accurate volume-measuring device, such as a box of 1-ft³ volume.

  c. Check proportioning often and whenever mortar tenders are changed.

2. *Refractory mortar and materials are required for pointing mortar in firebrick.*

3. Is mortar being used up within specified time limits?

  a. Time limit is *2½ hours*.

  b. Stiffened mortar can be retempered within that time limit, but mortar beginning to set must be discarded.

Brick

1. Has clay or shale brick been tested for rate of absorption?

  a. Test will be performed by approved laboratory.

  b. Brick will be wetted as indicated by test results.

  c. At time of laying, brick will be damp but with no visible water film on exterior surfaces.

2. Is brick being shoved into place?

  a. Joints should be filled solidly when and as the brick is laid.

  b. Either the "end buttering" or "pick and dip" method is acceptable.

  c. "Slushing" to fill head joints, after brick is laid, is not acceptable.

  d. Check to ensure that mortar bond is not broken between newly laid units and their mortar joints.

3. Is space between brick facing and backup masonry, in solid walls, completely filled with mortar?

4. Are structural header courses or metal ties installed between face and backup masonry?

  a. Are side joints filled with mortar for entire length of header brick?

  b. Are metal ties of specified material, shape, and size and at proper spacing?

5. Are all exposed joints of uniform width? Is a tolerance given in the specifications?

6. Is brick being covered and protected at the finish of each work day? Spread straw or use another protection measure to preclude rain splashing mud or clay on brick veneer.

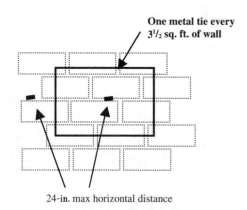

Fig. 5-21 *Brick wall ties.*

Veneer Ties

1. Must be minimum of No. 22 gage by ⅞ in.

2. In wind areas of 30 psf (or D seismic zones), one tie per 2 sq. ft. of wall area.

3. Ties around openings 3 ft O.C. and not more than 12 in. from the edge of opening.

Concrete Masonry Units (CMUs)

1. Are starting courses and other specified courses full-bedded in mortar under both face shells and webs?

2. Are all other courses face-shell-bedded only?

3. Are all units laid up with a full head joint for face-shell thickness?

4. Are units checked just prior to installation for chips, cracks, and defective units?

5. Are joints of uniform width and finished appearance? Correct type?

Fig. **5-22** *Masonry joints.*

6. Are all cuts being made by wet masonry saw?

7. Are sizes of units such that difference between vertical faces does not exceed ⅛ in.? (This applies to exposed-to-view and painted masonry in habitable rooms and spaces.)

8. Is felt paper provided on three sides of mortar key in control joints?

9. Are the special control joint and metal sash jamb CMU available in both full and half sizes?

10. Are bond beams constructed entirely of special U-shaped bond beam block? Is correct re-bar used?

11. Is reinforcing continuous, including bent corner bars, for full length of bond beam?

12. Is vertical cell reinforcing in place and the cells filled full with concrete?

13. Are all lintels of depth specified and with minimum of 4-in. bearing on each side? Bearing shall be greater for openings over 8 ft.

14. Are intersecting partition anchors being installed as exterior walls are erected?

15. Are ties provided in masonry furring for securing facing units?

16. Has face of exterior walls been damp-proofed?

17. Check prior to installing furring for plaster or gypsum board.

18. Are cuts for electric boxes and panels and other built-in items being made by masonry saws and sized so plate or frame will completely cover them?

19. Concealing electrical conduit in 4-in. exposed block partitions is not practical.

- Bring immediately to the attention of the Project Architect.

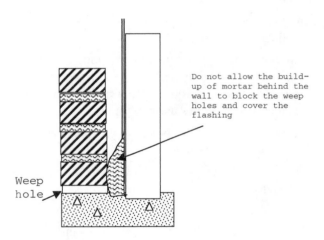

Do not allow the build-up of mortar behind the wall to block the weep holes and cover the flashing

Weep hole

Fig. **5-23** *Do not allow mortar to build up in wall and block weep holes.*

Structural Clay Facing Units

1. Facing tile shall be laid with full bed and head joints.

2. Layout will be planned to avoid using pieces shorter than 4 in.

3. Base units only may be two-face; other courses two-unit construction in walls with facing unit finish both sides.

4. Glazed tile wainscots: Use the number of full courses that will come nearest to specified height. If more than 2 in. below specified height, add another full course.

5. Joints in glazed tile shall be not less then ³⁄₁₆ in. nor more than ¼ in. wide.

6. Joints in showers and kitchens shall be raked back and filled with pointing mortar.

7. Faces of tile will be cleaned with damp rag as work progresses.

Cavity Wall Construction

1. Is cavity drainage provided by a step in the foundation wall so that exterior wythe is below finish floor elevations, by weep holes, or by means of flashing?

2. Are through-wall flashing and weep holes provided at base of wall and also over lintels, bond and spandrel beams?

   a. Are weep holes at specified spacing?

   b. Are flashings continuous with watertight joint?

3. Are cavities being kept clean?

   a. Is wood strip set across ties to catch mortar droppings?

   b. Is excess mortar, squeezed out of joints, cut off flush on cavity faces?

4. Are box-type wire ties, minimum width 4 in., being used? These ties may be an integral part of joint reinforcing wire, if required. If installed separately, do not place both in same bed joints.

   a. Is length of box ties proper to provide anchorage in face-shell mortar beds?

   b. Are box tie drips located within the air space of cavity?

   c. Is spacing of ties as specified?

   d. Have additional rows of ties been installed at jambs of openings, at either side of control joints, and at corners?

   e. Are solid masonry returns at jambs of openings detailed rather than extra ties?

Composite Wall Construction

1. The collar joint between wythes shall be completely filled with mortar or grout.

2. Is anchorage provided between wythes, either with ties or continuous-type joint reinforcement?

Chimneys and Fireplaces

1. Is flue sized correctly?

2. Is flue lining being carried up integral with masonry?

3. Is interior of the liner smooth and flush at mortar joints?

4. Is space between masonry and flue lining filled solid with mortar? If there is more than one flue in the chimney, have masonry wythes (partitions) been installed between flues?

5. Is thimble sized and located to meet approved smoke pipe?

6. Are fireplace throat and smoke chamber free of obstructions? Size?

7. Are damper, lintel angle, supply air, and ash clean-out installed?

8. Has correct type of refractory mortar been used?

9. Are required number of reinforcing metal ties installed for bonding face and fire brick? (Check seismic zone.)

10. Foundations for masonry fireplaces must be minimum of 12 in. thick.

11. Walls of the fireplace must have a minimum of 6 in. to the foundation edge on all sides.

GROUTING

Table 5-10 Site Mixing Grout Proportions by Volume

Type	Portland Cement	Hydrated Lime or Lime Putty	Aggregate Measured in a Damp, Loose Condition	
			Fine	Coarse
Fine	1	0–¹⁄₁₀	2¼–3 times the sum of the volume of the cementitious materials	
Coarse	1	0–¹⁄₁₀	2¼–3 times the sum of the volume of the cementitious materials	1–2 times the sum of the volumes of the cementitious materials

Grout Type	Maximum Height (ft)	Minimum Width of Grout Space (in.)	Minimum Grout Space Dimensions for Grouting Cells of Hollow Units (in. × in.)
Fine	1	0.75	1.5 × 2
	5	2	2 × 3
	12	2.5	2.5 × 3
	24	3	3 × 3
Coarse	1	1.5	1.5 × 3
	5	2	2.5 × 3
	12	2.5	3 × 3
	24	3	3 × 4

FIREPLACES

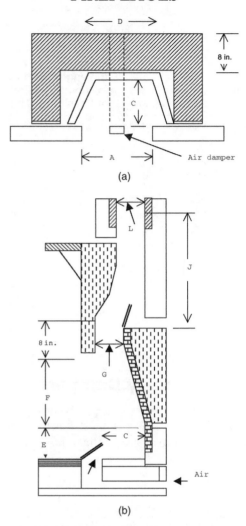

Fig. 5-24 *Fireplace measurements (typical).*

Fire Brick

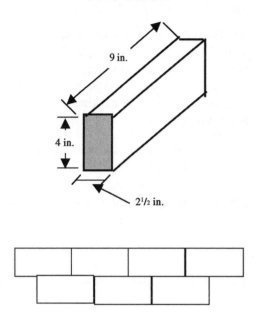

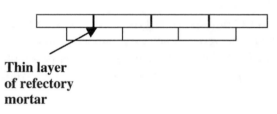

Fig. 5-25 *Standard fire brick; incorrect laying of brick.*

**Thin layer
of refectory
mortar**

Fig. 5-26 *Correct laying of brick.*

Note: Masonry fireplace foundations have different standards for foundations, usually a minimum of 12 in. instead of 6 in.

Table 5-11 *Conventional Fireplace Dimensions (in.)*

A	B	C	D	E	F	G
24	24	16	11	14	18	8¾
26	24	16	13	14	18	8¾
28	24	16	15	14	18	8¾
30	29	16	17	14	23	8¾
32	29	16	19	14	23	8¾
36	29	16	23	14	23	8¾
40	29	16	27	14	23	8¾
42	32	16	29	14	26	8¾
48	32	18	33	14	26	8¾
54	37	20	37	16	29	13
60	40	22	42	16	31	13
72	40	22	54	16	31	13

Masonry Chimneys

1. Chimneys are to be lined with approved clay flue lining, a listed liner, or other approved material that will resist corrosion, erosion, and weakening from the vent gases at temperatures up to 1,800°F.

2. If liners are installed in existing chimney structures (Type B), then the connection must be marked not to allow any solid or liquid burning appliances to be attached.

3. Chimneys are to extend at least 5 ft above the highest connected equipment draft hood outlet or flue collar.

4. Sizing of chimneys:

   a. The effective area of a chimney serving listed appliances with draft hoods: Category I appliances listed for use with Type B vents are to be sized using Tables 12-13 to 12-16.

b. An exception to using these tables for sizing a single appliance with a draft hood is that the vent connector and chimney flue will have an area not less than the appliance flue collar or draft hood and not greater than 7 times the draft hood outlet.

c. When two appliances with draft hoods are connected, then the flue area must be the same as the largest appliance outlet plus 50% of the smaller appliance outlet and not greater than 7 times the smaller draft hood outlet.

Example:

Largest outlet + 50% of smallest < chimney flue size < 7 × smallest

5. Chimneys previously used for liquid or solid fuels, and now using fuel gas, must have a cleanout. It is to be located so that its upper edge is 6 in. below the lowest edge of the lowest inlet opening.

6. Offsets of Type B or Type L are not to exceed 45° from the vertical; however, one angle must not exceed 60°. The horizontal distance of a vent plus the connector vent shall not exceed 75% of the vertical height of the vent.

Flue Liners

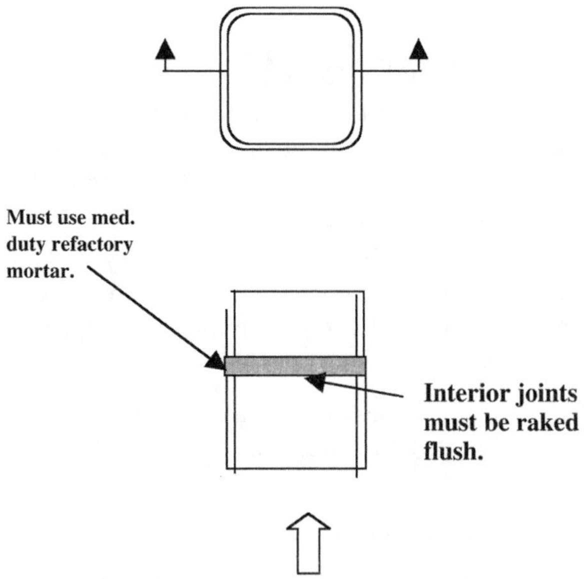

Must use med. duty refactory mortar.
Interior joints must be raked flush.

Fig. 5-27 *Flue liners.*

Table 5-11 *Fireplace Opening in Determining Flue Size*

Fireplace Opening (sq. in.)	Flue Shapes			
	Round	Square	Rectangle with Length to Width 2:1 or Less	Rectangle with Length to Width More Than 2:1
400	33⅓	40	40	50
450	37½	45	45	56¼
500	41⅔	50	50	62½
550	45⅚	55	55	68¾
600	50	60	60	75
650	54⅙	65	65	81¼
700	58⅓	70	70	87½
750	62½	75	75	93¾
800	66⅔	80	80	100
850	70⅚	85	85	106¼
900	75	90	90	112½
1000	83⅓	100	100	125
1100	91⅔	110	110	137½
1200	100	120	120	150
1300	108⅓	130	130	162½
1400	116⅔	140	140	175
1500	125	150	150	187½

Chimney Dampers

Where an unlisted decorative appliance is installed in a vented fireplace, the damper must have a permanent free opening equal to or greater than those listed in the tables below.

Table 5-12 *Damper Open Area from Unlisted Decorative Appliances*

Minimum Permanent Free Opening	Chimney Height (ft)		
	6	8	10
8	7800	8400	9000
13	14000	15200	16800
20	23200	25200	27600
29	34000	37000	40400
39	46400	50400	55800
51	62400	68000	74400
64	80000	86000	96400

Minimum Permanent Free Opening	Chimney Height (ft)		
	15	20	30
8	9800	10600	11200
13	18200	20200	21600
20	30200	32600	36600
29	44600	50400	55200
39	62400	68400	76800
51	84000	94000	105800
64	108800	122200	138600

Table 5-13 Code-Required Flue Sizes per Fireplace Openings

Fireplace Opening (sq. in.)	Flue Shapes: Round	Square	Rectangle with Length to Width 2:1 or Less	Rectangle with Length to Width More Than 2:1
400	33⅓	40	40	50
450	37½	45	45	56¼
500	41⅔	50	50	62½
550	45⅚	55	55	68¾
600	50	60	60	75
650	54⅙	65	65	81¼
700	58⅓	70	70	87½
750	62½	75	75	93¾
800	66⅔	80	80	100
850	70⅚	85	85	106¼
900	75	90	90	112½
1000	83⅓	100	100	125
1100	91⅔	110	110	137½
1200	100	120	120	150
1300	108⅓	130	130	162½
1400	116⅔	140	140	175
1500	125	150	150	187½

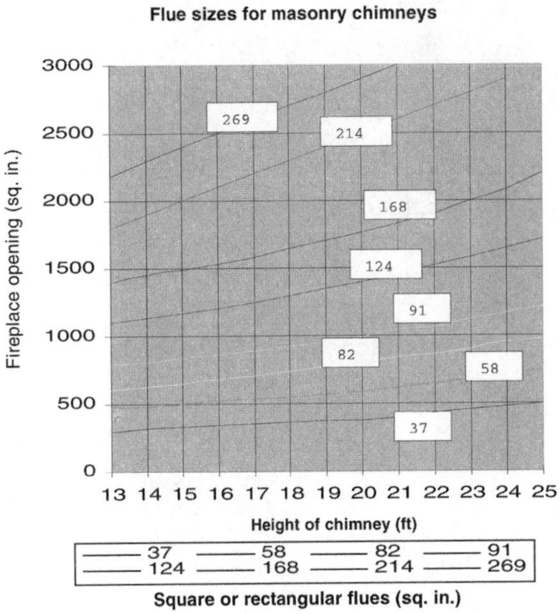

Fig. 5-28 *Chimney flue sizing.*

Table 5-14 Masonry Chimney Liner Dimensions with Circular Equivalents

Nominal Liner Size	Inside Liner Dimensions	Circular Equivalent in.	Circular Equivalent in.^{2}
4 × 8	2½ × 6½	4	12.2
		5	19.6
		6	28.3
		7	38.3
8 × 8	6¾ × 6¾	7.4	42.7
		8	50.3
8 × 12	6½ × 10½	9	63.6
		10	78.5
12 × 12	9¾ × 9¾	10.4	83.3
		11	95
12 × 16	9½ × 13½	11.8	107.5
		12	113.0
		14	153.9
16 × 16	13¼ × 13¼	14.5	162.9
		15	176.7
16 × 20	13 × 17	16.2	206.1
		18	254.4
20 × 20	16¾ × 16¾	18.2	260.2
		20	314.1
20 × 24	16½ × 20½	20.1	314.2
		22	380.1
24 × 24	20¼ × 20¼	22.1	380.1
		24	452.3

Roof Clearances

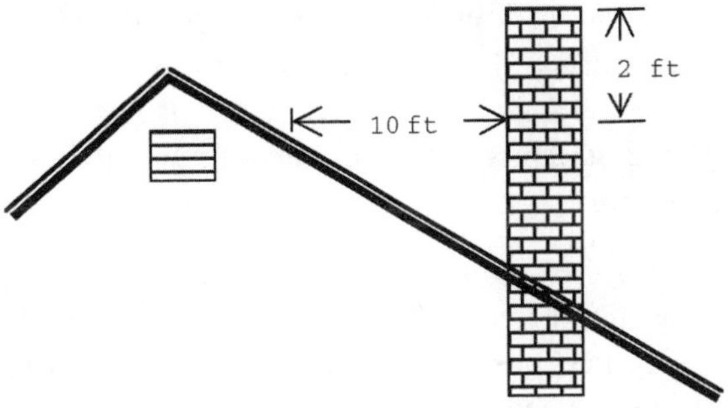

Fig. 5-29 *Roof terminations for chimneys and single-wall vents (no caps).*

Anchors, Ties, and Joint Reinforcement

1. Anchors and ties will be installed as the work progresses.
2. Do not use makeshift wall ties (i.e., 16p nails or others are not acceptable).
3. For the flexible ties between structural steel columns and masonry walls: Is clearance space also provided between column and masonry to allow for differential movement?
4. Openings require more ties.
5. Cells of CMU are required to be solidly filled with mortar where anchors and ties occur.
6. If in a seismic zone, is additional reinforcement being used?

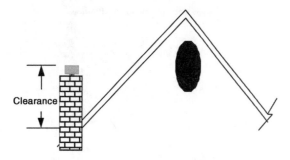

Roof Slope	Clearance
Flat–6/12	1–0 in.
6/12–7/12	1–3 in.
7/12–8/12	1–6 in.
8/12–9/12	2–0 in.
9/12–10/12	2–6 in.
10/12–11/12	3–3 in.
11/12–12/12	4–0 in.

Fig. 5-30 *Gas vent terminations for listed vent caps (12 in. or less in diameter and 8 ft from vertical walls).*

7. Is joint reinforcing installed with mortar above and below it?

8. Are sections of joint reinforcing lapped the specified amount?

Note: Required lap is greater for smooth wire than for deformed wire.

9. Check for the required use of preformed joint reinforcing around corners and at intersecting walls. The specified ties are required in addition to joint reinforcing when masonry bond is not provided.

Cleaning of Masonry

1. A little care during the laying of masonry, including removing mortar droppings, careful tooling of joints, and daily dry brushing, will keep the cleaning operations to a minimum.

2. A cleaning solution is specified for brick; however, the selection of detergent is verified by checking the sample panel for discoloration or stain before proceeding. (Remember that the sample panel was cleaned after erection.)

3. Make cleaning operation one of the last phases of job. Do not start before mortar is thoroughly set and cured.

4. Remove large particles of mortar with a putty knife before washing.

5. Stain or discoloration remaining on brick after cleaning is removed with a 6% solution of muriatic acid

applied with stiff fiber brushes. When acid is used, goggles, gloves, and other personnel protective equipment must be provided and used.

a. Soak area to be cleaned with plenty of water before applying acid.

b. The brickwork below the area being cleaned should be kept thoroughly soaked with water.

c. Clean only 10 to 20 sq. ft. at a time for each man.

d. Scrub the brick, not the mortar joints.

e. Wash the wall thoroughly with plenty of water immediately after scrubbing with acid.

Concrete Masonry Units

1. Remove excess mortar from joints and faces of units.

2. Brush all dust and foreign matter from faces of walls.

3. Never use the acid wash on concrete masonry.

4. If tooling has not produced uniform joints, it may be necessary to rub them with carborundum stones.

5. Repoint joints as necessary for watertightness and appearance.

Glazed Structural Tile and Prefaced Masonry

1. Masons should remove mortar smears from face of tile with clean damp rags immediately after laying.

2. Upon completion of walls, wash all surfaces of tile with soap powder and clean water, using stiff fiber brushes.

3. Remove hard lumps of mortar with wooden paddles.

4. Metal cleaning tools, metal brushes, and acid solution should not be used.

5. Repoint joints as necessary for watertightness and appearance.

REINFORCED MASONRY

Reinforced masonry construction uses different terms and methods not found in the material just presented.

Following are some of the common terms:

• Reinforced masonry uses embedded reinforcement, such that the materials act together in the wall to resist lateral forces.

• Reinforced composite masonry consists of solid facing units bonded to reinforced hollow masonry backing. The collar joint is filled with mortar or grout.

• Reinforced solid unit masonry also consists of two wythes separated by a collar joint. Both wythes are built of solid units, and the collar joint is reinforced and filled with grout.

1. High-lift grouting is the method used to fill masonry with grout in lifts from *2 ft–4 ft* high. *Masonry cleanouts are required for this method.*

2. Low-lift grouting includes lifts up to 2 ft and does not require cleanouts.

3. Vertical grout barriers are used to limit horizontal flow of grout to 25 ft for each high-lift grout pour. Construct grout barriers with solid masonry units.

4. Caging devices and centering clips are embedded in masonry to position vertical reinforcing either in collar joints or in the cells of hollow masonry.

5. Grout holes are provided in overhead construction such as slabs and spandrel beams, aligned with reinforcing in masonry below. Grout holes must be at least 4 in. in diameter or 3×4 in. in horizontal dimension.

6. Check for special tests and requirements for samples, certificates, test reports, shop drawings, and for the installation of the special materials in the sample panel.

7. Check for the proper grout mix. Check the specifications.

8. A low-alkali cement is usually used in reinforced masonry to reduce chances for efflorescence. *Masonry cement usually is not permitted. Review the specifications.*

Pointing and Cleaning

Pointing

Has the construction been checked for voids in the pointing defects and have defects been repaired?

Cleaning

Has all masonry been carefully and thoroughly cleaned as required? Efflorescence must be removed following the masonry manufacturer's recommended methods.

Joints

Tolerances (Load Bearing)

Head and bed	$-\frac{3}{8}$ in.
First course on footer	Not less than $\frac{1}{4}$ in. or more than $\frac{3}{4}$ in.
Bed joint	$\pm\frac{1}{8}$ in.
Head joint	$-\frac{1}{4}$ in., $+\frac{3}{8}$ in.
Collar joint	$-\frac{1}{4}$ in., $+\frac{3}{8}$ in.

Except for non-load-bearing veneer, there is no tolerance standard.

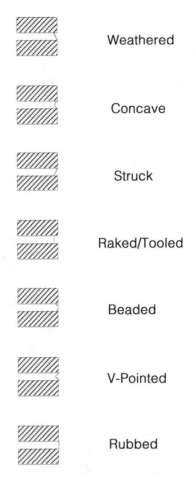

Weathered

Concave

Struck

Raked/Tooled

Beaded

V-Pointed

Rubbed

Fig. 5-31 *Typical masonry pointing.*

Wall Ties/Reinforcement

1. Hollow masonry—need to be embedded at least $\frac{1}{2}$ in.

2. Solid masonry—$1\frac{1}{2}$-in. embedded (*cannot be bent after being embedded*).

3. Interior non-load-bearing walls need to be anchored at their intersections at vertical interval of not more than 16 in. with 9-gage galvanized mesh.

4. At least $\frac{5}{8}$ in. mortar coverage at exposed face.

5. All other reinforcement shall have not less than $\frac{3}{4}$ in. except where exposed to weather or soil; then the minimum is 2 in.

6. For seismic zones 3 and 4, anchors need to be 4 ft on center.

7. Stack bond—unreinforced masonry shall have at least two wires in bed joints 16 in. O.C. vertically.

8. Openings in masonry walls require more ties.

Table 5-15 *Heights of Block and Brick Based on ⅜-in. Mortar Joint*

Block No. of Courses	Brick No. of Courses	Height of Course
4	12	2 ft.–8 in.
	13	2 ft.–10⅝ in.
	14	3 ft.–1⅜ in.
5	15	3 ft.–4 in.
	16	3 ft.–6⅝ in.
	17	3 ft.–9⅜ in.
6	18	4 ft.–0 in.
	19	4 ft.–2⅝ in.
	20	4 ft.–5⅜ in.
7	21	4 ft.–8 in.
	22	4 ft.–10⅝ in.
	23	5 ft.–1⅜ in.
8	24	5 ft.–4 in.
	25	5 ft.–6⅝ in.
	26	5 ft.–9⅜ in.
9	27	6 ft.–0 in.
	28	6 ft.–2⅝ in.
	29	6 ft.–5⅜ in.
10	30	6 ft.–8 in.
	31	6 ft.–10⅝ in.
	32	7 ft.–1⅜ in.
11	33	7 ft.–4 in.
	34	7 ft.–6⅝ in.
	35	7 ft.–9⅜ in.
12	36	8 ft.–0 in.
	37	8 ft.–2⅝ in.
	38	8 ft.–5⅜ in.
13	39	8 ft.–8 in.
	40	8 ft.–10⅝ in.
	41	9 ft.–1⅜ in.
14	42	9 ft.–4 in.
	43	9 ft.–6⅝ in.
	44	9 ft.–9⅜ in.
15	45	10 ft.–0 in.
	46	10 ft.–2⅝ in.
	47	10 ft.–5⅜ in.
16	48	10 ft.–8 in.

COLD WEATHER MORTAR

- Proper mortar temperature should be between 70 and 100°F. Heating the mixing water is one of the easiest and best ways of raising mortar temperatures; however, care should be taken not to raise the water temperature above 160°F. This prevents the danger of "flash" setting when the water comes into contact with the cement.

- In freezing temperatures wet sand will freeze and ice crystals will form in the sand, and will need to be thawed before using. Most advise against the using of antifreeze materials because such treatment can seriously impair the mortar strength. Adding calcium chloride to the mortar will resist freezing; however, care needs to be taken where mortar comes in con-

tact with metals such as re-bars and lintels, for they will be susceptible to accelerated rusting. Most experts suggest not using the "flake" form of the calcium chloride and using the solution instead. This will ensure even mixing. Masonry units need to be protected from freezing for at least 48 hours prior to their use. This includes the units that have already been laid and are ready for the new courses. Heavy poly sheets and heaters should be used to enclose the work area.

CMU Retaining Walls

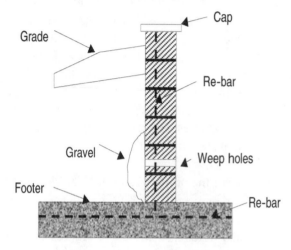

Fig. 5-32 *Cantilever retaining wall.*

Note: Most codes require an engineered design if wall is over 4 ft in height.

Table 5-16 *Typical 8-in. Walls*

Height of Wall	Width of Footer	Thickness of Footer	Dist. to Wall Face
3 ft–4 in.	2 ft–4 in.	9 in.	8 in.
4 ft–0 in.	2 ft–9 in.	9 in.	10 in.
4 ft–8 in.	3 ft–3 in.	10 in.	12 in.
5 ft–4 in.	3 ft–8 in.	10 in.	14 in.
6 ft–0 in.	4 ft–2 in.	12 in.	15 in.

Table 5-17 *Typical 12-in. Walls*

Height of Wall	Width of Footer	Thickness of Footer	Dist. to Wall Face
6 ft–8 in.	4 ft–6 in.	12 in.	16 in.
7 ft–4 in.	4 ft–10 in.	12 in.	18 in.
8 ft–0 in.	5 ft–5 in.	12 in.	20 in.
8 ft–8 in.	5 ft–10 in.	14 in.	22 in.
9 ft–4 in.	6 ft–4 in.	14 in.	24 in.

Table 5-18 *Soil Lateral Loads*

Soil Description	Unified Soil Classification	Design Lateral Soil Load (psf)
Well-graded, clean gravels; gravel-sand mixes	OW	30
Poorly graded clean gravels; gravel-sand mixes	OP	30
Silty gravels; poorly graded gravel-sand mixes	OM	45
Clayey gravels; poorly graded gravel-sand-clay mixes	OC	45
Well-graded, clean sands; gravelly sand mixes	SW	30
Poorly graded clean sands; sand-gravel mixes	SP	30
Silty sands; poorly graded sand-silt mixes	SM	45
Sand-silt-clay mix with plastic fines	SM-SC	45
Clayey sands; poorly graded sand-clay mixes	SC	60
Inorganic silts and clayey silts	ML	45
Mixture of inorganic silt and clay	ML-CL	60
Inorganic clays of low to medium plasticity	CL	60
Organic silts and silt-clays, low plasticity	CL	Check codes
Inorganic clayey silts; elastic silts	MH	60
Inorganic clays of high plasticity	CH	Check codes
Organic clays and silty clays	CH	Check codes

Table 5-19 *Reinforcement for Masonry Retaining Walls (30 psf)*

Nominal Wall Thickness (in.)	Wall Depth H [ft (m)]	Reinforcement Size and Spacing for Equivalent Fluid Weight of Soil (30 psf)
8	4.0 (1.2)	#4 @ 64 in.
	4.7 (1.4)	#4 @ 40 in.
	5.3 (1.6)	#4 @ 24 in.
	6.0 (1.8)	#5 @ 24 in.
	6.7 (2.0)	#5 @ 16 in.
10	4.0 (1.2)	#4 @ 72 in.
	4.7 (1.4)	#4 @ 56 in.
	5.3 (1.6)	#4 @ 40 in.
	6.0 (1.8)	#4 @ 24 in.
	6.7 (2.0)	#4 @ 16 in.
	7.3 (2.2)	#5 @ 24 in.
	8.0 (2.4)	#5 @ 16 in.
12	4.0 (1.2)	#4 @ 72 in.
	4.7 (1.4)	#4 @ 72 in.
	5.3 (1.6)	#4 @ 48 in.
	6.0 (1.8)	#4 @ 32 in.
	6.7 (2.0)	#4 @ 24 in.
	7.3 (2.2)	#4 @ 16 in.
	8.0 (2.4)	#5 @ 24 in.
	8.7 (2.7)	#5 @ 16 in.
	9.3 (2.8)	#6 @ 16 in.

Table 5-20 *Reinforcement for Masonry Retaining Walls (45 psf)*

Nominal Wall Thickness (in.)	Wall Depth H [ft (m)]	Reinforcement Size and Spacing for Equivalent Fluid Weight of Soil (45 psf)
8	4.0 (1.2)	#4 @ 40 in.
	4.7 (1.4)	#4 @ 24 in.
	5.3 (1.6)	#4 @ 16 in.
	6.0 (1.8)	#6 @ 16 in.
	6.7 (2.0)	#6 @ 8 in.
10	4.0 (1.2)	#4 @ 64 in.
	4.7 (1.4)	#4 @ 40 in.
	5.3 (1.6)	#4 @ 24 in.
	6.0 (1.8)	#4 @ 16 in.
	6.7 (2.0)	#5 @ 16 in.
	7.3 (2.2)	#6 @ 16 in.
	8.0 (2.4)	#6 @ 8 in.
12	4.0 (1.2)	#4 @ 72 in.
	4.7 (1.4)	#4 @ 48 in.
	5.3 (1.6)	#4 @ 32 in.
	6.0 (1.8)	#4 @ 24 in.
	6.7 (2.0)	#4 @ 16 in.
	7.3 (2.2)	#5 @ 16 in.
	8.0 (2.4)	#5 @ 16 in.
	8.7 (2.7)	#7 @ 16 in.
	9.3 (2.8)	#7 @ 8 in.

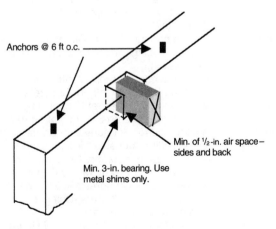

Anchors @ 6 ft o.c.

Min. of 1/2-in. air space— sides and back

Min. 3-in. bearing. Use metal shims only.

Fig. 5-33 *Beam pockets.*

Table 5-21 *Reinforcement for Masonry Retaining Walls (60 psf)*

Nominal Wall Thickness (in.)	Wall Depth H [ft (m)]	Reinforcement Size and Spacing for Equivalent Fluid Weight of Soil
8	4.0 (1.2)	#4 @ 32 in.
	4.7 (1.4)	#4 @ 16 in.
	5.3 (1.6)	#5 @ 16 in.
	6.0 (1.8)	#8 @ 16 in.
	6.7 (2.0)	Check codes/design
10	4.0 (1.2)	#4 @ 48 in.
	4.7 (1.4)	#4 @ 24 in.
	5.3 (1.6)	#4 @ 16 in.
	6.0 (1.8)	#5 @ 16 in.
	6.7 (2.0)	#6 @ 16 in.
	7.3 (2.2)	#6 @ 8 in.
	8.0 (2.4)	Check codes/design
12	4.0 (1.2)	#4 @ 64 in.
	4.7 (1.4)	#4 @ 40 in.
	5.3 (1.6)	#4 @ 24 in.
	6.0 (1.8)	#4 @ 16 in.
	6.7 (2.0)	#5 @ 16 in.
	7.3 (2.2)	#6 @ 16 in.
	8.0 (2.4)	#7 @ 16 in.
	8.7 (2.7)	#7 @ 8 in.
	9.3 (2.8)	Check codes/design

COMMON MASONRY DEFECTS/PROBLEMS

Visible Defects	Possible Causes
Bowing of outer and inner shell	Creep, shrinkage of building frame, thermal expansion, moisture, inadequate tying of bricks, faulty construction
Horizontal cracking at concrete floor level	Thermal expansion, moisture, lack of isolation joints
Dampness on inside face of inner wythe	Condensation, plumbing leaks, inadequate flashing, clogged or missing weep holes
Random cracking on internal finishes	Thermal expansion, moisture
Vertical, diagonal cracks following a zig-zag pattern	Differential foundation settlement and/or heave of heavy clay, frost heave, loss of support (footer)
Wall out of plumb	Foundation rotation truss/rafter failure, faulty construction overloading, eccentric loading
Cracking at window and door corners	Rusting of lintels, differential settlement
Brick facing coming off	Spalling, moisture, wrong grade of brick, chemical cleaning
Small cracks (not zig-zags)	Shrinkage of mortar on expansion joints, wrong type of mortar

STUCCO

Table 5-22 *Stucco Curing Times*

Coat	Keep Moist	Set (days)
Scratch	12 hours	2
Brown	12 hours	7
Finish	12 hours	2

ASTM CONCRETE STANDARDS

American Society for Testing and Materials documents related to aggregates, cement, and concrete are as follows.

C 29-87	Test Method for Unit Weight and Voids in Aggregate
C 31-87	Practice for Making and Curing Concrete Test Specimens in the Field
C 33-86	Specification for Concrete Aggregates
C 39-86	Test Method for Compressive Strength of Cylindrical Concrete Specimens
C 40-84	Test Method for Organic Impurities in Fine Aggregates for Concrete
C 42-85	Method of Obtaining and Testing Drilled Cores and Sawed Beams of Concrete
C70-79	Test Method for Surface Moisture in Fine Aggregate
C 78-84	Test Method for Flexural Strength of Concrete (Using Simple Beam with Third-Point Loading)
C 85-66	Test Method for Cement Content of Hardened Portland Cement Concrete
C 87-83	Test Method for Effect of Organic Impurities in Fine Aggregate on Strength of Mortar
C 88-83	Test Method for Soundness of Aggregates by Use of Sodium Sulfate or Magnesium Sulfate
C 91-87	Specification for Masonry Cement
C 94-86	Specification for Ready-Mixed Concrete
C 109-86	Test Method for Compressive Strength of Hydraulic Cement Mortars (Using 2-in. or 50-mm Cube Specimens)
C 114-85	Methods for Chemical Analysis of Hydraulic Cement

Stucco Mix

Material	Cubic Feet	Gallons	Pounds
Sand	2	15	200
Portland Cement	1/2	3 1/2	47
Lime	1/3	2 1/2	12
Water	3/4	6	48

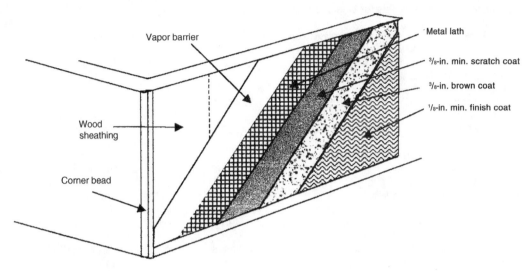

Fig. 5-34 Stucco applications.

Labels: Vapor barrier, Metal lath, 3/8-in. min. scratch coat, 3/8-in. brown coat, 1/8-in. min. finish coat, Wood sheathing, Corner bead

C 115-86	Test Method for Fineness of Portland Cement by the Turbidimeter	C 171-69	Specification for Sheet Materials for Curing Concrete
C 117-87	Test Method for Materials Finer than 75-*Jlm* (No. 200) Sieve in Mineral Aggregates by Washing	C 172-82	Method of Sampling Freshly Mixed Concrete
C 123-83	Test Method for Lightweight Pieces in Aggregate	C 173-78	Test Method for Air Content of Freshly Mixed Concrete by the Volumetric Method
C 125-86	Definitions of Terms Relating to Concrete and Concrete Aggregates	C 174-87	Test Method for Measuring Length of Drilled Concrete Cores
C 127-84	Test Method for Specific Gravity and Absorption of Coarse Aggregate	C 177-85	Test Method for Steady-State Heat Flux Measurements and Thermal Transmission Properties by Means of the Guarded-Hot-Plate Apparatus
C 128-84	Test Method for Specific Gravity and Absorption of Fine Aggregate		
C 131-81	Test Method for Resistance to Degradation of Small-Size Coarse Aggregate by Abrasion and Impact in the Los Angeles Machine	C 183-83	Methods of Sampling and Acceptance of Hydraulic Cement
		C 184-83	Test Method for Fineness of Hydraulic Cement by the 150-μm (No. 100) and 75-μm (No. 200) Sieves
C 136-84	Method for Sieve Analysis of Fine and Coarse Aggregates		
C 138-81	Test Method for Unit Weight, Yield, and Air Content (Gravimetric) of Concrete	C 185-85	Test Method for Air Content of Hydraulic Cement Mortar
C 141-85	Specification for Hydraulic Hydrated Lime for Structural Purposes	C 186-86	Test Method for Heat of Hydration of Hydraulic Cement
C 142-78	Test Method for Clay Lumps and Friable Particles in Aggregates	C 187-86	Test Method for Normal Consistency of Hydraulic Cement
C 143-78	Test Method for Slump of Portland Cement Concrete	C 188-84	Test Method for Density of Hydraulic Cement
C 150-86	Specification for Portland Cement	C 190-85	Test Method for Tensile Strength of Hydraulic Cement Mortars
C 151-84	Test Method for Autoclave Expansion of Portland Cement	C 191-82	Test Method for Time of Setting of Hydraulic Cement by Vicat Needle
C 156-80	Test Method for Water Retention by Concrete Curing Materials	C 192-81	Method of Making and Curing Concrete Test Specimens in the Laboratory
C 157-86	Test Method for Length Change of Hardened Hydraulic-Cement Mortar and Concrete	C 204-84	Test Method for Fineness of Portland Cement by Air Permeability Apparatus

C 215-85 Test Method for Fundamental Transverse, Longitudinal, and Torsional Frequencies of Concrete Specimens

C 219-84 Terminology Relating to Hydraulic Cement

C 226-86 Specification for Air-Entraining Additions for Use in the Manufacture of Air-Entraining Portland Cement

C 227-87 Test Method for Potential Alkali Reactivity of Cement-Aggregate Combinations (Mortar-Bar Method)

C 230-83 Specification for Flow Table for Use in Tests of Hydraulic Cement

C 231-82 Test Method for Air Content of Freshly Mixed Concrete by the Pressure Method

C 232-87 Test Methods for Bleeding of Concrete

C 233-87 Test Method for Air-Entraining Admixtures for Concrete

C 243-85 Test Method for Bleeding of Cement Pastes and Mortars

C 260-86 Specification for Air-Entraining Admixtures for Concrete

C 265-83 Test Method for Calcium Sulfate in Hydrated Portland Cement Mortar

C 266-87 Test Method for Time of Setting of Hydraulic Cement by Gillmore Needles

C 270-86 Specification for Mortar for Unit Masonry

C 289-87 Test Method for Potential Reactivity of Aggregates (Chemical Method)

C 293-79 Test Method for Flexural Strength of Concrete (Using Simple Beam with Center-Point Loading)

C 294-86 Descriptive Nomenclature for Constituents of Natural Mineral Aggregates

C 295-85 Practice for Petrographic Examination of Aggregates for Concrete

C 305-82 Method for Mechanical Mixing of Hydraulic Cement Pastes and Mortars of Plastic Consistency

C 309-81 Specification for Liquid Membrane-Forming Compounds for Curing Concrete

C 311-87 Test Methods for Sampling and Testing Fly Ash or Natural Pozzolans for Use as a Mineral Admixture in Portland Cement Concrete

C 330-87 Specification for Lightweight Aggregates for Structural Concrete

C 332-87 Specification for Lightweight Aggregates for Insulating Concrete

C 341-84 Test Method for Length Change of Drilled or Sawed Specimens of Cement Mortar and Concrete

C 342-79 Test Method for Potential Volume Change of Cement-Aggregate Combinations

C 348-86 Test Method for Flexural Strength of Hydraulic Cement Mortars

C 359-83 Test Method for Early Stiffening of Portland Cement (Mortar Method)

C 360-82 Test Method for Ball Penetration in Fresh Portland Cement Concrete

C 387-87 Specification for Packaged, Dry, Combined Materials for Mortar and Concrete

C 403-85 Test Method for Time of Setting of Concrete Mixtures by Penetration Resistance

C 418-81 Test Method for Abrasion Resistance of Concrete by Sandblasting

C 430-83 Test Method for Fineness of Hydraulic Cement by the 45-μm (No. 325) Sieve

C 441-81 Test Method for Effectiveness of Mineral Admixtures in Preventing Excessive Expansion of Concrete Due to Alkali-Aggregate Reaction

C 451-83 Test Method for Early Stiffening of Portland Cement (Paste Method)

C 452-85 Test Method for Potential Expansion of Portland Cement Mortars Exposed to Sulfate

C 457-82 Practice for Microscopical Determination of Air-Void Content and Parameters of the Air-Void System in Hardened Concrete

C 465-85 Specifications for Processing Additions for Use in the Manufacture of Hydraulic Cements

C 469-87 Test Method for Static Modulus of Elasticity and Poisson's Ratio of Concrete in Compression

C 470-87 Specification for Molds for Forming Concrete Test Cylinders Vertically

C 490-86 Specification for Apparatus for Use in Measurement of Length Change of Hardened Cement Paste, Mortar, and Concrete

C 494-86 Specification for Chemical Admixtures for Concrete

C 495-86 Test Method for Compressive Strength of Lightweight Insulating Concrete

C 496-87 Test Method for Splitting Tensile Strength of Cylindrical Concrete Specimens

C 511-85 Specification for Moist Cabinets, Moist Rooms, and Water Storage Tanks Used in the Testing of Hydraulic Cements and Concretes

C 512-87 Test Method for Creep of Concrete in Compression

C 513-86 Test Method for Obtaining and Testing Specimens of Hardened Lightweight Insulating Concrete for Compressive Strength

C 535-81 Test Method for Resistance to Degradation of Large-Size Coarse Aggregate by Abrasion and Impact in the Los Angeles Machine

C 566-84 Test Method for Total Moisture Content of Aggregate by Drying

C 567-85 Test Method for Unit Weight of Structural Lightweight Concrete

C 586-69 Test Method for Potential Alkali Reactivity of Carbonate Rocks for Concrete Aggregates (Rock Cylinder Method)

C 595-86 Specification for Blended Hydraulic Cements

C 597-83 Test Method for Pulse Velocity through Concrete

C 617-85 Practice for Capping Cylindrical Concrete Specimens

C 618-85 Specification for Fly Ash and Raw or Calcined Natural Pozzolan for Use as a Mineral Admixture in Portland Cement Concrete

C 637-84 Specification for Aggregates for Radiation-Shielding Concrete

C 638-84 Descriptive Nomenclature of Constituents of Aggregates for Radiation-Shielding Concrete

C 641-82 Test Method for Staining Materials in Lightweight Concrete Aggregates

C 642-82 Test Method for Specific Gravity, Absorption, and Voids in Hardened Concrete

C 666-84 Test Method for Resistance of Concrete to Rapid Freezing and Thawing

C 671-86 Test Method for Critical Dilation of Concrete Specimens Subjected to Freezing

C 672-84 Test Method for Scaling Resistance of Concrete Surfaces Exposed to Deicing Chemicals
C 682-87 Practice for Evaluation of Frost Resistance of Coarse Aggregates in Air-Entrained Concrete by Critical Dilation Procedures
C 684-81 Method of Making, Accelerated Curing, and Testing of Concrete Compression Test Specimens
C 685-86 Specification for Concrete Made by Volumetric Batching and Continuous Mixing
C 688-77 Specification for Functional Additions for Use in Hydraulic Cements
C 702-87 Practice for Reducing Field Samples of Aggregate to Testing Size
C 778-80a Specification for Standard Sand
C 779-82 Test Method for Abrasion Resistance of Horizontal Concrete Surfaces
C 786-83 Test Method for Fineness of Hydraulic Cement and Raw Materials by the 300-μm (No. 50), 150-μm (No. 100), and 75-μm (No. 200) Sieves by Wet Methods
C 796-87 Test Method for Foaming Agents for Use in Producing Cellular Concrete Using Preformed Foam
C 801-81 Practice for Determining the Mechanical Properties of Hardened Concrete under Triaxial Loads
C 803-82 Test Method for Penetration Resistance of Hardened Concrete
C 805-85 Test Method for Rebound Number of Hardened Concrete
C 806-75 Test Method for Restrained Expansion of Expansive Cement Mortar
C 807-83 Test Method for Time of Setting of Hydraulic Cement Mortar by Modified Vicat Needle
C 823-83 Practice for Examination and Sampling of Hardened Concrete in Constructions
C 827-87 Test Method for Change in Height of Early Ages of Cylindrical Specimens from Cementitious Mixtures
C 845-80 Specification for Expansive Hydraulic Cement
C 856-83 Practice for Petrographic Examination of Hardened Concrete
C 869-80 Specification for Foaming Agents Used in Making Preformed Foam for Cellular Concrete
C 873-85 Test Method for Compressive Strength of Concrete Cylinders Cast in Place in Cylindrical Molds
C 876-87 Test Method for Half-Cell Potentials of Uncoated Reinforcing Steel in Concrete
C 878-87 Test Method for Restrained Expansion of Shrinkage-Compensating Concrete
C 881-78 Specification for Epoxy-Resin-Base Bonding Systems for Concrete
C 900-87 Test Method for Pullout Strength of Hardened Concrete
C 917-82 Method for Evaluation of Cement Strength Uniformity from a Single Source
C 918-80 Method for Developing Early Age Compression Test Values and Projecting Later Age Strengths
C 928-80 Specification for Packaged, Dry, Rapid-Hardening Cementitious Materials for Concrete Repairs
C 937-80 Specification for Grout Fluidifier for Preplaced-Aggregate Concrete
C 938-80 Practice for Proportioning Grout Mixtures for Preplaced-Aggregate Concrete
C 939-87 Test Method for Flow of Grout for Preplaced-Aggregate Concrete (Flow Cone Method)
C 940-87 Test Method for Expansion and Bleeding of Freshly Mixed Grouts for Preplaced-Aggregate Concrete in the Laboratory
C 941-87 Test Method for Water Retentivity of Grout Mixtures for Preplaced-Aggregate Concrete in the Laboratory
C 942-86 Test Method for Compressive Strength of Grouts for Preplaced-Aggregate Concrete in the Laboratory
C 943-80 Practice for Making Test Cylinders and Prisms for Determining Strength and Density of Preplaced-Aggregate Concrete in the Laboratory
C 944-80 Test Method for Abrasion Resistance of Concrete or Mortar Surfaces by the Rotating-Cutter Method
C 953-87 Test Method for Time of Setting of Grouts for Preplaced-Aggregate Concrete in the Laboratory
C 979-82 Specification for Pigments for Integrally Colored Concrete
C 989-87 Specification for Ground Granulated Blast-Furnace Slag for Use in Concrete and Mortars
C 995-86 Test Method for Time of Flow of Fiber-Reinforced Concrete through Inverted Slump Cone
C 1012-87 Test Method for Length Change of Hydraulic-Cement Mortars Exposed to Sulfate Solution
C 1017-85 Specification for Chemical Admixtures for Use in Producing Flowing Concrete
C 1018-85 Test Method for Flexural Toughness and First-Crack Strength Fiber-Reinforced Concrete (Using Beam with Third-Point Loading)
C 1038-85 Test Method for Expansion of Portland Cement Mortar Bars Stored in Water
C 1040-85 Test Methods for Density of Unhardened and Hardened Concrete in Place by Nuclear Methods
C 1059-86 Specification for Latex Agents for Bonding Fresh to Hardened Concrete
C 1064-86 Test Method for Temperature of Freshly Mixed Portland Cement Concrete
C 1073-85 Test Method for Hydraulic Activity of Ground Slag by Reaction with Alkali
C 1074-87 Practice for Estimating Concrete Strength by the Maturity Method
C 1078-87 Test Methods for Determining Cement Content of Freshly Mixed Concrete
C 1079-87 Test Methods for Determining Water Content of Freshly Mixed Concrete
C 1084-87 Test Method for Portland Cement Content of Hardened Hydraulic-Cement Concrete
D 75-82 Practice for Sampling Aggregates
D 98-87 Specification for Calcium Chloride
D 345-80 Methods of Sampling and Testing Calcium Chloride for Roads and Structural Applications
D 448-86 Classification for Sizes of Aggregate for Road and Bridge Construction

D 558-82	Test Method for Moisture-Density Relations of Soil-Cement Mixtures
D 632-84	Specification for Sodium Chloride
D 2240-81	Test Method for Rubber Property-Durometer Hardness
D 3042-86	Test Method for Insoluble Residue in Carbonate Aggregates

D 3963-82	Specification for Epoxy-Coated Reinforcing Steel
E 11-87	Specification for Wire-Cloth Sieves for Testing Purposes
E 380-84	Metric Practice

ASTM MASONRY STANDARDS

C5	Specification for Quicklime for Structural Purposes
C31	Method of Making and Curing Concrete Test Specimens in the Field
C33	Specification for Concrete Aggregates
C39	Method of Test for Compressive Strength of Cylindrical Concrete Specimens
C55	Specification for Concrete Building Brick
C90	Specification for Hollow Load-Bearing Concrete Masonry Units
C91	Specification for Masonry Cement
C94	Specification for Ready-Mixed Concrete
C129	Specification for Nonload-Bearing Concrete Masonry Units
C139	Specification for Concrete Masonry Units for Construction of Catch Basins and Manholes
C140	Methods of Sampling and Testing Concrete Masonry Units
C143	Test Method for Slump of Hydraulic Cement Concrete
C144	Specification for Aggregate for Masonry Mortar
C145	Specification for Solid Load-Bearing Concrete Masonry Units
C150	Specification for Portland Cement
C207	Specification for Hydrated Lime for Masonry Purposes
C236	Test Method for Steady-State Thermal Performance of Building Assemblies by Means of a Guarded Hot Box
C270	Specification for Mortar for Unit Masonry
C315	Specification for Clay Flue Linings
C404	Specification for Aggregates for Masonry Grout
C423	Test Method for Sound Absorption and Sound Absorption Coefficients by the Reverberation Room Method
C426	Test Method for Drying Shrinkage of Concrete Block
C476	Specification for Grout for Masonry
C595	Specification for Blended Hydraulic Cements
C617	Practice for Capping Cylindrical Concrete Specimens
C631	Specification for Bonding Compounds for Interior Plastering
C634	Definitions of Terms Relating to Environmental Acoustics
C744	Specification for Prefaced Concrete and Calcium Silicate Masonry Units
C780	Method for Preconstruction and Construction Evaluation of Mortars for Plain and Reinforced Unit Masonry
C847	Specification for Metal Lath
C887	Specification for Packaged, Dry, Combined Materials for Surface Bonding Mortar
C897	Specification for Aggregate for Job-Mixed Portland Cement-Based Plasters
C901	Specification for Prefabricated Masonry Panels

C920	Specification for Elastomeric Joint Sealants
C926	Specification for Application of Portland Cement-Based Plaster
C932	Specification for Surface-Applied Bonding Agents for Exterior Plastering
C933	Specification for Welded Wire Lath
C936	Specification for Solid Concrete Interlocking Paving Units
C946	Practice for Construction of Dry-Stacked, Surface-Bonded Walls
C952	Test Method for Bond Strength of Mortar to Masonry Units
C962	Guide for Use of Elastomeric Joint Sealants
C1006	Test Method for Splitting Tensile Strength of Masonry Units
C1012	Test Method for Length Change of Hydraulic-Cement Mortars Exposed to a Sulfate Solution
C1019	Method of Sampling and Testing Grout
C1032	Specification for Woven Wire Plaster Base
C1038	Test Method for Expansion of Portland Cement Mortar Bars Stored in Water
C1063	Based Plaster
C1072	Method for Measurement of Masonry Flexural Bond Strength
C1093	Practice for the Accreditation of Testing Agencies for Unit Masonry
C1142	Specification for Ready Mixed Mortar for Unit Masonry
C1148	Test Method for Measuring the Drying Shrinkage of Masonry Mortar
D3665	Practice for Random Sampling of Construction Materials
D4258	Practice for Surface Cleaning Concrete for Coating
D4259	Practice for Abrading Concrete
D4260	Practice for Acid Etching Concrete
D4261	Practice for Surface Cleaning Concrete Unit Masonry for Coating
D4262	Test Method for pH of Chemically Cleaned or Etched Concrete Surfaces
D4263	Test Method for Indicating Moisture in Concrete by the Plastic Sheet Method
E72	Methods of Conducting Strength Tests of Panels for Building Construction
E90	Method for Laboratory Measurement of Airborne Sound Transmission Loss of Building Partitions
E119	Methods of Fire Tests of Building Construction and Materials
E336	Method for Measurement of Airborne Sound Insulation in Buildings
E380	Practice for Use of the International System of Units (SI) (the Modernized Metric System)
E413	Classification for Determination of Sound Transmission Class
E447	Test Methods for Compressive Strength of Masonry Prisms
E492	Method of Laboratory Measurement of Impact Sound Transmission Through Floor Ceiling Assemblies Using the Tapping Machine
E597	Practice for Determining a Single-Number Rating of Airborne Sound Isolation in Multiunit Building Specifications

6
CHAPTER

Carpentry

DELIVERY AND STORAGE

Fig. 6-1 *Wood trusses being stored incorrectly.*

LUMBER CHARACTERISTICS

Edge grain

Angle grain

Cross grain

Flat grain

Fig. 6-2 *Grain patterns.*

Defects

1. Check defects against the appropriate grading rules found in the appropriate inspection agency manuals.
2. Obtain copies of the grading rules and check lumber for:
   a. Tolerance of dimensions
   b. Imperfections in excess of those allowable, as regards:
   - **(1)** Checks, splits, shake, pockets
   - **(2)** Decay
   - **(3)** Grain structure
   - **(4)** Knots
   - **(5)** Correct grade and type
   - **(6)** Moisture content
   - **(7)** Percentage of hardwood or sapwood
   - **(8)** Wane (presence of bark or lack of wood)
   - **(9)** Warp, crook, bow, cup

Full definitions of the above properties or defects and other grading considerations are included in most of the grading rules handbooks. Some abbreviated definitions are listed below:

Burl: A distortion of the grain usually caused by a prior injury to the tree.

Bow: A flatlike deviation from a straight line drawn from end to end of a member.

Check: A separation of the wood across or through the rings of growth and usually a result of seasoning.

Crook: An edgewise deviation from a straight line drawn from end to end of a member.

Fig. 6-3 *Sheathing storage: The contractor has covered some of the materials, but the rest will soon become damaged and unusable.*

Knots: Lumber that has a portion of a limb or branch that has incorporated itself into the piece.

Pitch: An accumulation of the tree's resin. Sometimes referred to as a *streak of pitch*.

Pith: The soft core in the structural center of a log.

Pocket: An opening between the growth rings. It will usually contain bark or pitch.

Shake: A lengthwise separation of the member occurring between or through the rings.

Wane: A lake of wood or exposed bark on the edge or corner of the member.

Warp: A deviation from a true surface. This includes bows, cups, crooks, and twists.

Table 6-1 *Grading Standards for 2 × 4 (10 ft)*

Grade Category	Maximum Edge Knot (in.)	Wane	Warp (in.) Crook	Warp (in.) Twist
Structural Light Framing				
Select Structural	¾	¼ thickness, ¼ width	½	9/16
No. 1	1	¼ thickness, ¼ width	½	9/16
No. 2	1¼	⅓ thickness, ⅓ width	11/16	¾
No. 3	1¾	½ thickness, ½ width	1	1⅛
Construction	1½	¼ thickness, ¼ width	½	9/16
Standard	2	⅓ thickness, ⅓ width	11/16	¾
Utility	2½	½ thickness, ½ width	1	1⅛
Stud	1¾	⅓ thickness, ½ width	⅜	7/16

Source: American Softwood Lumber Standard.

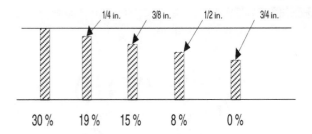

Fig. 6-4 *Shrinkage rate of typical 2 × 10.*

Note: Furniture is usually made from 15% moisture; 8% and 0% are unusually dry.

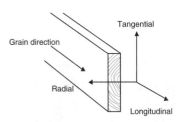

Fig. 6-5 *Wood grain terms.*

• Wood shrinks when allowed to dry and will swell again if it is allowed to come in contact with water. The largest amount of shrinkage will be tangential to the growth rings with the least amount occurring longitudinally to the rings.

Common Wood Engineering Terms

Five basic factors influence the strength of wood:

• Wood specific gravity

• Slope of grain

• Presence of knots or holes

• Moisture content

• Age

Modulus of rupture: This measurement shows the maximum bending load that a board can support. The number indicates the stress required to cause failure. The higher number means that a greater force is required to cause failure.

Modulus of elasticity: This is the measurement of stiffness that determines the deflection from a load. An example would be boards on a floor. They will recover to their original shape from a stress up to the proportional limit, but when stressed beyond this point, a permanent set will remain.

The modulus of elasticity is not a force number but a ratio of the stress applied up to the proportional limit divided by the strain (the deflection over a given area). In simple terms: take the force of 7200 psi and divide it by the amount of deflection over a given area (.0050 in.) and you have an MOE of 1.44. The higher the number on the chart, the greater the stiffness.

Stress: The force being exerted on a board in a given area. This force is typically measured in pounds per square inch (psi).

Strain: Shows how the piece of wood is affected by the stress (force). An example would be how much wood is compressed or deflected from this force. It is expressed in inches per inch.

Strength: The wood's ability to resist the applied stress (force) without failure. When the strength is equal to or greater than the stress, the strain will be relieved and the board will return to normal as the stress is removed.

Proportional limit: The balance of stress/strain/strength is constant up the proportional limit. Any force beyond this would cause the board to not return to its original shape. A permanent set remains (or structural damage occurs).

Compression parallel to grain: When used as studs, posts, or columns, the fibers are stressed uniformly parallel to and along the full length. In this application, the maximum strength of wood is at work. The numbers in Table 6-3 indicate the maximum crushing strength. The larger number indicates a stronger board.

Compression perpendicular to grain: When a joist or beam supports weight, it is important to determine this load factor so the side grain doesn't get crushed. Table 6-3 shows the load that was placed across the grain with the material stressed up to the proportional limit. Wood is considerably weaker in this test compared to compression parallel to grain. The larger numbers in Table 6-3 indicate greater strength to resist stress.

Specific gravity provides the relative weight of wood compared to an equal volume of water. For many engineering applications, the basis for specific gravity is generally the oven dry weight and volume at a 12% moisture content (MC). Specific gravity is used as a standard basis to compare species. A larger number indicates a heavier material.

As a general rule, the *greater* the specific gravity or density of a wood, the *greater* the strength.

Density is the weight of wood per cubic foot at a specified MC. Density is important to indicate strength in wood and may predict certain characteristics such as hardness, ease of machining, and nailing resistance. A larger number indicates a stronger wood.

Grade Stamps

Fig. 6-6 *Typical lumber grade stamp. ICC codes require that all lumber be stamped.*

Approved lumber grading organizations (up to date at the time of this printing). Check with the approved grading authority (Canadian or U.S.) if you have a stamp that is not listed.

California Lumber Inspection Service (CLIS)
P.O. Box 6989
San Jose, California 95150
Phone: (408) 993-1633
Fax: (408) 993-1642

Northeastern Lumber Manufacturers Association (NeLMA)
272 Tuttle Road, P.O. Box 87A
Cumberland Center, Maine 04021
Phone: (207) 829-6901
Fax: (207) 829-4293
Web: http://www.nelma.org

Northern Softwood Lumber Bureau (NSLB)
272 Tuttle Road, P.O. Box 87A
Cumberland Center, Maine 04021
Phone: (207) 829-6901
Fax: (207) 829-4293
email: nelma@javanet.com

Pacific Lumber Inspection Bureau (PLIB)
P.O. Box 7235
Bellevue, Washington 98008
Phone: (425) 746-6542
Fax: (425) 746-5522

Redwood Inspection Service (RIS)
405 Enfrente Drive, Suite 400
Novato, California 94949
Phone: (415) 382-0662
Fax: (415) 382-8531
email: cfgrover@worldnet.att.net
Web: http://www.calredwood.org

RR®
028 No 1 SYP KD19

Renewable Resource Associates, Inc. (RRA)
3091 Chaparral Place
Lithonia, Georgia 30038
Phone: (770) 482-9385
Fax: (770) 484-2541
email: rra.inc.@mindspring.com

SPIB®
KD19 No. 2 (7)

Southern Pine Inspection Bureau (SPIB)
4709 Scenic Highway
Pensacola, Florida 32504
Phone: (850) 434-2611
Fax: (850) 433-5594
email: spib@spib.org
Web: http://www.spib.org

AUDITED BY
TP®
000 NO.2 S-DRY SYP

Timber Products Inspection (TP)
P.O. Box 919
Conyers, Georgia 30012
Phone: (770) 922-8000
Fax: (770) 922-1290
email: tpinsp@mindspring.com
Web: http://www.tpinspection.com

West Coast Lumber Inspection Bureau (WCLIB)
Box 23145
Portland, Oregon 97281
Phone: (503) 639-0651
Fax: (503) 684-8928
email: info@wclib.org
Web: http://www.wclib.org

Western Wood Products Association (WWPA)
Yeon Building
522 SW Fifth Avenue
Portland, Oregon 97204-2122
Phone: (503) 224-3930
Fax: (503) 224-3934
email: info@wwpg.org
Web: http://www.wwpa.org

Canadian Approved Grading Agencies

A.F.P.A.® 00
S—P—F
S-DRY STAND

Alberta Forest Products Association (AFPA)
11738 Kingsway Avenue #200
Edmonton, Alberta T5G OX5
Phone: (403) 452-2841
Fax: (403) 455-0505
email: afpinfo@CODIPIJ?l11art.ab.ca
Web: http://www.abforestproc::l.org

CL®A 100
SPRUCE-PINE-FIR
NO. 1 S-DRY

Canadian Lumbermen's Association (CLA)
27 Goulburn Avenue
Ottawa, Ontario K1N 8C7
Phone: (613) 233-6205
Fax: (613) 233-1929
email: cla@sympatico.ca
Web: http://www.cla-ca.ca

Canadian Mill Services Association (CMSA)
Suite 1100-555 Burrard Street
Vancouver, British Columbia V7X 157
Phone: (604) 891-1200
Fax: (604) 682-8641
email: beatty@cofiho.cofi.org
Web: http://www.cofi.org

CSI.   No 1
        S-DRY
000 HEM-FIR(N)

Canadian Softwood Inspection Agency, Inc. (CSI)
a10-20226 Fraser Highway
Langley, British Columbia V2Z 1P1
Phone: (604) 532-7624
Fax: (604) 532-7625

Cariboo Lumber Manufacturers Association (CLMA)
205-197 North 2nd Avenue
Williams Lake, British Columbia V2G 1Z6
Phone: (250) 392-7778
Fax: (250) 392-4692
email: clma@wlake.com
Web: http://www.clma.com

CFPA® 00
S-P-F S-DRY
CONST

Central Forest Products Association (CFPA)
P.O. Box 1169
Hudson Bay, Saskatchewan SOE OYO
Phone: (306) 865-2595
Fax: (306) 865-3302

Coniferous Lumber Inspection Bureau (CLIB)
Kennedy Building–Suite 210
222 McIntyre Street West
North Bay, Ontario P1B 2Y8
Phone: (705) 476-2542
Fax: (705) 476-5899
email: clib@vianet.on.ca

Gateway Lumber Inspection Bureau (GLIB)
992 Burns Street
North Bay, Ontario P1B 3V4
Phone: (705) 474-9148
Fax: (705) 474-3644

Interior Lumber Manufacturers Association (ILMA)
360-1855 Kirschner Road
Kelowna, British Columbia V1 Y 4N7
Phone: (250) 860-9663
Fax: (250) 860-0009
email: ilma@silk.net
Web: http://www.ilma.com

Macdonald Inspection (MI)
112-1720 14th Avenue
Campbell River, British Columbia V9W 8B9
Phone: (250) 287-4422
Fax: (250) 287-8840
email: macinsp@island.net
Web: http://www.gradestamp.com

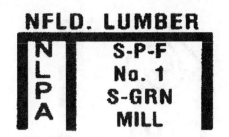

Newfoundland Lumber Producers Association (NLPA)
P.O. Box 8
Glovertown, Newfoundland A0G 2L0
Phone: (709) 533-2206
Fax: (709) 533-2611

Maritime Lumber Bureau (MLB)
P.O. Box 459
Amherst, Nova Scotia B4H 4A1
Phone: (902) 667-3889
Fax: (902) 667-0401
email: mlb@ns.sympatico.ca
Web: http://www.mlb.ca

Ontario Lumber Manufacturers Association (OLMA)
55 University Avenue, Suite 1105, Box 8
Toronto, Ontario M5J 2H7
Phone: (416) 367-9717
Fax: (416) 367-3415 9

Northern Forest Products Association (NFPA)
400-1488 Fourth Avenue
Prince George, British Columbia V21 4Y2
Phone: (250) 564-5136
Fax: (250) 564-3588
email: nfpa@pgweb.com
Web: http://www.nfpa.pc.ca

Pacific Lumber Inspection Bureau (PLIB)
British Columbia Division
P.O. Box 19118
Fourth Avenue Postal Outlet
Vancouver, British Columbia V6K 4R8
Phone: (425) 746-6542
Fax: (604) 732-1782

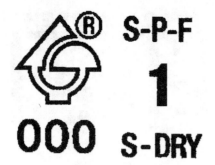

S-P-F
1
000 S-DRY

Quebec Lumber Manufacturers Association (QLMA)
5055 West Hamel Boulevard, Suite 200
Quebec City, Quebec G2E 2G6
Phone: (418) 872-5610
Fax: (418) 872-3062
email: info@sciage-lumber.qc.ca
Web: http://www.sciage-lumber.qc.ca

Table 6-2 *Lumber Grading Standards*

Grade Category	Maximum Edge Knot (in.)	Wane	Warp (in.)	
			Crook	Twist
Structural Light Framing				
Select Structural	¾	¼ thickness, ¼ width	½	9⁄16
No. 1	1	¼ thickness, ¼ width	½	9⁄16
No. 2	1¼	⅓ thickness, ⅓ width	11⁄16	¾
No. 3	1¾	½ thickness, ½ width	1	1⅛
Construction	1½	¼ thickness, ¼ width	½	9⁄16
Standard	2	⅓ thickness, ⅓ width	11⁄16	¾
Utility	2½	½ thickness, ½ width	1	1⅛
Stud	1¾	⅓ thickness, ½ width	⅜	7⁄16

Source: American Softwood Lumber Standard.

Wood Rot   If the wood is badly decayed, this will be quite visible. Two common visual results of decay are a bleached and stringy appearance to the wood, or a darkened surface with cubical cracking. If fungal growth is visible on the surface, the wood has probably already suffered strength loss, but do not rely on visual cues alone. Wood can appear stained and be sound, or can appear normal yet still have already suffered significant strength loss due to decay. Use the pick test to determine whether or not the wood is, in fact, sound. Insert the point of a knife at a shallow angle to the surface and attempt to lever up a thin splinter. If the wood splinters, it is sound. If instead it breaks just above the blade like a carrot snapping in half, it is decayed.

CRAWLSPACE FRAMING
Pressure-Treated

Pressure-Treated Properties

- Sills < 8 in. from ground
- Girders < 12 in. from ground
- Joists < 18 in. from ground
- All sills and sleepers on concrete.
- Ends of girders in concrete and masonry having less than ½-in. clearance on ends, sides, and top.

Note: Pressure-treated wood needs to be retreated in field when cut or drilled.

Treated lumber to conform to DOC PS 20-70.

Columns and Posts

- Metal post poles and columns in contact with concrete need to be primed.
- Wood columns, posts, and poles supporting structures and are embedded in concrete need to be pressure-treated.
- Cripple walls above 4 in. need to meet requirements for size for additional story.
- Columns
  a. *Wood* columns need to be at least 4 in. × 4 in. nominal.
  b. *Steel* columns need to be at least 3 in. in diameter (must be primed/painted inside as well as outside).

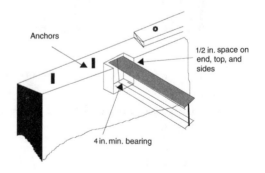

Fig. 6-7 *Beam pockets.*

Table 6-3 *Representative Working Stress Values (psi) for Lumber at 19% Moisture Content, Continuing or Prolonged Reuse*

Species and Grade	Extreme Fiber Bending	Compression Perpendicular to Grain	Compression Parallel to Grain	Modulus of Elasticity $\times 10^6$
Douglas Fir–Larch				
Range, all grades	275–2450	625–730	475–1850	1.3–1.9
No. 2, 4 × 4 and smaller	1450	625	1000	1.7
Constr., 4 × 4 and smaller	875–1050	625	1150	1.5
Eastern Spruce				
Range, all grades	175–1400	390	300–1050	1.0–1.5
No. 2, 4 × 4 and smaller	975	390	650	1.4
Constr., 4 × 4 and smaller	700	390	750	1.2
Southern Pine				
Range, all grades	200–2600	375–660	400–2300	1.2–1.9
No. 2, 4 × 4 and smaller	1150–1400	375–565	650–975	1.4–1.6
Constr., 4 × 4 and smaller	825–1000	375–565	725–1100	1.2–1.4
Hem–Fir				
Range, all grades	100–1650	405	375–1300	1.1–1.6
No. 2, 4 × 4 and smaller	1150	405	825	1.4
Constr., 4 × 4 and smaller	700–825	405	925	1.2
California Redwood				
Range, all grades	225–2300	425–650	500–2150	.9–1.4
No. 2, 4 × 4 and smaller	1400	650	1100	1.25
Constr., 4 × 4 and smaller	665–825	425	925	.9
Adjustment for moisture content greater than 19%: Use percentage shown (also applies to wood used wet)	86	67	70	97
Increase for load duration of 7 days or less, permitted for lumber and plywood	25%	25%	25%	0
Plywood sheathing used wet, plyform B-B, Class I (Grade stress level 5-2)	1545	(bearing on face) 210	—	1,500,000

GIRDERS

Steel

- The use of steel beams is becoming more and more popular among builders because of their ease of use and relative lower cost. The most common of the steel beams is the I-shaped beam thus called an I beam. In actuality the I beam is referred to as a W-shaped beam. Beams come in different sizes, shapes, and strengths. It is important that a competent engineer or architect provide the size required for your intended use.

- A typical beam would be denoted as

  W 16 × 36

- The W refers to the type of beam, the 16 is the nominal depth of the beam in inches, and the 36 is the weight of the beam per foot. The heavier the weight, the stronger the beam.

- Beams used as girders are called *simple beams* because the ends are usually not fixed to the pockets in which they rest. Thus, in theory the beams ends are free to rotate and/or flex.

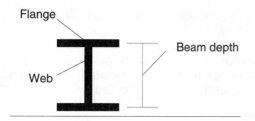

Fig. 6-8 *Typical I-beam section.*

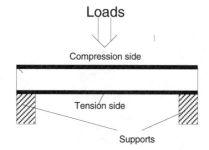

Fig. 6-9 *Steel beams.*

Table 6-4 *Maximum Steel Beam Loading*

Beam Sizes and Weights (kips)					
Spans	W10 × 21	W12 × 27	W14 × 30	W16 × 36	W18 × 50
10	29	45	56	75	119
12	24	38	46	63	99
14	21	32	40	54	85
16	17.9	28	35	47	74
18	15.9	25	31	42	66
20	14.3	23	28	38	59
22		21	25	34	54
24		19	24	31	49
26			21	29	46
28			19.6	27	42
30			18.6	25	40

Note: All loads are in kips (1000 lb).

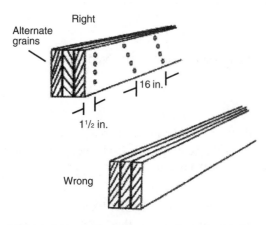

Fig. 6-10 *Job-site-built girders (see nailing schedule for correct size and spacing of nails).*

WOOD GIRDERS: EXTERIOR WALLS

Table 6-5 *Exterior Walls—Girders Supporting Roof and Ceiling; Ground Snow Load 30 psf*

	Building Widths (ft)					
	20		28		36	
Size	Span	No. Jacks	Span	No. Jacks	Span	No. Jacks
2-2 × 6	5-5	1	4-8	1	4-2	1
2-2 × 8	6-10	1	5-11	2	5-4	2
2-2 × 10	8-5	2	7-3	2	6-6	2
2-2 × 12	9-9	2	8-5	2	7-6	2
3-2 × 8	8-4	1	7-5	1	6-8	1
3-2 × 10	10-6	1	9-1	2	8-2	2
3-2 × 12	12-2	2	10-7	2	9-5	2
4-2 × 8	7-0	1	6-1	2	5-5	2
4-2 × 10	11-8	1	10-6	1	9-5	2
4-2 × 12	14-1	1	12-2	2	10-11	2

Table 6-6 *Exterior Walls—Girders Supporting Roof, Ceiling, and One Center-Bearing Floor; Ground Snow Load 30 psf*

	Building Widths (ft)					
	20		28		36	
Size	Span	No. Jacks	Span	No. Jacks	Span	No. Jacks
2-2 × 6	4-6	1	4-0	1	3-7	2
2-2 × 8	5-9	2	5-0	2	4-6	2
2-2 × 10	7-0	2	6-2	2	5-6	2
2-2 × 12	8-1	2	7-1	2	6-5	2
3-2 × 8	7-2	1	6-3	2	5-8	2
3-2 × 12	10-2	2	8-11	2	8-0	2
4-2 × 8	5-10	2	5-2	2	4-8	2
4-2 × 10	10-1	1	8-10	2	8-0	2
4-2 × 12	11-9	2	10-3	2	9-3	2

Table 6-7 *Exterior Walls—Girders Supporting Roof, Ceiling, and One Clear Span Floor; Ground Snow Load 30 psf*

	Building Widths (ft)					
	20		28		36	
Size	Span	No. Jacks	Span	No. Jacks	Span	No. Jacks
2-2 × 6	3-11	1	3-5	2	3-0	2
2-2 × 8	5-0	2	4-4	2	3-10	2
2-2 × 10	6-1	2	5-3	2	4-8	2
2-2 × 12	7-1	2	6-1	3	5-5	3
3-2 × 8	6-3	2	5-5	2	4-10	2
3-2 × 10	7-7	2	6-7	2	5-11	2
3-2 × 12	8-10	2	7-8	2	6-10	2
4-2 × 8	5-1	2	4-5	2	3-11	2
4-2 × 10	8-9	2	7-7	2	6-10	2
4-2 × 12	10-2	2	8-10	2	7-11	2

Table 6-8 Exterior Walls—Girders Supporting Roof, Ceiling, and Two Center-Bearing Floors; Ground Snow Load 30 psf

| | Building Widths (ft) | | | | | |
| | 20 | | 28 | | 36 | |
Size	Span	No. Jacks	Span	No. Jacks	Span	No. Jacks
2-2 × 6	3-9	2	3-3	2	2-11	2
2-2 × 8	4-9	2	4-2	2	3-9	2
2-2 × 10	5-9	2	5-1	2	4-7	3
2-2 × 12	6-8	2	5-10	3	5-3	3
3-2 × 8	5-11	2	5-2	2	4-8	2
3-2 × 12	8-5	2	7-4	2	6-7	2
4-2 × 8	4-10	2	4-3	2	3-10	2
4-2 × 10	8-4	2	7-4	2	6-7	2
4-2 × 12	9-8	2	8-6	2	7-8	2

Table 6-9 Exterior Walls—Girders Supporting Roof and Ceiling; Ground Snow Load 50 psf

| | Building Widths (ft) | | | | | |
| | 20 | | 28 | | 36 | |
Size	Span	No. Jacks	Span	No. Jacks	Span	No. Jacks
2-2 × 6	4-8	1	4-1	1	3-8	2
2-2 × 8	5-11	2	5-2	2	4-7	2
2-2 × 10	7-3	2	6-3	2	5-7	2
2-2 × 12	8-5	2	7-3	2	6-6	2
3-2 × 8	7-5	1	6-5	2	5-9	2
3-2 × 10	9-1	2	7-10	2	7-0	2
3-2 × 12	10-7	2	9-2	2	8-2	2
4-2 × 8	6-1	2	5-3	2	4-8	2
4-2 × 10	10-6	1	9-1	2	8-2	2
4-2 × 12	12-2	2	10-7	2	9-5	2

Table 6-10 Exterior Walls—Girders Supporting Roof, Ceiling, and One Center-Bearing Floor; Ground Snow Load 50 psf

| | Building Widths (ft) | | | | | |
| | 20 | | 28 | | 36 | |
Size	Span	No. Jacks	Span	No. Jacks	Span	No. Jacks
2-2 × 6	4-1	1	3-7	2	3-3	2
2-2 × 8	5-2	2	4-6	2	4-1	2
2-2 × 10	6-4	2	5-6	2	5-0	2
2-2 × 12	7-4	2	6-5	2	5-9	3
3-2 × 8	6-5	2	5-8	2	5-1	2
3-2 × 10	7-11	2	6-11	2	6-3	2
3-2 × 12	9-2	2	8-0	2	7-3	2
4-2 × 8	5-3	2	4-7	2	4-2	2
4-2 × 10	9-1	2	8-0	2	7-2	2
4-2 × 12	10-7	2	9-3	2	8-4	2

Table 6-11 Exterior Walls—Girders Supporting Roof, Ceiling, and One Clear Span Floor; Ground Snow Load 50 psf

| | Building Widths (ft) | | | | | |
| | 20 | | 28 | | 36 | |
Size	Span	No. Jacks	Span	No. Jacks	Span	No. Jacks
2-2 × 6	3-10	2	3-4	2	3-0	2
2-2 × 8	4-10	2	4-2	2	3-9	2
2-2 × 10	5-11	2	5-1	2	4-7	3
2-2 × 12	6-10	2	5-11	3	5-4	3
3-2 × 8	6-1	2	5-3	2	4-8	2
3-2 × 10	7-5	2	6-5	2	5-9	2
3-2 × 12	8-7	2	7-5	2	6-8	2
4-2 × 8	4-11	2	4-3	2	3-10	2
4-2 × 10	8-7	2	7-5	2	6-7	2
4-2 × 12	9-11	2	8-7	2	7-8	2

Table 6-12 Exterior Walls—Girders Supporting Roof, Ceiling, and Two Center-Bearing Floors; Ground Snow Load 50 psf

| | Building Widths (ft) | | | | | |
| | 20 | | 28 | | 36 | |
Size	Span	No. Jacks	Span	No. Jacks	Span	No. Jacks
2-2 × 6	3-8	2	3-2	2	2-10	2
2-2 × 8	4-7	2	4-0	2	3-8	2
2-2 × 10	5-8	2	4-11	2	4-5	3
2-2 × 12	6-6	2	5-9	3	5-2	3
3-2 × 8	5-9	2	5-1	2	4-7	2
3-2 × 10	7-1	2	6-2	2	5-7	2
3-2 × 12	8-2	2	7-2	2	6-5	3
4-2 × 8	4-9	2	4-2	2	3-9	2
4-2 × 10	8-2	2	7-2	2	6-5	2
4-2 × 12	9-5	2	8-3	2	7-5	2

INTERIOR GIRDERS

Table 6-13 Interior Girders—One Floor Only

| | Building Widths (ft) | | | | | |
| | 20 | | 28 | | 36 | |
Size	Span	No. Jacks	Span	No. Jacks	Span	No. Jacks
2-2 × 6	4-6	1	3-11	1	3-6	1
2-2 × 8	5-9	1	5-0	2	4-5	2
2-2 × 10	7-0	2	6-1	2	5-5	2
2-2 × 12	8-1	2	7-0	2	6-3	2
3-2 × 8	7-2	1	6-3	1	5-7	2
3-2 × 10	8-9	1	7-7	2	6-9	2
3-2 × 12	10-2	2	8-10	2	7-10	2
4-2 × 8	5-10	1	5-1	2	4-6	2
4-2 × 10	10-1	1	8-9	1	7-10	2
4-2 × 12	11-9	1	10-2	2	9-1	2

Table 6-14 Interior Girders Supporting Two Floors Only

| | Building Widths (ft) | | | | | |
| | **20** | | **28** | | **36** | |
Size	**Span**	**No. Jacks**	**Span**	**No. Jacks**	**Span**	**No. Jacks**
2-2 × 6	3-2	2	2-9	2	2-5	2
2-2 × 8	4-1	2	3-6	2	3-2	2
2-2 × 10	4-11	2	4-3	2	3-10	3
2-2 × 12	5-9	2	5-0	3	4-5	3
3-2 × 8	5-1	2	4-5	2	3-11	2
3-2 × 10	6-2	2	5-4	2	4-10	2
3-2 × 12	7-2	2	6-3	2	5-7	3
4-2 × 8	4-2	2	3-7	2	3-2	2
4-2 × 10	7-2	2	6-2	2	5-6	2
4-2 × 12	8-4	2	7-2	2	6-5	2

Table 6-15 Ledger Bolts

| | Bolt Size and Proper Spacing | |
Joist Span	**Roof**	**Floor**
10 ft	1/2 @ 2 ft-6 in. 7/8 @ 3 ft-6 in.	1/2 @ 2 ft-0 in. 7/8 @ 2 ft-9 in.
10 ft–15 ft	1/2 @ 1 ft-9 in. 7/8 @ 2 ft-6 in.	1/2 @ 1 ft-4 in. 7/8 @ 2 ft-0 in.
15 ft–20 ft	1/2 @ 1 ft-3 in. 7/8 @ 2 ft-0 in.	1/2 @ 1 ft-0 in. 7/8 @ 1 ft-6 in.

Note: Hollow concrete masonry units must be grouted full to receive ledger bolts.

Table 6-16 Design Deflections Limits

Construction	**Live Load**	**Snow or Wind Load**	**Dead plus Live Load**
Roof members:			
Supporting plaster ceiling	L/360	L/360	L/240
Supporting nonplaster ceiling	L/240	L/240	L/180
Not supporting ceiling	L/180	L/180	L/120
Floor members	L/360	—	L/240
Exterior walls and interior partitions:			
With brittle finishes	—	L/240	—
With flexible finishes	—	L/120	—
Farm buildings	—	—	L/180
Greenhouses	—	—	L/120

Table 6-17 Maximum Allowable Deflections of Structural Members

Span	L/180	L/240	L/360
15	1 in.	$^3/_4$ in.	$^1/_2$ in.
16	1$^1/_{16}$ in.	$^{13}/_{16}$ in.	$^{17}/_{32}$ in.
17	1$^1/_8$ in.	$^{27}/_{32}$ in.	$^9/_{16}$ in.
18	1$^3/_{16}$ in.	$^{29}/_{32}$ in.	$^{19}/_{32}$ in.
19	1$^9/_{32}$ in.	$^{15}/_{16}$ in.	$^5/_8$ in.
20	1$^{11}/_{32}$ in.	1 in.	$^{21}/_{32}$ in.
21	1$^{13}/_{32}$ in.	1$^1/_{16}$ in.	$^{11}/_{16}$ in.
22	1$^{15}/_{32}$ in.	1$^3/_{32}$ in.	$^{23}/_{32}$ in.
23	1$^{17}/_{32}$ in.	1$^5/_{32}$ in.	$^{35}/_{32}$ in.
24	1$^{19}/_{32}$ in.	1$^3/_{16}$ in.	$^{13}/_{16}$ in.
25	1$^{21}/_{32}$ in.	1$^1/_4$ in.	$^{27}/_{32}$ in.
26	1$^{23}/_{32}$ in.	1$^5/_{16}$ in.	$^7/_8$ in.
27	1$^{13}/_{16}$ in.	1$^{11}/_{32}$ in.	$^{29}/_{32}$ in.
28	1$^7/_8$ in.	1$^{13}/_{32}$ in.	$^{15}/_{16}$ in.
29	1$^{15}/_{16}$ in.	1$^7/_{16}$ in.	$^{31}/_{32}$ in.
30	2 in.	1$^1/_2$ in.	1 in.
31	2$^1/_{16}$ in.	1$^9/_{16}$ in.	1$^1/_{32}$ in.
32	2$^1/_8$ in.	1$^{19}/_{32}$ in.	1$^1/_{16}$ in.

Table 6-18 Minimum Design Loads for Occupancy Uses

Occupancy/Use	Uniform Load (psi)	Concentrated Load (lb)
Apartments (see Residential)	—	—
Access floor systems		
Office use	50	2,000
Computer use	100	2,000
Armories and drill rooms	150	—
Assembly areas and theaters		
Fixed seats (fastened to floor)	60	
Lobbies	100	
Movable seats	100	
Stages and platforms	125	—
Follow spot, projections and control rooms	50	
Catwalks	40	
Balconies (exterior)	100	—
On one- and two-family residences only, and not exceeding 100 ft^2	60	
Decks	Same as occupancy served	—
Bowling alleys	75	—
Cornices	60	—
Corridors, except as otherwise indicated	100	—
Dance halls and ballrooms	100	—

Table 6-18 (Continued)

Occupancy/Use	Uniform Load (psi)	Concentrated Load (lb)
Dining rooms and restaurants	100	—
Elevator machine room grating (on area of 4 in.^{2})	—	300
Finish light floor plate construction (on area of 1 in.^{2})	—	200
Fire escapes	100	
On single-family dwellings only	40	—
Garages (passenger vehicles only)	40	
Grandstands (see Stadiums and Arenas, Bleachers)	—	—
Gymnasiums, main floors and balconies	100	—
Hospitals		
Operating rooms, laboratories	60	1,000
Private rooms	40	1,000
Wards	40	1,000
Corridors above first floor	80	1,000
Hotels (see Residential)	—	—
Libraries		
Reading rooms	60	1,000
Stack rooms	150	1,000
Corridors above first floor	80	1,000
Manufacturing		
Light	125	2,000
Heavy	250	3,000
Marquees	75	—
Office buildings		
File and computer rooms shall be designed for heavier loads based on anticipated occupancy		
Lobbies and first-floor corridors	100	2,000
Offices	50	2,000
Corridors above first floor	80	2,000
Penal institutions		
Cell blocks	40	—
Corridors	100	
Residential		
One- and two-family dwellings:		
Uninhabitable attics without storage	10	
Uninhabitable attics with storage	20	—
Habitable attics and sleeping areas	30	
All other areas except balconies and decks	40	
Hotels and multifamily dwellings:		

Table 6-18 (Continued)

Occupancy/Use	Uniform Load (psi)	Concentrated Load (lb)
Private rooms and corridors serving them	40	
Public rooms and corridors serving them	100	
Schools		
Classrooms	40	1,000
Corridors above first floor	80	1,000
First-floor corridors	100	1,000
Scuttles, skylight ribs, and accessible ceilings	—	200
Sidewalks, vehicular driveways, and yards, subject to trucks	250	8,000
Skating rinks	100	—
Stadiums and arenas		
Bleachers	100	—
Fixed seats (fastened to floor)	60	
Stairs and exits		
One- and two-family dwellings	40	
All other	100	
Storage warehouses (shall be designed for heavier loads if required for anticipated storage)		
Light	125	
Heavy	250	
Stores		
Retail:		
First floor	100	1,000
Upper floors	75	1,000
Wholesale, all floors	125	1,000
Walkways and elevated platforms (other than exit ways)	60	—

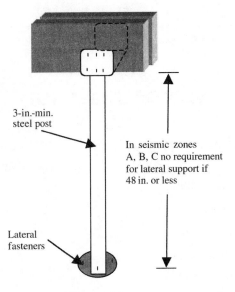

3-in.-min. steel post

In seismic zones A, B, C no requirement for lateral support if 48 in. or less

Lateral fasteners

Fig. 6-11 *Posts.*

PIPE POST LOADS

Table 6-19 *A 36 Standard Pipe (Load in kips)*

Nominal (in.)	6	5	4	3½	3
Wall Thickness	0.280	0.258	0.237	0.226	0.216
Weight per Foot	18.97	14.62	10.79	9.11	7.58
Length (ft)	A 36 Standard Pipe (Load in kips)*				
6	110	83	59	48	38
7	108	81	57	46	36
8	106	78	54	44	34
9	103	76	52	41	31
10	101	73	49	38	28
11	98	71	46	35	25
12	95	68	43	32	22
13	92	65	40	29	19
14	89	61	36	25	16
15	86	58	33	22	14
16	82	55	29	19	12
17	79	51	26	17	11
18	75	47	23	15	10
19	71	43	21	14	
20	67	39	19	12	
22	59	32	15	10	
24	51	27	13		
25	47	25	12		
26	43	23			
28	37	20			
30	32	17			
31	30				
32	29				
34	25				
36	23				
37	21				
38					

* Kips: Example 37 kips = 37,000 lb.

FLOORS (FRAMING)
Joist

- Blocking min. of utility grade.
- Joist to be doubled under load-bearing wall when running parallel.
- Joist bearings:

  Wood: 1½ in.

  Masonry: 3 in.
- Lap joist a min. of 3 in.
- Ledger must be at least 2 × 2.

Table 6-20 *Axial Compression Capacity of Solid Wood Post (kips)*

Size			Unbraced Length (ft)							
Desig-nation	Area of Section (in.²)	6	8	10	12	14	16	18	20
2 × 3	3.375	0.8							
2 × 4	5.25	1.3							
3 × 4	8.75	6.0	3.4	2.2					
3 × 6	13.75	9.4	5.3	3.4					
4 × 4	12.25	14.7	9.3	5.9	4.1	3.0			
4 × 6	19.25	23.1	14.6	9.3	6.5	4.8			
4 × 8	25.375	30.4	19.2	12.3	8.5	6.3			
6 × 6	30.25	35.4	33.5	29.6	22.5	16.6	12.7	10.0	8.1
6 × 8	41.25	48.3	45.7	40.3	30.6	22.6	17.3	13.6	11.0
6 × 10	52.25	61.2	57.9	51.1	38.8	28.6	21.9	17.2	14.0
6 × 12	63.25	74.1	70.1	61.8	47.0	34.7	26.5	20.9	17.0
8 × 8	56.25	67.5	66.0	63.9	60.0	53.6	43.8	34.6	28.0
8 × 10	71.25	85.5	83.6	80.9	75.9	67.9	55.4	46.9	35.5
8 × 12	86.25	103.5	101.2	98.0	91.9	82.2	67.1	53.0	42.9
8 × 14	101.25	121.5	118.9	115.0	107.9	96.5	78.8	62.3	50.4
10 × 10	90.25	108.3	108.3	106.0	103.6	99.6	93.5	84.5	72.1
10 × 12	109.25	131.1	131.1	128.4	125.4	120.6	113.2	102.4	87.3
10 × 14	128.25	153.9	153.9	150.7	147.2	141.6	132.9	120.2	102.5
10 × 16	147.25	176.7	176.7	173.0	169.0	162.5	152.5	138.0	117.7
12 × 12	132.25	158.7	158.7	158.7	155.5	152.7	148.6	142.5	134.1

Note: Wood used is dense No. 1 Douglas fir–larch.

- Must have header, or 2 × blocking.
- Bridging needed if depth-to-thickness ratio exceeds 6–1 intervals. Not to exceed 10 ft.
- Drilling and notching <⅙ the depth of joist. None allowed in middle third of joist on ledgers <¼ the depth of joist end.
- Holes. None within 2 in. of top or bottom and in dia. <⅓ the depth.
- Header joist <4 in. may be single. Must use hangers in more than 4 in.
- *Floor trusses cannot be altered!*
- Sawn beams (4 in. and more) cannot be notched, drilled, or cut, except at their ends for a ledger.

Engineered Joist

General (always check the specific manufacturer's guide when installing engineered joist)

- If more than one hole is to be cut, the minimum distance between the holes must be twice the longest dimension of the largest adjacent hole.

- Holes can be positioned vertically within the web. The flange cannot be cut.
- Holes with diameter of 1½ in. may be cut anywhere in the web as long as they are 3 in. away from all other holes.
- Do not hang joist by the top flange or web.

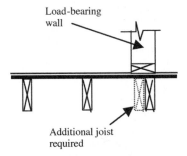

Fig. 6-12 *Joists supporting load-bearing wall.*

Doubled joists that are separated to allow for piping or vents are to be fully depth blocked by lumber not less than 2 in. and blocking is not to be spaced more than 4 ft O.C.

Notching and Cutting of Joist
- Notches cannot be deeper than ⅓ the depth of the ceiling joist.

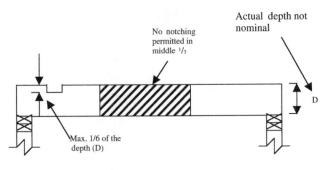

Fig. 6-13 *Floor joist notches.*

Table 6-21 *Drilled Hole Maximums in Joists*

Nominal	Actual (in.)	⅓ (33%) (in.)
2 × 6	1½ × 5¼	1¾
2 × 8	1½ × 7¼	2¹³⁄₃₂
2 × 10	1½ × 9¼	3³⁄₃₂
2 × 12	1½ × 11¼	3¾
2 × 14	1½ × 14¼	4¾

Table 6-22 *Notch Maximums in Joists*

Nominal	Actual (in.)	⅙ (17%) (in.)
2 × 6	1½ × 5¼	⅞
2 × 8	1½ × 7¼	1⁷⁄₃₂
2 × 10	1½ × 9¼	1¹⁷⁄₃₂
2 × 12	1½ × 11¼	1⅞
2 × 14	1½ × 14¼	2⅜

Table 6-23 *Notch Maximums in Ceiling Joists/Rafters*

Nominal	Actual (in.)	⅓ (33%) (in.)
2 × 6	1½ × 5¼	1¾
2 × 8	1½ × 7¼	2¹³⁄₃₂
2 × 10	1½ × 9¼	3³⁄₃₂
2 × 12	1½ × 11¼	3¾
2 × 14	1½ × 14¼	4¾

Table 6-24 *End Notch Maximums in Ceiling Joists/Rafters*

Nominal	Actual (in.)	¼ (25%) (in.)
2 × 6	1½ × 5¼	1⁵⁄₁₆
2 × 8	1½ × 7¼	1¹³⁄₁₆
2 × 10	1½ × 9¼	2⁵⁄₁₆
2 × 12	1½ × 11¼	2¹³⁄₁₆
2 × 14	1½ × 14¼	3⁹⁄₁₆

Note: Do not use pre-engineered joist with dimensional lumber as the band board. Differences in shrinking can cause structural problems or failures!

Span Tables—Loading Definitions
- The type of species and the grade of wood for the rafters and joists determine the maximum allowable *stress in bending* (f_b) and its *modulus of elasticity* (e). These two values determine how far a rafter or joist can span and still meet the minimum deflection requirements. Excessive deflection of these members can cause damage to drywall, finishes, and/or bouncy floors.
- The tables listed in the next section are simplified and do not show all the wood species available. Consult with your local code requirements to determine your exact requirements. All spans are considered clear horizontal simple beams with ends fixed.

How to Read the Code Span Tables
- Many times builders do not fully understand how to use the lumber span tables in the codes. Rafters and

joists obviously carry loads or are weighted down by something. These loads are commonly referred to as live loads, dead loads, snow loads, and wind loads.

- *Live loads:* These are the weights of such things as people, furniture, and others that are imposed by the particular use that the room or structure will be subjected to.

- *Dead loads:* These are the weights of the actual building materials and systems (such as the HVAC unit in the attic space).

- *Snow loads:* Weights of snow accumulation that can be expected in your area of the country. These are usually stipulated by the code enforcement department in your area.

- *Wind loads:* Same as the above. However, it may also depend on where the structure is to be located, such as at the top of a hill or in a forested area where it will be better protected from the force imposed by the wind.

- The code table expresses the framing member in terms of its strength and stiffness. Both are considered of equal importance. All lumber when loaded will bend or deflect. Codes limit the amount of this deflection depending on what the area is to be used for—a living room has a different limit than a bedroom. Roof rafters are limited as to their pitch or slope. The lower the pitch, the stronger they must be. The deflection is expressed as a fraction such as L/180 or L/360. The maximum allowable deflection in determined by taking the length of the "clear" span and dividing that number by the denominator, usually 180, 240, or 360.

- Stiffness of the member is expressed as the modulus of elasticity or E, and along with the bending design value or F_b. E values are expressed in millions of pounds per square inch or psi. A value in the table such as 1.1 is 1,100,000 psi. F_b is in pounds per square inch. The code tables will identify these two values when you have taken the span that you are working with and the spacing of the members, i.e., 12 in. O.C., 16 in. O.C., etc. Determining these minimum acceptable values is the first thing necessary in deciding on which type and grade of wood will meet the applicable codes.

- Once you have identified E and F_b, you can then go into the appropriate table (make sure you check the heading). *Note:* Chances are that you will not find a grade that the E and F_b numbers match exactly. Always use the next higher value available in the code table.

Table 6-25 Allowable Deflection of Structural Members

Structural Member	Allowable Deflection
Rafters having slopes greater than ³⁄₁₂ with no finished ceiling attached to rafters	L/180
Interior walls and partitions	H/180
Floors and plastered ceilings	L/360
All other structural members	L/240
Exterior walls with plaster or stucco finish	H/360
Exterior walls—wind loads with brittle finishes	L/240
Exterior walls—wind loads with flexible finishes	L/120

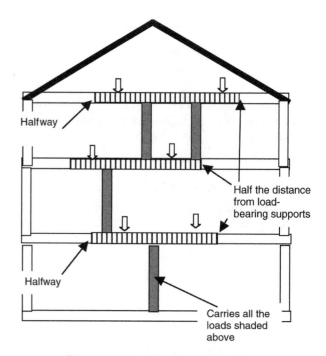

Fig. 6-14 *Loading structural members.*

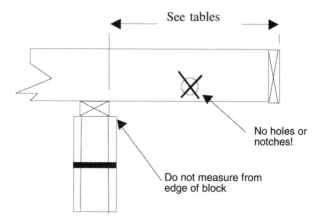

Fig. 6-15 *Cantilevered joist.*

Table 6-26 *Cantilever Spans for Floor Joists Supporting Light-Frame Exterior Bearing Wall and Roof Only*

Member and Spacing	Roof Width (ft)											
	Ground Snow Load <20 psf			Ground Snow Load 30 psf			Ground Snow Load 50 psf			Ground Snow Load 70 psf		
	24	32	40	24	32	40	24	32	40	24	32	40
2 × 8 @ 12 in.	20 in.	15 in.		18 in.								
2 × 10 @ 16 in.	29 in.	21 in.	16 in.	26 in.	18 in.		20 in.					
2 × 10 @ 12 in.	36 in.	26 in.	20 in.	34 in.	22 in.	16 in.	26 in.			19 in.		
2 × 12 @ 16 in.		32 in.	25 in.	36 in.	29 in.	21 in.	29 in.	20 in.		23 in.		
2 × 12 @ 12 in.		42 in.	31 in.		37 in.	27 in.	36 in.	27 in.	17 in.	31 in.	19 in.	
2 × 12 @ 8 in.		48 in.	45 in.		48 in.	38 in.		40 in.	26 in.	36 in.	29 in.	18 in.

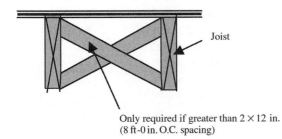

Joist

Only required if greater than 2 × 12 in.
(8 ft-0 in. O.C. spacing)

Fig. 6-16 *Floor/ceiling joist bracing.*

JOIST SPANS
Floor Joist Spans—
30-psf Live Load*

Deflection Limits

Table 6-27 *Design Deflection Requirements*

Construction	Live Load	Snow or Wind Load	Dead plus Live Load
Roof members:			
Supporting plaster ceiling	L/360	L/360	L/240
Supporting nonplaster ceiling	L/240	L/240	L/180
Not supporting ceiling	L/180	L/180	L/120
Floor members	L/360	—	L/240
Exterior walls and interior partitions:			
With brittle finishes	—	L/240	—
With flexible finishes	—	L/120	—
Farm buildings	—	—	L/180
Greenhouses	—	—	L/120

Table 6-28 *Maximum Allowable Deflections (Computed)*

Span	L/180	L/240	L/360
15	1 in.	¾ in.	½ in.
16	1¹⁄₁₆ in.	¹³⁄₁₆ in.	¹⁷⁄₃₂ in.
17	1⅛ in.	²⁷⁄₃₂ in.	⁹⁄₁₆ in.
18	1³⁄₁₆ in.	²⁹⁄₃₂ in.	¹⁹⁄₃₂ in.
19	1⁹⁄₃₂ in.	¹⁵⁄₁₆ in.	⅝ in.
20	1¹¹⁄₃₂ in.	1 in.	²¹⁄₃₂ in.
21	1¹³⁄₃₂ in.	1¹⁄₁₆ in.	¹¹⁄₁₆ in.
22	1¹⁵⁄₃₂ in.	1³⁄₃₂ in.	²³⁄₃₂ in.
23	1¹⁷⁄₃₂ in.	1⁵⁄₃₂ in.	³⁵⁄₃₂ in.
24	1¹⁹⁄₃₂ in.	1³⁄₁₆ in.	¹³⁄₁₆ in.
25	1²¹⁄₃₂ in.	1¼ in.	²⁷⁄₃₂ in.
26	1²³⁄₃₂ in.	1⁵⁄₁₆ in.	⅞ in.
27	1¹³⁄₁₆ in.	1¹¹⁄₃₂ in.	²⁹⁄₃₂ in.
28	1⅞ in.	1¹³⁄₃₂ in.	¹⁵⁄₁₆ in.
29	1¹⁵⁄₁₆ in.	1⁷⁄₁₆ in.	³¹⁄₃₂ in.
30	2 in.	1½ in.	1 in.
31	2¹⁄₁₆ in.	1⁹⁄₁₆ in.	1¹⁄₃₂ in.
32	2⅛ in.	1¹⁹⁄₃₂ in.	1¹⁄₁₆ in.

*Residential sleeping areas maximum allowed deflection L/360.

Table 6-29 *Floor Joist—30-psf Live Load;*
Dead Load = 10 psf

Joist Spacing (in.)	Species and Grade		2 × 6 (ft-in.)
	Douglas fir–larch	SS	12-6
	Douglas fir–larch	#1	12-0
	Douglas fir–larch	#2	11-10
	Douglas fir–larch	#3	9-8
	Hem-fir	SS	11-10
	Hem-fir	#1	11-7
	Hem-fir	#2	11-0
12	Hem-fir	#3	9-8
	Southern pine	SS	12-3
	Southern pine	#1	12-0
	Southern pine	#2	11-10
	Southern pine	#3	10-5
	Spruce-pine-fir	SS	11-7
	Spruce-pine-fir	#1	11-3
	Spruce-pine-fir	#2	11-3
	Spruce-pine-fir	#3	9-8
	Douglas fir–larch	SS	11-4
	Douglas fir–larch	#1	10-11
	Douglas fir–larch	#2	10-9
	Douglas fir–larch	#3	8-5
	Hem-fir	SS	10-9
	Hem-fir	#1	10-6
	Hem-fir	#2	10-0
16	Hem-fir	#3	8-5
	Southern pine	SS	11-2
	Southern pine	#1	10-11
	Southern pine	#2	10-9
	Southern pine	#3	9-0
	Spruce-pine-fir	SS	10-6
	Spruce-pine-fir	#1	10-3
	Spruce-pine-fir	#2	10-3
	Spruce-pine-fir	#3	8-5
	Douglas fir–larch	SS	9-11
	Douglas fir–larch	#1	9-7
	Douglas fir–larch	#2	9-1
	Douglas fir–larch	#3	6-10
	Hem-fir	SS	9-4
	Hem-fir	#1	9-2
	Hem-fir	#2	8-9
24	Hem-fir	#3	6-10
	Southern pine	SS	9-9
	Southern pine	#1	9-7
	Southern pine	#2	9-4
	Southern pine	#3	7-4
	Spruce-pine-fir	SS	9-2
	Spruce-pine-fir	#1	8-11
	Spruce-pine-fir	#2	8-11
	Spruce-pine-fir	#3	6-10

Table 6-30 *Floor Joist—30-psf Live Load;*
Dead Load = 10 psf

Joist Spacing (in.)	Species and Grade		2 × 8 (ft-in.)
	Douglas fir–larch	SS	16-6
	Douglas fir–larch	#1	15-10
	Douglas fir–larch	#2	15-7
	Douglas fir–larch	#3	12-4
	Hem-fir	SS	15-7
	Hem-fir	#1	15-3
	Hem-fir	#2	14-6
12	Hem-fir	#3	12-4
	Southern pine	SS	16-2
	Southern pine	#1	15-10
	Southern pine	#2	15-7
	Southern pine	#3	13-3
	Spruce-pine-fir	SS	15-3
	Spruce-pine-fir	#1	14-11
	Spruce-pine-fir	#2	14-11
	Spruce-pine-fir	#3	12-4
	Douglas fir–larch	SS	15-0
	Douglas fir–larch	#1	14-5
	Douglas fir–larch	#2	14-1
	Douglas fir–larch	#3	10-8
	Hem-fir	SS	14-2
	Hem-fir	#1	13-10
	Hem-fir	#2	13-2
16	Hem-fir	#3	10-8
	Southern pine	SS	14-8
	Southern pine	#1	14-5
	Southern pine	#2	14-2
	Southern pine	#3	11-6
	Spruce-pine-fir	SS	13-10
	Spruce-pine-fir	#1	13-6
	Spruce-pine-fir	#2	13-6
	Spruce-pine-fir	#3	10-8
	Douglas fir–larch	SS	13-1
	Douglas fir–larch	#1	12-4
	Douglas fir–larch	#2	11-6
	Douglas fir–larch	#3	8-8
	Hem-fir	SS	12-4
	Hem-fir	#1	12-0
	Hem-fir	#2	11-4
24	Hem-fir	#3	8-8
	Southern pine	SS	12-10
	Southern pine	#1	12-7
	Southern pine	#2	12-4
	Southern pine	#3	9-5
	Spruce-pine-fir	SS	12-1
	Spruce-pine-fir	#1	11-6
	Spruce-pine-fir	#2	11-6
	Spruce-pine-fir	#3	8-8

Table 6-31 *Floor Joist—30-psf Live Load; Dead Load = 10 psf*

Joist Spacing (in.)	Species and Grade		2 × 10 (ft-in.)
12	Douglas fir–larch	SS	21-0
	Douglas fir–larch	#1	20-3
	Douglas fir–larch	#2	19-10
	Douglas fir–larch	#3	15-0
	Hem-fir	SS	19-10
	Hem-fir	#1	19-5
	Hem-fir	#2	18-6
	Hem-fir	#3	15-0
	Southern pine	SS	20-8
	Southern pine	#1	20-3
	Southern pine	#2	19-10
	Southern pine	#3	15-8
	Spruce-pine-fir	SS	19-5
	Spruce-pine-fir	#1	19-0
	Spruce-pine-fir	#2	19-0
	Spruce-pine-fir	#3	15-0
16	Douglas fir–larch	SS	19-1
	Douglas fir–larch	#1	18-5
	Douglas fir–larch	#2	17-2
	Douglas fir–larch	#3	13-0
	Hem-fir	SS	18-0
	Hem-fir	#1	17-8
	Hem-fir	#2	16-10
	Hem-fir	#3	13-0
	Southern pine	SS	18-9
	Southern pine	#1	18-5
	Southern pine	#2	18-0
	Southern pine	#3	13-7
	Spruce-pine-fir	SS	17-8
	Spruce-pine-fir	#1	17-2
	Spruce-pine-fir	#2	17-2
	Spruce-pine-fir	#3	13-0
24	Douglas fir–larch	SS	16-8
	Douglas fir–larch	#1	15-0
	Douglas fir–larch	#2	14-1
	Douglas fir–larch	#3	10-7
	Hem-fir	SS	15-9
	Hem-fir	#1	14-8
	Hem-fir	#2	13-10
	Hem-fir	#3	10-7
	Southern pine	SS	16-5
	Southern pine	#1	16-1
	Southern pine	#2	14-8
	Southern pine	#3	11-1
	Spruce-pine-fir	SS	15-5
	Spruce-pine-fir	#1	14-1
	Spruce-pine-fir	#2	14-1
	Spruce-pine-fir	#3	10-7

Table 6-32 *Floor Joist—30-psf Live Load; Dead Load = 10 psf*

Joist Spacing (in.)	Species and Grade		2 × 12 (ft-in.)
12	Douglas fir–larch	SS	25-7
	Douglas fir–larch	#1	24-8
	Douglas fir–larch	#2	23-0
	Douglas fir–larch	#3	17-5
	Hem-fir	SS	24-2
	Hem-fir	#1	23-7
	Hem-fir	#2	22-6
	Hem-fir	#3	17-5
	Southern pine	SS	25-1
	Southern pine	#1	24-8
	Southern pine	#2	18-8
	Southern pine	#3	18-8
	Spruce-pine-fir	SS	23-7
	Spruce-pine-fir	#1	23-0
	Spruce-pine-fir	#2	23-0
	Spruce-pine-fir	#3	17-5
16	Douglas fir–larch	SS	23-3
	Douglas fir–larch	#1	21-4
	Douglas fir–larch	#2	19-11
	Douglas fir–larch	#3	15-1
	Hem-fir	SS	21-11
	Hem-fir	#1	20-9
	Hem-fir	#2	19-8
	Hem-fir	#3	15-1
	Southern pine	SS	22-10
	Southern pine	#1	22-5
	Southern pine	#2	21-1
	Southern pine	#3	16-2
	Spruce-pine-fir	SS	21-6
	Spruce-pine-fir	#1	19-11
	Spruce-pine-fir	#2	19-11
	Spruce-pine-fir	#3	15-1
24	Douglas fir–larch	SS	20-3
	Douglas fir–larch	#1	17-5
	Douglas fir–larch	#2	16-3
	Douglas fir–larch	#3	12-4
	Hem-fir	SS	19-2
	Hem-fir	#1	17-0
	Hem-fir	#2	16-1
	Hem-fir	#3	12-4
	Southern pine	SS	19-11
	Southern pine	#1	19-6
	Southern pine	#2	17-2
	Southern pine	#3	13-2
	Spruce-pine-fir	SS	18-9
	Spruce-pine-fir	#1	16-3
	Spruce-pine-fir	#2	16-3
	Spruce-pine-fir	#3	12-4

Table 6-33 *Floor Joist—30-psf Live Load; Dead Load = 20 psf*

Joist Spacing (in.)	Species and Grade		2 × 6 (ft-in.)
12	Douglas fir–larch	SS	12-6
	Douglas fir–larch	#1	12-0
	Douglas fir–larch	#2	11-6
	Douglas fir–larch	#3	8-8
	Hem-fir	SS	11-10
	Hem-fir	#1	11-7
	Hem-fir	#2	11-0
	Hem-fir	#3	8-8
	Southern pine	SS	12-3
	Southern pine	#1	12-0
	Southern pine	#2	11-10
	Southern pine	#3	9-4
	Spruce-pine-fir	SS	11-7
	Spruce-pine-fir	#1	11-3
	Spruce-pine-fir	#2	11-3
	Spruce-pine-fir	#3	8-8
16	Douglas fir–larch	SS	11-4
	Douglas fir–larch	#1	10-8
	Douglas fir–larch	#2	9-11
	Douglas fir–larch	#3	7-6
	Hem-fir	SS	10-9
	Hem-fir	#1	10-4
	Hem-fir	#2	9-10
	Hem-fir	#3	7-6
	Southern pine	SS	11-2
	Southern pine	#1	10-11
	Southern pine	#2	10-5
	Southern pine	#3	8-1
	Spruce-pine-fir	SS	10-6
	Spruce-pine-fir	#1	9-11
	Spruce-pine-fir	#2	9-11
	Spruce-pine-fir	#3	7-6
24	Douglas fir–larch	SS	9-11
	Douglas fir–larch	#1	8-8
	Douglas fir–larch	#2	8-1
	Douglas fir–larch	#3	6-2
	Hem-fir	SS	9-4
	Hem-fir	#1	8-6
	Hem-fir	#2	8-0
	Hem-fir	#3	6-2
	Southern pine	SS	9-9
	Southern pine	#1	9-7
	Southern pine	#2	8-6
	Southern pine	#3	6-7
	Spruce-pine-fir	SS	9-2
	Spruce-pine-fir	#1	8-1
	Spruce-pine-fir	#2	8-1
	Spruce-pine-fir	#3	6-2

Table 6-34 *Floor Joist—30-psf Live Load; Dead Load = 20 psf*

Joist Spacing (in.)	Species and Grade		2 × 8 (ft-in.)
12	Douglas fir–larch	SS	16-6
	Douglas fir–larch	#1	15-7
	Douglas fir–larch	#2	14-7
	Douglas fir–larch	#3	11-0
	Hem-fir	SS	15-7
	Hem-fir	#1	15-2
	Hem-fir	#2	14-4
	Hem-fir	#3	11-0
	Southern pine	SS	16-2
	Southern pine	#1	15-10
	Southern pine	#2	15-7
	Southern pine	#3	11-11
	Spruce-pine-fir	SS	15-3
	Spruce-pine-fir	#1	14-7
	Spruce-pine-fir	#2	14-7
	Spruce-pine-fir	#3	11-0
16	Douglas fir–larch	SS	15-0
	Douglas fir–larch	#1	13-6
	Douglas fir–larch	#2	12-7
	Douglas fir–larch	#3	9-6
	Hem-fir	SS	14-2
	Hem-fir	#1	13-1
	Hem-fir	#2	12-5
	Hem-fir	#3	9-6
	Southern pine	SS	14-8
	Southern pine	#1	14-5
	Southern pine	#2	13-6
	Southern pine	#3	10-3
	Spruce-pine-fir	SS	13-10
	Spruce-pine-fir	#1	12-7
	Spruce-pine-fir	#2	12-7
	Spruce-pine-fir	#3	9-6
24	Douglas fir–larch	SS	13-1
	Douglas fir–larch	#1	11-0
	Douglas fir–larch	#2	10-3
	Douglas fir–larch	#3	7-9
	Hem-fir	SS	12-4
	Hem-fir	#1	10-9
	Hem-fir	#2	10-2
	Hem-fir	#3	7-9
	Southern pine	SS	12-10
	Southern pine	#1	12-4
	Southern pine	#2	11-0
	Southern pine	#3	8-5
	Spruce-pine-fir	SS	12-1
	Spruce-pine-fir	#1	10-3
	Spruce-pine-fir	#2	10-3
	Spruce-pine-fir	#3	7-9

Table 6-35 *Floor Joist—30-psf Live Load; Dead Load = 20 psf*

Joist Spacing (in.)	Species and Grade		2 × 10 (ft-in.)
12	Douglas fir–larch	SS	21-0
	Douglas fir–larch	#1	19-0
	Douglas fir–larch	#2	17-9
	Douglas fir–larch	#3	13-5
	Hem-fir	SS	19-10
	Hem-fir	#1	18-6
	Hem-fir	#2	17-6
	Hem-fir	#3	13-5
	Southern pine	SS	20-8
	Southern pine	#1	20-3
	Southern pine	#2	18-7
	Southern pine	#3	14-0
	Spruce-pine-fir	SS	19-5
	Spruce-pine-fir	#1	17-9
	Spruce-pine-fir	#2	17-9
	Spruce-pine-fir	#3	13-5
16	Douglas fir–larch	SS	19-1
	Douglas fir–larch	#1	16-5
	Douglas fir–larch	#2	15-5
	Douglas fir–larch	#3	11-8
	Hem-fir	SS	18-0
	Hem-fir	#1	16-0
	Hem-fir	#2	15-2
	Hem-fir	#3	11-8
	Southern pine	SS	18-9
	Southern pine	#1	17-11
	Southern pine	#2	16-1
	Southern pine	#3	12-2
	Spruce-pine-fir	SS	17-8
	Spruce-pine-fir	#1	15-5
	Spruce-pine-fir	#2	15-5
	Spruce-pine-fir	#3	11-8
24	Douglas fir–larch	SS	16-2
	Douglas fir–larch	#1	13-5
	Douglas fir–larch	#2	12-7
	Douglas fir–larch	#3	9-6
	Hem-fir	SS	15-9
	Hem-fir	#1	13-1
	Hem-fir	#2	12-5
	Hem-fir	#3	9-6
	Southern pine	SS	16-5
	Southern pine	#1	14-7
	Southern pine	#2	13-1
	Southern pine	#3	9-11
	Spruce-pine-fir	SS	15-0
	Spruce-pine-fir	#1	12-7
	Spruce-pine-fir	#2	12-7
	Spruce-pine-fir	#3	9-6

Table 6-36 *Floor Joist—30-psf Live Load; Dead Load = 20 psf*

Joist Spacing (in.)	Species and Grade		2 × 12 (ft-in.)
12	Douglas fir–larch	SS	25-7
	Douglas fir–larch	#1	22-0
	Douglas fir–larch	#2	20-7
	Douglas fir–larch	#3	15-7
	Hem-fir	SS	24-2
	Hem-fir	#1	21-6
	Hem-fir	#2	20-4
	Hem-fir	#3	15-7
	Southern pine	SS	25-1
	Southern pine	#1	24-8
	Southern pine	#2	21-9
	Southern pine	#3	16-8
	Spruce-pine-fir	SS	23-7
	Spruce-pine-fir	#1	20-7
	Spruce-pine-fir	#2	20-7
	Spruce-pine-fir	#3	15-7
16	Douglas fir–larch	SS	23-0
	Douglas fir–larch	#1	19-1
	Douglas fir–larch	#2	17-10
	Douglas fir–larch	#3	13-6
	Hem-fir	SS	21-11
	Hem-fir	#1	18-7
	Hem-fir	#2	17-7
	Hem-fir	#3	13-6
	Southern pine	SS	22-10
	Southern pine	#1	21-4
	Southern pine	#2	18-10
	Southern pine	#3	14-6
	Spruce-pine-fir	SS	21-4
	Spruce-pine-fir	#1	17-10
	Spruce-pine-fir	#2	17-10
	Spruce-pine-fir	#3	13-6
24	Douglas fir–larch	SS	18-9
	Douglas fir–larch	#1	15-7
	Douglas fir–larch	#2	14-7
	Douglas fir–larch	#3	11-0
	Hem-fir	SS	18-5
	Hem-fir	#1	15-2
	Hem-fir	#2	14-4
	Hem-fir	#3	11-0
	Southern pine	SS	19-11
	Southern pine	#1	17-5
	Southern pine	#2	15-5
	Southern pine	#3	11-10
	Spruce-pine-fir	SS	17-5
	Spruce-pine-fir	#1	14-7
	Spruce-pine-fir	#2	14-7
	Spruce-pine-fir	#3	11-0

Joist Spans for Areas Requiring Maximum Deflection L/360*

Table 6-37 *Floor Joist—40-psf Live Load; Dead Load = 10 psf*

Joist Spacing (in.)	Species and Grade		2 × 6 (ft-in.)
12	Douglas fir–larch	SS	11-4
	Douglas fir–larch	#1	10-11
	Douglas fir–larch	#2	10-9
	Douglas fir–larch	#3	8-8
	Hem-fir	SS	10-9
	Hem-fir	#1	10-6
	Hem-fir	#2	10-0
	Hem-fir	#3	8-8
	Southern pine	SS	11-2
	Southern pine	#1	10-11
	Southern pine	#2	10-9
	Southern pine	#3	9-4
	Spruce-pine-fir	SS	10-6
	Spruce-pine-fir	#1	10-3
	Spruce-pine-fir	#2	10-3
	Spruce-pine-fir	#3	8-8
16	Douglas fir–larch	SS	10-4
	Douglas fir–larch	#1	9-11
	Douglas fir–larch	#2	9-9
	Douglas fir–larch	#3	7-6
	Hem-fir	SS	9-9
	Hem-fir	#1	9-6
	Hem-fir	#2	9-1
	Hem-fir	#3	7-6
	Southern pine	SS	10-2
	Southern pine	#1	9-11
	Southern pine	#2	9-9
	Southern pine	#3	8-1
	Spruce-pine-fir	SS	9-6
	Spruce-pine-fir	#1	9-4
	Spruce-pine-fir	#2	9-4
	Spruce-pine-fir	#3	7-6
24	Douglas fir–larch	SS	9-0
	Douglas fir–larch	#1	8-8
	Douglas fir–larch	#2	8-1
	Douglas fir–larch	#3	6-2
	Hem-fir	SS	8-6
	Hem-fir	#1	8-4
	Hem-fir	#2	7-11
	Hem-fir	#3	6-2
	Southern pine	SS	8-10
	Southern pine	#1	8-8
	Southern pine	#2	8-6
	Southern pine	#3	6-7
	Spruce-pine-fir	SS	8-4
	Spruce-pine-fir	#1	8-1
	Spruce-pine-fir	#2	8-1
	Spruce-pine-fir	#3	6-2

*Floor joist spans—40-psf live load.

Table 6-38 *Floor Joist—40-psf Live Load; Dead Load = 10 psf*

Joist Spacing (in.)	Species and Grade		2 × 8 (ft-in.)
12	Douglas fir–larch	SS	15-0
	Douglas fir–larch	#1	14-5
	Douglas fir–larch	#2	14-2
	Douglas fir–larch	#3	11-0
	Hem-fir	SS	14-2
	Hem-fir	#1	13-10
	Hem-fir	#2	13-2
	Hem-fir	#3	11-0
	Southern pine	SS	14-8
	Southern pine	#1	14-5
	Southern pine	#2	14-2
	Southern pine	#3	11-11
	Spruce-pine-fir	SS	13-10
	Spruce-pine-fir	#1	13-6
	Spruce-pine-fir	#2	13-6
	Spruce-pine-fir	#3	11-0
16	Douglas fir–larch	SS	13-7
	Douglas fir–larch	#1	13-1
	Douglas fir–larch	#2	12-7
	Douglas fir–larch	#3	9-6
	Hem-fir	SS	12-10
	Hem-fir	#1	12-7
	Hem-fir	#2	12-0
	Hem-fir	#3	9-6
	Southern pine	SS	13-4
	Southern pine	#1	13-1
	Southern pine	#2	12-10
	Southern pine	#3	10-3
	Spruce-pine-fir	SS	12-7
	Spruce-pine-fir	#1	12-3
	Spruce-pine-fir	#2	12-3
	Spruce-pine-fir	#3	9-6
24	Douglas fir–larch	SS	11-11
	Douglas fir–larch	#1	11-0
	Douglas fir–larch	#2	10-3
	Douglas fir–larch	#3	7-9
	Hem-fir	SS	11-3
	Hem-fir	#1	10-9
	Hem-fir	#2	10-2
	Hem-fir	#3	7-9
	Southern pine	SS	11-8
	Southern pine	#1	11-5
	Southern pine	#2	11-0
	Southern pine	#3	8-5
	Spruce-pine-fir	SS	11-0
	Spruce-pine-fir	#1	10-3
	Spruce-pine-fir	#2	10-3
	Spruce-pine-fir	#3	7-9

Table 6-39 *Floor Joist—40-psf Live Load; Dead Load = 10 psf*

Joist Spacing (in.)	Species and Grade		2 × 10 (ft-in.)
12	Douglas fir–larch	SS	19-1
	Douglas fir–larch	#1	18-5
	Douglas fir–larch	#2	17-9
	Douglas fir–larch	#3	13-5
	Hem-fir	SS	18-0
	Hem-fir	#1	17-8
	Hem-fir	#2	16-10
	Hem-fir	#3	13-5
	Southern pine	SS	18-9
	Southern pine	#1	18-5
	Southern pine	#2	18-0
	Southern pine	#3	14-0
	Spruce-pine-fir	SS	17-8
	Spruce-pine-fir	#1	17-3
	Spruce-pine-fir	#2	17-3
	Spruce-pine-fir	#3	13-5
16	Douglas fir–larch	SS	17-4
	Douglas fir–larch	#1	16-5
	Douglas fir–larch	#2	15-5
	Douglas fir–larch	#3	11-8
	Hem-fir	SS	16-5
	Hem-fir	#1	16-0
	Hem-fir	#2	15-2
	Hem-fir	#3	11-8
	Southern pine	SS	17-0
	Southern pine	#1	16-9
	Southern pine	#2	16-1
	Southern pine	#3	12-2
	Spruce-pine-fir	SS	16-0
	Spruce-pine-fir	#1	15-5
	Spruce-pine-fir	#2	15-5
	Spruce-pine-fir	#3	11-8
24	Douglas fir–larch	SS	15-2
	Douglas fir–larch	#1	13-5
	Douglas fir–larch	#2	12-7
	Douglas fir–larch	#3	9-6
	Hem-fir	SS	14-4
	Hem-fir	#1	13-1
	Hem-fir	#2	12-5
	Hem-fir	#3	9-6
	Southern pine	SS	14-11
	Southern pine	#1	14-7
	Southern pine	#2	13-1
	Southern pine	#3	9-11
	Spruce-pine-fir	SS	14-0
	Spruce-pine-fir	#1	12-7
	Spruce-pine-fir	#2	12-7
	Spruce-pine-fir	#3	9-6

Table 6-40 *Floor Joist—40-psf Live Load; Dead Load = 10 psf*

Joist Spacing (in.)	Species and Grade		2 × 12 (ft-in.)
12	Douglas fir–larch	SS	23-3
	Douglas fir–larch	#1	22-0
	Douglas fir–larch	#2	20-7
	Douglas fir–larch	#3	15-7
	Hem-fir	SS	21-11
	Hem-fir	#1	21-6
	Hem-fir	#2	20-4
	Hem-fir	#3	15-7
	Southern pine	SS	22-10
	Southern pine	#1	22-5
	Southern pine	#2	21-9
	Southern pine	#3	16-8
	Spruce-pine-fir	SS	21-6
	Spruce-pine-fir	#1	20-7
	Spruce-pine-fir	#2	20-7
	Spruce-pine-fir	#3	15-7
16	Douglas fir–larch	SS	21-1
	Douglas fir–larch	#1	19-1
	Douglas fir–larch	#2	17-10
	Douglas fir–larch	#3	13-6
	Hem-fir	SS	19-11
	Hem-fir	#1	18-7
	Hem-fir	#2	17-7
	Hem-fir	#3	13-6
	Southern pine	SS	20-9
	Southern pine	#1	20-4
	Southern pine	#2	18-10
	Southern pine	#3	14-6
	Spruce-pine-fir	SS	19-6
	Spruce-pine-fir	#1	17-10
	Spruce-pine-fir	#2	17-10
	Spruce-pine-fir	#3	13-6
24	Douglas fir–larch	SS	18-5
	Douglas fir–larch	#1	15-7
	Douglas fir–larch	#2	14-7
	Douglas fir–larch	#3	11-0
	Hem-fir	SS	17-5
	Hem-fir	#1	15-2
	Hem-fir	#2	14-4
	Hem-fir	#3	11-0
	Southern pine	SS	18-1
	Southern pine	#1	17-5
	Southern pine	#2	15-5
	Southern pine	#3	11-10
	Spruce-pine-fir	SS	17-0
	Spruce-pine-fir	#1	14-7
	Spruce-pine-fir	#2	14-7
	Spruce-pine-fir	#3	11-0

Table 6-41 Floor Joist—40-psf Live Load; Dead Load = 20 psf

Joist Spacing (in.)	Species and Grade		2 × 6 (ft-in.)
12	Douglas fir–larch	SS	11-4
	Douglas fir–larch	#1	10-11
	Douglas fir–larch	#2	10-6
	Douglas fir–larch	#3	7-11
	Hem-fir	SS	10-9
	Hem-fir	#1	10-6
	Hem-fir	#2	10-0
	Hem-fir	#3	7-11
	Southern pine	SS	11-2
	Southern pine	#1	10-11
	Southern pine	#2	10-9
	Southern pine	#3	8-6
	Spruce-pine-fir	SS	10-6
	Spruce-pine-fir	#1	10-3
	Spruce-pine-fir	#2	10-3
	Spruce-pine-fir	#3	7-11
16	Douglas fir–larch	SS	10-4
	Douglas fir–larch	#1	9-8
	Douglas fir–larch	#2	9-1
	Douglas fir–larch	#3	6-10
	Hem-fir	SS	9-9
	Hem-fir	#1	9-6
	Hem-fir	#2	8-11
	Hem-fir	#3	6-10
	Southern pine	SS	10-2
	Southern pine	#1	9-11
	Southern pine	#2	9-6
	Southern pine	#3	7-4
	Spruce-pine-fir	SS	9-6
	Spruce-pine-fir	#1	9-1
	Spruce-pine-fir	#2	9-1
	Spruce-pine-fir	#3	6-10
24	Douglas fir–larch	SS	9-0
	Douglas fir–larch	#1	7-11
	Douglas fir–larch	#2	7-5
	Douglas fir–larch	#3	5-7
	Hem-fir	SS	8-6
	Hem-fir	#1	7-9
	Hem-fir	#2	7-4
	Hem-fir	#3	5-7
	Southern pine	SS	8-10
	Southern pine	#1	8-8
	Southern pine	#2	7-9
	Southern pine	#3	6-0
	Spruce-pine-fir	SS	8-4
	Spruce-pine-fir	#1	7-5
	Spruce-pine-fir	#2	7-5
	Spruce-pine-fir	#3	5-7

Table 6-42 Floor Joist—40-psf Live Load; Dead Load = 20 psf

Joist Spacing (in.)	Species and Grade		2 × 8 (ft-in.)
12	Douglas fir–larch	SS	15-0
	Douglas fir–larch	#1	14-2
	Douglas fir–larch	#2	13-3
	Douglas fir–larch	#3	10-0
	Hem-fir	SS	14-2
	Hem-fir	#1	13-10
	Hem-fir	#2	13-1
	Hem-fir	#3	10-0
	Southern pine	SS	14-8
	Southern pine	#1	14-5
	Southern pine	#2	14-2
	Southern pine	#3	10-10
	Spruce-pine-fir	SS	13-10
	Spruce-pine-fir	#1	13-3
	Spruce-pine-fir	#2	13-3
	Spruce-pine-fir	#3	10-0
16	Douglas fir–larch	SS	13-7
	Douglas fir–larch	#1	12-4
	Douglas fir–larch	#2	11-6
	Douglas fir–larch	#3	8-8
	Hem-fir	SS	12-10
	Hem-fir	#1	12-0
	Hem-fir	#2	11-4
	Hem-fir	#3	8-8
	Southern pine	SS	13-4
	Southern pine	#1	13-1
	Southern pine	#2	12-4
	Southern pine	#3	9-5
	Spruce-pine-fir	SS	12-7
	Spruce-pine-fir	#1	11-6
	Spruce-pine-fir	#2	11-6
	Spruce-pine-fir	#3	8-8
24	Douglas fir–larch	SS	11-11
	Douglas fir–larch	#1	10-0
	Douglas fir–larch	#2	9-5
	Douglas fir–larch	#3	7-1
	Hem-fir	SS	11-3
	Hem-fir	#1	9-9
	Hem-fir	#2	9-3
	Hem-fir	#3	7-1
	Southern pine	SS	11-8
	Southern pine	#1	11-3
	Southern pine	#2	10-0
	Southern pine	#3	7-8
	Spruce-pine-fir	SS	11-0
	Spruce-pine-fir	#1	9-5
	Spruce-pine-fir	#2	9-5
	Spruce-pine-fir	#3	7-1

Table 6-43 *Floor Joist—40-psf Live Load;*
Dead Load = 20 psf

Joist Spacing (in.)	Species and Grade		2 × 10 (ft-in.)
12	Douglas fir–larch	SS	19-1
	Douglas fir–larch	#1	17-4
	Douglas fir–larch	#2	16-3
	Douglas fir–larch	#3	12-3
	Hem-fir	SS	18-0
	Hem-fir	#1	16-11
	Hem-fir	#2	16-0
	Hem-fir	#3	12-3
	Southern pine	SS	18-9
	Southern pine	#1	18-5
	Southern pine	#2	16-11
	Southern pine	#3	12-10
	Spruce-pine-fir	SS	17-8
	Spruce-pine-fir	#1	16-3
	Spruce-pine-fir	#2	16-3
	Spruce-pine-fir	#3	12-3
16	Douglas fir–larch	SS	17-4
	Douglas fir–larch	#1	15-0
	Douglas fir–larch	#2	14-1
	Douglas fir–larch	#3	10-7
	Hem-fir	SS	16-5
	Hem-fir	#1	14-8
	Hem-fir	#2	13-10
	Hem-fir	#3	10-7
	Southern pine	SS	17-0
	Southern pine	#1	16-4
	Southern pine	#2	14-8
	Southern pine	#3	11-1
	Spruce-pine-fir	SS	16-0
	Spruce-pine-fir	#1	14-1
	Spruce-pine-fir	#2	14-1
	Spruce-pine-fir	#3	10-7
24	Douglas fir–larch	SS	14-9
	Douglas fir–larch	#1	12-3
	Douglas fir–larch	#2	11-6
	Douglas fir–larch	#3	8-8
	Hem-fir	SS	14-4
	Hem-fir	#1	11-11
	Hem-fir	#2	11-4
	Hem-fir	#3	8-8
	Southern pine	SS	14-11
	Southern pine	#1	13-4
	Southern pine	#2	12-0
	Southern pine	#3	9-1
	Spruce-pine-fir	SS	13-8
	Spruce-pine-fir	#1	11-6
	Spruce-pine-fir	#2	11-6
	Spruce-pine-fir	#3	8-8

Table 6-44 *Floor Joist—40-psf Live Load;*
Dead Load = 20 psf

Joist Spacing (in.)	Species and Grade		2 × 12 (ft-in.)
12	Douglas fir–larch	SS	23-3
	Douglas fir–larch	#1	20-1
	Douglas fir–larch	#2	18-10
	Douglas fir–larch	#3	14-3
	Hem-fir	SS	21-11
	Hem-fir	#1	19-7
	Hem-fir	#2	18-6
	Hem-fir	#3	14-3
	Southern pine	SS	22-10
	Southern pine	#1	22-5
	Southern pine	#2	19-10
	Southern pine	#3	15-3
	Spruce-pine-fir	SS	21-6
	Spruce-pine-fir	#1	18-10
	Spruce-pine-fir	#2	18-10
	Spruce-pine-fir	#3	14-3
16	Douglas fir–larch	SS	21-0
	Douglas fir–larch	#1	17-5
	Douglas fir–larch	#2	16-3
	Douglas fir–larch	#3	12-4
	Hem-fir	SS	19-11
	Hem-fir	#1	17-0
	Hem-fir	#2	16-1
	Hem-fir	#3	12-4
	Southern pine	SS	20-9
	Southern pine	#1	19-6
	Southern pine	#2	17-2
	Southern pine	#3	13-2
	Spruce-pine-fir	SS	19-6
	Spruce-pine-fir	#1	16-3
	Spruce-pine-fir	#2	16-3
	Spruce-pine-fir	#3	12-4
24	Douglas fir–larch	SS	17-1
	Douglas fir–larch	#1	14-3
	Douglas fir–larch	#2	13-4
	Douglas fir–larch	#3	10-1
	Hem-fir	SS	16-10
	Hem-fir	#1	13-10
	Hem-fir	#2	13-1
	Hem-fir	#3	10-1
	Southern pine	SS	18-1
	Southern pine	#1	15-11
	Southern pine	#2	14-0
	Southern pine	#3	10-9
	Spruce-pine-fir	SS	15-11
	Spruce-pine-fir	#1	13-4
	Spruce-pine-fir	#2	13-4
	Spruce-pine-fir	#3	10-1

Ceiling Joist Spans

Table 6-45 Ceiling Joist Spans 2 × 6
(uninhabitable attics without storage;
live load = 10 psf, dead load = 5 psf, L/240)

Ceiling Joist Spacing (in.)	Species and Grade		2 × 6 (ft-in.)
12	Douglas fir–larch	SS	20-8
	Douglas fir–larch	#1	19-11
	Douglas fir–larch	#2	19-6
	Douglas fir–larch	#3	15-10
	Hem-fir	SS	19-6
	Hem-fir	#1	19-1
	Hem-fir	#2	18-2
	Hem-fir	#3	15-10
	Southern pine	SS	20-3
	Southern pine	#1	19-11
	Southern pine	#2	19-6
	Southern pine	#3	17-0
	Spruce-pine-fir	SS	19-1
	Spruce-pine-fir	#1	18-8
	Spruce-pine-fir	#2	18-8
	Spruce-pine-fir	#3	15-10
16	Douglas fir–larch	SS	18-9
	Douglas fir–larch	#1	18-1
	Douglas fir–larch	#2	17-8
	Douglas fir–larch	#3	13-9
	Hem-fir	SS	17-8
	Hem-fir	#1	17-4
	Hem-fir	#2	16-6
	Hem-fir	#3	13-9
	Southern pine	SS	18-5
	Southern pine	#1	18-1
	Southern pine	#2	17-8
	Southern pine	#3	14-9
	Spruce-pine-fir	SS	17-4
	Spruce-pine-fir	#1	16-11
	Spruce-pine-fir	#2	16-11
	Spruce-pine-fir	#3	13-9
24	Douglas fir–larch	SS	16-4
	Douglas fir–larch	#1	15-9
	Douglas fir–larch	#2	14-10
	Douglas fir–larch	#3	11-2
	Hem-fir	SS	15-6
	Hem-fir	#1	15-2
	Hem-fir	#2	14-5
	Hem-fir	#3	11-2
	Southern pine	SS	16-1
	Southern pine	#1	15-9
	Southern pine	#2	15-6
	Southern pine	#3	12-0
	Spruce-pine-fir	SS	15-2
	Spruce-pine-fir	#1	14-9
	Spruce-pine-fir	#2	14-9
	Spruce-pine-fir	#3	11-2

Note: Check availability of lumber over 20 ft in length.

Table 6-46 Ceiling Joist Spans 2 × 8
(uninhabitable attics without storage;
live load = 10 psf, dead load = 5 psf, L/240)

Ceiling Joist Spacing (in.)	Species and Grade		2 × 8 (ft-in.)
12	Douglas fir–larch	SS	See note
	Douglas fir–larch	#1	See note
	Douglas fir–larch	#2	25-8
	Douglas fir–larch	#3	20-1
	Hem-fir	SS	25-8
	Hem-fir	#1	25-2
	Hem-fir	#2	24-0
	Hem-fir	#3	20-1
	Southern pine	SS	See note
	Southern pine	#1	See note
	Southern pine	#2	25-8
	Southern pine	#3	21-8
	Spruce-pine-fir	SS	25-2
	Spruce-pine-fir	#1	24-7
	Spruce-pine-fir	#2	24-7
	Spruce-pine-fir	#3	20-1
16	Douglas fir–larch	SS	24-8
	Douglas fir–larch	#1	23-10
	Douglas fir–larch	#2	23-0
	Douglas fir–larch	#3	17-5
	Hem-fir	SS	23-4
	Hem-fir	#1	22-10
	Hem-fir	#2	21-9
	Hem-fir	#3	17-5
	Southern pine	SS	24-3
	Southern pine	#1	23-1
	Southern pine	#2	23-4
	Southern pine	#3	18-9
	Spruce-pine-fir	SS	22-10
	Spruce-pine-fir	#1	22-4
	Spruce-pine-fir	#2	22-4
	Spruce-pine-fir	#3	17-5
24	Douglas fir–larch	SS	21-7
	Douglas fir–larch	#1	20-1
	Douglas fir–larch	#2	18-9
	Douglas fir–larch	#3	14-2
	Hem-fir	SS	20-5
	Hem-fir	#1	19-7
	Hem-fir	#2	18-6
	Hem-fir	#3	14-2
	Southern pine	SS	21-2
	Southern pine	#1	20-10
	Southern pine	#2	20-1
	Southern pine	#3	15-4
	Spruce-pine-fir	SS	19-11
	Spruce-pine-fir	#1	18-9
	Spruce-pine-fir	#2	18-9
	Spruce-pine-fir	#3	14-2

Note: Check availability of lumber over 20 ft in length.

Table 6-47 *Ceiling Joist Spans 2 × 10*
(uninhabitable attics without storage;
live load = 10 psf, dead load = 5 psf, L/240)

Ceiling Joist Spacing (in.)	Species and Grade		2 × 10 (ft-in.)
12	Douglas fir–larch	SS	See note
	Douglas fir–larch	#1	See note
	Douglas fir–larch	#2	See note
	Douglas fir–larch	#3	24-6
	Hem-fir	SS	See note
	Hem-fir	#1	See note
	Hem-fir	#2	See note
	Hem-fir	#3	24-6
	Southern pine	SS	See note
	Southern pine	#1	See note
	Southern pine	#2	See note
	Southern pine	#3	25-7
	Spruce-pine-fir	SS	See note
	Spruce-pine-fir	#1	See note
	Spruce-pine-fir	#2	See note
	Spruce-pine-fir	#3	24-6
16	Douglas fir–larch	SS	See note
	Douglas fir–larch	#1	See note
	Douglas fir–larch	#2	See note
	Douglas fir–larch	#3	21-3
	Hem-fir	SS	See note
	Hem-fir	#1	See note
	Hem-fir	#2	See note
	Hem-fir	#3	21-3
	Southern pine	SS	See note
	Southern pine	#1	See note
	Southern pine	#2	See note
	Southern pine	#3	22-2
	Spruce-pine-fir	SS	See note
	Spruce-pine-fir	#1	See note
	Spruce-pine-fir	#2	See note
	Spruce-pine-fir	#3	21-3
24	Douglas fir–larch	SS	See note
	Douglas fir–larch	#1	24-6
	Douglas fir–larch	#2	22-11
	Douglas fir–larch	#3	17-4
	Hem-fir	SS	See note
	Hem-fir	#1	23-11
	Hem-fir	#2	22-7
	Hem-fir	#3	17-4
	Southern pine	SS	See note
	Southern pine	#1	See note
	Southern pine	#2	23-11
	Southern pine	#3	18-1
	Spruce-pine-fir	SS	25-5
	Spruce-pine-fir	#1	22-11
	Spruce-pine-fir	#2	22-11
	Spruce-pine-fir	#3	17-4

Note: Check availability of lumber over 20 ft in length.

Table 6-48 *Ceiling Joist Spans 2 × 6*
(uninhabitable attics with limited storage;
live load = 10 psf, dead load = 10 psf, L/240)

Ceiling Joist Spacing (in.)	Species and Grade		2 × 6 (ft-in.)
12	Douglas fir–larch	SS	16-4
	Douglas fir–larch	#1	15-9
	Douglas fir–larch	#2	14-10
	Douglas fir–larch	#3	11-2
	Hem-fir	SS	15-6
	Hem-fir	#1	15-2
	Hem-fir	#2	14-5
	Hem-fir	#3	11-2
	Southern pine	SS	16-1
	Southern pine	#1	15-9
	Southern pine	#2	15-6
	Southern pine	#3	12-0
	Spruce-pine-fir	SS	15-2
	Spruce-pine-fir	#1	14-9
	Spruce-pine-fir	#2	14-9
	Spruce-pine-fir	#3	11-2
16	Douglas fir–larch	SS	14-11
	Douglas fir–larch	#1	13-9
	Douglas fir–larch	#2	12-10
	Douglas fir–larch	#3	9-8
	Hem-fir	SS	14-1
	Hem-fir	#1	13-5
	Hem-fir	#2	12-8
	Hem-fir	#3	9-8
	Southern pine	SS	14-7
	Southern pine	#1	14-4
	Southern pine	#2	13-6
	Southern pine	#3	10-5
	Spruce-pine-fir	SS	13-9
	Spruce-pine-fir	#1	12-10
	Spruce-pine-fir	#2	12-10
	Spruce-pine-fir	#3	9-8
24	Douglas fir–larch	SS	13-0
	Douglas fir–larch	#1	11-2
	Douglas fir–larch	#2	10-6
	Douglas fir–larch	#3	7-11
	Hem-fir	SS	12-3
	Hem-fir	#1	10-11
	Hem-fir	#2	10-4
	Hem-fir	#3	7-11
	Southern pine	SS	12-9
	Southern pine	#1	12-6
	Southern pine	#2	11-0
	Southern pine	#3	8-6
	Spruce-pine-fir	SS	12-0
	Spruce-pine-fir	#1	10-6
	Spruce-pine-fir	#2	10-6
	Spruce-pine-fir	#3	

Note: Check availability of lumber over 20 ft in length.

Table 6-49 *Ceiling Joist Spans 2 × 8*
(uninhabitable attics with limited storage;
live load = 10 psf, dead load = 10 psf, L/240)

Ceiling Joist Spacing (in.)	Species and Grade		2 × 8 (ft-in.)
12	Douglas fir–larch	SS	21-7
	Douglas fir–larch	#1	20-1
	Douglas fir–larch	#2	18-9
	Douglas fir–larch	#3	14-2
	Hem-fir	SS	20-5
	Hem-fir	#1	19-7
	Hem-fir	#2	18-6
	Hem-fir	#3	14-2
	Southern pine	SS	21-2
	Southern pine	#1	20-10
	Southern pine	#2	20-1
	Southern pine	#3	15-4
	Spruce-pine-fir	SS	19-11
	Spruce-pine-fir	#1	18-9
	Spruce-pine-fir	#2	18-9
	Spruce-pine-fir	#3	14-2
16	Douglas fir–larch	SS	19-7
	Douglas fir–larch	#1	17-5
	Douglas fir–larch	#2	16-3
	Douglas fir–larch	#3	12-4
	Hem-fir	SS	18-6
	Hem-fir	#1	16-10
	Hem-fir	#2	16-0
	Hem-fir	#3	12-4
	Southern pine	SS	19-3
	Southern pine	#1	18-11
	Southern pine	#2	17-5
	Southern pine	#3	13-3
	Spruce-pine-fir	SS	18-1
	Spruce-pine-fir	#1	16-3
	Spruce-pine-fir	#2	16-3
	Spruce-pine-fir	#3	12-4
24	Douglas fir–larch	SS	17-1
	Douglas fir–larch	#1	14-2
	Douglas fir–larch	#2	13-3
	Douglas fir–larch	#3	10-0
	Hem-fir	SS	16-2
	Hem-fir	#1	13-10
	Hem-fir	#2	13-1
	Hem-fir	#3	10-0
	Southern pine	SS	16-10
	Southern pine	#1	15-10
	Southern pine	#2	14-2
	Southern pine	#3	10-10
	Spruce-pine-fir	SS	15-10
	Spruce-pine-fir	#1	13-3
	Spruce-pine-fir	#2	13-3
	Spruce-pine-fir	#3	

Note: Check availability of lumber over 20 ft in length.

Table 6-50 *Ceiling Joist Spans 2 × 10*
(uninhabitable attics with limited storage;
live load = 10 psf, dead load = 10 psf, L/240)

Ceiling Joist Spacing (in.)	Species and Grade		2 × 10 (ft-in.)
12	Douglas fir–larch	SS	See note
	Douglas fir–larch	#1	24-6
	Douglas fir–larch	#2	22-11
	Douglas fir–larch	#3	17-4
	Hem-fir	SS	See note
	Hem-fir	#1	23-11
	Hem-fir	#2	22-7
	Hem-fir	#3	17-4
	Southern pine	SS	See note
	Southern pine	#1	See note
	Southern pine	#2	23-11
	Southern pine	#3	18-1
	Spruce-pine-fir	SS	25-5
	Spruce-pine-fir	#1	22-11
	Spruce-pine-fir	#2	22-11
	Spruce-pine-fir	#3	17-4
16	Douglas fir–larch	SS	25-0
	Douglas fir–larch	#1	21-3
	Douglas fir–larch	#2	19-10
	Douglas fir–larch	#3	15-0
	Hem-fir	SS	23-8
	Hem-fir	#1	20-8
	Hem-fir	#2	19-7
	Hem-fir	#3	15-0
	Southern pine	SS	24-7
	Southern pine	#1	23-1
	Southern pine	#2	20-9
	Southern pine	#3	15-8
	Spruce-pine-fir	SS	23-1
	Spruce-pine-fir	#1	19-10
	Spruce-pine-fir	#2	19-10
	Spruce-pine-fir	#3	15-0
24	Douglas fir–larch	SS	20-11
	Douglas fir–larch	#1	17-4
	Douglas fir–larch	#2	16-3
	Douglas fir–larch	#3	12-3
	Hem-fir	SS	20-6
	Hem-fir	#1	16-11
	Hem-fir	#2	16-0
	Hem-fir	#3	12-3
	Southern pine	SS	21-6
	Southern pine	#1	18-10
	Southern pine	#2	16-11
	Southern pine	#3	12-10
	Spruce-pine-fir	SS	19-5
	Spruce-pine-fir	#1	16-3
	Spruce-pine-fir	#2	16-3
	Spruce-pine-fir	#3	12-3

Note: Check availability of lumber over 20 ft in length.

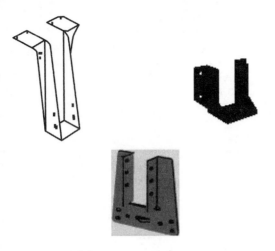

Fig. 6-17 *Typical joist/truss hangers.*

Note: The codes require that the hangers be installed as per the manufacturer's instructions. All require all nailing connections to be thorough and complete in order to comply with their load capabilities. When engineered lumber is used there are additional requirements that the hangers must meet.

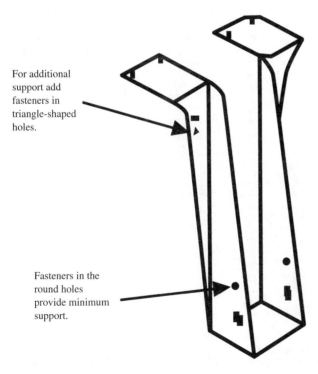

For additional support add fasteners in triangle-shaped holes.

Fasteners in the round holes provide minimum support.

Fig. 6-18 *Typical nailing pattern for joist hanger.*

Note: Special requirements are required when using engineered joists or rafters. Check the manufacturer's installation procedures.

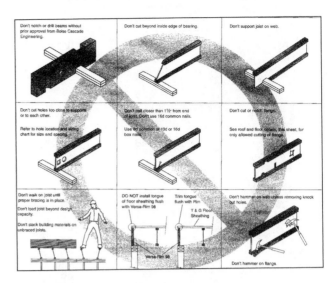

Fig. 6-19 *Typical installation "Don'ts" for engineered joists.*

Engineered Structural Wood

Note: Many builders have found that the wood I joists better suit their needs. Although the codes currently do not specifically address the engineered framing members, they do stipulate that they must be installed as per manufacturer's instructions. The individual builder needs to make sure that their supplier gives them a copy of the maximum allowable cuts, notches, and penetrations that are allowed. Check that the local code enforcement authority in their region has approved their use.

Determining Linear Loading

Square foot load divided by 12 = linear load

Example [40 psf LL + 10 psf DL × 24 (joist spacing)] divided by 12 = linear load

Squash blocks and web stiffeners are used for different purposes. Squash blocks are used to transfer vertical load, while stiffeners are used to increase bearing capacity at the supports.

Squash blocks are typically used when you have a load bearing perpendicular to a joist at an interior support. The squash blocks will transfer the vertical load from the top load-bearing wall to the bottom load-bearing wall, bypassing the joist. Squash blocks are not typically used on joists with load-bearing walls at exterior supports because they lack lateral resistance. Rim board

Table 6-51 AJS™ 20 Allowable Uniform Loads (plf)

Span (ft)	9½ in. Live Load	9½ in. Total Load	11⅞ in. Live Load	11⅞ in. Total Load	14 in. Live Load	14 in. Total Load	16 in. Live Load	16 in. Total Load
6	—	309	—	381	—	381	—	381
7	—	265	—	326	—	326	—	326
8	—	232	—	286	—	286	—	286
9	—	206	—	254	—	254	—	254
10	—	185	—	228	—	228	—	228
11	154	168	—	208	—	208	—	208
12	122	154	—	190	—	190	—	190
13	98	142	160	176	—	176	—	176
14	79	132	130	163	—	163	—	163
15	65	120	108	152	—	152	—	152
16	54	106	90	137	129	143	—	143
17	46	92	76	121	109	134	—	134
18	39	78	65	108	93	127	124	127
19	33	67	55	97	80	117	107	120
20	28	57	48	87	69	105	93	114
21	25	50	41	79	60	96	81	108
22	21	43	36	72	52	87	71	101
23	19	38	32	64	46	80	62	92
24	17	34	28	56	41	—	55	85
25	15	30	25	50	36	67	49	78

Courtesy of Boise Cascade Corporation.

Table 6-52 AJS™ 25 Allowable Uniform Loads (plf)

Span (ft)	9½ in. Live Load	9½ in. Total Load	11⅞ in. Live Load	11⅞ in. Total Load	14 in. Live Load	14 in. Total Load	16 in. Live Load	16 in. Total Load
6	—	309	—	381	—	381	—	381
7	—	265	—	326	—	326	—	326
8	—	—	—	286	—	286	—	286
9	—	206	—	254	—	254	—	254
10	—	185	—	228	—	228	—	228
11	—	168	—	208	—	208	—	208
12	—	154	—	190	—	190	—	190
13	131	142	—	176	—	176	—	176
14	10	132	—	163	—	163	—	163
15	88	123	144	152	—	152	—	152
16	—	116	121	143	—	143	—	143
17	62	109	102	134	—	134	—	134
18	—	103	87	127	124	127	—	127
19	45	91	75	120	107	120	—	120
20	39	79	65	—	93	—	—	114
21	34	68	56	108	81	108	—	108
22	30	60	49	99	71	104	95	104
23	26	52	43	87	63	99	84	99
24	—	46	38	—	—	95	—	95
25	20	41	34	69	49	91	66	91

Notes:

1. Total load values are limited by shear, moment, or total load deflection equal to L/240.
2. Live load values are limited by deflection equal to L/480. For deflection limited to L/360 or L/960, multiply live load value by 1.33 and 0.5, respectively.
3. Both the total load and live load columns must be checked. Where a live load is not shown, the total load value will control.
4. Table values assume no composite action provided by sheathing.
5. Table values assume no repetitive member increase in bending capacities.
6. Total load values assume minimum bearing lengths without web stiffeners for joist depths of 16 in. and less.
7. Table values apply to either simple or continuous span joists. Span is measured center to center of the minimum required bearing length. Analyze continuous span joists with the BC CALC® software if the length of any span is less than half the length of an adjacent span.
8. This table was designed to apply to a broad range of applications. It may be possible to exceed the limitations of this table by analyzing a specific application with the BC CALC® software. For more information visit www.BoiseBuilding.com/EWP.

Table and notes courtesy of Boise Cascade Corporation.

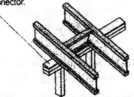

2x beveled plate for slope greater than 1/4"/12. For slope greater than 4/12. use birdsmouth cut or metal connector.

Simpson VPA or Kant-Sag TMP connectors or equal can be used in lieu of beveled plate for slopes from 3/12 to 12/12.

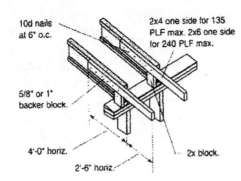

10d nails at 6" o.c.

2x4 one side for 135 PLF max. 2x6 one side for 240 PLF max.

5/8" or 1" backer block.

4'-0" horiz.

2'-6" horiz.

2x block.

Do not bevel-cut joist beyond inside face of wall.

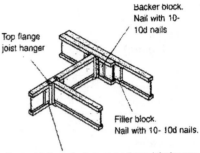

Web stiffener required each side.

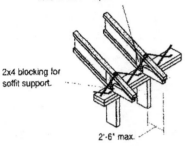

2x4 blocking for soffit support.

2'-6" max.

Web stiffener required each side.

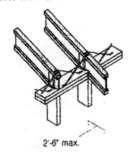

2'-6" max.

Backer block. Nail with 10-10d nails

Top flange joist hanger

Filler block. Nail with 10- 10d nails.

Backer block required where top flange joist hanger load exceeds 250 lbs. Install tight to top flange

Simpson MSTA36 or Kant-Sag MSTA36 strap with 26-10d nails where slope exceeds 7/12.

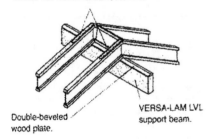

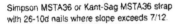

Double-beveled wood plate.

VERSA-LAM LVL support beam.

VERSA-LAM LVL support beam.

Simpson MSTA36 or Kant-Sag MSTA36 strap with 26-10d nails where slope exceeds 7/12.

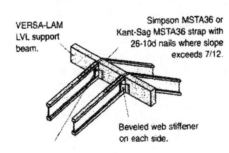

Beveled web stiffener on each side.

Web stiffener required each side.

Birdsmouth cut permitted at low end only.

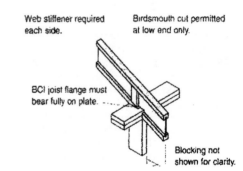

BCI joist flange must bear fully on plate.

Blocking not shown for clarity.

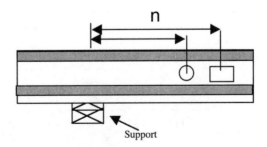

n

Support

Fig. 6-20 Engineered rafters.

are typically used at exterior supports because they have both a vertical and lateral resistive capacity.

Web stiffeners are required when a joist's bearing forces exceed its bearing capacity. For example, deep I joists will often be governed by bearing and not by deflection, bending, or shear. A deep I joist will have tremendous bending and stiffness capacity, but will still typically be bearing on the same 1¾-in. bearing length as the shallower I joist. If the joist is long enough, that bearing stress may be too much for the ⅜-in. unrein-forced thick web. Web stiffeners basically reinforce the web at these bearing locations.

Often, web stiffeners allow for a more efficient use of material. A deep unstiffened I joist may reach bearing capacity limit, while still having ample capacity in bending, shear, and stiffness. By stiffening the web, the bearing resistance is increased, thus permitting the lengthening of the span, which will provide economic benefits.

(The preceding four paragraphs courtesy of Boise Cascade Corporation.)

Table 6-53 *Minimum Distance (D) from Any Support to the Centerline of the Hole*

Round Hole Diameter (in.)	2	3	4	5	6	6½	7	8	8⅞	9	10	11	12	13
Rectangular Hole Side (in.)			2	4	6	6								
Any 9½-in. Joist — Span 8	1'–0'	1'–6'	2'–2'	2'–10'	3'–6'	3'–10"								
Span 12	1'–4'	2'–4'	3'–4'	4'–3'	5'–3'	5'–9'								
Span 16	1'–10'	3'–1'	4'–5'	5'–8'	T–0'	7'–8'								

Round Hole Diameter (in.)	2	3	4	5	6	6½	7	8	8⅞	9	10	11	12	13
Rectangular Hole Side (in.)				2	3	4	5	7	8					
Any 11⅞-in. Joist — Span 8	1'–0'	1'–1'	1'–4'	1'–10'	2'–4'	2'–7'	2'–10"	3'–4"	3'–9'					
Span 12	1'–0'	1'–3'	2'–0'	2'–9'	3'–6'	3'–11'	4'–3'	5'–0'	5'–8'					
Span 16	1'–0'	1'–9'	2'–9'	3'–8'	4'–8'	5'–2"	5'–8"	6'–8'	7'–6'					
Span 20	1'–0'	2'–2'	3'–5'	4'–8'	5'–10'	6'–6'	T–1'	8'–4'	9'–5'					

Round Hole Diameter (in.)	2	3	4	5	6	6½	7	8	8⅞	9	10	11	12	13
Rectangular Hole Side (in.)					2	3	3	5	6	6	8	9		
Any 14-in. Joist — Span 8	1'–0'	1'–1'	1'–2'	1'–3'	1'–8'	1'–10'	2'–1'	2'–6'	2'–10'	2'–11'	3'–4'	3'–9'		
Span 12	1'–0'	1'–1'	1'–3"	1'–11'	2'–6"	2'–10"	3'–2"	3'–9'	4'–4'	4'–4"	5'–0'	5'–7"		
Span 16	1'–0'	1'–1'	1'–9'	2'–7'	3'–4'	3'–9'	4'–2'	5'–0'	5'–9'	5'–10'	6'–8'	T–6'		
Span 20	1'–0'	1'–2"	2'–2'	3'–2'	4'–3"	4'–9"	5'–3'	6'–3"	7'–2"	7'–4'	8'–4'	9'–4'		
Span 24	1'–0'	1'–5'	2'–7'	3'–10'	5'–1'	5'–8'	6'–4'	T–6'	8'–7'	8'–9'	10'–0'	11'–3'		

Round Hole Diameter (in.)	2	3	4	5	6	6½	7	8	8⅞	9	10	11	12	13
Rectangular Hole Side (in.)							2	3	5	5	6	8	9	10
Any 16-in. Joist — Span 8	1'–0'	1'–1'	1'–2'	1'–2'	1'–3'	1'–3'	1'–6'	1'–10'	2'–2'	2'–2'	2'–7'	2'–11'	3'–3'	3'–8'
Span 12	1'–0'	1'–1'	1'–2'	1'–2'	1'–8'	1'–11'	2'–3'	2'–9"	3'–3'	3'–4"	3'–10'	4'–5'	4'–11'	5'–6'
Span 16	1'–0'	1'–1'	1'–2'	1'–6'	2'–3'	2'–7'	3'–0'	3'–9'	4'–4'	4'–5'	5'–2'	5'–11'	6'–7'	T–4'
Span 20	1'–0'	1'–1'	1'–2'	1'–11'	2'–10'	3'–3'	3'–9'	4'–8'	5'–5'	5'–7"	6'–6"	7'–5'	8'–3'	9'–2'
Span 24	1'–0'	1'–1'	1'–3'	2'–4'	3'–5'	3'–11'	4'–6'	5'–7'	6'–6'	6'–8"	T–9'	8'–10'	9'–11'	11'–1'

Table 6-53 *(Continued)*

Round Hole Diameter (in.)		2	3	4	5	6	6½	7	8	8⅞	9	10	11	12	13
Rectangular Hole Side (in.)									2	3	3	5	6	7	9
Any 18-in. Joist	Span (ft) 8	1'–0'	1'–1'	1'–2'	1'–2'	1'–3'	1'–5'	1'–6'	1'–10'	2'–1'	2'–1'	2'–5'	2'–8'	2'–11'	3'–3'
	12	1'–0'	1'–1'	1'–2'	1'–6'	1'–11	2'–1'	2'–4'	2'–9'	3'–1'	3'–2'	3'–7'	4'–0'	4'–5'	4'–10'
	16	1'–0'	1'–1'	1'–5'	2'–0'	2'–6'	2'–10'	3'–1'	3'–8'	4'–2'	4'–3'	4'–10'	5'–4'	5'–11'	6'–6'
	20	1'–0'	1'–1'	1'–9"	2'–6'	3'–2'	3'–6'	3'–11'	4'–7"	5'–3"	5'–4'	6'–0'	6'–9"	7'–5'	8'–2"
	24	1'–0'	1'–3'	2'–2'	3'–0'	3'–10'	4'–3'	4'–8'	5'–6'	6'–3'	6'–4'	T'–3'	8'–1'	8'–11'	9'–9'
	28	1'–0'	1'–6'	2'–6'	3'–6'	4'–6'	5'–0"	5'–5"	6'–5'	T'–4'	T'–5'	8'–5'	9'–5'	10'–5'	11'–5"

Round Hole Diameter (in.)		2	3	4	5	6	6½	7	8	8⅞	9	10	11	12	13
Rectangular Hole Side (in.)										2	2	3	5	6	7
Any 20-in. Joist	Span (ft) 8	1'–0'	1'–1'	1'–2"	1'–2'	1'–3'	1'–3'	1'–3"	1'–6'	1'–9'	1'–9'	2'–0'	2'–3'	2'–6'	2'–9'
	12	1'–0'	1'–1'	1'–2'	1'–2'	1'–7'	1'–9'	1'–11"	2'–4'	2'–8'	2'–8'	3'–1'	3'–5'	3'–10'	4'–2'
	16	1'–0'	1'–1'	I'–2'	1'–7'	2'–1'	2'–4'	2'–7"	3'–1'	3'–7'	3'–7'	4'–1"	4'–7'	5'–1"	5'–7'
	20	1'–0'	1'–1'	1'–5'	2'–0'	2'–8'	3'–0'	3'–3'	3'–11'	4'–5'	4'–6'	5'–2'	5'–9'	6'–5'	T'–0'
	24	1'–0'	1'–1'	1'–8'	2'–5'	3'–2'	3'–7'	3'–11'	4'–8'	5'–4'	5'–5"	6'–2'	6'–11'	7'–a"	8'–5'
	28	1'–0'	1'–1'	2'–0'	2'–10'	3'–9'	4'–2'	4'–7'	5'–6'	6'–3'	6'–4'	T'–3'	8'–1'	9'–0"	9'–10'

SHEATHING

Table 6-54 *Minimum Thickness of Floor Sheathing*

Joist Spacing	Minimum Thickness	
	Perpendicular to Joist	**Diagonal to Joist**
24-in. O.C.	1¹⁄₁₆ in.	¾ in.
16-in. O.C.	⅝ in.	⅝ in.
48-in. O.C.	1½ tongue and groove	N/A
54-in. O.C.	(Same as above)	N/A
60-in. O.C.	(Same as above)	N/A

Table 6-55 *Plywood Combination Subfloor Underlayment*

	Joist Spacing	
Identification	**16-in. O.C.**	**24-in. O.C.**
Species groups		
1	½ in.	¾ in.
2 and 3	⅝ in.	⅞ in.
4	¾ in.	1 in.

- *Particle board* cannot be less than ¼ in. thick.
- Needs to span at least *two supports*.
- *Subflooring* may be omitted if joist spacing is 16 in. or less and if 1-in. tongue and groove is used.

PLYWOOD
Plywood Classifications

Table 6-56 *Plywood Classes*

Group 1	Birch, Douglas fir, larch, pine, maple, southern pine, tanoak
Group 2	Cedar, cypress, fir, hemlock, lauan, black maple, pine-western white, spruce, sweet-gum, yellow poplar
Group 3	Red alder, birch, maple, ponderosa pine, redwood, spruce
Group 4	Aspen, cedar, cottonwood, sugar pine, eastern white pine
Group 5	Basswood, fir, balsam, poplar

Veneer quality (plywood)	
N	High quality intended for natural finish, allows some repairs, free of all open defects
A	Paintable and very smooth, can be used as natural finish with minimum repairs permissible
B	Solid surface with repair plugs and tight knots permitted. Can be painted.
C	Some sanding defects that do not affect the service of the panel, typical knot holes less than 1½ in. and splits less than ½ in.
C (plugged)	Higher quality than 'C' above. Surfaces are fully sanded.
D	Lesser quality, used in interior backing not seen. Knotholes up to 2½ in. permitted as well as limited splits.

Fig. 6-21 *Plywood grading.*

Note: When a sheet of plywood is rated A-C or C-D, for example, one side is A while the other exposed side is C. The better side is always the exposed (visible) side when installing, unless otherwise noted on the plans or specifications.

Plywood Exposure Ratings

Exterior: Fully waterproof bond. Designed for applications where panels are subject to permanent ongoing exposure to moisture.

Exterior—Exposure 1: Fully waterproof bond, but not intended for permanent ongoing exposure to moisture.

Exterior—Exposure 2: Interior type with intermediate glue. Intended for protected applications where only slight exposure to moisture is likely to occur.

Interior 2: Designed for interior applications only.

Grade Designation, Description, and Uses of Typical Plywoods

APA Rated Sheathing EXT Exterior sheathing panel for subflooring and wall and roof sheathing, siding on service and farm buildings, crating, pallets, pallet bins, cable reels, etc.; manufactured as conventional veneered plywood, as a composite, or as a nonveneered panel.

APA Structural 1 and 2 Rated Sheathing EXT For engineered applications in construction and industry where resistance to permanent exposure to weather or moisture is required; manufactured as conventional veneered plywood, as a composite, or as a nonveneered panel; unsanded, structural more commonly available.

APA Rated Sturd-I-Floor EXT For combination sub-floor-underlayment under carpet where severe moisture conditions may be present, as in balcony decks; high concentrated and impact load resistance; manufactured as conventional veneered plywood, as a composite, or as a nonveneered panel; available square-edge or tongue-and-groove.

APA A-C EXT For use where the appearance of only one side is important: soffits, fences, structural uses, boxcar and truck linings, farm buildings, tanks, trays, commercial refrigerators.

APA B-C EXT Utility panel for farm service and work buildings, boxcar and truck linings, containers, tanks, agricultural equipment; also as a base for exterior coatings for walls and roofs.

APA B-B EXT Utility panel with solid faces.

APA Underlayment C-C Plugged EXT For application over structural subfloor; smooth surface for application of carpet and high concentrated and impact load resistance; touch-sanded; for areas to be covered with thin resilient flooring (using panels with sanded face).

APA C-C Plugged EXT For use as an underlayment over structural subfloor, open soffits, and other similar applications where continuous or severe moisture may be present; smooth surface for carpet and high concentrated and impact load resistance; touch-sanded.

APA B-B Plyform Class 1 and Class 2 EXT Concrete form grades with high reuse factor; sanded on both sides and mill-oiled unless otherwise specified; special restrictions on species; also available in HDO for very smooth concrete finish, in structural 1 (all plies limited to group 1 species), and with special overlays.

APA Marine EXT Ideal for boat hulls; only of Douglas fir or western larch; special solid jointed core construction.

APA HDO EXT High-density overlay; hard semi-opaque resin-fiber overlay on both faces; abrasion resistant; for concrete forms.

APA MDO EXT Medium-density overlay; smooth, opaque, resin-fiber overlay on one or both faces; ideal base for paint, indoors and outdoors.

APA Rated Sheathing Exp 1 or 2 Specially designed for subflooring and wall and roof sheathing, but also used for a broad range of other applications; manufactured as conventional veneered plywood, as a composite, or as a nonveneered panel; exposure 1 for long construction delays.

APA Structural 1 & 2 Rated Sheathing Exp 1 Unsanded panel grades for use where strength is of maximum importance: structural diaphragms, box beams, gusset plates, and stressed-skin panels; manufactured as conventional veneered plywood, as a composite, or as a nonveneered panel.

APA Rated Sturd-I-Floor Exp 1 or 2 Specially designed as combination subfloor-underlayment; smooth surface for application of carpet and high concentrated and impact load resistance; manufactured as conventional plywood, as a composite, or as a reconstituted wood panel (waferboard, oriented strand board, structural particleboard); available square-edge or tongue-and-groove.

APA Rated Sturd-I-Floor 48 O.C. (2-4-1) Exp 1 For combination subfloor-underlayment on 32-in. and 48-in. spans and for heavy timber roof construction; manufactured only as conventional plywood; available square-edge or tongue-and-groove.

APA Underlayment INT For application over structural subfloor; smooth surface for application of carpet and high concentrated and impact load resistance; touch-sanded; for areas to be covered with thin resilient flooring (using panels with fully sanded face).

APA A-D INT For use where appearance of only one side is important: paneling, built-ins, shelving, and partitions.

APA B-D INT Utility panel with one solid side; good for backing, sides of built-ins, shelving, etc.

APA CoD Plugged INT For built-ins, wall and ceiling tile backing, cable reels, and walkways; not a substitute for underlayment or Sturd-I-Floor due to lack of their indentation resistance; touch-sanded; also available with exterior glue.

APA A-A INT For applications with both sides on view: built-ins, cabinets, furniture, partitions; smooth face, and suitable for painting.

APA A-B INT For use where appearance of one side is less important but where two solid surfaces are necessary.

APA B-B INT Utility panel with two solid surfaces.

WALLS (FRAMING)
Studs

Table 6-57 *Minimum Stud Spacing (for One Floor)*

Height Less Than	Spacing			
	24 in.	16 in.	12 in.	8 in.
10 ft	2 × 4	2 × 4	2 × 4	2 × 4
12 ft	2 × 6	2 × 4	2 × 4	2 × 4
14 ft	2 × 6	2 × 6	2 × 4	2 × 4
16 ft	2 × 6	2 × 6	2 × 6	2 × 4
18 ft	Design	2 × 6	2 × 6	2 × 6
20 ft	Design	Design	2 × 6	2 × 6
24 ft	Design	Design	Design	2 × 6

One floor.

Table 6-58 *Minimum Stud Spacing (for One Floor and Roof)*

Height Less Than	Spacing			
	24 in.	16 in.	12 in.	8 in.
10 ft	2 × 6	2 × 4	2 × 4	2 × 4
12 ft	2 × 6	2 × 6	2 × 6	2 × 4
14 ft	2 × 6	2 × 6	2 × 6	2 × 6
16 ft	Design	2 × 6	2 × 6	2 × 6
18 ft	Design	2 × 6	2 × 6	2 × 6
20 ft	Design	Design	2 × 6	2 × 6
24 ft	Design	Design	Design	2 × 6

One floor and roof.

Table 6-59 *Minimum Stud Spacing (for Two Floors and Roof)*

Height Less Than	Spacing			
	24 in.	16 in.	12 in.	8 in.
10 ft	2 × 6	2 × 4	2 × 4	2 × 4
10 ft	2 × 6	2 × 6	2 × 4	2 × 4
12 ft	2 × 6	2 × 6	2 × 6	2 × 6
14 ft	2 × 6	2 × 6	2 × 6	2 × 6
16 ft	Design	Design	2 × 6	2 × 6
18 ft	Design	Design	2 × 6	2 × 6
20 ft	Design	Design	Design	2 × 6
24 ft	Design	Design	Design	Design

Two floors and roof.
Snow less than 25 psf.
F_b > 1310 psi.
e > 1,600,000 psi.
Tributary dimensions for floors and roofs < 6 ft.
Maximum span not exceeding 12 ft.
Exterior sheathing.
Eaves less than 2 ft.

- Typical grading values of studs:

Select structural

No. 1

No. 2

No. 3

Stud grade

Construction grade

Standard grade

Utility grade

Strongest to weakest

- Studs need to be minimum No. 3, standard, or stud grade.
- Utility, standard, stud, or No. 3 grade may not be used in seismic zone D.
- May be utility if not supporting floors.
- For spacing, see Table 6-61 when not more than 10 ft in height.
- Double top plate (laps offset by at least 48 in.) may use single plate if a 3 in. by 6 in. gage plate is nailed to each wall segment if rafters or joist centered no more than 1 in. over studs.
- If joist or rafters are spaced more than 16 in. and studs are 24 in. they must rest within 5 in. of bearing studs (not if using 2 × 6 plates).
- Interior non-load-bearing wall may have single top plate.
- Nonload partitions
  - 2 × 4 (flat) if 16-in. O.C.; 2 × 3 if 24-in. O.C.
- Notching
- Any in exterior wall or load bearing < 25% of the width.
- Nonbearing < 40% of the width
- Bored or drilled
  - Any provided that < 40% of width
  - No closer than ⅝ in. to edge.
  - Cannot be located in the same section as another a cut or notch.
  - May be 60% if doubled and not more than two in a row.

Table 6-60 Holes/Notching in Load-Bearing Studs and Exterior Walls

Nominal	Actual	Holes 40%	Holes 60%*	Notching 25%
2 × 4	1½ × 3½	1¹³⁄₃₂	2³⁄₃₂	⅞
2 × 6	1½ × 5½	2³⁄₁₆	3⁵⁄₁₆	1⅜

*Stud must be doubled.

Table 6-61 Holes/Notching in Non-Load-Bearing Studs

Nominal	Actual	Holes 40%	Notching 40%
2 × 4	1½ × 3½	1¹³⁄₃₂	1¹³⁄₃₂
2 × 6	1½ × 5½	2³⁄₁₆	2³⁄₁₆

Table 6-62 Stud Spacing

Supporting	Studs 2 × 4	2 × 6
Roof and ceiling	24-in. O.C.	24-in. O.C.
One floor, roof and ceiling	16-in. O.C.	24-in. O.C.
Two floors, roof and ceiling	N/A	16-in. O.C.
One floor only	24-in. O.C.	24-in. O.C.

Wall Bracing

- 1-in. by 4-in. let-in (must run from plate to plate or structural sheathing).
- Located at each end and every 25 ft.
- Bracing is to between 45° and 60°.
- Special requirements for earthquake-prone areas.

Wall Bracing Methods

In seismic categories A and B (low probability), see map in Appendix.

Special considerations and attachments are required for seismic zones C, D1, and D2 or where winds exceed 100 mph.

Braced Wall Methods

1. 1 × 4 let-in bracing from bottom plate to top plate. Angled not more than 60° or less than 45°.
2. ⅝-in. wood boards applied diagonally spaced a max. of 24 in.
3. ⁵⁄₁₆-in. wood structural panel sheathing for studs on 16-in. O.C. Minimum of ⅜ in. for studs spaced on 24-in. O.C.
4. ½-in. or ²⁵⁄₃₂-in. structural fiberboard sheathing applied vertically for studs on 16-in. O.C.
5. ½-in. gypsum board on studs spaced 24-in. O.C. Fastened at 7-in. O.C.
6. Particle board installed in accordance to the International Code fastener schedule.
7. Portland cement plaster on studs 16-in. O.C. when installed as per International Code applications.

8. $\frac{7}{16}$-in. minimum hardboard panel siding when installed with fasteners penetrating $1\frac{1}{2}$ in. of the framing members on 6-in. O.C. for edges and 12-in. O.C. supplemental.

Particle Board (OSB) Wall Wind Bracing

In seismic zones A and B (low probability) and for wind speeds less than 100 mph. For other seismic zones and higher wind speeds see the ICC codes.

Table 6-63　*Acceptable Wall Bracing*

Area	Bracing Method	Location and Amount of Bracing
One story; top of two or three story	1,2,3,4,5,6,7,8	Located at each end and at least every 25 ft O.C. but not less than 16% of braced wall line.
First story of two story; second story of three story	1,2,3,4,5,6,7,8	Located at each end and at least every 25 ft but not less than 16% of braced wall line for method 3 and 25% for methods 2, 3, 4, 5, 6, 7, or 8.
First story of three story	2,3,4,5,6,7,8	Minimum of 48-in.-wide panels each end and at least every 25 ft O.C., but not less than 25% of braced wall for method 3 and 35% of braced wall line for methods 2, 3, 4, 5, 6, 7, or 8.

Table 6-64　*Spacing of Intermediate OSB Wall Sheathing for Wind Bracing, O.C. (ft)*

Level	Corners and % of Braced Wall Length	Braced Wall Length (ft)				
		20	30	40	50	60
One story	16%	3.2	4.8	6.4	8.0	9.6
Top floor of two or three story	16%	3.2	4.8	6.4	8.0	9.6
First story of two story	25%	5.0	7.5	10.0	12.5	15.0
Second story of three story	25%	5.0	7.5	10.0	12.5	15.0
First story of three story	35%	7.0	10.5	14.0	17.5	21.0

Table 6-65　*Minimum Thickness of Wall Sheathing*

Sheathing Type	Minimum Thickness	Maximum Wall Stud Spacing
Wood boards	$\frac{5}{8}$ in.	24 in. on center
Fiberboard	$\frac{1}{2}$ in.	16 in. on center
Wood structural panel (plywood)	In accordance with Table 6-66	—
Gypsum sheathing	$\frac{1}{2}$ in.	16 in. on center
Gypsum wallboard	$\frac{1}{2}$ in.	24 in. on center
Reinforced cement mortar	1 in.	24 in. on center

Table 6-66　*Wood Structural Panel Wall Sheathing (Not Exposed to the Weather)*

Minimum Thickness (in.)	Panel Span Rating	Stud Spacing (in.)		
			Nailable Sheathing	
		Siding Nailed to Studs	Sheathing Parallel to Studs	Sheathing Perpendicular to Studs
$\frac{5}{16}$	12/0, 16/0, 20/0; wall, 16 in. O.C.	16	—	16
$\frac{3}{8}$, $\frac{15}{32}$, $\frac{1}{2}$	16/0, 20/0, 24/0, 32/16; wall, 24 in. O.C.	24	16	24
$\frac{7}{16}$, $\frac{15}{32}$, $\frac{1}{2}$	24/0, 24/16, 32/16; wall, 24 in. O.C.	24	24	24

Plywood shall consist of four or more plies.

Table 6-67 *Typical Nailing Schedule for Plywood and Particleboard for Subfloor, Roof, and Wall Sheathing*

Thickness	Type Nails	Edges	Intermediate
⁵⁄₁₆ in.–¹⁄₂ in.	6d common		
	subfloor	6 in.	12 in.
	walls	6 in.	12 in.
	8d common		
	roof	6 in.	12 in.
¹⁹⁄₃₂ in.–1 in.	8d common	6 in.	12 in.
1¹⁄₈ in.–1¹⁄₄ in.	10d common	6 in.	12 in.

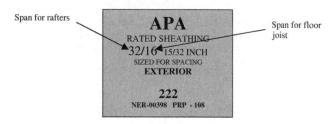

Span for rafters *Span for floor joist*

APA
RATED SHEATHING
32/16 15/32 INCH
SIZED FOR SPACING
EXTERIOR

222
NER-00398 PRP - 108

Fig. 6-22 *Typical plywood stamp.*

Table 6-68 *Allowable Spans for Particleboard Wall Sheathing (Not Exposed to the Weather)*

		Stud Spacing (in.)
Grade	Thickness (in.)	Siding Nailed to Studs
M-S exterior glue	³⁄₈	16
and M-2	¹⁄₂	16
exterior glue		

Nails ³⁄₈ in. from sheathing edge

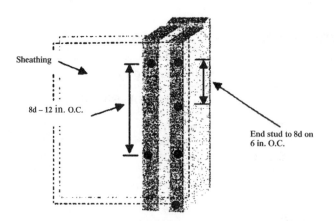

Sheathing

8d – 12 in. O.C.

End stud to 8d on 6 in. O.C.

Fig. 6-23 *Corner studs and sheathing.*

Note: Corner sheathing used as wind bracing requirement must be fastened to both the bottom and top plates.

Firestopping

- Requires cutting off all concealed vertical and horizontal openings as follows:
  - Between floors and roofs, soffits, drop ceilings, cove ceilings
  - Furred spaces at ceilings and floors
  - Around vents, pipes, ducts, chimneys, and fireplaces

Firestop Materials

- 2-in. nominal lumber
- ²³⁄₃₂-in. structural panel with joints backed with same
- ³⁄₄-in. particle board with joints backed with same
- ¹⁄₂-in. gypsum board
- ¹⁄₄-in. cement millboard
- Unfaced fiberglass for around vents, pipes, ducts, chimneys, and fireplaces

Unfaced fiberglass must fill the wall cavity a minimum of 16 in. vertically and packed around piping, conduit, etc.

HEADERS
Header Spans
(Exterior Walls)

Table 6-69 *Exterior Wall Headers Supporting Roof and Ceiling; Ground Snow Load 30 psf*

	Building Widths (ft)					
	20		28		36	
Size	Span	No. Jacks	Span	No. Jacks	Span	No. Jacks
2-2 × 6	5–5	1	4–8	1	4–2	1
2-2 × 8	6–10	1	5–11	2	5–4	2
2-2 × 10	8–5	2	7–3	2	6–6	2
2-2 × 12	9–9	2	8–5	2	7–6	2
3-2 × 8	8–4	1	7–5	1	6–8	1
3-2 × 10	10–6	1	9–1	2	8–2	2
3-2 × 12	12–2	2	10–7	2	9–5	2
4-2 × 8	7–0	1	6–1	2	5–5	2
4-2 × 10	11–8	1	10–6	1	9–5	2
4-2 × 12	14–1	1	12–2	2	10–11	2

Table 6-70 *Exterior Wall Headers Supporting Roof, Ceiling, and One Center-Bearing Floor; Ground Snow Load 30 psf*

| | Building Widths (ft) | | | | | |
| | 20 | | 28 | | 36 | |
Size	Span	No. Jacks	Span	No. Jacks	Span	No. Jacks
2-2 × 6	4–6	1	4–0	1	3–7	2
2-2 × 8	5–9	2	5–0	2	4–6	2
2-2 × 10	7–0	2	6–2	2	5–6	2
2-2 × 12	8–1	2	7–1	2	6–5	2
3-2 × 8	7–2	1	6–3	2	5–8	2
3-2 × 12	10–2	2	8–11	2	8–0	2
4-2 × 8	5–10	2	5–2	2	4–8	2
4-2 × 10	10–1	1	8–10	2	8–0	2
4-2 × 12	11–9	2	10–3	2	9–3	2

Table 6-71 *Exterior Wall Headers Supporting Roof, Ceiling, and One Clear Span Floor; Ground Snow Load 30 psf*

| | Building Widths (ft) | | | | | |
| | 20 | | 28 | | 36 | |
Size	Span	No. Jacks	Span	No. Jacks	Span	No. Jacks
2-2 × 6	3–11	1	3–5	2	3–0	2
2-2 × 8	5–0	2	4–4	2	3–10	2
2-2 × 10	6–1	2	5–3	2	4–8	2
2-2 × 12	7–1	2	6–1	3	5–5	3
3-2 × 8	6–3	2	5–5	2	4–10	2
3-2 × 10	7–7	2	6–7	2	5–11	2
3-2 × 12	8–10	2	7–8	2	6–10	2
4-2 × 8	5–1	2	4–5	2	3–11	2
4-2 × 10	8–9	2	7–7	2	6–10	2
4-2 × 12	10–2	2	8–10	2	7–11	2

Table 6-72 *Exterior Wall Headers Supporting Roof, Ceiling, and Two Center-Bearing Floors; Ground Snow Load 30 psf*

| | Building Widths (ft) | | | | | |
| | 20 | | 28 | | 36 | |
Size	Span	No. Jacks	Span	No. Jacks	Span	No. Jacks
2-2 × 6	3–9	2	3–3	2	2–11	2
2-2 × 8	4–9	2	4–2	2	3–9	2
2-2 × 10	5–9	2	5–1	2	4–7	3
2-2 × 12	6–8	2	5–10	3	5–3	3
3-2 × 8	5–11	2	5–2	2	4–8	2
3-2 × 12	8–5	2	7–4	2	6–7	2
4-2 × 8	4–10	2	4–3	2	3–10	2
4-2 × 10	8–4	2	7–4	2	6–7	2
4-2 × 12	9–8	2	8–6	2	7–8	2

Table 6-73 *Exterior Wall Headers Supporting Roof and Ceiling; Ground Snow Load 50 psf*

| | Building Widths (ft) | | | | | |
| | 20 | | 28 | | 36 | |
Size	Span	No. Jacks	Span	No. Jacks	Span	No. Jacks
2-2 × 6	4–8	1	4–1	1	3–8	2
2-2 × 8	5–11	2	5–2	2	4–7	2
2-2 × 10	7–3	2	6–3	2	5–7	2
2-2 × 12	8–5	2	7–3	2	6–6	2
3-2 × 8	7–5	1	6–5	2	5–9	2
3-2 × 10	9–1	2	7–10	2	7–0	2
3-2 × 12	10–7	2	9–2	2	8–2	2
4-2 × 8	6–1	2	5–3	2	4–8	2
4-2 × 10	10–6	1	9–1	2	8–2	2
4-2 × 12	12–2	2	10–7	2	9–5	2

Table 6-74 *Exterior Wall Headers Supporting Roof, Ceiling, and One Center-Bearing Floor; Ground Snow Load 50 psf*

| | Building Widths (ft) | | | | | |
| | 20 | | 28 | | 36 | |
Size	Span	No. Jacks	Span	No. Jacks	Span	No. Jacks
2-2 × 6	4–1	1	3–7	2	3–3	2
2-2 × 8	5–2	2	4–6	2	4–1	2
2-2 × 10	6–4	2	5–6	2	5–0	2
2-2 × 12	7–4	2	6–5	2	5–9	3
3-2 × 8	6–5	2	5–8	2	5–1	2
3-2 × 10	7–11	2	6–11	2	6–3	2
3-2 × 12	9–2	2	8–0	2	7–3	2
4-2 × 8	5–3	2	4–7	2	4–2	2
4-2 × 10	9–1	2	8–0	2	7–2	2
4-2 × 12	10–7	2	9–3	2	8–4	2

Table 6-75 *Exterior Wall Headers Supporting Roof, Ceiling, and One Clear Span Floor; Ground Snow Load 50 psf*

| | Building Widths (ft) | | | | | |
| | 20 | | 28 | | 36 | |
Size	Span	No. Jacks	Span	No. Jacks	Span	No. Jacks
2-2 × 6	3–10	2	3–4	2	3–0	2
2-2 × 8	4–10	2	4–2	2	3–9	2
2-2 × 10	5–11	2	5–1	2	4–7	3
2-2 × 12	6–10	2	5–11	3	5–4	3
3-2 × 8	6–1	2	5–3	2	4–8	2
3-2 × 10	7–5	2	6–5	2	5–9	2
3-2 × 12	8–7	2	7–5	2	6–8	2
4-2 × 8	4–11	2	4–3	2	3–10	2
4-2 × 10	8–7	2	7–5	2	6–7	2
4-2 × 12	9–11	2	8–7	2	7–8	2

Table 6-76 *Exterior Wall Headers Supporting Roof, Ceiling, and Two Center-Bearing Floors; Ground Snow Load 50 psf*

Size	Building Widths (ft)					
	20		28		36	
	Span	No. Jacks	Span	No. Jacks	Span	No. Jacks
2-2 × 6	3–8	2	3–2	2	2–10	2
2-2 × 8	4–7	2	4–0	2	3–8	2
2-2 × 10	5–8	2	4–11	2	4–5	3
2-2 × 12	6–6	2	5–9	3	5–2	3
3-2 × 8	5–9	2	5–1	2	4–7	2
3-2 × 10	7–1	2	6–2	2	5–7	2
3-2 × 12	8–2	2	7–2	2	6–5	3
4-2 × 8	4–9	2	4–2	2	3–9	2
4-2 × 10	8–2	2	7–2	2	6–5	2
4-2 × 12	9–5	2	8–3	2	7–5	2

Header Spans (Interior Walls)

Table 6-77 *Interior Header—One Floor Only*

Size	Building Widths (ft)					
	20		28		36	
	Span	No. Jacks	Span	No. Jacks	Span	No. Jacks
2-2 × 6	4–6	1	3–11	1	3–6	1
2-2 × 8	5–9	1	5–0	2	4–5	2
2-2 × 10	7–0	2	6–1	2	5–5	2
2-2 × 12	8–1	2	7–0	2	6–3	2
3-2 × 8	7–2	1	6–3	1	5–7	2
3-2 × 10	8–9	1	7–7	2	6–9	2
3-2 × 12	10–2	2	8–10	2	7–10	2
4-2 × 8	5–10	1	5–1	2	4–6	2
4-2 × 10	10–1	1	8–9	1	7–10	2
4-2 × 12	11–9	1	10–2	2	9–1	2

Headers in Joists or Rafters

- Openings larger than 4 ft, header must be doubled.
- Opening 6 ft or larger, metal hangers must be used.
- If nonbearing, then only need 2 × 4 laying flat (for up to 8 ft).

- Need to be No. 2 grade lumber.
- Bearing must be minimum 1½ in. on wood, 3 in. on masonry.
- Must have correct number of jack studs per size of opening and load imposed.

Table 6-78 *Interior Header—Two Floors Only*

Size	Building Widths (ft)					
	20		28		36	
	Span	No. Jacks	Span	No. Jacks	Span	No. Jacks
2-2 × 6	3–2	2	2–9	2	2–5	2
2-2 × 8	4–1	2	3–6	2	3–2	2
2-2 × 10	4–11	2	4–3	2	3–10	3
2-2 × 12	5–9	2	5–0	3	4–5	3
3-2 × 8	5–1	2	4–5	2	3–11	2
3-2 × 10	6–2	2	5–4	2	4–10	2
3-2 × 12	7–2	2	6–3	2	5–7	3
4-2 × 8	4–2	2	3–7	2	3–2	2
4-2 × 10	7–2	2	6–2	2	5–6	2
4-2 × 12	8–4	2	7–2	2	6–5	2

FASTENERS

Table 6-79 *Nailing Schedule*

Building Members		Number and Type	Spacing
Joist to sill or girder		3—8d	N/A
Sole plate to joist/blocking		16d	16 in. O.C.
Top plate/sole to stud	End nail	2—16d	N/A
Stud to sole plate	Toe nail	3—8d or 2—16d	N/A
Double stud	Face nail	10d	24 in. O.C.
Double top plate	Face nail	10d	24 in. O.C.
Double top plate at splice	Face nail	4—10d	N/A
Top plate at corners	Face nail	2—10d	N/A
Headers w/spacers along each side		16d	16 in. O.C.
Ceiling joist to top plate	Toe nail	3—8d	N/A
Ceiling joist lapped	Face nail	3—10d	N/A
Rafters to top plate	Face nail	2—16d	N/A
Corner studs		10d	24 in. O.C.
Built-up girders and beams		10d	32 in. O.C. (staggered)

Size	Length (in.)	Diam (in.)	Remarks	Where Used
2d	1	.072	Small Head	Finish Work, Shop Work.
2d	1	.072	Large Flathead	Small Timber, Wood Shingles, Lathes.
3d	1½	.08	Small Head	Finish Work, Shop Work.
3d	1½	.08	Large Flathead	Small Timber, Wood Shingles, Lathes.
4d	1½	.098	Small Head	Finish Work, Shop Work.
4d	1½	.098	Large Flathead	Small Timber, Lathes, Shop Work.
5d	1¾	.098	Small Head	Finish Work, Shop Work.
5d	1¼	.098	Large Flathead	Small Timber, Lathes, Shop Work.
6d	2	.113	Small Head	Finish Work, Casing, Stops, etc., Shop Work.
6d	2	.113	Large Flathead	Small Timber, Siding, Sheathing, etc., Shop Work.
7d	2¼	.113	Small Head	Casing, Base, Ceiling, Stops, etc.
7d	2¼	.113	Large Flathead	Sheathing, Siding, Subflooring, Light Framing.
8d	2½	.131	Small Head	Casing, Base, Ceiling, Wainscot, etc., Shop Work.
8d	2⅓	.131	Large Flathead	Sheathing, Siding, Subflooring, Light Framing, Shop Work.
8d	1¼	.131	Extra-Large Flathead	Roll Roofing, Composition Shingles.
9d	2¼	.131	Small Head	Casing, Base, Ceiling, etc.
9d	2½	.131	Large Flathead	Sheathing, Siding, Subflooring, Framing, Shop Work.
10d	3	.148	Small Head	Casing, Base, Ceiling, etc., Shop Work.
10d	3	.148	Large Flathead	Sheathing, Siding, Subflooring, Framing, Shop Work.
12d	3¼	.148	Large Flathead	Sheathing, Subflooring, Framing.
16d	3½	.162	Large Flathead	Framing, Bridges, etc.
20d	4	.192	Large Flathead	Framing, Bridges, etc.
30d	4½	.207	Large Flathead	Heavy Framing, Bridges, etc.
40d	5	.225	Large Flathead	Heavy Framing, Bridges, etc.
60d	5½	.244	Large Flathead	Extra-Heavy Framing, Bridges, etc.
60d	6	.262	Large Flathead	Extra-Heavy Framing, Bridges, etc.

Fig. 6-24 *Typical nails. This chart applies to wire nails, although it may be used to determine the length of cut nails.*

Note: Currently neither the ICC nor any other codes make a distinction between box or common nails except for rafter heal connections (16d common = 40d box) or some sheathing applications. Common nails in general have 30% more holding strength than box nails.

Pull-Out Strength per Inch of Penetration (Common Nails)

Species of Wood	Size of Nail, d									
	6	8	10	12	16	20	30	40	50	60
Redwood (open grain)	13	15	17	17	19	22	24	26	28	30
Eastern white pine	14	16	18	18	20	24	25	28	30	32
Idaho white pine	16	18	21	21	23	27	29	31	34	37
Eastern spruce	17	19	22	22	24	29	31	33	36	39
Redwood (close grain); pine—red, ponderosa, sugar; hem-fir	18	21	23	23	26	30	33	35	38	41
Lodgepole pine	20	23	26	26	29	34	37	40	43	47
Mountain hemlock	24	27	31	31	34	40	43	47	51	55
Douglas fir–larch	29	34	38	38	42	49	53	58	63	67
Southern pine	35	41	46	46	50	59	64	70	76	81

Notes:

1. The above values are for nails driven into seasoned or unseasoned wood that will remain wet or dry wood that will remain dry. If unseasoned wood will become seasoned under loaded conditions, then the allowable load is ¼ of the value shown.

2. Nails should not be loaded in withdrawal from end grain.

3. The allowable withdrawal load for nails in toenailed joints is ⅔ of the tabular value.

Lateral Strength (Common Nails)

Species of Wood	Size of Nail, *d*									
	6	8	10	12	16	20	30	40	50	60
Redwood (open grain) Cedar: western, northern white Fir, balsam Spruce: Engelmann and eastern Pine: eastern white, western white, Idaho white	41	51	61	61	70	91	102	115	130	146
Pine: lodgepole, northern, red, ponderosa, sugar Redwood (close grain) Hemlock: mountain and eastern Spruce: Sitka	51	64	77	77	88	114	127	144	163	182
Douglas fir–larch Southern pine	63	78	94	94	108	139	155	176	199	223

Data reproduced courtesy of National Forest Products Association.

Notes:

1. The above values are based on the assumption that the nail or spike penetrates the piece receiving the point for a distance not less than 14 diameters for species in the first group: not less than 13 diameters for species in the second group; and not less than 11 diameters for species in the third group. When penetration is less than that specified, the allowable load may be determined by straight-line interpolation between zero and the tabulated load, except that penetration must not be less than 1/3 of that specified.

2. The allowable lateral loads for nails or spikes driven into end grain are 2/3 of the tabular values.

3. If the nail or spike is driven into partially seasoned wood, or into dry wood that will be wet in service, the allowable load is 75% of the tabular values.

Staples

Table 6-80 *Using Staples for Wood Structural Subfloor Panels, Roof and Wall Sheathing to Framing, and Particleboard Wall Sheathing to Framing*

Thickness (in.)	Staple and Length (in.) (all crowns ⁷⁄₁₆ in. min.)	Spacing of Fasteners	
		Edges (in.)	Field (in.)
⁵⁄₁₆	Staple 15 ga. 1⅜ Staple 16 ga. 1¾	6	12

Table 6-80 *(Continued)*

Thickness (in.)	Staple and Length (in.) (all crowns ⁷⁄₁₆ in. min)	Spacing of Fasteners	
		Edges (in.)	Field (in.)
⅜	Staple 15 ga. 1⅜ Staple 16 ga. 1¾	6 6	12 12
¹⁵⁄₃₂ and ½	Staple 15 ga. 1½ Staple 16 ga. 1¾	6 6	12 12
¹⁹⁄₃₂ and ⅝	Staple 15 and 16 ga. 1⅝	6	12
²³⁄₃₂ and ¾	Staple 14 ga. 1¾ Staple 15 ga. 1¾ Staple 16 ga. 2	6 5 4	12 10 8
1	Staple 14 ga. 2 Staple 15 ga. 2	5 4	10 8

TOP PLATES

- Top plates are to be lapped at least 24 in.
- Corner top plates to be lapped.
- If cut more than 50%, top plate needs 24 ga. steel spanning between the two studs.
- Single top plates may be used under special conditions.
- Sheathing for "wind" bracing must reach and be fastened into the top plate.

Table 6-81 *Stud Spacing for Structural Wall Sheathing*

Span Ratings	Thickness	Max. Stud Spacing Siding Nailed to:	
		Stud	Sheathing
¹²⁄₀, ¹⁶⁄₀, ²⁰⁄₀; wall, 16-in. O.C.	⁵⁄₁₆, ⅜	16-in. O.C.	16-in. O.C.
⁴⁄₀, ²⁴⁄₁₆, ³²⁄₁₆; wall, 24-in. O.C.	⅜, ⁷⁄₁₆, ¹⁵⁄₃₂, ½	24-in. O.C.	24-in. O.C.

PARTICLEBOARD WALL SHEATHING

- Leave ¹⁄₁₆-in. gap at edges.
- Nail no closer than ⅜ in. to the edge.

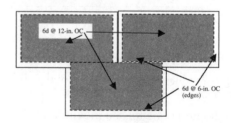

Fig. 6-25 *Nailing sheathing (wall and subflooring).*

STAPLES FOR WOOD STRUCTURAL PANELS

Using staples for wood structural subfloor panels, roof and wall sheathing to framing, and particleboard wall sheathing to framing.

Thickness (in.)	Staple and Length (in.) (all crowns ⁷⁄₁₆ in. min.)	Spacing of Fasteners	
		Edges (in.)	Field (in.)
⁵⁄₁₆	Staple 15 ga. 1⅜ Staple 16 ga. 1¾	6	12
⅜	Staple 15 ga. 1⅜ Staple 16 ga. 1¾	6 6	12 12
¹⁵⁄₃₂ and ½	Staple 15 ga. 1½ Staple 16 ga. 1¾	6 6	12 12
¹⁹⁄₃₂ and ⅝	Staple 15 and 16 ga. 1⅝	6	12
²³⁄₃₂ and ¾	Staple 14 ga. 1¾ Staple 15 ga. 1¾ Staple 16 ga. 2	6 5 4	12 10 8
1	Staple 14 ga. 2 Staple 15 ga. 2	5 4	10 8

RAFTERS

- Rafter ties shall be spaced no more than 4 ft on center.
- Ridge board shall be at least 1 in. and the same depth as the end cut of the rafter it supports.
- Hip and valley shall have a hip rafter or valley rafter of not less than 2 in. and of same depth as rafter it supports.
- If roof pitch is less than 3 vertical in. in 12 in., then the rafters and joist need to be designed as beams.
- Rafters and joists exceeding depth-to-thickness ratio by 5 to 1 need lateral support.
- Needs bridging if depth-to-thickness ratio exceeds 6 to 1, at 10 ft or less intervals.
- Headers (in rafters) need to be doubled if spanning more than 4 ft.
- Truss members cannot be cut or altered.

CUTTING AND NOTCHING (JOISTS AND RAFTERS)

1. Not exceeding ¼ the depth at the ends.
2. None located in middle ⅓ of the span.
3. Not exceeding ⅙ of depth at the top or bottom.
4. Tension side (bottom) of lumber (4 in.) shall not be notched except at the ends.

5. Cantilevered members cannot be notched!
6. They may have holes drilled if they are a minimum of 4 in. from the end.

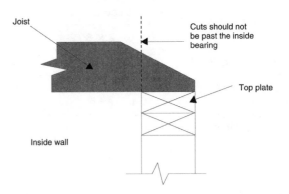

Fig. 6-26 *Cutting joist ends.*

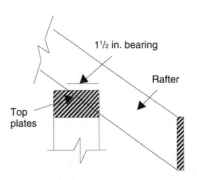

Fig. 6-27 *Birdsmouth cut.*

RAFTER SPANS

Table 6-82 *Rafter Spans for Common Lumber Species (roof live load = 20 psf, ceiling not attached to rafters, L/Δ = 180)*

Rafter Spacing 12 in.		Dead Load = 10 psf			
		2 × 6	2 × 8	2 × 10	2 × 12
Species and Grade		(ft-in.)	(ft-in.)	(ft-in.)	(ft-in.)
Doug. fir–larch	SS	18-0	23-9	Note	Note
Doug. fir–larch	#1	17-4	22-5	Note	Note
Doug. fir–larch	#2	16-7	21-0	25-8	Note
Doug. fir–larch	#3	12-6	15-10	19-5	22-6
Hem-fir	SS	17-0	22-5	Note	Note
Hem-fir	#1	16-8	21-10	Note	Note
Hem-fir	#2	15-11	20-8	25-3	Note
Hem-fir	#3	12-6	15-10	19-5	22-6
South. pine	SS	17-8	23-4	Note	Note
South. pine	#1	17-4	22-11	Note	Note
South. pine	#2	17-0	22-5	Note	Note
South. pine	#3	13-6	17-2	20-3	24-1
Spruce-pine-fir	SS	16-8	21-11	Note	Note
Spruce-pine-fir	#1	16-3	21-0	25-8	Note
Spruce-pine-fir	#2	16-3	21-0	25-8	Note
Spruce-pine-fir	#3	12-6	15-10	19-5	22-6

Note: Check availability of lumber over 20 ft-0 in.

Table 6-83 *Rafter Spans for Common Lumber Species (roof live load = 20 psf, ceiling not attached to rafters, L/Δ = 180)*

Rafter Spacing 12 in.		Dead Load = 20 psf			
		2 × 6	2 × 8	2 × 10	2 × 12
Species and Grade		(ft-in.)	(ft-in.)	(ft-in.)	(ft-in.)
Doug. fir–larch	SS	18-0	23-5	Note	Note
Doug. fir–larch	#1	15-4	19-5	23-9	Note
Doug. fir–larch	#2	14-4	18-2	22-3	25-9
Doug. fir–larch	#3	10-10	13-9	16-9	19-6
Hem-fir	SS	17-0	22-5	Note	Note
Hem-fir	#1	14-11	18-11	23-2	Note
Hem-fir	#2	14-2	17-11	21-11	25-5
Hem-fir	#3	10-10	13-9	16-9	19-6
South. pine	SS	17-8	23-4	Note	Note
South. pine	#1	17-3	21-9	25-10	Note
South. pine	#2	15-1	19-5	23-2	Note
South. pine	#3	11-8	14-10	17-6	20-11
Spruce-pine-fir	SS	16-8	21-9	Note	Note
Spruce-pine-fir	#1	14-4	18-2	22-3	25-9
Spruce-pine-fir	#2	14-4	18-2	22-3	25-9
Spruce-pine-fir	#3	10-10	13-9	16-9	19-6

Note: Check availability of lumber over 20 ft-0 in.

Table 6-85 *Rafter Spans for Common Lumber Species (roof live load = 20 psf, ceiling not attached to rafters, L/Δ = 180)*

Rafter Spacing 16 in.		Dead Load = 20 psf			
		2 × 6	2 × 8	2 × 10	2 × 12
Species and Grade		(ft-in.)	(ft-in.)	(ft-in.)	(ft-in.)
Doug. fir–larch	SS	16-0	20-3	24-9	Note
Doug. fir–larch	#1	13-3	16-10	20-7	23-10
Doug. fir–larch	#2	12-5	15-9	19-3	22-4
Doug. fir–larch	#3	9-5	11-11	14-6	16-10
Hem-fir	SS	15-6	19-11	24-4	Note
Hem-fir	#1	12-11	16-5	20-0	23-3
Hem-fir	#2	12-3	15-6	18-11	22-0
Hem-fir	#3	9-5	11-11	14-6	16-10
South. pine	SS	16-1	21-2	Note	Note
South. pine	#1	15-0	18-10	22-4	Note
South. pine	#2	13-0	16-10	20-1	23-7
South. pine	#3	10-1	12-10	15-2	18-1
Spruce-pine-fir	SS	14-10	18-10	23-0	Note
Spruce-pine-fir	#1	12-5	15-9	19-3	22-4
Spruce-pine-fir	#2	12-5	15-9	19-3	22-4
Spruce-pine-fir	#3	9-5	11-11	14-6	16-10

Note: Check availability of lumber over 20 ft-0 in.

Table 6-84 *Rafter Spans for Common Lumber Species (roof live load = 20 psf, ceiling not attached to rafters, L/Δ = 180)*

Rafter Spacing 16 in.		Dead Load = 10 psf			
		2 × 6	2 × 8	2 × 10	2 × 12
Species and Grade		(ft-in.)	(ft-in.)	(ft-in.)	(ft-in.)
Doug. fir–larch	SS	16-4	21-7	Note	Note
Doug. fir–larch	#1	15-4	19-5	23-9	Note
Doug. fir–larch	#2	14-4	18-2	22-3	25-9
Doug. fir–larch	#3	10-10	13-9	16-9	19-6
Hem-fir	SS	15-6	20-5	Note	Note
Hem-fir	#1	14-11	18-11	23-2	Note
Hem-fir	#2	14-2	17-11	21-11	25-5
Hem-fir	#3	10-10	13-9	16-9	19-6
South. pine	SS	16-1	21-2	Note	Note
South. pine	#1	15-9	20-10	25-10	Note
South. pine	#2	15-1	19-5	23-2	Note
South. pine	#3	11-8	14-10	17-6	20-11
Spruce-pine-fir	SS	15-2	19-11	25-5	Note
Spruce-pine-fir	#1	14-4	18-2	22-3	25-9
Spruce-pine-fir	#2	14-4	18-2	22-3	25-9
Spruce-pine-fir	#3	10-10	13-9	16-9	19-6

Note: Check availability of lumber over 20 ft-0 in.

Table 6-86 *Rafter Spans for Common Lumber Species (roof live load = 20 psf, ceiling not attached to rafters, L/Δ = 180)*

Rafter Spacing 24 in.		Dead Load = 10 psf			
		2 × 6	2 × 8	2 × 10	2 × 12
Species and Grade		(ft-in.)	(ft-in.)	(ft-in.)	(ft-in.)
Doug. fir–larch	SS	14-4	18-10	23-4	23-4
Doug. fir–larch	#1	12-6	15-10	19-5	19-5
Doug. fir–larch	#2	11-9	14-10	18-2	18-2
Doug. fir–larch	#3	8-10	11-3	13-8	13-8
Hem-fir	SS	13-6	17-10	22-9	22-9
Hem-fir	#1	12-3	15-6	18-11	18-11
Hem-fir	#2	11-7	14-8	17-10	17-10
Hem-fir	#3	8-10	11-3	13-8	13-8
South. pine	SS	14-1	18-6	23-8	23-8
South. pine	#1	13-9	17-9	21-1	21-1
South. pine	#2	12-3	15-10	18-11	18-11
South. pine	#3	9-6	12-1	14-4	14-4
Spruce-pine-fir	SS	13-3	17-5	21-8	21-8
Spruce-pine-fir	#1	11-9	14-10	18-2	18-2
Spruce-pine-fir	#2	11-9	14-10	18-2	18-2
Spruce-pine-fir	#3	8-10	11-3	13-8	13-8

Note: Check availability of lumber over 20 ft-0 in.

Table 6-87 Rafter Spans for Common Lumber Species (roof live load = 20 psf, ceiling not attached to rafters, L/Δ = 180)

Rafter Spacing 24 in.		Dead Load = 20 psf			
		2 × 6	2 × 8	2 × 10	2 × 12
Species and Grade		(ft-in.)	(ft-in.)	(ft-in.)	(ft-in.)
Doug. fir–larch	SS	13-1	16-7	20-3	23-5
Doug. fir–larch	#1	10-10	13-9	16-9	19-6
Doug. fir–larch	#2	10-2	12-10	15-8	18-3
Doug. fir–larch	#3	7-8	9-9	11-10	13-9
Hem-fir	SS	12-10	16-3	19-10	23-0
Hem-fir	#1	10-7	13-5	16-4	19-0
Hem-fir	#2	10-0	12-8	15-6	17-11
Hem-fir	#3	7-8	9-9	11-10	13-9
South. pine	SS	14-1	18-6	22-11	Note
South. pine	#1	12-3	15-4	18-3	21-9
South. pine	#2	10-8	13-9	16-5	19-3
South. pine	#3	8-3	10-6	12-5	14-9
Spruce-pine-fir	SS	12-2	15-4	18-9	21-9
Spruce-pine-fir	#1	10-2	12-10	15-8	18-3
Spruce-pine-fir	#2	10-2	12-10	15-8	18-3
Spruce-pine-fir	#3	7-8	9-9	11-10	13-9

Note: Check availability of lumber over 20 ft-0 in.

Table 6-89 Rafter Spans for Common Lumber Species (roof live load = 20 psf, ceiling attached to rafters, L/Δ = 240)

Rafter Spacing 12 in.		Dead Load = 20 psf			
		2 × 6	2 × 8	2 × 10	2 × 12
Species and Grade		(ft-in.)	(ft-in.)	(ft-in.)	(ft-in.)
Doug. fir–larch	SS	16-4	21-7	Note	Note
Doug. fir–larch	#1	15-4	19-5	23-9	Note
Doug. fir–larch	#2	14-4	18-2	22-3	25-9
Doug. fir–larch	#3	10-10	13-9	16-9	19-6
Hem-fir	SS	15-6	20-5	Note	Note
Hem-fir	#1	14-11	18-11	23-2	Note
Hem-fir	#2	14-2	17-11	21-11	25-5
Hem-fir	#3	10-10	13-9	16-9	19-6
South. pine	SS	16-1	21-2	Note	Note
South. pine	#1	15-9	20-10	25-10	Note
South. pine	#2	15-1	19-5	23-2	Note
South. pine	#3	11-8	14-10	17-6	20-11
Spruce-pine-fir	SS	15-2	19-11	25-5	Note
Spruce-pine-fir	#1	14-4	18-2	22-3	25-9
Spruce-pine-fir	#2	14-4	18-2	22-3	25-9
Spruce-pine-fir	#3	10-10	13-9	16-9	19-6

Note: Check availability of lumber over 20 ft-0 in.

Table 6-88 Rafter Spans for Common Lumber Species (roof live load = 20 psf, ceiling attached to rafters, L/Δ = 240)

Rafter Spacing 12 in.		Dead Load = 10 psf			
		2 × 6	2 × 8	2 × 10	2 × 12
Species and Grade		(ft-in.)	(ft-in.)	(ft-in.)	(ft-in.)
Doug. fir–larch	SS	16-4	21-7	Note	Note
Doug. fir–larch	#1	15-9	20-10	Note	Note
Doug. fir–larch	#2	15-6	20-5	25-8	Note
Doug. fir–larch	#3	12-6	15-10	19-5	22-6
Hem-fir	SS	15-6	20-5	Note	Note
Hem-fir	#1	15-2	19-11	25-5	Note
Hem-fir	#2	14-5	19-0	24-3	Note
Hem-fir	#3	12-6	15-10	19-5	22-6
South. pine	SS	16-1	21-2	Note	Note
South. pine	#1	15-9	20-10	Note	Note
South. pine	#2	15-6	20-5	Note	Note
South. pine	#3	13-6	17-2	20-3	24-1
Spruce-pine-fir	SS	15-2	19-11	25-5	Note
Spruce-pine-fir	#1	14-9	19-6	24-10	Note
Spruce-pine-fir	#2	14-9	19-6	24-10	Note
Spruce-pine-fir	#3	12-6	15-10	19-5	22-6

Note: Check availability of lumber over 20 ft-0 in.

Table 6-90 Rafter Spans for Common Lumber Species (roof live load = 20 psf, ceiling attached to rafters, L/Δ = 240)

Rafter Spacing 16 in.		Dead Load = 10 psf			
		2 × 6	2 × 8	2 × 10	2 × 12
Species and Grade		(ft-in.)	(ft-in.)	(ft-in.)	(ft-in.)
Doug. fir–larch	SS	14-11	19-7	25-0	Note
Doug. fir–larch	#1	14-4	18-11	23-9	Note
Doug. fir–larch	#2	14-1	18-2	22-3	25-9
Doug. fir–larch	#3	10-10	13-9	16-9	19-6
Hem-fir	SS	14-1	18-6	23-8	Note
Hem-fir	#1	13-9	18-1	23-1	Note
Hem-fir	#2	13-1	17-3	21-11	25-5
Hem-fir	#3	10-10	13-9	16-9	19-6
South. pine	SS	14-7	19-3	24-7	Note
South. pine	#1	14-4	18-11	24-1	Note
South. pine	#2	14-1	18-6	23-2	Note
South. pine	#3	11-8	14-10	17-6	20-11
Spruce-pine-fir	SS	13-9	18-1	23-1	Note
Spruce-pine-fir	#1	13-5	17-9	22-3	25-9
Spruce-pine-fir	#2	13-5	17-9	22-3	25-9
Spruce-pine-fir	#3	10-10	13-9	16-9	19-6

Note: Check availability of lumber over 20 ft-0 in.

Table 6-91 *Rafter Spans for Common Lumber Species (roof live load = 20 psf, ceiling attached to rafters, L/Δ = 240)*

Rafter Spacing 16 in.		Dead Load = 20 psf			
		2 × 6	2 × 8	2 × 10	2 × 12
Species and Grade		(ft-in.)	(ft-in.)	(ft-in.)	(ft-in.)
Doug. fir–larch	SS	14-11	19-7	24-9	Note
Doug. fir–larch	#1	13-3	16-10	20-7	23-10
Doug. fir–larch	#2	12-5	15-9	19-3	22-4
Doug. fir–larch	#3	9-5	11-11	14-6	16-10
Hem-fir	SS	14-1	18-6	23-8	Note
Hem-fir	#1	12-11	16-5	20-0	23-3
Hem-fir	#2	12-3	15-6	18-11	22-0
Hem-fir	#3	9-5	11-11	14-6	16-10
South. pine	SS	14-7	19-3	24-7	Note
South. pine	#1	14-4	18-10	22-4	Note
South. pine	#2	13-0	16-10	20-1	23-7
South. pine	#3	10-1	12-10	15-2	18-1
Spruce-pine-fir	SS	13-9	18-1	23-0	Note
Spruce-pine-fir	#1	12-5	15-9	19-3	22-4
Spruce-pine-fir	#2	12-5	15-9	19-3	22-4
Spruce-pine-fir	#3	9-5	11-11	14-6	16-10

Note: Check availability of lumber over 20 ft-0 in.

Table 6-93 *Rafter Spans for Common Lumber Species (roof live load = 20 psf, ceiling attached to rafters, L/Δ = 240)*

Rafter Spacing 24 in.		Dead Load = 20 psf			
		2 × 6	2 × 8	2 × 10	2 × 12
Species and Grade		(ft-in.)	(ft-in.)	(ft-in.)	(ft-in.)
Doug. fir–larch	SS	13-0	16-7	20-3	23-5
Doug. fir–larch	#1	10-10	13-9	16-9	19-6
Doug. fir–larch	#2	10-2	12-10	15-8	18-3
Doug. fir–larch	#3	7-8	9-9	11-10	13-9
Hem-fir	SS	12-3	16-2	19-10	23-0
Hem-fir	#1	10-7	13-5	16-4	19-0
Hem-fir	#2	10-0	12-8	15-6	17-11
Hem-fir	#3	7-8	9-9	11-10	13-9
South. pine	SS	12-9	16-10	21-6	Note
South. pine	#1	12-3	15-4	18-3	21-9
South. pine	#2	10-8	13-9	16-5	19-3
South. pine	#3	8-3	10-6	12-5	14-9
Spruce-pine-fir	SS	12-0	15-4	18-9	21-9
Spruce-pine-fir	#1	10-2	12-10	15-8	18-3
Spruce-pine-fir	#2	10-2	12-10	15-8	18-3
Spruce-pine-fir	#3	7-8	9-9	11-10	13-9

Note: Check availability of lumber over 20 ft-0 in.

Table 6-92 *Rafter Spans for Common Lumber Species (roof live load = 20 psf, ceiling attached to rafters, L/Δ = 240)*

Rafter Spacing 24 in.		Dead Load = 10 psf			
		2 × 6	2 × 8	2 × 10	2 × 12
Species and Grade		(ft-in.)	(ft-in.)	(ft-in.)	(ft-in.)
Doug. fir–larch	SS	13-0	17-2	21-10	Note
Doug. fir–larch	#1	12-6	15-10	19-5	22-6
Doug. fir–larch	#2	11-9	14-10	18-2	21-0
Doug. fir–larch	#3	8-10	11-3	13-8	15-11
Hem-fir	SS	12-3	16-2	20-8	25-1
Hem-fir	#1	12-0	15-6	18-11	21-11
Hem-fir	#2	11-5	14-8	17-10	20-9
Hem-fir	#3	8-10	11-3	13-8	15-11
South. pine	SS	12-9	16-10	21-6	Note
South. pine	#1	12-6	16-6	21-1	25-2
South. pine	#2	12-3	15-10	18-11	22-2
South. pine	#3	9-6	12-1	14-4	17-1
Spruce-pine-fir	SS	12-0	15-10	20-2	24-7
Spruce-pine-fir	#1	11-9	14-10	18-2	21-0
Spruce-pine-fir	#2	11-9	14-10	18-2	21-0
Spruce-pine-fir	#3	8-10	11-3	13-8	15-11

Note: Check availability of lumber over 20 ft-0 in.

Table 6-94 *Rafter Spans for Common Lumber Species (ground snow load = 30 psf, ceiling not attached to rafters, L/Δ = 180)*

Rafter Spacing 12 in.		Dead Load = 10 psf			
		2 × 6	2 × 8	2 × 10	2 × 12
Species and Grade		(ft-in.)	(ft-in.)	(ft-in.)	(ft-in.)
Doug. fir–larch	SS	15-9	20-9	Note	Note
Doug. fir–larch	#1	14-9	18-8	22-9	24-8
Doug. fir–larch	#2	13-9	17-5	21-4	18-8
Doug. fir–larch	#3	10-5	13-2	16-1	Note
Hem-fir	SS	14-10	19-7	25-0	25-9
Hem-fir	#1	14-4	18-2	22-2	24-4
Hem-fir	#2	13-7	17-2	21-0	18-8
Hem-fir	#3	10-5	13-2	16-1	Note
South. pine	SS	15-6	20-5	Note	Note
South. pine	#1	15-2	20-0	24-9	Note
South. pine	#2	14-5	18-8	22-3	20-0
South. pine	#3	11-2	14-3	16-10	Note
Spruce-pine-fir	SS	14-7	19-2	24-6	24-8
Spruce-pine-fir	#1	13-9	17-5	21-4	24-8
Spruce-pine-fir	#2	13-9	17-5	21-4	18-8
Spruce-pine-fir	#3	10-5	13-2	16-1	

Note: Check availability of lumber over 20 ft-0 in.

Table 6-95 *Rafter Spans for Common Lumber Species (ground snow load = 30 psf, ceiling not attached to rafters, L/Δ = 180)*

Rafter Spacing 12 in.		Dead Load = 20 psf			
		2 × 6	2 × 8	2 × 10	2 × 12
Species and Grade		(ft-in.)	(ft-in.)	(ft-in.)	(ft-in.)
Doug. fir–larch	SS	15-9	20-1	24-6	Note
Doug. fir–larch	#1	13-2	16-8	20-4	23-7
Doug. fir–larch	#2	12-4	15-7	19-1	22-1
Doug. fir–larch	#3	9-4	11-9	14-5	16-8
Hem-fir	SS	14-10	19-7	24-1	Note
Hem-fir	#1	12-10	16-3	19-10	23-0
Hem-fir	#2	12-2	15-4	18-9	21-9
Hem-fir	#3	9-4	11-9	14-5	16-8
South. pine	SS	15-6	20-5	Note	Note
South. pine	#1	14-10	18-8	22-2	Note
South. pine	#2	12-11	16-8	19-11	23-4
South. pine	#3	10-0	12-9	15-1	17-11
Spruce-pine-fir	SS	14-7	18-8	22-9	Note
Spruce-pine-fir	#1	12-4	15-7	19-1	22-1
Spruce-pine-fir	#2	12-4	15-7	19-1	22-1
Spruce-pine-fir	#3	9-4	11-9	14-5	16-8

Note: Check availability of lumber over 20 ft-0 in.

Table 6-97 *Rafter Spans for Common Lumber Species (ground snow load = 30 psf, ceiling not attached to rafters, L/Δ = 180)*

Rafter Spacing 16 in.		Dead Load = 20 psf			
		2 × 6	2 × 8	2 × 10	2 × 12
Species and Grade		(ft-in.)	(ft-in.)	(ft-in.)	(ft-in.)
Doug. fir–larch	SS	13-9	17-5	21-3	24-8
Doug. fir–larch	#1	11-5	14-5	17-8	20-5
Doug. fir–larch	#2	10-8	13-6	16-6	19-2
Doug. fir–larch	#3	8-1	10-3	12-6	14-6
Hem-fir	SS	13-6	17-1	20-10	24-2
Hem-fir	#1	11-1	14-1	17-2	19-11
Hem-fir	#2	10-6	13-4	16-3	18-10
Hem-fir	#3	8-1	10-3	12-6	14-6
South. pine	SS	14-1	18-6	23-8	Note
South. pine	#1	12-10	16-2	19-2	22-10
South. pine	#2	11-2	14-5	17-3	20-2
South. pine	#3	8-8	11-0	13-0	15-6
Spruce-pine-fir	SS	12-9	16-2	19-9	22-10
Spruce-pine-fir	#1	10-8	13-6	16-6	19-2
Spruce-pine-fir	#2	10-8	13-6	16-6	19-2
Spruce-pine-fir	#3	8-1	10-3	12-6	14-6

Note: Check availability of lumber over 20 ft-0 in.

Table 6-96 *Rafter Spans for Common Lumber Species (ground snow load = 30 psf, ceiling not attached to rafters, L/Δ = 180)*

Rafter Spacing 16 in.		Dead Load = 10 psf			
		2 × 6	2 × 8	2 × 10	2 × 12
Species and Grade		(ft-in.)	(ft-in.)	(ft-in.)	(ft-in.)
Doug. fir–larch	SS	14-4	18-10	23-9	Note
Doug. fir–larch	#1	12-9	16-2	19-9	22-10
Doug. fir–larch	#2	11-11	15-1	18-5	21-5
Doug. fir–larch	#3	9-0	11-5	13-11	16-2
Hem-fir	SS	13-6	17-10	22-9	Note
Hem-fir	#1	12-5	15-9	19-3	22-3
Hem-fir	#2	11-9	14-11	18-2	21-1
Hem-fir	#3	9-0	11-5	13-11	16-2
South. pine	SS	14-1	18-6	23-8	Note
South. pine	#1	13-9	18-1	21-5	25-7
South. pine	#2	12-6	16-2	19-3	22-7
South. pine	#3	9-8	12-4	14-7	17-4
Spruce-pine-fir	SS	13-3	17-5	22-1	25-7
Spruce-pine-fir	#1	11-11	15-1	18-5	21-5
Spruce-pine-fir	#2	11-11	15-1	18-5	21-5
Spruce-pine-fir	#3	9-0	11-5	13-11	16-2

Note: Check availability of lumber over 20 ft-0 in.

Table 6-98 *Rafter Spans for Common Lumber Species (ground snow load = 30 psf, ceiling not attached to rafters, L/Δ = 180)*

Rafter Spacing 24 in.		Dead Load = 10 psf			
		2 × 6	2 × 8	2 × 10	2 × 12
Species and Grade		(ft-in.)	(ft-in.)	(ft-in.)	(ft-in.)
Hem-fir	SS	11-10	15-7	19-1	22-1
Hem-fir	#1	10-2	12-10	15-8	18-2
Hem-fir	#2	9-7	12-2	14-10	17-3
Hem-fir	#3	7-4	9-4	11-5	13-2
South. pine	SS	12-3	16-2	20-8	25-1
South. pine	#1	11-9	14-9	17-6	20-11
South. pine	#2	10-2	13-2	15-9	18-5
South. pine	#3	7-11	10-1	11-11	14-2
Spruce-pine-fir	SS	11-7	14-9	18-0	20-11
Spruce-pine-fir	#1	9-9	12-4	15-1	17-6
Spruce-pine-fir	#2	9-9	12-4	15-1	17-6
Spruce-pine-fir	#3	7-4	9-4	11-5	13-2

Note: Check availability of lumber over 20 ft-0 in.

Table 6-99 *Rafter Spans for Common Lumber Species (ground snow load = 30 psf, ceiling not attached to rafters, L/Δ = 180)*

Rafter Spacing 24 in.		Dead Load = 20 psf			
		2 × 6	2 × 8	2 × 10	2 × 12
Species and Grade		(ft-in.)	(ft-in.)	(ft-in.)	(ft-in.)
Hem-fir	SS	11-0	13-11	17-0	19-9
Hem-fir	#1	9-1	11-6	14-0	16-3
Hem-fir	#2	8-7	10-10	13-3	15-5
Hem-fir	#3	6-7	8-4	10-2	11-10
South. pine	SS	12-3	16-2	19-8	23-0
South. pine	#1	10-6	13-2	15-8	18-8
South. pine	#2	9-2	11-9	14-1	16-6
South. pine	#3	7-1	9-0	10-8	12-8
Spruce-pine-fir	SS	10-5	13-2	16-1	18-8
Spruce-pine-fir	#1	8-8	11-0	13-6	15-7
Spruce-pine-fir	#2	8-8	11-0	13-6	15-7
Spruce-pine-fir	#3	6-7	8-4	10-2	11-10

Note: Check availability of lumber over 20 ft-0 in.

Table 6-101 *Rafter Spans for Common Lumber Species (ground snow load = 50 psf, ceiling not attached to rafters, L/Δ = 180)*

Rafter Spacing 12 in.		Dead Load = 20 psf			
		2 × 6	2 × 8	2 × 10	2 × 12
Species and Grade		(ft-in.)	(ft-in.)	(ft-in.)	(ft-in.)
Doug. fir–larch	SS	13-3	17-0	20-9	24-0
Doug. fir–larch	#1	11-2	14-1	17-3	20-0
Doug. fir–larch	#2	10-5	13-2	16-1	18-8
Doug. fir–larch	#3	7-10	10-0	12-2	14-1
Hem-fir	SS	12-6	16-6	20-4	23-7
Hem-fir	#1	10-10	13-9	16-9	19-5
Hem-fir	#2	10-3	13-0	15-10	18-5
Hem-fir	#3	7-10	10-0	12-2	14-1
South. pine	SS	13-0	17-2	21-11	Note
South. pine	#1	12-6	15-9	18-9	22-4
South. pine	#2	10-11	14-1	16-10	19-9
South. pine	#3	8-5	10-9	12-9	15-2
Spruce-pine-fir	SS	12-3	15-9	19-3	22-4
Spruce-pine-fir	#1	10-5	13-2	16-1	18-8
Spruce-pine-fir	#2	10-5	13-2	16-1	18-8
Spruce-pine-fir	#3	7-10	10-0	12-2	14-1

Note: Check availability of lumber over 20 ft-0 in.

Table 6-100 *Rafter Spans for Common Lumber Species (ground snow load = 50 psf, ceiling not attached to rafters, L/Δ = 180)*

Rafter Spacing 12 in.		Dead Load = 10 psf			
		2 × 6	2 × 8	2 × 10	2 × 12
Species and Grade		(ft-in.)	(ft-in.)	(ft-in.)	(ft-in.)
Doug. fir–larch	SS	13-3	17-6	22-4	26-0
Doug. fir–larch	#1	12-0	15-3	18-7	21-7
Doug. fir–larch	#2	11-3	14-3	17-5	20-2
Doug. fir–larch	#3	8-6	10-9	13-2	15-3
Hem-fir	SS	12-6	16-6	21-1	25-6
Hem-fir	#1	11-9	14-10	18-1	21-0
Hem-fir	#2	11-1	14-0	17-2	19-11
Hem-fir	#3	8-6	10-9	13-2	15-3
South. pine	SS	13-0	17-2	21-11	Note
South. pine	#1	12-10	16-10	20-3	24-1
South. pine	#2	11-9	15-3	18-2	21-3
South. pine	#3	9-2	11-8	13-9	16-4
Spruce-pine-fir	SS	12-3	16-2	20-8	24-1
Spruce-pine-fir	#1	11-3	14-3	17-5	20-2
Spruce-pine-fir	#2	11-3	14-3	17-5	20-2
Spruce-pine-fir	#3	8-6	10-9	13-2	15-3

Note: Check availability of lumber over 20 ft-0 in.

Table 6-102 *Rafter Spans for Common Lumber Species (ground snow load = 50 psf, ceiling not attached to rafters, L/Δ = 180)*

Rafter Spacing 16 in.		Dead Load = 10 psf			
		2 × 6	2 × 8	2 × 10	2 × 12
Species and Grade		(ft-in.)	(ft-in.)	(ft-in.)	(ft-in.)
Doug. fir–larch	SS	12-1	15-10	19-5	22-6
Doug. fir–larch	#1	10-5	13-2	16-1	18-8
Doug. fir–larch	#2	9-9	12-4	15-1	17-6
Doug. fir–larch	#3	7-4	9-4	11-5	13-2
Hem-fir	SS	11-5	15-0	19-1	22-1
Hem-fir	#1	10-2	12-10	15-8	18-2
Hem-fir	#2	9-7	12-2	14-10	17-3
Hem-fir	#3	7-4	9-4	11-5	13-2
South. pine	SS	11-10	15-7	19-11	24-3
South. pine	#1	11-7	14-9	17-6	20-11
South. pine	#2	10-2	13-2	15-9	18-5
South. pine	#3	7-11	10-1	11-11	14-2
Spruce-pine-fir	SS	11-2	14-8	18-0	20-11
Spruce-pine-fir	#1	9-9	12-4	15-1	17-6
Spruce-pine-fir	#2	9-9	12-4	15-1	17-6
Spruce-pine-fir	#3	7-4	9-4	11-5	13-2

Note: Check availability of lumber over 20 ft-0 in.

Table 6-103 *Rafter Spans for Common Lumber Species (ground snow load = 50 psf, ceiling not attached to rafters, L/Δ = 180)*

Rafter Spacing 16 in.		Dead Load = 20 psf			
		2 × 6	2 × 8	2 × 10	2 × 12
Species and Grade		(ft-in.)	(ft-in.)	(ft-in.)	(ft-in.)
Doug. fir–larch	SS	11-7	14-8	17-11	20-10
Doug. fir–larch	#1	9-8	12-2	14-11	17-3
Doug. fir–larch	#2	9-0	11-5	13-11	16-2
Doug. fir–larch	#3	6-10	8-8	10-6	12-3
Hem-fir	SS	11-5	14-5	17-8	20-5
Hem-fir	#1	9-5	11-11	14-6	16-10
Hem-fir	#2	8-11	11-3	13-9	15-11
Hem-fir	#3	6-10	8-8	10-6	12-3
South. pine	SS	11-10	15-7	19-11	23-10
South. pine	#1	10-10	13-8	16-2	19-4
South. pine	#2	9-5	12-2	14-7	17-1
South. pine	#3	7-4	9-4	11-0	13-1
Spruce-pine-fir	SS	10-9	13-8	15-11	19-4
Spruce-pine-fir	#1	9-0	11-5	13-11	16-2
Spruce-pine-fir	#2	9-0	11-5	13-11	16-2
Spruce-pine-fir	#3	6-10	8-8	10-6	12-3

Note: Check availability of lumber over 20 ft-0 in.

Table 6-105 *Rafter Spans for Common Lumber Species (ground snow load = 50 psf, ceiling not attached to rafters, L/Δ = 180)*

Rafter Spacing 24 in.		Dead Load = 20 psf			
		2 × 6	2 × 8	2 × 10	2 × 12
Species and Grade		(ft-in.)	(ft-in.)	(ft-in.)	(ft-in.)
Hem-fir	SS	9-4	11-9	14-5	16-8
Hem-fir	#1	7-8	9-9	11-10	13-9
Hem-fir	#2	7-3	9-2	11-3	13-0
Hem-fir	#3	5-7	7-1	8-7	10-0
South. pine	SS	10-4	13-8	16-7	19-5
South. pine	#1	8-10	11-2	13-3	15-9
South. pine	#2	7-9	10-0	11-11	13-11
South. pine	#3	6-0	7-7	9-0	10-8
Spruce-pine-fir	SS	8-10	11-2	13-7	15-9
Spruce-pine-fir	#1	7-4	9-4	11-5	13-2
Spruce-pine-fir	#2	7-4	9-4	11-5	13-2
Spruce-pine-fir	#3	5-7	7-1	8-7	10-0

Note: Check availability of lumber over 20 ft-0 in.

Table 6-104 *Rafter Spans for Common Lumber Species (ground snow load = 50 psf, ceiling not attached to rafters, L/Δ = 180)*

Rafter Spacing 24 in.		Dead Load = 10 psf			
		2 × 6	2 × 8	2 × 10	2 × 12
Species and Grade		(ft-in.)	(ft-in.)	(ft-in.)	(ft-in.)
Hem-fir	SS	9-11	12-9	15-7	18-0
Hem-fir	#1	8-3	10-6	12-10	14-10
Hem-fir	#2	7-10	9-11	12-1	14-1
Hem-fir	#3	6-0	7-7	9-4	10-9
South. pine	SS	10-4	13-8	17-5	21-0
South. pine	#1	9-7	12-0	14-4	17-1
South. pine	#2	8-4	10-9	12-10	15-1
South. pine	#3	6-5	8-3	9-9	11-7
Spruce-pine-fir	SS	9-6	12-0	14-8	17-1
Spruce-pine-fir	#1	7-11	10-1	12-4	14-3
Spruce-pine-fir	#2	7-11	10-1	12-4	14-3
Spruce-pine-fir	#3	6-0	7-7	9-4	10-9

Note: Check availability of lumber over 20 ft-0 in.

Table 6-106 *Rafter Spans for Common Lumber Species (ground snow load = 30 psf, ceiling attached to rafters, L/Δ = 240)*

Rafter Spacing 12 in.		Dead Load = 10 psf			
		2 × 6	2 × 8	2 × 10	2 × 12
Species and Grade		(ft-in.)	(ft-in.)	(ft-in.)	(ft-in.)
Doug. fir–larch	SS	14-4	18-10	24-1	Note
Doug. fir–larch	#1	13-9	18-2	22-9	Note
Doug. fir–larch	#2	13-6	17-5	21-4	24-8
Doug. fir–larch	#3	10-5	13-2	16-1	18-8
Hem-fir	SS	13-6	17-10	22-9	Note
Hem-fir	#1	13-3	17-5	22-2	25-9
Hem-fir	#2	12-7	16-7	21-0	24-4
Hem-fir	#3	10-5	13-2	16-1	18-8
South. pine	SS	14-1	18-6	23-8	Note
South. pine	#1	13-9	18-2	23-2	Note
South. pine	#2	13-6	17-10	22-3	Note
South. pine	#3	11-2	14-3	16-10	20-0
Spruce-pine-fir	SS	13-3	17-5	22-3	Note
Spruce-pine-fir	#1	12-11	17-0	21-4	24-8
Spruce-pine-fir	#2	12-11	17-0	21-4	24-8
Spruce-pine-fir	#3	10-5	13-2	16-1	18-8

Note: Check availability of lumber over 20 ft-0 in.

Table 6-107 *Rafter Spans for Common Lumber Species (ground snow load = 30 psf, ceiling attached to rafters, L/Δ = 240)*

Rafter Spacing 12 in.		Dead Load = 20 psf			
		2 × 6	2 × 8	2 × 10	2 × 12
Species and Grade		(ft-in.)	(ft-in.)	(ft-in.)	(ft-in.)
Doug. fir–larch	SS	14-4	18-10	24-1	Note
Doug. fir–larch	#1	13-2	16-8	20-4	23-7
Doug. fir–larch	#2	12-4	15-7	19-1	22-1
Doug. fir–larch	#3	9-4	11-9	14-5	16-8
Hem-fir	SS	13-6	17-10	22-9	Note
Hem-fir	#1	12-10	16-3	19-10	23-0
Hem-fir	#2	12-2	15-4	18-9	21-9
Hem-fir	#3	9-4	11-9	14-5	16-8
South. pine	SS	14-1	18-6	23-8	Note
South. pine	#1	13-9	18-2	22-2	Note
South. pine	#2	12-11	16-8	19-11	23-4
South. pine	#3	10-0	12-9	15-1	17-11
Spruce-pine-fir	SS	13-3	17-5	22-3	Note
Spruce-pine-fir	#1	12-4	15-7	19-1	22-1
Spruce-pine-fir	#2	12-4	15-7	19-1	22-1
Spruce-pine-fir	#3	9-4	11-9	14-5	16-8

Note: Check availability of lumber over 20 ft-0 in.

Table 6-109 *Rafter Spans for Common Lumber Species (ground snow load = 30 psf, ceiling attached to rafters, L/Δ = 240)*

Rafter Spacing 16 in.		Dead Load = 20 psf			
		2 × 6	2 × 8	2 × 10	2 × 12
Species and Grade		(ft-in.)	(ft-in.)	(ft-in.)	(ft-in.)
Doug. fir–larch	SS	13-0	17-2	21-3	24-8
Doug. fir–larch	#1	11-5	14-5	17-8	20-5
Doug. fir–larch	#2	10-8	13-6	16-6	19-2
Doug. fir–larch	#3	8-1	10-3	12-6	14-6
Hem-fir	SS	12-3	16-2	20-8	24-2
Hem-fir	#1	11-11	14-1	17-2	19-11
Hem-fir	#2	10-6	13-4	16-3	18-10
Hem-fir	#3	8-1	10-3	12-6	14-6
South. pine	SS	12-9	16-10	21-6	Note
South. pine	#1	12-6	16-2	19-2	22-10
South. pine	#2	11-2	14-5	17-3	20-2
South. pine	#3	8-8	11-0	13-0	15-6
Spruce-pine-fir	SS	12-0	15-10	19-9	22-10
Spruce-pine-fir	#1	10-8	13-6	16-6	19-2
Spruce-pine-fir	#2	10-8	13-6	16-6	19-2
Spruce-pine-fir	#3	8-1	10-3	12-6	14-6

Note: Check availability of lumber over 20 ft-0 in.

Table 6-108 *Rafter Spans for Common Lumber Species (ground snow load = 30 psf, ceiling attached to rafters, L/Δ = 240)*

Rafter Spacing 16 in.		Dead Load = 10 psf			
		2 × 6	2 × 8	2 × 10	2 × 12
Species and Grade		(ft-in.)	(ft-in.)	(ft-in.)	(ft-in.)
Doug. fir–larch	SS	13-0	17-2	21-10	Note
Doug. fir–larch	#1	12-6	16-2	19-9	22-10
Doug. fir–larch	#2	11-11	15-1	18-5	21-5
Doug. fir–larch	#3	9-0	11-5	13-11	16-2
Hem-fir	SS	12-3	16-2	20-8	25-1
Hem-fir	#1	12-0	15-9	19-3	22-3
Hem-fir	#2	11-5	14-11	18-2	21-1
Hem-fir	#3	9-0	11-5	13-11	16-2
South. pine	SS	12-9	16-10	21-6	Note
South. pine	#1	12-6	16-6	21-1	25-7
South. pine	#2	12-3	16-2	19-3	22-7
South. pine	#3	9-8	12-4	14-7	17-4
Spruce-pine-fir	SS	12-0	15-10	20-2	24-7
Spruce-pine-fir	#1	11-9	15-1	18-5	21-5
Spruce-pine-fir	#2	11-9	15-1	18-5	21-5
Spruce-pine-fir	#3	9-0	11-5	13-11	16-2

Note: Check availability of lumber over 20 ft-0 in.

Table 6-110 *Rafter Spans for Common Lumber Species (ground snow load = 30 psf, ceiling attached to rafters, L/Δ = 240)*

Rafter Spacing 24 in.		Dead Load = 10 psf			
		2 × 6	2 × 8	2 × 10	2 × 12
Species and Grade		(ft-in.)	(ft-in.)	(ft-in.)	(ft-in.)
Hem-fir	SS	10-9	14-2	18-0	21-11
Hem-fir	#1	10-2	12-10	15-8	18-2
Hem-fir	#2	9-7	12-2	14-10	17-3
Hem-fir	#3	7-4	9-4	11-5	13-2
South. pine	SS	11-2	14-8	18-9	22-10
South. pine	#1	10-11	14-5	17-6	20-11
South. pine	#2	10-2	13-2	15-9	18-5
South. pine	#3	7-11	10-1	11-11	14-2
Spruce-pine-fir	SS	10-6	13-10	17-8	20-11
Spruce-pine-fir	#1	9-9	12-4	15-1	17-6
Spruce-pine-fir	#2	9-9	12-4	15-1	17-6
Spruce-pine-fir	#3	7-4	9-4	11-5	13-2

Note: Check availability of lumber over 20 ft-0 in.

Table 6-111 *Rafter Spans for Common Lumber Species (ground snow load = 30 psf, ceiling attached to rafters, L/Δ = 240)*

Rafter Spacing 24 in.		Dead Load = 20 psf			
		2 × 6	2 × 8	2 × 10	2 × 12
Species and Grade		(ft-in.)	(ft-in.)	(ft-in.)	(ft-in.)
Hem-fir	SS	10-9	13-11	17-0	19-9
Hem-fir	#1	9-1	11-6	14-0	16-3
Hem-fir	#2	8-7	10-10	13-3	15-5
Hem-fir	#3	6-7	8-4	10-2	11-10
South. pine	SS	11-2	14-8	18-9	22-10
South. pine	#1	10-6	13-2	15-8	18-8
South. pine	#2	9-2	11-9	14-1	16-6
South. pine	#3	7-1	9-0	10-8	12-8
Spruce-pine-fir	SS	10-5	13-2	16-1	18-8
Spruce-pine-fir	#1	8-8	11-0	13-6	15-7
Spruce-pine-fir	#2	8-8	11-0	13-6	15-7
Spruce-pine-fir	#3	6-7	8-4	10-2	11-10

Note: Check availability of lumber over 20 ft-0 in.

Table 6-113 *Rafter Spans for Common Lumber Species (ground snow load = 50 psf, ceiling attached to rafters, L/Δ = 240)*

Rafter Spacing 12 in.		Dead Load = 20 psf			
		2 × 6	2 × 8	2 × 10	2 × 12
Species and Grade		(ft-in.)	(ft-in.)	(ft-in.)	(ft-in.)
Doug. fir–larch	SS	12-1	15-11	20-3	24-0
Doug. fir–larch	#1	11-2	14-1	17-3	20-0
Doug. fir–larch	#2	10-5	13-2	16-1	18-8
Doug. fir–larch	#3	7-10	10-0	12-2	14-1
Hem-fir	SS	11-5	15-0	19-2	23-4
Hem-fir	#1	10-10	13-9	16-9	19-5
Hem-fir	#2	10-3	13-0	15-10	18-5
Hem-fir	#3	7-10	10-0	12-2	14-1
South. pine	SS	11-10	15-7	19-11	24-3
South. pine	#1	11-7	15-4	18-9	22-4
South. pine	#2	10-11	14-1	16-10	19-9
South. pine	#3	8-5	10-9	12-9	15-2
Spruce-pine-fir	SS	11-2	14-8	18-9	22-4
Spruce-pine-fir	#1	10-5	13-2	16-1	18-8
Spruce-pine-fir	#2	10-5	13-2	16-1	18-8
Spruce-pine-fir	#3	7-10	10-0	12-2	14-1

Note: Check availability of lumber over 20 ft-0 in.

Table 6-112 *Rafter Spans for Common Lumber Species (ground snow load = 50 psf, ceiling attached to rafters, L/Δ = 240)*

Rafter Spacing 12 in.		Dead Load = 10 psf			
		2 × 6	2 × 8	2 × 10	2 × 12
Species and Grade		(ft-in.)	(ft-in.)	(ft-in.)	(ft-in.)
Doug. fir–larch	SS	12-1	15-11	20-3	24-8
Doug. fir–larch	#1	11-7	15-3	18-7	21-7
Doug. fir–larch	#2	11-3	14-3	17-5	20-2
Doug. fir–larch	#3	8-6	10-9	13-2	15-3
Hem-fir	SS	11-5	15-0	19-2	23-4
Hem-fir	#1	11-2	14-8	18-1	21-0
Hem-fir	#2	10-8	14-0	17-2	19-11
Hem-fir	#3	8-6	10-9	13-2	15-3
South. pine	SS	11-10	15-7	19-11	24-3
South. pine	#1	11-7	15-4	19-7	23-9
South. pine	#2	11-5	15-0	18-2	21-3
South. pine	#3	9-2	11-8	13-9	16-4
Spruce-pine-fir	SS	11-2	14-8	18-9	22-10
Spruce-pine-fir	#1	10-11	14-3	17-5	20-2
Spruce-pine-fir	#2	10-11	14-3	17-5	20-2
Spruce-pine-fir	#3	8-6	10-9	13-2	15-3

Note: Check availability of lumber over 20 ft-0 in.

Table 6-114 *Rafter Spans for Common Lumber Species (ground snow load = 50 psf, ceiling attached to rafters, L/Δ = 240)*

Rafter Spacing 16 in.		Dead Load = 10 psf			
		2 × 6	2 × 8	2 × 10	2 × 12
Species and Grade		(ft-in.)	(ft-in.)	(ft-in.)	(ft-in.)
Doug. fir–larch	SS	11-0	14-5	18-5	22-5
Doug. fir–larch	#1	10-5	13-2	16-1	18-8
Doug. fir–larch	#2	9-9	12-4	15-1	17-6
Doug. fir–larch	#3	7-4	9-4	11-5	13-2
Hem-fir	SS	10-4	13-8	17-5	21-2
Hem-fir	#1	10-2	12-10	15-8	18-2
Hem-fir	#2	9-7	12-2	14-10	17-3
Hem-fir	#3	7-4	9-4	11-5	13-2
South. pine	SS	10-9	14-2	18-1	22-0
South. pine	#1	10-7	13-11	17-6	20-11
South. pine	#2	10-2	13-2	15-9	18-5
South. pine	#3	7-11	10-1	11-11	14-2
Spruce-pine-fir	SS	10-2	13-4	17-0	20-9
Spruce-pine-fir	#1	9-9	12-4	15-1	17-6
Spruce-pine-fir	#2	9-9	12-4	15-1	17-6
Spruce-pine-fir	#3	7-4	9-4	11-5	13-2

Note: Check availability of lumber over 20 ft-0 in.

Table 6-115 *Rafter Spans for Common Lumber Species (ground snow load = 50 psf, ceiling attached to rafters, L/Δ = 240)*

Rafter Spacing 16 in.		Dead Load = 20 psf			
		2 × 6	2 × 8	2 × 10	2 × 12
Species and Grade		(ft-in.)	(ft-in.)	(ft-in.)	(ft-in.)
Doug. fir–larch	SS	11-0	14-5	17-11	20-10
Doug. fir–larch	#1	9-8	12-2	14-11	17-3
Doug. fir–larch	#2	9-0	11-5	13-11	16-2
Doug. fir–larch	#3	6-10	8-8	10-6	12-3
Hem-fir	SS	10-4	13-8	17-5	20-5
Hem-fir	#1	9-5	11-11	14-6	16-10
Hem-fir	#2	8-11	11-3	13-9	15-11
Hem-fir	#3	6-10	8-8	10-6	12-3
South. pine	SS	10-9	14-2	18-1	22-0
South. pine	#1	10-7	13-8	16-2	19-4
South. pine	#2	9-5	12-2	14-7	17-1
South. pine	#3	7-4	9-4	11-0	13-1
Spruce-pine-fir	SS	10-2	13-4	16-8	19-4
Spruce-pine-fir	#1	9-0	11-5	13-11	16-2
Spruce-pine-fir	#2	9-0	11-5	13-11	16-2
Spruce-pine-fir	#3	6-10	8-8	10-6	12-3

Note: Check availability of lumber over 20 ft-0 in.

Table 6-116 *Rafter Spans for Common Lumber Species (ground snow load = 50 psf, ceiling attached to rafters, L/Δ = 240)*

Rafter Spacing 24 in.		Dead Load = 10 psf			
		2 × 6	2 × 8	2 × 10	2 × 12
Species and Grade		(ft-in.)	(ft-in.)	(ft-in.)	(ft-in.)
Hem-fir	SS	9-1	11-11	15-2	18-0
Hem-fir	#1	8-3	10-6	12-10	14-10
Hem-fir	#2	7-10	9-11	12-1	14-1
Hem-fir	#3	6-0	7-7	9-4	10-9
South. pine	SS	9-5	12-5	15-10	19-3
South. pine	#1	9-3	12-0	14-4	17-1
South. pine	#2	8-4	10-9	12-10	15-1
South. pine	#3	6-5	8-3	9-9	11-7
Spruce-pine-fir	SS	8-10	11-8	14-8	17-1
Spruce-pine-fir	#1	7-11	10-1	12-4	14-3
Spruce-pine-fir	#2	7-11	10-1	12-4	14-3
Spruce-pine-fir	#3	6-0	7-7	9-4	10-9

Note: Check availability of lumber over 20 ft-0 in.

Table 6-117 *Rafter Spans for Common Lumber Species (ground snow load = 50 psf, ceiling attached to rafters, L/Δ = 240)*

Rafter Spacing 24 in.		Dead Load = 20 psf			
		2 × 6	2 × 8	2 × 10	2 × 12
Species and Grade		(ft-in.)	(ft-in.)	(ft-in.)	(ft-in.)
Hem-fir	SS	9-1	11-9	14-5	15-11
Hem-fir	#1	7-8	9-9	11-10	13-9
Hem-fir	#2	7-3	9-2	11-3	13-0
Hem-fir	#3	5-7	7-1	8-7	10-0
South. pine	SS	9-5	12-5	15-10	19-3
South. pine	#1	8-10	11-2	13-3	15-9
South. pine	#2	7-9	10-0	11-11	13-11
South. pine	#3	6-0	7-7	9-0	10-8
Spruce-pine-fir	SS	8-10	11-2	13-7	15-9
Spruce-pine-fir	#1	7-4	9-4	11-5	13-2
Spruce-pine-fir	#2	7-4	9-4	11-5	13-2
Spruce-pine-fir	#3	5-7	7-1	8-7	10-0

Note: Check availability of lumber over 20 ft-0 in.

Table 6-118 *Rafter Spans for 70-psf Ground Snow Load (ceiling not attached to rafters, L/Δ = 180)*

Rafter Spacing 12 in.		Dead Load = 10 psf			
		2 × 6	2 × 8	2 × 10	2 × 12
Species and Grade		(ft-in.)	(ft-in.)	(ft-in.)	(ft-in.)
Doug. fir–larch	SS	11-10	15-8	19-5	22-6
Doug. fir–larch	#1	10-5	13-2	16-1	18-8
Doug. fir–larch	#2	9-9	12-4	15-1	17-6
Doug. fir–larch	#3	7-4	9-4	11-5	13-2
Hem-fir	SS	11-3	14-9	18-10	22-1
Hem-fir	#1	10-2	12-10	15-8	18-2
Hem-fir	#2	9-7	12-2	14-10	17-3
Hem-fir	#3	7-4	9-4	11-5	13-2
South. pine	SS	11-8	15-4	19-7	23-10
South. pine	#1	11-5	14-9	17-6	20-11
South. pine	#2	10-2	13-2	15-9	18-5
South. pine	#3	7-11	10-1	11-11	14-2
Spruce-pine-fir	SS	11-0	14-6	18-0	20-11
Spruce-pine-fir	#1	9-9	12-4	15-1	17-6
Spruce-pine-fir	#2	9-9	12-4	15-1	17-6
Spruce-pine-fir	#3	7-4	9-4	11-5	13-2

Note: Check availability of lumber over 20 ft-0 in.

Table 6-119 *Rafter Spans for 70-psf Ground Snow Load (ceiling not attached to rafters, L/Δ = 180)*

Rafter Spacing 12 in.		Dead Load = 20 psf			
		2 × 6	2 × 8	2 × 10	2 × 12
Species and Grade		(ft-in.)	(ft-in.)	(ft-in.)	(ft-in.)
Doug. fir–larch	SS	11-10	15-0	18-3	21-2
Doug. fir–larch	#1	9-10	12-5	15-2	17-7
Doug. fir–larch	#2	9-2	11-8	14-2	16-6
Doug. fir–larch	#3	6-11	8-9	10-9	12-5
Hem-fir	SS	11-3	14-8	18-0	20-10
Hem-fir	#1	9-7	12-1	14-10	17-2
Hem-fir	#2	9-1	11-5	14-0	16-3
Hem-fir	#3	6-11	8-9	10-9	12-5
South. pine	SS	11-8	15-4	19-7	23-10
South. pine	#1	11-1	13-11	16-6	19-8
South. pine	#2	9-7	12-5	14-10	17-5
South. pine	#3	7-5	9-6	11-3	13-4
Spruce-pine-fir	SS	11-0	13-11	17-0	19-8
Spruce-pine-fir	#1	9-2	11-8	14-2	16-6
Spruce-pine-fir	#2	9-2	11-8	14-2	16-6
Spruce-pine-fir	#3	6-11	8-9	10-9	12-5

Note: Check availability of lumber over 20 ft-0 in.

Table 6-121 *Rafter Spans for 70-psf Ground Snow Load (ceiling not attached to rafters, L/Δ = 180)*

Rafter Spacing 16 in.		Dead Load = 20 psf			
		2 × 6	2 × 8	2 × 10	2 × 12
Species and Grade		(ft-in.)	(ft-in.)	(ft-in.)	(ft-in.)
Doug. fir–larch	SS	10-3	13-0	15-10	18-4
Doug. fir–larch	#1	8-6	10-9	13-2	15-3
Doug. fir–larch	#2	7-11	10-1	12-4	14-3
Doug. fir–larch	#3	6-0	7-7	9-4	10-9
Hem-fir	SS	10-1	12-9	15-7	18-0
Hem-fir	#1	8-3	10-6	12-10	14-10
Hem-fir	#2	7-10	9-11	12-1	14-1
Hem-fir	#3	6-0	7-7	9-4	10-9
South. pine	SS	10-7	14-0	17-10	21-0
South. pine	#1	9-7	12-0	14-4	17-1
South. pine	#2	8-4	10-9	12-10	15-1
South. pine	#3	6-5	8-3	9-9	11-7
Spruce-pine-fir	SS	9-6	12-0	14-8	17-1
Spruce-pine-fir	#1	7-11	10-1	12-4	14-3
Spruce-pine-fir	#2	7-11	10-1	12-4	14-3
Spruce-pine-fir	#3	6-0	7-7	9-4	10-9

Note: Check availability of lumber over 20 ft-0 in.

Table 6-120 *Rafter Spans for 70-psf Ground Snow Load (ceiling not attached to rafters, L/Δ = 180)*

Rafter Spacing 16 in.		Dead Load = 10 psf			
		2 × 6	2 × 8	2 × 10	2 × 12
Species and Grade		(ft-in.)	(ft-in.)	(ft-in.)	(ft-in.)
Doug. fir–larch	SS	10-9	13-9	16-10	19-6
Doug. fir–larch	#1	9-0	11-5	13-11	16-2
Doug. fir–larch	#2	8-5	10-8	13-1	15-2
Doug. fir–larch	#3	6-4	8-1	9-10	11-5
Hem-fir	SS	10-2	13-5	16-6	19-2
Hem-fir	#1	8-9	11-2	13-7	15-9
Hem-fir	#2	8-4	10-6	12-10	14-11
Hem-fir	#3	6-4	8-1	9-10	11-5
South. pine	SS	10-7	14-0	17-10	21-8
South. pine	#1	10-2	12-9	15-2	18-1
South. pine	#2	8-10	11-5	13-7	16-0
South. pine	#3	6-10	8-9	10-4	12-3
Spruce-pine-fir	SS	10-0	12-9	15-7	18-1
Spruce-pine-fir	#1	8-5	10-8	13-1	15-2
Spruce-pine-fir	#2	8-5	10-8	13-1	15-2
Spruce-pine-fir	#3	6-4	8-1	9-10	11-5

Note: Check availability of lumber over 20 ft-0 in.

Table 6-122 *Rafter Spans for 70-psf Ground Snow Load (ceiling not attached to rafters, L/Δ = 180)*

Rafter Spacing 24 in.		Dead Load = 10 psf			
		2 × 6	2 × 8	2 × 10	2 × 12
Species and Grade		(ft-in.)	(ft-in.)	(ft-in.)	(ft-in.)
Doug. fir–larch	SS	8-10	11-3	13-9	15-11
Doug. fir–larch	#1	7-4	9-4	11-5	13-2
Doug. fir–larch	#2	6-11	8-9	10-8	12-4
Doug. fir–larch	#3	5-2	6-7	8-1	9-4
Hem-fir	SS	8-8	11-0	13-6	13-11
Hem-fir	#1	7-2	9-1	11-1	12-10
Hem-fir	#2	6-9	8-7	10-6	12-2
Hem-fir	#3	5-2	6-7	8-1	9-4
South. pine	SS	9-3	12-2	15-7	18-2
South. pine	#1	8-3	10-5	12-5	14-9
South. pine	#2	7-3	9-4	11-1	13-0
South. pine	#3	5-7	7-1	8-5	10-0
Spruce-pine-fir	SS	8-3	10-5	12-9	14-9
Spruce-pine-fir	#1	6-11	8-9	10-8	12-4
Spruce-pine-fir	#2	6-11	8-9	10-8	12-4
Spruce-pine-fir	#3	5-2	6-7	8-1	9-4

Note: Check availability of lumber over 20 ft-0 in.

Table 6-123 *Rafter Spans for 70-psf Ground Snow Load (ceiling not attached to rafters, L/Δ = 180)*

Rafter Spacing 24 in.		Dead Load = 20 psf			
		2 × 6	2 × 8	2 × 10	2 × 12
Species and Grade		(ft-in.)	(ft-in.)	(ft-in.)	(ft-in.)
Doug. fir–larch	SS	8-4	10-7	12-11	15-0
Doug. fir–larch	#1	6-11	8-9	10-9	12-5
Doug. fir–larch	#2	6-6	8-3	10-0	11-8
Doug. fir–larch	#3	4-11	6-3	7-7	8-10
Hem-fir	SS	8-3	10-5	12-4	12-4
Hem-fir	#1	6-9	8-7	10-6	12-2
Hem-fir	#2	6-5	8-1	9-11	11-6
Hem-fir	#3	4-11	6-3	7-7	8-10
South. pine	SS	9-3	12-2	14-8	17-2
South. pine	#1	7-10	9-10	11-8	13-11
South. pine	#2	6-10	8-9	10-6	12-4
South. pine	#3	5-3	6-9	7-11	9-5
Spruce-pine-fir	SS	7-9	9-10	12-0	12-11
Spruce-pine-fir	#1	6-6	8-3	10-0	11-8
Spruce-pine-fir	#2	6-6	8-3	10-0	11-8
Spruce-pine-fir	#3	4-11	6-3	7-7	8-10

Note: Check availability of lumber over 20 ft-0 in.

Table 6-125 *Rafter Spans for 70-psf Ground Snow Load (ceiling attached to rafters, L/Δ = 240)*

Rafter Spacing 12 in.		Dead Load = 20 psf			
		2 × 6	2 × 8	2 × 10	2 × 12
Species and Grade		(ft-in.)	(ft-in.)	(ft-in.)	(ft-in.)
Doug. fir–larch	SS	10-9	14-3	18-2	21-2
Doug. fir–larch	#1	9-10	12-5	15-2	17-7
Doug. fir–larch	#2	9-2	11-8	14-2	16-6
Doug. fir–larch	#3	6-11	8-9	10-9	12-5
Hem-fir	SS	10-2	13-5	17-2	20-10
Hem-fir	#1	9-7	12-1	14-10	17-2
Hem-fir	#2	9-1	11-5	14-0	16-3
Hem-fir	#3	6-11	8-9	10-9	12-5
South. pine	SS	10-7	14-0	17-10	21-8
South. pine	#1	10-5	13-8	16-6	19-8
South. pine	#2	9-7	12-5	14-10	17-5
South. pine	#3	7-5	9-6	11-3	13-4
Spruce-pine-fir	SS	10-0	13-2	16-9	19-8
Spruce-pine-fir	#1	9-2	11-8	14-2	16-6
Spruce-pine-fir	#2	9-2	11-8	14-2	16-6
Spruce-pine-fir	#3	6-11	8-9	10-9	12-5

Note: Check availability of lumber over 20 ft-0 in.

Table 6-124 *Rafter Spans for 70-psf Ground Snow Load (ceiling attached to rafters, L/Δ = 240)*

Rafter Spacing 12 in.		Dead Load = 10 psf			
		2 × 6	2 × 8	2 × 10	2 × 12
Species and Grade		(ft-in.)	(ft-in.)	(ft-in.)	(ft-in.)
Doug. fir–larch	SS	10-9	14-3	18-2	22-1
Doug. fir–larch	#1	10-5	13-2	16-1	18-8
Doug. fir–larch	#2	9-9	12-4	15-1	17-6
Doug. fir–larch	#3	7-4	9-4	11-5	13-2
Hem-fir	SS	10-2	13-5	17-2	20-10
Hem-fir	#1	10-0	12-10	15-8	18-2
Hem-fir	#2	9-6	12-2	14-10	17-3
Hem-fir	#3	7-4	9-4	11-5	13-2
South. pine	SS	10-7	14-0	17-10	21-8
South. pine	#1	10-5	13-8	17-6	20-11
South. pine	#2	10-2	13-2	15-9	18-5
South. pine	#3	7-11	10-1	11-11	14-2
Spruce-pine-fir	SS	10-0	13-2	16-9	20-5
Spruce-pine-fir	#1	9-9	12-4	15-1	17-6
Spruce-pine-fir	#2	9-9	12-4	15-1	17-6
Spruce-pine-fir	#3	7-4	9-4	11-5	13-2

Note: Check availability of lumber over 20 ft-0 in.

Table 6-127 *Rafter Spans for 70-psf Ground Snow Load (ceiling attached to rafters, L/Δ = 240)*

Rafter Spacing 16 in.		Dead Load = 10 psf			
		2 × 6	2 × 8	2 × 10	2 × 12
Species and Grade		(ft-in.)	(ft-in.)	(ft-in.)	(ft-in.)
Doug. fir–larch	SS	9-10	12-11	16-6	19-6
Doug. fir–larch	#1	9-0	11-5	13-11	16-2
Doug. fir–larch	#2	8-5	10-8	13-1	15-2
Doug. fir–larch	#3	6-4	8-1	9-10	11-5
Hem-fir	SS	9-3	12-2	15-7	18-11
Hem-fir	#1	8-9	11-2	13-7	15-9
Hem-fir	#2	8-4	10-6	12-10	14-11
Hem-fir	#3	6-4	8-1	9-10	11-5
South. pine	SS	9-7	12-8	16-2	19-8
South. pine	#1	9-5	12-5	15-2	18-1
South. pine	#2	8-10	11-5	13-7	16-0
South. pine	#3	6-10	8-9	10-4	12-3
Spruce-pine-fir	SS	9-1	11-11	15-3	18-1
Spruce-pine-fir	#1	8-5	10-8	13-1	15-2
Spruce-pine-fir	#2	8-5	10-8	13-1	15-2
Spruce-pine-fir	#3	6-4	8-1	9-10	11-5

Note: Check availability of lumber over 20 ft-0 in.

Table 6-128 Rafter Spans for 70-psf Ground Snow Load (ceiling attached to rafters, L/Δ = 240)

Rafter Spacing 16 in.		Dead Load = 20 psf			
		2 × 6	2 × 8	2 × 10	2 × 12
Species and Grade		(ft-in.)	(ft-in.)	(ft-in.)	(ft-in.)
Doug. fir–larch	SS	9-10	12-11	15-10	18-4
Doug. fir–larch	#1	8-6	10-9	13-2	15-3
Doug. fir–larch	#2	7-11	10-1	12-4	14-3
Doug. fir–larch	#3	6-0	7-7	9-4	10-9
Hem-fir	SS	9-3	12-2	15-7	18-0
Hem-fir	#1	8-3	10-6	12-10	14-10
Hem-fir	#2	7-10	9-11	12-1	14-1
Hem-fir	#3	6-0	7-7	9-4	10-9
South. pine	SS	9-7	12-8	16-2	19-8
South. pine	#1	9-5	12-0	14-4	17-1
South. pine	#2	8-4	10-9	12-10	15-1
South. pine	#3	6-5	8-3	9-9	11-7
Spruce-pine-fir	SS	9-1	11-11	14-8	17-1
Spruce-pine-fir	#1	7-11	10-1	12-4	14-3
Spruce-pine-fir	#2	7-11	10-1	12-4	14-3
Spruce-pine-fir	#3	6-0	7-7	9-4	10-9

Note: Check availability of lumber over 20 ft-0 in.

Table 6-129 Rafter Spans for 70-psf Ground Snow Load (ceiling attached to rafters, L/Δ = 240)

Rafter Spacing 24 in.		Dead Load = 10 psf			
		2 × 6	2 × 8	2 × 10	2 × 12
Species and Grade		(ft-in.)	(ft-in.)	(ft-in.)	(ft-in.)
Doug. fir–larch	SS	8-7	11-3	13-9	15-11
Doug. fir–larch	#1	7-4	9-4	11-5	13-2
Doug. fir–larch	#2	6-11	8-9	10-8	12-4
Doug. fir–larch	#3	5-2	6-7	8-1	9-4
Hem-fir	SS	8-1	10-8	13-6	13-11
Hem-fir	#1	7-2	9-1	11-1	12-10
Hem-fir	#2	6-9	8-7	10-6	12-2
Hem-fir	#3	5-2	6-7	8-1	9-4
South. pine	SS	8-5	11-1	14-2	17-2
South. pine	#1	8-3	10-5	12-5	14-9
South. pine	#2	7-3	9-4	11-1	13-0
South. pine	#3	5-7	7-1	8-5	10-0
Spruce-pine-fir	SS	7-11	10-5	12-9	14-9
Spruce-pine-fir	#1	6-11	8-9	10-8	12-4
Spruce-pine-fir	#2	6-11	8-9	10-8	12-4
Spruce-pine-fir	#3	5-2	6-7	8-1	9-4

Note: Check availability of lumber over 20 ft-0 in.

Table 6-130 Rafter Spans for 70-psf Ground Snow Load (ceiling attached to rafters, L/Δ = 240)

Rafter Spacing 24 in.		Dead Load = 20 psf			
		2 × 6	2 × 8	2 × 10	2 × 12
Species and Grade		(ft-in.)	(ft-in.)	(ft-in.)	(ft-in.)
Doug. fir–larch	SS	8-4	10-7	12-11	15-0
Doug. fir–larch	#1	6-11	8-9	10-9	12-5
Doug. fir–larch	#2	6-6	8-3	10-0	11-8
Doug. fir–larch	#3	4-11	6-3	7-7	8-10
Hem-fir	SS	8-1	10-5	12-4	12-4
Hem-fir	#1	6-9	8-7	10-6	12-2
Hem-fir	#2	6-5	8-1	9-11	11-6
Hem-fir	#3	4-11	6-3	7-7	8-10
South. pine	SS	8-5	11-1	14-2	17-2
South. pine	#1	7-10	9-10	11-8	13-11
South. pine	#2	6-10	8-9	10-6	12-4
South. pine	#3	5-3	6-9	7-11	9-5
Spruce-pine-fir	SS	7-9	9-10	12-0	12-11
Spruce-pine-fir	#1	6-6	8-3	10-0	11-8
Spruce-pine-fir	#2	6-6	8-3	10-0	11-8
Spruce-pine-fir	#3	4-11	6-3	7-7	8-10

Note: Check availability of lumber over 20 ft-0 in.

Table 6-131   Rafter/Ceiling Joist Heel Joint Connections (Number of 16d Nails Required)

Rafter Slope	Rafter Spacing (in.)	Ground Snow Load (psf) 30				50				70			
		Roof Span (ft)											
		12	20	28	36	12	20	28	36	12	20	28	36
3:12	12	4	6	8	11	5	8	12	15	6	11	15	20
	16	5	8	11	14	6	11	15	20	8	14	20	26
	24	7	11	16	21	9	16	23	30	12	21	30	39
4:12	12	3	5	6	8	4	6	9	11	5	8	12	15
	16	4	6	8	11	5	8	12	15	6	11	15	20
	24	5	9	12	16	7	12	17	22	19	16	23	29
5:12	12	3	4	5	7	3	5	7	9	4	7	9	12
	16	3	5	7	9	4	7	9	12	5	9	12	16
	24	4	7	10	13	6	10	14	18	7	13	18	23
7:12	12	3	3	4	5	3	4	5	7	3	5	7	9
	16	3	4	5	6	3	5	7	9	4	6	9	11
	24	3	5	7	9	4	7	10	13	5	9	13	17
9:12	12	3	3	3	4	3	3	4	5	3	4	5	7
	16	3	3	4	5	3	4	5	7	3	5	7	9
	24	3	4	6	7	3	6	8	10	4	7	10	13
12:12	12	3	3	3	3	3	3	3	4	3	3	4	5
	16	3	3	3	4	3	3	4	5	3	4	5	7
	24	3	3	4	6	3	4	6	8	3	6	8	10

Notes:

a. 40d box nails shall be permitted to be substituted for 16d common nails.

b. Nailing requirements shall be permitted to be reduced 25% if nails are clinched.

c. Heel joint connections are not required when the ridge is supported by a load-bearing wall, header, or ridge beam.

d. When intermediate support of the rafter is provided by vertical struts or purlins to a load-bearing wall, the tabulated heel joint connection requirements shall be permitted to be reduced proportionally to the reduction in span.

e. Equivalent nailing patterns are required for ceiling joist to ceiling joist lap splices.

f. When rafter ties are substituted for ceiling joists, the heel joint connection requirement shall be taken as the tabulated heel joint connection requirement for 2/3 of the actual rafter slope.

GLUE-LAMINATED BEAMS

Table 6-132   Glue-Laminated Beams Designed for Deflections 1/180

Actual Size in Inches	Clear Spans (ft)						
	8	12	16	20	24	28	32
3 × 5.5	409	121	51	26			
3 × 6.9	679	237	100	51	30		
3 × 8.3	978	409	173	88	51	32	
3 × 9.6	1332	592	274	140	81	51	34
3 × 11.0	1641	773	409	210	121	76	51
3 × 12.4	1917	978	550	298	173	109	73
3 × 13.8	2216	1208	679	409	237	149	100
3 × 15.1	2540	1462	822	526	315	198	133

Actual Size in Inches	Clear Spans (ft)						
	8	12	16	20	24	28	32
5 × 9.6	2220	986	457	234	135	85	57
5 × 11.0	2735	1288	682	349	202	127	85
5 × 12.4	3196	1631	917	497	288	181	121
5 × 13.8	3693	2013	1132	682	395	249	167
5 × 15.1	4233	2436	1370	863	525	331	222
5 × 16.5	4819	2735	1628	1019	682	429	288
5 × 17.9	5459	3038	1895	1186	809	546	366
5 × 19.3	6160	3357	2181	1365	931	674	457

Table 6-132 (Continued)

Actual Size in Inches	Clear Spans (ft)						
	8	12	16	20	24	28	32
6.75 × 12.4	4314	2201	1230	671	388	245	164
6.75 × 13.8	4986	2718	1503	921	533	336	225
6.75 × 15.1	5714	3289	1801	1127	709	447	299
6.75 × 16.5	6506	3692	2125	1330	907	580	388
6.75 × 17.9	7370	4102	2474	1549	1056	737	494
6.75 × 19.3	8316	4532	2848	1783	1216	879	617
6.75 × 20.6	9358	4986	3247	2032	1386	1003	757
6.75 × 22.0	10509	5465	3671	2298	1567	1133	856
6.75 × 23.4	11790	5971	3997	2578	1758	1272	961

Source: AM Institute of Timber Construction.

Actual Size in Inches	Clear Spans (ft)						
	8	12	16	20	24	28	32
3 × 5.5	409	121	51	26			
3 × 6.9	679	237	100	51	30		
3 × 8.3	978	409	173	88	51	32	
3 × 9.6	1332	592	274	140	81	51	34
3 × 11.0	1641	773	409	210	121	76	51
3 × 12.4	1917	978	550	298	173	109	73
3 × 13.8	2216	1208	679	409	237	149	100
3 × 15.1	2540	1462	822	526	315	198	133

Source: AM Institute of Timber Construction.

Table 6-133 *Glue-Laminated Beams Designed for Deflections 1/360*

Actual Size in Inches	Clear Spans (ft)						
	8	12	16	20	24	28	32
3 × 5.5	256	76	32				
3 × 6.9	500	148	62	32			
3 × 8.3	851	256	108	55	32		
3 × 9.6	1158	406	171	88	51	32	
3 × 11.0	1427	606	256	131	76	48	32
3 × 12.4	1667	851	364	186	108	68	46
3 × 13.8	1927	1050	500	256	148	93	62
3 × 15.1	2208	1271	665	340	197	124	83

Actual Size in Inches	Clear Spans (ft)						
	8	12	16	20	24	28	32
5 × 9.6	1930	677	286	146	85	53	36
5 × 11.0	2378	1010	426	218	126	80	53
5 × 12.4	2779	1418	607	311	180	113	76
5 × 13.8	3212	1751	833	426	247	155	104
5 × 15.1	3681	2118	1108	567	328	207	139
5 × 16.5	4190	2378	1415	737	426	268	180
5 × 17.9	4747	2642	1648	936	542	341	229
5 × 19.3	5357	2919	1897	1170	677	426	286

Actual Size in Inches	Clear Spans (ft)						
	8	12	16	20	24	28	32
6.75 × 12.4	3752	1914	818	419	243	153	102
6.75 × 13.8	4336	2363	1124	575	333	210	140
6.75 × 15.1	4969	2860	1496	766	443	279	187
6.75 × 16.5	5657	3211	1848	994	575	362	243
6.75 × 17.9	6408	3567	2151	1264	732	461	309
6.75 × 19.3	7231	3941	2477	1550	914	575	385
6.75 × 20.6	8137	4336	2824	1767	1124	708	474
6.75 × 22.0	9138	4752	3192	1998	1362	859	575
6.75 × 23.4	10252	5192	3476	2242	1529	1030	690

ROOFS
Roof Framing

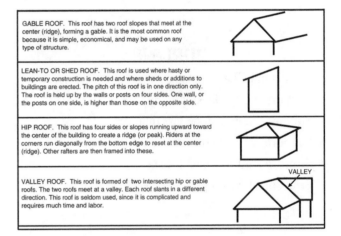

Fig. 6-28 *Typical roof types.*

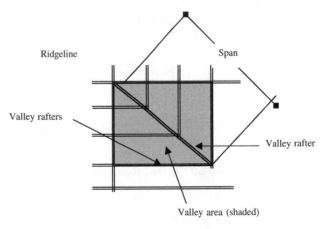

Fig. 6-29 *Valley roof (same for hip roof).*

Table Hip and Valley Beam Sizes

Hip or Valley Beam		Roof Live Load		Ground Snow Load					
		20 psf		30 psf		50 psf		70 psf	
		Roof Dead Load							
		10 psf	20 psf	10 psf	20 psf	10 psf	20 psf	10 psf	20 psf
Horizontal Span (ft-in.)	Hip or Valley Area (ft × ft)	Hip Rafter or Valley Beam Size							
5-8	4 × 4	1-2 × 6	1-2 × 6	1-2 × 6	1-2 × 6	1-2 × 6	1-2 × 6	1-2 × 6	1-2 × 6
8-6	6 × 6	1-2 × 6	1-2 × 6	1-2 × 6	1-2 × 6	2-2 × 6	2-2 × 6	2-2 × 6	2-2 × 6
11-4	8 × 8	2-2 × 6	2-2 × 6	2-2 × 6	2-2 × 8	2-2 × 8	2-2 × 8	2-2 × 10	2-2 × 10
14-2	10 × 10	2-2 × 8	2-2 × 10	2-2 × 10	2-2 × 10	2-2 × 12	2-2 × 12	3-2 × 10	3-2 × 12
17-0	12 × 12	2-2 × 10	2-2 × 12	2-2 × 12	3-2 × 10	3-2 × 12	4-2 × 12	4-2 × 12	4-2 × 12
19-10	14 × 14	3-2 × 12	4-2 × 12	3-2 × 12	4-2 × 12	4-2 × 12	—	—	—
22-8	16 × 16	4-2 × 12	—	—	—	—	—	—	—

Values are for #2 hem-fir, Douglas fir, Southern pine, or S-P-F.

PURLINS

- Purlins must be same size as supported rafters.
- Supported by at least 2 in. by 4 in. (struts).
- Supports cannot slope less than 45°.
- Supports spaced no more than 4 ft apart.
- Struts braced if over 8 ft long.
- Struts must be supported by load-bearing walls.

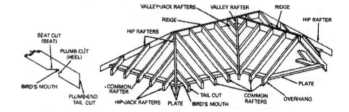

Fig. 6-31 *Roof framing elements.*

Roof Curbs

- 3/12 pitch or less at least 4 in. in height.

TRUSSES

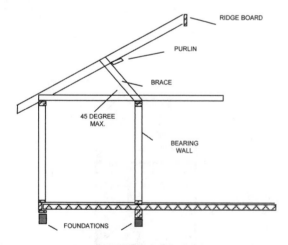

Fig. 6-30 *Roof purlin supports.*

Rafters and joist must bear:

- 1½ in. on wood
- 3 in. on masonry

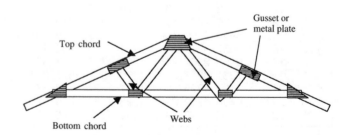

Fig. 6-32 *Typical parts of a truss.*

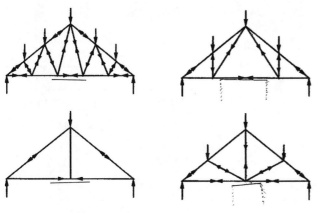

Fig. 6-33 *Forces acting on trusses.*

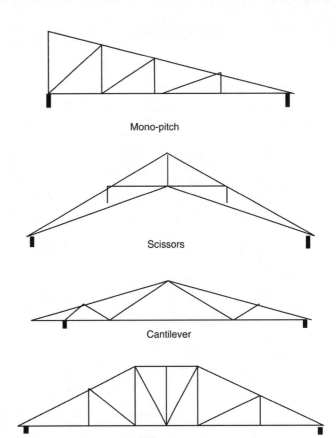

Mono-pitch

Scissors

Cantilever

Gable end

Fig. 6-34 *(Continued)*

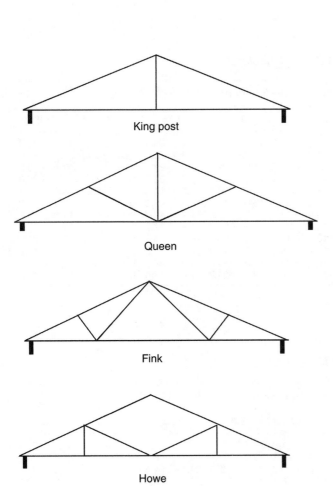

King post

Queen

Fink

Howe

Fig. 6-34 *Typical trusses.*

Roof Tiedowns (Hurricane Clips)

Tiedowns (hurricane clips) are required for roof ceiling construction whenever they are subjected to wind pressures of 20 psf or greater. Wind pressures are to be determined using zone 1 in the table and the effective wind area of 100 sq. ft.

Required Considerations

- What type of roof? Hip, gable, etc.
- Slope of roof (in degrees for code tables)
- Square footage exposed?
- Wind determine exposure rating (cladding loading)
- Wind zone
- Design wind load

Note: A continuous load path downward must be provided from the roof assembly to the bottom plate.

Table 6-138 *Component and Cladding Loads for a Building with a Mean Roof Height of 30 Feet Located in Exposure B (from ICC Building Codes)*

Roof 0–10 degrees (1:12–2:12 slope)

Zone	Wind Area	Basic Wind Speed (mph—3-second gust)								
		85	90	100	105	110	120	125	130	140
1	10	10.0 −13.0	10.0 −14.6	10.0 −18.0	10.0 −19.8	10.0 −21.8	10.5 −25.9	11.4 −28.1	12.4 −30.4	14.3 −35.3
1	20	10.0 −12.7	10.0 −14.2	10.0 −17.5	10.0 −19.3	10.0 −21.2	10.0 −25.2	10.7 −27.4	11.6 −29.6	13.4 −34.4
1	50	10.0 −12.2	10.0 −13.7	10.0 −16.9	10.0 −18.7	10.0 −20.5	10.0 −24.4	10.0 −28.4	10.6 −28.6	12.3 −33.2
1	100	10.0 −11.9	10.0 −13.3	10.0 −18.5	10.0 −18.2	10.0 −19.9	10.0 −23.7	10.0 −25.7	10.0 −27.8	11.4 −32.3
2	10	10.0 −21.8	10.0 −24.4	10.0 −30.2	10.0 −33.3	10.0 −36.5	10.5 −43.5	11.4 −47.2	12.4 −51.0	14.3 −59.2
2	20	10.0 −19.5	10.0 −21.8	10.0 −27.0	10.0 −29.7	10.0 −32.6	10.0 −38.8	10.7 −42.1	11.6 −45.6	13.4 −52.9
2	50	10.0 −16.4	10.0 −18.4	10.0 −22.7	10.0 −25.1	10.0 −27.5	10.0 −32.7	10.0 −35.5	10.6 −38.4	12.3 −44.5
2	100	10.0 −14.1	10.0 −15.8	10.0 −19.5	10.0 −21.5	10.0 −23.6	10.0 −28.1	10.0 −30.5	10.0 −33.0	11.4 −38.2
3	10	10.0 −32.8	10.0 −36.8	10.0 −45.4	10.0 −50.1	10.0 −55.0	10.5 −55.4	11.4 −71.0	12.4 −76.8	14.3 −89.0
3	20	10.0 −27.2	10.0 −30.5	10.0 −37.6	10.0 −41.5	10.0 −45.5	10.0 −54.2	10.7 −58.8	11.6 >3.6	13.4 −73.8
3	50	10.0 −19.7	10.0 −22.1	10.0 −27.3	10.0 −30.1	10.0 −33.1	10.0 −39.3	10.0 −42.7	10.6 −48.2	12.3 −53.5
3	100	10.0 −14.1	10.0 −15.8	10.0 −19.5	10.0 −21.5	10.0 −23.6	10.0 −28.1	10.0 −30.5	10.0 −33.0	11.4 −38.2

Roof 10–30 degrees (3:12–8:12 slope)

Zone	Wind Area	Basic Wind Speed (mph—3-second gust)								
		85	90	100	105	110	120	125	130	140
1	10	10.0 −11.9	10.0 −13.3	10.4 −16.5	11.4 −18.2	12.5 −19.9	14.9 −23.7	16.2 −25.7	17.5 −27.8	20.3 −32.3
1	20	10.0 −11.6	10.0 −13.0	10.0 −16.0	10.4 −17.6	11.4 −19.4	13.6 −23.0	14.8 −25.0	16.0 −27.0	18.5 −31.4
1	50	10.0 −11.1	10.0 −12.5	10.0 −15.4	10.0 −17.0	10.0 −18.6	11.9 −22.2	12.9 −24.1	13.9 −26.0	16.1 −30.2
1	100	10.0 −10.8	10.0 −12.1	10.0 −14.9	10.0 −16.5	10.0 −18.1	10.5 −21.5	11.4 −23.3	12.4 −25.2	14.3 −29.3
2	10	10.0 −25.1	10.0 −28.2	10.4 −34.8	11.4 −38.3	12.5 −42.1	14.9 −50.1	16.2 −54.3	17.5 −58.7	20.3 −56.1
2	20	10.0 −22.8	10.0 −25.6	10.0 −31.5	10.4 −34.8	11.4 −38.2	13.6 −45.4	14.8 −49.3	16.0 −53.3	18.5 −51.8
2	50	10.0 −19.7	10.0 −22.1	10.0 −27.3	10.0 −30.1	10.0 −33.0	11.9 −39.3	12.9 −42.7	13.9 −46.1	16.1 −53.5
2	100	10.0 −17.4	10.0 −19.5	10.0 −24.1	10.0 −26.6	10.0 −29.1	10.5 −34.7	11.4 −37.6	12.4 −40.7	14.3 −47.2
3	10	10.0 −25.1	10.0 −28.2	10.4 −34.8	11.4 −38.3	12.5 −42.1	14.9 −50.1	16.2 −54.3	17.5 −58.7	20.3 −56.1
3	20	10.0 −22.8	10.0 −25.6	10.0 −31.5	10.4 −34.8	11.4 −38.2	13.6 −45.4	14.8 −49.3	16.0 −53.3	18.5 −41.8
3	50	10.0 −19.7	10.0 −22.1	10.0 −27.3	10.0 −30.1	10.0 −33.0	11.9 −39.3	12.9 −42.7	13.9 −46.1	16.1 −53.5
3	100	10.0 −17.4	10.0 −19.5	10.0 −24.1	10.0 −26.6	10.0 −29.1	10.5 −34.7	11.4 −37.6	12.4 −40.7	14.3 −47.2

Roof 30–45 degrees (8:12–12:12 slope)

Zone	Wind Area	Basic Wind Speed (mph—3-second gust)								
		85	90	100	105	110	120	125	130	140
1	10	11.9 −13.0	13.3 −14.6	16.5 −18.0	18.2 −19.8	19.9 −21.8	23.7 −25.9	25.7 −28.1	27.8 −30.4	32.3 −35.3
1	20	11.6 −12.3	13.0 −13.8	16.0 −17.1	17.6 −18.8	19.4 −20.7	23.0 −24.6	25.0 −26.7	27.0 −28.9	31.4 −33.5
1	50	11.1 −11.5	12.5 −12.8	15.4 −15.9	17.0 −17.5	18.6 −19.2	22.2 −22.8	24.1 −24.8	26.0 −25.8	30.2 −31.1
1	100	10.8 −10.8	12.1 −12.1	14.9 −14.9	18.5 −16.5	18.1 −18.1	21.5 −21.5	23.3 −23.3	25.2 −25.2	29.3 −29.3
2	10	11.9 −15.2	13.3 −17.0	16.5 −21.0	18.2 −23.2	19.9 −25.5	23.7 −30.3	25.7 −32.9	27.8 −35.6	32.3 −41.2
2	20	11.6 −14.5	13.0 −16.3	16.0 −20.1	17.6 −22.2	19.4 −24.3	23.0 −29.0	25.0 −31.4	27.0 −34.0	31.4 −39.4
2	50	11.1 −13.7	12.5 −15.3	15.4 −18.9	17.0 −20.8	18.6 −22.9	22.2 −27.2	24.1 −29.5	26.0 −32.0	30.2 −37.1
2	100	10.8 −13.0	12.1 −14.6	14.9 −18.0	16.5 −19.8	18.1 −21.8	21.5 −25.9	23.3 −28.1	25.2 −30.4	29.3 −35.3
3	10	11.9 −15.2	13.3 −17.0	16.5 −21.0	18.2 −23.2	19.9 −25.5	23.7 −30.3	25.7 −32.9	27.8 −35.6	32.3 −41.2
3	20	11.6 −14.5	13.0 −16.3	18.0 −20.1	17.6 −22.2	19.4 −24.3	23.0 −29.0	25.0 −31.4	27.0 −34.0	31.4 −39.4
3	50	11.1 −13.7	12.5 −15.3	15.4 −18.9	17.0 −20.8	18.6 −22.9	22.2 −27.2	24.1 −29.5	26.0 −32.0	30.2 −37.1
3	100	10.8 −13.0	12.1 −14.6	14.9 −18.0	16.5 −19.8	18.1 −21.8	21.5 −25.9	23.3 −28.1	25.2 −30.4	29.3 −35.3

For Walls

Wind Zone	Wind Area	Basic Wind Speed (mph—3-second gust)																	
		85		90		100		105		110		120		125		130		140	
4	10	13.0	−14.1	14.6	−15.8	18.0	−19.5	19.8	−21.5	21.8	−23.6	25.9	−28.1	28.1	−30.5	30.4	−33.0	35.3	−38.2
4	20	12.4	−13.5	13.9	−15.1	17.2	−18.7	18.9	−20.6	20.8	−22.6	24.7	−26.9	28.8	−29.2	29.0	−31.6	33.7	−36.7
4	50	11.8	−12.7	13.0	−14.3	16.1	−17.8	17.8	−19.4	19.5	−21.3	23.2	−25.4	25.2	−27.5	27.2	−29.8	31.6	−34.6
4	100	11.1	−12.2	12.4	−13.6	15.3	−16.8	16.9	−18.5	18.5	−20.4	22.0	−242	23.9	−26.3	25.9	−28.4	30.0	−33.0
5	10	13.0	−17.4	14.6	−19.5	18.0	−24.1	19.8	−26.6	21.8	−29.1	25.9	−34.7	28.1	−37.6	30.4	−40.7	35.3	−47.2
5	20	12.4	−16.2	13.9	−18.2	17.2	−22.5	18.9	−24.8	20.8	−27.2	24.7	−32.4	26.8	−35.1	29.0	−38.0	33.7	−44.0
5	50	11.6	−14.7	13.0	−16.5	16.1	−20.3	17.8	−22.4	19.5	−24.6	23.2	−29.3	25.2	−31.8	27.2	−34.3	31.6	−39.8
5	100	11.1	−13.5	12.4	−15.1	15.3	−18.7	16.9	−20.6	18.5	−22.6	22.0	−26.9	23.9	−29.2	25.9	−31.6	30.0	−36.7

See Figure 6-35 for location of zones.
Plus and minus signs signify pressures acting toward and away from the building surfaces.
For wind speeds greater than 140 mph, see the codes.
Zones refer to the area of a structure such as the overhangs of the roof and are dependent on the type of roof, i.e., hip or gable construction.

Table 6-139 *Adjustments to Wind Loading Due to Exposure Zones*

Roof Height	Exposure Zone		
	B	C	D
15	1.00	1.21	1.47
20	1.00	1.29	1.55
25	1.00	1.35	1.61
30	1.00	1.40	1.66
35	1.05	1.45	1.70
40	1.09	1.49	1.74
45	1.12	1.53	1.78
50	1.16	1.56	1.81
55	1.19	1.59	1.84
60	1.22	1.62	1.87

Wind Exposure Categories

For each wind direction considered, an exposure category that adequately reflects the characteristics of ground surface irregularities shall be determined for the site at which the building or structure is to be constructed.

For a site located in the transition zone between categories, the category resulting in the largest wind forces shall apply.

Account shall be taken of variations in ground surface roughness that arise from natural topography and vegetation as well as from constructed features.

The ICC Building Code defines the exposures as:

1. *Exposure A.* Large city centers with at least 50% of the buildings having a height in excess of 70 ft. Use of this exposure category shall be limited to those areas for which terrain representative of exposure A prevails in the upwind direction for a distance of at least 0.5 mile or 10 times the height of the building or other structure, whichever is greater. Possible channeling effects or increased velocity pressures due to the building or structure being located in the wake of adjacent buildings shall be taken into account.

2. *Exposure B.* Urban and suburban areas, wooded areas, or other terrain with numerous closely spaced obstructions having the size of single-family dwellings or larger. *Exposure B shall be assumed unless the site meets the definition of another type of exposure.*

3. *Exposure C.* Open terrain with scattered obstructions, including surface undulations or other irregularities, having heights generally less than 30 ft extending more than 1500 ft from the building site in any quadrant. This exposure shall also apply to any building located within exposure B–type terrain where the building is directly adjacent to open areas of exposure C–type terrain in any quadrant for a distance of more than 600 ft. This category includes flat, open country, grasslands, and shorelines in hurricane-prone regions.

4. *Exposure D.* Flat, unobstructed areas exposed to wind flowing over open water (excluding shorelines in hurricane-prone regions) for a distance of at least 1 mile. Shorelines in exposure D include inland waterways, the Great Lakes, and coastal areas of California, Oregon, Washington, and Alaska. This exposure shall apply only to those buildings and other structures exposed to the wind coming from over the water. Exposure D extends inland from the shoreline a distance of 1500 ft or 10 times the height of the building or structure, whichever is greater.

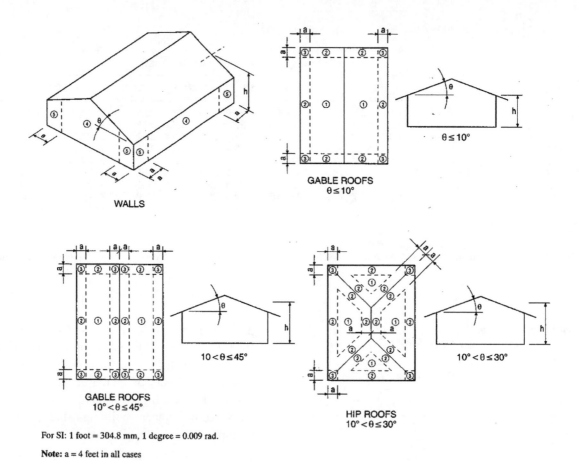

WALLS

GABLE ROOFS
θ ≤ 10°

GABLE ROOFS
10° < θ ≤ 45°

HIP ROOFS
10° < θ ≤ 30°

For SI: 1 foot = 304.8 mm, 1 degree = 0.009 rad.

Note: a = 4 feet in all cases

Fig. 6-35 *Wind zones on a typical structure.*

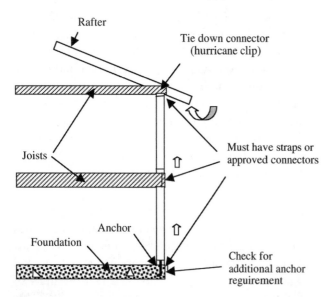

Fig. 6-36 *Roof tie-downs with connections to footer. The building code requires that the load imposed by the rafter/top plate connector be transferred down to the foundation of the structure.*

Wind Forces

Wind Speed	Force (lb per sq. ft.)	Wind Speed	Force (lb per sq. ft.)
1	.005	20	1.970
2	.020	25	3.075
3	.044	30	4.428
4	.079	35	6.027
5	.123	40	7.873
6	.177	45	9.963
7	.241	50	12.30
8	.315	55	14.9
9	.400	60	17.71
10	.492	65	20.85
12	.708	70	24.1
14	.964	75	27.7
15	1.107	80	31.49
16	1.25	100	49.2
18	1.55		

Roof Ventilation

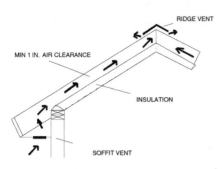

Fig. 6-37 *Roof ventilation.*

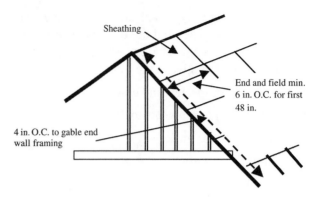

Fig. 6-38 *Nailing gable sheathing when basic wind speed is greater than 80 mph.*

- Need as a minimum 1 sq. in. of ventilation area to every 150 sq. ft. of the attic area.
- Can be *reduced* to 1 to 300 if:
  1. At least 50% but not more than 80% of venting is supplied by ventilators located in the upper space and at least 3 ft above cornice vents.
  2. The attic has a vapor barrier on warm side of ceiling.
- Vaulted ceilings with the drywall nailed directly to the rafter require each cavity to have cross-ventilation.
- Vents need corrosion-resistant mesh with openings less than ⅛ in.
- Insulation needs to be at least 1 in. away from all vents.
- Check dormers.

Attic Access

- Minimum of 22 in. by 30 in. opening.
- Check HVAC or WH—must be able to remove and or reinstall new ones.
- Clearance of 30 in. between rafters and opening (headspace).
- Check electrical wiring protection near opening (see electrical chapter).

Table 6-140 *Roof Sheathing (Wood Panels) Nailing*

Thickness (in.)	Type Nail	Edge Spacing	Field Spacing
⁵⁄₁₆ to ½	8d common	6	12
¹⁹⁄₃₂ to 1	8d common	6	12
1⅛ to 1¼	10d common or 8d deformed	6	12

Truss Installation

Fig. 6-39 *Trusses not adequately supported during transport.*

Truss Design (these items must be available at the site):

1. Slope, span, and spacing of trusses
2. Joint locations
3. Required bearings of trusses and locations
4. Design loads as applicable
   - Top chord live load (including snow loads)
   - Top chord dead load
   - Bottom chord live load
   - Bottom chord dead load
   - Concentrated loads and their points of application
   - Controlling wind and earthquake loads
   - Special loading for HVAC, WH, or others
5. Adjustments to lumber and joint connector design values for conditions of use
6. Each reaction force and direction

7. Joint connector type and description (e.g., size, thickness, or gage) and the dimensioned location of each joint connector except where symmetrically located relative to the joint interface

8. Lumber size, species, and grade for each member

9. Connection requirements for:
   - Truss-to-truss girder
   - Truss ply to ply
   - Field splices

10. Calculated deflection ratio and/or maximum description for live and total load

11. Maximum axial compression forces in the truss members to enable the building designer to design the size, connections, and anchorage of the permanent continuous lateral bracing; forces shall be shown on the truss design drawing or on supplemental documents

12. Required permanent truss member bracing location

Table 6-141 *Maximum Allowed Variances from Design*

Length of Truss*	Variance from Design
Up to 30 ft	½ in.
Over 30 ft	¾ in.
Height of Truss	**Variance from Design**
Up to 5 ft	¼ in.
Over 5 ft	½ in.

*Excludes overhangs/extensions.

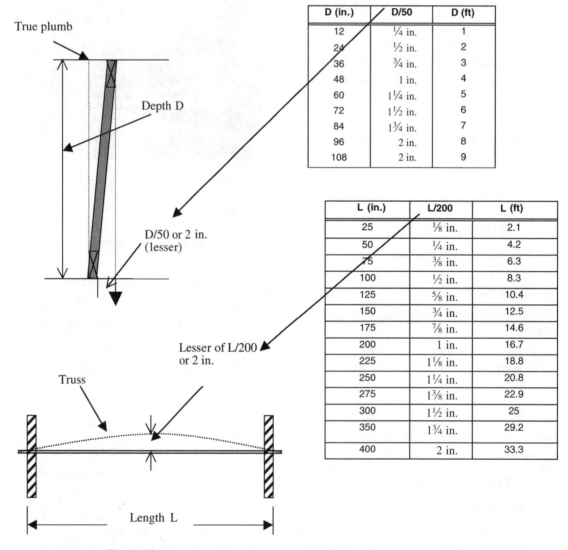

D (in.)	D/50	D (ft)
12	¼ in.	1
24	½ in.	2
36	¾ in.	3
48	1 in.	4
60	1¼ in.	5
72	1½ in.	6
84	1¾ in.	7
96	2 in.	8
108	2 in.	9

L (in.)	L/200	L (ft)
25	⅛ in.	2.1
50	¼ in.	4.2
75	⅜ in.	6.3
100	½ in.	8.3
125	⅝ in.	10.4
150	¾ in.	12.5
175	⅞ in.	14.6
200	1 in.	16.7
225	1⅛ in.	18.8
250	1¼ in.	20.8
275	1⅜ in.	22.9
300	1½ in.	25
350	1¾ in.	29.2
400	2 in.	33.3

True plumb

Depth D

D/50 or 2 in. (lesser)

Lesser of L/200 or 2 in.

Truss

Length L

Fig. 6-40 *Truss bow allowances as per HIB-91 Truss Plate Institute (TPI).*

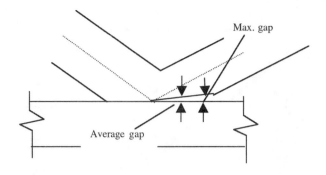

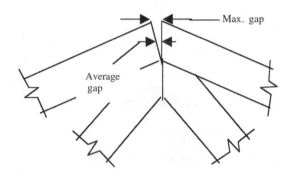

| Max. gap | 1/4 in. |
| Average gap | 1/8 in. |

Fig. 6-41 *Truss tolerances.*

Note: A uniform gap is equal to an average gap.

| Max. Gap | 1/8 in. |
| Average Gap | 1/16 in. |

Fig. 6-42 *Truss tolerances.*

Fig. 6-43 *This truss failure was due to only one web member being misplaced.*

Truss Inspections

Before Installation

- Verify sizes, design as per approved shop drawings, plans, and specifications
- Verify correct wood type and grade
- Correct metal plates, locations, and tolerances
- Correct web placements and within tolerances
- Stored correctly
- Do not allow the cutting of bands until ready to install
- Use correct methods of lifting

After Installation

- Has appropriate ground bracing been used to anchor the lateral bracing?
- Has lateral bracing been installed? Spaced correctly?
- Is lateral bracing lapped correctly?
- Are diagonal braces installed?
- Are trusses spaced correctly?
- Are metal plates correctly installed and sized?
- Are trusses laterally and vertically within tolerances?
- Has there been damage during installation?

Truss Repairs

Any correction which involves cutting, drilling, or relocating any truss member or metal connector plate is considered as a major correction, and should never be done without the written approval of the truss designer and/or the designer of record.

Truss Design Requirements

These items must be available at the site as per building codes.

1. Slope, span, and spacing of trusses
2. Joint locations
3. Required bearings of trusses and locations
4. Design loads as applicable
   - Top chord live load (including snow loads)
   - Top chord dead load
   - Bottom chord live load
   - Bottom chord dead load (check for HVAC or water heater)

- Concentrated loads and their points of application

- Controlling wind and earthquake loads

5. Adjustments to lumber and joint connector design values for conditions of use

6. Each reaction force and direction

7. Joint connector type and description (e.g., size, thickness, or gauge) and the dimensioned location of each joint connector except where symmetrically located relative to the joint interface

8. Lumber size, species, and grade for each member

9. Connection requirements for:
   - Truss-to-truss girder
   - Truss ply to ply
   - Field splices

10. Calculated deflection ratio and/or maximum description for live and total load

11. Maximum axial compression forces in the truss members to enable the building designer to design the size, connections, and anchorage of the permanent continuous lateral bracing; forces shall be shown on the truss design drawing or on supplemental documents

12. Required permanent truss member bracing location

Permanent Diagonal Braces*

Permanent diagonal bracing in the plane of the web members is also used to distribute unequal loading to adjacent trusses and to spread lateral forces to diaphragms or shear walls. Spacing of rows of permanent diagonal bracing in the plane of the webs is a matter of the building designer's judgment and will depend on the truss span, truss configuration, type of building, and the loading. Generally for pitched roof trusses, the spacing ranges from 12 to 16 ft, depending on how it relates to the bracing in the plane of the top chord. For parallel chord trusses, continuous cross and/or horizontal bridging between trusses should be provided at spacings of approximately 8 to 10 ft for floors and 12 to 16 ft for roofs. Cross-bridging should be a minimum of 1 × 3's with two 8d nails at each end. Horizontal bridging should be a minimum of 2 × 6 strongbacks (on edge) attached to each truss with three 10d nails. Strongbacks should be attached to walls at their outer ends or restrained by other means.

* The following section is from TPI—HIB-91.

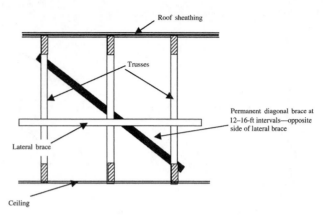

Fig. 6-44 *Permanent diagonal bracing.*

BEARING LOCATION

FOR THIS AND ALL SIMILAR TRUSSES

Truss design requires that this truss be installed on a support at this location.

Truss Plate Institute

**PLATE HERE
Bearing Location**

TEMPORARY LATERAL BRACING REQUIRED

Truss design requires temporary continuous lateral bracing on this chord member and similar chord members of adjacent trusses. Refer to Truss Plate Institute's guidelines for location of temporary lateral bracing.

Truss Plate Institute

Fig. 6-45 *Truss safety/information tags.*

Table 6-142 *Metal Plate Tolerances*

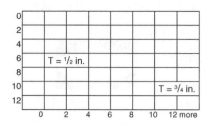

Example:

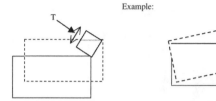

- Must leave a 1-in. gap between panel and masonry.
- Oversize all penetrations for roof.
- Must span two or more supports.
- Need to have $\frac{1}{16}$-in. gap between panels and nailed no closer than $\frac{3}{8}$ in. from the edges.

CHIMNEYS AND FIREPLACE FRAMING

Note: Framers need to pay particular attention to the clearances allowed by the codes for combustible framing materials.

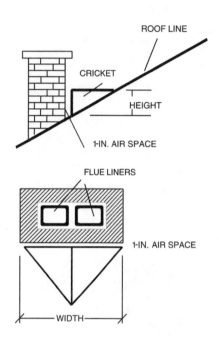

ROOF SHEATHING

Table 6-143 *Minimum Thickness for Lumber Roof Sheathing*

Rafter or Beam Spacing	Minimum Thickness
24 in. O.C.	$\frac{5}{8}$ in.
48 in. O.C.	
60 in. O.C.	$1\frac{1}{2}$ in. T & G
72 in. O.C.	

Table 6-144 *Minimum Thickness for Particleboard Sheathing*

Rafter or Beam Spacing	Minimum Thickness*
16 in. O.C.	$\frac{3}{8}$ in.
24 in. O.C.	$\frac{7}{16}$ in.

*$\frac{3}{8}$-in. and $\frac{7}{16}$-in. boards must be T&G or have clips or blocking at the unsupported edges.

Table 6-145 *Spans for C-D and C-C Plywood Sheathing*

		Maximum Spans	
Rated	Nominal Thickness	With Edge Support	Without Edge Support
$^{16}\!/_0$	$\frac{5}{16}, \frac{3}{8}$	16	16
$^{20}\!/_0$	$\frac{5}{16}, \frac{3}{8}$	20	20
$^{24}\!/_0$	$\frac{3}{8}, \frac{7}{16}, \frac{1}{2}$	24	20*
$^{24}\!/_{16}$	$\frac{7}{16}, \frac{1}{2}$	24	24
$^{32}\!/_{16}$	$\frac{15}{32}, \frac{1}{2}, \frac{5}{8}$	32	28
$^{40}\!/_{20}$	$\frac{19}{32}, \frac{5}{8}, \frac{3}{4}, \frac{7}{8}$	40	32
$^{48}\!/_{24}$	$\frac{23}{32}, \frac{3}{4}, \frac{7}{8}$	48	36

*24 for 1/2 in.

Roof Slope	Height of Cricket
12 to 12	$\frac{1}{2}$ of width
8 to 12	$\frac{1}{3}$ of width
6 to 12	$\frac{1}{4}$ of width
4 to 12	$\frac{1}{6}$ of width
3 to 12	$\frac{1}{8}$ of width

Fig. 6-46 *Cricket heights (all chimneys).*

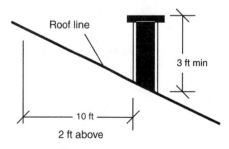

Fig. 6-47 *Fireplace chimney heights.*

INTERIOR TRIM/FRAMING
Kitchen Cabinets

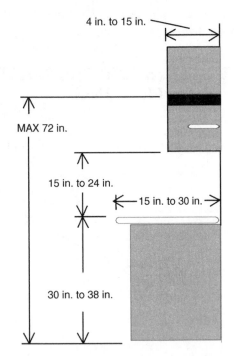

Fig. 6-48 *Minimum requirements for kitchens and vanities.*

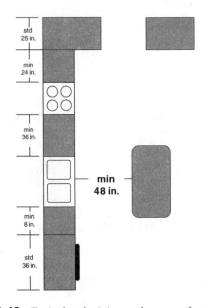

Fig. 6-49 *Typical and minimum clearances for kitchens.*

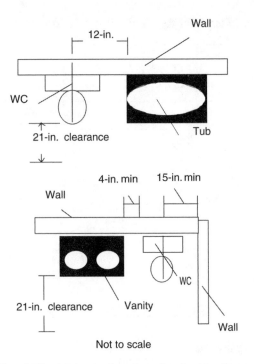

Not to scale

Fig. 6-50 *Minimum clearances for plumbing fixtures.*

RAMPS AND STAIRS
Ramps (Residential)*

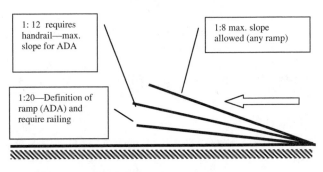

1:12 requires handrail—max. slope for ADA

1:8 max. slope allowed (any ramp)

1:20—Definition of ramp (ADA) and require railing

Fig. 6-51 *Ramp standards.*

New Construction (ADA)

- Any route with a slope greater than 1:20 is considered a ramp.
- Maximum slope is 1:12 (for ADA).
- Maximum rise for any run is 30 in.
- Handrails are required for:
  - Any horizontal rise greater than 6 in.
  - Any horizontal projection greater than 72 in.

*ADA Rules and Regulations, *New Federal Register*, Vol. 56, No. 144.

- Handrails on ramps must be 34 in. to 38 in. in height.
- Cross slope cannot exceed 1:50 (approx. ¼ in./ft)
- Changes in level cannot exceed ½ in.
- Clear width must be a minimum of 36 in.

Renovation/Existing Construction

- Slope between 1:10 and 1:12 for a maximum of 6-in. rise
- Slope between 1:8 and 1:10 for a maximum of 3-in. rise
- Slope greater than 1:8 is not allowed.

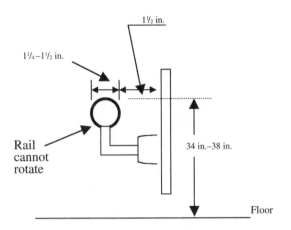

Fig. 6-52 *Handrails.*

Ramps (Commercial)

1. If used as egress—maximum slope of 1:12; all others—maximum slope of 1:8.
2. Runs: maximum rise is 30 in.
3. Must have handrail on both sides if rise greater than 1:6.
4. Must have landings at top and bottom and at turns.
5. Ramps are to be slip resistant (no trowel finish).

Stairs (Residential)

1. At least 36 in. in width.
2. With one handrail at least 32 in. With two handrails 28 in. (36 in. for ADA).
3. Risers not more than 7¾ in. in height.
4. Treads not less than 10 in. in depth; greatest vs. lesser by no more than ⅜ in.

Nosing

1. ¾ in.–1¼ in. except when depth of tread is at least 11.
2. Headroom must be at least 6 ft 8 in.

Spiral Stairs

1. Minimum width 26 in.
2. Minimum width of 7½ in. at 12 in. from narrow end.
3. Minimum headroom 6 ft 6 in.
4. Treads are identical no more than 9½ in.

Note: Spiral staircases need a handrail on the outside of the steps.

Circular Stairs

1. Minimum depth of tread is 6 in.
2. Smaller radius not less than twice the width of stairway.
3. Minimum tread depth of 10 in. measured 12 in. from narrow end.

Handrails

1. 34 in. to 38 in. in height.
2. Space next to wall not less than 1½ in.
3. Grip size 1¼ in. to 2 in.
4. Openings less than 4 in. apart.
5. Need to withstand a 200-psf force (from all directions).
6. Handrails are required with four or more risers.
7. Guardrails are required if more than 30 in. above grade.

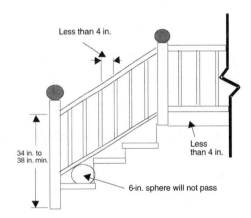

Fig. 6-53 *Stairs.*

Stairs (Commercial)

1. Minimum of 44 in. in width if more than 50 occupants, 36 in. if 50 or less.
2. Must have minimum headroom of 80 in.
3. Risers: minimum of 4 in. and maximum of 7 in.
4. Treads: 11 in. minimum.
5. Vertical rise limited to 12 ft.

Residential: 10 in.
Commercial: 11 in.
Residential: 7 3/4 in.
Commercial: 4 to 8 in.

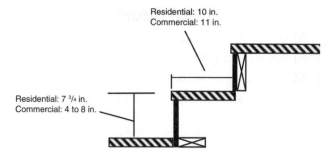

Fig. 6-54 *Stair treads and risers.*

Fireplace Trim

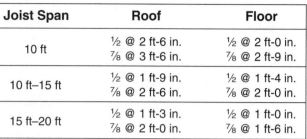

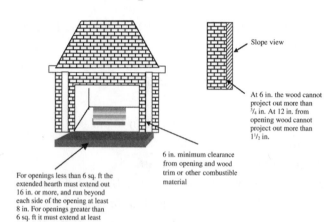

Slope view
At 6 in. the wood cannot project out more than 3/4 in. At 12 in. from opening wood cannot project out more than 1 1/2 in.
6 in. minimum clearance from opening and wood trim or other combustible material
For openings less than 6 sq. ft the extended hearth must extend out 16 in. or more, and run beyond each side of the opening at least 8 in. For openings greater than 6 sq. ft it must extend at least 20 in. in front and a min. of 12 in. on each side.

Fig. 6-55 *Masonry fireplace clearances.*

WOOD DECKS/BALCONIES

Table 6-153 Design Live Loads

Use	Min. Live Load (lb/sq. ft.)
Decks	40
Exterior balconies	60
Fire escapes	40
Attics without storage	10
Attics with storage	20
Sleeping rooms	30
All other rooms	40
Stairs	40
Guardrails/handrails	200

Note: The codes preclude masonry veneer from supporting any load other that its own.

Table 6-154 Ledger Bolt Sizes and Correct Spacing

Joist Span	Roof	Floor
10 ft	$\frac{1}{2}$ @ 2 ft-6 in. $\frac{7}{8}$ @ 3 ft-6 in.	$\frac{1}{2}$ @ 2 ft-0 in. $\frac{7}{8}$ @ 2 ft-9 in.
10 ft–15 ft	$\frac{1}{2}$ @ 1 ft-9 in. $\frac{7}{8}$ @ 2 ft-6 in.	$\frac{1}{2}$ @ 1 ft-4 in. $\frac{7}{8}$ @ 2 ft-0 in.
15 ft–20 ft	$\frac{1}{2}$ @ 1 ft-3 in. $\frac{7}{8}$ @ 2 ft-0 in.	$\frac{1}{2}$ @ 1 ft-0 in. $\frac{7}{8}$ @ 1 ft-6 in.

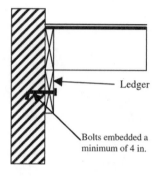

Ledger
Bolts embedded a minimum of 4 in.

Fig. 6-56 *Ledger bolts.*

Note: Building codes do not allow brick veneer to support any load other than itself. Therefore, ledgers supporting decks and or other loading must be supported by the load-bearing member of the structure or independently supported.

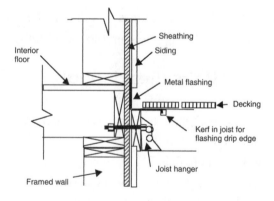

Sheathing
Interior floor
Siding
Metal flashing
Decking
Kerf in joist for flashing drip edge
Joist hanger
Framed wall

Exterior deck flashing

Fig. 6-57 *Deck flashing detail.*

Deck/Balcony Joist Spans

Table 6-155 *Joist Spans for Decks; 40-psf Live Load, 10-psf Dead Load, L/360*

Species No. 2 or better, L/360	Joist Size	Joist Spacing (in. on center) 40 lb/ft²		
		12 in.	16 in.	24 in.
Douglas fir, Southern pine	2 × 6	10 ft 4 in.	9 ft 5 in.	7 ft 10 in.
	2 × 8	13 ft 8 in.	12 ft 5 in.	10 ft 2 in.
	2 × 10	17 ft 5 in.	15 ft 5 in.	12 ft 7 in.
	2 × 12	20 ft 0 in.	17 ft 10 in.	14 ft 7 in.
Hem-fir, spruce-pine-fir	2 × 6	9 ft 2 in.	8 ft 4 in.	7 ft 3 in.
	2 × 8	12 ft 1 in.	10 ft 11 in.	9 ft 6 in.
	2 × 10	15 ft 4 in.	14 ft 0 in.	11 ft 7 in.
	2 × 12	18 ft 8 in.	16 ft 6 in.	13 ft 6 in.
Ponderosa pine, redwood, Western cedar	2 × 6	8 ft 10 in.	8 ft 0 in.	7 ft 0 in.
	2 × 8	11 ft 8 in.	10 ft 7 in.	8 ft 10 in.
	2 × 10	14 ft 10 in.	13 ft 3 in.	10 ft 10 in.
	2 × 12	17 ft 9 in.	15 ft 4 in.	12 ft 7 in.

Table 6-156 *Joist Spans for Decks/Balconies; 60-psf Live Load, 10-psf Dead Load*

Species No. 2 or better, L/360	Joist Size	Joist Spacing (in. on center) 60 lb/ft²		
		12 in.	16 in.	24 in.
Douglas fir, Southern pine	2 × 6	9 ft 0 in.	8 ft 2 in.	6 ft 8 in.
	2 × 8	11 ft 11 in.	10 ft 6 in.	8 ft 7 in.
	2 × 10	15 ft 0 in.	13 ft 0 in.	10 ft 7 in.
	2 × 12	17 ft 5 in.	15 ft 1 in.	12 ft 4 in.
Hem-fir, spruce-pine-fir	2 × 6	8 ft 0 in.	7 ft 3 in.	6 ft 3 in.
	2 × 8	10 ft 6 in.	9 ft 6 in.	8 ft 0 in.
	2 × 10	13 ft 5 in.	12 ft 0 in.	9 ft 10 in.
	2 × 12	16 ft 1 in.	14 ft 0 in.	10 ft 10 in.
Ponderosa pine, redwood, Western cedar	2 × 6	7 ft 9 in.	7 ft 0 in.	5 ft 11 in.
	2 × 8	10 ft 2 in.	9 ft 2 in.	7 ft 6 in.
	2 × 10	12 ft 11 in.	11 ft 2 in.	9 ft 2 in.
	2 × 12	15 ft 0 in.	13 ft 0 in.	10 ft 7 in.

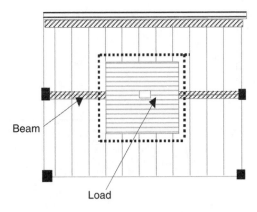

Fig. 6-58 *Tributary loading on decks.*

Maximum Beam Spans for Decks

Table 6-157 *40-psf Douglas Fir and Southern Pine (No. 2 or Better)*

Beam	Tributary Load Width (ft)												
	4	5	6	7	8	9	10	11	12	13	14	15	16
(2) 2 × 6	7	6											
(2) 2 × 8	9	8	7	7	6	6							
(2) 2 × 10	11	10	9	8	8	7	7	6	6	6	6		
(3) 2 × 8	12	11	10	9	8	7	7	7	6	6	6		
(2) 2 × 12	13	12	10	10	9	8	7	7	7	6	6	6	
(3) 2 × 10	15	13	12	11	10	10	9	9	8	8	8	7	7
(3) 2 × 12	16	15	14	13	12	11	11	10	10	9	9	8	8
4 × 6	7	7	6										
4 × 8	10	9	8	7	7	6	6	6					
6 × 8	12	10	9	9	8	8	7	7	6	6	6	6	

Table 6-158 *40-psf Hem-Fir, S-P-F (No. 2 or Better)*

Beam	Tributary Load Width (ft)												
	4	5	6	7	8	9	10	11	12	13	14	15	16
(2) 2 × 6	6	6											
(2) 2 × 8	8	7	6	6									
(2) 2 × 10	10	9	8	7	7	6	6						
(3) 2 × 8	11	10	9	8	7	7	6	6	6				
(2) 2 × 12	11	10	9	8	8	7	7	6	6	6			
(3) 2 × 10	13	12	11	10	9	8	8	8	7	7	6	6	
(3) 2 × 12	15	14	12	11	11	10	9	9	8	8	8	7	7
4 × 6	7	6	6										
4 × 8	9	8	7	6	6	6							
6 × 8	9	8	8	7	7	6	6	6					

Post Loading for Decks

Table 6-159 *Maximum Post Heights, Southern Pine–Douglas Fir Post (40-psf LL + 10-psf DL)*

Load Area (sq. ft.)	Maximum Post Height		
	4 × 4	4 × 6	6 × 6*
36	10 ft	14 ft	17 ft
48	10 ft	14 ft	17 ft
60	10 ft	13 ft	17 ft
72	9 ft	12 ft	17 ft
84	9 ft	11 ft	17 ft
96	8 ft	10 ft	17 ft
108	8 ft	10 ft	17 ft
120	7 ft	9 ft	17 ft
132	7 ft	8 ft	17 ft
144	6 ft	8 ft	17 ft
156	6 ft	8 ft	17 ft
168	6 ft	8 ft	17 ft
180	6 ft	7 ft	16 ft
192	5 ft	7 ft	16 ft
204	5 ft	7 ft	15 ft
216	5 ft	7 ft	15 ft
228	4 ft	6 ft	14 ft
240	4 ft	6 ft	14 ft
256	4 ft	6 ft	13 ft

*No. 1 grade

Table 6-160 Maximum Post Heights, Hem-Fir, S-P-F (40-psf LL + 10-psf DL)

Load Area (sq. ft.)	Maximum Post Height		
	4 × 4	4 × 6	6 × 6*
36	10 ft	14 ft	17 ft
48	10 ft	14 ft	17 ft
60	10 ft	13 ft	17 ft
72	9 ft	12 ft	17 ft
84	9 ft	11 ft	17 ft
96	8 ft	11 ft	17 ft
108	8 ft	10 ft	17 ft
120	7 ft	9 ft	17 ft
132	7 ft	9 ft	17 ft
144	6 ft	9 ft	17 ft
156	6 ft	8 ft	17 ft
168	6 ft	8 ft	16 ft
180	6 ft	8 ft	16 ft
192	5 ft	7 ft	15 ft
204	5 ft	7 ft	15 ft
216	5 ft	7 ft	14 ft
228	4 ft	7 ft	13 ft
240	4 ft	6 ft	13 ft
256	4 ft	6 ft	12 ft

* No. 1 grade

Table 6-162 Maximum Post Heights, Southern Pine–Douglas Fir Post (60-psf LL + 10-psf DL)

Load Area (sq. ft.)	Maximum Post Height		
	4 × 4	4 × 6	6 × 6*
36	10	14	17
48	10	12	17
60	9	11	17
72	8	10	17
84	7	9	17
96	7	9	16
108	6	8	15
120	6	8	14
132	5	7	13
144	5	7	12
156	5	7	11
168		6	9
180		6	6
192		6	
204		5	
216		5	
228		5	
240		5	
256			

* No. 1 grade

Table 6-161 Maximum Post Heights, Ponderosa Pine, Redwood, Western Cedar, S-P-F (South) (40-psf LL + 10-psf DL)

Load Area (sq. ft.)	Maximum Post Height		
	4 × 4	4 × 6	6 × 6*
36	10 ft	14 ft	17 ft
48	10 ft	13 ft	17 ft
60	9 ft	12 ft	17 ft
72	8 ft	11 ft	17 ft
84	7 ft	10 ft	17 ft
96	7 ft	9 ft	17 ft
108	6 ft	8 ft	17 ft
120	6 ft	8 ft	17 ft
132	5 ft	7 ft	16 ft
144	4 ft	7 ft	15 ft
156		7 ft	15 ft
168		6 ft	14 ft
180		6 ft	14 ft
192		5 ft	13 ft
204		5 ft	13 ft
216		4 ft	12 ft
228		4 ft	12 ft
240			11 ft
256			11 ft

* No. 1 grade

Table 6-163 Maximum Post Heights, Hem-Fir, S-P-F (60-psf LL + 10-psf DL)

Load Area (sq. ft.)	Maximum Post Height		
	4 × 4	4 × 6	6 × 6*
36	10	14	17
48	10	13	17
60	9	11	17
72	8	10	17
84	7	9	17
96	7	9	16
108	6	8	14
120	6	8	12
132	6	7	10
144	5	7	
156	5	7	
168		6	
180		6	
192		6	
204		5	
216		5	
228			
240			
256			

* No. 1 grade

Table 6-164 *Maximum Post Heights, Ponderosa Pine, Redwood, Western Cedar, S-P-F (South) (60-psf LL + 10-psf DL)*

Load Area (sq. ft.)	Maximum Post Height		
	4 × 4	4 × 6	6 × 6*
36	10	13	17
48	9	11	17
60	7	10	17
72	7	9	17
84	6	8	17
96	5	7	16
108		7	15
120		6	14
132		5	13
144		5	13
156			12
168			11
180			11
192			10
204			10
216			9
228			9
240			8
256			6

* No. 1 grade

Fasteners for Decks

Table 6-165 *Deck Limits Due to Bolting Only Fasteners*

Connections Using 6 × 6 Posts or 4 × 4 Posts and ½-in.-Diameter Bolts			
Tributary Load Area (ft²)			
Live Load	Douglas Fir, Southern Pine	Hem-Fir, Hem-Fir, S-P-F, S-P-F (South)	Ponderosa Pine, Redwood, Western Cedar
Two-Bolt Connection (2 × 6, 2 × 8)			
40	30	26	23
60	20	19	16
Three-Bolt Connection (2 × 10, 2 × 12)			
40	44	39	34
60	32	28	24

Table 6-166 *Connections Using 6 × 6 Posts and ⅝-in.-Diameter Bolts*

Connections Using 6 × 6 Posts and ⅝-in.-Diameter Bolts			
Tributary Load Area (ft²)			
Live Load	Douglas Fir, Southern Pine	Hem-Fir, Hem-Fir, S-P-F, S-P-F (South)	Ponderosa Pine, Redwood, Western Cedar
Two-Bolt Connection (2 × 8, 2 × 10)			
40	42	34	27
60	30	24	19
Three-Bolt Connection (2 × 12)			
40	63	51	40
60	45	37	29

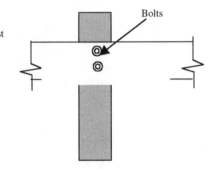

This type of fastener is the least desirable. The load is limited to the strength of the bolts, which greatly lessens the amount of tributary loading allowed

Fig. 6-59 *Bolts in post limits.*

Table 6-167 *Minimum Bolt Diameter for Joist to Post Connections*

Size of Joist Bolted to Post	Bolt Diameter	
	½ in.	⅝ in.
2 × 6	2	—
2 × 8	2	2
2 × 10	3	2
2 × 12	3	3

Deck Loading

Table 6-168   Average Person 160-lb Loading; 40-psf Live Load (10-psf Dead Load)

Width (ft)	Deck Length (ft)									
6	7	8	9	10	11	12	13	14	16	
7	12	14	16	18	19	21	23	25	28	
8	14	16	23	20	22	24	26	32	32	
9	16	18	20	23	25	27	29	32	36	
10	18	20	23	25	28	30	33	35	40	
11	19	22	25	28	30	33	36	39	44	
12	21	24	27	30	33	36	39	42	48	
13	23	26	29	33	36	39	42	46	52	
14	25	28	32	35	39	42	46	49	56	

Table 6-169   Average Person 160-lb Loading; 50-psf Live Load (10-psf Dead Load)

Width (ft)	Deck Length (ft)									
6	7	8	9	10	11	12	13	14	16	
7	15	18	20	22	24	26	28	31	35	
8	18	20	23	25	28	30	33	40	40	
9	20	23	25	28	31	34	37	39	45	
10	22	25	28	31	34	38	41	44	50	
11	24	28	31	34	38	41	45	48	55	
12	26	30	34	38	41	45	49	53	60	
13	28	33	37	41	45	49	53	57	65	
14	31	35	39	44	48	53	57	61	70	

7
CHAPTER

Structural Steel

GENERAL

This chapter covers the structural steel in buildings, either commercial or industrial construction projects. Welding is also covered. Steel construction in residential and light commercial use is covered in Chapter 6, "Carpentry."

The Inspector should have the following to assist in his inspections:

- American Institute of Steel Construction (AISC) Publications:

  Specification for the Design, Fabrication and Erection of Structural Steel for Buildings (with commentary), Nov. 1, 1978.

  Specification for Structural Joints Using ASTM A325 or A490 Bolts, Feb. 4, 1976; Errata July 1, 1976.

PRECONSTRUCTION INSPECTION

1. Receive and review approved shop drawings
2. Coordinate with other trades
3. Check mill test reports
4. Check welder certificates for appropriateness and expiration

5. Check to see if weld procedure is qualified or if using AWS prequalified welds
6. Have contractor inventory and inspect all steel deliveries
7. Check for high-strength bolting requirements
   - Type
   - Size
   - Bolt tightening methods
8. Check painting requirements
9. Check for erection procedure and handling requirements. Make sure all safety precautions are followed.

SHOP DRAWINGS

1. All critical connections are to be shown on the contract drawings and must be fabricated in accordance with the specifications and contract drawings. Connections not shown on contract drawings are to be detailed in accordance with AISC.
2. Approved shop drawings must be on hand prior to the start of steel erection.
3. Particular attention should be given to requirements and arrangement of temporary bolting and bracing, guylines, and fastenings.

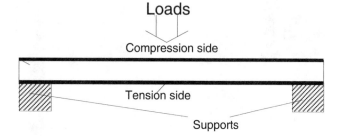

Fig. 7-1 *Steel beams.*

Table 7-1 *Steel Beam Spans*

Beam Sizes and Weights (kips)					
Spans	W10 × 21	W12 × 27	W14 × 30	W16 × 36	W18 × 50
10	29	45	56	75	119
12	24	38	46	63	99
14	21	32	40	54	85
16	17.9	28	35	47	74
18	15.9	25	31	42	66
20	14.3	23	28	38	59
22		21	25	34	54
24		19	24	31	49
26			21	29	46
28			19.6	27	42
30			18.6	25	40

Note: All loads are in kips (1000 lb).

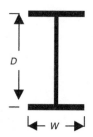

Fig. 7-2 *Wide flange steel (W).*

Table 7-2 *Steel Beams Sizes*

Designation	Depth (in.)	Flange (W) (in.)
W 36 × 135	35.55	11.95
W 30 × 99	29.65	10.45
W 24 × 84	24.10	9.02
W 24 × 55	23.57	7.01
W 21 × 68	21.13	8.27
W 21 × 44	20.66	6.50
W 18 × 65	18.35	7.59
W 18 × 46	18.06	6.06
W 18 × 35	17.70	6.00
W 16 × 45	16.13	7.04
W 16 × 36	15.86	6.99
W 14 × 68	14.04	10.04

Table 7-2 (Continued)

Designation	Depth (in.)	Flange (W) (in.)
W 14 × 43	13.66	8.00
W 14 × 26	13.91	5.03
W 14 × 22	13.74	5.00
W 12 × 79	12.38	12.08
W 12 × 58	12.19	10.01
W 12 × 30	12.34	6.62
W 12 × 16	11.99	3.99
W 10 × 45	10.10	8.02
W 10 × 26	10.33	5.77
W 10 × 15	9.99	4.00
W 10 × 12	9.87	3.96
W 8 × 48	8.50	8.11
W 8 × 24	7.93	6.25
W 8 × 18	8.14	5.25
W 8 × 10	7.89	3.94
W 6 × 25	6.38	6.08
W 6 × 16	6.28	4.03
W 6 × 12	6.03	4.00
W 6 × 9	5.90	3.94

STEEL ON THE JOB SITE

Check the following items of the structural steel upon arrival and prior to erection.

Sizes and Shapes

1. Check every member against the shop drawings for correct size, shape, and weight.

2. Check sizes and type, grade of bolts, rivets, washers, and welds as well as hole diameters.

3. Watch for beams made up of welded plates being substituted for a rolled beam.

Table 7-3 Hot-Rolled Steel Symbols

Hot-Rolled Steel	Symbol
Plate	PL
Flat bar	FL T
Square bar	BAR
Wide-flange beam the basic shape used for beams and columns	W
American standard beam used for beams with narrow flanges	S
Miscellaneous beam a lightweight beam	M
American standard channel used for lightweight beams, door jambs, purlins, and girts	C
Junior beam, a lightweight beam similar to the I-beam and used in secondary members	JR

Table 7-3 (Continued)

Hot-Rolled Steel	Symbol
Round, or rod used for cross-bracing in roofs and walls	ROD
Angle used in secondary members	L
Structural tube, square or rectangular, slit from flat-rolled steel, formed, fusion welded, and cut to length in one continuous operation. This shape is commonly used for columns.	TS
Standard pipe	STD PIPE
Extra strong pipe	X-STRONG PIPE
Double extra strong pipe similar to schedule 40, 80, and 120 steel pipe, and used for columns	XX-STRONG PIPE
Structural tees cut from wide-flange shapes	WT
American standard shapes	ST
Miscellaneous shapes	MT

Table 7-4 Chord Truss Spans

Typical Ratios of Truss Depths for Parallel Chord Trusses	
Depth (ft)	Span (ft)
2	20 to 30
3	35 to 45
4	50 to 60
5	65 to 75
6	80 to 90
7	95 to 110
8	120 to 200

Alignment and Damage

1. Members must be free of kinks, bends, or other damage.

2. Check the specifications for allowable tolerances.

3. No straightening of bent or misaligned members should be allowed in the field except as approved by the Project Manager.

New Steel

1. Check that the steel furnished is new.

2. Look for identifying mill markings and log.

3. Look for such tell-tale evidence as old rivet and bolt holes that may have been filled with weld material, ground smooth, and painted over.

4. Check that steel is free of all other defects.

Fig. 7-3 *Iron workers setting a column.*

Shop Fabrication

1. Has the steel been inspected in the shop by an inspector? Keep copies of the reports.

   a. If no shop inspection, then all shop connections must be inspected in the field with the same care required for field connections.

   b. Steel inspected in the shop should be examined upon arrival at the job site to determine if damage has been incurred during transportation or if errors and faulty workmanship may have gone undetected during shop inspection.

2. Check if column ends, scheduled to be milled, have been milled. Check to determine whether cap and base plates on columns have been correctly welded.

3. Shop connections are discussed in the Field Connection section.

Shop Painting

1. Inspect shop painting for abraded areas and loose mill scale or rust, making sure that all defects are satisfactorily corrected before erection.

2. Check the specifications to determine if contact surfaces for joints to be connected with high tensile strength bolts are not to be painted. Contact surfaces for friction type connections must be free of paint. Check the AISC for treatment permitted.

3. Check specifications for steel embedded in concrete and paint on steel surfaces to be field welded or on which fire proofing is spray applied.

Storage and Handling

1. Steel should be stored neatly in a pre-designated area and out of the way of the other trades.

2. Require steel members to be blocked off the ground to avoid corrosion and to aid in inspection. For prolonged storage, the steel should be properly protected against the weather and other construction activity.

TRUSS RIGGING

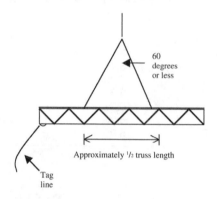

Fig. 7-4 *Trusses less than 30 ft.*

3. When unloading or during erection of long flexible steel members or trusses, require the contractor to use a double choker or double sling so as not to overstress the member by picking it up at only one point.

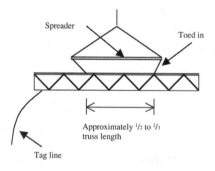

Fig. 7-5 *Trusses 30 ft to 60 ft.*

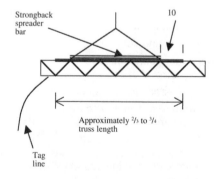

Fig. 7-6 *Trusses over 60 ft.*

4. Monitor the handling of steel to prevent distortion or damage during unloading and storage. Bent items must not be used—even if re-bent to original condition.

5. Check for adequate connections in partly fabricated units. When not completely welded in the shop, the units should be bolted or otherwise supported to prevent damage in shipment and handling.

COMMON CAUSES OF STEEL FAILURES

- Burnt or oversized bolt holes.
- Unequal stressing in gusset plates.
- Excessive bolt tension.
- Using nonconforming grade of bolts.
- High-strength bolts are not correct size, length, and/or incorrect washers or nuts are used.
- Machined bolt holes are not aligned properly, wrong size, or in wrong location or arrangement.

CONTRACTOR'S EQUIPMENT

1. Check cranes to ensure that they have been inspected, have been tested, and are of adequate capacity for the intended loads.

2. Check to ensure that the cables are new or are in good condition, not frayed or worn, and that necessary safety stops are installed. The provisions for steel handling and erection as well as equipment inspection in the Contractors Safety Manual should be carefully reviewed.

FOUNDATIONS ALIGNMENT

1. Dimensions and elevations of foundations should be checked against the contract drawings.

2. Check footings for spacing, elevations, and size.

3. Check the date of concrete pour for foundations to receive columns. Do not permit placement on green concrete (usually 7 days for normal concrete).

ANCHOR BOLTS

1. Check to ensure that sufficient length of bolt is protruding above the concrete to allow full engagement by the nut and allows for leveling nut.

2. Make sure the contractor maintains an accurate inventory of bolts. Do not permit any concrete piers or foundation caps to be scheduled until required bolts are identified on hand.

3. Prior to the erection of structural steel, the anchor bolt settings should be checked for accuracy of layout. Use templates to ensure accurate placement.

Fig. 7-7 *Damaged anchor bolts.*

4. Chipping of concrete and bending of anchor bolts to fit bearing plates is *not permitted.*

5. Bolts should be protected from concrete, grout, and other material.

6. Store bolts in protected areas to keep free of mud, dirt, and moisture.

7. Do not allow the contractor to re-install incorrectly anchors by epoxy unless prior approval is given by the Project Engineer.

Steel Erection

Base plates

1. See that temporary connections necessary to hold all steel in proper position are provided before permanent welds are accurately fitted, aligned, plumbed, and leveled.

2. Check that top of concrete is clear of dirt or foreign material.

3. Check that base plate is set at proper line and level or slope, as required for alignment of frame, and firmly anchored down over metal wedges, shims, and/or setting nuts. The space between top of concrete and bottom of base plate should be a minimum of $1/24$ base plate width.

4. Shims should be steel plates of varying thickness and not nuts or odd pieces of metal.

5. The frame must be plumbed and properly guyed before making final adjustments to setting. Setting shims and wedges should be snugly fitted so they cannot be easily dislodged.

6. Prior to grouting insist that the concrete bases are free of dirt or debris—cleaning with compressed air is desirable method. See Masonry chapter on grouting procedures and methods.

7. Check that the dry-pack bedding mortar or grout between top of concrete and bottom of bearing-plate is properly rammed and completely placed.

8. Check that provision is made for proper curing of exposed edge of mortar bedding.

9. Shims and wedges should remain in place. Projections beyond edges of bearing-plates should be cut off.

10. Separate setting plates are not permitted.

Fig. 7-8 *Column base with packed "dry" grout.*

Alignment

1. Check that all steel members are accurately fitted, leveled, plumbed, and guyed and adequate temporary connections made before permanent riveted, welded, or bolted connections are completed.

2. Do not permit rough handling of material, such as heavy pounding with sledges.

3. Driftpins may be used only to bring together several parts; they should not be used in such a manner as to distort or damage the metal.

4. Do not permit the use of a gas-cutting torch for correcting fabrication errors on any major member in the structural framing. Its use will be permitted on minor members when the member is not under stress and then only with the approval of the Project Manager.

Fig. 7-9 *Iron workers making connection.*

Guys and Supports

1. Check guys and supports for size and condition, adequacy of anchorage and suitability of anchorage points.

2. Guylines must be taut.

3. Check that contact between guylines or braces and erection equipment is avoided.

4. Procedures which might cause back-guys to break during plumbing up or erection operations should not be permitted.

Field Connections—Bolting, General

1. Check type, length and size of bolt, size and type of washers, and size of hole.

2. Check to ensure that all bolt heads and nuts are resting squarely against the metal, and that bolts have been drawn adequately tight.

3. Check for the requirements for upset threads or lockwashers and for compliance with these requirements.

4. Check for alignment of holes. Poor matching of holes should be cause for rejection of the members. *Burning to correct misalignment is not permitted.*

High-Strength Bolted Connection

The A325 high-strength bolt may be identified by three radial marks on the head and three long indented marks on the nut. The A490 bolt head is marked A490, and the nut is marked either 2H or DH. The bolt is used with a washer on the side of the element that is turned, except for A325 bolts when turn-of-nut tightening method is used. The inspector should make sure ordinary washers and nuts are not used and should have the AISC pamphlet *Specification for Structural Joints Using ASTM A325 or A490 Bolts.*

Recommendations on inspection in the pamphlet should be followed.

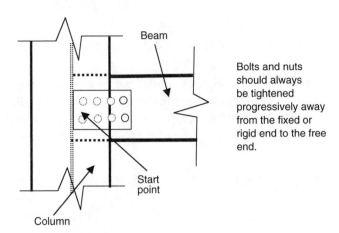

Fig. 7-10 *Bolt-tightening sequence.*

Some of the items to check in a high-tensile, bolted connection are as follows:

1. Unless noted otherwise in the specifications, contact surfaces of a high-tension–bolted connection should show only the normal tight mill scale and should be free of dirt, oil, loose scale, burrs, pits, and other defects that would prevent the solid seating of the parts.

2. Paint is permitted in bearing-type connections. Check the AISC specification for surface treatments permitted in friction type connections. The drawings will usually define these connections.

3. The contractor should provide the means and should calibrate *twice a day* all wrenches to be used for calibrated wrench-tightening method.

4. Check required bolt tension by use of a torque wrench furnished by the contractor. All high-strength bolts need not be checked. Normally 5–10% of the bolts should be checked.

5. Since AISC specifies bolt tightening in terms of bolt tension, it is necessary that the torque wrench be calibrated using a device which will indicate actual bolt tension.

Table 7-5 *ASTM A325 Bolt Tensions*

Size	Required Tension	Approximate Torque Needed
½ in.	10,850 lb	90 lb/ft
⅝ in.	17,250 lb	180 lb/ft
¾ in.	25,600 lb	320 lb/ft
⅞ in.	32,400 lb	470 lb/ft
1 in.	42,500 lb	710 lb/ft

Table 7-6 *ASTM A490 Bolt Tensions*

Bolt Diameter	Tension
½ in.	—
⅝ in.	—
¾ in.	35,000 lb
⅞ in.	49,000 lb
1 in.	64,000 lb
1⅛ in.	80,000 lb
1¼ in.	102,000 lb

6. An acceptable and preferred method of torqueing high-strength bolts is the "turn of nut" method described in the AISC pamphlet *Structural Joints Using ASTM A325 or A490 Bolts*. Be familiar with this method.

7. The AISC specification permits the use of direct tension indicators (indicator washers) providing the correct indication of tension has been achieved. In other words, the tension required must be determined by testing with a torque wrench.

8. *High-strength bolts cannot be reused.*

Turn-of-Nut (Bolt) Tightening Method

When the turn-of-nut method is used to tighten the bolt to the tension specified, first, enough bolts are to be brought to a "snug tight" condition to ensure that the parts of the joint are brought together and have good contact between them. *Snug tight* is defined as the tightness attained by a few impacts of an impact wrench or the full effort of a man using an ordinary spud wrench. Next, the remaining bolts shall be placed in the remaining holes and brought to snug tightness. All bolts then be tightened additionally by the applicable amount of nut rotation specified in the table below.

Table 7-7 *Turn-of-Nut (Bolt) Tightening Method*

	Disposition of Outer Faces of Bolted Ports		
	Both Faces Normal to Bolt Axis	One Face Normal to Bolt Axis, Other Face Sloped Not More Than 1:20	Both Faces Sloped Not More Than 1:20 from Normal to Bolt Axis
Up to and including 4 diameters	⅓ turn	½ turn	⅔ turn
Over 4 diameters but not exceeding 8 diameters	½ turn	⅔ turn	⅚ turn
Over 8 diameters but not exceeding 12 diameters	⅔ turn	⅚ turn	1 turn

Bolt length (as measured from underside of head to end of point).

Sequence of tightening is to be progressing from the most rigid part of the joint to its free edges. During tightening there shall be no rotation of the reverse side.

Unfinished Bolted Connections

1. Check to see if specifications require that bolts be dipped in red lead paint before installation.
2. Check that the same number of threads are exposed in any one connection and that the correct length of bolt is used.
3. Check for the contractors use of an approved welding procedure prior to the commencement of welding.

Turned Bolts

Turned or rivet bolts in reamed holes have the same value as rivets. The same checks should be made for turned bolts as for other bolts.

Ribbed Bolts

The ribbed bolt is the equivalent of a rivet and is used without a washer. The same checks should be made for ribbed bolts as for other bolts.

Welded Connections

Some items to check in a welded connection area follow:

1. Check on the qualifications of the welders and for qualified procedures in accordance with Section 5 of the Structural Welding Code, AWS D1.1.
2. Check to see that all of the welds called for on the approved shop drawings have actually been made, and that they are accurately located and of the specified sizes. Check to see that shop nondestructive tests (radiographing, magnifluxing) required by the specifications have been performed. Keep copies for your records.
3. Check finished welds for size, length, and standards of workmanship with respect to contour and appearance of the weld surface, surface defects, craters, undercutting, overlapping edges of welds, cracks, etc. Unacceptable welds should be removed, rewelded, and re-examined promptly.
4. Weld location is important; placing weld in the wrong location may be just as serious as omitting the welds altogether.
5. Over-welding either in size or length of welds is to be discouraged since such practices may introduce distortions.

6. Surfaces to be welded should be free from loose scale, slag, rust, grease, paint, and any other foreign material, except mill scale, which, as it withstands rigorous wire brushing, may remain.
7. Joint surfaces to be welded should be free from fins and tears.
8. Field welding requires similar checks to shop welding, and in addition the inspector must be aware of minimum ambient temperature in weld vicinity of 0°F (−18°C) and of the preheat requirements.

Fig. 7-11 *Welder: Field welds usually require certified welders.*

Inserts and Attachments

1. Structural steel should not be cut for passage of conduits, pipes, etc. unless shown on the approved shop drawings.
2. The burning of holes for attachment of supports is not permitted.
3. Identify and notify the project structural engineer if beams or columns are misfabricated with unused bolt holes. If the member is not rejected, make sure all unused holes are welded flush with engineer approval first.

Final Painting

1. Prior to final painting, the steel should be cleaned of all foreign matter and the prime coat touched up, including rivets, bolts, areas welded, etc.
2. Final coats of paint should be applied prior to surfaces being made inaccessible by masonry, roofing, etc.
3. Remember that steel to be encased in concrete or on which fireproofing is spray applied is not to be painted unless otherwise specifically required.

Open Web Steel Joists

1. Check to see if holes in bearing plate at one end have been slotted, where specified.

2. As soon as joists are in place, all bridging should be completely installed and the joists permanently fastened into place before the application of any loads.

3. Question conditions that cause excessive concentrated loads not indicated on structural drawings, including loads not located at panel points. Your supervisor should investigate.

4. The ends of all bridging lines terminating at walls or beams should be anchored at plane of top and bottom chords as noted on the drawings or as specified.

5. See that the principal tension members are the full length of joist without splicing or jointing.

6. Check the anchorage of the joist to its supports.

7. Do not allow the burning or enlargement of any holes in the joist.

8. Check to see that all rust, scale, weld flux, slag, and spatter have been removed and joist is clean before it is painted.

9. Check specifications to determine if steel joists over crawl spaces are required to have protective coatings.

STEEL DECKING

1. Do not place any loads on the joist girders until the joist bearing on the girder are in place.

2. Do not weld joist girder bottom chord braces until all dead loads are applied.

3. Check that all bridging is in place and secured according to the approved shop drawings.

4. Do not allow decking to be stacked on structural members. Make sure beams are securely fastened on both ends before setting the deck stack.

5. Prior to fastening the deck make sure the building or section of the building has been "racked" and is plumb.

6. Verify the manufacturers lapping requirements. All laps are to be at the beams only.

7. Check that the decking has the minimum amount of bearing at the ends (usually 1½ in.).

8. Roof decking should always be started at the low side so that the deck edges are lapped in a shingle fashion.

9. Check that decking is of the correct gage.

10. Decking is to be puddle welded to the beam supports at all points to provide a maximum average spacing of 12 in.

11. Do not allow for any loose deck sheets to be left overnight due to wind.

12. Ensure that all reinforcing and shoring is in place before pouring concrete.

13. Penetrations over 12 in. require additional reinforcing. A minimum is two #4s on each side of the opening and extending a minimum of 16 in. beyond.

14. Never allow the deck to be used as a working platform until it has been securely fastened.

15. Do not allow any other trades to work on the decking until it has been fastened.

STEEL TANKS

1. Field inspection of steel tank materials will be made upon delivery, as for structural steel.

2. Foundation pads, anchor bolts, or other supports should be checked before erection of tank starts.

3. Surfaces to be welded should be free from loose scale, slag, heavy rust, grease, paint, and any other foreign material excepting tightly adherent mill scale. Surfaces shall also be smooth, uniform and free from fins, tears, and other defects which adversely affect proper welding.

4. Damage to shop coat of paint both inside and outside of assembled tank should be touched up with specified paint prior to final painting.

5. Ladders and safety cages should be checked for rough or sharp edges, loose rungs, clearances, etc.

6. Field painting should not be permitted until all water, dirt, grease, etc., are removed and the tank surfaces are dry.

WELDING
General

1. This section covers welding and the inspector's duties in the inspection of welding. This covers all types of ferrous and nonferrous materials; and to welding processes—gas or electric.

2. Welding is a specialized trade. The checklist items that follow will assist the inspector in his duties; make him aware of possible poor quality workmanship, and show the need for promptly requesting technical assistance from a qualified welding specialist on questionable items.

3. The inspector should have a complete, basic knowledge of welding methods, practices, and procedures. His inspection of welding should ensure that quality welding is being obtained.

4. *Welding and cutting are still the greatest single cause of fire on construction projects.* Large fire losses are very common. The continuous occurrence of small fires and the presence of charred combustible material is indisputable evidence of improper and uncontrolled welding procedures and operations. Prior to approval of welding operations, combustible material must be removed or adequately protected. Combustible material such as low-density fiberboard, bituminous and plastic products, saturated products including vapor barriers, flammable liquids and vapors including paints, varnishes, petroleum, and other materials with high flame spread characteristics if ignited cannot be controlled by first aid firefighting equipment. Fire prevention and control must be a primary consideration on all welding operations.

5. Since there is no craft designation of "welder" in the construction industry, all crafts perform the welding on their own work. This requires that any person doing welding must be certified. It is the Inspector's job to check the certifications and to maintain a copy on file.

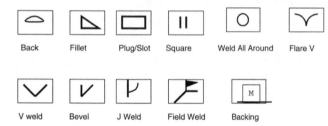

Fig. 7-12 *Basic weld symbols.*

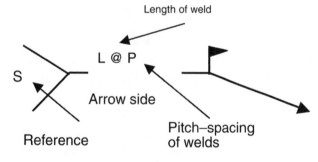

Fig. 7-13 *Welding symbol markings.*

Prior to Welding

1. Check whether welding procedure specifications have been submitted and approved. You should have in hand the approved procedure specifications, in the format required by Appendix E., AWS D1.1.

This specification guides your checking of material, process, position, rod specification and classification, number of passes, current polarity, and other needed information.

2. Check welder's certification. It must be submitted and approved prior to welding. The certification must state that he is qualified to weld as the procedure dictates. His qualification test result, represented by the certification, must be available from the contractor.

Welding Sequence and Procedure Drawings

1. Check for excessive distortion. Lay welds in prearranged pattern.

2. Check approved shop drawings against contract drawings, note any discrepancies, and advise the Project Manager or Site Superintendent.

3. Check weld symbols; interpret correctly.

4. Check placement of welds in designated sequence. Do not permit deviations.

Inspection Procedure

General

1. Be sure that a copy of the American Welding Society "Structural Welding Code" (AWS) D1.1 is available for your use. You should become familiar with Section 6, Inspection, which has been completely rewritten in the Code.

2. Ensure that the approved welding procedure is adhered to.

Specific

1. Process

  a. Identify welding process used, i.e., gas welding or metal arc welding.

  b. Check welding procedure specification for agreement as to correct process to be used.

  c. Carefully inspect the welding of the metals. Watch for burns.

2. Base metal

  • Check mill reports to see that necessary approval action has been taken on material prior to job fabrication.

3. Filler metal

   a. Look at container or color coding of electrodes (welding rods) for classification.

   b. Reject all coated electrodes that have been wet or on which the coating has been damaged.

   c. Low hydrogen covered electrodes require special handling, drying and storage. Read paragraph 4.5 of the AWS Structural Welding Code.

   d. Check diameter of electrodes.

4. Position

   • Ensure that no welder is welding in any position other than that for which he has been qualified.

5. Preparation of base metal

   Observe the joint preparation prior to welding.

   a. See that method of cutting bevel ensures parallel surfaces.

   b. Do not allow torch cutting unless special permission has been received.

   c. When torching overhead, a barricade or other acceptable means must be present to warn those below.

   d. Inspect surfaces for removal of all dirt, grease, loose scale, slag, or rust.

   e. Examine weld joint for root opening, bevel angle, root face, and groove face.

   f. Verify alignment of material.

   g. Determine allowable tolerances.

6. Nature of current (arc welding only)

   a. Check polarity if D.C. current is being used. Either straight polarity or reversed polarity may be used, depending on material welded and electrode used. Check approved welding procedure.

      (1) Check positive and negative leads at welding machine.

      (2) Use plates 1 and 2 to identify type of polarity (pages 5B-7 and 5B-8).

   b. Check frequency shown on nameplate if alternating current welders are used.

      (1) Does it agree with frequency shown on approved welding procedure schedule?

      (2) Does it require identical frequencies?

7. Size of welding tips (gas welding only)

   • Check tip size.

8. Nature of flame (gas welding only)

   a. Check flame adjustments and controls.

   b. Check weld's adjustment for application (reducing, oxidizing, or neutral).

9. Method of welding (gas welding only)

   • Check method of welding to be used (forehand or backhand)

10. Welding technique (Check actual technique being used.)

    a. Examine current and voltage-dial readings at which pointers have been set on welding machine. Require measurement by instruments.

    b. Identify number of passes or heads placed.

    c. Determine diameter size of electrode used for each pass of weld material placed.

    d. Ensure that all welds are quality welds, that techniques are such that there is no excessive weld pileups or spatter, no irregular weld contours, no undercut, or no off-center welds.

11. Cleaning

    • See that all slag or flux is removed before laying down the next successive weld bead.

12. Defects

    Check welding against method noted on welding procedure specifications.

    a. Ensure that defects are ground, chipped, or chiseled back to sound metal with no irregular edges or areas of stress concentration.

    b. Observe that metal is not rolled over a defect.

    c. Inspect for surface cracks in critical areas by magnetic particle testing.

13. Peening

    • Check degree of peening permitted and the suggested or approved types of tests.

14. Treatment of underside of weld groove

    • Check detail and sketches noted on welding procedure specifications.

16. Preheating

    a. Check requirements.

    b. Check methods of control.

Check to see that all weld flux, slag, and spatter is completely removed. Be sure each welder identifies his work by stamping his mark near each weld.

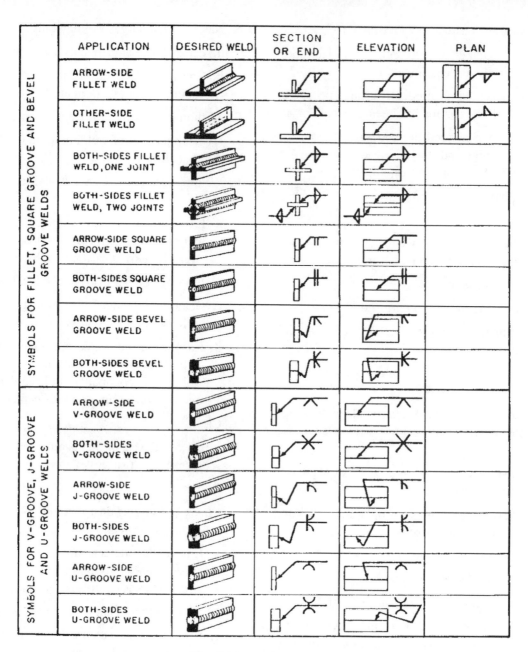

Fig. 7-14 *Welding symbols.*

Types of Welding Inspections

Eddy current (weld testing) Used for detecting surface breaking indications through coating thickness as great as 2 mm (0.08 in.), and it can be used on wet surfaces. Because, however, only the area under test is being inspected, several scans must be employed for complete coverage.

Liquid penetrant testing (weld testing) Detects flaws open to the surface using a dye that seeps into discontinuities.

Magnetic particle testing (*MT*) (weld testing) Used for detecting short length and shallow surface break-ing indications. Its sensitivity, however, is severely reduced in detection of indications through coatings (generally 0.2–0.4 mm [0.006–0.012 in.]), and MT is difficult to use outside on wet surfaces.

Radiographic testing (*RT*) (weld testing) Used for volumetric detection of indications. It cannot, however, detect lamellar indications.

Ultrasonic testing (weld testing) Detects location and size of discontinuities in the weld (inclusions, porosity, lack of fusion) using high-frequency sound waves that are reflected by the flaws.

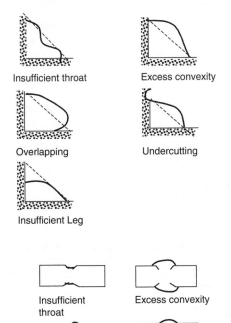

Fig. 7-15 *Sample welder's certification.*

Insufficient throat

Excess convexity

Overlapping

Undercutting

Insufficient Leg

Insufficient throat

Excess convexity

Undercutting

Satisfactory

Overlapping

Fig. 7-16 *Weld inspections.*

Protection

Table 7-8 *Minimum Cover of Lightweight Concrete on Steel Columns*

Steel Size	Fire Resistance Rating (hr)				
	1	1½	2	3	4
W14 × 233	1	1	1	1	1½
W14 × 193				1½	
W14 × 74					2
W14 × 61					2½
W14 × 43			1½	2	
W12 × 65	1	1	1	1½	2
W12 × 53				2	2½
W12 × 40			1½		
W10 × 112	1	1	1	1½	2
W10 × 88					
W10 × 60					
W10 × 33			1½	2	2½
W8 × 35	1	1		2	2½
W8 × 28			1½		
W8 × 24					3
W8 × 18		1½		2½	

STEEL ROOF DECKING
General

For permanent industrial construction, steel roof decking with board-type insulation or underlayment is most commonly used as the roof deck system. Steel roof decking is usually formed in U shapes with various depth and rib spacing profiles from 22-gage (0.0295) sheets. Steel decking is delivered either galvanized or with manufacturers standard shop coat paint. Fire resistance ratings for steel roof decking assemblies are discussed in the roofing manual. Steel forms remaining in place for lightweight concrete roof decks are discussed in the Concrete Manual, the chapter "Concrete for Structures".

Submittals

1. Check shop drawings for completeness and accuracy and determine that there are no conflicts with the plans and specifications.

2. Check to see that the design computations for the structural deck have been received and approved. The Steel Deck Institute (SDI) certification of design may substitute for the actual design computations.

3. The above items, any samples required, and the installation procedures should be available before work starts.

Storage

1. Check material for damage on delivery.

2. Check for ventilated storage and that units are elevated at one end. Touch up abraded surfaces.

3. Do not allow excessive concentrated storage on newly placed concrete.

Installation Procedures

1. You should have a copy of the SDI Design Manual for Floor Decks and Roof Decks. This information together with that in the contract specification should be reviewed.

2. For welded attachment, check on welder qualification.

3. Welder should demonstrate satisfactory welds before beginning actual installation.

4. Special tools are used with screw type fasteners. Tools and operators shall be checked for safety compliance.

5. Screw type fasteners should not be permitted in high-wind velocity areas of seismic zones or greater.

6. Spacing of fasteners should be shown on shop drawings. Check this with SDI manual spacing.

7. Check for damaged units or accessories. Deck units should be a minimum 22-gage (0.0295-in.) thickness; check the actual contract requirements. Most accessories require increased thickness. Burn holes from welds is cause for rejection.

8. All welded areas shall be brushed, cleaned, and then painted. Use same type as for actual shop coat. Use high-zinc dust paint for touch up on galvanized surfaces.

9. Check holes and openings in the deck for required reinforcing members. Check details in the shop drawings.

10. If decking is to receive concrete, check the need for shoring and the contractors shoring plan.

11. For decking to receive insulation and built-up roofing, a minimum of ¼-in. dent or damage across any three ribs is a cause for rejection.

12. Check for the correct placement, height, and size of studs.

Table 7-9   Type NR

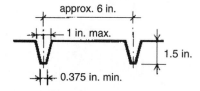

Deck Type/ Gage	Span Type	Weight (psi)	Total (Dead/Live) Safe Load for Spans Indicated in ft-in. (lb/ft²)												
			4-0	4-6	5-0	5-6	6-0	6-6	7-0	7-6	8-0	8-6	9-0	9-6	10
NR22	Simple	1.6	73	58	47										
NR20		2.0	91	72	58	48	40								
NR18		2.7	121	95	77	64	54	46							
NR22	Two	1.6	80	63	51	42									
NR20		2.0	96	76	61	51	43								
NR18		2.7	124	98	79	66	55	47	41						
NR22	Three or more	1.6	100	79	64	53	44								
NR20		2.0	120	95	77	63	53	45							
NR18		2.7	155	123	99	82	69	59	51	44					

Table 7-10 Type IR

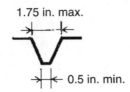

1.75 in. max.
0.5 in. min.

Deck Type/ Gage	Span Type	Weight (psi)	Total (Dead/Live) Safe Load for Spans Indicated in ft-in. (lb/ft^2)												
			4-0	4-6	5-0	5-6	6-0	6-6	7-0	7-6	8-0	8-6	9-0	9-6	10
IR22	Simple	1.6	86	68	55	45									
IR20		2.0	106	84	68	56	47	40							
IR18		2.7	142	112	91	75	63	54	46	40					
IR22	Two	1.6	93	74	60	49	41								
IR20		2.0	112	88	71	59	50	42							
IR18		2.7	145	115	93	77	64	55	47	41					
IR22	Three or more	1.6	117	92	75	62	52	44							
IR20		2.0	140	110	89	74	62	53	46	40					
IR18		2.7	181	143	116	96	81	69	59	52	45	40			

Table 7-11 Type WR

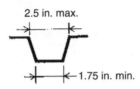

2.5 in. max.
1.75 in. min.

Deck Type/ Gage	Span Type	Weight (psi)	Total (Dead/Live) Safe Load for Spans Indicated in ft-in. (lb/ft^2)										
			5-0	5-6	6-0	6-6	7-0	7-6	8-0	8-6	9-0	9-6	10
WR20	Simple	1.6	89	70	56	46							
WR18		2.0	112	87	69	57	47	40					
WR22		2.7	154	119	94	76	63	53	45				
WR20	Two	1.6	98	81	68	58	50	43					
WR18		2.0	125	103	87	74	64	55	49	43			
WR22		2.7	165	137	115	98	84	73	65	57	51	46	41
WR20	Three or more	1.6	122	101	85	72	62	54	46	40			
WR18		2.0	156	129	108	92	80	67	57	49	43		
WR22		2.7	207	171	144	122	105	91	76	65	57	50	44

Table 7-12 Number and Spacing for U-Bolt Clips on Wire Ropes

Steel Rope Dia. (in.)	No. Drop Forged Clips	No. Other Material Clips	Min. Spacing (in.)
½	3	4	3
⅝	3	4	3¾
¾	4	5	4½
⅞	4	5	5¼
1	5	6	6
1⅛	6	6	6¾
1¼	6	7	7½
1⅜	7	7	8¼
1½	7	8	9

Note: Never Saddle a Dead Horse.

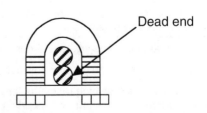

Dead end

Fig. 7-17 *Correct placement of bolts on cable.*

STRUCTURAL STEEL CHECKLIST

	1. Check the steel on the job with the plans and specifications.
	2. Verify previous inspections, such as excavations, foundations, and footings for corrections.
	3. Check all anchor bolts! Are damaged bolts corrected as per engineers instructions?
	4. Check mill certifications and test reports.
	5. Check dimensional tolerances.
	6. Check grade of steel for conformance to specifications.
	7. Check grade of steel pipe and tubing for conformance to specifications.
	8. Inspect material for compliance with specifications.
	9. Inspect structural steel members for distortion, excessive rust, flaws, and burned holes.
	10. Did you call for laboratory reports when in doubt?
	11. Check for proper priming and or special coating treatment.
	12. Are the approved plans on the job?
	13. Check that no changes appear on the approved field plans.
	14. Check for camber in beams and trusses if specified.
	15. Check steel members for size, thickness, and weight.
	16. Check splicing for conformance to plans.
	17. Check bolt holes as to number, alignment, location, and size.
	18. Check anchor bolts for size, length, plumbness, embedment, and protrusion of threaded end or nut engagement.
	19. Check rivet holes as to size, alignment, arrangement, and number.
	20. Check that the diameter of bolt holes are not more than $\frac{1}{16}$ in. larger than the bolt diameters. Inspect high tensile bolts for proper size, length, and type of bolts, washers, and nuts.
	21. Check bolt tightening for methods used in applying the required minimum tension, calibration of the wrenches used and damage to bolt threads, contact surfaces, and proper tightening of bolts.
	22. Check for hardened washer when required by specifications and beveled washers where the surfaces of nut and bolt head contacts are not sufficiently parallel.
	23. Check embedment, alignment, size, and length of all base anchors.
	24. Verify that unfinished bolts are used only in locations noted on the plans and specifications. Did you check bolt holes for size, misfit holes, number, location, spacing, and edge and end distances?
	25. Note any open holes to check for omission of required bolts.
	26. Check bolts for number, size, and location.
	27. Ensure that the type of bolts used is as indicated in the specifications.
	28. Inspect for loose or bent bolts.
	29. Verify that defective bolts were marked, removed, and replaced.
	30. Did you check bolt holes for size, number, location, and edge and end distances?
	31. Inspect for omission of bolts by marking any open holes.
	32. Ensure that sheet steel members are of the required gauge, weight, and thickness.
	33. Check columns for bearing surfaces, alignment, size and fit of base plates, splice plates, and bearing and embedment in masonry or concrete.
	34. Ensure that ends of beams and girders bearing on masonry or concrete conform to the details on the plans.
	35. Check the anchors, straps, and bolts for size, strength, and position.
	36. Inspect light steel–bearing members for proper gauge, location of splices, reinforcement when studs or plates are cut, and adequate bearing on supporting members.

	37. Inspect steel-joisted floors for plan compliance.
	38. Inspect steel trusses for proper fabrication, that they are installed according to the plans, and that permanent bracing is installed.
	39. Inspect steel-joisted roofs for adequate bridging, approved size and type of joist, and approved handling methods.
	40. Inspect compression members for size, type, adequate end anchorage, fabrication and alignment of splices, lateral support, and size and thickness of bearing plates.
	41. Inspect tension members for size and thickness of plate, size of rods, type of end connections, tightness, and alignment.
	42. Ensure that adequate temporary bracing was provided by the contractor.
	43. Inspect for unloading and storage of material on all steel members.
	WELDING
	1. Inspect against the approved plans for size and spacing, type, and location.
	2. Ensure that all welders are certified by a recognized agency.
	3. Ensure that base metal conforms to the specifications.
	4. Inspect welding rods for conformance to specifications.
	5. Inspect assembled materials before welding for rust, scabs, seams, scale, plate laminations, root openings, and proper edge preparation.
	6. Verify that the design engineer or a certified welding inspector is utilized to inspect welds. Ensure that welds are clean and free from slag.
	7. Inspect for dimensional defects, for size and shape of welds on the approved plans, warpage, and joint preparation.
	8. Inspect for voids resulting from improper chemical reaction.
	9. Inspect for cavities and incomplete penetration caused by several cavities.
	10. Ensure that no nonmetallic solids are trapped in the weld.
	11. Inspect for imperfect fusion.
	12. Inspect for undercutting.
	13. Inspect for weld cracks and crafters.
	14. Inspect for surface holes and other surface irregularities.
	15. Ensure that defective welds are clearly marked in accordance with known methods, marked in a distinct color, and marked clearly enough to be visible until repair is made.
	16. Inspect the repaired weld and mark if the repair is not satisfactory.

8
CHAPTER

Doors and Windows

METAL DOORS AND FRAMES
Submittals

Shop Drawings

1. Check catalogues cut sheets, drawings for material type size, finish, assembly, anchorage, connections, etc.

2. A door schedule with rough openings should be included.

3. Check for special assembles and equipment such as fire-rating hardware, reinforcement, noncombustible insulation as required.

4. Check for required ADA specifications, clearances, etc.

Certificates

1. Do certificates meet or exceed the specification requirements?

2. Special certificates of inspection are usually required for oversized fire-rated doors and for fire-rated doors without UL label.

Manufacturing Instructions

Check submittals for approval and use at installation.

Catalogue cuts may also he required to complete the instructions.

MATERIALS
General

1. Doors and frames usually have specific gauge or thickness specifications.

2. See the section Installation for items pertaining to specific types of doors and frames.

3. Check workmanship of joints and connections.

4. Check for closed top, finished flush and sealed, on exterior doors.

5. Are louvers permitted? Louvers must be non-removable from the locked side of doors for security.

6. Will door frame be set before masonry begins? Toothing masonry for later installation of metal frames is prohibited unless specifically approved.

7. Check for frame anchors in accordance with requirements.

8. Are guards provided at the hinge and strike areas to prevent filling with mortar as frames are installed? Is hardware reinforcement built into doors and frames?

9. Are special frames provided for the special doors? Soundproof? Lightproof? Lead lined?

Table 8-1 *U-Factor (Windows, Glazed Doors, and Skylights)*

Material and Product	Single Glazed	Double Glazed
Metal w/o Thermal Break		
Operable	1.27	0.87
Fixed	1.13	0.69
Garden Window	2.60	1.81
Curtain Wall	1.22	0.79
Skylight	1.98	1.31
Site assembled overhead	1.36	0.82
Metal with Thermal Break		
Operable	1.08	0.65
Fixed	1.07	0.63
Curtain Wall	1.11	0.68
Skylight	1.89	1.11
Site assembled overhead	1.25	0.70
Reinforced vinyl/metal clad wood		
Operable	0.90	0.57
Fixed	0.98	0.56
Skylight	1.75	1.05
Wood, Vinyl, Fiberglass		
Operable	0.89	0.55
Fixed	0.98	0.56
Garden Window	2.31	1.61
Skylight	1.47	0.84
Glass Block (no reinforcement)	0.60	

2000 International Energy Code

Finish

1. Is finish as specified? Mill? Satin? Anodic? Enameled? Aluminum?

2. Shop coat required on steel? Or is it galvanized? Damaged surfaces of protective coatings must be recoated when found (even if they are not on the visible side).

3. Is factory-supplied hardware finish as specified?

Most finish hardware is referenced according to the *U.S. Code System:*

US P	Prime paint coat
US 3	Polished brass
US 4	Satin brass
US 9	Polished bronze
US 10	Satin bronze
US 14	Polished nickel
US 15	Satin nickel
US 20	Statuary bronze
US 26	Polished chrome
US 26D	Satin chrome
US 28	Anodized aluminum
US 32	Polished stainless steel
US 32A	Satin stainless steel

Table 8-2 *Solar Heat Gain Coefficient (SHGC)*

Product	Single Glazed			
Metal	Clear	Bronze	Green	Gray
Operable	0.75	0.64	0.62	0.61
Fixed	0.78	0.67	0.65	0.64
Nonmetal				
Operable	0.63	0.54	0.53	0.52
Fixed	0.75	0.64	0.62	0.61

Product	Single Glazed			
Metal	Clear + Clear	Bronze + Clear	Green + Clear	Gray + Clear
Operable	0.66	0.55	0.53	0.52
Fixed	0.68	0.57	0.55	0.54
Nonmetal				
Operable	0.55	0.46	0.45	0.44
Fixed	0.66	0.54	0.53	0.52

Weather Stripping

1. All exterior doors require weather stripping.
2. Check type material. The elastomeric materials are required for door heads and jambs. Spring metal should not be used. Check specification for door bottom weather stripping. Has it been properly adjusted? Is daylight visible?

Hardware

1. Check for aluminum or stainless steel hardware on sliding glass doors. This includes compatible fasteners.
2. Accordion doors usually require either anodized aluminum or chrome-plated brass hardware. Check installation instructions and specifications.

Screens

1. Check type screen. Is bronze, aluminum, fiberglass, or plastic-coated specified?
2. Are splines removable and reusable? Are all fasteners in place?
3. Are guards provided at the hinge and strike areas to prevent filling with mortar as frames are installed?
4. Is hardware reinforcement built into doors and frames?
5. Are special frames provided for nonstandard doors? Soundproof? Lightproof? Lead-lined? Fire-rated?

6. Check frame size and stiffness for compliance.
7. Do the door louvers require insect screening?

Glazing

1. Sliding glass doors require safety glass. Check for etched (permanent) label in lower corner of glass.
2. Check AAMA 402.9 for required glass thickness.
3. Both lites of double-glazed sliding doors must be *safety glass.*
4. Are glazed peepholes required and provided in vestibule doors of cold storage facilities?
5. Are removable or snap-on glazing beads specified? Do type and removal meet Steel Door Institute specifications?

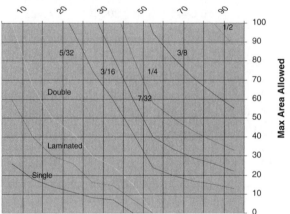

Fig. 8-1 *Wind pressure on glazing.*

Safety Glass

For windows, safety glass is needed in these locations:

- Bottom edge less than 18 in. above the floor
- Top edge greater than 36 in. above the floor
- Within 36 in. of a walking area
- Any individual pane greater than 9 sq. ft.
- Here's where you need safety glass for doors:
    - Entrance and exit doors (excluding jalousies)
    - Fixed and sliding panels of sliding glass doors
    - Panels in swinging doors
    - Storm doors
    - Doors and walls for showers, tubs, whirlpools, etc.
    - Panels that are within 2 ft of a door and are less than 5 ft above the floor

- Unframed swinging doors, with these exceptions:
    1. Openings in doors too small for a 3-in. sphere to pass through
    2. Leaded glass panels
    3. Faceted or decorative glass
- Safety glass is also required in these other areas:
    1. All glass in railings
    2. Walls and fences enclosing indoor and outdoor swimming pools with glass less than 5 ft above a walking surface and less than 3 ft measured horizontally from the walking area

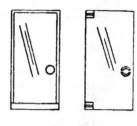

Ingress and egress doors

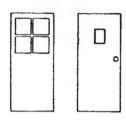

Glass doors
(framed and unframed)

Table 8-3 *Wind Forces*

Wind Speed	Force (lb. per sq. ft.)	Wind Speed	Force (lb. per sq. ft.)
1	0.005	20	1.970
2	0.020	25	3.075
3	0.044	30	4.428
4	0.079	35	6.027
5	0.123	40	7.873
6	0.177	45	9.963
7	0.241	50	12.30
8	0.315	55	14.9
9	0.400	60	17.71
10	0.492	65	20.85
12	0.708	70	24.1
14	0.964	75	27.7
15	1.107	80	31.49
16	1.25	100	49.2
18	1.55	—	—

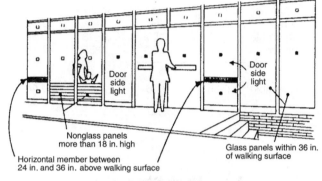

Door side light

Door side light

Nonglass panels more than 18 in. high

Horizontal member between 24 in. and 36 in. above walking surface

Glass panels within 36 in. of walking surface

☐ Ordinary glazing allowed
■ Safety glass required

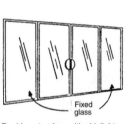

Fixed glass

Double entry door with sidelights

Glazed panel

Storm doors

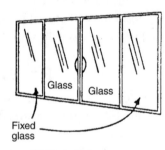

Glass   Glass

Fixed glass

Sliding-type doors

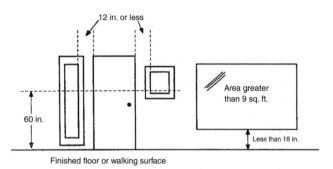

12 in. or less

Area greater than 9 sq. ft.

60 in.

Less than 18 in.

Finished floor or walking surface

Fig. 8-2 *Glass doors.*

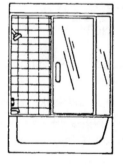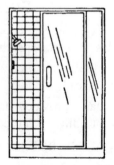

Tub enclosure   Shower enclosure

Fig. 8-2 *Glass doors (continued).*

ADA CLEARANCE REQUIREMENTS
Front Approaches

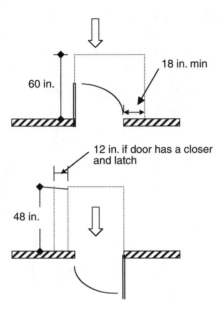

Fig. 8-3A   *ADA clearance requirements. Front approaches.*

Hinge Side Approach Doors

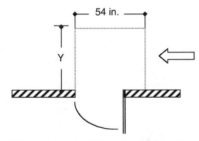

Y = 42 in.; if door has latch and closer then Y = 48 in.

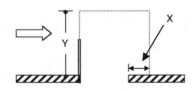

X = min 36 in. if Y = 60 in.; X = min 42 in. if Y = 54 in.

Fig. 8-3B   *ADA clearance requirements. Hinge side approach doors.*

Latch Side Approach

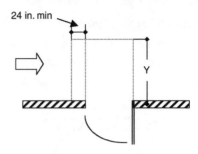

Y = 42 in.; if door has a closer then Y = min 48 in.

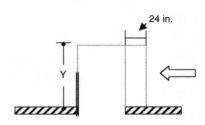

Y = 48 in.; if door has a closer then Y = 54 in. min

Fig. 8-3C   *ADA clearance requirements. Latch side approach.*

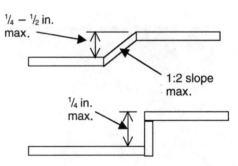

Fig. 8-4   *Changes in floor level.*

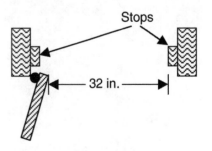

Fig. 8-5   *Minimum door openings.*

STORAGE

1. Units should be checked on arrival for damage, missing items, and comparison with samples and shop drawings.

2. Check for correct sizes and door swings.

3. Have contractor reorder damaged units ASAP.

4. Use off-ground storage protected from the weather.

5. Wood doors must be stored in a clean and dry space. *If unfinished the area must be humidity controlled!*

6. Make sure adequate security is provided.

INSTALLATION

General

1. Set door frames before erection of surrounding masonry. Toothing-out at missing frames is not permitted.

2. Check frame anchorage at floor.

3. Make sure the frame is securely braced with wood blocking to prevent warping and bowing when the concrete/grout is placed.

4. Leave all spreaders in place until wall is erected and frame anchored-in.

5. Fill hollow metal frames with concrete, mortar, or plaster, as appropriate, for stiffening.

Fig. 8-6 *Metal door frame supported and braced to prevent warping and/or movement during installation.*

6. Check for double stud at jambs in framed walls.

7. Leave required groove for sealant bead at exterior door frames. Other special doors may require sealant.

8. Operate units to determine the correct adjustments.

9. Are silencers installed in frames? Do not allow them to be painted.

10. Check fire-rated door frames immediately for required labels. *Make sure labels do not get painted!*

11. Check door swings and light switch locations, as well as handicap button locations.

12. Use shop drawings and manufacturer's instruction to verify installation.

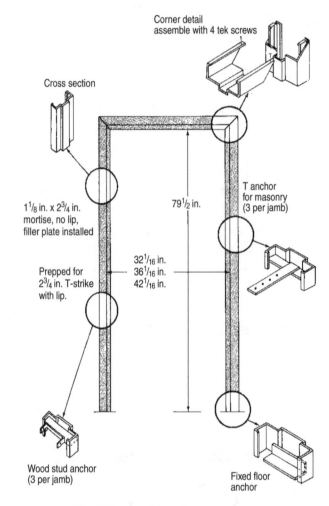

Fig. 8-7 *Metal door frame components.*

Aluminum Combination Doors

1. Is a residential-quality door being used for heavy traffic? Does it meet the specifications?

2. Check frame anchorage and use of compatible fasteners.

3. Check fit, and adjust as required for weatherproofness.

Aluminum Hinged Doors

1. These doors are usually glazed with stile and rail construction for entrance ways.
2. Be sure to make a timely check on back-priming for concealed surfaces against dissimilar materials.
3. Protect finish surfaces from damage, mortar stain, etc. with adequate protection.
4. Check weather stripping for tight fit.

Aluminum Sliding Glass Doors

1. Safety glass is required.
2. Is aluminum finish as specified?
3. Check for back-priming aluminum surfaces in contact with dissimilar materials.
4. Check for weather stripping at full perimeter and meeting rail. Adjust fit for weatherproofness.
5. Are fasteners aluminum or stainless steel?
6. Make a final check with requirements in AAMA publication 402.9. Check for AAMA quality certification label.

Steel-Hinged Doors

1. Do the fire-rated doors have required labels?
2. Do all exterior doors have thresholds and weather stripping?
3. Check the top of exterior doors for sealed and flush cap to prevent water entry into doors.
4. Make a final check of installation in accordance with the following information:

   The Installation of Commercial Steel Doors and Steel Frames

   Insulated Steel Doors in Wood Frames

   Builders Hardware Door and Hardware Institute (DHI)

   Standard Steel Doors and Frames, No. 100-078, Steel Door Institute

Steel Overhead Doors

1. Are exterior doors insulated? Fully weather stripped?
2. Is insulation required to be noncombustible type? Does it meet "U" value requirement?
3. These doors are for commercial application and have specific requirements for wind resistance and deflection. Do they comply?

4. Is guide and track adjustment correct for proper operation?
5. Are lites installed properly? Conform to approved shop drawings.
6. Are safety and limit switches operating properly?
7. Is the pilot door insulated? Weather stripped? Does it have safety stop for electric operator?

Steel Rolling Doors

1. These doors have interlocking slats. Are end locks provided as required? Are windlocks provided if required?
2. Check all features of installation and operation with shop drawings and manufacturing instructions.

Steel Sliding Doors

1. Are face panels the specified gauge?
2. Are operating cables and counter weights enclosed to 7-ft height?
3. Is specified operating force sufficient for manual operation?
4. Are safety features operable for electric power driven doors?

Accordion Doors

1. Check concealed supporting construction for adequacy. Review all shop drawings, catalog cuts, and manufacturing instructions.
2. Check for fire rating requirements.
3. Track sections shall be at least 6 ft long, minimum 14-gage aluminum or 16-gage steel. Check specs.
4. Check tract alignment, especially at joints.
5. Metal soffit is required at ceiling when track is recessed type.
6. Check for ball bearing carrier wheels.
7. Check panels (door) for label indicating flame spread rating not more than 25.
8. Check fit at bottom seal when closed.
9. Check speed, bottom seal retraction, and safety shutoff of electrically operated door.

Fire-Rated Doors

1. Check door schedule for location of fire-rated doors.
2. Check for appropriate label on edge of door and on door frame. Labels shall be permanently affixed. Do not paint.

3. *Oversized fire-rated* door will have a certificate of inspection instead of the label. Check National Fire Protection Association (NFPA) Standards No. 80 and 80A for certification requirements. (Do not allow this to be painted.)

4. Labeled door frames will have nonremovable anchors for attachment to wall construction.

5. Check for positive closure and latching devices.

Cold Storage Doors

1. Doors shall arrive factory assembled with templates for all attachment.

2. Check door frame anchorage and wireway for the recessed electric heater cable on freezer doors and exterior doors.

3. Heaters shall be thermostatically controlled.

4. Check armor plating for type material, gage, and finish.

5. Check for heavy duty hardware in specified material and finish.

6. Check door latch for safety release from inside box.

7. Is a door closer or padlock required?

8. Are gasket seals effective? Are the number of seals per door as required.

9. Is door construction vapor tight?

10. Are sliding door hangers adjustable? Check floor guides for location and adjustment for adequate gasket seal.

11. Hinge-type door shall arrive factory mounted in its frame for erection in an assembled and rigidly anchored frame.

12. Vestibule doors shall have reinforcement at doors and jambs as required, including specified wheel guards and bumpers.

13. Check for heavy duty steel supports for vestibule doors. Check for full closure.

ELECTRIC OPERATORS

General

1. Check submittal for compliance with requirements:
   a. Totally enclosed motor
   b. Required operating mechanism, emergency release, auxiliary operators, etc.

2. Safety device at bottom edge of door.

Installation

1. Check for conflicting items in the way of tracks, operating devices, and door extension.

2. Check weather stripping for tight seal at operator closure limit. Any daylight or air infiltration?

3. Is the operator performing as required?

WOOD DOORS AND FRAMES
Submittals

Shop Drawings

1. Check for the door schedule, which should include location, dimensions, and a full description of door type with required marked identification.

2. Check for correct door swings and ADA requirements.

3. All of the different type door elevations and specials, including weather stripping and thresholds, must be identified.

4. Show wood blocks as required for locks, louvers, etc.

Certificates

• Certificates of compliance are required for doors that do not bear identifying marks.

Materials

General

1. Standards of the National Woodwork Manufacturers Association (NWMA) are used for the specific requirements of wood door quality. You must have the applicable publications to adequately check the doors upon arrival.

2. Are the wood species and grade as specified?

3. Check for identifying marks required.

4. Check condition, including factory finish or prime coat. Are edges (top and bottom) sealed?

Exterior Doors (Type I)

Fig. 8-8 *Metal frames being stored outside without any protection.*

1. Check for water-repellent preservative treatment.
2. Are flush doors solid wood block core?
3. Is glue bond exterior type?

Interior Doors (Type II)

1. Is adhesive used with natural finish doors of the non-staining variety?
2. Panel or flush type?

Defects and Warp

1. Check quality of doors against the table of characteristics in the NWMA standard.
2. Reject doors of inferior quality.
3. Warp shall not exceed ¼ in. for standard size doors. Check NWMA applicable standard.

Left-handed door   Right-handed door

Fig. 8-9 *Door swings.*

- If the door opens toward you and the door knob is on the left, then it is a left-handed door.
- If the door opens toward you and the door knob is on the right, then it is a right-handed door.

Storage

1. After initial check for quality and fit, protect doors from damage and extremes in temperature and humidity.
2. Store doors upright to avoid damaging face finish.

Installation

Rough Openings

1. Observe limits so that dimensions do not exceed those for framed openings by more than specified amounts.
2. Check anchorage of rough buck. Is treated wood required? Are cut edges resealed?

Framed Openings

1. Check for blocking as required.
2. Is opening plumb?

Fitting and Hanging

1. Are required clearances provided? Usual clearances required are:
   - Head ⅛ in.
   - Sides ⅛ in.
   - Bottom ½ in. (¼ in. over thresholds)
2. Is lock edge of door beveled?
3. Be sure that cut edges of doors are resealed.
4. Check weather stripping on exterior doors. Surface mounted is best type as it is adjustable but spring type may still be required at heads and jambs.
5. Check weather stripping for anchorage, compatible fasteners, and proper adjustment.
6. Check hardware chapter for special type thresholds.
7. Check butts for size and shape.

Table 8-5 *U Factor (Energy Code) for Nonglazed Doors*

Door Type	With Foam Core	Without Foam Core
Steel doors (1.75 in. thick)	0.35	0.60
	Without Storm Door	With Storm Door
Wood doors (1.75 in. thick)		
Panel (0.438-in. panels)	0.54	0.36
Hollow core flush	0.46	0.32
Panel (1.125-in. panels)	0.39	0.28
Solid core flush	0.40	0.26

METAL AND WOOD WINDOWS
Submittals

Shop Drawings

1. Check for specifics on each different type window, as:
   a. Thickness and dimensions
   b. Weather stripping
   c. Hardware
   d. Finish/factory priming
   e. Fasteners, anchorage, and their compatibility with adjoining materials
2. Check for the window schedule and compare it with the schedule on the drawings.

Certificates/Labels

1. Certified test reports on air and water infiltration thermal conductivity, condensation resistance and load tests must be provided for environmental control windows.

2. An Architectural Aluminum Manufacturing Association (AAMA) quality certification label on aluminum windows and storm windows may replace the certificate.

3. Performance certification labels on wood windows indicate they must comply with ANSI A200.l provisions and requirements. Do they?

Materials

Screens

1. Check steel screens against Steel Window Institute (SWI) specifications.

2. Check aluminum screens against ANSI A134.l requirements.

3. Look for screens on buildings that don't have combination storm-screen units.

Storm Windows

1. Must comply with provisions and requirements of ANSI A134 .3.

2. Check for vertical or horizontal sliding operation.

3. Is factory-painted finish as specified or is aluminum mill finish?

4. Check for separation or isolation between steel prime windows and aluminum storm windows.

5. Check for compatible fasteners. Those fasteners exposed must be aluminum or nonmagnetic stainless steel.

Metal Prime Windows

1. Aluminum
   a. Must comply with ANSI A134.1.
   b. Check for certificate on minimum condensation factor when double glazed. See AAMA 1502.6 for this requirement.
   c. Check A-A2 of A134.1 for awning windows. Awning windows are hinged at the top.
   d. For basement windows and other fixed windows, check P-A2.
   e. Check C-A2 for casement windows.
   f. Check DH-A2 for double and single-hung type.
   g. Horizontal-sliding windows refer to HS-A2.
   h. Projected windows are similar to awning windows but have a different specification, P-A2. All sash or projected windows do not open as with awning type.
   i. Check TH-A2 for top-hinged windows.
   j. Vertically pivoted windows refer to VP-A2.
   k. Check window finish for factory painted or anodized treatment. Check anodizing for quality and color.

   Temporary protective coating on aluminum must be removed before the surfaces receive sealants.

2. Steel
   a. Check SWI specification for all types, including basement, casement, projected, classroom, security, and others.
   b. Check for protective finish, either factory prime coat of paint on steel or over hot-galvanized steel.

Wood Prime Windows

1. Check ANSI A200.1 for general and specific requirements.

2. Windows will usually be single or double-hung type, although awning, casement, or horizontal-sliding type may be specified.

3. Wood windows shall be factory primed for finish painting.

4. Check for extra hardware such as sash lifts, sash lock, or latch and sash pulls.

Environmental Control Windows

1. These are special aluminum windows that have a thermal break in the frame and are double glazed with a slat-type venetian blind between the glass panes.

2. Check thermal-break for ½-in. minimum separation. Barrier at break shall be weatherproof neoprene, rigid vinyl, or polyurethane.

3. Unit shall arrive fully assembled and glazed.

4. Check normal operation and key controlled operations required.

5. Check required finish.

Installation

1. Anchors as specified shall be of material that is compatible for metal windows.

2. Protect aluminum window surfaces in contact with dissimilar materials as required in AAMA 302.9 provisions.

3. Check for unit alignment and plumbness.

4. Check operation and require adjustments as necessary.

5. Check for removal of temporary protective coating from aluminum on surfaces to receive sealants.

6. Check for required performance certification labels (wood windows) and quality certification labels (aluminum windows).

7. Window cleaning anchors may be required. Watch for:

   a. Specified anchor material.

   b. Frame reinforcement at anchors and additional window anchorage.

   c. Requirement in ANSI A39.1.

8. Check AAMA 1302.5 for forced-entry resistant windows.

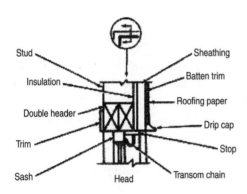

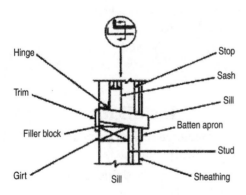

Fig. 8-10 *Window components.*

HARDWARE
Materials

Submittals

1. Make sure that the contractor obtains an early approval of hardware schedule and samples. An approvals list may also required. Hardware templates must be provided to door and frame manufacturers in a timely manner.

2. Double-check the schedule to ensure that no openings have been omitted or sized incorrectly.

3. Check for required certificates and test reports as per submittal list.

4. Be alert to hardware and keying requirements on such items as:

   a. Roof scuttles

   b. Sliding, rolling, and lift doors

   c. Refrigerator and other mechanical equipment doors

   d. Screens and doors

   e. Special master keying program

5. Hardware items such as astragals, silencers, stops, coordinators, holders, and thresholds need close observation because they are often overlooked.

6. Hardware finishes are identified in Builders Hardware Manufacturers Association (BHMA) Standard 1301. Check for required finish and base metal. Watch for restrictions on the use of aluminum.

Delivery of Materials

1. Materials will be received in original packages and not repackaged.

2. Packages should be opened for inspection and inventory and then resealed until time for attaching to the doors.

3. Examine items for the utilization of the correct materials at scheduled locations.

4. Check the keying. A keying schedule is required and keys must be tagged or otherwise identified with the door for which the lock is intended.

5. Are all keys stamped as required?

6. Check for and review security plan for all master keys. Insist on sign-out sheets.

Application

General

1. Check for quality workmanship and the proper installation of each item of hardware.

2. Compare installation with manufacturer's instructions.

3. Determine the proper installation height and location.

4. Examine the method of fastening. Evaluate for durability and rigidity.

5. Make sure that the proper size and type of hardware is being installed on each door. Use the hardware schedule for this check.

Installation Checks

1. Observe whether there are nonremovable pins in hinges installed on out-swinging exterior doors and on doors to secure areas that swing into corridors.

2. Check for nonferrous fasteners on hardware exposed to the weather.

3. Check for tamper-proof fasteners as required on surface-mounted hardware.

4. Ensure the use of proper closers and brackets. Note the installation of closer for adequate clearance. Closers on exterior should not be mounted exposed to the weather.

5. Look for the omission of stops and silencers. Watch for installations that will allow hardware to swing into parts of the structure or into other hardware. Each door requires a hardware stop.

6. Check for the matching of hardware finishes in each area.

7. See that each item of hardware functions properly after installation.

8. Check for installation of thresholds where scheduled.

9. There are special requirements for mortise-type locks and trim. Check your specifications.

10. Locksets for lead-shielded doors shall be lead-lined the factory. Thickness shall be not less than the door lead thickness.

11. Door pulls shall be through-bolted type.

12. Check for proper listing or label on hardware and detection devices for labeled fire-rated doors.

13. Is hardware on labeled doors properly installed?

14. Check for required kick plates when push plates are installed.

15. Is the key cabinet at a suitable location?

16. You will need the American National Standards Institute (ANSI) specific standard to fully check hardware items in question.

GLAZING
Submittals

Descriptive Data

• Manufacturer's descriptive data are required. See that manufacturer's installation instructions are provided and used for site-installed units, especially insulating, laminated, one-way, and control tower glass. Verify cleaning instructions for acrylic plastic glazing.

• *Certificates*. Certificates or labels with specified identification are required. Safety glass is required to have etched marking of identification at a corner of each pane.

• *Guarantee*. Check for *10-year* guarantee on insulating glass units (or what was required in contract documents).

Materials

General

1. Check thickness. Units to be clear and smooth on both sides.

2. Check for manufacturer's recommended backstop and sealant.

3. Is glazing tape proper type and size?

Glass

1. Check all types required: primary, figured, heat-absorbing, light-reducing, wire, insulating, laminated, one-way vision, tempered, and heat-strengthened glass.

2. Does wire glass in fire-rated doors comply with NFPA No. 80 requirements?

Glazing and Sealing Compounds

1. Check the Flat Glass Marketing Association (FGMA) Glazing Manual for recommended types.

2. Use aluminum color for glazing units of aluminum (natural color) material.

3. Use gray or neutral color otherwise and for painted materials.

Installation

1. Check for required sealant primed with sealant manufacturer's instructions.

2. Double prime wood and ferrous metal rabbets and beads before glazing.

3. Double-strength glass (⅛-in. thick) is usually required in openings up to and including 21 sq. ft.

4. Do not unpack acrylic plastic until ready to glaze.

5. Check for required shims, separators, etc. in accordance with drawing sand manufacturers instructions.

6. Are exposed fasteners for glazing corrosion-resistant type?

7. Check for removal of acrylic plastic protective cover immediately after installation. Manufacturer may recommend this requirement.

8. Check mirror frame, fasteners, anchorage, and location.

9. When in doubt about hazardous glaring locations, check the publication contents of the Consumer Product Safety Commission publication 16 CFR 1201, titled, Safety Standard for Architectural Glazing Materials.

9
CHAPTER

Finishes

METAL FRAMING AND FURRING AND LATH AND PLASTER (STUCCO)

General

The Inspector should be familiar with the reference publications for the finish materials specified in project plans and documents. Most are the ASTMs, American Society for Testing and Materials, and their contents are the criteria used for checking the approval and usage of materials. Equally important is to make sure the contractors involved also have these and the site management are knowledgeable of their contents. Needed references for installation include the following American National Standards Institute (ANSI) publications:

- A42.1 Gypsum Plastering
- A42.2 Portland Cement Plastering (Stucco)
- A42.3 Lathing and Furring for Portland Cement Plaster (Stucco)
- A42.4 Interior Lathing and Furring

Framing and Furring

Steel framing includes form and truss type studs for walls and 1½ in. channels for ceilings. Furring is ¾-in. channels or 18–20-gage hat-shaped channels for walls and ceilings. Check drawings and specifications for material requirements; gages differ from project to project.

Lathing

Both metal and gypsum lath are included in this booklet. Metal lath is expanded, welded, or woven; gypsum lath is solid or perforated.

Note: Perforated gypsum lath cannot be used on ceilings.

Plastering

There are many gypsum and portland cement plaster materials available. The mix ingredients and proportions, number of coats, and type of substrate are critical in quality plastering. Obtain a copy of the manufacturer's installation instructions and ensure the contractor follows them.

Note: Portland cement plaster is not applied to gypsum lath.

Stucco

Stucco is a mixture of portland cement, sand, and lime mix used mainly in exterior work. The ANSI A42.2 and A42.3 sections on proportioning and mixing and on application and curing must be followed.

Table 9-1 Stucco Mixes

Material	Cubic Feet	Gallons	Pounds
Sand	2	15	200
Portland cement	½	3½	47
Lime	⅓	2½	12
Water	¾	6	48

Veneer Plaster

Veneer plaster is a hard plaster finish provided over gypsum wallboard (GWB). A thin layer of specially formulated gypsum plaster is applied over GWB manufactured with an absorption face paper for bonding. Reinforcing mesh tape is applied over the joints in the installed GWB.

Submittals

Samples

Check for samples required. They usually include a section of each type of lath and accessory, such as casing and corner beads. A stucco panel showing the finish texture and color should be required.

Shop Drawing

Installation drawings for ceiling framing and details of the additional supports at ceiling and wall openings are usually required. Drawings for stucco work should include all details and information on mix proportions and thickness of coats.

Certification

Specifications may require certification for the bonding compound. This is in the form of a certified test report complying with provisions in the contract specifications.

Material List

A complete list of all materials and the intended use, specifically located, is required.

Materials

Ferrous steel items are either shop coated with an approved protective paint or galvanized. Stainless steel tie wire may be required in some ceiling applications.

Ceiling Framing and Furring

1. Hangers use 8-gage, galvanized steel wire or steel strap.

2. Framing is usually 1½-in. steel channel (check specifications).

3. Furring is either ¾-in. steel channel or 25-gage hat-shaped sheet-metal channel.

4. Tie wire is 16-gage. Stainless steel wire may be required for wet areas.

Wall Framing and Furring

1. Studs may be either 18-gage, sheet-metal type or the truss type formed with 7-gage wire. Stud width is shown on the drawings.

2. Furring is usually ¾-in. channel or 25-gage hat-shaped sheet-metal channel.

3. Furring brackets for attachment to concrete or masonry are 20-gage with a serrated edge for anchoring tie wire used to attach furring members.

4. Runners are 24-gage for attaching studs and furring to floors and ceilings.

5. Tie wire is minimum of 18-gage and clips used instead of tie wire must be at least 8-gage. Stainless steel tie wire may be required in special areas.

Lath

1. Metal lath is either expanded type, cut and expanded from steel sheets, or made with welded or woven wire. Lath made from wire must have an integral paper backing to help hold the plaster until it sets.

2. Gypsum lath is usually 16 × 48 in. and ½ in. thick for use on framing or furring. Larger sections, available for solid-type partitions, extend from floor to ceiling height. Gypsum lath can be supplied perforated for use only in walls.

3. The options for type of lath and weight (for metal) or thickness (for gypsum) depends on the spacing of the framing or furring to which the lath is directly attached.

Plaster

1. Gypsum basecoats are prepared with bagged and labeled gypsum mixed with aggregates in the proportions given in the specifications. Sand or a lightweight aggregate, either perlite or vermiculite, may be used. Check for required type aggregate in fire-rated partitions and ceilings. Check for special gypsum for plaster applied by machine method.

2. Gypsum—finish coat—use one of the following types:
   - Lime putty made from special finishing hydrated lime and gypsum plaster.
   - Ready-mix gypsum finishing plaster.
   - High-strength gypsum special plaster and lime are required for a hard, high-strength finish.

3. Portland cement plaster is proportioned as specified in the manufacturer's instructions.

Accessories

1. Items must be checked with the approved sample for thickness or gage, flange width, and configuration.

2. All steel items are galvanized except that cornerite and strip lath may be given a protective paint coating at the factory in lieu of galvanized finish.

Stucco

1. Lath reinforcement is usually welded or woven wire placed on wood or metal framing. Waterproof paper is required either integral with the lath or by separate application. Separate paper application requires separately applied wire backing. Lath should be spaced at least ¼ in. out from supports for embedment.

2. Stucco mix includes portland cement and sand with not more than 10% special finishing lime, by weight of cement, added as the plasticizing agent.

3. Stucco finish coat with integral color will require a mill mix material to which only water is added at the job site.

4. Accessories, except for cornerite and striplath, shall be either zinc or rigid vinyl.

Veneer Plaster   Veneer plaster is a mill-mixed gypsum plaster formulated for use over GWB.

Storage

1. Labeled materials will be checked for compliance with the specifications upon delivery. Material not in compliance or unidentified will be rejected.

2. Make sure the contractor follows the storage requirements posted on the containers or attached instructions.

3. Containers will be sealed.

4. Store materials in a dry and protected location to prevent dampness, deterioration, and damage from other contractors.

5. Shade gypsum lath and veneer plaster base from direct sunlight. Sunlight will deteriorate the absorptive paper face.

Preparation

Framing and Furring

1. Is ceiling to be suspended from the structure or directly attached?

2. Is furring required for direct attachment? All furring is required to be plumb.

3. How will suspended ceiling be leveled? By water tube? By laser?

4. Is wall framing long enough or high enough to require horizontal stiffeners?

5. Does layout provide for extra framing and furring at control joints?

6. Check the framing details for openings.

Lathing

1. Is lath material proper design and weight for the spacing interval of framing or furring?

2. Is metal lath application on walls set for required top to bottom laydown?

3. Is gypsum lath application planned for staggered joint in alternate courses?

4. Is stainless steel tie wire required?

5. Is self-furring metal lath being used over solid substrate?

Plastering and Stucco

1. Have lath and accessories been checked for secure fastening?

2. Are accessory grounds and screeds set for required plaster thickness?

3. For direct application, are the concrete and masonry surfaces clean and bondable?

4. Are control joint beads set and secured over control joints in the concrete and masonry?

5. Check plaster mixing equipment, batching method, and cleaning procedures.

6. Is temperature at least 55°F and will existing site ventilation be adequate for drying plaster?

7. Are required heating devices placed to exclude direct heat on plastered surfaces? Fans and baffles may be required.

8. Portland cement plaster must be damp cured. Is the planned curing method satisfactory?

9. Are all building openings closed? Are heaters properly vented to the outside?

Openings

1. Are the required extra supports and framing installed at ceiling openings such as for recessed light fixtures and access panels?

2. Are the metal door frames back-plastered?

3. Are strip lath corners required at corners of openings to reinforce against plaster corner cracking?

Testing

1. Are accurate thermometers available?

2. Stainless steel tie wire and zinc accessories for stucco should be nonmagnetic. Is a magnet available for testing?

3. Measure the depth of grounds and screeds from face of lath to determine plaster thickness. Will it be the specified thickness?

4. Do the specifications require a slump cone test to test machine the plaster? The slump of plaster is limited to between 2½ and 3 in. when tested in a 6-in.-high plaster slump cone.

INSTALLATION AND APPLICATION
Ceiling Framing and Furring

1. Check hanger wire or strap spacing. Must be 42 in. in each direction or a combination of 48 and 36 in., the 48 in. being along the framing (runner) channel.

2. Hangers must be plumb. Hangers at the perimeter must be within 6 in. of walls.

3. Check for runner and furring channel clearance at walls of unrestrained ceilings.

4. Check channels for specified splice interlock and lap. Splice location shall be staggered in adjacent members. Take two wire loops with each splice tie.

5. Are saddle ties correctly made?

6. Finish each tie with three loops or three twists, as appropriate.

7. Check wire tieing procedure; wire ends must be flattened so they will not protrude near or through plaster surface.

Wall Framing and Furring

1. Check carpentry chapter for wood framing requirements.

2. Check floor and ceiling runner anchorage. Runners shall be attached to furring members of continuous ceilings.

3. Require specified number of fasteners at runner-stud connections. Check for additional studs at each side of doorways and at corners and intersecting walls.

4. Wall stiffeners are provided with the ¾-in. channel or the 1½-in. channel, installed horizontally within the stud space. Check your specifications for location of these stiffeners.

5. Check furred walls for:

   • Direction; horizontal or vertical furring

   • Furring brackets locations

   • Furring brackets anchorage

   • Fastening furring to brackets

   • Floor and ceiling runner attachment

6. Check the required framing for solid plaster partitions.

7. Is a separate furring or framing member installed on each side of control joint?

Lathing

1. Type lath selected shall be compatible with the interval of spacing of the framing or furring to which the lath is directly attached.

2. Attach lath with long edge across supports.

3. Fasten metal lath at 6-in. intervals at supports and 9-in. intervals at laps. Fasten gypsum lath at 5-in. intervals.

4. Lap width depends on type metal lath used. Check the project specifications for the lap width.

5. Make end laps of metal lath at supports.

6. Lath on unrestrained ceilings shall terminate in casing beads. Do not attach casing bead to the wall.

7. Metal lath at restrained ceilings shall turn down at least 6 in. on walls or cornerite shall be used.

8. Check for cornerite on gypsum lath at the ceiling-wall intersection of restrained ceilings.

9. Metal lath on walls shall be applied from top of wall so that lower course laps upper course, except paper-backed lath is installed bottom to top of wall.

10. Check for metal lath orientation for maximum mechanical bond. Expanded metal lath on walls shall feel rough when wiped from top to bottom of wall.

11. Turn lath through corners for 6 in. or install cornerite. Attach only to underlying lath.

12. Check for strip-lath, oriented diagonally, at each corner of openings. Attach only to underlying lath.

13. Cut lath at control joints. Control joint will bridge lath opening with each wing attached to cut end of lath.

OPENINGS

1. Check for strip-lath at the corners of openings which are 12 in. or greater in any dimension.

2. Fasten strip-lath diagonally to plaster base without fastening to framing or furring.

3. Openings shall be framed with finish frames and plaster stops or with casing beads.

4. Check for additional hanger, framing, and furring supports for ceiling openings. Check the approved shop drawing for details.

5. Hollow steel frames in walls for doors and windows require back-plastering.

6. Form grooves in this plaster to receive lath.

7. A substitute for back-plastering is tieing each set of double studs together with at least four sets of column clips. Fasten frame securely to double stud sets.

8. Check for the runner channel section used as a header at the top of openings. Turn runner ends to member into jamb studs.

9. Don't forget the channel stiffener embedded in the wall, above the head of each opening.

10. Check for a separate knee brace extending from each jamb.

11. Studs are not anchored to structural supports.

ACCESSORIES

1. Check accessories for alignment, either level or plumb.

2. Check beads, screeds, grounds, and frames for required depth to develop the specified thickness of plaster.

3. Corner joints to exposed items shall be mitered. Butt joints shall be joined with splice plates.

4. Each corner bead shall be installed as a one-piece unit. Is the bull-nose bead required? Is a built-in corner guard required?

5. Use the casing bead to separate plaster at abutting dissimilar materials and also at the perimeter of restrained ceilings.

6. Check the detail for correct application of control joint bead. Lath is cut to enable the joint to work and prevent nearby cracking.

GYPSUM BASE COATS

1. Accurate proportioning by volume is required. Check the table in the specifications.

2. Check water content of machine applied plaster with a slump test.

3. Will there be two or three separate coats (including the finish coat)? Three coats are required on metal lath.

4. Each base coat is approximately ¼ in. thick. The single coat in two-coat plaster (including the finish coat) is ⅛ in. in the same operation to increase base coat thickness to ⅜ in.

5. Check for bond with a solid base such as smooth finish concrete. A bonding compound application may be required.

6. Check the specifications for plaster application sequence in solid partitions.

GYPSUM FINISH COAT

1. Finish coat mix proportions are given by weight.

2. Check for required finish coat material given in the finish schedule on the drawings.

3. If regular gypsum finish is indicated, either lime-putty or prepared gypsum may be used, except that prepared gypsum finish cannot be used over lightweight (perlite or vermiculite aggregated) base coats.

4. Check the specifications for finish proportions and mixing sequence.

5. The special, high-strength gypsum finish must be checked at the mixer location. It is extremely difficult to determine high-strength finish in place.

6. Do not apply high-strength gypsum over lightweight aggregate base coats.

7. The base coat surface is to be dampened immediately before applying the finish coat.

8. Normal tolerance in finish surface is ¹⁄₁₆ in. in 10 ft. Finish coat thickness is:

- Minimum ¹⁄₁₆ in.
- Maximum ⅛ in.

PORTLAND CEMENT PLASTER

1. Use portland cement plaster over gypsum plaster or over gypsum lath.

2. Check for curing setup before plastering begins. It is important that all coats be moist cured to control shrinkage.

3. Check for a requirement for groove joints on approximately 4-ft centers through the finish coat to control shrinkage crackling.

4. The foregoing groove joints will be in addition to normal control joint spacing on not more than 12-ft centers.

STUCCO

1. Stucco is portland cement plaster mix applied to the exterior of building walls.

2. Check screeds, grounds, and frames to produce ⅞-in. thick stucco measured from face of lath.

3. Check planned sequence of operation for continuous application to natural break lines such as openings, corners, and control joints.

4. Dampen masonry and concrete surfaces immediately before applying stucco.

5. Check during provisions before stucco application begins. Continuous moist curing is most important.

6. Finish coat must also be shaded from direct rays of the sun while curing.

Table 9-2 *Setting Times for Stucco*

Coat	Keep Moist	Set (days)
Scratch	12	2
Brown	12	7
Finish	12	2

7. Remember that stucco accessories such as casing beads, corner beads, control joints, and base screeds must be zinc or rigid vinyl material. Where these items are specified in galvanized steel, check the project's specifications.

8. Check finish texture and color for a match with the approved sample panel.

VENEER PLASTER

1. Plaster base is the same size and shape as gypsum wallboard. This board has an absorption face paper for bonding the veneer plaster coats.

2. Check the specifications for the one- or the two-coat system.

3. Cover all joints with mesh reinforcing tape. Do not overlap tape at joint intersections. Fasten tape with staples; see the system instructions.

4. A pretreatment at joints may be required before full surface application of plaster. Check manufacturer's instructions.

5. Plastering requirements are generally the same as regular plaster; however, temperature and ventilation requirements must be closely monitored. Veneer plaster is more sensitive to drafts and sudden changes in temperature.

6. Check veneer plaster for thickness between $\frac{1}{16}$ and $\frac{3}{32}$ in.

GYPSUM WALLBOARD (GWB)
General

References

Of all the indicated references, the GA-216 is most important. This is the Gypsum Association "Recommended Specifications for the Application and Finishing of Gypsum Board."

Framing

Generally, either wood or steel members are used. Industry standards with wood is that the stud or furring face should not vary more than $\frac{1}{8}$ in. from the plane of the faces of adjacent members.

Materials

Adhesives

1. Check joint treatment compound. Is it quick dry (1 day) or slow dry (3 day) for the complete, three-coat system?

2. Be sure that fastening adhesive is recommended by the wallboard manufacturer for intended use.

3. Fastening adhesive is not to be used to attach wallboard in fire-rated construction.

Fasteners and Hangers

1. Use only the special nail with annular rings. Nail length must be $\frac{3}{4}$ in. longer than wallboard thickness. Too long is as harmful as too short.

2. Use screws at least $1\frac{1}{8}$ in. long in wood and 1 in. long in steel members. The Type S screw is used with 25-gage steel studs and Type W is used with wood. Type S screws have drill points.

3. A pan head (flat and without shoulder) screw should be used for attaching steel stud in steel runner.

4. Check for 9-gage-minimum galvanized hanger wire and a minimum of 16-gage galvanized tie wire. Exception to tie wire is that 13-gage is used to splice furring and to tie studs, used as furring, to main channels. Check project specifications.

Table 9-3 *Fastener Schedule for Drywall*

Thickness Ceiling/ Wall	Long Dim. to Framing	Framing Spacing	Nail Spacing	Screw Spacing	Size of Nail
$\frac{3}{8}$ in. Ceiling Wall	Perpendicular Both directions	16 in. 16 in.	7 in. 8 in.	12 in. 16 in.	$1\frac{1}{4}$ in. long, 13 gage $1\frac{1}{4}$ in. annular ringed 4d cooler nail $1\frac{3}{8}$ in. long, $\frac{7}{32}$ in. head
$\frac{1}{2}$ in. Ceiling Ceiling Wall	Both directions Perpendicular Both directions	16 in. 24 in. 24 in.	7 in. 7 in. 8 in.	12 in. 12 in. 12 in.	$1\frac{3}{8}$ in. long, 13 gage $1\frac{1}{4}$ in. annular ringed 5d cooler nail $1\frac{5}{8}$ in. long, $\frac{15}{64}$ in. head Gyp. board nail, $1\frac{5}{8}$ in.
$\frac{5}{8}$ in. Ceiling Ceiling Wall	Both directions Perpendicular Both directions	16 in. 24 in. 24 in.	7 in. 7 in. 8 in.	12 in. 12 in. 12 in.	$1\frac{5}{8}$ in. long, 13 gage $1\frac{3}{8}$ in. annular ringed 6d cooler nail $1\frac{7}{8}$ in. long, $\frac{19}{64}$ in. head Gyp. board nail, $1\frac{7}{8}$ in.

Framing

1. Check Carpentry chapter for wood grade stamps, moisture, and type preservative treatment, when required. Studs (steel) and runner channels are a minimum 25-gage. Studs have knockouts or holes for utility lines. Do not allow any additional cutting of holes other than those supplied by the manufacturer. Check drawings for stud gage required.

2. Use full-length studs. Do not permit splicing steel studs.

3. All steel members have a lightweight electrogalvanized finish.

DRYWALL SCREWS

There are two types of drywall screws commonly used: type S and type W.

- *Type S*—Type S screws are designed for attachment to metal studs. The screws are self-tapping and very sharp, since metal studs can flex away. At least $\frac{3}{8}$ in. of the threaded part of the screw should pass through a metal stud. Although other lengths are available, 1-in. type S screws are commonly used for single-ply drywall.

- *Type W*—Type W screws hold drywall to wood. They should penetrate studs or joists at least $\frac{5}{8}$ in. If you are applying two layers of drywall, the screws holding the second sheet need to penetrate the wood beneath only $\frac{1}{2}$ in.

FIRE-RATED CONSTRUCTION

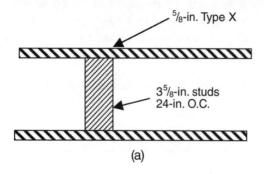

⁵⁄₈-in. Type X

3⁵⁄₈-in. studs
24-in. O.C.

(a)

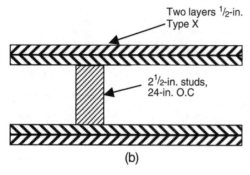

Two layers ¹⁄₂-in.
Type X

2¹⁄₂-in. studs,
24-in. O.C

(b)

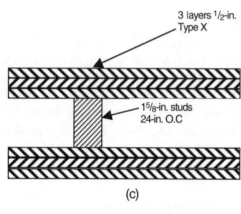

3 layers ¹⁄₂-in.
Type X

1⁵⁄₈-in. studs
24-in. O.C

(c)

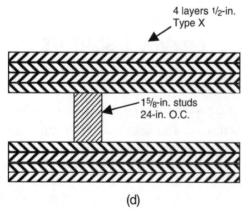

4 layers ¹⁄₂-in.
Type X

1⁵⁄₈-in. studs
24-in. O.C.

(d)

Fig. 9-1 *Fire-rated construction:*
(a) One-hour wall assembly.
(b) Two-hour wall assembly.
(c) Three-hour wall assembly (first layers are vertical, face layer horizontal).
(d) Four-hour wall assembly (first layers are vertical, face layer horizontal).

Table 9-4 *Time Assigned to Fire-Exposed Side of Finish Materials Wall*

Finish	Time (min)
Gypsum Wallboard	
³⁄₈ in.	10
¹⁄₂ in.	15
⁵⁄₈ in.	30
³⁄₈ in. (2 layers)	25
³⁄₈ in. plus ¹⁄₂ in.	35
³⁄₈ in. (2 layers)	40
Type X gypsum wallboard	
¹⁄₂ in.	25
⁵⁄₈ in.	40
Portland cement-sand plaster on metal lath	
³⁄₄ in.	20
⁷⁄₈ in.	25
1 in.	30
Gypsum-sand plaster on metal lath	
³⁄₄ in.	50
⁷⁄₈ in.	60
1 in.	80

Furring

1. Check chapter for wood furring requirements.
2. Hat-shaped steel furring is generally used. For long spans (over 4 ft), steel studs should be used.
3. Main member supporting is the 1½-in. steel channel.

Trim

1. All steel trim is galvanized, such as the corner bead, casing bead, edge bead, and control joint.
2. Zinc metal beads may be required for special use or location. Check specifications.

Storage

1. Weatherproof storage is required for all materials used.
2. Premixed adhesives also have temperature restrictions and limited pot life. Check the container label.
3. Stack GWB flat to prevent sagging. Don't permit use of damaged board.

Waterproofing

1. Check for specification requirement for waterproof-type board. This specially treated board is used as a base.
2. Caulk openings for pipes, etc., flush with specified waterproof material. Check for need to fireproof.

3. Water-resistant board on ceilings is prohibited.

4. A vapor barrier behind water resistant board is prohibited.

5. Where regular gypsum wallboard needs waterproofing, check for the following:

    a. Waterproof coating at cut edges; at edge and for 4 in. on each surface from cut edge.

    b. Waterproof coating over fastener heads.

    c. Coating at edge of board adjacent to shower or tub base. Remember that framing spacing should be less and more fasteners required in wallboard used for tile base. Check your specifications.

INSTALLATION: CEILING FRAMING AND FURRING
Wood

1. Check alignment of members.

2. Blocking is required to support ends of GWB with fasteners. All GWB edges must be supported.

3. Level furring as required.

Note: Make joints over directly framing members.

Steel Framing

1. Also see Carpentry chapter.

2. For attached ceilings: GWB is not attached directly to framing. See Steel Furring.

Suspended Ceilings

1. Check main runner channel spacing. Four foot is maximum spacing with hat-shaped furring.

2. Are wire hangers plumb?

3. Space parallel runners not more than 6 in. from walls.

4. Check for 12-in. lap at interlocking splices. Splices require a tie at each end with 16-gage wire.

Steel Furring

1. Attach hat-shaped furring to framing with saddle ties.

2. Maximum furring spacing is 16 in. on center.

3. Space parallel furring member not more than 2 in. from wall.

4. For spans greater than 4 ft, use studs as furring. Check the specifications for stud size and spacing.

5. Check for splice ties and staggering the lap in adjacent members. Splice lap 8 in.

INSTALLATION: WALL FRAMING AND FURRING

1. Wood framing and furring or walls and partitions shall be erected as described in Chapter 6 .

2. Check surface alignment of wood framing. Mark unsatisfactory member and require correction when tolerances are exceeded.

3. Check for required blocking at:

    a. End joints of GWB.

    b. At openings in GWB.

    c. Attached fixtures, door bumpers, lockers, hand rails, chair rails, curtain rails, etc.

4. Check to make sure the wood does not have excessive moisture (over 19%).

Steel Framing

1. Check alignment of floor and ceiling runner channels.

2. Support or runner channel at top of wall must be secure. Check specifications for details.

3. Screw attachment of studs to runners requires two screws at each end. One on either side of runner-stud joint before GWB is applied.

4. Spacing of studs is usually 16 in. on center. Where 24-in. spacing is permitted, the GWB fastener interval is reduced and more fasteners are required.

Steel Furring

1. Use saddle ties at the intersections with steel frame. Maximum furring span is feet.

2. Shim for plumb alignment over concrete and masonry. Attachment is through flanges of hat-shaped furring at 24 in. on center on alternate flanges.

Framed Openings

1. At ceiling openings that cut furring, use an additional runner to support furrings each side of opening.

2. Ceiling openings with cut framing—install additional hangers and framing to support furring.

3. Wall openings:

    a. Check specifications for double stud requirement at unframed openings.

    b. Runner channel is used as header at top of opening. Cut channel 24 in. longer than opening width and turn ends to member into jamb studs.

    c. Check for required knee braces at jamb studs of unsupported walls.

APPLICATION

1. Check preparation. Building must be weather tight before beginning GWB application.
2. Horizontal application on walls or ceilings is when GWB tapered edges lay across (perpendicular to) attachment members.
3. For vertical application, ensure that the tapered edges lay along (parallel to) attachment members.
4. Check for ceiling application ahead of wall application, except that suspended ceilings are placed after wall finish.

At the initial inspection, problems related to cutting, fitting, and fastener spacing and overdriving must be corrected.

   a. Plan application method for least length of end joints. Stagger all end joints.

   b. Joints on opposite sides of the same wall should not occur on same framing member.

5. Check fastener type, interval, and spacing requirements.
6. Remember that vertical application requires fastener attachment at the ends of GWB sheets.
7. For fire-rated construction, check the attachment method required in the fire-rated system.
8. Attachment fasteners shall be:

   a. Driven into ceilings beginning from the center of each GWB sheet and progressing outward.

   b. Driven into walls beginning from the top of sheets.

9. There are restrictions to the use of foil-backed GWB. For thermal effectiveness, leave at least a ¾-in. space behind foil surface.

Joint Treatment

1. Minimum temperature required is 50°F, beginning from 48 hours before treatment and until adhesive has dried.
2. Check type adhesive used. Is it the fast-drying type?
3. Require the person mixing adhesive powder to wear a respirator.
4. Check for three coats of adhesive at joints and fastener heads. Taper as required.
5. Sanding the paper cover of GWB is not allowed. This raises the nap of the paper which will create "high" spots in paint finish.

Control Joints

1. Check for control-joint requirement. These should be shown on the drawings to divide large areas of GWB surface.
2. Install a separate attachment member for each wing of the control joint bead.

Schedule of Inspections

Make job inspections at the following stages:

1. When job is almost ready for materials delivery, in order to check environmental conditions and plan for delivery.
2. When materials are delivered to the job.
3. When framing is erected but before board or lath application.
4. When gypsum board base layer and/or face layer are applied.
5. When joints are treated; when veneer plaster finish or conventional plaster is applied. When job is completed.

Delivery and Storage

When materials are delivered, check the following:

1. See that materials meet specifications and are in good condition.
2. Store gypsum boards flat on the floor; store plasters and bagged goods flat on a raised platform. Protect from moisture and damage by abuse.
3. Protect framing materials from damage and moisture.
4. Make sure the weight does not overload the flooring and structural supports.

Framing Inspection

Framing members, either wood or metal, must meet architect's specifications and be free of defects. During and after framing construction, make the following inspections:

1. See that wood and steel framing materials meet specifications as required by local building codes, regulations, and standards.
2. Check accuracy of alignment and position of framing, including bracing if required, according to plans and details. Make sure load-bearing studs are directly underneath the members they support.
3. See that partitions are straight and true and that ceilings are level.

4. Measure spacing of studs and joists. Spacing should not exceed maximum allowable for the system.

5. Look for protrusions of blocking, bridging or piping, and twisted studs and joists that would create an uneven surface. Correct situation before board attachment.

6. Make sure there is appropriate blocking and support for fixtures and board.

7. See that window and door frames and electrical and plumbing fixtures are set for the board thickness used.

8. Check for proper position and attachment of resilient and furring channels.

9. Review all wood and steel framing for compliance with minimum framing requirements.

10. Examine steel studs at corners, intersections, terminals, shelf-walls, and door and borrowed light frames for positive attachment to floor and ceiling runners. All load-bearing and curtain wall studs should sit tight against web of runner.

11. Inspect spliced steel components for proper assembly. (Shaft wall and curtain wall studs and load-bearing framing should not be spliced.)

12. See that steel stud flanges in field all face the same direction.

13. See that preset door frames are independently fastened to floor slab and that borrowed light frames are securely attached to stud and runner rough framing at all jamb anchors.

14. Make sure that door and borrowed light frames will be spot-grouted, as required.

Suspended Grillage

1. Measure spacing of hangers, channels, and studs to see that they are within allowable limits.

2. Check ends of main runner and furring channels. They should not be let into or supported by abutting walls, and should extend to within 6 in. of the wall to support a furring channel.

3. Make sure furring channel clips are alternated and that furring channel splices are properly made.

4. See that mechanical equipment is independently supported and does not depend upon the grillage for support.

5. Inspect construction around light fixtures and opening to see that recommended reinforced channel support is provided.

Inspecting Drywall and Veneer Plaster Installations

Base Layer

1. Verify that material being used complies with specifications and requirement of fire or sound rating.

2. Make sure that proper perpendicular or parallel application of board is being used and that end joints are staggered.

3. Check for cracked and damaged-edge panels; see that they are not used.

4. See that the recommended fasteners are being used, spaced, and set properly.

5. Check for proper use of acoustical sealant.

6. Inspect installation to make sure thermal insulating or sound attenuation fire blankets are properly attached and fitted.

7. Be certain vapor retarder is installed and sealed as required.

8. Review appropriate system construction and application, such as fire-rated assembles and inspect for compliance with laminating recommendations and other construction procedures.

9. See that required control joints are properly located and installed.

Face Layer

1. Verify material compliance.

2. Look for high-quality workmanship. Cracked or damaged-edge boards should not be used. Board surfaces should be free of defects; joints correctly butted and staggered.

3. Check for proper application method—perpendicular or parallel.

4. Examine fasteners for compliance with specifications, proper spacing, and application.

5. Review adhesive application method and see that recommendations and specifications are being followed. Under adverse drying conditions resulting from high humidity, at either high or low temperature, drying of the laminating compound could be prolonged.

6. Inspect trim, corner beads, and related components for alignment, grounds, secure attachment, and proper installation.

7. Make sure that acoustical sealant is applied around electrical outlets and other penetrations and that it completely seals the void.

Fasteners

1. Make sure recommended or specified fasteners are used.

2. See that fasteners are applied in such a manner that the board hangs flat against the framing without binding.

3. Observe whether board is held tightly against framing during application. Test for loose board by pushing adjacent to the fastener. See that face paper is not broken when fastener is driven. If necessary, a second fastener should be driven within 1½ in. of the faulty one.

4. Examine fastener positions. Fasteners should be at least ⅜ in. in from edges and ends.

5. Make sure that fastener heads in veneer plaster assemblies are flush with the gypsum base surface, not dimpled.

Adhesives

1. See that adhesive is applied to clean, dry surfaces only.

2. So proper bond can be obtained, make sure that board is erected within allowable time limit after adhesive is applied.

3. Measure size of bead and spacing, and see that a sufficient quantity is applied.

4. Observe impacting blows for proper spacing and positioning.

5. Make sure temporary fastening and shoring holds panel tightly in place.

6. Review appropriate adhesive application methods (see Chapter 3) and inspect for compliance.

Joint Treatment—Drywall

1. Make sure panel surface is ready for joint treatment. Fastener heads should be properly seated below panel surface. Protrusions should be sanded below level of surface. Joints between panels should be filled with joint compound before taping.

2. See that recommended mixing directions are followed. Only clean water and mixing equipment should be used. Joint compounds cannot be held over or retempered.

3. Inspect joints and corners to see that tape is properly embedded and covered promptly with a thin coat of joint compound. Only compounds suitable for embedding should be used. Avoid heavy fills.

4. Make sure compound is used at its heaviest workable consistency and not overthinned with water.

5. Make sure joint compound is allowed to dry thoroughly between coats (see drying time required on manufacturer's instructions).

6. Inspect second and third coats over joints for smoothness and proper edge feathering.

7. See that fastener heads and metal trim are completely covered.

8. See that the paper surface of the gypsum board has not been damaged by sanding.

9. Make sure that all finished joints are smooth, dry, dust free, and sealed before decoration.

Levels of Gypsum Board Finishing

Contract documents traditionally have used nonspecific terms such as "industry standards" or "workmanlike finish" to describe how finished gypsum board walls and ceilings should look. This practice often has led to misunderstandings about the degree of finishing sophistication required for any particular job.

A collective effort of four industry trade associations—Association of the Wall and Ceiling Industries-International (AWCI), Ceilings and Interior Systems Construction Association (CISCA), Gypsum Association (GA), and Painting and Decorating Contractors of America (PDCA)—has resulted in the adoption of industry-wide recommended specifications on levels of gypsum board finish. The work identifies five specific levels of finishing, enabling architects to more closely identify the sophistication required and allowing for better competitive bidding among contractors.

Key factors used in determining the sophistication level required include the location of the work to be done, type and angle of surface illumination (both natural and artificial lighting), and type of paint or wall covering to be used and method of application. Critical lighting conditions, gloss paints, and thin wall coverings require a high level of finish, while heavily textured and painted surfaces or surfaces that will be decorated with heavy-gage wall coverings require less sophistication.

The following level descriptions are taken from *GA-214-90 Levels of Gypsum Board Finish.*

Level 1 "Frequently specified in plenum areas above ceilings, in attics, in areas where the assembly would generally be concealed or in building corridors and other areas not normally open to public view. Accessories are optional at specifier discretion in corridors and other areas with pedestrian traffic. Some degree of sound and smoke control is obtained; this level of treatment is referred to as 'fire-taping' in some geographic areas. Where fire resistance rating is required for the gypsum board assembly, details of construction must be in accordance with reports of fire tests of assemblies that have met the fire-rating requirement."

Level 1 may be achieved with SHEETROCK Joint Treatment products by applying the first (embedding) coat to joints and to inside corners. Fire-taping may exclude the double-back of the first coat over the tape.

Level 2 "Specified where water-resistant gypsum backing board (ASTM I C630) is used as a substrate for tile; may be specified in garages, warehouse storage or other similar areas where surface appearance is not of primary concern."

Level 2 may be achieved with SHEETROCK Joint Treatment products by applying the first (embedding) and second (fill) coats to joints, to inside corners, and one coat of joint compound applied over all fasteners, metal bead, and trim.

Level 3 "Typically specified in appearance areas that are to receive heavy or medium texture (spray or hand applied) finishes before final painting, or where heavy grade wall coverings are to be applied as the final decoration. This level of finish is not recommended where smooth painted surfaces or light to medium weight wall coverings are specified."

Level 3 may be achieved with SHEETROCK Joint Treatment products by applying the first (embedding), second (fill), and third (finish) coats to joints. Inside corners should be treated and three coats of joint compound should be applied over all fasteners, metal bead, and trim. If low shrinkage compounds are used, only two coats are required over fasteners, metal bead, and trim. Surfaces should be primed with a flat latex paint with high solid content applied undiluted.

Level 4 "This level should be specified where light textures or wall coverings are to be applied, or economy is of concern. In critical lighting areas, flat paints applied over light textures tend to reduce joint photographing. Gloss, semigloss, and enamel paints are not recommended over this level of finish. The weight, texture, and sheen level of wall coverings applied over this level of finish should be carefully evaluated. Joints and fasteners must be adequately concealed if the wall covering material is lightweight, contains limited pattern, has a gloss finish, or any combination of these features is present. Unbacked vinyl wallcoverings are not recommended over this level of finish."

Level 4 may be achieved with the same joint finishing and priming recommendations shown above for Level 3.

Level 5 "This level of finish is recommended where gloss, semi-gloss, enamel, or nontextured flat paints are specified or where severe lighting conditions occur. This highest quality finish is the most effective method to provide a uniform surface and minimize the possibility of joint photographing and of fasteners showing through the final decoration."

Level 5 may be achieved by following the same joint finishing recommendations as shown for Level 3 followed by application of a thin skim coat of joint compound over the entire surface. After the skim coat has dried, the entire surface should be primed with a flat latex paint with high solid content applied undiluted.

Inspecting Joint Treatment and Finish—Veneer Plaster

1. See that corner bead is properly attached and aligned at all outside corners.

2. See that control joints are properly installed where required.

3. See that proper joint reinforcement is used—tape for normal conditions over wood framing. For abnormal job or weather conditions and jobs with steel stud framing, joint treatment must be of approved type. Check specifications.

4. Tape should not overlapped at intersections.

5. Be sure that all taped, preset base joints are set before finish application begins.

6. Be sure that no gypsum base with faded or marred face paper is installed.

Inspecting Conventional Plaster Installations

Plaster Base

1. See that material being used complies with specifications and fire or sound-tested construction.

2. Review appropriate system construction and application, and inspect for proper installation practices.

3. Check for proper application of base perpendicular to framing members, and see that end joints are staggered.

4. Check for cracked and damaged edges of plaster base. These should not be used.

5. Be sure recommended fasteners or clips are used and spaced properly.

6. Check for proper use of acoustical sealant.

7. Inspect installation to make sure that insulating blankets are properly attached and fitted.

8. Be sure adequate supports/blockings are in place for fixture and cabinet application.

Grounds for Plastering

The thickness of basecoat plaster is the most important element of a good plaster job. To ensure proper thickness of plaster, grounds should be properly set and followed. Check the following points:

1. All openings should have specified plaster grounds applied as directed. If plaster screeds are used, the dots and continuous strips of plaster forming the screed must be applied to the ground thickness to permit proper plumbing and leveling.

2. Grounds should be set for recommended minimum thickness for particular plaster base being used.

3. Control joints should be installed as required for materials and construction with lath separated behind joint.

Job Conditions for Plastering

This phase of inspection is also important. Periodically make an accurate check of the following points: At no time should plastering be permitted without proper heating and ventilation. Circulation of air is necessary to carry off excess moisture in the plaster, and a uniform temperature in a comfortable working range helps to avoid structural movement due to temperature differential.

• To prevent "dryouts," precautions must be taken against rapid drying before plaster set has occurred. Check temperature during damp, cold weather where artificial heat is provided. During hot, dry summer weather, cover window and door openings to prevent rapid drying due to uneven air circulation.

Plaster Application

The visible success of the job is at stake with the finish plaster coat, and required measures should be taken to finish correctly.

1. Check plaster type and mixing operation.

2. See that proper plaster thickness is maintained.

3. Inspect plaster surfaces during drying. Setting of basecoat plaster is indicated by hardening of plaster and darkening of surface as set takes place. Plaster that has set but not yet thoroughly dried will be darker in color than the unset portion. This accounts for the mottled effect as plaster sets.

4. Consult architect's specifications to see that proper surface finish method is being used.

5. Check temperature of building for proper finish plaster drying conditions.

Cleanup

For a complete job, cleanup is the final stage. All scaffolding, empty containers, and excess materials should be removed from the job site. Floors should be swept and the building site left in good condition for decoration and finishing.

TERRAZZO; CERAMIC AND QUARRY TILE
General

References

1. As noted, there is a variety of terrazzo materials that are described in the Materials section.

2. Likewise, the various methods and materials for setting and grouting ceramic and quarry tiles are given.

3. You should have the references describing tile installation available to determine and check the required methods for acceptable work. Most are American National Standards Institute (ANSI) publications.

4. The latest issue of common use references should be in the field office library. Your request for other needed publications should be made well in advance of the preparatory inspection meeting.

   a. Check section for the lath and plaster requirements for the wet wall base for ceramic tile.

   b. When a thin (⅛-in.) mortar bed such as dry-set or resinous material is planned for tile, the substrate must be within required smoothness tolerances.

Submittals

1. Samples shall be received as required in the colors and patterns given in the finish schedule on the drawings.

2. Bonded terrazzo application requires certificates of compliance for conductive and resinous mortars and grout.

3. Resinous terrazzos require certified teat reports, manufacturer's descriptive and application data, and maintenance literature.

4. Check for shop drawings that show layout of all accessories.

5. Check the applicator contractor qualifications as required by the specifications.

Materials

Bonded Terrazzo

This is portland cement base material with a total thickness of 1¾- to 1¼-in. underbed and a ½-in. topping.

Resinous Terrazzo

A thin (about ¼-in.) resinous base material that is applied to finished, hard rock concrete. The resinous flooring system specified could be one of the following:

- Epoxy
- Polyacrylate
- Polyester
- Synthetic latex mastic or resin emulsion

Conductive Resinous Terrazzo

Same as above except includes acetylene carbon black powder to impart conductance. Matrix is black color. Thickness is ¼ or ⅜ in. depending on resin system selected. Check your specifications.

Industrial Resinous Terrazzo

Same as for resinous terrazzo. The resin system specified will depend on exposure conditions. These systems are intended for floors of biological laboratories and similar hard wear areas.

Sparkproof Industrial Resinous Terrazzo

Similar to conductive resinous terrazzo except that formulation is intended for hard use areas in explosive or volatile flammable liquid atmospheres.

Ceramic Tile

Standard grade per Tile Council of America (TCA) standard specification. Check for required glazed or unglazed finish surface.

Quarry Tile

Check grade per specifications and whether smooth or abraded unglazed surface finish is required.

Mortar for Tile Setting

The following may be specified:

1. Plastic mortar bad of sand and portland cement mix. See ANSI A108.1.

2. Dry-set mortar of pre-mixed material, water added; for use over cured mortar (plaster) bed or required concrete or masonry. See ANSI A108.5.

3. Resinous; either epoxy or furan material for special use areas. Check the finish schedule.

Adhesive for Tile Setting

A premixed material conforming to ANSI A108.4 and used in dry areas over gypsum wallboard.

Grout

Premixed using white portland cement for ceramic tile. May be job mixed with gray cement for quarry tile.

Metal Lath

Use to reinforce the setting bed for wall tile. Expanded metal lath weighing 3.4 pounds per square yard.

Reinforcing Wire Fabric

Use to reinforce the concrete fill, when required, for floor setting bed—either 2×2 in., 16-gage, or 1½ in., 16- and 13-gage wire.

Terrazo Accessories

1. *Aggregate.* Check for blend of chips (⅛–¼) in accordance with NTMA No. 1 requirements. Marble chips usually specified except that granite chips may be specified to increase stain and acid resistance.

2. *Divider strips.* May be brass, white zinc alloy, or plastic. (Brass and plastic may react with resinous materials.) Check your specifications for material and gauge thickness.

3. *Control and expansion joint strips.* Special "sandwich" shapes for use at joint locations in the substrate. A neoprene filler material, or temporary filler removed for sealant, is part of the preformed joint material. Check NTMA Specifications for details.

4. *Primer, binder, and filler.* Materials required in resinous terrazzo mix as recommended by the binder manufacturer.

5. *Grout.* As required and recommended by the manufacturer of the resin.

6. *Curing materials.* Portland cement terrazzo cured with wet sand, waterproof sheet, or liquid membrane curing compound.

7. *Cleaner and sealer.* As recommended for terrazzo by the material manufacturer. Sealer is a penetrating type.

Preparation

Storage

Check container labels on arrival for matching information with that submitted in manufacturer's data. Storage must be in a protected location to prevent freezing.

Temperature

Check your specifications. Minimums may be 50°F or 60°F, depending on system specified.

Substrate

1. Check section for cement plaster application for wall tile.
2. Plaster finish will depend on tile setting method; rough finish for bond with plastic mortar bed and trowel finish to required tolerances for dry-set mortar bed.
3. Check for adequate curing of plaster.
4. Check for use of curing compound on the concrete base. It must be completely removed for proper bond.
5. *Correct defects in concrete. Allowable smoothness tolerance is* $\frac{1}{8}$ *in. in 10 ft to* receive the dry-set and thin-set systems. Has concrete aged for required period of time?
6. Check surface finish. It may be trowel, light broom, or float finish, depending on terrazzo system to be applied.
7. For tile, the substrate must be within 2 in. of finish floor elevation. If not, a reinforced concrete fill is required.
8. Check the specifications for concrete fill mix proportions and reinforcement laps.
9. Discontinue reinforcement fabric at control and expansion joints.
10. Check the shop drawing for grounding grid in conductive finish floors.
11. Check for low-slump mix for portland cement bonded terrazzo system.
12. Check divider strip layout for terrazzo from approved shop drawings. (Don't use strips over joints in the substrate.)
13. Have all preparations been made and the contractor is ready for installation?

Note: Certified test reports are usually required for the resinous flooring system.

Installation

Bonded Terrazzo

1. Check mix proportions and color. Will the topping thickness be the required minimum? Make a final check on divider strip depth.
2. Nest cement paste is required directly over underbed surfaces.
3. Do the specifications require seeding with aggregate chips? Rolling until excess water is removed? Trowel finish using divider strips as screeds?
4. Check curing requirements.
5. Finishing process is described in the specifications for rough grinding, grouting, curing, and fine grinding.
6. A smooth, level surface with a minimum of swirl marks should be the result of a first-class finish.
7. Check the cleaning and sealing and protection required.

Resinous Terrazzo

1. Requirements are given in the data submitted by the manufacturer.
2. Are divider strips at indicated location and depth to produce required thickness for these thin-set floor finishes?
3. Check preparation of cast-in-place cove base, where required.
4. Are the control and expansion strips placed exactly at the same joint locations in the substrate?
5. Check the mixing and placing instructions of the resin manufacturer for actual conformance with work to be performed. The sequence of grinding, grouting, curing, and finish grinding is important for quality work.

CERAMIC TILE

1. Install wall tile before floor tile.
2. Check for symmetrical layout such that no tile course is less than one-half tile width
3. Tile wainscot height shall be to nearest full course dimension.
4. Check for required caps, corners, and other trimmer tile. Check for accessories.

5. Where resinous grout is scheduled, rake joints clean and check grout manufacturer's instructions for neutralizing joints and application of grout.

6. Check for required conductive dry-set mortar. See *ANSI A118.2*.

7. Check size and height of marble thresholds. Fully grouted head joints at ends shall be not more than ¼ in. wide.

8. Check for required control joints in walls and floors.

9. Clean and protect finished work as specified.

QUARRY TILE

1. Check quarry tile layout for alignment and joint width.

2. Check for abrasive surface finish. See the finish schedule.

3. Resinous mortar and grout shall be mixed and applied in accordance with manufacturer's instructions.

ACCEPTANCE TESTING

1. Conductive tile and terrazzo will be tested in accordance with provisions in *National Fire Protection Association (NFPA) Standard No. 56A*.

2. The resistance test determines conductivity. A qualified technician shall perform the tests. Written test results are required.

3. Spark resistance tests and conditions are described in the specifications. Written test results are required.

RESILIENT FLOORING
General

References

1. The flooring company's installation instructions must be submitted. The Inspector needs to know these instructions.

2. A special conductivity test is required for the conductive vinyl tile installation. The test is described in NFPA Standard No. 56A.

Submittals

1. Check for receipt of floor installation instructions. The cleaning and maintenance instructions are also required.

2. Are flooring samples approved? Use these to check for approved colors of delivered flooring.

3. Test reports or certificates of compliance, as applicable, are required.

Materials

Conductive Vinyl

- Must be layed in special conductive epoxy cement.

Vinyl Composition

1. Tile can be either ³⁄₃₂ or ⅛ in. thick. Check your specifications and the tile with a thickness gage.

2. Check pattern color distribution. They must continue through tile thickness.

3. Same tile lot number, as stamped on containers, must be used in same area.

4. Additional tiles from every lot and or area need to be available for turnover to the client. All must be clearly marked.

Sheet Vinyl

Check the referenced Specifications. A 72-in. minimum width is required.

Adhesives

Use only the tile manufacturer's recommended material.

Wall Base

Check finish schedule for color. Check height and thickness for conformance.

Storage

Require a clean and dry location with temperature above 70°F for 2 days before installation. Read accompanying instructions and follow if a conflict exists.

Preparation

1. Is concrete floor ready for installation? Check the following:
   a. Has area for flooring been above 70°F for 2 days prior to application?
   b. Is concrete surface clean and level (except for required slopes)?
   c. Are all defects and damage repaired?
   d. Make dryness test as described in the specification.
   e. Has any noncompatible curing compound been removed?
   f. Is all other work complete?

2. The adhesive may not bond where certain curing compounds were used on the concrete surface.

- Wax base compound must be completely removed before adhesive is applied.

3. All types of curing compound must be completely removed before applying conductive epoxy cement for conductive vinyl tile flooring.

4. Spills must be completely cleaned and checked for compatibility with the adhesive.

5. If lightweight concrete (less than 90 pcf density), is a topping required?

6. For wood substrate, check joints and fasteners for smoothness.

7. Does contractor have barriers to prohibit traffic on newly installed floor?

8. Protection is required until client turnover.

Installation

1. Check manufacturer's instructions. Require installation as instructed.

2. Check layout at initial inspection. Perimeter tile must be not less than one-half full size tile.

3. Do not allow for the excessive use of adhesives.

4. Check sheet flooring for trapped air bubbles at substrate. Roller must be used from center, outward to edges.

5. Check wall base for good adhesion. Preformed corners may be required by the specifications.

Cleaning and Protection

1. Clean as required.
   a. Dry clean vinyl and vinyl composition floors immediately after installation.
   b. Wash, clean, and rinse after 5 days as per printed care instructions.

2. Polish as specified at project's end. Make sure of the compatibility of the wax with that the client will be using.

3. Protect all flooring surfaces with a covering of heavy-duty building paper until turnover to the client.

4. Check for any dropped nails or screws, or any other object that when stepped on will cause damage to the floor.

ACOUSTICAL TREATMENT
General

References

1. This chapter covers acoustical suspended ceilings.

2. Details that require inspection:
   a. Check the suspension system requirements in *ASTM C636*.
   b. There are many submittal requirements to check at the preparatory inspection. See Submittals.
   c. Temperature and humidity limits must be maintained to avoid warping.
   d. Check the requirements and locations for systems required to have a sound transmission class (STO) and a fire-resistive rating.

Submittals

1. Check for ceiling manufacturer's installation instructions. These should not conflict with contract specifications.

2. Samples of the different tiles are required.

3. A shop drawing with details of the suspension system must be approved, as well as a reflected ceiling plan, when specified.

4. Certified test reports or approved test data will be necessary for special systems for sound transmission and fire resistance. Be sure ceiling openings are occupied by approved lighting fixtures, etc. Can light fixture lens be removed?

Materials

Acoustical Units

1. Has the tile proposed been approved?

2. Should you have that responsibility, a copy of *SS-S-118* will be necessary to check out the requirements and compare with descriptive data and label information.

Grid Systems

1. Use approved shop drawing to check system installation.

2. The 12-gage galvanized hanger wire is the minimum size permitted.

3. Do not allow the contractor to "double" up on the edges. Start at least 6 in. away from wall uniformly and then go to full panels.

Storage

1. Check labels upon arrival and special labels if required.

2. Before installing the materials must be stored at same climate conditions for 24 hours as encountered

at installation. Maximum 75% relative humidity and temperature between 60 and 80°F.

Preparation

1. Make a final check for interferences and resolve or report them to the Site Superintendent.

2. Temperature and humidity conditions in the installation areas must be as given above.

3. Check hanger wire structural attachments. They cannot be attached to steel deck, nor fire piping or HVAC ducts or runs.

4. Check for required access panels.

Instruction

1. Hanger wires shall be hung plumb. When an angle or splay is necessary because of obstruction, and additional hanger will be used to compensate.

2. Check hangers for clearance from duct and pipe insulation.

3. Wire hangers with kinks must be replaced.

4. Supports cannot be attached to steel decks.

5. Check perimeter molding for required attachment to walls.

6. Springs are required between tile edge and molding except at lay-in systems.

7. Check the special construction requirements for main member splices, tile hold down clips, etc.

8. Are access panels properly located and identified?

9. Check the level surface of ceiling for conformance to tolerances

10. Extra support hangers may be required, such as at heavy light fixtures, to eliminate detection beyond tolerances permitted.

11. Replace damaged or dirty tile as required.

12. Check for moisture resistant panels in areas requiring its use.

PAINTING
General

References

Should you have to examine the test reports, the referenced publications for those type paints and coatings must be used to:

1. Compare and determine conformance.

2. Decide to approve or reject the material.

3. Request additional sampling and testing.

Safety

1. Check the requirements for storage of paints, brushes, and rags; ventilation in confined spaces; and protection when spray painting.

2. Check working platforms, scaffolds, and swing stages for protective devices.

3. Review and keep on file all Material Safety Data Sheets for all materials.

Submittals

1. *Certificates.* Check for the certificate attesting to not more than 0.06% lead in any and all materials provided. (Except for lead-base primers to be used in concealed locations.)

2. Manufacturer's instructions are required for:
   a. Textured coatings
   b. Epoxy
   c. Polyurethane
   d. Liquid glaze
   e. Floor coatings

3. Samples
   a. Be sure material is well mixed before sample is drawn.
   b. Mark quart samples and include represented quantity and batch number.
   c. Sample each type representing more than 25 gallons.
   d. Store samples at specified temperature range for future testing.
   e. Check for approved proprietary brands substituted for specified type in quantities not exceeding 25 gallons.
   f. Are the sample panels representing each type of liquid glaze coating approved? Check for specified coating thickness.
   g. A sample finished room may be required in the specifications. It will be important to observe paint application and the finishes to determine acceptance.

Materials
General

1. Check containers for proper labeling and storage.

2. Examine material in damaged containers for possible rejection.

3. The 5-gallon container is maximum size for pigmented paints.

4. Water-thinned paints must be kept at above freezing temperature.

Cement-Emulsion Filler Coat

1. Use either acrylic or polyvinyl acetate (PVA) exterior emulsion; do not intermix or interchange.

2. Check the dry ingredients, e.g., cement and sand, for specification compliance.

3. Mixing of the five ingredients is done just prior to application.

Solvent-Thinned Filler Coat

Comes premixed for immediate use.

Vinyl Wash Coat

Two component. Must be mixed at jobsite. For use as prime coat on painted, galvanized steel, or nonferrous surfaces.

Vinyl System

1. Uses *Steel Structures Paint Council Specification SSPC-Paint 9-64* material.

2. Used to protect ferrous metal surfaces exposed in severe chemical or salt atmospheres.

3. Do not use over conventional paint, including primed metal surfaces.

Fungicide

1. Check for labeling and do not accept an "overstamp" unless validated by manufacturer.

2. For all paint coats where specified. Check for specified use over pipe insulation.

3. Check for use over painted formboard ceilings.

Mixing and Thinning

1. Check for complete mixing by observing consistency and color.

2. Are base coats tinted?

3. Job mix must be in accordance with manufacturer's instructions.

4. Check pre-mix and mixing cycle for cement-emulsion fill coats.

5. Is vinyl wash coat used same day it is mixed?

6. Maximum thinning is 1 pint per gallon of paint; immediately before application and at application temperature.

7. Do not allow the contractor to intermix different types/grades of paints or different manufacturers' paints.

Surface Preparation

General

1. Check for protection of unpainted adjacent surfaces.

2. Are ferrous metal surfaces, including fastener heads, primed before coating with water-thinned paints?

3. Check for oil and grease. Remove same from surface with a low toxicity solvent.

4. Concrete, stucco, and masonry must age for *30 days* before beginning painting.

5. Before applying to concrete, make sure an approved moisture test is done and that the surface has been properly prepped.

For Cement-Emulsion Filler

1. Check for uniformly damp masonry surface immediately before painting.

2. No standing water permitted.

For Primers

1. Check ferrous metal and remove all rust and loose mill scale. Solvent clean before priming.

2. Galvanized surfaces must be solvent cleaned and a vinyl wash coat applied within 24 h before priming.

3. Painted nonferrous metals receive same treatment as galvanized metal.

4. Check for immediate cleaning and priming of abraded shop coating.

For Washable Paint Systems

1. Check the specified paint system to determine preparation.

2. Finish coating may be enamel semigloss or gloss type for the epoxy or polyurethane over masonry surfaces.

3. Check manufacturer's instructions for base coat preparation for epoxy, polyurethane, and liquid glaze coatings.

4. Check for acid etch treatment to concrete for the epoxy and polyurethane systems.

5. Check for use of solvent-thinned filler as preparation for enamel undercoats, epoxy, or polyurethane over masonry surfaces.

6. Seal plaster and gypsum board with latex paint coat before proceeding with enamel, epoxy, or polyurethane washable paint systems.

Plaster

1. Must satisfy two requirements prior to painting:
   a. Age for at least 30 days
   b. Contain not more than 5% moisture
2. Use a moisture meter with plaster calibration. Use probes in hard to see locations.

Wood

1. Check for treatment of knots and other breaks that bleed pitch.
2. Have nails and other fasteners been set in finish surfaces in preparation for primer? Touch-up is still required even if the wood was previously primed.
3. Sand smooth the finished wood surfaces of millwork.
4. Remember to seal wood adjacent to surfaces about to receive water-thinned paints.
5. Check moisture content of wood before painting. A maximum of 12% is permitted for painting. Use a moisture meter.

Moisture Test for Concrete Slabs

Moisture test should be conducted on all new concrete floors as well as older existing ones. Visual inspection is not an adequate check for the presence of moisture that may be migrating toward the surface of the concrete.

Vapor Barrier Test

Place a piece of vapor barrier (6-mil) poly that is at least 3 ft × 3 ft in size directly on the concrete. Tape all sides and corners tightly with duct tape to seal it completely. After a period from 48 to 72 h, any moisture should be visible on the sheet of poly. If moisture is present, then the slab needs more time to fully cure or there may be a water table problem forcing the water up through the slab. This is possible if the vapor barrier was installed incorrectly (gaps, tears, missed areas, etc.) or in some cases if it was omitted all together.

Calcium Chloride Test

Visual testing. The calcium chloride is poured directly onto the concrete, then covered with a piece of poly. Duct tape should be used to tightly seal the plastic to the concrete floor. After 60 hours, the plastic is to be removed for a visual examination of the calcium chloride. A small amount of moisture will cause the calcium to cake or darken in color. More moisture will cause moisture drops to form. Severe moisture will cause the calcium chloride to dissolve.

Weight testing. A much more accurate test using calcium chloride is to determine how much moisture it has absorbed by weighing it. Usually the test procedures will tell you how much calcium to place on the slab; this is usually done by calcium tablets as opposed to using powdered calcium. Either by weighing the calcium before placement or by having the known weight and then reweighing after the test is complete, an exact moisture amount can be determined. Most flooring applications require less than 3 lb of moisture per 1000 sq. ft. before being applied.

Application

Temperature

1. Check the different requirements for ambient temperature such as:
   a. A 50 to 90°F range for applying water-thinned paints.
   b. A 45 to 95°F for most other paints. Note that liquid glaze, epoxy, and polyurethane manufacturers may have other temperature requirements.
2. Check for minimum humidity during polyurethane application—usually 3%.

Methods

1. Permit use of brush, roller, or spray except:
   a. Stiff-bristle type brush application required for cement-emulsion filler coat.
   b. Brush out solvent-thinned filler coat, then squeegee off the excess when tacky.
   c. Brush on the first coating on metal surfaces.
   d. Brush on solvent-type stains.
   e. Check for textured coating manufacturer's special application instructions.
2. Check coverage for uniformity in texture and color. Remember the base coats must be tinted.
3. Your system for checking color, number of coats, and quality should be worked out with your supervisor in advance.
4. Be especially alert for uniformity of coating appearance. Touch-up may be required for suction spots on porous surfaces.
5. Check for coverage in hard to reach locations.

6. Check for dryness before applying additional coats or removing required temporary heat. Different type paints have different dryness characteristics.

Note: Generally, if a finger rub does not mar the painted surface, the paint coat is dry.

Coverage and Thickness

1. Refer to manufacturer's instructions for epoxy, polyurethane, and liquid glaze coatings.

2. Check coating thickness for liquid glaze. Required base coat is *5 mil* minimum, and the top or glaze coat is *3 mil* minimum. Use a thickness gage suitable to the surface coated to make these checks.

3. Film thicknesses are specified for paint on ferrous metal surfaces. Spot check these thicknesses for primer coat and total system with a thickness gage.

Estimates

1. Vinyl-wash coat film thickness requirements are usually specified.

Table 9-5 *Approximate Paint Coverage Using a Brush*

Paint/Surface	Sq. Ft/Gal
Interior	
Flat paints on smooth walls	450–500
Flat paints on textured walls	300–350
Gloss on smooth walls	400–450
Gloss on textured walls	250–300
Enamel on floors	400–450
Shellac on wood floors	500–550
Exterior	
Flat/gloss on wood siding	450–500
Oil stain on siding	200–300
Latex on brick veneer	200–300

2. Check painting applicator for uniform coverage. The paint being used must be mixed frequently to maintain consistency and color.

Natural Finish

1. Check exterior wood surfaces to be stained. Rough surface requires about double the amount of stain.

2. Check varnished surfaces for smoothness. Sand smooth after each coat of varnish.

3. Use wood filler coat for smooth surfacing open grain wood such as oak.

4. Check putty on wood filler color tinting to match natural finish.

Inspection of Dry Paint Coatings

Coating Thickness

1. Dry coating thickness readings on steel substrates are commonly taken using magnetic gages. Nonmagnetically operated equipment is used for nonferrous metallic substrates. Calibration of all coating thickness gages and measurement of coating thickness should be performed in accordance with *ASTM D1186* or *ASTM D1400.*

2. Determination of the thickness of each coat in a multicoat system should be an inspection point, especially when each coat is generically different. For example, if an inorganic zinc primer/epoxy intermediate/urethane topcoat system is specified, each layer should be measured to ensure proper thickness, because coating thickness gages will not yield individual layer thickness after subsequent coats are applied. When using nondestructive gages to measure multicoat systems, the average thickness of the first coat must be determined prior to application of the second coat. Readings taken after the second coat is applied obviously will be the total thickness of the two coats combined, and the specific thickness of the second coat can only be determined by subtracting the average thickness obtained from the first coat reading.

3. It is a good idea, where practical, to provide a means to indicate coating thickness in areas where it is either thin or thick so appropriate repair can be done by the coating applicator. Possible methods are brush application of a light tinted coat of the same paint, compatible felt tip marking pens, chalk, or other material that can be readily removed. Wax crayons or incompatible spray paints should not be used.

4. Thickness readings are taken to provide reasonable assurance that the specified thickness has been achieved. However, it is not possible to measure every square in. of the surface. Both *ASTM D1186* and *D1400* state that, when using coating thickness gages, five separate spot measurements should be made over every 9.3-m^2 (100-ft^2) area. Each spot measurement consists of an average of three gage readings taken within a 12.7-mm-diameter (½-in.) circle.

Nondestructive dry film thickness measurement instruments fall into three basic categories:

- Magnetic pulloff
- Electromagnetic probe
- Eddy current probe

Cleanliness and Time (Cure) Between Coats When more than one coat is to be applied, a determination of the cleanliness of the surface immediately prior to application of the next coat is required. In addition to dirt and dust, dry spray or overspray may cause a problem. All dirt, dust, and other contaminants should be removed because their presence can result in reduced adhesion between coats and porosity in the subsequent coat, which could render the coating less resistant to environmental effects. The surface also should be inspected for any adverse contamination from the environment. In addition to intercoat cleanliness, the recoat window also must be observed. Recoating too soon may cause solvent entrapment, wrinkling, and other film defects; exceeding the recoat window may result in intercoat adhesion difficulties (common with moisture cure urethane systems).

Holiday/Pinhole Detection A holiday is a skip or miss on the coating film, while a pinhole is typically a microscopic hole in the coating film. Holiday, pinhole, or spark testing can be used to find the nicks, scrapes, and pinholes in the coating film. Pinholes can be present in any coating layer and should be closed before the next coat is applied. Pinhole testing is common when the coating is intended for immersion service. Holiday testing may be required after the application of either the next to last or the last coat of paint. Usually when such testing is specified, the test is done when the coating is sufficiently dry but before final cure has occurred so that repair material will successfully bond to the underlying coats.

Assessing Compressed Air Cleanliness Compressed air used for blast cleaning, blow down, and coating spray atomization must be free from oil and moisture contamination. Contaminants of this type are effectively transferred to the surface with the air and blast-cleaning media (abrasive) or by mixing it with the coating during application. Adequate moisture and oil traps should be used on all lines to ensure that the air is dry and adequately oil-free so that it does not interfere with the quality of the work. A simple test for determining air cleanliness is outlined in *ASTM D4285* and requires holding a clean piece of white blotter paper or a white cloth approximately 457.2 mm (18 in.) from the air supply, downstream of moisture and oil separators. The air is permitted to blow on the blotter paper for a minimum of 1 minute, then the blotter is inspected for signs of detrimental amounts of moisture or oil contamination.

WALL COVERING

Submittals

1. Check for sample color and pattern in accordance with finish schedule requirements on the drawings.
2. Additional information required from the wall covering manufacturer is as follows:
   - Installation instructions
   - Descriptive data
   - Fire and smoke rating
   - Cleaning instructions
   - Maintenance data

Materials

1. Wall covering shall conform to Contract Specifications.
2. Is wall covering weight as specified? Type indicates weight, as Type I, 7 oz/sy; Type II, 13 oz/sy; or Type III, 22 oz/sy.
3. Is a factory applied polyvinyl fluoride protective film required?
4. Is primer and adhesive mildew resistant? Check the container labels.
5. Check material type and design of wainscot cap.
6. Install exterior corner guards.
7. Store wall covering flat in a dry location at temperature of not less than 50°F.

Preparation

1. Wall surfaces of GWB and plaster shall be clean and dry. Check plaster for not more than 5 percent moisture content before application. Check with a moisture meter.
2. Surface shall be within specified smoothness tolerance.
3. Become familiar with wall covering manufacturer's surface preparation requirements, which usually include the following:
   - GWB joint and fastener treatment
   - Sanding rough and glossy surfaces
   - Coating of primer sealer
4. Is the minimum temperature of 50°F satisfied in areas to receive wall covering?

Installation

1. Apply as directed in wall covering manufacturer's instructions.

2. Use material in exact order as cut from the roll. Look for special instructions.

3. When wall-cutting (double-cut) procedure is used to match joints, do not cut substrate.

4. Do not make joints closer than 6 in. to corners.

5. Extend wall covering at least ½ in. behind base, trim, electric plates, etc.

6. Check pattern and color and lot number for match. Should variations occur, corrective action is required.

7. Finished surfaces shall be free of air pockets, wrinkles, open joints, tears, or other defects.

TOILET PARTITIONS AND ACCESSORIES
Submittals

Shop Drawings

1. Toilet partition shop drawings must be approved. Check partitions on arrival and compare features with those shown on the shop drawings. Especially compare the following:
   - Gages of metal
   - Reinforcing for accessories
   - Fitting
   - Anchoring
   - Hardware finish

2. Style of partition shall be as specified:
   - Style A—floor supported
   - Style B—ceiling hung
   - Style C—overhead braced

3. Check screens for adequate anchorage requirements.

Samples

1. Accessory samples must be submitted and approved. Check accessories on delivery and compare to approved samples. A listing of accessories follows:
   - Facial tissue dispenser
   - Grab bar
   - Medicine cabinet
   - Glass mirror
   - Metal mirror
   - Paper towel dispenser
   - Sanitary napkin dispenser
   - Shower curtain
   - Shower curtain rod
   - Soap dispenser
   - Soap holder
   - Glass shelf
   - Metal shelf
   - Soap and grab bar combination
   - Towel bar
   - Towel pin
   - Toilet tissue dispenser
   - Toothbrush and tumbler holder
   - Waste receptacle

2. Descriptive data should accompany each accessory sample. Copies are to be made and handed over to the client at part of the close-out documents.

Materials

Partitions

For verification of type, style, quality, size, etc., the requirements in the contract specifications must be checked. Also check for partition and screen panel reinforcement where accessory attachment is required.

Accessories

Check the specification for detailed description of accessories.

Installation and Application

1. Check for damaged units and reject. All units are to be in *new* condition.

2. Metal fasteners and fittings shall be of the same or compatible metal for cathotic protection. Check for required stainless steel fasteners.

3. Check the anchors for plumbness and level attachment.

4. Check for required through-bolting.

5. Are exposed fasteners of tamper-proof design?

6. Check the mounting height for accessories which should be shown on the room detail elevation on the

7. Drawings (check ADA details closely).

8. Check the partition door clearance and for adjustment to 30 degree open in the unlatched position.

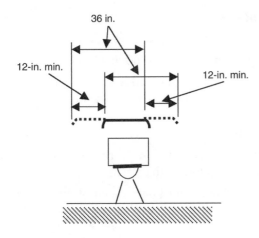

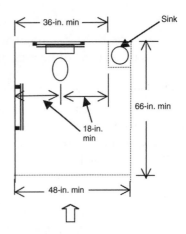

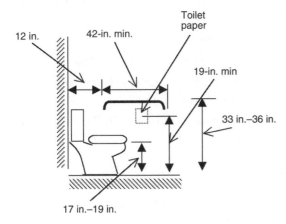

Fig. 9-2 *Required clearances for fixtures and accessories.*

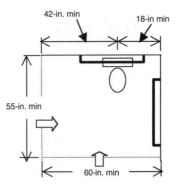

Fig. 9-3 *Plumbing fixture and partition clearances.*

Water Closets

- The height of the seat will be 17 to 19 in. from the finish floor.
- The grab bar directly behind the water closet is a minimum of 36 in.
- Flush controls are to be either hand operated or automatic. They are mounted no more than 44 in. above the finish floor.

Toe Clearances   In a standard stall, at least one of the side partitions and the front partition will have a minimum of 9 in. May be omitted if the stall is greater than 60 in. in depth.

Lavatories   The rim or counter surface cannot be located more than 34 in. from the finish floor.

A minimum of 29 in. is required to the underside of the apron to the finish floor.

Faucets may be push type, lever, or electronic. If electronic, they must run for a minimum of 10 s.

Knee (from wheelchair) clearance is to be a minimum of 8 in. and toe clearance from the wall is a minimum of 6-in. clearance.

Mirrors   The bottom edge of the actual reflective surface is to be a maximum of 40 in. above finish flooring.

RAISED FLOORS
Submittals

Descriptive Data

Check floor manufacturer's data, including installation, cleaning, and maintenance instructions.

Shop Drawings

1. Check for approved shop drawings, which should include the following:
   - Layout and elevations for the system
   - Component materials in detail
   - Grounding
   - Shop coating and finishes
2. Installation methods may also be included on the shop drawings.

Samples

A floor panel with the finish flooring and samples of manufactures standard colors of flooring are required.

Design Calculations

Either calculations or certified test reports for floor loading, air leakage, grounding, and bond strength of adhesive used for pedestals and for finish flooring are required for approval if requested in the contract documents.

Certificate

Check for receipt of the manufacturer's certificate, signed by an officer of the company, indicating compliance with the contract requirements.

Materials

Types

1. Extruded aluminum frame.
2. Zinc-coated steel frame.

Floor Panels

1. Die-cast aluminum.
2. Die-cast steel with baked enamel finish.
3. Combination: Wood core of particleboard encapsulated in steel or aluminum. Flame spread rating of 25 or less is required.
4. Finish floor may be resilient tile of plastic laminate. Check the requirements as conductive vinyl tile may be required.
5. Check for rubber or vinyl cove base specified. Molded external and internal corners may be required.

Steps and Ramps

1. Check the shop drawings for materials, sizes, and details.
2. Are the nonslip traffic surfaces located as required?
3. Are ADA requirements being met?

ADA Requirements

Ramps

1. Any route with a slope greater than 1:20 is considered to be a ramp, and must meet all ADA requirements.
2. The maximum slope allowed for ramps is 1:12, one unit of rise for every 12 units of run.
3. The maximum rise for any run is 30 in.
4. The minimum clear width of ramps is to be 36 in.
5. Cross slope of ramps maximum of 1:50.

Landings

1. Must be as wide as the ramp leading to it.
2. Length must be at least 60 in. clear.
3. When the landing is used to change direction of the ramp, then it must at least 60×60 in.

Handrails

1. Handrails are required if the rise is greater than 6 in. or the run is longer than 72 in.
2. Any 1:20 ramp must have handrails and guards.
3. Clear space between the handrail and wall is to be $1\frac{1}{2}$ in.
4. Top of handrail to be mounted between 34 in. and 38 in.
5. Required if four or more risers.
   a. Check the shop drawings for details.
   b. Check finishes on rails and standards, anodized, satin finish, aluminum tubing, etc.
6. Spiral staircases need a handrail on the outside on the steps.

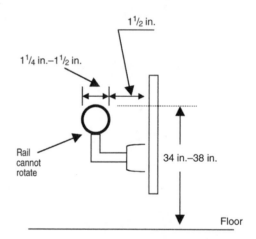

Fig. 9-4 *Handrails.*

Installation

Preparation

1. Are the shop drawings and installation instructions available?
2. Concrete subfloor must be clean before beginning and cleaned again after installation of the floor system.
3. Is subfloor to be painted? Check for the presence of curing compound or other bond-breaker. Be sure surface is clean and unpainted before adhesive applications for pedestal bases.

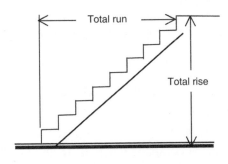

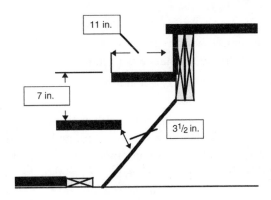

Fig. 9-8 *Stair treads and risers (commercial).*

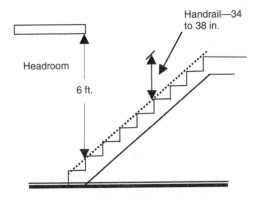

Fig. 9-5 *Headroom for stairs.*

4. Check for required temperature and humidity conditions before installation.

Framing

1. Check pedestal alignment and elevation. Finish floor smoothness tolerance must be not more than $\frac{1}{16}$ in. in 10 ft.

2. Is the pedestal base anchored with mechanical fasteners? Don't attach fasteners until base adhesive has set. Check adhesive container label for set time.

3. Check stringer interlock, or panel interlock at pedestals when stringers are not required.

4. Check for installation of required auxiliary framing wherever panels are cut or terminated.

5. Coating damage and abrasions must be repaired when discovered.

Floor Panels

1. Check for required interlock and fit.

2. Check for level installation. Check for smoothness without projecting edges and rocking panels.

3. If wood core panels are cut, they must be covered with metal skin at the cut edges.

4. All cutouts for electric conductors and cables must be bushed and closed as detailed.

5. Floor panels shall be removable except for perimeter panels and cut panels which must be anchored to framing. At least two lifting devices for removing panels shall be provided.

Finish Flooring

1. Check for loose flooring material. Plug cracks and voids before application of cove base.

2. Check for continuous grounding of all metal parts of raised floor.

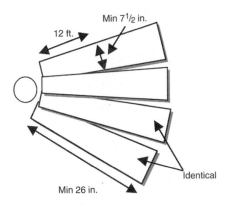

Fig. 9-6 *Spiral stairs.*

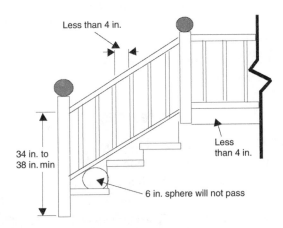

Fig. 9-7 *Minimum and maximum stair measurements.*

Testing

1. You should be available to witness. Keep a copy of the electrical resistance test report.
2. Check for humidity and temperature conditions required for the test.
3. Obtain a copy of the National Fire Protection Association (NFPA) *Standard No. 56A* and become familiar with the test requirements and the modifications given in the raised floor specification. Required test values are given in the specification.
4. Require a written report of the test results.

Protection

1. Clean the finish floor in accordance with the flooring manufacturer's instructions.
2. Be alert for restrictions to cleaners permitted for conductive flooring
3. All damaged materials must be replaced with new, so insist on adequate protection for the finished floor, using paper, fiberboard, and/or plywood as necessary.

Spare Parts

1. Check the specifications for the number of required lifting devices to remove floor panels.
2. Check for required spare floor panels.
3. Check for required spare pedestal assemblies and stringers.

WINDOW TREATMENT
General

1. Approval action on shop drawings and manufacturer's descriptive data will require a check on provisions in the contract specifications.
2. Proper fit is the responsibility of the contractor. Field measurements should be taken after trim work is complete.

Materials

1. Check sample for required operation, smooth traverse, rotation, and access for cleaning the window glass.
2. There are special requirements for audiovisual and lightproof items. Check the operation through light traps.
3. Cloth curtains will have straight, French seams. A French seam is described as a seam stitched first on the right side and then turned in and stitched on the wrong side so that the raw edges are enclosed in the seam.

Installation

1. Check approved shop drawing for installation requirements.
2. Check for complete finishing, including all painting before beginning installation.
3. Is the item centered and level with the covered opening?
4. Are hold down brackets required?
5. Are audiovisual and light proof items, including the light traps, closely fitted to prevent outside light from infiltrating the room?

CABINETS AND CASEWORK
General

1. Shop drawings are required. View the chapter Carpentry for typical clearances and installations. Check for approval and necessary information, which should include the following:
   - Plan and elevation details
   - Layout
   - Gage of metal, thickness of wood
   - Mounting and anchorage
   - Hardware type and finish
   - Reinforcing for hardware
2. Check American National Standards Institute (ANSI) *Standard A161.1* for kitchen cabinets and *A156.9* for cabinet hardware.
3. Check for receipt of required samples and the Architect's approval.
4. A certificate indicating casework material compliance with specific requirements in the specification will be required.
5. Check ADA requirements in all designated handicap areas/rooms.

Materials

Metal

1. Casework is usually made of carbon steel with a baked enamel finish. Check your specifications as stainless steel may be required.
2. Cabinets are made of carbon steel with baked enamel finish.

3. Check for good workmanship in fit-up and fastenings. Exposed welds are to be ground smooth and refinished.
4. Should a workmanship question occur, check the quality of the approved sample.

Wood

1. Casework shall be finished with plastic laminate over plywood or particleboard. Check for delaminating at edges and joints.
2. Cabinets shall be natural, stained, or paint finish.
3. Check cabinet construction, reinforcing, and finish by comparison with the approved sample cabinet.
4. Check for drawer stops.

Hardware

1. Check cabinet hardware for specified type and finish. specified.
2. Check for through-bolted hardware attached to units with particleboard core.
3. Drawer guides shall be firmly and adequately fastened to framework.

Countertop and Backsplash

1. Check items with approved sample.

2. Laminated material shall comply with the LD3 Standard of the National Electrical Manufacturers Association (NEMA).
3. Verify caulking specification (type, color, etc.).

Delivery and Storage

1. Check for damage at delivery and reject nonrepairable units or items.
2. Store units in a protected location to prevent damage.

Installation

1. Precautions shall be taken to prevent damage to room finishes during installation of casework and cabinets.
2. Check alignment for level and plumb installation.
3. Verify the humidity levels, temperatures, etc. are within specifications.
4. In multiple configurations, make sure the sequence is correct.
5. Anchors and fasteners shall be at the required interval and locations specified. Check fastening and anchor effectiveness.
6. Check that door and drawer are aligned and have smooth operation.
7. Check that drawers, when opened, do not interfere with door operation.

10
CHAPTER

Thermal and Moisture Protection

DAMPPROOFING AND WATERPROOFING
Submittals

1. The required certificates of compliance and material manufacturer's installation instructions must be approved *before the work is started.*

2. Specifications permitting the use of either asphalt or coal tar pitch materials (either cold or hot) require the contractor to indicate the method to be used. This should be included in the submittals.

Fig. 10-1 *Worker installing asphalt dampproofing compound.*

Surface Preparations
Cleanliness and Smoothness

1. Masonry surfaces are required to be pointed flush.

2. All excess mortar or concrete is to be removed from surfaces before dampproofing or waterproofing.

3. Have rough or high spots been ground smooth?

4. Is surface free from all foreign matter including sand, mud, dirt, and dust?

5. If the area has been washed down, it must be dry before applying waterproofing application.

Dampproofing
Plans and Specifications

Check plans, specifications, and manufacturer's instructions for all locations of dampproofing. Check that the height of dampproofing on exterior of walls below grade is to the correct height.

Note: At no time may dampproofing be substituted for waterproofing.

Application

1. See that the ambient temperature is above 40°F.

2. Check for application of approved prime coat for both tar and asphalt dampproofing systems, and for an asphalt waterproofing system. Check temperatures of materials.

3. Always apply dampproofing, *before* furring, on interior of walls.

4. Check coating for breaks or application that was too thin after a surface has been dampproofed. Repair all areas if disturbed.

   a. Check for air voids in concrete.

   b. Reseal all voids not sealed by original application.

   c. Both hot or cold systems require *two coatings.*

Waterproofing
General

1. Check the requirement for primer application.

2. See that the ambient temperature is above 40°F.

3. Review contractor's plan for work to ensure timely and organized completion.

4. Review the plan for backfill materials. Do not allow backfilling until the application has fully cured.

Fig. 10-2 *Workers installing membrane-type waterproofing material. Note: The face has been primed.*

Waterproofing Systems

Coal Tar Polyurethane Coal tar–modified polyurethane is a cold-applied liquid waterproofing system. It is applied as a liquid at the rate of 10–15 mils/coat. The coating dries hard but has some elasticity. This material may be attacked by acids in groundwater but can be defended by a protection board.

Polymer-Modified Asphalt Polymer-modified asphalt is a cold-applied liquid waterproofing system, but it is difficult to achieve an even coating on a vertical surface. High-grade, polymer-modified asphalt is superior to coal tar–modified polyurethane in elasticity, crack-spanning ability, and resealability but inferior in its resistance to chemicals.

Membrane Waterproofing Systems Waterproofing applied as a solid-sheet membrane has an advantage over liquid-applied systems in that quality control over thickness is ensured by the manufacturing process. Most membrane systems are chemically stable and have good crack-spanning ability. Thermoplastic membranes may be applied in various ways: affixed to walls or laid beneath slabs. Thermoplastic membranes are rated for resistance to chemicals and longevity. Seals and overlaps must be carefully and completely closed in order for membranes to function as radon barriers.

Bentonite Bentonite clay expands when moist and thereby creates a waterproof barrier. Bentonite is not as resistant to chemicals as the thermoplastic membranes. The major flaw of this material as a radon barrier, however, is that it is only expanded when wet. This is acceptable for a waterproofing material but not for a gas barrier.

FOUNDATION DAMPPROOFING

Masonry is to be parged with ⅜-in. portland cement, then one of the following:

1. Bituminous coating
2. Acrylic modified cement—3 lb/sq. yd.
3. ⅛-in. surface bonding mortar
4. Any approved waterproofing method

FOUNDATION WATERPROOFING

One of the following:

1. Membrane of 2-ply hot-mopped felts
2. 55-lb roll roofing
3. 6-mil polyvinyl chloride
4. 6-mil polyethylene
5. 40-mil polymer-modified asphalt

All laps must be sealed with approved material.

Table 10-1 *Dew Point Temperatures*

Dry Bulb or Room Temperature (°F)	Dew Point (°F) Based on Relative Humidity									
	10%	20%	30%	40%	50%	60%	70%	80%	90%	100%
40	9	5	13	19	24	28	31	34	37	40
45	−5	9	17	23	28	32	36	39	42	45
50	1	13	21	27	32	37	41	44	47	50
55	3	17	25	31	37	41	45	49	52	55
60	6	20	29	36	41	46	50	54	57	60
65	10	24	33	40	46	51	55	58	62	65
70	13	28	37	45	51	56	60	63	67	70
75	17	31	42	49	55	60	65	68	72	75
80	20	36	46	54	60	65	69	73	77	80
85	23	40	50	58	65	70	74	78	82	85
90	27	44	55	62	69	74	79	82	86	90

Example: If an office area has a room temperature of 70°F and relative humidity of 30%, the wall temperature should not fall below 37°F, or condensation will form on its surface.

Exterior Flashing/House Wraps

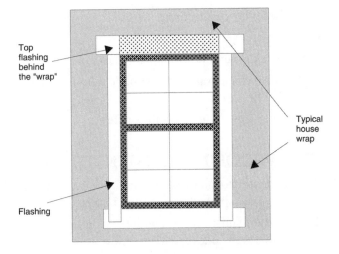

Fig. 10-3 *Flashing around windows.*

Fig. 10-4 *House wrap.*

House wrap must be lapped a minimum of 6 in. horizontally and 12 in. on the corners and sealed with an approved tape. House wraps are not a substitute for flashings.

Application—Metallic Oxide Waterproofing

1. Test area.
   a. Selection of test location is important for a workmanship demonstration.
   b. Access required until all waterproofing is complete.
2. Special surface preparation.
   a. Roughen concrete surfaces for better contact.
   b. Patching shall be as specified. Roughen all patched areas.
   c. Check patching at construction joints.
   d. Check caulking at penetrations. Correct type?
   e. Check for required continuous grooves at intersections.
3. Check for adequate curing.
4. Protection of waterproofing.
   a. Check grout mix formula for each coating.
   b. Finish of the top coating will be to receive specified finish material.
   c. Seven-day curing as with concrete.

FIREPROOFING (CEMENTITIOUS)

1. The contractor must be certified by the manufacturer of the sprayed fireproofing material.
2. Thickness must conform with the plans and specifications. All codes are to be followed.
3. Manufacturer's application procedures and data sheets are to be followed and kept on file.

4. Delivered materials must be in their original, unopened packages.
5. Do the specifications require a UL label and listing?
6. Do not apply when ambient temperature or surface temperature is less than 40°F.
7. Is material stored aboveground, dry, and protected from the weather?
8. Check expiration dates.
9. Check to ensure that all surfaces are free of all dirt, oil, paints, rust, scale, water, etc. before application.
10. Is there appropriate ventilation to allow controlled drying?
11. Are all hangers, clips, sleeves, and supports in place before application?
12. Re-check after all trades have completed their work. Repair and reseal all damaged areas.
13. Do the specifications require an independent testing lab? The standard is set forth in ASTM E605, "Standard Test Methods for Thickness and Density of Sprayed Fire Resistive Materials Applied to Structural Members."

BUILDING INSULATION
Submittals

1. Is insulation material approved for both composition and thickness? Does it meet the U- or R-value requirements? Check the plans and specs.
2. Have the vapor barrier and method of installation been approved?
3. Has the contractor presented the approved samples?

Table 10-2 *Typical Home Air Leakage*

Wall outlet	20%
Windows	12%
Recessed lights	5%
Bath vent	1%
Exterior doors	5%
Sliding door	2%
Dryer vent	3%
Fireplace	5%
Range vent	5%
Duct system	14%
Soleplate	25%
Other	3%
	100%

Source: Department of Energy.

COMMON THERMAL TERMS

BTU (British thermal unit)   The amount of heat that it takes to raise the temperature of 1 lb of water 1°F (about 252 calories).

Calories The amount of heat needed to raise the temperature of 1 g of water 1°C.

K The number of BTUs per hour, per square foot, per Fahrenheit degree difference, per each inch of thickness moving through any particular given material.

U Sum of Ks for an assembly such as a wall or roof.

R Denotes the resistance to flow of heat. R is the reciprocal of K or U.

$$R = 1/K$$
$$U = 1/(\text{sum of all Rs})$$

Design Temperature

Degree day One day times the number of degrees Fahrenheit that the mean temperature is below 65°F.

MATERIALS

1. Are the materials approved as specified?

2. Are the materials stored in a dry, protected environment? No wet or damp insulation shall be used in any work.

Installation

1. Check vapor barrier. It must be installed on the "warm in winter" side of the wall or ceiling.

2. Roof insulation must be protected from moisture by being covered with roofing immediately after being placed. It must never be left unprotected overnight.

3. Building insulation should be installed only after the building is closed in from weather, and construction has advanced to the point where no damage will result to either the insulation or vapor barrier. Vapor barriers are often damaged by other trades after installation.

4. Secure edges of batts or blankets to supporting members. Follow the manufacturer's installation instructions on proper spacing and fastening schedules.

   a. Fill all areas at tops against frames, jambs, and headers, etc. for a continuous seal against air infiltration. Install insulation around cold sides of electric boxes, ducts, pipes, vents, etc.

   b. Lap and seal edges and ends of vapor barrier or use separate sheet membrane vapor barrier.

   c. Check loose-fill insulation for required thickness after application.

d. Information on insulation for masonry walls is in Chapter 5.

e. Information on perimeter insulation is in Chapter 4.

Table 10-3 *R-Values of Insulations*

Materials	R-Value per Inch	R-Value per Unit
Fiberglass		
3½ in.		11
3⅝ in.		13
6½ in.		19
7 in.		22
9 in.		30
13 in.		38
Rock wool		
3½ in.		11
3⅝ in.		13
6½ in.		19
7 in.		22
Loose fill		
Cellulous	2.8–3.7	
Perlite	2.8	
Rock wool	3.1	
Vermiculite	2.2	
Rigid board		
Molded polystyrene	3.6–4.4	
Extruded polystyrene	5	

CONFIGURATED ROOFING AND SIDING
Shop Drawings and Samples

Material Approval

1. Has the contractor received approval of layout drawings and material certification for the galvanized or the aluminum coated steel; the aluminum or the factory color finished metal; or the asbestos cement corrugated sheets, sealant, fasteners, special shapes, and accessories?

2. Design calculations shall also be submitted for approval.

3. Check for certified test results on factory color finish. Is a high-performance finish specified?

4. Does sheet configuration (depth) match up with roof slope?

On-site Checking of Materials Approved shop drawings, samples, and installation instructions including FM's must be used by the inspector to check the roofer's operation.

STORAGE AND PROTECTION

Storage

1. Inspect bundles on arrival at the jobsite. Check galvanized and aluminum for white rust. This condition is cause for rejection.

2. See that materials are properly stacked and protected from traffic and weather.

3. See that material is stacked in a manner that will provide drainage and prevent abuse.

Protection

- Handle at the site for any defects and reject defective material.
- Check material for:
  - Breaks
  - Cracks
  - Wetness
  - Mud and dirt
  - Chipping
  - Marred surfaces or other defects

INSTALLATION

Fastening

1. Check the sealant for color, type, and method of application. Sealant is required at all joints of roof sheets and should be specified for side laps of wall sheets in locations where wind-driven rain is common.

2. Check fasteners for specified type, size, and spacing.

3. Use aluminum fasteners with aluminum sheets.

4. Check contractor's correction procedures for notching or drilled holes in roofing or siding sheets.

5. Check for washers for correct type and size.

6. Fasteners must be driven with sufficient depth to seat the washer.

Application

1. Check length of end laps. Lay side laps away from the prevailing wind.

2. Check for proper drilling and cutting.

3. See that all accessories and special shapes are provided in conformance with shop drawings.

4. Check for molded closure strips.

5. Expansion joints should be provided as detailed.

6. Is specified insulation used? Is application in accordance with manufacturer's instruction? Will thickness satisfy U value required?

7. Is a rigid steel or plywood wall liner or wainscot used? Check for configuration, attachment, and finish. Is the plywood required to be fire resistance? Verify all grade stamps.

Asbestos—Cement Sheets

1. Check for latest EPA safety and health requirement for cutting and drilling asbestos.

2. Is vacuum required? Is water jet required?

3. Are workers knowledgeable on the potential hazards?

INSULATION FOR BUILT-UP ROOFING

Pre-Installation Inspection

1. The Project Manager, Superintendent, Roofing Contractor, Manufacturer's Representative, and Inspector must attend and participate as well as any other contractors that may be involved, such as the HVAC for rooftop unit installations.

2. The roof deck is visually inspected for readiness. All deficiencies are to be noted and corrected before work begins.

Fig. 10-5 *Typical metal roofing.*

3. All matters relating to the total roofing operations are to be discussed: insulations, built-up roofing, flashings, safety, etc.

4. All requirements must be clearly understood before work can begin.

Material

1. See that only approved materials are used.

   a. Check for use of the proper type of asphalt for roof slope involved.

   b. Do not allow the temperature to vary more than ±25°F at point of application.

   c. The insulation must be the approved thickness and type, and treated or faced as required. All multiple layers of insulation are required to have the joints offset. In the event EVT is not furnished by the manufacturer, the following maximum temperatures may be used:

• Dead level asphalt	Type I	475°F
• Flat grade asphalt	Type II	500°F
• Steep grade asphalt	Type III	525°F
• Special steep asphalt	Type IV	525°F

Note: Label information must include the equiviscous temperature (EVT). EVT is the temperature at which the asphalt will attain a viscosity of 125 centistokes. This is the optimum temperature for wetting, spreading, and fusion to surface.

Fig. 10-6 *Roofing asphalt.*

NONCOMBUSTIBLE ROOF MATERIALS

- Exposed concrete slab
- Cement shingles
- Copper/ferrous shingles or sheets
- Slate shingles
- Clay/concrete tiles

FIRE-RETARDANT ROOFING

Class A. Assemblies not readily flammable. Afford a high degree of fire protection to the roof deck.

Class B. Assemblies effective against moderate fire exposures. Provides a moderate level of protection to the roof deck.

Class C. Assemblies effective against light fire exposures. Provides a measurable level of protection to the roof deck.

NONRATED ROOFING

Roofing materials that are not listed as a Class A, B, or C roofing assemblies are called nonrated.

- Have insulation thickness computations for the system been submitted and approved?
- Check roof slope. Both insulation and vapor barrier must be mechanically fastened when slope is more than ½ in./ft. Check fastener types required and approved.
- What type of vapor barrier membrane will be used? Check lapping requirements.
- Are wood nailers treated? Use only waterborne, pressure-treated wood. Are ends being retreated when cut?

SPECIAL REQUIREMENTS OVER STEEL DECKS

1. Check for use of urethane insulation on steel deck. Urethane cannot be used directly on steel decks. Use composite board with a Factory Mutual Research Corp, Class I rating.

2. If isocyanurate is selected by the contractor, a Class I rating is required on steel decks.

3. Is adhesive for use on steel deck fire rated?

4. See plan detail for fastening nailers to steel decks.

5. On acoustic-type steel decks, check for an applied vapor barrier.

6. Check insulation board for square edges.

7. Check for tapered insulation. Fitup is extremely important for smooth surfaces.

PREPARATION OF THE ROOF DECK

1. See that the entire section of roof deck construction is complete before vapor barrier and insulation application begin.

2. See that the roof is dry, smooth, firm, and free of dirt, projections, and foreign materials.

3. Check metal roof decks for holes, rust, or repair of paint, especially where deck has been welded.

4. Note preparation and safety protection around roof openings.

5. Run moisture test on the concrete deck.

6. Protect roof drains and vents during roofing operations. Check for proper drainage.

APPLICATION OF VAPOR BARRIER

1. Are weather conditions suitable?

2. If the deck is concrete, has it been primed?

3. Is bitumen kettle safely located? Fire extinguisher?

4. Does kettle have an operable thermometer?

5. *Kettle must be attended at all times when bitumen is heated.*

6. Check for asphalt temperature within 25°F of EVT at the point of application.

7. Are joints in precast decks covered as required?

8. Check for solid mopping and brooming for the 2-ply, 15-pound felt over concrete.

9. Are fasteners for base sheet–type vapor barrier the approved type for gypsum deck? For insulating concrete deck? Check fastened materials for specified fastening.

10. Ensure that felts are maintained at a minimum temperature of 50°F for not less than 24 hours prior to laying.

11. Record ambient temperature prior to placing the vapor barrier.

12. Does vapor barrier seal edge of insulation at openings? Do not seal with vapor barrier if edge of insulation is vented.

13. Check for felt edge envelope formed with vapor barrier where insulation is vented. Install envelope in steep asphalt or bituminous cement at roof edges.

14. Inspect the vapor barrier to ensure that it provides a complete seal over the deck. See that the method of brooming ensures complete adhesion to deck, ensures complete adhesion between plies, and does not leave air pockets.

Wood Nailers and Vents

1. Nailers flush with the deck will be used with nailable insulations.

a. On slopes more than ½ in./ft, nail vapor barrier to nailers.

b. Nail first layer of insulation.

c. Nailers are installed as concrete is cast. Install parallel to the slope of the roof.

d. Check for flush nailers to fasten flashings for roofing applied to the deck.

2. Use surface mounted nailers at edges of insulation. Slot nailers for venting insulation, except on steel decks.

3. Nonnailable insulation needs surface mounted nailers, parallel to the slope, when slope is more than ½ in./ft. Check nailable securement requirements from the manufacturer's instructions.

4. Use 1-in.-thick nailers on edge behind base flashings.

Application of Insulation

1. On slopes up to ½ in./ft.

a. Check for solid moppings of hot bitumen over vapor barrier or directly to concrete deck.

b. Limit bitumen to 12–15 lb per square on steel deck flutes. Use steep slope (Type III) asphalt.

Fig. 10-7 *Sloped insulation around roof drain.*

2. On slopes more than ½ in./ft:

a. Check for fastener requirements.

b. Use treated surface nailers between insulation section, parallel to slope.

c. Is the nailer thickness same as insulation?

3. Use only dry insulation. Has wet insulation been removed from the work site?

4. The roofing contractor must plan to cover all insulation on the same day it is applied with full roofing system (or provide a temporary approved covering).

5. Apply insulation in at least two layers. Always stagger joints.

6. Lay top layer so that continuous insulation joint is parallel to the roof slope. Be sure this joint is not over flute openings of steel decks.

7. Lay units with close joints. Be sure that no voids are built in by damaged boards or open joints.

8. Remember to protect insulation at end of workday. Check for wet insulation.

9. Underlayment supports roofing on steel decks not requiring insulation. Same application as for insulation. Use insulation manufacturer's recommended thickness.

BUILT-UP ROOFING

Preconstruction Inspection

1. The Project Manager, Superintendent, Roofing Contractor, Manufacturer's Representative, and Inspector must attend and participate as well as any other contractors that may be involved, such as the HVAC for rooftop unit installations.

2. Check the schedule. The insulation, roofing, and sheetmetal phases should be held together because all this work must be coordinated.

3. Discuss types of machines to be used on the roof. The deck and installed materials cannot be subject to damage.

4. Check deck conditions for loading with materials—do not allow overloading.

Material

1. Use only asphalt felts with hot asphalt or coal tar felts with hot cool tar.

2. Check for labels on all materials. Labels must identify specified and approved materials.

3. Contractor must prove specified material without proper labels meet specifications. Test if necessary.

4. Check surface treatment materials.

5. Are the special type IV glass-fibered felts specified in cold climatic locations?

Preparation of the Roof Deck

1. Bitumen kettles are not allowed on the roof deck.

2. Do not overload deck. Remember that all material must be protected from weather.

3. The system of roofing application should provide for free drainage at all temporary terminations.

Note: Remember the moisture test for concrete decks. Remember the air-dry density test for insulating concrete decks.

Fig. 10-8 *Preparing roof for coatings.*

Application of Roofing

1. Check felt temperature from storage.

2. Check bitumen temperature control to prevent overheating.

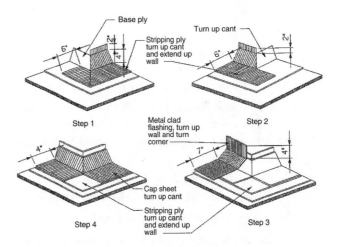

Fig. 10-9 *Typical corner flashing procedures.*

3. Check hot asphalt supply system for specified EVT at point of use. A maximum of 25°F variation from EVT is permitted. *No more at any time.*

4. Are ambient weather conditions suitable? Is the temperature at least 40°F? Too windy? Is there a threat of rain?

5. Note the method of laying the felt that is immediately behind the mopping of bitumen and ensure that the felt is broomed-in so that the layer will be

free of air pockets, wrinkles, and buckles. Most manufacturers will not certify any roof if the ridges can be pushed over with a finger.

6. Check the requirements for and the installation of base sheet. This is the only occasion when hot coal-tar could be applied to an asphalt base sheet.

7. Are cant strips installed as required?

8. Are all felts at specified lap?

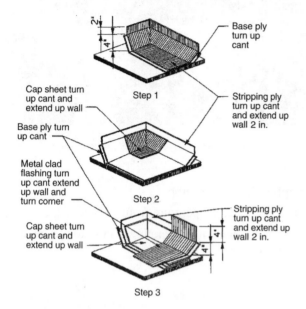

Fig. 10-10 *Typical corner (inside) flashing procedures.*

9. Check for two extra plies of felt at eaves and rakes for envelope bitumen stop. Check for application to deck or insulation in steep slope asphalt or bituminous cement. Use only organic or asbestos felts for these envelopes.

10. For fiberglass felt system, the edge envelopes must be separately placed. Fiberglass felts cannot be used.

11. Check aggregates to be used for surfacing:

   a. Has aggregate been sampled and approved for use?

   b. Is aggregate dry and free from dust, sand, loam, and other foreign material?

   c. Is stone water-worn and free from sharp, flat, and angular pieces?

   d. Is slag crushed, blast-furnace slag? If you cannot tell visually, check certificate of compliance.

   e. Is aggregate spread while bitumen is still hot? Is it thoroughly and evenly embedded in hot bitumen? Have aggregates and bitumen been applied at the specified weights per unit area?

   f. Check for the removal of loose aggregate. Are there bare spots?

   g. Check method of transporting and storing aggregate on roof to ensure that felt and flashing have not been damaged and to prevent excessive loading of roof in localized areas.

12. Cap sheet may be specified instead of the flood coat and aggregate surface. Check for special requirements. Cap sheet should be rolled into hot asphalt to prevent blistering.

13. Use a glaze coating of hot bitumen when rain is about to occur.

14. Glaze coat is only an emergency treatment.

15. Check to see that the roof drains have been set at proper location and elevation, that they are properly flashed, and that they are clean and provided with gratings when roofing is completed.

16. Are roofing samples being taken? Check sample immediately for free water, bitumen skips, and weight. Record results and replace sample unless a deficiency exists. Sample may be replaced depending on nature of deficiency provided a firm understanding can be reached prior to replacement.

17. If finished or unfinished roof sections are used for traffic, be sure that roofing is protected by temporary runways.

18. Do not allow the contractor to use the approved walk pads as his work runway.

19. Check for felt fastenings requirements on roof slopes more than ½ in./ft. *Do not* use coal tar on these slopes.

Application—Bituminous System

1. The felt or fabric plies and pitch or asphalt waterproofing are applied in the same manner as for built-up roofing.

2. Do not allow hot bitumen vapors near open flames and other sources of ignition.

3. Adequate ventilation must be provided, and operations are prohibited in enclosed areas.

4. Adequate personal protective measures must be taken.

5. Asphalt and tar kettles are not to be permitted in enclosed structures. Kettle temperature must be thermostatically controlled.

6. Check the application of felt, especially at all locations requiring two (or more) additional fabric reinforcing plies.

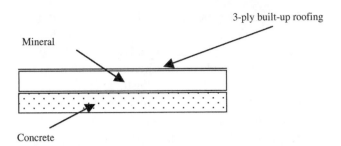

Mineral

3-ply built-up roofing

Concrete

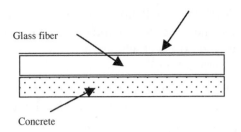

Glass fiber

Concrete

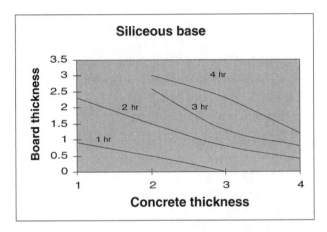

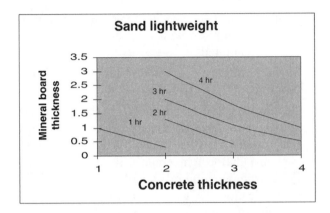

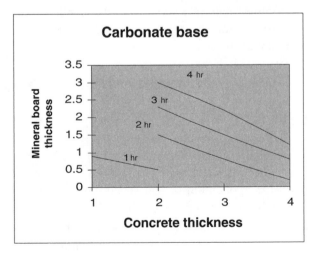

Fig. 10-11 *Roof fire rating assemblies for mineral board insulation.*

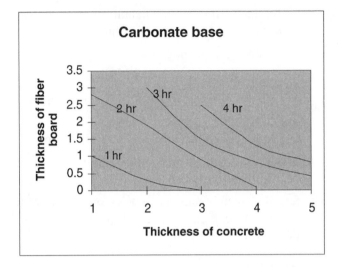

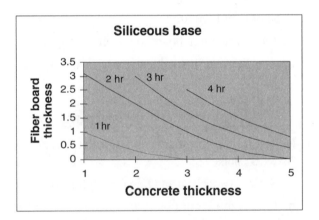

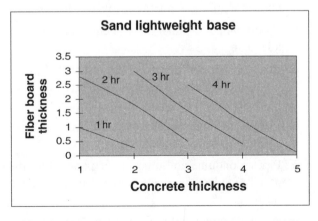

Fig. 10-12 *Roof fire rating for glass fiberboard assemblies.*

Built-up Roofing   319

7. Check the installation of flashing and the lapping and mopping of waterproofing into flashing and around all penetrating items passing through the waterproofing.

8. Check the application of the waterproofing for exact conformance with the specification regarding:

   a. Weight of moppings and final coating.

   b. Bitumen—follow the manufacturer's recommended application temperature.

   c. Brooming in the membrane.

   d. Required nailers on vertical surfaces.

   e. Flash receivers at top of walls to eliminate any exposed joint.

   f. Requirement for reinforcing at control joints.

9. Make sure that all waterstops, flashings, etc. have been correctly installed.

10. See that membranes are always protected from damage. Check the requirement for board protection during backfill.

Check for:

1. Type of board required

2. Method of bonding board to waterproofing

3. Correct fill material and method of installing

MEMBRANE ROOFING

1. Before roofing contractor is allowed to commence its work, make sure:

   a. Surfaces are clean and free from foreign material.

   b. Excess mortar or concrete is removed; all holes, joints, and cracks are pointed; and rough or high spots are ground smooth on concrete decks.

   c. Wood nailers or other attachment conditions are adequate.

   d. Surfaces are dry to receive heated asphalt, coal tar, and petroleum solvent asphalt mastics. Surfaces are tested for dampness if necessary.

   e. Slope is as required. If roof surfaces do not have sufficient slope, contact architect.

   f. Pipes, conduits, and other items penetrating the membrane are in place and ready to receive flashing.

   g. All sheet metal and roof accessories are in place or on hand to be installed in conjunction with roofing as required.

2. Materials of types required should be provided. Softening point of bitumen is as required. Materials are identifiable and comply with ASTM or FS standards. Stand roll roofing on end and keep free of contact with earth or moisture. Protective coverings of stored roll roofing should be vented so that condensation will not occur.

3. Nails and fasteners should be of length, shank, head, and coating required.

4. Felts for use with asphalt should be asphalt saturated; felts for use with coal-tar pitch should be coal-tar saturated.

5. Surface to receive roofing should be primed, if required.

6. Asphalt or pitch should not be overheated. Check kettle thermometer. Methods to transport heated material are provided to avoid overcooling. Measure installation temperature. If asphalt is being used, heating requirement is EVT, ±25°F, at point of application. EVT is the temperature at which asphalt will attain a viscosity of 125 centistokes, which is the practical and optimum temperature for wetting and fusion at the point of application. In the event EVT information is not furnished by the manufacturer, the following maximum heating temperatures should be used as guidelines:

Dead level asphalt	Type I	475°F
Flat grade asphalt	Type II	500°F
Steep grade asphalt	Type III	525°F
Special steep asphalt	Type IV	525°F

Note: In no case should the kettle or tanker be heated above flash point. Do not exceed final blowing temperature for more than 4 hours.

7. Roofing materials should not be applied unless correct bitumen application temperatures can be maintained.

8. Observe lap, nailing, and quantity of pitch or asphalt applied. In no case should felt touch felt; not bare spots.

9. See that felts are laid so that each layer is free of air pockets, wrinkles, and buckles. Brooming may be required. Glass fiber felts should not be broomed. Do not allow "flopping" of roofing felts, except in the application of cap sheets. See that no felt touches felt. Mopping is full to ply lines.

10. All surfaces should be kept moisture free. *Under no condition allow exposure of insulation or felts overnight without a mopping.* Protect stored material from moisture.

11. When felt layer equipment is used, observe that jets are clear and an adequate and uniform layer of bitumen is deposited.

12. Observe installation of roofing at cant strips, vertical surfaces, reglets, and penetration. Observe sealing of roofing membrane envelopes where use of envelopes is required.

13. All concrete walls to receive roofing should be primed. All wall membranes are properly prepared and attached or fastened as specified.

14. Are aggregates for surfacing of type, color, and size specified and clean and dry?

15. Are aggregates in quantity required spread evenly over flood coat while bitumen is hot?

16. Roll roofing or cap sheet, if utilized, should be of weight, selvage, finish, color, as required. Cap sheet installed as required.

17. Operations should be performed in a manner to avoid plugging of drains, weeps holes, etc. and do not damage adjoining surfaces.

18. Observe that roof drains are set to permit proper drainage.

19. Roofing plies are to be mopped into clamping ring. Lead collar flashing is installed and stripped in, if required.

20. Roofing should be protected from damage by other trades or by general contractor during installation and following completion. If subject to heavy traffic, movement of equipment, storage, or materials, or use as a work surface, runways, plywood sheets, or other protection should be provided.

21. Observe and/or cut samples if required. Patching is properly performed where samples are cut. Samples are to be taken before finish surface (e.g., aggregate, cap sheet, emulsion) is applied. Make sure contract provisions allow for the cutting of a sample and required patching procedures.

22. Clean up is provided after installation, drain clearance, and debris removal.

FLASHINGS

Preconstruction Inspection

1. Shop drawings for sheet metal roof flashings are reviewed.

2. Flashings for preconstruction inspection include the felt strip flashings and plastic base flashings and their requirements.

3. Will flashing work be another's scope of work? Coordinated with roofing?

4. Check for same-day installation to completely waterproof the roofing area begun each day.

5. A copy of the roofing felt manufacturer's published flashing recommendations is required.

6. Check for flashings at all projections through roofing.

Material

1. Check that the asbestos flashing sheet has a built-in reinforcing fabric. This is required even though not in manufacturer's recommendations.

2. Where the glass fiber system is to be installed, use the mineral (glass-fibered) cap sheet. See label for conformance to SS-R-630, Class 3.

3. Check label on bituminous cement for asphalt base Type I, per SS-C-153.

Base Flashing

1. Check for correct selection of two-ply or three-ply system.

Table 10-4 *Typical Flashing*

Material	Minimum Thickness	Advantages	Disadvantages
Stainless steel	0.01 in. (0.25 mm)	Extremely durable, nonstaining	Difficult to solder and form
Cold-rolled copper	10 oz/sq. ft.	Durable, easily formed, easily joined	Stains adjacent masonry
EPDM	30 mils (0.8 mm)	Flexible, easy to form, easy to join, nonstaining	Metal drip edge required, more easily torn
Rubberized asphalt	30 mils (0.8 mm)	Self-healing, flexible, easy to form, easy to join	Dimensional instability, incompatibility with joint sealants, metal drip edge required
Copper laminates	5 oz/sq. ft.	Easy to form, easy to join, nonstaining	Metal drip edge required, more easily torn
PVC	30 mils (0.8 mm)	Easy to form, easy to join, nonstaining, low cost	Questionable durability, easily torn, metal drip edge required
Galvanized steel	0.015 in. (0.38 mm)	Easy to paint, relatively easy to form	Difficult to solder, subject to early corrosion at bends

2. Be sure the manufacturer's published recommendations are available and used by the contractor.

3. Check installation for loose plies. Embed all sheets fully into adhesive and press into position. Are laps correct?

4. Are plies mechanically fastened with term metal at top of vertical leg?

5. Check for felt strip over horizontal joint with roofing.

Strip Flashing

1. Two-ply strip flashing required.

2. Check for solid coatings of bituminous cement.

3. Install strip flashings, before surfacing treatment, over all horizontal edges of sheet metal gravel stops, roof drain and pipe flashing flanges, and metal base flashings.

ROOF WALKWAYS AND LADDERS

Wood Walkways

1. Check for pressure-treated wood.

2. Are cut edges being treated?

3. Are pads of premolded filler strips being used beneath wood bases? Locate these before roofing surface treatment.

Composition Type Walkways

1. Is material of specified design and thickness?

2. Is material pressed into hot bitumen over top roofing ply?

3. Is space provided between sections for drainage?

Precast Concrete Walkways

Check the requirements for size, location, and spacing. Be sure roofing surface is clean. Precast concrete units are usually set loose over the waterproofed surface.

Ladders

1. Are ladders located with walkways?

2. If ladders are anchored into roofing, check for relocation to sidewalls to avoid penetrations.

3. Are they the correct finish? Galvanized?

SINGLE-PLY ROOFING

Although there are several different generic types of single-ply roofing materials, and many more systems, only the EPDM (ethylene propylene diene monomer) type is specified in this chapter. Some jurisdictions such as the Corps of Engineers allow only the EPDM Roofing System. This is a synthetic rubber material. The following section deals with systems using that material.

Submittals

1. Check for receipt of the certificate attesting to material compliance. Remember the certificate must be signed by a representative of the manufacturer's firm.

2. The following must be received and approved before roofing can begin:

   a. Manufacturer's installation instructions.

   b. Samples of the membrane, joint cement, and sealant.

   c. Layout drawings and all flashing details.

Materials

1. Check the EPDM material labels closely for specification and certificate compliance.

2. Check storage site for temperature and weather protection. Adhesives and sealant are especially sensitive to these conditions.

3. Ballast for surface covering must be clean and well graded.

4. Check waterproofing treatment for wood nailers and rants; same as for built-up roofing—material should have a grade stamp.

Application of Roofing

1. A preconstruction inspection *must* be held before roofing begins.

   a. Roof deck must be in same condition as for built-up roofing. This includes a positive air-dry density test for insulating concrete roof deck.

   b. Check manufacturer's instructions.

   c. Are the lap joints between sheets of EPDM at least 3 in. wide?

   d. Are laps made to shed water?

   e. Check special treatment at expansion joints for drainage and waterproofing.

   f. Check for perimeter nailers and adequate fastening of the membrane.

   g. Have all joints been carefully inspected before concealing with ballast?

   h. Flashings must be installed the same day as roofing membrane to waterproof area covered.

   i. Remember cutoffs at end of day or when rain is imminent. Roof must be made weather tight at the end of each day.

j. See board insulation and vapor barrier checklists. Board insulation may be loose laid instead of usual adhesion method for built-up roofing. Check the specs.

FLUID-APPLIED ROOFING

The system given in the specs includes spray-applied urethane foam insulation applied to broom finish concrete roof decks. Two coats of spray-applied silicone rubber cover the urethane.

Submittals

1. Check applicator's experience for satisfactory performance.
2. Check for manufacturer's application instructions and material certificates of compliance.
3. Have samples been examined?
4. Does roofing system meet the Underwriters Laboratories UL 790 test for fire resistance?
5. Has insulation thickness computation been approved?

Materials

1. Check labels for compliance.
2. Is there enough coating material to cover all areas to specified dry film thickness?

Application of Urethane Insulation

1. Check the complete plan of application during the preconstruction inspection.
2. Has equipment been calibrated to ensure even coverage? At the beginning? Daily?
3. Is thickness as determined for specified R or U value?
4. Are layers lapped?
5. Check surface smoothness and slope for drainage.

Application of Coatings

1. Protective coating must be applied the same day to the urethane foam.
2. Check the dry film thickness.
3. Finish coating must be free of pinholes.
4. Check for sheet elastomeric base flashings.
5. Is a granule finish required? Are walkways included? It is extremely important that walkways be provided where traffic is expected, such as to perform maintenance on rooftop HVAC units.

STRIP SHINGLE ROOFING

Preparation for Installation

1. Have the required samples been submitted and approved?
2. Do shingles on site match the approved samples? Are they labeled as UL approved? Do they require a fire rating? Are they wind resistant?
3. Is roof clean, dry, and otherwise ready for roofing? Check to cover knot holes and splits with sheet-metal plates.
4. Check the roofing substrate for squareness.
5. Check the moisture content of the wood substrate and required spacings and nailing patterns and types.

Fig. 10-13 *Installing starter strip with ice dam protection.*

6. Are flashings installed or on hand to be installed concurrently with roofing? Check specifications for type of materials.
7. Check for proper installation of under layment and metal edge drips. Edge drip strips are installed over the underlayment.
8. Check slope as double layer underlayment (two layers of 90 lb felt or galvanized metal) is required on slopes to 4 in./ft.
9. Check for special requirements if in cold climate where there is a habit of ice building up at the eaves (ice damming). Either a sheet metal eave flashing or layer of bituminous cement should be required.

Installation

1. Check starter course of shingles, at the eaves. Is it a double or triple layer of shingles? Does this starter course extend ¾ in. beyond eave line to form a drip?

2. Check alignment of layers and rows of shingles. Start rows at center of roof for spans over 30 ft and lay to chalk lines or other guide for a neat job.

3. Check exposure of shingles on hips and ridges. Are all nails concealed?

4. Check that each shingle tab is cemented in place with bituminous cement with a contact area of at least 1 sq. in. Check the manufacturer's instructions for self-sealing type shingles. They must be followed.

5. Self-sealing shingles are usually required, and the manufacturer's warranty furnished by the contractor provides insurance against unit blow-off. The contractor shall be responsible for replacement of blown-off or damaged shingles. Keep at least one bundle for turn over to the client at project closeout.

6. Are correct nailing procedures followed? Size, type, penetrations into the decking?

Fig. 10-15 *Wood shingle/shake exposure.*

Table 10-6 Wood Shake Weather Exposure and Roof Slope

			Exposure (in.)
Roofing Material	Length (in.)	Grade	4:12 Pitch or Steeper
Shakes of naturally durable wood	18	No. 1	7½
	24	No. 1	10
Preservative-treated taper sawn shakes	18	No. 1	7½
	24	No. 1	10
	18	No. 2	5½
	24	No. 2	7½
Taper-sawn shakes of naturally durable southern yellow pinewood	18	No. 1	7½
	24	No. 1	10
	18	No. 2	5½
	24	No. 2	7½

Table 10-5 Roof Coverings

Roof Type	Min. Slope
Composite asphalt shingle	4*
Composite asphalt roll roof	2
Composite asphalt sheet roof	1
Wood shingle	3
Wood shakes	3
Slate	5
Built-up	0

*May be 2/12 under certain conditions.

Table 10-7 Wood Shingle Weather Exposure and Roof Slopes

			Exposure (in.)	
Roofing Material	Length (in.)	Grade	3:12 Pitch to < 4:12	4:12 Pitch or Steeper
Shingles of naturally durable wood	16	No. 1	3¾	5
		No. 2	3½	4
		No. 3	3	3½
	18	No. 1	4¼	5½
		No. 2	4	4½
		No. 3	3½	4
	24	No. 1	5¾	7½
		No. 2	5½	6½
		No. 3	5	5½

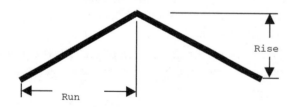

Slope	Pitch
2 in 12	1/12
3 in 12	1/8
4 in 12	1/6
5 in 12	5/24
6 in 12	1/4
7 in 12	7/24
8 in 12	1/3
10 in 12	5/12
12 in 12	1/2

Fig. 10-14 *Slope and pitch.*

VENTILATION

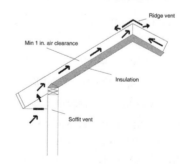

Fig. 10-16 *Roof ventilation.*

1. Need as a minimum 1 to 150 of the area.
2. Can be reduced to 1 to 300 if:
   - At least 50% but not more than 80% of venting is supplied by ventilators located in the upper space and at least 3 ft above cornice vents. Or if the attic has a vapor barrier on warm side of ceiling.
3. Vents need corrosion-resistant mesh with openings less than ⅛ in.

Table 10-8   *Ventilation Required (sq. in.)*

	Width of Structure										
Length	20	22	24	26	28	30	32	34	36	38	40
20	192	211	230	269	269	288	307	326	356	365	384
22	211	232	253	275	296	317	338	359	380	401	422
24	230	253	276	300	323	346	369	392	415	438	461
26	250	275	300	324	349	374	399	424	449	474	499
28	269	296	323	349	376	403	430	457	484	511	538
30	288	317	346	374	403	432	461	490	518	547	576
32	307	338	369	399	430	461	492	522	553	584	614
34	326	359	392	424	457	490	522	555	588	620	653
36	346	380	415	449	484	518	553	588	622	657	691
38	365	401	438	474	511	547	584	620	657	693	730
40	384	422	461	499	538	576	614	653	691	730	768
42	403	444	484	524	564	605	645	685	726	766	806
44	422	465	507	549	591	634	676	718	760	803	845
46	442	486	530	574	618	662	707	751	795	839	883
48	461	507	553	599	645	691	737	783	829	876	922
50	480	528	576	624	672	720	768	816	864	912	960

Note: Use the above table if you meet the requirement to provide 1/300 ventilation of the ceiling area.

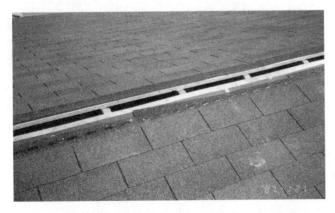

Fig. 10-17   *Preparation of roof for ridge vent.*

- Insulation needs to be at least 1 in. away from all vents.

VALLEY FLASHINGS

1. Valley flashing must be 28-gage metal; 8-in. each side with 4-in. end laps.
2. Roll roofing used in valleys must be at least 30 lb felt. Installed 10 in. up each side, or two layers of 90-lb mineral-surface material.

Fig. 10-18   *Installation of valley flashing.*

FASTENERS

1. Nails to be corrosion resistant and at least 12-gage, with ⅜ in. head.
2. Nails must penetrate ¾ in. into sheathing or thickness (whichever is less).
   - 4 nails per 36–40-in. shingle
   - 2 nails per 9–18-in. shingle

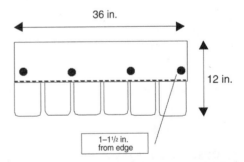

Fig. 10-19   *Typical nailing pattern on shingles.*

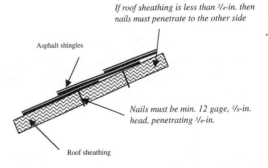

Fig. 10-20   *Minimum nailing penetration in roof sheathings.*

TILE ROOFING

- Must be 3/12 pitch or greater need two layers of 15 lb. felt, or one 30 lb. felt.

Wood Shingles

1. Install on solid sheathing or 1 × 4 in. strips not spaced more than actual weather exposure of shingles.

2. Spacing not to exceed ¼ in.

3. Lap side not less than 1½ in.

4. Cannot be used on slopes less than 3/12.

5. Flashing at least 28-gage metal.

6. Valley metal to run up each side at least 10 in.

7. Each bundle requires a grade label.

Underlayment for Low Slope Roof

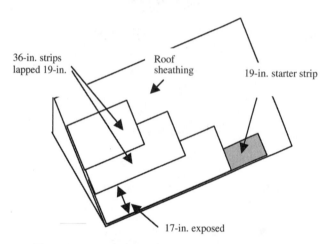

Fig. 10-21 *Low slope (2:12–3:12) roof underlayment.*

FLASHING AND SHEET METAL
Preparation for Inspection of Sheet Metal Work

Shop Drawings and Samples

1. Do the construction and the installation comply with requirements in the plans and specifications and or approved shop drawings for shape, joining, fastening?

2. Factory fabricated internal and external corners should be shown or indicated.

3. Do the materials match the approved samples?

4. Compare detail information with specifications.

5. Metal base flashing must detail wood nailers (pressure treated) for fastening the roof flange.

   a. *Expansion joints.* Examine specifications for spacing these joints in all sheet metal work. Check plan, specifications, and shop drawings for design of the expansion joints.

   (1) Check the specification table for joints and spacing of expansion joints.

   (2) Inspect the location of joints with respect to corners, end spacing, and locations such as gutters and such items as midpoints from downspouts.

   (3) Check drawings for details of expansion joints. See if space has been allowed for expansion.

Dissimilar Materials

1. Evaluate the entire job to see that all *dissimilar metal* materials in contact, which may support galvanic action, have been isolated from each other. Some typical examples to watch for are:

   a. Copper and aluminum flashings in contact with each other, or with ferrous material.

   b. Copper, stainless steel, and aluminum flashings fastened with ferrous material.

   c. Aluminum bases set on pressure-treated wood.

   d. Different metal fasteners used on metals.

2. Determine specification requirement for method of isolating dissimilar materials.

Installation

Fastening

1. Attachment by direct nailing or cleating, for spacing and for location. Are screw shank nails required? What is the minimum allowable penetration? Check codes or manufacturer's recommendations.

2. Check all soldering, welding, bolting, riveting, etc.

3. Check detail on drawing for fastening or securing ends or edges in concrete or masonry construction.

Gravel Stop Fascia

1. Has 6-in.-wide nailer been provided for attaching flange to roof deck? Must be pressure treated.

2. Check flange for 4-in. width applied in bituminous cement over roofing felt.

3. Are screw shank nails of compatible material? Are nails driven within 1 in. of edge at 3 in. on center as a minimum?

4. Mop two plies of roofing felt, one 9 in. wide and one 12 in. wide, over inner flange. This is referred to as *strip flashing.*

5. Check for continuous cleat anchoring lower edge of fascia (not required for fascia membering into gutters).

6. Do butt joints have the ½-in. separation? Are the joint cover plates also set in bituminous cement?

7. Check approved shop drawing design of extruded aluminum gravel stop fascia. Same for the manufacturer's installation method.

Metal Base Flashing

1. Base flashing should be installed the same day as the roofing installation.

2. Check for flat-locked and soldered or sealed joints.

3. Check the location of lapped expansion joints.

4. Is roof flange set in bituminous cement? Is vertical leg long enough for at least 3-in. lap with cap flashing?

5. See that roof flange is covered with two plies of felt strip flashing after nailing at 3 in. on center.

6. Corners, interior and exterior: Are they factory fabricated?

Cap Flashings

1. Cap flashing system will be either the separate cap in reglet or a two-piece combination (cap in receiver) unit.

2. Check the fabrication shown on the shop drawing for:

   a. Vertical location above finished roof surface.

   b. Shape for drainage away from anchorage point.

   c. Shape for pressure fit against base flashing.

3. Is lower edge of flashing folded back ½ in.?

4. Check for 3-in. lap joints for cap and for receiver sections.

5. Corners, interior, and exterior: Are they factory fabricated?

Through-Wall Flashing

1. Carefully check for locations requiring through-wall flashing. All should be shown on the shop drawing.

2. Ensure that the flashing is being installed in the middle of the mortar joint. Assure that it extends to within ½ in. of face of wall.

3. Check the design and installation requirement for the various locations of metal flashing, such as: above the roof line, below the roof line in cavities more than ¾-in. wide, at lintels and sills.

4. Does flashing extend at least 4 in. beyond the ends of each sill?

5. Check for the smooth copper slip joint in the bed joint at the end of lintels adjacent to control joint.

6. Is the metal through-wall factory deformed for bonding with mortar?

7. Do joints between sections of lightweight flashing consist of at least 3-in. laps with approved sealants?

8. Check anchor holes such as for parapet cap anchors to see that they are completely filled with plastic cement at the flashing course.

Valley Flashing

1. Check installation for coverage, lap, and material beneath roof covering.

2. Check cleating operation for adequate anchoring.

Stepped Base Flashing

1. Check for neat installation with a separate flashing section for each shingle course. Do not accept unsightly uneven appearance.

2. Are sections sized to lap 3 in. and run 4 in. each way?

3. Are cap flashings used? If not, the stepped sections must be fitted beneath siding.

4. Cap flashing are mandatory for fireplace chimneys.

Edge Strip

1. The strips are provided continuously at bottom edge of fascia and act as a drip and continuous cleat.

2. Check fastening size and type to supporting construction and fascia.

3. Check for the required washers, which are electrolytically compatible, to hold the strips away from vented gravel stops.

Louvers

1. Check fabrication for first-class workmanship. Check for approved/compatible fasteners.

2. Check to see that louvers are installed right-side up.

3. Check louvers after installation for water tightness.

4. Examine specifications for requirement miscellaneous items as screens, movable shutters, etc.

5. Additional information is provided in Chapter 15.

Reglets

1. Make sure that polyvinyl chloride reglets are used with aluminum cap flashings.

2. Check the setting of reglets in concrete and masonry to assure a method of firm and secure anchorage at the required elevations.

3. Check the Subcontractor-proposed provision for anchoring the cap in reglets. Also check the actual firmness of the flashing as installed.

4. Is the receiver of the two-piece combination unit used as planned instead of the reglet? Eliminate flat spots. Be sure receiver slopes from face of wall.

Gutters

1. Recheck approved gutters for type, shape, general design, and layout. Make sure that the continuous cleat or bracket supports permit freedom of movement. Make sure back of gutter is higher than front.

2. Check slope of gutter to provide drainage to outlets.

3. Check brackets and spacers for size, type, location and spacing.

4. Check basket strainers for gutter openings into downspouts.

5. Do expansion joints limit runs with the specified distances? Are these joints at highpoints? Do joint covers have diverters?

Downspouts

1. Check downspouts for being factory fabricated and corrugated longitudinally in approximately 10-ft lengths.

2. Check for the requirement for specials, such as downspout leaders, scuppers, overflow scuppers, conductor heads, etc. (See the *Architectural Sheet Metal Manual* by SMACCMA.)

3. Check that all interior roof drains and leaders have at least a 1% slope.

4. Check to see that the downspouts are plumb, that they clear the wall by at least 1 inch, and that they are firmly secured with approved straps; one strap anchor located at the top of each downspout section.

5. Downspout sections are telescoped together except that the leader downspout joint should be riveted. Make sure inside ends have been cut.

6. Check downspouts terminating in drainage line. They should be neatly fitted and secured with a portland cement mortar cap, or have a rectangle to round approved connector.

PARAPET COVERS

1. Does shop drawing show anchorage and joints?

   a. Both sides must be cleated at lower edge.

   b. Flat lock joints are required between all sections.

2. Is top of cover sloped for drainage? Drip edges?

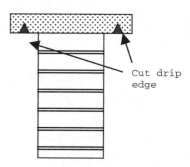

Cut drip edge

Fig. 10-22 *Drip cuts on top of parapet wall.*

MISCELLANEOUS

1. Check for miscellaneous sheet metal items, especially those shown on the plan but omitted from the specifications. (See the *Architectural Sheet Metal Manual* by SMACCMA.)

2. Check those items that have been included in the specifications. Check items such as snow guards, splash pans, radiator-recess linings, perimeter insulation covers, etc. for type required, fabrication, and method of installation. Shop drawings are required.

CAULKING AND SEALANTS

Submittals

1. Are the certified laboratory test reports acceptable?

2. Is the descriptive data approved?

3. Have the samples been approved? Will testing be necessary? Are the colors as required?

Material

1. Check grade, color, and the other required label information and compare with samples and test reports.

2. Check storage protection, exposure temperatures, and shelf-life limits.

3. Area requiring caulking or sealant joint symbols and details are shown on the drawings. The contractor will indicate in his submittals where each type

and color will be used. Joints must be constructed as detailed.

Preparation

1. Check to ensure that material used is from batch tested.
2. Have grooves of adequate depth been provided? Are they clean? This includes removal of the temporary protective coating.
3. Has the required primer been coated over the surface to receive caulking? Has the test been made on sample surfaces?

4. Has the backstop or bond-preventative material been installed?
5. Check for masking tape to protect adjacent surfaces.

Application

1. Make certain that the workmen have the proper equipment.
2. See that grooves are the indicated shape. Check that the proper depth is used.
3. See that appearance is uniform and relatively smooth.
4. Do not allow smears of caulking.

Table 10-9 *Approved Caulking Applications*

Wood to wood	All acrylics, unless gap is greater than ⅜ in. Silicone for gaps greater than ⅜ in.
Wood to masonry	Butyl rubber for less than ½-in. gaps
Wood to metals	All acrylics, unless gap is greater than ⅜ in. Butyl rubber for less than ½-in. gaps Silicone for gaps up to 1 in. Urethane foam for gaps larger than 1 in.
Masonry to masonry	Butyl rubber for less than ½-in. gaps Grouts and special water stop fillers for gaps over ¾ in.

Table 10-10 *Typical Water and Moisture Problems and the Possible Causes*

Problem	Due to	Solution
Ceiling spotting	Roof leaks Ice damming A/C condensate in attic Cathedral ceiling penetrations (recessed light fixtures, exhaust fans) Duct condensation (cooling season) Wind-blown precipitation through vents and louvers Uninsulated (cold) spots Plumbing condensation	Roof repairs Roof ventilation Clear condensate line, install backup pan Install fixtures designed for air-tight installation, good workmanship Rewrap ducts with insulation and vapor retarder Select vent design for water exclusion Add insulation to bare spots Gasket between vent pipe and top plate
Roof leaks	Workmanship, products	Roof repair
Leaking around fireplace	No rain cap Flashing	Install rain cap Caulk or redo flashing around chimney
Damp ceilings at edges near outside wall	Incorrect insulation installation	Reposition insulation, install air chutes and blocking
Mold on walls (heating season)	High indoor humidity	Find and remove excess moisture source, clean with dilute bleach solution
Mold on walls (cooling season)	Cold-side vapor retarder (should be installed on the warm side)	Use vapor permeable interior finish, avoid depressurization of interior
Damp exterior walls	Settled insulation, ice dam leakage	Correct insulation, install eave flashing

Table 10-10 (Continued)

Problem	Due to	Solution
Window condensation	High indoor humidity	Find and remove excess moisture source, place heat source beneath window, open drapes and blinds
Frost or ice on window glass	Single glazing	Use double-glazing, install storm windows
Rust on bathroom lights, hardware	Fan not working or being run as needed	Replace fan and instruct others to use it
Moisture dripping from light fixtures, heating/cooling registers	Fixtures or registers are cold metal	Make sure insulation covers duct work, avoid recessed fixtures
Mold or decay on floor framing	High humidity in basement or crawl space	Place ground cover in crawl space, correct site drainage
Roof sheathing: frosting mold, delamination	High humidity in attic	Close holes in ceiling plane, add balanced ventilation
Exterior paint peeling	Moisture transport to outside. Poor paint prep (workmanship)	Reduce interior moisture level, allow moisture to escape behind siding
Mildew on exterior walls	Natural conditions	Remove by scrubbing, repaint with mildicide-containing paint
Mildew on interior walls or in closets	No heat source or inadequate air circulation	Add insulation, install louvered doors, reduce humidity. Cut ½ in. off bottom of doors.
Mildew on bathroom tile, grout and shower curtains	High bathroom humidity	Remove mildew, use exhaust ventilation
Water in basement/crawl space	Site damage. Plumbing leaks. Rising water table. A/C condensate. Trees/scrubs	Correct gutters, downspouts, and drainage. Repair plumbing. Drain to outside. Sump pump, consult geotechnical engineer
Efflorescence on masonry and concrete	Moisture movement through materials	Reduce leak or moisture source
Mold on framing or trim at windows near window	Window condensation	Reduce high humidity or locate heat source

Table 10-11 *Converting Pitch to Slope to Degrees*

Pitch	Slope, %	Degrees
1:12	8.33	3.75
2:12	16.67	7.5
3:12	25.00	11.25
4:12	33.33	15
5:12	41.67	18.75
6:12	50.00	22.5
7:12	58.33	26.25
8:12	66.67	30
9:12	75.00	33.75
10:12	83.33	37.5
11:12	91.67	41.25
12:12	100.00	45

Note: Most roofing applications are expressed in slope or pitch. However, sometimes degrees are used.

INSULATIONS
Mineral Wool

The term mineral wool includes three products—rock wool, slag wool, and fiberglass. These three products have essentially the same properties. They are formed by melting the base material and spinning it into fine threads. Rock wool is made from limestone; fiberglass is made from glass; and slag wool is made from steel mill slag.

Mineral wool insulations do not absorb moisture, but a leaking roof or condensation in a wall cavity will saturate the wool and cause settling. A facing material, either foil or kraft facing, is sometimes needed to support the fiberglass in wall cavities. However, unfaced batts, used with a continuous vapor retarder, can be used just as easily. The foil facing on batt insulation is supposed to provide a vapor retarder. Faced batts should not be relied on to provide vapor retarders where these are called for.

Mineral wool batts and blankets are about 99% air. The remaining 1% is spun fiber and phenolic binder. Because the mineral wools are made from common materials, this type of insulation is relatively inexpensive.

Where fireproof construction is required, mineral wool formed into semirigid fiberglass panels can be used. Panels can be faced on one side with an asphalted vapor retarder or aluminum foil.

Unlike fiberglass batts and blankets, semirigid fiberglass panels, developed in Canada or cold-climate basement insulation, can be used below ground to insulate basement or crawlspace walls. The fibers in the panels are oriented vertically to channel water down to the footing drain tile.

All types of mineral fibers are also available in the form of loose fill, which can be blown into closed cavities or spread over horizontal surfaces. During the blowing process, an adhesive can be added that sets up and effectively forms a batt of insulation that will not settle. Mineral fiber insulation also can be applied to vertical surfaces in this manner.

Wood Products

Fiberboard A commonly used exterior sheathing material, wood fiberboard is made from the by-products of wood, sugar cane, or cellulose processing, coated with asphalt or other binder, and formed into a rigid board. The board provides rigidity so that a wall can be constructed without diagonal bracing. Fiberboard can also be used as a nail base for the siding. It does have some insulating value as well. The material is treated to provide maximum fire, termite, and rot resistance.

Cellulose Cellulose is most commonly available as a loose fill. It is manufactured from shredded newspaper or wood products and treated with fire-retardant chemicals. The greatest threat to cellulose is moisture. Cellulose performs adequately as long as any moisture stays in vapor form. However, water that leaks into the insulation or forms in it by condensation can saturate the fibers, reducing the thermal resistance of the material. The additional weight may also cause the insulation to settle, producing uninsulated areas.

The most common chemicals used to make cellulose insulation fire retardant are forms of boric acid. If humidity is high, the fire-retardant chemicals in the insulation may cause corrosion of truss plates, electrical conduit, or other metals.

The R-value per inch of thickness is greater than that of the mineral wools because the cellulose fibers are poor conductors of heat. The insulating value of mineral fiber insulation varies with the density of the product. As density increases, the size of the air spaces formed by the fibers get smaller, increasing the insulating value. However, the contact area between the fibers increases, increasing conduction loss. Insulation should be installed at the optimum density, as specified by the manufacturer.

Insulating Foams

All rating of rigid foams are based on tests of aged materials at 75°F. Most foams have higher R-values at the time of manufacture but decrease in R-values as they age. Aging affects polystyrene, polyurethane, and polyisocyanurate. R-values are higher at lower temperatures.

Extruded Polystyrene (PS) Polystyrene is produced from petrochemicals. Under high temperatures, polystyrene pellets are fed into an extruder and mixed with a blowing agent. Gas is trapped in the cells during the foaming process. The foam comes out of a slotted opening and expands to 30 times its original size. The foam is usually manufactured to the desired thickness. This creates cells with closed walls. However, thick blocks can be manufactured and then cut to expose the cells. This type of insulation can be stuccoed to provide insulation on the exterior of the building.

Because of its closed-cell structure, extruded polystyrene is an effective vapor retarder. It is also one of the few insulating products that can be used for exterior foundation insulation. Although it retains its insulating value during in-ground use, it must be protected from sunlight and garden equipment.

If the foam is installed inside the house, most codes require a 15-min fire barrier (equivalent to ½-in. gypsum drywall) to protect occupants from the smoke produced from burning polystyrene.

Expanded Polystyrene (EPS) Expanded polystyrene is made in a two-step process. The expanded polystyrene pellets are expanded into a form called prepuff. The pellets are fed into a tank, where steam heats and expands the beads. Second, the expanding pellets are fed into molds where they fuse into a solid block. After cooling and aging, the block is cut with hot wires into the desired shapes. Because the beads are cut, the expanded polystyrene will absorb water. Therefore, it should not be used in contact with the soil. Also, the R-value of the foam, per inch of thickness, is less than that of extruded polystyrene.

Phenolic Foam Like other rigid, closed-cell foams, phenolic foam has a high R-value. Aging has little or no effect on its insulating value. However, it is brittle, and edges of panels are easily broken.

For those concerned about fire safety, phenolic foam has low flame spread and smoke characteristics. Because it shatters into tiny, glass-like particles when sawed, eye protection and gloves should be worn during handling. Rigid foam insulations are made of tiny cells in close contact with one another. The air between the cells and the air (or other gas) trapped within the cell walls slows the flow of heat.

Polyisocyanurate Polyisocyanurate foam is basically a urethane that has been modified to provide greater fire resistance, less smoke emission, and more flexibility. Polyisocyanurate panels are usually reinforced with glass fibers. Because they are less brittle than polyurethane but have similarly high insulating values, polyisocyanurate foams are often used as a core material in composite panels. Composite panels are particularly useful above open-beamed ceilings. They provide a finished ceiling surface, insulation, and a surface to which roofing can be nailed. Polyisocyanurate foam should not be used in contact with the soil.

Polyurethane Polyurethane is formed when isocyanate (aniline and formaldehyde) react with a polyol (polyester), either in a factory to form board material or on a surface when the materials are mixed in a spray. The resulting foam is rigid and adhesive. The foam is often used in composite panels or as an exterior, above-ground insulation.

The foam cells are filled with a fluorocarbon gas, which is less conductive than air. The gas trapped in the cells can dissipate over time and cause some loss of R-value. To obtain an accurate estimate of long-term thermal performance, look for an aged R-value. In panels the gas is often kept from escaping by a foil facing. Since foil is an effective vapor retarder, care must be taken in cold climates to avoid condensation problems.

Although hard to ignite, polyurethane foam gives off poisonous cyanogen gas while burning. Because polyurethane foam also produces higher-than-average amounts of smoke when it burns, the foam should not be left exposed in an occupied area. When the foam is installed inside the house, most codes require the equivalent of ½-in. gypsum drywall to provide 15-min fire protection.

Table 10-12 *Thermal Resistivities (per Inch)*

Material	R-Value
Batt. (mineral wool)	3.12
Loosefill (mineral wool)	3.7
Perlite	2.78
Glass fiber boards	4.17
Exp. polystyrene	4
Fiberboard	2.94

11
CHAPTER

Piping
Systems

GENERAL

Coordination of Work

1. This chapter covers piping for the water, gas, drainage, heating, fire sprinkler and refrigeration/air conditioning systems, and condensate (drainage) pipelines and site underground piping systems. Piping is also covered in the Sitework chapter. Refrigerator/air conditioning piping includes refrigerant, condenser and chilled water pipelines.

2. Drawings indicate general layout. Pipe and equipment space and schedule for installation must be coordinated between the various subcontractors doing the work.

3. Check and eliminate interference between electrical, mechanical, architectural, and structural features, especially in equipment rooms and ceiling areas. This is especially important in hallway ceilings where the piping and equipment become congested.

Layout

1. The contractor should provide equipment and mechanical room layout drawings, which must be reviewed and approved. Coordination is required with other trades.

2. Pipe sleeve layout drawings should be required (see specifications). Check for clearances and proper sleeve sizes to include the pipe insulation thickness.

3. Check layout for space to allow access and operation of all valves.

4. Check layout for space to maintain and repair piping, especially at equipment locations.

5. Check space for anchors and expansion loops.

6. Check space for support of hangers for piping.

7. Check for proper slope in pipe lines.

8. Check that minimum overhead clearances are observed and ceiling heights are sufficient.

9. Check for proper ADA restrictions for groundwork and rough-ins.

Note: Remember that all piping systems carrying liquids must be drainable.

10. Pipe lines (except in sleeves) should not pass through footings; locate beneath footings before the footings are placed.

11. Check equipment dimension to ensure all equipment can be removed and replaced through the doorways provided, once ceiling/roof is installed.

MATERIALS

Submittals

1. These usually include information on compliance with specifications using labels, listings, or certificates. Shop drawings are required for layout of mechanical rooms and should include any special support for heavy piping and fittings.

2. The mechanical design engineer will check submittals for compliance with requirements.

3. After determining that the submittal is in compliance, use its descriptive information to check the material at delivery. Use the layout drawings to check actual installation.

4. Record all field changes if different from the layout.

Storage and Handling

1. Ensure that materials are handled safely and carefully to prevent damage.

    a. Reject damaged materials. Mark to make sure they are not used.

    b. Have damaged coatings repaired.

2. Ensure proper handling for coated pipe.

3. Check for storage off of the ground and weathertight storage when required.

4. Store pipe and fittings to eliminate entry of dust, dirt, etc.

5. Refrigerant pipe is cleaned and capped at the factory, and must remain capped until ready for use.

6. Check for piping that is factory cleaned and purged with inert gas and capped. Check for gas-tight capping.

WATER PIPE AND FITTINGS

1. Pipe materials differ greatly for aboveground cold water pipelines. Many are plastic materials. Plastic pipes cannot be used in water systems for buildings greater than two stories in height.

2. Plastic type pipe cannot extend through the roof or through fire-rated walls or floors.

3. Seamless copper water tube must be hard drawn: Type M above ground and Type L or K for belowground. Check specifications as well as the governing codes.

FUEL GAS PIPE AND FITTINGS

1. Comply with all code requirements to include the Fuel Gas Code as given in National Fire Protection Association (NFPA) Standard No. V54.

2. Check for permitted pipe options; either all or only steel, aluminum alloy, metal tubing, and plastic materials may be specified.

3. Check for specific materials required in insulating couplings.

4. Aluminum alloy tubing and pipe is not permitted underground or at exterior locations.

5. Plastic pipe is not permitted in or under the building and is permitted only underground outside of the building.

6. Check the specifications for ambient temperature limitations to the use of plastic pipe.

DRAINAGE PIPE AND FITTINGS

These consist of the waste system, the storm drains and rainwater conductors, and the condensate drainage pipelines from air conditioning and refrigeration units.

1. There are many optional pipe materials; their use is dependent on locations in the building and in the drainage system.

2. Use the pipe material submittal for identification or the pipe material table in the specifications.

3. Check for drainage pattern type fittings as they are required in the wet pipe portion of the waste system.

4. Hubless cast iron pipe cannot be used underground and may not be permitted in crawlspaces—check the codes and specifications.

5. Check for use of proper pipe and fittings in corrosive waste and vent systems.

HEATING PIPE AND FITTINGS

1. Check for use of black steel pipe or copper tubing for low temperature hot water pipelines.

2. Steam piping must be black steel: vent piping must be the same type.

3. Check for use of Schedule 40, black steel, in high temperature pipelines of 2 in. and larger.

4. Welded joints are normally used for high temperature water pipelines over ¾ in. diameter. Check the code and project specifications.

REFRIGERATION AND AIR CONDITIONING PIPE AND FITTINGS

1. Check the steel pipe or the copper or steel tubing and fittings for intended service. Refrigerant service rating is required for lines carrying any type of refrigerant.

2. Check for galvanized steel pipe or hard drawn copper tubing for condenser water lines. Lines 4 in. and larger require black steel that must be coated and wrapped for underground use.

Table 11-1 *Approved Piping Materials*

Welded and seamless steel pipe (black or galvanized)	ASTM A 53
Cast iron soil pipe and fittings (hub and spigot)	ASTM A 74
Cast iron fittings (threaded)	ASTM A 126
Malleable iron fittings (threaded)	ASTM A 197
Seamless copper pipe	ASTM B 42
Seamless red brass pipe	ASTM B 43
Seamless copper tubing	ASTM B 75
Seamless copper water tubing (Type K, L, M)	ASTM B 88
ABS-DWV pipe and fittings	ASTM D 2661
PVC-DWV pipe and fittings	ASTM D 2665
3.25-in.-O.D. PVC-DWV pipe and fittings	ASTM D 2949
ABS-DWV schedule 40 with cellular core	ASTM F 628
Co-extruded PVC plastic pipe with cellular core	ASTM F 891
Co-extended composite ABS-DWV pipe and fittings	ASTM F 1488
Cast iron soil pipe and fittings (hubless)	CISPI 301
Copper drainage tube (DWV)	ASTM B 306
Mechanical couplings	CSA B 602M
Solvent cement for ABS-DWV pipe and fittings	ASTM D 2235
Solvent cement for PVC-DWV pipe and fittings	ASTM D 2564
Socket bell for PVC-DWV pipe and fittings	ASTM D 2672
Primers for solvents	ASTM F 656
Hubless cast iron soil pipe and fittings	ASTM A 888
Couplings used with hubless	CISPI 310-95
Shielded couplings	ASTM C 1277
Co-extruded composite ABS DWV sch. 40 IPS pipe solvent cement fittings	ASTM F 1488 ASTM D 2235 ASTM D 2661 ASTM F 628
Co-extruded composite PVC DWV sch. 40 IPS pipe solvent cement fittings	ASTM F 1488 ASTM D 2564 ASTM D 2665 ASTM F 891
Co-extruded composite PVC DWV IPS pipe—DR-PS140 PS200 solvent cement fittings	ASTM F 1488 ASTM D 2564 ASTM D 2665 ASTM F 891

Table 11-2 *Hydronic Piping*

Materials	Approved Uses
Brass pipe	Aboveground
Brass tubing	Aboveground
Chlorinated poly(vinyl chloride) (CPVC) pipe and tubing	1. Aboveground 2. Embedded in radiant system 3. Temp <180°F
Copper pipe	1. Aboveground
Copper tubing (type K, L, or M)	1. Aboveground 2. Embedded in radiant system
Cross-linked polyethylene (PEX) tubing	1. Embedded in radiant system 2. Temp <180°F
Polybutylene (PB) pipe and tubing	1. Aboveground 2. Embedded in radiant system 3. Temp <180°F
Polyethylene (PE) pipe	1. Embedded in radiant system 2. Temp <180°F 3. Low temp <130°F
Steel pipe	1. Aboveground 2. Embedded in radiant system
Steel tubing	1. Aboveground

Fig. 11-1 *Multiple piping system (should be marked).*

3. Check the type of piping specified for chilled water lines.

4. The drainage lines for condensate water are usually given in the plumbing section of the specifications or notes on the drawings.

5. Check for the correct use and placement of air vents.

FIRE SPRINKLER PIPE AND FITTINGS

1. Ensure that materials are in accordance with approved submittals.

2. The type of system is designed to use a specific water supply and distribution for specific occupancy. More information can be found in National Fire Protection Association (NFPA) Standard No. 13.

3. Contractor's working plans shall be approved and are to be used when installing the system. All changes are to be reflected on the record set of drawings kept by the contractor.

INSTALLATION OF PIPING SYSTEMS
General

1. Laying underground pipe lines is covered in the site piping system section.

2. Installation of exposed pipelines inside the building should follow building lines.

3. The building structure cannot be cut or otherwise weakened for pipelines without written approval.

4. Check for required slope in horizontal runs; liquid systems must be drainable. Check for drains at low points.

5. Check for air cocks at high points.

6. Check for required access to drains, air cocks, and valves.

7. Check for contact between dissimilar metals such as copper to iron or steel. Isolation (separation) will be required. Dissimilar pipe must be coupled with a dielectric connection.

8. Are hangers proper style and size, and at required intervals? Are ferrous hangers coated where used against copper pipe? Size hangers to encompass the pipe insulation.

9. Are pipelines restrained from lateral movement at trapeze.

10. Wall or floor supports must also restrain the pipeline from lateral movement.

11. Check for support needs at each floor but not more than 15-ft intervals. Support is not necessary at the floor slab on grade hangers with U bolts or other type clips.

12. Check for extra hangers or supports required at fittings and devices. A hanger is usually required within 1 ft of each change of direction.

13. Suspended heavy pipelines must have proper support without overloading support points. Check:

    a. Excess loads on steel bar joints or beams.

    b. A hanger load or multiple hangers at the same location with more than 100 lb of load. Where you have a suspicious condition, request a structural evaluation from the design engineer.

14. Check for required anchors and expansion loops or joints, especially on long pipelines. Also check for approved guides at the expansion points.

15. Check for union or flanged connections at equipment and elsewhere in order to break and repair or replace piping, etc.

16. Check for proper size pipe sleeves. Sleeves shall be large enough for the pipe insulation thickness when required.

17. Pipe sleeves through waterproofing must have a clamping device to hold the flashing.

18. Sleeves must protrude above finished floor surfaces in wet areas. The annular pace between pipe and sleeve must be sealed.

19. Check for proper fireproofing of openings between pipes and fire-rated construction.

20. Check that escutcheons are used around pipes penetrating finished surfaces.

21. Make sure when piping passes through fire wall assemblies that it is appropriately caulked or sealed.

22. Use soft drawn copper tubing, as permitted, when not using fittings.

23. Steel pipe bending with proper equipment is permitted in sizes to 4-in. diameter. Bend radius must be at least 6 times pipe diameter.

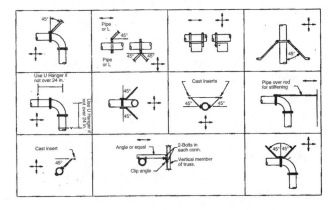

Fig. 11-2 *Piping supports.*

Fig. 11-3 *Copper piping being supported and separated from metal studs.*

Table 11-3 Hydronic Piping Hanger Spacing

Materials	Max. Horizontal	Max. Vertical
ABS	4	10
CPVC less than or equal to 1¼-in. pipe or tubing	3	5
CPVC greater than or equal to 1-in. pipe or tubing	4	10
Copper pipe	12	10
Copper tubing (Type K, L, or M)	6	10
Polyethylene (PEX) tubing	2.67	4
Polybutylene (PB) pipe and tubing	2.67	4
Polyethylene (PE) pipe	2.67	4
Steel pipe	12	15
Steel tubing	8	10
PVC	4	10

PIPE CONNECTIONS
Screwed

1. Examine the threading operation for:

   a. Square cut pipe.

   b. Proper reaming before threading.

   c. Sharp cutters so that threads are not shaved.

   d. Tapered threads, not running threads.

   e. Thread run; no more than three threads should be exposed after connection is tight. The specifications may have a threading table you can refer to.

   f. Use of cutting oil. Pipe shall be cleaned of oil and metal "filings." This is critical for refrigerant lines.

   g. Protect all floor surfaces. Use a sandbox or other adequate protection under the threading/cutting operation.

   h. Plastic pipe and metallic tubing are not to be threaded.

2. Examine screwed pipe connections for:

   a. Use of approved thread lubricant or tape applied to male threads only. Some piping may not permit use of tape at screwed joints; check for requirements.

   b. Measure threads to ensure that they are the minimum length required by code.

   c. Tighten connection, but do not overtighten.

3. Check for distorted valves. See that wrenches rather than pliers are used on the end of valves being

screwed onto the pipes in order to prevent damage to the valve bore. Do not screw pipes against the web of globe valves or against the underside of seat rings of gate valves.

4. Use threaded connections to angle stops at plumbing fixtures.

Mechanical

1. Check the gasket material; it must be compatible with the liquid or gas in the pipeline.

2. Check proper alignment of flanges, couplings, and gaskets.

3. Gaskets with high-temperature water should be metallic asbestos type.

4. Do not use the drift pin or spud wrench handle (or other unapproved method) to align flanges.

5. Mechanical couplings and fittings must be compatible and manufactured by the same concern.

6. Dissimilar metal connections must have cathodetic protection from galvanic action.

7. Mechanical couplings are usually permitted on ferrous metal pipelines in the building for domestic hot and cold water systems. Check the specifications and approved shop drawings.

Hub and Hubless Types

1. Check for proper rubber gasket installation in the hub or bell. Spigot end must be seated into the hub.

2. When molten lead is used to make the joint, check for:

   • Jute compacted into base of joint to seal the end, and center the spigot end in the hub.

   • Depth of joint.

   • Pouring the molten lead joint in a continuous operation.

   • Caulking the lead with proper size irons.

   • Caulking each joint at least three times around.

3. Hubless joint uses a rubber sleeve with stainless steel band; the assembly must be approved by the Cast Iron Soil Pipe Institute (CISPI).

4. Check for proper torque wrench set to 5 ft-lb for tightening the stainless steel band in hubless joints.

Soldered

1. Surfaces of the fitting and pipe must be cleaned to bright metal with an abrasive material before the joint is made.

2. The 50/50 solder is half tin/half lead and can be used in drainage, waste, and vent (DWV) pipelines.

3. Check current allowable lead solder percentages in water piping.

4. Silver solder is 95/5, 95% tin and 5% antimony, and must be used in all other pipelines.

5. Approximately 400°F for soft solder and 115°F for silver solder.

6. Check for use of a multiflame torch for uniformly heating joints where 2½-in.-diameter and larger pipe are soldered.

Solvent Cement (Adhesive)

1. For plastic pipe connections use compatible materials.

2. Use in accordance with the pipe manufacturer's instructions.

3. Do not join different kinds of plastic pipe together unless they are approved compatible.

4. Only heat-fusion connection is used to join polyethylene pipe, tubing, or fittings.

Welded

1. Check for use of welding fittings.

2. Making fittings by notching or mitering pipe is not permitted.

3. Check for the approved welding procedures before welding begins.

4. Check for the individual welder's certification in the type welding each welder must perform.

5. Check welding of refrigerant pipe as the fittings and pipe must be filled with inert gas, such as nitrogen, during welding. This prevents the formation of scale inside the pipe.

6. Welding for fire sprinkler systems must be performed in a shop and in accordance with NFPA 13 requirements. Job-site welding is not permitted.

FITTINGS AND VALVES

1. Check riser diagrams and floor plans on drawings for proper valve locations.

2. Are valves proper type?

3. Valves must be oriented with stems in horizontal position or above. Only the horizontal position is allowed for refrigerant pipelines.

4. Check and globe valves have an arrow cast in housing to indicate direction of flow. Check these valves for proper orientation in the pipeline flow.

5. Check for access to all valves. Are access locations marked on ceiling panels? Also make any changes to the record set of construction drawings.

6. Use dielectric connectors where required at locations where different metals connect together in the pipeline.

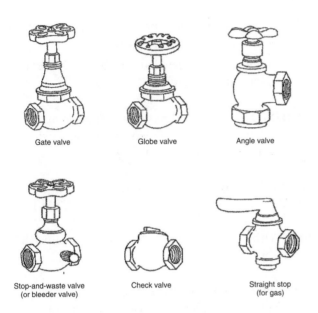

Fig. 11-4 Common valves.

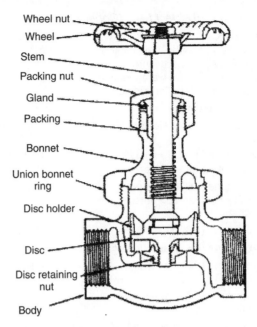

Fig. 11-6 Globe valve.

PIPELINES
Water Pipelines

a. Are air chambers installed at fixtures?

b. Are water hammer arrestors shown instead of air chambers? Check your riser diagrams on the drawings for locations and sizes of these arrestors.

c. Are valves located as shown? Are they accessible?

d. Does the water service have a gate valve and drain at its point of building entry?

e. Check for use of a backflow prevention device in each branch waterline connected to another system.

f. Check for a vacuum breaker to prevent back-siphonage at each fitting or fixture with hose connection.

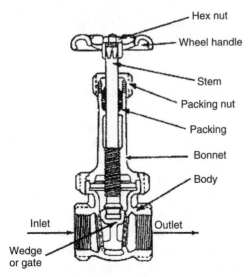

Fig. 11-5 Sample gate valve.

Table 11-4 Water Supply and Distribution Piping

Material	Standard
ABS plastic pipe (SDR-PR)	ASTM D 2282
ABS plastic pipe schedule 40 and 80	ASTM D 1527
CPVC plastic hot and cold water distribution systems	ASTM D 2846
CPVC plastic pipe schedule 40 and 80	ASTM F 441
CPVC plastic pipe schedule (SDR-PR)	ASTM F 442
Crosslinked PE plastic hot and cold water distribution	ASTM F 877
Crosslinked polyethylene (PEX) tubing	ASTM F 876

Table 11-4 *(Continued)*

Crosslinked polyethylene/aluminum/ crosslinked polybutylene (PEX-AL-PEX) for water service and water distribution piping	ASTM F 1281
Ductile iron pressure pipe	ASTM A 377
PB plastic hot water distribution systems	ASTM D 3309
Polybutylene/aluminum/polyethylene (PE-AL-PE) for water service piping	ASTM F 1282
Polybutylene (PB) plastic pipe (SDR-PR) based on outside diameter	ASTM D 3000
Polybutylene (PB) plastic tubing	ASTM D 2666
Polybutylene (PE) plastic tubing	ASTM D 2737
Polyethylene (PE) plastic pipe (SDR-PR)	ASTM D 3000
Polyethylene (PE) plastic pipe controlled OD	ASTM D 2447
Polyethylene plastic pipe, schedule 40	ASTM D 2104
Polyethylene plastic pipe (SDR-PR) controlled ID	ASTM D 2239
PVC plastic pipe schedule 40, 80, and 120	ASTM D 1785
PVC pressure rated pipe (SDR Series)	ASTM D 2241
Seamless brass type	ASTM B 135
Seamless copper tube	ASTM B 75
Seamless copper watertube Type K, L, and M	ASTM B 88
Seamless red brass pipe, standard sizes	ASTM B 43
Specification for polybutylene (PB) plastic pipe (SIDR-PR) based on controlled inside diameter	ASTM D 2662
Welded copper water tube (WK, WL, WM)	ASTM B 447

Fuel Gas Pipelines

The following items are code approved or disapproved.

Cast Iron Cast-iron pipe shall not be used.

Steel Steel and wrought-iron pipe shall be at least of standard weight (Schedule 40) and shall comply with one of the following standards:

1. ASME B 36.10, 10M
2. ASTM A 53
3. ASTM A 106

Copper and Brass Copper and brass pipe shall not be used if the gas contains more than an average of 0.3 grains of hydrogen sulfide per 100 standard cubic feet

of gas. Threaded copper, brass, or aluminum alloy pipe in iron pipe sizes shall be permitted to be used with gases not corrosive to such material.

Aluminum Aluminum-alloy pipe shall comply with ASTM B 210 or ASTM B 241 (except that the use of alloy 5456 is prohibited), and shall be marked at each end of each length indicating compliance.

Aluminum-alloy pipe shall be coated to protect against external corrosion in the following circumstances:

1. Where it is in contact with masonry, plaster, or insulation.

2. Where it is subject to repeated wettings by such liquids as water, detergent, or sewage.

3. Aluminum-alloy pipe shall not be used in exterior locations or underground.

Metallic Tubing Seamless copper, aluminum alloy, or steel tubing shall be permitted to be used with gases not corrosive to such material.

Copper Tubing Copper tubing shall comply with Standard Type K or L of ASTM B 88 or ASTM B 280.

Steel Tubing Steel tubing shall comply with ASTM A 254 or ASTM A 539.

Corrugated Stainless Steel Tubing Corrugated stainless steel tubing shall be tested and listed in compliance with the construction, installation, and performance requirements of ANSI/AGA LC 1.

Plastic Pipe, Tubing, and Fittings Plastic pipe, tubing, and fittings shall be used outside underground only and shall conform with ASTM D 2513. Pipe shall be marked "gas" and "ASTM D 2513."

Anodeless Risers Plastic pipe, tubing, and anodeless risers must comply with the following:

1. Factory-assembled anodeless risers shall be recommended by the manufacturer for the gas used and shall be leak tested by the manufacturer in accordance with written procedures.

2. Service head adapters and field-assembled anodeless risers incorporating service head adapters shall be recommended by the manufacturer for the gas used by the manufacturer and shall be designed certified to meet the requirements of Category I of ASTM D 2513.

3. The manufacturer shall provide the user qualified installation instructions as prescribed by the U.S. Department of Transportation, Code of Federal Regulations, Title 49, Part 192.283(b).

LP-Gas Systems The use of plastic tubing, pipe and fittings in undiluted liquefied petroleum gas piping systems shall be in accordance with NFPA 58.

Defects in pipe, tubing, or fittings shall not be repaired. Defective pipe, tubing, and fittings shall be replaced.

Where in contact with material or atmosphere exerting a corrosive action, metallic piping and fittings coated with a corrosion-resistant material shall be used. See section on Corrosions.

Damaged Threads

1. Pipe with threads that are stripped, chipped, corroded, or otherwise damaged shall not be used.

2. If a weld is damaged during the operation of cutting or threading, that portion of the pipe shall be rejected (not repaired).

3. Number of threads. Field threading of metallic pipe is shown in Table 11.6.

Workmanship and Defects Pipe or tubing and fittings shall be clear and free from cutting burrs and defects in structure or threading, and shall be thoroughly brushed, and scale/chip blown.

Used Materials Pipe, fittings, valves, or other materials shall not be used again unless they have been approved for the service intended.

1. Avoid installation under buildings. Fuel gas service should be installed below grade on the outside. Do not install service pipeline in the trench with other utilities.

2. Do not permit soldered joints. Use pressure-threaded joints for copper pipe.

3. When piping is to be embedded in concrete, check for special requirements such as:
   - Should be acceptable to the gas service company.
   - Check concrete mix for compatibility with pipe material.
   - Do not allow piping to touch dissimilar material such as rebar.
   - Certain concrete additives and aggregates may not be compatible.

4. Don't embed gas pipelines in solid walls and partitions.

5. Check for protective coating requirements on underground metallic pipelines.

6. Where piping must be buried under the building, it should be encased in a gas-tight conduit for its full length of run. Space between the pipe and conduit must be safely vented to the atmosphere. Check the codes and specifications.

7. Check for pipe slope and for the presence of drains at low points.

8. Check for required pipeline bonding and grounding in accordance with the National Electric Code.

9. Check for shutoff valves as required.

10. Make sure that all fuel lines are visibly marked.

Table 11-5 Gas Piping Support

Type	Spacings
Rigid ¾ or under	10 ft
Rigid 1 in. or over	12 ft
Tubing 1½ in. and under	6 ft

Table 11-6 Fuel Gas Threading Specifications for Metallic Pipe

Iron Pipe (in.)	Length of Threaded Portion (in.)	Approximate No. of Threads to Cut
½	¾	10
¾	¾	10
1	⅞	10
1¼	1	11
1½	1	11

Gas Pipe Sizing

- Find length to most remote fixture from the gas meter. This will be the figure that you enter into the table.

- Find the most remote demand from the manufacturer's date plate. If unknown, you can use Table 11-7, which lists some of the more typical gas burning appliances.

- Then work back picking up additional gas demands.

- Add up the values for the branch you are working on and then divide that number by the heating value (average Btu per cubic foot of gas). This value can be obtained from the supplier.

- Repeat the above steps for any piping branching off.

Table 11-7 *Typical Gas Demands*

Appliance	Btu Input (Approximate)
Range	65,000
Oven (built-in)	25,000
Top unit (built-in)	40,000
Water heater, 30–40 gal	45,000
Water heater, 50 gal	55,000
Automatic water heaters	
2 gal/min	142,800
4 gal/min	285,000
6 gal/min	428,400
Clothes dryer	35,000
Gas light	2,500

Note: For smooth-wall semirigid tubing and corrugated stainless steel tubing, consult the additional tables in the international codes.

Table 11-8 *Approximate Pipe Sizing*

Pipe Length	Btu			
	½ in.	¾ in.	1 in.	1¼ in.
10	174	363	684	1404
20	119	249	470	965
30	96	200	377	775
40	82	171	323	663
50	73	152	286	588
60	66	138	259	532
70	61	127	239	490
80	56	118	222	456
90	53	111	208	428
100	50	104	197	404
125	44	93	174	358
150	40	84	158	324
200	34	72	135	278
250	30	64	120	246

Table 11-9 *Maximum Gas Capacity (ft³) of Pipe for Gas*

Pipe Length	Nominal Iron Pipe Size (in.)					
	¼	⅜	½	¾	1	1¼
10	43	95	175	360	680	1400
20	29	65	120	250	465	950
30	24	52	97	200	375	770
40	20	45	82	170	320	660
50	18	40	73	151	285	580
60	16	36	66	138	260	530
70	15	33	61	125	240	490
80	14	31	57	118	220	460
90	13	29	53	110	205	430
100	12	27	50	103	195	400

For gas pressure of 0.5 psi or less, .60 specific gravity gas.

Note: The International Fuel Gas Code will allow the above table to be used for specific gravity of .70 or less. If it is greater than .60 the cubic foot of gas values in the table above need to be adjusted by the multiplier identified in the table below.

Table 11-10 *Multipliers to Be Used When Specific Gravity Is Greater Than 0.60*

Gas Specific Gravity	Multiplier
.65	.96
.70	.93
.75	.90
.80	.87
.85	.84
.90	.82
1.00	.78
1.10	.74
1.20	.71
1.30	.68
1.40	.66
1.50	.63
1.60	.61
1.70	.59
1.80	.58
1.90	.56
2.00	.55
2.10	.54

Table 11-11 *Pipe Sizing for 2-psi-Capacity Pipes of Different Sizes in Cubic Feet per Hour for an Initial Pressure of 2 psi with a 1-psi Pressure Drop*

Pipe Length	Pipe Size (Schedule 40)			
	½	¾	1	1¼
10	1506	3041	5561	11415
20	1065	2150	3932	8072
30	869	1756	3211	6591
40	753	1521	2781	5708
50	673	1360	2487	5105
60	615	1241	2270	4660
70	569	1150	2102	4315
80	532	1075	1966	4036
90	502	1014	1854	3805
100	462	934	1708	3508

Table 11-12 *Piping Bends Allowed for Metallic Fuel Gas Piping*

Pipe Diameter (in.)	Min. Bend Radius Six Times the Diameter (in.)
⅜	2¼
½	3
¾	4½
1	6
1¼	7½
1½	9
2	12
2½	15
3	18
3½	21
4	24
5	30
6	36

Table 11-13 *Plastic Pipe Minimum Bending Radiuses*

Pipe Diameter (in.)	Min. Bend Radius 25 Times the Diameter (in.)
⅜	9⅜
½	12½
¾	18¾
1	25
1¼	31¼
1½	37½
2	50
2½	62½
3	75
3½	87½
4	100
5	125
6	150

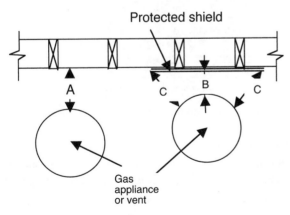

A is equal to clearance allowed with no protection.
B is the "reduced clearance" as shown in Table 11-14.
C is the distance the protective method must extend and equals the original unprotected distance A.

Fig. 11-7 *Clearance from combustionable materials.*

APPLIANCE INSTALLATIONS
Types of Protection(s)

1. 3.5-in.-thick masonry without air space.

2. 0.5-in.-thick insulation board over 1-in. glass fiber or mineral wool.

3. 0.024-in.-thick sheet metal over 1-in. glass fiber or mineral wool reinforced with wire on the rear face and with a ventilated air space. (Spacers are to be noncombustionable and not located directly behind the appliance or vent.)

4. 3.5-in.-thick masonry with air space.

5. 0.024-in.-thick sheet metal with ventilating air space (at least 1-in. ventilating air space).

6. 0.5-in.-thick insulation board with at least 1 in. air space.

7. 0.024-in. sheet metal with 1-in. air space over additional 0.024 piece of sheet metal.

8. 1-in. glass fiber or mineral wool sandwiched between two sheets of 0.024-in.-thick sheet metal with ventilating air space.

Note: Mineral wool batts are to have a density of 8 lb/ft^3 and a minimum melting point of 1500°F (816°C).

Table 11-14 *Approved Reductions in Clearances for Each Protection Method*

Type of Protection	Above (in.)	Sides and Rear (in.)
0	N/A	24
1	24	18
2	18	12
3	N/A	12
4	18	12
5	18	12
6	18	12
7	18	12

Original required clearance is 36 in.

Type of Protection	Above (in.)	Sides and Rear (in.)
0	N/A	12
1	12	9
2	9	6
3	N/A	6
4	9	6
5	9	6
6	9	6
7	9	6

Original required clearance is 18 in.

Type of Protection	Above (in.)	Sides and Rear (in.)
0	N/A	9
1	9	6
2	6	4
3	N/A	6
4	6	4
5	6	4
6	6	4
7	6	4

Original required clearance is 12 in.

Type of Protection	Above (in.)	Sides and Rear (in.)
0	N/A	6
1	6	5
2	5	3
3	N/A	6
4	5	3
5	5	3
6	5	3
7	5	3

Original required clearance is 9 in.

Type of Protection	Above (in.)	Sides and Rear (in.)
0	N/A	5
1	4	3
2	3	3
3	N/A	6
4	3	2
5	3	3
6	3	3
7	3	3

Original required clearance is 6 in.

VENTING GAS APPLIANCES

Vents that pass through insulation require a shield of at least 26-gage sheet metal. In attics the shield is to extend at least 2 in. above the level of insulation.

Mechanical draft vents must be at least 7 ft above grade if located adjacent to public walkways.

MASONRY CHIMNEYS

1. Chimneys are to be lined with approved clay flue lining, a listed liner, or other approved material that will resist corrosion, erosion, and weakening from the vent gases at temperatures up to 1800°F.

2. If liners are installed in existing chimney structures (Type B), then the connection must be marked not to allow any solid or liquid burning appliances to be attached.

3. Chimneys are to extend at least 5 ft above the highest connected equipment draft hood outlet or flue collar.

4. Sizing of chimneys:

   a. The effective area of a chimney serving listed appliances with draft hoods: Category I appliances listed for use with Type B vents are to be sized using Tables 12-13 to 12-16.

   b. An exception to using these tables for sizing a single appliance with a draft hood is that the vent connector and chimney flue will have an area not less than the appliance flue collar or draft hood and not greater than 7 times the draft hood outlet.

   c. When two appliances with draft hoods are connected, then the flue area must be the same as the largest appliance outlet plus 50% of the smaller appliance outlets and not greater than 7 times the smaller draft hood outlet.

Example

Largest outlet + 50% of smallest < chimney
flue size < 7 × smallest

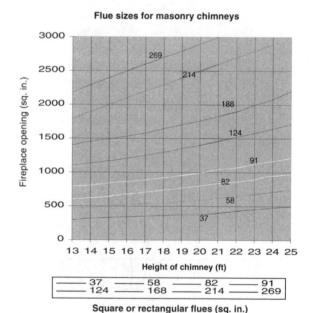

Fig. 11-8 *Approved flue sizing for chimneys.*

5. Chimneys previously used for liquid or solid fuels, and now using fuel gas, must have a cleanout. It is to be located so that its upper edge is 6 in. below the lowest edge of the lowest inlet opening.

6. Offsets of Type B or Type L are not to exceed 45° from the vertical; however, one angle must not exceed 60°. The horizontal distance of a vent plus the connector vent shall not exceed 75% of the vertical height of the vent.

Table 11-15 *Fireplace Opening in Determining Flue Size*

Fireplace Opening (sq. in.)	Flue Shapes			
	Round	Square	Rectangle with Length to Width 2:1 or Less	Rectangle with Length to Width More Than 2:1
400	33⅓	40	40	50
450	37½	45	45	56¼
500	41⅔	50	50	62½
550	45⅚	55	55	68¾
600	50	60	60	75
650	54⅙	65	65	81¼
700	58⅓	70	70	87½
750	62½	75	75	93¾
800	66⅔	80	80	100
850	70⅚	85	85	106¼
900	75	90	90	112½
1000	83⅓	100	100	125
1100	91⅔	110	110	137½
1200	100	120	120	150
1300	108⅓	130	130	162½
1400	116⅔	140	140	175
1500	125	150	150	187½

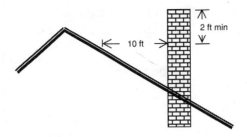

Fig. 11-9 *Roof terminations for chimneys and single wall vents (no caps).*

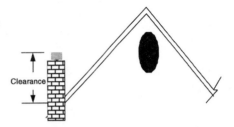

Roof Slope	Clearance
Flat–6/12	1 ft–0 in.
6/12–7/12	1 ft–3 in.
7/12–8/12	1 ft–6 in.
8/12–9/12	2 ft–0 in.
9/12–10/12	2 ft–6 in.
10/12–11/12	3 ft–3 in.
11/12–12/12	4 ft–0 in.

Fig. 11-10 *Gas vent terminations for listed vent caps 12 in. or less in diameter and 8 ft from vertical walls.*

CHIMNEY DAMPERS

Where an unlisted decorative appliance is installed in a vented fireplace, the damper must have a permanent free opening equal to or greater than those listed in the tables below.

Table 11-16 *Damper Open Area from Unlisted Decorative Appliances*

Min. Permanent Free Opening	Chimney Height (ft)		
	6	8	10
8	7 800	8 400	9 000
13	14 000	15 200	16 800
20	23 200	25 200	27 600
29	34 000	37 000	40 400
39	46 400	50 400	55 800
51	62 400	68 000	74 400
64	80 000	86 000	96 400

Min. Permanent Free Opening	Chimney Height (ft)		
	15	20	30
8	9 800	10 600	11 200
13	18 200	20 200	21 600
20	30 200	32 600	36 600
29	44 600	50 400	55 200
39	62 400	68 400	76 800
51	84 000	94 000	105 800
64	108 800	122 200	138 600

Table 11-17 *Masonry Chimney Liner Dimensions with Circular Equivalents*

Nominal Liner Size	Inside Liner Dimensions	Circular Equivalent	
		in.	in.²
4 × 8	2½ × 6½	4	12.2
		5	19.6
		6	28.3
		7	38.3
8 × 8	6¾ × 6¾	7.4	42.7
		8	50.3
8 × 12	6½ × 10½	9	63.6
		10	78.5
12 × 12	9¾ × 9¾	10.4	83.3
		11	95
12 × 16	9½ × 13½	11.8	107.5
		12	113.0
		14	153.9
16 × 16	13¼ × 13¼	14.5	162.9
		15	176.7

Table 11-17 (Continued)

Nominal Liner Size	Inside Liner Dimensions	Circular Equivalent	
		in.	in.²
16 × 20	13 × 17	16.2	206.1
		18	254.4
20 × 20	16¾ × 16¾	18.2	260.2
		20	314.1
20 × 24	16½ × 20½	20.1	314.2
		22	380.1
24 × 24	20¼ × 20¼	22.1	380.1
		24	452.3

See Chap. 12 for sizing single- or multiple-vent configurations.

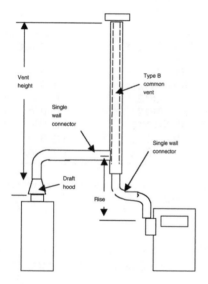

Fig. 11-11 *Typical vent/connector—two single walls connectors into type B vent.*

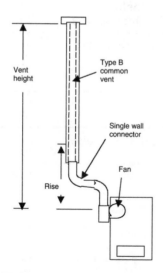

Fig. 11-12 *Fan-assisted vent.*

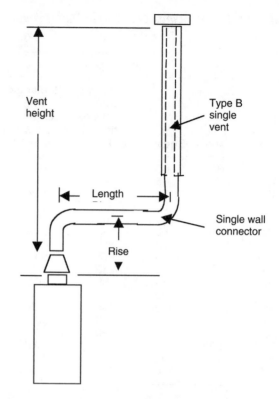

Fig. 11-13 *Single appliance vent connector to type B vent.*

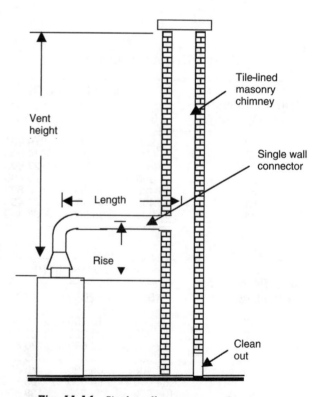

Fig. 11-14 *Single wall connector to chimney.*

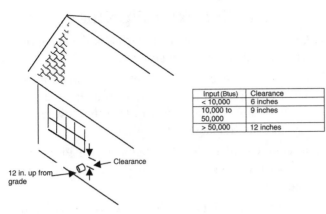

Input (Btus)	Clearance
< 10,000	6 inches
10,000 to 50,000	9 inches
> 50,000	12 inches

Fig. 11-15 *Clearance for direct vent appliances.*

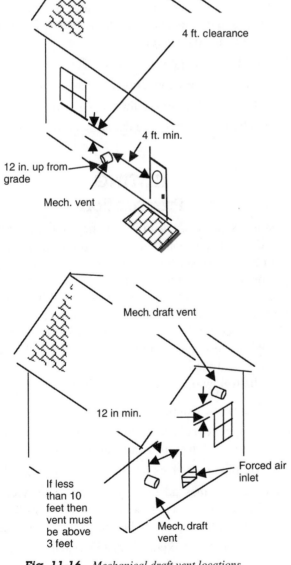

Fig. 11-16 *Mechanical draft vent locations.*

Wall venting for Categories II and IV appliances or other condensing types of venting cannot terminate over other equipment that could be damaged by the condensation or terminate over public walkways.

Table 11-18 *Clearances from Combustionable Materials for Connectors: For Listed Type B Vent*

Equipment	Clearance Required
Equipment with draft hoods and those listed for use with Type B vents.	As listed
Residential boilers, furnaces with listed gas conversion and draft hood.	6 in.
Residential appliances listed for use with Type L vents.	Not permitted
Unlisted residential appliances with a draft hood.	Not permitted
Residential and low-heat equipment other than ones listed above.	Not permitted

Table 11-19 *For Listed Type L Vent*

Equipment	Clearance Required
Equipment with draft hoods and those listed for use with Type B vents.	As listed
Residential boilers, furnaces with listed gas conversion and draft hood.	6 in.
Residential appliances listed for use with Type L vents.	As listed
Unlisted residential appliances with a draft hood.	6 in.
Residential and low-heat equipment other than ones listed above.	9 in.

Table 11-20 *For Single-Wall Metal Pipe*

Equipment	Clearance Required
Equipment with draft hoods and those listed for use with Type B vents.	6 in.
Residential boilers, furnaces with listed gas conversion and draft hood.	in.
Residential appliances listed for use with Type L vents.	in.
Unlisted residential appliances with a draft hood.	in.
Residential and low-heat equipment other than ones listed above.	18 in.

For factory-built chimneys—as per the manufacturer's installation instructions.

CLOTHES DRYER EXHAUST (GAS)

Ducts must be galvanized steel or aluminum if passing through any fire-rated assembly. They must terminate outside and not be connected to any other vent assembly. Ducts cannot exceed 25 ft in length. Reduce:

- 2½ ft for each 45° bend
- 5 ft for each 90° bend

The duct must be a minimum of 4 in. in diameter. Joints must be in the direction of the flow.

Drainage Lines

- Hubless cast-iron pipelines require support next to each joint.
- Hub-type pipelines require support at 10-ft intervals and within 3 ft of each fitting.
- Check for required expansion joint at floors in plastic pipeline risers.
- Install cleanouts so they are flush with finish surfaces. Close each cleanout with a (brass or PVC) plug.
- Check the elevation of each floor drain before finished floor is placed to ensure drainage slope.
- Check floor drain for type specified. Does it require a special item such as a sediment basket, a backwater valve, or a self-priming valve?
- On roof drains check for the clamping ring to hold the metal flashing and for the cast iron strainer.
- Interior roof drains/leaders require a backup system. Must have a minimum 1% slope.

Heating Pipelines

1. Check for slope of at least 1 in. in 10 ft.
2. Reducing fittings on horizontal lines must be eccentric type with bottom of pipelines flat for positive drainage flow.
3. Check for proper branch line take off from the high temperature pipeline supply and return. Should be from the upper half of pipeline, at a 45° angle in direction of flow.
4. Check for special piping from high-temperature waterline air vents to funnel drain.

Refrigeration and Air Conditioning Pipelines

1. Refrigerant steel pipeline joints should be welded. Check specifications.
2. Refrigerant tubing of copper or steel are to have brazed joints.

Fire Sprinkler Pipelines

1. Check the approved shop drawings for the fire sprinkler system layout and pipe sizes.
2. Check for possible conflict between final sprinkler head location and user items, such as large equipment or high shelving, that restrict the flow coverage or cause damage to the system.
3. Review Chapter 3 of the National Fire Protection Association Standard 13 for supports, hangers, slope, and drainage.
4. Do not allow paint on sprinkler heads. Check heads for proper temperature rating indicated by color code or stamped numbers.
5. Where required, outside connection shall be the size indicated and shall mate with fire department hose.
6. Check for required sprinklers in concealed spaces, such as elevator shafts and under stairs.
7. Check for special protection against freezing, corrosion, and earthquakes, and for sprinkler head clearance from heat sources.
8. Check electric power and alarm for:
   - Electric power correction ahead of the main switch.
   - Effective location of the local alarm.
   - Alarm tie-in with fire department, if required.

TESTING
Preparation

Testing is the responsibility of the contractor unless stated as owner responsibility in the specifications. Check with the supervisor for recommended presence of user personnel during certain testing such as sprinkler, etc. The system or portion of the system will be prepared for testing by the contractor who installed the pipeline. The Inspector will be responsible for verifying the extent of the test. The method and results which will be reported and filed.

The following items must be checked:

1. Determine extent of test.
2. Is pipeline isolated at limits of the test with valves closed and the plugs and caps tightly in place?
3. Are pipeline valves open within the test area?
4. Are pipelines adequately blocked and anchored for pressure tests? Pipelines should be in the permanent, fixed position before the test is permitted.
5. Will joints be exposed for the visual or soap test requirements?

6. When testing pipeline to be concealed, does extent of test include all of the affected pipelines?

7. For a pressure test, have diaphragms or other internal parts of valves, regulations, etc., which may be damaged by the pressure, removed.

8. Review the test method to be used.

9. Inspect the test instruments and apparatus for proper type, calibration, and operation.

10. When flushing to clean the pipeline, check to determine that coils for heating, air conditioning, and refrigerant lines are bypassed to prevent flushing water from passing through coils.

Performing Tests

Water Pipelines

1. Pneumatic or hydrostatic test shall be used. Check codes for the correct pressure and length of time for the test.

2. Check ambient temperature at beginning and end of test period for temperature differential and the correction factor for the final gauge reading.

3. For the hydrostatic test, was the tested segment vented to ensure it was completely filled with water?

Fuel Gas Pipelines

1. An air pressure test, similar to the waterline test, is usually done. Do not use oxygen.

2. Refer to National Fire Protection Association (NFPA) Bulletin 565 test requirements for nitrous oxide and oxygen system test requirements.

3. Check the gas system for leakage immediately when beginning the test using fuel gas.

Gas Piping Inspection Methods

- Approved gases:
  a. Air
  b. CO_2
  c. Nitrogen
- Must withstand a pressure of 10 lb not less than 15 min.
- Welded pipe with pressures exceeding 14-in. water column require a test pressure of 60 lb psi for a minimum of 30 min.

Gravity Drainage Lines

1. Is the test stack high enough to provide the 10-ft head for all of the tested line?

2. Must be able to maintain 5-lb pressure for 15 min.

3. Check each joint for leakage.

4. The final testing is done with smoke or the peppermint test. All fixtures are to be attached.

Fig. 11-17 *Pressure check for gas piping.*

Heating Pipelines

1. Hydrostatic pressure testing is required. Usually 45 psig for 4 hours for low temperature waterlines.

2. High pressure waterlines are tested at $1\frac{1}{2}$ times design pressure.

Refrigeration and Air Conditioning Pipelines

1. Pneumatic pressure test used on refrigerant pipelines using dry nitrogen. Check each joint with soap solution.

2. Refrigerant pipelines also are charged with refrigerant gas and joints checked for leaks with a halide torch.

3. Refrigerant pipelines also require an evacuation test. Check the specifications for details.

4. Check the hydrostatic pressure test on water pipelines for use of appropriate pressure and time requirements.

Fire Sprinkler Pipelines

1. Refer to Chapter 1, NFPA 13 for specific test requirements.

2. Ensure that feeder piping has been flushed before testing.

3. Check for approved testing procedures and adequate monitoring of the tests by a qualified professional.

4. Check the adequacy of contractor's required material and test certificates to be submitted after completion of tests.

5. Test blanks used in the system during testing shall be approved type, and each blank shall be numbered and accounted for at activation of the system.

CLEANING, ADJUSTING, AND OPERATION

Cleaning

1. Pipelines constructed with properly stored and protected pipe should need very little cleaning.

2. Close ends of unfinished lines during work stoppages.

3. Check the specification for flushing requirements. Flushing may be required for all pipelines.

4. The completed potable water system must be sterilized by chlorinating. Specification may require a test.

5. Heating pipelines must be cleaned with a chemical solution after successful completion of the pressure tests. Check for proper solution, temperature, and time.

6. Fire sprinkler systems must be flushed and disinfected after testing.

Adjusting

1. When beginning the operating phase, each piping system must be closely inspected for necessary adjustment and proper operation.

2. Adjust flow and flush valves.

3. Check air cocks for leakage; clean and adjust as required.

4. Condenser and chilled water pipelines must be balanced after testing.

5. Check for heating system approved balancing procedure. This must be performed by a qualified technician.

6. Maintain a copy of all reports for your records.

Operation

1. Specifications require that user personnel be instructed in proper system operation. Record the attendees and copy of instructions given.

2. Check the posted operating instructions. Are posting requirements met? Do they include the required diagrams?

3. Are pipelines coded as required? If piping is prepainted, make sure markings are not on the hidden side.

4. Check for required spare parts and OEM manuals.

PLUMBING SYSTEMS
General

This chapter covers plumbing fixtures, materials, and good workmanship practices for plumbing systems.

Fixtures and Materials

Inspections

Ensure that all plumbing fixtures and materials have been submitted and approved prior to fabrication and installation. During subsequent inspections, check to see that contract requirements and all ADA requirements were complied with during installation. Inspections will be made as the installation of the plumbing systems progresses throughout the facility under construction or renovation. Obtain and review manufacturer's installation information.

Storage and Handling

1. Ensure that all materials and equipment are handled carefully, properly stored, and protected to prevent damage.

2. Reject damaged materials and equipment and mark them. Have them removed from the site as soon as possible.

3. Inspect the plumbing fixtures upon arrival at the job site for conformance with contract requirements. Require proper storage and protection from damage before and after installation.

4. Ensure that fixtures are installed in compliance with contract requirements and all ADA requirements are satisfied.

Coordination of Work

Check for interferences between electrical, mechanical, architectural, and structural features—especially in toilet and baths, room walls, floors, door swings, and pipe chases.

Installation

General

1. Review the total plumbing system and how it fits into the total job and where the specific items are to be installed. Prior to installing plumbing fixtures, check to ensure that all testing of water supply lines, vents, and drains have been completed.

2. Check size, spacing, elevation, and location of wall and floor stub outs to receive plumbing equipment. Do not allow plumbing fixtures to be stained, or supply lines to be undersized. Ensure that the stub outs are corrected as necessary prior to setting plumbing fixtures.

3. Check location and firmness of the installation of specified equipment supports, holders, and tie down flanges.

4. Check setting or attaching plumbing fixtures, for required seals, traps, grouting, and caulking. Check each fixture for alignment, height, anchorage, and plumbness.

5. Check for use of approved finish such as chrome plating on exposed piping, valves, escutcheons, cover plates, and drains.

6. Check for surge arrestors on lines having quick closing valves. Check for positioning of access opening to allow maintenance of surge arrestors and operation of control and shut-off valves. Check for individual shut-off valves at each piece of plumbing equipment. (Check drawings and specifications.)

7. Check for connection of hot water piping to the left-hand side of showers, lavatories, and sinks. Also make sure only cold water is provided to toilets and urinals.

8. Check for specified trim, materials, screws, and bolts.

Protection

1. Keep trash and debris out of fixtures and drains. Check fixtures for damage during installation.

2. Have contractor cover and protect fixtures after installation to prevent future breakage, staining, or contractor's use.

3. Check workmanship on all bolting, grouting, caulking, shimming, and leveling after work in toilet and bath area has been completed. All fixtures, whether wall or floor mounted, must be firmly attached.

4. Check all ADA requirements for proper locations and required distances for all fixtures.

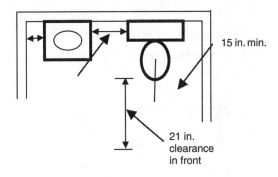

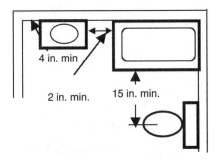

Fig. 11-18 *Minimum fixture clearances.*

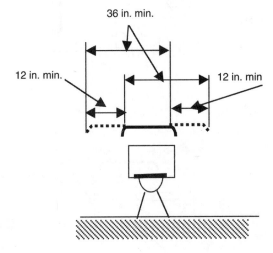

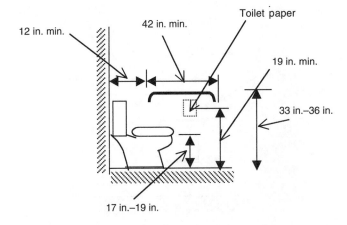

Fig. 11-19 *ADA requirements for plumbing fixtures.*

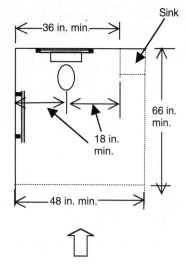

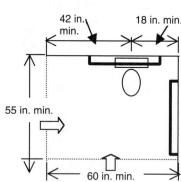

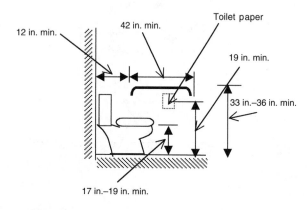

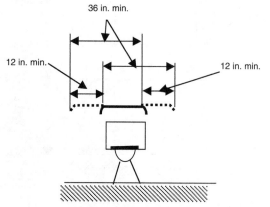

Fig. 11-19 *(Continued)*

ADA Requirements

Water Closets

- The height of the seat will be 17 to 19 in. from the finish floor.
- The grab bar directly behind the water closet is a minimum of 36 in.
- Flush controls are to be either hand operated or automatic. They are mounted no more than 44 in. above the finish floor.

Toe Clearances

In a standard stall, at least one of the side partitions and the front partition will have a minimum of 9 in. (may be omitted if the stall is greater than 60 in. in depth).

Lavatories

1. The rim or counter surface cannot be located more than 34 in. from the finish floor.
2. A minimum of 29 in. is required from the underside of the apron to the finish floor.
3. Knee clearance (from wheelchair) is to be a minimum of 8 in. and toe clearance from the wall a minimum of 6 in.

PIPELINES, DRAINS, VENT STACKS, AND INSULATION

Table 11-21 *Maximum Distances for Trap Arms*

Size of Trap (in.)	Slope	Distance from Trap to Vent
1¼	¼	5
1½	¼	6
2	¼	8
3	¼	12
4	⅛	16

Cleaning, Adjusting, and Operating

Cleaning

1. Inspect all surfaces for damage or stains. Replace or clean as necessary. Clean equipment before running water through it.
2. See that all grease, paint, plaster, spackle, spots, and debris are removed. See that anchorage and seals are firm. See that equipment is still undamaged. Accept only properly working, undamaged equipment.

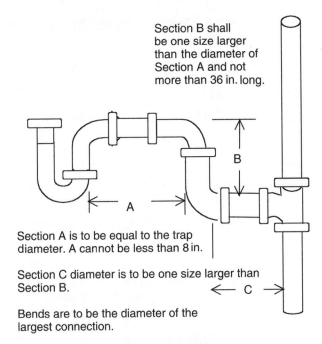

Section B shall be one size larger than the diameter of Section A and not more than 36 in. long.

B

A

Section A is to be equal to the trap diameter. A cannot be less than 8 in.

Section C diameter is to be one size larger than Section B.

← C →

Bends are to be the diameter of the largest connection.

Fig. 11-20 *Vertical leg fixture.*

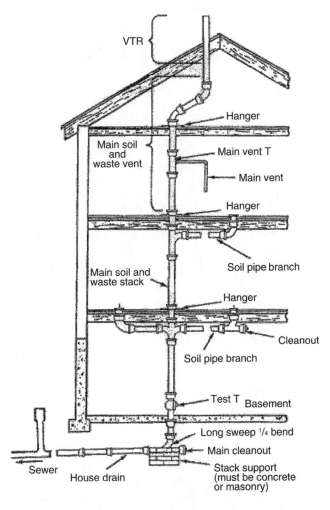

VTR

Hanger

Main soil and waste vent

Main vent T

Main vent

Hanger

Soil pipe branch

Main soil and waste stack

Hanger

Cleanout

Soil pipe branch

Test T — Basement

Long sweep ¼ bend

Main cleanout

Sewer

House drain

Stack support (must be concrete or masonry)

Fig. 11-21 *Typical vent stacks.*

Adjusting and Operating

1. Flush, turn on, or otherwise run water through the complete system. Check flow, water levels, quietness of operation, leakage, and shut-off capability. Repeat many times.

2. Reject equipment that is damaged, does not operate properly, is not installed properly, and is not in new condition.

RESIDENTIAL PLUMBING REQUIREMENTS
Fuel Piping

Gas Piping Inspection Methods

- Approved gases:
  a. Air
  b. CO_2
  c. Nitrogen
- Approved gases must withstand a pressure of 10 lb not less than 15 min.
- Welded pipe with pressures exceeding 14-in. water column require a test pressure of 60 lb psi for a minimum of 30 min.
- Gas meters need to be at least 3 ft away from sources of ignition when installed indoors.
- Used piping may be used for gas if free from defects.

Gas Pipes

- Cannot use plastic in or under a house.
- Gas shutoff valves need to be within 6 ft of the appliance and in same area.
- All fuel-gas appliances need a cut-off valve.
- Fireplace gas shut offs need to be within 4 ft.
- Pipe joints need tape or joint compound (on male only).
- Fittings for steel pipe need to be:
  a. Copper
  b. Brass
  c. Bronze
- Connectors cannot be over 3 ft except dryers and ranges where they may reach 6 ft.
- Outdoor appliances may have a gas hose not to exceed 15 ft.
- Metallic gas piping needs to be buried at least 12 in. below the grade.

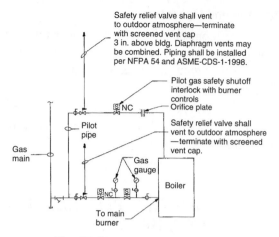

Fig. 11-22 *Typical boiler piping.*

- Plastic piping needs to be buried at least 16 in. below grade.

- Also must have a no. 18 AWG yellow wire with the ends exposed.

- Dissimilar piping need to be joined by approved dialectic fittings and couplings.

- Plastic to metal connections:

  a. Made only underground.

  b. Only outside the house with approved fittings.

- Piping through concrete or masonry walls need to be enclosed in a sleeve.

- Need "dirt" leg (sediment trap) installed as close to appliance as possible.

- Dirt leg not needed with:

  a. Ranges

  b. Clothes dryers

  c. Outdoor grills

- Gas piping cannot run through air plenums, air ducts, dumbwaiters, elevator shafts.

- Suitable for combustible air ducts.

- Gas pipe unions are not allowed in concealed areas.

- Piping in concrete slabs needs a minimum of 1½-in. concrete coverage and cannot come in contact with rebars and or wire mesh.

- All gas piping needs to supported by fabricated materials compatible with the piping material.

- Field wrap piping in contact with material that will corrode the material.

- Fuel piping cannot be located in a concrete slab that contains quick-set additive such as calcium.

- Tanks require a minimum of 10 ft from any part of the dwelling.

Metallic Tubing

- Free of all buckling when bent.

- Inside radius of bend less than 6 times the tubing outside diameter.

Plastic Piping

- Inside bend radius not less than 25 times the outside diameter of pipe.

- Tubing in studs, joist, or any framing member needs shielding by 16-gage plate if within 5 in. of each side of the framing member.

- All gas piping needs to be purged and have caps placed on them until they are attached to the appliance.

- Must be marked if not black steel piping.

- Not required in same room as appliance.

- Marked at 5-ft intervals where exposed.

- Gas piping needs to be sized accordingly to the required demand of the appliance(s).

Liquid Petroleum Tanks

Table 11-22 *Minimum Separation between Containers and Public Ways, Buildings, or Lot Lines of Adjoining Property*

Container Capacity (Water Gallons)	Minimum Separation between Containers and Public Ways, Buildings, or Lot Lines of Adjoining Property	
	Mounded or Underground Container (ft)	Aboveground Container (ft)
Less than 125	10	5
125–250	10	10
251–500	10	10
501–2,000	10	25
2,001–30,000	50	50
30,001–70,000	50	75
70,001–90,000	50	100
90,001–120,000	50	125

Location of LP-Gas Containers

1. Minimum distance for underground containers shall be measured from the pressure relief device and the filling or liquid-level gauge vent connection at the

container, except that all parts of an underground container shall be 10 ft or more from a building or lot line of adjoining property that can be built upon.

2. For other than installations in which the overhanging structure is 50 ft or more above the relief-valve discharge outlet: In applying the distance between buildings and ASME containers with a water capacity of 125 gallons or more, a minimum of 50% of this horizontal distance shall also apply to all portions of the building that project more than 5 ft from the building wall and that are higher than the relief valve discharge outlet. This horizontal distance shall be measured from a point determined by projecting the outside edge of such overhanging structure vertically downward to grade or other level upon which the container is installed. Distances to the building wall shall not be less than those prescribed in Table 11-22.

3. Containers of less than a 125-gal water capacity are allowed next to the building they serve when in compliance.

Oil Lines/Tanks

- Maximum amount stored in the building or aboveground is limited to 660 gallons (residential).
- Underground tanks not less than 1 ft away from property lines, foundations, and/or basement walls must be protected.
- Aboveground tanks must be at least 5 ft from property lines.
- Need at least 1 ft of covering.
- Inside tanks require a gage.
- Connections of combustible materials are not permitted within the building or aboveground outside the building.
- Oil piping to appliances can not be less than ⅜-in. diameter.
- Vent piping not less than 1¼-in. diameter.
- Vent piping cannot terminate within 2 ft of any building opening.
- Need shutoff valves between the tank and appliance.
- Oil pressure not to exceed 3 psi at inlet to appliances.

Types of Fuel Oils

Fuel oils for heating are broadly classified as distillate fuel oils (lighter oils) or residual fuel oils (heavier oils). ASTM has established specifications for fuel oil prop-

erties that subdivide the oils into various grades. Grades 1 and 2 are distillate fuel oils. Grades 4, 5 (light), 5 (heavy), and 6 are residual fuel oils. Specifications for the grades are based on required characteristics of fuel oils for use in different types of burners. The ANSI standard specification for fuel oils is ASTM Standard 0396-86.

Grade 1 is a light distillate intended for vaporizing-type burners. High volatility is essential to continued evaporation of the fuel oil with minimum residue.

Grade 2 is a heavier (API gravity) distillate than 1. Grade 2 is used primarily with pressure-atomizing (gun) burners that spray the oil into a combustion chamber. The atomized oil vapor mixes with air and burns. This grade is used in most domestic burners and many medium-capacity commercial-industrial burners.

Grade 4 is an intermediate fuel that is considered either a light residual or a heavy distillate. Intended for burners that atomize oils of higher viscosity than domestic burners can handle, its permissible viscosity range allows it to be pumped and atomized at relatively low storage temperatures.

Grade 5 (light) is a residual fuel of intermediate viscosity for burners that handle fuel more viscous than Grade 4 without preheating. Preheating may be necessary in some equipment for burning and, in colder climates, for handling.

Grade 5 (heavy) is a residual fuel more viscous than Grade 5 (light), but intended for similar purposes. Preheating is usually necessary for burning and, in colder climates, for handling.

Grade 6, sometimes referred to as Bunker C, is a high-viscosity oil used mostly in commercial and industrial heating. It requires preheating in the storage tank to permit pumping, and additional preheating at the burner.

Table 11-23 *Typical API Gravity, Density, and Healing Value or Standard Grades of Fuel Oil*

Grade No.	API Gravity	Density, lb/gal	Healing Value, Btu/gal
1	38–45	6.950–6.675	137,000–132,900
2	30–38	7.296–6.960	141,800–137,000
4	20–28	7.787–7.396	148,100–143,100
5L	17–22	7.940–7.686	150,000–146,800
5H	14–18	8.080–7.890	152,000–149,400
6	8–15	8.448–8.053	155,900–151,300

Table 11-24 Recommended Nominal Size for Fuel Oil Suction Lines from Tank to Pump (Grades 1 and 2)

Pumping Rate, gph	Length of Run in Feet at Maximum Suction Lift of 10									
	25	50	75	100	125	150	175	100	250	300
10	½	½	½	½	½	½	½	¾	¾	
40	½	½	½	½	½	¾	¾	¾	¾	
70	½	½	¾	¾	¾	¾	¾	1	1	
100	½	¾	¾	¾	¾	1	1	1	1	1¼
130	½	¾	¾	1	1	1	1	1	1¼	1¼
160	¾	¾	¾	1	1	1	1	1¼	1¼	1¼
190	¾	¾	1	1	1	1	1¼	1¼	1¼	
220	¾	1	1	1	1	1¼	1¼	1¼	1¼	

Table 11-25 Recommended Nominal Size for Fuel Oil Suction Lines from Tank to Pump (Grades 5 and 6)

Pumping Rate, gph	Length of Run in Feet at Maximum Suction Lift of 15									
	15	50	75	100	125	150	175	200	250	300
10	1½	1½	1½	1½	1½	1½	2	2	2½	2½
40	1½	1½	1½	2	2	2½	2½	2½	2½	
70	1½	2	2	2	2	2½	2½	2½		
100	2	2	2	2½	2½	3	3	3		
130	2	2	2½	2½	2½	3	3	3	3	4
160	2	2	2½	2½	2½	3	3	3	4	4
190	2	2½	2½	2½	3	3	3	4	4	4
220	2½	2½	2½	3	3	3	4	4	4	4

Notes:
1. Pipe sizes smaller than 1½ are not recommended for use with residual-grade fuel oils.
2. Lines conveying fuel oil from discharge pump to burners and tank return may be reduced by one or two sizes depending on piping length and pressure losses.

DRILLING AND NOTCHING OF STRUCTURAL MEMBERS FOR ALL LINES

Fig. 11-23 *Holes in joist for plumbing.*

Studs

- Load bearing
  a. Holes less than 40%
  b. Notches less than 25%
- Non-load-bearing
  a. Holes less than 60%
  b. Notches less than 40%

Joists

- Notches less than ⅙ the depth
- None allowed in middle third.
- Not within 2 in. of top or bottom drilled holes less than ⅓ the depth.

Notching and Boring Studs

Table 11-26 Holes/Notching in Load-Bearing Studs

Nominal	Actual	Holes		Notching
		40%	60%	25%
2 × 4	1½ × 3½	1¹³⁄₃₂	2³⁄₃₂	⅞
2 × 6	1½ × 5½	2³⁄₁₆	3⁵⁄₁₆	1⅜

Table 11-27 Holes/Notching in Non-Load-Bearing Studs

Nominal	Actual	Holes		Notching
		40%	60%	40%
2 × 4	1½ × 3½	1¹³⁄₃₂	2³⁄₃₂	1¹³⁄₃₂
2 × 6	1½ × 5½	2³⁄₁₆	3⁵⁄₁₆	2³⁄₁₆

Table 11-28 Drilled Hole Maximums in Joists

Nominal	Actual	⅓ (33%) in.
2 × 6	1½ × 5¼	1¾
2 × 8	1½ × 7¼	2¹³⁄₃₂
2 × 10	1½ × 9¼	3³⁄₃₂
2 × 12	1½ × 11¼	3¾
2 × 14	1½ × 14¼	4¾

Table 11-29 Notch Maximums in Joists

Nominal	Actual	⅙ (17%) in.
2 × 6	1½ × 5¼	⅞
2 × 8	1½ × 7¼	1⁷⁄₃₂
2 × 10	1½ × 9¼	1¹⁷⁄₃₂
2 × 12	1½ × 11¼	1⅞
2 × 14	1½ × 14¼	2⅜

Table 11-30 Notch Maximums in Ceiling Joists/Rafters

Nominal	Actual	⅓ (33%) in.
2 × 6	1½ × 5¼	1¾
2 × 8	1½ × 7¼	2¹³⁄₃₂
2 × 10	1½ × 9¼	3³⁄₃₂
2 × 12	1½ × 11¼	3¾
2 × 14	1½ × 14¼	4¾

Table 11-31 End Notch Maximums in Ceiling Joists/Rafters

Nominal	Actual	¼ (25%) in.
2 × 6	1½ × 5¼	1⁵⁄₁₆
2 × 8	1½ × 7¼	1¹³⁄₁₆
2 × 10	1½ × 9¼	2⁵⁄₁₆
2 × 12	1½ × 11¼	2¹³⁄₁₆
2 × 14	1½ × 14¼	3⁹⁄₁₆

Table 11-32 Approved Water Piping

Name	Chemical Name	Typ. Uses
ABS	Acrylonitrile butadiene styrene	Rigid black used for drain waste and vents
CPVC	Chlorinated polyvinyl chloride	Like PVC, also can be used for hot water
PB	Polybutylene	Used for water lines, both hot and cold
PE	Polyethylene	Flexible plastic tubing for cold water
PP	Polypropylene	Rigid plastic for traps and drain lines
PVC	Polyvinyl chloride	Rigid plastic used in cold water and DWV lines
SR	Styrene rubber	Rigid pipe for underground use

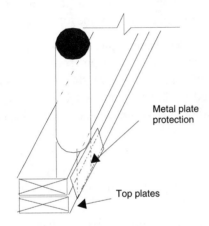

Fig. 11-24 *Protection for piping in top plates.*

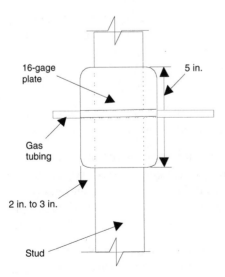

Fig. 11-25 *Gas tubing protection in framing members.*

WATER LINES

- Test 30 min at 100 psi using potable water only.
- Maximum run—60 ft.
- Requires pressure-reducing valve if pressure is over 80 psi.
- Minimum pressure is 40 psi (for wells also). Water not to be tested less than the working pressure; tested with air—not less than 50 psi.

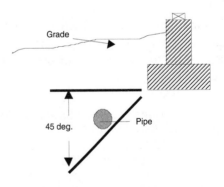

Fig. 11-26 *Footer and piping clearance.*

- Underground piping cannot be supported by blocks or on rocks at any point.
- Backfill placed in 6-in. layers and tamped.
- Trenches need to be kept open until inspected.
- No rocks or other such type fill allowed until after 12 in. of fill.
- May install water in same trench as sewer providing it is to the side and 12 in. separates them.

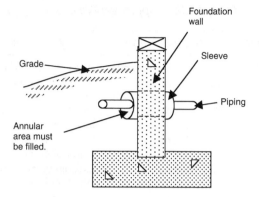

Fig. 11-27 *Sleeve in foundation wall.*

Copper Pipes

Type K: Has the thickest walls of the three types, usually used in underground locations.

Type L: Has medium wall thickness. Mostly used as service to a home and for use in the interior distribution system.

Type M: Has the thinnest wall and only available in rigid hard tempered. Used as general water distribution systems.

Plastic Water Lines

- Only ABS, PVC, or PE can be used for cold water piping.
- Only CPVC, PB, or PE can be used by either hot or cold water.
- Air gaps are required at the discharge point of a relief valve or piping. Minimum air gap is measured vertically from the lowest end of the water supply outlet to the flood rim or receptor.

Table 11-33 *Recommended Sizing for Supply, Drains, and Vents**

Fixture	Supply	Drain/Trap	Vent
Main	1 in.	N/A	N/A
House service	¾ in.	N/A	N/A
Supply risers	¾ in.	N/A	N/A
House sewer	N/A	4 in.	N/A
House drain	N/A	3 in.	N/A
Soil stack	N/A	3 in.	N/A
Branch drain/vent	N/A	1½ in.	1¼ in.
Water closet	½ in.	3½ in.	2 in.
Bathtub	½ in.	1½ in.	1¼ in.
Lavatory	½ in.	1½ in.	2¼ in.
Kitchen sink	½ in.	1½ in.	1¼ in.
Clothes washer	½ in.	2 in.	1¼ in.
Dishwasher	½ in.	1½ in.	1¼ in.
Shower	½ in.	2 in.	1¼ in.

*Based on two-family dwelling.

Table 11-34 *Maximum Fixture Units Allowed to Be Connected to Branches and Stacks*

Pipe Sizes	Horizontal Branch	One Vertical Branch	Special Conditions
1¼			Limited to a single fixture
1½	3	4	No water closets
2	6	10	
2½	12	20	No water closets
3	20 (max. of three water closets)	48 (max. of six water closets)	
4	160	240	

Determining Required Water Supply and Pipe Sizes

Step 1 Obtain the daily static service pressure from the local water company or from the developer. This number requires adjustment for the following conditions.

- If the elevation of the highest water supply is higher than the water meter location (source of the determined water static pressure), then the pressure is to be reduced by 0.5 psi for each foot in height variance. If the meter is higher than the furthest source, then add 0.5 psi per foot of difference.

- If a water pressure reducing valve is installed, then the static pressure is to be reduced by 80% or the set pressure downstream of the reducing valve, whichever is smaller.

- Deduct for water softeners, backflow preventers, water filters, or other special equipment as per the manufacturer of these devices.

- Deduct the pressure in excess of 8 psi for special fixtures, such as flushometer tanks for water closets or temperature-controlled showers; for example, if the fixture has a psi deduction of 10 psi, you would deduct 2 psi for the static pressure (10 psi − 8 psi).

Step 2 Using the resulting pressure from the adjustments above, find corresponding Table 11-37.

Step 3 Determine the maximum developed length from the supply source and the most remote fixture for both hot and cold. This number is then multiplied by 1.2 to make adjustments for pressure loss due to pipe fittings. Use this number to enter the table chosen from Step 2.

Step 4 To determine the size of the water service pipe, follow down the column "Max. Developed Length" to a fixture unit equal to or greater than all the fixture units (use the combined column for both the hot and cold runs) calculated by using the table corresponding to the calculated water pressure. Read to the left for the required water service piping size and water meter.

Step 5 To determine the size of each branch line (either hot or cold), start at the most remote water demand and work back along the line to the main distribution, adding up each fixture unit value from Table 11-35 for either the hot or the cold column. Using the appropriate table for water pressure as in Step 4 above, identify the same or next-smaller water meter size and read the column to the right labeled "distribution" for the correct size of the branch. At no time is the branch line required to be larger than the main distribution line established in Step 4. Repeat this step for the remaining branch lines.

Note: Piping for "future fixtures" such as an unfinished basement must also be figured into the total.

Table 11-35 Water Supply Fixture Units

Fixture or Groups	Fixture Units		
	Hot	Cold	Combined
Bathtub	1.0	1.0	1.4
Clothes washer	1.0	1.0	1.4
Dishwasher	1.4	—	1.4
Hose bibb		2.5	2.5
Kitchen sink	1.0	1.0	1.4
Lavatory	0.5	0.5	0.7
Laundry tub	1.0	1.0	1.4
Shower stall	1.0	1.0	1.4
Water closet	—	2.2	2.2
Full bath group	1.5	2.7	3.6
Half bath group	0.5	2.5	2.6
Kitchen group (w/o garbage disposal)	1.9	1.0	2.5
Laundry group	1.8	1.8	2.5

Table 11-36 Minimum Water Piping Size Based on Water Supply Fixture Units

30–39-psi Pressure						
Service Pipe	Distribution Pipe	Max. Developed Length				
		40	60	80	100	150
¾	½	2.5	2	1.5	1.5	1
¾	¾	9.5	7.5	6	5.5	4
¾	1	32	25	20	16.5	11
1	1	32	32	27	21	13.5
¾	1¼	32	32	32	32	30
1	1¼	80	80	70	61	45
1½	1¼	80	80	80	75	54
1	1½	87	87	87	87	84
1½	1½	151	151	151	151	117

Table 11-36 (Continued)

40–49-psi Pressure						
Service Pipe	Distribution Pipe	Max. Developed Length				
		40	60	80	100	150
¾	½	3	2.5	2	1.5	1.5
¾	¾	9.5	9.5	8.5	7	5.5
¾	1	32	32	32	26	18
1	1	32	32	32	32	21
¾	1¼	32	32	32	32	32
1	1¼	80	80	80	80	65
1½	1¼	80	80	80	80	75
1	1½	87	87	87	87	87
1½	1½	151	151	151	151	151

50–60-psi Pressure						
Service Pipe	Distribution Pipe	Max. Developed Length				
		40	60	80	100	150
¾	½	3	3	2.5	2	1.5
¾	¾	9.5	9.5	9.5	8.5	6.5
¾	1	32	32	32	32	25
1	1	32	32	32	32	30
¾	1¼	32	32	32	32	32
1	1¼	80	80	80	80	80
1½	1¼	80	80	80	80	80
1	1½	87	87	87	87	87
1½	1½	151	151	151	151	151

Over 60-psi Pressure						
Service Pipe	Distribution Pipe	Max. Developed Length				
		40	60	80	100	150
¾	½	3	3	3	2.5	2
¾	¾	9.5	9.5	9.5	9.5	7.5
¾	1	32	32	32	32	32
1	1	32	32	32	32	32
¾	1¼	32	32	32	32	32
1	1¼	80	80	80	80	80
1½	1¼	80	80	80	80	80
1	1½	87	87	87	87	87
1½	1½	151	151	151	151	151

Note: A pressure-reducing valve is required for static pressures exceeding 80 psi.

Table 11-37 Minimum Fixture Flow Capacities at Point of Discharge

Fixture	Flow Rate (gpm)	Flow Pressure (psi)
Bidet	2	4
Water closet	1.6	15
Water closet, tank, one piece	6	20
Bathtub	4	8
Dishwasher	2.75	8
Laundry tub	4	8
Lavatory	2	8
Sink	2.5	8
Shower	3	20
Hose bibb	5	8

Table 11-38 Maximum Flow Rates

Plumbing Fixture	Max. Flow Rate
Lavatory faucet	2.2 gpm @ 60 psi
Shower head	2.5 gpm @ 80 psi
Sink faucet	2.2 gpm @ 60 psi
Water closet	1.6 gal per flush

Water Pipe Corrosion

- Plumbing systems act very much like a battery. The metal piping acts as the anode while water is the oxygen carrying solution. In a reaction the water and pipe try to reach equilibrium. In doing so, the metal ions from the pipe go into the water; thus oxidation commonly known as corrosion or rust occurs. Different metals corrode at different rates. Copper corrodes very slowly and makes an excellent supply vessel for water. Magnesium, zinc, and iron corrode faster.
- Galvanized pipe is the process of coating the iron pipe with zinc, where the zinc will enter the water first before the iron, thus prolonging the decay or corrosion of the iron.

Note: Hot water tanks must not exceed 180° at 100 psi.

Other Causes of Pipe Corrosion

- Stray electric current.
- Bacteria in water supply.
- Acidic water levels.
- Contact between dissimilar metals.
- Soil, waste, and drains passing under a footing or through a foundation wall need to be placed in an iron pipe sleeve two sizes larger; or the wall shall have a relieving arch.
- Need to protect water, soil, and waste piping from freezing.
- Max. water line length is 60 ft.
- Min. water line diameter is ¾ in.
- Must be rated at 160 psi at 73°F.

Table 11-39 Piping Supports

Type	Max. Horizontal Supports	Max. Vertical Supports
Cast iron	5 ft or 10 ft if 10-ft pipe is used	Each story not to exceed 15 ft
Steel	¾ in.–10 ft-0 in. 1 in.–12 ft-0 in.	15 ft-0 in.
Copper	1¼ in.–6 ft-0 in. 1½ in.–10 ft	10 ft-0 in.
Plastic (DWV)	4 ft-0 in.	Each story and a midway guide
Plastic rigid	3 ft-0 in.	Each story and a midway guide

PLUMBING FIXTURES

- All except water closet need strainers.
- Tail pieces for sinks, dishwashers, laundry tubs, and bathtubs must be at least 1½ in. O.D.
- Fixture with concealed tubular traps need an access panel 12 in. in its least dimension.
- Joints that are screwed, solvent-cemented, and fused or withstand 25 psi do not need an access panel.
- Cannot have more than 8% lead content for water pipings/joints.
- Bolts and screws to mount fixtures need to be copper, brass, or corrosion resistant material.
- Joints must be water tight at floors and walls.
- Water closets not less than 15 in. from walls or partitions.

Showers

Showers must have the following:

1. 900 sq. in. of floor area.
2. Must deliver a rate of 2½ gpm at 80 psi.

3. Must be set at 120° or less.

4. Be able to have a clear radius of 30 in. on floor.

5. Door must open outward.

6. Shower riser must be secured to the structure.

7. Shower head must be energy conserving with a maximum flow of 2½ gpm at 80 psi.

8. Require a high limit stop of 120° max.

9. Floor drains must be min of 2 in. and have a strainer.

SANITARY DRAINAGE

Table 11-40 *Approved Sanitary Drainage Materials*

Welded and seamless steel pipe (black or galvanized)	ASTM A 53
Cast iron soil pipe and fittings (hub and spigot)	ASTM A 74
Cast iron fittings (threaded)	ASTM A 126
Malleable iron fittings (threaded)	ASTM A 197
Seamless copper pipe	ASTM B 42
Seamless red brass pipe	ASTM B 43
Seamless copper tubing	ASTM B 75
Seamless copper water tubing (Type K, L, M)	ASTM B 88
ABS-DWV pipe and fittings	ASTM D 2661
PVC-DWV pipe and fittings	ASTM D 2665
3.25-in.-O.D. PVC-DWV pipe and fittings	ASTM D 2949
ABS-DWV schedule 40 with cellular core	ASTM F 628
Co-extruded PVC plastic pipe with cellular core	ASTM F 891
Co-extended composite ABS-DWV pipe and fittings	ASTM F 1488
Cast iron soil pipe and fittings (hubless)	CISPI 301
Copper drainage tube (DWV)	ASTM B 306
Mechanical couplings	CSA B602M
Solvent cement for ABS-DWV pipe and fittings	ASTM D 2235
Solvent cement for PVC-DWV pipe and fittings	ASTM D 2564
Socket bell for PVC-DWV pipe and fittings	ASTM D 2672
Primers for solvents	ASTM F 656
Hubless cast iron soil pipe and fittings	ASTM A 888
Couplings used with hubless shielded couplings	CISPI 310-95 ASTM C 1277
Co-extruded composite ABS DWV sch. 40 IPS pipe solvent cement fittings	ASTM F 1488 ASTM D 2235 ASTM D 2661 ASTM F 628

Table 11-40 *(Continued)*

Co-extruded composite PVC DWV sch. 40 IPS pipe solvent cement fittings	ASTM F 1488 ASTM D 2564 ASTM D 2665 ASTM F 891
Co-extruded composite PVC DWV IPS pipe; DR-PS140 PS200 solvent cement fittings	ASTM F 1488 ASTM D 2564 ASTM D 2665 ASTM F 891

Determining Drainage Capacity

Drain Pipe Sizing

Step 1. Starting with the most remote fixture, add up all the fixture units downstream to the building drain.

Step 2. Using the total fixture value from above, use Table 11-42 for sizing branches and stacks.

Step 3. Use Table 11-43 to determine the pipe diameter and slope for the building sewer/drain.

Fixture Branch and Stack Sizing

1. Determine the fixture units for the branch in question and use Table 11-42.

2. Below-grade drain piping cannot be less than 1½ in. in diameter.

3. Drain stacks may not be smaller than the largest horizontal branch. (Code allows for exceptions.)

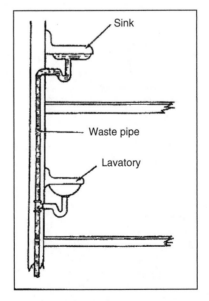

Fig. 11-28 *Indirect siphonage.*

Table 11-41 *Drainage Fixture Units*

Fixture Type/Group	Drainage Unit
Bar sink	1
Bathtub	2
Bidet	1
Clothes washer	2
Dishwasher	2
Floor drain	Only used if used as a receptor, then use the value of the fixture discharging into it
Kitchen sink	2
Lavatory	1
Laundry tub	2
Shower stall	2
Water closet (1.6 gal)	3
Water closet (greater than 1.6)	4
Full bath	5
Full bath (with WC using more than 1.6 gal)	6
Half bath	4
Half bath (with WC using more than 1.6 gal)	
Kitchen	3
Laundry	3
Multiple baths	
1.5 baths	7
2 baths	8
2.5 baths	9
3 baths	10
3.5 baths	11

Table 11-42 *Maximum Fixture Units Connected to Branches and Stacks*

Pipe Size (Nominal)	Horizontal Branch	Any One Vertical Branch or Drain
1¼ (Note a)	—	—
1½ (Note b)	3	4
2	6	10
2½ (Note b)	12	20
3	20	48
4	160	240

Note a: 1¼-in. pipe is limited to a single fixture drain or trap arm.
Note b: No water closets.

Table 11-43 *Max. Fixture Units Allowed to Building Drain, Sewer, or Building Drain Branch*

Pipe Diameter, in.	Slope per Foot		
	⅛ in.	¼ in.	½ in.
1½ (Notes a, b)	—	— (Note a)	— (Note a)
2 (Note b)	—	21	27
2½ (Note b)	—	24	31
3	36	42	50
4	180	218	250

Note a: Limited to branch not serving more than two fixtures, one if serving a pumped discharge or garbage disposal.
Note b: Number of water closets.

Cleanouts

- Installed at not more than 100 intervals.
- Installed at each change of direction exceeding 45°. Except not more than one cleanout required in each 40 ft regardless of the changes in direction.
- Cleanouts are to have a minimum front clearance of 18 in. for pipes 3 in. or larger. Pipes less than 3 in. must have 12-in. clearance.

Table 11-44 *Cleanout Sizes*

Pipe Size	Cleanout Size
1½ in.	1½
2 in.	1½
3 in.	2½
4 in. and larger	3½

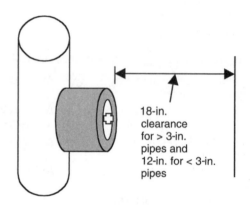

18-in. clearance for > 3-in. pipes and 12-in. for < 3-in. pipes

Fig. 11-29 *Required minimum clearances in front of cleanouts.*

Fittings

- Drainage fittings are to be designed to maintain a slope of ¼ vertical unit to each horizontal unit.

Drains

- 3-in. diameter or less must slope at least 2% or a ¼ vertical for each 12 horizontal.
- 4-in. diameter or more must slope at least 1% or a ⅛ vertical for each 12 horizontal.

Roof Vents

- Penetrate through the roof a minimum of 6 in. high side.
- Shall vent downward if through a wall or building overhang.

Traps

- Slip joints may be used in drainage piping on both sides of the trap and in the trap seal.

Table 11-45 *Trap Arm Lengths*

Diameter	Length
1¼	5 in.
1½	6 in.
2	8 in.
3	12 in.
4	16 in.

Septic Tanks

Perk Test

- Perk tests are basically an evaluation of the absorption rate of the soils in your area to adequately dispose of the used water and waste in your system. Although the tests are sometimes carried out differently from location to location, they are all basically the same. It is advisable to check with your local county health department and/or code officials to determine exactly what test they require.

- Begin by digging three holes at different locations within the area proposed as the leach field. Each hole should have a diameter of at least 6 in. and be at a depth of the proposed drain pipes. Clean and scrape the sides of the holes to remove any fallen dirt. Place on the bottom of each hole approximately ½ to ¾ in. crushed stone. Fill each hole with at least 12 in. of water. Maintain the 12 in. depth for at least 4 hours. Keep in mind that the purpose is to try to simulate the actual conditions once the drain field is actually installed.

- Sometimes when sandy soils are encountered the authorities will forgo the saturation process; if not, the perk tests should be taken within 15 h and not later than 30 h.

- Fill each hole with 6 in. of water and measure the amount of absorbing that happens with the level of each hole. The purpose of the test is to measure the amount of time it takes 1 in. of water to be absorbed into the soil. By dividing the time interval used between each measurement in each individual hole, you will then have a rate of drop with each of the three holes. A typical figure might be a 1 in. drop per each hour. Average the three test holes together and then you will have developed the rate of absorption (peck test) for that particular area.

Table 11-46 *Absorption Rate*

Soil Type	Required Leaching Area (sq. ft.)/ 100 gal of Tank Capacity	Max. Absorption Capacity (gal/sq. ft. Leaching Area)
Sand/gravel	20	5
Fine sand	25	4
Sandy loam and clay	40	2.5
Sandy clay	60	1.66
Clay with small amounts of sand/gravel	90	1.11

Table 11-47 *Capacity Requirements in Residential Construction*

Number of Bedrooms	Tank Capacity
1 or 2	750 gal
3	1000 gal
4	1200 gal
5 or 6	1500 gal

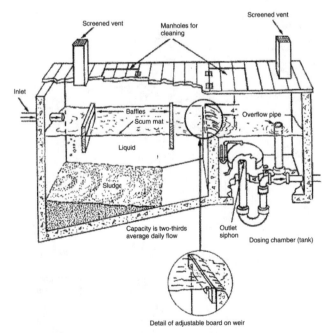

Notes:
1. Use the board cover only to retain heat in cold climate or to control fly nuisance.
2. When not required for dosing the drain system, the dosing chamber and siphon are omitted

Fig. 11-30 *Typical septic tank.*

Table 11-48 *Separation Requirements*

Minimum Horizontal Clearance	Septic Tank	Disposal Fields
Buildings	5 ft	8 ft
Property line	5 ft	5 ft
Water well	50 ft	50 ft
Streams	50 ft	50 ft
Large trees	10 ft	None
Water line	5 ft	5 ft

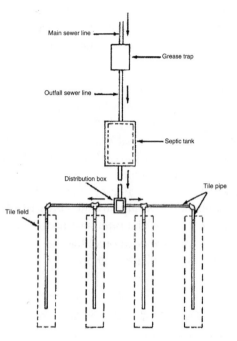

Fig. 11-31 *Septic system leach field.*

Water Heaters

- Fuel burning water heaters shall not be installed in a room used as a storage area.

- Direct vent water heaters are not required to be installed within an enclosure.

- Only full-bore type valves allowed on cold water supply side only.

- If installed in garage the burner must be 18 in. above finish floor grade.

Table 11-49 *Clearances for Water Heaters*

Type	Top	Front	Back	Sides
Oil	6 in.	6 in.	36 in.	36 in.
Gas	6 in.	18 in.	36 in.	36 in.
Elect	6 in.	6 in.	36 in.	48 in.

Table 11-50 *Required Supply (Residential)*

No. Baths	Gas	Electric	Oil
1–1½ gal	30 gal	40 gal	30 gal
2–2½ gal	40 gal	50 gal	30 gal
3–3½ gal	50 gal	66 gal	30 gal

Based on three-bedroom home.
Gas and oil water heaters are prohibited in bedrooms, bathrooms, and clothes closets.

Boiler/Water Heaters

Table 11-51 *Expansion Tank Minimum Capacities (Water Temperature 195°F, Fill Pressure 12 psig, Minimum Operating Pressure 30 psig)*

System Volume	Diaphragm Type	Nonpressurized Type
10	1.0	1.5
20	1.5	3.0
30	2.5	4.5
40	3.0	6.0
50	4.0	7.5
60	5.0	9.0
70	6.0	10.5
80	6.5	12.0
90	7.5	13.5
100	8.0	15.0

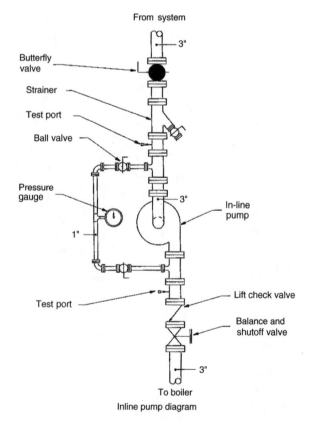

Fig. 11-32 *Inline pump.*

DOMESTIC WATER WELLS

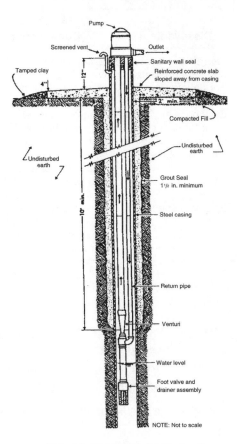

Fig. 11-33 *Typical drilled well.*

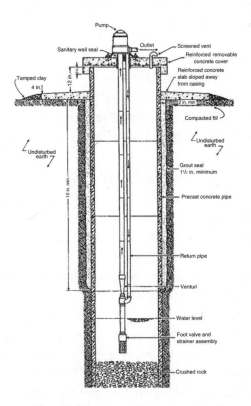

Fig. 11-34 *Typical dug or bored well.*

Table 11-52 *Well Pumps*

Type of Pump	Suction Lift (ft)	Usual Pumping Depths (ft)	Pressure Heads
Reciprocating			
Shallow well	22–26	22–26	100–200
Deep well	22–25	Up to 600	Up to 600
Centrifugal			
Shallow well single stage straight centrifugal	20	10–20	100–150
Regenerative vane turbine	28	28	100–200
Deep well vertical line turbine (multistage)		50–300	100–800

Disinfecting of Wells

Every well should be properly disinfected after construction or repair. This can be effectively accomplished by providing dosage of 50 to 100 ppm available chlorine to a well, pump, pressure tank, and distribution system. After the well is chlorinated, each outlet is allowed to flow until chlorine appears (chlorine detected by odor or orthotolidine test). The outlet is then turned off and the solution allowed to stand in the system 12 h and then pumped to waste. Sodium hypochlorite, which is available as household bleach with 5.25% available chlorine, used at the rate of 1 pint per 100 gal water will do the job. Dilute household bleach with four parts water, pour into the well, operate pump until solution is in contact with all parts of water system. Let treated water stand in system as described above.

FIRE PROTECTION SYSTEMS
General

Definition

This section covers materials, equipment, and installation procedures for fire protection systems.

Approvals

1. Review Submittal Register and ensure that all material equipment and shop drawings are approved prior to preparatory inspection, and prior to either fabrication or installation. Obtain any helpful manufacturer's installation information.

Table 11-53 *Typical Wells*

Type	Diameter	Maximum Depth (ft)	Lining or Casing	Suitability	Disadvantages	Method of Construction
Dug	3–20 in.	40	Wood, masonry, concrete, or metal	Water near surface may be hand dug	Large number of man hours, dangerous	Excavation from within well
Driven	2–4 in.	50	Pipe	Simple using hand tools	Formations must be soft and boulder free	Hammered a pipe into ground
Jetted	3 or 4 in.	200	Pipe	Small diameter wells on sand	Only possible if loose sand formations	High-pressure water pumped through pipe
Bored	Up to 36 in.	50	Pipe	Useful in clay soils	Difficult on loose sand or cobbles	Rotating earth auger
Collector	15 ft	130	Reinforced concrete caisson	Used adjacent to surface recharge such as lake or river		Caisson is sunk into aquifer
Drilled	Up to 60 in.	4000	Pipe	Suitable for variety of soils	Requires special tools	a. Hydraulic rotary b. Cable tool percussion c. Reverse circulation rotary

2. Ensure that seismic restraints (if required) are shown on shop drawings.

Storage and Handling

1. Ensure that all materials and equipment are handled carefully to prevent damage.

   a. Reject damaged material and equipment. Mark such items and have them removed from the site.

   b. Have damaged coatings repaired.

2. In handling heavy pipe use wide belt slings to avoid damage to pipe coatings.

3. Check storage facilities for adequate weather protection, possible damage, and safety hazard.

4. When outside storage is necessary, store materials and equipment aboveground and protected for vehicle traffic.

Coordination of Work

Continually check for interferences among electrical, mechanical, architectural, and structural features such as cranes, especially in ceiling area and along walls where a fire protection system is to be installed.

Sprinkler Systems

General

1. Ensure that fire protection systems serving occupied buildings are not shut off for repairs without advance notice being given to proper authorities and/or owners.

2. Note valves and equipment proposed for location within reach of flood waters.

3. Do not take water from fire mains for domestic use.

4. Identify painting and coding requirements.

5. Check that sprinkler heads are not painted or blocked in any way.

6. Identify areas to client that have a high likelihood of being used as unauthorized storage and thus block sprinkler coverage.

Materials

1. Coordinate fire department hose connections to ensure compatibility with local fire department.

2. Inspect pipe, fittings, and valves. Pipe is to be reamed free from all burrs and fins.

Water Supply

1. Evaluate contractor's plan of work to minimize interruption of water service.

2. Witness all flow tests and maintain a copy for your records.

3. Ensure that water line is located below frost line and meets the code in the area.

4. Block off ends of supply lines terminating in building or valve house.

5. Be certain that pipe joints are left exposed and uninsulated until final inspection and tests are made.

6. See that turns in supply line are braced, blocked, or clamped.

Aboveground Piping

1. Verify size of pipe. Check to ensure all hangers are tight.

   a. Run parallel to building lines, with slope to drain.

   b. See that branch piping is off top of main.

   c. Where impossible to obtain an even slope, plugs should be provided at low points so that the entire system may be drained. Check for inspection test connections required by NFPA and local jurisdiction.

2. Check that no cutting or notching of structural members for support or passage of pipe is allowed.

3. Ensure that holes through fire walls are provided with sleeves and plates and are properly resealed with approved fire-retardant sealer. Sleeves should be provided where pipe passes through walls and floors.

4. Check that installation of seismic restraints are installed (if required) as approved.

Sprinkler Heads

1. Be sure that heads in accordance with NFPA 13 are installed in upright position with recommended clearance to roof or ceiling surfaces.

   a. When in pendant position, return bends will be used if water is subject to sedimentation.

   b. Where subject to mechanical injury, heads will be provided with approved guards.

   c. All heads will be new and should not be painted.

2. Determine sprinkler head temperature ratings as proper for ambient temperatures anticipated in the area (e.g., near heaters, skylights, in compressor rooms). Notify the Project Manager in instances where sprinkler head temperature ratings appear to be inconsistent with anticipated ambient temperatures.

3. Spare heads should be provided and arrangements made to transfer them to the client at closeout.

4. Where sprinkler heads are shown to be installed in special hazard areas, such as computer shops, confirm that installation will be in conformance with area usage.

Drains

- See that valves or plugs are provided to ensure drainage of the entire system. Ensure that the discharger from all drain valves is visible. They should be arranged so that a wide-open valve position under normal pressure will not cause any damage to any surrounding feature.

Wet Pipe Systems

1. Check that piping layout is in accordance with approved drawings.

2. Alarm check-valve assembly must conform with connection diagram.

3. Observe installation of waterflow indicators for conformance with connection diagram.

4. Confirm insulation and painting and labeling requirements.

5. Check water flow alarm signal.

Dry Pipe Systems

1. Determine that piping layout is in strict accordance with approved drawings.

2. Note dry pipe valve installation for conformance with connection diagram.

3. Inspect installation of air compressors. Air supply line should include flexible connection and orifice plate. Check motor controller operation. If compressor is equipped with an air storage tank, ensure that condensate water drain is provided at bottom of tank.

4. Examine locations and operation of condensate chambers, i.e., drum drips.

5. Check water flow alarm signal time and dry valve trip test time. Be present to witness the test.

6. Where dry pipe valve accelerators are provided, check for proper operation.

Sterilization

- Witness dosage, distribution, retention, and final flushout. Request copy of lab inspection report if required.

Alarm Facilities

1. Check installations to ensure that all alarm devices have been provided and are in operating condition.

2. Be sure that electric power for alarm signals is taken from the house current supply line ahead of the main switch.

3. Examine alarm system for tie-in with local fire department. Request a visit by the local fire marshall.

4. Check alarm to ensure that it works as intended with no defects.

Testing

1. Review test procedure and witness all tests.

2. Protect dry pipe valves against damage during the tests.

3. In testing extensions to the existing system, ensure that self-indicating blanks are used. Remove upon completion of tests.

4. Ensure that all sprinkler contractor's certificates covering materials and tests are on record and that you have copies.

5. Ensure that flushing and hydrostatic tests are made in accordance with the accepted tests specified in Standard 13 of the NFPA.

6. Ensure that all lines and controls are properly color-coded painted, identified, tagged, and with directional flow markings and are correctly spaced and visible.

7. Make sure the user/fire marshall is present as needed during any testing.

Fire Protection Checklist

1. Is the sprinkler system installed in accordance with the approved plans?

2. Is the water pressure as specified in the approved plans?

3. Do all valves operate?

4. Have you followed the inspector's test?

5. Has paint been inadvertently applied to the sprinkler heads?

6. Is shelving, a structure, or a fixture obstructing any sprinkler head?

7. Are tamper switches and flow detector switches electrically connected to the fire department?

UNDERGROUND PIPE SYSTEMS
General

This chapter covers excavation, trenching, backfilling, and laying of underground pipe systems. The types of underground pipe systems are as follows:

- Water
- Storm drainage
- Sanitary
- Fuel
- Steam, high and low temperature hot water

Plans, Specifications, and Layout

Prior to the start of field construction, the plans and specifications should be thoroughly reviewed. The Inspector must check and review isolation of any utility lines that are to be worked on. Also, check and review the permanent disconnection and capping of critical utility lines such as natural gas, fuel oil, and LPG that are to be abandoned.

Note: Make sure contractor purges all fuel lines before abandoned.

1. Observe existing utilities and all possible interference with existing systems.

2. Confer with local utility companies to ascertain that all utilities are indicated on the contract drawings. Utilities not shown on contract drawings should be entered on record drawings.

3. Check all electrical facilities, both aerial and underground.

Accessibility of Valves, Hydrants, and Manholes

All valves, hydrants, and manholes should be constructed in such manner that they can be utilized in the future. Hydrants should be accessible for operation.

Lines and Grades

Lines and grades should be established and staked, and reference benchmarks should be set before any excavation or pipe-laying operations.

1. Check each type of utility being installed within a project for conflict as to the layout and elevations at each point of crossing.

2. Check for conflict with existing utilities.

3. Review codes for possible conflicts with specifications and plans.

Connections to Existing Utilities

Plan and coordinate connections to existing utilities. Under no conditions will an existing utility service be interrupted without full coordination with the owners and utility company involved.

Interference

Hold traffic interference to a minimum when installing utilities in or under walks, streets, or railroads. The contractor should ensure that jacking and boring of pipe, where required by the contract, are carried out in a manner that does not disrupt traffic or other activities.

1. Determine that materials are on hand and that work is organized, so that interference is held to a minimum.
2. Ensure that warning signs, barricades, and obstruction lights are placed and that regular traffic flows smoothly.
3. Traffic interruptions and detours must be coordinated with the proper road departments responsible for the service.

Damages

See that completed pipe installations are not damaged by movement of construction equipment over or near pipe.

Testing

Pressure tests shall be performed prior to backfilling for visual inspection of joints. Alignment tests on all pipes and drain lines are made before backfill is completed. Test results shall be recorded. Check to:

1. Inspect every joint.
2. Ensure that corrective action is in accordance with requirements.

PIPES AND FITTINGS
Material Compliance

1. Determine the quality of all material delivered to the work site for specification compliance.
   • Pipe, pipe fittings, valves, and other components should be checked to ensure that they carry the appropriate stamp and standards organization designations such as ASTM or ASME.
2. Compare submittals with material brought to the job. Check labeling for type, grade, strength, and classification and determine size and condition of materials. Also check pipe fittings, such as tees, ells, and couplings.
3. Verify the quality of miscellaneous items such as valves, service boxes, stops, special connections, and tapped tees.

Handling and Storage

1. See that pipes and fittings are handled with the proper tools and equipment. Do not permit dragging and handling of pipe with chains, wire ropes, etc.

2. Check for damaged pipes, fittings, and pipe coating. Reject all damaged materials promptly, and have rejected materials removed from the jobsite immediately.
3. Make sure adequate and accessible storage area has been provided.
4. Determine requirements for repairing damaged surface coatings.

Field Coating

1. Check the availability of an approved coating test device.
2. Check for breaks and abrasions of pipe coating.
3. Implement requirements for cleaning of surfaces before coating.
4. Follow the requirement for painting with primer and sealer.
5. Check for the requirement to coat edges or ends of pipe and bolt threads.

Laying Pipes—General

1. Check the gradient, line, and grade of the pipeline trench or bed before laying proceeds and after completion of each section.
2. Observe method of jointing permitted.
3. Use pipe manufacturer's installation information. Where there is a difference between this information and the contract specifications, this difference should be called to the attention of the Project Manager.
4. Check for cleanliness of pipe (especially joints) during placement. Cover pipe openings with temporary protection.
5. Ensure that all pipe to be placed on earth is placed on dry, firm soil.
6. Check for obstructions in pipe, such as pipe plugs, and debris.
7. Do not allow pipes to be left open overnight.

Water Lines

1. Grade lines to avoid high points as much as possible. Where high points occur, check specifications for requirements for vacuum and relief valves.
2. See that fire hydrants are plumb with the pumper nozzle facing the roadway. Check location of hydrant shutoff valve and post indicator valve (no

Fig. 11-35 *Pipe in trench (no stable bedding).*

shutoff valve between the PIV and the building it serves).

3. Measure height of the lowest nozzle above finish grade. An 18-in. clearance is usually a required standard.

4. Check that fire hydrant threads conform and fit the hose or firefighting equipment that will be connected to them.

5. Observe the hydrant barrel drain.

   a. Plug the drain in locations of high ground water where the hydrant is specified to have no drain. Check hydrant valves to see if they are required to sit on a 4-in.-thick concrete pad.

   b. In area where the ground water is low, the drain plug must be removed and drainage aggregate (18 in. of crushed stone) provided.

   c. Check thrust blocking and/or tie rods.

   d. Check for movement at joints, bands, dead ends, and hydrants.

   e. Check wedging at all fittings.

6. Require the hydrostatic pressure test and specified leakage tests.

7. Ensure that the contractor sterilizes all phases of water lines that the construction worker may have contaminated—not just the new piping runs.

   a. Main lines require thorough flushing with water until all mud and debris have been removed.

   b. Add disinfecting agent as required and in recommended quantities.

   c. Solution to remain in the line at least 8 and preferably 24 h.

   d. There should be no less than 10 ppm residual at extreme end of line at end of contact period.

   e. Flush entire system thoroughly.

8. Ensure that valves are accessible; check the valve nut after backfilling is completed.

9. Check distance requirements between parallel and crossing water and waste piping.

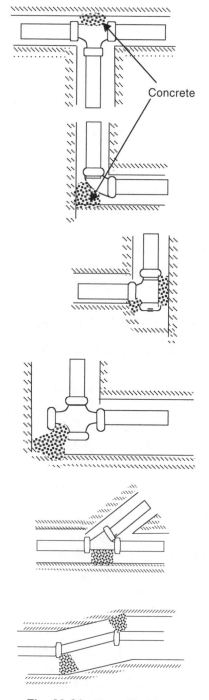

Fig. 11-36 *Thrust blockings.*

Thrust Block Area of Bearing

Table 11-54 Amounts of Concrete for Typical Thrust Bearings

Pipe Size (in.)	Square Feet of Bearing			
	¼ Bend	⅛ Bend	¹⁄₁₆ Bend	Ts, Caps, Plugs
6 or less	6	3	2	4
8	10	5	3	7
10	15	8	4	11
12	21	11	6	15
14	28	15	8	20
16	36	19	10	25
18	44	24	13	32
20	53	29	15	38
24	75	41	21	53

Fig. 11-37 *Water valve (not protected).*

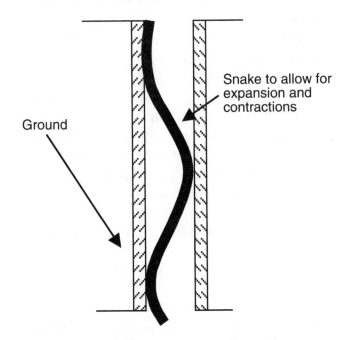

Fig. 11-38 *Plastic pipe in utility trench.*

(Labels: Ground; Snake to allow for expansion and contractions)

Table 11-55 *Expansion Characteristics of PVC*

Temperature Change (°F)	Length Change of PVC Conduit (in./100 ft)	Temperature Change (°F)	Length Change of PVC Conduit (in./100 ft)
5	0.2	105	4.2
10	0.4	110	4.5
15	0.6	115	4.7
20	0.8	120	4.9
25	1.0	125	5.1
30	1.2	130	5.3
35	1.4	135	5.5
40	1.6	140	5.7
45	1.8	145	5.9
50	2.0	150	6.1
55	2.2	155	6.3
60	2.4	160	6.5
65	2.6	165	6.7
70	2.8	170	6.9
75	3.0	175	7.1
80	3.2	180	7.3
85	3.4	185	7.5
90	3.6	190	7.7
95	3.8	195	7.9
100	4.1	200	8.1

Fuel Gas Lines

1. Do not permit lines to be buried under buildings, nor in trenches with other utilities, unless approved.

2. Enforce safety regulations rigidly during construction of gas and all other fuel lines.

3. Continuously check the area with a detector for an explosive atmosphere. Record all readings.

4. When there is indication of an explosive condition, do not commence work until the explosive condition has been identified and cleared.

5. Install gas pipes above other utilities which they cross, and with a minimum cover of 2 ft. Pipe under pavements or heavily traveled areas will be encased or located deep enough so that there will be no damage from heavy traffic. Verify local codes.

6. Check cleanliness of pipe before lowering into trench.

7. Check pipe coating for damage during connection, laying, and backfilling operations. Permit coated piping to be handled only by hand or with non-metallic flexible slings.

8. Keep pipe clean during installation by careful handling and by keeping ends of pipe closed.

9. Make sure contractor uses the correct marking tape over the pipe and at the prescribed depth.

Sanitary Sewers

1. Check distance separating sewers from water line. Always install sewer or force main below water line if the lines are within 6 ft horizontally, unless special provisions are taken at crossings; otherwise spacing must be at least 10 ft horizontally. Check for special code requirements where sewer lines or force mains cross above water lines. Require leakage tests for sanitary sewers and force mains. Check to see that spigot end of pipe is pointed downstream in pipeline.

2. Check that the designed grade is maintained between manholes.

3. Ensure that top elevation of manhole is flush with paving grades or higher than finished grade of ground surrounding area, as specified.

4. Check that the contractor is following specific safety precautions to be taken when working in sewers. Sewer gas is extremely dangerous. Review the contractor's safety plan.

Storm Sewers

1. Check that installation is performed by proceeding upgrade with spigot or tongue end of pipes pointing in the direction of flow.

2. Check the installation of all fittings, joints, connections at manholes, and connections to existing facilities.

3. Check grade, elevation, and finish of paved inverts.

4. Check that elliptical pipe sections are handled carefully in transporting, storing, and installing.

5. Check for installation of all subdrainage tile as shown on plans.

6. Where watertight joints are required, see that hydrostatic test requirements are met, and that rubber gaskets are not affixed more than 24 hours prior to pipe installation and are protected from sun, dust, and other deleterious agents.

7. Cover openings to prevent the entrance of dirt, debris, or animals into the pipe.

8. Require shaping the trench bottom as detailed in either the plans or shop drawings.

9. In rocky soils, overexcavate at least two pipe diameters and fill with suitable backfill material before placing pipe.

Heat Distribution Lines

1. All heat distribution piping is subject to expansion and contraction. Check that all lines are straight, both vertically and horizontally.

2. Expansion of piping will be absorbed by expansion joints or fabricated pipe loops. There must be room for the pipe loop to move as well as for maintenance.

3. Verify strength, security, and proper placement of anchors and supports.

4. Inspect rigid installation of anchors.

5. Require uniform pitch of steam pipe. Trap all low points.

6. Follow the manufacturer's recommended installation procedure for the insulation materials, unless there are specific changes on the approved shop drawings. Log and report all discrepancies to the Proj-ect Manager.

7. Store and protect insulation from the weather.

8. Keep underground pipe conduit system dry during and after construction.

9. Examine waterproofing carefully. Check shop drawing details for both field applied and factory applied waterproofing to protect the insulation.

10. Valve pits should be watertight and have sumps or drains. Check for proper valves, fittings, supports, seals around pit openings, casing, drain, vents, sump, aluminum jacketing over insulation, ladder, etc.

11. Valve pits should also be checked to ensure that they are of the required size and that valves, flanges, and other components have been located as to be accessible and to provide sufficient space for ease of maintenance. Is there a requirement for future work?

12. Check welding of pipe lines for compliance with specification requirements and the applicable codes.

13. Ensure that all changes in direction are done with approved type fittings.

14. Check welds or metal casing on underground steam lines for leaks or damaged asphalt coatings.

15. See that the proper class of underground system materials have been tested for acceptability.

16. Require that all low points in the system are drained and high points are vented.

17. Ensure that the field testing is satisfactorily performed, including hydrostatic, visual, and holiday detector tests.

18. Check for drainage of groundwater from system.

Fuel Lines

Note: Fuel lines in this section pertain to underground liquid petroleum systems.

1. Check drain connections at low points and air releases at high points.
2. Check that field application of covering on joints is not done until the pneumatic pressure test has been conducted.
3. Check if screens and filter elements are installed; check mesh and material; check installation for proper direction of flow; and check clearances for removal of screen and access to drain connection.
4. Check with an approved instrument for fuel vapors that may accumulate in pits or enclosed areas and can cause explosions.
   a. Provide adequate ventilation during operation in a liquid fuel area.
   b. Prohibit open fires, sparks, or static electricity in the vicinity of vapors which may be explosive.
   c. Check by use of a detector for explosive atmosphere.

Jointing of Pipes

General

1. Check to see that all jointing surfaces are kept clean. Check to ensure that pipes of different materials, densities, or manufacturers can and are being properly joined. For example, heat fusion of plastic pipe of different densities is problematic. This piping should be joined with mechanical couplings to ensure a leakproof connection. Also be aware of metal piping of different materials for cathodic protection.
2. Do not join pipes in mud and water.
3. Check tightness of joints.

Hot-Pour Joints

1. Hot-pour joints must be clean and dry. The presence of moisture may cause explosion and possible injury.
2. Check for uniformity of annular space.
3. Check method of application and make sure all joints are adequately filled.
4. Check temperature of the compound.

Poured Lead Joints

1. Check packing for uniformity and tightness.
2. Check depth and amount of lead being placed in joints.
3. Check the pouring operation; it should be done in one continuous pour.

4. Check driving during caulking. If lead is permitted to be displaced to a depth greater than $\frac{1}{4}$ in., the joint should be remade.

Flexible Joints

1. Check for approved material, make, type, and number of splices.
2. Check placing and positioning of flexible gasket.
3. Check depth of gasket with a gauge.
4. Check use of approved lubricant.
5. Do not cover until a hydrostatic test is conducted, as soon as possible.

Tapered End Couplings

- Drive tapered end couplings up tight when joining bituminous fiber pipe.

Cement Mortar Joints

1. Determine specific requirements for types of joints, whether oakum, diaper band, etc.
2. Ensure that mortar meets requirements of contract specifications.
3. Observe that the jointing operation will completely fill joints and form a bond on the outside.
4. Cure cement mortar joints.
5. Remove excess grout from inside and outside of pipe.
6. Protect from weather conditions until fully cured.

Pipe Threads

1. Cut pipe threads with the appropriate tools.
2. Provide proper length thread; the pipe taper is lost by overlength threading.
3. Ream pipe flush on the inside surface.
4. Apply joint compound to the threads on the pipe, not to the fittings.
5. Make up all joints tightly.

Copper Tubing Joints

1. Check types of pipes and fittings used against types required.
2. Cut copper tubing off square and remove burrs.
3. Ensure clean tubing before fluxing and soldering.
4. Check type of tools used for flaring compression type joints.

Welded Joints

1. Inspect contractors qualifications and approved procedure.
2. Fabricate and weld as much as possible before lowering pipe into trench.
3. Check against possible cave-in when in trench.
4. Explore for explosive gases within pipes and before welding in fueling areas.
5. Check pipe ends for bevel.
6. Make a very careful inspection of welds in hard to reach areas.
7. Remove all welding slag before visual inspection.
8. Do not cover until all testing has been satisfactory completed.

Mechanical Joints in Manholes

• Install in accordance with manufacturer's instructions.

Flanged Joints in Manholes

• Install gaskets and bolts and ensure that flanges are not damaged. Use proper bolt torquing procedures.

Corrugated Banding

1. Laps of all circumferential joints in the pipe should provide that the outside lap be on the downstream side of the joint with the longitudinal laps on the side of the in-place pipe.
2. All markings indicating the top of the pipe should coincide with the specified alignment of the pipe.
3. While the connecting band is being placed, ensure that the band is adjusted correctly.
4. Check the specifications or necessity to use bituminous material at the joint after jointing.

Caps or Plugs

1. Close open ends of pipe when work is not in progress and always at the end of each work day.
2. Keep pipelines clean of all debris, rodents, and water.

Manholes and Concrete Encasements

Materials

• Check material requirements with delivered materials at the preparatory inspection.

Construction

1. Check dimensions and layout.
2. Check invert elevations and details of the invert channels in manholes.

3. Check placement of material such as concrete, reinforcement, brick, block, plaster, frames and covers, and rungs.
4. See that manholes are not obstructed by dumped waste concrete or other construction material.

Excavation and Backfilling

Excavation Existing underground utilities will be carefully marked by the appropiate utility company before excavated. Keep them protected for the duration of the work. Existing utilities will be suitably supported to prevent damage to them and to prevent transferring any direct load on to the new piping system below.

1. Check need for shoring or excavate to required side slope as per OSHA (see appendix on OSHA requirements).
2. Report all damaged existing utilities immediately.
3. Note location of all unknown or unreported utilities for inclusion on revised utility plan.
4. Determine that access steps or ladders are provided in trenches, where necessary, and that they are maintained in safe condition. Check that all OSHA guidelines are strictly followed.

Trenching

1. Begin trench excavation for sewers at the lower end of the line and proceed upgrade to protect the work from possible flooding, unless job conditions prohibit.
2. Check specifications and job requirements for maximum width of trench and minimum depth of pipe.
3. Check bed of the trench for grade and suitability of materials before any pipe is laid. If the trench is overexcavated, bring the bed to grade and compact. When encountering rock excavations, check the minimum overdepth specified and check that backfilling is performed with select bedding material.
4. Keep water from the trenches during construction. Use pumps or a well point system.
5. Check that final hand grading precedes pipe laying by no more than the amount of pipe that can be installed the same day.
6. Check excavation of bottom of trench. Is it graded and shaped to bottom quadrant of sewer pipe, and has excavation under all bells been performed as

specified? Has approved gravel bedding material been used?

7. Inspect distance between potable water lines and sanitary sewer trenches for minimum allowable clearance.

8. Check pipe-handling procedures and do not allow loads to be swung over the heads of workmen.

9. Are thrust blocks being used? Are they in the correct locations? Record all approved deviations from plans and specs.

Backfilling Ensure that special care is taken when backfilling around ductile iron. Recheck alignment after backfill operations.

Polyethylene Sleeve

1. Require leakage tests for sanitary sewers. Verify that specific backfill and compaction requirements for plastic pipe have been followed.

2. Permit placement of backfill only between pipe joint locations until all lines have been tested and/or approved, unless job conditions require otherwise. In the case of pressure testing, place sufficient backfill material to prevent pipes from moving out of place. In the case of wrapped and coated piping, do not permit any backfilling until the coating at welds and fittings has been completed and the entire coating tested for holidays. Ensure that backfill in contact with the piping does not damage protective coatings. Make sure that all lines are located on as-built drawings before backfilling.

3. Check backfill material, and inspect the placement operation for uniform layers (6–8 in.) on each side of the pipeline.

4. Check that the contractor keeps foreign materials and large stones out of the backfill material. Backfill operation check:

   a. Thickness of each layer for moisture content and compaction.

   b. Do not machine compact fill on top of a pipeline until required minimum cover has been placed.

   c. That there are no large or sharp rocks used.

   d. Have contractor check soil density testing as required.

   e. Check sewer lines to manhole after the backfilling operation. Check from manhole for broken pipe, settlement in the line, lateral movement, and cleanliness.

Summary

1. The plans and specifications must always be followed unless the Project Architect or Project Manager approves changes. All changes must have an appropriate paper trail.

2. The Inspector must ensure that the contractor red-lined as built drawings and system O&M manuals are submitted to the owner as soon as possible after completion of all or each section of the system if the construction is phased. In any case the appropriate (recorded) red-lined drawings and O&M manuals should be given to the owner before any portion of the system is placed in operation by the client or the facility is occupied.

3. All items that are questionable should be reported to the Project Manager or appropriate site management. Follow up on their disposition.

4. Maintain records of all training classes given to the client and owners.

5. Refer to the applicable OSHA requirements for excavations.

CORROSIONS

Forms of Corrosion Almost all corrosion problems and failures encountered can be associated with one or more of the eight basic forms of corrosion: (1) general corrosion, (2) galvanic corrosion, (3) concentration-cell (crevice) corrosion, (4) pitting corrosion, (5) intergranular corrosion, (6) stress corrosion cracking, (7) dealloying, and (8) erosion corrosion.

1. *General corrosion.* With general corrosion (sometimes called uniform corrosion), anodic dissolution is uniformly distributed over the entire metallic surface. The corrosion rate is nearly constant at all locations. Microscopic anodes and cathodes are continuously changing their electrochemical behavior from anode to cathode cells for a uniform attack. The general corrosion rates for metals in a wide variety of environments are known, and common practice is to select materials with rates that are acceptable for the application.

2. *Galvanic corrosion.* Galvanic (dissimilar metals) corrosion occurs when two electrochemically dissimilar metals are metallically connected and exposed to a corrosive environment. The less-noble metal (anode) suffers accelerated attack, and the more noble metal (cathode) is cathodically protected by the galvanic current. The tendency of a metal to corrode in a galvanic cell is determined by its position in the "galvanic series" of metals and alloys as listed in Table 11.56.

The metal order listed is only appropriate for seawater at 25°C (77°F). The order may vary with both temperature and composition of the electrolyte (water or soil). In fact, under some conditions, two metals may reverse their water respective order (potentials). For example, iron may become anodic with respect to zinc in fresh water at a temperature above 66°C (150°F). A common galvanic corrosion cell occurs when copper lines are connected to galvanized steel water mains. In this example, the soil is the electrolyte, the copper line is the cathode, and the water main is the anode.

Table 11-56 *Galvanic Series in Seawater at 25°C (77°F)*

Corroded end (anodic, or least noble)
Magnesium
Magnesium alloys
Zinc
Galvanized steel or galvanized wrought iron
Aluminum alloys—5052, 3004, 3003, 1100, 6053, in this order
Low-carbon steel
Wrought iron
Cast iron
Ni-Resist (high-nickel cast iron)
Type 410 stainless steel (active)
50-50 lead-tin solder
Type 450 stainless steel (active)
Type 304 stainless steel (active)
Type 316 stainless steel (active)
Lead
Tin
Copper alloy C28000 (muntz metal, 60% Cu)
Copper alloy C67500 (manganese bronze)
Copper alloys C46400, C46500, C46600
Alloy 200 (active)
Alloy 6700 (active)
Alloy B
Chlorimet 2
Copper alloy C27000 (yellow brass, 65% Cu)
Copper alloys C44300, C44400, C44500 (admiralty brass)
Copper alloys C60800, C61400 (aluminum bronze)
Copper alloy C23000 (red brass, 85% Cu)
Copper C11000 (ETP copper)
Copper alloys C65100, C65500 (silicon bronze)
Copper alloy C71500 (copper nickel, 30% Ni)
Copper alloy C92300, cast (leaded tin bronze G)
Copper alloy C92200, cast (leaded tin bronze M)
Alloy 200 (passive)
Alloy 600 (passive)
Alloy 400
Type 410 stainless steel (passive)
Type 304 stainless steel (passive)
Type 3316 stainless steel (passive)
Alloy 825
Alloy 62
Alloy C
Chlorimet 3
Silver
Titanium
Graphite
Gold
Platinum
Protected end (cathodic, or most noble)

3. *Concentration cell corrosion.* Concentration cell corrosion occurs because of differences in the environment surrounding the metal. This form of corrosion is sometimes referred to as "crevice corrosion," "gasket corrosion," and "deposit corrosion" because it commonly occurs in localized areas where small volumes of stagnant solution exist. Normal mechanical construction can create crevices at sharp corners, spot welds, lap joints, fasteners, flanged fittings, couplings, threaded joints, and tube sheet supports. At least five types of concentration cells exist; the most common are the "oxygen" and "metal ion" cells. Areas on a surface in contact with an electrolyte having a high oxygen concentration generally will be cathodic relative to those areas where less oxygen is present (oxygen cell). Areas on a surface where the electrolyte contains an appreciable quantity of the metal's ions will be cathodic compared to locations where the metal ion concentration is lower (metal ion cell).

4. *Pitting corrosion.* Pitting corrosion is a randomly occurring, highly localized form of attack on a metal surface, characterized by the fact that the depth of penetration is much greater than the diameter of the area affected. Pitting is one of the most destructive forms of corrosion, yet its mechanism is not completely understood. Steel and galvanized steel pipes and storage tanks are susceptible to pitting corrosion and tuberculation by many potable waters. Various grades of stainless steel are susceptible to pitting corrosion when exposed to saline environments.

5. *Intergranular corrosion.* Intergranular corrosion is a localized condition that occurs at, or in narrow zones immediately adjacent to, the grain boundaries of an alloy. Although a number of alloy systems are susceptible to intergranular corrosion, most problems encountered in service involve austenitic stainless steels (such as 304 and 316) and the 2000 and 7000 series aluminum alloys. Welding, stress relief annealing, improper heat treating, or overheating in service generally establish the microscopic, compositional inhomogeneities that make a material susceptible to intergranular corrosion.

6. *Stress corrosion cracking.* Stress corrosion cracking (environmentally induced–delayed failure) describes the phenomenon that can occur when many alloys are subjected to static, surface tensile stresses, and are exposed to certain corrosive environments. Cracks are initiated and propagated by the combined effect of a surface tensile stress and the envi-

ronment. When stress corrosion cracking occurs, the tensile stress involved is often much less than the yield strength of the material; the environment is usually one in which the material exhibits good resistance to general corrosion.

7. *Dealloying.* Dealloying is a corrosion process in which one element is preferentially removed from an alloy. This occurs without appreciable change in the size or shape of the component; but the affected area becomes weak, brittle, and porous. The two most important examples of dealloying are the preferential removal of zinc from copper zinc alloys (dezincification), and the preferential removal of iron from gray cast iron (graphitic corrosion). Graphitic corrosion sometimes occurs on underground cast iron water mains and leads to splitting of the pipe when the water pressure is suddenly increased.

8. *Erosion corrosion.* Erosion corrosion refers to the repetitive formation (a corrosion process) and destruction (a mechanical process) of the metal's protective surface film. This typically occurs in a moving liquid. Erosion may be impinging (in the case of a pipe ell) or sliding (pipe wall) when it occurs. An example is the erosion corrosion of copper water tubes in a hot, high-velocity, soft-water environment. Cavitation is a special form of erosion corrosion.

Corrosion Mitigation Corrosion mitigation can be accomplished by design considerations, by employing corrosion-resistant materials of construction and cathodic protection, by using protective coatings, or by using inhibitors.

Design Considerations The use of acceptable engineering practices to minimize corrosion is fundamental to corrosion control. This is accomplished by engineering design. One of the most important factors in designing for corrosion control is to avoid crevices where deposits of water-soluble compounds and moisture can accumulate and are not accessible for maintenance. Any region where two surfaces are loosely joined, or come into proximity, also qualifies as a crevice site. Joining geometries also present various crevice corrosion problems. Examples include: bolting, back-to-back angles, rough welds, weld spatter, sharp edges, corners, discontinuities, and intermittent welding.

a. *Crevice corrosion.* Crevice corrosion relies on establishing a crevice geometry to allow water or other liquids or deposits to enter the crevice. One

form of corrosion prevention is to eliminate crevice geometry by design. Joints and fastenings should be arranged to give clean, uninterrupted lines; therefore, welded joints are preferable to bolted or riveted joints. Sound welds and complete weld penetration will help to avoid porosity and crevice development that often result from intermittent welding, rough welds, and weld spatter. Grinding sharp edges, corners, welds, and weld spatter will help prevent crevice corrosion, as well as paint striping procedures over similar surfaces. Striping is a procedure that entails brush or spray application of the primer or, in some instances, the entire coating system over potential corrosion sites. Striping is designed to give additional barrier protection from the exposure, and it is common when the service environment includes some degree of immersion or splash.

b. *Stainless steel coupled to carbon steel.* The galvanic series listed in Table 11-56 illustrates some of the common metals in seawater. The further apart the metals are in the series, the more rapid will be the corrosion of the more anodic metal. That is, a metal tends to corrode when connected to a more cathodic metal. For example, carbon steel will corrode more rapidly when connected to stainless steel.

Stainless Steel—Active and Passive States Several grades of stainless steel appear toward the anodic (upper) end of the galvanic series when they are in the "active" condition, and at the cathodic (lower) end when they are in the "passive" condition. The corrosion-resistant nature of stainless steel is related to its inherent ability to form a protective oxide film in the presence of oxygen or various oxidizing chemicals such as nitric or sulfuric acid. If the protective oxide film is destroyed, the stainless steel is subjected to rapid corrosion (the active condition) in the presence of oxygen-free acids such as hydrochloric acid. Therefore, the correct application of a specific grade of stainless steel should include a determination if the oxidation level of the environment will result in a passive or active state.

Stainless steels, particularly the 300 series, are subject to a heat treating effect called "sensitization" during welding and stress relieving between 427°C (800°F) and 760°C (1400°F). During welding, these stainless steels may form chromium carbides (at temperatures of 427°C (800°F) to 760°C (1400°F). Therefore, the chromium near the grain boundaries is tied up and no longer forms the protective oxide film (chromium oxide). Thus, the grain boundaries are susceptible to intergranular corrosion and the stainless steel is no longer in the passive state. Sensitized stainless steels can deteriorate in acidic soil or water. This type of corrosion can be prevented by a solution treatment and repassivation process after welding.

a. *Unfavorable area differences.* The rate of corrosion resulting from galvanic action frequently will depend on the relative exposed areas of the two metals in contact. For example, zinc will corrode when connected to iron. The zinc will "protect" the iron by making it the cathode of the galvanic cell. This is the principle behind a zinc-rich coating on steel. Small anode areas, in combination with large cathode areas, should be avoided whenever possible. A small piece of zinc will corrode rapidly when coupled to a large area of iron, yet the iron will receive little protection. Coating less noble metals and leaving the more noble metal uncoated is not recommended. A poor coating application can reduce the service life of the metal significantly because of local defects that will cause accelerated anodic corrosion resulting from a galvanic action. Examples of these coating defects are pinholes, scratches, skips, and physical damage.

b. *Isolation of dissimilar metals.* Galvanic attack may be prevented by using an insulator to prevent contact (completion of electrical circuit) between dissimilar metals. The more noble metal can be insulated from the less noble metal through the use of plastic washers for fasteners. Ceramics or nonconductive insulating materials also may be used.

c. *Connection of old and new materials.* Galvanic corrosion is not limited to cells in which totally dissimilar metals are in contact and exposed to an electrolyte. Differences in the composition or surface condition of "similar" metals frequently can result in galvanic corrosion cells. For example, clean steel is typically anodic to corroded steel. Therefore, it is common in pipeline operations to find new pipeline installed in a repaired section or branch line corroding more rapidly than the old line to which it is connected. The older pipe causes accelerated corrosion of the new piping because of galvanic action. Local galvanic anode installation or the application of an insulator may prevent this problem.

d. *Electrical grounding.* Steel pipe in soil or water, electrically connected to rebar in concrete, is another corrosion-related problem associated with galvanic cells. Steel pipe always should be prevented from contacting the reinforcing steel in concrete because the reinforcing steel is passive and will cause accelerated corrosion of the steel piping.

e. *Galvanized piping* in 60°C (140°F) to 77°C (170°F) water. At normal ambient temperatures, galvanized steel is anodic to unprotected steel. The sacrificial action of the zinc is caused by the relative potential difference of zinc and iron at normal temperatures. However, in hot water applications, the potential of zinc decreases (becomes more cathodic) with an increase in temperature and actually may have the anodes and cathodes reversed. The steel would become anodic to the zinc. Therefore, galvanized piping should not be used when water immersion temperatures are in the 60°C (140°F) to 77°C (170°F) range because the steel may become sacrificial to the zinc.

Cathodic Protection   Cathodic protection is an electrical method of mitigating corrosion on metallic structures that are exposed to electrolytes such as soils and waters. Corrosion control is achieved by forcing a quantity of direct current to flow from auxiliary anodes, through the electrolyte, and onto the metal structure to be protected.

Theoretically, corrosion of the structure is completely eliminated when the open-circuit potentials of the cathodic sites are polarized to the open-circuit potentials of the anodic sites. The entire protected structure becomes cathodic relative to the auxiliary anodes. Therefore, corrosion of the metal structure will cease when the applied cathodic current equals the corrosion current. There are two basic methods of corrosion control by cathodic protection. One involves the use of current that is produced when two electrochemically dissimilar metals or alloys are metallically connected and exposed to the electrolyte. This is commonly referred to as a sacrificial or galvanic cathodic protection system. The other method of cathodic protection involves the use of a direct current power source and auxiliary anodes, which is commonly referred to as an impressed current cathodic protection system.

Sacrificial (Galvanic) Systems   Sacrificial-anode-type cathodic protection systems provide cathodic current by galvanic corrosion. The current is generated by metallically connecting the structure to be protected to a metal/alloy that is electrochemically more active than the material to be protected. Both the structure and the anode must be in contact with the electrolyte. Current discharges from the expendable anode through the electrolyte and onto the structure to be protected. The anode corrodes in the process of providing protection to the structure. The basic components of a single, sacrificial-anode-type cathodic protection installation are the structure to be protected, the anode, and the means of connecting the structure to the anode.

a. The cathodic current generated by the sacrificial anode depends on the inherent potential between the anode and the structure to be protected. Theoretically, any metal or alloy more electrochemically active than another would be capable of cathodically protecting the more noble material. In practice, only Type 2 zinc (99.9% Zn conforming to ASTM B418) and alloys of magnesium are used for the protection of steel in soils. Although zinc has a higher current output efficiency, most sacrificial anodes installed for the protection of underground steel structures are fabricated from magnesium alloys because magnesium alloys provide a higher driving potential.

b. Sacrificial-anode-type cathodic protection systems have a number of advantages:

- No external power is required.
- No regulation is required.
- Easy to install.
- Minimum of cathodic interference problems.
- Anodes can be readily added.
- Minimum of maintenance required.
- Uniform distribution of current.
- Minimum right-of-way/easement costs.
- Efficient use of protective current.
- Installation can be inexpensive if installed at time of construction.

c. Sacrificial-anode-type systems also have disadvantages that limit their application:

- Limited driving potential.
- Lower/limited current output.
- Poorly coated structures may require many anodes.
- Can be ineffective in high-resistivity environments.
- Installation can be expensive if installed after construction.

Impressed Current Systems Impressed-current-type cathodic protection systems provide cathodic current from an external power source. A direct current (DC) power source forces current to discharge from expendable anodes through the electrolyte and onto the structure to be protected. Although the current is not generated by the corrosion of a sacrificial metal/alloy, the energized materials used for the auxiliary anodes do corrode.

a. The basic components of an impressed-current-type cathodic protection system are the structure to be protected, a DC power source, a group of auxiliary anodes (ground bed or anode bed), and insulated lead wires connecting the structure to be protected to the negative terminal of the power source and the ground bed to the positive terminal of the power source.

b. The DC power source is usually a rectifier, although current also can be obtained using engine-driven generators, batteries, solar cells, fuel cells, wind-powered generators, and thermoelectric generators. High-silicon chromium-bearing cast iron anodes and ceramic-coated anodes are commonly used materials for auxiliary anodes when impressed-current-type cathodic protection systems are used to mitigate corrosion on underground steel structures.

c. Impressed-current-type cathodic protection systems have a number of advantages:

- Can be designed for a wide range of voltage and current
- High ampere-year output is available from single ground bed
- Large areas can be protected by a single installation
- Variable voltage and current output
- Applicable in high-resistivity environments
- Effective in protecting uncoated and poorly coated structures

4. Impressed-current-type systems also have disadvantages that limit their application:

- Can cause cathodic interference problems
- Are subject to power failure and vandalism
- Have right-of-way restrictions
- Require periodic inspection and maintenance
- Require external power, resulting in monthly power costs
- Overprotection can cause coating damage

Systematic Cathodic Protection Design Procedure

a. The systematic cathodic protection design procedure provides the corrosion engineer an opportunity to evaluate the technical and economical benefits that result when several cathodic protection system designs are considered for a given project. The engineer is provided an opportunity to select the most advantageous system. Basically, the systematic cathodic protection design procedure is an optimization of the various existing methods. The procedure simultaneously considers both types of cathodic protection systems; it is applicable to both proposed and existing underground structures. Most important, the procedure provides flexibility in evaluating the alternatives, which are available in selecting the optimum cathodic protection system for the structure involved.

b. During the predesign phase, basic information is obtained regarding the structure and its external environment. This information is collected by conducting and evaluating the results of selected field tests and considering the corrosion-control experience of other operations in the general area. The objective of the predesign phase is to determine the viability of cathodic protection as an effective means of corrosion control.

c. The design phase sizes the cathodic protection system components. Initial iterations in the design phase, however, should be considered tentative. Once the tentative system components are selected, technical and economical life cycle costs must be calculated. Comparison of the various alternatives then can be made by evaluating each system's technical/economical benefits. Plans and specifications can be developed after design analysis; the system then can be installed. Following installation, the design procedure requires that the corrosion engineer conduct further field surveys to ensure that the protection criterion selected from NACE RP-0l-69 is satisfied. The systematic design procedure also requires that, with an impressed-current-type cathodic protection system, additional field tests be conducted to ensure that no stray current corrosion problems exist. The procedure also requires that the corrosion engineer outline a cathodic protection system reoccurring maintenance program.

Monitoring Effectiveness of Cathodic Protection Systems After a cathodic protection system is installed, the system needs to be monitored. The system should be evaluated periodically to ensure that it is providing corrosion protection to the metallic structure. Criteria have been developed to determine if adequate corrosion protection is being achieved on the structure in question. For example, some of the indications of a cathodic protection problem include changes in operating conditions of the rectifier output and any noted corrosion increase of the structures.

Criteria for Cathodic Protection Structure-to-electrolyte potential measurements are analyzed to determine whether or not a structure is cathodically protected; these measurements are made by the use of cathodic protection criteria. Unfortunately, no one simple criterion has been accepted by all cathodic protection engineers that can be practicably measured in the field under all circumstances. Guidelines for selecting the proper criterion under various circumstances will be provided below. Guidance concerning the criteria of cathodic protection for external corrosion control on underground structures is found in two recommended practices (RPs) published by NACE. These are RP-01-69 and RP-02-85. A summary of the criteria for steel and cast iron structures follows.

a. One criterion is a negative (cathodic) potential of at least 850 millivolts (mV) with the cathodic protection applied. This potential is measured with respect to a saturated copper/copper sulfate reference electrode contacting the electrolyte. Voltage drops other than those across the structure-to-electrolyte boundary must be considered for valid interpretation of this voltage measurement.

b. A negative polarized potential of at least 850 mV relative to a saturated copper/copper sulfate reference electrode is another criterion. Polarized potential is defined as the potential across the structure/electrolyte interface that is the sum of the corrosion potential and the cathodic polarization.

c. Another criterion is defined as a minimum of 100 mV of cathodic polarization between the structure surface and a stable reference electrode contacting the electrolyte. The formulation or decay of polarization can be measured to satisfy this criterion. The −0.85-volt (V) potential criterion states that voltage drops other than those across the structure to electrolyte boundary must be considered when interpreting the measurements. Two criteria, "polarization" and "polarized potential," need to be considered. This is of utmost concern when evaluating potential measurements because only polarization provides cathodic protection. No protection is provided by the voltage drops other than those across the structure-to-electrolyte (i.e., structure-to-soil) boundary.

Dielectric Isolation It may be desirable to electrically isolate a cathodically protected structure from all other metallic structures, such as connecting lines, pump stations, and terminals. If the installation is not isolated, these connections also will be cathodically protected, and current requirements frequently will be excessive. Electrical insulation of pipelines and other structures is accomplished by dielectric isolation. Small lines may be insulated by insulating couplings or unions. If feasible, insulated flanges should be assembled and electrically tested with an ohmmeter before being connected into a line.

Inhibitors   Any substance, when added in small quantities to a corrosive environment containing carbon steel or an alloy that will decrease the corrosion rate is called an inhibitor. Inhibitors function in various ways and are beyond the scope of this manual. Additions of soluble hydroxides, chromates, phosphates, silicates, and carbonates are used to decrease the corrosion rate of carbon steel and alloys in various corrosive environments. The concentration of a given inhibitor needed to protect a metal will depend on a number of factors such as composition of the environment, temperature, velocity of the liquid, the presence or absence in the metal of internal or external stresses, composition of the metal, and the presence of any other metal contact. The type and quantity of inhibitors required for a given metal may be determined by experiments. These experiments should include measurements on the location and degree of corrosive attack as a function of inhibitor type and concentration. Corrosive attacks may occur even if experimentation shows that adequate levels and the correct type of inhibitor are used. Small anode areas and increased attack may develop under loose scale, under deposits of foreign matter, in crevices, and in similar locations relatively inaccessible to the inhibitor.

Protective Coatings   Coatings and linings play a significant role in corrosion prevention and are used extensively for this purpose. Coatings also can perform other valuable functions such as easier cleanability, decon-tamination or graffiti removal, color or a pleasing aesthetic appearance, more light reflectance for a better working environment or for safety purposes, and a color marking or safety warning. There are many different types of coatings. Organic coatings are most commonly applied by brush, roller, or airless or conventionally atomized air-spray equipment. These coatings consist of an organic binder or film with inhibitive, barrier, and sacrificial pigments for corrosion protection. Because of the concerns regarding worker and environmental protection, many coatings are changing to the use of nontoxic, nonhazardous pigments and/or solvents, using water-based or high-solids binders. Metallic coatings such as thermal sprayed zinc, aluminum or aluminum-zinc alloys, stainless steel, and chromium can be used to protect against corrosion or provide increased wear or abrasion resistance. Zinc-rich coatings are widely used to provide galvanic corrosion protection to steel. Galvanizing (either strip or hot-dip) is another way of applying zinc to a steel surface for corrosion protection.

12
CHAPTER

Mechanics

GENERAL

This chapter covers ductwork for air conditioning, heating, ventilating, exhaust systems, and energy conservation systems as it pertains to the codes. It is important that the Inspector have a thorough knowledge of the job plans, specifications, and potential obstructions in the area in which the ductwork is to be installed, including locations of fire-rated walls that the duct must penetrate. Check the following:

1. That all equipment has identification nameplates, and the unit is as specified.

2. That approved vibration isolators and flexible connections are furnished and installed if required. (Check seismic zones in the Appendix.)

3. That using building equipment for temporary heat is understood and/or approved.

4. That provisions are made for proper mounting and anchorage of equipment pads, hangers, etc. (special for seismic zone areas).

5. That equipment operates as intended.

SHOP DRAWINGS

1. It is the Project Architect/Engineer's responsibility to determine that all ductwork is approved well in advance so that it will not delay the progress of the job.

2. Check ductwork delivered to the site for conformance with approved shop drawings.

3. Make sure delivered and stored items are properly stored with tags, so that they will not be installed in a wrong location.

DUCTWORK
Fabrication

See SMACNA duct manual appropriate to material and service requirements.

1. Inspect for type, thickness, and shape of sheet material; check fiberglass boards used for ductwork.

2. Check workmanship and observe lock seams and breaks in ductwork for cracks of sheet metal ducts. Check fiberglass ducts for broken or damaged edges, joints, and seams.

3. Inspect all joint connections for correct type and adequate sealing to prevent movement and air loss.

4. Make sure that the joints are neatly finished and that the duct is smooth on the inside. Any laps should be made in the directions of the flow of air. Internal

insulation will be securely fastened and coated as specified.

5. Provide adequate bracing and reinforcement of the larger ducts.

6. Compare the radius of curved duct with the specification requirements.

7. Check the slope ratio of all transitions. Provide turning vanes and extractors to eliminate abrupt turns of air which cause noticeable turbulence.

8. Check the need for and construction of splitter dampers. Make sure the operating mechanism is accessible; if exposed in a room, the mechanism is to be finished.

9. Make sure that fire and/or smoke dampers are provided in ducts as required by NEPA and SMACNA fire damper guide and codes. Check for fire-safety switch on return air ducts of circulation system.

10. Check duct for the required test holes and covers. Are they accessible?

11. Make sure that the ducts are sealed and protected during the construction period.

12. Check the fabrication of flexible connections.

13. All equipment serviced by the ductwork is required to be fully accessible for maintenance, repairs, oiling, cleaning, and for filter changing.

Ductwork Code Requirements

- Plastic duct may not exceed 150°.

- Metal ducts to be supported by 1-in. straps of 18- or 12-gage galvanized metal wire.

- Supports not to exceed 10-ft intervals.

- All ductwork in nonconditioned areas need to be insulated.

- Cooling ducts passing through nonconditioned areas also need a vapor retarder.

- No gas or plumbing waste cleanouts can be located at or pass through plenums.

Erection

1. Examine all fabricated ducts, rejecting any which are not smooth or any which are damaged.

2. Examine duct hangers for specified material, thickness, and spacing.

3. Check specification requirements for the need for stiffeners for wide ducts. Also check for need of trapeze hangers under wide ducts.

4. Provide approved flexible connections between ducts and for fan units.

Table 12-1 *ASHRAE Recommended Design Criteria*

Area		Inside Design Conditions		Air Movement	Air Changes (per hr)
		Winter	Summer		
Dining and entertainment	Cafeterias	70–74°F 20–30% rh	78°F 50% rh	50 fpm at 6 ft above floor	12–15
	Restaurants	70–74°F 20–30% rh	74–78°F 33–60% rh	25–30 fpm	8–12
	Bars	70–74°F 20–30% rh	74–78°F 30–60% rh	30 fpm at 6 ft above floor	15–20
	Nightclubs	70–74°F 20–30% rh	74–78°F 30–60% rh	Below 23 fpm at 3 ft above floor	20–30
	Kitchen	70–74°F	85–88°F	30–50 fpm	12–15
Office building		70–74°F 20–30% rh	74–78°F 50–60 rh	25–45 fpm	4–10
Libraries and museums	Average		61–72°F 30–33% rh	Below 23 fpm	8–12
	Archival	Special considerations		Below 23 fpm	8–12
Bowling		70–74°F 20–30% rh	73–78°F 30–33% rh	50 fpm at 6 ft above floor	10–13
Communication centers	Telephone terminal rooms	72–78°F 20–30% rh	72–78°F 20–30% rh	25–30 fpm	8–20
	Teletype centers	70–74°F 20–30% rh	74–78°F 20–30% rh	25–30 fpm	8–20
	Radio and television stations	74–78°F 30–40% rh	74–78°F 30–33% rh	Below 23 fpm at 12 ft above floor	15–40
Transportation centers	Airport terminals	70–74°F 20–30% rh	74–78°F 30–60% rh	25–30 fpm at 6 ft above floor	8–12
	Ship docks	70–74°F 20–30% rh	74–78°F 30–60% rh	23–30 fpm 6 ft above floor	8–12
	Bus terminal	70–74°F 20–30% rh	74–78°F 30–60% rh	25–30 fpm at 6 ft above floor	8–12
	Garages	20–33°F	80–100°F	30–75 fpm	4–6 (NFPA)
Warehouses		Inside designs often depend on the materials stored.			1–4

rh = relative humidity.

5. Check rigidity and tightness of field installed items as dampers and defectors.

6. Provide access doors at all fire dampers, automatic dampers, coils, filters, heaters, thermostats, or at any item that requires servicing. Doors are to be airtight, securely fastened, accessible, and able to be fully opened. Refer to SMACNA and specifications for size of access doors required.

7. Inspect goose necks and rain hoods for method of fastening, flashing, and bracing. Goose necks are to be turned away from the prevailing wind. Check specifications for screens on open end of goose necks.

8. Provide proper size sleeves where insulated duct passes through wall openings. Future requirements?

9. When obstructions cannot be avoided, the duct area should never be decreased more than 10%, and then a streamlined collar should be used. Larger obstructions require an increase in the duct size in order to maintain as nearly uniform velocity as possible. Notify the Project Manager.

10. Have contractor test metal duct for air tightness before insulating.

11. All ducts, plenums, and casings must be thoroughly cleaned of debris and blown free of small particles and dust before supply outlets are installed.

Diffusers, Registers, and Grilles

1. Ensure that the contractor furnishes a schedule showing all air inlets and outlets.

2. Inspect diffusers and registers for accessible volume control operator.

3. Examine specification and installation for integral anti-smudge rings for diffusers.

4. Check for loose or bent vanes.

5. Inspect each item for fit, and see that gaskets are provided when required.

6. Inspect for the proper operation of registers, dampers, and grille vent controls.

Installation

1. Ductwork layout is coordinated with other trades to avoid congestion and interference. A ductwork drawing coordinating plumbing, electrical, sprinklers, etc. is recommended on complex work.

2. Type, material, thickness, and shape are as required. Field changes are approved before installation.

3. Joint connections are of required type. Check seams and breaks for cracks. Joint provides a smooth surface on interior of duct, and laps are in direction of air flow.

4. Slope ratio of transitions, radius of curved duct, air turns, and deflectors are provided as required.

5. Bracing, reinforcement, stiffeners, hangers, etc. are provided and ductwork is installed as plans and specifications.

6. Verify that all volume dampers, branch duct dampers, register or diffuser dampers, and splitter dampers are provided as required and an operating mechanism is accessible.

7. Fire dampers and smoke dampers of type required are furnished and installed as required by NFPA. Verify that access is provided to dampers.

8. Flexible connectors are fabricated and provided where required.

9. Access doors and/or access space is provided at all items requiring servicing, such as fire dampers, automatic dampers, manual dampers, coils, heaters, filters, and thermostats. Size is sufficient for access and maintenance.

10. Proper sleeves and openings through walls and floors are provided as required and are sealed as required. Allow no cutting of structural members without approval.

11. Ductwork is properly taped or sealed as required by the codes and the contract specifications.

Duct Insulation

1. Ducts are tested for air tightness, if required, before installation of insulation.

2. Type, thickness, material, extent, and method of fastening and installation are as required.

3. Sound deadening and vapor barrier are provided as required.

4. Insulation subject to damage is protected as required.

5. Materials are fire retardant or incombustible as required.

6. Vapor barrier integrity is maintained.

Diffusers, Registers, and Grilles

1. All ducts, plenums, and equipment are thoroughly cleaned of all debris before supply outlets are installed.

2. All items are furnished and installed as required, and approved. Finishes in areas match as required.

3. Volume control devices are provided as required and are accessible.

4. Gaskets are provided and installed as required.

5. Items are securely attached and supported as required.

Note: Insulation for metal ductwork is covered in the section "Mechanical Insulation."

Balancing and Testing

- Balancing and testing air supplies is covered in "Ventilating, Air Supply, and Distribution Systems."

MECHANICAL INSULATION
General

This section covers field-applied insulation. Factory-applied insulation is specified under the equipment, duct, or piping to be installed, or as detailed in the specifications and plans.

Identification of Material

All packages or standard containers of insulation, jacket material, cements, adhesives, and coatings delivered for use, and all samples have a manufacturer's stamp or label attached giving the name of the manufacturer, brand, and a description of the material.

Shop Drawings

1. It is the inspector's responsibility to determine that all insulation-related materials are approved well in advance of their actual need on the job.

2. After approval of materials and prior to insulating any pipe, the contractor will submit for approval sample insulation boards or approved standards showing his proposed methods of mechanical insulation, including cut-a-way sections, insulation, coverings, and finish of completed work. Approved sample boards will be maintained by the contractor at the job site for the duration of the work.

Ductwork Insulation

1. Distinguish between areas requiring flexible type insulation and those requiring rigid or semirigid type insulation.

2. Check the type and thickness of insulation and requirements for vapor barrier.

3. Check the method of fastening insulation to exterior or interior of duct.

a. If metal pins are used, check the type and spacing.

b. If wire is used, see that corners of insulation are protected from possible damage.

c. Verify that adhesive materials are correct, and that the area specified receives proper coverage.

4. Make a careful check for breaks in insulation and vapor barriers.

5. See that materials are fire-retardant or noncombustible as required by the specifications.

6. When equipment casings are required to be insulated, check for proper application. See that application is firm.

7. Where insulation is subject to mechanical damage, check for protection requirements.

8. Check for continuity of insulation through walls and floor, if required.

9. Check for proper sealing of insulation to diffusers, grills, and fire dampers.

Pipe Insulation

1. Determine whether the material on the job has been approved for the particular piping being installed. Make sure insulations, vapor barriers, adhesives, and sealers are noncombustible or fire retardant as specified.

2. Note that heated water piping is insulated differently from chilled water piping and from combined chilled and heated water piping.

3. Check thickness of insulation and of vapor barrier.

4. Determine if insulation jackets which are exposed to view are required to be painted.

5. Examine the requirements for the insulation of flanges, fittings, and valves, and ensure compliance with the requirements and specifications of the project.

6. Check the lap and the sealing at joints.

7. Be very careful to see that there are no breaks in the vapor barrier. Watch for later damages during construction.

8. Check specification requirements for extending through sleeves in walls, floors, and ceilings; chilled water lines.

9. Inside cabinets of fan coil units should be covered as required to prevent condensate dripping on floor.

10. Make sure that pipe hangers are installed over insulation. Metal shields to be provided between hanger ring and insulation. High-density insulation

inserts shall be installed with a length equal to length of metal shield.

11. Check for the neat termination and seal of insulation at the end of insulation.

12. Know the special requirements for insulation and jacketing of piping exposed to weather.

13. Check the installation, the width, and the spacing of the bands used on pipe jacketing.

14. In chilled-water and hot-water combination piping, check for vapor seal requirement on boiler piping.

Ducts Generally Not Requiring Insulation

- Site-erected casings and plenums constructed of factory-insulated sheet metal panels.

- Ducts shown to be acoustically lined, provided sufficient thickness of liner is specified.

- Supply and return ducts in air conditioned or heated spaces, unless otherwise shown.

- Return ducts in ceiling spaces when roofing is insulated. Ceiling space shall be defined as those spaces between the ceiling and bottom of floor deck or roof deck inside the heated space insulated envelope.

- Supply and return ducts made out of faced fiberglass insulating board. Check on sealing joints between individual duct sections, thickness, and connections.

Insulation for Rectangular and Round Ducts

1. Check flexible-type insulation used on concealed ducts for specified minimum density, usually ¾ pcf for rectangular ducts.

2. Check rigid-type insulation used on exposed ducts for specified minimum density, usually 3 pcf for rectangular ducts.

3. Check for flexible-type insulation specified for round duct, usually a minimum density ¾ pcf.

4. Check for specified vapor barrier jacket on exposed insulation, either factory applied or field applied.

5. Check specification for requirement for factory applied or field-applied vapor barrier on insulation on concealed duct.

6. Check rigid fiberglass duct installation method to ensure accessibility for maintenance of coils, vanes, and fan motors used in the HVAC duct system.

Insulation for Hot Equipment

1. Check specification to determine if insulation is required to be rigid block or semi-rigid board.

2. Check for specified type of material and thickness of insulation being installed.

3. Form or fabricate insulation to fit equipment.

4. On round equipment insulation, edges will be beveled to ensure tight joints.

5. Check joints for being tightly butted and for being filled with mineral fiber or insulation cement.

6. Check specifications and manufacturer's recommendation on spacing of bands. Spacing will not be less than 12 in. on centers.

7. Check for excessive use of wires in lieu of bands. Check for insulation corner protectors under wires.

8. Check hot ducts and equipment for specified finish.

9. Check for continuity of insulation through walls and floors.

Insulation for Cold Equipment

1. Check dual temperature equipment, which operates at 60°F or below at any time, for insulation as specified for cold equipment. Check specification for pump insulation. It may vary from flexible-, rigid-, or semirigid-type insulation. Check all other equipment for specified insulation.

2. Check insulation for thickness specified.

3. Check installation of vapor barrier.

4. Check drain pans under pumps for insulation underneath.

5. Check cold duct and equipment insulation and finish, in accordance with specifications.

Aboveground Pipe Insulation

1. Check contract specifications to determine type of insulation required on pipelines within the structure.

   a. Normally, domestic hot water, steam, condensate, hot water heating, heated oil, and water defrost lines are insulated as hot pipelines.

   b. Normally, domestic cold water, interior roof drains, refrigerant suction lines, chilled water and dual temperature water lines, air-conditioner condensate drain pipelines, exposed-to-weather drainage piping, and piping which operates at 60°F or below at any time are insulated as cold pipelines.

2. Check exterior piping for being insulated as required by specifications for piping exposed to weather.

3. Check specifications for areas which are to receive factory-applied vapor barrier jackets, field-applied aluminum jackets, and field-applied vapor barrier.

Piping Exposed to Weather

1. Check to see that pipe is insulated and jacketed for applicable service. Note that the vapor barrier is not normally specified for hot pipelines.

2. Check to see if specified jacket is aluminum.

3. Check to see if jacket is required to be factory applied or field applied.

   a. Check to see if aluminum jacket laps not less than 2 in. at all joints.

   b. Check banding requirements for the jacket.

   c. Check to see that horizontal joints are lapped downward to shed water, and that vertical joints are sealed with a waterproof coating.

4. Check specifications for special treatment of flanges, couplings, unions, valves, fittings, and anchors.

Underground Pipe Insulation

- Check all belowground domestic hot water heating, heating hot water to 200°F, dual temperature water, and chilled water piping for specified insulation. Generally the insulation is 1½-in. thick cellular glass.

Cellular Glass Insulation

1. Check to see that bore surfaces of insulation are coated with a thin application of high-strength gypsum cement, as recommended by manufacturer.

2. Check to see that insulation joints are:

   a. Staggered, one-half overlapping the next opposite half section.

   b. All joints are tightly butted and seated with bedding compound.

   c. Insulation secured with two stainless steel bands per section of insulation.

   d. Insulation termites at anchor blocks.

   e. Insulation is continuous through sleeves and manhole.

   f. Backfill around and 3 in. above the insulation to be free of stones larger than ¼ in. in any dimension.

   g. Insulation extends 2 in. inside of building interior and tightly butted, scaled, and vapor barrier coated to interior piping.

h. Check for special insulation requirements for flanges, couplings, unions, valves, and fittings.

i. Check finish of insulation for two coats of mastic with glass cloth or tape embedded between coats. Check for proper overlap at all joints.

3. Check that wet film thickness of both coats of mastic meets specification requirements.

4. Check termination points to see that mastic and cloth or tape covers the end of the insulation and extends along the base pipe as required by the specifications.

HEATING SYSTEMS
General

- This section covers material, equipment, and good workmanship practices for the installation of heating systems.

Materials and Equipment

General

1. Make sure that each piece of material and each item of equipment has been approved well in advance of its need. When the material and equipment arrive on the job, inspect them very carefully, comparing them with the approved shop drawing and samples. Check and record nameplate data on all equipment.

2. Determine that there is adequate space in the room for proper functioning and maintenance of all the equipment.

3. Reject all damaged materials and equipment and have them removed from the site.

4. Check the electrical features of equipment and coordinate with the mechanical features.

5. Determine that provisions have been made for access panels.

6. Check specification provisions for necessary spare parts and tools for all of the equipment.

7. Require proper storage and protection of all materials and equipment.

8. Check the required controls and valves for compliance with contract requirements.

9. Check the noise level of all equipment.

10. Verify requirements for the installation of flexible pipe connections and vibration eliminators for equipment.

11. Check the installation of all equipment for compliance with manufacturer's recommendations.

12. See that operations and maintenance instructions are with equipment and are posted on the wall upon completion of installation.

Boilers, Furnaces, and Accessory Equipment

1. Examine pressure boilers for conformance with the ASME Code.

2. Check for all necessary connections on the boiler.

3. Check cast iron boilers, if field assembled, for tightness of joints. All joints shall be sealed. Reject cracked sections.

4. Inspect refractory furnaces built up on the job for materials and workmanship.

   a. Require expansion joints to be provided. Piping on both sides of expansion joints should be properly guided.

   b. Ensure packing to prevent gas or air leakage.

   c. Reject all cracked, chipped or otherwise damaged brick and tile.

   d. Check plastic refractories for placement, thorough ramming, and consistency.

   e. Require refractories to be kept dry.

   f. Inspect for use of refractory mortar in construction of combustion chamber.

   g. Check for air circulation under the combustion chamber floors.

5. Inspect the application of insulation after all joints are tightly sealed. Check material, thickness, and finish.

6. Observe accessory equipment operation such as feedwater controllers, dampers, pressure and draft gages, flow and pressure recorders, soot blowers, water columns, and boiler blowdown. Check the pressurestat differential.

7. Check requirement for expansion joint in floor around the boiler.

Fuel-Burning Equipment

1. Coal, hand-fired: Verify installation of grates and operation of dumping mechanism.

2. Coal, stoker-fired: Confirm capacity and operation of feeder, grates, and ash removal.

3. Oil burners: Check

   a. Size and type of burner tips.

   b. Location of electrodes to ensure spark in oil spray cone.

   c. Position of gas or oil pilot.

   d. Clearances for removal of burner from furnace.

   e. Burner adjustments.

   f. Carbon dioxide in flue gas.

4. Inspect gas burners for cleanliness, adjustments, position of pilot flame, and sensing element. Check regulator and controls.

   a. Blow out gas line before connecting to burner or regulator.

   b. Install regulator in vertical position.

   c. Pipe gas vents to the outdoors.

Table 12-2 *Clearances for Central Furnaces*

Type	Top	Front	Back	Sides
Oil	24 in.	24 in.	12 in.	36 in.
Gas	18 in.	18 in.	12 in.	36 in.
Elect	18 in.	18 in.	24 in.	36 in.

Appliance Types

Category I   Appliances operate with a nonpositive vent connection pressure and with a flue gas temperature of at least 140°F above its dewpoint.

Category II   Appliances operate with a nonpositive vent connection pressure and with a flue gas temperature less than 140°F above its dewpoint.

Category III   Appliances operate with a positive vent pressure and with a flue gas temperature at least 140°F above its dewpoint.

Category IV   Appliances operate with a positive vent pressure and with a flue gas temperature less than 140°F above its dewpoint.

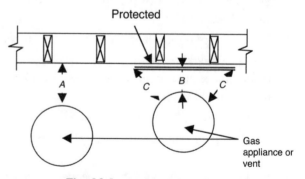

Fig. 12-1 *Appliance installations.*

A is equal to clearance allowed with no protection.
B is the "reduced clearance" as shown in Table 12-3.
C is the distance the protective method must extend and equals the original unprotected distance *A*.

Types of Protection(s)

1. 3.5-in.-thick masonry without air space.

2. 0.5-in.-thick insulation board over 1-in. glass fiber or mineral wool.

3. 0.024-in.-thick sheet metal over 1-in. glass fiber or mineral wool reinforced with wire on the rear face and with a ventilated air space. (Spacers are to be noncombustionable and not located directly behind the appliance or vent.)

4. 3.5-in.-thick masonry with air space.

5. 0.024-in.-thick sheet metal with ventilating air space (at least 1-in. ventilating air space).

6. 0.5-in.-thick insulation board with at least 1-in. air space.

7. 0.024-in. sheet metal with 1-in. air space over additional 0.024 piece of sheet metal.

8. 1-in. glass fiber or mineral wool sandwiched between two sheets of 0.024-in.-thick sheet metal with ventilating air space.

Note: Mineral wool batts are to have a density of 8 lb/ft^3 and a minimum melting point of 1500°F (816°C).

Table 12-3 *Approved Reductions in Clearances as per Type of Protection Used*

Type of Protection	Above (in.)	Sides and Rear (in.)
0	N/A	24
1	24	18
2	18	12
3	N/A	12
4	18	12
5	18	12
6	18	12
7	18	12

Original required clearance is 36 in.

Type of Protection	Above (in.)	Sides and Rear (in.)
0	N/A	12
1	12	9
2	9	6
3	N/A	6
4	9	6
5	9	6
6	9	6
7	9	6

Original required clearance is 18 in.

Table 12-3 *(Continued)*

Type of Protection	Above (in.)	Sides and Rear (in.)
0	N/A	9
1	9	6
2	6	4
3	N/A	6
4	6	4
5	6	4
6	6	4
7	6	4

Original required clearance is 12 in.

Type of Protection	Above (in.)	Sides and Rear (in.)
0	N/A	6
1	6	5
2	5	3
3	N/A	6
4	5	3
5	5	3
6	5	3
7	5	3

Original required clearance is 9 in.

Type of Protection	Above (in.)	Sides and Rear (in.)
0	N/A	5
1	4	3
2	3	3
3	N/A	6
4	3	2
5	3	3
6	3	3
7	3	3

Original required clearance is 6 in.

VENTING GAS APPLIANCES

Vents that pass through insulation require a shield of at least 26-gage sheet metal. In attics the shield is to extend at least 2 in. above the level of insulation. Mechanical draft vents must be at least 7 ft above grade if located adjacent to public walkways.

Masonry Chimneys

1. Chimneys are to be lined with approved clay flue lining, a listed liner, or other approved material that will resist corrosion, erosion, and weakening from the vent gases at temperatures up to 1800°F.

2. If liners are installed in existing chimney structures (Type B), then the connection must be marked not to

Heat Pumps Cooling Mode		
Size	**Type**	**Minimum Efficiency**
Less than 65,000 Btu/h	Split system	10.0 SEER
	Single package	9.7 SEER
65,000 Btu/h to less than 135,000 Btu/h	Split system and single package	8.9 EER
135,000 Btu/h to less than 240,000 Btu/h	Split system and single package	8.5 EER
240,000 Btu/h to less than 760,000 Btu/h	Split system and single package	8.5 EER
Less than 760,000 Btu/h	Split system and single package	8.2 EER

Heat Pumps Heating Mode		
Size	**Type**	**Minimum Efficiency**
Less than 65,000 Btu/h	Split system	6.8 HSPF
	Single package	6.6 HSPF
65,000 Btu/h to less than 135,000 Btu/h	47°F db/43°F db	3.0 COP
	17°F db/15°F db	2.0 COP
135,000 Btu/h to less than 240,000 Btu/h	47°F db/43°F db	2.9 COP
	17°F db/15°F db	2.0 COP
More than 240,000 Btu/h	47°F db/43°F db	2.9 COP

allow any solid or liquid burning appliances to be attached.

3. Chimneys are to extend at least 5 ft above the highest connected equipment draft hood outlet or flue collar.

4. Sizing of chimneys:

   a. The effective area of a chimney serving listed appliances with draft hoods: Category I appliances listed for use with Type B vents are to be sized using the tables located in the Vent and Connector Tables section of this chapter.

   b. An exception to using these tables for sizing a single appliance with a draft hood is that the vent connector and chimney flue will have an area not less than the appliance flue collar or draft hood and not greater than seven times the draft hood outlet.

   c. When two appliances with draft hoods are connected, then the flue area must be the same as the largest appliance outlet plus 50% of the smaller appliance outlets and not greater than 7 times the smaller draft hood outlet.

Example:

Largest outlet + 50% of smallest < chimney flue size < 7 × smallest

5. Chimneys previously used for liquid or solid fuels and now using fuel gas must have a cleanout. It is to be located so that its upper edge is 6 in. below the lowest edge of the lowest inlet opening.

6. Offsets of Type B or Type L are not to exceed 45° from the vertical—one angle must not exceed 60°. The horizontal distance of a vent plus the connector vent shall not exceed 75% of the vertical height of the vent.

Chimney Dampers

Where an unlisted decorative appliance is installed in a vented fireplace, the damper must have a permanent free opening equal to or greater than those listed in Table 12-5.

Table 12-5 *Damper Open Area from Unlisted Decorative Appliances*

Minimum Permanent Free Opening	Chimney Height (ft)		
	6	**8**	**10**
8	7800	8400	9000
13	14000	15200	16800
20	23200	25200	27600
29	34000	37000	40400
39	46400	50400	55800
51	62400	68000	74400
64	80000	86000	96400

Table 12-5 (Continued)

Minimum Permanent Free Opening	Chimney Height (ft)		
	15	20	30
8	9800	10600	11200
13	18200	20200	21600
20	30200	32600	36600
29	44600	50400	55200
39	62400	68400	76800
51	84000	94000	105800
64	108800	122200	138600

Table 12-6 Flue Liner Sizes

Nominal Liner Size	Inside Liner Dimensions	Circular Equivalent	
		in.	in.^{2}
4 × 8	2½ × 6½	4	12.2
		5	19.6
		6	28.3
		7	38.3
8 × 8	6¾ × 6¾	7.4	42.7
		8	50.3
8 × 12	6½ × 10½	9	63.6
		10	78.5
12 × 12	9¾ × 9¾	10.4	83.3
		11	95
12 × 16	9½ × 13½	11.8	107.5
		12	113.0
		14	153.9
16 × 16	13¼ × 13¼	14.5	162.9
		15	176.7
16 × 20	13 × 17	16.2	206.1
		18	254.4
20 × 20	16¾ × 16¾	18.2	260.2
		20	314.1
20 × 24	16½ × 20½	20.1	314.2
		22	380.1
24 × 24	20¼ × 20¼	22.1	380.1
		24	452.3

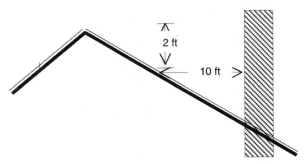

Fig. 12-2 *Roof terminations for chimneys and single wall vents (no caps).*

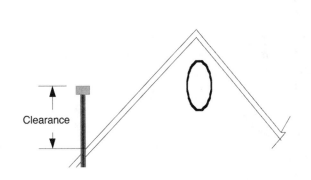

Roof Slope	Clearance
Flat–6/12	1 ft–0 in.
6/12–7/12	1 ft–3 in.
7/12–8/12	1 ft–6 in.
8/12–9/12	1 ft–0 in.
9/12–10/12	2 ft–6 in.
10/12–11/12	3 ft–3 in.
11/12–12/12	4 ft–0 in.

Fig. 12-3 *Gas vent terminations for listed vent caps (12 in. or less in diameter and 8 ft from vertical walls).*

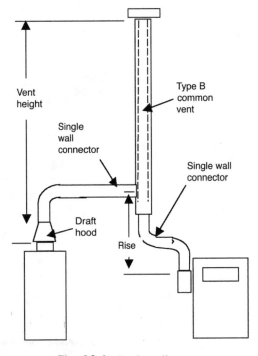

Fig. 12-4 *Single wall vent.*

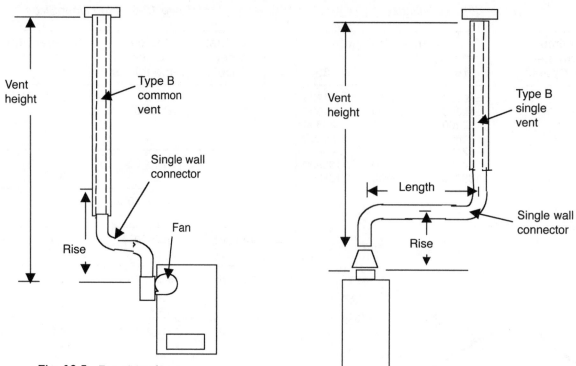

Fig. 12-5 *Fan-assisted vent.*

Fig. 12-6 *Single wall connector.*

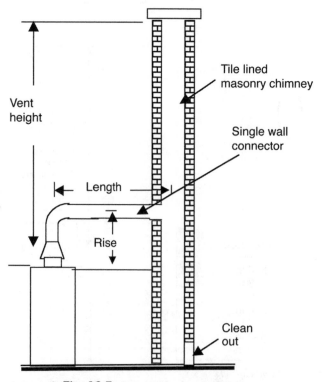

Fig. 12-7 *Vents with masonry chimney.*

Vent and Connector Tables

Table 12-7 *Capacity of Type B Double-Wall Gas Vents When Connected Directly to a Single Category I Appliance*

Height H (ft)	Lateral L (ft)	Vent Diameter D (in.)								
		3			4			5		
		Appliance Input Rating in Thousands of Btu/h								
		FAN		NAT	FAN		NAT	FAN		NAT
		Min	Max	Max	Min	Max	Max	Min	Max	Max
6	0	0	78	46	0	152	86	0	251	141
	2	13	51	36	18	97	67	27	157	105
	4	21	49	34	30	94	64	39	153	103
	6	25	46	32	36	91	61	47	149	100
8	0	0	84	50	0	165	94	0	276	155
	2	12	57	40	16	109	75	25	178	120
	5	23	53	38	32	103	71	42	171	115
	8	28	49	35	39	98	66	51	164	109
10	0	0	88	53	0	175	100	0	295	166
	2	12	61	42	17	118	81	23	194	129
	5	23	57	40	32	113	77	41	187	124
	10	30	51	36	41	104	70	54	176	115
15	0	0	94	58	0	191	112	0	327	187
	2	11	69	48	15	136	93	20	226	150
	5	22	65	45	30	130	87	39	219	142
	10	29	59	41	40	121	82	51	206	135
	15	35	53	37	48	112	76	61	195	128
20	0	0	97	61	0	202	119	0	349	202
	2	10	75	51	14	149	100	18	250	166
	5	21	71	48	29	143	96	38	242	160
	10	28	64	44	38	133	89	50	229	150
	15	34	58	40	46	124	84	59	217	142
	20	48	52	35	55	116	78	69	206	134
30	0	0	100	64	0	213	128	0	374	220
	2	9	81	56	13	166	112	14	283	185
	5	21	77	54	28	160	108	36	275	176
	10	27	70	50	37	150	102	48	262	171
	15	33	64	NA	44	141	96	57	249	163
	20	56	58	NA	53	132	90	66	237	154
	30	NA	NA	NA	73	113	NA	88	214	NA
50	0	0	101	67	0	216	134	0	397	232
	2	8	86	61	11	183	122	14	320	206
	5	20	82	NA	27	177	119	35	312	200
	10	26	76	NA	35	168	114	45	299	190
	15	59	70	NA	42	158	NA	54	287	180
	20	NA	NA	NA	50	149	NA	63	275	169
	30	NA	NA	NA	69	131	NA	84	250	NA

(continued)

Table 12-7 *(Continued)*

Height H (ft)	Lateral L (ft)	Vent Diameter D (in.)							
		6			7			8	
		Appliance Input Rating in Thousands of Btu/h							
		FAN		NAT	FAN		NAT	FAN		NAT
		Min	Max	Max	Min	Max	Max	Min	Max	Max
6	0	0	375	205	0	524	285	0	698	370
	2	32	232	157	44	321	217	53	425	285
	4	50	227	153	66	316	211	79	419	279
	6	59	223	149	78	310	205	93	413	273
8	0	0	415	235	0	583	320	0	780	415
	2	28	263	180	42	365	247	10	483	322
	5	53	255	173	70	356	237	83	473	313
	8	64	247	165	84	347	227	99	463	303
10	0	0	447	255	0	631	345	0	847	450
	2	26	289	195	40	402	273	48	533	355
	5	52	280	188	68	392	263	81	522	346
	10	67	267	175	88	376	245	104	504	330
15	0	0	502	285	0	716	390	0	970	525
	2	22	339	225	38	475	316	45	633	414
	5	49	330	217	64	463	300	76	620	403
	10	64	315	208	84	445	288	99	600	386
	15	76	301	198	98	429	275	115	580	373
20	0	0	540	307	0	776	430	0	1057	575
	2	20	377	249	33	531	346	41	711	470
	5	47	367	241	62	519	337	73	697	460
	10	62	351	228	81	499	321	95	675	443
	15	73	337	217	94	481	308	111	654	427
	20	84	322	206	107	464	295	125	634	410
30	0	0	587	336	0	853	475	0	1173	650
	2	18	432	280	27	613	394	33	826	535
	5	45	421	273	58	600	385	69	811	524
	10	59	405	261	77	580	371	91	788	507
	15	70	389	249	90	560	357	105	765	490
	20	80	374	237	102	542	343	119	743	473
	30	104	346	219	131	507	321	149	702	444
50	0	0	633	363	0	932	518	0	1297	708
	2	15	497	314	22	715	445	26	975	615
	5	43	487	308	55	702	438	65	960	605
	10	56	471	298	73	681	426	86	935	589
	15	66	455	288	85	662	413	100	911	572
	20	76	440	278	97	642	401	113	888	556
	30	99	410	259	123	605	376	141	844	522

Table 12-8 *Capacity of Type B Double-Wall Vents with Single-Wall Metal Connectors Serving a Single Category I Appliance*

Height H (ft)	Lateral L (ft)	Vent Diameter D (in.)									
		3			4			5			6	
		Appliance Input Rating in Thousands of Btu/h										
		FAN		NAT	FAN		NAT	FAN		NAT	FAN		NAT
		Min	Max	Max	Min	Max	Max	Min	Max	Max	Min	Max	Max
6	0	38	77	45	59	151	85	85	249	140	126	373	204
	2	39	51	36	60	96	66	85	156	104	123	231	156
	4	NA	NA	33	74	92	63	102	152	102	146	225	152
	6	NA	NA	31	83	89	60	114	147	99	163	220	148
8	0	37	83	50	58	164	93	83	273	154	123	412	234
	2	39	56	39	59	108	75	83	176	119	121	261	179
	5	NA	NA	37	77	102	69	107	168	114	151	252	171
	8	NA	NA	33	90	95	64	122	161	107	175	243	163
10	0	37	87	53	57	174	99	82	293	165	120	444	254
	2	39	61	41	59	117	80	82	193	128	119	287	194
	5	52	56	39	76	111	76	105	185	122	148	277	186
	10	NA	NA	34	97	100	68	132	171	112	188	261	171
15	0	36	93	57	56	190	111	80	325	186	116	499	283
	2	38	69	47	57	136	93	80	225	149	115	337	224
	5	51	63	44	75	128	86	102	216	140	144	326	217
	10	NA	NA	39	95	116	79	128	201	131	182	308	203
	15	NA	NA	NA	NA	NA	72	158	186	124	220	290	192
20	0	35	96	60	54	200	118	78	346	201	114	537	306
	2	37	74	50	56	148	99	78	248	165	113	375	248
	5	50	68	47	73	140	94	100	239	158	141	363	239
	10	NA	NA	41	93	129	86	125	223	146	177	344	224
	15	NA	NA	NA	NA	NA	80	155	208	136	216	325	210
	20	NA	NA	NA	NA	NA	NA	186	192	126	254	306	196
30	0	34	99	63	53	211	127	76	372	219	110	584	334
	2	37	80	56	55	164	111	76	281	183	109	429	279
	5	49	74	52	72	157	106	98	271	173	136	417	271
	10	NA	NA	NA	91	144	98	122	255	168	171	397	257
	15	NA	NA	NA	115	131	NA	151	239	157	208	377	242
	20	NA	NA	NA	NA	NA	NA	181	223	NA	246	357	228
	30	NA	NA	NA	NA	NA	NA	NA	NA	NA	NA	NA	NA
50	0	33	99	66	51	213	133	73	394	230	105	629	361
	2	36	84	61	53	181	121	73	318	205	104	495	312
	5	48	80	NA	70	174	117	94	308	198	131	482	305
	10	NA	NA	NA	89	160	NA	118	292	186	162	461	292
	15	NA	NA	NA	112	148	NA	145	275	174	199	441	280
	20	NA	NA	NA	NA	NA	NA	176	257	NA	236	420	267
	30	NA	NA	NA	NA	NA	NA	NA	NA	NA	315	376	NA

(continued)

Table 12-8 (Continued)

Height H (ft)	Lateral L (ft)	Vent Diameter D (in.)											
		7			8			9			10		
		Appliance Input Rating in Thousands of Btu/h											
		FAN		NAT	FAN		NAT	FAN		NAT	FAN		NAT
		Min	Max	Max	Min	Max	Max	Min	Max	Max	Min	Max	Max
6	0	165	522	284	211	695	369	267	894	469	371	1,118	569
	2	159	320	213	201	423	284	251	541	368	347	673	453
	4	187	313	208	237	416	277	295	533	360	409	664	443
	6	207	307	203	263	409	271	327	526	352	449	656	433
8	0	161	580	319	206	777	414	258	1,002	536	360	1,257	658
	2	155	363	246	197	482	321	246	617	417	339	768	513
	5	193	352	235	245	470	311	305	604	404	418	754	500
	8	223	342	225	280	458	300	344	591	392	470	740	486
10	0	158	628	344	202	844	449	253	1,093	584	351	1,373	718
	2	153	400	272	193	531	354	242	681	456	332	849	559
	5	190	388	261	241	518	344	299	667	443	409	834	544
	10	237	369	241	296	497	325	363	643	423	492	808	520
15	0	153	713	388	195	966	523	244	1,259	681	336	1,591	838
	2	148	473	314	187	631	413	232	812	543	319	1,015	673
	5	182	459	298	231	616	400	287	795	526	392	997	657
	10	228	438	284	284	592	381	349	768	501	470	966	628
	15	272	418	269	334	568	367	404	742	484	540	937	601
20	0	149	772	428	190	1,053	573	238	1,379	750	326	1,751	927
	2	144	528	344	182	708	468	227	914	611	309	1,146	754
	5	178	514	334	224	692	457	279	896	596	381	1,126	734
	10	222	491	316	277	666	437	339	866	570	457	1,092	702
	15	264	469	301	325	640	419	393	838	549	526	1,060	677
	20	309	448	285	374	616	400	448	810	526	592	1,028	651
30	0	144	849	472	184	1,168	647	229	1,542	852	312	1,971	1056
	2	139	610	392	175	823	533	219	1,069	698	296	1,346	863
	5	171	595	382	215	806	521	269	1,049	684	366	1,324	846
	10	213	570	367	265	777	501	327	1,017	662	440	1,287	821
	15	255	547	349	312	750	481	379	985	638	507	1,251	794
	20	298	524	333	360	723	461	433	955	615	570	1,216	768
	30	389	477	305	461	670	426	541	895	574	704	1,147	720
50	0	138	928	515	176	1,292	704	220	1,724	948	295	2,223	1,189
	2	133	712	443	168	971	613	209	1,273	811	280	1,615	1,007
	5	164	696	435	204	953	602	257	1,252	795	347	1,591	991
	10	203	671	420	253	923	583	313	1,217	765	418	1,551	963
	15	244	646	405	299	894	562	363	1,183	736	481	1,512	934
	20	285	622	389	345	866	543	415	1,150	708	544	1,473	906
	30	373	573	NA	442	809	502	521	1,086	649	674	1,399	848

Table 12-9 *Vent Connector Capacity of Type B Double-Wall Vents with Type B Double-Wall Connectors Serving Two or More Category I Appliances*

Vent Height H (ft)	Connector Rise R (ft)	Type B Double-Wall Vent and Connector Diameter D (in.)											
		3			4			5			6		
		Appliance Input Rating in Thousands of Btu/h											
		FAN		NAT	FAN		NAT	FAN		NAT	FAN		NAT
		Min	Max	Max	Min	Max	Max	Min	Max	Max	Min	Max	Max
6	1	22	37	26	35	66	46	46	106	72	58	164	104
	2	23	41	31	37	75	55	48	121	86	60	183	124
	3	24	44	35	38	81	62	49	132	96	62	199	139
8	1	22	40	27	35	72	48	49	114	76	64	176	109
	2	23	44	32	36	80	57	51	128	90	66	195	129
	3	24	47	36	37	87	64	53	139	101	67	210	145
10	1	22	43	28	34	78	50	49	123	78	65	189	113
	2	23	47	33	36	86	59	51	136	93	67	206	134
	3	24	50	37	37	92	67	52	146	104	69	220	150
15	1	21	50	30	33	89	53	47	142	83	64	220	120
	2	22	53	35	35	96	63	49	153	99	66	235	142
	3	24	55	40	36	102	71	51	163	111	68	248	160
20	1	21	54	31	33	99	56	46	157	87	62	246	125
	2	22	57	37	34	105	66	48	167	104	64	259	149
	3	23	60	42	35	110	74	50	176	116	66	271	168
30	1	20	62	33	31	113	59	45	181	93	60	288	134
	2	21	64	39	33	118	70	47	190	110	62	299	158
	3	22	66	44	34	123	79	48	198	124	64	309	178
50	1	19	71	36	30	133	64	43	216	101	57	349	145
	2	21	73	43	32	137	76	45	223	119	59	358	172
	3	22	75	48	33	141	86	46	229	134	61	366	194

(continued)

Table 12-9 *(Continued)*

Vent Height H (ft)	Connector Rise R (ft)	Type B Double-Wall Vent and Connector Diameter D (in.)											
		7			8			9			10		
		Appliance Input Rating in Thousands of Btu/h											
		FAN		NAT	FAN		NAT	FAN		NAT	FAN		NAT
		Min	Max	Max	Min	Max	Max	Min	Max	Max	Min	Max	Max
6	1	77	225	142	92	296	185	109	376	237	128	466	289
	2	79	253	168	95	333	220	112	424	282	131	526	345
	3	82	275	189	97	363	248	114	463	317	134	575	386
8	1	84	243	148	100	320	194	118	408	248	138	507	303
	2	86	269	175	103	356	230	121	454	294	141	564	358
	3	88	290	198	105	384	258	123	492	330	143	612	402
10	1	89	257	154	106	341	200	125	436	257	146	542	314
	2	91	282	182	109	374	238	128	479	305	149	596	372
	3	94	303	205	111	402	268	131	515	342	152	642	417
15	1	88	298	163	110	389	214	134	493	273	162	609	333
	2	91	320	193	112	419	253	137	532	323	165	658	394
	3	93	339	218	115	445	286	140	565	365	167	700	444
20	1	86	334	171	107	436	224	131	552	285	158	681	347
	2	89	354	202	110	463	265	134	587	339	161	725	414
	3	91	371	228	113	486	300	137	618	383	164	764	466
30	1	83	391	182	103	512	238	125	649	305	151	802	372
	2	85	408	215	105	535	282	129	679	360	155	840	439
	3	88	423	242	108	555	317	132	706	405	158	874	494
50	1	78	477	197	97	627	257	120	797	330	144	984	403
	2	81	490	234	100	645	306	123	820	392	148	1014	478
	3	83	502	263	103	661	343	126	842	441	151	1043	538

Table 12-10 *Common Vent Capacity of Type B Double-Wall Vents with Type B Double-Wall Connectors Serving Two or More Category I Appliances*

Vent Height H (ft)	Type B Double-Wall Common Vent Diameter D (in.)								
	4			5			6		
	Combined Appliance Input Rating in Thousands of Btu/h								
	FAN +FAN	FAN +NAT	NAT +NAT	FAN +FAN	FAN +NAT	NAT +NAT	FAN +FAN	FAN +NAT	NAT +NAT
6	92	81	65	140	116	103	204	161	147
8	101	90	73	155	129	114	224	178	163
10	110	97	79	169	141	124	243	194	178
15	125	112	91	195	164	144	283	228	206
20	136	123	102	215	183	160	314	255	229
30	152	138	118	244	210	185	361	297	266
50	167	153	134	279	244	214	421	353	310

Vent Height H (ft)	Type B Double-Wall Common Vent Diameter D (in.)								
	7			8			9		
	Combined Appliance Input Rating in Thousands of Btu/h								
	FAN +FAN	FAN +NAT	NAT +NAT	FAN +FAN	FAN +NAT	NAT +NAT	FAN +FAN	FAN +NAT	NAT +NAT
6	309	248	200	404	314	260	547	434	335
8	339	275	223	444	348	290	602	480	378
10	367	299	242	477	377	315	649	522	405
15	427	352	280	556	444	365	753	612	465
20	475	394	310	621	499	405	842	688	523
30	547	459	360	720	585	470	979	808	605
50	641	547	423	854	706	550	1164	977	705

Table 12-11 *Vent Connector Capacity of Type B Double-Wall Vent with Single-Wall Connectors Serving Two or More Category I Appliances*

Vent Height H (ft)	Connector Rise R (ft)	Single-Wall Metal Vent Connector Diameter D (in.)											
		3			4			5			6		
		Appliance Input Rating in Thousands of Btu/h											
		FAN		NAT	FAN		NAT	FAN		NAT	FAN		NAT
		Min	Max	Max	Min	Max	Max	Min	Max	Max	Min	Max	Max
6	1	NA	NA	26	NA	NA	46	NA	NA	71	NA	NA	102
	2	NA	NA	31	NA	NA	55	NA	NA	85	168	182	123
	3	NA	NA	34	NA	NA	62	121	131	95	175	198	138
8	1	NA	NA	27	NA	NA	48	NA	NA	75	NA	NA	106
	2	NA	NA	32	NA	NA	57	125	126	89	184	193	127
	3	NA	NA	35	NA	NA	64	130	138	100	191	208	144
10	1	NA	NA	28	NA	NA	50	119	121	77	182	186	110
	2	NA	NA	33	84	85	59	124	134	91	189	203	132
	3	NA	NA	36	89	91	67	129	144	102	197	217	148
15	1	NA	NA	29	79	87	52	116	138	81	177	214	116
	2	NA	NA	34	83	94	62	121	150	97	185	230	138
	3	NA	NA	39	87	100	70	127	160	109	193	243	157
20	1	49	56	30	78	97	54	115	152	84	175	238	120
	2	52	59	36	82	103	64	120	163	101	182	252	144
	3	55	62	40	87	107	72	125	172	113	190	264	164
30	1	47	60	31	77	110	57	112	175	89	169	278	129
	2	51	62	37	81	115	67	117	185	106	177	290	152
	3	54	64	42	85	119	76	122	193	120	185	300	172
50	1	46	69	34	75	128	60	109	207	96	162	336	137
	2	49	71	40	79	132	72	114	215	113	170	345	164
	3	52	72	45	83	136	82	119	221	123	178	353	186

Table 12-11 *(Continued)*

Vent Height H (ft)	Connector Rise R (ft)	Single-Wall Metal Vent Connector Diameter D (in.)										
		7			8			9			10		
		Appliance Input Rating in Thousands of Btu/h											
		FAN		NAT	FAN		NAT	FAN		NAT	FAN		NAT
		Min	Max	Max	Min	Max	Max	Min	Max	Max	Min	Max	Max
6	1	207	223	140	262	293	183	325	373	234	447	463	286
	2	215	251	167	271	331	219	334	422	281	458	524	344
	3	222	273	188	279	361	247	344	462	316	468	574	385
8	1	226	240	145	285	316	191	352	403	244	481	502	299
	2	234	266	173	293	353	228	360	450	292	492	560	355
	3	241	287	197	302	381	256	370	489	328	501	609	400
10	1	240	253	150	302	335	196	372	429	252	506	534	308
	2	248	278	183	311	369	235	381	473	302	517	589	368
	3	257	299	203	320	398	265	391	511	339	528	637	413
15	1	238	291	158	312	380	208	397	482	266	556	596	324
	2	246	314	189	321	411	248	407	522	317	568	646	387
	3	255	333	215	331	438	281	418	557	360	579	690	437
20	1	233	325	165	306	425	217	390	538	276	546	664	336
	2	243	346	197	317	453	259	400	574	331	558	709	403
	3	252	363	223	326	476	294	412	607	375	570	750	457
30	1	226	380	175	296	497	230	378	630	294	528	779	358
	2	236	397	208	307	521	274	389	662	349	541	819	425
	3	244	412	235	316	542	309	400	690	394	555	855	482
50	1	217	460	188	284	604	245	364	768	314	507	951	384
	2	226	473	223	294	623	293	376	793	375	520	983	458
	3	235	486	252	304	640	331	387	816	423	535	1013	518

Table 12-12 *Common Vent Capacity of Type B Double-Wall Vent with Single-Wall Connectors Serving Two or More Category I Appliances*

Vent Height H (ft)	Type B Double-Wall Common Vent Diameter D (in.)								
	4			5			6		
	Combined Appliance Input Rating in Thousands of Btu/h								
	FAN +FAN	FAN +NAT	NAT +NAT	FAN +FAN	FAN +NAT	NAT +NAT	FAN +FAN	FAN +NAT	NAT +NAT
6	NA	78	64	NA	113	99	200	158	144
8	NA	87	71	NA	126	111	218	173	159
10	NA	94	76	163	137	120	237	189	174
15	121	108	88	189	159	140	275	221	200
20	131	118	98	208	177	156	305	247	223
30	145	132	113	236	202	180	350	286	257
50	159	145	128	268	233	208	406	337	296

Vent Height H (ft)	Type B Double-Wall Common Vent Diameter D (in.)								
	7			8			9		
	Combined Appliance Input Rating in Thousands of Btu/h								
	FAN +FAN	FAN +NAT	NAT +NAT	FAN +FAN	FAN +NAT	NAT +NAT	FAN +FAN	FAN +NAT	NAT +NAT
6	304	244	196	398	310	257	541	429	332
8	331	269	218	436	342	285	592	473	373
10	357	292	236	467	369	309	638	512	398
15	416	343	274	544	434	357	738	599	456
20	463	383	302	606	487	395	824	673	512
30	533	446	349	703	570	459	958	790	593
50	622	529	410	833	686	535	1139	954	689

Table 12-13 *Vent Connector Capacity of Masonry Chimney with Type B Double-Wall Connectors Serving Two or More Category I Appliances*

Vent Height H (ft)	Connector Rise R (ft)	Type B Double-Wall Vent Connector Diameter D (in.)									
		3			4			5			6		
		Appliance Input Rating in Thousands of Btu/h											
		FAN		NAT	FAN		NAT	FAN		NAT	FAN		NAT
		Min	Max	Max	Min	Max	Max	Min	Max	Max	Min	Max	Max
6	1	24	33	21	39	62	40	52	106	67	65	194	101
	2	26	43	28	41	79	52	53	133	85	67	230	124
	3	27	49	34	42	92	61	55	155	97	69	262	143
8	1	24	39	22	39	72	41	55	117	69	71	213	105
	2	26	47	29	40	87	53	57	140	86	73	246	127
	3	27	52	34	42	97	62	59	159	98	75	269	145
10	1	24	42	22	38	80	42	55	130	71	74	232	108
	2	26	50	29	40	93	54	57	153	87	76	261	129
	3	27	55	35	41	105	63	58	170	100	78	284	148
15	1	24	48	23	38	93	44	54	154	74	72	277	114
	2	25	55	31	39	105	55	56	174	89	74	299	134
	3	26	59	35	41	115	64	57	189	102	76	319	153
20	1	24	52	24	37	102	46	53	172	77	71	313	119
	2	25	58	31	39	114	56	55	190	91	73	335	138
	3	26	63	35	40	123	65	57	204	104	75	353	157
30	1	24	54	25	37	111	48	52	192	82	69	357	127
	2	25	60	32	38	122	58	54	208	95	72	376	145
	3	26	64	36	40	131	66	56	221	107	74	392	163
50	1	23	51	25	36	116	51	51	209	89	67	405	143
	2	24	59	32	37	127	61	53	225	102	70	421	161
	3	26	64	36	39	135	69	55	237	115	72	435	180

(continued)

Table 12-13 *(Continued)*

Vent Height H (ft)	Connector Rise R (ft)	Type B Double-Wall Vent Connector Diameter D (in.)										
		7			**8**			**9**			**10**		
		Appliance Input Rating in Thousands of Btu/h											
		FAN		NAT	FAN		NAT	FAN		NAT	FAN		NAT
		Min	Max	Max	Min	Max	Max	Min	Max	Max	Min	Max	Max
6	1	87	274	141	104	370	201	124	479	253	145	599	319
	2	89	324	173	107	436	232	127	562	300	148	694	378
	3	91	369	203	109	491	270	129	633	349	151	795	439
8	1	94	304	148	113	414	210	134	539	267	156	682	335
	2	97	350	179	116	473	240	137	615	311	160	776	394
	3	99	383	206	119	517	276	139	672	358	163	848	452
10	1	101	324	153	120	444	216	142	582	277	165	739	348
	2	103	366	184	123	498	247	145	652	321	168	825	407
	3	106	397	209	126	540	281	147	705	366	171	893	463
15	1	100	384	164	125	511	229	153	658	297	184	824	37
	2	103	419	192	128	558	260	156	718	339	187	900	432
	3	105	448	215	131	597	292	159	760	382	190	960	486
20	1	98	437	173	123	584	239	150	752	312	180	943	397
	2	101	467	199	126	625	270	153	805	354	184	1011	452
	3	104	493	222	129	661	301	156	851	396	187	1067	505
30	1	96	504	187	119	680	255	145	883	337	175	1,115	432
	2	99	531	209	122	715	287	149	928	378	179	1,171	484
	3	101	554	233	125	746	317	152	968	418	182	1,220	535
50	1	92	582	213	115	798	294	140	1,049	392	168	1,334	506
	2	95	604	235	118	827	326	143	1,085	433	172	1,379	558
	3	98	624	260	121	854	357	147	1,118	474	176	1.421	611

Table 12-14 *Common Vent Connector Capacity of Masonry Chimney with Type B Double-Wall Connectors Serving Two or More Category I Appliances*

Vent Height H (ft)	Minimum Internal Area of Masonry Chimney Flue (sq. in.)											
	12			19			28			38		
	Combined Appliance Input Rating in Thousands of Btu/h											
	FAN +FAN	FAN +FAN	NAT +NAT	FAN +FAN	FAN +FAN	NAT +NAT	FAN +FAN	FAN +FAN	NAT +NAT	FAN +FAN	FAN +FAN	NAT +NAT
6	NA	74	25	NA	119	46	NA	178	71	NA	257	103
8	NA	80	28	NA	130	53	NA	193	82	NA	279	119
10	NA	84	31	NA	138	56	NA	207	90	NA	299	131
15	NA	NA	36	NA	152	67	NA	233	106	NA	334	152
20	NA	NA	41	NA	NA	75	NA	250	122	NA	368	172
30	NA	NA	NA	NA	NA	NA	NA	270	137	NA	404	198
50	NA	NA	NA	NA	NA	NA	NA	NA	NA	NA	NA	NA

Vent Height H (ft)	Minimum Internal Area of Masonry Chimney Flue (sq. in.)											
	50			63			78			113		
	Combined Appliance Input Rating in Thousands of Btu/h											
	FAN +FAN	FAN +FAN	NAT +NAT	FAN +FAN	FAN +FAN	NAT +NAT	FAN +FAN	FAN +FAN	NAT +NAT	FAN +FAN	FAN +FAN	NAT +NAT
6	NA	351	143	NA	458	188	NA	582	246	1,041	853	NA
8	NA	384	163	NA	501	218	724	636	278	1,144	937	408
10	NA	409	177	606	538	236	776	686	302	1,226	1,010	454
15	523	467	212	682	611	283	874	781	365	1,374	1,156	546
20	565	508	243	742	668	325	955	858	419	1,513	1,286	648
30	615	564	278	816	747	381	1,062	969	496	1,702	1.473	749
50	NA	620	328	879	831	461	1,165	1,089	606	1,905	1,692	922

Table 12-15 *Vent Connector Capacity of Masonry Chimney with Single-Wall Connectors Serving Two or More Category I Appliances*

Vent Height H (ft)	Connector Rise R (ft)	Type B Double-Wall Vent Connector Diameter D (in.)											
		3			4			5			6		
		Appliance Input Rating in Thousands of Btu/h											
		FAN		NAT	FAN		NAT	FAN		NAT	FAN		NAT
		Min	Max	Max	Min	Max	Max	Min	Max	Max	Min	Max	Max
6	1	NA	NA	21	NA	NA	39	NA	NA	66	179	191	100
	2	NA	NA	28	NA	NA	52	NA	NA	84	186	227	123
	3	NA	NA	34	NA	NA	61	134	153	97	193	258	142
8	1	NA	NA	21	NA	NA	40	NA	NA	68	195	208	103
	2	NA	NA	28	NA	NA	52	137	139	85	202	240	125
	3	NA	NA	34	NA	NA	62	143	156	98	210	264	145
10	1	NA	NA	22	NA	NA	41	130	151	70	202	225	106
	2	NA	NA	29	NA	NA	53	136	150	86	210	255	128
	3	NA	NA	34	97	102	62	143	166	99	217	277	147
15	1	NA	NA	23	NA	NA	43	129	151	73	199	271	112
	2	NA	NA	30	92	103	54	135	170	88	207	295	132
	3	NA	NA	34	96	112	63	141	185	101	215	315	151
20	1	NA	NA	23	87	99	45	128	167	76	197	303	117
	2	NA	NA	30	91	111	55	134	185	90	205	325	136
	3	NA	NA	35	96	119	64	140	199	103	213	343	154
30	1	NA	NA	24	86	108	47	126	187	80	193	347	124
	2	NA	NA	31	91	119	57	132	203	93	201	366	142
	3	NA	NA	35	95	127	65	138	216	105	209	381	160
50	1	NA	NA	24	85	113	50	124	204	87	188	392	139
	2	NA	NA	31	89	123	60	130	218	100	196	408	158
	3	NA	NA	35	94	131	68	136	231	112	205	422	176

Table 12-15 (Continued)

Vent Height H (ft)	Connector Rise R (ft)	Type B Double-Wall Vent Connector Diameter D (in.)											
		7			8			9			10		
		Appliance Input Rating in Thousands of Btu/h											
		FAN		NAT	FAN		NAT	FAN		NAT	FAN		NAT
		Min	Max	Max	Min	Max	Max	Min	Max	Max	Min	Max	Max
6	1	231	271	140	292	366	200	362	474	252	499	594	316
	2	239	321	172	301	432	231	373	557	299	509	696	376
	3	247	365	202	309	491	269	381	634	348	519	793	437
8	1	250	298	146	313	407	207	387	530	263	529	672	331
	2	258	343	177	323	465	238	397	607	309	540	766	391
	3	266	376	205	332	509	274	407	663	356	551	838	450
10	1	267	316	151	333	434	213	410	571	273	558	727	343
	2	276	358	181	343	489	244	420	640	317	569	813	403
	3	284	389	207	352	530	279	430	694	363	580	880	459
15	1	268	376	161	349	502	225	445	646	291	623	808	366
	2	277	411	189	359	548	256	456	706	334	634	884	424
	3	286	439	213	368	586	289	466	755	378	646	945	479
20	1	265	425	169	345	569	235	439	734	306	614	921	387
	2	274	455	195	355	610	266	450	787	348	627	986	443
	3	282	481	219	365	644	298	461	831	391	639	1,042	496
30	1	259	492	183	338	665	250	430	864	330	600	1,089	421
	2	269	518	205	348	699	282	442	908	372	613	1,145	473
	3	277	540	229	358	729	312	452	946	412	626	1,193	524
50	1	252	567	208	328	778	287	417	1,022	383	582	1,302	492
	2	262	588	230	339	806	320	429	1,058	425	596	1,346	545
	3	271	607	255	349	831	351	440	1,090	466	610	1,386	597

Table 12-16 *Common Vent Capacity of Masonry Chimney with Single-Wall Connectors Serving Two or More Category I Appliances*

Vent Height H (ft)	Minimum Internal Area of Masonry Chimney Flue (sq. in.)								
	12			19			28		
	Combined Appliance Input Rating in Thousands of Btu/h								
	FAN +FAN	FAN +NAT	NAT +NAT	FAN +FAN	FAN +NAT	NAT +NAT	FAN +FAN	FAN +NAT	NAT +NAT
6	NA	NA	25	NA	118	45	NA	176	71
8	NA	NA	28	NA	128	52	NA	190	81
10	NA	NA	31	NA	136	56	NA	205	89
15	NA	NA	36	NA	NA	66	NA	230	105
20	NA	NA	NA	NA	NA	74	NA	247	120
30	NA	NA	NA	NA	NA	NA	NA	NA	135
50	NA	NA	NA	NA	NA	NA	NA	NA	NA

Vent Height H (ft)	Minimum Internal Area of Masonry Chimney Flue (sq. in.)											
	38			50			63			78		
	Combined Appliance Input Rating in Thousands of Btu/h											
	FAN +FAN	FAN +NAT	NAT +NAT	FAN +FAN	FAN +NAT	NAT +NAT	FAN +FAN	FAN +NAT	NAT +NAT	FAN +FAN	FAN +NAT	NAT +NAT
6	NA	255	102	NA	348	142	NA	455	187	NA	579	245
8	NA	276	118	NA	380	162	NA	497	217	NA	633	277
10	NA	295	129	NA	405	175	NA	532	234	771	680	300
15	NA	335	150	NA	400	210	677	602	280	866	772	360
20	NA	362	170	NA	503	240	765	661	321	947	849	415
30	NA	398	195	NA	558	275	808	739	377	1052	957	490
50	NA	NA	NA	NA	612	325	NA	821	456	1152	1076	600

Direct Venting

In direct vent installations, combustion air is drawn into a sealed firebox from outside the house through coaxial intake/exhaust pipe. This eliminates depressurization, resulting in a warmer, healthier home environment. Direct venting also eliminates the need to extend the exhaust vent through the roof, making installation easier and less expensive.

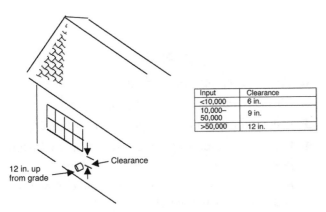

Input	Clearance
<10,000	6 in.
10,000–50,000	9 in.
>50,000	12 in.

Fig. 12-8 *Clearance for direct vent appliances.*

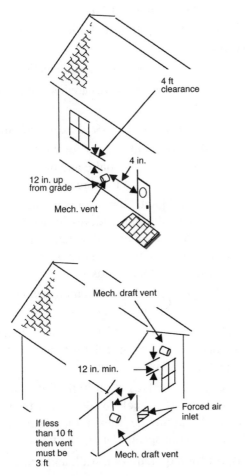

Fig. 12-9 *Mechanical draft vent locations.*

Through-wall venting for Category II and Category IV appliances or other condensing types of venting cannot terminate over other equipment that could be damaged by the condensation or terminate over public walkways.

Clearances from Combustionable Materials for Connectors

Table 12-17 *Clearances from Combustionable Materials for Connectors for Listed Type B Vent*

Equipment	Clearance Required
Equipment with draft hoods and those listed for use with Type B vents.	As listed
Residential boilers, furnaces with listed gas conversion and draft hood.	6 in.
Residential appliances listed for use with Type L vents.	Not permitted
Unlisted residential appliances with a draft hood.	Not permitted
Residential and low-heat equipment other than ones listed above.	Not permitted

Table 12-18 *Clearances from Combustionable Materials for Connectors for Listed Type L Vent*

Equipment	Clearance Required
Equipment with draft hoods and those listed for use with Type B vents.	As listed
Residential boilers, furnaces with listed gas conversion and draft hood.	6 in.
Residential appliances listed for use with Type L vents.	As listed
Unlisted residential appliances with a draft hood.	6 in.
Residential and low-heat equipment other than ones listed above.	9 in.

Table 12-19 *Clearances from Combustionable Materials for Connectors for Single-Wall Metal Pipe*

Equipment	Clearance Required
Equipment with draft hoods and those listed for use with Type B vents.	6 in.
Residential boilers, furnaces with listed gas conversion and draft hood.	9 in.
Residential appliances listed for use with Type L vents.	9 in.
Unlisted residential appliances with a draft hood.	9 in.
Residential and low-heat equipment other than ones listed above.	18 in.

Draft Fans

1. Check fans and drivers for anchorage, alignment, and rotation.
2. Check accessibility of lubrication fittings.
3. Inspect dampers for operation in compliance with contract requirements.
4. Inspect bearings for smoothness and overheating.
5. Check vibration and vibration-absorbing mounts.
6. Inspect insulation application to induced draft fan.
7. Examine safety control interlocks and sic-flow switches.

OIL STORAGE TANK

1. Check for underwriter's approval.
2. Check tank capacity and calibration.
3. See that tanks have the required openings and the means for proper anchorage.
4. Check for tank heaters, when required.
5. Examine paint coating and examine holiday testing.
6. Check manufacturer's instructions for proper installation.

Circulating, Condensate, and Vacuum Return Pumps

Inspect for capacity and for method of mounting.

Miscellaneous Fittings and Equipment

Inspect valves, drips, traps, coils, elements, convectors, radiators, etc., as they are brought on the job to make sure that they are of the correct capacity and that they have been approved.

Inspection

Planning

1. Check the codes, reference data, and manufacturer's recommendations.
2. Check with contractor for its detail layouts of equipment and piping, which are normally made to coordinate work of the various trades.
3. Compare nameplate data, piping markings, etc. with requirements.
4. Provide the proper spacing of equipment to make sure that there is adequate room for piping, duct-

work, accessibility for maintenance, and that walls behind ductwork can be finished without duct removal. Check for adequate clearance for removal of air filters and strainers.
5. Verify how the heating system fits into the total job.
6. Be sure that sleeves of the correct size and material are properly located in floors and walls before they are built.

PIPING

1. Compare piping workmanship.
2. Check storage and handling procedures.
3. Inspect for the required type and size of pipe.
4. Examine the cutting of construction to install piping.
5. Require provisions for expansion and contraction, and proper anchorage of pipe.
6. Check the installation of mechanical expansion joints. Do not remove spacers until expansion joints are ready to be installed.
7. Verify that the pitch of the horizontal runs are correct.
8. Check the position of branch connections.
9. Be sure that required valves are installed in the correct positions.
10. Check the method and procedure of jointing pipes.
    a. On threaded joints, check for the use of tapered threads. See that graphite and oil, or an equivalent, are applied to the threads.
    b. On welded joints, check for compliance with approved welding procedures; inspect for defective welds; check type of material of the welding rod; make sure welders have been qualified and are stamping their welds.
11. See that piping is properly supported and aligned and that there is no strain on joints.
12. See that proper grade and alignment are maintained and that proper fittings are provided to eliminate air pockets and restrictions.
13. Check for air valves at all high points and at the ends of mains. Check for drips and traps at low points. Examine the lines to make sure that condensate cannot accumulate in the lines.
14. Inspect for required floor, wall, and ceiling plates.
15. Check for type, size, material, and finish.

16. Watch for the use and proper installation of eccentric fittings.

17. See that interconnecting piping between boilers conforms to shop drawings and ASME Code. Watch for adequate valves and other special fittings. Cut-off valves shall be provided to isolate each boiler from the steam header.

18. Be sure that lift fittings are provided where the gravity flow of vacuum returns is interrupted by a change to a higher elevation.

19. Clean all supply and return lines before putting them into operation. Check whether contractor has cleaned all traps and strainers after pipe cleaning and before system operation.

20. Check safety valve discharge pipe for number of ells (restriction).

21. Check bent pipe for kinks, wrinkles, or other malformations. Be sure that approved radius bends are not exceeded.

Pipe Insulation

1. Know locations of pipes required to be insulated.

2. See that insulation has been approved.

3. Check width and type of material and the spacing of bands.

4. Be sure that all fittings except unions and flanges are insulated.

5. Be sure that insulation is being correctly installed.

6. See the section "Mechanical Insulation" for additional checks.

7. Check for continuity of insulation through walls and floors.

8. Check that proper thickness of insulation is being applied.

9. On chilled-water and hot-water combination piping and boiler piping check for vapor seal requirement.

Hot Water Systems

1. Note the installation of balancing valves or orifices in the return connection of each radiator or heating device.

2. See that contractor balances system as required by plans or specifications.

3. Ensure that threaded openings are provided on converters. See that safety devices and temperature controls are furnished and are in working order. Check coil for tightness and clearance for its removal. Note drain pipe to outside atmosphere or floor drain from blow-off safety valves.

4. Check for automatic and manual vents.

5. Examine expansion tanks for size, conformance to code, protective paint coating, insulation, water level gage, drain, and air charging valves.

High-Temperature Hot Water

1. Check pumps for:
   a. Leveling, alignment, and stability on foundation.
   b. Lubrication.
   c. Seals for leaks.
   d. Packing adjustment and type.
   e. Pressure retention.
   f. Correct rotation.
   g. Seal coolant service installed.

2. Ensure that radiant heating coils are accurately placed, firmly secured, and absolutely tight under a hydrostatic test pressure of one and one-half times the operating pressure prior to encasement in construction.

MECHANICAL VAULTS

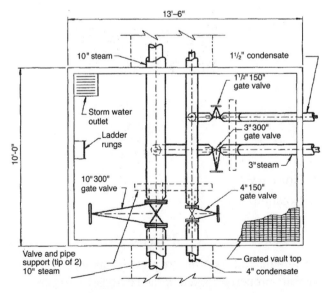

Fig. 12-10 *Valve manhole vault.*

Table 12-20 *Manhole Clearances*

Min. Distance	Conduit or Pipe Insulations	Valve Stem End or Body	Electrical Equipment	Ladder	Sump or Bottom of Trap Drain
Wall	18 in.	18 in.	—	6 in.	18 in.
Floor	24 in.	24 in.	36 in.	12 in.	12 in.
Top of manhole	18 in.	12 in.	6 in.	6 in.	36 in.

STEAM SYSTEMS

1. Know details of the type of system required.
2. Check the operation of supply valves to radiator and convector.
3. Check radiator run-out for pitch.

Hot Air Heating

1. Ensure that contractor follows NFPA criteria for installation of oil or gas equipment.
2. Be sure that return air has free passage to heater unit.
3. Note damper setting balance of the flow of air.
4. Check that flexible connections have been installed between furnace and duct system.

Heating and Ventilating Units

1. Require that all component parts operate satisfactorily.
2. Note access doors for tightness and clearance.
3. Determine that noise level is within acceptable limits.
4. Check flexible pipe connections and/or vibration eliminators.
5. Check rotation.

Unit Heaters

Check:

1. Clearances
2. Controls
3. Air distribution
4. Noise level
5. Rotation

Controls

Be sure that the controls are provided as specified, that they are properly hooked up, and that they will perform the required operation.

BOILERS AND BOILER PLANTS
General Requirements

1. Before rolling in, check the cleaning of ends of tubes and the surfaces of tube holes in drums and headers. Check to ensure that new boilers exposed to weather are covered to prevent corrosion.
2. See that tube-rolling is done by experienced workmen and that all precautions are taken to prevent either under- or over-rolling. At this stage of erection request technical assistance.
3. Ensure that the boiler inspector is notified when it is time for the hydrostatic test. Obtain Certificate of Inspection. Do not permit the installation of any baffles or the setting of refractories until after the boiler has passed inspection.
4. Affirm that baffles of steel, refractory tile, or monolithic construction are installed gas-tight but with provision for expansion, and that they will resist dislodgment by "puffs."
5. Ensure that boiling-out operations for the removal of grease, oil, and other foreign matter are performed before boiler is placed in operation.
6. Ensure that space is provided for tube removal and cleaning and for general maintenance of all equipment.
7. Check to ensure that during periods of operation by contractor chemical treatment and blowdown are provided to prevent scale deposits and corrosion.

SETTINGS

1. Be sure that all settings are constructed with provision for expansion and contraction of both the refractories and the pressure parts. See that expansion joints are sealed to prevent passage of air or gases but are flexible enough to maintain their seal under movement of the structure. Check the entire setting for leaks.
2. Check solid refractory walls for plumb, level courses and dipped joints. Check grades of refractories used.

Chipped, cracked, wet, or broken refractory materials will be rejected.

3. Ensure that refractory tile and setting casings are constructed to prevent the escape of gases or the infiltration of air, and that they are installed in accordance with the recommendations of the manufacturer.

4. Insist that all openings through setting walls are accurately located and of proper size. Check temperature of boiler setting surface against room temperature. Verify that pipe sleeves for draft gages are clean and flush with interior face of wall.

5. Inspect uptake damper for correct location, bearing material, and freedom of operation when hot.

FUEL-BURNING EQUIPMENT

1. Correlate coal stokers with stationary grates for accurate placement and support of the grate bars. See that shaking and dumping mechanism will work freely under operating temperatures.

2. Evaluate traveling and moving grates for alignment of running parts and guides, tightness of seals, and provision for expansion and contraction.

3. Note lubrication and protection of motors, gears, and bearings.

4. Examine all moving parts for operation under temperatures encountered and for loads specified.

5. Ensure that grate design and coal sizing are suitable for each other.

6. See that stoker feeding mechanism is adjusted to distribute the coat evenly over the grates.

7. Verify that pulverizers are constructed and installed as nearly dust-tight as possible. Be sure the equipment is firmly secured to foundation. Check units for proper balance and quiet operation at normal operating speeds.

8. See if pulverizers are adjusted for proper coal fineness. Notice whether heat is applied to the coal in the pulverizer or if temperatures are obtained prior to the entrance of coal to ensure satisfactory dryness of coal.

9. Ensure that burners are adjusted for efficient operation, minimum excess air, stable ignition at low rating, and no impingement on furnace walls. Use a boiler test kit when required.

10. Evaluate the coal feeder for accurate and even operation.

11. Examine the installation of access and inspection doors.

12. View magnetic separators for location ahead of pulverizers.

13. All safety precautions are to be observed in the installation of gas burners and piping. Arrangement of gas valves should be in accordance with ASA Standard Z 21.33.

14. Burners should be arranged to permit ready inspection and servicing.

15. Note location of pilot flame. Provision shall be made to facilitate manual lighting of pilot flame. A hand torch and receptacle should be provided for each boiler.

16. See that mixing dampers or valves are adjusted to proportion air and fuel for the most efficient combustion with minimum excess air and stable operation of low rating, with no impingement on furnace walls. Check the manufacturer's setting requirements.

17. Compare all dimensions of the combustion chamber during construction for agreement with manufacturer's approved shop drawings. Check all materials of construction for compliance with specifications and approved shop drawing. Take physical samples of all tile, insulating plastic, firebrick, etc. for future reference.

18. Check type and capacity of heaters for grade of oil.

19. Check relief of excess pressure in pumps.

20. Test oil piping for leaks.

DRAFT FANS AND DUCTWORK

1. See that induced draft fans are provided with clean-out doors.

2. Verify the operation of dampers at high flue gas temperatures.

BLOW DOWN SYSTEM

1. Insist that work conforms to applicable codes.

2. Observe location of vent and discharge lines.

3. Require that piping provides for expansion and contraction.

COMBUSTION CONTROLS

1. Inspect equipment for type, capacity, installation, and operation.

2. Be sure that operating devices are firmly secured to floor, foundations, or other supports and that they

operate freely. They should have sufficient power to easily perform their duties.

3. Check the location and stability of sleeves in setting walls, ducts, or breechings for draft piping, thermometers, and gages.

4. Pipe, tubing, and wiring should run neatly and parallel to the lines of building or structure. They should be firmly secured and have proper pitch. See that draft piping is provided with means for removing accumulations of ash and soot.

5. Verify the operation of safety controls.

6. Check that flame-sensing device is installed in position to sense both pilot and main flame.

7. Determine that instrument panels are firmly anchored and set plumb. Be sure that wiring, tubing, and piping are neatly arranged in rear of panel. See that nameplates, indicating the function of each instrument, are mounted on the face of the pane.

8. Secure a written statement from the manufacturer's representative to the effect that all equipment of the control system is properly installed and in perfect operating condition before acceptance.

FLAME TYPES (FUEL GAS)
Yellow-Tipped Flame

- A yellow-tipped flame with a small inner bluish flame at the burner ports usually indicates incomplete combustion of the gas due to insufficient supply of primary air. Soot will usually form on vents and heat exchangers.

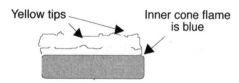

Fig. 12-11A *Yellow-tipped flame.*

Lazy-Soft Flame

- This flame occures when the primary is sufficient enough to eliminate the yellow tips on the outer portion of the flame. Both the inner and outer flames are not well defined.

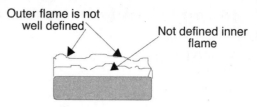

Fig. 12-11B *Lazy-soft flame.*

Floating Flame

- Indicates insufficient secondary air supply that is caused by a restricted air flow, bad venting, or a combination of the two. This flame usually gives an odor because of the unburned gas by-products.

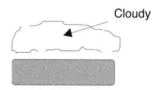

Fig. 12-11C *Floating flame.*

Uniform Lifting Flame

- Caused by excessive amounts of primary air being supplied to the burner usually can also be heard as a blowing noise.

Fig. 12-11D *Uniform lifting flame.*

Orange-Colored Flame

- Usually caused by dust burning in the flame—not a problem unless it's excessive.

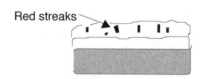

Fig. 12-11E *Orange-colored flame.*

Sharply Defined Flame

- Good combustion: A sharp, crisp flame indicates proper mixture of gas, secondary, and primary airs.
- Both inner and outer are have straight sides with the inner flame resting on the burner ports with no clearance between them.

APPLIANCE TYPES

Category I Appliances that operate with a nonpositive vent connection pressure and with a flue gas temperature of at least 140°F above its dewpoint.

Category II Appliances that operate with a nonpositive vent connection pressure and with a flue gas temperature less than 140°F above its dewpoint.

Category III Appliances that operate with a positive vent pressure and with a flue gas temperature at least 140°F above its dewpoint.

Category IV Appliances that operate with a positive vent pressure and with a flue gas temperature less than 140°F above its dewpoint.

Appliance Installation Codes: Requirements

1. Shall be accessible without moving permanent structure.
2. Shall have a 30-ft platform (working space) in front of control side of appliance.
3. Exception: Room heaters need only 18 in. of working space.
4. Not less than 1-in. clear air space from combustible materials.
5. *All must have label.*
6. Appliances installed in earthquake-prone areas need to be anchored to prevent lateral movement if using nonrigid water connections over 4 ft.
7. Appliances that generate any type of ignitable source must have that source a minimum of 18 in. above the floor.
8. Open burner appliances such as a cooking range do not need automatic shutoff device for use if the pilot light fails.
9. Forced air furnaces need a control limit that prevents outlet air from exceeding 250°F.
10. Electric heater ducts need a limit of 200°F.

HEATING AND COOLING EQUIPMENT

1. Need to be installed in such a manner as to allow their replacement and or repair.
2. Need a power receptacle within 25 ft.
3. Need to be sized in accordance with ACCA Manual J.
4. Attic installation needs to provide a min of 22 ft wide by 30 ft long. Also requires a passage to the area.
5. Also needs a permanent light switch and outlet with the switch located at the passageway opening.
6. Units installed on the ground, in the crawl space need to be on a slab or masonry units at least 3 in. high and level.
7. Units suspended from the floor need a clearance of at least 6 in. from the ground.
8. If equipment is installed in an excavation, it will have at least 6-in. clearance on the bottom and 12 in. on the sides; the control side still needs a minimum of 30-in. clearance.
9. If the excavation exceeds 12 in., then it needs concrete or masonry units installed to a height of 4 in. above the ground height.
10. Fuel-burning furnaces will not be installed in rooms used for storage.

ECONOMIZERS AND AIR HEATERS

Check for tightness of tubes or plates and for evidence of erosion or corrosion whether integral with the boiler or separate units. Observe working condition.

FLY ASH COLLECTORS

Check:

1. Inspection and cleanout doors for location and adequacy.
2. Dampers for free operation under all temperature conditions.
3. Discharge grates for leakage of either ash or air.

BOILER SPECIALTIES

1. Verify all trimmings such as water column, steam gage, safety valves, blow-off valves, nonreturn valves, stop and check feed valves, and vent valves for type and size. Inspect for installation and setting.
2. Check that safety valve discharge piping is anchored so that it does not impose a strain on the valve.

Table 12-21 *Expansion Tank Minimum Capacities (Water Temperature 195°F, Fill Pressure 12 psig, Minimum Operating Pressure 30 psig)*

System Volume	Diaphragm Type	Nonpressurized Type
10	1.0	1.5
20	1.5	3.0
30	2.5	4.5
40	3.0	6.0
50	4.0	7.5
60	5.0	9.0
70	6.0	10.5
80	6.5	12.0
90	7.5	13.5
100	8.0	15.0

SOOT BLOWERS

1. Determine operating pressure of steam-operated unit.

2. Note materials of elements and bearings.

3. See that wall boxes are accurately and firmly set and that the operating heads are securely fastened. Ensure that each element operates freely and that it may be removed without disturbing tubes or setting.

4. Check clearance for the removal of soot blowers.

5. Ensure that drainage is provided to prevent moisture from being blown into the furnace.

6. Check for correct location and installation of test holes in breechings and stacks to allow for periodic measurement of fly ash and other particulate matter for air pollution control.

   a. Inspect breechings for gauge (thickness) of metal, supports, and insulation.

   b. Examine cleanout doors for tightness, location, and size.

   c. Check expansion joints for tightness and location.

   d. Check caulked joint at opening around breaching entering masonry chimneys.

   e. Check guys, bracing, or other supports.

   f. Reject damaged or unsuitable brick and radial block.

   g. See that all courses are brought up together and bonded.

   h. In reinforcement operation inspect materials and accuracy of placement. Observe especially the lapping of bars.

   i. Evaluate the material and the setting of embedded items for securing ladders, platforms, cables, lights, doors, or other equipment.

   j. Check openings and locations of test holes in breaching. Check cleanout door for size and location.

   k. Check closing and latching of cleanout doors.

   l. See that firebrick lining covers the chimney area and that weep holes are provided at bottom.

   m. Check continuous-pour type concrete chimneys for a smooth, jointless exterior finish.

   n. Determine if ladders are sturdy, securely anchored, and provided with safety cages where required.

   o. Verify that metal vent cap, when required, is firmly secured and coated for prevention of corrosion.

   p. Identify requirement for obstruction lights and lightning protection. Check access to them for servicing.

   q. Ensure that chimney is plumb, concentric, and has uniform taper from top to bottom.

BOILER FEEDWATER

Check:

1. Type of water treatment for water available.

2. Pressures and temperatures to be obtained in boiler. Materials and installation.

3. Scales, proportioning devices, and mixing valves for accuracy and operation. Installation of tanks and piping for types of material and supports, workmanship, and conformance with contract requirements.

4. Pressure tanks for conformance with the applicable codes and ASME stamp.

5. Control apparatus for the installation and operation of all components. Check should be done by the manufacturer's service engineer. Refer to job specifications for necessary tests and reports required, and determine from service engineer the sequence of testing.

6. Open heaters for the installation of pans, trays, plates, sprays, and other internal parts, as well as for the setting of the control for water level in storage compartment.

7. That heater vent operates and that the heater reduces the oxygen content in the water to the specified amounts before acceptance. Checking should be done by manufacturer's service engineer.

8. Closed heaters for compliance with code governing unfired pressure vessels.

9. That clearance is provided for the removal of tubes. Evaluate performance.

10. Thermometers and gages for accuracy and operation.

TURBINES

1. Inspect equipment for the pressures and temperatures to he applied. Compare with approved shop drawings.

2. Examine all drains, drips, leakoffs, relief valves, and other required safety devices for operation.

3. Ensure that turbines are firmly secured to foundation, are accurately aligned with driven equipment, and operate without vibration.

4. Check that piping is installed to impose no strain on turbine connections.

5. Verify that provision is made for expansion when aligning couplings.

6. Be certain that field-assembled turbines are installed by the manufacturer's erectors only.

7. Reduction gears must mesh perfectly and operate smoothly and without noise or vibration. Check dwelling after turbines and gears are in perfect alignment.

8. Evaluate the operation of governors.

9. Check capacity and steam consumption under various load conditions.

SMOKE CONNECTIONS

1. Examine the size and construction of stacks and flues.

2. Check the clearance space between stacks, flues, and adjacent building materials.

3. Inspect the method of supporting and anchoring all smoke connections.

4. See that cleanout is provided which will allow cleaning of the entire smoke connection without dismantling.

FUEL STORAGE AND CONVEYING

1. Inspect overhead bunkers for capacity in conformance with specifications. See that all gates are installed dust-tight and that they operate freely. Note the sealing of spaces around top of bunkers and elevators.

2. Be sure that silos are erected plumb and concentric.

3. See that courses in tile, brick, or block silos are carried up evenly, that horizontal joints are level, and that reinforcement is welded and thoroughly embedded.

4. Tight joints and reinforcement bands for concrete stave silos must be pulled up tightly.

5. Check continuous-pour-type concrete silo for a smooth, jointless exterior finish.

6. Determine whether pneumatic conveyers are installed with air and dust-tight joints.

7. Examine materials and installation of mechanical coal conveyers.

8. Ensure that screw flights do not ride on bottom of trough.

9. See that bucket, chain, and belt conveyor guides and bearings are carefully aligned.

10. Evaluate skip hoists for capacity and proper installation, with particular attention to operation of the top and bottom limit stops.

11. Make sure that housings for all conveyors and elevators are installed with dust-tight joints.

12. Access doors and connections with chutes and discharge gates should be tightly fitted.

13. Observe that chutes are installed with sufficient slope to ensure free gravity flow of coal.

14. Check weighing lorries for capacity, accuracy of weight, and ease of operation.

15. Verify that vibrating feeders are accurately positioned and adjusted for specified flow of coal.

16. Be sure that coal crushers are securely anchored to foundation or supports and that grids are adjusted to proper coal size. Ascertain the direction of rotation.

17. Check coal scales for accuracy of weight and for operation of component parts.

18. Track and truck hoppers—ensure provision for removing water from pita. Inspect hopper grids for size opening and materials.

19. Note flow of coal of entire conveying system, from unloading hoppers to boilers.

PAINTING

1. See that equipment contains the correct finish. Watch for abrasions.

2. Watch for miscellaneous ferrous metal items that are not primed.

3. Require finish painting as specified.

4. Identify all pipe runs as specified.

TESTING

Make sure that all required tests of heating equipment are accurately recorded. See that tests are performed by manufacturer's representatives where required. Check tests and verify that tests meet all requirements before acceptance. Report unsatisfactory test results to the supervisor.

OPERATING INSTRUCTIONS AND GUARANTIES

1. See that equipment guaranties and instructions for the operation of equipment are furnished for hand-over to the client.

2. Notify the site supervisor of the readiness of the construction for test and subsequent operation for instructing personnel. Videotaping is an excellent tool.

VENTILATING, AIR SUPPLY, AND DISTRIBUTION SYSTEM
General

Since the ventilating system is largely dependent on associated equipment, the Inspector must closely coordinate this chapter with all the additional chapters in this inspection manual.

Equipment

General

1. It is the PM's responsibility, in concert with the Inspector, to determine that all equipment is approved well in advance of its actual need on the job.

2. Check all equipment delivered to the site for conformance with approved shop drawings. Make sure the necessary rating and test certificates have been furnished.

3. Closely examine material for any damages. Minor abrasions or rust spots must be cleaned and repainted to match original paint in appearance and in quality. Reject damaged items.

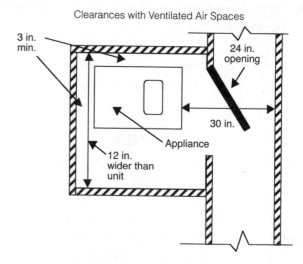

Fig. 12-12 *Appliance clearances.*

4. Be certain that approved vibration isolators and flexible connections will be furnished as specified.

5. Examine the mounting of each piece of equipment for secure installation. Check codes for maximum spacing of supports.

6. Check equipment for excess noise and vibration.

7. Do not use dissimilar materials, especially screws, fasteners, and flashings with different equipment bases and housing materials.

Clothes Dryers

1. Exhaust vents need a backdraft damper.

2. Ducts to be of rigid metal with no screws penetrating to the interior of the duct.

3. Length cannot exceed 25 ft.

4. Reduce overall length by 2.5 ft for every 45° bend and 5 ft for each 90° bend.

5. Gas dryers cannot be located in room with other fuel-burning appliances.

Clothes Dryer Exhaust (Fuel Burning)

1. Ducts must be galvanized steel or aluminum if passing through any fire-rated assembly.

2. Must terminate outside and not connected to any other vent assembly

3. Ducts cannot exceed 25 ft in length. Reduce:
   a. 2½ ft for each 45° bend
   b. 5 ft for each 90° bend

4. The duct must be minimum 4-in. diameter.

5. Joints must be in the direction of the flow.

FANS AND AIR HANDLING UNITS

1. Check rotation of fan before permanent power connection is made.
2. Check method of drive. If belt driven, check means provided to adjust the motor.
3. Check the type of motor enclosure.
4. See that specified seals, sleeves, and bearings are provided; and when lubricating type bearings are allowed, provide accessibility for lubricating without dismantling fan or disconnecting duct.
5. Provide a fire-safety switch on return air ducts of circulation systems.
6. Check for pulley and belt alignment.
7. See that adequate guards are provided for rotating equipment and belts.
8. Check for installation of smoke detectors when required.

Power Roof Ventilators

1. Provide service accessibility.
2. Flashing at curbs must be water tight.
3. Discharged air is not to be directed toward air intakes.
4. Check for required disconnect switch, which should be visible and properly marked.

Gravity Ventilators

1. Examine installation for rigidity and weather tightness.
2. Make sure units are oiled and properly adjusted.
3. Check the actual freedom of rotation of the blades.

Dampers

1. Backdraft dampers should be installed for each exhaust fan.
2. Check the actual operation of the dampers. See that dampers do not rattle and that felt strips are provided for backdraft dampers.
3. Ensure that a separate frame is provided in openings on which the dampers will be mounted.
4. Check for correct installation of fire dampers in accordance with SMACNA Fire Damper Guide.

Filters

1. Make sure the proper type of filter is furnished and installed.

2. Check thickness and method of mounting and supporting.
3. Provide proper amount of adhesive and washing tank for viscous medium type filters.
4. Inspect sealing strips.
5. Provide accessibility for removal and replacement of filters.
6. Ensure that air stream is distributed uniformly over all filter areas.
7. Observe electrostatic-type filters for operation of warning lights and door interlocks. Check ionizers for loose wires, sparking, and free access.
8. Inspect automatic sprays for complete washing and spray coverage.
9. On traveling screen-type filters, note the operation of screen and oil charge.
10. On renewable roll media-type filters, inspect:
    a. Tracking of roll
    b. Media runout switch
    c. Timer setting
    d. Static pressure control
    e. Tension on media
11. See that clean filters are installed upon completion of final tests.
12. Check specifications regarding requirements for spare filters. This requirement is sometimes expressed as a percentage of the total of each kind required. Check on the transfer of the spares to the operating agency.

Screens

1. Provide bird or insect screens if required.
2. Check fabric material and installation of dissimilar materials.
3. Check mesh size.

Return Air

- It can be diluted with outdoor air.
- Return air openings shall not be less than 2 sq. in. for each 1000 Btu/h input rating of the furnace (for warm-air furnace).
- Return air for heat pumps and central AC units requires a minimum of 6 sq. in. for each 1000 Btu/h of nominal cooling output.

Prohibited:

- Return air for warm air furnaces from garages, bathrooms, kitchens, and other dwelling areas.
- Outdoor air not to be taken from within 10 ft from either appliance or plumbing exhaust vents that are located less than 3 ft above the inlet.
- Outdoor inlets are to be covered with ¼ mesh with openings less than ½ in.

Supply Air Venting

- Requires 2 sq. in./1000 Btu/h for warm air furnaces.
- For central air and heat pumps, supply air shall be at least 6 sq. in. per 1000 Btu/h cooling output.

Combustible Air

- Does not apply to direct vent appliances, listed and labeled appliances, and domestic clothes dryers.
- Buildings of unusually tight construction require combustible air from outside.
- Buildings of ordinary tightness require a volume of 50 cu. ft. per 1000 Btu/h input.
- Air requirements needed for other systems such as exhaust fans, fireplaces, and clothes dryers. Need to be factored in when computing the required air space required.

Openings for Air (Reductions)

- Metal louvers—75% of gross area
- Wood louvers—25% of gross area

Air from Inside Building

- Each opening shall have 1 sq. in. per 1000 Btu/h, but not less than 100 sq. in.
- If area does not meet 50 sq. ft per 1000 Btu/h, then there shall be two openings to adjacent areas: one 12 in. from the top of the space and one 12 in. from the bottom.

Air from Outdoors

- Requires two openings, one 12 in. from top of enclosure and one 12 in. from the bottom.

- Can be connected to crawl or attic if they are ventilated.
- Vertical ducts must have minimum 1 sq. in. per 4000 Btu/h for all appliances in the space.
- Horizontal ducts must have minimum 1 sq. in. per 2000 Btu/h.
- Ducts in attic must extend at least 6 in. above the ceiling joist and insulation.
- Ducts in attic shall not be screened.
- Ducts supplying combustible air from under floor areas require twice the required air opening.
- All outside openings require a corrosion-resistant screen with openings at least ¼ in. and not larger than ½ in.

Combustion and Vent Air

1. All air from inside the building.
   a. A confined space with two openings.
      - Each opening to have a min. free area of not less than 1 sq. in./1000 Btu of the total gas input of all the units together.
      - But not less than 100 sq. in.
      - One 12 in. from the top, one 12 in. from the bottom.
      - Minimum dimension of at least 3 in.
2. All air from outdoors.
   a. Two opening methods.
      - Ducts must be same size as opening.
      - Opening a min. of 3 in.
      - One 12 in. from the top, one 12 in. from the bottom.
      - If a vertical duct is used: 1 sq. in. of free area for each 4000 Btu of all the units combined.
      - If a horizontal duct is used: All the same as the vertical except the free opening shall be 1 sq. in./2000 Btu of the total units in the space.

One Opening Method:

- 12 in. from the top of the enclosure.
- 1-in. clearance from the sides and back.
- 6-in. clearance from the front of the appliance.
- 1 sq. in./3000 Btu of total input of all the units.
- Not less than the sum of all vent connections.

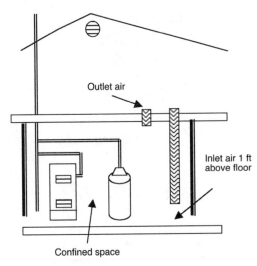

Fig. 12-13 *Inlet and outlet air from attic.*

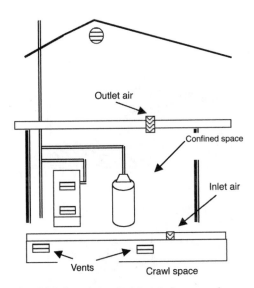

Fig. 12-14 *Inlet and outlet air from crawlspace.*

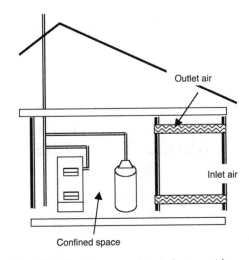

Fig. 12-15 *Inlet and outlet air from outside.*

VENTS
General

1. Metal duct clearance to ground at least 6 in.
2. Ducts in concrete—min. 2-in. coverage.
3. Joints must be taped or have gaskets (airtight).
4. Connectors require a minimum of ¼ in./ft.
5. Supported with 1½-in. straps every 4 ft.
6. Insulated if in unconditioned areas.

Types of Vents

Type B. All approved gas units with draft hoods and all other category I type appliances.

Type BW. Approved wall furnaces labeled for BW vents.

Type L. For approved oil burning appliances and gas appliances approved for type B vents.

Ductwork and Mechanical Insulation

Diffusers, Registers, and Grilles

1. See that the contractor furnishes a schedule showing all air inlets and outlets.
2. Inspect diffusers and registers for accessible volume control operator.
3. Examine specification and installation for integral antismudge rings for diffusers.
4. Check for loose or bent vanes.
5. Inspect each item for fit, and see that sponge-rubber gaskets are provided when required.
6. Inspect for the proper operation of registers, dampers, and grille directional controls.

Balancing and Testing

General check for any required certification of HVAC test and balance subcontractor/agent, prior to their arrival at site.

Cleaning and Adjusting

1. All ducts, plenums, and casings must be thoroughly cleaned of debris and blown free of small particles and dust before supply outlets are installed.

2. Clean equipment of oil, dust, dirt, and paint spots.

3. Replace sectional throwaway filters after ductwork is blown out and cleaned.

4. Lubricate all bearings.

5. Check tension on all belts and the adjustment of fan pulleys.

6. Check that all fan and belt guards are in place.

7. Install temporary filters for testing purposes.

Testing

1. Before insulating duct, test it for air tightness. Contractor must provide necessary equipment for air-flow measurements and coefficients for registers and diffusers.

2. Review contractor's method for recording test data, including comparison to the design air flows.

3. Test each outlet for the amount of air quantities required.

4. Final air flows must be recorded after all adjustments are made.

5. If actual air flows result in objectional velocities or distribution, notify the Project Manager.

6. Check all dampers for proper operation.

Air Movement from Type A Outlets (Ceiling)

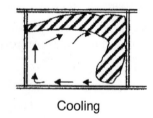
Cooling

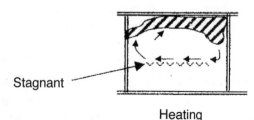
Heating

Fig. 12-16A *Air movement from Type A outlets (high side wall).*

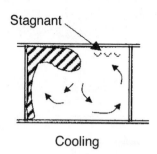
Cooling

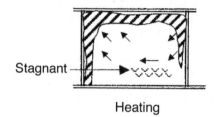
Heating

Fig. 12-16B *Air movement from Type B outlets.*

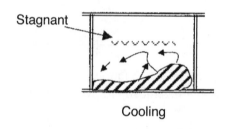
Cooling

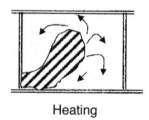
Heating

Fig. 12-16C *Air movement from Type D outlets.*

REFRIGERATION AND AIR CONDITIONING
General

This section covers refrigeration and air conditioning for both the central and unitary type systems. Since there is generally a duplication in the requirements for piping and ductwork for this subject and for plumbing and air handling, and since those areas have been covered in previous chapters, it will be necessary for the inspector to be very familiar with the piping section and the ductwork section.

Piping

Refrigerator Piping

1. Determine where copper or black steel will be used, and the type required.
2. Make sure the piping and fittings have been approved.
3. Check the method of installing piping.
4. Make sure piping is stored as prescribed in specifications.

Water Piping

1. Check the type of piping required for chilled water and condenser water systems.
2. Determine weight and class of piping.
3. Make sure the specified and approved piping, fittings, and jointing materials are being used.

Installation

1. Check for defects in fabricating and installing piping. Watch specifically for workmanship, supports, and sleeves.
2. Be especially careful to:
   a. Make sure the specified solder is used. Check soldering of joints.
   b. See that internal valve parts are removed from valves, and that valves are wet wrapped before soldering.
   c. See that joints are thoroughly cleaned before soldering.
   d. Check on the removal of excess flux and acid after joints are made.
3. Make sure the proper types of flexible connections are installed in the required locations.
4. See that unions or flanges are installed at all equipment, at control valves, and at other points that will facilitate maintenance.
5. Check carefully for the proper slope of all lines. Ensure slope of refrigerant lines to provide movement of oil through the system.
6. Check installation for improper configuration of piping. Make sure the installation conforms with the approved drawing. If there is any question about the requirement for the arrangement of piping and if there is no approved drawing, obtain the drawing before allowing the contractor to proceed.
7. Make sure air vents are installed at high points in water lines and that drains are installed at low points.
8. Do not allow gate valves to be installed where globe valves are required.
9. Be sure balancing cocks are installed as required to permit proper balancing.
10. Do not install swing check valves in vertical lines with a downward flow of water.
11. Check for the installation of such required items as pressure gauges, thermal elements, and thermometer wells.
12. Provide adequate number and type of hangers. Hangers on uninsulated copper pipe must be electrolytically coated or made of solid compatible nonferrous metals.
13. Check for the proper installation of oil traps and double risers in refrigerant lines.
14. Check valves for pressure setting and discharge locations.
15. Be sure that refrigerant system is evacuated prior to charging and accomplished according to job specifications.
16. Make sure the system is charged with the required type and amount of refrigerant.
17. See that the system is completely checked for leaks. Dry nitrogen should be used for pressure tests unless another system has been approved.
18. Double-check to see that there are no unnecessary oil traps.
19. Vacuum should be broken by charging the system with dry refrigerant for which the system is designed.

DRILLING AND NOTCHING OF STRUCTURAL MEMBERS
Studs

- Load bearing: holes less than 40%; notches less than 25%.
- Non-load-bearing: holes less than 60%; notches less than 40%.

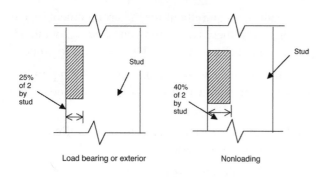

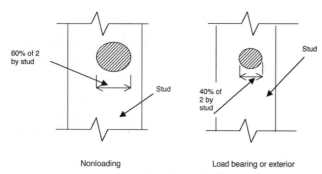

Fig. 12-17 *Notching and boring studs.*

Table 12-22 *Holes/Notching in Load-Bearing Studs*

Nominal	Actual	Holes		Notching
		40%	60%	25%
2 × 4	1½ × 3½	1¹³⁄₃₂	2³⁄₃₂	⁷⁄₈
2 × 6	1½ × 5½	2³⁄₁₆	3⁵⁄₁₆	1³⁄₈

Table 12-23 *Holes/Notching in Non-Load-Bearing Studs*

Nominal	Actual	Holes		Notching
		40%	60%	40%
2 × 4	1½ × 3½	1¹³⁄₃₂	2³⁄₃₂	1¹³⁄₃₂
2 × 6	1½ × 5½	2³⁄₁₆	3⁵⁄₁₆	2³⁄₁₆

Joist Specs (Notching or Drilling)

1. Notches less than ⅙ the depth.
2. None allowed in middle third.
3. Not within 2 in. of top or bottom.
4. Drilled holes less than ⅓ the depth.

Table 12-24 *Drilled Hole Maximums in Joists*

Nominal	Actual	⅓ (33%) in.
2 × 6	1½ × 5¼	1¾
2 × 8	1½ × 7¼	2¹³⁄₃₂
2 × 10	1½ × 9¼	3³⁄₃₂
2 × 12	1½ × 11¼	3¾
2 × 14	1½ × 14¼	4¾

Table 12-25 *Notch Maximums in Joists*

Nominal	Actual	⅙ (17%) in.
2 × 6	1½ × 5¼	⁷⁄₈
2 × 8	1½ × 7¼	1⁷⁄₃₂
2 × 10	1½ × 9¼	1¹⁷⁄₃₂
2 × 12	1½ × 11¼	1⁷⁄₈
2 × 14	1½ × 14¼	2³⁄₈

Table 12-26 *Notch Maximums in Ceiling Joists/Rafters*

Nominal	Actual	⅓ (33%) in.
2 × 6	1½ × 5¼	1¾
2 × 8	1½ × 7¼	2¹³⁄₃₂
2 × 10	1½ × 9¼	3³⁄₃₂
2 × 12	1½ × 11¼	3¾
2 × 14	1½ × 14¼	4¾

Table 12-27 *End Notch Maximums in Ceiling Joists/Rafters*

Nominal	Actual	¼ (25%) in.
2 × 6	1½ × 5¼	1⁵⁄₁₆
2 × 8	1½ × 7¼	1¹³⁄₁₆
2 × 10	1½ × 9¼	2⁵⁄₁₆
2 × 12	1½ × 11¼	2¹³⁄₁₆
2 × 14	1½ × 14¼	3⁹⁄₁₆

Notch and Hole Spacing and Sizes Allowed for Joists

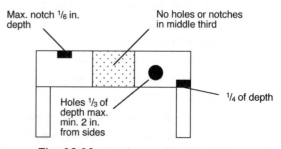

Fig. 12-18 *Notching and boring of joists.*

INSULATION

1. Determine whether the material on the job has been approved for the particular piping being installed. Make sure insulations, vapor barriers, adhesives, and sealers are noncombustible or fire retardant as specified.

2. Note that heated water piping is insulated differently from both chilled water piping and combination chilled and heated water piping.

3. Check thickness of insulation and of vapor barrier finish.

4. Determine that insulation jackets which are exposed to view are paintable.

5. Examine the requirements for the insulation of flanges, fittings, and valves, and ensure compliance with the specifications.

6. Check the lap and the sealing at joints.

7. Be very careful to see that there are no breaks in the vapor barrier. Watch for later damages during construction.

8. Check specification requirements for extending insulation through sleeves in walls, floors, and ceilings; chilled water lines inside cabinets of fan coil units should be insulated as required to prevent condensation from dripping on floor.

9. Make sure that pipe hangers are installed over insulation. Metal shields are to be provided between hanger ring and insulation. High-density insulation insert shall be installed with a length equal to the length of metal shield.

10. Know the special requirements for insulation and jacketing of piping exposed to weather.

11. Check for the neat termination and seal of insulation at the end of insulation.

12. Check the installation, the width, and the spacing of the bands used on pipe jacketing.

EQUIPMENT
General

1. All equipment should be checked to see that it is approved before it is needed on the job. When equipment arrives on the job, it should be checked against the shop drawing.

2. During installation, the contractor's work should be checked against the contract plans and specifications, the approved shop drawing, and the manufacturer's recommendations. Be sure that no damaged equipment is installed.

3. See that equipment is stored and protected until installed.

4. Be sure that all refrigeration equipment is installed strictly in accordance with the code.

5. Check on space requirements for equipment. Obtain an equipment room layout drawing and make sure that adequate clearances are provided for installation, maintenance, and operation. Doors?

6. Determine the need for access panels. A common error is the failure to provide the means for pulling condenser and chiller tubes.

7. Check the type of motors on equipment, the type of motor starter, heaters in the motor starters, and voltage of motor.

8. Make sure that all rotating parts, such as belts, chains, sheaves, shaft couplings, etc., are covered to protect personnel.

9. Make sure all equipment is lubricated according to manufacturer's instructions.

Condensers

1. See that air flow is not obstructed and that wind deflectors are installed, if required, in air cooled condensers.

2. Inspect water cooled condensers for leaks and proper flow.

3. Check evaporative condensers for:
   - Spray coverage.
   - Float valve operation without chatter.
   - Water level.
   - Fan rotation and speed.
   - Pump suction strainer.
   - Liquid discharge line carried full size to first elbow, with a 12-in. to 18-in. drop to receiver.
   - Mesh size of inlet screens.
   - Pan, casing, eliminators, fan corrosion protection, and complete drainage.
   - Provision for and adjustment of constant bleeding.

4. For all season air-cooled condensers, manufacturer's recommended installation should be adhered to. Check project plans, specifications, and manufacturer's recommended installation to see if condenser flooding or air volume control is required.

Reciprocating Compressors

Check for:

1. Oil, suction, and discharge pressures.
2. Shaft alignment on direct-driven machines.
3. Operation of high pressurestat, low pressurestat, and oil pressure failure switch.
4. Proper level viscosity of oil.
5. Installation of required gages.
6. Amount, correct type, and dryness of refrigerant charge.
7. Pressure holding ability upon pump-down.
8. Isolator deflection and compressor vibration.
9. Suction strainer screen mesh and the removal of startup belts.
10. Unloader action.
11. Compressor speed.
12. Belt tension and alignment.
13. Motor amperage under maximum load.
14. Refrigerant flood back and oil foaming.
15. Cylinder head overheating.
16. Rotation.
17. Automatic oil heater in crank case. Heater should work during shutdown.
18. Loops in refrigerant piping, as loops will permit oil to be trapped.
19. Damage to equipment compressor—if so, should not be run during vacuum tests.

Centrifugal Compressors

Check for:

1. Alignment of compressor, drive, and gear box.
2. Suction damper or inlet vane operation.
3. Safety control circuit operation.
4. Purge compressor operation.
5. Float valve operation, if furnished.
6. Oil pump and cooler operation.
7. Noise and vibration.
8. Required gauges.

Receivers

Check for:

1. Location, if installed on the outside of the building.
2. Do not place in direct rays of sun.

3. Relief valves are adequate size.
4. ASME stamp.
5. Drain, purge valve, liquid level indication, and shut-off valves.

Water Chillers

1. Examine water drains, vents, and correct pass arrangement in direct-expansion-type chillers.
2. Inspect for freeze protection safety devices.
3. Check strength of liquid bleed-off at bottom of flooded chillers. Check adjustment of level control.
4. Check tubes and shell in brine chiller for type of material.

Evaporative Coolers

- Inspect for adequate spray coverage, nonsagging media, water carry-through, correct water level in sump, and lack of float valve "chatter."

Unit Coolers

Check for:

1. Corrosion protected pan and casing.
2. Water defrost units for spray coverage with no carry-over.
3. Electric defrost units, for cycle timing in accordance with the job conditions.
4. Hot gas defrost, for suction pressures and refrigerant charge in accordance with manufacturer's instructions.
5. Drainage during defrost cycle.
6. Cycle timing.
7. Check that drain lines are properly trapped on the warm end.

Refrigeration Specialties

Check:

1. Superheat setting of expansion valves and that bulb and equalizer position is in accordance with the manufacturer's recommendations.
2. Solenoid valve for vertical stem, correct direction of refrigerant flow, and manual opener disengaged.
3. Unobstructed view of sight glass.
4. Operation of evaporator pressure regulator under light load.
5. Operation of hold-back value upon start-up.

6. Float valves or switches are mounted level and at a height which will ensure correct liquid level in the evapoess before opening of refrigerant drier canisters.

7. Air tightness before opening of refrigerant drier cannisters.

8. Drier; if it is the replaceable type, piping will be arranged to facilitate replacement three-valve by-pass.

9. Piping connections of liquid-suction heat exchanger.

10. That direct expansion coils are installed as recommended by manufacturer.

11. That pans of fan-coil units are protected against corrosion.

12. That drain pans are installed under all units, or as needed, to collect condensate.

Package-Type Air Conditioners

Check the following:

1. High-pressure cutout setting.

2. Compressor hold-down bolts (for shipping) removed.

3. Drip pan should be watertight and connected to open drain.

4. Water regulator valve operation, if used.

5. Installation of air filters and strainers.

6. Operation of thermostat.

7. Suction and discharge pressures of refrigeration compressors.

Heat Pumps

Table 12-28 *Typical Return and Supply Duct Sizing for Heat Pumps*

Btu/h	50,000	60,000	80,000	100,000	125,000
sq. in.	300	360	480	600	750
Round/dia.	20 in.	22 in.	26 in.	28 in.	32 in.

Heat pumps require 6 sq. in. per 1000 Btu/h.

• Outdoor unit needs to have a level supporting foundation at least 3 in. above the ground.

• Units also need to be secured to prevent displacement.

Table 12-29 *Minimum Heat Pump Efficiency*

Equipment	Type	Minimum Performance
Air-cooled heat pump <65,000 Btu/h (heat mode)	Split unit	6.8 HSPF
	Single unit	6.6 HSPF
Air-cooled heat pump <65,000 Btu/h (cooling mode)	Split unit	10.0 SEER
	Single unit	9.7 SEER
Gas/oil furnace <225,000 Btu/h	—	AFUE 78%
Gas/oil steam or hot water boilers <225,000 Btu/h	—	AFUE 80%

Washers

1. Check the following features of the spray-type air washers:

   a. All nozzles discharging water spray.

   b. No water should carry over from eliminators.

   c. Eliminators must not rattle, and they must be removable for maintenance.

   d. Float valve should not "chatter" on opening or closing.

2. Check the following features of the capillary-type washers:

   a. Media should not sag in frames.

   b. Wetting of all media.

   c. Water level is at correct height.

Humidifiers and Dehumidifiers

1. Examine the humidifiers for supported coil and corrosion-protected pan.

2. Check refrigeration-type dehumidifiers for frosting of cooling coil and for water carry-over.

3. Check absorption type dehumidifiers for the following:

   a. Solution level and temperature controls.

   b. No solution should carry over from eliminators.

   c. Regenerator duct must be drained of specified material, and correctly sealed.

Absorption Refrigeration Machine

Check the following:

1. Cleanliness of all parts during erection.

2. Proper materials.

3. Access for removing tubes from absorber-evaporator and generator-condenser.

4. Control operation, especially high- and low-limit temperature cutouts or condenser water pump interlock.

5. Operation of purge system.

6. Unit to be fully charged with water and a nontoxic absorber after installation.

7. Services of a factory representative for charging, testing, starting the plant, and providing instruction.

Cooling Towers and Ponds

1. Check mechanical-draft cooling towers for unobstructed air intake, fan rotation and speed, belt tension, stacked fill, and weather protection of motor. (Do not allow open fan motors when totally enclosed motors are specified.) Ensure that water-flow-through outlet does not form a vortex which draws air in with the water. Check operation of water temperature control and drainage devices.

2. Observe spray ponds for evenness of sprays and for water drift.

3. Ensure provision for an adjustment of constant bleed.

4. See that mist eliminators are installed when specified.

5. Ensure the installation of overflow and drain piping.

6. See that the water is at an adequate level after operation and that the spray pump operates.

7. Check belt alignment and tension.

8. Verify seasonal chemical treatments if required.

Pumps

1. Ensure that manufacturer's nameplates, equipment, serial numbers, or code stamps are not covered or hidden from view after installation.

2. Check for anchorage of pump in compliance with contract.

3. Check alignment of pump with motor and piping.

4. Make sure that all gages and meters are provided.

5. See that eccentric reducers, in lieu of concentric reducers, are used in suction piping, and that the flat side is turned up.

6. Check for adequate support of piping around pump.

7. Be sure check valve is installed in discharge piping.

8. Check pump packing. Make sure adequate packing is installed to allow gland take-up.

9. Check for excess vibration and flexible piping connections if required.

10. Make sure that the pump motor is weatherproof when specified, and that it is connected to rotate correctly.

11. Recheck oil sumps after operation, if applicable.

Insulation

1. Check for:
   a. Proper insulation of chilled water pumps.
   b. Insulated converters and expansion tanks.
   c. Insulated condensate drain pans of air handling units.
   d. Protective finish over such items as pumps, converters tanks, fans, etc.

2. Ensure that all insulating materials have been approved and that they are of the specified thickness.

3. Check the method of attaching insulation to equipment.

4. Make sure that specified reinforcing is provided in adhesive plaster finish.

5. See that corner angle beads are installed at the specified corners.

6. See that the adhesive finish coat has a smooth, pleasing finish.

7. Check on the application of vapor barriers to see that they effectively seal out all moisture.

Controls

1. Review all control installations with approved control shop drawings to ensure that they are being installed in strict conformance with the drawings.

2. See that dampers are mounted securely on rigid supports and that the correct bearings are provided on the blade axles.

3. Note damper motors while fan is on, and check linkage between damper and motor.

4. Examine valve operations for tight closing.

5. Examine electrical equipment for interlocking.

6. Check on the installation of all required alarm bells.

7. See that freeze-stats are installed as specified.

8. Check for proper electrical current and voltage in the control system. Carefully check the operation of solenoid valves.

9. Check that air compressor location will permit tank drain operation, and check for the cycle time with all operating controls.

10. Verify clean elements in humidistats when the system is started.

11. Evaluate pneumatic systems for air-tightness, restrictions caused by flattening of the tubing, and cleanliness of the system.

12. Inspect electronic systems for grounded shielded cable, and location of amplifiers with respect to magnetic fields, such as large transformers.

13. View graphic panels for damaged plastic, dirt between plastic and back plate, lacing of control wires, and access for service to all controls.

14. Verify control instructions, including sequence of operations, and control drawing furnished by the contractor when conducting final acceptance test. Check each function of the controls.

Testing

Submittals

Be sure the contractor obtains approval of test procedures and other pertinent information prior to testing.

Procedures

1. Make a record of all tests, including such information as who attended, methods and procedures of test, results, and conclusions. Check specifications to determine that the contractor is recording sufficient data to comply with requirements.

2. Before tests are scheduled, see that contractor has proper tools, equipment, and instruments; gages should be certified and pretested.

3. See that equipment is thoroughly checked and prepared for tests.

4. Make sure strainers and filters are clean immediately prior to the test.

Types

1. Check the testing of refrigerant piping. See that specified pressure is put on the lines. Make sure all joints are checked and that leaks are detected, repaired, and retested until found satisfactory. Isolate all items which may be damaged by high pressure.

2. See that the hydrostatic test is performed on all water piping. Carefully check to see if there is a loss in pressure during the test.

3. See that a performance test on the system is run for the duration specified. Make sure needed corrections and adjustments are made as determined during the test. See that the contractor records all data required for the performance test.

4. After successful tests, install a new oil charge in compressor. Change oil filters and socks, and provide new cartridge in refrigerant drier. (Oil charge is not required for factory-sealed units.)

Painting

1. See that equipment is furnished with the correct finish. Watch for abrasions.

2. Watch for miscellaneous ferrous metal items that are not primed.

3. Require touching up, priming, and finish painting as specified.

4. Apply asphaltic varnish on all hangers and other items not to be painted. Require piping identification on coding as specified.

Operating Instructions and Guaranties

1. See that equipment guaranties, schematic flow diagrams, and instructions for the operation of equipment are furnished and posted.

2. Arrange for future operating personnel to be instructed on the operation of equipment. Make a record of instruction periods, including any complications, instructing personnel, and personnel instructed. Videotaping such training is a good practice.

Table 12-30 *Estimates of Service Lives of Various HVAC System Components*

Equipment	Years	Equipment	Years	Equipment	Years
Air conditioners		Air terminals		Air-cooled condensers	20
Window unit	10	Diffusers, grilles, and registers	27	Evaporative condensers	20
Residential single or split package	15	Induction and fan-coil units	20	Insulations	
Commercial through-the-wall	15	VAV and double-duct boxes	20	Molded	20
Water-cooled package	15	Air washers	17	Blanket	24
Heat pumps		Ductwork	30	Pumps	
Residential air-to-air	15	Dampers	20	Base-mounted	20
Commercial air-to-air	15	Fans		Pipe-mounted	10
Commercial water-to-air	19	Centrifugal	25	Sump and well	10
Rooftop air conditioners		Axial	20	Condensate	15
Single-zone	15	Propeller	15	Reciprocating engines	20
Multizone	15	Ventilating roof mounted	20	Steam turbines	30
Boilers		Coils		Electric motors	
Hot water (steam)	24	Dx. water or steam	20	Motor starters	17
Steel	25	Electric	15	Electric transformers	30
Cast iron	35	Heat exchangers		Controls	
Electric	15	Shell-and-tube	24	Pneumatic	20
Burners	21	Reciprocating compressors	20	Electric	16
Furnaces		Package chillers		Electronic	15
Gas- or oil-fired	18	Reciprocating	20	Valve actuators	
Unit heaters		Centrifugal	23	Hydraulic	15
Gas or electric	13	Absorption	23	Pneumatic	20
Hot water or steam	20	Cooling towers		Self-contained	10
Radiant heaters		Galvanized metal	20		
Electric	10	Wood	20		
Hot water or steam	25	Ceramic	34		

Carbon Monoxide

A by-product of burning fuels, carbon monoxide (CO) is a deadly gas that kills in a matter of minutes once it is inhaled into the lungs where it attaches to the hemoglobin and moves into the blood stream. Hemoglobin has a much greater attraction to CO than oxygen and forms a very strong bond with the CO. Hemoglobin that has bonded with CO is unable to carry oxygen to the body, so its victim suffers from a lack of oxygen, thus actually suffocating.

Symptoms of CO Poisoning

- Flu-like symptoms
- Tightness across forehead
- Headache
- Partial loss of muscular control
- Increased pulse and respiration
- Dizziness
- Weakness
- Nausea

Table 12-31 *Allowable CO Levels in Appliances*

Range	800 ppm
Dryer	400 ppm
Water heater	200 ppm
Unvented heater	200 ppm
Vented space heater	200 ppm

Suspect CO when:

- Condensation on windows
- Plants are dying
- Odor of aldehyde
- Owners complain of headaches, nausea
- Other CO symptoms

ENERGY CONSERVATION
Insulation

Insulation material must bear the R-Value or a certification of the R-Value must be provided at the job site

Table 12-32 *Climate Zones*

Heating Degree Days (HDDs)	Climate Zone
0–499	1
500–999	2
1000–1499	3
1500–1999	4
2000–2499	5
2500–2999	6
3000–3499	7
3500–3999	8
4000–4499	9
4500–4999	10
5000–5499	11
5500–5999	12
6000–6499	13
6500–6999	14
7000–8499	15
8500–8999	16
9000–12999	17

Note: See Appendix for climate zones.

Table 12-33 *Maximum Glazing U-Factors*

Heating Degree Days (HDDs)	Max. U-Factors
0–499	Any
500–999	0.90
1000–1499	0.75
1500–1999	0.75
2000–2499	0.65
2500–2999	0.60
3000–3499	0.55
3500–3999	0.50
4000–4499	0.45
4500–4999	0.45
5000–5499	0.45
5500–5999	0.40
6000–6499	0.35
6500–6999	0.35
7000–8499	0.35
8500–8999	0.35
9000–12999	0.35

Note: See Appendix for HDDs.

by the insulation installer. Blown-in insulation and/or sprayed-on insulation, the installer is to provide:

1. Initial installed thickness
2. Settled thickness
3. Coverage area
4. Number of bags installed

Markers are required to be installed for attic insulation. Markers are to be attached to trusses, rafters, or joists and divided into 1-in. increments.

Appliances

All mechanical and plumbing systems that require preventive maintenance for efficient operation are to be attached to the appliance, or a label will be attached to the appliance showing the location of the maintenance instructions.

Exterior Wall R-Values

The R-value is to be arrived by the sum of the R-values of the insulation material and not by the framing members, drywall, structural sheathings, or exterior siding materials.

Table 12-34 *Minimum Required R-Values (Ceilings)*

Heating Degree Days (HDDs)	Minimum R-Value
0–499	R-13
500–999	R-19
1000–1499	R-19
1500–1999	R-26
2000–2499	R-30
2500–2999	R-30
3000–3499	R-30
3500–3999	R-30
4000–4499	R-38
4500–4999	R-38
5000–5499	R-38
5500–5999	R-38
6000–6499	R-38
6500–6999	R-49
7000–8499	R-49
8500–8999	R-49
9000–12999	R-49

Note: See Appendix for HDDs.

Note: Where the construction allows insulation to be installed over the top plate, the R-values may be adjusted as follows:

• R-30 can be used where R-38 is specified.

• R-38 can be used where R-49 is specified.

Table 12-35 *Minimum Required R-Values (Walls)*

Heating Degree Days (HDDs)	Minimum R-Value
0–499	R-11
500–999	R-11
1000–1499	R-11
1500–1999	R-13
2000–2499	R-13
2500–2999	R-13
3000–3499	R-13
3500–3999	R-13
4000–4499	R-13
4500–4999	R-16
5000–5499	R-18
5500–5999	R-18
6000–6499	R-18
6500–6999	R-21
7000–8499	R-21
8500–8999	R-21
9000–12999	R-21

Note: See Appendix for HDDs.

Table 12-37 *Minimum Required R-Values (Basement Walls)*

Heating Degree Days (HDDs)	Minimum R-Value
0–499	R-0
500–999	R-0
1000–1499	R-0
1500–1999	R-5
2000–2499	R-5
2500–2999	R-6
3000–3499	R-7
3500–3999	R-8
4000–4499	R-8
4500–4999	R-9
5000–5499	R-9
5500–5999	R-10
6000–6499	R-10
6500–6999	R-11
7000–8499	R-11
8500–8999	R-18
9000–12999	R-19

Note: See Appendix for HDDs.

Table 12-36 *Minimum Required R-Values (Floors)*

Heating Degree Days (HDDs)	Minimum R-Value
0–499	R-11
500–999	R-11
1000–1499	R-11
1500–1999	R-11
2000–2499	R-11
2500–2999	R-19
3000–3499	R-19
3500–3999	R-19
4000–4499	R-19
4500–4999	R-19
5000–5499	R-19
5500–5999	R-21
6000–6499	R-21
6500–6999	R-21
7000–8499	R-21
8500–8999	R-21
9000–12999	R-21

Note: See Appendix for HDDs.

Table 12-38 *Minimum Required R-Values (Slab Perimeter)*

Heating Degree Days (HDDs)	Minimum R-Value/Depth
0–499	R-0
500–999	R-0
1000–1499	R-0
1500–1999	R-0
2000–2499	R-0
2500–2999	R-4/2 ft
3000–3499	R-4/2 ft
3500–3999	R-5/2 ft
4000–4499	R-5/2 ft
4500–4999	R-6/2 ft
5000–5499	R-6/2 ft
5500–5999	R-9/4 ft
6000–6499	R-9/4 ft
6500–6999	R-11/4 ft
7000–8499	R-13/4 ft
8500–8999	R-14/4 ft
9000–12999	R-18/4 ft

Note: See Appendix for HDDs.

Table 12-39 *Minimum Required R-Values (Crawlspace Walls)*

Heating Degree Days (HDDs)	Minimum R-Value
0–499	R-0
500–999	R-4
1000–1499	R-5
1500–1999	R-5
2000–2499	R-6
2500–2999	R-7
3000–3499	R-8
3500–3999	R-10
4000–4499	R-11
4500–4999	R-17
5000–5499	R-17
5500–5999	R-19
6000–6499	R-20
6500–6999	R-20
7000–8499	R-20
8500–8999	R-20
9000–12999	R-20

Note: See Appendix for HDDs.

Table 12-40 *Mass Wall Assembly (R-Values)*

Type	No Insulation	Insulated
6-in. lightweight	2.3	5.0
6-in. medium weight	2.1	4.2
6-in. normal	1.9	3.3
8-in. lightweight	2.6	6.7
8-in. medium weight	2.3	5.3
8-in. normal	2.1	4.2
12-in. lightweight	2.9	9.1
12-in. medium weight	2.6	7.1
12-in. normal	2.3	5.6

Table 12-41 *CMU Cells Not Grouted*

Type	Insulated-Grouted 10 ft O.C.	Insulated-Grouted <10 ft O.C.
6-in. lightweight	4.5	3.8
6-in. medium weight	3.8	3.2
6-in. normal	3.1	2.7
8-in. lightweight	5.9	4.8
8-in. medium weight	4.8	4.0
8-in. normal	3.8	3.3
12-in. lightweight	7.9	6.3
12-in. medium weight	6.4	5.2
12-in. normal	5.1	4.3

FOUNDATION INSULATION

Vertical insulation is to be expanded polystyrene or extruded polystyrene. Horizontal insulation is to be extruded polystyrene. Horizontal insulation placed less than 12 in. below the ground or the portion extending outward from the foundation edge more than 24 in. requires protection. Protection consists of:

1. Concrete slab
2. Asphalt paving
3. Cementitous board
4. Rated plywood
5. Other approved materials

Insulation Checklist

1. Insulation in heavily termite-infested areas has restrictions.
2. Extruded and expanded polystyrene, polyisocyanurate, and other foam plastics are not to be installed on exterior faces or under interior or exterior foundations or slabs below grade.
3. Clearances between the foam plastic insulation installed above grade and exposed earth is to be at least 6 in.

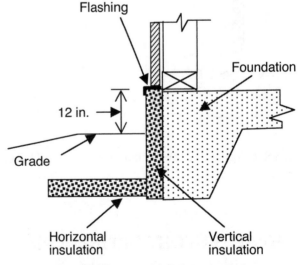

Fig. 12-19 *Typical foundation insulation.*

Table 12-42 *R-Values for Foundation Insulation*

Air Freezing Index	Vertical Insulation R-Value	Horizontal R-Value along Walls	Horizontal R-Value at Corners
1500 or less	4.5	NR	NR
2000	5.6	NR	NR
2500	6.7	1.7	4.9
3000	7.8	6.5	8.6
3500	9.0	8.0	11.2
4000	10.1	10.5	13.1

Table 12-43 *Insulation Measurements for Foundation Insulation*

Air Freezing Index	Horizontal Insulation Dimensions		
	A	B	C
1500 or less	NR	NR	NR
2000	NR	NR	NR
2500	12	24	40
3000	12	24	40
3500	24	30	60
4000	24	36	60

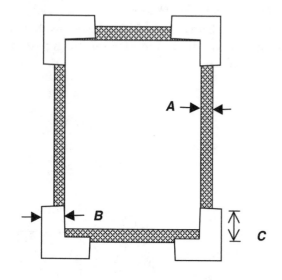

Note: See Appendix for climate zones in the United States.

HVAC/ENERGY DEFINITIONS

Annual Fuel Utilization Efficiency Factor (AFUE). The ratio of annual output energy to annual input energy, which includes any nonheating pilot input loss for gas- or oil-fired furnaces or boilers. It does not include electrical energy.

British Thermal Unit (Btu). Btu is the standard of measurement for heat energy. One Btu is the amount of heat to raise the temperature of one pound of water one degree Fahrenheit.

Cooling Degree Day (CDD). Cooling degree days are based upon a difference in temperature and time. Usually it is an indicator in measuring the energy consumption in the region that you are currently building. It is basically the difference between the mean temperature of the region (usually 65°F) and those days with a temperature different from that standard. For example, a day with a temperature of 76°F has a mean temperature of 11 CDD (76°F minus the mean of 65°F equals 11). Thus, the annual degree-days would be the total sum of days difference for a total of the entire year.

Coefficient of Performance (COP). The ratio between heat output and power input. For example, 1 kW of straight electric heat provides 3,412 Btuh. If a heat pump's COP is 3.00, the same kW delivers 10,236 Btuh. The COP ratio is calculated by dividing the total heat pump heating capacity by the total electrical input (W) and multiply the result by 3.412.

$$\frac{Btuh}{(W)\,3.412} = COP \quad or \quad \frac{Btuh}{(kW)\,3,412} = COP$$

Coefficient of Performance (COP)—Cooling. The ratio of the rate of heat removal to the rate of energy input in consistent units, for a complete cooling system.

Coefficient of Performance (COP)—Heating. The ratio of the rate of heat delivered to the rate of energy input in consistent units, for a complete heat pump system.

Energy Efficiency Ratio (EER). The ratio of net equipment cooling capacity in Btu/h (W) to total rate of electric input in watts under designed operating conditions.

Heating Seasonal Performance Factor (HSPF). The total heating output of a heat pump during its normal annual usage period for heating, in Btu, divided by the total electric energy input for the same period, in watt hours.

Heating Degree Day (HDD). As with the cooling degree day (CDD), the heating degree day is also used in estimating the amount of energy consumed as opposed to the amount of energy consumed for cooling. As with CDD, take the difference between the actual temperature and the mean temperature and add the sums of the days together to get the annual HDD days for the calendar year.

Seasonal Energy Efficiency Ratio (SEER). The total cooling output of an air conditioner during its normal annual usage period for cooling, in Btu/h (W), divided by the total electric energy input during the same period of time in watt hours.

Thermal Transmittance (U). The coefficient of heat transmission (air to air). It is the time rate of heat flow per unit area and unit temperature difference between the warm side and the cool side air films (Btu/h $\times$ ft^2 $\times$ °F). The U-factor applies to combinations of different materials used in series along a heat path, single materials that comprise a build-

ing section, cavity air spaces, and surface air films on both sides of the building element. In roofing applications it is the rate of time the heat flow (per square feet) from the warm side of the roof to the cool side, per unit temperature difference between the two sides. That is, the lower the U-value, the slower and less loss of heat flow occurs through the roof membrane.

Thermal Conductance. The time rate of heat flow through a body from one of its bounding surfaces to the other for a unit temperature difference between the two surfaces under steady conditions.

Thermal Resistance (R). The reciprocal of thermal conductance.

13

CHAPTER

Electrical

INTERIOR ELECTRICAL

This section is designed to assist the Inspector in obtaining quality installation and construction of the electrical installation required by the contract specifications. It is recognized that specialized technical aspects of this subject may require the services of an electrical engineer or technician. When the work appears to be beyond the scope of the Inspector, assistance should be requested promptly from the immediate supervisor. During the preliminary inspection of each phase of work, make an inspection of materials prior to installation for conformance with specification, plans, and approved shop drawings. The submittal register, which lists approved materials, is essential to this inspection. Components for interior electrical work will be inspected before they are installed and energized.

General Requirements

1. The electrical installation must conform to the applicable rules of the current National Electrical Code (NEC), except where expressly modified by the plans and specifications. The appropriate edition of the code will be listed in the specifications. A copy of the applicable NEC should be readily available to the general inspector, and he or she should be prepared to use it as a reference and an authority. However, the NEC is a minimum standard intended to ensure a safe installation. Project specifications may require a higher-quality installation than that which is required by the minimum standards of the NEC.

2. A substitution or change to the requirements of the project specification proposed on the basis of being "Okay under the Code" should not be accepted unless approved by the Project Manager. NEC paragraph references in this text are to assist the Inspector in using the Code and to lend authority to his demands for features not spelled out in the project specifications.

3. Watch job conditions at all times to ensure that the electrical work is done at the proper time in relation to other parts of the building construction.

4. Determine the existence, extent, and classification of hazardous locations as noted in the contract documentation. If such locations exist, the installation therein should be strictly in accordance with appropriate sections of the NEC.

5. Inspect materials and equipment and approved shop drawings. If materials are in accord with approved shop drawing but appear to be contrary to specifications, inform the Project Manager. Do not approve any doubtful material or workmanship (NEC 500-503).

6. Examine both contractor- and owner-furnished equipment for damage in shipment. Promptly report defective equipment and accept or reject such equipment, as directed.

7. Shop inspection by the Inspector may have been required for some equipment and material. Copies of reports of such shop inspections should be on hand before acceptance of material or equipment.

8. Storage of electrical equipment will be done per manufacturer's requirements, and in dry locations, free of dirt and dust, and with protection from physical damage. Storage of switchgear, and engine generator units will usually require indoor storage. Temporary heaters may be required or specified to keep equipment free from effects of condensation. Equipment installed during construction phases should be protected from dirt and moisture. A requirement for this protection may be found in the general conditions of the contract (also NEC 110-11).

9. Require the contractor to furnish all layout drawings required by the specifications. Electrical contract drawings should be reviewed and compared with architectural, structural, and mechanical drawings for possible conflicts. Examples are:

   a. Are the wall switches located with proper respect to door swing?

   b. Does location of wall outlets conflict with installation of baseboard heating units, casework, tile, cabinets, or lockers?

   c. Do cabinets and panels have the required working clearances?

   d. Is there interference with other building construction, such as pipes, ducts, overhead doors, sliding doors, and accessibility? Especially check equipment room layout. Is there ample space with correct clearances?

   e. Are all cable trays clear of other trades? Accessible?

   f. Is relocation of ceiling lighting outlets required, especially in utility and boiler rooms, to avoid interference with mechanical equipment?

   g. Check if ceiling access will be needed in "pulling" wires through the conductors.

   h. Will transformers, bus duct, or switchgear be subjected to moisture from inadequate overhead flooring?

i. Have suspended ceilings been lowered, making lighting fixture clearance from floor inadequate? Will it interfere with the required foot-candles specified?

Temporary electric service will generally be required during the construction period for lighting, power, and sometimes heat. The contractor should make early arrangements for such service to prevent construction delays; temporary installations will be located so as not to interfere with operation of existing facilities or permanent construction. The contractor should arrange for frequent inspection and rehabilitation of temporary installation during the course of the contract to keep it in good repair (NEC-305).

1. Adherence to OSHA requirements and the overall Project Safety Manual is a general provision requirement for all projects.

   a. Temporary open wiring should be guarded or isolated by elevation. Types NM in dry locations and/or NMC in damp locations (Romex) are suitable for temporary wiring when guarded or isolated by elevation (NEC 320, 336).

   b. Portable and extension cords shall be an Underwriters Laboratory (UL) listed type for the usage. Hard service cords Type S, SJ, SJO, SJT, SJTO, STO, or ST are recommended for this service. Types NM or NMC are not approved as portable cables or covers (NEC 400).

   c. Ground fault circuit protection for construction sites is required on all 120-V, single-phase, 15- and 20-amp receptacles per NEC 305-4.

2. Use by the contractor of equipment and facilities permanently incorporated in the structure should be carefully watched to see that circuits and equipment are not overloaded and that all work is left in essentially new condition. All protected safety and working lamps used for temporary lighting shall be removed when construction is completed, and new lamps shall be installed in permanent light fixtures.

3. The submittal register should be prepared and included in the contract specifications prior to bidding the work. This list of required equipment will ensure timely approval and will alert the Inspector if the Contractor has not procured all equipment. Generally, electrical construction materials and equipment must be built and tested according to UL requirements. Listed materials and equipment will bear the UL label.

4. Check shop drawings for all equipment having electrical connections to be sure that rough-in conduits and circuits are correctly sized and located.

5. Manufacturer's representatives are sometimes required to assist field and contractor personnel in the installation, assembly, testing, and/or initial operation of electrical equipment. Maintain a complete record of all adjustments and tests made during installation and startup, and of any peculiarities of the equipment which may be of use to those responsible for its operation and maintenance. Turn a copy of the record over to your supervisor for delivery to the using agency. Retain a copy of all records for the job file.

6. The client's representative should be required to witness tests. The presence or absence of the client's personnel should be noted on the test report.

7. Fire ratings of structures shall not be compromised by electrical installations [NEC 300-21; Grounding (NEC 250)].

Drawings and Specifications

Drawings and specifications should be examined carefully to determine the nature and extent of the grounding system and the requirements for separate grounding of equipment and structures. Automatic Data Processing (ADP) and Communications and Health Care facilities may have special or separately derived lightning protection or grounding requirements.

Temporary Electric

1. Temporary open wiring should be guarded or isolated by elevation. Types NM in dry locations and/or NMC in damp locations (Romex) are suitable for temporary wiring when guarded or isolated by elevation.

2. Portable and extension cords shall be an Underwriters Laboratory (UL) listed type for the usage. Hard service cords Type S, SJ, SJO, SJT, SJTO, STO, or ST are recommended for this service. Types NM or NMC are not approved as portable cables or covers.

3. Ground fault circuit protection for construction sites is required on all 120-V, single-phase, 15- and 20-amp receptacles per NEC 305-4.

   • Use by the contractor of equipment and facilities permanently incorporated in the structure should be carefully watched to see that circuits and equipment are not overloaded and that all work is left in essentially new condition. All protected safety and working lamps used for temporary lighting shall be removed when construction is completed, and new lamps shall be installed in permanent light fixtures.

Visual Inspection

Visual inspection should be made of all ground-system conductors, connections, and electrodes as the work progresses. Ground resistance test: The resistance of all electrodes must be tested to ensure resistance to ground of 25 ohm or less (Project Specifications or NEC 250-84).

Grounds to Metallic Water-Piping System

Grounds to metallic water piping systems should be made on the street side of the meter. Where this is impracticable, full-size jumper connections should be made around any piping system elements which can be removed (NEC 250-112).

1. Make sure that when the water piping system is used for a ground, the water pipe is a metallic pipe and that no insulating fitting has been interposed in the pipe between the ground wire connection and earth (NEC 250-81). An additional ground electrode shall supplement the connection to the water pipe system (NEC 250-81 or NEC 250-83).

2. Where a metallic water main is not available, driven ground electrodes will be provided in conformance with specifications (NEC 250-83 and Project Specifications: Ground Rods).

3. Interior metallic water piping shall always be grounded [NEC 250-80(a)].

Bolted Connections

Bolted connections should be examined to make sure that they are tight and that contact surfaces are cleaned and dry. Contact surfaces will be metal-to-metal. Painted surfaces should be cleaned to bare metal (NEC 250-75).

Exothermic Welding Connections

Exothermic welding connections will be made in strict accordance with the manufacturer's instructions and will employ the proper type and size of mold for the type and size of connection made.

Metallic Enclosures

Metallic enclosures for ground wires shall be electrically continuous from the point of attachment to cabinets or equipment to the grounding electrode and shall be securely fastened to the ground clamp or fitting [NEC 250-92(a)].

Incoming Service Conduit

Incoming service conduit must be grounded by logs, pressure connectors, or clamps. Locknuts and bushings are *not* acceptable for grounding service conduit [NEC 250-32, -71(a) and -72].

Grounding Connection

Ground clamps for connection to water pipe or grounding electrode should be compatible with the pipe or electrode and UL approved for the purpose (NEC 250-115).

Ground Rods

1. Check size, length, and material of ground rods or electrodes against contract drawings and specifications (NEC 250-83, Project Specifications: Grounding).

2. If suitable water pipe is not available, and if ground rods cannot be driven to a minimum depth of 8 ft, other means of establishing a ground must be utilized (NEC 250-83 and 250-84).

System Neutral and Equipment Grounds

Grounding electrode conductor should be joined to grounding electrodes as shown on drawings (NEC 250-112). Some special electronic facilities may require additional isolated grounding electrodes and conductors.

System Neutral

System neutral (grounded circuit conductor) should be grounded (connected to the grounding conductor) on the *supply side* of the service disconnecting means [main service switch(es)]. This connection should be made within the service entrance equipment enclosure (NEC 250-23, 250-50).

Multiple Connections

The connecting of more than one grounding conductor to an electrode by a single clamp is prohibited, unless the clamp or fitting is of a type of specifically designed and approved by the UL for such use (NEC 250-115).

Fig. 13-1 *Grounding loop welded to ground rod.*

Grounding Resistance

Grounding resistance should be verified by instrument measurement (Job Specification or NEC 250-84).

Electrical Continuity

Electrical continuity should be verified throughout the system, usually by visual inspection.

Wiring Methods (NEC 300)

Rigid Metal Conduit, Intermediate Metal Conduit (IMC), and Electrical Metallic Tubing (EMT)

Check to determine requirements and limitations on the use of rigid conduit, IMC, or EMT and special finishing or coating material (steel with zinc coating or galvanizing is standard). Other materials may be allowed or required (Project Specifications: Wiring Methods; NEC-345, 346, 347, and 348).

1. The project specifications generally require the service entrance raceway to be rigid metal conduit.

2. Check size of installed conduit against plans and specifications and determine adequacy for number and size of conductors to be installed (Project Specifications and NEC 345-7, 346-6, and 348-6).

3. Check minimum size of conduit permitted by specifications for both electrical system and communication system (Project Specifications: Telephone and Signal System Raceways; NEC 345-6, 346-5, 347-11, and 348-5).

4. Check to be sure that all required conduits are in place before on-grade slabs are placed. Check stub-up locations against equipment shop drawings.

    a. Generally, for slab-on-grade, construction conduit must be placed under the slab and must be rigid type. (Check plans and specifications.)

    b. Check project specifications for requirement that for stub-ups, couplings should be installed at finished floor level for free-standing equipment (Project Specifications).

    c. Exposed conduit should be installed so that bent portion of stub-up will not extend above floor level.

    d. Be sure that all buried conduit has been surface treated as required by specifications (Project Specifications: Conduit and Tubing Systems).

5. Inspect for damage to the conduit systems (Project Specifications and NEC 345-10, 356-10, 347-13, and 348-9).

6. Is conduit system to be installed concealed or exposed? Check project specifications and plans.

7. Check for the use of the proper type of conduit fittings, i.e., concrete-tight, rain-tight cast fittings; expansion joints, water tight (NEC 345-9, 346-9, 347-6, and 348-8).

8. Check for installation of sleeves for future work in foundation walls and floors during correct stage of construction.

9. Check maximum number of bends in any single conduit run.

10. Make sure that all the conduit required for circuits involving equipment furnished by other sections of the specifications and approved shop drawings, as well as the electrical sections, is installed prior to placing of concrete, closing the walls, ceilings, etc.

11. Check for bushings on ends of conduit. Bushings are not usually required on EMT fittings, because EMT connectors should have smooth internal surfaces (NEC 345-15, 346-8, 347-12).

    a. Check for use of insulating bushings and double lock nuts [NEC 373-6(c)].

    b. Check for use of double locknuts for circuits over 250 V to ground [NEC 250-76(b)].

    c. See that locknuts, bushings, couplings, and connectors are made up tight to ensure ground continuity [NEC 250-92(b)].

12. See that field cuts of conduits and EMT are made square, ends reamed or filed, and cleaned of oil and filings (Project Specifications; NEC 345-8, 346-7, and 348-11). Unreamed ends are very sharp and will damage the wire.

13. Use of running threads is not permitted at couplings (NEC 346-9).

14. Correlate location of conduit terminations against approved shop drawings, equipment, and building plans.

15. Tubing and conduit should be securely fastened in place at intervals required. Means of support provided should be in accord with specifications and NEC requirements (Project Specifications; NEC 348-12, 348-12, 347-8, 346-12, and 345-12).

Table 13-1 *Supports for Rigid Metal Conduits*

Conduit Size (in.)	Max. Distance between Supports (ft)
½ to ¾	10
1	12
1¼ to 1½	14
2 to 2½	16
3 and larger	20

Table 13-2 *Supports for Rigid Nonmetallic Conduits*

Conduit Size	Max. Distance between Supports (ft)
½–1	3
1¼–2	5
2½–3	6
3½–5	7
6	8

Table 13-3 *Supports for EMT Conduits*

Conduit Size	Max. Distance between Supports (ft)
All sizes	10

16. Exposed conduit runs are to be installed parallel or perpendicular to walls and structural members. Vertical conduit runs should be plumb.

17. Conduit runs in wet areas shall be mounted so that there is at least ¼ in. air space between it and the wall or support surface [NEC 300-6(c)].

18. Minimum radius of bends of conduit should be in accordance with the table in the NEC (NEC 346-10, 348-9, 345-10). This table is based on utilizing conductors with 600-V insulation. For cables with higher voltage ratings, and special cables such as telephone cable, consult manufacturer's recommendations for minimum radius of bend.

19. Check for supporting of vertical raceways at each floor level of multistory buildings (Project Specifications).

20. Install galvanized pull wires in empty conduits when required by designs or specifications.

21. Verify the use of corrosion-resistant materials in areas where corrosive influences exist (NEC 300-6; Project Specifications).

22. Require means for prevention of entrance of foreign matter in conduits during construction.

23. Use UL-listed flexible conduit, standard or liquid tight, for connections to motors installed on slide rails, resilient mounts, those subject to vibration, and elsewhere as specified (NEC 350, 351; Project Specifications). Minimum size is ½ in. except as allowed in NEC 350-3, and a bonding jumper may be required.

24. In areas classified as hazardous, be sure that installation is strictly in accord with project specifications and applicable to NEC articles 500 through 517. All questions should be referred to qualified personnel. For Class 1, Division 1 areas, the following items should be carefully verified:

   a. Only threaded steel IMC or threaded rigid metallic conduit, or MI cable with approved connectors, can be used [NEC 501-4(a); threaded joints must be up wrench tight (NEC 500-1) unless a bonding jumper is installed].

   b. At least *five full threads* must be engaged at each threaded joint [NEC 501-4(a)]. All field-made threads must be tapered (NEC 500-1).

   c. All fittings, fixtures, boxes, and enclosures must be specifically involved. An underwriter's approval seal is generally affixed to the equipment. If not, secure other firm verification of approval.

   d. Explosion proof fittings, boxes, and enclosures have screw or ground joints at openings. Be sure that the surface of the ground joints is clean, unscratched, and smooth, so that the mating surfaces make intimate contact throughout their area. Covers must be tight, and gaskets are not to be used.

   e. Be sure that all required seals are installed in the correct location and that they are of the correct type (NEC 501-5 and 502-5). Be sure seals are the correct type of application: vertical or horizontal.

   f. Check the mounting method of equipment to be sure that no holes have been drilled into the interior chamber of an explosion-proof enclosure.

   g. Be sure that all flexible conduits bear the underwriter's listing seal for the hazard involved.

   h. See that proper approved type sealing compound has been installed in all sealing fittings. Follow manufacturer's recommendations [NEC 501-5(c)2].

25. Where rigid nonmetallic conduits are installed under the specification, they should be installed in accordance with NEC 347 and all special requirements of the project specifications.

26. Provide conductor support in long vertical conduit runs (NEC 300-19).

27. Pull wires are provided and are of type specified.

Table 13-4 *Allowable Conduit Bending Radiuses*

Size of Conduit (in.)	Minimum Allowed Radius
½ in.	4
¾ in.	5
1 in.	6
1¼ in.	8
1½ in.	10
2 in.	12
2½ in.	15
3 in.	18
3½ in.	21
4 in.	24
5 in.	30
6 in.	36

Cable Systems

1. Mineral-insulated metal sheathed cable, Type MI, will be installed in accordance with Article 330 of the NEC and project specifications.

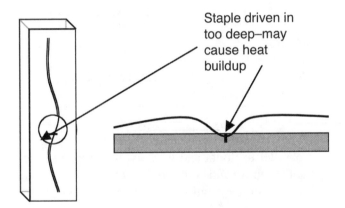

Staple driven in too deep–may cause heat buildup

Fig. 13-2 *Incorrectly driven staple for conductor.*

2. Metal-clad cable Types MC and AC (commonly called "BX") should be installed in accord with project specification requirements and Articles 333 and 334 of the NEC. See that insulating bushings or equivalent protection are provided between the conductors and the armor at terminations.

3. Nonmetallic sheathed cables, Types NM and NMC commonly called "Romex," should be installed in accord with project specifications and Article 336 of the NEC.

a. Type NM cable must not be used when nonmetallic sheathed cable is installed in the cells of masonry block walls which are exposed or which are subject to excessive moisture or dampness. This includes exterior masonry walls. In dry, noncorrosive locations, type MN may be used. NMC is applicable in wet locations (NEC 336-3).

b. See that nails or staples are not driven into cable or driven too tight. Protecting plates may be required (NEC 300-4).

c. Inspect ground wire for proper fastening at terminating points and outlet boxes. Attach to each box of fitting by securely fastening the wire to the intended screw or with an approved grounding device (NEC 25C-114).

d. See that cable is secured as required by the National Electrical Code, within 12 in. of every cabinet, outlet box, or fitting and otherwise at intervals not exceeding 4½ ft (NEC 336-5). See also NEC 370-7(c) for support of cable entering nonmetallic boxes.

4. When required by the project specification, service entrance cable types SE and USE should be installed in accord with NEC 338.

CABLE SYSTEMS

Check that:

- Metal-clad cable (BS) is installed where specified. Cutting is performeabd without conductor damage, and bushings are installed.

- Do not allow staples to be driven excessively to hold the cable.

- Prevent driving of nails into cable. Code gage protection plates are provided where specified.

- NMC cable is used in wet locations or areas exposed to dampness (including exterior masonry walls).

- Nonmetallic cable is installed in areas allowed by contract documents and permitted by codes. Located so cable is protected unless otherwise protected by elevation and/or nonaccessible spaces.

- Cables are secured within 12 in. of box or fitting and otherwise at intervals not exceeding 4½ ft.

Table 13-5 Approved Wiring Applications

Wiring Method	Abbr.	Underground	Wet Locations	Damp Locations	Embedded in Concrete	Embedded in Masonry	Run Exposed	Special Conditions
Armored cable	AC	N	N	N	N	N	Y	
Elect. metallic tubing	EMT	Y*	Y	Y	Y	Y	Y	*Must be protected from corrosion
Elect. nonmetallic tubing	ENT	N	Y*	Y	Y	Y	Y	*Sunlight resistant
Flexible metal conduit	FMC	N	Y*	Y*	N	N	Y	*Must be approved for wet/damp
Intermediate metal conduit	IMC	Y*	Y	Y	Y	Y	Y	*Must be protected from corrosion
Liquid-tight flexible conduit	LFC	Y	Y	Y	N	Y	Y	Not more than 6 ft in length
Metal-clad cable	MC	Y	Y	Y	N	Y	Y	
Nonmetallic sheathed cable	NM	N	N	N	N	N	Y	
Rigid nonmetallic conduit	RNC	Y*	Y	Y	Y	Y	Y	*Must be protected from corrosion and must be sch. 80 if subject to damage
Rigid metallic conduit	RMC	Y*	Y	Y	Y	Y	Y	*Must be protected from corrosion
Service entrance cable	SE	N	Y	Y	N	N	Y	
Surface raceways	SR	N	N	N	N	N	Y	
Underground feeder cable	UF	Y	Y*	Y	N	N	Y	*Sunlight resistant
Underground service cable	USE	Y	Y	Y	N	N	Y	

Table 13-6 Maximum Number of Wires Allowed in Conduit

Wire Size	Maximum Number of Wires Permitted per Conduit Size (in.)							
	1	2	3	4	5	6	7	8
14	½	½	½	½	¾	¾	1	1
12	½	½	½	¾	¾	1	1	1
10	½	¾	¾	¾	1	1	1	1
8	½	¾	¾	1	1¼	1¼	1¼	1¼

Busway Systems (NEC 364; Project Specifications)

1. Support busways at specified intervals (NEC 364-5).

2. Install sway braces when needed to limit lateral movement of busway (Project Specifications).

3. Busway position, vertical or horizontal, will determine whether plugs are installed on the sides or on top and bottom. If plans do not indicate desired position, determination of appropriate location should be made.

4. Install busway runs securely in straight alignment, parallel to floors and walls, with sufficient space either above and below, or on both sides, to permit installation, operation and servicing of bus plugs.

5. Check to be sure that types of duct furnished are in accord with specification. Check conductor metal, enclosure type, duct type, wall flanges, and fire stops.

6. Ground duct housing (NEC 250-33).

7. Vertical riser sections up to 6 ft above the floor must be unventilated (NEC 364-6).

8. Check plug-in features and tap off devices against specification.

9. Check on trolley busways, trolleys, brushes, contact rollers, and flexible cables for no binding and good contact.

10. Component sections should be legibly marked with voltage and current ratings and manufacturer's name (NEC 364-15).

11. Installation and furnishing of busways usually require that the contractor verify field dimensions. Be sure that timely ordering of busway is not delayed.

12. Provide for expansion as required by the manufacturer.

Busways

1. Proper support is provided at specified intervals. Sway braces are provided as required to prevent lateral movement.

2. Provision for expansion is in accordance with manufacturer's instructions.

3. Plug-in features and top of devices are as approved and specified.

4. Component sections are legibly identified and marked with voltage, amperage, and name of manufacturer (as per NEC 364-15).

5. Joints are tightened in strict accordance with manufacturer's instructions.

6. Busway is accessible as specified.

7. Busway housing is grounded.

8. Trolley busways, trolleys, brushes, contact rollers, and flexible cables have good contact and move freely.

9. Busway expansion joints must be provided at all building expansion joint locations.

10. Seismic bracing has been provided per contract documents (depending on the zone).

Underfloor Raceways

1. Raceways are parallel with floor construction, firmly supported at proper elevation, and in straight alignment.

2. No damaged joints are allowed.

3. All joints are tight and sealed in accordance with manufacturer's instructions between sections and to junction boxes.

4. Cross-sectional dimensions are as specified.

5. Sufficient setting depth has been provided at junction boxes.

6. Inserts both pre-set and after-set are or will be secure to raceways and set flush with floor.

Continuous Rigid Cable Supports or Cable Trays

Cable trays are installed to support cables. Only certain specified cables may be installed, and loading of support is limited. Cable trays should be installed in accordance with project specifications and NEC 318. Tray system with cable installed must not downgrade fire barriers [NEC 318-5(g), 300-21].

Wireways

Wireways or enclosed troughs are installed to house and protect wire and cable. In general, wires of the building wire type, such as TW, may be installed in approved wireways. The installation should be made in accordance with project specifications and NEC 362. Particular attention should be paid to NEC 362-5, which limits the number of conductors approved for wireway installation.

Underfloor Duct Systems (NEC 354, 356)

1. Install underfloor raceways of steel construction parallel with floor construction and in straight alignment.

2. Check to see that sufficient setting depth is available for junction boxes. These are the deepest elements of underfloor raceway systems.

3. Check for tight joints between underfloor raceway sections and at junction boxes to keep water out of raceway systems (NEC 354-13, 356-9).

4. Inserts of both the preset and after-set type will be mechanically secured to the underfloor raceway and set level with the floor (NEC 354-14, 356-10).

5. Splices and tapes in underfloor raceway systems will not be made in outlets at inserts, but only at junction boxes to keep water out of raceway systems (NEC 354-13, 356-9).

6. Provide markers at ends of underfloor raceway runs as a minimum. Plans and specifications may require more markings (NEC 354-9, 356-8).

7. Install end caps at ends of all underfloor raceway systems (NEC 354-10).

8. Check tap-off locations to cabinets, panel boards, and receptacles against drawings.

9. Verify from shop drawings relative positions of services in compartments; should be uniform throughout system.

10. Check cross-sectional dimensions for adequate size (NEC 354-5, 356-5; Project Specifications).

11. Be sure that grounding continuity is maintained at all connections in the system (NEC 250-75).

Movable Partition

Movable partitions and similar enclosures, unless specifically listed as raceways, cannot be used as enclosures for general wiring conductors. Instead, raceways (such as conduit) must be installed, or cable (such as type MI) appropriate for the application must be installed. See NEC restrictions for kitchen vent hoods (NEC 410-9).

Conductors (NEC 310)

1. Check type of insulation and jacket, conductor material, conductor size, and stranding in each circuit (Project Specifications and NEC).

2. Observe pulling of wires and cables to detect damage to sheaths, jackets, and insulation. This damage is usually caused when runs are "paid out" in a debris-laden area and then stepped on, or by raceways having sharp edges or contamination. Pulling-eyes or cable-gripping devices will be required for large cables.

3. Install all conductors of a circuit, including neutral, in same raceway in conformance with NEC limitations (NEC 300-20, 215-4).

4. Connections and joints will be clean and tight, with listed pressure-type connectors, and made in junction and outlet boxes, not in raceways (NEC 110-14, 300-15).

5. Connectors, lugs, and clamps used to connect copper and aluminum conductors must be suitable for use with the conductor material to prevent galvanic corrosion (NEC 110-14).

6. All aluminum conductors must be covered with antioxidant before connection.

7. Use only white or natural grey identified conductors for the grounded circuit conductor. Neutral (white or grey) conductor of the wiring system will be insulated throughout (NEC 200-7). Conductors having white or grey identified coverings shall only be used as the grounded circuit conductor except as allowed in exceptions 1–3 in NEC 200-7. Generally, use the same white color for the entire system grounded conductors.

8. When a grounding conductor for equipment is run with circuit conductors it shall be bare, or green covered [NEC 250-57(b)]. Project specifications may require insulated conductors.

9. Enforce color coding of conductors of branch circuits when required by project specifications.

10. Branch-circuit conductors within 3 in. of a ballast within the ballast compartment shall be recognized for use at temperatures not lower than 90°C (194°F) (NEC 410-31).

11. Check that branch circuit wiring is not undersized. Specification may require increased wire size when runs from panel board to center of load equal or exceed 100 ft for 120-V circuits or 230 ft for 277-V circuit.

12. See that correct fixture wiring installation is made (NEC 410-22–34).

Table 13-7 *2% Voltage Drops for 240 V*

Amps	Watts (240 V)	One-Way Distance (ft)			
		No. 14	No. 12	No. 10	No. 8
5	1200	180	285	455	720
10	2400	90	140	225	360
15	3600	60	95	150	240
20	4800	45	70	115	180
25	6000	35	55	90	140
30	7200	30	48	75	120
40	9600		36	56	90
50	12000			45	70
60	14400				60

Table 13-8 *2% Voltage Drops for 120 V*

Amps	Watts (120 V)	One-Way Distance (ft)			
		No. 14	No. 12	No. 10	No. 8
5	600	90	143	228	360
10	1200	45	70	113	180
15	1800	30	47.5	75	120
20	2400	22.5	35	57.5	90
25	3000	17.5	27.5	45	70
30	3600	15	24	37.5	60
40	4800		18	28	45
50	6000			22.5	35
60	7200				30

OUTLETS

1. Check for requirements of cast boxes in exposed work, exterior work, wet locations, damp locations, and hazardous locations.

2. Require hub-type cast boxes when specified.

3. Check size of junction and pull boxes (NEC 370-6, 18, 20). Do not permit overcrowding of boxes with excessive number of conductors (NEC 370-6).

General Receptacles

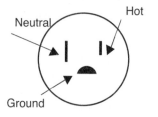

Fig. 13-3 *Typical 15-amp, 125-volt outlet.*

Color Coding

- *Black.* Hot, connects to the darker screw terminal of the switch or receptacle.

- *Red.* Second hot wire when it is a 240-V circuit.

- *White.* Neutral wire, or grounding wire, connects to the lighter or silver terminal of switch or receptacle.

- *Green or Bare.* Grounding wire, connects to the green screw.

The NEC does allow white-colored wires to be used as hot leads provided that the visible part of the wire is painted or taped black.

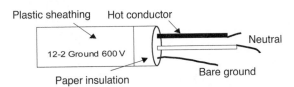

Fig. 13-4 *Typical wire components.*

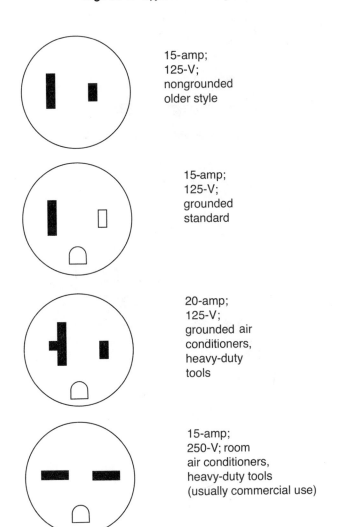

Fig. 13-5A *Typical NEMA receptacles.*

15-amp;
125-V;
nongrounded
older style

15-amp;
125-V;
grounded
standard

20-amp;
125-V;
grounded air
conditioners,
heavy-duty
tools

15-amp;
250-V; room
air conditioners,
heavy-duty tools
(usually commercial use)

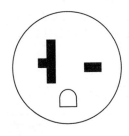

20-amp;
250-V;
grounded air
conditioners, heavy-1-
duty tools

15-amp;
277-V;
grounded
commercial lighting

30-amp;
125/250-V;
dryers and heavy-duty
equipment

20-amp;
125/250-V;
commercial and
industrial use

50-amp;
125/250-V;
home ranges,
commercial
and industrial use

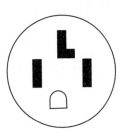

30-amp;
125/250-V;
grounded dryers and
heavy-duty equipment

Fig. 13-5A *(Continued)*

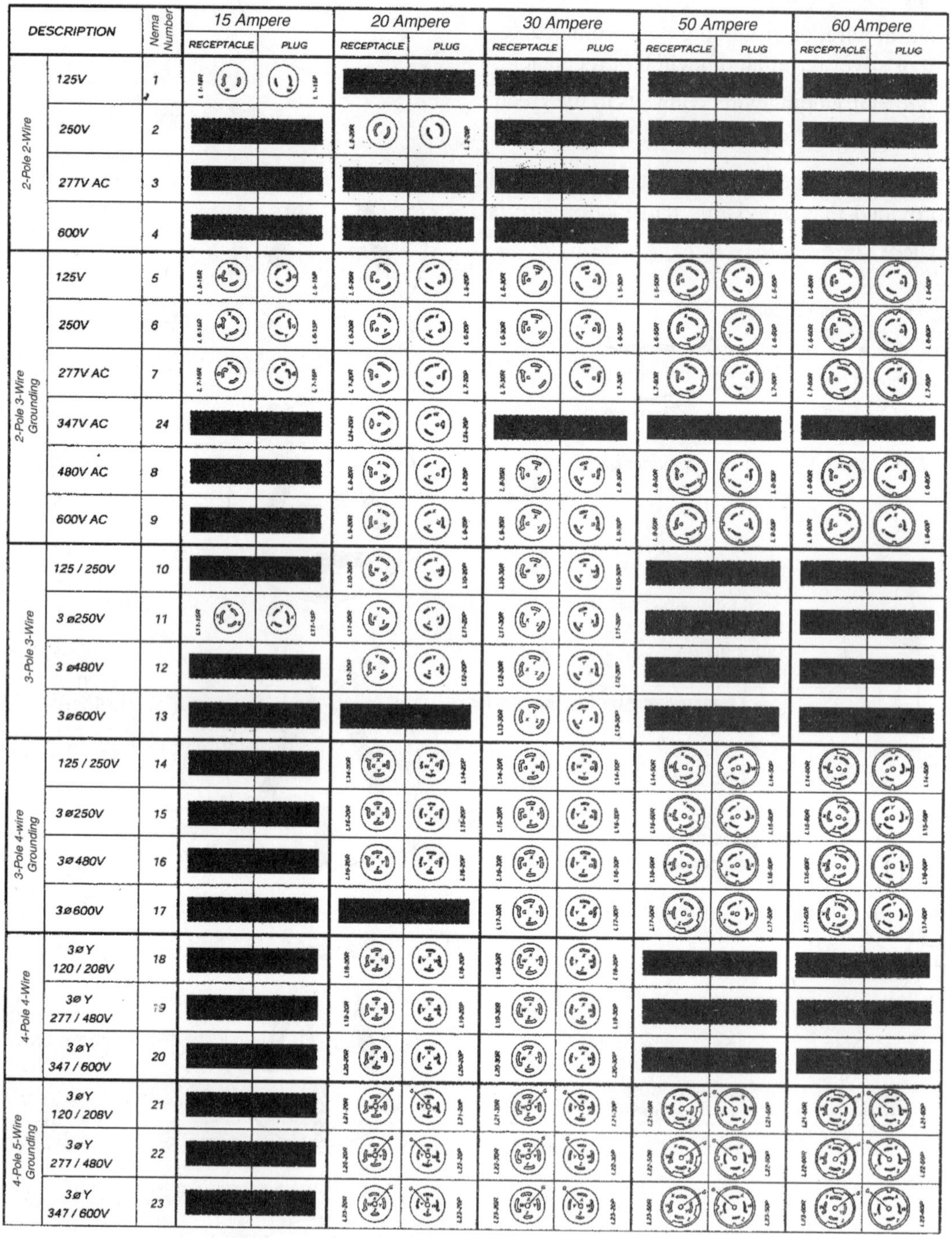

DESCRIPTION		Nema Number	15 Ampere		20 Ampere		30 Ampere		50 Ampere		60 Ampere	
			RECEPTACLE	PLUG	RECEPTACLE	PLUG	RECEPTACLE	PLUG	RECEPTACLE	PLUG	RECEPTACLE	PLUG
2-Pole 2-Wire	125V	1										
	250V	2										
	277V AC	3										
	600V	4										
2-Pole 3-Wire Grounding	125V	5										
	250V	6										
	277V AC	7										
	347V AC	24										
	480V AC	8										
	600V AC	9										
3-Pole 3-Wire	125 / 250V	10										
	3 ø250V	11										
	3 ø480V	12										
	3ø600V	13										
3-Pole 4-wire Grounding	125 / 250V	14										
	3 ø250V	15										
	3 ø 480V	16										
	3ø600V	17										
4-Pole 4-Wire	3 ø Y 120 / 208V	18										
	3 ø Y 277 / 480V	19										
	3 ø Y 347 / 600V	20										
4-Pole 5-Wire Grounding	3 ø Y 120 / 208V	21										
	3 ø Y 277 / 480V	22										
	3 ø Y 347 / 600V	23										

Note: Blank spaces reserved for future configurations.

Fig. 13-5B   NEMA configurations for locking plugs and receptacles.

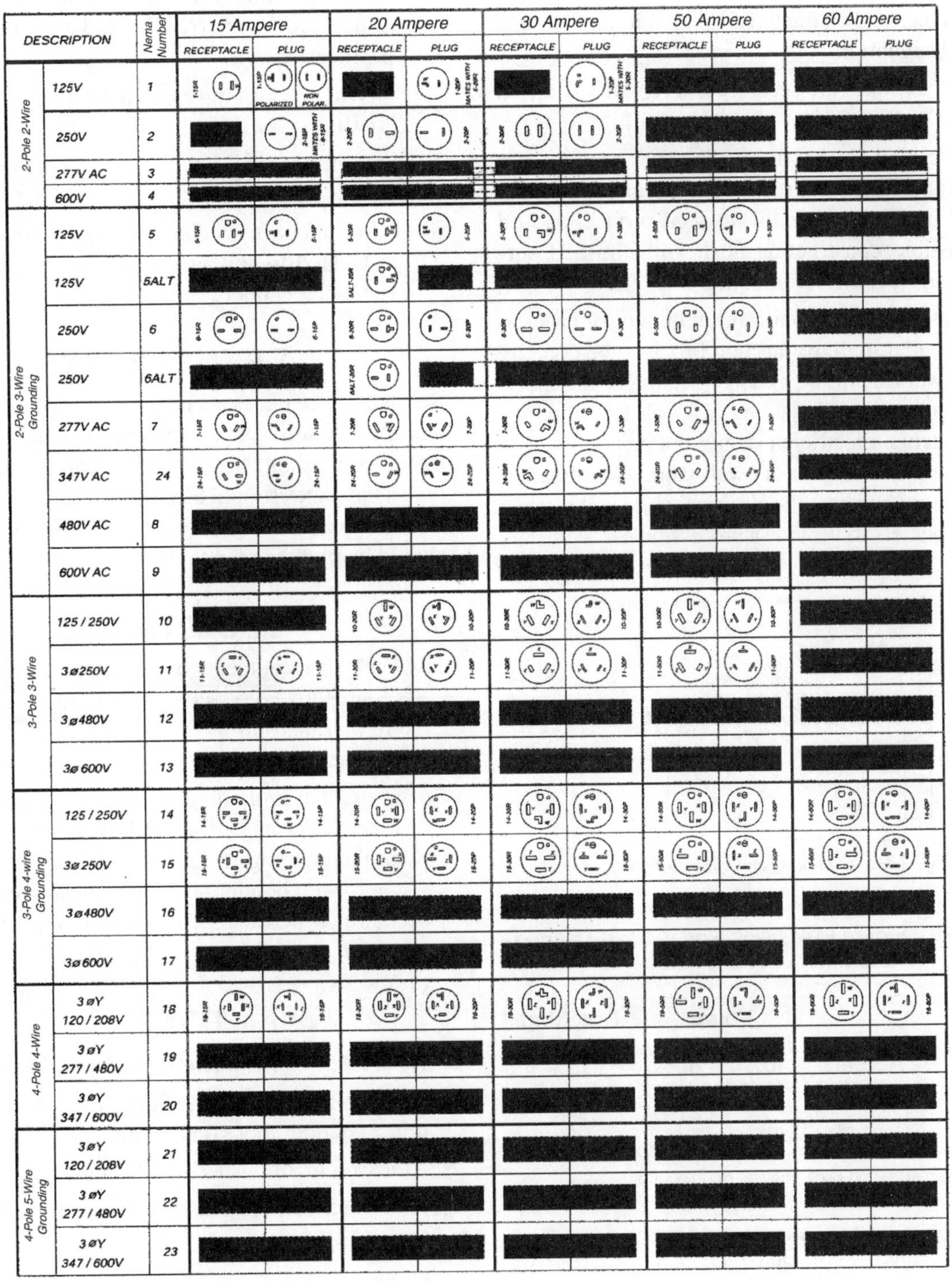

DESCRIPTION		Nema Number	15 Ampere		20 Ampere		30 Ampere		50 Ampere		60 Ampere	
			RECEPTACLE	PLUG	RECEPTACLE	PLUG	RECEPTACLE	PLUG	RECEPTACLE	PLUG	RECEPTACLE	PLUG
2-Pole 2-Wire	125V	1										
	250V	2										
	277V AC	3										
	600V	4										
2-Pole 3-Wire Grounding	125V	5										
	125V	5ALT										
	250V	6										
	250V	6ALT										
	277V AC	7										
	347V AC	24										
	480V AC	8										
	600V AC	9										
3-Pole 3-Wire	125 / 250V	10										
	3ø250V	11										
	3ø480V	12										
	3ø 600V	13										
3-Pole 4-wire Grounding	125 / 250V	14										
	3ø 250V	15										
	3ø480V	16										
	3ø600V	17										
4-Pole 4-Wire	3 øY 120 / 208V	18										
	3 øY 277 / 480V	19										
	3 øY 347 / 600V	20										
4-Pole 5-Wire Grounding	3 øY 120 / 208V	21										
	3 øY 277 / 480V	22										
	3 øY 347 / 600V	23										

Note: Blank spaces reserved for future configurations.

Fig. 13-5C NEMA configurations for straight-blade plugs and receptacles.

Check

1. Check identification requirements of power and control conductors at terminals and in pull boxes and junction boxes. Fenders should be tagged to indicate electrical characteristics, circuit number, and panel designation.

2. Check that boxes are securely and rigidly supported (NEC 370-13).

3. Fit concealed boxes into walls and ceilings. On noncombustible construction, the front edge of box should be within ¼ in. of finished surface, and on combustible construction flush with finished surface or project therefrom (NEC 370-10).

4. Any masonry or dry wall work required for installation of outlet, pull, or junction box is to be done by skilled workmen. The masonry section of the specifications requires the cutting of block for fitting installed items. Electrician should not be permitted to chop away masonry or dry wall work. Coordination is necessary between the electrical trade and masons and carpenters to provide a professional system.

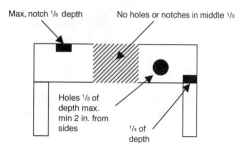

Fig. 13-6 *Notching and boring of joists.*

Table 13-9 *Figure Holes/Notching in Load-Bearing and Exterior Wall Studs*

| Nominal | Actual | Holes | | Notching |
		40%	*60%	25%
2 × 4	1½ × 3½	1¹³⁄₃₂	2³⁄₃₂	⅞
2 × 6	1½ × 5½	2³⁄₁₆	3⁵⁄₁₆	1⅜

*Holes between 40% and 60% must be double stud.

Table 13-10 *Figure Holes/Notching in Non-Load-Bearing Studs*

| Nominal | Actual | Holes | | Notching |
		40%	*60%	40%
2 × 4	1½ × 3½	1¹³⁄₃₂	2³⁄₃₂	1¹³⁄₃₂
2 × 6	1½ × 5½	2³⁄₁₆	3⁵⁄₁₆	2³⁄₁₆

*Holes between 40% and 60% must be double stud.

5. Check for air space between box and wall or supporting surface in wet locations where surface-type units are used (NEC 300-6).

6. Are outlets that are exposed to the weather a weather-proof type (NEC 370-5 and 300-6; Project Specifications)?

7. Pull and junction boxes shall have free access (NEC 370-19).

8. Floor outlets shall be of required type and properly located.

9. Light outlets in mechanical and equipment rooms are located to suit servicing and maintenance and extend below ducts.

DEVICE PLATES

See that device plates are of specified material and finish and that all surfaces are in contact with wall (Project Specifications and NEC 410-56). On surface-mounted boxes the plates should be compatible with the box and without overhanging corners, and NEC 380-0. Plates should be plumb and not dished or bowed.

RECEPTACLES

1. Check all receptacles to be sure that specified voltage, ampere, color, slots, etc. are furnished. Also be sure that the plug is furnished if specified (Project Specifications).

2. Be sure that grounding continuity is maintained between the grounded metal box and receptacle and that the bonding jumper is installed when required or approved bonding type receptacle. Some designs require ground wire from panel to receptacle (NEC 250-74).

BOXES

- No greater than ⅛ in. between drywall and box shell.

- At least ¼ in. of sheathing showing at cable entrance, but not more than ¾ in.

- At least 6 in. of "extra" conductor required in boxes.

- At wet areas the receptacle needs to be GFCI protected.
  - Garages
  - Outside
  - Unfinished basements
  - Kitchens
  - Bathrooms

- Regular sunsported boxes are not to be used for ceiling fans.

- A 3-in. box is too small for ¼ Romex cable.
- Conduit bends shall not exceed 360° total bends in-between stations.
- Walls 2 ft or wider need receptacles.
- Halls longer than 10 ft need receptacle(s).
- Placed every 6 ft along walls.

Table 13-11 *Wire Sizes*

Wire Size	Cubic Inches
#14	2.00
#12	2.25
#10	2.50
#8	3.00
#6	5.00

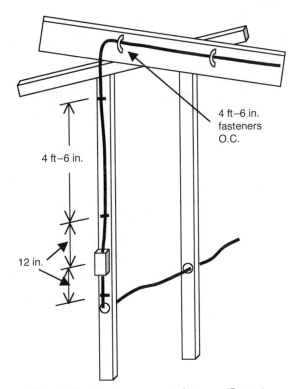

Fig. 13-7 *Maximum support distances (Romex).*

WALL SWITCHES

1. Check wall switches for proper ampere rating, voltage rating, and type. Usually "AC only" is required. AC-only switches are marked "AC" or "AC only" on yoke, never "AC/DC." They can be used for alternating current only. Wall switches will be in hot leg of circuit, not in neutral, and should be installed with the "on" position "up" (NEC 380-6).

2. Check for requirements of installing pilot lights on switches (project specifications).

OUTLETS

1. Architectural drawings are referred to for comparison of all conditions affecting layout of outlets. Coordinate work with other trades.

2. Special equipment outlets have been roughed in as per manufacturer's rough-in drawings and/or approved shop drawings.

3. Floor outlets of approved type are properly located. Verify dimensions if indicated or critical. Review with the approved equipment and furniture layout.

4. Wall receptacles, switch outlets, cable/communication, and fixture outlets are mounted at height and location specified.

5. Light outlets in mechanical and equipment rooms are located to suit servicing and maintenance and extend below ducts and ceiling. Door swings, equipment, and other features are not in conflict for convenience of use.

6. Junction, pull, and outlet boxes are of type, size, and location specified. Are they properly identified?

7. Boxes are securely and rigidly supported and do not rely on conduits for this support, except as permitted by code.

8. Ground fault receptacles are provided in locations specified by the NEC, such as areas near water or outside.

9. Cast boxes and special boxes are provided as specified in fire rated areas, exposed areas, exterior areas, wet locations, and hazardous locations. All boxes exposed to the elements are weatherproof.

10. Do not allow an excessive number of conductors in boxes.

11. Plaster rings, extension rings, etc., are provided. Incombustible surfaces allow ¼ in. of space from finish, and combustible shall be flush. No combustible material is exposed to interior of box.

12. Inspections are conducted from the local jurisdiction before covering.

13. Unused openings are sealed.

14. Boxes are accessible.

15. Grounding continuity is maintained, including jumpers. Installed devices are of specified type, voltage, amperage, color, etc.

16. Switches are installed in hot leg of circuit (not neutral) and with "on" position up, except for momentary contact, three-way and four-way switches.

SERVICE EQUIPMENT

1. Check to be sure that the proper type of enclosure is furnished (such as drip-proof, totally enclosed, etc.) (Project Specifications).

2. Standard NEMA (KS-1) designations are used to describe various enclosures for switches. The designations are as follows:

Type 1	Indoor—general purpose
Type 2	Outdoor—dust-tight, raintight, and sleet (ice) resistant
Type 4	Indoor/outdoor—watertight and dust-tight
Type 5	Indoor dustproof
Type 7	Class I, Groups A, B, C and/or D—indoor hazardous locations—airbreak equipment
Type 9	Indoor hazardous locations—airbreak equipment
Type 12	Indoor—industrial use, dust-tight and drip-tight with knockouts

Note: "Weatherproof" is defined in the NEC as so constructed or protected that exposure to the weather will not interfere with successful operation (NEC 100) and raintight, rainproof, or watertight equipment can fulfill the requirements for weatherproof.

1. Check whether fusible-type or circuit-breaker type of service switch is required (Project Specifications).

2. Check that the service-switch enclosure is bonded to the ground system (NEC 230-62, 63).

3. Check voltage rating and ampere rating of switch. Check also circuit breaker trip and fuse sizes and interrupting capacities (Project Specifications and Plans).

4. Check ground fault protection of service equipment when required by NEC 230-95 or Project Specifications.

5. Check meter location when specified.

Panelboards

1. Be sure to inspect plug-in panel board devices to determine tightness of fit.

2. Check loads on panels to be sure of approximate balance among the phases. This is best done by use of clamp-on-type ammeters on feeders while panel is carrying its normal load (operational test).

3. Be sure the panelboards typed directory is properly filled out so that area and devices served can be quickly identified.

4. Circuit breakers, switches, and fuses in panelboards should be inspected to determine that they have correct number of poles, proper voltage, current-rating, and proper interrupting capacity. Refer to contract drawings and project specifications.

5. Check panelboards for inclusion of blanked-off spaces for future circuit breaker installation. Space to be adequately sized for the rating of future circuit breaker. Also see that spare breakers required are in place in addition to blanked-off spaces.

6. Check mounting height of top switch or circuit breaker. It should be less than 6 ft, 6 in.

Cabinets

1. Check on size of gutter space. A minimum of 5 in. is required for panelboards with through feeders. Load centers should be in accordance with NEC 373-6(a). Telephone cabinets are to be checked for inclusion of backboard painted with insulation varnish.

2. Compare size of telephone cabinets against contract drawings.

3. Mounting is to be rigid and independent of the support by conduits. In damp locations, there should be ¼-in. minimum air space at back of panel (NEC 373-2).

4. Connections to conduits are to be tight (NEC 250-71–79).

5. Look for special features of construction and installation for areas other than normal, such as hazardous, wet, exposed to fumes, etc. (NEC 110-11).

6. Examine for galvanized metal construction.

7. Check mounting height of panelboard cabinets. Distance from the highest position of top switch or circuit-breaker to floor should not exceed 6 ft, 6 in. (Project Specifications).

8. Cabinets must be UL approved (with label or stamp present).

Fuses

Inspect for the following:

1. Specified voltage rating.

2. Specified amperage and interrupting rating.

3. Nonrenewable cartridge types for over 30-amp capacity

4. Are dual element time-delay fuses or current limiting fuses with special "reject" holders required?

5. Do not allow "piggy back" connections.

6. Are GFCI breakers installed if required?

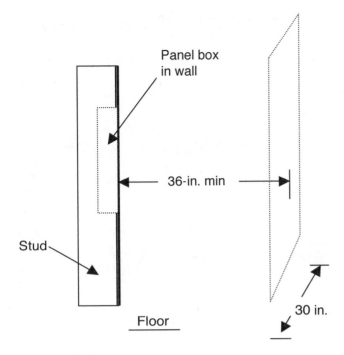

Fig. 13-8A *Panel box clearances.*

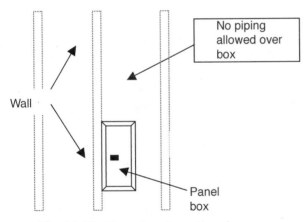

Fig. 13-8B *Front view of panel box clearances.*

Table 13-12 *Branch-Circuit Requirements*

Circuit Rating:	15 A	20 A	30 A	40 A	50 A
Copper Conductors (Min. Size)					
Circuit wires	14	12	10	8	6
Taps	14	14	14	12	12
Overcurrent protection	15 A	20 A	30 A	40 A	50 A
Receptacle rating	15 A max.	15 or 20 A	30 A	40 or 50 A	50 A
Maximum load	15 A	20 A	30 A	40 A	50A

Underground Service Conduits

1. Check detail requirements of plans and specifications.

2. Check requirement for painting or coating of conduits.

3. Check method and location of termination of conduit ends and grounding (NEC 230-55). Seal building ends of raceways entering from distribution system (NEC 230-48).

Lamps and Lighting Fixtures

Lighting fixtures should be examined for:

1. Cracked glass, chipped porcelain, and plastics, bent louvers, overall finish, detachable sockets on RLM dome fixtures (when specified) and "push type" sockets on open fluorescent fixtures (when specified) (OCE standard fixture drawings).

2. Required lamp type, wattage, and color characteristics.

3. Ballasts for fluorescent and mercury-vapor lamps suitable for circuit voltage and of high power-factor type; overload protection for ballasts, if specified ballasts should be suitable for low-temperature operation. Ballasts for fixtures to be recessed in fire-rated or insulated ceiling construction may be required to be "low loss" type to hold ambient temperature down.

4. Stairways:
   - 850 lumens at landings
   - Switch at both levels
   - 850 lumens at top landing on exterior stairs

Table 13-13 *Lumens to Watts Conversions*

Watts	Lumens	Watts	Lumens
15	125	150	2880
25	235	200	4010
40	455	300	6360
60	870	500	10850
75	1190	750	17040
100	1750	1000	23740

5. Plumb installation and horizontal and vertical alignment.

6. End-caps, canopies, louvers, side panel guards, globes in place, and tight-glass side panels, if specified; acrylic plastic lens when specified.

7. Aiming of floodlights and all other adjustable fixtures.

8. Lamps that are to be installed for the project shall be new and installed just prior to completion.

9. Storage battery–powered emergency lighting sets should be checked against applicable codes and specifications for requirements of the underwriter's listing and other features. They should be permanently installed strictly in accordance with project specifications and NEC Article 700.

10. Emergency lighting circuits should be installed in accordance with project specifications and NEC Article 700.

11. Circuit wiring should be kept independent of all other wiring (NEC 700-17).

12. End-to-end mounted flourescent fixtures must have the Underwriter's approval for mounting end-to-end (NEC 410-31) when used as raceways.

13. Required characteristics specified.

14. Grounded properly.

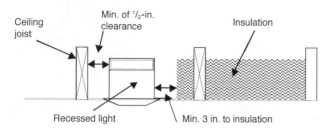

Fig. 13-9 *Recessed lighting clearances from insulation.*

Equipment Connections

1. Refer to applicable paragraphs of this chapter.

2. Check plans and specifications for any special features.

3. If client-furnished equipment is involved, ensure the timely availability of all connection drawings.

TRANSFORMER STATIONS
Dry-Type Transformers

Check enclosure for indoor or outdoor service. Install so that air circulation will not be restricted around the transformers. Close-to-ceilings installations should be avoided.

Transformer Taps

Connect to produce specified voltage under normal load.

Liquid-Filled Transformers

Fig. 13-10 *Transformer.*

Check to see that they are filled to proper level. The level mark is indicated on transformer.

Nameplate Data

Check against specification requirements and approved shop drawings (NEC 450-11).

Accessories

Check liquid-filled transformers for compliance with specifications or with specified standards. Such include: connections for sampling, draining, and filtering of insulating liquid; level gage; thermometer; pressure and vacuum gages; external tap changer; provisions for jacking, rolling and lifting; provisions for pole, platform, or slab mounting; provision grounding of case and windings; and alarm devices actuated by abnormal liquid level, temperature, or pressure; and automatic control devices for operation of forced air or other oil-cooling equipment which will permit operation of transformers at higher-than-normal ratings.

Bushings

Check to see that bushings are free of moisture and dirt, and that they are not chipped and cracked.

Insulating Liquid

Check against requirements. Nonflammable fluid-insulated power transformers are generally required indoors.

Grounding

Check grounding connections of metal housing, neutrals of primary and secondary winding to the grounding system (NEC 450-9 and 250-26).

Ventilation

See that ventilation is adequate (NEC 450-45).

SWITCHGEAR

Check for:

1. Anchor bolts and floor plates in proper location. Consult approved shop drawings and contract drawings.
2. Level floor location for gear and any roll-out equipment.
3. Conduit entrances and wiring trenches in proper location.
4. Bus duct connection provisions suitable for duct attachment.
5. Ground bus connections brought to proper location. Consult approved shop drawings.
6. Plumb and level installation of gear. Installation in accordance with manufacturer's instructions.
7. All blocking is removed from instrument and relays.
8. Adjustments made where required; taps and plugs at proper settings. Consult manufacturer's installation instructions.
9. Fuses in place and of proper type—voltage, current, interrupting capacity, current limiting.
10. Indicating lamps with proper color caps in place.
11. Furnishing of spare fuses and lamps and any operating handles or cranks.
12. Manufacturer's instruction books, wiring diagrams, etc., delivered to responsible individual accepting installation. Make a list and have it signed and filed.
13. Terminals marked in accordance with approved shop drawings and specifications.
14. Are all wiring connections made up tight?
15. If switchgear is to be installed in any hazardous locations, check the specifications and drawings for any required special construction features.
16. Check for sufficient clearance between back of switchboard and wall. Minimum of 30 in. is required if equipment or wiring is accessible only from back. Additional clearance may be required (NEC 110-16 and 34).
17. Check that switchboard frames are properly grounded.
18. Check to be sure conduit stub-ups have coupling installed at floor level if required by project specifications.
19. Check to be sure that proper phase relationship and identification of connections including instrumentation have been accomplished.
20. Special requirements, such as seismic conditions.

ENGINE GENERATOR SETS

Inspect for overall compliance with the specifications as to type and rating of components—kVA, kW, horsepower, rpm, voltage—and in particular as to the following:

1. Engine will be suitable for operation on the fuel specified.
2. Voltage ratings of starter, battery, and battery charger will be the same. Voltage regulator may need to be reset if nickel cadmium batteries are furnished.
3. Check spare parts provided with unit to see that the supply is complete and that they fit the unit furnished.
4. Installation should be in accord with NFPA 30, 31, and 37, as required by project specifications. Check for proper calibration of gage stick.
5. That ventilation is adequate.
6. See that operation and maintenance manuals are posted in engine room.
7. Check operation of transfer switches.
8. Check governor operation.
9. Check cranking cycle for reset.
10. Check to determine that emergency shutdown prevents recycling.
11. Required field tests have been satisfactorily completed.
12. Check automatic transfer switch, lab test reports, operation, and settings.

ELEVATOR INSTALLATIONS

1. Check voltage rating of hoisting machinery.
2. Provide safety interlocks as specified and check operation.
3. Record all performance of specified tests.

SPECIALTY SYSTEMS

Includes:

- Several types of audible and visual paging systems
- Nurses call
- Central dictation
- Intercommunication systems of loudspeaker and telephone type
- Fire alarm systems
- Clock systems
- Supervisory systems
- Those which combine more than one function in a single system

Products of various manufacturers of like systems may differ greatly. Manufacturer's installation instructions will be rigidly adhered to. The following will apply generally to all systems:

1. Master sets and main or central station equipment and switchboards of miscellaneous systems will be so placed as to be easily accessible for operation and maintenance in locations having adequate ventilation.
2. Generally, component parts of miscellaneous systems will be products of one manufacturer.
3. Wiring between system components may be of special character. Inspect for requirement for use of optical fiber cable, shielded cables, twisted pairs, and isolation of any system from another.
4. Check installation of miscellaneous systems equipment to see that the proper type and sizes of fuses have been used, that leads are connected to proper terminals and that the equipment is designed to operate on the available supply voltage.

TESTS
All Testing

1. When testing of any electrical equipment or system is required, advise the electrical inspector or engineer and obtain his assistance. The following paragraphs cover a wide range of testing, and it will be your responsibility to obtain assistance when such testing is beyond your capabilities or knowledge.
2. Unless otherwise specified, testing should be performed by the contractor when the inspector is present. All arrangements for tests should be made by the contractor. For tests of major equipment and high-voltage cables, the contractor should also notify the manufacturers so they may witness the tests.

3. The client should be notified when any unusual testing is to be performed so that they may be present to witness the test. Client cooperation should be obtained well in advance for any tests which may affect their facilities or operations.

Precautions

Precautions should be taken to ensure that test voltages are applied only to equipment or circuits under test, and that all instrument and control circuits are disconnected during the test. Verify that all electrical equipment can be Lock-Out/Tag-Out.

Electrical Tests

Electrical tests should not be conducted under ambient conditions unsuitable for testing, such as excessively high humidity conditions.

Records of Tests

Each testing record is to include but not be limited to:

1. Ambient temperatures.
2. Weather conditions.
3. Circuit designation and extent of wiring systems being tested; name and serial number of the machine tested.
4. Signatures of those witnessing the tests.
5. Date of testing.

Description of Tests

1. De-energized operational testing will determine that moving parts do not bind, rotating parts work freely and are not obstructed by foreign materials, that they are lubricated as required, and that such limits or stops as may be necessary to restrict the motion of moving parts are in place and functioning.
2. Operational testing will show that the equipment performs all functions for which it is designed in accordance with the design and manufacturer's specifications.
3. Continuity testing will determine that circuits are continuous throughout the circuit.
4. High potential testing will determine that the insulation has sufficient dielectric strength to withstand the surges to which it might be subjected and to ensure freedom from pinholes and any other possible damage.
5. Megger tests determine that the wiring system and equipment are free from short circuits and grounds

and measure the insulation resistances of the circuit and/or equipment under test.

Megger Tests

Megger tests of insulation resistance should be made when specified and approved if satisfactory.

Method of Testing

1. High-potential field tests should be made in strict compliance with the applicable standards listed in the specifications and with the recommendations of the manufacturer of the equipment.

   a. Tests should not be repeated unless the necessity for repetition has been determined by an electrical engineer or specified.

   b. Make only after all safety precautions relative to grounding of the test equipment have been checked.

2. Insulation resistance and high-potential tests of wiring systems should be made when required between one conductor and ground with all other conductors and sheath or conduit connected to the same ground. Tests should be made on each conductor in this manner.

3. Rotating equipment operational tests should include an inspection for alignment with driven machine, proper lubrication, freedom from excessive vibration in operation, proper direction of rotation, voltage and current drain check against motor nameplate ratings, check of rpm, and excessive heating.

4. Rotating equipment operational tests should include an inspection for alignment with driven machine, proper lubrication, freedom from excessive vibration in operation, proper direction of rotation, voltage and current drain check against motor nameplate ratings, check of rpm, and excessive heating.

5. Switch and manual motor starter operational tests should include an examination for proper operation, alignment of contacts, and contact pressure.

6. Motor-starter operational tests should include manually operating the armature or plunger and contact-bar to determine that movement is free, contacts are in alignment, contact pressure is adequate, and auxiliary contacts function properly. The starter should be energized from all control points, and the operation of all control-circuit interlocks should be checked.

7. Reduced-voltage starters should be checked for correct sequence and timing of application of incremental and full voltages.

8. Variable- and adjustable-speed motor controls should be checked to see that operating speeds correspond to the position of the speed control device.

9. Circuit-breaker operational tests for large air circuit breakers operating and test positions under manual operation and through control circuits from each control point. Checking of breaker mechanisms for alignment; freedom of motion and adequate pressure of contacts; tripping, devices; inspection to ensure that breaker cannot be moved from operating position while closed. Indicating lights, targets, annunciators, and alarms should be observed for operation in connection with associated circuit breakers, control switches, and other operating devices to ensure that the signal indication corresponds to the switch position of the indicating device.

10. Protective relays should be checked to see that time and current settings have been made as specified.

11. Operational tests of relays should include checking of operation at specified current or voltage and time values; checking of peak current of instantaneous elements; checking of differential elements for operation only under condition of proper direction of power flow.

12. Rod electrodes should be tested for resistance to ground. If resistance is greater than the specified resistance, or a maximum of 25 ohms, additional rods or longer rods should be installed. Consult specifications.

13. Miscellaneous systems for intercommunication, paging, clock-control fire alarms, etc. shall be given operational tests at all operating points to demonstrate that they will perform all specified functions. In particular, it shall be demonstrated that sounding devices are audible under normal ambient sound-level conditions in areas for which coverage is specified, that false signals cannot be transmitted over fire alarm systems specified to be of the noninterfering type, that reserve-power attachments for clock systems will operate for the specified length of time, and that all special features and accessories specified for each system have been incorporated therein.

14. Engine-generator tests include, but may not be limited to, the following:

    a. If diesel-engine driven, be sure all factory or shop tests are completed as specified.

b. Demonstrate starting all units from all manual control points and from automatic control as specified.

c. Demonstrate voltage and frequency regulation are within specified limits under all load conditions.

d. Establish load requirements for testing of units. Either connected load or created load such as obtained with salt water rheostat or other satisfactory method. Determine who will furnish load banks, if required.

e. Engine-generator tests should incorporate full load tests. Specifications will at times require 110% load testing for a limited time.

f. Satisfactory operation of transfer switch installation in accordance with specification requirements should be demonstrated.

g. Operational check of all safety controls should be made. This will include operation of safety stop switches, operation of high water temperature, low oil pressure, overspeed, and any other safety circuit required by the specifications.

h. Demonstrate full load continuous operation without overheating the engine.

i. Be sure all field tests specified are performed and recorded.

15. Transformers should be checked for shipping damage, leakage, proper voltage and tap settings, grounding, and for signs of water in the oil.

16. Service equipment should be tested for ground fault protection as specified and NEC 230-95.

17. Operational tests should be made on all switches, dimmers, lighting, battery units, and miscellaneous equipment.

EXTERIOR ELECTRICAL
General

This section covers exterior electrical distribution systems, aerial and underground, and transformer stations. Make an inspection of materials prior to installation for conformance with specifications, plans, and approved shop drawings. The Submittal Register, which should list approved materials, is essential to this inspection. Components for distribution systems will be inspected before they are installed and energized. Initial inspection and follow-up inspections will follow work as required by the contract documents.

AERIAL DISTRIBUTION
Wood Poles

Note: If concrete or steel poles are provided, be sure that the poles meet the strength and other criteria provided in the specifications.

1. Check strength (class), length, conditions, and treatment of poles against design requirements. (A current edition of ANSI Standard 05.1, "Specifications and Dimensions for Wood Poles," should be available to the inspector.) Be sure that certification of compliance with applicable AWPA preservation specification has been submitted.

2. Be sure that provisions for storage and handling of poles are in accordance with specification requirements.

3. Usually, specifications require poles to be full treated rather than butt treated. The preservation specification should be checked for verification.

4. Poles should be turned, chamfered, trimmed, roofed, gained, and bored prior to pressure treatment. When field boring or gaining is necessary, additional preservation should be applied to bared surfaces.

5. Examine type of handling tools.

6. Be sure that gains have been made for all crossarms.

7. A site check of the pole line route and pole locations should be made to be sure that pole lengths furnished will be suitable to carry all intended circuits (including communications) and still maintain required vertical and horizontal clearances from the ground and other obstructions. (A current edition of ANSI-C2, National Electrical Safety Code, should be available to the inspector.)

8. Be sure that the depths of pole holes are equal to minimum specification requirements, and that the width of each hole is adequate for backfilling and tamping in 6-in. lifts when required by the specifications. Surplus earth should be piled around the pole and tightly tamped to assist in drainage away from the pole and to compensate for shrinkage of the backfill.

9. If design requires numbering of poles, see that this is done correctly.

10. See that the grading of pole tops is even.

11. When it is necessary to shorten a pole, see that the cut is made at the top and that it is treated with hot preservative.

Crossarms

1. Check that the material meets specification requirements.
2. Verify that wooden crossarms use proper preservation treatment.
3. Examine fastening
   a. Inspect installation, bolting, setting angle, number, type, and length of crossarm and secureness obtained.
   b. Check vertical spacing of multiple crossarms.
   c. Check pinhole spacing.

Hardware

1. Be sure that all ferrous hardware (braces, bolts, lamps, pins, nuts, washers, screws, etc.) is standard pole line galvanized hardware.
2. Be sure that all hardware is of the specified strength size and length.
3. Be sure that crossarm pins are of the specified strength and height.
4. Bolts should not protrude more than approximately 2 in. or less than ⅛ in. beyond the nut.

Insulators

1. Check furnished insulators against specification requirements.
2. Inspect for damage.
3. Check types and spacing of pins.
4. Determine location of guy insulators.

Conductors (Aerial)

1. Compare furnished supports with plans and specifications:
   a. Stranded or solid.
   b. Copper, aluminum, or combinations of copper and steel or aluminum and steel sized according to the specifications. Bare, weatherproof covered, or insulated conductors. Ensure that insulation meets the project specifications.
   c. If messengers are used to support cables, check to see that they are sized, attached, and grounded properly.
2. Check during installation:
   a. Tree trimming.
   b. Line sag and tension are within the specified requirements of the contract or NESC.

c. Handling watch for methods which will produce twists, kinks, abrasions, or cuts.
d. Method of dead ending.
e. Connectors and treatment of conductors at connectors or splices.
f. Armor rod and/or armor tapes on aluminum conductors at supports.
g. Tie wires and methods of securing conductors to insulators.
h. Installations requiring racks and utilization of same.
i. Horizontal and vertical clearance between conductors (ANSI C2).
j. Installation and location of drip loops.
k. Connectors on service drops. If dissimilar metals are connected, be sure that the approved connector is used.
l. Dead ending with approved clamps with strength not less than that of the conductor.
m. Area requiring special protection.
n. Requirements for neutrals.

Giving

1. Compare the type of guy with its intended use.
2. Check type and size of anchors against ground conditions.
3. Check materials to be used, especially in areas where anchor rod corrosion may be a problem.
   a. Check for protective thimbles and thimble eye bolts.
   b. Examine three-bolt clamps at guy terminals.

RESIDENTIAL SERVICES

- Only one service is permitted for each dwelling.
- No service can pass through another dwelling.
- Each occupant shall have access to the main disconnect for their unit.
- No more than six switches or circuit breakers shall be permitted as a means of service disconnection.

SERVICE CLEARANCES

- At least 3 ft from sides of openings, such as operable windows (bottoms as well), doors, decks, and balconies.
- At least 8 ft above roof surface.

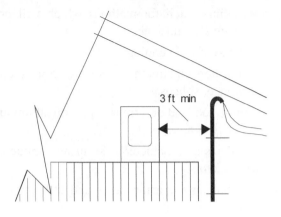

Fig. 13-11   *Service conduit/conductors clearances to openings.*

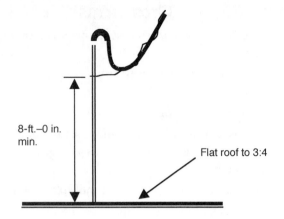

Flat roof to 3:4

8-ft.–0 in. min.

- At least a 3-ft vertical distance in all directions from the roof, but not where the conductor is attached to the side of the building.
- For roof with slope of 4 in., 12 in., or greater the minimum distance is 3 ft.
- At least 18 in. above the overhanging portion of the roof.

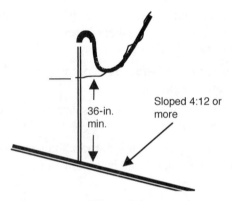

36-in. min.

Sloped 4:12 or more

Fig. 13-13   *Service to roof clearances.*

Table 13-14   Overhead Service Clearances

Walks	Min. 10 ft above
Driveway	Min. 12 ft above
Roadway	Min. 18 ft above

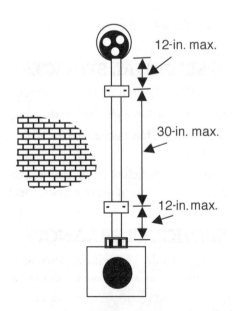

12-in. max.

30-in. max.

12-in. max.

Fig. 13-12   *SE cable supports.*

CHECK DURING INSTALLATION

1. Anchor distance from poles. (Anchor and guy strength is based on 1 to 1 slope. If the distance between pole and anchor rods has to be decreased, strengths must be increased.)
2. Location of guy insulator if required.
3. Point of attachment on pole.
4. Installation of rock anchors.
5. Location of expansion anchors and log anchor rods.
6. Need for additional guys.
7. Installation of guy protectors.
8. Gaining of poles for push braces.
9. Identification of primary phases stamped on all transition poles and at all substations entering and leaving.
10. Length of anchor rods.
11. Grounding and bonding of guys when specified.
12. Guy markers are in place.

PRIMARY AND SECONDARY FUSE CUTOUTS

1. See that approved type is used. Is it indicating or dropout; enclosed or open?

2. Check current and voltage rating and short circuit interrupting capacity against design requirements.

3. Be sure that fuse links are of the capacity and delay specified and that they do not exceed the capacity of connected conductors. (Capacity tables for conductors may be found in NFPA Handbook 70, National Electrical Code.)

4. Check connection points of line conductors and load conductors.

5. Examine type of bracket. Be sure bracket is secure, clear of adjoining structure, and convenient for operation.

LIGHTNING ARRESTORS

Check the following:

1. Location.

2. Voltage rating and type against specification requirement.

3. Mounting bracket.

4. Grounding connectors.

5. Ground resistance prior to energizing the line.

6. Arrestors are not used as insulators to support conductors.

POLETOP SWITCHES

1. Compare switches with approval, making sure that correct current and voltage-rated ones are used.

2. Ensure that contact surfaces will operate under ice conditions.

3. Watch arcing horns for contact during operation.

4. See that operating rods are provided with an insulator in the rod if specified.

5. Make sure operating handle is equipped with lock and keys. If interlocking keying is specified, be sure it is furnished. Check out interlocking.

6. Examine location of operating handle for convenience and safety.

GROUNDING

1. Check type of ground conductors against design.

2. Inspect exothermic welded ground connections for size rod, connector, and powder charge against manufacturer's recommendations.

3. Verify that ground rods are properly spaced relative to the pole.

4. Examine mechanical grounding connectors.

5. Check connectors to aluminum conductors. Connectors must be approved for aluminum.

6. See that grounding conductors are protected from mechanical injury.

7. Determine and record ground resistance; also determine need for additional ground rods.

8. Record number and each driven depth of ground rods.

9. Ensure that all noncurrent carrying metal parts on pole are grounded when specified.

10. Check for separate grounding conductors and rods for lightning arrestor and equipment when required by the specifications or drawings.

Table 13-15 *Minimum Grounding Requirements*

Conductors			Grounding	
Copper	Aluminum	Amps	Copper	Aluminum
4	2	100	8	6
3	1	110	8	6
2	1/O	125	8	6
1	2/O	150	6	4
1/O	3/O	175	6	4
2/O	4/O	200	4	2
3/O	250 kcmil	225	4	2
4/O	300 kcmil	250	2	1/O
250 kcmil	350 kcmil	300	2	1/O
350 kcmil	500 kcmil	350	2	1/O
400 kcmil	600 kcmil	400	1/O	3/O

STREET LIGHTING

1. Examine all street lighting components.

   a. Check lighting bracket.

   b. When inspecting fixtures, watch for:
   - Light diffusing pattern.
   - Open or enclosed type.
   - Gaskets to protect the globe.
   - Film cutouts on series systems.
   - Free access for maintenance.
   - Insulating transformers.

   c. Inspect regulator for kW rating, input voltage, and output current.

   d. Verify protector and control equipment voltage rating.

2. Check during installation:

   a. Height of fixture. Supporting base?

   b. Lightning arrestors and fused cutouts installed on each phase of the supply to the protector.

   c. All ferrous surfaces hot dip galvanized.

   d. Each fixture will be secured with required number of through bolts of correct size.

UNDERGROUND RISERS

1. Examine conduit clamps for size and number.

2. Check duct seal at the conduit terminations.

3. Look for listed insulated bushings at the conduit termination.

4. Check cable terminations.

5. Inspect during installation:

   a. Lag screws used on the conduit clamps.

   b. Cable supports to eliminate weight on the cable terminations.

   c. Metallic conduit below grade has approved protective finish as required.

   d. Stress cones on shielded cable.

   e. Safe climbing space.

UNDERGROUND DISTRIBUTION
Duct System

1. Check:

   a. Materials.

   b. Method of encasement.

   c. Painting.

   d. Duct supports and spacers for size to maintain duct spacing.

2. Check during installation:

   a. End bells and bushings at duct terminations.

   b. Ground bushings at all conduit terminations.

   c. Strength of concrete and presence of reinforcing steel where required under roads, paved areas, etc.

   d. Compacted subgrade.

   e. Spacers and spacing between ducts and minimum concrete cover all sides of ductbank.

   f. Spacing between electric and signal ducts.

   g. Alignment and grade of conduits, especially during encasement with concrete.

   h. Staggering of conduit joints.

   i. Adapters for joining dissimilar types of duct (see that they are not field fabricated).

   j. Changes in direction made with factory fabricated devices.

   k. Ducts secured in the forms.

   l. Ducts pitched to drain.

   m. Duct plugs used during construction and on all spare ducts.

   n. Cleaning of ducts.

   o. Seal duct entrances into manholes.

   p. Cover over ducts.

   q. Pull wires in place.

   r. Minimum curve radius of duct line in accordance with specification.

   s. Installation of marker if required by specifications.

Manholes and
Underground Vaults

1. Verify size according to specifications.

2. Check that duct entrances are located to avoid sharp cable bends or sufficient space is allotted to permit a reverse cable bend.

3. Determine strength of concrete.

4. Check quantity and size of reinforcing steel.

5. Check strength of cover and frame, marking of cover, and machine finished joint between frame and cover.

6. Be sure that approved cable racks, pulling irons, steps, ground rod, etc. are provided in the specified quantity.

7. Check during installation:

   a. Sequence of concrete placement (construction joints are undesirable between the base and walls).

   b. Seal around duct entrances and plug unused ducts.

   c. Pull irons are located opposite duct entrances.

   d. Waterproofing.

   e. Sump or drain.

   f. Quantity and location of cable racks, hooks, and insulators.

   g. Ground rod and ground cable.

   h. Grounding of cable racks and lead cable sheaths.

Primary Cables

1. Inspect splicing kits and methods.

2. Check qualification of cable splicer.

3. Check cables for insulation, shielding, stranding, jacket or sheath, and voltage rating.

4. Examine potheads and pothead compounds.

5. Check during installation that proper cable limits, pulling techniques, and equipment are used to prevent cable damage.

   a. Type of pulling compounds: Verify that the compound is compatible with the cable and does not affect the flame retardation of the cable.

   b. Setup of reels (do not kink).

   c. Cables sealed for pulling.

   d. Abrasion to sheaths on manhole frames.

   e. Even tension used in cable pulling.

   f. Cable routing in manhole.

   g. Splicing or terminating of cable.

   h. Conductor identification tags.

   i. Stress cones at splices and terminations.

   j. Ground shielding at splices and potheads.

   k. Abrasion or damage to cable by dragging on ground.

   l. Fireproofing cables in manhole when specified.

   m. Required tests.

Direct Burial Cable

1. Verify cable burial depth.

2. Check protective covering or armor. Check manufacturer's designation for use. Compare material with approval data.

3. Check during installation:

   a. Type of bedding and covering (should be smooth and free of stones and sharp objects).

   b. Use of untreated plank over cable when specified.

   c. Method of laying.

   d. Weaving of cable in trench.

   e. Radius of bends.

   f. Splices (minimization).

   g. Use of approved splicing kits.

   h. Installation of concrete cable markers with letter and arrow or tape markers as specified.

   i. Concrete-encased conduits with bushings under traffic crossings.

   j. Spacing between cables.

   k. Compaction over cables.

Table 13-16   *Minimum Burial Depths (in.) and Cover*

Location	UF	Rigid Metal	PVC	GFCI 20 Amp
General	24	6	18	12
2-in. concrete	18	6	12	6
Under building	N/A	0	0	N/A
Under 4-in. concrete*	18	4	4	6
Street	24	24	24	24
Driveways	18	18	18	12

*No vehicle traffic.

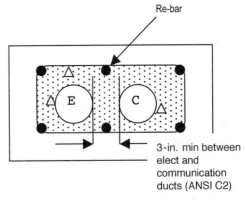

Fig. 13-14 *Joint trench with electric and communications.*

Potheads

1. Check the size of the conductors or cables.

2. Check the stuffing box or wiping sleeve.

3. Verify that the compound is approved and installed as required.

4. Make sure that the installer is a qualified splicer.

5. Check the stress cones.

6. Test the compound for correct pouring temperature.

Transformers in Fenced Enclosures

1. See that ferrous materials are protected with galvanized finish or are painted per specifications.

2. Ensure that transformers, potheads, fused cutouts, and lightning arrestors conform with the electrical characteristics specified and/or approved.

3. Check installation of primary and secondary cabling for stress cones, waterproof connections, and insulators.

4. Check during installation:

- Swing of gates.

- Drainage of transformer pad.

- Elevation of transformer off pad.

- Grounding of all noncurrent carrying metal within the enclosure.

- Grounding of the fence and gate.

- Proper grounding of primary (e.g., surge arresters) and secondary (e.g., neutral) equipment.

- Space available in the transformer enclosure.

- Bonding of all metal conduits terminating in the transformer enclosure to the ground system.

- Proper warning signs affixed to enclosure fence.

- Welds on fence structure are protected in accordance with specifications.

- Pad-mounted transformers without fenced enclosures.

- See that tamper-proof enclosure has not exposed bolts, nuts, or fittings, the removal of which would give access to live internal parts; that meters, valves, and other accessories are within locked enclosure or otherwise resistant to tampering; and that ventilation openings are so protected that a wire cannot be inserted to contact a live part.

- Verify that accessories such as lightning arrestors, switches, gages, etc., are furnished as specified.

- Make sure the contractor(s) are fully familiar with Lock-Out/Tag-Out procedure before any testing.

Cathodic Protection

General

1. Cathodic protection is provided to preserve underground or underwater metallic structures including submerged interior surface of water storage tanks from corrosion. Corrosion takes place at points where electrical current leaves the metal and travels through the ground or electrolyte to another metal or to a different place on the same pipe or structure. Corrosion is arrested when an electromotive force is impressed on an underground or underwater metallic structure in such a way as to make the entire structure cathodic with respect to the adjacent soil or water.

2. Cathodic protection can be provided as described above or in the following manner: Sacrificial galvanic anodes are used having a difference of potential with respect to the structure to be protected. The anodes are made of a material, such as magnesium

or zinc, which is anodic with respect to the protected structure. The galvanic–anode system is designed to deliver relatively small current from a large number of anodes.

Shop Drawings

1. The following items, if required in the work, must be approved prior to installation:

- Anodes—electrical boxes

- Conductors—splicing materials

- Rectifiers—anode hanger for tanks

- Conduit—transformer

2. Check material brought to the job site against approved shop drawings.

Anodes

1. Be sure the anodes are not broken while being installed (some anodes are very brittle).

2. Do not vary the spacing of the anodes more than 5% either way.

3. The location of the anode bed should not be changed without consulting your supervisor.

4. Be sure the anodes are installed in accordance with design and specifications.

Conductors

The insulation on the conductors must not be damaged during construction on impressed current systems. If it is damaged, the conductor may be soon be destroyed by electrolytic action.

Conductor Connections

Ensure that joints are mechanically secure and that they are water tight.

Insulating Joints

Determine if insulating joints in pipe structures are required. Install in accordance with construction drawings. The insulating joints are used to accomplish the following: Isolate dissimilar metals; sectionalize pipe lines with dissimilar coatings; sectionalize one cathodic protection systems from another.

Bonding

1. See that pipe joints are bonded (if called for in the contract) before the pipeline is backfilled.

2. Be sure that bonds to other piping systems or structures are installed. If they are the resistor type, see that they are adjusted.

Test Points

- Test points must be located exactly as shown on contract drawings.

Foreign Pipes and Structures

1. Foreign pipes and structures may require cathodic protection.
2. If you should discover, in the vicinity of the cathodic protection system, underground metal pipes or tanks that were unknown to the designer, bring them to your supervisor's attention.

Backfill for Underground Metallic Structure

1. Backfill of pipes and tanks must not contain rock or materials which would damage the coating on the structure or pipe.
2. Check to see that only specified type of backfill is used. Cinder backfill should never be used.

Auxiliary Equipment

- Check the installation of the rectifiers, transformers, conduit, and other electrical equipment.

Electrical Measurements

1. Impressed current system—inform your supervision when the installation is complete.
2. Sacrificial type anode system (using metallic anodes without external power supply)—inform your supervisor when system is complete, prior to bonding the anodes to the structure.

Starting and Adjusting

Do not start the system to make adjustments. Request a qualified person in cathodic protection systems to perform these functions.

Record of Testing

Obtain a copy of the readings taken by the cathodic protection expert, including the potential measurements of the pipe before and after protection is applied; rectifier current; and voltage readings for each set of potential measurements after the system is connected. These readings should be kept in the job records and turned over to the client when the work has been completed.

ELECTRICAL HEATING
General

Definition

This section covers materials, equipment, and good workmanship practices for the installation of electrical heating system.

Approvals

Ensure that all material, equipment, and shop drawings are approved prior to installation of the electrical heating equipment. Obtain helpful manufacturer's installation information.

Storage and Handling

1. Ensure that all materials and equipment are handled carefully to prevent damage.
2. Reject damaged material and equipment. Have it removed from the site.
3. Check storage facility for adequate weather protection, possible damage, and safety hazard.
4. When outside storage is necessary, store materials and equipment aboveground.

Coordination of Work

- Continually check for interferences between electrical, mechanical, architectural, and structural features.

Layout of Work

1. The contractor must provide equipment and mechanical room layout drawings, which include location of hot water heater, for review and approval.
2. Check location of water heater for accessibility for mechanical and electrical, maintenance, and future replacement if necessary.
3. The contractor must coordinate installation of electric heaters with work of other trades to avoid obstruction to heating pattern and overheatings of adjacent surfaces. Coordinate changes in heater layout with supervisor.

Electric Water Heaters

1. Check for the required number of heating elements.
2. Check to determine that each heating element is controlled by a separate thermostat.
3. Check for manual-reset-type high-limit cutout. High-limit cutout to open all electrical connects to all heating elements.

4. Voltage rating of heaters must be in accordance with specification requirements. 240 volt units, if operated on 208 V, will only deliver approximately 75% of design heating capacity.

Electric Heaters

1. Check voltage rating of equipment furnished.

2. Check wattage rating of heater (project specifications or design). Check to see whether a high-limit switch is required.

3. Check physical requirements of heater. Embedded elements are usually specified.

4. Heaters for hazardous areas are to bear a tag indicating UL approval.

5. A functional test is required on electric heaters.

6. Check thermostats for range of operation, differential, locking facilities, thermometer, and lock-shield requirements.

Coordination with Mechanical Work for Electric Water Heaters

Pressure–Temperature Relief Valve

1. Check to see that the relief valve is stamped for the specified pressure and temperature.

2. Check to see that the relief valve is correctly positioned and piped to safely discharge.

3. Check to see if relief valve will reset after being manually activated. Relief valves may be separate or combination pressure and relief on equipment used for heating water or storing hot water.

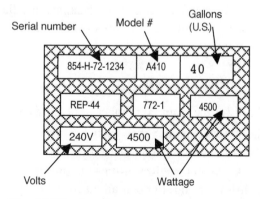

Fig. 13-15 *Typical electrical appliance data plate.*

ALARM AND DETECTION SYSTEMS
General

Definition

This chapter covers materials, equipment, and good workmanship practices for the installation of fire alarm and detector systems. It is important that the inspector have a thorough knowledge of the NEC and applicable NFPA codes, contract specifications, and the fire protection plan for the whole building. Any missing or inconsistent application of the various fire protection parts should be called to the attention of your supervisor.

Approvals

Ensure that all materials, equipment, and shop drawings are approved prior to preparatory inspection and installation. Obtain helpful manufacturer's installation information.

Storage and Handling

1. Ensure that all materials and equipment are new and handled carefully to prevent damage. Reject damaged materials or equipment and have it removed from the site.

2. Check storage facility for adequate weather protection, possible damage, and safety hazard.

Layout of Work

1. Check equipment requirements and locations on contract drawings and specifications.

2. Check approved shop drawings for complete wiring and schematic diagram for equipment furnished, equipment layout, and other details required to demonstrate that the system has been coordinated and will function as a unit.

3. Check contract specification for requirements for contractor to furnish spare parts and spare parts data, operating instruction manual, maintenance instructions manual, and performance test reports. Note in specifications which items are to be turned over and which items are to be posted permanently in the building.

Coordination of Work

1. Continually check for interference between electrical, mechanical, architectural, and structural features. Ensure that paint, fireproofing, or other material is not accidentally applied to sensors, nameplates on equipment, or on posted operating instructions.

2. Electrical work is to be installed under the guidance of section "Interior Electrical." Other coordination requirements are with fire protection systems and piping systems. Mechanical installation will normally be in accordance with NFPA 13 unless otherwise specified in the contract specifications.

Fire Detecting Devices

Fire detecting devices will be located as shown or otherwise directed by fire officials. Unless otherwise shown, the devices will be surface mounted. Smoke detectors will not be located in direct supply air flow nor closer than 3 ft from an air supply diffuser.

Smoke Detectors, Ionization Types

Check for dual chamber design. Check for sensitive adjustment. Check for correct operating voltage and type of current (AC or DC). Check for indicator lamp. Check duct-mounted detector to see if the air sampling tube length is equal to width of duct. Smoke detectors located in the underfloor spaces will only be mounted in upper portion of the space with the detector facing downward or mounted sideways.

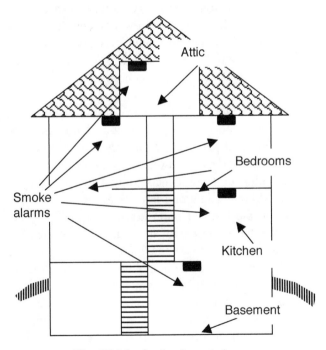

Fig. 13-16 *Smoke alarms in homes.*

Smoke Detectors, Photoelectric Type

Check for factor calibration and not field adjustment. Check for light source lamp or LED of specified voltage.

Heat Detectors

1. Check heat detector requirements for fixed temperature or combination fixed temperature and rate-of-rise ratings. Check for replaceable fixable elements. Check for specified locations of detectors.

2. Heat detectors located in spaces where the ambient temperature can be over 100°F will be rated higher than ordinary temperature; e.g., detectors located in attic spaces should have an intermediate temperature rating.

Fire Alarm Stations

Check for type of station specified. Check for coded or noncoded requirement. Check for test key requirement. Check locks for being keyed alike with fire alarm control panel. Check mounting requirements.

Signaling Devices

Check for locations as indicated on contract documents. Bells are normally mounted on removable adapter plates over electrical outlet boxes. For exterior bells, check for weatherproof-type bells with metal housing and protection grills. Visual fire alarm indicators are mounted same as bells. Trouble indicators are normally mounted in flush-mounted panels.

Control Units

Check control unit for complying with approved shop drawings. Check for proper operating voltage. Check to see that upon failure of power supply that system shall operate from backup power supply. Check panel for metal construction, with factory-applied red enamel finish, accessible from the front, and surface mounted unless otherwise indicated. Check for proper labeling of control panels such as descriptive labeling of zones.

Smoke Detector Panel

Check for proper voltage power supply. Check for backup power system, panel fabrication, paint color, and mounting.

Annunciation Panel

Check annunciation panel for complying with approved unit. Check to see if it is tamperproof.

Power Supply

Check specifications for power feed, overload protection, and conductor hook-up equipment. Check specifications for backup power requirements, i.e., primary, batteries, and generators.

Testing

Test to be conducted in the presence of clients or an authorized representative. Check specification for description of tests to be conducted. Check to see that all quality control records, test reports, and records of corrective actions are furnished to the client.

LIGHTNING PROTECTION
General

Lightning Phenomena   The planet earth is similar to a huge battery continuously losing electrons to the atmosphere. These electrons can be lost in less than an hour unless the supply is continually replenished. It is widely agreed among physicists and scientists that thunderstorms occurring thousands of times daily around the earth return electrons to earth to maintain normal magnitude of electrons at or near the surface of the earth. The rate of electron loss from earth, called the "air–earth ionic current," has been calculated to be 9 microampere for every square mile of earth's surface. Thunderstorms supply electrons back to earth by an opposite electron potential gradient of perhaps 10 kV/m within a thundercloud. This feedback forms a potential difference of from 10 to 100 MV in a single discharge between the center of a cloud and earth.

These lightning discharges carry currents varying from 10 to 345 kA to earth at an average rate of 100 times per second with a duration of less than ½ second per flash. Each flash consists of up to 40 separate strokes; each stroke of lightning lasting for this brief instant releases about 250 kilowatt-hours of energy—enough to operate a 100-watt lightbulb continuously for more than 3 months at the rated voltage of the lamp.

Lightning discharges do not always bring electrons to earth, because so-called positive ground-to-cloud strokes consist of low-power energy transmissions from earth to small negative charge pockets in a thunder cloud. However, magnitudes of discharge voltages and currents are approximately the same from cloud to earth, and all occur within the same discharge timeframes. Just before the lightning flash, the ground within a radius of several miles below the cloud becomes deficient in electrons.

Repelled by the army of electrons in the cloud base, many of the free electrons on the ground are pushed away. The result is that the ground beneath the cloud base becomes more positively charged. As the cloud moves, the positive charge region below moves like its shadow. As the cloud charge balloons, the pressure becomes so great that a chain reaction of ionized air occurs. Ionization is the process of separating air molecules into positive ions and negative electrons. This air, which is normally a good electrical insulator, becomes a good conductor and allows the cloud electrons to pierce the faulted insulation and descend this newly created ionized air path between cloud and earth. The lightning flash starts when a quantity of electrons from the cloud heads toward earth in a succession of steps, pulsing forward with an additional step every 50 ms, creating a faintly luminous trail called the initial or stepped leader. As the leader nears the ground, its effects create an ionized streamer, which rises to meet the advancing leader. When the two join, the ionized air path between cloud and earth is completed, and the leader blazes a faint trail to earth. Immediately a deluge of electrons pour from this lightning discharge channel creating the brilliant main or return stroke that produces most of the light we see. The motions of the leader and the main or return stroke appear to move in opposite directions, but lightning is not an alternating current, because the transferred electrical recharge current moves back to earth.

Code Applicability   NFPA No. 78 is intended to apply to the protection of ordinary buildings, special occupancies, stacks, and facilities housing flammable liquids and gases. The lightning protection code will be utilized where lightning damage to buildings and structures would cause large economic loss.

Nature of Damage   Damage may range from minor defacement to the building to serious foundation upheaval, fire, and personnel casualties. Damage control can be effective dependent on the extent of fireproofing and lightning protection incorporated into the project design. Although lightning strokes generate static discharges in the form of radio noise, it is generally accepted that these cause only an instant of interference to man-made electronic systems. Increased heating effects are also a factor since a lightning bolt increases the temperature of the lightning channel to about 15,000°C. This sudden increase in temperature and pressure causes such an abrupt expansion of air that any hazard type of atmosphere which comes within the ionized air path of the lightning bolt becomes explosive. The explosive nature of the air expansion of bolt channels can cause physical disruption of structures located near the lightning stroke. Lightning discharges below the earth surface sometimes fuse sand into fulgurates which appear like glass tubes. Trees of 40 ft or more in height are especially vulnerable targets for attraction of lightning discharges and are susceptible to being totally destroyed.

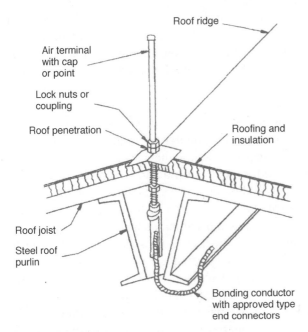

Fig. 13-17 *Sample detail of lightning protection.*

Effective Resistance to Ground   The lightning protection system will be designed to provide an electrical path to ground from any point in the system, and that point will be of considerably lower resistance than that otherwise available by use of the unprotected facility.

Low resistance to ground is desirable but not essential for any lightning protection system. Where low resistance to ground is mandatory, grounding electrode patterns as described herein will furnish ample length of electrical path in contact with earth to dissipate each lightning discharge without damage to the protected building.

Limitations in Use of Lightning Protection

General   Lightning protection will be installed as part of the initial construction project, particularly in view of long replacement time and the high cost of structures. Installation cost of lightning protection systems during project construction is small when compared to the cost of the installation as a whole. Economic and operational considerations will be made in determining the need for lightning protection system, unless otherwise directed by the using agency.

Air Terminals

The purpose of air terminals is to intercept lightning discharges above facilities. Air terminals will be in accordance with UL 96, 96A, and NFPA No. 78. Where

the building roof is not metal and building construction includes steel framing, air terminal connection assemblies will conform generally to Fig. 13-17.

Ground Rods   Ground rods will be not less than 10 ft in length, nor less than ¾-in.-diameter pipe or equivalent solid rod. Ground rods will be located clear of paved surfaces, walkways, and roadways. Rods will be driven so that tops are at least six in. below finished grade, and 3 to 8 ft beyond the perimeter of the building foundation. Where ground rods are used with a counterpoise, tops will be driven to the same elevation as counterpoise below finished grade. Exact location of rods must give preference to use of moist earth. Contact with chemically injurious waste water or other corrosive soils will be avoided. Where avoidance of chemically injurious or buried metal pipes enter a building, the nearest ground rod will be connected thereto.

Earth Electrode Subsystem   Each earth electrode subsystem or counterpoise will consist of one or more closed loops or grid arrangement of No. 1/0 AWG bare copper conductors installed around facility perimeter not less than 2 ft below the earth surface. Larger conductors should be used when installed in highly corrosive soils. A second loop, if used, should not be less than 10 ft beyond the first and inner loop. At least two ground rods should be provided at each corner of each counterpoise loop where earth-seeking currents tend to concentrate.

Roof Conductors

Roof conductors shall be connected directly to the roof or ridge roll. Sharp bends or turns in conductors shall be avoided. Necessary turns shall have a radius of not less than 200 mm (8 in.). Conductors shall preserve a downward or horizontal course and shall be rigidly fastened every 900 mm (3 ft) along the roof and down the building to the ground. Metal ventilators shall be rigidly connected to the roof conductor at three places. All connections shall be electrically continuous. Roof conductors shall be coursed along the contours of flat roofs; ridges; parapets, and edges; and where necessary, over flat surfaces, in such a way as to join each air terminal to all the rest. Roof conductors surrounding tank tops, decks, flat surfaces, and flat roofs shall be connected to form a closed loop.

Fences

Except as indicated below, metal fences that are electrically continuous with metal posts extending at least 600 mm (2 ft) into the ground require no additional grounding. Other fences shall be grounded on each side of every gate. Fences shall be grounded by means of ground rods every 300 to 450 m (1000 to 1500 ft) of length when fences are located in isolated places, and every 150 to 225 m (500 to 750 ft) when in proximity [30 m (100 ft) or less] to public roads, highways, and buildings. (Where the fence consists of wooden posts and horizontal metal strands only, down conductors consisting of No. 8 copper wire or equivalent shall be run from the ground rod the full height of the fence and fastened to each wire, so as to be electrically continuous.) The connection to ground shall be made from the post where it is of metal and is electrically continuous with the fencing. All metal fences shall be grounded at or near points crossed by overhead lines in excess of 600 V and at distances not exceeding 45 m (150 ft) on each side of line crossings.

Copper

Copper conductors used on nonmetallic stacks shall weigh not less than 170 kg per 300 m (375 lb per 1000 ft), and the size of any wire in the cable shall be not less than No. 15 AWG. The thickness of any web or ribbon used on stacks shall be not less than No. 12 AWG. Counterpoise shall be copper conductors no smaller than No. 1/0 AWG.

Aluminum

Aluminum shall not contact the earth nor shall it be used in any other manner that will contribute to rapid deterioration of the metal. Appropriate precautions shall be observed at connections with dissimilar metals. Aluminum conductors for bonding and interconnecting metallic bodies to the main cable shall be at least equivalent to the strength and cross-sectional area of a No. 4 AWG aluminum wire. When perforated strips are used, they must be wider than solid strips. A strip width that is at least twice that of the diameter of the perforations shall be used. Aluminum strip for connecting exposed water pipes shall be not less than No. 12 AWG in thickness and at least 38.1 mm (1½ in.) wide.

Down Conductors

Down conductors shall be electrically continuous from air terminals and roof conductors to grounding electrodes. Down conductors shall be coursed over extreme outer portions of the building, such as corners, with consideration given to the location of ground connections and air terminals. Each building or structure shall have not less than two down conductors located as widely separated as practicable, at diagonally opposite corners.

On rectangular structures having gable, hip, or gambrel roofs more than 35 m (110 ft) long, there shall be at least one additional down conductor for each additional 15 m (50 ft) of length or fraction thereof. On rectangular structures having French, flat, or sawtooth roofs exceeding 75 m (250 ft) in perimeter, there shall be at least one additional down conductor for each 30 m (100 ft) of perimeter or fraction thereof. On an L- or T-shaped structure, there shall be at least one additional down conductor; on an H-shaped structure, at least two additional down conductors; and on a wing-built structure, at least one additional down conductor for each wing. On irregularly shaped structures, the total number of down conductors shall be sufficient to make the average distance between them along the perimeter not greater than 30 m (100 ft). On structures exceeding 15 m (50 ft) in height, there shall be at least one additional down conductor for each additional 18 m (60 ft) of height or fraction thereof, except that this application shall not cause down conductors to be placed about the perimeter of the structure at intervals of less than 15 m (50 ft). Additional down conductors shall be installed when necessary to avoid "dead ends" or branch conductors ending at air terminals, except where the air terminal is on a roof below the main protected level and the "dead end" or branch conductor is less than 5 m (16 ft) in length and maintains a horizontal or downward coursing. Down conductors shall be equally and symmetrically spaced about the perimeter of the structure. [Down conductors shall be protected by placing in (PVC) (rigid steel) conduit for a minimum distance of 1800 mm (72 in.) above finished grade level.] If the conduit is metal, the down conductor shall be bonded at the top and bottom of the conduit.

The complete installation shall have a total resistance to ground of not more than 25 ohms if a counterpoise is not used. Ground rods shall be tested individually prior to connection to the system, and the system as a whole shall be tested not less than 24–48 hours after rainfall. When the resistance of the complete installation exceeds the specified value or two ground rods individually exceed 25 ohms, the Project Manager shall be notified immediately. A counterpoise, where required, shall be of No. 1/0 copper cable or equivalent material having suitable resistance to corrosion and shall be laid around the perimeter of the structure in a trench not less than 600 mm (2 ft) deep at a distance not less than 900 mm (3 ft) nor more than 2.5 m (8 ft) from the nearest point of the structure. All connections between ground connectors and grounds or counterpoise, and between counterpoise and grounds shall be electrically continuous. Where so indicated on the drawings, an alternate method for grounding electrodes in shallow soil shall be provided by digging trenches radially from the building. The lower ends of the down conductors (or their equivalent in the form of metal strips or wires) are then buried in the trenches.

Metal Roofs

Metal roofs which are in the form of sections insulated from each other shall be made electrically continuous by bonding. Air terminals shall be connected to, and made electrically continuous with, the metal roof as well as the roof conductors and down conductors. Ridge cables and roof conductors shall be bonded to the roof at the upper and lower edges of the roof and at intervals not to exceed 30 m (100 ft). The down conductors shall be bonded to roof conductors and to the lower edge of the metal roof. Where the metal of the roof is in small sections, the air terminals and down conductors shall have connections made to at least four of the sections. All connections shall have electrical continuity and have a surface contact of at least 1935 mm^2 (3 in.^{2}).

ALUMINUM CONDUCTORS
General

The information included is important because of recurring and serious problems in public and private construction where aluminum conductors are used in the wiring system. We permit a limited use of aluminum conductors. Special skills and tools are required when making connections and terminations with aluminum conductors.

Materials

Conductors

The electrical systems shown on drawings indicate copper wire size given in gage number, American Wire Gauge (AWG). Aluminum wire size substitutions for copper wire must have amperage of not less than the copper wire size shown. The tables in Article 310 of the NEC show the allowable ampacities of insulated copper and insulated aluminum conductors. The correct size aluminum wire can be determined by using the amperage value for copper wire in a given size in the aluminum conductor table. The equivalent temperature rating of the conductor must match-up with the conductor being installed.

Table 13-17 *American Wire Gauge (AWG) Wire Sizes*

Gage Number	Diameter (mils)	Cross Section Circular mils	sq. in.	lb/1000 ft
4/0	460.0	212,000.0	0.166	641.0
3/0	410.0	168,000.0	.132	508.0
2/0	365.0	133,000.0	.105	403.0
1/0	325.0	106,000.0	.0829	319.0
1	289.0	83,700.0	.0657	253.0
2	258.0	66,400.0	.0521	201.0
3	229.0	52,600.0	.0413	159.0
4	204.0	41,700.0	.0328	126.0
5	182.0	33,100.0	.0260	100.0
6	162.0	26,300.0	.0206	79.5
7	144.0	20,800.0	.0164	63.0
8	128.0	16,500.0	.0130	50.0
9	114.0	13,100.0	.0103	39.6
10	102.0	10,400.0	.00815	31.4
11	91.0	8,230.0	.00647	24.9
12	81.0	6,530.0	.00513	19.8
13	72.0	5,180.0	.00407	15.7
14	64.0	4,110.0	.00323	12.4
15	57.0	3,260.0	.00256	9.86
16	51.0	2,580.0	.00203	7.82
17	45.0	2,050.0	.00161	6.20
18	40.0	1,620.0	.00128	4.92
19	36.0	1,290.0	.00101	3.90
20	32.0	1,020.0	.000802	3.09
21	28.5	810.0	.000636	2.45
22	25.3	642.0	.000505	1.94
23	22.6	509.0	.000400	1.54
24	20.1	404.0	.000317	1.22
25	17.9	320.0	.000252	0.970
26	15.9	254.0	.000200	0.769
27	14.2	202.0	.000158	0.610
28	12.6	160.0	.000126	0.484
29	11.3	127.0	.0000995	0.384
30	10.0	101.0	.0000789	0.304
31	8.9	79.7	.0000626	0.241
32	8.0	63.2	.0000496	0.191
33	7.1	50.1	.0000394	0.152
34	6.3	39.8	.0000312	0.120
35	5.6	31.5	.0000248	0.0954
36	5.0	25.0	.0000196	0.0757
37	4.5	19.8	.0000156	0.0600
38	4.0	15.7	.0000123	0.0476
39	3.5	12.5	.0000098	0.0377
40	3.1	9.9	.0000078	0.0299

Bolts, Nuts, and Washers

1. Check these materials for proper alloy and finish. An anodized finish may be required.

2. Plain, standard series flat washers are required; narrow series washers cannot be used.

3. Antioxidant joint compound use approved oxide-inhibiting joint compound when making-up aluminum conductor/pressure fitting connections and at bus bar connections.

4. Connectors

a. Pressure connectors must be tinned aluminum bodies.

b. Must be rated for use with aluminum conductors.

5. Must be required size, material, and tightened to specified torque.

Installation

Conductor Size

• Check for the equivalent aluminum gage size as the size shown on the drawings is for copper.

Removing Insulation

1. Check removal or stripping method; wire should not be damaged. Recommended methods are:

   Whittling. Using a knife as in sharpening a pencil.

   Peeling. Using a knife from the end of the conductor to peel back and cut off the insulation, cutting away from the wire.

   Stripping. Using the proper size stripping tool. A tool that will nick or ring the wire shall not be used. ("Ringing" is to cut the wire over its circumference.)

2. Wire conductors which are nicked or ringed should have damaged portion removed and the conductor properly prepared.

3. A nick or ring reduces conductor ampacity and introduces a weak point.

Surface Preparation

1. Check for clean surface.

2. Wire may require wire brushing to ensure aluminum oxide is removed.

3. Cleaning may require a coating of antioxidant joint compound and a second wire brushing.

4. Check for the required costing of antioxidant joint compound on wire immediately before the connection is made.

5. On aluminum bus bars, check for silver plating at connection point surfaces.

6. Also check for a light coating of antioxidant joint compound at bus bar connections.

Connections

1. Are bolted connections tightened with an approved calibrated torque wrench? Check that compression connectors are applied with the proper tool and force.

2. Are screw connections properly torqued?

3. Are terminal lugs and connectors made from approved materials? They must be made of aluminum and tin and so labeled. Also, cap must be nickel-plated copper.

4. Are compression terminals and connectors tightened with the special tool?

5. Screws of bolt-type terminals and connectors must be tightened with an approved, calibrated torque wrench.

6. Check torque wrenches for calibration by an approved testing firm. These wrenches are designed to slip when the present torque is exceeded.

Table 13-18   *Wires per Electrical Box*

Shape	Dimensions	Wire Size				
		#6	#8	#10	#12	#14
Square	4 × 1¼		6	7	8	9
	4 × 1½	4	7	8	9	10
	4 × 2⅛	6	10	12	13	15
Round and octagonal	4 × 1¼		4	5	5	6
	4 × 1½		5	6	6	7
	4 × 2⅛	4	7	8	9	10
Rectangular	2 × 3 × 2¼		3	4	4	5
	2 × 3 × 2½		4	5	5	6
	2 × 3 × 2¾		4	5	6	7
	2 × 3 × 3½	3	6	7	8	9

Connection to Vibrating or Cycling Equipment

Aluminum conductors are not recommended for this equipment. Use standard or solid copper conductors as specified.

1. Check for use of aluminum conductors to vibrating equipment. Extreme movement and vibration induces stresses in aluminum wire. Aluminum wire has poor workability.

2. Check for use of aluminum conductors in cycling equipment. The aluminum conductor receives high current and stress each time equipment is energized. This causes connections to loosen.

Environmental Conditions

Conditions Which Can Affect
Aluminum Conductors

1. Salt water, air pollution, and high relative humidity conditions or corrosive soil will accelerate corrosion of unprotected aluminum wire.

2. Extreme changes in the ambient temperature will adversely affect workability and the extent of creep and oxidation.

3. When any of these conditions are present, check for use of aluminum conductors. When used, check for a protection tape wrap for the exposed bare aluminum wire. Apply an oxide-inhibiting joint compound to the surface of exposed connectors and terminals.

Inspection and Analysis

1. Wrong wire size? See Article 310, NEC for aluminum equivalent size for copper size shown in Table 13-20.

2. Is the conductor ringed or nicked? Disapprove and require a new section of undamaged conductor be prepared using proper methods.

3. Terminal material must be bimetallic when copper and aluminum are used on the same terminal or bus. Check for stamped letters "AL-CU" for an approved bimetallic terminal. Check for both proper size and type of terminals and connectors.

4. Is aluminum bus silver plated at the connection point surfaces? If not, disapprove, as it must be factory plated.

5. Is aluminum wire cleaned and coated with oxide-inhibiting joint compound immediately before making connections?

6. Is an approved, calibrated torque wrench used to tighten bolted and screwed connections? Check for recent calibration date.

7. Check for proper crimping tool use in compression connections.

8. Is connection loose or otherwise poorly made? After electrical system is activated, check for:
   a. Voltage drop across the connection (there is no voltage drop across a good connection).
   b. Discoloration of the aluminum wire and/or insulation at the connection: gray-white color coating on the wire indicates aluminum oxide corrosion. If a brown-black color appears on the insulation, or if the insulation is brittle, a failure is indicated.

9. A "hot spot check" with an infrared scan will indicate thermal buildup at points of failure.

10. Scope of codes are limited to 400 amps and 120/240 V for one- and two-family homes/dwellings.

11. All electrical equipment must bear the label of an approved agency and be installed according to the manufacturer's instructions.

12. Equipment that is only approved for dry locations must be protected from the weather during construction.

13. All must be firmly mounted.

14. Electrical equipment must be identifiable and marked with the voltage, current, wattage, and other pertinent markings.

15. All disconnects must be marked and arranged so that their purpose is evident.

Working Clearances

- Not less than 36 in. in depth.
- Not less than 30-in. wide in front of the equipment.
- Not less than the width of the equipment.
- Not less than 6½ ft from the floor.
- The equipment doors must be able to open to 90°.
- Areas directly above the equipment must be keep clear; this includes all piping, ducts, and unrelated equipment.
- Must have lights for working spaces, including panelbars and service equipment.

Terminals

- If more than one conductor is used on one terminal, then it needs to be marked approving such an application.
- No. 10 and smaller connections need to be made by wire binding screws and nuts having upturned lugs or the equivalent.

Table 13-19 Copper and Aluminum Wire Comparisons

Amps	Copper	Aluminum
15	14 ga	12 ga
20	12 ga	10 ga
30	10 ga	8 ga
40	8 ga	6 ga
60	4 ga	4 ga

Grounded Conductors

- No. 6 and smaller shall only be white or grey.
- Grounding conductors shall be identified by a continuous green color or green with one or more yellow stripes on the insulation, or can be bare.
- Must have at least 6 in. of free conductor at each outlet, each junction, switches, and splices.

Table 13-20 *Conduit Abbreviations*

Allowable Wiring	Abbr.
Armored cable	AC
Elec. metallic tubing	EMT
Elec. nonmetallic tubing	ENT
Flexible metal conduit	FMC
Intermediate metal conduit	IMC
Liquidtight flex conduit	LFC
Metal-clad cable	MC
Nonmetallic sheathed cable	NMSC
Rigid nonmetallic conduit	RNC
Rigid metallic conduit	RMC
Service entrance cable	SEC
Surface raceways	SR
Underground feeder cable	UF
Underground service cable	USE

Grounding of Service

- If a no. 8 conductor (or less) is used, then it must be protected.

- If nonprotected no. 6 is used, then it must follow the wall snugly. It requires that a support be within 12 in. of termination and 24 in. throughout the length.

- If the sole grounding system is a rod or pipe, then the conductor may be no. 6 copper or no. 4 aluminum.

- At no time may gas piping be used as a grounding electrode.

- Aluminum electrodes cannot be used.

- Grounding connections cannot be on "load" side of service disconnection means.

- Underground metal water piping in contact with at least 10 ft of earth (without the use of a water meter) may be used as a ground.

- Rod and pipe electrodes need to be at least 8 ft in length and pipe shall not be less than ¾ in. diameter.

- Steel and iron need to be treated for corrosion protection.

- Rods of steel or iron shall be at least ⅝ in. in diameter.

- Rods or pipes must be driven their entire length; if rock is encountered, then they may be driven at an angle not to exceed 45° or buried in a trench at least 2½ ft in depth.

- Single electrodes need to have a resistance to ground of at least 25 ohms.

- Insulated (or bare) aluminum or copper-clad aluminum conductors cannot be used in contact with earth or direct contact with masonry.

- Must be at least 18 in. away from ground when installed outside.

- Connections to grounding electrodes must be of approved means.

- Only one conductor per clamp or fitting.

- Must be accessible.

Subpanels and Fuse Boxes

- All breakers and fuses need to be clearly and permanently marked.

- Unused openings need to be closed.

- Cannot be installed in clothes closets or bathrooms.

- Maximum height of breaker is 6 ft 6 in.

- Disconnects must be in sight and not more than 50 ft from the equipment serviced.

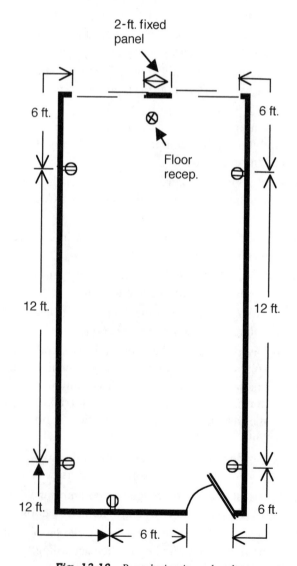

Fig. 13-18 *Branch circuits and outlets.*

RESIDENTIAL REQUIREMENTS BY ROOMS
Kitchens

- Must have a minimum of two 20-amp circuits.
- Ranges in excess of 8¾ kVA need a circuit of at least 40 amps.
- Water-heating appliances need a circuit rated at least 125% of that found on the equipment data plate.

Laundry Area

- Need at least one 20-amp designated circuit/receptacle.

Attics

- Cables must be protected within 6 ft of opening(s) with strip guards at least the same height of the cable.
- All cables subject to damage need to be protected.

Basements

- Cables need protection if exposed to physical damage.
- Schedule 80 PVC rigid metal conduit or other approved means.
- Panels require ¼-in. clearance from basements with damp walls.

LIGHTING

- Recessed lighting must have at least 3 in. clear from insulation and ½ in. from combustibles (for non-approved types).

Table 13-21 *Cord Lengths*

Appliance	Minimum Cord Lengths	Maximum Cord Lengths
Sink disposal	18	36
Built-in dishwasher	36	48
Trash compactor	36	48

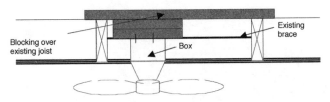

Fig. 13-19 *Ceiling fan support.*

Minimum Service Load Calculation Procedures for Residential Use

1. First, multiply the square-foot area by 3 volt-amps to determine the general lighting and receptacle outlets.
2. Multiply 1500 volt-amps by the total number of 20-amp-rated circuits (kitchen, laundry, etc.). Add to 1.
3. Add the volt-amps listed on all permanently fastened appliances such as cooking units, ranges, ovens, clothes dryers, and water heaters. The minimum allowed is 100% of the above sum if 10,000 volt-amps or less. If greater than 10,000 volt-amps, then also take 40% of the portion above the 10,000 and add the two together. Next add the largest-value one of the following:

- Rating on data plate for air conditioners, heat pump equipment.
- Rating on data plate for electric thermal storage.
- 65% of data-plate rating for central space heating, including supplemental heating unit for heat pump.
- 65% of data-plate rating of electric space heating units (if less than four separately controlled units.)
- 40% of data-plate rating of electric space heating units for four or more separately controlled units.

4. Take the total load (volt-amps) and divide by 240 V to arrive at the amperage (amps) required.

OHM'S LAW

Ohm's law states that there is a fixed relationship that exists between voltage (E), current (I), and resistance (R) such that the current flowing in a circuit is directly proportional to the applied voltage, and inversely proportional to the resistance. This formula can be stated three ways, but first, for mathematical purposes, the following symbols are used:

Electrical current in amperes $= I$

Electrical pressure in volts $= E$

Electrical resistance in ohms (Ω) $= R$

1. The current in amperes is equal to the pressure in volts divided by the resistance in ohms:

$$I = E/R$$

2. The resistance in ohms is equal to the pressure in volts divided by the current in amperes:

$$R = E/I$$

3. The pressure in volts is equal to the current in amperes multiplied by the resistance in ohms:

$$E = I \times R$$

With any two factors known, the third can easily be calculated by either division or multiplication. All that is necessary is to keep track of when to multiply and when to divide. The following diagrams are often helpful:

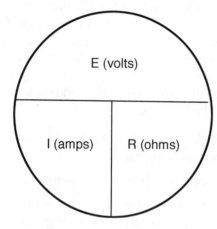

I = E / R
R = E / I
E = I × R

Fig. 13-20   *Ohm's law.*

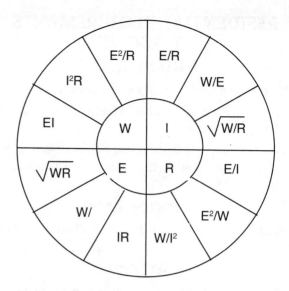

Fig. 13-21   *Ohm's law broken down further.*

14
CHAPTER

OSHA

GENERAL
Prime Contractor/ Subcontractor Relationship

1. Regardless of the agreements entered into by the prime contractor with its subcontractors, the prime contractor shall not be relieved of the overall responsibility for OSHA compliance.

2. When the subcontractor agrees to perform a part of the contract, it will also accept the responsibility for the OSHA requirements for that portion of the work. The prime contractor and subcontractor will have joint responsibility.

3. No employee shall be allowed to work in surroundings or under working conditions which are unsanitary, hazardous, or dangerous to their health or safety.

4. It is the responsibility on the Contractor to initiate and maintain an accident prevention program. Programs are to provide for frequent and regular inspections of job sites, materials, and equipment by a "competent person."

5. A "competent person" has been trained and is capable of identifying existing and predictable hazards in the surroundings or working conditions which are unsanitary, hazardous, or dangerous. This person must also have the necessary authority to correct the problem promptly.

6. Faulty machinery, tools, materials, and equipment will be tagged or have the controls locked to render them inoperable or removed from the job site.

7. Employees required to handle dangerous substances such as flammable liquids, gases, poisons, and caustics shall be instructed regarding their safe handling and use and protective measures.

8. Employees required to enter into confined areas are to be instructed in the hazards involved, appropriate precautions, and the correct use of protective and emergency equipment.

Fire Protection and Prevention

- The employer is responsible for the development and maintenance of a fire protection and prevention program throughout all phases of the work.

Housekeeping

1. During construction, the contractor shall keep all debris and scrapes cleared from work areas, stairs, and passageways.

2. Containers are to be supplied for trash and oily and used rags. Those used for flammable and/or hazardous wastes must have a cover.

3. Dropping debris more than 20 ft on the outside of the structure requires the use of chutes. The bottom area must be barricaded with warning signs posted.

Illumination

- Construction areas, ramps, corridors, offices, field shops, stairwells, and storage areas are required to be lighted to not less than the table below. This lighting is required at all times when work is in progress.

Table 14-1 Required Lighting for Areas

Foot Candles	Area(s)
5	General construction areas.
3	General construction areas, concrete work, excavation, access ways, active storage areas, loading areas, refueling, field-maintenance areas.
5	Indoors: warehouses, corridors, hallways, and exit ways.
5	Underground tunnels, shafts.
10	Tunnels and shaft heading during drilling, mucking, and scaling.
10	General construction plant and shop areas, electrical and mechanical rooms, indoor toilets, store rooms.
30	First-aid stations, infirmaries, and offices.

FIRST AID

1. If the project does not have an infirmary, clinic, hospital, or physician reasonably accessible, then the contractor must have a person trained and certified in first aid (documented) available at the job site when work is in progress.

2. Telephone numbers of the physicians, hospitals, and clinics are to be posted in a conspicuously located position.

3. Where the worker's eyes or body may be exposed to injurious corrosive materials, the contractor must provide a suitable facility for a quick flushing of the eyes and/or body.

4. First-aid kits are to be easily accessible and inspected weekly to ensure expended items are replaced promptly.

Sanitation

1. An adequate supply of potable water is to be provided at the job site.

2. Containers are to be marked, have a tightly closing lid, and be equipped with a tap. Dipping is not allowed.

3. Common drinking cups are not permitted. Disposable cups must have a trash receptacle provided for the used cups.

Toilets

Table 14-2 Minimum Number of Facilities on Construction Sites

No. of Employees	Minimum Number of Facilities
20 or less	1
20 to 200	1 toilet seat and urinal per 40 workers
200 or more	1 toilet seat and urinal per 50 workers

Contractors are required to provide washing facilities for workers engaged in painting, coating, or other operations where contaminants may be harmful to the worker. The facility is to be located close to the work site and equipped to be able to remove the substances in question.

Noise Exposure

Table 14-3 Personal Protection Required for dBa Levels

Duration per Day (hr)	dBa Sound Level
8	90
6	92
4	95
3	97
2	100
1½	102
1	105
½	110
¼ or less	115

Note: Exposure to impulsive or impact noise must not exceed 140-dB sound pressure level.

1. In all cases where levels exceed those in Table 14-3, the contractor will administer an effective hearing conservation program.

2. Ear protective measures inserted into the ear are to be fitted or determined individually by a competent person. Plain cotton is not acceptable.

PERSONAL PROTECTIVE EQUIPMENT (PPE)
Head Protection

1. Workers in areas where there is a possible danger from falling or flying objects or from electrical hazards are required to were approved protective helmets.

2. Helmets must meet the specifications of the American National Standards Institute (ANSI) document Z89.1-1971.

3. Helmets for high-voltage protection from burns and shock are required to meet ANSI Z89.2-1971.

Eye and Face Protection

1. Eye protection is required for workers when work from machines or operations present a potential eye or face injury from physical, chemical, or radiation agents.

2. Persons wearing corrective eyewear are required to wear goggles or spectacles that have protective lenses installed or goggles that are designed to be worn over workers' eyewear.

3. OSHA provides a table for special consideration for eye and face protective measures under differing circumstances.

Table 14-4 Filter Lens Requirements for Welding and Cutting

Operation	Lens Shade
Shield metal-arc welding: ¹⁄₁₆, ³⁄₃₂, ⅛, ⁵⁄₃₂ dia. electrodes	10
Gas shielded-arc welding (nonferrous): ¹⁄₁₆, ³⁄₃₂, ⅛, ⁵⁄₃₂ dia. electrodes	11
Gas shielded-arc welding (ferrous): ¹⁄₁₆, ³⁄₃₂, ⅛, ⁵⁄₃₂ dia. electrodes	12
	12
Shielded metal-arc welding: ³⁄₁₆, ⁷⁄₃₂, ¼, ⁵⁄₁₆, ⅜ dia. electrodes	14
Atomic hydrogen welding	10–14
Carbon-arc welding	14
Soldering	2
Torch brazing	3–4
Light cutting (to 1 in.)	3–4
Medium cutting (1–6 in.)	4–5
Heavy cutting (over 6 in.)	5–6
Gas welding (up to ⅛ in.)	4–5
Gas welding (⅛ to ½ in.)	5–6
Gas welding (over ½ in.)	6–8

Fall Protection

1. Every worker on a walking or working surface on an unprotected side or edge more than 6 ft above the next lower level is to be protected by the use of guardrail systems, safety net systems, or personal fall arrest systems.

2. Warning lines are a barrier erected on a roof to warn workers (roofers) they are approaching an area that does not have a protection system in place. Warning lines are required to:

   • Be erected around all sides of the roof work area.

   • Erected not less than 6 ft from the edge when mechanical equipment is not being used.

   • Shall consist of rope, wire, or chains with flagging at not less than 6-ft intervals.

   • The rope, wire, or chain shall have a tensile strength of 500 lb.

   • Stanchions must be capable of withstanding a force of 16 lb without tipping over.

Control Lines

1. Control lines are to be used to mark a controlled access zone.

2. Control lines are to be erected not less than 6 ft nor more than 25 ft from the unprotected leading edge except in the case for erecting precast concrete panels. Then the control line shall be erected not less than 6 ft nor more than 60 ft or ½ the length of the precast piece from the leading edge.

3. Control lines are to be made from rope, wire, tapes, or other equivalent materials. Bright flagging is to be no more than 6 ft on center.

4. The control lines sag must not be more than 39 in. nor can the highest point be more than 45 in., unless when laying brick then it can be no higher than 50 in.

Holes in Decks

• All penetrations and holes shall be protected by the use of guardrail systems and safety net systems, or personal fall arrest systems if more than 6 ft above the lower level.

Safety Belts, Lanyards, and Lifelines

1. Safety belts, lanyards, and lifelines shall not be used for any other loading except for their original intent. If used, they must be removed from service immediately.

2. An anchorage for a lifeline must be capable of supporting a minimum dead load of 5400 lb.

3. Safety belts are to be a minimum of ½ in. of nylon or equivalent approved material. The maximum length will provide a fall no greater than 6 ft and a minimum of 5400 lb.

4. Hardware for lanyards and safety belts are to be able to withstand a tensile loading of 4000 lb.

SAFETY NET

1. Safety nets are required when the workers are above 25 ft above ground or water where the use of ladders, scaffolds, safety lines, and safety belts is impractical.

2. Nets shall extent 8 ft beyond the edge and as close in height to the work area as possible.

3. The net's mesh will not be larger than 6 in. × 6 in. and will be capable of withstanding 17,500 ft-lb as a minimum. The net shall have the manufacturer's label attached.

FIRE PROTECTION

The contractor is responsible for developing and following a fire protection program throughout all phases of the construction. The contractor is also responsible for providing the required fire-fighting equipment.

• Equipment is to be located in conspicuous locations.

• A temporary or permanent water supply is required as soon as combustible materials accumulate.

• A fire extinguisher, rated not less than 2A, is to be provided for each 3000 sq. ft. of the protected area.

• Fire extinguishers are to be located so that the distance to the nearest extinguisher does not exceed 100 ft.

• One open 55-gal drum with two fire pails may be substituted for a 2A fire extinguisher. Water is to be protected from freezing.

• A ½ garden hose not exceeding 100 ft, with a hose horizontal discharge stream of 30 ft, may be substituted for a 2A fire extinguisher.

• In multistory construction sites one 2A fire extinguisher is to be located adjacent to each stairway.

• A fire extinguisher of 10B is to be provided within 5 gal or more of combustible liquids or 5 lb of flammable gas. (This does not apply to the fuel tanks of motor vehicles.)

• Fire alarm codes and procedures are to be posted at phones at employee entrances.

- Combustible storage areas shall not be located within 10 ft of a building or structure, and access is to be provided with drives being at least 15 ft in width.
- No more than 25 gal of flammable and combustible liquids inside the structure unless stored in an approved storage cabinet.
- Not more than 60 gal of flammable liquids or 120 gal of combustible liquids may be stored in one cabinet. No more than three cabinets may be located in a single storage area.
- Cabinets are to be labeled "Flammable—Keep Fire Away."

MATERIAL STORAGE

1. Maximum safe load limits must be posted on floors used as storage areas, except for floors and concrete slabs on grade.
2. Bagged materials are to be staked by stepping back the layers and then "cross-keying" the bags at least every 10-bag level.
3. Lumber is to have all nails removed before stacking.
4. Lumber stacks shall not be piled higher than 20 ft and if handled manually, not more than 16-ft high.
5. Lumber storage is to be keep free of hazards from tripping, fire, explosion, and pest harborage.

RIGGING

1. Rigging equipment is to be inspected before each shift of workers. Defective equipment should be removed immediately.
2. Alloy steel chain slings are to be inspected by a competent person on a regular basis. Inspection records are to be kept, and at no time should the inspections be made in more than 12-month intervals.
3. The basis of inspection is to include:
   a. Frequency of the slings used
   b. Severity of the working conditions
   c. Nature of lifts made
   c. Past sling experience of service lives

Wire Ropes

- The eye splice shall not have less than three full tucks.
- Wire is considered defective if any length of eight diameters (for the full length) has more than 10 visible broken wires.

- U-bolts are to have the U section on the dead end of the rope.
- Slings are to be protected and padded from the sharp edges of the lifted load.

Table 14-5 *Number and Spacing for U-bolt Clips on Wire Ropes*

Steel Rope Dia. (in.)	No. Drop-Forged Clips	No. Other Materials Clips	Min. Spacing (in.)
½	3	4	3
⅝	3	4	3¾
¾	4	5	4½
⅞	4	5	5¼
1	5	6	6
1⅛	6	6	6¾
1¼	6	7	7½
1⅜	7	7	8¼
1½	7	8	9

TOOLS

If the tools were to accommodate a guard, the guard must be in place in order to be used. Guarded tools include:

1. Guillotine cutters
2. Shears
3. Alligator shears
4. Power presses
5. Milling machines
6. Power saws
7. Jointers
8. Grinders
9. Portable power tools

Power Tools

1. All power tools are to be double insulated or grounded.
2. Power tool cords are not to be used for lowering or hoisting power tools.
3. Compressed air can only be used for cleaning if the pressure is less than 30 psi. Exception: Concrete form work, mill scale, and similar cleaning.
4. Hoses shall not be used to hoist or lower tools.
5. Only workers who have been trained in power-actuated tool use may be approved for their use.
6. Tools are to only be loaded just prior to use. Loaded tools should never be left unintended.

Gas Welding and Cutting

1. Valve caps must be in place on compressed gas cylinders during transporting, moving, and storage.

2. A suitable cylinder truck, chain, or other steadying device is to be used to keep the cylinders from being knocked over while in use.

3. Cylinders must be in the upright position at all times unless during short periods during movement.

4. Oxygen cylinders are to be stored separately from fuel-gas cylinders a minimum distance of 25 ft, or have a noncombustible barrier of at least 5-ft high and with a fire-resistance rating of at least ½ hr.

ELECTRICAL
Generators

Portable generators need not be grounded by their frame and may serve as the grounding electrode for a system that is supplied by the generator if the following conditions are met.

1. The generator supplies only the equipment mounted on the generator.

2. The non-current-carrying metal parts of the equipment and the equipment grounding conductor terminals of the receptacles are bonded to the frame of the generator.

Vehicle-Mounted Generators

The frame of the vehicle may serve as the grounding electrode for the system supplied by the generator if the following conditions are met:

1. The frame of the generator is bonded to the frame of the vehicle.

2. The generator supplies only equipment located on the vehicle.

3. The non-current-carrying metal parts of the equipment and the equipment grounding conductor terminals of the receptacles are bonded to the frame of the generator.

SCAFFOLDS

1. Employers are required to have competent person designated to determine the feasibility and safety of providing fall protection for workers erecting and dismantling scaffolds.

2. Scaffolds must be capable of supporting their own weight and at least four times the maximum intended load.

3. Each working platform is required to be fully planked except when erecting or dismantling.

4. The maximum allowable open space between the planking and the uprights is not to exceed 9½ in.

5. Toe boards are required when the working platform is greater than 10 ft in height. Toe boards must be a minimum of 3½ in. in height, fastened securely, and not have more than ¼-in. clearance above the walking/working surface.

Table 14-6 *Minimum Clearances between Scaffolds and Power Lines*

Voltage	Minimum Distance	Alternatives
<300 V	3 ft	
300 to 50 kV	10 ft	
>50 kV	10 ft plus .4 in. for each 1 kV over 50	2 times the length of the line insulator but never less than 10 ft

Insulated lines.

Voltage	Minimum Distance	Alternatives
<50 kV	10 ft	
>50 kV	10 ft plus .4 in. for each 1 kV over 50	2 times the length of the line insulator but never less than 10 ft

Uninsulated lines.

6. The maximum distance from the face of work and the scaffolding shall not be more than 14 in. unless guardrail systems are used or personal fall arrest systems are used. Maximum distance when using outrigger scaffolding is 3 in.

7. Scaffolds greater than 35 ft in height must have a rest area each 35 ft in height.

8. Cross-bracing is not to be used for access or egress.

Table 14-7 *Spans for Wood Planks (2 × 10 Lumber or 2 × 9 Rough Sawn)*

Maximum (lb/sq. ft.)	Maximum Span Using Full Thickness Undressed Lumber (ft)	Maximum Span Using Nominal Dimensioned Lumber (ft)
25	10	8
50	8	6
75	6	

EXCAVATIONS
Definitions

Cohesive soils. Refers to clay (finely graded soils) or soils with a high clay content. Cohesive soils do not crumble and in excavation activities can have vertical slope. Cohesive soils are "plastic" when moist, and hard to break when dry.

Plastic soils. A soil property which allows the soil to be molded and deformed without cracking or an appreciable volume change.

Stable rock. Means natural solid mineral matter that can be excavated with vertical sides and remain intact when exposed.

Fissured soil. Refers to soil material that has a tendency to break along definite planes with little resistance. The soil may have open cracks.

Granular soil. Refers to gravel, sands, or silts (coarse-grained soil) with very little clay content. Granular soils have no cohesive strength when dry and crumbles easily when dry.

Types of Soils

Type A

Cohesive soils with an unconfined compressive strength of 1.5 tons/sq. ft. or more. Examples are clay, silty clay, sandy clay, and clay loam. Cemented soils such as caliche and hardpan are also considered Type A soils. Soils are disqualified as Type A if:

- Soil is subject to heavy vibrations or heavy traffic.
- Soil has been previously disturbed.
- Soil is part of a layered system with a slope of four horizontal to one vertical or greater.

Type B

Cohesive soils with an unconfined compressive strength greater than 0.5 ton/sq. ft. but less than 1.5 tons/sq. ft. Or type A soils with the above disqualifications or granular cohesionless soils including angular gravels, silt, silt loam, and sandy loam. Type B also includes dry rock that is not stable.

Type C

Cohesive soils with an unconfined compressive strength of less than 0.5 ton/sq. ft.; granular soils such as gravel, sand and loamy sand; soils in which water is seeping; or unstable submerged rock. OSHA requires that classifications be based on at least one visual and one manual analysis by a competent person.

Manual Tests

Plasticity Test

In your hand, mold a moist or wet clump of soil into a ball and attempt to roll it into a thread as thin as 1/8 in. in diameter. Cohesive soils are plastic and can be rolled without crumbling. If at least a 2-in. length of 1/8-in. diameter can be held at one end without breaking, it is considered cohesive.

Dry Strength

When a sample crumbles in your hands with only moderate pressure into fine powder or individual grains, it is considered granular—any combination of gravel, silt, or sand. If the soil breaks into clumps which do not do not break up easily and there is no visual indication of fissured then the soil can be considered unfissured.

Thumb Test

Used to estimate the unconfined compressive strengths of soils. This test is to be conducted on an undisturbed clump as soon as possible after or during the excavation to minimize the effects of exposure to the elements that will dry the sample. Type A soils can be readily indented with the thumb; however, this is accomplished only with great effort. Type C soils can easily be penetrated several inches by the thumb. It also can be molded by light finger pressure. If the excavation is exposed to rain after the initial testing, then the soil should be retested and classified accordingly. Other approved tests may be conducted such as a pocket penetrometer or a hand-operated shearvane.

Visual Analysis

- Carefully observe the excavation as it is taking place, especially the sides. Check the size and amounts of the soil. Finely grained soils are generally cohesive. Soils composed primarily of coarsely grained material are gravel and or granular materials.
- Observe the soils falling from the excavator; soil that remains in clumps when removed from the hole are cohesive.
- Check the sides of the excavation. Cracks of spaces could indicate fissured material. Chunks of material falling from the vertical sides are signs of fissured material; even small amounts are potentially hazardous.

- Check the opening for signs of water.
- Look for layered soils and determine if they slope toward the excavation. Estimate the vertical fall per unit for each horizontal unit. Layers exceeding four horizontal to one vertical are grounds for reclassification.

Sloping and Benching

Excavations remaining open for 24 h or less are considered "short term" and have separate protection requirements.

Table 14-8 *Maximum Slopes for Excavations 20 ft or Less*

Soil Types	Maximum Slope
Stable rock	Vertical
Type A	¾ : 1
Type B	1 : 1
Type C	1½ : 1

Note: Sloping and benching for excavation in excess of 20 ft must be designed by a registered professional engineer.

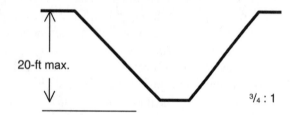

Fig. 14-1 *Simple slope (Type A soils).*

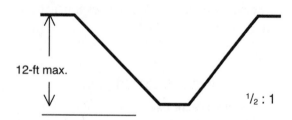

Fig. 14-2 *Simple slope: short term—less than 24 h (Type A soils).*

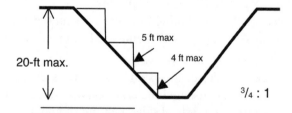

Fig. 14-3 *Multiple bench slope (Type A soils).*

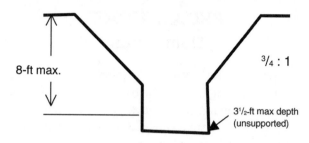

Fig. 14-4 *Unsupported lower portion (Type A soils).*

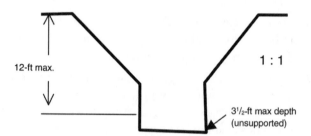

Fig. 14-5 *Unsupported lower portion: 8–12 ft max. (Type A soils).*

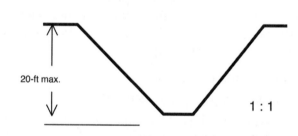

Fig. 14-6 *Simple slope (Type B soils).*

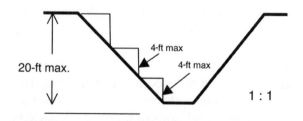

Fig. 14-7 *Multiple bench slope (Type B soils).*

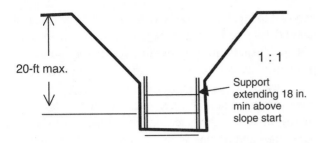

Fig. 14-8 *Supported lower portion: 20-ft max. (Type B soils).*

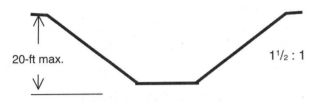

Fig. 14-9 *Simple slope (Type C soils).*

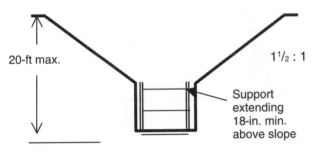

Fig. 14-10 *Supported lower slope (Type C soils).*

Note: OSHA regulations provide for approved alterations to the above when layered soils are encountered.

STAIRWAYS AND LADDERS

• Stairways constructed for construction use and that are not part of the permanent structure shall have landings not less than 30 in. in the direction of travel and extend 22 in. in width at every 12 ft (or less) of vertical rise.

• Stairs are to be installed between 30° and 50° from horizontal.

• Riser heights and stair tread depth must be uniform with neither varying more than ¼ in.

• If a door opens on the stairway, a platform must be provided large enough to still provide clearance when the door is opened.

• Bare metal pans are not to be used as stairs until either the concrete is placed or the pans are filled with other temporary suitable material such as wood.

Stair Rails and Handrails

Stairways with four or more risers or rising more than 30 in. must have as a minimum:

1. At least one handrail.

2. One stair rail system along each unprotected side.

3. Height of the stair rail must not exceed 36 in. from the tread.

4. If balusters are used, they must not exceed 19 in. O.C.

5. Handrails and stair rails must be capable of withstanding a 200-lb force applied on the top edge in any outward or downward direction.

6. When the top edge of the stairwell also serves as the handrail then the top edge height cannot exceed 37 in. nor less than 36 in. from the thread.

7. Handrails are to have a minimum of 3-in. clearance between them and adjacent walls, or other objects.

Ladders

1. Must be able to support 4 times the maximum intended loads, except heavy-duty Type 1A, which must carry 3.3 times the maximum loads.

2. Each rung must be capable of supporting a single concentrated loading of 250 lb applied in the middle of the rung.

3. Rungs, cleats, or steps must not be spaced more than 14 in. apart and no closer than 10 in. for portable ladders.

4. Stepladders must be equipped with a metal spreader or locking device to hold the ladder in the open position.

5. The minimum distance between the back or the ladder, its rungs, cleats, or steps is 7 in.

6. Ladders shall extend 42 in. above the access level or landing platform.

7. Ladders are to be placed on level, secure surfaces unless they are otherwise secured, to prevent accidental displacement.

8. Single-rail ladders are prohibited from use.

LEAD IN CONSTRUCTION

Pure lead is a heavy metal and is one of the basic chemical elements. When absorbed into the body in certain doses it is considered toxic. It can be absorbed either by breathing in its dust or by ingestion into the body. Studies have also shown that certain organic lead compounds can actually be absorbed through the skin. This amount is considered insignificant.

Most often, lead is inhaled by the lungs and upper respiratory tract; however, a significant portion is ingested. Once in the bloodstream, lead is circulated through the body and is stored in various body organs and tissues. Some makes its way out of the body; however, as the exposure continues, the lead level will increase and will slowly cause irreversible damage to the person's health. Even short-term exposures can cause seizures, coma, and even death from cardiorespiratory arrest. Long-term exposure may result in severe damage to the blood and nervous, urinary, and reproductive systems. Children born of parents who were exposed to excess levels of lead are more likely to have birth defects such as mental retardation, behavioral disorders, or even death during the first year.

Common symptoms of lead poisoning include:

- Headaches
- Tremors
- Constipation
- Loss of appetite
- Excessive tiredness
- Weakness
- Metallic taste
- Anxiety
- Insomnia
- Numbness
- Hyperactivity
- Dizziness

Standards

OSHA standards aim to reduce the workers exposure for lead by identifying the hazard and limiting the exposure from the permissible rate of 200 $\mu g/m^3$ to an 8-h time-weighted average of 50 μg.

Most workers will come into contact with lead by:

1. Demolition of older structures.
2. Working with products with lead.
3. Routine maintenance.
4. Transportation or disposal of site debris.
5. Painting and paint prepping.

Limits of Exposure It is the employer's responsibility to establish and maintain an accurate record documenting the nature and relevancy of the exposure. Until the employer performs or has a lab perform an exposure assessment and documents that his or her workers are not exposed to levels of lead above the Permissible Exposure Limit (PEL), he must treat them as if they were exposed. This will usually mean providing respiratory protection, protective work clothing, change areas, hand-washing facilities, biological monitoring, and training. The contractor is responsible for keeping a written record of the survey, including the date, location in the work site, and the names and Social Security numbers of the workers involved.

If the worker's exposure is above the PEL, the contractor must perform monitoring at least every 6 months and continue until at least two consecutive measurements taken at 7-day intervals are below the permissible limit.

Compliance Plan

OSHA requires that any contractor who will be working in and around lead paint have a written compliance plan. This plan is the contractor's strategy for minimizing the risk of exposure for his or her employes. As a minimum, the plan is to include:

1. Written documentation.
2. Implementation prior to the start of the work.
3. Identity of each construction activity that would emit lead.
4. Method to be used to limit/control the exposure.
5. Technology to be used.
6. Engineering plans and studies to control air monitoring.
7. Schedule.
8. Inspections by a trained, competent person.
9. Availability to all affected employees.
10. Revised and updated reports every 6 months.

LEAD PAINT

- Inside the house as well as outside.
- In the soil around the structure.
- Windows and window sills.
- Doors and door frames.
- Stairs, railings, and banisters.
- Porches and fences.

Protective Measures

1. Do not use dry scraper, belt sander, propane torches, or heat guns to remove lead-based paints. These will create a large amount of lead dust and/or fumes.

2. Do not allow food, beverages, tobacco products, and cosmetics in lead-contaminated work areas.

3. Provide a clean change area to change into protective clothing and then back to street clothes.

4. Provide shower facilities and handwashing stations.

5. Provide respirators and training in their use. Make sure the correct type is used based on the level of airborn contamination.

Conduct training at regular intervals.

RECORD KEEPING

The contractor is responsible for establishing and maintaining three exposure assessment records. As a minimum, they are to include:

1. Dates, number, duration, locations, and results of each sample taken.

2. A description on the sampling and analytical methods used.

3. Types of respiratory protection used.

4. Names, Social Security numbers, job titles, and title classifications of the person(s) doing the monitoring.

5. Environmental conditions.

6. Accurate records for any employee subject to medical surveillance. This includes:

   • Name, Social Secutiry number, and duty description of employee.

   • Copy of doctors notes, reports, and prescriptions.

   • Lead monitoring reports.

   • Description of the laboratory testing procedures.

   • All medical examination records.

   • Dates the employee was removed from the lead exposure and returned.

7. All records must be keep indefinitely and make available upon request to:

   • The affected employee.

   • All former employees.

   • OSHA.

   • Director of NIOSH.

OSHA Reporting

Per OSHA, any injury or illness resulting in one or more of the following must be reported:

• Death.

• Days away from work.

• Restricted work.

• Transfer to another position.

• Medical treatment beyond first aid.

• Loss of consciousness.

Cases not meeting the above requirements but involving a significant injury or illness diagnosed by a physician or other licensed health care professional should also be reported.

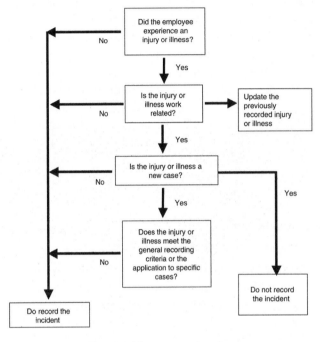

Fig. 14-11 *OSHA reporting.*

OSHA CIVIL PENALTIES POLICY

A sevenfold increase in the maximum limits for OSHA civil monetary penalties was stipulated in the Budget Reconciliation Act passed by the 101st Congress. The maximum allowable penalty is now $70,000 for each willful or repeated violation; and $7,000 for each serious or other-than-serious violation as well as $7,000 for each day beyond a stated abatement date for failure to correct a violation. These amounts are ceilings—not floors. However, in order to ensure that the most flagrant violators are in fact fined at an effective level, a minimum penalty of $5,000 for a willful violation of the OSHA Act was adopted. The new penalty policy will be applicable to all citations issued as a result of inspections initiated after March 1, 1991, for violations occurring after November 5, 1990—the effective date of the Budget Reconciliation Act.

The new policy also applies to those states with OSHA-approved state occupational safety and health programs, under the congressional direction that these state plans must be "at least as effective" as the national plan. The participating states are being given a reasonable period to implement the new penalty structure which takes into account the states' legislative calendars.

The basic penalty process will not change—it still follows the criteria set forth in the OSHA Act, which is to determine penalties based on the gravity of the violation and the size, good faith, and history of the employer. Gravity determines the base amount; the other factors determine appropriate reductions.

As in the past, all penalty amounts are proposed penalties issued with the citation. The employer may contest the penalty amount as well as the citation within the statutory 15-day contest period. Thereafter, the penalty may be adjudicated by the independent Occupational Safety and Health Review Commission, or OSHA may negotiate with the employer to settle for a reduced penalty amount if this will lead to speedy abatement of the hazard.

Here is how the new system for proposing penalties will operate.

Adjustment Factors

The size adjustment factor is as follows: For an employer with only one to 25 workers, the penalty will be reduced 60%; 26–100 workers, the reduction will be 40%; 101–250 workers, a 20% reduction; and more than 250 workers, there will be no reduction in the penalty. There may be up to an additional 25% reduction for evidence that the employer is making a good-faith effort to provide good workplace safety and health, and an additional 10% reduction if the employer has not been cited by OSHA for any serious, willful, or repeat violations in the past 3 years.

In order to qualify for the full 25% "good faith" reduction, an employer must have a written and implemented safety and health program such as given in OSHA's voluntary "Safety and Health Management Guidelines" (Federal Register, Vol. 54, No. 16, January 26, 1989, pp. 3904–3916) and that includes programs required under the OSHA standards, such as Hazard Communication, Lockout/Tagout, or safety and health programs for construction required in CPR 29 1926.20.

Serious Violations

The typical range of proposed penalties for serious violations, before adjustment factors are applied, will be $1,500–$5,000, although the Regional Administrator may propose up to $7,000 for a serious violation when warranted.

A serious violation is defined as one in which there is substantial probability that death or serious physical harm could result, and the employer knew or should have known of the hazard. Serious violations will be categorized in terms of severity—high, medium, or low—and the probability of an injury or illness occurring greater or lesser.

Base penalties for serious violations will be assessed as follows:

Severity	Probability	Penalty
High	Greater	$5,000
Medium	Greater	3,500
Low	Greater	2,500
High	Lesser	2,500
Medium	Lesser	2,000
Low	Lesser	1,500

Penalties for serious violations that are classified as high in both severity and greater in probability will only be adjusted for size and history.

Other-Than-Serious Violations

If an employer is cited for an other-than-serious violation which has a low probability of resulting in an injury or illness, there will be no proposed penalty. However, the violation must still be corrected. If the other-than-serious violation has a greater probability of resulting in an injury or illness, then a base penalty of $1,000 will be used, to which appropriate adjustment factors will be applied. The OSHA Regional Administrator may use a base penalty of up to $7,000 if circumstances warrant.

Regulatory Violations

Regulatory violations involve violations of posting, injury and illness reporting and recordkeeping requirements, and not telling employees about advance notice of an inspection. OSHA will be applying adjustments only for the size and history of the establishments. Here are the base penalties, before adjustments, to be proposed for posting requirement violations: OSHA notice, $1,000; annual summary, $1,000; and failure to post citations, $3,000.

Base reporting and record-keeping penalties are as follows: Failure to maintain OSHA 200 and OSHA 101 forms, $1,000; failure to report a fatality or catastrophe within 48 hours, $5,000 (with a provision that the OSHA Regional Administrator could adjust that up to

$7,000, in exceptional circumstances); denying access to records, $1,000; and not telling employees about advance notice of an inspection, $2,000.

Willful Violations

In the case of willful serious violations, the initial proposed penalty has to be between $5,000 and $70,000. OSHA calculates the penalty for the underlying serious violation, adjusts it for size and history, and multiplies it by 7. The multiplier of 7 can be adjusted, upward or downward, at the OSHA Regional Administrator's discretion, if circumstances warrant. The minimum willful serious penalty is $5,000. *Willful violations* are those committed with an intentional disregard of, or plain indifference to, the requirements of the OSHA and regulations.

Repeat Violations

A *repeat violation* is a violation of any standard, regulation, rule, or order where, upon reinspection, a substantially similar violation is found. Repeat violations will only be adjusted for size, and the adjusted penalties will then be multiplied by 2, 5, or 10. The multiplier for small employers—250 employees or fewer—is 2 for the first instance of a repeat violation, and 5 for the second repeat. However, the OSHA Regional Administrator has the authority to use a multiplication factor of up to 10 on a case involving a repeat violation by a small employer to achieve the necessary deterrent effect.

The multiplier for large companies—250 or more employees—is 5 for the first instance of repeat violation, and 10 for the second repeat. If the initial violation was other-than-serious, without a penalty being assessed, then the penalty will be $200 for the first repetition of that violation, $500 for the second repeat, and $1,000 for the third repeat.

Failure to Abate

Failure to correct a prior violation within the prescribed abatement period could result in a penalty for each day the violation continues beyond the abatement date. In these failure-to-abate cases, the daily penalty will be equal to the amount of the initial penalty (up to $7,000) with an adjustment for size only. This failure to abate penalty may be assessed for a maximum of 30 days by the OSHA area office. In cases of partial abatement of the violation, the OSHA Regional Administrator has authority to reduce the penalty by 25–75%.

If the failure to abate is more than 30 days, it may be referred to the OSHA national office in Washington where a determination may be made to assess a daily penalty beyond the initial 30 days.

OSHA CHECKLIST
Review for Items That Apply

We encourage you to use this checklist. You will find it a useful tool in helping to identify hazards on the project. Employers who are developing an occupational safety and health program on their own will find this checklist especially helpful. However, this is not meant to be a replacement for a comprehensive occupational safety and health program. To develop such a program requires more than a checklist. To be successful, the program must be integrated into your daily operations. This self-inspection checklists section contains the most common hazards found in workplaces and covers issues that need to be addressed to prevent accidents and decrease costs resulting from occupational injuries, illnesses, and fatalities.

Self-Inspection Checklists

Employer Posting

- Is the OSHA poster, *Job Safety and Health*, displayed in a prominent location where all employees are likely to see it? Are other required posters or notices properly displayed, such as:
- Field Sanitation Notice for workers?
- Safety Committee meeting minutes?
- OSHA 200 Summary?
- Notice of compensation guarantee contract?
- Are emergency telephone numbers posted where they can be readily used in case of emergency?
- Where employees may be exposed to any toxic substances or harmful physical agents, have appropriate information concerning employee access to medical and exposure records and Material Safety Data Sheets (MSDSs) been made readily available to affected employees?
- Are signs regarding exits from buildings, room capacity, floor loading, exposure to X-ray, microwave, or other harmful radiation or substances posted where required?

Recordkeeping

- Are all occupational injuries and illnesses, including those involving loss of life, loss of consciousness, loss of time from work, and those requiring treatment other than first aid, being recorded as required on the *OSHA Form 200?*
- Are copies of *OSHA Form 200* and First Report of Injury, Form 801, kept for five years?

- Are employee medical records and records of employee exposures to hazardous substances or harmful physical agents current?
- Have arrangements been made to maintain required records for the legal period of time for each specific type of record? (Some records must be maintained for at least 40 years.)
- Are operating permits and records current for such items as elevators, pressure vessels, and liquefied petroleum gas tanks?
- Are employee safety and health training records maintained?
- Is documentation of safety inspections and corrections maintained?

Safety and Health Program

- Do you have top management commitment?
- Have you established labor and management accountability?
- Do you have a system in place for hazard identification and control?
- Do you investigate all incidents and accidents?
- Do you encourage employee involvement in health and safety matters?
- Do you provide occupational safety and health training for your workers and supervisors?
- Do you perform periodic evaluations of the plan?

Medical Services and First Aid

- Has an emergency medical plan been developed?
- Are emergency phone numbers posted?
- Are first-aid kits easily accessible to each work area, with necessary supplies available; periodically inspected; and replenished as needed?
- Are means provided for quick drenching or flushing of the eyes and body in areas where caustic or corrosive liquids or materials are handled?

Safety Committees

- Do you have an active safety committee with equal numbers of employer and employee representatives?
- Are records kept documenting safety and health training for each employee by name or other identifier, training dates, type(s) of training, and training provider?
- Does the committee meet at least monthly, or quarterly for office-type environments?

- Is a written record of safety committee meetings distributed to affected employees, and maintained for OSHA review?
- Does the safety committee conduct quarterly hazard identification surveys?
- Does the committee review results of periodic, scheduled work site inspections?
- Does the committee review accident and near-miss investigations and, where necessary, submit recommendations for prevention of future incidents?
- Does the committee involve all workers in the safety and health program?
- Are safety committee minutes kept for 3 years, and are each month's minutes posted?
- Has your safety committee developed an accident investigation procedure?
- Has the committee reviewed your safety and health program and made recommendations for possible improvements?
- Have committee members been trained and instructed in safety committee purpose and operation, methods of conducting meetings, OSHA rules which apply to the workplace, hazard identification, and accident investigation principles?

Fire Protection

- If you have 11 or more empoyees, do you have a written fire-prevention plan?
- Does your plan describe the type of fire protection equipment and/or systems (if any) that are available for use?
- Have you established practices and procedures to control potential fire hazards and ignition sources?
- Are employees aware of the fire hazards of the materials and processes to which they are exposed?
- If you have a fire alarm system, is it tested at least annually?
- Are sprinkler heads protected by metal guards when exposed to physical damage?
- Is proper clearance maintained below sprinkler heads?
- Are portable fire extinguishers provided in adequate numbers and types?
- Are fire extinguishers mounted in readily assessable locations?
- Are fire extinguishers recharged regularly and then noted on the inspection tag?
- If employees are expected to use fire extinguishers and fire protection procedures, are they trained?

- If employees are not trained to use fire extinguishers, are they trained to immediately evacuate the building?

Personal Protective Equipment (PPE) and Clothing

- Has there been an assessment of the hazards that might require PPE, including a review of injuries?
- Has the assessment been verified through written certification?
- Does it identify the workplace evaluated?
- Has training been provided to each employee required to wear PPE?
- Has the training been verified through written certification?
- Are protective goggles or face shields provided and worn when there is any danger of flying material or caustic or corrosive materials?
- Are ANSI-approved safety glasses worn at all times in areas where there is risk of eye injury?
- Are protective gloves, aprons, shields, or other protection provided against cuts, corrosive liquids, and chemicals?
- Are hard hats provided and worn where danger of falling objects exists?
- Are hard hats inspected periodically for damage to the shell and suspension system?
- Do workers who are exposed to vehicular traffic wear garments that make them stand out from their surroundings?
- Do workers wear reflective garments at night?
- Are approved respirators provided for regular or emergency use where needed?
- Is there a written respirator program?
- Are the respirators inspected before and after each use?
- Is a written record kept of all inspection dates and findings?
- Have all employees been trained in adequate work procedures, use and maintenance of protective clothing, and proper use of equipment when cleaning up spilled toxic or other hazardous materials or liquids?
- Is a spill kit available to clean up spilled toxic or hazardous materials?
- Where employees are exposed to conditions that could cause foot injury, are safety shoes required to be worn?
- Is all protective equipment maintained in a sanitary condition and ready for use?

- Do you have eyewash facilities and a quick-drench shower within a work area where employees are exposed to caustic or corrosive materials?
- When lunches are eaten on the premises, are they eaten in areas where there is no exposure to toxic materials or other health hazards?
- Is protection against the effects of occupational noise exposure provided when sound levels exceed those of the OSHA noise and hearing conservation standard?

General Work Environment

- Are all worksites clean and orderly?
- Are walking surfaces kept dry or appropriate means taken to ensure that surfaces are slip-resistant?
- Are all spilled materials or liquids cleaned up immediately?
- Is combustible scrap, debris, and waste stored safely and removed from the worksite promptly?
- Are covered metal waste cans used for oily and paint-soaked waste?
- Are the minimum number of toilets and washing facilities provided?
- Are toilets and washing facilities sanitary?
- Are all work areas adequately lighted?

Walkways

- Are aisles and passageways kept clear and are they at least 22 in. wide?
- Are aisles and walkways appropriately marked?
- Are wet surfaces covered with non-slip materials?
- Are openings or holes in the floors or other treading surfaces repaired or otherwise made safe?
- Is there safe clearance for walking in aisles where vehicles are operating?
- Are materials or equipment stored so sharp objects cannot obstruct the walkway?
- Are changes of direction or elevations readily identifiable?
- Are aisles or walkways that pass near moving or operating machinery, welding operations, or similar operations arranged so employees will not be subjected to hazards?
- Is adequate headroom (of at least 6.5 ft) provided for the entire length of any walkway?
- Are standard guardrails provided wherever aisle or walkway surfaces are elevated more than 4 ft above any adjacent floor or the ground?

- Are bridges provided over conveyors and similar hazards?

Floor and Wall Openings

- Are floor holes or openings guarded by a cover, guardrail, or equivalent on all sides (except at entrance to stairways or ladders)?
- Are toeboards installed around the edges of a permanent floor opening (where persons may pass below the opening)?
- Are skylight screens of such construction and mounting that they will withstand a load of at least 200 lb?
- Is the glass in windows, doors, and glass walls (which may be subject to human impact) of sufficient thickness and type for all conditions of use?
- Are grates or similar covers over floor openings, such as floor drains, of such design that foot traffic or rolling equipment will not be caught by the grate spacing?
- Are unused portions of service pits and pits not actually in use covered or protected by guardrails or equivalent?

Stairs and Stairways

- Are standard stair rails and handrails present on all stairways having four or more risers?
- Are all stairways at least 22 in. wide?
- Do stairs have at least 6.5 ft of overhead clearance?
- Do stairs angle no more than 50° and no less than 30°?
- Are step risers on stairs uniform from top to bottom, with no riser spacing greater than 9.5 in.?
- Are steps on stairs and stairways designed or provided with a surface that renders them slip resistant?
- Are stairway handrails located between 30–42 in. above the leading edge of stair treads?
- Do stairway handrails have at least 3-in. clearance between handrails and the wall or surface they are mounted on?
- Are stairway handrails capable of withstanding a load of 200 lbs applied in any direction?
- Where stairs or stairways exit directly into any area where vehicles may be operated, are adequate barriers and warnings provided to prevent employees from stepping into the path of traffic?

Elevated Surfaces

- Are signs posted, when appropriate, showing elevated floor load capacity?

- Are elevated surfaces (more than 4 ft above the floor or ground) provided with standard guardrails?
- Are all elevated surfaces (beneath which people or machinery could be exposed to falling objects) provided with standard toeboards?
- Is a permanent means of access/egress provided to elevated work surfaces?
- Is material on elevated surfaces piled, stacked, or racked in a manner to prevent it from tipping, falling, collapsing, rolling, or spreading?
- Are dock boards or bridge plates used when transferring materials between docks and trucks or railcars?
- When in use, are dock boards or bridge plates secured in place?

Exit or Egress

- Are all exits marked with an exit sign and illuminated by a reliable light source if possibly used in the dark?
- Are the directions to exits, if not immediately apparent, marked with visible signs?
- Are doors, passageways, or stairways that are neither exits nor access to exits, and which could be mistaken for exits, appropriately marked "NOT AN EXIT," or "TO BASEMENT," "STOREROOM," and the like?
- Are exit signs provided with the word "EXIT" in lettering at least 6 in. high and the stroke of the lettering at least ¾ in. wide?
- Are exit doors side-hinged?
- Are all exits kept free of obstructions and unlocked?
- Are at least two means of egress provided from elevated platforms, pits, or rooms where the absence of a second exit would increase the risk of injury from hot, poisonous, corrosive, suffocating, flammable, or explosive substances?
- Are there sufficient exits to permit prompt escape in case of emergency?
- Are the number of exits from each floor of a building and the number of exits from the building itself appropriate for the building occupancy load?
- When workers must exit through glass doors, storm doors and such, are the doors fully tempered and meeting safety requirements for human impact?

Exit Doors

- Are doors required to serve as exits designed and constructed so that the way of exit travel is obvious and direct?

- Are windows (which could be mistaken for exit doors) made inaccessible by barriers or railing?

- Are exit doors able to open from the direction of exit travel without the use of a key or any special knowledge or effort?

- Is a revolving, sliding, or overhead door prohibited from serving as a required exit door?

- When panic hardware is installed on a required exit door, will it allow the door to open by applying a force of 15 lb or less in the direction of the exit traffic?

- Are doors on cold-storage rooms provided with an inside release mechanism that will release the latch and open the door even if it is padlocked or otherwise locked on the outside?

- Where exit doors open directly onto a street, alley, or other area where vehicles may be operated, are adequate barriers and warnings provided to prevent employees from stepping directly into the path of traffic?

- Are doors that swing in both directions between rooms in which there is frequent traffic, provided with viewing panels in each door?

Portable Ladders

- Are all ladders in good condition, joints between steps and side rails tight, all hardware and fittings securely attached, and moveable parts operating freely without binding or undue play?

- Are nonslip safety feet on all ladders except step ladders?

- Are ladder rungs and steps free of grease and oil?

- Are employees prohibited from placing a ladder in front of doors opening toward the ladder except when the door is blocked open, locked, or guarded?

- Are employees prohibited from placing ladders on boxes, barrels, or other unstable bases to obtain additional height?

- Are employees instructed to face the ladder when ascending/descending?

- Are employees prohibited from using ladders that are broken; are missing steps, rungs, or cleats; or have broken side rails or other faulty equipment?

- Are employees instructed not to use the top step of ordinary stepladders as a step?

- When portable rung ladders are used to gain access to elevated platforms, roofs, and the like, does the ladder always extend at least 3 ft above the elevated surface?

- Is it required that when portable rung or cleat-type ladders are used, the base is so placed that slipping will not occur, or it is lashed or otherwise held in place?

- Are portable metal ladders legibly marked with signs reading "CAUTION—Do Not Use Around Electrical Equipment" or equivalent wording?

- Are the rungs of ladders uniformly spaced at 12 in., center to center?

Hand Tools and Equipment

- Are all tools and equipment (both company- and employee-owned) in good working condition?

- Are hand tools such as chisels or punches (that develop mushroomed heads) reconditioned or replaced as necessary?

- Are broken or fractured handles on hammers, axes, or similar equipment replaced promptly?

- Are appropriate handles used on files and similar tools?

- Are appropriate safety glasses, face shields, and similar equipment used while using hand tools or equipment which might produce flying materials or be subject to breakage?

- Are jacks checked periodically to assure that they are in good operating condition?

- Are tool handles wedged tightly in the head of all tools?

- Are tool-cutting edges kept sharp so the tool will move smoothly without binding or skipping?

- Are eye and face protection used when driving hardened or tempered tools, bits, or nails?

Portable (Power-Operated) Tools and Equipment

- Are grinders, saws, and similar equipment provided with appropriate safety guards?

- Are power tools used with the shield or guard recommended by the manufacturer?

- Are portable circular saws equipped with guards above and below the base shoe?

- Are circular saw guards checked to ensure guarding of the lower blade portion?

- Are rotating or moving parts of equipment guarded to prevent physical contact?

- Are all cord-connected, electrically operated tools and equipment effectively grounded or of the approved double-insulated type?

- Are effective guards in place over belts, pulleys, chains, and sprockets on equipment such as concrete mixers, air compressors, and the like?

- Are portable fans provided with full guards having openings of ½ in. or less?
- Is hoisting equipment available and used for lifting heavy objects, and are hoist ratings and characteristics appropriate for the task?
- Are ground-fault circuit interrupters (provided on all temporary electrical 15-, 20-, and 30-ampere circuits) used during periods of construction?

Or

- Do you have an assured equipment-grounding conductor program in place in construction?
- Are pneumatic and hydraulic hoses on power-operated tools checked regularly for deterioration or damage?

Abrasive Wheel Equipment Grinders

- Is the work rest used and kept adjusted to within ⅛ in. of the wheel?
- Is the adjustable tongue on the top side of the grinder used and kept adjusted to within ¼ in. of the wheel?
- Do side guards cover the spindle, nut, flange, and 75% of the wheel diameter?
- Are bench and pedestal grinders permanently mounted?
- Are ANSI-approved goggles or face shields always worn when grinding?
- Is the maximum RPM rating of each abrasive wheel compatible with the RPM rating of the grinder motor?
- Are fixed or permanently mounted grinders connected to their electrical supply system with metallic conduit or by another permanent wiring method?
- Does each grinder have an individual on/off switch?
- Is each electrically operated grinder effectively grounded?
- Before mounting new abrasive wheels, are they visually inspected and ring tested?
- Are dust collectors and powered exhausts provided on grinders used in operations that produce large amounts of dust?
- To prevent coolant from splashing workers, are splash guards mounted on grinders that use coolant?
- Is cleanliness maintained around grinders?

Machine Guarding

- Is there an employee training program for safe methods of machine operation?
- Is there adequate supervision to ensure that employees are following safe machine-operating procedures?

- Is there a regular program of safety inspection for machinery and equipment?
- Is all machinery and equipment clean and properly maintained?
- Is sufficient clearance provided around and between machines to allow for safe operations, set up and servicing, material handling, and waste removal?
- Is equipment and machinery securely placed and anchored when necessary to prevent tipping or other movement that could result in personal injury?
- Is there a power shut-off switch within reach of the operator's position at each machine?
- Are the noncurrent-carrying metal parts of electrically operated machines bonded and grounded?
- Are foot-operated switches guarded or arranged to prevent accidental actuation by personnel or falling objects?
- Are manually operated valves and switches (controlling the operation of equipment and machines) clearly identified and readily accessible?
- Are all emergency stop buttons colored red?
- Are all pulleys and belts (that are located within 7 ft of the floor or working level) properly guarded?
- Are all moving chains and gears properly guarded?
- Are methods provided to protect the operator and other employees in the machine area from hazards created at the point of operation, ingoing nip points, rotating parts, flying chips, and sparks?
- Are machinery guards secured and arranged so they do not present a hazard in their use?
- If special hand tools are used for placing and removing material, do they protect the operator's hands?
- Are revolving drums, barrels, and containers (required to be guarded by an enclosure that is interlocked with the drive mechanism so that revolution cannot occur) guarded?
- Do arbors and mandrels have firm and secure bearings, and are they free from play?
- Are provisions made to prevent machines from automatically starting when power is restored (following a power failure or shut down)?
- Are machines constructed so as to be free from excessive vibration (when the largest size tool is mounted and run at full speed)?
- If machinery is cleaned with compressed air, is air pressure controlled and personal protective equipment or other safeguards used to protect operators and other workers from eye and body injury?

- Are fan blades protected with a guard having openings no larger than ½ in. when operating within 7 ft of the floor?
- Are saws used for ripping equipped with anti-kickback devices and spreaders?
- Are radial arm saws guarded and so arranged that the cutting head will gently return to the back of the table when released?

Lockout/Tagout Procedures

- Is all machinery or equipment (capable of movement) required to be de-energized or disengaged and locked out during cleaning, servicing, adjusting, or setting-up operations?
- Is it prohibited to lock out control circuits in lieu of locking out main power disconnects?
- Are all equipment control-valve handles provided with a means of lockout?
- Does the lockout/tagout procedure require that stored energy (i.e., mechanical, hydraulic, air) be released or blocked before equipment is locked out for repairs?
- Are appropriate employees provided with individually keyed personal safety locks?
- Are employees required to keep personal control of their key(s) while they have safety locks in use?
- Is it required that employees check the safety of the lockout by attempting to start up after making sure no one is exposed? Where the power disconnecting means for equipment does not also disconnect the electrical control circuit:
  - Are the appropriate electrical enclosures identified?
  - Are means provided to assure the control circuit can also be disconnected and locked out?

Welding, Cutting, and Brazing

- Are only authorized and trained personnel permitted to use welding, cutting, or brazing equipment?
- Are compressed gas cylinders regularly examined for signs of defect, deep rusting, or leakage?
- Are cylinders kept away from sources of heat?
- Are employees prohibited from using cylinders as rollers or supports?
- Are empty cylinders appropriately marked, their valves closed, and valve-protection caps placed on them?
- Are signs reading: "DANGER—NO SMOKING, MATCHES OR OPEN LIGHTS," or the equivalent posted?

- Are cylinders, cylinder valves, couplings, regulators, hoses, and apparatus kept free of oily or greasy substances?
- Unless secured on special trucks, are regulators removed and valve-protection caps put in place before moving cylinders?
- Do cylinders without fixed hand wheels have keys, handles, or nonadjustable wrenches on stem valves when in service?
- Are liquefied gases stored and shipped with the valve end up and with valve covers in place?
- Before a regulator is removed, is the valve closed, and then gas released from the regulator?
- Is open circuit (no load) voltage of arc welding and cutting machines as low as possible and not in excess of the recommended limit?
- Are electrodes removed from the holders when not in use?
- Are employees required to shut off the electric power to the welder when no one is in attendance?
- Is suitable fire-extinguishing equipment available for immediate use?
- Are welders forbidden to coil or loop welding electrode cable around their bodies?
- Are work and electrode lead cables frequently inspected for wear and damage and replaced when needed?
- Do means for connecting cable lengths have adequate insulation?
- When the object to be welded cannot be moved and fire hazards cannot be removed, are shields used to confine heat, sparks, and slag?
- Are fire watchers assigned when welding or cutting is performed in locations where a serious fire might develop?
- When welding is done on metal walls, are precautions taken to protect combustibles on the other side?
- Before hot work begins, are drums, barrels, tanks, and other containers so thoroughly cleaned and tested that no substances remain that could explode, ignite, or produce toxic vapors?
- Do eye-protection helmets, hand shields, and goggles meet appropriate standards?
- Are employees exposed to the hazards created by welding, cutting, or brazing operations protected with personal protective equipment and clothing?
- Is a check made for adequate ventilation where welding or cutting is performed?

- When employees work in confined spaces, is the atmosphere monitored and are means provided for quick removal of welders in case of an emergency?

Compressors and Compressed Air

- Are compressors equipped with pressure-relief valves and pressure gages?
- Are compressor air intakes installed and equipped to ensure that only clean, uncontaminated air enters the compressor?
- Are air filters installed on the compressor intake?
- Are compressors operated and lubricated according to the manufacturer's recommendations?
- Are safety devices on compressed-air systems checked frequently?
- Before any repair work is done on the pressure systems of the compressor, is the pressure bled off and the system locked out?
- Are signs posted to warn of the automatic starting feature of the compressors?
- Is the belt drive system totally enclosed to provide protection on the front, back, top, and sides?
- Is it strictly prohibited to direct compressed air toward a person?
- Are employees prohibited from using compressed air at over 29 PSI for cleaning purposes unless they use an approved nozzle with pressure relief and clip guard?
- Are employees prohibited from cleaning clothing with compressed air?
- When using compressed air for cleaning, do employees use personal protective equipment?
- Are high-pressure hoses and connections in good repair?
- Before compressed air is used to empty containers of liquid, is the safe working pressure of the container checked?
- When compressed air is used with abrasive blast cleaning equipment, is the operating valve a type that must be held open manually?
- Is it prohibited to use compressed air to move combustible dust if such action could cause the dust to be suspended in the air and cause a fire or explosion?
- If plastic piping is used, is the plastic approved for air line service? (Some ABS is OK—PVC is not.)

Compressed Gas and Cylinders

- Are cylinders with water-weight capacity over 30 lb equipped (with means for connecting a valve protector or device, or with a collar or recess) to protect the valve?
- Are cylinders legibly marked to clearly identify the gas contained?
- Are compressed-gas cylinders stored in areas that are protected from external heat sources (such as flames, intense radiant heat, electric arcs, or high-temperature lines)?
- Are cylinders located or stored in areas where they will not be damaged by passing or falling objects or be subject to tampering by unauthorized persons?
- Are cylinders stored or transported in a manner to prevent them from creating a hazard by tipping, falling, or rolling?
- Are cylinders containing liquefied fuel gas stored or transported in a position so that the safety relief device is always in direct contact with the vapor space in the cylinder?
- Are valve protectors always placed on cylinders when the cylinders are not in use or connected for use?
- Are all valves closed off before a cylinder is moved, when the cylinder is empty, and at the completion of each job?
- Are low-pressure fuel-gas cylinders checked periodically for corrosion, general distortion, cracks, or any other defect that might indicate a weakness or render them unfit for service?
- Does the periodic check of low-pressure fuel-gas cylinders include inspection of the bottom of each cylinder?

Industrial Trucks/Forklifts

- Do industrial truck operators meet the new industrial truck operator training requirements adopted in May 1999?
- Is substantial overhead protective equipment provided on high-lift rider equipment?
- Are the required lift-truck operating rules posted and enforced, and is the capacity rating posted in plain view of the operator?
- Is directional lighting provided on each industrial truck that operates in an area with less than two foot-candles per square foot of general lighting?
- Does each industrial truck have a warning horn, whistle, gong, or other device that can be clearly heard above the normal noise in the operation area?
- Are the brakes on each industrial truck capable of bringing the vehicle to a complete and safe stop when fully loaded?

- Will the industrial truck's parking brake effectively prevent the vehicle from moving when unattended?
- Are industrial trucks operating in areas of flammable gases or vapors, combustible dust, or ignitable fibers approved for such locations?
- Are motorized hand and hand/rider trucks so designed that the brakes are applied and power to the drive motor shuts off when the operator releases his/her grip on the device that controls the travel?
- Are industrial trucks with internal combustion engines, that are operated in buildings or enclosed areas, checked to ensure such operations do not cause harmful concentrations of dangerous gases or fumes?

Spray Finishing Operations

- Is adequate ventilation ensured before spray operations are started?
- Is mechanical ventilation provided when spraying is performed in enclosed areas?
- When mechanical ventilation is provided during spraying operations, is it arranged so that it will not circulate contaminated air?
- Is the spray area free of hot surfaces?
- Is the spray area at least 20 ft from flames, sparks, operating electrical motors, and other ignition sources?
- Are the portable lamps used to illuminate spray areas suitable for use in a hazardous location?
- Is approved respiratory equipment provided and used during spraying operations?
- Do solvents used for cleaning have a flash point of 10°F or more?
- Are fire control sprinkler heads kept clean?
- Are "NO SMOKING" signs posted in the spray areas, paint rooms, paint booths, and paint storage areas?
- Is the spray area kept clean of combustible residue?
- Are spray booths constructed of metal, masonry, or other substantial noncombustible material?
- Are spray booth floors and baffles noncombustible and easily cleaned?
- Is infrared drying apparatus kept out of the spray area during spraying operations?
- Is the spray booth completely ventilated before the drying apparatus is used? Is the electric drying apparatus properly grounded? Do all drying spaces have adequate ventilation?
- Are lighting fixtures for spray booths located outside the booth, and the interior lighted through sealed clear panels?

- Are the electric motors for exhaust fans placed outside booths or ducts?
- Are belts and pulleys inside the booth fully enclosed?
- Do ducts have access doors to allow cleaning?

Confined Spaces

- Is there a written permit-confined-space program?
- Is the program available for inspection?
- Are confined spaces thoroughly emptied of any corrosive or hazardous substances, such as acids or caustics, before entry?
- Before entry, are all pipelines to a confined space containing inert, toxic, flammable, or corrosive materials valved off and blanked or disconnected and separated?
- Are all impellers, agitators, or other moving equipment inside confined spaces locked out if they present a hazard?
- Is either natural or mechanical ventilation provided prior to confined-space entry?
- Before entry, are appropriate atmospheric tests performed to check for oxygen deficiency, toxic substances, and explosive concentrations in the confined space?
- Is adequate lighting provided for the work being performed in the confined space?
- Is the atmosphere inside the confined space frequently tested or continuously monitored during the work process?
- Is there an attendant outside the confined space whose sole responsibility is to watch the work in progress, sound an alarm if necessary, and help render assistance?
- Are attendants or other employees prohibited from entering the confined space without lifelines and respiratory equipment if there is an emergency?
- In addition to the attendant, is there at least one other trained rescuer in the vicinity?
- Are all rescuers appropriately trained and using approved, recently inspected equipment?
- Does all rescue equipment allow for lifting employees vertically through a top opening?
- Are rescue personnel trained in first aid and CPR, and are they immediately available?
- Is there an effective communication system for whenever respiratory equipment is used and the employee in the confined space is out of sight of the attendant?

- Is approved respiratory equipment required if the atmosphere inside the confined space cannot be made acceptable?
- Is all portable electrical equipment used inside confined spaces either grounded and insulated or equipped with ground-fault protection?
- Before gas welding or burning is begun in a confined space, are hoses checked for leaks, compressed-gas bottles removed, and torches lighted only outside the confined space area, to be returned to the confined space only after testing for explosive atmosphere?
- When using oxygen-consuming equipment (such as salamanders, torches, furnaces) in a confined space, is air provided to ensure combustion without reducing the oxygen concentration of the atmosphere below 19.5% by volume?
- Whenever combustion-type equipment is used in a confined space, are provisions made to ensure that the exhaust gases are vented outside the enclosure?
- Is each confined space checked for decaying vegetation or animal matter that may produce methane?
- Is the confined space checked for possible industrial waste that could contain toxic properties?
- If the confined space is below the ground and near areas where motor vehicles are operating, is it possible for vehicle exhaust or carbon monoxide to enter the space?

Environmental Controls

- Are all work areas properly lighted?
- Are hazardous substances identified that may cause harm by inhalation, ingestion, skin absorption, or contact?
- Are employees aware of the hazards involved with the various chemicals they may be exposed to in their work environment, such as ammonia, chlorine, epoxies, and caustics?
- Is employee exposure to chemicals in the workplace kept within acceptable levels? Can a less harmful method or product be used?
- Is the work area's ventilation system appropriate for the work being performed?
- Are proper precautions taken by employees handling asbestos and other fibrous materials?
- Are caution labels and signs used to warn of asbestos?
- Is the possible presence of asbestos determined prior to the beginning of any repair, demolition, construction, or reconstruction work?

- Are asbestos-covered surfaces kept in good repair to prevent release of fibers?
- Are wet methods used (when practicable) to prevent emission of airborne asbestos fibers, silica dust, and similar hazardous materials?
- Is vacuuming with appropriate equipment conducted, rather than blowing or sweeping dust?
- Are grinders, saws, and other machines that produce respirable dust vented to an industrial collector or a central-exhaust system?
- Are all local-exhaust ventilation systems designed and operated properly (at the airflow and volume necessary) for the application? Are the ducts free of obstructions? Have you ensured that belts are not slipping?
- Is personal protective equipment provided, used, and maintained whenever required?
- Are there written standard operating procedures for the selection and use of respirators?
- Are restrooms and washrooms kept clean and sanitary?
- Is all water provided for drinking, washing potable?
- Are all outlets for water that is not suitable for drinking clearly identified?
- Are employees instructed how to properly lift heavy objects?
- Where heat is a problem, have all fixed work areas been provided with a proper means of cooling?
- Are employees working on streets and roadways, where they are exposed to the hazards of traffic, required to wear high-visibility clothing?
- Are exhaust stacks and air intakes located so that contaminated air will not be recirculated within a building or other enclosed area?

Flammable and Combustible Materials

- Are combustible scrap, debris, and waste materials stored in covered metal receptacles and removed from the worksite promptly?
- Are proper storage methods used to minimize the risk of fire and spontaneous combustion?
- Are approved containers and tanks used for the storage and handling of flammable and combustible liquids?
- Are all connections on drums and combustible liquid piping (vapor and liquid) tight?
- Are all flammable liquids kept in closed containers when not in use?

- Are bulk drums of flammable liquids grounded and bonded to containers during dispensing?
- Do storage rooms for flammable and combustible liquids have explosion-proof lights?
- Do storage rooms for flammables and combustible liquids have mechanical or gravity ventilation?
- Are safe practices followed when liquid petroleum gas is stored, handled, and used?
- Are liquefied petroleum storage tanks guarded to prevent damage from vehicles?
- Are all solvent wastes and flammable liquids kept in fire-resistant, covered containers until they are removed from the work site?
- Is vacuuming used whenever possible, rather than blowing or sweeping combustible dust?
- Are fire separators placed between stacked containers of combustibles or flammables to ensure their support and stability?
- Are fuel-gas cylinders and oxygen cylinders separated by distance, fire-resistant barriers, or other means while in storage?
- Are fire extinguishers provided for the type of materials they will extinguish, and placed in areas where they are to be used?

  Class A. Ordinary combustible materials fires

  Class B. Flammable liquid, gas, or grease fires

  Class C. Energized-electrical equipment fires
- If a Halon 1301 fire extinguisher is used, can employees evacuate within the specified time (for that extinguisher)?
- Are appropriate fire extinguishers mounted within 75 ft of outside areas containing flammable liquids, and within 10 ft of any inside storage area for such materials?
- Is the transfer/withdrawal of flammable or combustible liquids performed by trained personnel?
- Are fire extinguishers mounted so that employees do not have to travel more than 75 ft for a Class A fire or 50 ft for a Class B fire?
- Are employees trained in the use of fire extinguishers?
- Are all extinguishers serviced, maintained, and tagged at intervals not to exceed 1 year? Is a record maintained of required monthly checks of extinguishers?
- Are all extinguishers fully charged and in their designated places? Are extinguishers free from obstruction or blockage?
- Where sprinkler systems are permanently installed, are the nozzle heads directed or arranged so that water will not be sprayed into operating electrical switchboards and equipment?
- Are "NO SMOKING" signs posted in areas where flammable or combustible materials are used or stored?
- Are "NO SMOKING" signs posted on liquefied petroleum gas tanks?
- Are "NO SMOKING" rules enforced in areas involving storage and use of flammable materials?
- Are safety cans used for dispensing flammable or combustible liquids?
- Are all spills of flammable or combustible liquids cleaned up promptly?

Hazardous Chemical Exposures

- Is employee exposure to chemicals kept within acceptable levels?
- Are eyewash fountains and safety showers provided in areas where caustic corrosive chemicals are handled?
- Are all employees required to use personal protective clothing and equipment (gloves, eye protection, respirators) when handling chemicals?
- Are flammable or toxic chemicals kept in closed containers when not in use?
- Where corrosive liquids are frequently handled in open containers or drawn from storage vessels or pipelines, are adequate means provided to neutralize or dispose of spills or overflows (properly and safely)?
- Have standard operating procedures been established, and are they being followed when chemical spills are cleaned up?
- Are respirators stored in a convenient and clean location?
- Are emergency-use respirators adequate for the various conditions under which they may be used?
- Are employees prohibited from eating in areas where hazardous chemicals are present?
- Is personal protective equipment provided, used, and maintained whenever necessary?
- Are there written standard operating procedures for selecting and using respirators where needed?
- If you have a respirator protection program, are your employees instructed on the correct usage and limitations of the respirators?
- Are the respirators NIOSH-approved for particular applications?
- Are respirators inspected and cleaned, sanitized, and maintained regularly?

- Are you familiar with the Threshold Limit Value (TLV) or Permissible Exposure Limit (PEL) of airborne contaminants and physical agents used in your workplace?

- Have you considered having an industrial hygienist or environmental health specialist evaluate your work operations?

- If internal combustion engines are used, is carbon monoxide kept within acceptable levels?

- Is vacuuming used rather than blowing or sweeping dusts whenever possible for cleanups?

Hazard Communication

- Have you compiled a list of hazardous substances that are used in your workplace?

- Is there a written hazard communication program dealing with material safety data sheets (MSDSs), labeling, and employee training?

- Is someone responsible for MSDSs, container labeling, and employee training?

- Is each container for a hazardous substance (vats, bottles, storage tanks) labeled with product identity and a hazard warning that communicates specific health and physical hazards?

- Is there an MSDS readily available for each hazardous substance used?

- Do you inform other employers whose employees share a work area with your employees, where hazardous substances are used?

- Do you have an employee training program for hazardous substances? Does this program include:

  - An explanation of what an MSDS is, and how to obtain and use one? An explanation of "Right to Know"?

  - The contents of the MSDS for each hazardous substance or class of substances?

  - Informing employees where they can review the employer's written hazard communication program, and where hazardous substances are located in work areas?

  - Explaining the physical and health hazards of substances in the work area, how to detect their presence, and specific protective measures to be used?

  - Hazard communication program details including labeling system and MSDS use?

  - How employees will be informed of hazards of non-routine tasks and hazards of unlabeled pipes?

Electrical Safety

- Are your workplace electricians familiar with OSHA electrical safety rules?

- Do you require compliance with OSHA rules on all contract electrical work?

- Are all employees required to report (as soon as practical) any obvious hazard to life or property observed in connection with electrical equipment or lines?

- Are employees instructed to make preliminary inspections and/or appropriate tests to determine what conditions exist before starting work on electrical equipment or lines?

- When electrical equipment or lines are to be serviced, maintained, or adjusted, are necessary switches opened, locked out, and tagged?

- Are portable, hand-held electrical tools and equipment grounded or are they of the double-insulated type?

- Are electrical appliances such as vacuum cleaners, polishers, and vending machines grounded?

- Do extension cords have a grounding conductor? Are multiple plug adapters prohibited?

- Are ground-fault circuit interrupters installed on each temporary 15-, 20-, or 30-amp, 125-V AC circuit at locations where construction, demolition, modifications, alterations, or excavations are being performed? Or

- Do you have an assured equipment-grounding conductor program in place?

- Are all temporary circuits protected by suitable disconnecting switches or plug connectors at the junction with permanent wiring?

- Is exposed wiring and cords with frayed or deteriorated insulation repaired or replaced promptly?

- Are flexible cords and cables free of splices or taps?

- Are clamps or other securing means provided on flexible cords or cables at plugs, receptacles, tools, equipment, and is the cord jacket securely held in place?

- Are all cords, cable, and raceway connections intact and secure?

- In wet or damp locations, are electrical tools and equipment appropriate for the use or locations (or otherwise protected)?

- Are electrical power lines and cables located (overhead, underground, underfloor, other side of walls) before digging, drilling, or similar work begins?

- Is the use of metal measuring tapes, ropes, hand lines, or similar devices with metallic thread woven into the fabric prohibited where these could come into contact with energized parts of equipment or circuit conductors?

- Is the use of metal ladders prohibited in areas where the ladder or the person using the ladder could come into contact with energized parts of equipment, fixtures, or circuit conductors?
- Are all disconnecting switches and circuit breakers labeled to indicate their use or equipment served?
- Are disconnecting means always opened before fuses are replaced?
- Do all interior wiring systems include provisions for grounding metal parts or electrical raceways, equipment, and enclosures?
- Are all electrical raceways and enclosures securely fastened in place?
- Are all energized parts of electrical circuits and equipment guarded against accidental contact by approved cabinets or enclosures?
- Is sufficient access and working space provided and maintained around all electrical equipment to permit ready and safe operations and maintenance?
- Are all unused openings (including conduit knockouts) of electrical enclosures and fittings closed with appropriate covers, plugs, or plates?
- Are electrical enclosures such as switches, receptacles, and junction boxes provided with tight-fitting covers or plates?
- Are employees prohibited from working alone on energized lines or equipment over 600 volts?
- Are employees forbidden from working closer than 10 ft from high-voltage (over 750 volts) lines?

Noise

- Are there areas in your workplace where continuous noise levels exceed 85 dBa? (To determine maximum allowable levels for intermittent or impact noise, see OSHA's noise and hearing conservation rules.)
- Are noise levels measured using a sound-level meter or an octave band analyzer, and are you keeping records of these levels?
- Have you tried isolating noisy machinery from the rest of your operation? Have engineering controls been used to reduce excessive noise?
- Where engineering controls are not feasible, are administrative controls (worker rotation) being used to minimize individual employee exposure to noise?

- Is there a preventive health program that educates employees about safe levels of noise and exposure, effects of noise on their health, and use of personal protection?
- Are employees who are exposed to continuous noise above 85 dBa retrained annually?
- Have work areas in which noise levels make voice communication difficult been identified and posted?
- Is approved hearing protection equipment (noise attenuating devices) used by every employee working in areas where noise levels exceed 90 dBa?
- Are employees properly fitted and instructed in the proper use and care of hearing protection?
- Are employees who are exposed to continuous noise above 85 dBa given periodic audiometric testing to ensure that you have an effective hearing-protection system?

Identification of Piping Systems

- When nonpotable water is piped through a facility, are outlets or taps posted to alert employees that the water is unsafe and not to be used for drinking, washing, or personal use?
- When hazardous substances are transported through above-ground piping, is each pipeline identified?
- Have asbestos-covered pipelines been identified?
- When pipelines are identified by colored paint, are all visible parts of the line well identified?
- When pipelines are identified by color-painted bands or tapes, are these located at reasonable intervals, and at each outlet, valve, or connection?
- When pipelines are identified by color, is the color code posted at all locations where confusion could introduce hazards to employees?
- When the contents of pipelines are identified by name or abbreviations, is the information readily visible on the pipe near each valve or outlet?
- When pipelines carrying hazardous substances are identified by tags, are the tags constructed of durable material, the message clearly and permanently distinguishable, and tags installed at each valve or outlet?
- When pipelines are heated by electricity, steam, or other external source, are suitable warning signs or tags placed at unions, valves, or other serviceable parts of the system?

Materials Handling

- Are materials stored in a manner to prevent sprain or strain injuries to employees when retrieving the materials?

- Is there safe clearance for equipment through aisles and doorways?
- Are aisleways permanently marked and kept clear to allow safe passage?
- Are motorized vehicles and mechanized equipment inspected daily or prior to use?
- Are vehicles shut off and brakes set prior to loading and unloading?
- Are containers of combustibles or flammables, when stacked while being moved, always separated by dunnage sufficient to provide stability?
- Are dock boards (bridge plates) used when loading and unloading operations are taking place between vehicles and docks?
- Are trucks and trailers secured from movement during loading and unloading?
- Are dock plates and loading ramps constructed and maintained with sufficient strength to support imposed loading?
- Are hand trucks maintained in safe operating condition?
- Are chutes equipped with side boards of sufficient height to prevent materials from falling off?
- Are chutes and gravity-roller sections firmly placed or secured to prevent displacement?
- At the delivery end of rollers or chutes, are provisions made to brake the movement of materials?
- Are materials handled at a uniform level to prevent lifting or twisting injuries?
- Are material-handling aids used to lift or transfer heavy or awkward objects?
- Are pallets usually inspected before loading or moving?
- Are hooks with safety latches or other devices used when hoisting materials so that slings or load attachments won't accidentally slip off the hoist hooks?
- Are securing chains, ropes, chokers or slings adequate for the job being performed?
- When equipment or materials are being hoisted, do you ensure that no one will be passing under suspended loads?

Cranes and Hoists

- Are cranes visually inspected for defective components prior to the start of any work shift?
- Are all electrically operated cranes effectively grounded?
- Is a crane preventive maintenance program established?

- Is the load chart clearly visible to the operator?
- Are all operators trained, and provided with the operator's manual for the particular crane being operated?
- Have operators of construction industry cranes of 5-ton or greater capacity been issued a valid operator's card?
- Are operating controls clearly identified?
- Is a fire extinguisher provided at the operator's station?
- Is the rated capacity visibly marked on each crane?
- Is an audible warning device mounted on each crane?
- Is sufficient lighting provided for the operator to perform the work safely?
- Are cranes with booms that could fall backward equipped with boomstops?
- Does each crane have a certificate indicating that required testing and examinations have been performed?
- Are crane inspection and maintenance records maintained and available for inspection?

Transporting Employees and Materials

- Do employees operating vehicles on public thoroughfares have operator licenses?
- Are motor-vehicle drivers trained in defensive driving and proper use of the vehicle?
- Are seat belts provided and are employees required to use them?
- Does each van, bus, or truck used to transport employees have an adequate number of seats?
- When employees are transported by truck, are provisions provided to prevent their falling from the vehicle?
- When transporting employees, are vehicles equipped with lamps, brakes, horns, mirrors, windshields, and turn signals that are in good repair?
- Are transport vehicles provided with handrails, steps, stirrups, or similar devices that have been placed and arranged so employees can safely mount or dismount?
- Is a fully charged fire extinguisher, in good condition, with at least "4 B:C" rating maintained in each employee transport vehicle?
- When sharp-edged cutting tools are carried in passenger compartments of employee transport vehicles, are they placed in closed boxes or containers that are secured in place?
- Are employees prohibited from riding on top of any load that can shift, topple, or otherwise become unstable?

- Are materials that could shift and enter the cab secured or barricaded?

Infection Control

- Are employees potentially exposed to infectious agents in body fluids?
- Have occasions of potential occupational exposure been identified and documented?
- Has a training and information program been provided for employees exposed to or potentially exposed to blood and/or regulated body fluids?
- Have infection-control procedures been instituted where appropriate, such as ventilation, universal precautions, workplace practices, and personal protective equipment?
- Are employees aware of specific workplace practices for handwashing, handling sharp instruments, handling laundry, disposal of contaminated materials, reusable equipment, etc.?
- Is personal protective equipment provided for and available to employees?
- Is the necessary equipment (mouthpieces, resuscitation bags, other ventilation devices) provided for administering mouth-to-mouth resuscitation on potentially infected patients?
- Are supplies and equipment available to allow employees to comply with workplace practices, e.g., handwashing sinks, biohazard tags and labels, sharps containers, and detergents/disinfectants to clean up spills?
- Are environmental and working surfaces and equipment cleaned and disinfected after contact with blood or potentially infectious materials?
- Is infectious waste placed in closable, leak-proof containers, bags, or puncture-resistant holders with proper labels?
- Has medical surveillance including HBV evaluation, antibody testing, and vaccination been made available to potentially exposed employees?
- How often is training done and does it cover:
  - Universal precautions?
  - Personal protective equipment?

- Workplace practices, which should include blood drawing, room cleaning, laundry handling, and cleanup of blood spills?
- Needlestick exposure/management?
- Hepatitis B vaccination?

Split Rim and Multipiece Wheel Tire Inflation

- In areas where tires are mounted and/or inflated on drop-center wheels, is a safety procedure posted and enforced?
- Where tires are mounted and/or inflated on wheels with split rims and/or retainer rings, is a safety procedure posted and enforced?
- Does each tire inflation hose have a clip-on chuck with at least 24 in. of hose between the chuck and an inline valve and gage?
- Does the tire-inflation control valve automatically shut off the air flow when the valve is released?
- Is a tire-restraining device such as a cage rack used while inflating tires mounted on split rims or rims using retainer rings?
- Are employees forbidden from being directly over or in front of a tire while it is being inflated?

Emergency-Action Plan

- Have you developed an emergency-action plan?
- Have emergency-escape procedures and routes been developed and communicated to all employees?
- Do employees who must complete critical plant operations before evacuating know the proper procedures?
- Is the employee alarm system that provides warning for emergency action recognizable and perceptible above ambient conditions?
- Are alarm systems properly maintained and tested regularly?
- Is the emergency-action plan reviewed and revised periodically?
- Do employees know their responsibilities:
  - For reporting emergencies?
  - During an emergency?
  - For performing rescue and medical duties?

Appendices

A. Referenced Trade Associations

B. Typical Blueprint Symbols

C. Common Blueprint Abbreviations

D. Common Lumber Abbreviations

E. Useful Equations

F. Climate Zones by States and Counties

APPENDIX A.   REFERENCED TRADE ASSOCIATIONS

AA
Aluminum Association
900 19th St., NW, Suite 300
Washington, DC 20006
www.aluminum.org
(202) 862-5100

AABC
Associated Air Balance Council
1518 K St., NW, Suite 503
Washington, DC 20005
www.aabchq.com
(202) 737-0202

AAMA
American Architectural
Manufacturers Association
1827 Walden Office Sq., Suite 104
Schaumburg, IL 60173-4268
www.aamanet.org
(847) 303-5664

AASHTO
American Association of
State Highway and
Transportation Officials
444 North Capitol St., NW
Suite 249
Washington, DC 20001
www.aashto.org
(202) 624-5800

AATCC
American Association of Textile
Chemists and Colorists
P.O. Box 12215
One Davis Dr.
Research Triangle Park,
NC 27709-2215
www.aatcc. org
(919) 549-8141

ABMA
American Bearing Manufacturers
Association
(Formerly: Anti-Friction Bearing
Manufacturers Association)
1200 19th St., NW, Suite 300
Washington, DC 20036-2401
www.abma-dc.org
(202) 429-5155

ABMA
American Boiler Manufacturers
Association
950 North Glebe Rd., Suite 160
Arlington, VA 22203-1824
www.abma.com
(703) 522-7350

ACI
American Concrete Institute
P.O. Box 9094
Farmington Hills, MI 48333-9094
www.aci-int.org
(248) 848-3700

ACIL
ACIL: The Association
of Independent Scientific,
Engineering, and
Testing Firms
1629 K St., NW, Suite 400
Washington, DC 20006
www.acil.org
(202) 887-5872

ACPA
American Concrete Pipe
Association
222 West Las Colinas Blvd.
Suite 641
Irving, TX 75039-5423
www.concrete-pipe.org
(972) 506-7216

ADC
Air Diffusion Council
11 South LaSalle St., Suite 1400
Chicago, IL 60603
(312) 201-0101

ABIC
Association of Edison
Illuminating Companies
600 N. 18th St.
P.O. Box 2641
Birmingham, AL 35291-0992
(205) 250-2530

AFPA
American Forest and Paper
Association (Formerly: National
Forest Products Association)
1111 19th St., NW, Suite 800
Washington, DC 20036
(202) 463-2700

AGA
American Gas Association
1515 Wilson Blvd.
Arlington, VA 22209
www.aga.com
(703) 841-8400

AHA
American Hardboard Association
1210 W. Northwest Hwy
Palatine, IL 60067-1897
(847) 934-8800

AHAM
Association of Home
Appliance Manufacturers
20 N. Wacker Dr., Suite 1500
Chicago, IL 60606
www.aham.org
(312) 984-5800

AI
Asphalt Institute
Research Park Dr.
P.O. Box 14052
Lexington, KY 40512-4052
www.asphaltinstitute.org
(606) 288-4960

AIA
The American Institute of
Architects
1735 New York Ave., NW
Washington, DC 20006-5292
www.aia.org
(202) 626-7300

AIA
American Insurance Association
1130 Connecticut Ave., NW
Suite 1000
Washington, DC 20036
(202) 828-7100

AISC
American Institute of Steel
Construction
One East Wacker Dr., Suite 3100
Chicago, IL 60601-2001
(800) 644-2400
(312) 670-2400

AISI
American Iron and Steel Institute
1101 17th St., NW
Washington, DC 20036-4700
www.steel.org
(202) 452-7100

AITC
American Institute of Timber
Construction
7012 S. Revere Pkwy, Suite 140
Englewood, CO 80112
www.aitc-glulam.org
(303) 792-9559

ALCA
Associated Landscape
Contractors of America
12200 Sunrise Valley Dr.
Suite 150
Reston, VA 20191
www.alca.org
(703) 620-6363

ALI
Associated Laboratories, Inc.
P.O. Box 152837
1323 Wall St.
Dallas, TX 75315
(214) 565-0593

ALSC	American Lumber Standards Committee P.O. Box 210 Germantown, MD 20875	(301) 972-1700
AMCA	Air Movement and Control Association International, Inc. 30 W. University Dr. Arlington Heights, IL 60004-1893 www.amca.org	(847) 394-0150
ANLA	American Nursery and Landscape Association (Formerly: American Association of Nurserymen) 1250 Eye St., NW, Suite 500 Washington, DC 20005	(202) 789-2900
ANSI	American National Standards Institute 11 West 42nd St., 13th Floor New York, NY 10036-8002 www.ansi.org	(212) 642-4900
AOAC	AOAC International 481 N. Frederick Ave. Suite 500 Gaithersburg, MD 20877	(301) 924-7077
AOSA	Association of Official Seed Analysts 201 N. 8th St., Suite 400 P.O. Box 81152 Lincoln, NE 68501-1152	(402) 476-3852
APA	APA—The Engineered Wood Association (Formerly: American Plywood Association) P.O. Box 11700 Tacoma, WA 98411-0700 www.apawood.org	(206) 565-6600
APA	Architectural Precast Association P.O. Box 08669 Fort Myers, FL 33908-0669	(941) 454-6989
API	American Petroleum Institute 1220 L St., NW, Suite 900 Washington, DC 20005-8029	(202) 682-8000
ARI	Air-Conditioning and Refrigeration Institute 4301 Fairfax Dr., Suite 425 Arlington, VA 22203 www.ari.org	(703) 524-8800
ARMA	Asphalt Roofing Manufacturers Association Center Park 4041 Powder Mill Rd., Suite 404 Calverton, MD 20705	(301) 231-9050
ASA	Acoustical Society of America 500 Sunnyside Blvd. Woodbury, NY 11797	(516) 576-2360
ASC	Adhesive and Sealant Council 1627 K St., NW, Suite 1000 Washington, DC 20006-1707	(202) 452-1500
ASCA	Architectural Spray Coaters Association 230 W. Wells St. Suite 311 Milwaukee, WI 53203	(414) 273-3430

ASCE	American Society of Civil Engineers—World Headquarters 1801 Alexander Bell Dr. Reston, VA 20191-4400 www.asce.org.	(800) 548-2723
ASHES	Amer. Society for Healthcare Environmental Services (Division of the American Hospital Assoc.) One North Franklin, Suite 2700 Chicago, IL 60606	(800) 424-2626 (312) 422-3860
ASHRAE	American Society of Heating, Refrigerating and Air Conditioning Engineers 1791 Tullie Circle, NE Atlanta, GA 30329-2305 www.ashrae.org	(800) 527-4723
ASLA	American Society of Landscape Architects 4401 Connecticut Ave. NW 5th Floor Washington, DC 20008-2369 www.asla.org	(202) 686-2752
ASME	American Society of Mechanical Engineers 345 East 47th St. New York, NY 10017-2392 www.asme.org	(800) 434-2763
ASPE	American Society of Plumbing Engineers 3617 Thousand Oaks Blvd. Suite #210 Westlake Village, CA 91362-3649	(805) 495-7120
ASQC	American Society for Quality Control 611 East Wisconsin Ave. Milwaukee, WI 53201-3005 www.asqc.org	(800) 248-1946 (414) 272-8575
ASSE	American Society of Sanitary Engineering 28901 Clemens Rd. Westlake, OH 44145 www.asse-plumbing.org	(216) 835-3040
ASTM	American Society for Testing and Materials 100 Barr Harbor Dr. West Conshohocken, PA 19428-2959 www.astln.org	(610) 832-9500
ATIS	Alliance for Telecommunications Industry Solutions (Formerly: Exchange Carriers Standards Association) 1200 G St., NW, Suite 500 Washington, DC 20005	(202) 628-6380
AWCI	Association of the Wall and Ceiling Industries— International 307 E. Annandale Rd., Suite 200 Falls Church, VA 22042-2433 www.awci.org	(703) 534-8300
AWCMA	American Window Covering Manufacturers Association (See WCMA)	

AWI	Architectural Woodwork Institute 1952 Isaac Newton Sq. Reston, VA 20190 www.awinet.org	(703) 733-0600
AWPA	American Wood Preservers' Association 3246 Fall Creek Hwy, Suite 1900 Granbury, TX 76049-7979	(817) 326-6300
AWS	American Welding Society 550 NW Lejeune Rd. Miami, FL 33126 www.amweld.org	(800) 443-9353 (305) 443-9353
AWWA	American Water Works Association 6666 W. Quincy Ave. Denver, CO 80235 www.awwa.org	(800) 926-7337 (303) 794-7711
BANC	Brick Association of North Carolina P.O. Box 13290 Greensboro, NC 27415-3290	(800) 622-7425 (910) 273-5566
BHMA	Builders Hardware Manufacturers Association 355 Lexington Ave., 17th Floor New York, NY 10017-6603	(212) 661-4261
BIA	Brick Institute of America 11490 Commerce Park Dr. Reston, VA 22091-1525 www.bia.org	(703) 620-0010
BIFMA	The Business and Institutional Furniture Manufacturer's Association 2680 Horizon Dr., SE, Suite A1 Grand Rapids, MI 49546-7500 www.bifma.com	(616) 285-3963
CAGI	Compressed Air and Gas Institute c/o Thomas Associates, Inc. 1300 Sumner Ave. Cleveland, OH 44115-2851 www.cagi.org	(216) 241-7333
CAUS	Color Association of the United States 409 W. 44th St. New York, NY 10036-4402	(212) 582-6884
CBM	Certified Ballast Manufacturers Association 1422 Euclid Ave., Suite 402 Cleveland, OH 44115-2094	(216) 241-0711
CCC	Carpet Cushion Council P.O. Box 546 Riverside, CT 06878-0546	(203) 637-1312
CDA	Copper Development Association New York, NY www.copper.org	(800) 232-3282 (212) 251-7200
CFFA	Chemical Fabrics & Film Association, Inc. c/o Thomas Associates, Inc. 1300 Sumner Ave. Cleveland, OH 44115-2851 www.chemicalfabricsandfilm.com	(216) 241-7333
CGA	Compressed Gas Association 1725 Jefferson Davis Hwy Suite 1004 Arlington, VA 22202-4102 www.cganet.com	(703) 412-0900
CISCA	Ceilings and Interior Systems Construction Association 1500 Lincoln Hwy, Suite 202 St. Charles, IL 60174 www.cisca.org	(630) 584-1919
CISPI	Cast Iron Soil Pipe Institute 5959 Shallowford Rd., Suite 419 Chattanooga, TN 37421	(423) 892-0137
CLFMI	Chain Link Fence Manufacturers Institute 9891 Broken Land Pkwy Suite 300 Columbia, MD 21046	(301) 596-2584
CPPA	Corrugated Polyethylene Pipe Association 432 N. Superior St. Toledo, OR 43604	(800) 510-2772 (419) 241-2221
CRI	Carpet and Rug Institute 310 S. Holiday Ave. Dalton, GA 30722-2048 www.carpet-rug.com	(800) 882-8846
CRSI	Concrete Reinforcing Steel Institute 933 N. Plum Grove Rd. Schaumburg, IL 60173-4758 www.crsi.org	(847) 517-1200
CSSB	Cedar Shake and Shingle Bureau 515 116th Ave., NE Suite 275 Bellevue, WA 98004-5294	(206) 453-1323
CTI	Ceramic Tile Institute of America 12061 West Jefferson Blvd. Culver City, CA 90230-6219	(310) 574-7800
CTI	Cooling Tower Institute P.O. Box 73383 Houston, TX 77273	(281) 583-4087
DASMA	Door and Access Systems Manufacturers Association— International (Formerly: National Association of Garage Door Manufacturers) c/o Thomas Associates, Inc. 1300 Sumner Ave. Cleveland, OH 44115-2851 www.dasma.com	(216) 241-7333
DHI	Door and Hardware Institute (Formerly: National Builders Hardware Association) 14170 Newbrook Dr. Chantilly, VA 20151-2223 www.dhi.org	(703) 222-2010
DIPRA	Ductile Iron Pipe Research Association 245 Riverchase Pkwy East Suite 0 Birmingham, AL 35244	(205) 988-9870
EIA	Electronic Industries Association 2500 Wilson Blvd. Arlington, VA 22201	(703) 907-7500

EIMA	EIFS Industry Members Association 402 N. Fourth St., Suite 102 Yakima, WA 98901-2470 www.eifsfacts.com	(800) 294-3462 (509) 457-3500
EJMA	Expansion Joint Manufacturers Association 25 N. Broadway Tarrytown, NY 10591-3201	(914) 332-0040
FCI	Fluid Controls Institute c/o Thomas Associates, Inc. 1300 Sumner Ave. Cleveland, OH 44115-2851 www.fluidcontrolsinstitute.org	(216) 241-7333
FCICA	Floor Covering Installation Contractors Association (Formerly: Floor Covering Installation Board) P.O. Box 948 Dalton, GA 30722-0948	(706) 226-5488
FM	Factory Mutual System 1151 Boston-Providence Tnpk P.O. Box 9102 Norwood, MA 02062-9102 www.factorymutual.com	(781) 762-4300
FTI	Facing Tile Institute c/o Stark Ceramics P.O. Box 8880 Canton, OH 44711	(330) 488-1211
GA	Gypsum Association 810 First St., NE, Suite 510 Washington, DC 20002 www.usg.com	(202) 289-5440
OANA	Glass Association of North America (Formerly: Flat Glass Marketing Association) 3310 SW Harrison St. Topeka, KS 66611-2279 www.glasswebsite.com	(913) 266-7013
GRI	Geosynthetic Research Institute 33rd and Lancaster Walk Rush Building, West Wing Philadelphia, PA 19104 www.drexel.edu/gri	(215) 895-2343
HEI	Heat Exchange Institute c/o Thomas Associates, Inc. 1300 Sumner Ave. Cleveland, OH 44115-2851 www.heatexchange.org	(216) 241-7333
HI	Hydraulic Institute 9 Sylvan Way Parsippany, NJ 07054-3802	(201) 267-9700
HID	Hydronics Institute Division of Gas Appliance Manufacturers Association P.O. Box 218 35 Russo Place Berkeley Heights, NJ 07922 www.gamanet.org	(908) 464-8200
HMA	Hardwood Manufacturers Association (Formerly: Southern Hardwood Lumber Manufacturers Association) 400 Penn Center Blvd., Suite 530 Pittsburgh, PA 15235-5605 www.hardwood.org	(412) 829-0770
HPVA	Hardwood Plywood and Veneer Association 1825 Michael Farraday Dr. P.O. Box 2789 Reston, VA 22195-0789 www.hpva.org	(703) 435-2900
IAS	International Approval Services 8504 East Pleasant Valley Rd. Cleveland, OH 44131 www.iasapprovals. org	(216) 524-4990
ICBA	Insulated Cable Engineers Association, Inc. P.O. Box 440 South Yarmouth, MA 02664	(508) 394-4424
IEC	International Electrotechnical Commission 11 West 42nd St. 13th Floor New York, NY 10036-8002	(212) 642-4900
IEEE	Institute of Electrical and Electronics Engineers 345 E. 47th St. New York, NY 10017-2394 www.ieee. org	(800) 678-4333 (212) 705-7900
IESNA	Illuminating Engineering Society of North America 120 Wall St., 17th Floor New York, NY 10005-4001 www.iesna.org	(212) 248-5000
IIDA	International Interior Design Association 341 Merchandise Mart Chicago, IL 60654-1104	(312) 467-1950
ILI	Indiana Limestone Institute of America Stone City Bank Building Suite 400 Bedford, IN 47421	(812) 275-4426
IMSA	International Municipal Signal Association P.O. Box 539 165 E. Union St. Newark, NY 14513	(800) 723-4672 (315) 331-2182
INCE	Institute of Noise Control Engineering P.O. Box 3206 Arlington Branch Poughkeepsie, NY 12603	(914) 462-4006
IRI	Industrial Risk Insurers P.O. Box 5010 85 Woodland St. Hartford, CT 06102-5010	(860) 520-7300
ISA	ISA—International Society for Measurement and Control P.O. Box 12277 67 Alexander Dr. Research Triangle Park, NC 27709 www.isa.org	(919) 549-8411
ISS	Iron and Steel Society 410 Commonwealth Dr. Warrendale, PA 15086-7512 www.issource.org	(412) 776-1535

ISWA   Insect Screening Weavers   (914) 962-9052
Association
P.O. Box 1018
Ossining, NY 10562

ITS   Intertek Testing Services   (800) 345-3851
(Formerly: Inchcape Testing   (607) 753-6711
Services)
P.O. Box 2040
3933 US Route 11
Cortland, NY 13045-7902
www.itsglobal.com

KCMA   Kitchen Cabinet Manufacturers   (703) 264-1690
Association (Formerly: National
Kitchen Cabinet Association)
1899 Preston White Dr.
Reston, VA 22091-4326
www.kema.org

LGSI   Light Gage Structural Institute   (972) 625-4560
c/o Loseke Technologies, Inc.
P.O. Box 560746
The Colony, TX 75056

LIA   Lead Industries Association, Inc.   (800) 422-5323
295 Madison Ave.   (212) 578-4750
New York, NY 10017
www.leadinfo.com

LMA   Laminating Materials   (201) 664-2700
Association (Formerly:
American Laminators
Association)
116 Lawrence St.
Hillsdale, NJ 07642-2730
www.lma.org

LPI   Lightning Protection Institute   (800) 488-6864
3335 N. Arlington Heights Rd.   (847) 577-7200
Suite E
Arlington Heights, IL 60004-7700

MBMA   Metal Building Manufacturers   (216) 241-7333
Association
c/o Thomas Associates, Inc.
1300 Sumner Ave.
Cleveland, OH 44115-2851
www.mbma.com

MCAA   Mechanical Contractors   (301) 869-5800
Association of America
1385 Piccard Dr.
Rockville, MD 20850-4329

MFMA   Maple Flooring Manufacturers   (847) 480-9138
Association
60 Revere Dr., Suite 500
Northbrook, IL 60062
www.maplefloor.com

MFMA   Metal Framing Manufacturers   (312) 644-6610
Association (Formerly: Wood
and Synthetic Flooring Institute)
401 N. Michigan Ave.
Chicago, IL 60611

MHI   Material Handling Institute   (800) 345-1815
(A Division of the Material   (704) 522-8644
Handling Industry)
8720 Red Oak Blvd.
Suite 201
Charlotte, NC 28217-3992
www.mhi.org

MIA   Marble Institute of America   (614) 228-6194
30 Eden Alley, Suite 301
Columbus, OH 43215
www.marble-institute.com

MIA   Masonry Institute of America   (213) 388-0472
2550 Beverly Blvd.
Los Angeles, CA 90057
www.masonryinstitute.org

ML/SFA   Metal Lath/Steel Framing   (312) 456-5590
Association
8 South Michigan Ave.
Suite 1000
Chicago, IL 60603

MRCA   Midwest Roofing Contractors   (800) 879-4448
Association   (913) 843-4888
4840 W. 15th St., Suite 1000
Lawrence, KS 66049

MSS   Manufacturers Standardization   (703) 281-6613
Society of the Valve and
Fittings Industry
127 Park St., NE
Vienna, VA 22180-4602

NAA   National Arborist Association   (800) 733-2622
P.O. Box 1094   (603) 673-3311
Amherst, NH 03031-1094
www.natlarb.com

NAAMM   National Association of   (312) 456-5590
Architectural Metal Manufacturers
8 South Michigan Ave., Suite 1000
Chicago, IL 60603
www.gss.net/naamm

NAIMA   North American Insulation   (703) 684-0084
Manufacturers Association
(Formerly: Thermal Insulation
Manufacturers Association)
44 Canal Center Plaza, Suite 310
Alexandria, VA 22314
www.naima. org

NAMI   National Accreditation &   (757) 594-8658
Management Institute, Inc.
11870 Merchants Walk
Suite 202
Newport News, VA 23606

NAPA   National Asphalt Pavement   (301) 731-4748
Association
5100 Forbes Blvd.
Lanham, MD 20706-4413

NAPM   National Association of   (914) 698-7603
Photographic Manufacturers
550 Mamaroneck Ave.
Harrison, NY 10528

NCAC   National Coil Coaters Association   (312) 321-6894
401 N. Michigan Ave.
Chicago, IL 60611

NCCA   National Concrete Masonry   (703) 713-1900
Association
2302 Horse Pen Rd.
Herndon, VA 20171-3499
www.ncma.org

NCPI   National Clay Pipe Institute   (414) 248-9094
P.O. Box 759, 253-80 Center St.
Lake Geneva, WI 53147

NCRPM	National Council on Radiation Protection and Measurements 7910 Woodmont Ave., Suite 800 Bethesda, MD 20814-3095 www.ncrp.com	(800) 229-2652 (301) 657-2652
NCSPA	National Corrugated Steel Pipe Association 1255 23rd St., NW, Suite 850 Washington, DC 20037 www.ncspa.org	(202) 452-1700
NEBB	Natural Environmental Balancing Bureau 8575 Grovemont Circle Gaithersburg, MD 20877-4121	(301) 977-3698
NECA	National Electrical Contractors Association 3 Bethesda Metro Center Suite 1100 Bethesda, MD 20814-5372	(301) 657-3110
NEI	National Elevator Industry 185 Bridge Plaza North Suite 310 Fort Lee, NJ 07024	(201) 944-3211
NELMA	Northeastern Lumber Manufacturers Association 272 Tuttle Rd. P.O. Box 87A Cumberland Center, ME 04021	(207) 829-6901
NEMA	National Electrical Manufacturers Association 1300 N. 17th St., Suite 1847 Rosslyn, VA 22209 www.nema.org	(703) 841-3200
NETA	InterNational Electrical Testing Association P.O. Box 687 106 Stone St. Morrison, CO 80465-1526 www.netaworld.org	(303) 697-8441
NFPA	National Fire Protection Association One Batterymarch Park P.O. Box 9101 Quincy, MA 02269-9101 www.nfpa.org	(800) 344-3555 (617) 770-3000
NFPA	National Forest Products Association (See AFPA)	
NFRC	National Fenestration Rating Council Incorporated 1300 Spring St., Suite 120 Silver Spring, MD 20910 www.nfrc.org	(301) 589-NFRC
NHLA	National Hardwood Lumber Association P.O. Box 34518 Memphis, TN 38184-0518 www.natlhardwood.org	(901) 377-1818
NIA	National Insulation Association (Formerly: National Insulation and Abatement Contractors Association) 99 Canal Center Plaza, Suite 222 Alexandria, VA 22314 www.insulation.org	(703) 683-6422

NLGA	National Lumber Grades Authority #406 First Capital Pl. 960 Quayside Dr. New Westminster, BC V3M 6G2	(604) 524-2393
NOFMA	National Oak Flooring Manufacturers Association P.O. Box 3009 Memphis, TN 38173-0009	(901) 526-5016
NPA	National Particleboard Association 18928 Premiere Ct. Gaithersburg, MD 20879-1569 www.pbmdf.com	(301) 670-0604
NPCA	National Paint and Coatings Association 1500 Rhode Island Ave., NW Washington, DC 20005-5597 www.paint.org	(202) 462-6272
NRCA	National Roofing Contractors Association O'Hare International Center 10255 W. Higgins Rd., Suite 600 Rosemont, IL 60018-5607 www.roofonline.org	(800) 323-9545 (847) 299-9070
NRMCA	National Ready Mixed Concrete Association 900 Spring St. Silver Spring, MD 20910 www.nrmca.org	(301) 587-1400
NSA	National Stone Association 1415 Elliot Pl., NW Washington, DC 20007 www.aggregates.org	(202) 342-1100
NTMA	National Terrazzo and Mosaic Association 3166 Des Plaines Ave. Suite 121 Des Plaines, IL 60018 www.ntma.com	(800) 323-9736 (847) 635-7744
NWWDA	National Wood Window and Door Association (Formerly: National Woodwork Manufacturers Association) 1400 E. Touhy Ave., G-54 Des Plaines, IL 60018 www.nwwda.org	(800) 223-2301 (847) 299-5200
PATMI	Power Actuated Tool Manufacturers Institute, Inc. 1603 Boonslick Rd. St. Charles, MO 63301-2244	(314) 947-6610
PCA	Portland Cement Association 5420 Old Orchard Rd. Skokie, IL 60077-1083 www.portcement.org.	(847) 966-6200
PCI	Precast/Prestressed Concrete Institute 175 W. Jackson Blvd. Chicago, IL 60604 www.pci.org	(312) 786-0300
PDCA	Painting and Decorating Contractors of America 3913 Old Lee Hwy, Suite 33-B Fairfax, VA 22030 www.pdca.com	(800) 332-7322 (703) 359-0826

PDI	Plumbing and Drainage Institute 45 Bristol Dr., Suite 101 South Easton, MA 02375	(800) 589-8956 (508) 230-3516
PEI	Porcelain Enamel Institute 4004 Hillsboro Pike, Suite 224-B Nashville, TN 37215 www.porcelainenamel.com	(615) 385-5357
POI	PVC Geomembrane Institute P.O. Box 4226 Traverse City, MI 49685 users.aol.com/forPVCl	(616) 933-6373
PPFA	Plastic Pipe and Fittings Association 800 Roosevelt Rd., Building C Suite 20 Glen Ellyn, IL 60137-5833	(630) 858-6540
PPI	Plastic Pipe Institute (The Society of the Plastics Industry, Inc.) 1801 K St., NW, Suite 600L Washington, DC 20006 www.plasticpipe.org	(202) 974-5306
RCMA	Roof Coatings Manufacturers Association Center Park 4041 Powder Mill Rd. Suite 404 Calverton, MD 20705	(301) 230-2501
RCSC	Research Council on Structural Connections Sargent & Lundy 55 E. Monroe St. Chicago, IL 60603	(312) 269-2424
RFCI	Resilient Floor Covering Institute 966 Hungerford Dr., Suite 12-B Rockville, MD 20850-1714	(301) 340-8580
RMA	Rubber Manufacturers Association 1400 K St., NW, Suite 900 Washington, DC 20005 www.rma.org	(800) 220-7620 (202) 682-4800
SAE	SAE International 400 Commonwealth Dr. Warrendale, PA 15096-0001	(412) 776-4841 (412) 776-4910
SDI	Steel Deck Institute P.O. Box 25 Fox River Grove, IL 60021 www.sdi.org	(847) 462-1930
SDI	Steel Door Institute 30200 Detroit Rd. Cleveland, OH 44145-1967	(216) 889-0010
SEFA	Scientific Equipment and Furniture Association 1028 Duchess Dr. McLean, VA 22102-2010 www.sefalabfurn.com	(703) 790-8661
SEGD	Society for Environmental Graphic Design 401 F St., NW, Suite 333 Washington, DC 20001-2728	(202) 638-5555

SHLMA	Southern Hardwood Lumber Manufacturers Association (See HMA)	
SIGMA	Sealed Insulating Glass Manufacturers Association 401 N. Michigan Ave. Chicago, IL 60611-4267	(312) 644-6610
SJI	Steel Joist Institute 3127 10th Ave., North Ext. Myrtle Beach, SC 29577-6760	(803) 626-1995
SMA	Screen Manufacturers Association 2850 S. Ocean Blvd., Suite 114 Palm Beach, FL 33480-5535	(561) 533-0991
SMACNA	Sheet Metal and Air Conditioning Contractors National Association, Inc. 4201 Lafayette Center Dr. P.O. Box 221230 Chantilly, VA 20151-1209 www.smacna.org	(703) 803-2980
SPI	Society of the Plastics Industry, Inc. Spray Polyurethane Division 1801 K St., NW, Suite 600K Washington, DC 20006 www.socplas.org	(800) 951-2001 (202) 974-5200
SPIB	Southern Pine Inspection Bureau 4709 Scenic Hwy Pensacola, FL 32504-9094	(904) 434-2611
SPRI	SPRI (Formerly: Single Ply Roofing Institute) 175 Highland Ave. Needham Heights, MA 02194-3034	(617) 444-0242
SSINA	Specialty Steel Industry of North America c/o Collier, Shannon Rill & Scott 3050 K St., NW, Suite 400 Washington, DC 20007 www.ssina.com	(800) 982-0355 (202) 342-8630
SSPC	Steel Structures Painting Council 40 24th St., 6th Floor Pittsburgh, PA 15222-4643	(412) 281-2331
STI	Steel Tank Institute 570 Oakwood Rd. Lake Zurich, IL 60047-1559	(847) 438-8265
SWI	Steel Window Institute c/o Thomas Associates, Inc. 1300 Sumner Ave. Cleveland, OH 44115-2851 www.steelwindows.com	(216) 241-7333
SWPA	Submersible Wastewater Pump Association 1806 Johns Dr. Glenview, IL 60025-1657	(847) 729-7972
SWRI	Sealant, Waterproofing and Restoration Institute 2841 Main Kansas City, MO 64108	(816) 472-7974
TCA	Tile Council of America 100 Clemson Research Blvd. Anderson, SC 29625	(864) 646-8453

TPI	Truss Plate Institute 583 D'Onofrio Dr., Suite 200 Madison, WI 53719	(608) 833-5900
TPI	Turfgrass Producers International (Formerly: American Sod Producers Association) 1855-A Hicks Rd. Rolling Meadows, IL 60008	(800) 405-8873 (847) 705-9898
UL	Underwriters Laboratories Inc. 333 Pfingsten Rd. Northbrook, IL 60062 www.ul.com	(800) 704-4050 (847) 272-8800
UNI	Uni-Bell PVC Pipe Association 2655 Villa Creek Dr., Suite 155 Dallas, TX 75234 www.uni-bell.org	(972) 243-3902
USITT	USITT: The American Association of Design and Production Professionals in the Performing Arts 6443 Ridings Rd. Syracuse, NY 13206-1111	(800) 938-7488 (315) 463-6463
USP	U.S. Pharmacopeia (Formerly: U.S. Pharmacopoeial Convention) 12601 Twinbrook Pkwy Rockville, MD 20852-1790	(800) 227-8772 (301) 881-0666
WA	Wallcoverings Association 401 N. Michigan Ave. Chicago, IL 60611-4267	(312) 644-6610
WCLIB	West Coast Lumber Inspection Bureau P.O. Box 23145 Portland, OR 97281-3145	(503) 639-0651

WCMA	Window Covering Manufacturers Association (Formerly: American Window Covering Manufacturers Association) 355 Lexington Ave., 17th Floor New York, NY 10017-6603	(212) 661-4261
WEF	Water Environment Federation (Formerly: Water Pollution Control Federation) 601 Wythe St. Alexandria, VA 22314-1994	(703) 684-2400
WIC	Woodwork Institute of California P.O. Box 980247 West Sacramento, CA 95798-0247	(916) 372-9943
WMMPA	Wood Moulding & Millwork Producers Association 507 First St. Woodland, CA 95695 www.wmmpa.com	(800) 550-7889 (916) 661-9591
WRI	Wire Reinforcement Institute 203 Loudoun St., SW Leesburg, VA 20175-2718	(703) 779-2339
WSC	Water Systems Council Building C, Suite 20 800 Roosevelt Rd. Glen Ellyn, IL 60137	(630) 545-1762
WWPA	Western Wood Products Association Yeon Building 522 SW 5th Ave. Portland, OR 97204-2122	(503) 224-3930

APPENDIX B. TYPICAL BLUEPRINT SYMBOLS

Electrical Abbreviations

A.F.F.	Above Finished Floor
A.F.G.	Above Finished Grade
AMP	Amperes
AL	Aluminum
AHU	Air Handling Unit
BLDG	Building
CKT	Circuit
C	Conduit
CONN	Connection
COND	Conductor
CU	Copper
DET	Detail
DN	Down
DISC	Disconnect
DP	Distribution Panel
EA	Each
ELEC	Electrical
ELEV	Elevator
EM	Emergency
EMT	Electrical Metallic Tube
EWC	Electric Water Cooler
F	Fuse
FLA	Full Load Amps
FLEX	Flexible
FLR	Floor
FLUOR	Fluorescent
G	Ground
GALV	Galvanized
HID	High-Intensity Discharge
HP	Horsepower
H	Height
IG	Isolated Ground
IN.	Inch
INC	Incandescent
JB	Junction Box
KCMIL	1000 Circular Mils
KVA	Kilovolt Amps
KVAR	Kilovolt Amps Reactive
KW	Kilowatt
KWH	Kilowatt Hour

LA	Lightning Arrester
LTG	Lighting
LV	Low Voltage
MAX	Maximum
MCB	Main Circuit Breaker
MCC	Motor Control Center
MDP	Main Distribution Panel
MFG	Manufacturer
MG	Motor Generator
MH	Manhole, Metal Holide, Mo.
MIC	Microphone
MIN	Minimum
MLO	Main Lugs Only
MTD	Mounted
N/A	Not Applicable
NEC	National Electrical Code
NEMA	National Electrical Manufacturers Association
NFPA	National Fire Protection
NIC	Not in Contract
NTS	Not to Scale
NO	Normally Open, Number
PB	Pull Box, Push Button
PH	Phase
PNL	Panel
POC	Point of Connection
PS	Pull Switch
QTY	Quantity
RGS	Rigid Galvanized Steel
RCPT	Receptacle
SCH	Schedule
SQ. FT.	Square Foot
SW	Switch
SYS	System
TEL	Telephone
TYP	Typical
UH	Unit Heater
UPS	Uninterruptible Power Sup
V	Voltage
W	Wire
W/	With

Exterior Electrical

Existing		New
$O_{35/3}$	Pole, length, and class as indicated	$\bullet_{35/3}$
$\underline{8M-20}$ <	Down guy; noted as 8000-pound strength, anchor at 20 feet from pole	$\underline{8M-20}$ <
$\underset{\triangledown\triangle\triangledown}{3-25}$	Transformer bank pole-mounted: shown as three-phase 25-kVA transformers	$\underset{\blacktriangledown\blacktriangle\blacktriangledown}{3-25}$
$\triangle_{25}$	Single-phase transformer; pole-mounted 25 kVA noted	$\blacktriangle_{25}$
$\boxed{T}_{100}$	Pad-mounted transformer indicated as 100 kVA	$\boxed{T}_{100}$
$\underset{EOP}{4\#6 \quad 4160V}$	Overhead primary—shown as 4 #6 conductors, 4160 V	$\underset{OHP}{4\#6 \quad 4160V}$
— EUP —	Underground primary	— UP —
— EOS —	Overhead secondary	— OHS —
— EUS —	Underground secondary	— US —
— EUT —	Underground telephone conduit	— UT —
— EOT —	Overhead telephone	— OT —
— EUC —	Underground communication	— UC —
○⊐	Pole-mounted lighting fixture	●✱
— EG —	Buried ground wire	— G —
----- EG -----	Ground wire exposed	- - - G - - -
—•—	Ground connection or equipment bond	—•—
··— EG ··—	Roof conductor	— ·· G — ·· —
$\odot_W$	Ground rod 10 ft long and ¾ in. diameter (W denotes installation in well)	$\odot_W$
✳	Lightning rod, 24 in. high	✳
☐	Manhole; subscript denotes the following: EMH = electrical, TMH = telephone, CMH = communications	☐
⑤	Pad-mounted sectionalizing switch	

Communication

◀ W — Voice/data outlet, 2 in. × 4 in. deep outlet box with two modular category 5 RJ-45 jacks. Service will consist of two 4-pair plenum rated category 5 unshielded twisted pair #24 AWG cable in 1 in. conduit to cable tray and then in cable tray to nearest communications room. Contractor provides box, raceway, and pull string; owner provides cabling and connectors mounted

18 in. AFF unless otherwise noted. Subscript denotes the following:

W: Wall mounted at 54 in. AFF

◁ W — Telephone outlet, 2 in. × 2 in. deep outlet box with one modular category 5 RJ-45 jack. Service will consist of one 4-pair plenum rated category 5 unshielded twisted pair #24 AWG cable in 1 in. conduit to cable tray and then in cable tray to nearest communications room. Contractor provides box, raceway, and pull string; owner provides cabling and connectors mounted at 18 in. AFF unless otherwise noted. Subscript denotes the following:

W: Wall mounted at 54 in. AFF

⊣Ⓢ Speaker

Ⓢ Speaker (ceiling mounted)

[TV] TV outlet, 2 in. × 4 in. deep outlet box with one F-type connector, service shall be one plenum rated RG-coaxial cable in 1 in. conduit to cable tray and then in cable tray to nearest communications room. Contractor provides box, raceway, and pull string; owner provides cabling and connectors. Mount 24 in. AFF unless otherwise noted.

[B]○ Classroom bell

Dual service floor bow with one 20 amp duplex outlet and two modular category 5 RJ-45 jacks with service equivalent to a voice/data outlet. Walker RC2001-A-BL20A or equal.

[CR]$_{WP}$ Card reader mount 42 in. AFF. Subscript denotes weatherproof

Ⓑ Balanced magnetic switch

[ACAS] Access control and alarm system control valve

Fire Alarm

[FA] Fire alarm control panel

[F] Fire alarm manual station—mount 48 in. AFF

[F]◁ Fire alarm horn/strobe light—mount 80 in. AFF

⊣(F) Wall-mounted fire alarm strobe light—mount 80 in. AFF

[S]$_S$ Smoke detector; subscript denotes the following: S: Single station

[D] Duct-mounted smoke detector

[H]$_F$ Heat detector; subscript denotes the following:

F: Fixed temperature

R: Rate of rise

RF: Combination rate of rise and fixed temperature

[TS] Tamper switch

[FS] Flow switch

[SD] Smoke damper

⊣Ⓓ Door holder

ⓈⓋ Solenoid valve connection

ⓁⓈ Limit switch connection

Ⓣ Thermostat connection

ⓅⒺ Pneumatic/electric connection

ⓅⒸ Photocell

ⓅⓈ Pressure switch connection

Power

Ⓖ Floor grounding plate

Ⓡ Relay control unit

☐ Contactor

⬛◻ Emergency power off, red mushroom head pushbutton station

⦚ Pushbutton station, 2 buttons

⦚ Pushbutton station, 3 buttons

☐Ⓖ Generator set

⬓ Automatic transfer switch

⊖ Duplex receptacle; subscript denotes the following:

WP: Weatherproof

GFI: Integral Ground Fault Interrupt

⊖$^{(6-6Ø)}_{GFI}$ Special purpose receptacle, number denotes NEMA configuration

⊕ Quadruplex receptacle

Ⓢ Floor-mounted receptacle

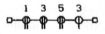

Multi-outlet surface raceway, size and number of conductors as indicated. Superscripts denote circuit numbers. Subscripts denote the following for all receptacles:

WP: Weatherproof

GFI: Integral Ground Fault Interrupt

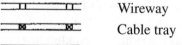

Wireway

Cable tray

Plug in or feeder bus

⊣Ⓒ$_D$ Wall-mounted single face clock or double face clock

$$3 Wall switch 120–277 volt, 20 amp, single pole. Subscripts denote the following:

HP: Motor rated with overload protection

D,600: Dimmer switch, 600 watt noted

a: Switching designation

3: Three way

4: Four way

K: Key operated

P: Pilot light

F: Fan

Motor connection (5 HP indicated)

Switchboard

Panelboard, surface mounted

Panelboard, recessed

Transformer

Lighting

Ceiling Mounted   **Wall Mounted**

Fluorescent lighting fixture.
  A: Indicates type
  b: Denotes switch designation

Fluorescent lighting fixture wired for individual switching of inside and outside lamps, letter indicates type

Emergency fluorescent lighting fixture, letter indicates type

Fluorescent one by four lighting fixture, letter indicates type

Strip fluorescent lighting fixture, letter indicates type

Emergency self-contained lighting unit with two light fixture heads, letter indicates type

Exit light with arrow; letter indicates type, number of faces shown:
  X1: 120 V
  X2: 277 V

Self-contained emergency lighting unit and exit light, letter indicates type

Emergency remote head

Incandescent or HID lighting fixture, letter indicates type

Emergency incandescent or HID lighting fixture, letter indicates type

Vanity light

Conduits and Wire

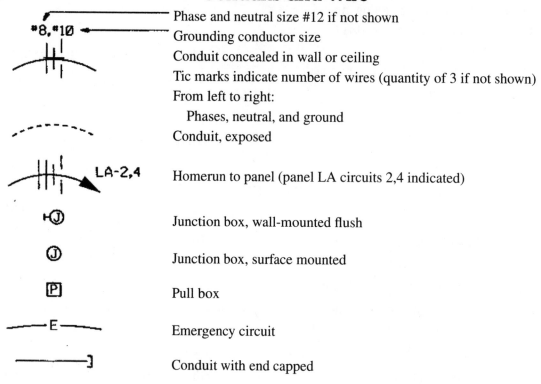

Phase and neutral size #12 if not shown

#8, #10 ← Grounding conductor size

Conduit concealed in wall or ceiling

Tic marks indicate number of wires (quantity of 3 if not shown)

From left to right:

    Phases, neutral, and ground

Conduit, exposed

LA-2,4 Homerun to panel (panel LA circuits 2,4 indicated)

Junction box, wall-mounted flush

Junction box, surface mounted

Pull box

—E— Emergency circuit

Conduit with end capped

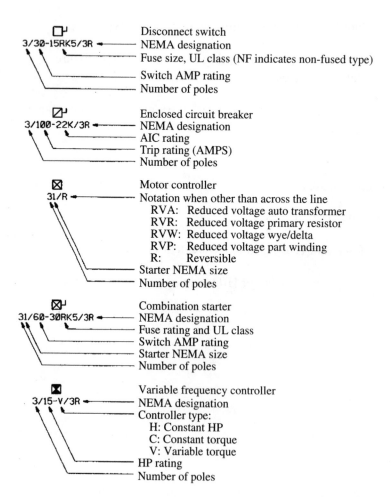

Disconnect switch
3/30-15RK5/3R ← NEMA designation
— Fuse size, UL class (NF indicates non-fused type)
— Switch AMP rating
— Number of poles

Enclosed circuit breaker
3/100-22K/3R ← NEMA designation
— AIC rating
— Trip rating (AMPS)
— Number of poles

Motor controller
31/R ← Notation when other than across the line
    RVA: Reduced voltage auto transformer
    RVR: Reduced voltage primary resistor
    RVW: Reduced voltage wye/delta
    RVP: Reduced voltage part winding
    R: Reversible
— Starter NEMA size
— Number of poles

Combination starter
31/60-30RK5/3R ← NEMA designation
— Fuse rating and UL class
— Switch AMP rating
— Starter NEMA size
— Number of poles

Variable frequency controller
3/15-V/3R ← NEMA designation
— Controller type:
    H: Constant HP
    C: Constant torque
    V: Variable torque
— HP rating
— Number of poles

Plumbing

Symbol	Name	Symbol	Name
—HWS—	Hot water supply	Plug valve
—HWR—	Hot water return	Two-way control valve
—CWS—	Condenser water supply	Three-way control valve
—CWR—	Condenser water return	Check valve
—CHWS—	Chilled water supply	Needle valve
—CHWR—	Chilled water return	Pressure reducing
—CD—	Condensate drain	Relief or safety valve
—G—	Gas	Temperature and pressure valve
—MU—	Makeup water	Solenoid valve
—S—	Storm or roof leader	Square head cock valve
	Soil or waste	Balancing valve
	Vent	Union
	Cold water	Tee, outlet down
	Hot water	Cap
	Hot water recirculation	Elbow
—F—	Fire water	Elbow, turned up
HB	Hose bibb	Elbow, turned down
△	Revision	Reducer, concentric
⬡	Sheet notes	Reducer, eccentric
✳	Pipe through floor	Tee
⊘	Pumps	Tee, outlet up
Ⓟ	Pressure gage and cock	Man. air eliminator
PS	Pressure switch	Auto air eliminator
	Strainer	Alignment guide
	Strainer, blow off	Anchor
	Ball valve	Expansion joint
	Butterfly valve	Temp. gage
	Diaphragm	CO Wall cleanout
	Gate valve	CO Floor cleanout
	Globe valve	
	Angle valve	

APPENDIX C. COMMON BLUEPRINT ABBREVIATIONS

Architectural

A	ACT	Acoustical tile ceiling
	ADD	Addition
	AFF	Above finished floor
	ASTM	American Society for Testing and Materials
B	BD	Board
	BDF	Board foot
	BLK	Block
	BM	Beam
	B.O.	By others
	BRG	Bearing
	BRK	Brick
	BUR	Built-up roof
C	C.F.M.	Cubic feet per minute
	Cu. Ft.	Cubic foot
	CHNL	Channel
	CJ	Control joint
	CLG	Ceiling
	CLKG	Caulking
	CLO	Closet
	CLR	Clear, clearance
	CMU	Concrete masonry unit
	C.O.	Clean out
	CONC	Concrete
	CPT	Carpet
	CRS	Course(s)
	CT	Ceramic tile
	CTR	Center
	CU	Cubic
D	DIA.	Diameter
	DBL	Double
	DEMO	Demolish
	DN	Down
	DR	Door
	DW	Dishwasher
E	EA	Each
	EJ	Expansion joint
	EL	Elevation/grade
	ELEV	Elevator
	EP	Electric panel
	ETR	Existing to remain
	EWC	Electric water cooler
	EXP	Exposed
	EXT	Exterior
F	FT	Foot
	FBRGL	Fiberglass
	FCU	Fan coil unit
	FD	Floor drain
	FF	Finish floor
	FL/FLR	Floor
	FLSHG	Flashing
	FLOUR	Fluorescent
	FND	Foundation
	FTG	Footing
	F.R.	Fire resistive
G	GA	Gage (Gauge)
	GAL	Gallon
	GALV	Galvanized
	GFI	Ground fault interrupter
	GL	Glass
	GND	Ground
	GWB	Gypsum wall board
	GYP	Gypsum
H	HC	Hollow core
	HDR	Header
	HDWR	Hardware
	HDWD	Hardwood
	HM	Hollow metal
	HP	Horsepower
	HT	Height
	HTR	Heater
	HVAC	Heating, ventilation, and air conditioning
	HW	Hot water
I	IN	Inch
	INCL	Include
	INCAN	Incandescent
	INSIL	Insulation
	INT	Interior
J	JT	Joint
K	K/KIP	1000 pounds
	KITCH	Kitchen
	KW	Kilowatt
L	LAM	Laminate
	LAV	Lavatory
	LH	Left hand
	LIBR	Library
	LIN. FT.	Linear foot
	LL	Live load
	LTG	Lighting
M	MM	Millimeter
	M	Men, mortar
	MATL	Material
	MAX	Maximum
	MDO	Medium density overlay
	MECH	Mechanical
	MEMB	Membrane
	MTL	Metal
	MLDG	Molding
	MO	Masonry opening
	MTD	Mounted
N	NO	Number
	N	North
	N.I.C.	Not in contract
	NOM	Nominal
	NTS	Not to scale
O	OA	Overall
	OC	On center
	OFF	Office
	OPNG	Opening
	OPP	Opposite

P	PART	Partition
	PERIM	Perimeter
	PL	Plate
	P. LAM.	Plastic laminate
	PLEX	Plexiglas
	PLMB	Plumbing
	PLYWD	Plywood
	PR	Pair
	PREFAB	Prefabricated
	P.S.I.	Pounds per square inch
	P.S.F.	Pounds per square foot
	PT	Point
	PTD	Painted
	PVC	Polyvinyl chloride
	PVMT	Pavement
Q	QT	Quarry tile
	QTY	Quantity
R	R	Radius, riser
	RECP	Receptacle
	REINF	Reinforcing
	REV	Revision
	RH	Right hand
	RM	Room
	RO	Rough opening
S	SQ. FT.	Square foot
	S	South
	SAN	Sanitary
	SC	Solid core
	SECT	Section
	SHTHG	Sheathing
	SIM	Similar
	SOV	Shut-off valve
	SP	Standpipe
	S.STL	Stainless steel
	STD	Standard
	STL	Steel
	STOR	Storage
	SUBFL	Subfloor
	SUSP	Suspend
	SYM	Symmetrical
	S & V	Stain and varnish
T	T & G	Tongue and groove
	T	Tread
	TBS	To be specified
	THK	Thickness
	T.O.	Top of
	TP	Toilet paper
	TYP	Typical
U	UL	Underwriters laboratory
	UTIL	Utility
	U.O.N.	Unless otherwise noted
V	V	Volt
	VCT	Vinyl composition tile
	VERT	Vertical
	VIF	Verify in field
	VT	Vinyl tile

W	W/	With
	W/O	Without
	W	Watt, west, women, water
	WC	Water closet
	WD	Wood
	WP	Working point
	WT	Weight
	WTR	Water
	WWM	Welded wire mesh
	WDW	Window

Plumbing

D	Dryer
W	Washer
V.T.R.	Vent through roof
FD	Floor drain
C.O.	Clean out
TPV	Trap primer valve
SAN	Sanitary waste piping
CW	Domestic cold water
HW	Hot water piping
HWR	Hot water recirculating piping
GD	Garbage disposal
W.H.	Wall hydrant
BFP	Backflow preventer

Electrical

A	Amperes
AFF	Above finished floor
AHU	Air handling unit
AWG	American wire gauge
C	Conduit
G.	Ground wire
HD	Heavy duty
HP	Horse power
KW	Kilowatt (1000 watts)
LTG	Lighting
MAX	Maximum
MCB	Main circuit breaker
MH	Mounting height
NEMA	National Electric Manufacturer Code
P	Pole
PNL	Panel
REC	Receptacle
SW	Switch
UL	Underwriters lab
V	Voltage
W	Watts, wires
WH	Water heater
TELE	Telephone

HVAC

CU #	Condensing unit
AHU #	Air handling unit
ZD #	Zone damper
RL	Refrigerant line

APPENDIX D. COMMON LUMBER ABBREVIATIONS

AD	Air dried	EE	Eased edge edged
AD	After deduction freight	EG	Edge (vertical) grain
ALS	American Lumber Standards	EM	End matched
AVG	Average	ES	Englemann spruce
AW&L	All widths and lengths	f	Allowable fiber stress in bending (also FB)
BD	Board		
BD FT	Board feet	FAS	Free alongside (vessel)
BDL	Bundle	FG	Flat or slash grain
BEV	Bevel	FLG	Flooring
BH	Boxed heart	FOB	Free on board (named point)
B/L, BL	Bill of lading	FOHC	Free of heart center
BM	Board measure	FRT	Freight
B&S	Beams & stringers	FT	Foot
BSND	Bright Sapwood no defect	FT.BM	Feet board measure (also FBM)
BTR	Better	Ft.SM	Feet surface measure
CB	Center beaded	H.B.	Hollow back
CF	Cost and freight	HEM	Hemlock
C/F	Cost, insurance and freight	H&M	Hit and miss
C/FE	Cost, insurance, freight, exchange	H or M	Hit or miss
C/L	Carload	IC	Incense cedar
CLG	Ceiling	IN	Inch or inches
CLR	Clear	IND	Industrial
CM	Center matched	IWP	Idaho white pine
CS	Caulking seam	J&P	Joists and planks
CSG	Casing	JTD	Jointed
CV	Center V	KD	Kiln-dried
DET	Double end trimmed	L	Larch
DF	Douglas Fir	LBR	Lumber
DF-L	Douglas Fir-Larch	LCL	Less than carload
DIM	Dimension	LF	Light framing
DKG	Decking	LFVC	Loaded full visible capacity
D/S DS	Drop siding	LGR	Longer
D&M	Dressed & matched	LGTH	Length
E	Edge or modulus of elasticity	LIN	Lineal
EB1S	Edge bead one side	LNG	Lining
EB2S	Edge bead two sides	LP	Lodgepole pine
E&CB2S	Edge & center bead two sides	M	Thousand
EV1S	Edge vee one side	M.BM	Thousand (ft) board measure
EV2S	Edge vee two sides	MC	Moisture content
E&CV1S	Edge & center vee one side	MG	Mixed grain
E&CV2S	Edge & center vee two sides	MLDG	Molding

MOE	Modulus of elasticity or "E"
MOR	Modulus of rupture
MSR	Machine stress rated
NBM	Net board measure
N1E	Nose one edge
PAD	Partly air dried
PARA	Paragraph
PART	Partition
PAT	Pattern
PET	Precision end trimmed
PP	Ponderosa pine
P&T	Posts and timbers
RC	Red cedar
RDM	Random
REG	Regular
RGH	Rough
R/L, RL	Random length
R/S	Resawn
R/W, RW	Random width
SB1S	Single bead one side
SDG	Siding
SEL	Select
SG	Slash or flat grain
S/L, SL	Shiplap
STD. M	Standard matched
SM	Surface measure
SP	Sugar pine
SQ	Square
STK	Stock
STPG	Stepping
STR	Structural
S&E	Side and edge
S1E	Surfaced one edge
S2E	Surfaced two edges
S1S	Surfaced one side
S2S	Surfaced two sides
S4S	Surfaced four sides
S1S&CM	Surfaced one side and center matched
S2S&CM	Surfaced two sides and center matched
S4S&CS	Surfaced four sides and caulking seam
S1S1E	Surfaced one side, one edge
S1S2E	Surfaced one side, two edges
S2S1E	Surfaced one side, one edge
TBR	Timber
T&G	Tongued and grooved
VG	Vertical (edge) grain
WDR	Wider
WF	White Fir
WT	Weight
WTH	Width
WRC	Western Red Cedar
WWPA	Western Wood Products Association

Symbols

″	inch or inches
′	foot or feet
×	×, as 4 × 4
4/4, 5/4, 8/4, etc.	Nominal thickness expressed in fractions

Lumber in Board Feet

Sizes	8 ft	10 ft	12 ft	14 ft
1 × 2	1⅓	1⅔	2	2⅓
1 × 4	2⅔	3⅓	4	4⅔
1 × 6	4	5	6	7
1 × 8	5⅓	6⅔	8	9⅓
1 × 10	6⅔	8⅓	10	11⅔
1 × 12	8	10	12	14
1 × 16	10⅔	13⅓	16	18⅔
5/4 × 4	3⅓	4⅙	5	5⅚
5/4 × 6	5	6¼	7½	8¾
5/4 × 8	6⅔	8⅓	10	11⅔
5/4 × 12	10	12½	15	17½
2 × 4	5⅓	6⅔	8	9⅓
2 × 6	8	10	12	14
2 × 8	10⅔	13⅓	16	18⅔
2 × 10	13⅓	16⅔	20	23⅓
2 × 12	16	20	24	28
2 × 14	18⅔	23⅓	28	32⅔
2 × 16	21⅓	26⅔	32	37⅓

APPENDIX E. USEFUL EQUATIONS

Circumference of a circle:

3.1416 times the diameter

Area of a square:

length times width

Area of a rectangle:

length times width

Area of a triangle:

½ base times perpendicular height

Volume of cube/rectangle:

length times length times height

Volume of cylinder:

3.1416 times radius squared times height

Weights and Measures (U.S. System)

1 mile = 320 rods = 1,760 yd. = 5,280 ft

1 mile = 640 acres = 102,400 sq. rods = 3,097,600 sq. yd.

1 acre = 160 sq. rods = 4,840 sq. yd. = 43,560 sq. ft.

1 cu. yd. = 27 cu. ft. = .211 cord

1 gal = 4 qt = 8 pints = .13337 cu. ft.

1 ton = 2,000 lb = 32,000 oz

U.S. to Metric Conversions

From U.S.	To Metric	Multiply by
mile	km	1.609344
yard	m	0.9144
foot	m	0.3048
inch	mm	25.4
square mile	km^2	2.59000
acre	m^2	4046.87
square yard	m^2	0.836127
square foot	m^2	0.092903
square inch	mm^2	645.16
cubic yard	m^3	0.764555
cubic foot	m^3	0.02831685
pound	kg	0.453
plf	kg/m	1.488

Decimal to Inch Equivalents

.0625	1/16
.1250	1/8
.1875	3/16
.2500	1/4
.3125	5/16
.3750	3/8
.4375	7/16
.5000	1/2
.5625	9/16
.6250	5/8
.6875	11/16
.7500	3/4
.8125	13/16
.8750	7/8
.9375	15/16
1.0000	1

How to Interpolate

Many times when dealing with the tables in the codes, the number that you have may lie in-between the two values in the table. If the codes allow for interpolation from the table, it will say so in the form of a note at the bottom of the footer.

Sample Table

Size (in.) O.D.	Maximum Pressure (psi) Length (ft)			
	10	15	20	25
4	56	69	97	104
6	74	86	112	135
8	89	102	136	156

The above table is fictional and is only used as an example.

The size you are determining the max pressure for is 6 in. O.D., and the length is 16 ft. Because the lengths are in increments of 5 ft, there is no value available for 16 ft.

From the table:

6 in. @ 15 ft = 86

6 in. @ 20 ft = 112

112 − 86 = 26

20 − 15 = 5

26/5 = 5.2

We know that there are five increments between 15 and 20.

Each increment is equal to 5.2 (assuming all are equal).

Because 16 is one increment above 15, we would take the value of 15, 86 psi, and add 5.2 psi to it for the value of a 16-ft length.

$$86 \text{ psi} + 5.2 \text{ psi} = 91.2 \text{ psi}$$

Converting Decimals to Fractions

Example: 13.642 ft equals?

1. Subtract 13 from the figure (you know this is the number of feet).

2. The remainder .642 is still in feet and needs to be converted to inches. Knowing there are 12 in. in a foot,

$$.642 \text{ ft} \times 12 \text{ in.} = 7.704 \text{ in.}$$

3. Subtract the 7 from the figure to leave the decimal .704 in. The .704 now needs to be converted into a fraction of an inch. We assume your tape measure is in fractions and not decimals.

4. Knowing that there are 16 sixteenths in 1 in., multiply the $.704 \times 16 = 11.264$ or $^{11}/_{16}$. If you are working at extremely close tolerances, you may want to use $^{1}/_{32}$ of an inch or even $^{1}/_{64}$. Using $^{1}/_{64}$, $.704 \times 64 = 45.056$, or rounded off to $^{45}/_{64}$.

5. So, 13.642 ft equals 13 ft, 6 in. and $^{45}/_{64}$ of an inch, or 13 ft, $6^{45}/_{64}$ in.

$$13.642 \text{ ft} = 13 \text{ ft}, 6^{45}/_{64} \text{ in.}$$

Common Conversions Table

To Convert from	to	Multiply by
acres	square feet	43,560.0
acres	square yards	4,047.00
cubic feet	cubic inches	1,728.0
cubic feet	cubic yards	0.037
cubic feet	gallons (USA)	7.481
cubic feet of water	pounds	62.37
cubic inches	cubic feet	0.00058
cubic inches	cubic yards	0.000214
cubic inches	gallons	0.00433
cubic yards	cubic inches	46,656.00
cubic yards	cubic feet	27
feet	yards	0.333
feet	miles	0.000189
inches	feet	0.08333
inches	yards	0.02778
miles	feet	5,280.00
miles	yards	1,760.00
yards	miles	0.000568
square inches	square feet	0.00694
square inches	square yards	0.0007716
square feet	square inches	144
square feet	square yards	0.111
square feet	acres	0.000023
square yards	square inches	1,296.00
square yards	square feet	9

Weights of Building Materials

Weights of Building Materials

Item	Weight (lb/sq. ft.) Dead Load
Floor Area	
Ceramic tile (¾ in.) on 1 in. mortar bed	16
Hardwood flooring (⅞ in.)	4
Linoleum	1
Asphalt tile	1
Marble on concrete fill	33
Slate (1 in.)	15
Subflooring (¾ in.)	3
Terrazzo (1½ in.)	19
Wood joist	
2 × 6 (16 in. O.C.)	5
2 × 8 (16 in. O.C.)	6
2 × 10 (16 in. O.C.)	6
2 × 12 (16 in. O.C.)	7
Frame Walls	
Ext. stud 2 × 4, 16 in. OC, ⅝ in. drywall, insulation, ⅜ in. ext. siding	11
Ext. stud 2 × 6, 16 in. OC, ⅝ in. drywall, insulation, ⅜ in. ext. siding	12
Ext. stud w/brick veneer	48
Windows, glass, frame, sash	8
Masonry Partitions	
Concrete block, heavy aggregate	
4 in.	30
6 in.	42
8 in.	55
12 in.	85
Concrete block, light aggregate	
4 in.	20
6 in.	28
8 in.	38
12 in.	55
Clay tile	
4 in.	18
6 in.	24
8 in.	34

Weights of Building Materials (Continued)

Item	Weight (lb/sq. ft.) Dead Load
Masonry Walls	
Clay	
4 in.	39
8 in.	79
12½ in.	115
17 in.	155
22 in.	194
Concrete block (light)	
8 in.	35
12 in.	55
Concrete block (heavy)	
8 in.	55
12 in.	85
Glass block	
3⅞ in.	20
3⅛ in.	16
Wall coverings	
Gypsum sheathing (½ in.)	2
Rigid insulation, ½ in.	0.75
Fiberboard, ½ in.	0.75
Ceilings	
Gypsum board (per ⅛ in.)	0.55
Mech. ductwork	4
Plaster on wood lath	8
Suspended steel channel system	2
Wood furring suspended system	2.5
Roof Systems	
Asphalt shingles	2
Cement tile	16
Clay tile	20
Composition four-ply felt w/gravel	6
Metal deck, 20-gage	2.5
Slate, 3/16 in.	7
Slate, ¼ in.	10
Wood shingles	3
Wood sheathing (per in.)	3

Generalized Geologic Radon Potential of the United States by the U.S. Geological Survey

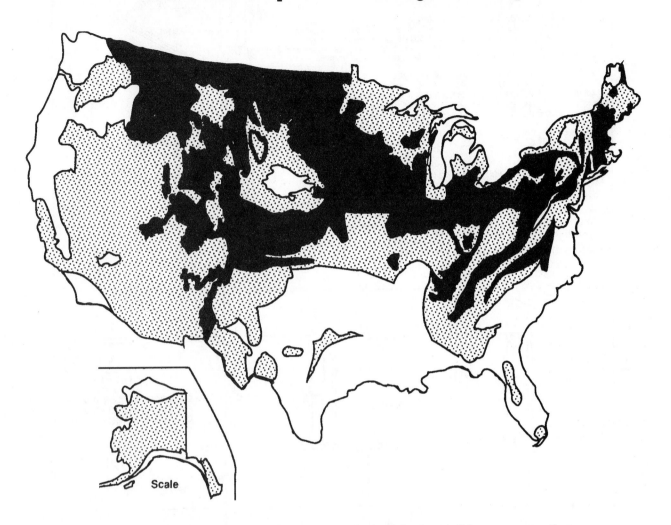

Geologic Radon Potential (Predicted Average Measurement)

☐	Low (less than 2 pCI/L)
▨	Moderate (2–4 pCI/L)
■	High (more than 4 pCI/L)

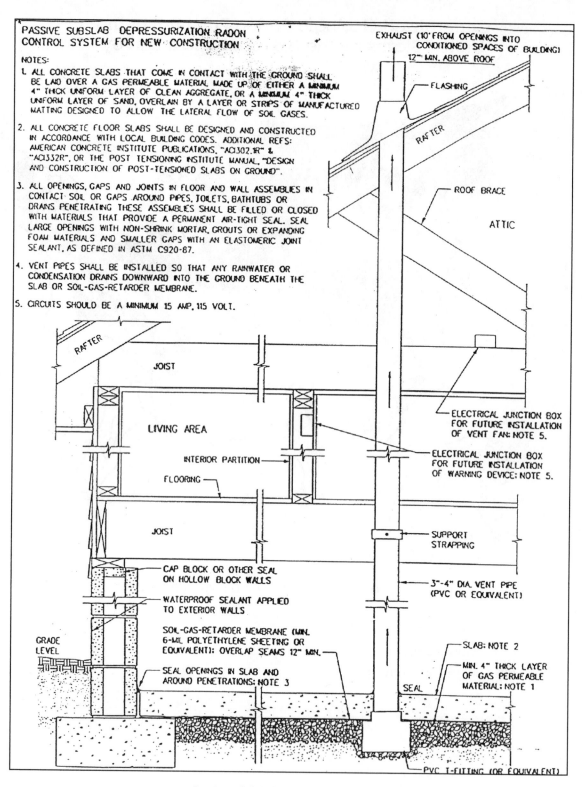

PASSIVE SUBSLAB DEPRESSURIZATION RADON CONTROL SYSTEM FOR NEW CONSTRUCTION

NOTES:

1. ALL CONCRETE SLABS THAT COME IN CONTACT WITH THE GROUND SHALL BE LAID OVER A GAS PERMEABLE MATERIAL MADE UP OF EITHER A MINIMUM 4" THICK UNIFORM LAYER OF CLEAN AGGREGATE, OR A MINIMUM 4" THICK UNIFORM LAYER OF SAND, OVERLAIN BY A LAYER OR STRIPS OF MANUFACTURED MATTING DESIGNED TO ALLOW THE LATERAL FLOW OF SOIL GASES.

2. ALL CONCRETE FLOOR SLABS SHALL BE DESIGNED AND CONSTRUCTED IN ACCORDANCE WITH LOCAL BUILDING CODES. ADDITIONAL REFS: AMERICAN CONCRETE INSTITUTE PUBLICATIONS, "ACI302.1R" & "ACI332R", OR THE POST TENSIONING INSTITUTE MANUAL, "DESIGN AND CONSTRUCTION OF POST-TENSIONED SLABS ON GROUND".

3. ALL OPENINGS, GAPS AND JOINTS IN FLOOR AND WALL ASSEMBLIES IN CONTACT SOIL OR GAPS AROUND PIPES, TOILETS, BATHTUBS OR DRAINS PENETRATING THESE ASSEMBLIES SHALL BE FILLED OR CLOSED WITH MATERIALS THAT PROVIDE A PERMANENT AIR-TIGHT SEAL. SEAL LARGE OPENINGS WITH NON-SHRINK MORTAR, GROUTS OR EXPANDING FOAM MATERIALS AND SMALLER GAPS WITH AN ELASTOMERIC JOINT SEALANT, AS DEFINED IN ASTM C920-87.

4. VENT PIPES SHALL BE INSTALLED SO THAT ANY RAINWATER OR CONDENSATION DRAINS DOWNWARD INTO THE GROUND BENEATH THE SLAB OR SOIL-GAS-RETARDER MEMBRANE.

5. CIRCUITS SHOULD BE A MINIMUM 15 AMP, 115 VOLT.

EXHAUST (10' FROM OPENINGS INTO CONDITIONED SPACES OF BUILDING)
12" MIN. ABOVE ROOF

FLASHING

RAFTER

ROOF BRACE

ATTIC

RAFTER

JOIST

LIVING AREA

INTERIOR PARTITION

FLOORING

JOIST

ELECTRICAL JUNCTION BOX FOR FUTURE INSTALLATION OF VENT FAN: NOTE 5.

ELECTRICAL JUNCTION BOX FOR FUTURE INSTALLATION OF WARNING DEVICE: NOTE 5.

SUPPORT STRAPPING

CAP BLOCK OR OTHER SEAL ON HOLLOW BLOCK WALLS

WATERPROOF SEALANT APPLIED TO EXTERIOR WALLS

3"-4" DIA. VENT PIPE (PVC OR EQUIVALENT)

SOIL-GAS-RETARDER MEMBRANE (MIN. 6-MIL POLYETHYLENE SHEETING OR EQUIVALENT): OVERLAP SEAMS 12" MIN.

GRADE LEVEL

SEAL OPENINGS IN SLAB AND AROUND PENETRATIONS: NOTE 3

SLAB: NOTE 2

MIN. 4" THICK LAYER OF GAS PERMEABLE MATERIAL: NOTE 1

SEAL

PVC T-FITTING (OR EQUIVALENT)

Passive subslab depressurization system.

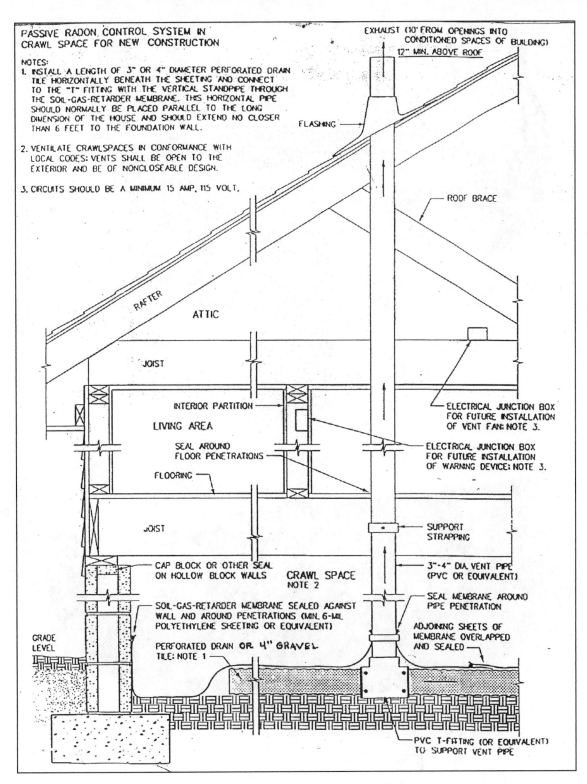

NOTES:

1. INSTALL A LENGTH OF 3" OR 4" DIAMETER PERFORATED DRAIN TILE HORIZONTALLY BENEATH THE SHEETING AND CONNECT TO THE "T" FITTING WITH THE VERTICAL STANDPIPE THROUGH THE SOIL-GAS-RETARDER MEMBRANE. THIS HORIZONTAL PIPE SHOULD NORMALLY BE PLACED PARALLEL TO THE LONG DIMENSION OF THE HOUSE AND SHOULD EXTEND NO CLOSER THAN 6 FEET TO THE FOUNDATION WALL.

2. VENTILATE CRAWLSPACES IN CONFORMANCE WITH LOCAL CODES; VENTS SHALL BE OPEN TO THE EXTERIOR AND BE OF NONCLOSEABLE DESIGN.

3. CIRCUITS SHOULD BE A MINIMUM 15 AMP, 115 VOLT.

Passive crawlspace depressurization system.

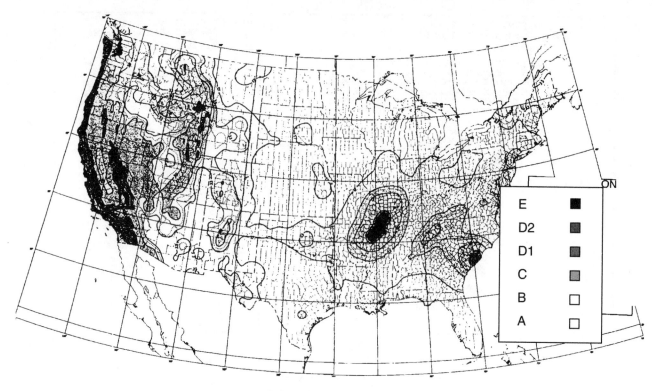

Seismic design categories.

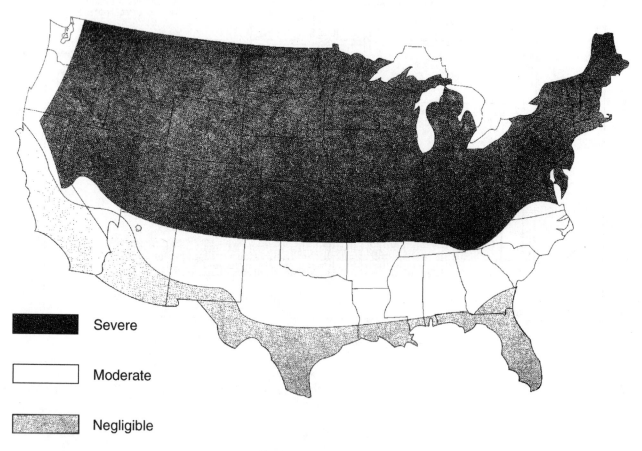

Severe

Moderate

Negligible

Weathering severity map.

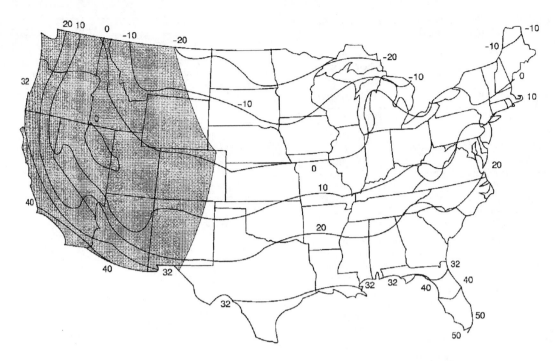

Design temperatures in this area must be based on analysis of local climate and topography.

Isolines for design temperatures for months of December, January, and Feburary.

Maximum Floor Allowances

Maximum Floor Area Allowances per Occupant

Occupancy	Floor Area in Sq. Ft. per Occupant
Agricultural building	300 gross
Aircraft hangars	500 gross
Airport terminal	
Concourse	100 gross
Waiting areas	15 gross
Baggage claim	20 gross
Baggage handling	300 gross
Assembly	
Gaming floors (keno, slots, etc.)	11 gross
Assembly with fixed seats	IBC Sec. 1003.2.2.9
Assembly without fixed seats	
Concentrated (chairs only, not fixed)	7 net
Standing space	5 net
Unconcentrated (tables and chairs)	15 net
Bowling centers, allow five persons for each lane including 15 ft of runway, and for additional areas	7 net
Business areas	100 gross
Courtrooms—other than fixed seating areas	40 net
Dormitories	50 gross

(continued)

Occupancy	Floor Area in Sq. Ft. per Occupant
Educational	
Classroom area	20 net
Shops and other vocational room areas	50 net
Exercise rooms	50 gross
H-5 fabrication and manufacturing areas	200 gross
Industrial areas	100 gross
Institutional areas	
Inpatient treatment areas	240 gross
Outpatient areas	100 gross
Sleeping areas	120 gross
Kitchens, commercial	200 gross
Library	
Reading rooms	50 net
Stack area	100 gross
Locker rooms	50 gross
Mercantile	
Basement and grade floor areas	30 gross
Areas on other floors	60 gross
Storage, stock, shipping areas	300 gross
Parking garages	200 gross
Residential	200 gross
Skating rinks, swimming pools	
Rink and pool	50 gross
Decks	15 gross
Stages and platforms	15 net
Accessory storage areas, mechanical equipment room	300 gross
Warehouses	500 gross

Occupancy/Use	Uniform Load (psi)	Concentrated Load (lb)
Apartments (see Residential)	—	—
Access floor systems		
Office use	50	2,000
Computer use	100	2,000
Armories and drill rooms	150	—
Assembly areas and theaters		
Fixed seats (fastened to floor)	60	
Lobbies	100	
Movable seats	100	
Stages and platforms	125	—
Follow spot, projections, and control rooms	50	
Catwalks	40	
Balconies (exterior)	100	
On one- and two-family residences only, and not exceeding 100 ft^2	60	—

Occupancy/Use	Uniform Load (psi)	Concentrated Load (lb)
Decks	Same as occupancy served	—
Bowling alleys	75	—
Cornices	60	—
Corridors, except as otherwise indicated	100	—
Dance halls and ballrooms	100	—
Dining rooms and restaurants	100	—
Elevator machine room grating (on area of 4 in.^{2})	—	300
Finish light floor plate construction (on area of 1 in.^{2})	—	200
Fire escapes	100	
On single-family dwellings only	40	—
Garages (passenger vehicles only)	40	
Grandstands (see Stadiums and Arenas, Bleachers)	—	—
Gymnasiums, main floors and balconies	100	—
Handrails, guards, and grab bars	IBC Sec. 1607.7	
Hospitals		
Operating rooms, laboratories	60	1,000
Private rooms	40	1,000
Wards	40	1,000
Corridors above first floor	80	1,000
Hotels (see Residential)	—	—
Libraries		
Reading rooms	60	1,000
Stack rooms	150	1,000
Corridors above first floor	80	1,000
Manufacturing		
Light	125	2,000
Heavy	250	3,000
Marquees	75	—
Office buildings		
File and computer rooms shall be designed for heavier loads based on anticipated occupancy		
Lobbies and first-floor corridors	100	2,000
Offices	50	2,000
Corridors above first floor	80	2,000

(continued)

Occupancy/Use	Uniform Load (psi)	Concentrated Load (lb)
Penal institutions		
Cell blocks	40	—
Corridors	100	
Residential		
One- and two-family dwellings		
Uninhabitable attics without storage	10	
Uninhabitable attics with storage	20	
Habitable attics and sleeping areas	30	
All other areas except balconies and decks	40	—
Hotels and multifamily dwellings		
Private rooms and corridors serving them	40	
Public rooms and corridors serving them	100	
Schools		
Classrooms	40	1,000
Corridors above first floor	80	1,000
First-floor corridors	100	1,000
Scuttles, skylight ribs, and accessible ceilings	—	200
Sidewalks, vehicular driveways, and yards, subject to trucks	250	8,000
Skating rinks	100	—
Stadiums and arenas		
Bleachers	100	—
Fixed seats (fastened to floor)	60	
Stairs and exits	100	
One- and two-family dwellings	40	
All other	100	
Storage warehouses (shall be designed for heavier loads if required for anticipated storage)		
Light	125	
Heavy	250	
Stores		
Retail		
First floor	100	1,000
Upper floors	75	1,000
Wholesale, all floors	125	1,000
Walkways and elevated platforms other than exit ways	60	—

Wind Forces

Wind Speed	Force (lb/sq. ft.)	Wind Speed	Force (lb/sq. ft.)
1	.005	20	1.970
2	.020	25	3.075
3	.044	30	4.428
4	.079	35	6.027
5	.123	40	7.873
6	.177	45	9.963
7	.241	50	12.30
8	.315	55	14.9
9	.400	60	17.71
10	.492	65	20.85
12	.708	70	24.1
14	.964	75	27.7
15	1.107	80	31.49
16	1.25	100	49.2
18	1.55		

Slope Conversions

Inch Rise per Foot	Slope	Percent Slope
1/16	0.0052	0.52
1/8	0.0104	1.04
3/16	0.0156	1.56
1/4	0.0208	2.08
5/16	0.0260	2.60
3/8	0.0313	3.13
7/16	0.0365	3.65
1/2	0.0417	4.17
9/16	0.0469	4.69
5/8	0.0521	5.21
11/16	0.0573	5.73
3/4	0.6350	6.25
13/16	0.0677	6.77
7/8	0.0729	7.29
15/16	0.0781	7.81
1	0.0833	8.33

APPENDIX F. CLIMATE ZONES BY STATES AND COUNTIES

Climate Zones by States and Counties

County	Zone	County	Zone	County	Zone
Alabama		St Clair	6	Navajo	10
Autauga	6	Sumter	5	Pima	4
Baldwin	4	Talladega	6	Pinal	4
Barbour	5	Tallapoosa	6	Santa Cruz	6
Bibb	6	Tuscaloosa	6	Yavapai	10
Blount	7	Walker	6	Yuma	3
Bullock	5	Washington	5		
Butler	5	Wilcox	5	**Arkansas**	
Calhoun	6	Winston	7	Arkansas	6
Chambers	6			Ashley	6
Cherokee	7	**Alaska Buroughs**		Baxter	9
Chilton	6	**and REAAs**		Benton	9
Choctaw	5	Adak Region	16	Boone	9
Clarke	5	Alaska Gateway	19	Bradley	6
Clay	7	Aleutian Region	17	Calhoun	6
Cleburne	7	Aleutians East	17	Carroll	9
Coffee	4	Anchorage	17	Chicot	6
Colbert	8	Annette Island	15	Clark	6
Conecuh	5	Bering Straits	19	Clay	8
Coosa	6	Bristol Bay	17	Cleburne	8
Covington	4	Chatham	16	Cleveland	6
Crenshaw	5	Chugach	17	Columbia	6
Cullman	7	Copper River	18	Conway	7
Dale	4	Delta/Greely	18	Craighead	8
Dallas	5	Denali	18	Crawford	8
De Kalb	8	Fairbanks N. Star	18	Crittenden	7
Elmore	6	Haines	16	Crosse	7
Escambia	4	Iditarod Area	19	Dallas	6
Etowah	7	Juneau	16	Desha	6
Fayette	7	Kashunamiut	18	Drew	6
Franklin	8	Kenai Peninsula	17	Faulkner	7
Geneva	4	Ketchikan Gateway	15	Franklin	8
Greene	5	Kodiak Island	16	Fulton	8
Hale	5	Kuspuk	18	Garland	7
Henry	4	Lake & Peninsula	17	Grant	6
Houston	4	Lower Kuskokwim	18	Greene	8
Jackson	8	Lower Yukon	18	Hempstead	7
Jefferson	6	Matanuska-Susitna	17	Hot Spring	7
Lamar	7	North Slope	19	Howard	7
Lauderdale	8	Northwest Arctic	19	Independence	8
Lawrence	8	Pribilof Islands	17	Izard	8
Lee	6	Sitka	15	Jackson	8
Limestone	8	Southeast Island	15	Jefferson	6
Lowndes	5	Southwest Region	17	Johnson	8
Macon	6	Yakutat	17	Lafayette	6
Madison	8	Yukon Flats	19	Lawrence	8
Marengo	5	Yukon-Koyukuk	19	Lea	7
Marion	7	Yupiit	18	Lincoln	6
Marshall	8			Little Rivera	6
Mobile	4	**Arizona**		Logan	7
Monroe	5	Apache	13	Lonoke	7
Montgomery	6	Cochise	6	Madison	9
Morgan	8	Coconino	14	Marion	9
Perry	5	Gila	8	Milleara	6
Pickens	6	Graham	6	Mississippi	8
Pike	5	Greenlee	6	Monroe	7
Randolph	7	La Paz	3	Montgomery	8
Russell	5	Maricopa	3	Nevada	6
Shelby	6	Mohave	7	Newton	9

County	Zone	County	Zone	County	Zone
Ouachita	6	San Diego	3	Mesa	13
Perry	7	San Francisco	6	Mineral	17
Phillips	7	San Joaquin	6	Moffat	15
Pike	7	San Luis Obispo	6	Montezuma	15
Poinsett	8	San Mateo	6	Montrose	13
Polk	8	Santa Barbara	5	Morgan	13
Pope	8	Santa Clara	6	Otero	11
Prairie	7	Santa Cruz	6	Ouray	15
Pulaski	7	Shasta	6	Park	17
Randolph	8	Sierra	11	Phillips	13
Saline	7	Siskiyou	11	Pitkin	17
Scott	7	Solano	6	Prowers	11
Searcy	9	Sonoma	6	Pueblo	11
Sebastian	8	Stanislaus	6	Rio Blanco	15
Sevier	7	Sutter	6	Rio Grande	17
Sharp	8	Tehama	6	Routt	17
St Francis	7	Trinity	9	Saguache	16
Stone	9	Tulare	6	San Juan	17
Union	6	Tuolumne	8	San Miguel	15
Van Buren	8	Ventura	4	Sedgwick	13
Washington	9	Yolo	6	Summit	17
White	7	Yuba	6	Teller	13
Woodruff	7			Washington	13
Yell	7	**Colorado**		Weld	13
		Adams	13	Yuma	13
California		Alamosa	16		
Alameda	6	Arapahoe	13	**Connecticut**	
Alpine	15	Archuleta	16	Fairfield	12
Amador	8	Baca	11	Hartford	13
Butte	6	Bent	11	Litchfield	14
Calaveras	8	Boulder	13	Middlesex	12
Colusa	6	Chaffee	16	New Haven	12
Contra Costa	6	Cheyenne	13	New London	12
Del Norte	9	Clear Creek	17	Tolland	14
El Dorado	8	Conejos	16	Windham	14
Fresno	6	Costilla	16		
Glenn	6	Crowley	11	**Delaware**	
Humboldt	9	Custer	16	Kent	9
Imperial	3	Delta	13	New Castle	10
Inyo	9	Denver	13	Sussex	9
Kern	5	Dolores	15		
Kings	6	Douglas	13	**DC**	
Lake	8	Eagle	15	Washington	10
Lassen	13	El Paso	13		
Los Angeles	4	Elbert	13	**Florida**	
Madera	6	Fremont	11	Alachua	3
Marin	6	Garfield	15	Baker	3
Mariposa	8	Gilpin	13	Bay	4
Mendocino	8	Grand	17	Bradford	3
Merced	6	Gunnison	17	Brevard	2
Modoc	15	Hinsdale	17	Broward	1
Mono	15	Huerfano	11	Calhoun	4
Monterey	6	Jackson	17	Charlotte	2
Napa	6	Jefferson	13	Citrus	2
Nevada	11	Kiowa	13	Clay	3
Orange	4	Kit Carson	13	Collier	1
Placer	8	La Plata	15	Columbia	3
Plumas	13	Lake	17	Dada	1
Riverside	4	Larimer	13	De Soto	2
Sacramento	6	Las Animas	11	Dixie	3
San Benito	6	Lincoln	13	Duvall	3
San Bernardino	4	Logan	13	Escambia	4

County	Zone	County	Zone	County	Zone
Flagler	3	Bibb	5	Hart	7
Franklin	4	Bleckley	5	Heard	6
Gadsden	4	Brantley	4	Henry	7
Gilchrest	3	Brooks	4	Houston	5
Glades	1	Bryan	4	Irwin	5
Gulf	4	Bulloch	5	Jackson	7
Hamilton	3	Burke	6	Jasper	6
Hardee	2	Butts	7	Jeff Davis	4
Hendry	1	Calhoun	5	Jefferson	6
Hernando	2	Camden	4	Jenkins	5
Highlands	2	Candler	5	Johnson	5
Hillsborough	2	Carroll	7	Jones	6
Holmes	4	Catoosa	8	Lamar	6
Indian Rivera	2	Charlton	4	Lanier	4
Jackson	4	Chatham	4	Laurens	5
Jefferson	4	Chattahoochee	5	Lea	5
Lafayette	3	Chattooga	8	Liberty	4
Lake	2	Cherokee	8	Lincoln	6
Lea	1	Clarke	7	Long	4
Leona	4	Clay	5	Lowndes	4
Levy	2	Clayton	7	Lumpkin	8
Liberty	4	Clinch	4	Macon	5
Madison	3	Cobb	7	Madison	7
Manatee	2	Coffee	5	Marion	5
Marion	2	Colquitt	4	McDuffie	6
Martina	1	Columbia	6	McIntosh	4
Monroe	1	Cook	4	Meriwether	6
Nassau	3	Coweta	7	Milleara	4
Okaloosa	4	Crawford	5	Mitchell	4
Okeechobee	2	Crisp	5	Monroe	6
Orange	2	Dade	8	Montgomery	5
Osceola	2	Dawson	8	Morgan	6
Palm Beach	1	De Kalb	7	Murray	8
Pasco	2	Decatur	4	Muscogee	5
Pinellas	2	Dodge	5	Newton	7
Polka	2	Dooly	5	Oconee	7
Putnam	3	Dougherty	5	Oglethorpe	7
Santa Rosa	4	Douglas	7	Paulding	7
Sarasota	2	Early	5	Peach	5
Seminole	2	Echols	4	Pickens	8
St Johns	3	Effingham	4	Pierce	4
St Lucie	2	Elbert	7	Pike	6
Sumter	2	Emanuel	5	Polk	7
Suwannee	3	Evans	4	Pulaski	5
Taylor	3	Fannin	8	Putnam	6
Union	3	Fayette	7	Quitman	5
Volusia	2	Floyd	7	Rabun	8
Wakulla	4	Forsyth	8	Randolph	5
Walton	4	Franklin	7	Richmond	6
Washington	4	Fulton	7	Rockdale	7
		Gilmer	8	Schley	5
Georgia		Glascock	6	Screven	5
Appling	4	Glenna	4	Seminole	4
Atkinson	4	Gordon	8	Spalding	7
Bacon	4	Grady	4	Stephens	7
Baker	4	Greene	6	Stewart	5
Baldwin	6	Gwinnett	7	Sumter	5
Banks	7	Habersham	8	Talbot	5
Barrow	7	Hall	7	Taliaferro	6
Bartow	7	Hancock	6	Tattnall	4
Ben Hill	5	Haralson	7	Taylor	5
Berrien	4	Harris	6	Telfair	5

County	Zone	County	Zone	County	Zone
Terrell	5	Latah	14	Kane	14
Thomas	4	Lemhi	15	Kankakee	13
Tift	5	Lewis	15	Kendall	13
Toombs	4	Lincoln	15	Knox	13
Towns	8	Madison	16	La Salle	13
Treutlen	5	Minidoka	15	Lake	14
Troupe	6	Nez Perce	12	Lawrence	11
Turner	5	Oneida	15	Lee	14
Twiggs	5	Owyhee	12	Livingston	13
Union	8	Payette	12	Logan	12
Upson	5	Power	15	Macon	12
Walker	8	Shoshone	14	Macoupin	11
Walton	7	Teton	16	Madison	10
Ware	4	Twin Falls	14	Marion	11
Warren	6	Valley	16	Marshall	13
Washington	6	Washington	13	Mason	12
Wayne	4			Massac	10
Webster	5	**Illinois**		McDonough	13
Wheeler	5	Adams	12	McHenry	14
White	8	Alexander	10	McLean	12
Whitfield	8	Bond	11	Menard	12
Wilcox	5	Boone	14	Mercer	13
Wilkes	7	Brown	12	Monroe	10
Wilkinson	5	Bureau	13	Montgomery	11
Worth	5	Calhoun	11	Morgan	12
		Carroll	14	Moultrie	12
Hawaii		Cass	12	Ogle	14
Hawaii	1	Champaign	12	Peoria	13
Honolulu	1	Christian	11	Perry	10
Kalawao	1	Clark	12	Piatt	12
Kauai	1	Clay	11	Pike	12
Maui	1	Clinton	10	Pope	10
		Coles	12	Pulaski	10
Idaho		Cook	14	Putnam	13
Ada	12	Crawford	11	Randolph	10
Adams	15	Cumberland	12	Richland	11
Bannock	15	De Kalb	14	Rock Island	13
Bear Lake	15	De Witt	12	Saline	10
Benewah	14	Douglas	12	Sangamon	12
Bingham	15	Du Page	14	Schuyler	12
Blaine	15	Edgar	12	Scott	12
Boise	15	Edwards	11	Shelby	11
Bonner	15	Effingham	11	St Clair	10
Bonneville	15	Fayette	11	Stark	13
Boundary	15	Ford	13	Stephenson	14
Butte	16	Franklin	10	Tazewell	12
Camas	15	Fulton	13	Union	10
Canyon	12	Gallatin	10	Vermilion	12
Caribou	15	Greene	11	Wabash	11
Cassia	14	Grundy	13	Warren	13
Clark	15	Hamilton	10	Washington	10
Clearwater	12	Hancock	13	Wayne	11
Custer	16	Hardin	10	White	10
Elmore	13	Henderson	13	Whiteside	14
Franklin	15	Henry	13	Will	13
Fremont	16	Iroquois	13	Williamson	10
Gem	13	Jackson	10	Winnebago	14
Gooding	13	Jasper	11	Woodford	13
Idaho	15	Jefferson	11		
Jefferson	16	Jersey	10	**Indiana**	
Jerome	14	Jo Daviess	14	Adams	13
Kootenai	14	Johnson	10	Allen	13

County	Zone	County	Zone	County	Zone
Bartholomew	11	Posey	10	Fayette	15
Benton	13	Pulaski	13	Floyd	15
Blackford	13	Putnam	12	Franklin	15
Boone	12	Randolph	13	Fremont	13
Brown	11	Ripley	11	Greene	14
Carroll	13	Rush	12	Grundy	15
Cass	13	Scott	11	Guthrie	14
Clark	10	Shelby	12	Hamilton	15
Clay	12	Spencer	10	Hancock	15
Clinton	13	St Joseph	13	Hardin	15
Crawford	11	Starke	13	Harrison	14
Daviess	11	Steuben	14	Henry	13
De Kalb	13	Sullivan	11	Howard	15
Dearborn	11	Switzerland	10	Humboldt	15
Decatur	12	Tippecanoe	13	Ida	15
Delaware	13	Tipton	13	Iowa	14
Dubois	11	Union	12	Jackson	14
Elkhart	13	Vanderburgh	10	Jasper	14
Fayette	12	Vermillion	12	Jefferson	13
Floyd	10	Vigo	12	Johnson	13
Fountain	12	Wabash	14	Jones	14
Franklin	12	Warren	12	Keokuk	13
Fulton	14	Warrick	10	Kossuth	15
Gibson	10	Washington	11	Lee	13
Grant	13	Wayne	12	Linn	14
Greene	11	Wells	13	Louisa	13
Hamilton	12	White	13	Lucas	13
Hancock	12	Whitley	14	Lyon	15
Harrison	10			Madison	14
Hendricks	12	**Iowa**		Mahaska	13
Henry	12	Adair	14	Marion	13
Howard	13	Adams	13	Marshall	14
Huntington	14	Allamakee	15	Mills	13
Jackson	11	Appanoose	13	Mitchell	15
Jasper	13	Audubon	14	Monona	14
Jay	13	Benton	14	Monroe	13
Jefferson	10	Black Hawk	15	Montgomery	13
Jennings	11	Boone	14	Muscatine	13
Johnson	12	Bremer	15	Obrien	15
Knox	11	Buchanan	15	Osceola	15
Kosciusko	14	Buena Vista	15	Page	13
La Porte	13	Butler	15	Palo Alto	15
Lagrange	14	Calhoun	15	Plymouth	15
Lake	13	Carroll	14	Pocahontas	15
Lawrence	11	Cass	14	Polk	14
Madison	13	Cedar	14	Pottawattamie	14
Marion	12	Cerro Gordo	15	Poweshiek	14
Marshall	13	Cherokee	15	Ringgold	13
Martin	11	Chickasaw	15	Sac	15
Miami	14	Clarke	13	Scott	13
Monroe	11	Clay	15	Shelby	14
Montgomery	12	Clayton	15	Sioux	15
Morgan	12	Clinton	13	Story	14
Newton	13	Crawford	14	Tama	14
Noble	14	Dallas	14	Taylor	13
Ohio	11	Davis	13	Union	13
Orange	11	Decatur	13	Van Buren	13
Owen	12	Delaware	15	Wapello	13
Parke	12	Des Moines	13	Warren	14
Perry	10	Dickinson	15	Washington	13
Pike	11	Dubuque	14	Wayne	13
Porter	13	Emmet	15		

County	Zone	County	Zone	County	Zone
Webster	15	Logan	12	Boyd	11
Winnebago	15	Lyon	11	Boyle	10
Winneshiek	15	Marion	11	Bracken	11
Woodbury	15	Marshall	12	Breathitt	10
Worth	15	Mcpherson	11	Breckenridge	9
Wright	15	Meade	10	Bullitt	10
		Miami	10	Butler	9
Kansas		Mitchell	12	Caldwell	9
Allen	10	Montgomery	9	Calloway	9
Anderson	10	Morris	11	Campbell	11
Atchison	11	Morton	10	Carlisle	9
Barber	9	Nemaha	11	Carroll	10
Barton	11	Neosho	9	Carter	11
Bourbon	10	Ness	12	Casey	10
Brown	11	Norton	13	Christian	9
Butler	10	Osage	10	Clark	10
Chase	10	Osborne	12	Clay	10
Chautauqua	9	Ottawa	11	Clinton	10
Cherokee	9	Pawnee	11	Crittenden	9
Cheyenne	13	Phillips	12	Cumberland	9
Clark	10	Pottawatomie	11	Daviess	9
Clay	11	Pratt	10	Edmonson	9
Cloud	12	Rawlins	13	Elliot	11
Coffey	10	Reno	11	Estill	10
Comanche	9	Republic	12	Fayette	10
Cowley	9	Rice	11	Fleming	11
Crawford	9	Riley	11	Floyd	10
Decatur	13	Rooks	12	Franklin	10
Dickinson	11	Rush	11	Fulton	9
Doniphan	11	Russell	11	Gallatin	11
Douglas	10	Saline	11	Garrard	10
Edwards	11	Scott	12	Grant	11
Elk	9	Sedgwick	10	Graves	9
Ellis	12	Seward	10	Grayson	9
Ellsworth	11	Shawnee	11	Green	9
Finney	11	Sheridan	12	Greenup	11
Ford	11	Sherman	13	Hancock	9
Franklin	10	Smith	12	Hardin	9
Geary	11	Stafford	11	Harlan	10
Gove	12	Stanton	11	Harrison	11
Graham	12	Stevens	10	Hart	9
Grant	11	Sumner	9	Henderson	9
Gray	11	Thomas	13	Henry	10
Greeley	12	Trego	12	Hickman	9
Greenwood	10	Wabaunsee	11	Hopkins	9
Hamilton	11	Wallace	12	Jackson	10
Harper	9	Washington	12	Jefferson	10
Harvey	11	Wichita	12	Jessamine	10
Haskell	11	Wilson	9	Johnson	11
Hodgeman	11	Woodson	10	Kenton	11
Jackson	11	Wyandotte	11	Knott	10
Jefferson	11			Knox	10
Jewell	12	**Kentucky**		Larue	9
Johnson	11	Adair	9	Laurel	10
Kearny	11	Allen	9	Lawrence	11
Kingman	10	Anderson	10	Lee	10
Kiowa	10	Ballard	9	Leslie	10
Labette	9	Barren	9	Letcher	10
Lane	12	Bath	11	Lewis	11
Leavenworth	11	Bell	10	Lincoln	10
Lincoln	11	Boone	11	Livingston	9
Linn	10	Bourbon	10	Logan	9

County	Zone	County	Zone	County	Zone
Lyon	9	Cameron	4	Lincoln	15
Madison	10	Catahoula	5	Oxford	16
Magoffin	10	Claiborne	6	Penobscot	15
Marion	10	Concordia	5	Piscataquis	17
Marshall	9	De Soto	5	Sagadhoc	15
Martin	11	East Baton Rouge	4	Somerset	17
Mason	11	East Carroll	6	Waldo	15
McCracken	9	East Feliciana	4	Washington	15
McCreary	10	Evangeline	4	York	15
McLean	9	Franklin	6		
Meade	9	Grant	5	**Maryland**	
Menifee	10	Iberia	4	Allegany	12
Mercer	10	Iberville	4	Anne Arundel	9
Metcalfe	9	Jackson	6	Baltimore	10
Monroe	9	Jefferson	3	Baltimore City	9
Montgomery	10	Jefferson Davis	4	Calvert	9
Morgan	10	La Salle	5	Caroline	9
Muhlenberg	9	Lafayette	4	Carroll	11
Nelson	10	Lafourche	3	Cecil	10
Nicholas	11	Lincoln	6	Charles	9
Ohio	9	Livingston	4	Dorchester	9
Oldham	10	Madison	6	Frederick	11
Owen	10	Morehouse	6	Garrett	13
Owsley	10	Natchitoches	5	Harford	10
Pendleton	11	Orleans	3	Howard	10
Perry	10	Ouachita	6	Kent	10
Pike	10	Plaquemines	3	Montgomery	10
Powell	10	Pointe Coupee	4	Prince George's	10
Pulaski	10	Rapides	5	Queen Anne's	9
Robertson	11	Red River	5	Somerset	9
Rockcastle	10	Richland	6	St Marys	9
Rowan	11	Sabine	5	Talbot	9
Russell	10	St Bernard	3	Washington	11
Scott	11	St Charles	3	Wicomico	9
Shelby	10	St Helena	4	Worcester	9
Simpson	9	St James	3		
Spencer	10	St John the Baptist	3	**Massachusetts**	
Taylor	9	St Landry	4	Barnstable	12
Todd	9	St Martin	4	Berkshire	14
Trigg	9	St Mary	3	Bristol	12
Trimble	10	St Tammany	4	Dukes	12
Union	9	Tangipahoa	4	Essex	13
Warren	9	Tensas	5	Franklin	14
Washington	10	Terrebonne	3	Hampden	14
Wayne	10	Union	6	Hampshire	14
Webster	9	Vermilion	4	Middlesex	13
Whitley	10	Varson	5	Nantucket	12
Wolfe	10	Washington	4	Norfolk	13
Woodford	10	Webster	6	Plymouth	12
		West Baton Rouge	4	Suffolk	13
Louisiana		West Carroll	6	Worcester	14
Acadia	4	West Feliciana	4		
Allen	4	Winn	5	**Michigan**	
Ascension	4			Alcona	15
Assumption	3	**Maine**		Alger	16
Avoyelles	5	Androscoggin	15	Allegan	14
Beauregard	4	Aroostook	17	Alpena	15
Bienville	6	Cumberland	15	Antrim	15
Bossier	6	Franklin	16	Arenac	15
Caddo	6	Hancock	15	Baraga	17
Calcasieu	4	Kennebec	15	Barry	14
Caldwell	6	Knox	15	Bay	15

County	Zone	County	Zone	County	Zone
Benzie	15	Roscommon	15	Mille Lacs	16
Berrien	14	Saginaw	14	Morrison	16
Branch	14	Sanilac	14	Mower	15
Calhoun	14	Schoolcraft	16	Murray	15
Cass	14	Shiawassee	14	Nicollet	15
Charlevoix	15	St Clair	14	Nobles	15
Cheboygan	15	St Joseph	14	Norman	17
Chippewa	16	Tuscola	14	Olmsted	15
Clare	15	Van Buren	14	Otter Tail	17
Clinton	14	Washtenaw	13	Pennington	17
Crawford	15	Wayne	13	Pine	16
Delta	16	Wexford	15	Pipestone	15
Dickinson	16			Polk	17
Eaton	14			Pope	16
Emmet	15	**Minnesota**		Ramsey	15
Genesee	14	Aitkin	17	Red Lake	17
Gladwin	15	Anoka	16	Redwood	15
Gogebic	17	Becker	17	Renville	15
Grand Traverse	15	Beltrami	17	Rice	15
Gratiot	14	Benton	16	Rock	15
Hillsdale	14	Big Stone	16	Roseau	17
Houghton	17	Blue Earth	15	Scott	15
Huron	14	Brown	15	Sherburne	16
Ingram	14	Carlton	17	Sibley	15
Ionia	14	Carver	15	St Louis	17
Iosco	15	Cass	17	Stearns	16
Iron	17	Chippewa	16	Steele	15
Isabella	15	Chisago	16	Stevens	16
Jackson	14	Clay	17	Swift	16
Kalamazoo	14	Clearwater	17	Todd	16
Kalkaska	15	Cook	17	Traverse	16
Kent	14	Cottonwood	15	Wabasha	15
Keweenaw	17	Crow Wing	17	Waseca	15
Lake	15	Dakota	15	Washington	15
Lapeer	14	Dodge	15	Watonwan	15
Leelanau	15	Douglas	16	Wilkin	17
Lenawee	14	Faribault	15	Winona	15
Livingston	14	Fillmore	15	Wright	16
Luce	16	Freeborn	15	Yellow Medicine	15
Mackinac	16	Goodhue	15		
Macomb	14	Grant	16		
Manistee	15	Hennepin	15	**Mississippi**	
Marquette	16	Houston	15	Adams	5
Mason	15	Hubbard	17	Alcorn	7
Mecosta	15	Isanti	16	Amite	4
Menominee	16	Itasca	17	Attala	6
Midland	15	Jackson	15	Benton	7
Missaukee	15	Kanabec	16	Bolivar	6
Monroe	13	Kandiyohi	16	Calhoun	6
Montcalm	14	Kittson	17	Carroll	6
Montmorency	15	Koochiching	17	Chickasaw	6
Muskegon	14	Lac Qui Parle	15	Choctaw	6
Newaygo	15	Lake	17	Claiborne	5
Oakland	14	Lake of the Woods	17	Clarke	5
Oceana	15	Le Sueur	15	Clay	6
Ogemaw	15	Lincoln	15	Coahoma	7
Ontonagon	17	Lyon	15	Copiah	5
Osceola	15	Mabnomen	17	Covington	5
Oscoda	15	Marshall	17	De Soto	7
Otsego	15	Martin	15	Forrest	5
Ottawa	14	McLeod	15	Franklin	5
Presque Isle	15	Meeker	16	Georgia	4

County	Zone	County	Zone	County	Zone
Greene	5	**Missouri**		Maries	11
Grenada	6	Adair	12	Marion	12
Hancock	4	Andrew	12	McDonald	9
Harrison	4	Atchison	13	Mercer	13
Hinds	6	Audrain	12	Miller	11
Holmes	6	Barry	9	Mississippi	9
Humphreys	6	Barton	10	Moniteau	11
Issaquena	6	Bates	11	Monroe	12
Itawamba	7	Benton	11	Montgomery	11
Jackson	4	Bollinger	10	Morgan	11
Jasper	5	Boone	11	New Madrid	9
Jefferson	5	Buchanan	12	Newton	9
Jefferson Davis	5	Butler	9	Nodaway	13
Jones	5	Caldwell	12	Oregon	9
Kemp era	6	Callaway	11	Osage	11
Lafayette	7	Camden	11	Ozark	9
Lamar	4	Cape Girardeau	9	Pemiscot	9
Lauderdale	6	Carroll	12	Perry	10
Lawrence	5	Carter	10	Pettis	11
Leaked	6	Cass	11	Phelps	10
Lee	7	Cedar	11	Pike	12
Leflore	6	Chariton	12	Platte	11
Lincoln	5	Christian	10	Polk	10
Lowndes	6	Clark	13	Pulaski	10
Madison	6	Clay	11	Putnam	13
Marion	4	Clinton	12	Ralls	12
Marshall	7	Cole	11	Randolph	12
Monroe	6	Cooper	11	Ray	11
Montgomery	6	Crawford	10	Reynolds	10
Neshoba	6	Dade	10	Ripley	9
Newton	6	Dallas	10	Saline	11
Noxubee	6	Daviess	12	Schuyler	13
Oktibbeha	6	De Kalb	12	Scotland	13
Panola	7	Dent	10	Scott	9
Pearl Rivera	4	Douglas	10	Shannon	10
Perry	5	Dunklin	9	Shelby	12
Pike	4	Franklin	10	St Charles	10
Pontotoc	7	Gasconade	11	St Clair	11
Prentiss	7	Gentry	13	St Francois	10
Quitman	7	Greene	10	St Louis	10
Rankin	6	Grundy	12	St Louis City	10
Scott	6	Harrison	13	Ste Genevieve	10
Starkey	6	Henry	11	Stoddard	9
Simpson	5	Hickory	11	Stone	9
Smith	5	Holt	12	Sullivan	12
Stone	4	Howard	11	Taney	9
Sunflower	6	Howell	9	Texas	10
Tallahatchie	7	Iron	10	Vernon	11
Tate	7	Jackson	11	Warren	11
Tippah	7	Jasper	9	Washington	10
Tishomingo	7	Jefferson	10	Wayne	10
Tunica	7	Johnson	11	Webster	10
Union	7	Knox	12	Worth	13
Walthall	4	Laclede	10	Wright	10
Warren	6	Lafayette	11		
Washington	6	Lawrence	10	**Montana**	
Wayne	5	Lewis	12	Beaverhead	15
Webster	6	Lincoln	11	Big Horn	15
Wilkinson	4	Linn	12	Blaine	16
Winston	6	Livingston	12	Broadwater	15
Yalobusha	7	Macon	12	Carbon	15
Yazoo	6	Madison	10	Carter	15

County	Zone	County	Zone	County	Zone
Cascade	15	Box Butte	15	Phelps	13
Chouteau	15	Boyd	14	Pierce	14
Custer	15	Brown	14	Platte	13
Daniels	16	Buffalo	13	Polk	13
Dawson	15	Burt	14	Red Willow	13
Deer Lodge	16	Butler	13	Richardson	13
Fallon	15	Cass	13	Rock	14
Fergus	15	Cedar	14	Saline	13
Flathead	16	Chase	13	Sarpy	13
Gallatin	15	Cherry	14	Saunders	13
Garfield	15	Cheyenne	14	Scotts Bluff	14
Glacier	16	Clay	13	Seward	13
Golden Valley	15	Colfax	13	Sheridan	15
Granite	16	Cuming	14	Sherman	14
Hill	16	Custer	14	Sioux	15
Jefferson	15	Dakota	14	Stanton	14
Judith Basin	15	Dawes	15	Thayer	13
Lake	15	Dawson	13	Thomas	14
Lewis and Clark	15	Deuel	14	Thurston	14
Liberty	16	Dixon	14	Valley	14
Lincoln	15	Dodge	13	Washington	13
Madison	15	Douglas	13	Wayne	14
McCone	15	Dundy	13	Webster	13
Meagher	15	Fillmore	13	Wheeler	14
Mineral	15	Franklin	13	York	13
Missoula	15	Frontier	13		
Musselshell	15	Furnas	13	**Nevada**	
Park	15	Gage	13	Carson City	12
Petroleum	15	Garden	14	Churchill	12
Phillips	16	Garfield	14	Clark	5
Pondera	16	Gosper	13	Douglas	13
Powder River	15	Grant	14	Elko	15
Powell	16	Greeley	14	Esmeralda	12
Prairie	15	Hall	13	Eureka	15
Ravalli	15	Hamilton	13	Humboldt	13
Richland	15	Harlan	13	Lander	13
Roosevelt	16	Hayes	13	Lincoln	12
Rosebud	15	Hitchcock	13	Lyon	13
Sanders	15	Holt	14	Mineral	12
Sheridan	16	Hooker	14	Nye	12
Silver Bow	16	Howard	14	Pershing	12
Stillwater	15	Jefferson	13	Storey	12
Sweet Grass	15	Johnson	13	Washoe	12
Teton	15	Kearney	13	White Pine	15
Toole	16	Keith	14		
Treasure	15	Keya Paha	14	**New Hampshire**	
Valley	16	Kimball	14	Belknap	15
Wheatland	15	Knox	14	Carroll	15
Wibaux	15	Lancaster	13	Cheshire	15
Yellowstone	15	Lincoln	14	Coos	16
Yellowstone		Logan	14	Grafton	15
National Park	15	Loup	14	Hillsborough	15
		Madison	14	Merrimack	15
Nebraska		Mcpherson	14	Rockingham	15
Adams	13	Merrick	13	Strafford	15
Antelope	14	Morrill	14	Sullivan	15
Arthur	14	Nance	13		
Banner	14	Nemaha	13	**New Jersey**	
Blaine	14	Nuckolls	13	Atlantic	10
Boone	14	Otoe	13	Bergen	12
		Pawnee	13	Burlington	11
		Perkins	13	Camden	10

County	Zone	County	Zone	County	Zone
Cape May	10	Chenango	15	Beauport	6
Cumberland	10	Clinton	15	Bertie	7
Essex	11	Columbia	13	Bladen	6
Gloucester	10	Cortland	15	Brunswick	6
Hudson	11	Delaware	15	Buncombe	9
Hunterdon	12	Dutchess	13	Burke	8
Mercer	11	Erie	14	Cabarrus	7
Middlesex	11	Essex	16	Caldwell	8
Monmouth	11	Franklin	16	Camden	7
Morris	12	Fulton	15	Carteret	6
Ocean	11	Genesee	14	Caswell	8
Passaic	12	Greene	14	Catawba	8
Salem	10	Hamilton	16	Chatham	8
Somerset	12	Herkimer	15	Cherokee	9
Sussex	13	Jefferson	15	Chowan	7
Union	11	Kings	10	Clay	9
Warren	12	Lewis	15	Cleveland	7
		Livingston	14	Columbus	6
New Mexico		Madison	14	Craven	6
Bernalillo	9	Monroe	14	Cumberland	7
Catron	11	Montgomery	14	Currituck	7
Chaves	7	Nassau	11	Dare	6
Cibola	12	New York	10	Davidson	8
Colfax	13	Niagara	14	Davie	8
Curry	9	Oneida	15	Duplin	6
De Baca	9	Onondaga	14	Durham	8
Dona Ana	7	Ontario	14	Edgecombe	7
Eddy	7	Orange	12	Forsyth	8
Grant	9	Orleans	14	Franklin	8
Guadalupe	9	Oswego	14	Gaston	7
Harding	11	Otsego	15	Gates	7
Hidalgo	7	Putnam	12	Graham	9
Lea	7	Queens	10	Granville	8
Lincoln	9	Rensselaer	14	Greene	7
Los Alamos	13	Richmond	11	Guilford	8
Luna	7	Rockland	12	Halifax	7
Mckinley	13	Saratoga	14	Harnett	7
Mora	15	Schenectady	14	Haywood	9
Otero	7	Schoharie	15	Henderson	9
Quay	8	Schuyler	15	Hertford	7
Rio Arriba	12	Seneca	14	Hake	7
Roosevelt	8	St Lawrence	15	Hyde	6
San Juan	12	Steuben	15	Iredell	8
San Miguel	12	Suffolk	11	Jackson	9
Sandoval	13	Sullivan	15	Johnston	7
Santa Fe	13	Tioga	15	Jones	6
Sierra	8	Tompkins	15	Lee	7
Socorro	9	Ulster	15	Lenoir	7
Taos	15	Warren	15	Lincoln	7
Torrance	11	Washington	15	Macon	9
Union	11	Wayne	14	Madison	9
Valencia	10	Westchester	12	Martin	7
		Wyoming	14	Mcdowell	8
New York		Yates	14	Mecklenburg	7
Albany	14			Mitchell	11
Allegheny	15	**North Carolina**		Montgomery	7
Bronx	11	Alamance	8	Moore	7
Broome	15	Alexander	8	Nash	7
Cattaraugus	15	Allegheny	11	New Hanover	6
Cayuga	14	Anson	7	Northampton	7
Chautauqua	13	Ashe	11	Onslow	6
Chemung	15	Avery	11	Orange	8

County	Zone	County	Zone	County	Zone
Pamlico	6	Mercer	16	Highland	11
Pasquotank	7	Morton	16	Hocking	12
Pondera	6	Mountrail	17	Holmes	13
Perquimans	7	Nelson	17	Huron	13
Person	8	Oliver	16	Jackson	11
Pitt	7	Pembina	17	Jefferson	13
Polk	7	Pierce	17	Knox	13
Randolph	8	Ramsey	17	Lake	13
Richmond	7	Ransom	16	Lawrence	11
Robeson	7	Renville	17	Licking	12
Rockingham	8	Richland	16	Logan	13
Rowan	7	Rolette	17	Lorain	13
Rutherford	7	Sargent	16	Lucas	14
Sampson	6	Sheridan	17	Madison	12
Scotland	7	Sioux	16	Mahoning	13
Stanly	7	Slope	16	Marion	13
Stokes	9	Stark	16	Medina	13
Surry	9	Steele	17	Meigs	11
Swain	9	Stutsman	17	Mercer	13
Transylvania	9	Towner	17	Miami	13
Tyrrell	6	Traill	17	Monroe	12
Union	7	Walsh	17	Montgomery	12
Vance	8	Ward	17	Morgan	12
Wake	7	Wells	17	Morrow	13
Warren	8	Williams	17	Muskingum	12
Washington	7			Noble	12
Watauga	11	**Ohio**		Ottawa	13
Wayne	7	Adams	11	Paulding	14
Wilkes	9	Allen	13	Perry	12
Wilson	7	Ashland	13	Pickaway	12
Yadkin	8	Ashtabula	13	Pike	11
Yancey	11	Athens	11	Portage	13
		Auglaize	13	Preble	12
North Dakota		Belmont	12	Putnam	13
Adams	16	Brown	11	Richland	13
Barnes	17	Butler	12	Ross	12
Benson	17	Carroll	13	Sandusky	13
Billings	16	Champaign	13	Scioto	11
Bottineau	17	Clark	13	Seneca	13
Bowman	16	Clermont	11	Shelby	13
Burke	17	Clinton	12	Stark	13
Burleigh	16	Columbiana	13	Summit	13
Cass	17	Coshocton	12	Trumbull	13
Cavalier	17	Crawford	13	Tuscarawas	13
Dickey	16	Cuyahoga	13	Union	13
Divide	17	Darke	13	Van Wert	13
Dunn	16	Defiance	14	Vinton	11
Eddy	17	Delaware	13	Warren	12
Emmons	16	Erie	13	Washington	11
Foster	17	Fairfield	12	Wayne	13
Golden Valley	16	Fayette	12	Williams	14
Grand Forks	17	Franklin	12	Wood	14
Grant	16	Fulton	14	Wyandot	13
Griggs	17	Gallia	11		
Hettinger	16	Geauga	13	**Oklahoma**	
Kidder	17	Greene	12	Adair	8
La Moure	16	Guernsey	12	Alfalfa	9
Logan	16	Hamilton	11	Atoka	7
McHenry	17	Hancock	13	Beaver	10
McIntosh	16	Hardin	13	Beckham	8
McKenzie	16	Harrison	13	Blaine	8
McLean	17	Henry	14	Bryan	7

County	Zone	County	Zone	County	Zone
Caddo	8	Texas	10	Centre	13
Canadian	8	Tillman	7	Chester	11
Carter	6	Tulsa	8	Clarion	14
Cherokee	8	Wagoner	8	Clearfield	15
Choctaw	6	Washington	9	Clinton	13
Cimarron	10	Washita	8	Columbia	13
Cleveland	7	Woods	9	Crawford	14
Coal	7	Woodward	9	Cumberland	12
Comanche	7			Dauphin	12
Cotton	7	**Oregon**		Delaware	10
Craig	9	Baker	15	Elk	15
Creek	8	Benton	10	Erie	14
Custer	8	Clackamas	10	Fayette	12
Delaware	8	Clatsop	11	Forest	15
Dewey	9	Columbia	11	Franklin	11
Ellis	9	Coos	9	Fulton	12
Garfield	8	Crook	14	Greene	12
Garvin	7	Curry	9	Huntingdon	12
Grady	7	Deschutes	14	Indiana	13
Grant	9	Douglas	9	Jefferson	15
Greer	7	Gilliam	12	Juniata	12
Harmon	7	Grant	15	Lackawanna	14
Harper	9	Harney	15	Lancaster	11
Haskell	7	Hood River	12	Lawrence	14
Hughes	7	Jackson	11	Lebanon	12
Jackson	7	Jefferson	13	Lehigh	12
Jefferson	6	Josephine	9	Luzerne	13
Johnston	6	Klamath	14	Lycoming	13
Kay	9	Lake	15	McKean	15
Kingfisher	8	Lane	10	Mercer	14
Kiowa	7	Lincoln	11	Mifflin	12
Latimer	7	Linn	10	Monroe	13
Le Flore	7	Malheur	12	Montgomery	11
Lincoln	7	Marion	10	Montour	13
Logan	8	Morrow	12	Northampton	12
Love	6	Multnomah	10	Northumberland	13
Major	9	Polk	10	Perry	12
Marshall	6	Sherman	13	Philadelphia	10
Mayes	8	Tillamook	11	Pike	13
McClain	7	Umatilla	12	Potter	15
McCurtain	7	Union	13	Schuylkill	13
McIntosh	7	Wallowa	15	Snyder	13
Murray	7	Wasco	13	Somerset	13
Muskogee	7	Washington	10	Sullivan	14
Noble	8	Wheeler	13	Susquehanna	15
Nowata	9	Yamhill	10	Tioga	15
Okfuskee	7			Union	13
Oklahoma	8			Venango	14
Okmulgee	8	**Pennsylvania**		Warren	14
Osage	8	Adams	11	Washington	12
Ottawa	9	Allegheny	12	Wayne	15
Pawnee	8	Armstrong	13	Westmoreland	13
Payne	8	Beaver	12	Wyoming	14
Pittsburg	7	Bedford	13	York	11
Pontotoc	7	Berks	12		
Pottawatomie	7	Blair	13		
Pushmataha	6	Bradford	15	**Rhode Island**	
Roger Mills	9	Bucks	11	Bristol	12
Rogers	9	Butler	14	Kent	12
Seminole	7	Cambria	13	Newport	12
Sequoyah	7	Cameron	15	Providence	14
Stephens	7	Carbon	13	Washington	12

County	Zone	County	Zone	County	Zone
South Carolina		Codington	16	Cannon	9
Abbeville	7	Corson	15	Carroll	9
Aiken	6	Custer	15	Carter	10
Allendale	5	Davison	15	Cheatham	9
Anderson	7	Day	16	Chester	8
Bamberger	5	Deuel	16	Claiborne	10
Barnwell	5	Dewey	15	Clay	9
Beauport	5	Douglas	14	Cocke	9
Berkeley	5	Edmunds	15	Coffee	8
Calhoun	6	Fall River	15	Crockett	8
Charleston	5	Faulk	15	Cumberland	9
Cherokee	7	Grant	16	Davidson	8
Chester	7	Gregory	14	De Kalb	9
Chesterfield	7	Haakon	15	Decatur	8
Clarendon	6	Hamlin	16	Dickson	9
Colleton	5	Hand	15	Dyer	8
Darlington	6	Hanson	15	Fayette	7
Dillon	6	Harding	15	Fentress	10
Dorchester	5	Hughes	15	Franklin	8
Edgefield	6	Hutchinson	14	Gibson	9
Fairfield	7	Hyde	15	Giles	8
Florence	6	Jackson	14	Grainger	9
Georgetown	5	Jerauld	15	Greene	9
Greenville	7	Jones	15	Grundy	9
Greenwood	7	Kingsbury	15	Hamblen	9
Hampton	5	Lake	15	Hamilton	8
Horry	5	Lawrence	15	Hancock	10
Jasper	5	Lincoln	15	Hardeman	8
Kershaw	7	Lyman	15	Hardin	8
Lancaster	7	Marshall	16	Hawkins	9
Laurens	7	McCook	15	Haywood	8
Lea	6	McPherson	16	Henderson	8
Lexington	6	Meade	15	Henry	9
Marion	6	Mellette	14	Hickman	9
Marlboro	6	Miner	15	Houston	9
McCormick	6	Minnehaha	15	Humphreys	9
Newberry	6	Moody	15	Jackson	9
Oconee	7	Pennington	15	Jefferson	9
Orangeburg	6	Perkins	15	Johnson	10
Pickens	7	Potter	15	Knox	8
Richland	6	Roberts	16	Lake	9
Saluda	6	Sanborn	15	Lauderdale	8
Spartanburg	7	Shannon	15	Lawrence	8
Sumter	6	Spink	15	Lewis	8
Union	7	Stanley	15	Lincoln	8
Williamsburg	6	Sully	15	Loudon	8
York	7	Todd	14	Macon	9
		Tripp	14	Madison	8
South Dakota		Turner	15	Marion	8
Aurora	15	Union	14	Marshall	8
Beadle	15	Walworth	15	Maury	9
Bennett	14	Yankton	14	McMinn	8
Bon Homme	14	Ziebach	15	McNairy	8
Brookings	16			Meigs	8
Brown	16	**Tennessee**		Monroe	8
Brule	15	Anderson	9	Montgomery	9
Buffalo	15	Bedford	8	Moore	8
Butte	15	Benton	9	Morgan	10
Campbell	15	Bledsoe	8	Obion	9
Charles Mix	14	Blount	8	Overton	9
Clark	16	Bradley	8	Perry	8
Clay	14	Campbell	10	Pickett	10

County	Zone	County	Zone	County	Zone
Polk	8	Castro	9	Hamilton	5
Putnam	9	Chambers	4	Hansford	9
Rhea	8	Cherokee	5	Hardeman	7
Roane	9	Childress	7	Hardin	4
Robertson	9	Clay	6	Harris	4
Rutherford	8	Cochran	8	Harrison	6
Scott	10	Coke	6	Hartley	9
Sequatchie	8	Coleman	5	Haskell	6
Sevier	9	Collin	5	Hays	4
Shelby	7	Collingsworth	7	Hemphill	8
Smith	9	Coloradoan	4	Henderson	5
Stewart	9	Comal	4	Hidalgo	2
Sullivan	9	Comanche	5	Hill	5
Sumner	9	Concho	5	Hockley	8
Tipton	8	Cooke	6	Hood	5
Trousdale	9	Coryell	5	Hopkins	6
Unicoi	10	Cottle	7	Houston	5
Union	9	Crania	5	Howard	6
Van Buren	9	Crockett	5	Hudspeth	6
Warren	9	Crosby	7	Hunt	6
Washington	9	Culberson	6	Hutchinson	9
Wayne	8	Dallam	9	Irion	5
Weakley	9	Dallas	5	Jack	6
White	9	Dawson	7	Jackson	3
Williamson	8	De Witt	3	Jasper	4
Wilson	9	Deaf Smith	9	Jeff Davis	6
		Delta	6	Jefferson	4
Texas		Denton	5	Jim Hogg	3
Anderson	5	Dickens	7	Jim Wells	3
Andrews	6	Dimmit	3	Johnson	5
Angelina	4	Donley	8	Jones	6
Aransas	3	Duvall	3	Karnes	3
Archer	6	Eastland	6	Kaufman	5
Armstrong	9	Ector	6	Kendall	5
Atascosa	3	Edwards	4	Kennedy	2
Austin	4	El Paso	6	Kent	7
Bailey	9	Elisa	5	Kerr	5
Bandera	4	Erath	5	Kimble	5
Bastrop	4	Falls	5	King	7
Baylor	7	Fannin	6	Kinney	4
Berea	3	Fayette	4	Kleberg	2
Bella	5	Fisher	6	Knox	7
Bexar	4	Floyd	8	La Sale	3
Blanco	5	Foard	7	Lamar	6
Borden	7	Fort Banda	4	Lamb	8
Bosque	5	Franklin	6	Lampasas	5
Bowie	6	Freestone	5	Lavaca	4
Brazoria	3	Friona	3	Lea	4
Brazos	4	Gaines	7	Leona	5
Brewster	5	Galveston	3	Liberty	4
Briscoe	8	Garza	7	Limestone	5
Brooks	3	Gillespie	5	Lipscomb	9
Browne	5	Glasscock	6	Live Osaka	3
Burleson	4	Goliad	3	Llano	5
Burnet	5	Gonzales	4	Loving	6
Caldwell	4	Gray	9	Lubbock	7
Calhoun	3	Grayson	6	Lynn	7
Callahan	6	Gregg	6	Madison	4
Cameron	2	Grimes	4	Marion	6
Camp	6	Guadalupe	4	Martin	6
Carson	9	Hale	8	Mason	5
Cass	6	Hall	8	Matagorda	3

County	Zone	County	Zone	County	Zone
Maverick	3	Taylor	6	Washington	10
McCulloch	5	Terrell	5	Wayne	14
McLennan	5	Terry	7	Weber	12
McMullen	3	Throckmorton	6		
Medina	4	Titus	6	**Vermont**	
Menarda	5	Tom Green	5	Addison	15
Midland	6	Travis	4	Bennington	15
Milam	4	Trinity	4	Caledonia	16
Mills	5	Tyler	4	Chittenden	15
Mitchell	6	Upshur	6	Essex	16
Montague	6	Upton	5	Franklin	15
Montgomery	4	Uvalde	4	Grand Isle	15
Moore	9	Val Verde	4	Lamoille	16
Morris	6	Van Zandt	5	Orange	16
Motley	7	Victoria	3	Orleans	16
Nacogdoches	5	Walker	4	Rutland	15
Navarro	5	Waller	4	Washington	16
Newton	4	Ward	6	Windham	15
Nolan	6	Washington	4	Windsor	15
Nueces	3	Webb	3		
Ochiltree	9	Wharton	3	**Virginia (counties)**	
Oldham	9	Wheeler	8	Accomack	8
Orange	4	Wichita	7	Albemarle	9
Palo Pinto	6	Wilbarger	7	Allegheny	10
Panola	5	Willacy	2	Amelia	9
Parker	5	Williamson	4	Amherst	9
Parmer	9	Wilson	4	Appomattox	9
Pecos	5	Winkler	6	Arlington	10
Polka	4	Wise	5	Augusta	11
Potter	9	Wood	6	Bath	11
Presidia	5	Yoakum	8	Bedford	9
Rains	6	Young	6	Bland	11
Randall	9	Zapata	2	Botetourt	9
Reagan	5	Zavala	3	Brunswick	8
Real	4			Buchanan	10
Red River	6	**Utah**		Buckingham	9
Reeves	6	Beaver	14	Campbell	9
Refugio	3	Box Elder	12	Caroline	9
Roberts	9	Cache	15	Carroll	11
Robertson	4	Carbon	14	Charles City	8
Rockwall	5	Daggett	15	Charlotte	9
Runnels	5	Davis	12	Chesterfield	9
Rusk	5	Duchesne	15	Clarke	11
Sabine	5	Emery	14	Craig	10
San Augustine	5	Garfield	14	Culpeper	10
San Jacinto	4	Grand	10	Cumberland	9
San Patricio	3	Iron	12	Dickenson	10
San Saba	5	Juab	12	Dinwiddie	8
Schleichera	5	Kane	10	Essex	9
Scurry	7	Millard	13	Fairfax	10
Shackelford	6	Morgan	15	Fauquier	10
Shelby	5	Piute	13	Floyd	11
Sherman	9	Rich	15	Fluvanna	9
Smith	5	Salt Lake	12	Franklin	10
Somervell	5	San Juan	13	Frederick	11
Starr	2	Sanpete	14	Giles	10
Stephens	6	Sevier	13	Gloucester	8
Sterling	6	Summit	15	Goochland	9
Stonewall	7	Tooele	12	Grayson	11
Sutton	5	Uintah	15	Greene	10
Swisher	9	Utah	12	Greensville	8
Tarrant	5	Wasatch	15	Halifax	9

County	Zone	County	Zone	County	Zone
Hampton	8	Bedford	9	Lewis	11
Hanover	9	Bristol	11	Lincoln	15
Henrico	8	Buena Vista	9	Mason	11
Henry	10	Charlottesville	9	Okanogan	15
Highland	11	Chesapeake	8	Pacific	11
Isle of Wight	8	Clifton Forge	10	Pend Oreille	15
James City	8	Colonial Hts	9	Pierce	11
King and Queen	9	Covington	10	San Juan	12
King George	9	Danville	9	Skagit	11
King William	9	Emporia	8	Skamania	11
Lancaster	8	Fairfax	10	Snohomish	11
Lee	10	Falls Church	10	Spokane	14
Loudoun	10	Franklin	8	Stevens	15
Louisa	9	Fredericksburg	10	Thurston	11
Lunenburg	9	Galax	11	Wahkiakum	11
Madison	11	Hampton	8	Walla Walla	11
Mathews	8	Harrisonburg	11	Whatcom	12
Mecklenburg	9	Hopewell	8	Whitman	14
Middlesex	8	Lexington	9	Yakima	12
Montgomery	11	Lynchburg	9		
Nansemond	8	Manassas	10	**West Virginia**	
Nelson	9	Manassas Park	10	Barbour	13
New Kent	8	Martinsville	10	Berkeley	11
Newport News	8	Newport News	8	Boone	10
Norfolk	8	Norfolk	8	Braxton	11
Northampton	8	Norton	10	Brooke	12
Northumberland	8	Petersburg	8	Cabell	10
Nottoway	9	Poquoson	8	Calhoun	11
Orange	10	Portsmouth	8	Clay	11
Page	11	Radford	11	Doddridge	12
Patrick	10	Richmond	8	Fayette	12
Pittsylvania	9	Roanoke	9	Gilmer	11
Powhatan	9	Salem	9	Grant	13
Prince Edward	9	South Boston	9	Greenbrier	12
Prince George	8	Staunton	11	Hampshire	11
Prince William	10	Suffolk	8	Hancock	12
Pulaski	11	Virginia Beach	8	Hardy	12
Rappahannock	11	Waynesboro	11	Harrison	12
Richmond	8	Williamsburg	8	Jackson	11
Roanoke	9	Winchester	11	Jefferson	11
Rockbridge	9			Kanawha	10
Rockingham	11	**Washington**		Lewis	12
Russell	10	Adams	12	Lincoln	10
Scott	10	Asotin	12	Logan	10
Shenandoah	11	Benton	11	Marion	12
Smyth	11	Chelan	12	Marshall	12
Southampton	8	Clallam	12	Mason	11
Spotsylvania	10	Clark	11	McDowell	11
Stafford	10	Columbia	12	Mercer	11
Surry	8	Cowlitz	11	Mineral	12
Sussex	8	Douglas	14	Mingo	10
Tazewell	11	Ferry	15	Monongalia	12
Virginia Beach	8	Franklin	11	Monroe	11
Warren	11	Garfield	12	Morgan	11
Washington	11	Grant	12	Nicholas	12
Westmoreland	8	Grays Harbor	11	Ohio	12
Wise	10	Island	12	Pendleton	13
Wythe	11	Jefferson	11	Pleasants	11
York	8	King	10	Pocahontas	13
		Kitsap	11	Preston	13
Virginia (cities)		Kittitas	14	Putnam	10
Alexandria	10	Klickitat	12	Raleigh	12

County	Zone	County	Zone	County	Zone
Randolph	13	Green	15	Taylor	17
Ritchie	11	Green Lake	15	Trempealeau	15
Roane	11	Iowa	15	Vernon	15
Summers	12	Iron	17	Vilas	17
Taylor	12	Jackson	15	Walworth	15
Tucker	13	Jefferson	15	Washburn	17
Tyler	11	Juneau	15	Washington	15
Upshur	12	Kenosha	15	Waukesha	15
Wayne	10	Kewaunee	15	Waupaca	15
Webster	12	La Crosse	15	Waushara	15
Wetzel	12	Lafayette	15	Winnebago	15
Wirt	11	Langlade	17	Wood	15
Wood	11	Lincoln	17		
Wyoming	11	Manitowoc	15	**Wyoming**	
		Marathon	15	Albany	16
Wisconsin		Marinette	15	Big Horn	15
Adams	15	Marquette	15	Campbell	15
Ashland	17	Menominee	15	Carbon	16
Barron	16	Milwaukee	15	Converse	15
Bayfield	17	Monroe	15	Crook	15
Brown	15	Oconto	15	Fremont	15
Buffalo	15	Oneida	17	Goshen	14
Burnett	17	Outagamie	15	Hot Springs	15
Calumet	15	Ozaukee	15	Johnson	15
Chippewa	15	Pepin	15	Laramie	15
Clark	15	Pierce	15	Lincoln	17
Columbia	15	Polk	16	Natrona	15
Crawford	15	Portage	15	Niobrara	15
Dane	15	Price	17	Park	15
Dodge	15	Racine	15	Platte	14
Door	15	Richland	15	Sheridan	15
Douglas	17	Rock	15	Sublette	17
Dunn	15	Rusk	16	Sweetwater	16
Eau Claire	15	Sauk	15	Teton	17
Florence	17	Sawyer	17	Uinta	16
Fond du Lac	15	Shawano	15	Washakie	15
Forest	17	Sheboygan	15	Weston	15
Grant	15	St Croix	15		

Glossary

A/C   An abbreviation for air conditioner or air conditioning.

A/C condenser   The outside fan unit of the air conditioning system. It removes the heat from the freon gas and "turns" the gas back into a liquid and pumps the liquid back to the coil in the furnace.

A/C disconnect   The main electrical ON–OFF switch near the A/C condenser.

Absolute humidity   The ratio of the mass of water vapor to the volume occupied by a mixture of water vapor and dry air.

Absorbent   A material that extracts one or more substances from a fluid (gas or liquid) medium on contact, and changes physically and/or chemically in the process. The less volatile of the two working fluids in an absorption cooling device.

Absorber   The component of a solar thermal collector that absorbs solar radiation and converts it to heat, or, as in a solar photovoltaic device, the material that readily absorbs photons to generate charge carriers (free electrons or holes).

Absorption   The passing of a substance or force into the body of another substance.

Absorption chiller   A type of air cooling device that uses absorption cooling to cool interior spaces.

Absorption coefficient   In reference to a solar energy conversion device, the degree to which a substance will absorb solar energy. In a solar photovoltaic device, the factor by which photons are absorbed as they travel a unit distance through a material.

Absorption cooling   A process in which cooling of an interior space is accomplished by the evaporation of a volatile fluid, which is then absorbed in a strong solution, then desorbed under pressure by a heat source, and then recondensed at a temperature high enough that the heat of condensation can be rejected to a exterior space.

Absorption refrigeration   A system in which a secondary fluid absorbs the refrigerant, releasing heat, then releases the refrigerant and reabsorbs the heat. Ammonia or water is used as the vapor in commercial absorption cycle systems; and water or lithium bromide is the absorber.

Absorptivity   In a solar thermal system, the ratio of solar energy striking the absorber that is absorbed by the absorber to that of solar energy striking a black body (perfect absorber) at the same temperature. The absorptivity of a material is numerically equal to its emissivity.

Accessible   Access thereto, but which first requires opening an access panel, door, or similar obstruction. "Readily accessible" means direct access without the use of tools for removing or moving any such obstruction.

Accessible, readily   Capable of being reached quickly for operation, renewal, or inspections without requiring those for whom ready access is requisite to climb over or remove obstacles or to resort to portable ladders, chairs, etc. (See "Accessible.")

Accessible (as applied to equipment)   Admitting close approach; not guarded by locked doors, elevation, or other effective means. (See "Accessible, readily.")

Accessible (as applied to wiring methods)   Capable of being removed or exposed without damaging the building structure or finish, or not permanently closed in by the structure or finish of the building. (See "Concealed" and "Exposed.")

Accumulator   A component of a heat pump that stores liquid and keeps it from flooding the compressor. The accumulator takes the strain off the compressor and improves the reliability of the system.

Acid rain   A term used to describe precipitation that has become acidic (low pH) due to the emission of sulfur oxides from fossil fuel burning power plants.

Acoustical materials   Types of tile, plaster, and other materials which absorb sound waves. Generally applied to interior wall surfaces to reduce reverberation or reflection of the waves.

Active cooling   The use of mechanical heat pipes or pumps to transport heat by circulating heat transfer fluids.

Active power   The power (in watts) used by a device to produce useful work. Also called input power.

Active solar heater   A solar water or space-heating system that uses pumps or fans to circulate the fluid (water- or heat-transfer-fluid-like diluted antifreeze) from the solar collectors to a storage tank subsystem.

Adhesive   A substance capable of holding material together by surface attachment. A general term that includes glue, cement mastic, and paste.

Adiabatic   Without loss or gain of heat to a system. An adiabatic change is a change in volume and pressure of a parcel of gas without an exchange of heat between the parcel and its surroundings. In reference to a steam turbine, the adiabatic efficiency is the ratio of the work done per pound of steam, to the heat energy released and theoretically capable of transformation into mechanical work during the adiabatic expansion of a unit weight of steam.

Adjustable speed drive   An electronic device that controls the rotational speed of motor-driven equipment such as fans, pumps, and compressors. Speed control is achieved by adjusting the frequency of the voltage applied to the motor.

Adobe   A building material made from clay, straw, and water, formed into blocks, and dried; used traditionally in the southwestern United States.

Aerator The round screened screw-on tip of a sink spout. It mixes water and air for a smooth flow.

Aerobic bacteria Microorganisms that require free oxygen, or air, to live, and contribute to the decomposition of organic material in soil or composting systems.

Aggregate A mixture of sand and stone and a major component of concrete.

Air The mixture of gases that surrounds the earth and forms its atmosphere, composed of, by volume, 21 percent oxygen, 78 percent nitrogen.

Air admittance valve A one-way valve designed to allow air into the plumbing drainage system when a negative pressure develops in the piping. This device shall close by gravity and seal the terminal under conditions of positive internal pressure.

Air break, drainage system An arrangement in which a discharge pipe from a fixture, appliance or device drains indirectly into a receptor below the flood level rim of the receptor.

Air change A measure of the rate at which the air in an interior space is replace by outside (or conditioned) air by ventilation and infiltration; usually measured in cubic feet per time interval (hour), divided by the volume of air in the room.

Air circulation, forced A means of providing space conditioning utilizing movement of air through ducts or plenums by mechanical means.

Air collector In solar heating systems, a type of solar collector in which air is heated in the collector.

Air conditioner A device for conditioning air in an interior space. A room air conditioner is a unit designed for installation in the wall or window of a room to deliver conditioned air without ducts. A unitary air conditioner is composed of one or more assemblies that usually include an evaporator or cooling coil, a compressor and condenser combination, and possibly a heating apparatus. A central air conditioner is designed to provide conditioned air from a central unit to a whole house with fans and ducts.

Air conditioning The control of the quality, quantity, and temperature-humidity of the air in an interior space.

Air-conditioning system An air-conditioning system consists of heat exchangers, blowers, filters, supply, exhaust, and return-air systems and shall include any apparatus installed in connection therewith.

Air diffuser An air distribution outlet, typically located in the ceiling, which mixes conditioned air with room air.

Air dried Wood seasoned by exposure to the atmosphere, in the open or under cover, without artificial heat.

Air-entraining agents Chemical additives which improve the workability and freeze-thaw durability of mortar as it ages.

Air gap, drainage system The unobstructed vertical distance through free atmosphere between the outlet of a waste pipe and the flood level rim of the fixture or receptor into which it is discharging.

Air gap, water distribution system The unobstructed vertical distance through free atmosphere between the lowest opening from a water supply discharge to the flood level rim of a plumbing fixture.

Air infiltration measurement A building energy auditing technique used to determine and/or locate air leaks in a building shell or envelope.

Airlock entry A building architectural element (vestibule) with two airtight doors that reduces the amount of air infiltration and exfiltration when the exterior most door is opened.

Air pollution The presence of contaminants in the air in concentrations that prevent the normal dispersive ability of the air, and that interfere with biological processes and human economics.

Air pollution control The use of devices to limit or prevent the release of pollution into the atmosphere.

Air quality standards The prescribed level of pollutants allowed in outside or indoor air as established by legislation.

Air register The component of a combustion device that regulates the amount of air entering the combustion chamber.

Air retarder/barrier A material or structural element that inhibits air flow into and out of a building's envelope or shell. This is a continuous sheet composed of polyethylene, polypropylene, or extruded polystyrene. The sheet is wrapped around the outside of a house during construction to reduce air in—and exfiltration—yet allow water to easily diffuse through it.

Air-source heat pump A type of heat pump that transfers heat from outdoor air to indoor air during the heating season, and works in reverse during the cooling season.

Air space The area between insulation facing and interior of exterior wall coverings. Normally a 1-in. air gap.

Airtight drywall approach (ADA) A building construction technique used to create a continuous air retarder that uses the drywall, gaskets, and caulking. Gaskets are used rather than caulking to seal the drywall at the top and bottom. Although it is an effective energy-saving technique, it was designed to keep airborne moisture from damaging insulation and building materials within the wall cavity.

Air-to-air heat pump See "Air-source heat pump."

Air-to-water heat pump A type of heat pump that transfers heat in outdoor air to water for space or water heating.

Albedo   The ratio of light reflected by a surface to the light falling on it.

Alcohol   A group of organic compounds composed of carbon, hydrogen, and oxygen; a series of molecules composed of a hydrocarbon plus a hydroxyl group; includes methanol, ethanol, isopropyl alcohol, and others.

Algae   Primitive plants, usually aquatic, capable of synthesizing their own food by photosynthesis.

Allowance(s)   A sum of money set aside in the construction contract for items which have not been selected and specified in the construction contract. For example, selection of tile as a flooring may require an allowance for an underlayment material, or an electrical allowance which sets aside an amount of money to be spent on electrical fixtures.

Alteration   A change in an air-conditioning, heating, ventilating or refrigeration system that involves an extension, addition or change to the arrangement, type or purpose of the original installation.

Alternating current (AC)   A type of electrical current, the direction of which is reversed at regular intervals or cycles; in the United States the standard is 120 reversals or 60 cycles per second.

Alternative fuels   A popular term for "nonconventional" transportation fuels derived from natural gas (propane, compressed natural gas, methanol, etc.) or biomass materials (ethanol, methanol).

Alternator   A generator producing alternating current by the rotation of its rotor, and which is powered by a primary mover.

Ambient air   The air external to a building or device.

Ambient temperature   The temperature of a medium, such as gas or liquid, which comes into contact with or surrounds an apparatus or building element.

Ammonia   A colorless, pungent gas (NH_3) that is extremely soluble in water and may be used as a refrigerant; a fixed nitrogen form suitable as fertilizer.

Ampacity   The current in amperes that a conductor can carry continuously under the conditions of use without exceeding its temperature rating.

Ampere (amp)   A unit of measure for an electrical current; the amount of current that flows in a circuit at an electromotive force of 1 volt and at a resistance of 1 ohm.

Amp-hours   A measure of the flow of current (in amperes) over 1 hour.

Anaerobic bacteria   Microorganisms that live in oxygen-deprived environments.

Anaerobic digester   A device for optimizing the anaerobic digestion of biomass and/or animal manure, and possibly to recover biogas for energy production. Digester types include batch, complete mix, continuous flow (horizontal or plug-flow, multiple-tank, and vertical tank), and covered lagoon.

Anaerobic digestion   The complex process by which organic matter is decomposed by anaerobic bacteria. The decomposition process produces a gaseous by-product often called "biogas" primarily composed of methane, carbon dioxide, and hydrogen sulfide.

Anaerobic lagoon   A holding pond for livestock manure that is designed to anaerobically stabilize manure and may be designed to capture biogas, with the use of an impermeable, floating cover.

Anchor bolts   Bolts embedded in concrete used to hold structural members in place.

Anchor straps   Strap fastener which is embedded in concrete or masonry walls to hold sills in place.

Anemometer   An instrument for measuring the force or velocity of wind; a wind gage.

Angle of incidence   In reference to solar energy systems, the angle at which direct sunlight strikes a surface; the angle between the direction of the sun and the perpendicular to the surface. Sunlight with an incident angle of 90° tends to be absorbed, while lower angles tend to be reflected.

Angle of inclination   In reference to solar energy systems, the angle that a solar collector is positioned above horizontal.

Angstrom unit   A unit of length named for A. J. Angstrom, a Swedish spectroscopist, used in measuring electromagnetic radiation equal to 0.00000001 centimeters.

Anhydrous ethanol   One hundred percent alcohol; neat ethanol.

Annual fuel utilization efficiency (AFUE)   The measure of seasonal or annual efficiency of a residential heating furnace or boiler. It takes into account the cyclic on/off operation and associated energy losses of the heating unit as it responds to changes in the load, which in turn is affected by changes in weather and occupant controls.

Annual load fraction   That fraction of annual energy demand supplied by a solar system.

Annual percentage rate (APR)   Annual cost of credit over the life of a loan, including interest, service charges, points, loan fees, mortgage insurance, and other items.

Annual rings   Rings or layers of wood which represent one growth period of a tree. In cross section the rings may indicate the age of the tree.

Annual solar savings   The annual solar savings of a solar building is the energy savings attributable to a solar feature relative to the energy requirements of a nonsolar building.

Anode   The positive pole or electrode of an electrolytic cell, vacuum tube, etc. (See "Sacrificial anode.")

Anthracite (coal)   A hard, dense type of coal that is hard to break, clean to handle, and difficult to ignite, and that burns with an intense flame and with the virtual absence of smoke because it contains a high percentage of fixed carbon and a low percentage of volatile matter.

Anthropogenic   Referring to alterations in the environment due to the presence or activities of humans.

Antifreeze solution   A fluid, such as methanol or ethylene glycol, added to vehicle engine coolant, or used in solar heating system heat transfer fluids, to protect the systems from freezing.

Antireflection coating   A thin coating of a material applied to a photovoltaic cell surface that reduces the light reflection and increases light transmission.

Antisiphon   A term applied to valves or mechanical devices that eliminate siphonage.

Aperture   An opening; in solar collectors, the area through which solar radiation is admitted and directed to the absorber.

Appliance   (a) A device for converting one form of energy or fuel into useful energy or work. (b) A device or apparatus that is manufactured and designed to utilize energy and for which code provides specific requirements.

Appliance energy efficiency ratings   The ratings under which specified appliances convert energy sources into useful energy, as determined by procedures established by the U.S. Department of Energy.

Appraisal   An expert valuation of property.

Approved   Acceptable to the authority having jurisdiction.

Apron   A piece of horizontal trim applied against the wall immediately below the stool. Conceals rough edge of plaster.

Architect   One who has completed a course of study in building and design, and is licensed by the state as an architect. One who draws up plans.

Area wells   Corrugated metal or concrete barrier walls installed around a basement window to hold back the earth.

Area-way   An open space around a basement window or doorway. Provides light, ventilation, and access.

Argon   A colorless, odorless, inert gas sometimes used in the spaces between the panes in energy efficient windows. This gas is used because it will transfer less heat than air. Therefore, it provides additional protection against conduction and convection of heat over conventional double-pane windows.

Array (solar)   Any number of solar photovoltaic modules or solar thermal collectors or reflectors connected together to provide electrical or thermal energy.

Ash   The noncombustible residue of a combusted substance composed primarily of alkali and metal oxides.

ASHRAE   Abbreviation for the American Society of Heating, Refrigeration, and Air-Conditioning Engineers.

Asphalt   A residue from evaporated petroleum. It is insoluble in water but is soluble in gasoline and melts when heated.

Assessment   A tax levied on a property, or a value placed on the worth of a property.

Assumption   Allows a buyer to assume responsibility for an existing loan instead of getting a new loan.

ASTM   Abbreviation for the American Society for Testing and Materials, which is responsible for the issue of many standard methods used in the energy industry.

Astragal   A molding attached to one of a pair of swinging double doors against which the other door strikes.

Asynchronous generator   A type of electric generator that produces alternating current that matches an existing power source.

Atmospheric pressure   The pressure of the air at sea level; one standard atmosphere at zero degrees Celsius is equal to 14.695 pounds per square inch (1.033 kilograms per square centimeter).

Atrium   An interior court to which rooms open.

Attachment plug   A device that, by insertion in a receptacle, establishes connection between the conductors of the attached flexible cord and the conductors connected permanently to the receptacle.

Attic   The usually unfinished space above a ceiling and below a roof.

Attic access   An opening that is placed in the drywalled ceiling of a home providing access to the attic.

Attic fan   A fan mounted on an attic wall used to exhaust warm attic air to the outside.

Attic vent   A passive or mechanical device used to ventilate an attic space, primarily to reduce heat buildup and moisture condensation.

Audit (energy)   The process of determining energy consumption, by various techniques, of a building or facility.

Automatic (or remote) meter reading system   A system that records the consumption of electricity, gas, water, etc. and sends the data to a central data accumulation device.

Automatic damper   A device that cuts off the flow of hot or cold air to or from a room as controlled by a thermostat.

Automatic   Self-acting, operating by its own mechanism when actuated by some impersonal influence as, for example, a change in current strength, pressure, temperature, or mechanical configuration.

Auxiliary energy or system   Energy required to operate mechanical components of an energy system, or a source of energy or energy supply system to back up another.

Availability   Describes the reliability of power plants. It refers to the number of hours that a power plant is available to produce power divided by the total hours in a set time period, usually a year.

Available heat   The amount of heat energy that may be converted into useful energy from a fuel.

Average cost   The total cost of production divided by the total quantity produced.

Average demand   The demand on, or the power output of, an electrical system or any of its parts over an interval of time, as determined by the total number of kilowatt-hours divided by the units of time in the interval.

Average wind speed (or velocity)   The mean wind speed over a specified period of time.

Avoided cost   The incremental cost to an electric power producer to generate or purchase a unit of electricity or capacity or both.

AWG   The abbreviation for American Wire Gauge; the standard for gauging the size of wires (electrical conductors).

Awning   An architectural element for shading windows and wall surfaces placed on the exterior of a building; can be fixed or movable.

Axial fans   Fans in which the direction of the flow of the air from inlet to outlet remains unchanged; includes propeller, tubaxial, and vaneaxial type fans.

Axial flow compressor   A type of air compressor in which air is compressed in a series of stages as it flows axially through a decreasing tubular area.

Axial flow turbine   A turbine in which the flow of a steam or gas is essentially parallel to the rotor axis.

Azimuth (solar)   The angle between true south and the point on the horizon directly below the sun.

Back charge   Billings for work performed or costs incurred by one party that, in accordance with the agreement, should have been performed or incurred by the billed party. Owners bill back charges to general contractors, and general contractors bill back charges to subcontractors. Examples of back charges include charges for cleanup work or to repair something damaged by another subcontractor, such as a tub chip or broken window.

Backband   A narrow rabbeted molding applied to the outside corner and edge of interior window and door casing to create a "heavy trim" appearance.

Backdrafting   The flow of air down a flue/chimney and into a house caused by low indoor air pressure that can occur when using several fans or fireplaces and/or if the house is very tight.

Backfill   The replacement of earth around foundations after excavating.

Backflow preventer, reduced-pressure zone type   A backflow-prevention device consisting of two independently acting check valves, internally force loaded to a normally closed position and separated by an intermediate chamber (or zone) in which there is an automatic relief means of venting to atmosphere, internally loaded to a normally open position between two tightly closing shutoff valves and with means for testing for tightness of the checks and opening of relief means.

Backflow preventer   A device or means to prevent backflow.

Backflow, drainage   A reversal of flow in the drainage system.

Backflow, water distribution   The flow of water or other liquids into the potable water supply piping from any sources other than its intended source. Back siphonage is one type of backflow.

Backing board (backer board)   In a two-layer drywall system, the base panel of gypsum drywall. It uses gray liner paper as facing and is not suitable as a top surface.

Backing   Frame lumber installed between the wall studs to give additional support for drywall or an interior trim–related item, such as handrail brackets, cabinets, and towel bars. In this way, items are screwed and mounted into solid wood rather than weak drywall that may allow the item to break loose from the wall. Carpet backing holds the pile fabric in place.

Backout   Work the framing contractor does after the mechanical subcontractors (heating-plumbing-electrical) finish their phase of work at the "rough" (before insulation) stage to get the home ready for a municipal frame inspection. Generally, the framing contractor repairs anything disturbed by others and completes all framing necessary to pass a "rough" frame inspection.

Backsiphonage   The flowing back of used or contaminated water from piping into a potable water supply pipe caused by a negative pressure in such pipe.

Backup energy system   A reserve appliance; for example, a stand-by generator for a home or commercial building.

Backwater valve   A device installed in a drain or pipe to prevent backflow of sewage.

Bacteria   Single-celled organisms—free-living or parasitic—that break down the wastes and bodies of dead organisms, making their components available for reuse by other organisms.

Baffle   A device, such as a steel plate, used to check, retard, or divert a flow of a material.

Baghouse   An air pollution control device used to filter particulates from waste combustion gases; a chamber containing a bag filter.

Balance point   An outdoor temperature, usually 20 to 45 degrees Fahrenheit, at which a heat pump's output equals the heating demand. Below the balance point, supplementary heat is needed.

Balance-of-system   In a renewable energy system, refers to all components other than the mechanism used to harvest the resource (such as photovoltaic panels or a wind turbine). Balance-of-system costs can include design, land, site preparation, system installation, support structures, power conditioning, operation and maintenance, and storage.

Baling   A means of reducing the volume of a material by compaction into a bale.

Ball cock   A valve that is used inside a gravity-type water closet flush tank to control the supply of water into the tank. It is also called a flush-tank fill valve or water control.

Ballast   A transformer that steps up the voltage in a florescent lamp.

Ballast efficacy factor   The measure of the efficiency of fluorescent lamp ballasts. It is the relative light output divided by the power input.

Ballast factor   The ratio of light output of a fluorescent lamp operated on a ballast to the light output of a lamp operated on a standard or reference ballast.

Balloon   A loan that has a series of monthly payments with the remaining balance due in a large lump-sum payment at the end.

Balloon framing   A type of building construction with upright studs that extend from the foundation sill to the rafter plate. Its use is decreasing in favor of platform framing and other construction styles.

Balusters   Vertical members in a railing used between a top rail and bottom rail or the stair treads. Sometimes referred to as "pickets" or "spindles."

Balustrade   A railing consisting of a series of balusters resting on a base, usually the treads, which supports a continuous stair or hand rail.

Band gap   In a semiconductor, the energy difference between the highest valence band and the lowest conduction band.

Band gap energy   The amount of energy (in electron volts) required to free an outer shell electron from its orbit about the nucleus to a free state, and thus promote it from the valence to the conduction level.

Barge   Horizontal beam rafter that supports shorter rafters.

Barge board   A decorative board covering the projecting rafter (fly rafter) of the gable end. At the cornice, this member is a fascia board.

Barrel (petroleum)   42 U.S. gallons (306 pounds of oil, or 5.78 million Btu).

Basal metabolism   The amount of heat given off by a person at rest in a comfortable environment; approximately 50 Btu per hour (Btu/h).

Base (baseboard)   A trim board placed against the wall around the room next to the floor.

Base power   Power generated by a power generator that operates at a very high capacity factor.

Base shoe   Small, narrow molding used around the perimeter of a room where the baseboard meets the finish floor.

Baseboard radiator   A type of radiant heating system where the radiator is located along an exterior wall where the wall meets the floor.

Baseload capacity   The power output of a power plant that can be continuously produced.

Baseload demand   The minimum demand experienced by a power plant.

Basement   (a) The conditioned or unconditioned space below the main living area or primary floor of a building. (b) The part of a house that is partly or wholly in the ground.

Basement window insert   The window frame and glass unit that is installed in the window buck.

Bat   A half brick.

Batch heater   This simple passive solar hot water system consists of one or more storage tanks placed in an insulated box that has a glazed side facing the sun. A batch heater is mounted on the ground or on the roof (make sure your roof structure is strong enough to support it). Some batch heaters use "selective" surfaces on the tank(s). These surfaces absorb sun well but inhibit radiative loss. (See "Bread box systems" and "Integral collector storage systems.")

Bathroom   An area including a basin with one or more of the following: a toilet, a tub, or a shower.

Batt/blanket   A flexible roll or strip of insulating material in widths suited to standard spacings of building structural members (studs and joists). They are made from glass or rock wool fibers. Blankets are continuous rolls. Batts are precut to 4- or 8-ft lengths.

Batten   A strip of wood placed across a surface to cover joints.

Batter   The slope, or inclination from the vertical, of a wall or other structure or portion of a structure.

Batter board   A temporary framework used to assist in locating corners when laying out a foundation.

Battery   An energy storage device composed of one or more electrolyte cells.

Battery energy storage   Energy storage using electrochemical batteries. The three main applications for battery energy storage systems include spinning reserve at generating stations, load leveling at substations, and peak shaving on the customer side of the meter.

Bay   One of the intervals or spaces into which a building plan is divided by columns, piers, or division walls.

Bay window   A rectangular, curved, or polygonal window or group of windows usually supported on a foundation extending beyond the main wall of a building.

Beadwall™   A form of movable insulation that uses tiny polystyrene beads blown into the space between two window panes.

Beam   A structural member transversely supporting a load. A structural member carrying building loads (weight) from one support to another. A principal structural member used between posts, columns, or walls. Sometimes called a "girder."

Beam radiation   Solar radiation that is not scattered by dust or water droplets.

Bearing header   (a) A beam placed perpendicular to joists and to which joists are nailed in framing for a chimney, stairway, or other opening. (b) A wood lintel. (c) The horizontal structural member over an opening (for example, over a door or window).

Bearing partition   A partition which supports a vertical load in addition to its own weight.

Bearing point   A point where a bearing or structural weight is concentrated and transferred to the foundation.

Bearing wall   A wall that supports any vertical load in addition to its own weight.

Bed molding   A molding applied where two surfaces come together at an angle. Commonly used in cornice trim especially between the plancier and frieze.

Bedding   A filling of mortar, putty, or other substance used to secure a firm bearing.

Bedrock   A subsurface layer of earth that is suitable to support a structure.

Bench mark   A mark on a permanent object fixed to the ground from which land measurements and elevations are taken.

Bend   A drainage fitting, designed to provide a change in direction of a drain pipe of less than the angle specified by the amount necessary to establish the desired slope of the line. (See "Elbow" and "Sweep.")

Bevel siding   Used as finish covering on the exterior of a structure. It is usually manufactured by "re-sawing"

dry, square-surfaced boards diagonally to produce two wedge-shaped pieces.

Bevel   To cut to an angle other than a right angle, such as the edge of a board or door.

Bid   A formal offer by a contractor, in accordance with specifications for a project, to do all or a phase of the work at a certain price in accordance with the terms and conditions stated in the offer.

Bid bond   A bond issued by a surety on behalf of a contractor that provides insurance to the recipient of the contractor's bid that, if the bid is accepted, the contractor will execute a contract and provide a performance bond. Under the bond, the surety is obligated to pay the recipient of the bid the difference between the contractor's bid and the bid of the next lowest responsible bidder if the bid is accepted and the contractor fails to execute a contract or to provide a performance bond.

Bid shopping   A practice by which contractors, both before and after their bids are submitted, attempt to obtain prices from potential subcontractors and material suppliers that are lower than the contractors' original estimates on which their bids are based, or after a contract is awarded, seek to induce subcontractors to reduce the subcontract price included in the bid.

Bidding requirements   The procedures and conditions for the submission of bids. The requirements are included in documents, such as the notice to bidders, advertisements for bids, instructions to bidders, invitations to bid, and sample bid forms.

Bifold door   Doors that are hinged in the middle for opening in a smaller area than standard swing doors. Often used for closet doors.

Bimetal   Two metals of different coefficients of expansion welded together so that the piece will bend in one direction when heated, and in the other when cooled, and can be used to open or close electrical circuits, as in thermostats.

Bin method   A method of predicting heating and/or cooling loads using instantaneous load calculation at different outdoor dry-bulb temperatures, and multiplying the result by the number of hours of occurrence of each temperature.

Binary cycle   Combination of two power plant turbine cycles utilizing two different working fluids for power production. The waste heat from the first turbine cycle provides the heat energy for the operation of the second turbine, thus providing higher overall system efficiencies.

Binder   A receipt for a deposit to secure the right to purchase a home at agreed-upon terms by a buyer and seller.

Bipass doors   Doors that slide by each other, commonly used as closet doors.

Bird's-mouth   A notch cut on the underside of a rafter to fit it to the top plate. Not a full notch if rafter ends flush with top plate instead of overhanging.

Blankets   Fiberglass or rock-wool insulation that comes in long rolls 15 or 23 in. wide.

Blemish   Any defect, scar, or mark that tends to detract from the appearance of wood.

Blind nailing   Refers to tongue-and-groove flooring. Nails are placed at the root of the tongue where they will be hidden. The nails pierce the subfloor at a 45 degree angle.

Blind stop   A member applied to the exterior edge of the side and head jamb of a window to serve as a stop for the top sash and to form a rabbet for storm sash, screens, blinds, and shutters.

Block out   To install a box or barrier within a foundation wall to prevent the concrete from entering an area. For example, foundation walls are sometimes "blocked" in order for mechanical pipes to pass through the wall, to install a crawlspace door, and to depress the concrete at a garage door location.

Blocked (door blocking)   Wood shims used between the door frame and the vertical structural wall framing members.

Blocked (rafters)   Short 2 by 4s used to keep rafters or joists from twisting, and installed at the ends and at midspan.

Blocking   Small wood pieces to brace framing members or to provide a nailing base for gypsum board or paneling.

Blow insulation   Fiber insulation in loose form and used to insulate attics and existing walls where framing members are not exposed.

Blower   The device in an air conditioner that distributes the filtered air from the return duct over the cooling coil/heat exchanger. This circulated air is cooled/heated and then sent through the supply duct, past dampers, and through supply diffusers to the living/working space.

Blower door   A device used by energy auditors to pressurize a building to locate places of air leakage and energy loss.

Blown-in insulation   An insulation product composed of loose fibers or fiber pellets that are blown into building cavities or attics using special pneumatic equipment.

Blueprint(s)   A type of copying method often used for architectural drawings. Usually used to describe the drawing of a structure which is prepared by an architect or designer for the purpose of design and planning, estimating, securing permits, and actual construction.

Blue stain   A stain caused by a fungus growth in unseasoned lumber—especially pine. It does not affect the strength of the wood.

Blue stake   Another phrase for "utility notification." This is when a utility company (telephone, gas, electric, cable TV, sewer and water, etc.) comes to the job site and locates and spray paints the ground and/or installs little flags to show where their service is located underground.

Board foot   A unit of measure for lumber equal to 1 in. thick by 12 in. wide by 12 in. long. Examples: $1'' \times 12'' \times 16' = 16$ board ft, $2'' \times 12'' \times 16' = 32$ board feet.

Board   Lumber less than 2 in. thick.

Boiler   A vessel or tank where heat produced from the combustion of fuels such as natural gas, fuel oil, or coal is used to generate hot water or steam for applications ranging from building space heating to electric power production or industrial process heat.

Boiler feedwater   The water that is forced into a boiler to take the place of that which is evaporated in the generation of steam.

Boiler horsepower   A unit of rate of water evaporation equal to the evaporation per hour of 34.5 lb of water at a temperature of 212°F into steam at 212°F.

Boiler pressure   The pressure of the steam or water in a boiler as measured; usually expressed in pounds per square inch gauge (psig).

Boiler rating   The heating capacity of a steam boiler; expressed in Btu per hour (Btu/h), or horsepower, or pounds of steam per hour.

Boiler, hot water heating   A self-contained appliance from which hot water is circulated for heating purposes and then returned to the boiler, and which operates at water pressures not exceeding 160 pounds per square inch gauge (psig) (1102 kPa gauge) and at water temperatures not exceeding 250°F (121°C) near the boiler outlet.

Bond or bonding   An amount of money which must be on deposit with a governmental agency in order to secure a contractor's license. The bond may be used to pay for the unpaid bills or disputed work of the contractor. Not to be confused with a performance bond. Such bonds are rarely used in residential construction; they are an insurance policy which guarantees proper completion of a project.

Bonding jumper, circuit   The connection between portions of a conductor in a circuit to maintain the required ampacity of the circuit.

Bonding jumper, equipment   The connection between two or more portions of the equipment grounding conductor.

Bonding jumper, main   The connection between the grounded circuit conductor and the equipment grounding conductor at the service.

Bonding jumper   A reliable conductor to ensure the required electrical conductivity between metal parts required to be electrically connected.

Bonding   The permanent joining of metallic parts to form an electrically conductive path that will ensure electrical continuity and the capacity to conduct safely any current likely to be imposed.

Bone (oven) dry   In reference to solid biomass fuels, such as wood, having zero moisture content.

Bone dry unit   A quantity of (solid) biomass fuel equal to 2400 lb bone dry.

Boom   A truck used to hoist heavy material up and into place. To put trusses on a home or to set a heavy beam into place.

Booster pump   A pump for circulating the heat transfer fluid in a hydronic heating system.

Boot   In heating and cooling system distribution ductwork, the transformation pieces connecting horizontal round leaders to vertical rectangular stacks.

Boron   The chemical element commonly used as the dopant in solar photovoltaic device or cell material.

Bottled gas   A generic term for liquefied and pressurized gas, ordinarily butane, propane, or a mixture of the two, contained in a cylinder for domestic use.

Bottom chord   The lower or bottom horizontal member of a truss.

Bottom plate   The 2 by 4s or 6s that lay on the subfloor upon which the vertical studs are installed. Also called a "sole plate."

Bottoming-cycle   A means to increase the thermal efficiency of a steam electric generating system by converting some waste heat from the condenser into electricity. The heat engine in a bottoming cycle would be a condensing turbine similar in principle to a steam turbine but operating with a different working fluid at a much lower temperature and pressure.

Brace   An inclined piece of framing lumber applied to wall or floor to strengthen the structure. Often used on walls as temporary bracing until framing has been completed.

Bracket   A projecting support for a shelf or other structure.

Branch   Any part of the piping system other than a riser, main, or stack.

Branch circuit   The circuit conductors between the final overcurrent device protecting the circuit and the outlet(s).

Branch circuit, appliance   A branch circuit supplying energy to one or more outlets to which appliances are to be connected; such circuits to have no permanently connected lighting fixtures not a part of an appliance.

Branch circuit, general purpose   A branch circuit that supplies a number of outlets for lighting and appliances.

Branch circuit, individual   A branch circuit that supplies only one utilization equipment.

Branch circuit, multiwire   A branch circuit consisting of two or more ungrounded conductors having a potential difference between them, and a grounded conductor having equal potential difference between it and each ungrounded conductor of the circuit, and that is connected to the neutral or grounded conductor of the system.

Branch interval   A distance along a soil or waste stack corresponding to a story height, but not less than 8 ft (2438 mm), within which the horizontal branches from one floor or story of a building are connected to the stack.

Branch main   A water distribution pipe which extends horizontally off a main or riser to convey water to branches or fixture groups.

Branch vent   A vent connecting two or more individual vents with a vent stack or stack vent.

Brazed joints   A joint obtained by the joining of metal parts with metals or alloys that melt at a temperature above 1000°F (538°C) but lower than the melting temperature of the parts to be joined.

Bread box system   This simple passive solar hot water system consists of one or more storage tanks placed in an insulated box that has a glazed side facing the sun. A bread box system is mounted on the ground or on the roof (make sure your roof structure is strong enough to support it). Some systems use "selective" surfaces on the tank(s). These surfaces absorb sun well but inhibit radiative loss. (See "Batch heaters" and "Integral collector storage systems.")

Breaker panel   The electrical box that distributes electric power entering the home to each branch circuit (each plug and switch) and composed of circuit breakers.

Brick construction   A type of construction in which the exterior walls are bearing walls made of brick.

Brick ledge   Part of the foundation wall where brick (veneer) will rest.

Brick lintel   The metal angle iron that brick rests on, especially above a window, door, or other opening.

Brick molding   A molding for window and exterior door frames. Serves as the boundary molding for brick or other siding material and forms a rabbet for the screens and/or storm sash or combination door.

Brick mold   Trim used around an exterior door jamb that siding butts to.

Brick tie A small, corrugated metal strip @ 1″ × 6″–8″ long nailed to wall sheeting or studs. They are inserted into the grout mortar joint of the veneer brick, and holds the veneer wall to the sheeted wall behind it.

Brick veneer A vertical facing of brick laid against and fastened to sheathing of a framed wall or tile wall construction.

Brick veneer construction A type of construction in which a wood-frame construction has an exterior surface of single brick.

Bridging Pieces fitted in pairs from the bottom of one floor joist to the top of adjacent joists, and crossed to distribute the floor load. Sometimes pieces of solid stock of a width equal to the joist are used.

Brine Water saturated or strongly impregnated with salt.

British thermal unit (Btu) The amount of heat required to raise the temperature of 1 lb of water 1°F; equal to 252 calories.

Btu/h The listed maximum capacity of any appliance, absorption unit, or burner expressed in British thermal units input per hour.

Buck Often used in reference to rough frame opening members. Door bucks used in reference to metal door frame. (See "Window bucks.")

Builder's risk insurance Insurance coverage on a construction project during construction, including extended coverage that may be added for the contract for the customer's protections.

Building codes Community ordinances governing the manner in which a home may be constructed or modified.

Building drain The lowest piping that collects the discharge from all other drainage piping inside the house and conveys it to the building sewer 30 in. (762 mm) outside the building wall.

Building energy ratio The space-conditioning load of a building.

Building envelope The structural elements (walls, roof, floor, foundation) of a building that encloses conditioned space; the building shell.

Building heat-loss factor A measure of the heating requirements of a building expressed in Btu per degree-day.

Building insurance Insurance covering the structure of the building.

Building orientation The relationship of a building to true south, as specified by the direction of its longest axis.

Building overall energy loss coefficient-area product The factor, when multiplied by the monthly degree days, that yields the monthly space heating load.

Building overall heat loss rate The overall rate of heat loss from a building by means of transmission plus infiltration, expressed in Btu's per hour, per degree temperature difference between the inside and outside.

Building paper A general term for papers, felts, and similar sheet materials used in buildings without reference to their properties or uses. Generally comes in long rolls.

Building permit Authorization to build or modify a structure.

Building sewer That part of the drainage system that extends from the end of the building drain and conveys its discharge to a public sewer, private sewer, individual sewage-disposal system, or other point of disposal.

Built-up roof A roofing composed of several layers of rag felt or jute saturated with coal tar, pitch, or asphalt. The top is finished with crushed slag or gravel. Generally used on flat- or low-pitched roofs.

Bulb The transparent or opaque sphere in an electric light that the electric light transmits through.

Bulb turbine A type of hydro turbine in which the entire generator is mounted inside the water passageway as an integral unit with the turbine. These installations can offer significant reductions in the size of the powerhouse.

Bulk density The weight of a material per unit of volume compared to the weight of the same volume of water.

Bull nose (drywall) Rounded drywall corners.

Bundle A package of shingles. Normally, there are three bundles per square and 27 shingles per bundle.

Burner capacity The maximum heat output (in Btu per hour) released by a burner with a stable flame and satisfactory combustion.

Burning point The temperature at which a material ignites.

Bus (electrical) An electrical conductor that serves as a common connection for two or more electrical circuits; may be in the form of rigid bars or stranded conductors or cables.

Busbar The power conduit of an electric power plant; the starting point of the electric transmission system.

Butt Type of door hinge. One leaf is fitted into space routed into the door frame jamb and the other into the edge of the door.

Butt edge The lower edge of the shingle tabs.

Butt hinge The most common type. One leaf attaches to the door's edge, the other to its jamb.

Butt joint The junction where the ends of two timbers meet, and also where sheets of drywall meet on the 4-ft edge. To place materials end-to-end or end-to-edge without overlapping.

Buy down   A subsidy (usually paid by a builder or developer) to reduce monthly payments on a mortgage.

By-fold door   Doors that are hinged in the middle for opening in a smaller area than standard swing doors. Often used for closet doors.

Bypass doors   Doors that slide by each other and commonly used as closet doors.

Bypass   An alternative path. In a heating duct or pipe, an alternative path for the flow of the heat transfer fluid from one point to another, as determined by the opening or closing of control valves both in the primary line and the bypass line.

Cabinet   (a) An enclosure designed either for surface or flush mounting and provided with a frame, mat or trim in which a swinging door or doors are or may be hung. (b) Case or box-like assembly consisting of shelves, doors, and drawers, used primarily for storage.

Cabinet drawer guide   A wood strip used to guide the drawer as it slides in and out of its opening.

Cabinet drawer kicker   Wood cabinet member placed immediately above and generally at the center of a drawer to prevent tilting down when pulled out.

Cage   The component of an electric motor composed of solid bars (of usually copper or aluminum) arranged in a circle and connected to continuous rings at each end. This cage fits inside the stator in an induction motor in channels between laminations, thin flat discs of steel in a ring configuration.

Caisson   A hole drilled into the earth and embedded into bedrock 3 to 4 ft. The structural support for a type of foundation wall, porch, patio, monopost, or other structure. Two or more "sticks" of reinforcing bars (rebar) are inserted into and run the full length of the hole, and concrete is poured into the caisson hole.

Calorie   The amount of heat required to raise the temperature of a unit of water, at or near the temperature of maximum density, one degree Celsius (or Centigrade; C), expressed as a "small calorie" (the amount of heat required to raise the temperature of 1 gram of water one degree C), or as a "large calorie" or "kilogram calorie" [the amount of heat required to raise one kilogram (1000 grams) of water one degree C]; capitalization of the word "calorie" indicates a kilogram calorie.

Calorific value   The heat liberated by the combustion of a unit quantity of a fuel under specific conditions; measured in calories.

Camber   A slight arch in a beam or other horizontal member which prevents it from bending into a downward or concave shape due to its weight or load it is to carry.

Candela   A unit of luminous intensity; the magnitude to the candela is such that the luminance of the total radiator, at the temperature of solidification of platinum, is 60 candelas per square centimeter.

Candle power   The illuminating power of a standard candle employed as a unit for determining the illuminating quality of an illuminant.

Cant strip   A triangular-shaped strip of wood used under shingles at gable ends or under the edges of roofing on flat decks.

Cantilever   An overhang. Where one floor extends beyond and over a foundation wall, for example, at a fireplace location or bay window cantilever. Normally, not extending over 2 ft.

Cantilevered void   Foundation void material used in unusually expansive soils conditions. This void is "trapezoid" shaped and has vertical sides of 6 in. and 4 in., respectively.

Cap   The upper member of a column, pilaster, door cornice, molding, or fireplace.

Cap flashing   The portion of the flashing attached to a vertical surface to prevent water from migrating behind the base flashing.

Capability   The maximum load that a generating unit, power plant, or other electrical apparatus can carry under specified conditions for a given period of time, without exceeding its approved limits of temperature and stress.

Capability margin   The difference between net electrical system capability and system maximum load requirements (peak load); the margin of capability available to provide for scheduled maintenance, emergency outages, system operating requirements, and unforeseen loads.

Capacitance   A measure of the electrical charge of a capacitor consisting of two plates separated by an insulating material.

Capacitor   An electrical device that adjusts the leading current of an applied alternating current to balance the lag of the circuit to provide a high power factor.

Capacity   The load that a power generation unit or other electrical apparatus or heating unit is rated by the manufacturer to be able to meet or supply.

Capacity (condensing unit)   The refrigerating effect in Btu/h produced by the difference in total enthalpy between a refrigerant liquid leaving the unit and the total enthalpy of the refrigerant vapor entering it. Generally measured in tons or Btu/h.

Capacity (effective, of a motor)   The maximum load that a motor is capable of supplying.

Capacity (heating, of a material)   The amount of heat energy needed to raise the temperature of a given mass of a substance by one degree Celsius. The heat required to raise the temperature of 1 kg of water by 1 degree Celsius is 4186 joules.

Capacity factor   The ratio of the average load on (or power output of) a generating unit or system to the capacity rating of the unit or system over a specified period of time.

Capital   The principal part of a loan, i.e., the original amount borrowed.

Capital and interest   A repayment loan and the most conventional form of home loan. The borrower pays an amount each month to cover the amount borrowed (or capital or principal) *plus* the interest charged on capital.

Capital costs   The amount of money needed to purchase equipment, buildings, tools, and other manufactured goods that can be used in production.

Capped rate   The mortgage interest rate will not exceed a specified value during a certain period of time, but it will fluctuate up and down below that level.

Carbon dioxide   A colorless, odorless noncombustible gas with the formula CO_2 that is present in the atmosphere. It is formed by the combustion of carbon and carbon compounds (such as fossil fuels and biomass), by respiration, which is a slow combustion in animals and plants, and by the gradual oxidation of organic matter in the soil.

Carbon monoxide   A colorless, odorless but poisonous combustible gas with the formula CO. Carbon monoxide is produced in the incomplete combustion of carbon and carbon compounds such as fossil fuels (i.e., coal, petroleum), their products (e.g., liquefied petroleum gas, gasoline), and biomass.

Carbon zinc cell battery   A cell that produces electric energy by the galvanic oxidation of carbon; commonly used in household appliances.

Cased opening   An interior opening without a door that is finished with jambs or trim.

Casement   Frames of wood or metal enclosing part (or all) of a window sash. May be opened by means of hinges affixed to the vertical edges.

Casement window   A window with hinges on one of the vertical sides. It swings open like a normal door.

Casing   The trimming around a door or window, outside or inside, or the finished lumber around a post or beam.

Catalytic converter   An air pollution control device that removes organic contaminants by oxidizing them into carbon dioxide and water through a chemical reaction using a catalysis, which is a substance that increases (or decreases) the rate of a chemical reaction without being changed itself; required in all automobiles sold in the United States, and used in some types of heating appliances.

Cathedral ceiling/roof   A type of ceiling and roof assembly that has no attic.

Cathode   The negative pole or electrode of an electrolytic cell, vacuum tube, etc., where electrons enter (current leaves) the system; the opposite of an anode.

Cathode disconnect ballast   An electromagnetic ballast that disconnects a lamp's electrode heating circuit once is has started; often called "low-frequency electronic" ballasts.

Cathodic protection   A method of preventing oxidation of the exposed metal in structures by imposing between the structure and the ground a small electrical voltage.

Caulking   (1) A flexible material used to seal a gap between two surfaces, e.g., between pieces of siding or the corners in tub walls. (2) To fill a joint with mastic or asphalt plastic cement to prevent leaks.

CCA (chromated copper arsenate)   A pesticide that is forced into wood under high pressure to protect it from termites, other wood-boring insects, and decay caused by fungus.

Ceiling   The downward facing structural element that is directly opposite the floor.

Ceiling fan   A mechanical device used for air circulation and to provide cooling.

Ceiling joist   One of a series of parallel framing members used to support ceiling loads and supported in turn by larger beams, girders or bearing walls. (Also called "roof joist.")

Cell   A component of a electrochemical battery. A primary cell consists of two dissimilar elements, known as electrodes, immersed in a liquid or paste known as the electrolyte. A direct current of 1–1.5 V will be produced by this cell. A secondary cell or accumulator is a similar design but is made useful by passing a direct current of correct strength through it in a certain direction. Each cell will produce 2 V; a 12-V car battery contains six cells.

Cellulose   The fundamental constituent of all vegetative tissue; the most abundant material in the world.

Cellulose insulation   A type of insulation composed of waste newspaper, cardboard, or other forms of waste paper.

Celotex™   Black fibrous board that is used as exterior sheething.

Cement   The gray powder that is the "glue" in concrete. Portland cement. Also, any adhesive.

Central heating system   A system where heat is supplied to areas of a building from a single appliance through a network of ducts or pipes.

Central power plant   A large power plant that generates power for distribution to multiple customers.

Central receiver solar power plants   Also known as "power towers," these use fields of two-axis tracking mirrors known as heliostats. Each heliostat is individually positioned by a computer control system to reflect the sun's rays to a tower-mounted thermal receiver. The effect of many heliostats reflecting to a common point creates the combined energy of thousands of suns, which produces high-temperature thermal energy. In the receiver, molten nitrate salts absorb the heat energy. The hot salt is then used to boil water to steam, which is sent to a conventional steam turbine generator to produce electricity.

Ceramic tile   A man- or machine-made clay tile used to finish a floor or wall. Generally used in bathtub and shower enclosures and on counter tops.

Cetane number   A measure of a fuel's (liquid) ease of self-ignition.

CFM (cubic feet per minute)   A rating that expresses the amount of air a blower or fan can move. The volume of air (measured in cubic feet) that can pass through an opening in one minute.

Chair rail   Interior trim material installed about 3–4 ft up the wall, horizontally.

Chalk line   A line made by snapping a taut string or cord dusted with chalk. Used for alignment purposes.

Chamfer   Corner of a board beveled at a 45° angle. Two boards butt-jointed and with chamfered edges form a V-joint.

Change order   A written document which modifies the plans and specifications and/or the price of the construction contract.

Charcoal   A material formed from the incomplete combustion or destructive distillation (carbonization) of organic material in a kiln or retort, and having a high energy density, being nearly pure carbon. (If produced from coal, it is coke.) Used for cooking, the manufacture of gunpowder and steel (notably in Brazil), as an absorbent and decolorizing agent, and in sugar refining and solvent recovery.

Charge carrier   A free and mobile conduction electron or hole in a semiconductor.

Charge controller   An electronic device that regulates the electrical charge stored in batteries so that unsafe, overcharge conditions for the batteries are avoided.

Chase   A framed, enclosed space around a flue pipe or a channel in a wall, or through a ceiling for something to lie in or pass through.

Check rails   Meeting rails of a double-hung window which are made thicker to fill the opening between the top and bottom sash. They are usually beveled.

Chemical energy   The energy liberated in a chemical reaction, as in the combustion of fuels.

Chiller   A device for removing heat from a gas or liquid stream for air conditioning/cooling.

Chimney   (a) A masonry or metal stack that creates a draft to bring air to a fire and to carry the gaseous byproducts of combustion safely away. (b) One or more passageways, vertical or nearly so, for conveying flue gases to the outside atmosphere. (See "Vent.")

Chimney connector   A pipe that connects a fuel-burning appliance to a chimney.

Chimney effect   The tendency of heated air or gas to rise in a duct or other vertical passage, such as in a chimney, small enclosure, or building, due to its lower density compared to the surrounding air or gas.

Chink   To install fiberglass insulation around all exterior door and window frames, wall corners, and small gaps in the exterior wall.

Chipboard   A manufactured wood panel made out of 1–2-in. wood chips and glue. Often used as a substitute for plywood in the exterior wall and roof sheathing. Also called OSB (oriented strand board) or wafer board.

Chlorofluorocarbon (CFC)   A family of chemicals composed primarily of carbon, hydrogen, chlorine, and fluorine whose principal applications are as refrigerants and industrial cleansers and whose principal drawback is the tendency to destroy the Earth's protective ozone layer.

Circuit   (a) A device, or system of devices, that allows electrical current to flow through it and allows voltage to occur across positive and negative terminals. (b) The path of electrical flow from a power source through an outlet and back to ground.

Circuit breaker   A device designed to open and close a circuit by nonautomatic means and to open the circuit automatically on a predetermined overcurrent without damage to itself when properly applied within its rating.

Circuit lag   As time increases from zero at the terminals of an inductor, the voltage comes to a particular value on the sine function curve ahead of the current. The voltage reaches its negative peak exactly 90° before the current reaches its negative peak, thus the current lags behind by 90°.

Circulating fluidized bed   A type of furnace or reactor in which the emission of sulfur compounds is lowered by the addition of crushed limestone in the fluidized bed thus obviating the need for much of the expensive stack gas cleanup equipment. The particles are collected and recirculated, after passing through a conventional bed, and cooled by boiler internals.

Class "A"   Optimum fire rating issued by Underwriters' Laboratories on roofing. The building codes in some areas require this type of roofing for fire safety.

Class "C"   Minimum fire rating issued by the Underwriters' Laboratories for roofing materials.

Clean power generator A company or other organizational unit that produces electricity from sources that are thought to be environmentally cleaner than traditional sources. Clean, or green, power is usually defined as power from renewable energy that comes from wind, solar, biomass energy, etc. There are various definitions of clean resources. Some definitions include power produced from waste-to-energy and wood-fired plants that may still produce significant air emissions.

Cleanout An accessible opening in the drainage system used for the removal of possible obstruction.

Cleat A strip of wood fastened across a door to add strength. Also a strip fastened to a wall to support a shelf, fixture, or other objects.

Clerestory A window located high in a wall near the eaves that allows daylight into a building interior and may be used for ventilation and solar heat gain.

Climate The prevailing or average weather conditions of a geographic region.

Clip ties Sharp, cut metal wires that protrude out of a concrete foundation wall (that at one time held the foundation form panels in place).

Close coupled An energy system in which the fuel production equipment is in close proximity, or connected to, the fuel using equipment.

Closed cycle A system in which a working fluid is used over and over without introduction of new fluid, as in a hydronic heating system or mechanical refrigeration system.

Closed-loop geothermal heat pump systems Closed-loop (also known as "indirect") systems circulate a solution of water and antifreeze through a series of sealed loops of piping. Once the heat has been transferred into or out of the solution, the solution is recirculated. The loops can be installed in the ground horizontally or vertically, or they can be placed in a body of water, such as a pond. See horizontal ground loop, vertical ground loop, slinky ground loop, and surface water loop for more information on the different types of closed-loop geothermal heat pump systems.

Closet A small room or chamber used for storage.

Closet pole A round molding installed in clothes closets to accommodate clothes hangers.

CO An abbreviation for "Certificate of Occupancy." This certificate is issued by the local municipality and is required before anyone can occupy and live within the home. It is issued only after the local municipality has made all inspections and all monies and fees have been paid.

Codes Legal documents that regulate construction to protect the health, safety, and welfare of people. Codes establish minimum standards but do not guarantee efficiency or quality.

Coefficient of heat transmission (U-value) A value that describes the ability of a material to conduct heat. The number of Btu that flow through 1 square foot of material, in one hour. It is the reciprocal of the R-value (U-value = 1/R-value).

Coefficient of performance (COP) A ratio of the work or useful energy output of a system versus the amount of work or energy inputted into the system as determined by using the same energy equivalents for energy in and out. Is used as a measure of the steady-state performance or energy efficiency of heating, cooling, and refrigeration appliances. The COP is equal to the Energy Efficiency Ratio (EER) divided by 3.412. The higher the COP, the more efficient the device.

Coefficient of utilization (CU) A term used for lighting appliances; the ratio of lumens received on a flat surface to the light output, in lumens, from a lamp; used to evaluate the effectiveness of luminaries in delivering light.

Cogeneration The generation of electricity or shaft power by an energy conversion system and the concurrent use of rejected thermal energy from the conversion system as an auxiliary energy source.

Cogenerator A class of energy producer that produces both heat and electricity from a single fuel.

Coil As a component of a heating or cooling appliance, rows of tubing or pipe with fins attached through which a heat transfer fluid is circulated and to deliver heat or cooling energy to a building.

Coincidence factor The ratio of the coincident, maximum demand or two or more loads to the sum of their noncoincident maximum demand for a given period; the reciprocal of the diversity factor, it is always less than or equal to one.

Coincident demand The demand of a consumer of electricity at the time of a power supplier's peak system demand.

Cold air return The ductwork (and related grills) that carries room air back to the furnace for reheating.

Cold night sky The low effective temperature of the sky on a clear night.

Collar beam A tie beam connecting rafters considerably above the wall plate. It is also called a rafter tie.

Collar Preformed flange placed over a vent pipe to seal the roofing above the vent pipe opening. Also called a vent sleeve.

Collector The component of a solar energy heating system that collects solar radiation, and that contains components to absorb solar radiation and transfer the heat to a heat transfer fluid (air or liquid).

Collector efficiency   The ratio of solar radiation captured and transferred to the collector (heat transfer) fluid.

Collector fluid   The fluid, liquid (water or water/antifreeze solution), or air used to absorb solar energy and transfer it for direct use, indirect heating of interior air or domestic water, and/or to a heat storage medium.

Collector tilt   The angle that a solar collector is positioned from horizontal.

Color rendering or rendition   A measure of the ability of a light source to show colors, based on a color rendering index.

Color Rendition (Rendering) Index (CRI)   A measure of light quality. The maximum CRI value of 100 is given to natural daylight and incandescent lighting. The closer a lamp's CRI rating is to 100, the better its ability to show true colors to the human eye.

Color temperature   A measure of the quality of a light source by expressing the color appearance correlated with a black body.

Column   Upright supporting member circular or rectangular in shape.

Combined-cycle power plant   A power plant that uses two thermodynamic cycles to achieve higher overall system efficiency; e.g., the heat from a gas-fired combustion turbine is used to generate steam for heating or to operate a steam turbine to generate additional electricity.

Combustible material   Any material not defined as noncombustible.

Combustion   The process of burning; the oxidation of a material by applying heat, which unites oxygen with a material or fuel.

Combustion air   The air provided to fuel-burning equipment including air for fuel combustion, draft hood dilution and ventilation of the equipment enclosure.

Combustion chamber   The part of a boiler, furnace or woodstove where the burn occurs; normally lined with firebrick or molded or sprayed insulation.

Combustion gases   The gaseous byproducts of the combustion of a fuel.

Combustion power plant   A power plant that generates power by combusting a fuel.

Combustion turbine   A turbine that generates power from the combustion of a fuel.

Comfort zone   A frequently used room or area that is maintained at a more comfortable level than the rest of the house; also known as a "warm room."

Commercial building   A building with more than 50% of its floor space used for commercial activities, which include stores, offices, schools, churches, libraries, museums, health care facilities, warehouses, and government buildings, except those on military bases.

Commercial sector   Consists of businesses that are not engaged in transportation or manufacturing or other types of industrial activities. Standard Industrial Classification (SIC) codes for commercial establishments are 50 through 87, 89, and 91 through 97.

Commissioning   The process by which a power plant, apparatus, or building is approved for operation based on observed or measured operation that meets design specifications.

Common vent   A single pipe venting two trap arms within the same branch interval, either back-to-back or one above the other.

Compact fluorescent   A smaller version of standard fluorescent lamps which can directly replace standard incandescent lights. These lights consist of a gas-filled tube, and a magnetic or electronic ballast.

Complete mix digester   A type of anaerobic digester that has a mechanical mixing system and where temperature and volume are controlled to maximize the anaerobic digestion process for biological waste treatment, methane production, and odor control.

Composting   The process of degrading organic material (biomass) by microorganisms in aerobic conditions.

Composting toilet   A self-contained toilet that uses the process of aerobic decomposition (composting) to break down feces into humus and odorless gases.

Compound paraboloid collector   A form of solar concentrating collector that does not track the sun.

Compressed air storage   The storage of compressed air in a container for use to operate a prime mover for electricity generation.

Compressed natural gas (CNG)   Natural gas (methane) that has been compressed to a higher pressure gaseous state by a compressor; used in CNG vehicles.

Compression chiller   A cooling device that uses mechanical energy to produce chilled water.

Compression web   A member of a truss system which connects the bottom and top chords and which provides downward support.

Compressor   A mechanical device that pressurizes a gas in order to turn it into a liquid, thereby allowing heat to be removed or added. A compressor is the main component of conventional heat pumps and air conditioners. In an air-conditioning system, the compressor normally sits outside and has a large fan (to remove heat).

Concealed gas piping   Piping that is enclosed in the building construction without means of access.

Concealed   Rendered inaccessible by the structure or finish of the building. Wires in concealed raceways are considered concealed, even though they may become accessible by withdrawing them. [See "Accessible (as applied to wiring methods")].]

Concentrating (solar) collector A solar collector that uses reflective surfaces to concentrate sunlight onto a small area, where it is absorbed and converted to heat or, in the case of solar photovoltaic (PV) devices, into electricity. Concentrators can increase the power flux of sunlight hundreds of times. The principal types of concentrating collectors include: compound parabolic, parabolic trough, fixed reflector moving receiver, fixed receiver moving reflector, Fresnel lens, and central receiver. A PV concentrating module uses optical elements (Fresnel lens) to increase the amount of sunlight incident onto a PV cell. Concentrating PV modules/arrays must track the sun and use only the direct sunlight because the diffuse portion cannot be focused onto the PV cells. Concentrating collectors for home or small business solar water heating applications are usually parabolic troughs that concentrate the sun's energy on an absorber tube (called a receiver), which contains a heat-transfer fluid.

Concrete The mixture of Portland cement, sand, gravel, and water. Used to make garage and basement floors, sidewalks, patios, foundation walls, etc. It is commonly reinforced with steel rods (rebar) or wire screening (mesh).

Concrete block A hollow concrete brick often 8 in. × 8 in. × 16 in. in size.

Concrete board A panel made out of concrete and fiberglass usually used as a tile backing material.

Condensate The liquid resulting when water vapor contacts a cool surface; also the liquid resulting when a vaporized working fluid (such as a refrigerant) is cooled or depressurized.

Condensate line The copper pipe that runs from the outside air conditioning condenser to the inside furnace (where the A/C coil is located).

Condensation The process by which water in air changes from a vapor to a liquid due to a change in temperature or pressure; occurs when water vapor reaches its dew point (condensation point); also used to express the existence of liquid water on a surface.

Condenser The device in an air conditioner or heat pump in which the refrigerant condenses from a gas to a liquid when it is depressurized or cooled.

Condenser coil The device in an air conditioner or heat pump through which the refrigerant is circulated and releases heat to the surroundings when a fan blows outside air over the coils. This will return the hot vapor that entered the coil into a hot liquid upon exiting the coil.

Condensing appliance An appliance that condenses water generated by the burning of fuels.

Condensing furnace A type of heating appliance that extracts so much of the available heat content from a combusted fuel that the moisture in the combustion gases condenses before it leaves the furnace. Also, this furnace circulates a liquid to cool the furnace's heat exchanger. The heated liquid may either circulate through a liquid-to-air heat exchanger to warm room air or it may circulate through a coil inside a separate indirect-fired water heater.

Condensing unit The outdoor component of a central air conditioner that is designed to remove heat absorbed by the refrigerant and transfer it outside the conditioned space.

Conditioned air Air treated to control its temperature, relative humidity, or quality.

Conditioned space The space contained within an insulated building enclosure which is conditioned directly or indirectly by heating or cooling systems.

Conditioned space The space contained within an insulated building enclosure which is conditioned directly or indirectly by heating or cooling systems.

Conditions, convenants, and restrictions The standards that define how a property may be used and the protections the developer makes for the benefit of all owners in a subdivision.

Conduction The transfer of heat through a material by the transfer of kinetic energy from particle to particle; the flow of heat between two materials of different temperatures that are in direct physical contact.

Conduction band An energy band in a semiconductor in which electrons can move freely in a solid, producing a net transport of charge.

Conductivity (thermal) This is a positive constant, k, that is a property of a substance and is used in the calculation of heat transfer rates for materials. It is the amount of heat that flows through a specified area and thickness of a material over a specified period of time when there is a temperature difference of one degree between the surfaces of the material.

Conductor The material through which electricity is transmitted, such as an electrical wire, or transmission or distribution line.

Conductors Pipes for conducting water from a roof to the ground or to a receptacle or drain; downspout.

Conduit body A separate portion of a conduit or tubing system that provides access through a removable cover(s) to the interior of the system at a junction of two or more sections of the system or at a terminal point of the system. Boxes such as FS and FD or larger cast or sheet metal boxes are not classified as conduit bodies.

Conduit, electrical   A pipe, usually metal, in which wire is installed.

Confined space   A room or space having a volume less than 50 cu. ft. per 1000 Btu/h of the aggregate input rating of all fuel-burning appliances installed in that space.

Connected load   The sum of the ratings of the electricity consuming apparatus connected to a generating system.

Connection charge   An amount paid by a customer for being connected to an electricity supplier's transmission and distribution system.

Connector, pressure (solderless)   A device that establishes a connection between two or more conductors or between one or more conductors and a terminal by means of mechanical pressure and without the use of solder.

Conservation   To reduce or avoid the consumption of a resource or commodity.

Conservation cost adjustment   A means of billing electric power consumers to pay for the costs of demand side management/energy conservation measures and programs. (See "Benefits charge.")

Constant dollars   The value or purchasing power of a dollar in a specified year carried forward or backward.

Constant-speed wind turbines   Wind turbines that operate at a constant rotor revolutions per minute (RPM) and are optimized for energy capture at a given rotor diameter at a particular speed in the wind power curve.

Construction contract   A legal document which specifies the what-when-where-how-how much and by whom in a construction project.

Construction drywall   A type of construction in which the interior wall finish is applied in a dry condition, generally in the form of sheet materials or wood paneling as contrasted to plaster.

Construction, frame   A type of construction in which the structural components are wood or depend on a wood frame for support.

Consumption charge   The part of a power provider's charge based on actual energy consumed by the customer; the product of the kilowatt-hour rate and the total kilowatt-hours consumed.

Contact cement   Neoprene rubber-based adhesive which bonds instantly upon contact of parts being fastened.

Contact resistance   The resistance between metallic contacts and the semiconductor.

Continuity tester   A device that tells whether a circuit is capable of carrying electricity.

Continuous fermentation   A steady-state fermentation process.

Continuous load   A load where the maximum current is expected to continue for at least 3 hr.

Continuous waste   A drain from two or more similar adjacent fixtures connected to a single trap.

Contractor   A company licensed to perform certain types of construction activities. In most states, the generals contractor's license and some specialty contractor's licenses don't require of compliance with bonding, workmen's compensation, and similar regulations. Some of the specialty contractor licenses involve extensive training, testing and/or insurance requirements. There are various types of contractors.

Contrast   The difference between the brightness of an object compared to that of its immediate background.

Control joint   Tooled, straight grooves made on concrete floors to "control" where the concrete should crack

Control, limit   An automatic control responsive to changes in liquid flow or level, pressure, or temperature for limiting the operation of an appliance.

Control, primary safety   A safety control responsive directly to flame properties that senses the presence or absence of flame and, in the event of ignition failure or unintentional flame extinguishment, automatically causes shutdown of mechanical equipment.

Convector   A system incorporating a heating element in an enclosure in which air enters an opening below the heating element, is heated, and leaves the enclosure through an opening located above the heating element.

Convenience outlet, gas   A permanently mounted hand-operated device for connecting and disconnecting an appliance to the gas supply piping conforming to AGA 7. The device includes an integral, manually operated gas valve so that the appliance is capable of being disconnected only when the valve is in the closed position.

Conventional fuel   The fossil fuels: coal, oil, and natural gas.

Conventional heat pump   This type of heat pump is known as an air-to-air system.

Conventional loan   A mortgage loan not insured by a government agency (such as FHA or VA).

Conventional power   Power generation from sources such as petroleum, natural gas, or coal. In some cases, large-scale hydropower and nuclear power generation are considered conventional sources.

Conversion efficiency   The amount of energy produced as a percentage of the amount of energy consumed.

Converter   A device for transforming the quality and quantity of electrical energy; also an inverter.

Convertibility   The ability to change a loan from an adjustable-rate schedule to a fixed-rate schedule.

Cooking unit, counter-mounted   A cooking appliance designed for mounting in or on a counter and consisting of one or more heating elements, internal wiring, and built-in or separately mountable controls. (See "Oven, wall-mounted.")

Cooling capacity   The quantity of heat that a cooling appliance is capable of removing from a room in 1 hr.

Cooling degree day   A value used to estimate interior air cooling requirements (load) calculated as the number of degrees per day (over a specified period) that the daily average temperature is above 65°F (or some other, specified base temperature). The daily average temperature is the mean of the maximum and minimum temperatures recorded for a specific location for a 24-h period.

Cooling load   That amount of cooling energy to be supplied (or heat and humidity removed) based on the sensible and latent loads.

Cooling pond   A body of water used to cool the water that is circulated in an electric power plant.

Cooling tower   A structure used to cool power plant water; water is pumped to the top of the tubular tower and sprayed out into the center; it is then cooled by evaporation as it falls, and then is either recycled within the plant or is discharged.

Cope   To cut or shape the end of a molded wood member so it will cover and fit the contour of an adjoining piece of molding.

Coped   Removing the top and bottom flange of the end(s) of a metal I-beam. This is done to permit it to fit within, and be bolted to, the web of another I-beam in a "T" arrangement.

Coped joint   Cutting and fitting woodwork to an irregular surface.

Copper-clad aluminum conductors   Conductors drawn from a copper-clad aluminum rod with the copper metallurgically bonded to an aluminum core. The copper forms a minimum of 10 percent of the cross-sectional area of a solid conductor or each strand of a stranded conductor.

Coproducts   The potentially useful byproducts of ethanol fermentation process.

Corbel   The triangular, decorative and supporting member that holds a mantel or horizontal shelf.

Corbel out   To extend outward from the surface of a masonry wall one or more courses to form a supporting ledge.

Cord (of wood)   A stack of wood 4 ft by 4 ft by 8 ft.

Corner bead   (a) A strip of formed sheet metal placed on outside corners of drywall before applying drywall 'mud.' (b) Molding used to protect corners. Also a metal reinforcement placed on corners before plastering.

Corner boards   Used as trim for the external corners of a house or other frame structure against which the ends of the siding are finished.

Corner braces   Diagonal braces let into studs to reinforce corners of frame structures.

Cornice   Overhang of a pitched roof, usually consisting of a fascia board, a soffit, and appropriate trim moldings.

Cornice   Exterior trim of a structure at the meeting of the roof and wall; usually consists of panels, boards, and moldings.

Coulomb   A unit for the quantity of electricity transported in 1 second by a current of 1 ampere.

Counterflashing   Flashing used on chimneys at the roof-line to cover shingle flashing and prevent moisture entry.

Counterflow heat exchanger   A heat exchanger in which two fluids flow in opposite directions for transfer heat energy from one to the other.

Counterfort   A foundation wall section that strengthens (and generally perpendicular to) a long section of foundation wall.

Course   A row of shingles or roll roofing running the length of the roof. Parallel layers of building materials such as bricks, or siding laid up horizontally.

Cove molding   Molding with a concave profile used primarily where two members meet at a right angle.

Covenants   Restrictions on the use of a property.

Crawlspace   The unoccupied and usually unfinished and unconditioned space between the floor, foundation walls, and the slab or ground of a building.

Creosote   A liquid byproduct of wood combustion (or distillation) that condenses on the internal surfaces of vents and chimneys, which if not removed regularly, can corrode the surfaces and fuel a chimney fire.

Cricket   A second roof built on top of the primary roof to increase the slope of the roof or valley. A saddle-shaped, peaked construction connecting a sloping roof with a chimney. Designed to encourage water drainage away from the chimney joint.

Cripple jack (cripple rafter)   A rafter which intersects neither the plate nor the ridge and is terminated at each end by hip and valley rafters.

Cripple stud   A stud used above a wall opening. Extends from the header above the opening to the top plate. Also used beneath a wall opening between sole plate and rough sill.

Critical compression pressure   The highest possible pressure in a fuel-air mixture before spontaneous ignition occurs.

Cross bridging   Diagonal bracing between adjacent floor joists, placed near the center of the joist span to prevent joists from twisting.

Cross connection Any connection between two otherwise separate piping systems whereby there may be a flow from one system to the other.

Cross tee Short metal "T" beam used in suspended ceiling systems to bridge the spaces between the main beams.

Crown molding A molding used on cornice or wherever an interior angle is to be covered, especially at the roof and wall corner.

Crystalline silicon photovoltaic cell A type of photovoltaic cell made from a single crystal or a polycrystalline slice of silicon. Crystalline silicon cells can be joined together to form a module (or panel).

Cube law In reference to wind energy, for any given instant, the power available in the wind is proportional to the cube of the wind velocity; when wind speed doubles, the power availability increases eight times.

Cubic foot (of natural gas) A unit of volume equal to 1 cubic foot at a pressure base of 14.73 pounds standard per square inch absolute and a temperature base of 60 degrees Fahrenheit.

Culvert Round, corrugated drain pipe (normally 15-in. or 18-in. diameter) that is installed beneath a driveway and parallel to and near the street.

Cupola Small vented four-sided structure installed on a roof. Adds decoration to the building and provides ventilation for the attic.

Cupping A type of warping that causes boards to curl up at their edges.

Curb The short elevation of an exterior wall above the deck of a roof. Normally a 2 by 6 box (on the roof) on which a skylight is attached.

Curb stop Normally a cast iron pipe with a lid (5-in. diameter) that is placed vertically into the ground, situated near the water tap in the yard, and where a water cut-off valve to the home is located (underground). A long pole with a special end is inserted into the curb stop to turn off/on the water.

Current (electrical) The flow of electrical energy (electricity) in a conductor, measured in amperes.

Curtain wall A wall, usually nonbearing, between piers or columns.

Customer charge An amount to be paid for energy periodically by a customer without regard to demand or energy consumption.

Customer class Categories of energy consumers, as defined by consumption or demand levels, patterns, and conditions, and generally included residential, commercial, industrial, agricultural.

Cut-in brace Nominal 2-in.-thick members, usually 2 by 4s, cut in between each stud diagonally.

Cut-in speed The lowest wind speed at which a wind turbine begins producing usable power.

Cutout bo An enclosure designed for surface mounting and having swinging doors or covers secured directly to and telescoping with the walls of the box proper. (See "Cabinet.")

Cutout speed The highest wind speed at which a wind turbine stops producing power.

Cycle In alternating current, the current goes from zero potential or voltage to a maximum in one direction, back to zero, and then to a maximum potential or voltage in the other direction. The number of complete cycles per second determines the current frequency; in the United States, the standard for alternating current is 60 cycles.

Cycling losses The loss of heat as the water circulates through a water heater tank and inlet and outlet pipes.

Cyclone burner A furnace/combustion chamber in which finely ground fuel is blown in spirals in the combustion chamber to maximize combustion efficiency.

Dado (a) A groove cut into a board or panel intended to receive the edge of a connecting board or panel. (b) A rectangular groove cut in wood across the grain.

Dam A structure for impeding and controlling the flow of water in a water course, and which increases the water elevation to create the hydraulic head. The reservoir creates, in effect, stored energy.

Damper A movable plate used to control air flow; in a wood stove or fireplace, used to control the amount and direction of air going to the fire.

Damper, volume A device that will restrict, retard or direct the flow of air in any duct, or the products of combustion of heat-producing equipment, vent connector, vent, or chimney.

Dampproofing The black, tar-like waterproofing material applied to the exterior of a foundation wall.

Darrius (wind) machine A type of vertical-axis wind machine that has long, thin blades in the shape of loops connected to the top and bottom of the axle; often called an "eggbeater windmill."

Daylight The end of a pipe (the terminal end) that is not attached to anything.

Daylighting The use of direct, diffuse, or reflected sunlight to provide supplemental lighting for building interiors.

Dead bolt (also called a dead lock) Special door security consisting of a hardened steel bolt and a lock. Lock is operated by a key on the outside and by either a key or handle on the inside.

Dead end A branch leading from a DWV system terminating at a developed length of 2 ft (610 mm) or more. Dead ends shall be prohibited except as an approved part of a rough-in for future connection.

Dead front   Without live parts exposed to a person on the operating side of the equipment.

Dead light   The fixed, nonoperable window section of a window unit.

Dead load   The weight of permanent, stationary construction included in a building.

Decay   Disintegration of wood substance due to action of wood-destroying fungi.

Decentralized (energy) system   Energy systems supply individual, or small groups, of energy loads.

Deck, decked   To install the plywood or wafer board sheeting on the floor joists, rafters, or trusses.

Declining block rate   An electricity supplier rate structure in which the per-unit price of electricity decreases as the amount of energy increases. Normally only available to very large consumers.

Decommissioning   The process of removing a power plant, apparatus, equipment, building, or facility from operation.

Decomposition   The process of breaking down organic material; reduction of the net energy level and change in physical and chemical composition of organic material.

Decorative gas appliance, vented   A vented appliance installed for the aesthetic effect of the flames rather than functional effects.

Decorative gas appliances for installation in vented fireplaces   A vented, gas-fired appliance designed for installation within the fire chamber of a vented fireplace, wherein the primary function lies in the aesthetic effect of the flames.

Dedicated circuit   An electrical circuit that serves only one appliance (e.g., dishwasher) or a series of electric heaters or smoke detectors.

De-energize(d)   To disconnect a transmission and/or distribution line; a power line that is not carrying a current; to open a circuit.

Deep discharge   Discharging a battery to 20% or less of its full charge capacity.

Default   Breach of a mortgage contract (not making the required payments).

Degree day   A unit for measuring the extent that the outdoor daily average temperature (the mean of the maximum and minimum daily dry-bulb temperatures) falls below (in the case of heating, see "Heating degree day"), or falls above (in the case of cooling, see "Cooling degree day") an assumed base temperature, normally taken as 65°F, unless otherwise stated. One degree day is counted for each degree below (for heating) or above (in the case of cooling) the base, for each calendar day on which the temperature goes below or above the base.

Degree hour   The product of 1 h, and usually the number of degrees Fahrenheit the hourly mean temperature is above a base point (usually 65°F); used in roughly estimating or measuring the cooling load in cases where processed heat, heat from building occupants, and humidity are relatively unimportant compared to the dry-bulb temperature.

Dehumidifier   A device that cools air by removing moisture from it.

Dehumidistat   A control mechanism used to operate a mechanical ventilation system based upon the relative humidity in the home.

Delamination   Separation of the plies in a panel due to failure of the adhesive. Usually caused by excessive moisture.

Demand   The rate at which electricity is delivered to or by a system, part of a system, or piece of equipment expressed in kilowatts, kilovoltamperes, or other suitable unit, at a given instant or averaged over a specified period of time.

Demand charge   A charge for the maximum rate at which energy is used during peak hours of a billing period. That part of a power provider service charged for on the basis of the possible demand as distinguished from the energy actually consumed.

Demand factor   The ratio of the maximum demand of a system, or part of a system, to the total connected load of a system or the part of the system under consideration.

Demand (tankless) water heater   A type of water heater that has no storage tank thus eliminating storage tank stand-by losses. Cold water travels through a pipe into the unit, and either a gas burner or an electric element heats the water only when needed.

Demand(ed) factor   The ratio of the maximum demand on an electricity generating and distribution system to the total connected load on the system; usually expressed as a percentage.

Demand-side management (DSM)   The process of managing the consumption of energy, generally to optimize available and planned generation resources.

Demolition permit   Authorization to tear down and remove an existing structure.

Dendrite   A slender, threadlike spike of pure crystalline material, such as silicon.

Dendritic web technique   A method for making sheets of polycrystalline silicon in which silicon dendrites are slowly withdrawn from a melt of silicon whereupon a web of silicon forms between the dendrites and solidifies as it rises from the melt and cools.

Department of Agriculture (USDA)   A federal government agency involved in rural development, marketing and regulatory programs, food safety, research, education and economics, food, nutrition and consumer service, farm and foreign agricultural services, and natural resources and environment programs.

Department of Energy (DOE)   A federal government agency, created in 1977, that is entrusted to contribute to the welfare of the United States by providing technical information, and a scientific and educational foundation for technology, policy, and institutional leadership to achieve efficiency in energy use, diversity in energy sources, a more productive and competitive economy, improved environmental quality, and a secure national defense.

Dependable capacity   The load-carrying ability of an electric power plant during a specific time interval and period when related to the characteristics of the load to be/being supplied; determined by capability, operating power factor, and the portion of the load the station is to supply.

Derating   The production of energy by a system or appliance at a level less than its design or nominal capacity.

Deregulation   The process of changing regulatory policies and laws to increase competition among suppliers of commodities and services. The process of deregulating the electric power industry was initiated by the Energy Policy Act of 1992. (See also "Restructuring.")

Desiccant   A material used to desiccate (dry) or dehumidify air.

Desiccant cooling   To condition/cool air by dessication.

Desiccation   The process of removing moisture; involves evaporation.

Design cooling load   The amount of conditioned air to be supplied by a cooling system; usually the maximum amount to be delivered based on a specified number of cooling degree days or design temperature.

Design heating load   The amount of heated air, or heating capacity, to be supplied by a heating system; usually the maximum amount to be delivered based on a specified number of heating degree days or design outside temperature.

Design life   Period of time a system or appliance (or component of) is expected to function at its nominal or design capacity without major repair.

Design temperature   The temperature that a system is designed to maintain (inside) or operate against (outside) under the most extreme conditions.

Design tip speed ratio   For a wind turbine, the ratio of the speed of the tip of a turbine blade for which the power coefficient is at maximum.

Design voltage   The nominal voltage for which a conductor or electrical appliance is designed; the ref-erence voltage for identification and not necessarily the precise voltage at which it operates.

Desuperheater   An energy-saving device in a heat pump that, during the cooling cycle, recycles some of the waste heat from the house to heat domestic water.

Developed length   The length of a pipeline measured along the centerline of the pipe and fittings.

Device   A unit of an electrical system that is intended to carry but not utilize electric energy.

Dewpoint   The temperature to which air must be cooled, at constant pressure and water vapor content, in order for saturation or condensation to occur; the temperature at which the saturation pressure is the same as the existing vapor pressure. (Also called "saturation point.")

Diameter   Unless specifically stated, the term "diameter" is the nominal diameter as designated by the approved material standard.

Difference of potential   The difference in electrical pressure (voltage) between any two points in an electrical system or between any point in an electrical system and the earth.

Differential thermostat   A type of automatic thermostat (used on solar heating systems) that responds to temperature differences (between collectors and the storage components) so as to regulate the functioning of appliances (to switch transfer fluid pumps on and off).

Diffuse solar radiation   Sunlight scattered by atmospheric particles and gases so that it arrives at the earth's surface from all directions and cannot be focused.

Diffusion   The movement of individual molecules through a material; permeation of water vapor through a material.

Diffusion length   The mean distance a free electron or hole moves before recombining with another hole or electron.

Digester (anaerobic)   A device in which organic material is biochemically decomposed (digested) by anaerobic bacteria to treat the material and/or to produce biogas.

Dilution air   Air that enters a draft hood or draft regulator and mixes with flue gases.

Dimension lumber   Lumber 2 to 5 in. thick, and up to 12 in. wide.

Dimensional stability   The ability of a material to resist changes in its dimensions due to temperature, moisture, and physical stress.

Dimmer   A light control device that allows light levels to be manually adjusted. A dimmer can save energy by reducing the amount of power delivered to the light while consuming very little themselves.

Diode   An electronic device that allows current to flow in one direction only.

Dip tube   A tube inside a domestic water heater that distributes the cold water from the cold water supply line into the lower area of the water heater where heating occurs.

Direct access   The ability of an electric power consumer to purchase electricity from a supplier of his or her choice without being physically inhibited by the owner of the electric distribution and transmission system to which the consumer is connected. (See "Open access.")

Direct beam radiation   Solar radiation that arrives in a straight line from the sun.

Direct current   A type of electricity transmission and distribution by which electricity flows in one direction through the conductor; usually relatively low voltage and high current; typically abbreviated as dc.

Direct gain   The process by which sunlight directly enters a building through the windows and is absorbed and stored in massive floors or walls.

Direct gain system   Passive solar construction in which the sun shines directly into living space to heat it.

Direct solar water heater   This system uses water as the fluid that is circulated through the collector to the storage tank. (Also known as "open-loop" system.)

Direct vent appliance   A fuel-burning appliance with a sealed combustion system that draws all air for combustion from the outside atmosphere and discharges all flue gases to the outside atmosphere.

Direct vent heater   A type of combustion heating system in which combustion air is drawn directly from outside and the products of combustion are vented directly outside. These features are beneficial in tight, energy-efficient homes because they will not depressurize a home and cause air infiltration and backdrafting of other combustion appliances.

Direct water heater   A type of water heater in which heated water is stored within the tank. Hot water is released from the top of the tank when a hot water faucet is turned. This water is replaced with cold water that flows into the tank and down to just above the bottom plate under which are the burners.

Disconnecting means   A device, or group of devices, or other means by which the conductors of a circuit can be disconnected from their source of supply.

Discount rate   The interest rate at which the Federal Reserve System stands ready to lend reserves to commercial banks. The rate is proposed by the 12 Federal Reserve banks and determined with the approval of the Board of Governors.

Discounting   A method of financial and economic analysis used to determine present and future values of investments or expenses.

Dispatchability   The ability to dispatch power.

Dispatching   To schedule and control the generation and delivery of electric power.

Displacement power   A source of power (electricity) that can displace power from another source so that source's power can be transmitted to more distant loads.

Distributed generation   A term used by the power industry to describe localized or on-site power generation.

Distribution   The process of distributing electricity; usually defines that portion of a power provider's power lines between a power provider's power pole and transformer and a customer's point of connection/meter.

Distribution feeder   See "Feeder."

Distribution line   One or more circuits of a distribution system on the same line or poles or supporting structures usually operating at a lower voltage relative to the transmission line.

Distribution system   That portion of an electricity supply system used to deliver electricity from points on the transmission system to consumers.

District heating   A heating system in which steam or hot water for space heating or hot water is piped from a central boiler plant or electric power/heating plant to a cluster of buildings.

Diversity factor   The ratio of the sum of the noncoincidental maximum demands of two or more loads to their coincidental maximum demands for the same period.

Dome (geodesic)   An architectural design invented by Buckminster Fuller with a regular polygonal structure based on radial symmetry.

Domestic hot water   Water heated for residential washing, bathing, etc.

Donor   In a solar photovoltaic device, an *n*-type dopant, such as phosphorus, that puts an additional electron into an energy level very near the conduction band; this electron is easily exited into the conduction band where it increases the electrical conductivity over that of an undoped semiconductor.

Door frame   An assembly of wood parts that form an enclosure and support for a door. Door frames are classified as exterior and interior.

Door operator   An automatic garage door opener.

Door stop   A molding nailed to the faces of the door frame jambs to prevent the door from swinging through.

Doorjamb, interior   The surrounding case into which and out of which a door closes and opens. It consists of two upright pieces, called side jambs, and a horizontal head jamb. These three jambs have the "door stop" installed on them.

Doping   The addition of dopants to a semiconductor.

Dormer   A projecting structure built out from a sloping roof. Usually includes one or more windows.

Double glass   Window or door in which two panes of glass are used with a sealed air space between. (Also known as "insulating glass.")

Double hung window   A window with two vertically sliding sashes, both of which can move up and down.

Double-pane or glazed window   A type of window having two layers (panes or glazing) of glass separated by an air space. Each layer of glass and surrounding air space reradiates and traps some of the heat that passes through, thereby increasing the windows resistance to heat loss (R-value).

Double wall heat exchanger   A heat exchanger in a solar water heating system that has two distinct walls between the heat transfer fluid and the domestic water, to ensure that there is no mixing of the two.

Downspout   A pipe, usually metal, for carrying rainwater down from the roof's horizontal gutters.

Downwind wind turbine   A horizontal axis wind turbine in which the rotor is downwind of the tower.

Draft   (a) A column of burning combustion gases that are so hot and strong that the heat is lost up the chimney before it can be transferred to the house. A draft brings air to the fire to help keep it burning. (b) The flow of gases or air through chimney, flue, or equipment caused by pressure differences. A *mechanical or induced* draft is developed by fan, air, steam jet, or other mechanical means. A *natural* draft is developed by the difference in temperature of hot gases and outside atmosphere.

Draft diverter   A door-like device located at the mouth of a fireplace chimney flue for controlling the direction and flow of the draft in the fireplace as well as the amount of oxygen that the fire receives.

Draft hood   A device built into or installed above a combustion appliance to ensure the escape of combustion byproducts, to prevent backdrafting of the appliance, or to neutralize the effects of the stack action of the chimney or vent on the operation of the appliance.

Draft regulator   A device that functions to maintain a desired draft in the appliance by automatically reducing the draft to the desired value.

Drag   Resistance caused by friction in the direction opposite to that of movement (i.e., motion) of components such as wind turbine blades.

Drain   Any pipe that carries soil and water-borne wastes in a building drainage system.

Drain tile   A perforated, corrugated plastic pipe laid at the bottom of the foundation wall and used to drain excess water away from the foundation. It prevents ground water from seeping through the foundation wall. (Also called "perimeter drain.")

Drainage fitting   A pipe fitting designed to provide connections in the drainage system which have provisions for establishing the desired slope in the system. These fittings are made from a variety of both metals and plastics. The methods of coupling provide for required slope in the system. (See "Durham fitting.")

Drainback (solar) systems   A closed-loop solar heating system in which the heat transfer fluid in the collector loop drains into a tank or reservoir whenever the booster pump stops to protect the collector loop from freezing.

Draw   The amount of progress billings on a contract that is currently available to a contractor under a contract with a fixed payment schedule.

Drip   (a) A member of a cornice or other horizontal exterior finish course that has a projection beyond the other parts for throwing off water. (b) A groove in the underside of a sill or drip cap to cause water to drop off on the outer edge instead of drawing back and running down the face of the building.

Drip cap   A molding or metal flashing placed on the exterior topside of a door or window frame to cause water to drip beyond the outside of the frame.

Drip groove   Semicircular groove on the underside of a drip cap or the lip of a window sill which prevents water from running back under the member.

Drop siding   Siding, usually ¾ in. thick and machined into various patterns. Drop siding has tongue-and-groove or shiplap joints.

Dry bulb temperature   The temperature of the air as measured by a standard thermometer.

Dry in   To install the black roofing felt (tar paper) on the roof.

Dry rot   A term loosely applied to many types of decay but especially to that which, when in an advanced stage, permits the wood to be easily crushed to a dry powder.

Dry steam geothermal plants   Conventional turbine generators are used with the dry steam resources. The steam is used directly, eliminating the need for boilers and boiler fuel that characterizes other steam-power-generating technologies. This technology is limited because dry-steam hydrothermal resources are extremely rare. The Geysers, in California, is the nation's only dry steam field.

Drywall [gypsum wallboard (GWB)]   A manufactured panel made out of gypsum plaster and encased in a thin cardboard. Usually ½ in. thick and 4 ft by 8 ft or 4 ft by 12 ft in size. The panels are nailed or screwed onto the framing and the joints are taped and covered with a joint compound. Green board–type drywall has a greater resistance to moisture than regular (white) plasterboard and is used in bathrooms and other "wet areas." Also known as "sheet rock" or "plasterboard." (See "Wallboard.")

Dual duct system   An air-conditioning system that has two ducts—one is heated, and the other is cooled—so that air of the correct temperature is provided by mixing varying amounts of air from each duct.

Duct fan   An axial flow fan mounted in a section of duct to move conditioned air.

Duct system   A duct system is a continuous passageway for the transmission of air which, in addition to ducts, includes but is not limited to duct fittings, dampers, plenums, fans, and accessory air-handling equipment.

Ducts   The heating system. Usually round or rectangular metal pipes installed for distributing warm (or cold) air from the furnace to rooms in the home. Also a tunnel made of galvanized metal or rigid fiberglass, which carries air from the heater or ventilation opening to the rooms in a building.

Dura board, dura rock   A panel made out of concrete and fiberglass usually used as a ceramic tile backing material. Commonly used on bathtub decks. (Sometimes called "Wonder board.")

Durham fitting   A special type of drainage fitting for use in the "Durham systems" installations in which the joints are made with recessed and tapered threaded fittings, as opposed to bell and spigot lead/oakum or solvent/cemented or soldered joints. The tapping is at an angle [not 90° (1.57 rad)] to provide for proper slope in otherwise rigid connections.

Durham system   A term used to describe soil or waste systems where all piping is of threaded pipe, tube or other such rigid construction using recessed drainage fittings to correspond to the types of piping.

Duty cycle   The duration and periodicity of the operation of a device.

Dwelling unit   One or more rooms for the use of one or more persons as a housekeeping unit with space for eating, living, and sleeping, and permanent provisions for cooking and sanitation.

DWV (drain–waste–vent)   The section of a plumbing system that carries water and sewer gases out of a home.

Dynamic head   The pressure equivalent of the velocity of a fluid.

Dynamo   A machine for converting mechanical energy into electrical energy by magnetoelectric induction; may be used as a motor.

Dynamometer   An apparatus for measuring force or power, especially the power developed by a motor.

Dyne   The absolute centimeter-gram-second unit of force; that force that will impart to a free mass of one gram an acceleration of one centimeter per second per second.

Earnest money   A sum paid to the seller to show that a potential purchaser is serious about buying.

Earth beam   A mound of dirt next to exterior walls to provide wind protection and insulation.

Earth cooling tube   A long, underground metal or plastic pipe through which air is drawn. As air travels through the pipe it gives up some of its heat to the soil, and enters the house as cooler air.

Earth-coupled ground source (geothermal) heat pump   A type of heat pump that uses sealed horizontal or vertical pipes, buried in the ground, as heat exchangers through which a fluid is circulated to transfer heat.

Earth sheltered houses   Houses that have earth berms around exterior walls.

Earth-ship   A registered trademark name for houses built with tires, aluminum cans, and earth.

Earthquake strap   A metal strap used to secure gas hot water heaters to the framing or foundation of a house. Intended to reduce the chances of having the water heater fall over in an earthquake and causing a gas leak.

Eased edge   Corner slightly rounded or shaped to a slight radius.

Easement   A formal contract which allows a party to use another party's property for a specific purpose; e.g., a sewer easement might allow one party to run a sewer line through a neighbor's property.

Eaves   The lower part of a roof that projects over an exterior wall. (Also called "the overhang.")

Eccentric   A device for converting continuous circular motion into reciprocating rectilinear motion.

Economizer   A heat exchanger for recovering heat from flue gases for heating water or air.

Effective capacity   The maximum load that a device is capable of carrying.

Effective opening   The minimum cross-sectional area at the point of water supply discharge, measured or expressed in terms of (1) the diameter of a circle, or (2) the diameter of a circle of equivalent cross-sectional area, if the opening is not circular (this is applicable to an air gap).

Efficacy   The amount of energy service or useful energy delivered per unit of energy input. Often used in reference to lighting systems, where the visible light output of a luminary is relative to power input; expressed in lumens per watt; the higher the efficacy value, the higher the energy efficiency.

Efficiency   Under the First Law of Thermodynamics, efficiency is the ratio of work or energy output to work or energy input, and cannot exceed 100%. Efficiency under the Second law of thermodynamics is determined by the ratio of the theoretical minimum energy that is required to accomplish a task relative to the energy actually consumed to accomplish the task. Generally, the measured efficiency of a device, as defined by the First law, will be higher than that defined by the Second law.

Efficiency (appliance) ratings   A measure of the efficiency of an appliance's energy efficiency.

Egress   A means of exiting the structure. An egress window is required in every bedroom and basement.

Elasticity of demand   The ratio of the percentage change in the quantity of a good or service demanded to the percentage change in the price.

Elbow   A pressure pipe fitting designed to provide an exact change in direction of a pipe run. An elbow provides a sharp turn in the flow path. (See "Bend" and "Sweep.")

Electric circuit   The path followed by electrons from a generation source, through an electrical system, and returning to the source.

Electric energy   The amount of work accomplished by electrical power, usually measured in kilowatt-hours (kWh). One kilowatt-hour is 1000 watts and is equal to 3413 Btu.

Electric furnace   An air heater in which air is blown over electric resistance heating coils.

Electric lateral   The trench or area in the yard where the electric service line (from a transformer or pedestal) is located, or the work of installing the electric service to a home.

Electric moisture meter   Meter used to determine the moisture content of wood. Action is based on electrical resistance or capacitance which varies with change in moisture content.

Electric power plant   A facility or piece of equipment that produces electricity.

Electric power sector   Those privately or publicly owned establishments that generate, transmit, distribute, or sell electricity.

Electric power transmission   The transmission of electricity through power lines.

Electric rate   The unit price and quantity to which it applies as specified in a rate schedule or contract.

Electric rate schedule   A statement of the electric rate(s), terms, and conditions for electricity sale or supply.

Electric resistance coils   Metal wires that heat up when electric current passes through them and are used in baseboard heaters and electric water heaters.

Electric resistance heating   A heating system in which heat, resulting when electric current flows through an "element" or conductor, such as Nichrome, which has a high resistance, is radiated to a room.

Electric system   The physically connected generation, transmission, and distribution facilities and components operated as a unit.

Electric system loss(es)   The total amount of electric energy loss in an electric system between the generation source and points of delivery.

Electric utility   A corporation, person, agency, authority, or other legal entity that owns and/or operates facilities for the generation, transmission, distribution, or sale of electricity primarily for use by the public. (Also known as a "power provider.")

Electrical charge   A condition that results from an imbalance between the number of protons and the number of electrons in a substance.

Electrical energy   The energy of moving electrons.

Electrical entrance package   The entry point of the electrical power including: (1) the 'strike' or location where the overhead or underground electrical lines connect to the house; (2) the meter which measures how much power is used; and (3) the panel or circuit breaker box (or fuse box) where the power can be shut off and where overload devices such a fuses or circuit breakers and located.

Electrical permit   A separate permit required for most electrical work.

Electrical rough   Work performed by the electrical contractor after the plumber and heating contractor are complete with their phase of work. Normally all electrical wires, and outlet, switch, and fixture boxes are installed (before insulation).

Electrical system energy losses   A measure of the amount of energy lost during the generation, transmission, and distribution of electricity.

Electrical trim   Work performed by the electrical contractor when the house is nearing completion. The electrician installs all plugs, switches, light fixtures, smoke detectors, appliance "pig tails," and bath ventilation fans; wires the furnace; and makes up the electric house panel. The electrician does all work necessary to get the home ready for and to pass the municipal electrical final inspection.

Electricity generation   The process of producing electricity by transforming other forms or sources of energy into electrical energy; measured in kilowatt-hours.

Electricity grid   A common term referring to an electricity transmission and distribution system.

Electrochemical cell   A device containing two conducting electrodes—one positive, and the other negative—made of dissimilar materials (usually metals) that are immersed in a chemical solution (electrolyte) that transmits positive ions from the negative to the positive electrode and thus forms an electrical charge. One or more cells constitute a battery.

Electrode   A conductor that is brought in conducting contact with a ground.

Electrodeposition   Electrolytic process in which a metal is deposited at the cathode from a solution of its ions.

Electrolysis   A chemical change in a substance that results from the passage of an electric current through an electrolyte. The production of commercial hydrogen by separating the elements of water, hydrogen, and oxygen by charging the water with an electrical current.

Electrolyte   A nonmetallic (liquid or solid) conductor that carries current by the movement of ions (instead of electrons) with the liberation of matter at the electrodes of an electrochemical cell.

Electromagnetic energy   Energy generated from an electromagnetic field produced by an electric current flowing through a superconducting wire kept at a specific low temperature.

Electromagnetic field (emf)   The electrical and magnetic fields created by the presence or flow of electricity in an electrical conductor or electricity consuming appliance or motor.

Electromotive force   The amount of energy derived from an electrical source per unit quantity of electricity passing through the source.

Electron   An elementary particle of an atom with a negative electrical charge and a mass of 1/1837 of a proton; electrons surround the positively charged nucleus of an atom and determine the chemical properties of an atom.

Electron volt   The amount of kinetic energy gained by an electron when accelerated through an electric potential difference of 1 V; equivalent to 1.603×10^{-12}; a unit of energy or work; abbreviated as eV.

Electronic ballast   A device that uses electronic components to regulate the voltage of fluorescent lamps.

Elevation sheet   The page on the blueprints that depicts the house or room as if a vertical plane were passed through the structure.

Elevation   The height of an object above grade level. Also means a type of drawing which shows the front, rear, and sides of a building.

Ellipsoidal reflector lamp   A lamp with a light beam focused 2 in. ahead of the lamp, reducing the amount of light trapped in the fixture.

Emission factor   A measure of the average amount of a specified pollutant or material emitted for a specific type of fuel or process.

Emission(s)   A substance(s) or pollutant emitted as a result of a process.

Emissivity   The ratio of the radiant energy (heat) leaving (being emitted by) a surface to that of a black body at the same temperature and with the same area; expressed as a number between 0 and 1.

Enclosed   Surrounded by a case, housing, fence or walls that will prevent persons from accidentally contacting energized parts.

Enclosure   The case or housing of apparatus, or the fence or walls surrounding an installation, to prevent personnel from accidentally contacting energized parts or to protect the equipment from physical damage.

End use   The purpose for which useful energy or work is consumed.

Endothermic   A heat-absorbing reaction or a reaction that requires heat.

Energize(d)   To send electricity through an electricity transmission and distribution network; a conductor or power line that is carrying current.

Energized   Electrically connected to a source of potential difference.

Energy   The capability of doing work; different forms of energy can be converted to other forms, but the total amount of energy remains the same.

Energy audit   A survey that shows how much energy you use in your house or apartment. It will help you find ways to use less energy.

Energy charge   That part of an electricity bill that is based on the amount of electrical energy consumed or supplied.

Energy density   The ratio of available energy per pound; usually used to compare storage batteries.

Energy efficiency ratio (EER)   The measure of the instantaneous energy efficiency of room air conditioners; the cooling capacity in Btu/hr divided by the watts of power consumed at a specific outdoor temperature (usually 95°F).

Energy-efficient mortgages   A type of home mortgage that takes into account the energy savings of a home that has cost-effective energy saving improvements that will reduce energy costs thereby allowing the homeowner to more income to the mortgage payment. A borrower can qualify for a larger loan amount than otherwise would be possible.

Energy factor (EF)   The measure of overall efficiency for a variety of appliances. For water heaters, the energy factor is based on three factors: (1) the recovery efficiency, or how efficiently the heat from the energy source is transferred to the water; (2) stand-by losses, or the percentage of heat lost per hour from the stored water compared to the content of the water; and (3) cycling losses. For dishwashers, the energy factor is defined as the number of cycles per kWh of input power. For clothes washers, the energy factor is defined as the cubic foot capacity per kWh of input power per cycle. For clothes dryers, the energy factor is defined as the number of pounds of clothes dried per kWh of power consumed.

Energy guide labels   The labels placed on appliances to enable consumers to compare appliance energy efficiency and energy consumption under specified test conditions as required by the Federal Trade Commission.

Energy intensity   The relative extent that energy is required for a process.

Energy storage   The process of storing, or converting energy from one form to another, for later use; storage devices and systems include batteries, conventional and pumped storage hydroelectric, flywheels, compressed gas, and thermal mass.

Enthalpy   A thermodynamic property of a substance, defined as the sum of its internal energy plus the pressure of the substance times its volume, divided by the mechanical equivalent of heat. The total heat content of air; the sum of the enthalpies of dry air and water vapor, per unit weight of dry air; measured in Btu per pound (or calories per kilogram).

Entrained bed gasifier   A gasifier in which the feedstock (fuel) is suspended by the movement of gas to move it through the gasifier.

Entropy   A measure of the unavailable or unusable energy in a system; energy that cannot be converted to another form.

Environment   All the natural and living things around us. The earth, air, weather, plants, and animals all make up our environment.

Equilibrium moisture content   The moisture content at which wood neither gains nor loses moisture when surrounded by air at a given relative humidity and temperature.

Equinox   The two times of the year when the sun crosses the equator and night and day are of equal length; usually occurs on March 21 (spring equinox) and September 23 (fall equinox).

Equipment   A general term including material, fittings, devices, appliances, fixtures, apparatus and the like used as a part of, or in connection with, an electrical installation.

Equity   The "valuation" that you own in your home, i.e., the property value less the mortgage loan outstanding.

Equivalent length   For determining friction losses in a piping system, the effect of a particular fitting equal to the friction loss through a straight piping length of the same nominal diameter.

Erg   A unit of work done by the force of 1 dyne acting through a distance of 1 cm.

Escrow   The handling of funds or documents by a third party on behalf of the buyer and/or seller.

Escutcheon   (a) An ornamental plate that fits around a pipe extending through a wall or floor to hide the cutout hole. (b) In builders' hardware, a protective plate or shield containing a keyhole.

Estimate   The amount of labor, materials, and other costs that a contractor anticipates for a project as summarized in the contractor's bid proposal for the project.

Estimating   The process of calculating the cost of a project. This can be a formal and exact process or a quick and imprecise process.

Ethanol   Ethyl alcohol (C_2H_5OH)   A colorless liquid that is the product of fermentation used in alcoholic beverages, industrial processes, and as a fuel additive. (Also known as "grain alcohol.")

Ethyl tertiary butyl ether (ETBE)   A chemical compound produced in a reaction between ethanol and isobutylene (a petroleum-derived by-product of the refining process). ETBE has characteristics superior to other ethers: low volatility, low water solubility, high octane value, and a large reduction in carbon monoxide and hydrocarbon emissions.

Eutectic   A mixture of substances that has a melting point lower than that of any mixture of the same substances in other proportions.

Eutectic salts   Salt mixtures with potential applications as solar thermal energy storage materials.

Evacuated-tube collector   A collector is the mechanism in which fluid (water or diluted antifreeze, for example) is heated by the sun in a solar hot water system. Evacuated-tube collectors are made up of rows of parallel, transparent glass tubes. Each tube consists of a glass outer tube and an inner tube, or absorber. The absorber is covered with a selective coating that absorbs solar energy well but inhibits radiative heat loss. The air is withdrawn ("evacuated") from the space between the tubes to form a vacuum, which eliminates conductive and convective heat loss. Evacuated-tube collectors are used for active solar hot water systems.

Evaporation   The conversion of a liquid to a vapor (gas), usually by means of heat.

Evaporative cooler   A device used for reducing air temperature by the process of evaporating water into an airstream.

Evaporative cooling   The physical process by which a liquid or solid is transformed into the gaseous state. For this process a mechanical device uses the outside air's heat to evaporate water that is held by pads inside the cooler. The heat is drawn out of the air through this process, and the cooled air is blown into the home by the cooler's fan.

Evaporator coil   The inner coil in a heat pump that, during the cooling mode, absorbs heat from the inside air and boils the liquid refrigerant to a vapor, which cools the house.

Excess air   Air that passes through the combustion chamber and the appliance flue in excess of that which is theoretically required for complete combustion.

Excitation   The power required to energize the magnetic field of a generator.

Exhaust hood, full opening   An exhaust hood with an opening at least equal to the diameter of the connecting vent.

Existing work   A plumbing system or any part thereof which has been installed prior to the effective date of this code.

Exothermic   A reaction or process that produces heat; a combustion reaction.

Expanded polystyrene   A type of insulation that is molded or expanded to produce coarse, closed cells containing air. The rigid cellular structure provides thermal and acoustical insulation, strength with low weight, and coverage with few heat loss paths. Often used to insulate the interior of masonry basement walls.

Expansion joint   A bituminous fiber strip used to separate blocks or units of concrete to prevent cracking due to dimensional change caused by shrinkage and variation in temperature.

Expansion tank   A tank used in a closed-loop solar heating system that provides space for the expansion of the heat transfer fluid in the pressurized collector loop.

Expansion valve   The device that reduces the pressure of liquid refrigerant thereby cooling it before it enters the evaporator coil in a heat pump.

Expansive soils   Earth that swells and contracts depending on the amount of water that is present. Betonite is an expansive soil.

Exposed aggregate finish   A method of finishing concrete which washes the cement/sand mixture off the top layer of the aggregate—usually gravel. Often used in driveways, patios, and other exterior surfaces.

Exposed (as applied to live parts)   Capable of being inadvertently touched or approached nearer than a safe distance by a person. It is applied to parts not suitably guarded, isolated or insulated. (See "Accessible" and "Concealed.")

Exposed (as applied to wiring methods)   On or attached to the surface or behind panels designed to allow access. [See "Accessible (as applied to wiring methods)."]

External combustion engine   An engine in which fuel is burned (or heat is applied) to the outside of a cylinder; a Stirling engine.

Externality   The environmental, social, and economic impacts of producing a good or service that are not directly reflected in the market price of the good or service.

Externally operable   Capable of being operated without exposing the operator to contact with live parts.

Extras   Additional work requested of a contractor, not included in the original plan, which will be billed separately and will not alter the original contract amount but will increase the cost of building the home.

Extruded polystyrene   A type of insulation material with fine, closed cells, containing a mixture of air and refrigerant gas. This insulation has a high R-value, good moisture resistance, and high structural strength compared to other rigid insulation materials.

Facade   Main or front elevation of a building.

Face nail   To install nails into the vertical face of a bearing header or beam.

Faced concrete   To finish the front and all vertical sides of a concrete porch, step(s), or patio. Normally the "face" is broom finished.

Facing brick   The brick used and exposed on the outside of a wall. Usually these have a finished texture.

Factory and shop lumber   Lumber intended to be cut up for use in further manufacture. It is graded on the basis of the percentage of the area which will produce a limited number of cuttings of a specified or a given minimum, size, and quality.

Factory-built chimney   A chimney composed of listed and labeled factory-built components assembled in accordance with the manufacturer's installation instructions to form the completed chimney.

Factory-built fireplace   A listed and labeled fireplace and chimney system composed of factory-made components, and assembled in the field in accordance with the manufacturer's instructions and the conditions of the listing.

Fan   A device that moves and/or circulates air and provides ventilation for a room or a building.

Fan coil   A heat exchanger coil in which a fluid such as water is circulated and a fan blows air over the coil to distribute heat or cool air to the different rooms.

Fan velocity pressure   The pressure corresponding to the outlet velocity of a fan; the kinetic energy per unit volume of flowing air.

Farad   A unit of electrical capacitance; the capacitance of a capacitor between the plates of which there appears a difference of 1 V when it is charged by one coulomb of electricity.

Fascia   Horizontal boards attached to rafter/truss ends at the eaves and along gables. Roof drain gutters are attached to the fascia.

Federal Energy Management Program (FEMP)   A program of the U.S. Department of Energy (DOE) that implements energy legislation and presidential directives. FEMP provides project financing, technical guidance and assistance, coordination and reporting, and new initiatives for the federal government. It also helps federal agencies identify the best technologies and technology demonstrations for their use.

Federal Energy Regulatory Commission (FERC)   This is an independent regulatory agency within the U.S. DOE that has jurisdiction over interstate electricity sales, wholesale electric rates, natural gas pricing, oil pipeline rates, and gas pipeline certification. It also licenses and inspects private, municipal, and state hydroelectric projects and oversees related environmental matters.

Feeder   All circuit conductors between the service equipment or the source of a separately derived system and the final branch-circuit overcurrent device.

Feedstock   A raw material that can be converted to one or more products.

Felt-tar paper   Installed under the roof shingles. Normally 15 or 30 lb.

Female   Any part, such as a nut or fitting, into which another (male) part can be inserted. Internal threads are female.

Fenestration   The placement or arrangement and sizes of the windows and exterior doors of a building.

Fermentation   The decomposition of organic material to alcohol, methane, etc. by organisms, such as yeast or bacteria, usually in the absence of oxygen.

Ferrule   Metal tubes used to keep roof gutters "open." Long nails (ferrule spikes) are driven through these tubes and hold the gutters in place along the fascia of the home.

FHA strap   Metal straps that are used to repair a bearing wall "cut-out," and to "tie together" wall corners, splices, and bearing headers. Also, they are used to hang stairs and landings to bearing headers.

Fiber board   A broad term used to describe sheet material of widely varying densities; manufactured from wood, cane, or other vegetable fibers.

Fiber saturation point   The stage in the drying or wetting of wood at which the cell walls are saturated and the cell cavities are free from water. It is assumed to be 30% moisture content, based on oven dry weight, and is the point below which shrinkage occurs.

Fiberglass insulation   A type of insulation, composed of small diameter pink, yellow, or white glass fibers, formed into blankets or batts, or used in loose-fill and blown-in applications.

Field measure   To take measurements (cabinets, countertops, stairs, shower doors, etc.) in the home itself instead of using the blueprints.

Filament   A coil of tungsten wire suspended in a vacuum or inert gas-filled bulb. When heated by electricity the tungsten "filament" glows.

Fill factor   The ratio of a photovoltaic cell's actual power to its power if both current and voltage were at their maxima. A key characteristic in evaluating cell performance.

Filter (air)   A device that removes contaminants, by mechanical filtration, from the fresh air stream before the air enters the living space. Filters can be installed as part of a heating/cooling system through which air flows for the purpose of removing particulates before or after the air enters the mechanical components.

Fin   A thin sheet of material (metal) of a heat exchanger that conducts heat to a fluid.

Finger joint   A manufacturing process of interlocking two shorter pieces of wood end to end to create a longer piece of dimensional lumber or molding. Often used in jambs and casings and are normally painted (instead of stained).

Finish   Both a noun and a verb to describe the exterior surface of building elements (walls, floors, ceilings, etc.) and furniture, and the process of applying it.

Fire block   Short horizontal members sometimes nailed between studs, usually about halfway up a wall. (See also "Fire stop.")

Fire brick   Brick made of refractory ceramic material which will resist high temperatures. Used in a fireplace and boiler.

Fire classification   Classifications of fires developed by the National Fire Protection Association.

Fire retardant chemical   A chemical or preparation of chemicals used to reduce the flammability of a material or to retard the spread of flame.

Fire stop   A solid, tight closure of a concealed space, placed to prevent the spread of fire and smoke through such a space. In a frame wall, this will usually consist of 2 by 4 cross blocking between studs. Work performed to slow the spread of fire and smoke in the walls and ceiling (behind the drywall). Includes stuffing wire holes in the top and bottom plates with insulation, and installing blocks of wood between the wall studs at the drop soffit line. This is integral to passing a rough frame inspection. (See also "Fire block.")

Fire wall   A wall which subdivides a building to restrict the spread of fire.

Fireplace   A wood- or gas-burning appliance that is primarily used to provide ambiance to a room. Conventional masonry fireplaces without energy-saving features often take more heat from a space than they put into it.

Fireplace chase flashing pan   A large sheet of metal that is installed around and perpendicular to the fireplace flue pipe. Its purpose is to confine and limit the spread of fire and smoke to a small area.

Fireplace insert   A wood- or gas-burning heating appliance that fits into the opening or protrudes on to the hearth of a conventional fireplace.

Fireplace stove   A freestanding, chimney-connected solid-fuel-burning heater with or without doors connected to the chimney.

Fireplace   An assembly consisting of a hearth and fire chamber of noncombustible material and provided with a chimney, for use with solid fuels.

Fire-resistive (fire-rated)   Applies to materials that are not combustible in the temperatures of ordinary fires and will withstand such fires for at least 1 h. Drywall used in the garage and party walls are to be fire-rated, ⅝-in. Type X.

Firing rate   The amount of BTUs/h or kWs produced by a heating system from the burning of a fuel.

First law of thermodynamics   States that energy cannot be created or destroyed, but only changed from one form to another. First law efficiency measures the fraction of energy supplied to a device or process that it delivers in its output. Also called the law of conservation of energy.

Fiscal year (FY)   The U.S. government's 12-month financial year, from October to September of the following calender year; e.g., FY 1998 extends from Oct. 1, 1997, to Sept. 30, 1998.

Fish tape   A long strip of spring steel used for fishing cables and for pulling wires through conduit.

Fishplate (gusset)   A wood or plywood piece used to fasten the ends of two members together at a butt joint with nails or bolts. Sometimes used at the junction of opposite rafters near the ridge line. Sometimes called a gang nail plate.

Fitting   An accessory such as a locknut, bushing or other part of a wiring system that is intended primarily to perform a mechanical rather than an electrical function.

Fixture   See "Plumbing fixture."

Fixture branch, drainage   A drain serving one or more fixtures which discharges into another portion of the drainage system.

Fixture branch, water supply   A water supply pipe between the fixture supply and a main water distribution pipe or fixture group main.

Fixture drain   The drain from the trap of a fixture to the junction of that drain with any other drain pipe.

Fixture fitting   Any device to control or guide the flow of water into, or convey water from, fixtures.

Fixture group main   The main water distribution pipe (or secondary branch) serving a plumbing fixture grouping such as a bath, kitchen or laundry area to which two or more individual fixture branch pipes are connected.

Fixture supply   The water supply pipe connecting a fixture or fixture fitting to a fixture branch.

Fixture unit, drainage (d.f.u.)   A measure of probable discharge into the drainage system by various types of plumbing fixtures; used to size DWV piping systems. The drainage fixture unit value for a particular fixture depends on its volume rate of drainage discharge, the time duration of a single drainage operation, and the average time between successive operations.

Fixture unit, water supply (w.s.f.u.)   A measure of the probable hydraulic demand on the water supply by various types of plumbing fixtures used to size water piping systems. The water supply fixture unit value for a particular fixture depends on its volume rate of supply, the time duration of a single supply operation and the average time between successive operations.

Flagstone (flagging or flags)   Flat stones (1 to 4 in. thick) used for walks, steps, floors, and vertical veneer (in lieu of brick).

Flakeboard   A manufactured wood panel made out of 1–2-in. wood chips and glue. Often used as a substitute for plywood in the exterior wall and roof sheathing. (Also called "OSB" or "waferboard.")

Flame-retention burner   An oil burner designed to hold the flame near the nozzle surface. Generally the most efficient type for residential use.

Flame-spread rating   A measure of the relative flame spread, and smoke development, from a material being tested. The flame spread rating is a single number comparing the flame spread of a material with red oak, arbitrarily given the number 100, and asbestos cement board with a flame spread of 0. Building codes require a maximum flame spread of 25 for insulation installed in exposed locations.

Flame-spread index   A numerical index indicating the relative surface-burning behavior of a material tested in accordance with ASTM E 84.

Flashing   Sheet metal or other material used in roof and wall construction (especially around chimneys and vents) to prevent rain or other water from entering.

Flashpoint   The minimum temperature at which sufficient vapor is released by a liquid or solid (fuel) to form a flammable vapor–air mixture at atmospheric pressure.

Flat mold   Thin wood strips installed over the butt seam of cabinet skins.

Flat paint   An interior paint that contains a high proportion of pigment and dries to a flat or lusterless finish.

Flat plate solar thermal/heating collectors   Large, flat boxes with glass covers and dark-colored metal plates inside that absorb and transfer solar energy to a heat transfer fluid. This is the most common type of collector used in solar hot water systems for homes or small businesses.

Flat roof   A roof which is level, or pitched only enough to provide for drainage.

Flatwork   Common word for concrete floors, driveways, basements, and sidewalks.

Floating   The next-to-last stage in concrete work, when you smooth off the job and bring water to the surface by using a hand float or bull float.

Floating wall   A nonbearing wall built on a concrete floor. It is constructed so that the bottom two horizontal plates can compress or pull apart if the concrete floor moves up or down. Normally built on basements and garage slabs.

Float-zone process   In reference to solar photovoltaic cell manufacture, a method of growing a large-size, high-quality crystal whereby coils heat a polycrystalline ingot placed atop a single-crystal seed. As the coils are slowly raised the molten interface beneath the coils becomes a single crystal.

Flood level rim   The edge of the receptor or fixture from which water overflows.

Floor drain   A plumbing fixture for recess in the floor having a floor-level strainer intended for the purpose of the collection and disposal of waste water used in cleaning the floor and for the collection and disposal of accidental spillage to the floor.

Floor furnace   A self-contained furnace suspended from the floor of the space being heated, taking air for combustion from outside such space, and with means for lighting the appliance from such space.

Floor space   The interior area of a building, calculated in square feet or meters.

Flow condition   In reference to solar thermal collectors, the condition where the heat transfer fluid is flowing through the collector loop under normal operating conditions.

Flow pressure   The static pressure reading in the water supply pipe near the faucet or water outlet while the faucet or water outlet is open and flowing at capacity.

Flow restrictor   A water and energy conserving device that limits the amount of water that a faucet or shower head can deliver.

Flue   (a) The structure (in a residential heating appliance, industrial furnace, or power plant) into which combustion gases flow and are contained until they are emitted to the atmosphere. (b) Large pipe through which fumes escape from a gas water heater, furnace, or fireplace. Normally these flue pipes are double-walled, galvanized sheet metal pipe and sometimes referred to as a "B vent." Fireplace flue pipes are normally triple walled. In addition, nothing combustible shall be within 1 in. from the flue pipe. (c) The space or passage in a chimney through which smoke, gas, or fumes rise. Each passage is called a flue, which with the surrounding masonry makes up the chimney.

Flue, appliance   The passages within an appliance through which combustion products pass from the combustion chamber to the flue collar.

Flue collar   The portion of a fuel-burning appliance designed for the attachment of a draft hood, vent connector, or venting system.

Flue damper   An automatic door located in the flue that closes it off when the burner turns off; purpose is to reduce heat loss up the flue from the still-warm furnace or boiler.

Flue gases   Products of combustion plus excess air in appliance flues or heat exchangers.

Flue lining   Two-foot lengths of fire clay or terra-cotta pipe (round or square) and usually made in all ordinary flue sizes. Used for the inner lining of chimneys with the brick or masonry work done around the outside. Flue linings in chimneys run from 1 foot below the flue connection to the top of the chimney.

Fluffing   The practice of installing blow-in, loose-fill insulation at a lower density than is recommended to meet a specified R-value.

Fluidized bed combustion (FBC)   A type of furnace or reactor in which fuel particles are combusted while suspended in a stream of hot gas.

Fluorescent lighting   A fluorescent lamp is a gas-filled glass tube with a phosphur coating on the inside. Gas inside the tube is ionized by electricity which causes the phosphur coating to glow. Normally with two pins that extend from each end.

Flush   Adjacent surfaces even, or in same plane (with reference to two structural pieces).

Flush valve   A device located at the bottom of a flush tank that is operated to flush water closets.

Flushometer tank   A device integrated within an air accumulator vessel, which is designed to discharge a predetermined quantity of water to fixtures for flushing purposes.

Flushometer valve   A device that discharges a predetermined quantity of water to fixtures for flushing purposes and is actuated by direct water pressure.

Fly ash   The fine particulate matter entrained in the flue gases of a combustion power plant.

Fly rafters   End rafters of the gable overhang supported by roof sheathing and lookouts.

Flywheel effect   The damping of interior temperature fluctuations by massive construction.

Foam (insulation)   A high R-value insulation product usually made from urethane that can be injected into wall cavities, or sprayed onto roofs or floors, where it expands and sets quickly.

Foam board   A plastic foam insulation product, pressed or extruded into board-like forms, used as sheathing and insulation for interior basement or crawl-space walls or beneath a basement slab; can also be used for exterior applications inside or outside foundations, crawlspaces, and slab-on-grade foundation walls.

Foam core panels   A type of structural, insulated product with foam insulation contained between two facings of drywall, or structural wood composition boards such as plywood, waferboard, and oriented strand board.

Foot candle   A unit of illuminance; equal to one lumen per square foot.

Foot pound   The amount of work done in raising one pound one foot.

Footer, footing   Continuous 8-in. or 10-in. thick concrete pad installed before and supports the foundation wall or monopost.

Footing   The spreading course or courses at the base or bottom of a foundation wall, pier, or column.

Force   The push or pull that alters the motion of a moving body or moves a stationary body; the unit of force is the dyne or poundal; force is equal to mass times velocity divided by time.

Forced air heating   A common form of heating with natural gas, propane, oil or electricity as a fuel. Air is heated in the furnace and distributed through a set of metal ducts to various areas of the house.

Forced air system or furnace   A type of heating system in which heated air is blown by a fan through air channels or ducts to rooms.

Forced ventilation   A type of building ventilation system that uses fans or blowers to provide fresh air to rooms when the forces of air pressure and gravity are not enough to circulate air through a building.

Form   Temporary structure erected to contain concrete during placing and initial hardening.

Formaldehyde   A chemical used as a preservative and in bonding agents. It is found in household products such as plywood, furniture, carpets, and some types of foam insulation. It is also a by-product of combustion and is a strong-smelling, colorless gas that is an eye irritant and can cause sneezing, coughing, and other health problems.

Fossil fuels   Fuels formed in the ground from the remains of dead plants and animals. It takes millions of years to form fossil fuels. Oil, natural gas, and coal are fossil fuels.

Foundation   The supporting portion of a structure below the first-floor construction, or below grade, including the footings.

Foundation ties   Metal wires that hold the foundation wall panels and rebar in place during the concrete pour.

Foundation waterproofing   High-quality, below-grade moisture protection. Used for below-grade exterior concrete and masonry wall damp-proofing to seal out moisture and prevent corrosion. Normally looks like black tar.

Fractional horse power motor   An electric motor rated at less than 1 horse power (hp).

Frame (window)   The outer casing of a window that sits in a designated opening of a structure and holds the window panes in place.

Frame inspection   The act of inspecting a home's structural integrity and its compliance with local municipal codes.

Framer   The carpenter contractor who installs the lumber and erects the frame, flooring system, interior walls, backing, trusses, rafters, decking, installs all beams, stairs, soffits, and all work related to the wood structure of the home. The framer builds the home according to the blueprints and must comply with local building codes and regulations.

Framing   The timber structure of a building which gives it shape and strength; including interior and exterior walls, floor, roof, and ceilings.

Freon   A registered trademark for a cholorfluorocarbon (CFC) gas that is highly stable and that has been historically used as a refrigerant.

Frequency   The number of cycles through which an alternating current passes per second; in the United States the standard for electricity generation is 60 cycles per second (60 Hertz).

Friction head   The energy lost from the movement of a fluid in a conduit (pipe) due to the disturbances created by the contact of the moving fluid with the surfaces of the conduit, or the additional pressure that a pump must provide to overcome the resistance to fluid flow created by or in a conduit.

Frieze   A boxed cornice wood trim member attached to the structure where the soffit (plancier) and wall meet.

Frost lid   Round metal lid that is installed on a water meter pit.

Frost line   The depth of frost penetration in soil and/or the depth at which the earth will freeze and swell. This depth varies in different parts of the country.

Fuel   Any material that can be burned to make energy.

Fuel cell   An electrochemical device that converts chemical energy directly into electricity.

Fuel efficiency   The ratio of heat produced by a fuel for doing work to the available heat in the fuel.

Fuel-grade alcohol   Usually refers to ethanol to 160 to 200 proof.

Fuel oil   Any liquid petroleum product burned for the generation of heat in a furnace or firebox, or for the generation of power in an engine. Domestic (residential) heating fuels are classed as Nos. 1, 2, 3; and industrial fuels as Nos. 4, 5, and 6.

Fuel-piping system   All piping, tubing, valves, and fittings used to connect fuel utilization equipment to the point of fuel delivery.

Fuel rate   The amount of fuel necessary to generate 1 kilowatt-hour of electricity.

Full sun   The amount of power density in sunlight received at the earth's surface at noon on a clear day (about 1000 W/m^2).

Fullway valve   A valve that in the full open position has an opening cross-sectional area equal to a minimum of 85 percent of the cross-sectional area of the connecting pipe.

Fungi   Plant-like organisms with cells with distinct nuclei surrounded by nuclear membranes, incapable of photosynthesis. Fungi are decomposers of waste organisms and exist as yeast, mold, or mildew.

Furling   The process of forcing, either manually or automatically, a wind turbine's blades out of the direction of the wind in order to stop the blades from turning.

Furnace (residential)   A combustion heating appliance in which heat is captured from the burning of a fuel for distribution, comprised mainly of a combustion chamber and heat exchanger.

Furnace, warm-air   A vented heating appliance designed or arranged to discharge heated air into a conditioned space.

Furring   Narrow strips of wood spaced to form a nailing base for another surface. Furring is used to level, to form an air space between the two surfaces, and to give a thicker appearance to the base surface.

Fuse   A safety device consisting of a short length of relatively fine wire, mounted in a holder or contained in a cartridge and connected as part of an electrical circuit. If the circuit source current exceeds a predetermined value, the fuse wire melts (i.e., the fuse "blows"), breaking the circuit and preventing damage to the circuit protected by the fuse.

Gable   That portion of a wall contained between the slopes of a double-sloped roof or that portion contained between the slope of a single-sloped roof and a line projected horizontally through the lowest elevation of the roof construction.

Gain   Notch or mortise cut to receive the end of another structural member or a hinge and other hardware.

Gallium arsenide   A compound used to make certain types of solar photovoltaic cells.

Gambrel roof   A roof slope formed as if the top of a gable (triangular) roof were cut off and replaced with a less steeply sloped cap. This cap still has a peaked ridge in the center.

Gang nail plate   A steel plate attached to both sides at each joint of a truss. Sometimes called a fishplate or gussett.

Gas   Fuel gas, such as natural gas, manufactured gas, undiluted liquefied petroleum gas (vapor phase only), liquefied petroleum gas–air mixture or mixtures of these gases.

Gas lateral   The trench or area in the yard where the gas line service is located, or the work of installing the gas service to a home.

Gas turbine   A type of turbine in which combusted, pressurized gas is directed against a series of blades connected to a shaft, which forces the shaft to turn to produce mechanical energy.

Gasification   The process in which a solid fuel is converted into a gas; also known as pyrolitic distillation or pyrolysis. Production of a clean fuel gas makes a wide variety of power options available.

Gasifier   A device for converting a solid fuel to a gaseous fuel.

Gasket/seal   A seal used to prevent the leakage of fluids, and also maintain the pressure in an enclosure.

Gasohol   A registered trademark of an agency of the state of Nebraska for an automotive fuel containing a blend of 10% ethanol and 90% gasoline.

Gasoline   A refined petroleum product suitable for use as a fuel in internal combustion engines.

Gate valve   A valve that lets you completely stop— but not modulate—the flow within a pipe.

Gauss   The unit of magnetic field intensity equal to 1 dyne per unit pole.

General contractor   Responsible for the execution, supervision, and overall coordination of a project and may also perform some of the individual construction tasks. Most general contractors are not licensed to perform all specialty trades and must hire specialty contractors for such tasks, e.g., electrical and plumbing.

Generator   A device for converting mechanical energy to electrical energy.

Geothermal energy   Energy produced by the internal heat of the earth; geothermal heat sources include: hydrothermal convective systems, pressurized water reservoirs, hot dry rocks, manual gradients, and magma. Geothermal energy can be used directly for heating or to produce electric power.

Geothermal heat pump   A type of heat pump that uses the ground, ground water, or ponds as a heat source and heat sink, rather than outside air. Ground or water temperatures are more constant and are warmer in winter and cooler in summer than air temperatures. Geothermal heat pumps operate more efficiently than conventional or air source heat pumps.

Geothermal power station   An electricity-generating facility that uses geothermal energy.

Gigawatt (GW)   A unit of power equal to 1 billion watts, 1 million kilowatts, or 1,000 megawatts.

Gin pole   A pole used to assist in raising a tower.

Girder   A large or principal beam of wood or steel used to support concentrated loads at particular points along its length.

Glare   The discomfort or interference with visual perception when viewing a bright object against a dark background.

Glazing   A term used for the transparent or translucent material in a window. This material (i.e. glass, plastic films, coated glass) is used for admitting solar energy and light through windows.

Glazing compound   A plastic substance of such consistency that it tends to remain soft and rubbery when used in glazing sash and doors.

Global warming   A popular term used to describe the increase in average global temperatures due to the greenhouse effect.

Globe valve   A valve that lets you adjust the flow of water to any rate between fully on and fully off. (See "Gate valve.")

Gloss enamel   A finishing paint material. Forms a hard coating with maximum smoothness of surface and dries to a sheen or luster (gloss).

Glue block   A wood block, triangular or rectangular in shape, which is glued into place to reinforce a right-angle butt joint. Sometimes used at the intersection of the tread and riser in a stairs.

Glued-laminated beam (glulam)   A structural beam composed of wood laminations or lams. The lams are pressure bonded with adhesives to attain a typical thickness of 1½ in. (It looks like five or more 2 × 4s are glued together.)

Governor   A device used to regulate motor speed or, in a wind energy conversion system, to control the rotational speed of the rotor.

Grade   Ground level, or the elevation at any given point. Also the work of leveling dirt. Also the designated quality of a manufactured piece of wood.

Grade, piping   See "Slope."

Grade beam   Thickened and reinforced section of a slab foundation designed to rest on supporting piling.

Grading permit   Authorization to change the contour of the land.

Grain   The direction, size, arrangement, appearance, or quality of the fibers in wood.

Grain alcohol   Ethanol.

Green certificates   Green certificates represent the environmental attributes of power produced from renewable resources. By separating the environmental attributes from the power, clean power generators are able to sell the electricity they produce to power providers at a competitive market value. The additional revenue generated by the sale of the green certificates covers the above-market costs associated with producing power made from renewable energy sources. Also known as green tags, renewable energy certificates, or tradeable renewable certificates.

Green power   A popular term for energy produced from clean, renewable energy resources.

Green pricing   A practice engaged in by some regulated utilities (i.e., power providers) where electricity produced from clean, renewable resources is sold at a higher cost than that produced from fossil or nuclear power plants, supposedly because some buyers are willing to pay a premium for clean power.

Greenhouse effect   A popular term used to describe the heating effect due to the trapping of long-wave (length) radiation by greenhouse gases produced from natural and human sources.

Greenhouse gases   Those gases, such as water vapor, carbon dioxide, tropospheric ozone, methane, and low-level ozone, that are transparent to solar radiation but opaque to long-wave radiation, and which contribute to the greenhouse effect.

Greenwood Freshly cut, unseasoned, wood.

Greywater Waste water from a household source other than a toilet. This water can be used for landscape irrigation depending upon the source of the greywater.

Grid The completed assembly of main and cross tees in a suspended ceiling system before the ceiling panels are installed. Also the decorative slats (munton) installed between glass panels.

Grid-connected system Independent power systems that are connected to an electricity transmission and distribution system (referred to as the electricity grid) such that the systems can draw on the grid's reserve capacity in times of need, and feed electricity back into the grid during times of excess production.

Ground (a) A device used to protect the user of any electrical system or appliance from shock. (b) Refers to electricity's habit of seeking the shortest route to earth. Neutral wires carry it there in all circuits. An additional grounding wire or the sheathing of the metal-clad cable or conduit—protects against shock if the neutral leg is interrupted. (c) A conducting connection, whether intentional or accidental, between an electrical circuit or equipment and the earth, or to some conducting body that serves in place of the earth.

Ground fault circuit interrupter (GFCI, GFI) (a) An ultrasensitive plug designed to shut off all electric current. Used in bathrooms, kitchens, exterior waterproof outlets, garage outlets, and "wet areas." Has a small reset button on the plug. (b) A device intended for the protection of personnel that functions to deenergize a circuit or portion thereof within an established period of time when a current to ground exceeds some predetermined value that is less than that required to operate the overcurrent protective device of the supply circuit.

Ground iron The plumbing drain and waste lines that are installed beneath the basement floor. Cast iron was once used, but black plastic pipe (ABS) is now widely used.

Ground loop In geothermal heat pump systems, a series of fluid-filled plastic pipes buried in the shallow ground, or placed in a body of water, near a building. The fluid within the pipes is used to transfer heat between the building and the shallow ground (or water) in order to heat and cool the building.

Ground reflection Solar radiation reflected from the ground onto a solar collector.

Ground-source heat pump See "Geothermal systems."

Grounded, effectively Intentionally connected to earth through a ground connection or connections of sufficiently low impedance and having sufficient current-carrying capacity to prevent the buildup of voltages that may result in undue hazards to connected equipment or to persons.

Grounded conductor A system or circuit conductor that is intentionally grounded.

Grounding A system used for electrical safety. An electrical wire runs from the exposed metal of a power tool to a third prong on the power plug. When used with a grounded receptacle, this wire directs harmful currents away from the operator.

Grounding conductor, equipment The conductor used to connect the non-current-carrying metal parts of equipment, raceways and other enclosures to the system grounding conductor, the grounding electrode conductor, or both at the service equipment or at the source of a separately derived system.

Grounding electrode conductor The conductor used to connect the grounding electrode to the equipment grounding conductor, the grounding conductor, or both at the service equipment or at the source of a separately derived system.

Groundwater Water from an aquifer or subsurface water source.

Grout A wet mixture of cement, sand and water that flows into masonry or ceramic crevices to seal the cracks between the different pieces. Mortar made of such consistency (by adding water) that it will flow into the joints and cavities of the masonry work and fill them solid.

Guarded Covered, shielded, fenced, enclosed, or otherwise protected by means of suitable covers, casings, barriers, rails, screens, mats, or platforms to remove the likelihood of approach or contact by persons or objects to a point of danger.

Gusset A panel or bracket of either wood or metal attached to the corners or intersections of a frame to add strength and stiffness.

Gutter Wood or metal trough attached to the edge of a roof to collect and conduct water from rain or melting snow.

Guy wire Cable used to secure a wind turbine tower to the ground in a safe, stable manner.

Gypsum plaster Gypsum formulated to be used with the addition of sand and water for base-coat plaster.

Gypsum wallboard Wall covering panels consisting of a gypsum core with facing and backing of paper.

H clip Small metal clips formed like an "H" that fits at the joints of two plywood (or wafer board) sheets to stiffen the joint. Normally used on the roof sheeting.

HVAC An abbreviation for heat, ventilation, and air conditioning.

Half story That part of a building situated wholly or partly within the roof frame, finished for occupancy.

Hangers See "Supports."

Hardboard A board material manufactured of wood fiber, formed into a panel having a density range of approximately 50 to 80 lb/cu. ft.

Hardware All of the "metal" fittings that go into the home when it is near completion. For example, door knobs, towel bars, handrail brackets, closet rods, house numbers, door closers, etc. The interior trim carpenter installs the "hardware."

Harmonic(s) A sinusoidal quantity having a frequency that is an integral multiple of the frequency of a periodic quantity to which it is related.

Haunch An extension, knee-like protrusion of the foundation wall that a concrete porch or patio will rest upon for support.

Hazard insurance Protection against damage caused by fire, windstorms, or other common hazards. Many lenders require borrowers to carry it in an amount at least equal to the mortgage.

Hazardous location Any location considered to be a fire hazard for flammable vapors, dust, combustible fibers, or other highly combustible substances.

Head A unit of pressure for a fluid, commonly used in water pumping and hydro power to express height a pump must lift water or the distance water falls. Total head accounts for friction head losses, etc.

Header Horizontal structural member that supports the load over an opening, such as a window or door. (Also called a "lintel.")

Headroom The clear space between floor line and ceiling, as in a stairway.

Hearth The fireproof area directly in front of a fireplace. The inner or outer floor of a fireplace, usually made of brick, tile, or stone.

Heartwood The wood extending from the pith or center of the tree to the sapwood, the cells of which no longer participate in the life processes of the tree.

Heat A form of thermal energy resulting from combustion, chemical reaction, friction, or movement of electricity. As a thermodynamic condition, heat, at a constant pressure, is equal to internal or intrinsic energy plus pressure times volume.

Heat-absorbing window glass A type of window glass that contains special tints that cause the window to absorb as much as 45% of incoming solar energy and reduce heat gain in an interior space. Part of the absorbed heat will continue to be passed through the window by conduction and reradiation.

Heat balance Energy output from a system that equals energy input.

Heat content The amount of heat in a quantity of matter at a specific temperature and pressure.

Heat engine A device that produces mechanical energy directly from two heat reservoirs of different temperatures. A machine that converts thermal energy to mechanical energy, such as a steam engine or turbine.

Heat exchanger A device used to transfer heat from a fluid (liquid or gas) to another fluid where the two fluids are physically separated.

Heat gain The amount of heat introduced to a space from all heat producing sources, such as building occupants, lights, appliances, and from the environment, mainly solar energy.

Heat loss The heat that flows from the building interior through the building envelope to the outside environment.

Heat meter An electrical municipal inspection of the electric meter breaker panel box.

Heat pipe A device that transfers heat by the continuous evaporation and condensation of an internal fluid.

Heat pump A mechanical device which uses compression and decompression of gas to heat and/or cool a house.

Heat pump water heaters A water heater that uses electricity to move heat from one place to another instead of generating heat directly.

Heat rate The ratio of fuel energy input as heat per unit of net work output; a measure of a power plant thermal efficiency, generally expressed as Btu per net kilowatt-hour.

Heat recovery ventilator A device that captures the heat from the exhaust air from a building and transfers it to supply fresh air entering the building to preheat the air and increase overall heating efficiency.

Heat register The grilled opening into a room by which the amount of warm air from a furnace can be directed or controlled; may include a damper.

Heat rough Work performed by the heating contractor after the stairs and interior walls are built. This includes installing all duct work and flue pipes. Sometimes, the furnace and fireplaces are installed at this stage of construction.

Heat sink A structure or media that absorbs heat.

Heat source A structure or media from which heat can be absorbed or extracted.

Heat storage A device or media that absorbs heat for storage for later use.

Heat storage capacity The amount of heat that a material can absorb and store.

Heat transfer The flow of heat from one area to another by conduction, convection, and/or radiation. Heat flows naturally from a warmer to a cooler material or space.

Heat transfer fluid   A gas or liquid used to move heat energy from one place to another; a refrigerant.

Heat transmission coefficient   (a) Any coefficient used to calculate heat transmission by conduction, convection, or radiation through materials or structures. (b) Hourly rate of heat transfer for 1 ft^2 of surface when there is a temperature difference of 1°F of the air on the two sides of the surface.

Heat trim   Work done by the heating contractor to get the home ready for the municipal final heat inspection. This includes venting the hot water heater; installing all vent grills, registers, and air-conditioning services; turning on the furnace; installing thermostats; venting ranges and hoods; and all other heat-related work.

Heating capacity   The quantity of heat necessary to raise the temperature of a specific mass of a substance by 1°. (See "Specific heat.")

Heating degree day(s) (HDD)   The number of degrees per day that the daily average temperature (the mean of the maximum and minimum recorded temperatures) is below a base temperature, usually 65°F, unless otherwise specified; used to determine indoor space heating requirements and heating system sizing. Total HDD is the cumulative total for the year/heating season. The higher the HDD for a location, the colder the daily average temperature(s).

Heating fuel units   Standardized weights or volumes for heating fuels.

Heating fuels   Any gaseous, liquid, or solid fuel used for indoor space heating.

Heating load   The rate of heat flow required to maintain a specific indoor temperature; usually measured in Btu per hour.

Heating season   The coldest months of the year, months where average daily temperatures fall below 65°F, creating a demand for indoor space heating.

Heating seasonal performance factor (HSPF)   The measure of seasonal or annual efficiency of a heat pump operating in the heating mode. It takes into account the variations in temperature that can occur within a season and is the average number of Btu of heat delivered for every watt-hour of electricity used by the heat pump over a heating season.

Heating value   The amount of heat produced from the complete combustion of a unit of fuel. The higher (or gross) heating value is that when all products of combustion are cooled to the precombustion temperature, water vapor formed during combustion is condensed, and necessary corrections have been made. Lower (or net) heating value is obtained by subtracting from the gross heating value the latent heat of va-

porization of the water vapor formed by the combustion of the hydrogen in the fuel.

Heating, ventilation, and air-conditioning (HVAC) system   All the components of the appliance used to condition interior air of a building.

Heel cut   A notch cut in the end of a rafter to permit it to fit flat on a wall and on the top, doubled, exterior wall plate.

Heliochemical process   The utilization of solar energy through photosynthesis.

Heliodon   A device used to simulate the angle of the sun for assessing shading potentials of building structures or landscape features.

Heliostat   A device that tracks the movement of the sun; used to orient solar concentrating systems.

Heliothermal   Any process that uses solar radiation to produce useful heat.

Heliothermic   Site planning that accounts for natural solar heating and cooling processes and their relationship to building shape, orientation, and siting.

Heliothermometer   An instrument for measuring solar radiation.

Heliotropic   Any device (or plant) that follows the sun's apparent movement across the sky.

Hemispherical bowl technology   A solar energy concentrating technology that uses a linear receiver that tracks the focal area of a reflector or array of reflectors.

Hertz   A measure of the number of cycles or wavelengths of electrical energy per second; U.S. electricity supply has a standard frequency of 60 hertz.

Heterojunction   A region of electrical contact between two different materials.

High-temperature (H.T.) chimney   A high-temperature chimney complying with the requirements of UL 103. A Type H.T. chimney is identifiable by the markings "Type H.T." on each chimney pipe section.

Higher heating value (HHV)   The maximum heating value of a fuel sample, which includes the calorific value of the fuel (bone dry) and the latent heat of vaporization of the water in the fuel. (See "Moisture content.")

High-intensity discharge lamp   A lamp that consists of a sealed arc tube inside a glass envelope, or outer jacket. The inner arc tube is filled with elements that emit light when ionized by electric current. A ballast is required to provide the proper starting voltage and to regulate current during operation.

Highlights   A light spot, area, or streak on a painted surface.

High-pressure sodium lamp   A type of high-intensity discharge (HID) lamp that uses sodium under high pressure as the primary light-producing element. These high-efficiency lights produce a golden white color and are used for interior industrial applications, such as in warehouses and manufacturing, and for security, street, and area lighting.

Hip   A roof with four sloping sides. The external angle formed by the meeting of two sloping sides of a roof.

Hip roof   A roof that rises by inclined planes from all four sides of a building.

Hole   The vacancy where an electron would normally exist in a solid; behaves like a positively charged particle.

Hollow-back   Removal of a portion of the wood on the unexposed face of a wood member to more properly fit any irregularity in bearing surface.

Hollow core door   Flush door with a core assembly of strips or other units which support the outer faces.

Home energy rating systems (HERS)   A nationally recognized energy rating program that gives builders, mortgage lenders, secondary lending markets, homeowners, sellers, and buyers a precise evaluation of energy losing deficiencies in homes. Builders can use this system to gauge the energy quality of their homes and also to have star ratings to compare to other homes.

Home run (electrical)   The electrical cable that carries power from the main circuit breaker panel to the first electrical box, plug, or switch in the circuit.

Honeycombs   The appearance concrete makes when rocks in the concrete are visible and where there are void areas in the foundation wall, especially around concrete foundation windows.

Horizontal branch, drainage   A drain pipe extending laterally from a soil or waste stack or building drain, which receives the discharge from one or more fixture drains.

Horizontal ground loop   In this type of closed-loop geothermal heat pump installation, the fluid-filled plastic heat exchanger pipes are laid out in a plane parallel to the ground surface. The most common layouts either use two pipes, one buried at 6 ft, and the other at 4 ft, or two pipes placed side-by-side at 5 ft in the ground in a 2-ft-wide trench. The trenches must be at least 4 ft deep. Horizontal ground loops are generally most cost effective for residential installations, particularly for new construction where sufficient land is available. (See "Closed-loop geothermal heat pump systems.")

Horizontal pipe   Any pipe or fitting that makes an angle of less than 45° (0.79 rad) with the horizontal.

Horizontal-axis wind turbines   Turbines in which the axis of the rotor's rotation is parallel to the wind stream and the ground.

Horn   The extension of a stile, jamb, or sill.

Horsepower (hp)   A unit of rate of operation. Electrical hp: A measure of time rate of mechanical energy output; usually applied to electric motors as the maximum output; 1 electrical hp is equal to 0.746 kW or 2545 Btu/h. Shaft hp: a measure of the actual mechanical energy per unit time delivered to a turning shaft; 1 shaft hp is equal to 1 electrical hp or 550 ft lb/sec. Boiler hp: a measure to the maximum rate to heat output of a steam generator; 1 boiler hp is equal to 33,480 Btu per hour of steam output.

Horsepower hour (hph)   One horsepower provided over 1 hour; equal to 0.745 kilowatt-hour or 2545 Btu.

Hose bib   An exterior water faucet (sill cock).

Hot air furnace   A heating unit where heat is distributed by means of convection or fans.

Hot dry rock   A geothermal energy resource that consists of high-temperature rocks above 300°F (150°C) that may be fractured and have little or no water. To extract the heat, the rock must first be fractured, then water is injected into the rock and pumped out to extract the heat. In the western United States, as much as 95,000 square miles (246,050 square kilometers) have hot dry rock potential.

Hot water   Water that is supplied to plumbing fixtures and appliances at a temperature between 120°F (49°C) and 140°F (60°C).

Hot wire   The wire that carries electrical energy to a receptacle or other device, in contrast to a neutral, which carries electricity away again; normally the black wire. (See "Ground.")

House Water and Power Committee   This committee has oversight over the generation and marketing of electric power from federal water projects by federally charted or Federal RPM authorities, measures and matters concerning water resources planning, compacts relating to use and apportionment of interstate waters, water rights or power movement programs, measures and matters pertaining to irrigation and reclamation projects, and other water resources development programs.

Hub height   The height above the ground where a horizontal axis wind turbine's hub is located.

Humidifier   An appliance normally attached to the furnace, or portable unit device designed to increase the humidity within a room or a house by means of the discharge of water vapor.

Humidity   A measure of the moisture content of air; may be expressed as absolute, mixing ratio, saturation deficit, relative, or specific.

Hurricane clip   Metal straps that are nailed and secure the roof rafters and trusses to the top horizontal wall plate. (Sometimes called a "Teco clip.")

Hydrogen   A chemical element that can be used as a fuel because it has a very high energy content.

Hydrogenated amorphous silicon Amorphous silicon with a small amount of incorporated hydrogen. The hydrogen neutralizes dangling bonds in the amorphous silicon, allowing charge carriers to flow more freely.

I-beam A steel beam with a cross section resembling the letter I. It is used for long spans as basement beams or over wide wall openings, such as a double garage door, when wall and roof loads bear down on the opening.

Identified (as applied to equipment) Recognizable as suitable for the specific purpose, function, use, environment, application, etc., where described in a particular code requirement. (See "Equipment.")

Ignite To heat a gaseous mixture to the temperature at which combustion takes place.

Ignition point The minimum temperature at which combustion of a solid or fluid can occur.

I-joist Manufactured structural building component resembling the letter "I." Used as floor joists and rafters. I-joists include two key parts: flanges and webs. The flange or form of the I-joist may be made of laminated veneer lumber or dimensional lumber, usually formed into a 1½ in. width. The web or center of the I-joist is commonly made of plywood or oriented strand board (OSB). Large holes can be cut in the web to accommodate duct work and plumbing waste lines. I-joists are available in lengths up to 60 ft long.

Illuminance A measure of the amount of light incident on a surface; measured in foot-candles or Lux.

Impoundment A body of water confined by a dam, dike, floodgate or other artificial barrier.

Impulse turbine A turbine that is driven by high velocity jets of water or steam from a nozzle directed to vanes or buckets attached to a wheel. (A pelton wheel is an impulse hydro turbine.)

Incandescent These lights use an electrically heated filament to produce light in a vacuum or inert gas-filled bulb.

Incandescent lamp A lamp employing an electrically charged metal filament that glows at white heat; a typical light bulb.

Incident solar radiation The amount of solar radiation striking a surface per unit of time and area.

Incinerator A device which consumes household waste by burning.

Independent power producer A company or individual that is not directly regulated as a power provider. These entities produce power for their own use and/or sell it to regulated power providers.

Indirect gain system Passive solar construction in which solar heat is stored in structures of masonry, water, or other medium and then passed along to living space by radiation, conduction, or convection.

Indirect solar water heater These systems circulate fluids other than water (such as diluted antifreeze) through the collector. The collected heat is transferred to the household water supply using a heat exchanger. (Also known as "closed-loop" systems.)

Indirect waste pipe A waste pipe that discharges into the drainage system through an air gap into a trap, fixture, or receptor.

Individual sewage disposal system A system for disposal of sewage by means of a septic tank or mechanical treatment, designed for use apart from a public sewer to serve a single establishment or building.

Individual vent A pipe installed to vent a single-fixture drain that connects with the vent system above or terminates independently outside the building.

Individual water supply A supply other than an approved public water supply which serves one or more families.

Induction The production of an electric current in a conductor by the variation of a magnetic field in its vicinity.

Induction generator A device that converts the mechanical energy of rotation into electricity based on electromagnetic induction. An electric voltage (electromotive force) is induced in a conducting loop (or coil) when there is a change in the number of magnetic field lines (or magnetic flux) passing through the loop. When the loop is closed by connecting the ends through an external load, the induced voltage will cause an electric current to flow through the loop and load. Thus rotational energy is converted into electrical energy.

Induction motor A motor in which a three-phase (or any multiphase) alternating current (i.e., the working current) is supplied to iron-cored coils (or windings) within the stator. As a result, a rotating magnetic field is set up, which induces a magnetizing current in the rotor coils (or windings). Interaction of the magnetic field produced in this manner with the rotating field causes rotational motion to occur.

Industrial process heat The thermal energy used in an industrial process.

Inert gas A gas that does not react with other substances; e.g. argon or krypton; sealed between two sheets of glazing to decrease the U-value (increase the R-value) of windows.

Infiltration The passage of air from indoors to outdoors and vice versa; term is usually associated with drafts from cracks, seams, or holes in buildings.

Inside corner The point at which two walls form an internal angle, as in the corner of a room.

Insolation   The solar power density incident on a surface of stated area and orientation, usually expressed as watts per square meter or Btu per square foot per hour.

Instantaneous efficiency (of a solar collector)   The amount of energy absorbed (or converted) by a solar collector (or photovoltaic cell or module) over a 15-min period.

Insulating glass   Window or door in which two panes of glass are used with a sealed air space between. (Also known as "double glass.")

Insulation   Any material high in resistance to heat transmission that, when placed in the walls, ceiling, or floors of a structure, will reduce the rate of heat flow.

Insulation blanket   A pre-cut layer of insulation applied around a water heater storage tank to reduce stand-by heat loss from the tank.

Insulation board, rigid   A structural building board made of coarse wood or cane fiber in ½- and $^{25}/_{32}$-in. thickness. It can be obtained in various size sheets and densities.

Insulation (thermal)   Any material high in resistance to heat transmission that is placed in structures to reduce the rate of heat flow.

Insulator   A device or material with a high resistance to electricity flow.

Integral collector storage system   This simple passive solar hot water system consists of one or more storage tanks placed in an insulated box that has a glazed side facing the sun. An integral collector storage system is mounted on the ground or on the roof (make sure your roof structure is strong enough to support it). Some systems use "selective" surfaces on the tank(s). These surfaces absorb sun well but inhibit radiative loss. Also known as bread box systems or batch heaters.

Integrated heating systems   A type of heating appliance that performs more than one function, for example space and water heating.

Interconnection   A connection or link between power systems that enables them to draw on each other's reserve capacity in time of need.

Interior finish   Material used to cover the interior framed areas of walls and ceilings.

Interior trim   General term for all the molding, casing, baseboard, and other trim items applied within the building by finish carpenters.

Internal gain   The heat produced by sources of heat in a building (occupants, appliances, lighting, etc.).

Internal mass   Materials with high thermal energy storage capacity contained in or part of a building's walls, floors, or free-standing elements.

Inverter   A device that that converts direct current electricity (e.g., from a solar photovoltaic module or array) to alternating current for use directly to operate appliances or to supply power to a electricity grid.

Ion   An electrically charged atom or group of atoms that has lost or gained electrons; a loss makes the resulting particle positively charged; a gain makes the particle negatively charged.

Ionizer   A device that removes airborne particles from breathable air. Negative ions are produced and give up their negative charge to the particles. These new negative particles are then attracted to the positive particles surrounding them. This accumulation process continues until the particles become heavy enough to fall to the ground.

Irradiance   The direct, diffuse, and reflected solar radiation that strikes a surface.

Isolated solar gain system   A type of passive solar heating system where heat is collected in one area for use in another.

Isolated   Not readily accessible to persons unless special means for access are used.

J channel   Metal edging used on drywall to give the edge a better finished appearance when a wall is not "wrapped." Generally, basement stairway walls have drywall only on the stair side. J channel is used on the vertical edge of the last drywall sheet.

Jack leg   An unskilled and untrained contractor or tradesperson.

Jack post   A type of structural support made of metal, which can be raised or lowered through a series of pins and a screw to meet the height required. Basically used as a replacement for an old supporting member in a building. (See "Monopost.")

Jack rafter   A short rafter framing between the wall plate and a hip rafter; or a hip or valley rafter and ridge board.

Jacket   The enclosure on a water heater, furnace, or boiler.

Jalousie   A series of small horizontal overlapping glass slats, held together by an end metal frame attached to the faces of window frame side jambs or door stiles and rails. The slats or louvers move simultaneously like a Venetian blind.

Jamb   The top and two sides of a door or window frame which contact the door or sash; top jamb and side jambs.

Jig   A device used to position material for accurate cutting or assembly. Most often used in factories making prefabricated building components.

Joinery   A term used by woodworkers when referring to the various types of joints used in a structure.

Joint   The location between the touching surfaces of two members or components joined and held together by nails, glue, cement, mortar, or other means.

Joint cement, joint compound A powder that is usually mixed with water and used for joint treatment in gypsum-wallboard finish. Often called spackle or drywall mud.

Joint trench When the electric company and telephone company dig one trench and "drop" both of their service lines in.

Joist hanger A metal U-shaped item used to support the end of a floor joist and attached with hardened nails to another bearing joist or beam.

Joist One of a series of parallel framing members used to support floor and ceiling loads, and supported in turn by larger beams, girders, or bearing walls.

Joule A metric unit of energy or work; the energy produced by a force of 1 newton operating through a distance of 1 m; 1 joule per second equals 1 watt or 0.737 foot-pound; 1 Btu equals 1055 joules.

Joule's law The rate of heat production by a steady current in any part of an electrical circuit that is proportional to the resistance and to the square of the current, or, the internal energy of an ideal gas depends only on its temperature.

Jumpers Water pipe installed in a water meter pit (before the water meter is installed), or electric wire that is installed in the electric house panel meter socket before the meter is installed. This is sometimes illegal.

Keeper The metal latch plate in a door frame into which a doorknob plunger latches.

Kerfing Longitudinal saw cuts or grooves of varying depths (dependent on the thickness of the wood member) made on the unexposed faces of millwork members to relieve stress and prevent warping; members are also kerfed to facilitate bending.

Kerosene A type of heating fuel derived by refining crude oil that has a boiling range at atmospheric pressure from 400 to 550°F.

Keyway A slot formed and poured on a footer or in a foundation wall when another wall will be installed at the slot location. This gives additional strength to the joint/meeting point.

Kiln-dried Wood seasoned in a kiln by means of artificial heat, controlled humidity, and air circulation.

Kilovolt-ampere (kVa) A unit of apparent power, equal to 1000 volt-amperes; the mathematical product of the volts and amperes in an electrical circuit.

Kilowatt (kW) A standard unit of electrical power equal to 1000 watts, or to energy consumption at a rate of 1000 joules per second.

Kilowatt-hour A unit or measure of electricity supply or consumption of 1000 W over the period of one hour; equivalent to 3412 Btu.

Kinetic energy Energy available as a result of motion that varies directly in proportion to an object's mass and the square of its velocity.

King stud The vertical 2 Xs frame lumber (left and right) of a window or door opening, and runs continuously from the bottom sole plate to the top plate.

Kneewall A wall usually about 3 to 4 ft high that is placed in the attic of a home, anchored with plates between the attic floor joists and the roof joist. Sheathing can be attached to these walls to enclose an attic space.

Knocked down Unassembled; refers to structural units requiring assembly after being delivered to the job.

Knot In lumber, the portion of a branch or limb of a tree that appears on the edge or face of the piece.

Kraft paper A brown building paper which resists puncturing. Kraft paper is used to face some blanket insulation materials.

Labeled Equipment or materials to which has been attached a label, symbol or other identifying mark of an organization acceptable to the authority having jurisdiction and concerned with product evaluation that maintains periodic inspection of production of labeled equipment or materials and by whose labeling the manufacturer indicates compliance with appropriate standards or performance in a specified manner.

Lagoon In wastewater treatment or livestock facilities, a shallow pond used to store wastewater where sunlight and biological activity decompose the waste.

Lally column A cylindrically shaped steel member used to support beams and girders. Sometimes filled with concrete.

Laminated shingles Shingles that have added dimensionality because of extra layers or tabs, giving a shake-like appearance. May also be called "architectural shingles" or "three-dimensional shingles."

Laminating Bonding together two or more layers of materials.

Lamp A light source composed of a metal base, a glass tube filled with an inert gas or a vapor, and base pins to attach to a fixture.

Landing A platform between flights of stairs or at the termination of a flight of stairs. Often used when stairs change direction. Normally no less than 3 ft × 3 ft square.

Landscaping Features and vegetation on the outside of or surrounding a building for aesthetics and energy conservation.

Langley A unit or measure of solar radiation; 1 calorie per square centimeter or 3.69 Btu per square foot.

Lap To cover the surface of one shingle or roll with another.

Latch   A beveled metal tongue operated by a spring-loaded knob or lever. The tongue's bevel lets you close the door and engage the locking mechanism, if any, without using a key. Contrasts with dead bolt.

Latent cooling load   The load created by moisture in the air, including from outside air infiltration and that from indoor sources such as occupants, plants, cooking, showering, etc.

Latent heat   The change in heat content that occurs with a change in phase and without change in temperature.

Lateral (electric, gas, telephone, sewer, and water)   The underground trench and related services (i.e., electric, gas, telephone, sewer, and water lines) that will be buried within the trench.

Lath   A building material of wood, metal, gypsum, or insulating board, fastened to frame of building to act as a plaster base.

Lattice   An open framework of crisscrossed wood or metal strips that form regular, patterned spaces.

Law(s) of Thermodynamics   The first law states that energy cannot be created or destroyed; the second law states that when a free exchange of heat occurs between two materials, the heat always moves from the warmer to the cooler material.

Lazy Susan   A circular revolving cabinet shelf used in corner kitchen cabinet unit.

Leader   Vertical pipe that carries rainwater from the gutter to the ground or a drain (also downspout).

Ledger   A strip attached to vertical framing or structural members to support joists or other horizontal framing. Similar to a ribbon strip.

Leech field   A method used to treat/dispose of sewage in rural areas not accessible to a municipal sewer system. Sewage is permitted to be filtered and eventually discharged into a section of the lot called a leech field.

Let in   Refers to any kind of notch in a stud, joist, block, or other piece which holds another piece. Somewhat like log cabin construction. The item which is supported in the notch is said to be "let in."

Lethe   A measure of air purity that is equal to one complete air change (in an interior space).

Let-in brace   Nominal 1-in.-thick board applied to notched stud diagonally. Also, an L-shaped, long (@ 10 ft) metal strap that is installed by the framer at the rough stage to give support to an exterior wall or wall corner.

Level   True horizontal. Also a tool used to determine level.

Level-transit   A surveying instrument used to check the plumb of walls in new structures. The telescope tube can swing in a vertical arc for comparing forward and backward readings.

Lien   An encumbrance that usually makes real or personal property the security for payment of a debt or discharge of an obligation.

Life-cycle cost   The sum of all the costs both recurring and nonrecurring, related to a product, structure, system, or service during its life span or specified time period.

Lift   The force that pulls a wind turbine blade, as opposed to drag.

Light   Space in a window sash for a single pane of glass. Also, a pane of glass.

Light construction   Construction generally restricted to conventional wood stud walls, floor and ceiling joists, and rafters. Primarily residential in nature, although it does include small commercial buildings.

Light quality   A description of how well people in a lighted space can see to do visual tasks and how visually comfortable they feel in that space.

Light trapping   The trapping of light inside a semiconductor material by refracting and reflecting the light at critical angles; trapped light will travel further in the material, greatly increasing the probability of absorption and, hence, of producing charge carriers.

Lighting outlet   An outlet intended for the direct connection of a lampholder, a lighting fixture, or a pendant cord terminating in a lampholder.

Limit switch   A safety control that automatically shuts off a furnace if it gets too hot. Most also control blower cycles.

Line loss (or drop)   Electrical energy lost due to inherent inefficiencies in an electrical transmission and distribution system under specific conditions.

Lineal foot   Having length only, pertaining to a line one foot long as distinguished from a square foot or cubic foot.

Lintel   A horizontal structural member which supports the load over an opening such as a door or window.

Liquid-based solar heating system   A solar heating system that uses a liquid as the heat transfer fluid.

Liquid-to-air heat exchanger   A heat exchanger that transfers the heat contained in a liquid heat transfer fluid to air.

Liquid-to-liquid heat exchanger   A heat exchanger that transfers heat contained in a liquid heat transfer fluid to another liquid.

Listed and listing   Terms referring to equipment which is shown in a list published by an approved testing agency qualified and equipped for experimental testing and maintaining an adequate periodic inspection of current productions and whose listing states that the equipment complies with nationally recognized standards when installed in accordance with the manufacturer's installation instructions.

Lithium-sulfur battery   A battery that uses lithium in the negative electrode and a metal sulfide in the positive electrode, and the electrolyte is molten salt; can store large amounts of energy per unit weight.

Live load   The total of all moving and variable loads that may be placed upon a building.

Live parts   Electric conductors, buses, terminals, or components that are uninsulated or exposed and a shock hazard exists.

Live steam   Steam available directly from a boiler under full pressure.

Load   The power required to run a defined circuit or system, such as a refrigerator, building, or an entire electricity distribution system.

Load analysis   Assessing and quantifying the discrete components that comprise a load. This analysis often includes time of day or season as a variable.

Load-bearing wall   Includes all exterior walls and any interior wall that is aligned above a support beam or girder. Normally, any wall that has a double horizontal top plate.

Load-duration curve   A curve that displays load values on the horizontal axis in descending order of magnitude against the percent of time (on the vertical axis) that the load values are exceeded.

Load factor   The ratio of average energy demand (load) to maximum demand (peak load) during a specific period.

Local solar time   A system of astronomical time in which the sun crosses the true north-south meridian at 12 noon, and which differs from local time according to longitude, time zone, and equation of time.

Location definitions   *Damp locations* are partially protected locations under canopies, marquees, roofed open porches and like locations, and interior locations subject to moderate degrees of moisture, such as some basements, some barns, and some cold-storage warehouses. *Dry locations* are locations not normally subject to dampness or wetness. A location classified as dry may be temporarily subject to dampness or wetness, as in the case of a building under construction. *Wet locations* are installations underground, in concrete slabs or masonry in direct contact with the earth, or locations subject to saturation with water or other liquids, such as vehicle-washing areas and locations exposed to weather and unprotected.

Lock block   A block of wood which is joined to the inside edge of the stile of a hollow core door and to which the lock is fitted. Flush doors have a lock block on each stile.

Log law   In reference to a wind energy conversion system, the wind speed profile in which wind speeds increase with the logarithmic of the height of the wind turbine above the ground.

Log lighter, gas-fired   An unlisted, manually operated gas-fired solid-fuel ignition device for installation in a vented solid-fuel-burning fireplace.

Long ton   A unit that equals 20 long hundredweights or 2240 lb. Used mainly in England.

Long-wave radiation   Infrared or radiant heat.

Lookout   Structural member running between the lower end of a rafter and the outside wall. Used to carry the underside of the overhang; plancier or soffit.

Loose fill insulation   Insulation made from rock wool fibers, fiberglass, cellulose fiber, vermiculite, or perlite minerals; loose fibers or granules can be applied by pouring directly from the bag or with a blower.

Louver   A vented opening into the home that has a series of horizontal slats and arranged to permit ventilation but to exclude rain, snow, light, insects, or other living creatures.

Low Btu gas   A fuel gas with a heating value between 90 and 200 Btu per cubic foot.

Low-E coatings and (window) films   A coating applied to the surface of the glazing of a window to reduce heat transfer through the window.

Low-emissivity windows and (window) films   Energy-efficient windows that have a coating or film applied to the surface of the glass to reduce heat transfer through the window.

Low-flush toilet   A toilet that uses less water than a standard one during flushing for the purpose of conserving water resources.

Lower (net) heating value   The lower or net heat of combustion for a fuel that assumes that all products of combustion are in a gaseous state.

Low-flow solar water heating systems   The flow rate in these systems is $\frac{1}{8}$ to $\frac{1}{5}$ the rate of most solar water heating systems. The low-flow systems take advantage of stratification in the storage tank and theoretically allows for the use of smaller diameter piping to and from the collector and a smaller pump.

Low-pressure gas supply system   A gas supply system with gas pressure at or below 0.5 psig (3.44 kPa gage).

Low-pressure sodium lamp   A type of lamp that produces light from sodium gas contained in a bulb operating at a partial pressure of 0.13 to 1.3 Pa. The yellow light and large size make them applicable to lighting streets and parking lots.

LP gas   Liquefied petroleum gas composed predominately of propane, propylene, butanes or butylenes, or mixtures thereof, which are gaseous under normal atmospheric conditions but are capable of being liquefied under moderate pressure at normal temperatures.

Lumber   The product of the saw and planing mill not further manufactured than by sawing, resawing, passing lengthwise through a standard planing machine, and crosscutting to length. Some matching of ends and edges may be included.

Lumens   Unit of measure for total light output. The amount of light falling on a surface of one square foot.

Lumens/watt (lpw)   A measure of the efficacy (efficiency) of lamps. It indicates the amount of light (lumens) emitted by the lamp for each unit of electrical power (watts) used.

Luminaire   A complete lighting unit consisting of a lamp(s), housing, and connection to the power circuit.

Luminance   The physical measure of the subjective sensation of brightness; measured in lumens.

Lux   The unit of illuminance equivalent to 1 lumen per square meter.

Macerating toilet systems   A system comprising a sump with a macerating pump which is designed to grind and discharge the waste from a bathroom group consisting of a water closet, lavatory, and bathtub or shower.

Magnetic ballast   A type of florescent light ballast that uses a magnetic core to regulate the voltage of a florescent lamp.

Main   The principal pipe artery to which branches are capable of being connected.

Make-up air   Air brought into a building from outside to replace exhaust air.

Male   Any part, such as a bolt, designed to fit into another (female) part. External threads are male.

Manifold water distribution systems   A fabricated piping arrangement in which a large supply main is fitted with multiple branches in close proximity, in which water is distributed separately to fixtures from each branch.

Mansard roof   A type of curb roof in which the pitch of the upper portion of a sloping side is slight and that of the lower portion steep. The lower portion is usually interrupted by dormer windows.

Mantel   The shelf above a fireplace opening. Also used in referring to the decorative trim around a fireplace opening.

Manual J   The standard method for calculating residential cooling loads developed by the Air-Conditioning and Refrigeration Institute (ARI) and the Air Conditioning Contractors of America (ACCA) based largely on the American Society of Heating, Refrigeration, and Air-Conditioning Engineer's (ASHRAE) "Handbook of Fundamentals."

Manufactured wood   A wood product such as a truss, beam, gluelam, microlam or joist which is manufactured out of smaller wood pieces and glued or mechanically fastened to form a larger piece. Often used to create a stronger member which may use less wood. (See "Oriented strand board.")

Manufacturer's installation instructions   Printed instructions included with equipment as part of the conditions of listing and labeling.

Manufacturer's specifications   The written installation and/or maintenance instructions which are developed by the manufacturer of a product and which may have to be followed in order to maintain the product warrantee.

Marginal cost   The cost of producing one additional unit of a product.

Masonry   Stone, rock, brick, hollow tile, concrete block, or tile, and sometimes poured concrete and gypsum block, or other similar materials, or a combination of same, bonded together with mortar to form a wall, pier, buttress, etc.

Masonry chimney   A field-constructed chimney of masonry units, bricks, stones, labeled masonry chimney units, or reinforced portland cement concrete, lined with suitable chimney flue liners.

Masonry fireplace   A field-constructed fireplace composed of solid masonry units, bricks, stones or concrete.

Masonry stove   A type of heating appliance similar to a fireplace but much more efficient and clean burning. They are made of masonry and have long channels through which combustion gases give up their heat to the heavy mass of the stove, which releases the heat slowly into a room. Often called Russian or Finnish fireplaces.

Mastic   A pasty material used as a cement (as for setting tile) or a protective coating (as for thermal insulation or waterproofing).

Matched lumber   Lumber that is edge dressed and shaped to make a close tongue-and-groove joint at the edges or ends. Also generally includes lumber with rabbeted edges.

MCF   An abbreviation for one thousand cubic feet of natural gas, which has a heat content of 1,000,000 Btus, or 10 therms.

Mean power output (of a wind turbine)   The average power output of a wind energy conversion system at a given mean wind speed based on a Raleigh frequency distribution.

Mean wind speed   The arithmetic wind speed over a specified time period and height above the ground (the majority of U.S. National Weather Service anemometers are at 20 ft (6.1 m).

Mechanical equipment   In architectural and engineering practice: All equipment included under the general heading of plumbing, heating, air conditioning, gas fitting, and electrical work.

Mechanical exhaust system   Equipment installed in a venting system to provide an induced draft.

Mechanical system   A system specifically addressed and regulated in this code and composed of components, devices, appliances, and equipment.

Mechanics lien   A lien on real property, created by statue in many years, in favor of persons supplying labor or materials for a building or structure, for the value of labor or materials supplied by them. In some jurisdictions, a mechanics lien also exists for the value of professional services. Clear title to the property cannot be obtained until the claim for the labor, materials, or professional services is settled. Timely filing is essential to support the encumbrance, and prescribed filing dates vary by jurisdiction.

Medallion   A raised decorative piece, sometimes used on flush doors.

Median wind speed   The wind speed with 50 percent probability of occurring.

Medium Btu gas   Fuel gas with a heating value of between 200 and 300 Btu/cu. ft.

Medium pressure   For valves and fittings, implies that they are suitable for working pressures between 125 to 175 lb/sq. in.

Medium-pressure gas supply systems   A gas supply system with gas pressure exceeding 0.5 psig (3.44 kPa gage) but not exceeding 5 psig (34 kPa gage).

Meeting rail   The bottom rail of the upper sash, and the top rail of the lower sash of a double-hung window.

Megawatt   One thousand kilowatts, or 1 million watts; standard measure of electric power plant generating capacity.

Megawatt-hour   One thousand kilowatt-hours or 1 million watt-hours.

Mercury vapor lamp   A high-intensity discharge lamp that uses mercury as the primary light-producing element. Includes clear, phosphor coated, and self-ballasted lamps.

Met   An approximate unit of heat produced by a resting person, equal to about 18.5 Btu per square foot per hour.

Metal halide lamp   A high-intensity discharge lamp type that uses mercury and several halide additives as light-producing elements. These lights have the best Color Rendition Index (CRI) of the high-intensity discharge lamps. They can be used for commercial interior lighting or for stadium lights.

Metal lath   Sheets of metal that are slit to form openings within the lath. Used as a plaster base for walls and ceilings and as reinforcing over other forms of plaster base.

Methane   A colorless, odorless, tasteless gas composed of one molecule of carbon and four of hydrogen, which is highly flammable. It is the main constituent of "natural gas," which is formed naturally by methanogenic, anaerobic bacteria or can be manufactured, and which is used as a fuel and for manufacturing chemicals.

Methanol (CH$_3$OH)   A clear, colorless, very mobile liquid that is flammable and poisonous; used as a fuel and fuel additive, and to produce chemicals. Also called "methyl alcohol" or "wood alcohol."

Metric ton   A unit of mass equal to 1000 kilograms or 2204.6 pounds.

Microclimate   The local climate of specific place or habitat, as influenced by landscape features.

Microgroove   A small groove scribed into the surface of a solar photovoltaic cell which is filled with metal for contacts.

Microlam   A manufactured structural wood beam. It is constructed of pressure and adhesive bonded wood strands of wood. They have a higher strength rating than solid sawn lumber. Normally comes in 1½ in. thickness and 9½ in., 11½ in., and 14 in. widths

Micrometer   One millionth of a meter (10^{-6} m).

Milar (mylar)   Plastic, transparent copies of a blueprint.

Mill   A common monetary measure equal to one-thousandth of a dollar or a tenth of a cent.

Millwork   The term used to describe products which are primarily manufactured from lumber in a planing mill or woodworking plant; including moldings, door frames and entrances, blinds and shutters, sash and window units, doors, stairwork, kitchen cabinets, mantels, cabinets, and porch work.

Minority carrier   A current carrier, either an electron or a hole, that is in the minority in a specific layer of a semiconductor material; the diffusion of minority carriers under the action of the cell junction voltage is the current in a photovoltaic device.

Minority carrier lifetime   The average time a minority carrier exists before recombination.

Miter joint   The joint of two pieces at an angle that bisects the joining angle. For example, the miter joint at the side and head casing at a door opening is made at a 45° angle.

Mixing valve   A valve operated by a thermostat that can be installed in solar water heating systems to mix cold water with water from the collector loop to maintain a safe water temperature.

Modified degree-day method   A method used to estimate building heating loads by assuming that heat loss and gain is proportional to the equivalent heat-loss coefficient for the building envelope.

Module   The smallest self-contained, environmentally protected structure housing interconnected photovoltaic cells and providing a single dc electrical output; also called a panel.

Moisture content   The water content of a substance (a solid fuel) as measured under specified conditions. *Dry basis:* equals the weight of a wet sample minus the weight of a (bone) dry sample divided by the weight of the dry sample times 100 (to get percent). *Wet basis:* equals the weight of a wet sample minus the weight of a (bone) dry sample divided by the weight of the wet sample times 100.

Molding   A relatively narrow strip of wood, usually shaped to a curved profile throughout its length. Used to accent and emphasize the ornamentation of a structure and to conceal surface or angle joints.

Monoculture   The planting, cultivation, and harvesting of a single species of crop in a specified area.

Monolithic   Term used for concrete construction poured and cast in one unit without joints.

Monopost   Adjustable metal column used to support a beam or bearing point. Normally 11 gauge or Schedule 40 metal, and determined by the structural engineer.

Mortar   A mixture of cement (or lime) with sand and water used in masonry work.

Mortise   A slot cut into a board, plank, or timber, usually edgewise, to receive the tenon (or tongue) of another board, plank, or timber to form a joint.

Motor   A machine supplied with external energy that is converted into force and/or motion.

Motor speed   The number of revolutions that the motor turns in a given time period (i.e., revolutions per minute, rpm).

Moulder   A woodworking machine designed to run moldings and other wood members with regular or irregular profiles. (See "Stickers.")

Movable insulation   A device that reduces heat loss at night and during cloudy periods and heat gain during the day in warm weather. A movable insulator could be an insulative shade, shutter panel, or curtain.

MR (moisture-resistant) wallboard   A type of gypsum wallboard processed to resist the effects of moisture and high humidity. It is used as a base under ceramic tile and other nonabsorbent finishes used in showers and tub alcoves.

Mudsill   Bottom horizontal member of an exterior wall frame which rests on top of a foundation; sometimes called "sill plate." (See "Sole plate.")

Mullion   A slender bar or pier forming a division between units of windows, screens, or similar frames; generally nonstructural.

Multijunction device   A high-efficiency photovoltaic device containing two or more cell junctions, each of which is optimized for a particular part of the solar spectrum.

Multi-outlet assembly   A type of surface or flush raceway designed to hold conductors and receptacles, assembled in the field or at the factory.

Multizone system   A building heating, ventilation, and/or air conditioning system that distributes conditioned air to individual zones or rooms.

Municipal solid waste (MSW)   Waste material from households and businesses in a community that is not regulated as hazardous.

Muntin   Vertical member between two panels of the same piece of panel work. The vertical and horizontal sashbars separating the different panes of glass in a window.

Muriatic acid   Commonly used as a brick cleaner after masonry work is completed.

Mushroom   The unacceptable occurrence when the top of a caisson concrete pier spreads out and hardens to become wider than the foundation wall thickness.

Nacelle   The cover for the gear box, drive train, generator, and other components of a wind turbine.

Nail inspection   An inspection made by a municipal building inspector after the drywall material is hung with nails and screws (and before taping).

Name plate   A metal tag attached to a machine or appliance that contains information such as brand name, serial number, voltage, power ratings under specified conditions, and other manufacturer supplied data.

National Electrical Code (NEC)   The NEC is a set of regulations that have contributed to making the electrical systems in the United States one of the safest in the world. The intent of the NEC is to ensure safe electrical systems are designed and installed. The National Fire Protection Association has sponsored the NEC since 1911. The NEC changes as technology evolves and component sophistication increases. The NEC is updated every 3 years. Following the NEC is required in most locations.

Natural cooling   Space cooling achieved by shading, natural (unassisted, as opposed to forced) ventilation, conduction control, radiation, and evaporation. (Also called "passive cooling.")

Natural draft   Draft that is caused by temperature differences in the air.

Natural finish   A transparent finish which does not seriously alter the original color or grain of the natural wood. Natural finishes are usually provided by sealers, oils, varnishes, water repellent preservatives, and other similar materials.

Natural gas   A hydrocarbon gas obtained from underground sources, often in association with petroleum and coal deposits. It generally contains a high percentage of methane, varying amounts of ethane, and inert gases; used as a heating fuel.

Natural gas steam reforming production   A two-step process where in the first step natural gas is exposed to a high-temperature steam to produce hydrogen, carbon monoxide, and carbon dioxide. The second step is to convert the carbon monoxide with steam to produce additional hydrogen and carbon dioxide.

Natural ventilation   Ventilation that is created by the differences in the distribution of air pressures around a building. Air moves from areas of high pressure to areas of low pressure with gravity and wind pressure affecting the airflow. The placement and control of doors and windows alter natural ventilation patterns.

Net floor area   The gross floor area, less the area of the partitions, columns, stairs, and other floor openings.

Net generation   Equal to gross generation less electricity consumption of a power.

Net present value   The value of a personal portfolio, product, or investment after depreciation and interest on debt capital are subtracted from operating income. It can also be thought of as the equivalent worth of all cash flows relative to a base point called the present.

Neutral wire   Usually color-coded white, this carries electricity from an outlet back to the service panel. (See "Hot wire" and "Ground.")

Newel   The main post at the start of the stairs and the stiffening post at the landing; a stair newel.

Nitrogen dioxide   This compound of nitrogen and oxygen is formed by the oxidation of nitric oxide (NO), which is produced by the combustion of solid fuels.

Nocturnal cooling   The effect of cooling by the radiation of heat from a building to the night sky.

Nominal capacity   The approximate energy producing capacity of a power plant, under specified conditions, usually during periods of highest load.

Nominal size   As applied to timber or lumber, the ordinary commercial size by which it is known and sold.

Nonbearing partition   A partition extending from floor to ceiling which supports no load other than its own weight.

Noncombustible material   Materials that pass the test procedure for defining noncombustibility of elementary materials set forth in ASTM E 136.

Nonconditioned space   A space that is isolated from conditioned space by insulated walls, floors or ceilings.

Nonrenewable fuels   Fuels that cannot be easily made or "renewed," such as oil, natural gas, and coal.

Nonutility generator/power producer   A class of power generator that is not a regulated power provider and that has generating plants for the purpose of supplying electric power required in the conduct of their industrial and commercial operations.

Normal recovery capacity   A characteristic applied to domestic water heaters that is the amount of gallons raised 100°F/hr (or min) under a specified thermal efficiency.

Nosing   The part of a stair tread which projects over the riser, or any similar projection; a term applied to the rounded edge of a board.

Notch   A crosswise groove at the end of a board.

Nozzle   The part of a heating system that sprays the fuel of fuel–air mixture into the combustion chamber.

Nuclear energy   Energy that comes from splitting atoms of radioactive materials, such as uranium, and which produces radioactive wastes.

Oakum   Loose hemp or jute fiber that's impregnated with tar or pitch and used to caulk large seams or for packing plumbing pipe joints.

Occupancy sensor   An optical, ultrasonic, or infrared sensor that turns room lights on when they detect a person's presence and off after the space is vacated.

Occupied space   The space within a building or structure that is normally occupied by people, and that may be conditioned (heated, cooled and/or ventilated).

Off-peak   The period of low energy demand, as opposed to maximum, or peak, demand.

Offset   A combination of fittings that makes two changes in direction bringing one section of the pipe out of line but into a line parallel with the other section.

Ohms   A measure of the electrical resistance of a material equal to the resistance of a circuit in which the potential difference of 1 volt produces a current of 1 ampere.

Ohm's law   In a given electrical circuit, the amount of current in amperes (I) is equal to the pressure in volts (E) divided by the resistance in ohms (R).

Oil (fuel)   A product of crude oil that is used for space heating, diesel engines, and electrical generation.

On center (O.C.)   A method of indicating the spacing of framing members by stating the measurement from the center of one member to the center of the succeeding one.

One-axis tracking   A system capable of rotating about one axis.

One-family dwelling   A building consisting solely of one dwelling unit.

On-peak energy   Energy supplied during periods of relatively high system demands as specified by the supplier.

On-site generation   Generation of energy at the location where all or most of it will be used.

Open access   The ability to send or wheel electric power to a customer over a transmission and distribution system that is not owned by the power generator (seller).

Open-hole inspection   When an engineer (or municipal inspector) inspects the open excavation and examines the earth to determine the type of foundation (caisson, footer, wall on ground, etc.) that should be installed in the hole.

Open-circuit voltage   The maximum possible voltage across a photovoltaic cell; the voltage across the cell in sunlight when no current is flowing.

Open-grain wood   Woods with large pores, such as oak, ash, chestnut, and walnut.

Open-loop geothermal heat pump system   Open-loop (also known as "direct") systems circulate water drawn from a ground or surface water source. Once the heat has been transferred into or out of the water, the water is returned to a well or surface discharge (instead of being recirculated through the system). This option is practical where there is an adequate supply of relatively clean water, and all local codes and regulations regarding groundwater discharge are met.

Operating cycle   The processes that a work input/output system undergoes and in which the initial and final states are identical.

Oriel window   A window that projects from the main line of an enclosing wall of a building and is carried on brackets, corbels, or a cantilever.

Orientation   The alignment of a building along a given axis to face a specific geographical direction. The alignment of a solar collector, in number of degrees east or west of true south.

Oriented strand board   A formed panel consisting of layers of compressed strand-like particles arranged at right angles to each other.

Outage   A discontinuance of electric power supply.

Outgassing   The process by which materials expel or release gasses.

Outlet   A point on the wiring system at which current is taken to supply utilization equipment.

Outrigger   An extension of a rafter beyond the wall line. Usually a smaller member nailed to a larger rafter to form a cornice or roof overhang.

Outside air   Air that is taken from the outdoors.

Outside coil   The heat-transfer (exchanger) component of a heat pump, located outdoors, from which heat is collected in the heating mode, or expelled in the cooling mode.

Outside corner   The point at which two walls form an external angle, one you usually can walk around.

Oven, wall-mounted   An oven for cooking purposes designed for mounting in or on a wall or other surface and consisting of one or more heating elements, internal wiring, and built-in or separately mountable controls. (See "Cooking unit, countermounted.")

Overcurrent   Any current in excess of the rated current of equipment or the ampacity of a conductor. It may result from overload (see definition), short circuit or ground fault.

Overhang   A building element that shades windows, walls, and doors from direct solar radiation and protects these elements from precipitation.

Overload   Operation of equipment in excess of normal, full-load rating, or of a conductor in excess of rated ampacity that, when it persists for a sufficient length of time, would cause damage or dangerous overheating. A fault, such as a short circuit or ground fault, is not an overload. (See "Overcurrent.")

Ovonic   A device, invented by Standford Ovshinsky, that converts heat or sunlight directly to electricity and has a unique glass composition that changes from an electrically nonconducting state to a semiconducting state.

Oxygenates   Gasoline fuel additives such as ethanol, ETBE, or MTBE that add extra oxygen to gasoline to reduce carbon monoxide pollution produced by vehicles.

P trap   Curved "U" section of drain pipe that holds a water seal to prevent sewer gases from entering the home through a fixture's water drain.

P/N   A semiconductor (photovoltaic) device structure in which the junction is formed between a p-type layer and an n-type layer.

Packing factor   The ratio of solar collector array area to actual land area.

Pad out, pack out   To shim out or add strips of wood to a wall or ceiling in order that the finished ceiling/wall will appear correct.

Padding   A material installed under carpet to add foot comfort, isolate sound, and to prolong carpet life.

Paint   A combination of pigments with suitable thinners or oils to provide decorative and protective coatings. Can be oil based or latex water based.

Pallets   Wooden platforms used for storing and shipping material. Forklifts and hand trucks are used to move these wooden platforms around.

Pane (window)   The area of glass that fits in the window frame.

Panel   A thin, flat piece of wood, plywood, or similar material, framed by stiles and rails as in a door (or cabinet door), or fitted into grooves of thicker material with molded edges for decorative wall treatment.

Panel (solar)   A term generally applied to individual solar collectors, and typically to solar photovoltaic collectors or modules.

Panel radiator   A mainly flat surface for transmitting radiant energy.

Panelboard   A single panel or group of panel units designed for assembly in the form of a single panel, including buses and automatic overcurrent devices, and equipped with or without switches for the control of light, heat, or power circuits, designed to be placed in a cabinet or cutout box placed in or against a wall or partition and accessible only from the front.

Panemone   A drag-type wind machine that can react to wind from any direction.

Paper, building   A general term for papers, felts, and similar sheet materials used in buildings without reference to their properties or uses. Generally comes in long rolls.

Parabolic aluminized reflector lamp   A type of lamp having a lens of heavy durable glass that focuses the light. They have longer lifetimes with less lumen depreciation than standard incandescent lamps.

Parabolic dish   A solar energy conversion device that has a bowl-shaped dish covered with a highly reflective surface that tracks the sun and concentrates sunlight on a fixed absorber, thereby achieving high temperatures, for process heating or to operate a heat (Stirling) engine to produce power or electricity.

Parabolic trough   A solar energy conversion device that uses a trough covered with a highly reflective surface to focus sunlight onto a linear absorber containing a working fluid that can be used for medium temperature space or process heat or to operate a steam turbine for power or electricity generation.

Parallel   A configuration of an electrical circuit in which the voltage is the same across the terminals. The positive reference direction for each resistor current is down through the resistor with the same voltage across each resistor.

Parallel connection   A way of joining photovoltaic cells or modules by connecting positive leads together and negative leads together; such a configuration increases the current, but not the voltage.

Parapet   A low wall or railing along the edge of a roof, balcony, or bridge. The part of a wall that extends above the roof line.

Pargeting   Thin coat of plaster applied to stone or brick to form a smooth or decorative surface.

Particleboard   A formed panel consisting of particles of wood flakes, shavings, slivers, etc., bonded together with a synthetic resin or other added binder.

Particulates   The fine liquid or solid particles contained in combustion gases. The quantity and size of particulates emitted by cars, power and industrial plants, wood stoves, etc. are regulated by the U.S. Environmental Protection Agency.

Parting stop or strip   A small wood piece used in the side and head jambs of double hung windows to separate the upper sash from the lower sash.

Partition   A wall that subdivides space within any story of a building.

Party wall   A wall used jointly by two parties under easement agreement and erected at or upon a line separating two parcels of land that may be held under different ownership.

Passivation   A chemical reaction that eliminates the detrimental effect of electrically reactive atoms on a photovoltaic cell's surface.

Passive solar (building) design   A building design that uses structural elements of a building to heat and cool a building, without the use of mechanical equipment, which requires careful consideration of the local climate and solar energy resource, building orientation, and landscape features, to name a few. The principal elements include proper building orientation, proper window sizing and placement and design of window overhangs to reduce summer heat gain and ensure winter heat gain, and proper sizing of thermal energy storage mass (for example, a Trombe wall or masonry tiles). The heat is distributed primarily by natural convection and radiation, but fans can also be used to circulate room air or ensure proper ventilation.

Passive solar construction   Structures of glass, wood, and masonry, which collect, transport, and store heat from the energy of the sun.

Passive solar heater   A solar water or space-heating system in which solar energy is collected, and/or moved by natural convection without using pumps or fans. Passive systems are typically integral collector/storage (ICS; or batch collectors) or thermosyphon systems. The major advantage of these systems is that they do not use controls, pumps, sensors, or other mechanical parts, so little or no maintenance is required over the lifetime of the system.

Passive solar home   A house built using passive solar design techniques.

Passive/natural cooling   To allow or augment the natural movement of cooler air from exterior, shaded areas of a building through or around a building.

Paver, paving Materials—commonly masonry—laid down to make a firm, even surface.

Peak demand/load The maximum energy demand or load in a specified time period.

Peak power Power generated that operates at a very low capacity factor; generally used to meet short-lived and variable high demand periods.

Peak shifting The process of moving existing loads to off-peak periods.

Peak sun hours The equivalent number of hours per day when solar irradiance averages $1 kW/m^2$. For example, six peak sun hours means that the energy received during total daylight hours equals the energy that would have been received had the irradiance for six hours been $1 kW/m^2$.

Peak watt A unit used to rate the performance of a solar photovoltaic (PV) cells, modules, or arrays; the maximum nominal output of a PV device, in watts (Wp) under standardized test conditions, usually 1000 watts per square meter of sunlight with other conditions, such as temperature specified.

Peak wind speed The maximum instantaneous wind speed (or velocity) that occurs within a specific period of time or interval.

Peaking capacity Power generation equipment or system capacity to meet peak power demands.

Peaking hydropower A hydropower plant that is operated at maximum allowable capacity for part of the day and is either shut down for the remainder of the time or operated at minimal capacity level.

Pedestal A metal box installed at various locations along utility easements that contain electrical, telephone, or cable television switches and connections.

Pellet fuel-burning appliance A closed-combustion, vented appliance equipped with a fuel-feed mechanism for burning processed pellets of solid fuel of a specified size and composition.

Pellet stove A space heating device that burns pellets; is more efficient, clean burning, and easier to operate than conventional cord wood–burning appliances.

Pellet vent A listed vent conforming to the pellet vent requirements of UL 641 for venting pellet fuel-burning appliances listed for use with pellet vents.

Pellets Solid fuels made from primarily wood sawdust that is compacted under high pressure to form small (about the size of rabbit feed) pellets for use in a pellet stove.

Pelton turbine A type of impulse hydropower turbine where water passes through nozzles and strikes cups arranged on the periphery of a runner, or wheel, which causes the runner to rotate, producing mechanical energy. The runner is fixed on a shaft, and the rota-

tional motion of the turbine is transmitted by the shaft to a generator. Generally used for high-head, low-flow applications.

Penalty clause A provision in a contract that provides for a reduction in the amount otherwise payable under a contract to a contractor as a penalty for failure to meet deadlines or for failure of the project to meet contract specifications.

Penny Term used to indicate nail length; abbreviated by the letter d. Applies to common, box, casing, and finishing nails.

Penstock A component of a hydropower plant; a pipe that delivers water to the turbine.

Percolation test, perc. test Tests that a soil engineer performs on earth to determine the feasibility of installing a leech field–type sewer system on a lot. A test to determine if the soil on a proposed building lot is capable of absorbing the liquid affluent from a septic system.

Perfluorocarbon Tracer-Gas Technique (PFT) An air infiltration measurement technique developed by the Brookhaven National Laboratory to measure changes over time (1 week to 5 months) when determining a building's air infiltration rate. This test cannot locate exact points of infiltration, but it does reveal long-term infiltration problems.

Performance bond An amount of money (usually 10% of the total price of a job) that a contractor must put on deposit with a governmental agency as an insurance policy that guarantees the contractor's proper and timely completion of a project or job.

Perimeter drain 3- or 4-in. perforated plastic pipe that goes around the perimeter (either inside or outside) of a foundation wall (before backfill) and collects and diverts ground water away from the foundation. Generally, it is "daylighted" into a sump pit inside the home, and a sump pump is sometimes inserted into the pit to discharge any accumulation of water.

Perimeter heating A term applied to warm-air heating systems that deliver heated air to rooms by means of registers or baseboards located along exterior walls.

Permeability A measure of the ease with which water penetrates a material.

Permeance A unit of measurement for the ability of a material to retard the diffusion of water vapor at $73.4°F$ ($23°C$). A perm, short for permeance, is the number of grains of water vapor that pass through a square foot of material per hour at a differential vapor pressure equal to 1 in. of mercury.

Permit A governmental municipal authorization to perform a building process. *Building permit:* Authorization to build or modify a structure (a separate permit is required for most electrical work and for new plumbing and larger modifications of existing plumbing systems); authorization to change the contour of the land; a health department authorization to build or modify a septic system. *Demolition permit:* Authorization to tear down and remove an existing structure. *Zoning use permit:* Authorization to use a property for a specific use, e.g., a garage, a single-family residence, and so on.

Phantom load   Any appliance that consumes power even when it is turned off. Examples of phantom loads include appliances with electronic clocks or timers, appliances with remote controls, and appliances with wall cubes (a small box that plugs into an AC outlet to power appliances).

Phase   Alternating current is carried by conductors and a ground to residential, commercial, or industrial consumers. The waveform of the phase power appears as a single continuous sine wave at the system frequency whose amplitude is the rated voltage of the power.

Phase change   The process of changing from one physical state (solid, liquid, or gas) to another, with a necessary or coincidental input or release of energy.

Phase-change materials   Material which changes from solid to liquid to gaseous state and which can store a great amount of heat energy.

Photocurrent   An electric current induced by radiant energy.

Photoelectric cell   A device for measuring light intensity that works by converting light falling on, or reach it, to electricity, and then measuring the current; used in photometers.

Photovoltaic device   A solid-state electrical device that converts light directly into direct current electricity of voltage-current characteristics that are a function of the characteristics of the light source and the materials in and design of the device. Solar photovoltaic devices are made of various semi-conductor materials including silicon, cadmium sulfide, cadmium telluride, and gallium arsenide, and in single-crystalline, multicrystalline, or amorphous forms.

Photovoltaic (solar) module or panel   A solar photovoltaic product that generally consists of groups of PV cells electrically connected together to produce a specified power output under standard test conditions, mounted on a substrate, sealed with an encapsulant, and covered with a protective glazing. Maybe further mounted on an aluminum frame. A junction box, on the back or underside of the module is used to allow for connecting the module circuit conductors to external conductors.

Photovoltaic (solar) system   A complete PV power system composed of the module (or array), and balance-of-system (BOS) components including the array supports, electrical conductors/wiring, fuses, safety disconnects, and grounds, charge controllers, inverters, battery storage, etc.

Photovoltaic-thermal (PV/T) systems   A solar energy system that produces electricity with a PV module, and collects thermal energy from the module for heating. There are no commercially available systems available (as of November 1997).

Physical vapor deposition   A method of depositing thin semiconductor photovoltaic) films. With this method, physical processes, such as thermal evaporation or bombardment of ions, are used to deposit elemental semiconductor material on a substrate.

Pier   A column of masonry, usually rectangular in horizontal cross section. Used to support other structural members.

Pigment   A powdered solid used in paint or enamel to give it a color.

Pigtails, electrical   The electric cord that the electrician provides and installs on an appliance such as a garbage disposal, dishwasher, or range hood.

Pilaster   A part of a wall that projects not more than one-half of its own width beyond the outside or inside face of a wall. Chief purpose is to add strength but may also be decorative.

Pile   A heavy timber, or pillar of metal or concrete, forced into the earth or cast in place to form a foundation member.

Pilot hole   A small-diameter, predrilled hole that guides a nail or screw.

Pilot light   A small, continuous flame (in a hot water heater, boiler, or furnace) that ignites gas or oil burners when needed.

Pitch   The incline slope of a roof or the ratio of the total rise to the total width of a house, i.e., a 6-ft rise and 24-ft width is a one-fourth pitch roof. Roof slope is expressed in the inches of rise, per foot of horizontal run.

Pitch control   A method of controlling a wind turbine's speed by varying the orientation, or pitch, of the blades, and thereby altering its aerodynamics and efficiency.

Plan view   Drawing of a structure with the view from overhead, looking down.

Plan   A drawing representing any one of the floors or horizontal cross sections of a building, or the horizontal plane of any other object or area.

Plancier   The underside of an eave or cornice, usually horizontal.

Plaster   A mixture of lime, cement, and sand used to cover outside and inside wall surfaces.

Plat A map, plan, or chart of a city, town, section, or subdivision indicating the location and boundaries of individual properties.

Plate A horizontal structural member placed on a wall or supported on posts, studs, or corbels to carry the trusses of a roof or to carry the rafters directly. Also a sole or base member of a partition or other frame.

Platform framing A system of framing a building where the floor joists of each story rest on the top plates of the story below (or on the foundation wall for the first story) and the bearing walls and partitions rest on the subfloor of each story.

Plenum A compartment or chamber to which one or more air ducts are connected and that forms part of the air distribution system.

Plot plan A view from above a building site. The plan shows distances from a structure to property lines. Sometimes called a site plan.

Plough, plow To cut a lengthwise groove in a board or plank. An exterior handrail normally has a ploughed groove for hand gripping purposes

Plug flow digester A type of anaerobic digester that has a horizontal tank in which a constant volume of material is added and forces material in the tank to move through the tank and be digested.

Plumb Exactly perpendicular or vertical; at right angles to the horizon or floor.

Plumb bob A lead weight attached to a string. It is the tool used in determining plumb.

Plumbing The work or business of installing pipes, fixtures, and other apparatus for bringing in the water supply and removing liquid and water-borne wastes. This term is used also to denote the installed fixtures and piping of a building.

Plumbing appliance An energized household appliance with plumbing connections, such as a dishwasher, food waste grinder, clothes washer, or water heater.

Plumbing appurtenance A device or assembly which is an adjunct to the basic plumbing system and demands no additional water supply nor adds any discharge load to the system. It is presumed that it performs some useful function in the operation, maintenance, servicing, economy, or safety of the plumbing system. Examples include filters, relief valves, and aerators.

Plumbing boots Metal saddles used to strengthen a bearing wall/vertical stud(s) where a plumbing drain line has been cut through and installed.

Plumbing fixture A receptor or device which requires both a water supply connection and a discharge to the drainage system, such as water closets, lavatories, bathtubs, and sinks. Plumbing appliances as a special class of fixture are further defined.

Plumbing ground The plumbing drain and waste lines that are installed beneath a basement floor.

Plumbing jacks Sleeves that fit around drain and waste vent pipes at and are nailed to the roof sheeting.

Plumbing permit A separate permit required for new plumbing and larger modifications of existing plumbing systems.

Plumbing rough Work performed by the plumbing contractor after the rough heat is installed. This work includes installing all plastic ABS drain and waste lines, copper water lines, bath tubs, shower pans, and gas piping to furnaces and fireplaces.

Plumbing stack A general term for the vertical main of a system of soil, waste, or vent piping.

Plumbing system Includes the water supply and distribution pipes, plumbing fixtures, supports and appurtenances; soil, waste and vent pipes; sanitary drains and building sewers to an approved point of disposal.

Plumbing trim Work performed by the plumbing contractor to get the home ready for a final plumbing inspection. Includes installing all toilets (water closets), hot water heaters, and sinks, and connecting all gas pipes to appliances, disposal, dishwasher, and all plumbing items.

Plumbing waste line Plastic pipe used to collect and drain sewage waste.

Plunge cutting A cutting method used to make a starting hole for a saber saw. The saw is held with the blade teeth almost flush with the wood surface. A cut is made completely through as the saw is tilted to a normal position.

Ply A term to denote the number of layers of roofing felt, veneer in plywood, or layers in built-up materials in any finished piece of such material.

Plywood A panel (normally 4 ft × 8 ft) of wood made of three or more layers of veneer, compressed and joined with glue, and usually laid with the grain of adjoining plies at right angles to give the sheet strength.

Point load A point where a bearing/structural weight is concentrated and transferred to the foundation.

Polyethylene A registered trademark for plastic sheeting material that can be used as a vapor retarder. This plastic is used to make grocery bags. It is a long chain of carbon atoms with two hydrogen atoms attached to each carbon atom.

Polystyrene See "Foam insulation."

Polystyrene panels Rigid insulation manufactured from expanded beads of plastic.

Polyvinyl resin emulsion glue Wood adhesive intended for interiors. Made from polyvinyl acetates which are thermoplastic and not suited for temperatures over 165°F. (Also known as "white glue.")

Porous media A solid that contains pores; normally, it refers to interconnected pores that can transmit the flow of fluids. (The term refers to the aquifer geology when discussing sites for CAES.)

Portico A porch or covered walk consisting of a roof supported by columns. A porch with a continuous row of columns.

Portland cement Cement made by heating clay and crushed limestone into a brick and then grinding to a pulverized powder state.

Post A vertical framing member usually designed to carry a beam. Often a 4 in. × 4 in., a 6 in. × 6 in., or a metal pipe with a flat plate on top and bottom.

Post-and-beam A basic building method that uses just a few hefty posts and beams to support an entire structure. Contrasts with stud framing.

Potable water Water that is suitable for drinking, as defined by local health officials.

Potential energy Energy available due to position.

Pound of steam One pound of water in vapor phase; is *not* steam pressure, which is expressed as pounds per square inch (psi).

Pound per square inch absolute (psia) A unit of pressure [hydraulic (liquid) or pneumatic (gas)] that does not include atmospheric pressure.

Power Energy that is capable or available for doing work; the time rate at which work is performed, measured in horsepower, watts, or Btu per hour. Electric power is the product of electric current and electromotive force.

Power outlet An enclosed assembly that may include receptacles, circuit breakers, fuseholders, fused switches, buses and watt-hour meter mounting means, intended to supply and control power to mobile homes, recreational vehicles or boats, or to serve as a means for distributing power required to operate mobile or temporarily installed equipment.

Power provider A company or other organizational unit that sells and distributes electrical power (e.g., private or public electrical utility), either to other distribution and wholesale businesses or to end users. Sometimes power providers also generate the power they sell.

Power transmission line An electrical conductor/cable that carries electricity from a generator to other locations for distribution.

Power vent A vent that includes a fan to speed up air flow. Often installed on roofs.

Prefabricated construction Type of construction so designed as to involve a minimum of assembly at the site, usually comprising a series of large units manufactured in a plant.

Preheater (solar) A solar heating system that preheats water or air that is then heated more by another heating appliance.

Preservative Substance that will prevent the development and action of wood-destroying fungi, borers of various kinds, and other harmful insects that deteriorate wood.

Pressure drop The loss in static pressure of a fluid (liquid or gas) in a system due to friction from obstructions in pipes; from valves, fittings, regulators, burners, etc.; or from a breech or rupture of the system.

Pressure relief valve A pressure-actuated valve held closed by a spring or other means and designed to relieve pressure automatically at the pressure at which it is set.

Pressure-treated wood Lumber that has been saturated with a preservative.

Pressurization testing A technique used by energy auditors, using a blower door, to locate areas of air infiltration by exaggerating the defects in the building shell. This test only measures air infiltration at the time of the test. It does not take into account changes in atmospheric pressure, weather, wind velocity, or any activities the occupants conduct that may affect air infiltration rates over a period of time.

Primary air The air that is supplied to the combustion chamber of a furnace.

Prime mover Any machine capable of producing power to do work.

Primer The first base coat of paint when a paint job consists of two or more coats. A first coating formulated to seal raw surfaces and holding succeeding finish coats.

Process heat Thermal energy that is used in agricultural and industrial operations.

Producer gas Low or medium Btu content gas, composed mainly of carbon monoxide, nitrogen (2), and hydrogen (2) made by the gasification of wood or coal.

Products of combustion The elements and compounds that result from the combustion of a fuel.

Programmable thermostat A type of thermostat that allows the user to program into the devices' memory a preset schedule of times (when certain temperatures occur) to turn on HVAC equipment.

Projected area The net south-facing glazing area projected on a vertical plane. Also, the solid area covered at any instant by a wind turbine's blades from the perspective of the direction of the windstream (as opposed to the swept area).

Propane A hydrocarbon gas, C_3H_8, occurring in crude oil, natural gas, and refinery cracking gas. It is used as a fuel, a solvent, and a refrigerant. Propane liquefies under pressure and is the major component of liquefied petroleum gas (LPG).

Propeller (hydro) turbine A turbine that has a runner with attached blades similar to a propeller used to drive a ship. As water passes over the curved propeller blades, it causes rotation of the shaft.

Property survey A survey to determine the boundaries of your property. The cost depends on the complexity of the survey.

Proximate analysis A commonly used analysis for reporting fuel properties; may be on a dry (moisture free) basis, as "fired," or on an ash- and moisture-free basis. Fractions usually reported include: volatile matter, fixed carbon, moisture, ash, and heating value (higher heating value).

Psi Pounds of pressure per square inch.

Psia Pounds of force per square inch absolute.

Psig Pounds of force per square inch gauge.

Psychrometer An instrument for measuring relative humidity by means of wet and dry-bulb temperatures.

Psychrometrics The analysis of atmospheric conditions, particularly moisture in the air.

P-type semiconductor A semiconductor in which holes carry the current; produced by doping an intrinsic semiconductor with an electron acceptor impurity (e.g., boron in silicon).

Public sewer A common sewer directly controlled by public authority.

Public water main A water supply pipe for public use controlled by public authority.

Pulse-width-modulated (pwm) wave inverter A type of power inverter that produces a high-quality (nearly sinusoidal) voltage, at minimum current harmonics.

Pump mix Special concrete that will be used in a concrete pump. Generally, the mix has smaller rock aggregate than regular mix.

Pumped storage facility A type of power generating facility that pumps water to a storage reservoir during off-peak periods, and uses the stored water (by allowing it to fall through a hydro turbine) to generate power during peak periods. The pumping energy is typically supplied by lower-cost-base power capacity, and the peaking power capacity is of greater value, even though there is a net loss of power in the process.

Punch list A list of discrepancies that need to be corrected by the contractor.

Punch out To inspect and make a discrepancy list.

Purge To clear of air, gas or other foreign substances.

Purlins Horizontal roof members used to support rafters between the plate and ridge board.

Push stick A pole or strip used to push a workpiece when cutting with power saws, jointers, and other power tools. Pushing a board by hand is usually unsafe with power equipment.

Putty A type of dough used in sealing glass in the sash, filling small holes and crevices in wood, and for similar purposes.

PVC or CPVC (polyvinyl chloride) A type of white or light gray plastic pipe sometimes used for water supply lines and waste pipe.

Pyranometer A device used to measure total incident solar radiation (direct beam, diffuse, and reflected radiation) per unit time per unit area.

Pyrheliometer A device that measures the intensity of direct beam solar radiation.

Pyrolysis The transformation on a compound or material into one or more substances by heat alone (without oxidation); often called destructive distillation. Pyrolysis of biomass is the thermal degradation of the material in the absence of reacting gases, and occurs prior to or simultaneously with gasification reactions in a gasifier. Pyrolysis products consist of gases, liquids, and char generally. The liquid fraction of pyrolisized biomass consists of an insoluble viscous tar, and pyroligneous acids (acetic acid, methanol, acetone, esters, aldehydes, and furfural). The distribution of pyrolysis products varies depending on the feedstock composition, heating rate, temperature, and pressure.

Quad One quadrillion Btu (1,000,000,000,000,000 Btu).

Qualifying facility A category of electric power producer established under the Public Utility Regulatory Policy Act (PURPA) of 1978, that includes small-power producers (SPP) who use renewable sources of energy such as biomass, geothermal, hydroelectricity, solar (thermal and photovoltaic), and wind, or cogenerators who produce both heat and electricity using any type of fuel. PURPA requires utilities to purchase electricity from these power producers at a rate approved by a state utility regulatory agency under federal guidelines. PURPA also requires power providers to sell electricity to these producers. Some states have developed their own programs for SPPs and utilities.

Quarry tile A man- or machine-made clay tile used to finish a floor or wall. Generally 6 in. × 6 in. × ¼ in. thick.

Quarter round Small molding with a cross section of one-fourth of a cylinder.

Quarter-sawed Lumber that has been cut at about a 90° angle to the annular growth rings.

Quick-closing valve A valve or faucet that closes automatically when released manually or controlled by mechanical means for fast-action closing.

Quick-disconnect device   A hand-operated device that provides a means for connecting and disconnecting an appliance to a gas supply and that is equipped with an automatic means to shut off the gas supply when the device is disconnected.

Rabbet   A rectangular shape consisting of two surfaces cut along the edge or end of a board.

Raceway   An enclosed channel of metal or nonmetallic materials designed expressly for holding wires, cables, or busbars, with additional functions as permitted in this code. Raceways include, but are not limited to, rigid metal conduit, rigid nonmetallic conduit, intermediate metal conduit, liquidtight flexible conduit, flexible metallic tubing, flexible metal conduit, electrical nonmetallic tubing, electrical metallic tubing, underfloor raceways, cellular concrete floor raceways, cellular metal floor raceways, surface raceways, wireways, and bus ways.

Radiant barrier   A thin, reflective foil sheet that exhibits low radiant energy transmission and under certain conditions can block radiant heat transfer; installed in attics to reduce heat flow through a roof assembly into the living space.

Radiant ceiling panels   Ceiling panels that contain electric resistance heating elements embedded within them to provide radiant heat to a room.

Radiant energy   Energy that transmits away from its source in all directions.

Radiant floor   A type of radiant heating system where the building floor contains channels or tubes through which hot fluids such as air or water are circulated. The whole floor is evenly heated. Thus, the room heats from the bottom up. Radiant floor heating eliminates the draft and dust problems associated with forced air heating systems.

Radiant heating system   A heating system where heat is supplied (radiated) into a room by means of heated surfaces, such as electric resistance elements, hot water (hydronic) radiators, etc.

Radiation   Energy transmitted from a heat source to the air around it. Radiators actually depend more on convection than radiation.

Radiative cooling   The process of cooling by which a heat-absorbing media absorbs heat from one source and radiates the heat away.

Radiator   A room heat delivery (or exchanger) component of a hydronic (hot water or steam) heating system; hot water or steam is delivered to it by natural convection or by a pump from a boiler.

Radiator vent   A device that releases pressure within a radiator when the pressure inside exceeds the operating limits of the vent.

Radioactive waste   Materials left over from making nuclear energy. Radioactive waste can living organisms if it is not stored safely.

Radon   A naturally occurring, heavier than air, radioactive gas common in many parts of the country. Radon gas exposure is associated with lung cancer. Mitigation measures may involve crawl space and basement venting and various forms of vapor barriers.

Radon system   A ventilation system beneath the floor of a basement and/or structural wood floor and designed to fan exhaust radon gas to the outside of the home.

Rafter   One of a series of structural members of a roof designed to support roof loads. The rafters of a flat roof are sometimes called roof joists.

Rafter, hip   A rafter that forms the intersection of an external roof angle.

Rafter, valley   A rafter that forms the intersection of an internal roof angle. The valley rafter is normally made of double 2-in.-thick members.

Rail   Cross members of panel doors or of a sash. Also, a wall or open balustrade placed at the edge of a staircase, walkway bridge, or elevated surface to prevent people from falling off. Any relatively lightweight horizontal element, especially those found in fences (split rail).

Railroad tie   Black tar and preservative impregnated, 6 in. × 8 in. and 6- to 8-ft-long wooden timber that was used to hold railroad track in place. Normally used as a member of a retaining wall.

Rainproof   So constructed, protected or treated as to prevent rain from interfering with the successful operation of the apparatus under specified test conditions.

Raintight   So constructed or protected that exposure to a beating rain will not result in the entrance of water under specified test conditions.

Rake   The trim members that run parallel to the roof slope and form the finish between the roof and wall at a gable end.

Rake fascia   The vertical face of the sloping end of a roof eave.

Rake siding   The practice of installing lap siding diagonally.

Rammed earth   A construction material made by compressing earth in a form; used traditionally in many areas of the world and widely throughout North Africa and the Middle East.

Ranch   A single-story, one-level home.

Rankine cycle   The thermodynamic cycle that is an ideal standard for comparing performance of heat engines, steam power plants, steam turbines, and heat pump systems that use a condensable vapor as the working fluid; efficiency is measured as work done divided by sensible heat supplied.

Rated life The length of time that a product or appliance is expected to meet a certain level of performance under nominal operating conditions; in a luminaire, the period after which the lumen depreciation and lamp failure is at 70% of its initial value.

Rated power The power output of a device under specific or nominal operating conditions.

Rayleigh frequency distribution A mathematical representation of the frequency or ratio that specific wind speeds occur within a specified time interval.

Reactive power The electrical power that oscillates between the magnetic field of an inductor and the electrical field of a capacitor. Reactive power is never converted to nonelectrical power. Calculated as the square root of the difference between the square of the kilovolt-amperes and the square of the kilowatts. Expressed as reactive volt-amperes.

Ready-mixed concrete Concrete mixed at a plant or in trucks en route to a job and delivered ready for placement.

Real price The unit price of a good or service estimated from some base year in order to provide a consistent means of comparison.

Rebar, reinforcing bar Ribbed steel bars installed in foundation concrete walls, footers, and poured in place concrete structures designed to strengthen concrete. Comes in various thickness and strength grade.

Receiver The component of a central receiver solar thermal system where reflected solar energy is absorbed and converted to thermal energy.

Receptacle An electrical outlet. A typical household will have many 120-V receptacles for plugging in lams and appliances and 240-V receptacles for the range, clothes dryer, air conditioners, etc.

Receptacle outlet An outlet where one or more receptacles are installed.

Receptor A fixture or device that receives the discharge from indirect waste pipes.

Recirculated air Air that is returned from a heated or cooled space, reconditioned and/or cleaned, and returned to the space.

Recirculation systems A type of solar heating system that circulate warm water from storage through the collectors and exposed piping whenever freezing conditions occur; obviously a not very efficient system when operating in this mode.

Rectifier An electrical device for converting alternating current to direct current. The chamber in a cooling device where water is separated from the working fluid (e.g., ammonia).

Recuperator A heat exchanger in which heat is recovered from the products of combustion.

Recycling The process of converting materials that are no longer useful as designed or intended into a new product.

Redline, red-lined prints Blueprints that reflect changes and that are marked with red pencil.

Reducer A fitting with different size openings at either end and used to go from a larger to a smaller pipe.

Reflectance The amount (percent) of light that is reflected by a surface relative to the amount that strikes it.

Reflective coatings Materials with various qualities that are applied to glass windows before installation. These coatings reduce radiant heat transfer through the window and also reflect outside heat and a portion of the incoming solar energy, thus reducing heat gain. The most common type has a sputtered coating on the inside of a window unit. The other type is a durable "hard-coat" glass with a coating baked into the glass surface.

Reflective glass A window glass that has been coated with a reflective film and is useful in controlling solar heat gain during the summer.

Reflective insulation An aluminum foil–fabricated insulator with backings applied to provide a series of closed air spaces with highly reflective surfaces. (See "Radiant barrier.")

Reflective insulation Sheet material with one or both faces covered with aluminum foil.

Reflective window films A material applied to window panes that controls heat gain and loss, reduces glare, minimizes fabric fading, and provides privacy. These films are retrofitted on existing windows.

Reflector lamps A type of incandescent lamp with an interior coating of aluminum that reflects light to the front of the bulb. They are designed to spread light over specific areas.

Refraction The change in direction of a ray of light when it passes through one media to another with differing optical densities.

Refrigerant The compound (working fluid) used in air conditioners, heat pumps, and refrigerators to transfer heat into or out of an interior space. This fluid boils at a very low temperature enabling it to evaporate and absorb heat.

Refrigerant compressor A specific machine, with or without accessories, for compressing a given refrigerant vapor.

Refrigerating system A combination of interconnected parts forming a closed circuit in which refrigerant is circulated for the purpose of extracting, then rejecting, heat. A direct refrigerating system is one in which the evaporator or condenser of the refrigerating system is in direct contact with the air or other substances to be cooled or heated. An indirect refrigerating system is one in which a secondary coolant cooled or heated by the refrigerating system is circulated to the air or other substance to be cooled or heated.

Refrigeration The process of the absorption of heat from one location and its transfer to another for rejection or recuperation.

Refrigeration capacity A measure of the effective cooling capacity of a refrigerator, expressed in Btu per hour or in tons, where 1 ton of capacity is equal to the heat required to melt 2000 lb of ice in 24 hr or 12,000 Btu per hour.

Refrigeration cycle The complete cycle of stages (evaporation and condensation) of refrigeration or of the refrigerant.

Regenerative cooling A type of cooling system that uses a charging and discharging cycle with a thermal or latent heat–storage subsystem.

Regenerative heating The process of using heat that is rejected in one part of a cycle for another function or in another part of the cycle.

Register A grill placed over a heating duct or cold air return.

Reglaze To replace a broken window.

Regulator A device for reducing, controlling and maintaining the pressure in a portion of a piping system downstream of the device.

Regulator vent The opening in the atmospheric side of the regulator housing permitting the movement of air to compensate for the movement of the regulator diaphragm.

Reinforced-concrete construction A type of construction in which the principal structural members, such as floors, columns, and beams, are made of concrete poured around steel bars or steel meshwork in such a manner that the two materials act together to resist force.

Relamping The replacement of a nonfunctional or ineffective lamp with a new, more efficient lamp.

Relative humidity A measure of the percent of moisture actually in the air compared with what would be in it if it were fully saturated at that temperature. When the air is fully saturated, its relative humidity is 100%.

Reliability This is the concept of how long a device or process can operate properly without needing maintenance or replacement.

Relief valve, pressure A safety device that, because of an excess buildup of pressure, automatically releases water from a supply system.

Relief valve, vacuum A device to prevent excessive buildup of vacuum in a pressure vessel.

Remote Remote electrical, gas, or water meter digital readouts that are installed near the front of the home in order for utility companies to easily read the home owners usage of the service.

Renewable energy Energy derived from resources that are regenerative or for all practical purposes can not be depleted. Types of renewable energy resources include moving water (hydro, tidal and wave power), thermal gradients in ocean water, biomass, geothermal energy, solar energy, and wind energy. Municipal solid waste (MSW) is also considered to be a renewable energy resource.

Resilient The ability of a material to withstand temporary deformation, the original shape being assumed when the stresses are removed.

Resistance The inherent characteristic of a material to inhibit the transfer of energy. In electrical conductors, electrical resistance results in the generation of heat. Electrical resistance is measured in ohms. The heat transfer resistance properties of insulation products are quantified as the R-value.

Resistance heating A type of heating system that provides heat from the resistance of an electrical current flowing through a conductor.

Resistive voltage drop The voltage developed across a cell by the current flow through the resistance of the cell.

Resistor An electrical device that resists electric current flow.

Retaining wall A structure that holds back a slope and prevents erosion.

Retrofit The process of modifying a building's structure.

Return air Air removed from a conditioned space through openings, ducts, plenums, or concealed spaces to the heat exchanger of a heating, cooling, or ventilating system.

Return duct The central heating or cooling system contains a fan that gets its air supply through these ducts, which ideally should be installed in every room of the house. The air from a room will move towards the lower pressure of the return duct.

Reverse thermosiphoning When heat seeks to flow from a warm area (e.g., heated space) to a cooler area, such as a solar air collector at night without a reverse flow damper.

Reversing valve A component of a heat pump that reverses the refrigerant's direction of flow, allowing the heat pump to switch from cooling to heating or heating to cooling.

R-factor See "R-value."

Ribbon   A narrow board attached to studding or other vertical members of a frame that adds support to joists or other horizontal members.

Ribbon (girt)   Normally, a 1 × 4 board let into the studs horizontally to support the ceiling or second-floor joists.

Ribbon (photovoltaic) cells   A type of solar photovoltaic device made in a continuous process of pulling material from a molten bath of photovoltaic material, such as silicon, to form a thin sheet of material.

Ridge   The horizontal line at the junction of the top edges of two sloping roof surfaces.

Ridge board   The board placed on the ridge of the roof onto which the upper ends of other rafters are fastened.

Ridge shingles   Shingles used to cover the ridge board.

Rigid insulation board   An insulation product made of a fibrous material or plastic foams, pressed or extruded into board-like forms. It provides thermal and acoustical insulation strength with low weight, and coverage with few heat loss paths.

Rim joist   A joist that runs around the perimeter of the floor joists and home.

Rise   The vertical distance from the eaves line to the ridge. Also the vertical distance from stair tread to stair tread.

Riser   (a) A water pipe that extends vertically one full story or more to convey water to branches or to a group of fixtures. (b) The vertical stair member between two consecutive stair treads.

Riser and panel   The exterior vertical pipe (riser) and metal electric box (panel) the electrician provides and installs at the "rough electric" stage.

Road base   An aggregate mixture of sand and stone.

Rock   When referring to drywall, this means to install drywall to the walls and ceilings (with nails and screws), and before taping is performed.

Rock bin   A container that holds rock used as the thermal mass to store solar energy in a solar heating system.

Rock wool   A type of insulation made from virgin basalt, an igneous rock, and spun into loose fill or a batt. It is fire resistant and helps with soundproofing.

Roll roofing   Consists of mineral granules on asphalt saturated felt or fiberglass. Roll roofing is the uncut form of mineral surfaced shingle material.

Roll, rolling (framing)   To install the floor joists or trusses in their correct place. (To "roll the floor" means to install the floor joists.)

Romex   A name brand of nonmetallic sheathed electrical cable that is used for indoor wiring.

Roof   A building element that provides protection against the sun, wind, and precipitation.

Roof jack   Sleeves that fit around the black plumbing waste vent pipes at, and are nailed to, the roof sheeting.

Roof joist   The rafters of a flat roof. Lumber used to support the roof sheeting and roof loads. Generally, 2 × 10s and 2 × 12s are used.

Roof pond   A solar energy collection device consisting of containers of water located on a roof that absorb solar energy during the day so that the heat can be used at night or that cools a building by evaporation at night.

Roof ridge   The horizontal line at the junction of the top edges of two roof surfaces where an external angle greater than 180 degrees is formed.

Roof sheathing or sheeting   The wood panels or sheet material fastened to the roof rafters or trusses on which the shingle or other roof covering is laid.

Roof valley   The V created where two sloping roofs meet.

Roof ventilator   A stationary or rotating vent used to ventilate attics or cathedral ceilings; usually made of galvanized steel or polypropylene.

Roofing   The materials applied to the structural parts of a roof to make it waterproof.

Room heater   A freestanding heating appliance installed in the space being heated and not connected to ducts.

Rotary cut veneer   Veneer cut on a lathe which rotates the log against a broad cutting knife. The veneer is cut in a continuous sheet much the same as paper is unwound from a roll.

Rotor   An electric generator consists of an armature and a field structure. The armature carries the wire loop, coil, or other windings in which the voltage is induced, whereas the field structure produces the magnetic field. In small generators, the armature is usually the rotating component (rotor) surrounded by the stationary field structure (stator). In large generators in commercial electric power plants the situation is reversed. In a wind energy conversion device, the rotor is the blades and rotating components.

Rough lumber   Lumber that has been cut to rough size with saws but has not been dressed or surfaced.

Rough opening   The horizontal and vertical measurement of a window or door opening before drywall or siding is installed.

Rough sill   The framing member at the bottom of a rough opening for a window. It is attached to the cripple studs below the rough opening.

Roughing-in   The initial stage of a plumbing, electrical, heating, carpentry, and/or other project, when all components that won't be seen after the second finishing phase are assembled. (See "Heat rough," "Plumbing rough," and "Electrical rough.")

Run, roof   The horizontal distance from the eaves to a point directly under the ridge. One-half the span.

Run, stair   The horizontal distance of a stair tread from the nose to the riser.

R-value   A measure of the capacity of a material to resist heat transfer; a measure of insulation. The R-value is the reciprocal of the conductivity of a material (U-value). The larger the R-value of a material, the greater its insulating properties.

Sack mix   The amount of portland cement in a cubic yard of concrete mix. Generally, five- or six-sack is required in a foundation wall.

Sacrificial anode   A metal rod placed in a water heater tank to protect the tank from corrosion. Anodes of aluminum, magnesium, or zinc are the more frequently used metals. The anode creates a galvanic cell in which magnesium or zinc will be corroded more quickly than the metal of the tank giving the tank a negative charge and preventing corrosion.

Saddle   A small second roof built behind the back side of a fireplace chimney to divert water around the chimney. Also, the plate at the bottom of some—usually exterior—door openings. Sometimes called a threshold.

Safety disconnect   An electronic (automatic or manual) switch that disconnects one circuit from another circuit. These are used to isolate power generation or storage equipment from conditions such as voltage spikes or surges, thus avoiding potential damage to equipment.

Salt gradient solar ponds   Consist of three main layers. The top layer is near ambient and has low salt content. The bottom layer is hot, typically 160–212°F (71–100°C), and is very salty. The important gradient zone separates these zones. The gradient zone acts as a transparent insulator, permitting the sunlight to be trapped in the hot bottom layer (from which useful heat is withdrawn). This is because the salt gradient, which increases the brine density with depth, counteracts the buoyancy effect of the warmer water below (which would otherwise rise to the surface and lose its heat to the air). An organic Rankine cycle engine is used to convert the thermal energy to electricity.

Sand float finish   Lime that is mixed with sand, resulting in a textured finish on a wall.

Sanitary sewer   A sewer system designed for the collection of waste water from the bathroom, kitchen, and laundry drains, and usually not designed to handle storm water.

Sapwood   The layers of wood next to the bark, usually lighter in color than the heartwood, that are actively involved in the life processes of the tree. More susceptible to decay than heartwood. Sapwood is not essentially weaker or stronger than heartwood of the same species.

Sash   A single light frame containing one or more lights of glass. The frame that holds the glass in a window, often the movable part of the window.

Sash balance   A device, usually operated by a spring and designed to hold a single-hung window vent up and in place.

Saturated felt   A felt which is impregnated with tar or asphalt.

Scaffold   A temporary structure or platform used to support workers and materials during building construction.

Scale   A term which specifies the size of a reduced size drawing. For example, a plan is drawn to ¼-in. scale if every ¼ in. represents l ft on the real structure.

Scantling   Lumber with a cross section ranging from 2 in. × 4 in. to 4 in. × 4 in.

Scarfing   Joining the ends of stock together with a sloping lap-joint so they appear to be a single piece.

Schedule (window, door, mirror)   A table on the blueprints that list the sizes, quantities, and locations of the windows, doors, and mirrors.

Scotia   A concave molding consisting of an irregular curve. Used under the nosing of stair treads and for cornice trim.

Scrap out   The removal of all drywall material and debris after the home is "hung out" (installed) with drywall.

Scratch coat   The first coat of plaster, which is scratched to form a bond for a second coat.

Screed   A tool used in concrete work to level and smooth a horizontal surface. Consists of a 3- to 5-ft wood or metal strip attached to a pole.

Screed, concrete   To level off concrete to the correct elevation during a concrete pour.

Screed, plaster   A small strip of wood, usually the thickness of the plaster coat, used as a guide for plastering.

Scribing   The cutting of a grid pattern of grooves in a semiconductor material, generally for the purpose of making interconnections.

Scupper   (a) An opening for drainage in a wall, curb or parapet. (b) The drain in a downspout or flat roof, usually connected to the downspout.

Scuttle   An opening in a ceiling which provides access to the attic.

Sealed combustion heating system A heating system that uses only outside air for combustion and vents combustion gases directly to the outdoors. These systems are less likely to backdraft and to negatively affect indoor air quality.

Sealer A finishing material, either clear or pigmented, that is usually applied directly over raw wood for the purpose of sealing the wood surface.

Seasonal energy efficiency ratio (SEER) A measure of seasonal or annual efficiency of a central air conditioner or air conditioning heat pump. It takes into account the variations in temperature that can occur within a season and is the average number of Btu of cooling delivered for every watt-hour of electricity used by the heat pump over a cooling season.

Seasonal performance factor (SPF) Ratio of useful energy output of a device to the energy input, averaged over an entire heating season.

Seasoned wood Wood, used for fuel, that has been air dried so that it contains 15 to 20 percent moisture content (wet basis).

Seasoning Drying and removing moisture from green wood in order to improve its usability.

Second law efficiency The ratio of the minimum amount of work or energy required to perform a task to the amount actually used.

Second law of thermodynamics This law states that no device can completely and continuously transform all of the energy supplied to it into useful energy.

Section drawing A type of drawing which shows how a part of a structure looks when cut by a vertical plane. The face remaining after a real cut would look like the drawing.

Seebeck effect The generation of an electric current, when two conductors of different metals are joined at their ends to form a circuit, with the two junctions kept at different temperatures.

Selectable load Any device, such as a light, television, and power tool, which is plugged into your central power source and used only intermittently.

Selective absorber A solar absorber surface that has high absorbence at wavelengths corresponding to that of the solar spectrum and low emittance in the infrared range.

Selective surface coating A material with high absorbence and low emittance properties applied to or on solar absorber surfaces.

Self-sealing shingles Shingles containing factory-applied strips or spots of self-sealing adhesive.

Selvage The part of the width of roll roofing which is smooth. For example, a 36-in. width has a granular surfaced area 17-in. wide and a 19-in.-wide selvage area.

Semiconductor Any material that has a limited capacity for conducting an electric current. Certain semiconductors, including silicon, gallium arsenide, copper indium diselenide, and cadmium telluride, are uniquely suited to the photovoltaic conversion process.

Semigloss paint or enamel A paint or enamel made so that its coating, when dry, has some luster but is not very glossy. Bathrooms and kitchens are normally painted semigloss.

Sensible cooling effect The difference between the total cooling effect and the dehumidifying effect.

Sensible cooling load The interior heat gain due to heat conduction, convection, and radiation from the exterior into the interior, and from occupants and appliances.

Sensible heat The heat absorbed or released when a substance undergoes a change in temperature.

Sensible heat storage A heat storage system that uses a heat storage medium, and where the additional or removal of heat results in a change in temperature.

Septic permit A health department authorization to build or modify a septic system.

Septic system An on-site waste water treatment system. It usually has a septic tank which promotes the biological digestion of the waste, and a drain field which is designed to let the left over liquid soak into the ground. Septic systems and permits are usually sized by the number of bedrooms in a house.

Septic tank A water-tight receptor that receives the discharge of a building sanitary drainage system and is constructed so as to separate solids from the liquid, digest organic matter through a period of detention, and allow the liquids to discharge into the soil outside of the tank through a system of open joint or perforated piping or a seepage pit.

Series A configuration of an electrical circuit in which the positive lead is connected to the negative lead of another energy producing, conducting, or consuming device. The voltages of each device are additive, whereas the current is not.

Service The conductors and equipment for delivering energy from the electricity supply system to the wiring system of the premises served.

Service conductors The conductors from the service point or other source of power to the service disconnecting means.

Service drop The overhead service conductors from the last pole or other aerial support to and including the splices, if any, connecting to the service-entrance conductors at the building or other structure.

Service-entrance conductors, overhead system The service conductors between the terminals of the service equipment and a point usually outside the building, clear of building walls, where joined by tap or splice to the service drop.

Service-entrance conductors, underground system The service conductors between the terminals of the service equipment and the point of connection to the service lateral.

Service-entrance panel Main power cabinet where electricity enters a home wiring system.

Service equipment The necessary equipment, usually consisting of a circuit breaker or switch and fuses, and their accessories, located near the point of entrance of supply conductors to a building or other structure, or an otherwise defined area, and intended to constitute the main control and means of cutoff of the supply.

Service lateral The underground service conductors between the street main, including any risers at a pole or other structure or from transformers, and the first point of connection to the service-entrance conductors in a terminal box or meter or other enclosure with adequate space, inside or outside the building wall. Where there is no terminal box, meter, or other enclosure with adequate space, the point of connection shall be considered to be the point of entrance of the service conductors into the building.

Service piping The piping and equipment between the street gas main and the gas-piping system inlet, which is installed by and is under the control and maintenance of the serving gas supplier.

Service point Service point is the point of connection between the facilities of the serving utility and the premises wiring.

Setback thermostat A thermostat with a clock which can be programmed to come on or go off at various temperatures and at different times of the day/week. Usually used as the heating or cooling system thermostat.

Setting block A wood block placed in the glass groove or rabbet of the bottom rail of an insulating glass sash to form a base or bed for the glass.

Settlement Shifts in a structure, usually caused by freeze-thaw cycles underground.

Sewage Any liquid waste containing animal matter, vegetable matter, or other impurity in suspension or solution.

Sewage ejector A pump used to lift waste water to a gravity sanitary sewer line. Usually used in basements and other locations which are situated bellow the level of the side sewer.

Sewage pump A permanently installed mechanical device for removing sewage or liquid waste from a sump.

Sewer lateral See "Side sewer."

Sewer stub The junction at the municipal sewer system where the home's sewer line is connected.

Sewer tap The physical connection point where the home's sewer line connects to the main municipal sewer line.

Shading coefficient A measure of window glazing performance that is the ratio of the total solar heat gain through a specific window to the total solar heat gain through a single sheet of double-strength glass under the same set of conditions; expressed as a number between 0 and 1.

Shake A wood roofing material, normally cedar or redwood. Produced by splitting a block of the wood along the grain line. Modern shakes are sometimes machine sawn on one side. See shingle.

Shall The term, when used in the code, is construed as mandatory.

Shear block Plywood that is face nailed to short (2 × 4 or 2 × 6) wall studs (above a door or window, for example). This is done to prevent the wall from sliding and collapsing.

Sheathing The structural covering. Consists of boards or prefabricated panels that are attached to the exterior studding or rafters of a structure.

Sheathing paper A building material used in wall, floor, and roof construction to resist the passage of air.

Shed roof A roof containing only one sloping plane.

Sheet metal duct work The heating system. Usually round or rectangular metal pipes and sheet metal (for return air) and installed for distributing warm (or cold) air from the furnace to rooms in the home.

Sheet metal work All components of a house employing sheet metal, such as flashing, gutters, and downspouts.

Sheet rock See "Drywall."

Shim A thin strip of wood sometimes wedgeshaped, for plumbing or leveling wood members. Especially helpful when setting door and window frames.

Shingles Roof covering of asphalt, asbestos, wood, tile, slate, or other material cut to stock lengths, widths, and thicknesses.

Shingles, siding Various kinds of shingles, used over sheathing for exterior wall covering of a structure.

Shiplap Lumber with edges that have been rabbeted to form a lap joint between adjacent pieces.

Shoring Lumber and timbers used to prevent the sliding of earth adjoining an excavation. Also the timbers used as temporary bracing or support.

Short circuit A situation that occurs when hot and neutral wires come in contact with each other. Fuses and circuit breakers protect against fire that could result from a short.

Short circuit current The current flowing freely through an external circuit that has no load or resistance; the maximum current possible.

Shunt load An electrical load used to safely use excess generated power when not needed for its primary uses. A shunt load in a residential photovoltaic system might be domestic water heating, such that when power is not needed for typical building loads, such as operating lights or running HVAC system fans and pumps, it still provides value and is used in a constructive, safe manner.

Shutter (a) Usually lightweight louvered decorative frames in the form of doors located on the sides of a window. Some shutters are made to close over the window for protection. (b) A wood assembly of stiles and rails to form a frame which encloses panels used in conjunction with door and window frames. Also may consist of vertical boards cleated together.

Side of trim Trim required to finish one side of a door or window opening.

Side sewer The portion of the sanitary sewer which connects the interior waste water lines to the main sewer lines. The side sewer is usually buried in several feet of soil and runs from the house to the sewer line. It is usually "owned" by the sewer utility, must be maintained by the owner and may only be serviced by utility-approved contractors. Sometimes called "sewer lateral."

Side vent A vent connecting to the drain pipe through a fitting at an angle less than 45 degrees (0.79 rad) to the horizontal.

Siding The finished exterior covering of the outside walls of a frame building.

Siding, lap siding Slightly wedge-shaped boards used as horizontal siding in a lapped pattern over the exterior sheathing. Varies in butt thickness from ½ to ¾ in. and in widths up to 12 in.

Sigma heat The sum of sensible heat and latent heat in a substance above a base temperature, typically 32 degrees Fahrenheit.

Silicon A chemical element, of atomic number 14, that is semimetallic, and an excellent semiconductor material used in solar photovoltaic devices; commonly found in sand.

Sill (a) The 2 × 4 or 2 × 6 wood plate framing member that lays flat against and bolted to the foundation wall (with anchor bolts) and upon which the floor joists are installed. Normally the sill plate is treated lumber. (b) The member forming the lower side of an opening, as a door sill or window sill.

Sill cock An exterior water faucet (hose bib).

Sill plate (mudsill) Bottom horizontal member of an exterior wall frame which rests on top a foundation, sometimes called mudsill. Also sole plate, bottom member of an interior wall frame.

Sill seal Fiberglass or foam insulation installed between the foundation wall and sill (wood) plate. Designed to seal any cracks or gaps.

Simple CS (caulk and seal) A technique for insulating and sealing exterior walls that reduces vapor diffusion through air leakage points by installing precut blocks of rigid foam insulation over floor joists, sheet subfloor, and top plates before drywall is installed.

Single glaze or pane One layer of glass in a window frame. It has very little insulating value (R-1) and provides only a thin barrier to the outside and can account for considerable heat loss and gain.

Single hung window A window with one vertically sliding sash or window vent.

Single-package system A year-round heating and air conditioning system that has all the components completely encased in one unit outside the home. Proper matching of components can mean more energy-efficient operation compared to components purchased separately.

Single-phase A generator with a single armature coil, which may have many turns, and the alternating current output consists of a succession of cycles.

Sizing The process of designing a solar system to meet a specified load given the solar resource and the nominal or rated energy output of the solar energy collection or conversion device.

Skylight A window located on the roof of a structure to provide interior building spaces with natural daylight, warmth, and ventilation.

Skylight Glazing framed into a roof.

Slab A concrete pad that sits on gravel or crushed rock; well-compacted soil either level with the ground or above the ground.

Slab, door A rectangular door without hinges or frame.

Slag Concrete cement that sometimes covers the vertical face of the foundation void material.

Sleeper Usually, a wood member embedded in concrete, as in a floor, that serves to support and to fasten the subfloor or flooring.

Sleeve(s) Pipe installed under the concrete driveway or sidewalk that will be used later to run sprinkler pipe or low-voltage wire.

Slinky™ ground loop In this type of closed-loop, horizontal, geothermal, heat-pump installation, the fluid-filled plastic heat exchanger pipes are coiled like a Slinky™ to allow more pipe in a shorter trench.

This type of installation cuts down on installation costs and makes horizontal installation possible in areas it would not be with conventional horizontal applications. (See "Closed-loop geothermal heat pump systems.")

Slip joint   A mechanical-type joint used primarily on fixture traps. The joint tightness is obtained by compressing a friction-type washer such as rubber, nylon, neoprene, lead or special packing material against the pipe by the tightening of a (slip) nut.

Slope (also fall, grade, pitch)   The fall of a line of pipe in reference to a horizontal plane. In plumbing, it is expressed as the fall in a fraction of an inch per length of pipe.

Slump   The "wetness" of concrete. A 3-in. slump is dryer and stiffer than a 5-in. slump.

Smart window   A term used to describe a technologically advanced window system that contains glazing that can change or switch its optical qualities when a low-voltage electrical signal is applied to it, or in response to changes in heat or light.

Smoke-developed index   A numerical index indicating the relative density of smoke produced by burning assigned to a material tested in accordance with ASTM E 84.

Sodium lights   A type of high intensity discharge light that has the most lumens per watt of any light source.

Soffit   The underside of the members of a building, such as staircases, cornices, beams, and arches. Relatively minor in size as compared with ceilings. Also called drop ceiling and furred-down ceiling.

Softwoods   The botanical group of trees that have needle- or scalelike leaves and are evergreen for the most part, cypress, larch, and tamarack being exceptions. The term has no reference to the actual hardness of the wood. Softwoods are often referred to as conifers, and botanically they are called gymnosperms.

Soil stack   A general term for the vertical main of a system of soil, waste, or vent piping.

Solar air heater   A type of solar thermal system where air is heated in a collector and either transferred directly to the interior space or to a storage medium, such as a rock bin.

Solar altitude angle   The angle between a line from a point on the earth's surface to the center of the solar disc, and a line extending horizontally from the point.

Solar array   A group of solar collectors or solar modules connected together.

Solar azimuth   The angle between the sun's apparent position in the sky and true south, as measured on a horizontal plane.

Solar cell   A solar photovoltaic device with a specified area.

Solar collector   A device used to collect, absorb, and transfer solar energy to a working fluid. Flat plate collectors are the most common type of collectors used for solar water or pool heating systems. In the case of a photovoltaics system, the solar collector could be crystalline silicon panels or thin-film roof shingles, for example.

Solar cooling   The use of solar thermal energy or solar electricity to power a cooling appliance. There are five basic types of solar cooling technologies: absorption cooling, which can use solar thermal energy to vaporize the refrigerant; desiccant cooling, which can use solar thermal energy to regenerate (dry) the desiccant; vapor compression cooling, which can use solar thermal energy to operate a Rankine-cycle heat engine; and evaporative coolers ("swamp" coolers), and heat pumps and air conditioners that can be powered by solar photovoltaic systems.

Solar declination   The apparent angle of the sun north or south of the earth's equatorial plane. The earth's rotation on its axis causes a daily change in the declination.

Solar distillation   The process of distilling (purifying) water using solar energy. Water can be placed in an air-tight solar collector with a sloped glazing material, and as it heats and evaporates, distilled water condenses on the collector glazing, and runs down where it can be collected in a tray.

Solar energy   Electromagnetic energy transmitted from the sun (solar radiation). The amount that reaches the earth is equal to one billionth of total solar energy generated, or the equivalent of about 420 trillion kilowatt-hours.

Solar energy collector   See "Solar collector."

Solar Energy Industries Association (SEIA)   A national trade association of solar energy equipment manufacturers, retailers, suppliers, installers, and consultants.

Solar Energy Research Institute (SERI)   A federally funded institute, created by the Solar Energy Research, Development and Demonstration Act of 1974, that conducted research and development of solar energy technologies. Became the National Renewable Energy Laboratory (NREL) in 1991.

Solar film   A window glazing coating, usually tinted bronze or gray, used to reduce building cooling loads, glare, and fabric fading.

Solar fraction   The percentage of a building's seasonal energy requirements that can be met by a solar energy device(s) or system(s).

Solar furnace   A device that achieves very high temperatures by the use of reflectors to focus and concentrate sunlight onto a small receiver.

Solar module (panel) A solar photovoltaic device that produces a specified power output under defined test conditions, usually composed of groups of solar cells connected in series, in parallel, or in series-parallel combinations.

Solar noon The time of the day, at a specific location, when the sun reaches its highest, apparent point in the sky; equal to true or due, geographic south.

Solar one A solar thermal electric central receiver power plant ("power tower") located in Barstow, California, and completed in 1981. The solar one had a design capacity of 10,000 peak kilowatts, and was composed of a receiver located on the top of a tower surrounded by a field of reflectors. The concentrated sunlight created steam to drive a steam turbine and electric generator located on the ground.

Solar space heater A solar energy system designed to provide heat to individual rooms in a building.

Solar spectrum The total distribution of electromagnetic radiation emanating from the sun. The different regions of the solar spectrum are described by their wavelength range. The visible region extends from about 390 to 780 nanometers (a nanometer is one billionth of one meter). About 99% of solar radiation is contained in a wavelength region from 300 nm (ultraviolet) to 3000 nm (near-infrared). The combined radiation in the wavelength region from 280 nm to 4000 nm is called the broadband, or total, solar radiation.

Solar thermal parabolic dishes A solar thermal technology that uses a modular mirror system that approximates a parabola and incorporates two-axis tracking to focus the sunlight onto receivers located at the focal point of each dish. The mirror system typically is made from a number of mirror facets, either glass or polymer mirror, or can consist of a single stretched membrane using a polymer mirror. The concentrated sunlight may be used directly by a Stirling, Rankine, or Brayton cycle heat engine at the focal point of the receiver or to heat a working fluid that is piped to a central engine. The primary applications include remote electrification, water pumping, and grid-connected generation.

Solar thermal systems Solar energy systems that collect or absorb solar energy for useful purposes. Can be used to generate high temperature heat (for electricity production and/or process heat), medium temperature heat (for process and space/water heating and electricity generation), and low temperature heat (for water and space heating and cooling).

Solar time The period marked by successive crossing of the earth's meridian by the sun; the hour angle of the sun at a point of observance (apparent time) is corrected to true (solar) time by taking into account the variation in the earth's orbit and rate of rotation. Solar time and local standard time are usually different for any specific location.

Solar transmittance The amount of solar energy that passes through a glazing material, expressed as a percentage.

Solarium A glazed structure, such as greenhouse or "sunspace."

Sole plate The lowest horizontal strip on wall and partition framing. The sole plate for a partition is supported by a wood subfloor, concrete slab, or other closed surface.

Solenoid An electromechanical device composed of a coil of wire wound around a cylinder containing a bar or plunger, that when a current is applied to the coil, the electromotive force causes the plunger to move; a series of coils or wires used to produce a magnetic field.

Solenoid valve An automatic valve that is opened or closed by an electromagnet.

Solid bridging A solid member placed between adjacent floor joists near the center of the span to prevent joists or rafters from twisting.

Solid fuels Any fuel that is in solid form, such as wood, peat, lignite, coal, and manufactured fuels such as pulverized coal, coke, charcoal, briquettes, pellets, etc.

Solidity In reference to a wind energy conversion device, the ratio of rotor blade surface area to the frontal, swept area that the rotor passes through.

Solstice The two times of the year when the sun is apparently farthest north and south of the earth's equator; usually occurring on or around June 21 (summer solstice in northern hemisphere, winter solstice for southern hemisphere) and December 21 (winter solstice in northern hemisphere, summer solstice for the southern hemisphere).

Sonotube Round, large cardboard tubes designed to hold wet concrete in place until it hardens.

Sound attenuation Sound proofing a wall or subfloor, generally with fiberglass insulation.

Space heat Heat supplied to the living space, for example, to a room or the living area of a building.

Space heater A movable or fixed heater used to heat individual rooms.

Spacer (window) Strips of material used to separate multiple panes of glass within the windows.

Spacing The distance between individual members or shingles in building construction.

Span The clear distance that a framing member carries a load without support between structural supports. The horizontal distance from eaves to eaves.

Spec home   A house built before it is sold. The builder speculates that he can sell it at a profit.

Specialty contractor   Licensed to perform a specialty task, e.g., electrical, side sewer, and asbestos abatement.

Specific gravity   The ratio of the weight of a body to the weight of an equal volume of water at some standard temperature.

Specific heat   The amount of heat required to raise a unit mass of a substance through one degree, expressed as a ratio of the amount of heat required to raise an equal mass of water through the same range.

Specific heat capacity   The quantity of heat required to change the temperature of one unit weight of a material by one degree.

Specific humidity   The weight of water vapor, per unit weight of dry air.

Specific volume   The volume of a unit weight of a substance at a specific temperature and pressure.

Specifications or specs   A narrative list of materials, methods, model numbers, colors, allowances, and other details which supplement the information contained in the blue prints. Written elaboration in specific detail about construction materials and methods. Written to supplement working drawings.

Spectral energy distribution   A curve illustrating the variation or spectral irradiance with wavelength.

Spectral irradiance   The monochromatic irradiance of a surface per unit bandwidth at a particular wavelength, usually expressed in watts per square meter-nanometer bandwidth.

Spectrally selective coatings   A type of window glazing films used to block the infrared (heat) portion of the solar spectrum but admit a higher portion of visible light.

Spillway   A passage for surplus water to flow over or around a dam.

Spinning reserve   Electric power provider capacity on line and running at low power in excess of actual load.

Splash block   Portable concrete (or vinyl) channel generally placed beneath an exterior sill cock (water faucet) or downspout in order to receive roof drainage from downspouts and to divert it away from the building.

Spline   A small strip of wood that fits into a groove or slot of both members to form a joint.

Split spectrum photovoltaic cell   A photovoltaic device where incident sunlight is split into different spectral regions, with an optical apparatus, that are directed to individual photovoltaic cells that are optimized for converting that spectrum to electricity.

Split system air conditioner   An air conditioning system that comes in two to five pieces: one piece contains the compressor, condenser, and a fan; the others have an evaporator and a fan. The condenser, installed outside the house, connects to several evaporators, one in each room to be cooled, mounted inside the house. Each evaporator is individually controlled, allowing different rooms or zones to be cooled to varying degrees.

Spreader stocker   A type of furnace in which fuel is spread, automatically or mechanically, across the furnace grate.

Sputtering   A process used to apply photovoltaic semi-conductor material to a substrate by a physical vapor deposition process where high-energy ions are used to bombard elemental sources of semiconductor material, which eject vapors of atoms that are then deposited in thin layers on a substrate.

Square   A unit of measure—100 sq. ft.—usually applied to roofing and siding material. Also, a situation that exists when two elements are at right angles to each other. Also a tool for checking this.

Square wave inverter   A type of inverter that produces square wave output; consists of a DC source, four switches, and the load. The switches are power semiconductors that can carry a large current and withstand a high-voltage rating. The switches are turned on and off at a correct sequence, at a certain frequency. The square wave inverter is the simplest and the least expensive to purchase, but it produces the lowest quality of power.

Square-tab shingles   Shingles on which tabs are all the same size and exposure.

Squeegie   Fine pea gravel used to grade a floor (normally before concrete is placed).

Squirrel cage motors   This is another name for an induction motor. The motors consist of a rotor inside a stator. The rotor has laminated, thin flat steel discs, stacked with channels along the length. If the casting composed of bars and attached end rings were viewed without the laminations the casting would appear similar to a squirrel cage.

Stack   (a) A smokestack or flue for exhausting the products of combustion from a combustion appliance. (b) Any main vertical DWV line, including offsets, that extends one or more stories as directly as possible to its vent terminal.

Stack (heat) loss   Sensible and latent heat contained in combustion gases and vapor emitted to the atmosphere.

Stack (trusses)   To position trusses on the walls in their correct location.

Stack vent   The extension of soil or waste stack above the highest horizontal drain connected.

Stack venting   A method of venting a fixture or fixtures through the soil or waste stack without individual fixture vents.

Stair carriage or stringer Supporting member for stair treads. Usually a 2 × 12 in. plank notched to receive the treads; sometimes called a "rough horse."

Stair landing A platform between flights of stairs or at the termination of a flight of stairs. Often used when stairs change direction. Normally no less than 3 ft × 3 ft square.

Stair rise The vertical distance from stair tread to stair tread (and not to exceed 7½ in.).

Stairwell The framed opening which receives the stairs.

Stall In reference to a wind turbine, a condition when the rotor stops turning.

Standalone generator A power source/generator that operates independently of or is not connected to an electric transmission and distribution network; used to meet a load(s) physically close to the generator.

Standalone inverter An inverter that operates independent of or is not connected to an electric transmission and distribution network.

Standard air Air with a weight of 0.075 pound per cubic foot with an equivalent density of dry air at a temperature of 86 degrees Fahrenheit and standard barometric pressure of 29.92 inches of mercury.

Standard conditions In refrigeration, an evaporating temperature of 5°F, a condensing temperature of 86°F, liquid temperature before expansion of 77°F, and suction temperature of 12°F.

Standard cubic foot A column of gas at standard conditions of temperature and pressure (32°F and one atmosphere).

Standard Industrial Classification (SIC) Code Standardized codes used to classify businesses by type of activity they engage in.

Standard practices of the trade(s) One of the more common basic and minimum construction standards. This is another way of saying that the work should be done in the way it is normally done by the average professional in the field.

Stand-by heat loses A term used to describe heat energy lost from a water heater tank.

Stand-by power For the consumer, this is the electricity that is used by your TVs, stereos, and other electronic devices that use remote controls. When you press "off" to turn off your device, minimal power (dormant mode) is still being used to maintain the internal electronics in a ready, quick-response mode. This way, your device can be turned on with your remote control and be immediately ready to operate.

Starter strip Asphalt roofing applied at the eaves that provides protection by filling in the spaces under the cutouts and joints of the first course of shingles.

Starting surge Power, often above an appliance's rated wattage, required to bring any appliance with a motor up to operating speed.

Starting torque The torque at the bottom of a speed (rpm) versus torque curve. The torque developed by the motor is a percentage of the full-load or rated torque. At this torque, the speed, i.e., the rotational speed of the motor as a percentage of synchronous speed, is zero. This torque is what is available to initially get the load moving and begin its acceleration.

Static pressure The force per unit area acting on the surface of a solid boundary parallel to the flow.

Static vent A vent that does not include a fan.

STC (Sound Transmission Class) The measure of sound stopping of ordinary noise.

Steam Water in vapor form; used as the working fluid in steam turbines and heating systems.

Steam boiler A type of furnace in which fuel is burned and the heat is used to produce steam.

Steam turbine A device that converts high-pressure steam, produced in a boiler, into mechanical energy that can then be used to produce electricity by forcing blades in a cylinder to rotate and turn a generator shaft.

Steel inspection A municipal and/or engineers inspection of the concrete foundation wall, conducted before concrete is poured into the foundation panels. Done to ensure that the rebar (reinforcing bar), rebar nets, void material, beam pocket plates, and basement window bucks are installed and wrapped with rebar and complies with the foundation plan.

Steel-frame construction A type of construction in which the structural parts are of steel or are dependent on a steel frame for support.

Step flashing Flashing application method used where a vertical surface meets a sloping roof plane. 6 in. × 6 in. galvanized metal bent at a 90 degree angle, and installed beneath siding and over the top of shingles. Each piece overlaps the one beneath it the entire length of the sloping roof (step by step).

Stepped footing A footing that changes grade levels at intervals to accommodate a sloping site.

Stick built A house built without prefabricated parts. Also called "conventional building."

Stickers Strips of wood used to separate the layers in a pile of lumber so air can circulate.

Stile The upright or vertical outside pieces of a sash, door, blind, or screen.

Stool A molded interior trim member serving as a sash or window frame sill cap. Stools may be beveled rabbeted or rabbeted to receive the window frame sill.

Stoop A small porch, veranda, or platform, or a stairway, outside an entrance to a building.

Stop box   Normally a 5-in.-diameter cast iron pipe with a lid that is placed vertically into the ground, situated near the water tap in the yard, and where a water cutoff valve to the home is located (underground). A long pole with a special end is inserted into the curb stop to turn off/on the water.

Stop order   A formal, written notification to a contractor to discontinue some or all work on a project for reasons such as safety violations, defective materials or workmanship, or cancellation of the contract.

Stop valve   A device installed in a water supply line, usually near a fixture, that permits an individual to shut off the water supply to one fixture without interrupting service to the rest of the system.

Stops   Moldings along the inner edges of a door or window frame. Also valves used to shut off water to a fixture.

Storage capacity   The amount of energy an energy storage device or system can store.

Storage hydropower   A hydropower facility that stores water in a reservoir during high-inflow periods to augment water during low-inflow periods. Storage projects allow the flow releases and power production to be more flexible and dependable. Many hydropower project operations use a combination of approaches.

Storage tank   The tank of a water heater.

Storage water heater   A water heater that releases hot water from the top of the tank when a hot water tap is opened. To replace that hot water, cold water enters the bottom of the tank to ensure a full tank.

Storm door   An exterior door that protects the primary door.

Storm sash or storm window   An extra window usually placed outside of an existing one, as additional protection against cold weather.

Storm sewer   A sewer system designed to collect storm water and is separated from the waste water system.

Storm sewer (drain)   A pipe used for conveying rainwater, surface water, condensate, cooling water or similar liquid wastes.

Storm windows   Glass, plastic panels, or plastic sheets that reduce air infiltration and some heat loss when attached to either the interior or exterior of existing windows.

Story   That part of a building between any floor or between the floor and roof.

Story pole   A strip of wood used to lay out and transfer measurements for door and window openings, siding and shingle courses, and stairways. (Also called a "rod.")

Straightedge   A straight strip of wood or metal used to layout or check the accuracy of work.

Stressed skin   Two facings, one glued to one side and the other to the opposite side of an inner structural framework to form a panel. Facings may be of plywood or other suitable material.

Strike plate   A metal piece mortised into or fastened to the face of a door frame side jamb to receive the latch or bolt when the door is closed.

String, stringer   A timber or other support for cross members in floors or ceilings. In stairs, the supporting member for stair treads. Usually a 2 × 12 in. plank notched to receive the treads.

Strip flooring   Wood flooring consisting of narrow, matched strips.

Strong back   L-shaped wooden support attached to tops of ceiling joists to strengthen them, maintain spacing, and bring them to same level.

Structural floor   A framed lumber floor that is installed as a basement floor instead of concrete. This is done on very expansive soils.

Structural window wall panel   A window unit framed into a wall panel at the factory. Also called a factory-assembled structural wall panel.

Stub, stubbed   To push through.

Stucco   An outside plaster finish made with Portland cement as its base.

Stud   A vertical wood framing member, also referred to as a wall stud, attached to the horizontal sole plate below and the top plate above. Normally 2 × 4s or 2 × 6s, and 8 ft long (sometimes 92⅝ in.). One of a series of wood or metal vertical structural members placed as supporting elements in walls and partitions.

Stud framing   A building method that distributes structural loads to each of a series of relatively lightweight studs. Contrasts with post and beam.

Stud shoe   A metal, structural bracket that reinforces a vertical stud. Used on an outside bearing wall where holes are drilled to accommodate a plumbing waste line.

Subcontractor   A general or specialty contractor who works for another general contractor.

Subfloor   The framing components of a floor to include the sill plate, floor joists, and deck sheeting over which a finish floor is to be laid.

Substation   An electrical installation containing power conversion (and sometimes generation) equipment, such as transformers, compensators, and circuit breakers.

Substrate   The physical material upon which a photovoltaic cell is applied.

Sump   (a) Pit or large plastic bucket/barrel inside the home designed to collect ground water from a perimeter drain system. (b) A tank or pit which receives sewage or waste, located below the normal grade of the gravity system and which is required to be emptied by mechanical means.

Sump pump   A pump installed to empty a sump. The pump is chosen to handle the type material to be pumped—either clear-water waste or soil-type sewage. The pump is selected for the specific head and volume of the load and is usually operated by level controllers.

Sun path diagram   A circular projection of the sky vault onto a flat diagram used to determine solar positions and shading effects of landscape features on a solar energy system.

Sun-tempered building   A building that is elongated in the east-west direction, with the majority of the windows on the south side. The area of the windows is generally limited to about 7% of the total floor area. A sun-tempered design has no added thermal mass beyond what is already in the framing, wallboard, and so on. Insulation levels are generally high.

Sunspace   A room that faces south (in the northern hemisphere), or a small structure attached to the south side of a house.

Super insulated houses   A type of house that has massive amounts of insulation, airtight construction, and controlled ventilation without sacrificing comfort, health, or aesthetics.

Super window   A popular term for highly insulating window with a heat loss so low it performs better than an insulated wall in winter, since the sunlight that it admits is greater than its heat loss over a 24-hour period.

Superconductivity   The abrupt and large increase in electrical conductivity exhibited by some metals as the temperature approaches absolute zero.

Supplementary heat   A heat source, such as a space heater, used to provide more heat than that provided by a primary heating source.

Supply air   Air delivered to a conditioned space through ducts or plenums from the heat exchanger of a heating, cooling or ventilating system.

Supply duct   The duct(s) of a forced air heating/cooling system through which heated or cooled air is supplied to rooms by the action of the fan of the central heating or cooling unit.

Supports   Devices for supporting, hanging and securing pipes, fixtures, and equipment.

Surface water loop   In this type of closed-loop geothermal heat pump installation, the fluid-filled plastic heat exchanger pipes are coiled into circles and submerged at least eight feet below the surface of a body of surface water, such as a pond or lake. The coils should only be placed in a water source that meets minimum volume, depth, and quality criteria. Also see closed-loop geothermal heat pump systems.

Surfaced lumber   Lumber that is dressed or finished by running it through a planer.

Suspended ceiling   A ceiling system supported by hanging it from the overhead structural framing.

Swamp cooler   A popular term used for an evaporative cooling device.

Sway brace   Metal straps or wood blocks installed diagonally on the inside of a wall from bottom to top plate, to prevent the wall from twisting, racking, or falling over "domino" fashion.

Sweep   A drainage fitting designed to provide a change in direction of a drain pipe of less than the angle specified by the amount necessary to establish the desired slope of the line. Sweeps provide a longer turning radius than bends and a less-turbulent flow pattern. (See "Bend" and "Elbow.")

Switches   A *general-use snap switch* is a form of general-use switch constructed so that it can be installed in device boxes or on box covers or otherwise used in conjunction with wiring systems recognized by this code. A *general-use switch* is a switch intended for use in general distribution and branch circuits. It is rated in amperes and is capable of interrupting its rated current at its rated voltage. An *isolating switch* is a switch intended for isolating an electric circuit from the source of power. It has no interrupting rating and is intended to be operated only after the circuit has been opened by some other means. A *motor-circuit switch* is a switch, rated in horsepower, capable of interrupting the maximum operating overload current of a motor of the same horsepower rating as the switch at the rated voltage.

Synchronous generator   An electrical generator that runs at a constant speed and draws its excitation from a power source external or independent of the load or transmission network it is supplying.

Synchronous inverter   An electrical inverter that inverts direct current electricity to alternating current electricity, and that uses another alternating current source, such as an electric power transmission and distribution network (grid), for voltage and frequency reference to provide power in phase and at the same frequency as the external power source.

Synchronous motor   A type of motor designed to operate precisely at the synchronous speed with no slip in the full-load speeds (rpm).

System mix   The proportion of electricity distributed by a power provider that is generated from available sources such as coal, natural gas, petroleum, nuclear, hydropower, wind, or geothermal.

T & G (tongue and groove)   A joint made by a tongue (a rib on one edge of a board) that fits into a corresponding groove in the edge of another board to make a tight flush joint. Typically, the subfloor plywood is T & G.

T bar   Ribbed, T-shaped bars with a flat metal plate at the bottom that are driven into the earth. Normally used chain link fence poles, and to mark locations of a water meter pit.

Tab   The exposed portion of strip shingles defined by cutouts.

Tail beam   A relatively short beam or joist supported in a wall on one end and by a header at the other.

Termite shield   A shield, usually made of sheet metal, placed in or on a foundation wall or around pipes to keep termites out of the structure.

Take off   The material necessary to complete a job.

Tankless water heater   A water heater that heats water before it is directly distributed for end use as required; a demand water heater.

Taping   The process of covering drywall joints with paper tape and joint compound.

Task lighting   Any light source designed specifically to direct light a task or work performed by a person or machine.

Teco   Metal straps that are nailed and secure the roof rafters and trusses to the top horizontal wall plate. (Also called a "hurricane clip.")

Tee   A T-shaped plumbing fitting.

Temperature and pressure (T & P) relief valve   A combination relief valve designed to function as both a temperature relief and pressure relief valve.

Temperature coefficient (of a solar photovoltaic cell)   The amount that the voltage, current, and/or power output of a solar cell changes due to a change in the cell temperature.

Temperature humidity index   An index that combines sensible temperature and air humidity to arrive at a number that closely responds to the effective temperature; used to relate temperature and humidity to levels of comfort.

Temperature relief valve   A temperature-actuated valve designed to discharge automatically at the temperature at which it is set.

Temperature zones   Individual rooms or zones in a building where temperature is controlled separately from other rooms or zones.

Temperature/pressure relief valve   A component of a water heating system that opens at a designated temperature or pressure to prevent a possible tank, radiator, or delivery pipe rupture.

Tempered   Strengthened. Tempered glass will not shatter nor create shards, but will "pelletize" like an au-tomobile window. Required in tub and shower enclosures and locations, entry door glass and sidelight glass, and in a windows when the window sill is less than 16 in. to the floor.

Tempering valve   A valve used to mix heated water with cold in a heating system to provide a desired water temperature for end use.

Tennessee Valley Authority (TVA)   A federal agency established in 1933 to develop the Tennessee River Valley region of the southeastern United States, and which is now nation's largest power producer.

Termite shield   A construction element that inhibits termites from entering building foundations and walls.

Termites   Wood-eating insects that superficially resemble ants in size and general appearance, and live in colonies.

Terra cotta   A ceramic material molded into masonry units.

Terrazzo flooring   A floor produced by embedding small chips of marble or colored stone in concrete an-then grinding and polishing the surface.

Therm   A unit of heat containing 100,000 British thermal units (Btu).

Thermal balance point   The point or outdoor temperature where the heating capacity of a heat pump matches the heating requirements of a building.

Thermal capacitance   The ability of a material to absorb and store heat for use later.

Thermal efficiency   A measure of the efficiency of converting a fuel to energy and useful work; useful work and energy output divided by higher heating value of input fuel times 100 (for percent).

Thermal energy   The energy developed through the use of heat energy.

Thermal energy storage   The storage of heat energy during power provider off-peak times at night, for use during the next day without incurring daytime peak electric rates.

Thermal envelope houses   An architectural design (also known as the double envelope house), sometimes called a "house-within-a-house," that employs a double envelope with a continuous airspace of at least 6 to 12 in. on the north wall, south wall, roof, and floor, achieved by building inner and outer walls, a crawlspace or sub-basement below the floor, and a shallow attic space below the weather roof. The east and west walls are single, conventional walls. A buffer zone of solar-heated, circulating air warms the inner envelope of the house. The south-facing airspace may double as a sunspace or greenhouse.

Thermal mass   Materials that store heat.

Thermal resistance (R-value)   This designates the resistance of a material to heat conduction. The greater the R-value the larger the number.

Thermal storage walls (masonry or water)   A thermal storage wall is a south-facing wall that is glazed on the outside. Solar heat strikes the glazing and is absorbed into the wall, which conducts the heat into the room over time. The walls are at least 8 in. thick. Generally, the thicker the wall, the less the indoor temperature fluctuates.

Thermocouple   A device consisting of two dissimilar conductors with their ends connected together. When the two junctions are at different temperatures, a small voltage is generated.

Thermodynamic cycle   An idealized process in which a working fluid (water, air, ammonia, etc.) successively changes its state (from a liquid to a gas and back to a liquid) for the purpose of producing useful work or energy, or transferring energy.

Thermodynamics   A study of the transformation of energy from one form to another, and its practical application. [See "Law(s) of Thermodynamics."]

Thermoelectric conversion   The conversion of heat into electricity by the use of thermocouples.

Thermography   A building energy auditing technique for locating areas of low insulation in a building envelope by means of a thermographic scanner.

Thermophotovoltaic cell   A device where sunlight concentrated onto a absorber heats it to a high temperature, and the thermal radiation emitted by the absorber is used as the energy source for a photovoltaic cell that is designed to maximize conversion efficiency at the wavelength of the thermal radiation.

Thermopile   A large number of thermocouples connected in series.

Thermoply™   Exterior laminated sheathing nailed to the exterior side of the exterior walls. Normally ¼ in. thick, 4 × 8 or 4 × 10 sheets with an aluminumized surface.

Thermosiphon system   This passive solar hot water system relies on warm water rising, a phenomenon, known as natural convection, to circulate water through the collectors and to the tank. In this type of installation, the tank must be above the collector. As water in the collector heats, it becomes lighter and rises naturally into the tank above. Meanwhile, cooler water in the tank flows down pipes to the bottom of the collector, causing circulation throughout the system. The storage tank is attached to the top of the collector so that thermosiphoning can occur.

Thermostat   A device used to control temperatures; used to control the operation of heating and cooling devices by turning the device on or off when a specified temperature is reached.

Three-dimensional shingles   Laminated shingles that have added dimensionality because of extra layers or tabs, giving a shake-like appearance. (Also called "architectural shingles.")

Three-phase current   Alternating current in which three separate pulses are present, identical in frequency and voltage, but separated 120 degrees in phase.

Three-way switch   A switch designed to operate in conjunction with a similar switch to control one outlet from two points.

Threshold   A wood member, beveled or tapered on each side, used to close the space between the bottom of a door and the sill or floor underneath. (Also called a "saddle.")

Tidal power   The power available from the rise and fall of ocean tides. A tidal power plant works on the principal of a dam or barrage that captures water in a basin at the peak of a tidal flow, then directs the water through a hydroelectric turbine as the tide ebbs.

Tie beam (collar beam)   A beam so situated that it ties the principal rafters of a roof together and preventsthem from thrusting the plate out of line.

Tilt angle (of a solar collector or module)   The angle at which a solar collector or module is set to face the sun relative to a horizontal position. The tilt angle can be set or adjusted to maximize seasonal or annual energy collection.

Timbers   Lumber 5 in. or larger in least dimension.

Time and materials contract (T & M)   A construction contract which specifies a price for different elements of the work such as cost per hour of labor, overhead, profit, etc.; a contract which may not have a maximum price, or may state a "price not to exceed."

Timer   A device that can be set to automatically turn appliances (lights) off and on at set times.

Tinner   Another name for the heating contractor.

Tip speed ratio   In reference to a wind energy conversion device's blades, the difference between the rotational speed of the tip of the blade and the actual velocity of the wind.

Tip up   The downspout extension that directs water (from the home's gutter system) away from the home. They typically swing up when mowing the lawn, etc.

Title   Evidence (usually in the form of a certificate or deed) of a person's legal right to ownership of a property.

TJI or TJ   Manufactured structural building component resembling the letter "I." Used as floor joists and rafters. I-joists include two key parts: flanges and webs. The flange or from of the I joist may be made of laminated veneer lumber or dimensional lumber, usually formed into a 1½ in. width. The web or center of the I-joist is commonly made of plywood or oriented strand board (OSB). Large holes can be cut in the web to accommodate duct work and plumbing waste lines. I-joists are available in lengths up to 60 in. long.

Toe space   A recessed space at the floor line of a base kitchen cabinet or other built-in units. Permits one to stand close without striking the vertical space with the toes.

Toeboard   A board fastened horizontally slightly above planking to keep tools and materials from falling on workers below. Can be used on scaffolds or at an access hole. Board must be at least 4 in. wide. Not needed for scaffolds under 10 ft.

Toenailing   To drive a nail at a slant with the initial surface in order to permit it to penetrate into a second member.

Ton (of air conditioning)   A unit of air cooling capacity; 12,000 Btu/hr.

Top chord   The upper or top member of a truss.

Top plate   Top horizontal member of a frame wall supporting ceiling joists, rafters, or other members.

Topping cycle   A means to increase the thermal efficiency of a steam electric generating system by increasing temperatures and interposing a device, such as a gas turbine, between the heat source and the conventional steam-turbine generator to convert some of the additional heat energy into electricity.

Torque (motor)   The turning or twisting force generated by an electrical motor in order for it to operate.

Total harmonic distortion   The measure of closeness in shape between a waveform and it's fundamental component.

Total heat   The sum of the sensible and latent heat in a substance or fluid above a base point, usually 32°F.

Transformer   An electromagnetic device that changes the voltage of alternating current electricity. It consists of an induction coil having a primary and secondary winding and a closed iron core.

Transformer   A device for transforming the voltage characteristics of an electric current.

Transmission   The process of sending or moving electricity from one point to another; usually defines that part of an electric power provider's electric power lines from the power plant buss to the last transformer before the customer's connection.

Transmission and distribution losses   The losses that result from inherent resistance in electrical conductors and transformation inefficiencies in distribution

transformers in a transmission and distribution network.

Transmission lines   Transmit high-voltage electricity from the transformer to the electric distribution system.

Transmitter (garage door)   The small, push-button device that causes the garage door to open or close.

Transom   A small opening above a door separated by a horizontal member (transom bar). Usually contains a sash or a louver panel hinged to the transom bar.

Trap   (a) A plumbing fitting that holds water to prevent air, gas, and vermin from backing up into a fixture. (b) A fitting, either separate or built into a fixture, which provides a liquid seal to prevent the emission of sewer gases without materially affecting the flow of sewage or waste water through it.

Trap arm   That portion of a fixture drain between a trap weir and the vent fitting.

Trap primer   A device or system of piping to maintain a water seal in a trap, typically installed where infrequent use of the trap would result in evaporation of the trap seal, such as floor drains.

Trap seal   The trap seal is the maximum vertical depth of liquid that a trap will retain, measured between the crown weir and the top of the dip of the trap.

Traveling grate   A furnace grate that moves fuel through the combustion chamber.

Tread   The horizontal part of a step on which the foot is placed.

Treated lumber   A wood product which has been impregnated with chemical pesticides such as CCA (chromated copper arsenate) to reduce damage from wood rot or insects. Often used for the portions of a structure which are likely to be in contact with soil and water.

Trellis   An architectural feature used to shade exterior walls; usually made of a lattice of metal or wood; often covered by vines to provide additional summertime shading.

Trickle (solar) collector   A type of solar thermal collector in which a heat transfer fluid drips out of header pipe at the top of the collector, runs down the collector absorber and into a tray at the bottom where it drains to a storage tank.

Trim   *Interior:* The finish materials in a building, such as moldings applied around openings (window trim, door trim) or at the floor and ceiling of rooms (baseboard, cornice, and other moldings). Also, the physical work of installing interior doors and interior woodwork, to include all handrails, guardrails, stairway balustrades, mantles, light boxes, base, door casings, cabinets, countertops, shelves, window sills, and aprons, etc. *Exterior:* The finish materials on the exterior a building, such as moldings applied around openings (window trim, door trim), siding, windows, exterior doors, attic vents, crawlspace vents, shutters, etc. Also, the physical work of installing these materials.

Trim (plumbing, heating, electrical) The work that the mechanical contractors perform to finish their respective aspects of work, and when the home is nearing completion and occupancy.

Trimmer stud A stud which supports the header for a wall opening. The stud extends from the sole plate to the bottom of the header. It is parallel to and in contact with a full length stud that extends from sole plate to top plate.

Trimmer The beam or floor joist into which a header is framed. Adds strength to the side of the opening.

Triple pane (window) This represents three layers of glazing in a window with an airspace between the middle glass and the exterior and interior panes.

Triple wall A type of chimney flue made with three metal pipes, each inside another. The concentric arrangement provides safety from fire while its light weight makes installation easy.

Tripod A support for a builder's level consisting of three sloping legs. Friction of the legs with the ground keeps them in place.

Trombe wall Thick wall of masonry placed next to exterior glazing to store solar energy in passive solar construction. Named for a French physicist Felix Trombe.

True power The actual power rating that is developed by a motor before losses occur.

True south The direction, at any point on the earth that is geographically in the northern hemisphere, facing toward the South Pole of the earth. Essentially a line extending from the point on the horizon to the highest point that the sun reaches on any day (solar noon) in the sky.

Truss A structural unit consisting of such members as beams, bars, and ties; usually arranged to form triangles. Provides rigid support over wide spans with a minimum amount of material.

Tub trap Curved, U-shaped section of a bath tub drain pipe that holds a water seal to prevent sewer gasses from entering the home through tubs water drain.

Tube (fluorescent light) A fluorescent lamp that has a tubular shape.

Tube-in-plate absorber A type of solar thermal collector where the heat transfer fluid flows through tubes formed in the absorber plate.

Tube-type collector A type of solar thermal collector that has tubes (pipes) that the heat transfer fluid flows through that are connected to a flat absorber plate.

Tungsten halogen lamp A type of incandescent lamp that contains a halogen gas in the bulb, which re-

duces the filament evaporation rate increasing the lamp life. The high operating temperature and need for special fixtures limits their use to commercial applications and for use in projector lamps and spotlights.

Turbine A device for converting the flow of a fluid (air, steam, water, or hot gases) into mechanical motion.

Turn down ratio The ratio of a boiler's or gasifier's maximum output to its minimum output.

Turnkey A term used when the subcontractor provides all materials (and labor) for a job.

Turpentine A petroleum, volatile oil used as a thinner in paints and as a solvent in varnishes.

Two-family dwelling A building consisting solely of two dwelling units.

Two-tank solar system A solar thermal system that has one tank for storing solar heated water to preheat the water in a conventional water heater.

Type B vent A listed and labeled vent conforming to UL 441 for venting gas appliances with draft hoods and other gas appliances listed for use with Type B vents.

Type BW vent A listed and labeled vent conforming to UL 441 for venting gas-fired vented wall furnaces listed for use with Type BW vents.

Type L vent A listed and labeled vent conforming to UL 641 for venting oil-burning appliances listed for use with Type L vents or with listed gas appliances.

UL (Underwriters' Laboratories) An independent testing agency that checks electrical devices and other components for possible safety hazards.

Ultimate analysis A procedure for determining the primary elements in a substance (carbon, hydrogen, oxygen, nitrogen, sulfur, and ash).

Ultraviolet Electromagnetic radiation in the wavelength range of 4 to 400 nanometers.

Unconfined space A space having a volume not less than 50 cu. ft. (1.42 m^3) per 1000 Btu/h (293 W) of the aggregate input rating of all appliances installed in that space. Rooms communicating directly with the space, in which the appliances are installed, through openings not furnished with doors, are considered a part of the unconfined space.

Undercoat A coating applied prior to the finishing or top coats of a paint job. It may be the first of two or the second of three coats. (Also called the "prime coat.")

Underground home A house built into the ground or slope of a hill, or which has most or all exterior surfaces covered with earth.

Underground plumbing The plumbing drain and waste lines that are installed beneath a basement floor.

Underlayment A ¼-in. material placed over the subfloor plywood sheeting and under finish coverings, such as vinyl flooring, to provide a smooth, even surface. Also a secondary roofing layer that is waterproof or water-resistant, installed on the roof deck and beneath shingles or other roof-finishing layer.

Unglazed solar collector   A solar thermal collector that has an absorber that does not have a glazed covering. Solar swimming pool heater systems usually use unglazed collectors because they circulate relatively large volumes of water through the collector and capture nearly 80% of the solar energy available.

Union   A plumbing fitting that joins pipes end-to-end so that they can be dismantled.

Unitary air conditioner   An air conditioner consisting of one or more assemblies that move, clean, cool, and dehumidify air.

Unprotected-metal construction   A type of construction in which the structural parts are of metal unprotected by fireproofing.

Unusually tight construction   Construction in which (a) walls and ceilings exposed to the outside atmosphere have a continuous water vapor retarder with a rating of 1 perm [57 mg/(s · m^2 Pa)] or less with openings gasketed or sealed; and (b) weather-stripping has been added on operable windows and doors, and caulking or sealant is applied to areas such as joints around window and door frames, between sole plates and floors, between wall-ceiling joints, between wall panels, at penetrations for plumbing, electrical, and gas lines, and at other openings.

Unvented heater   A combustion heating appliance that vents the combustion by-products directly into the heated space. The latest models have oxygen sensors that shut off the unit when the oxygen level in the room falls below a safe level.

Urea-formaldehyde resin glue   Moisture resistant glue which hardens through chemical action when water is added to the powdered resin.

Useful heat   Heat stored above room temperature (in a solar heating system).

Utility   A regulated entity which exhibits the characteristics of a natural monopoly (also referred to as a power provider). For the purposes of electric industry restructuring, "utility" refers to the regulated, vertically integrated electric company. "Transmission utility" refers to the regulated owner/operator of the transmission system only. "Distribution utility" refers to the regulated owner/operator of the distribution system which serves retail customers.

Utility easement   The area of the earth that has electric, gas, or telephone lines. These areas may be owned by the homeowner, but the utility company has the legal right to enter the area as necessary to repair or service the lines.

Utilization equipment   Equipment that utilizes electric energy for electronic, electromechanical, chemical, heating, lighting, or similar purposes.

U-value   The reciprocal of R-value. The lower the number, the greater the heat transfer resistance (insulating) characteristics of the material. (See "Coefficient of heat transmission.")

Vacuum breakers   A device which prevents back-siphonage of water by admitting atmospheric pressure through ports to the discharge side of the device.

Vacuum evaporation   The deposition of thin films of semiconductor material by the evaporation of elemental sources in a vacuum.

Valley   The V-shaped area of a roof where two sloping roofs meet. Water drains off the roof at the valleys.

Valley flashing   Sheet metal that lays in the V area of a roof valley.

Valley rafter   A rafter which forms the intersection of an internal roof angle.

Valuation   An inspection carried out for the benefit of the mortgage lender to ascertain if a property is a good security for a loan.

Valuation fee   The fee paid by the prospective borrower for the lender's inspection of the property. Normally paid upon loan application.

Vapor barrier   A building product installed on exterior walls and ceilings under the drywall and on the warm side of the insulation. It is used to retard the movement of water vapor into walls and prevent condensation within them. Normally, polyethylene plastic sheeting is used.

Vapor retarder   A material that retards the movement of water vapor through a building element (e.g., walls, ceilings) and prevents insulation and structural wood from becoming damp and metals from corroding. Often applied to insulation batts or separately in the form of treated papers, plastic sheets, and metallic foils.

Variable rate   An interest rate that will vary over the term of the loan.

Variable-speed wind turbines   Turbines in which the rotor speed increases and decreases with changing wind speed, producing electricity with a variable frequency.

Veneer   Extremely thin sheets of wood. Also a thin slice of wood or brick or stone covering a framed wall.

Veneer plaster   Interior wall covering consisting of a gypsum lath base and surfacing of ⅛-in. gypsum plaster.

Veneered wall   A frame building wall with a masonry facing (e.g., single brick). A veneered wall is nonload bearing.

Vent   (a) A passageway for conveying flue gases from fuel-fired appliances, or their vent connectors, to the outside atmosphere. (b) A pipe installed to provide a flow of air to or from a drainage system or to provide a circulation of air within such system to protect trap seals from siphonage and back pressure.

Vent connector   That portion of a venting system that connects the flue collar or draft hood of an appliance to a vent.

Vent damper device, automatic   A device intended for installation in the venting system, in the outlet of or downstream of the appliance draft hood, of an individual, automatically operated fuel-burning appliance and which is designed to automatically open the venting system when the appliance is in operation and to automatically close off the venting system when the appliance is in a standby or shutdown condition.

Vent gases   Products of combustion from fuel-burning appliances, plus excess air and dilution air, in the venting system above the draft hood or draft regulator.

Vent stack   A vertical vent pipe installed to provide circulation of air to and from the drainage system and which extends through one or more stories.

Vent system   Piping installed to equalize pneumatic pressure in a drainage system to prevent trap seal loss or blowback caused by siphonage or backpressure.

Vented gas appliance categories   The following categories are used to differentiate gas utilization equipment according to vent pressure and flue gas temperature: A *Category I* appliance operates with a non-positive vent connector pressure and with a flue gas temperature at least 140°F (60°C) above its dewpoint. A *Category II* appliance operates with a nonpositive vent connector pressure and with a flue gas temperature less than 140°F (60°C) above its dewpoint. A *Category III* appliance operates with a positive vent pressure and with a flue gas temperature at least 140°F (60°C) above its dewpoint. A *Category IV* appliance operates with a positive vent pressure and with a flue gas temperature less than 140°F (60°C) above its dewpoint.

Vented heater   A type of combustion heating appliance in which the combustion gases are vented to the outside, either with a fan (forced) or by natural convection.

Ventilated   Provided with a means to permit circulation of air sufficient to remove an excess of heat, fumes, or vapors.

Ventilation   The process of moving air (changing) into and out of an interior space either by natural or mechanically induced (forced) means.

Ventilation air   That portion of supply air that is drawn from outside, plus any recirculated air that has been treated to maintain a desired air quality.

Ventilation   The process of supplying or removing air by natural or mechanical means. Such air may or may not have been conditioned.

Venting   Removal of combustion products to the outdoors.

Vermiculite   Mineral closely related to mica, with the faculty of expanding on heating to form lightweight material with insulating qualities. Used as bulk insulation, also as aggregate in insulating and acoustical plaster, and in insulating concrete floors.

Vertical ground loop   In this type of closed-loop geothermal heat pump installation, the fluid-filled plastic heat exchanger pipes are laid out in a plane perpendicular to the ground surface. For a vertical system, holes (approximately 4 in. in diameter) are drilled about 20 ft apart and 100–400 ft deep. Into these holes go two pipes that are connected at the bottom with a U-bend to form a loop. The vertical loops are connected with horizontal pipe (i.e., manifold), placed in trenches, and connected to the heat pump in the building. Large commercial buildings and schools often use vertical systems because the land area required for horizontal ground loops would be prohibitive. Vertical loops are also used where the soil is too shallow for trenching, or for existing buildings, as they minimize the disturbance to landscaping. (See "Closed-loop geothermal heat pump systems.")

Vertical pipe   Any pipe or fitting which makes an angle of 45 degrees (0.79 rad) or more with the horizontal.

Visible light transmittance   The amount of visible light that passes through the glazing material of a window, expressed as a percentage.

Visible radiation   The visible portion of the electromagnetic spectrum with wavelengths from 0.4 to 0.76 microns.

Visqueen   A 4-mil or 6-mil plastic sheeting.

Void   Cardboard rectangular boxes that are installed between the earth (between caissons) and the concrete foundation wall. Used when expansive soils are present.

Volt   A unit of electrical force equal to that amount of electromotive force that will cause a steady current of one ampere to flow through a resistance of one ohm.

Voltage   A measure of electrical potential. Most homes are wired with 110- and 220-V lines. The 110-V power is used for lighting and most of the other circuits. The 220-V power is usually used for the kitchen range, hot water heater, and dryer.

Voltage (of a circuit)   The greatest root-mean-square (effective) difference of potential between any two conductors of the circuit concerned.

Voltage to ground   For grounded circuits, the voltage between the given conductor and that point or conduc-

tor of the circuit that is grounded. For ungrounded circuits, the greatest voltage between the given conductor and any other conductor of the circuit.

Volt-ampere A unit of electrical measurement equal to the product of a volt and an ampere.

WC An abbreviation for water closet (toilet).

Wafer A thin sheet of semiconductor (photovoltaic) material made by cutting it from a single crystal or ingot.

Waferboard (waferwood) Construction panels made up of long, thin chips of wood. Wafers are coated with a waterproof resin and wax and then bonded with heat and pressure.

Wainscot A lower interior wall surface (usually 3–4 ft above the floor) that contrasts with the wall surface above. May consist of solid wood or plywood.

Wale A horizontal wood or metal strip used on the outside of forms for concrete. Wales are used to keep the form walls from bending outward under the weight of poured concrete.

Walk-through A final inspection of a home before "closing" to look for and document problems that need to be corrected.

Wall A vertical structural element that holds up a roof, encloses part or all of a room, or stands by itself to hold back soil.

Wall orientation The geographical direction that the primary or largest exterior wall of a building faces.

Wall out When a painter pray paints the interior of a home.

Wall tie Metal strip or wire used to bind tiers of masonry in cavity wall construction, or to bind brick veneer to a wood frame wall.

Wallboard Wood pulp, gypsum, or other materials made into large, rigid sheets that may be fastened to the frame of a building to provide a surface finish.

Warp Any variation from a true or plane surface. Warp includes bow, crook, cup, and twist, or any combination thereof.

Warping Any distortion in a material.

Warranty In construction there are two general types of warranties. One is provided by the manufacturer of a product such as roofing material or an appliance. The second is a warranty for the labor. For example, a roofing contract may include a 20-year material warranty and a 5-year labor warranty. Many new homebuilders provide a 1-year warranty. Any major issue found during the first year should be communicated to the builder immediately. Small items can be saved up and presented to the builder for correction periodically through the first year after closing.

Waste Liquid-borne waste free of fecal matter.

Waste pipe (or stack) Piping that conveys only liquid sewage not containing fecal material.

Water board Water-resistant drywall to be used in tub and shower locations. Normally green or blue colored.

Water closet Another name for toilet.

Water distribution system Piping that conveys water from the service to the plumbing fixtures, appliances, appurtenances, equipment, devices, or other systems served, including fittings and control valves.

Water heater A closed vessel in which water is heated by the combustion of fuels, electricity, or other energy source and withdrawn for use external to the vessel at pressures not exceeding 160 psig (1103-kPa gage), including the apparatus by which heat is generated and all controls and devices necessary to prevent water temperatures from exceeding 210°F (99°C).

Water jacket A heat exchanger element enclosed in a boiler. Water is circulated with a pump through the jacket where it picks up heat from the combustion chamber after which the heated water circulates to heat distribution devices. A water jacket is also an enclosed water-filled chamber in a tankless coiled water heater. When a faucet is turned on water flows into the water heater heat exchanger. The water in the chamber is heated, transfers heat to the cooler water in the heat exchanger, and is then sent through the hot water outlet to the appropriate faucet.

Water main A water supply pipe for public use.

Water meter pit (or vault) The box cast iron bonnet and concrete rings that contains the water meter.

Water outlet A valved discharge opening, including a hose bibb, through which water is removed from the potable water system supplying water to a plumbing fixture or plumbing appliance which requires either an air-gap or backflow prevention device for protection of the supply system.

Water repellent A solution, primarily paraffin wax and resin in mineral spirits, which upon penetrating wood retards changes in its moisture content.

Water service pipe The outside pipe from the water main or other source of potable water supply to the water distribution system inside the building, terminating at the service valve.

Water source heat pump A type of (geothermal) heat pump that uses well (ground) or surface water as a heat source. Water has a more stable seasonal temperature than air thus making for a more efficient heat source.

Water supply system The water service pipe, the water distributing pipes and the necessary connecting pipes, fittings, control valves, and all appurtenances in or adjacent to the building or premises.

Water table The location of the underground water, and the vertical distance from the surface of the earth to this underground water.

Water tap The connection point where the home water line connects to the main municipal water system.

Water tight Constructed to prevent moisture from entering an enclosure under specified test conditions.

Water turbine A turbine that uses water pressure to rotate its blades; the primary types are the Pelton wheel, for high heads (pressure); the Francis turbine, for low to medium heads; and the Kaplan for a wide range of heads. Primarily used to power an electric generator.

Water wall An interior wall made of water-filled containers for absorbing and storing solar energy.

Water wheel A wheel that is designed to use the weight and/or force of moving water to turn it, primarily to operate machinery or grind grain.

Water-repellent preservative A liquid applied to wood to give wood water-repellant properties.

Watt A measure of the electrical requirement of an appliance calculated by multiplying the voltage times the amperage. For example: a 150-W light bulb which uses 110-V power needs a little less than 1 amp (110 V × 1 amp × 110 W).

Watt-hour A unit of electricity consumption of 1 W/hr.

Wattmeter A device for measuring power consumption.

Wave form The shape of the phase power at a certain frequency and amplitude.

Wave power The concept of capturing and converting the energy available in the motion of ocean waves to energy.

Wavelength The distance between similar points on successive waves.

Weathering The mechanical or chemical disintegration and discoloration of the surface of wood. It can be caused by exposure to light, the action of dust and sand carried by winds, and the alternate shrinking and swelling of the surface fibers that come with the continual variation in moisture content brought by changes in the weather. Weathering does not include decay.

Weatherization Work on a building exterior in order to reduce energy consumption for heating or cooling. Work involving adding insulation, installing storm windows and doors, caulking cracks, and putting on weather stripping.

Weatherproof So constructed or protected that exposure to the weather will not interfere with successful operation.

Weather-strip Narrow strips of metal, vinyl plastic, or other material so designed that when installed at doors or windows, they will retard the passage of air, water, moisture, or dust around the door or window sash.

Weephole A small hole, as in a retaining wall, to drain water to the outside. Commonly used at the lower edges of masonry cavity walls.

Wet vent A vent that also receives the discharge of wastes from other fixtures.

Wet wall An interior wall finish surface usually consisting of ⅜-in. gypsum plaster lathe and ½-in. gypsum plaster applied to the lath surface.

Whaler (waler) A horizontal member used in concrete form construction to stiffen and support the walls of the form.

Wheeling The process of transmitting electricity over one or more separately owned electric transmission and distribution systems. (See "Wholesale" and "Retail wheeling.")

Whole house fan A mechanical/electrical device used to pull air out of an interior space; usually located in the highest location of a building, in the ceiling, and venting to the attic or directly to the outside.

Wholesale wheeling The wheeling of electric power in amounts and at prices that generally have been negotiated in long-term contracts between the power provider and a distributor or very large power customer.

Wind ("i" pronounced as in kind) A term used to describe the warp in a board when twisted (winding). It will rest upon two diagonally opposite corners, if laid upon a perfectly flat surface.

Wind bracing Metal straps or wood blocks installed diagonally on the inside of a wall from bottom to top plate, to prevent the wall from twisting, racking, or falling over in "domino" fashion.

Wind energy Energy available from the movement of the wind across a landscape caused by the heating of the atmosphere, earth, and oceans by the sun.

Wind energy conversion system (WECS) An apparatus for converting the energy available in the wind to mechanical energy that can be used to power machinery (grain mills, water pumps) and to operate an electrical generator.

Wind power plant A group of wind turbines interconnected to a common power provider system through a network of transformers, distribution lines, and (usually) one substation. Operation, control, and maintenance functions are often centralized through a network of computerized monitoring systems, supplemented by visual inspection. This is a term commonly used in the United States. In Europe, it is called a generating station.

Wind resource assessment The process of characterizing the wind resource, and its energy potential, for a specific site or geographical area.

Wind rose   A diagram that indicates the average percentage of time that the wind blows from different directions, on a monthly or annual basis.

Wind speed   The rate of flow of the wind undisturbed by obstacles.

Wind speed duration curve   A graph that indicates the distribution of wind speeds as a function of the cumulative number of hours that the wind speed exceeds a given wind speed in a year.

Wind speed profile   A profile of how the wind speed changes with height above the surface of the ground or water.

Wind turbine   A term used for a wind energy conversion device that produces electricity—typically having one, two, or three blades.

Wind turbine rated capacity   The amount of power a wind turbine can produce at its rated wind speed, e.g., 100 kW at 20 mph. The rated wind speed generally corresponds to the point at which the conversion efficiency is near its maximum. Because of the variability of the wind, the amount of energy a wind turbine actually produces is a function of the capacity factor (e.g., a wind turbine produces 20% to 35% of its rated capacity over a year).

Wind velocity   The wind speed and direction in an undisturbed flow.

Window buck   Square or rectangular box that is installed within a concrete foundation or block wall. A window will eventually be installed in this "buck" during the siding stage of construction.

Window frame   The stationary part of a window unit; window sash fits into the window frame.

Window sash   The operating or movable part of a window; the sash is made of window panes and their border.

Window unit   Consists of a combination of the frame, window, weather-stripping, and sash activation device. May also include screens and/or storm sash. All parts are assembled as a complete operating unit.

Wing   A lateral extension of a building from the main portion; one of two or more coordinate portions of a building, which extend from a common junction.

Wingwall   A building structural element that is built onto a building's exterior along the inner edges of all the windows, and extending from the ground to the eaves. Wingwalls help ventilate rooms that have only one exterior wall which leads to poor cross-ventilation. Wingwalls cause fluctuations in the natural wind direction to create moderate pressure differences across the windows. They are only effective on the windward side of the building.

Wire (electrical)   A generic term for an electrical conductor.

Wire glass   Glass having a layer of meshed wire incorporated approximately in the center of the sheet.

Wire nut   A plastic device used to connect bare wires together.

Wonderboard™   A panel made out of concrete and fiberglass usually used as a ceramic tile backing material. Commonly used on bathtub decks.

Wood stove   A wood-burning appliance for space and/or water heating and/or cooking.

Working fluid   A fluid used to absorb and transfer heat energy.

Wound rotor motors   A type of motor that has a rotor with electrical windings connected through slip rings to the external power circuit. An external resistance controller in the rotor circuit allows the performance of the motor to be tailored to the needs of the system and to be changed with relative ease to accommodate system changes or to vary the speed of the motor.

Wrapped drywall   Areas that get complete drywall covering, as in the doorway openings of bifold and bipass closet doors.

Y   A Y-shaped plumbing fitting.

Yard of concrete   One cubic yard of concrete is 3 ft × 3 ft × 3 ft in volume, or 27 cu. ft. One cu. yd. of concrete will pour 80 sq. ft. of 3½-in. sidewalk or basement/garage floor.

Yaw   The rotation of a horizontal axis wind turbine around its tower or vertical axis.

Yoke   The location where a home's water meter is sometimes installed between two copper pipes, and located in the water meter pit in the yard.

Yurt   An octagonal-shaped shelter that originated in Mongolia, and traditionally made from leather or canvas for easy transportation.

Z-bar flashing   Bent, galvanized metal flashing that's installed above a horizontal trim board of an exterior window, door, or brick run. It prevents water from getting behind the trim/brick and into the home.

Zone   An area within the interior space of a building, such as an individual room(s), to be cooled, heated, or ventilated. A zone has its own thermostat to control the flow of conditioned air into the space.

Zone valve   A device, usually placed near the heater or cooler, which controls the flow of water or steam to parts of the building; it is controlled by a zone thermostat.

Zoning (government)   A governmental process and specification which limits the use of a property (e.g., single-family use, high-rise residential use, industrial use). Zoning laws may limit where you can locate a structure. (See "Building codes.")

Index

ABOUT THE AUTHOR

Gil L. Taylor has worked in the construction industry for more than 24 years, holding such positions as Project/Construction Manager for the Design/Build Division of Mason & Hanger Engineering, Kentucky State Resident Inspector, and Project Engineer for Takenaka International USA—one of *Engineering News-Record's* "Top 25" design/build firms. He belongs to several professional construction organizations, including the International Code Council (ICC). He is an ICC-certified building inspector as well as an ICC-certified inspector in electrical, plumbing, mechanical, and residential one- and two-family codes. He is the author of several books and manuals on construction and code issues, including the Up to Code series, published by McGraw-Hill in 2005. He lives in Lexington, Kentucky.